CHOICES IN SEXUALITY

CHOICES IN SEXUALITY

Second Edition

Susan L. McCammon
David Knox
Caroline Schacht

East Carolina University

Cincinnati, Ohio
www.atomicdog.com

Cover photos: © Stockbyte

Photos on pp. 5, 40, 151, 162, 185, 186, 245, 265, 280, 372, 404, 458, 484, 548 courtesy of David Knox.

ISBN 1-59260-050-6

Library of Congress Control Number: 2003107011

Printed in the United States of America by Atomic Dog Publishing, 1148 Main Street, Third Floor,
Cincinnati, OH 45202.

10 9 8 7 6 5 4 3 2

To our families,
Who have been among our very best choices,

Mike, Andrew, and Reagin,
Lisa, Dave, and Isabelle

Brief Contents

Contents

Chapter 8
Sexuality Across the Lifespan 241

Chapter 9
Cultural Diversity in Sexuality 273

Chapter 10
Partner Communication and Sexuality 297

Chapter 11
Planning Children and Birth Control 323

Chapter 12
Abortion and Adoption 355

Chapter 13
Pregnancy, Childbirth, and Transition to Parenthood 383

Chapter 14
Sexually Transmitted Diseases 409

Chapter 15
Sexual Dysfunctions and Sex Therapy 443

Chapter 16
Variant Sexual Behavior and the Commercialization of Sex 475

Chapter 17
Sexual Coercion 509

Preface

Sexuality is at the core of our existence. We are conceived as the product of sexual expression, identified for gender programming at birth by our genitals, find direction for our hormones during adolescence, experience sexual partners or mate, may be involved in reproduction/parenting a new generation, and experience the changes in sexuality as we age. For most of our lives we are confronted with sexual choices. Our choices are outcomes of biological directives, social influences, and interactions of the two, although the relative contribution of each component remains in debate.

Human sexuality is not just an academic course in psychology, sociology, health education, and biology; it is also a study of how you live your life and the accompanying level of satisfaction and meaning. We hope that you will develop a fundamental understanding of what human sexuality is and how it impacts you, your relationships, and society. The theme of *Choices in Sexuality* is to provide an understanding of how biological, social, and cultural influences impact your sexual choices and to encourage you to take charge of your life by making deliberate, informed sexual choices.

We have selected the theme of choices because students sometimes do not consider the alternatives of their choices. Nor do students often realize the consequences of their sexual choices to their long-term psychological and physical health, their relationships, and the quality of their lives. Several features of the text are provided to facilitate the process of making sexual choices. These various features include

- *Personal Choices*—These sections, indicated in the text by the icon to the right, discuss specific sexual choices relevant to each chapter that you might face. Examples include "Considerations for having intercourse with a new partner," "Share your sexual fantasies with your partner," "Sex with or without love," and "Use of a vibrator."
- *Self-Assessments*—These boxes provide a scale for you to measure a particular aspect of your sexuality and to compare your score with other adults who have completed the assessment. An example is the "Student Sexual Risks Scale" in Chapter 8. Each of the 18 chapters includes a scale.
- *Social Choices*—These boxes identify social issues with which our society is confronted. Examples include "Should Same-Sex Marriages Be Legal?" "Content of Sex Education in the Public Schools," and "How Old Is Too Old to Be a Parent?"
- *Think About It*—These paragraphs ask you to think critically about an issue presented in the chapter. For example, the following "Think About It" paragraph is presented in Chapter 14.

Think About It

How might educational programs go about informing people of the potential seriousness of untreated STDs without fueling fear that is out of proportion?

- *National and International Data*—To replace speculation with facts, numbers are presented to reflect empirical reality. In addition to data from *The Statistical Abstract of the United States: 2002,* the American Council on Education, and University of California provide representative data on colleges and universities throughout the United States every fall. Similarly, the National Health and Social Life Survey reflects information from individuals (of different ages, races, educations) throughout the United States.
- *Cultural Diversity*—Paragraphs distributed throughout the text reveal sexual phenomena in other societies and cultures. The material emphasizes that we tend to be ethnocentric unless we are reminded that other cultures often think and behave differently. Even within our own culture, there are variations, as in race and ethnicity.

ONLINE AND IN PRINT

Choices in Sexuality, Second Edition, is available online as well as in print. The online chapters demonstrate how the interactive media components of the text enhance presentation and understanding. For example,

- Animated illustrations help clarify concepts.
- Self-report questionnaires show you how specific text material relates to your own life.
- *QuickCheck* interactive questions and chapter quizzes test your knowledge of various topics and provide immediate feedback.
- Clickable glossary terms provide immediate definitions of key concepts.
- The search function allows you to quickly locate discussions of specific topics throughout the text.
- Highlighting capabilities allow you to emphasize main ideas. You can also add personal notes in the margin.

You may choose to use just the online version of the text, or both the online and the print versions together. This gives you the flexibility to choose which combination of resources works best for you. To assist those who use the online and print versions together, the primary heads and subheads in each chapter are numbered the same. For example, the first primary head in Chapter 1 is labeled 1-1, the second primary head in this chapter is labeled 1-2, and so on. The subheads build from the designation of their corresponding primary head: 1-1a, 1-1b, etc. This numbering system is designed to make moving between the online and print versions as seamless as possible.

Finally, next to a number of figures and boxes in the print version of the text, you will see icons similar to the ones on the left. These icons indicate that these figures or boxes in the online version of the text are interactive in a way that applies, illustrates, or reinforces the concept.

ACKNOWLEDGMENTS

Choices in Sexuality is the result of the work of many people. We would like to acknowledge Beth Credle, health educator at East Carolina University, for ensuring state-of-the-art information on contraception. Also at East Carolina University, we would like to thank Dr. Hubert Burden for his consultation on the anatomy illustrations, Carmen Gragnani, Sandra Galliani, Sarah Ramby, Kristen McGinty, Gloria Amend, Bill Robbins, Sarah Raji for library research, Eddie Fernandez for sharing resources, and Kristen McGinty for her organization/work on the glossary.

At Atomic Dog Publishing, we are indebted to Tom Doran and Ed Laube for their faith and support for the project and to the entire team who worked in sync to bring to life a state-of-the-art product both online and in print. Our principal guide through this process has been Christine Abshire, whom we feel is the absolute best of developmental editors. But those supporting her have also been superb—Vickie Putman, vice president of production; Kathy Davis, production coordinator; Joe Devine, director of interactive media and design; Daniel Brewer and Alaine Ahrens, interactive media designers;

Roger Kammerer, for his extraordinary sketches; Barb McDermott, editorial proofreader; and Chuck Hutchinson, the copy editor, whose talent is reflected throughout the manuscript.

Finally, we are indebted to the professors who teach human sexuality and have shared their vision of and suggestions for what a text for undergraduates should be. Their names and affiliations follow:

Veanne N. Anderson, Indiana State University
M. Betsy Bergen, Kansas State University
Victoria E. Bisorca, California State University, Long Beach
Robert B. Castleberry, University of South Carolina-Sumter Campus
Rodney E. Fowers, Highline Community College
Anne Goshen, California Polytechnic State University
Gordon Hammerle, Adrian College
Gary D. Hampe, University of Wyoming
Clement Handron, East Carolina University
Irene Hanson Frieze, University of Pittsburgh
Pamela B. Hill, San Antonio College
Lindette Lent, Arizona Western College
Laura Madson, New Mexico State University
Lynda Mae, University of Southern Mississippi
Donald Matlosz, Fresno State University
Leslie Minor-Evans, Central Oregon Community College
Jill M. Norvilitis, SUNY College at Buffalo
Howard A. Starr, Austin College
Terry S. Trepper, Purdue University-Calumet
Martin S. Weinberg, Indiana University
Judy Zimmerman, Portland Community College

We are always interested in ways to improve the text, and invite your feedback and suggestions for new ideas and material to include in subsequent editions. We are also interested in dialogue with professors and students about sexuality issues and invite you to e-mail us:

Susan McCammon mccammons@mail.ecu.edu
David Knox knoxd@mail.ecu.edu
Caroline Schacht schacthc@mail.ecu.edu

About the Authors

Susan L. McCammon, Ph.D., is Professor of Psychology at East Carolina University, where she has been teaching a Psychology of Sexual Behavior course during most semesters for the past 22 years. She also teaches in the Master of Arts Program in Clinical Psychology and is Chair and Director, Behavioral/Social Sciences Committee of the University and Medical School Institutional Review Board (for the protection of human subjects in research). She also directs the ECU Social Sciences Training Consortium, which is part of a national initiative to improve services for children with serious emotional problems and their families. Her professional publications include articles and book chapters on the impact of traumatic events, and the effects for trauma responders, teaching about trauma, homonegativity, and preparation of child mental health professionals. Her husband is a professor in Exercise Physiology; they have two teenage sons.

David Knox, Ph.D., is Professor of Sociology at East Carolina University and teaches Sociology of Human Sexuality as well as marriage and family courses. He is the author or co-author of more than 50 research publications and 10 books. He is a marriage/family therapist and married to Caroline Schacht; they have three children. He loves big band music.

Caroline Schacht, MA, is Instructor of Sociology at East Carolina University and emphasizes in her classes the importance of social and cultural forces on making choices. Her clinical work includes marriage, family, and sex therapy. She has won the Sociology Department's teaching award for lower division courses, is a divorce mediator, and is the co-author of several books, including *Choices in Relationships* (8th Edition) and *Understanding Social Problems* (3rd Edition). She is a graduate of clown school at the Barnum and Bailey Circus. Her passion is finding treasures at yard sales.

1

Choices in Sexuality: An Introduction

Chapter Outline

Sex cannot be contained within a definition of physical pleasure; it cannot be understood as merely itself for it has stood for too long as a symbol of profound connection between human beings.

—*Elizabeth Janeway, Between Myth and Morning*

Everyone remembers what he or she labels as his or her first sexual experience—whether it was early sex play with peers, masturbation, pornography, sexual fantasy, intercourse or whatever, it is marked in one's mind as sexual. And not too much later the person becomes aware that making choices about sexuality was part of growing up. Hence, the twin factors of sex and choices were part of our very existence and are the themes we have chosen for this text.

Sexuality is pervasive in our society—sexuality on the Internet, sex in the media (e.g., sex abuse of young boys by Catholic priests), and sexually explicit lyrics in music are but a few of the recurring aspects of sexuality in our society. And, just as our society is responding to economic and national security concerns, we are discovering new challenges to sexual issues in our society. In his call to action to promote sexual health and responsible sexual behavior, former Surgeon General David Satcher (2001) noted that

> *Sexuality is an integral part of human life. It carries the awesome potential to create new life. It can foster intimacy and bonding as well as shared pleasure in our relationships. It fulfills a number of personal and social needs and we value the sexual part of our being for the pleasure and benefits it affords us (p. 1).*

With its potential to contribute to our physical and mental health, sexuality is important throughout the entire lifespan, not just during the reproductive years. It is also important, Satcher observed, that individuals and communities recognize their responsibilities in making choices to protect sexual health. He cautioned that when irresponsible choices are made, sexuality can have negative consequences, including sexually transmitted diseases, unwanted pregnancy, and violent or coercive behavior. Satcher says that doing nothing (e.g., making no choices) to address these problems is unacceptable. His vision for promoting sexual health and responsible sexual behavior includes three fundamental goals of increasing public awareness/education, strengthening health/social interventions, and broadening the research base/providing information that is available from science.

A primary goal of this text is to emphasize the importance of making deliberate and informed sexuality choices. They include not only personal choices but also social choices in the form of enacting social policies or laws and making funding decisions that will impact sexual health and the well-being of our communities and society. Such informed decision making involves knowledge of the psychological, physiological, and social components of sexual functioning, and their interaction with the cultural and social context.

Sexual choices remain at the core of who we are as individuals (our sexual values) and as a nation (our governmental policies about sex on the Internet, sex education in the public school system, abortion, response to the AIDS pandemic, etc.). In this chapter we provide an overview of the text's theme—choices in sexuality. We begin by looking at the elements of human sexuality because making a sexual choice implies an understanding of what is meant by sexuality. We follow this by examining the nature of sexual choices (e.g., "no decision is a decision"), the various factors that influence our sexual choices, and specific steps in making a sexual choice. We then look at how our society is constantly changing and impacts our sexual choices as we prepare for Chapter 2 on sexual values. First, let's examine the various factors that make up human sexuality.

Human sexuality Complex term that includes the elements of thoughts, sexual self-concept, values, emotions, anatomy/physiology, reproduction, and behaviors.

1-1 ELEMENTS OF HUMAN SEXUALITY

Human sexuality is a complex and multifaceted concept. The various elements of human sexuality include thoughts, sexual self-concept, values, emotions, anatomy/physiology, reproduction, and behaviors. They typically occur in interpersonal relationships and are diverse within and between individuals.

1-1a Thoughts

The thoughts we have about sexual phenomena are a major component of human sexuality. Indeed, the major "sex organ" of our body is our brain. The thoughts in terms of interpretation and meaning an individual attaches to a particular sexual act (e.g., intercourse) will influence the subsequent emotions to that sexual behavior. Birnbaum (2003) noted that when intercourse is perceived as a sinful and shameful act, stress and negative affect occur. Homosexuals and heterosexuals may have different thoughts about the genitals of one's same or other sex. One's culture is also influential in determining the interpretations or meanings one has about sexual anatomy.

CULTURAL DIVERSITY 

Americans, for example, are taught to think of the naked breasts of adult women as erotic and inappropriate to display in public. In other societies, such as the Chavantez Indian tribe in Brazil, women's breasts have a neutral erotic meaning associated with them.

Sexual fantasies are thoughts or "stories told to ourselves that are embedded in sexual feelings" (Friedman and Downey, 2000). Engaging in sexual fantasies, alone and together, is sometimes (see section 7-4, "Sexual Fantasies, Sexual Cognitions, and Sexual Dreams") an enjoyable aspect of sexual behavior for some individuals and couples. Indeed, 87% of a sample of 349 university students and employees reported having sexual fantasies in the past two months (Hicks & Leitenbrg, 2001).

1-1b Sexual Self-Concept

Your **sexual self-concept** is the way you think or feel about your body and evaluate your level of interest in sex (highly sexual, asexual) and your value as a sexual partner (accomplished lover, lousy lover). *Body image* refers to the perception of one's own physical appearance and is influenced by cultural definitions of attractiveness. Various industries encourage Americans to feel bad about their weight, breast size, loss of hair, wrinkles, and varicose veins. Weight is a major commercial focus such that individuals are encouraged to think they are less valuable and attractive if their weight does not approximate the cultural ideal. Although both men and women have thoughts about their bodies, Wiederman (2000) developed a scale for women to assess the degree to which they think self-conscious thoughts about their body image when with a partner (see Box 1-1). Men might also take the scale (we predict their concerns will be lower).

Sexual self-concept The way an individual thinks and feels about his or her body, self-evaluation of one's interest in sex, and self-evaluation as a sexual partner.

Think About It 

In considering body image self-consciousness, it is important to keep in mind that in U.S. culture, women's thoughts about themselves as sex partners are influenced by their perception of their physical appearance (Wiederman, 2000). Wiederman's measure looks at body image self-consciousness during physical intimacy with a partner. Actual body size and general body dissatisfaction may not affect sexual enjoyment in the same way. In fact, Wiederman noted that only 7 to 12% of the samples of college women in his studies were obese according to criteria established by the National Center for Health Statistics. He suggested that some of the women with high body image self-consciousness during physical intimacy might have internalized some of our culture's unrealistic standards for female beauty and sex appeal. Cohen and Tannenbaum (2001) found that lesbian and bisexual women were less concerned that their partners be thin and may have rejected the societal fixation on excessive thinness. How would you explain the finding of Cohen and Tannenbaum?

Box 1-1 Self-Assessment

Body Image, Self-Consciousness Scale

To assess your body image and self-consciousness about your body, read each statement and indicate (by selecting a number) how often you agree with each statement or how often you think it would be true for you. The term *partner* refers to someone with whom you are romantically or sexually intimate.

0—Never 1—Rarely 2—Sometimes 3—Often 4—Usually 5—Always

___ 1. I would feel very nervous if a partner were to explore my body before or after having sex.
___ 2. The idea of having sex without any covers over my body causes me anxiety.
___ 3. While having sex I am (would be) concerned that my hips and thighs would flatten out and appear larger than they actually are.
___ 4. During sexual activity, I am (would be) concerned about how my body looks to my partner.
___ 5. The worst part of having sex is being nude in front of another person.
___ 6. If a partner were to put a hand on my buttocks I would think, "My partner can feel my fat."
___ 7. During sexual activity it is (would be) difficult not to think about how unattractive my body is.
___ 8. During sex I (would) prefer to be on the bottom so that my stomach appears flat.
___ 9. I would feel very uncomfortable walking around the bedroom, in front of my partner, completely nude.
___ 10. The first time I have sex with a new partner, I (would) worry that seeing my body without clothes will turn off my partner.
___ 11. If a partner were to put an arm around my waist, I would think, "My partner can tell how fat I am."
___ 12. I (could) only feel comfortable enough to have sex if it were dark so that my partner could not clearly see my body.
___ 13. I (would) prefer having sex with my partner on top so that my partner is less likely to see my body.
___ 14. I (would) have a difficult time taking a shower or bath with a partner.
___ 15. I (would) feel anxious receiving a full-body massage from a partner.

Scoring: Add the numbers you assigned for each of the statements. Possible score could range from zero to 75 with the higher the score, the greater the body image self-consciousness.

Norms: Two-hundred and nine undergraduate women ranging in age from 18 to 21 and mostly (90.9%) White completed the scale. Those who were currently in a dating relationship, had ever had vaginal intercourse, had ever received oral sex from a male and who had ever performed oral sex for a male scored a mean of 20.28, 22.23, 22.18, and 22.34 respectively, in contrast to those who were not in a dating relationship, had never had vaginal intercourse, had never received oral sex from a male, and who had never performed oral sex for a male who had mean scores of 32.29, 36.77, 41.08, and 37.66 respectively. Clearly, those who experienced or predicted the greatest degree of body image self-consciousness during physical intimacy with a partner had less heterosexual experience; conversely, increased heterosexual experience as a woman was associated with lower levels of being self-consciousness about one's body.

Source: Republished with permission of The Society for the Scientific Study of Sex, from *The Journal of Sex Research* from "Women's body image self-consciousness during physical intimacy with a partner" by M. W. Wiederman, (2000). 37, 60–68. Scale from page 68. Permission conveyed through Copyright Clearance Center, Inc.

Wiederman's (2000) data revealed that the woman's body image and sexual activity are linked in that respondents with more negative body images reported fewer sexual experiences. Specifically, even after statistically controlling for actual body size, general body satisfaction, and general sexual anxiety (negative expectations, regarding sexual interaction), women who experienced the greatest degree of body image self-consciousness during physical intimacy with a partner had less heterosexual experience, were less sexually assertive with partners, and reported more avoidance of sexual activity with a partner (p. 66).

Cultural Diversity

Body image concerns are not unique to the United States. Haavio-Mannila and Purhonen (2001) studied women and men in Finland and Russia and found that trim women feel that they are more sexually attractive than stout women and that women more than men feel that their sexual attractiveness is affected by their weight.

Box 1-2 Up Close

Body Piercing

Body piercing, as well as tattooing, is one way of enhancing one's thoughts about one's body. No longer a highly stigmatized practice carried out in the back rooms of adult bookstores or a practice specific to primitive societies, body piercing has become increasingly fashionable (Ed Bradley of CBS's *60 Minutes* has an earring on his left lobe). Although body mutilation in primitive societies is ritualistic and is considered a sign of social position, body piercing in the United States is more a function of providing individuals a strong sense of self and a connection with others, by enhancing people's feeling about their bodies, by providing the rush of the piercing experience, by giving people a way to rebel against mainstream society, and marking relationship events in commitment ceremonies or marking personal triumphs.

Meri Linn Emerson is an example of someone who marked an event by piercing in that she pierced her nose the first time she told her story of being raped to a support group. "They are physical marks of the positive steps I've taken," she noted (Starling, 2001). Other researchers have noted that the motivations for body piercing (anywhere from lobes to labia) also include sexual excitement, pain, aesthetics, mysticism, and shock value (Hanif, Frosh, Marnane, & Ghufoor, 2001). It appears that the most popular places for body piercing are the face or ears with fewer individuals piercing their tongues, nipples, abdomen, buttocks, and genitals.

Although health risks associated with body piercing are small, they should not be discounted. "Tattooing and body piercing has been associated with infections such as Hepatitis B, Hepatitis C, warts, and skin infections. In order to pierce the body or tattoo the skin, you must puncture the skin with a needle or sharp instrument. If the instrument or ink used in tattooing is contaminated with an infection, the person receiving the tattoo or piercing can become infected" (Pinette, 2002, p. 27). Precautions include determining the following:

1. Are the tattoo pigments (coloring) dispensed from single-use containers (which reduce the chance of catching an infection from another person)?
2. Are disposable sterile needles used for each tattoo?

This woman reported that she feels that tattoos and piercings improve her appearance and help screen the type men that she is interested in. "A guy with a lot of piercings and tattoos is the one I'm most attracted to."

3. Is all the equipment sterilized after each use? (Sterilization requires special machines called an autoclave or dry heat sterilizer.)
4. Does the professional tattooer wear disposable latex gloves for each customer and reglove when he or she leaves the area during the procedure?

Physician Pinette recommends, "Take time to evaluate the shops. You will have to live with your decision for the rest of your life" (p. 27).

One's sexual self-image may change in reference to the context. McKenna, Green, and Smith (2001) found that persons who felt stigmatized about certain aspects of their sexual self in general felt a new level of self-acceptance when they connected online with others who were similar. "The anonymity of the Internet interactions allowed these individuals to find others who shared the stigmatized aspect (e.g. homosexuality, bondage, fringe political groups), where finding similar others in non-anonymous real-life settings is virtually impossible" (p.303).

We have been discussing one's thoughts and feelings about one's body. Some people change their body and the way they feel about it by piercing. Box 1-2 on body piercing reflects this cultural phenomenon.

1-1c Values

Remember that sex is not out there, but in here, in the deepest layer of your own being.

—*Jacob Heusner, Words of Wisdom*

Values are moral guidelines for behavior regarded as right and wrong. Sexual values influence one's choices and sexual behavior.

NATIONAL DATA In a national study of college students, 55% of the men and 32% of adult women agreed with the statement "If two people really like each other, it's all right for them to have sex even if they've known each other for only a very short time" (Bartlett, 2002).

Relativism, a value system emphasizing that sexual decisions should be made in reference to the situation (hence, values are relative), is the predominant sexual value among college students. Seventy-three percent of 230 men and 84% of 388 women selected "relativism" as their prevailing sexual value. For most of these undergraduates, if they were in a secure, mutual love relationship, they felt that sexual intercourse was justified (Knox, Cooper, & Zusman, 2001).

Sexual values not only guide individual sexual behavior, but they also guide social policies related to sexual issues. Policies concerning sex with a minor, prostitution, sex on the Internet, sex education, same-sex marriage, abortion, and other sexually related issues are largely shaped by public values concerning sexuality. Alma Golden (2002, p. 97), editor of the journal *Adolescent and Family Health*, observed that in the past two decades Americans "seemed to focus on the value of personal satisfaction and the rights of individuals to pursue their own happiness and interests over the needs of society or family." Efforts directed toward personal fulfillment have sometimes not balanced self-gratification with self-esteem and respect for others. However, in the wake of the terrorist attack in New York, Golden suggests, "The fall of 2001 will be seen as a conclusion to the celebration of self-focus. The heroes and heroines of September are not remembered for their large homes, the size of their bank accounts, their personal independence, their wardrobes, personal fitness or sexual prowess." Their obituaries honored their devotion to work, spouses, family and friends, and compassion for those in need. Out of tragedy's stark reality, Golden discerns an opportunity for those who serve teens and families to educate and encourage, and offer a vision of cherished relationships, compassion, and integrity.

1-1d Emotions

Love and affection are increasingly the only glue that binds couples together.

—*Stephen Nock, sociologist*

Emotions are feelings and an important element of human sexuality. The following poem by Erin Brantley (2002) captures the feelings of emotional desire between two lovers.

LOVER'S HEAT
Racing hearts
Flesh on fire
Two wet bodies
DESIRE
Gazing eyes
Starry looks
Wild feelings
Innocence took
Deep emotion
Temperatures rising
Cravings endured

APPETIZING
Soft touches
Kisses sweet
Shadows of night
Lover's Heat
—Erin Brantley, used by permission

Fisher (2001) noted that humans have an innate attraction system (termed *passionate love*), which is characterized by increased energy and focused attention on a mating partner. These feelings are those of "exhilaration, intrusive thinking about the partner, and a craving for emotional union with the partner" (p. 96).

Although love is a common emotion, guilt, shame, anger, frustration, fear, and disappointment are other emotions that may occur in reference to human sexuality. Goodson, McCormick, and Evans (2001) confirmed a range of emotions college students experience when viewing sexually explicit materials online. They included excitement and anticipation about the activity (34%), guilt for engaging in the activity (29%), and anxiety (31%) about being caught. Feeling entertained (49%) and sexually aroused (33.9%) were the predominant emotions. More than half (51%) of the women and 31% of the men felt "disgusted with what I see" (p. 255).

1-1e Anatomy/Physiology

The idea of sex often brings to mind the thought of naked bodies or anatomy. Hence, the term *human sexuality* implies sexual anatomy, which refers to the external genitalia, secondary sex characteristics (such as a deepened voice in males), and internal reproductive organs of women (e.g., ovaries) and men (e.g., testes). *Physiology* refers to how the parts work or the functioning of the genitals and reproductive system.

1-1f Reproduction

The term *human sexuality* includes reproduction of the species. Sociobiologists, who believe that social behavior has a biological basis, emphasize that much of the sexual interaction that occurs between women and men has its basis in the drive to procreate. Indeed, the perpetuation of the species depends on the sperm and egg uniting. Fisher (2001) pointed out the importance of lust in human reproduction. She noted that **lust** (also known as the **sex drive** or **libido**) is the craving for sexual gratification (biologically driven by estrogen and androgens), which is necessary to "motivate individuals to seek sexual union with any appropriate member of the species" (p. 96).

Lust The craving for sexual gratification (biologically driven by estrogen and androgens) that motivates individuals to seek sexual union. See also **sex drive** and **libido.**

Sex drive The craving for sexual gratification (biologically driven by estrogen and androgens) that motivates individuals to seek sexual union. See also **lust** and **libido.**

Libido The craving for sexual gratification (biologically driven by estrogen and androgens) that motivates individuals to seek sexual union. See also **sex drive** and **lust.**

Think About It

Mackay (2001) noted that sexual reproduction is a relatively recent phenomenon. "Sexual reproduction in animals started only 300 million years ago. Life on earth got on pretty well for 300 million years before that with asexual reproduction. Why do you think there was a change from asexual to sexual reproduction? Biologists came up with a surprising answer: sexual reproduction reduces susceptibility to parasites and also creates new variants making extinction less likely through better adaptation to changing environments and it dilutes disadvantageous genes" (p. 623).

1-1g Behaviors

The term *human sexuality* implies a variety of behaviors. Although people commonly associate the word *sex* with *intercourse*, vaginal intercourse is only one of many sexual behaviors. Masturbation, oral sex, breast stimulation, manual genital stimulation, and anal intercourse are also sexual behaviors. However, the definition of what is *sex* is sometimes illusive. A team of researchers (Bogart, Cecil, Pinkerton, & Abramson, 2000) studied 223 undergraduates (both women and men) and found that while 97% considered vaginal intercourse and 93% considered anal intercourse as *sex*, only 44% considered oral intercourse as *sex*. The gender of the respondent and whether orgasm occurred were also operative in whether a behavior was identified as sex. Women were more likely to report a behavior as *sex* and the term *sex* was more likely to be used if an orgasm occurred.

Some behaviors may or may not be experienced as sexual, depending on the context and the definitions used by the respective partners. For example, kissing, touching, and caressing may be considered sexual behaviors with a lover, but not with a friend.

1-1h Interpersonal Relationships

It's not the men in your life that count, it's the life in your men.

—Mae West, 1930s actress

Although masturbation and sexual fantasies can occur outside the context of a relationship, much of sexuality occurs in the context of an interpersonal relationship. Such relationships may be heterosexual or homosexual; nonmarital, marital, or extramarital; casual or intimate; personal or business-related (as in phone sex and prostitution); and brief or long-term. The type of emotional and social relationship a couple has affects the definition and quality of their sexual relationship.

NATIONAL DATA Anderson, Wilson, Doll, Jones, and Baker (2000) analyzed a national sample of U.S. adults and noted that only 19% of those in an ongoing love relationship used a condom, whereas 62% used a condom if their partner was not someone they were seeing regularly.

1-1i Diversity

Sexual behaviors, thoughts, emotions, and values vary within the same person, between people, and between cultures. For example, the same person may have multiple sex partners at one age, but may be monogamous or celibate at another age. The more diverse the population of a society, the more the members of that society vary in the types of sexual behaviors they engage in and in their sexual thoughts, feelings, values, and relationships. As we have seen, even the definition of sex is such that there is no universal meaning of the term *sex* (Mackay, 2001). Given the ethnic, racial, and religious diversity of the population in the United States, the sexual diversity and variability among members of the U.S. population are not surprising.

CULTURAL DIVERSITY

When a cross-cultural perspective is considered, variations in sexuality become even more extensive. For example, although homosexual behavior is viewed as a variant sexual lifestyle in the United States, in the New Guinea Highlands, it is regarded as a pathway to heterosexuality (Herdt, 1981, 1989). Among the Sambia (New Guinea Highlands), preadolescent boys are taught to perform fellatio (oral sex) on older unmarried males and ingest their sperm. They do this believing it enables them to produce their own sperm in adulthood, thereby ensuring their ability to impregnate their wives.

Evidence of cultural diversity is also illustrated when comparing the sexual behavior of adults in France and the United States. A team of researchers (Gagnon, Giami, Michaels, & DeColomby, 2001) examined national data and found that the French are more likely to be monogamous than persons living in the United States.

Definitions of what is a family are also changing. Traditional heterosexual marriage is giving way to a diverse set of family patterns: single parents, gay/lesbian parents, divorced and blended families (Ferguson, 2001).

1-1j Personal Choices: Why Take a Course in Human Sexuality?

College students take courses in human sexuality for a variety of academic, personal, and career-related reasons. Some students sign up for human sexuality courses because they fulfill social science or elective requirements for graduation. Others take such courses to examine their own sexuality and gain knowledge that may help them make informed sexual choices. Still other students study human sexuality in preparation for careers as sex educators or therapists. Knowledge about sexuality is also very important for persons in a variety of occupational fields, including psychology, nursing, health education, and medicine. Michael (2001) noted that sexual activity has at least six "products": physical pleasure, emotional satisfaction, intimate bonding with one's partner that may promote love, reputation or peer judgment, the probability of pregnancy, and the probability of contracting a sexually transmitted disease. These products are of interest to individuals, academics, and researchers. Who wouldn't want to take a course in human sexuality? The fact that human sexuality courses are among the first to fill is not surprising.

You may wonder how your values or behavior might be influenced by taking a human sexuality course. In one community in the northeastern United States, a concerned group claimed that the sexuality education courses offered at the local community college were promoting early sexual activity and undermining the students' morals. The faculty surveyed 1,825 students taking human sexuality and health courses at the beginning and end of the courses. They found no evidence of changes in the basic moral system of students; student attitudes on the issues of abortion and premarital, casual, or oral sex had not changed by the end of the course. However, they did find some decrease in the students' risk for health-related problems. Following the course, the students who were sexually active reported fewer sexual partners and more frequent use of birth control (Feigenbaum & Weinstein, 1995).

Voss and Kogan (2001) also reported data on undergraduate university students who took a human sexuality course. Although the students who took the course did not increase their sexual experimentation, they were just as likely to take sexual risks (e.g., no condom use) when compared with students who did not take such a course. However, students who took the sexuality course were more likely to engage in health-promoting behaviors such as regularly conducting breast or testicular self-exams.

1-2 NATURE OF SEXUAL CHOICES

Having examined the various elements of the term *human sexuality*, we look at the nature of sexual choices—the theme of our text.

1-2a Not to Decide Is to Decide

The only time we really do not have a choice is when it never occurs to us that we do.
—Michael Schwalbe, sociologist

Not making a decision is a decision by default. For example, if you are having oral, vaginal, or anal intercourse and do not make a conscious decision or choice to use a latex condom (or dental dam), you have inadvertently made a decision or choice to increase your risk for contracting a sexually transmitted disease including HIV. If you are having vaginal intercourse and do not decide to use birth control, you have decided to risk pregnancy. If you do not monitor and restrict your alcohol or drug use at parties or in a new relationship, you have made a decision to drift toward unprotected sex. Indeed, if you don't make explicit sexual decisions about what you will and will not do and act on these decisions, you may have already made a decision to contract a sexually transmitted disease by default.

1-2b Choices Involve Trade-Offs

People can choose to nurture a positive, long-term vision of their relationship.
—Scott Stanley, W. C. Lobitz, Fran Dickson, researchers

All the choices you make will involve trade-offs or disadvantages, as well as advantages. The choice to cheat on your partner may provide excitement, but it may also produce feelings of guilt and may lead to the breakup of your relationship. The choice to tell your partner of an indiscretion may deepen your feelings of intimacy, but by doing so, you may risk your partner's leaving you. The choice to have an abortion may enable you to avoid the hardship of continuing an unwanted pregnancy, but it may also involve feelings of guilt, anxiety, or regret. Likewise, the choice to continue an unwanted pregnancy may enable you to experience the joy of having a child and allow you to avoid the guilt associated with having an abortion, but it may also involve the hardships of inopportune parenting or placing the baby for adoption.

1-2c Choices Include Selecting a Positive or Negative View

Regardless of your circumstances, you can choose to view a situation in positive terms. The skill of developing a positive view can be used in unlimited situations. The discovery of your partner having an affair can be viewed as an opportunity to open channels of communication with your partner and strengthen your relationship. One woman reported that dealing with her diagnosis of genital herpes helped her avoid potential partners who were not willing to work through the complications in the relationship. Being rejected by one's family members because of sexual orientation may be viewed positively as an opportunity to develop closer relationships with those family members who accept homosexuality.

1-2d Choices Produce Ambivalence and Uncertainty

Listen to your senses and make your decision.
—Jack Turner, psychologist

Ambivalence Conflicting feelings that coexist, producing uncertainty or indecisiveness about a person, object, idea, or course of action.

Choosing among options often creates **ambivalence**—conflicting feelings that produce uncertainty or indecisiveness about the next course of action. Many sexual choices involve ambivalence. For example, consider the conflicting feelings and uncertainty that would accompany the following decisions:

- When and with whom should I become sexually active?
- Should I report a family member who has sexually abused me?
- Should I have an abortion or continue an unwanted pregnancy?
- Should I keep an unplanned child that was conceived in a casual relationship or place the baby for adoption?
- Should I come out of the closet and tell my family that I am gay?
- Should I accept my co-worker's invitation to spend the night together at a conference (which means cheating on my partner)?
- Should I forgive my partner for having an affair or should I terminate the relationship?

Ambivalence occurs when one has many options to choose from. In the United States, for example, a young unmarried pregnant woman has the option of choosing to have an abortion, to rear the baby in a single-parent home, to place the baby for an adoption, and maybe to marry the biological father and keep the baby. A woman choosing any one of these options may forever reconsider if she made the right decision and blame herself for whatever decision she made. "If only I had," she may think.

Ambivalence may also occur when there are conflicting norms and values. For example, in the United States, individuals may be ambivalent about abortion because there are conflicting values regarding abortion, as evidenced by the pro-choice and antiabortion movements. Similarly, the decision of whether to engage in nonmarital sex may produce ambivalence because of the conflicting norms and values regarding nonmarital sex. One's parents and religion may convey that nonmarital sex is wrong, whereas one's peers and the media may indicate that it is acceptable and desirable.

1-2e Some Choices Are Revocable; Some Are Not

Some sexual choices are revocable; that is, they can be changed. For example, a person who has chosen to have sex with multiple partners can subsequently decide to be faithful to one partner or to abstain from sexual relations. An individual who, in the past, has chosen to accept being sexually unsatisfied in an ongoing relationship ("I never told him how to get me off," said one woman) can decide to address the issue or seek sex therapy with the partner.

Although many sexual choices can be modified or changed, some cannot. You cannot eliminate the effects of some sexually transmissible diseases, undo an abortion, or be a virgin after you have had intercourse.

1-2f Sexual Choices Are Learned

The movie *Monster's Ball* (for which Halle Berry won the best actress award in 2002) depicted how one's choice of a sexual partner is learned. Billy Bob Thornton played the role of a racist who is emotionally devastated when his son (who befriends Blacks) commits suicide. Thornton quits his job as a corrections officer in charge of executions, is lonely, and in grief. He stops to pick up a woman (played by Halle Berry) whose child has just been hit by a car and takes them to the hospital. The son dies and Thornton responds to help the grieving mother. They spend time together, drink, and have sex. Feelings develop on both sides as they navigate Thornton's racist father and his own climb from racism. Sex is embedded in the context of two people who need each other, and a loving relationship is formed. Their developing relationship shows how individuals who are reared to avoid each other can forge an emotional/sexual relationship given a particular set of environmental contexts.

1-3 INFLUENCES ON SEXUAL CHOICES

Whenever we make a sexual choice, we are being influenced by a myriad of factors. They include those described in sections 1-3a through 1-3h.

1-3a Emotional Influences

Arthur Schopenhauer, the German philosopher (1788–1860), noted that rather than wanting something because we have reasons for it, we tend to find reasons for something because we want it (Durant, 1962). In effect, Schopenhauer believed that we are driven by emotions and that we construct explanations for what we do as an afterthought. Love is a powerful emotion that influences sexual choices.

NATIONAL DATA Based on a national probability sample of 1,511 men between the ages of 18 and 59, the odds of their reporting that their last sexual experience was physically pleasurable were 7.4 times higher if they had sex to express love for their partner. Of 1,921 women between the ages of 18 and 59, the odds were 8.6 times higher (Waite & Joyner, 2001, p. 263).

1-3b Cultural Constraints

The society in which you live affects the attitudes you develop about sexuality. A team of researchers (Weinberg, Lottes, & Shaver, 2000) compared American and Swedish university students and found that the latter were less negative and more permissive about sexual expression. Indeed, the acceptance of a naturalistic view of sexuality among the Swedes leads to a more tolerant attitude toward sexual expression.

Social and cultural values, roles, norms, and laws also influence sexual choices. For example, the current emphasis on the social value of safe sex has increased the number of individuals who are choosing to use condoms. Traditional gender roles taught women that they should not initiate sexual intimacy and taught men to be the initiator in relationships. The changing roles of women and men have led to more women choosing to initiate sex in their relationships. Finally, governmental laws and policies may affect sexual choices by restricting or allowing, for example, access to abortion, prostitution, and certain methods of birth control. Additionally, sexual harassment laws and policies influence individuals' choices about how to interact with their employees, co-workers, and students.

1-3c Previous Decisions

Sexual choices are often affected by previous sexual choices. A partner who has chosen not to use pregnancy prevention may be faced with a choice about whether to continue or terminate an unwanted pregnancy. An individual in a committed relationship who has chosen to have an affair must also decide whether to disclose the affair to the partner. A person who has chosen to engage in unprotected, high-risk sexual behavior may then be faced with the choice of whether to be tested for HIV and other sexually transmitted diseases, and whether to disclose this infection to his or her partner.

1-3d Alcohol and Drug Use

Alcohol and drug use affect one's mood, judgment, and sexual choices. LaBrie and Earleywine (2000) found that 65% of 244 undergraduates reported having had intercourse without a condom after drinking. Alcohol consumption not only impairs judgment but also lowers inhibitions and often results in individuals making sexual choices that they would not have made if they were sober. Indeed, when we (the authors of your text) ask our students to identify the sexual choice they most regret, a frequent comment is "I got drunk and had unprotected sex."

Alcohol and other drugs affect not only what choices one makes, but whether one makes a choice at all. How can a person choose to have sex or not, or to use a condom or not, if that person is impaired or has passed out from alcohol or other drug use?

1-3e Peers

Our lives are shaped by the choices and actions of others around us.
—Lorne Tepperman, Susannah Wilson, sociologists

Peers are a major source of sexual knowledge. A sample of 269 high school students reported that their sexual knowledge was gathered from friends (70%), television (62%), parents (51%), books and sex education at school (47% each), with only 16% referring to siblings as informants. Fifteen percent, nearly all boys, had obtained sexual knowledge from pornography (Larsson & Svedin, 2002).

In addition to providing knowledge, peers influence sexual choices. A team of researchers (Nahom et al., 2001) asked a sample of more than 300 tenth graders, "How much pressure do you feel from others to have sex?" The respondents answered on a four-point continuum where 1 = none and 4 = a lot. The mean response was 2.18, with the girls feeling more pressure than the boys. Although direct pressure from peers in mid-adolescence does not appear to be extensive on sexual choices, the more subtle influence may be the perception of the sexual behavior of one's peers. For example, the tenth graders were also asked, "How many of your friends who are your age are having sexual intercourse?" On a seven-point continuum from 1= none of them to 7 = all of them, those tenth graders who had already had sex predicted a mean of 5.10 (five = more than half), whereas those teens who had not had sex predicted a mean of 3.18 (three = less than half). Clearly, those who perceived that their peers had already had sex tended to mirror similar sexual behavior in their own choices.

1-3f Family Factors

Various family factors, including family composition and relationships, values, and economic resources, influence sexual choices. For example, your family's economic resources may influence your choices about what type of birth control to use, whether to seek sexual health care (such as Pap tests and mammograms), and whether to continue an unplanned pregnancy. If your parents are an interracial couple or have values that are accepting of interracial couples, you may be more open to date and/or marry individuals of various races. Conversely, if your parents disapprove of interracial couples, you may feel less freedom to date individuals of a different race. If you already have two children of the same sex, you may be more likely to choose to have a third child than you would if you already had one child of each sex.

Family members can also influence your choices by giving directives such as, "If you are going to have sex, use a condom every time" or "Before you decide to have sex, tell me and I'll take you to a doctor and get you birth control pills." A student in the authors' class talked about how her parents pressured her to have an abortion when she was 17: "My parents told me to have an abortion or they would disown me. While I could have had the baby (and sometimes wish I had), I felt like the abortion was the thing to do."

Although it is sometimes assumed that family structure such as growing up in a single-parent, step, or cohabiting family would impact adolescent sexual behavior, Davis and Friel (2001) analyzed data on 6,261 girls and 6,106 boys ages 11 and 18 and found that structure does not automatically influence when an adolescent first has intercourse. Rather, the researchers found that the relationship mothers have with their daughters, their interaction, and the mothers' attitudes toward and discussion of sex was related to the age at which daughters began having sexual intercourse. Table 1-1 presents examples of factors and the decisions that may occur as a result of their influence.

TABLE 1-1

How Various Factors Can Influence a Sexual Decision

Factors	Decisions
Emotional influences	The more a couple is in love, the greater the chance of sexual intercourse occurring.
Cultural influences	Liberal, individualistic sexual norms in the United States increase the chance that a couple will choose to have intercourse as compared to conservative, familistic sexual norms in countries such as Japan and China.
Alcohol/drug use	Being "high" on alcohol or other drugs increases the chance of sexual intercourse.
Peer influence	Having peers who are sexually active and a partner who encourages sexual behavior increases the chance of deciding to have intercourse.
Family factors	Having liberal parents who encourage their son or daughter to take birth control measures and to "be safe" increases the likelihood that sexually active offspring will do so.

1-3g Locus of Control

Locus of control An individual's beliefs about the source or cause (internal or external) of his or her successes and failures.

Internal locus of control Belief that the successes and failures in life are attributable to one's own abilities and efforts.

External locus of control Perspective that successes and failures are determined by fate, chance, or some powerful external source.

Many psychological constructs are believed to influence sexuality, including self-esteem, attachment style, personality characteristics and styles (impulsiveness, sensation-seeking, dependency, etc.), and locus of control. In this section we focus on locus of control because it is especially relevant to decision making. The term **locus of control** refers to an individual's beliefs about the source or cause of his or her successes and failures. A person with an **internal locus of control** believes that successes and failures in life are attributable to his or her own abilities and efforts. A person with an **external locus of control** believes that successes and failures are determined by fate, chance, or some powerful external source (such as other individuals). In section 1-3h we consider the degree to which one is "free" to make sexual choices versus the degree to which external or social forces are operative.

1-3h Personal Choices: Do You or Other Factors Control Your Sexual Choices?

What do the following questions have in common?

- Is sex with an attractive stranger worth the risk of contracting HIV or other sexually transmitted disease?
- How and when do I bring up the issue of using a condom with a new partner?
- Can I find dating partners who will honor my value of being abstinent until marriage?
- How much do I tell my new partner about my previous sexual experiences (masturbation, number of sexual partners, homosexual encounters)?
- Do I disclose to my partner that I have fantasies about sex with other people?
- What type of birth control should my partner and I use?

Each of these questions involves making a sexual choice. One of the main goals of this text is to emphasize the importance of making deliberate and informed choices about your sexuality. The alternative is to let circumstances and others decide for you. Informed decision making involves knowledge of the psychological, physiological, and social components of sexual functioning, personal values, and the interaction between cultural values and sexual behaviors.

Free will Belief that although heredity and environment may influence our choices, individuals are ultimately in charge of their own destinies.

Determinism Belief that one's choices are largely determined by heredity and environment.

Choices may be the result of **free will.** The belief in free will implies that although heredity and environment may influence our choices, individuals are ultimately in charge of their own destinies. Even when our lives are affected by circumstances or events that we do not choose, we can still choose how to view and respond to those circumstances and events.

An alternative and competing assumption of making deliberate choices is **determinism**—the idea that our choices are largely determined by heredity and environment. Being born with a particular sexual orientation reflects determinism in the sense that sexual orientation may have a biological or genetic base. Determinism may also have a social basis. Sociologists emphasize that choices are heavily influenced by social forces such as the society in which one lives, one's family, and one's peers. This is a social context view of choices. Hence, most people are not free to live a homosexual lifestyle because of social disapproval. Similarly, the fact that less than one half of one percent of all marriages in the United States consist of a Black and White spouse (*Statistical Abstract of the United States: 2002*, Table 47) suggests that social factors may be operative in mate selection (social approval for selecting same race individuals and disapproval for selecting other race individuals).

Rather than view sexual choices as something we control or as something that is controlled by other factors, each view contributes to an understanding of sexual choices. In Table 1-2, we present some of the advantages and disadvantages of these two views.

♦

TABLE 1-2

Who Controls Our Choices? Advantages and Disadvantages of Different Views

Views	Advantages	Disadvantages
View 1: We Control Our Choices	Gives individuals a sense of control over their lives. Encourages individuals to take responsibility for their choices.	Blames individuals for their unwise sexual choices. Fails to acknowledge the influence of social and cultural factors on sexual choices.
View 2: Other Factors Influence Our Choices	Recognizes how emotions, peers, and cultural factors influence our lives and choices. Implies that making changes in our social and cultural environment may be necessary to help us make better choices.	Blames social and cultural factors for our own sexual choices. Discourages individuals from responsibility for their behaviors and choices.

1-4 MAKING SEXUAL CHOICES

Having identified the various elements that comprise the concept of human sexuality, reviewed the nature of sexual choices, and examined the influences on them, we look at what is involved in making wise sexual decisions. Although few of us carefully think out each sexual decision we make, we might benefit from following basic decision-making steps. Willingness to learn from previous decisions is also important for making wise sexual choices.

1-4a Basic Decision-Making Steps

The basic steps in decision making include the following. We will use the example of a couple facing the issue of the future of their relationship.

1. *Clarify values and goals*. Assess the degree to which the partners agree on whether they want to continue the relationship with the goal of a permanent relationship, including marriage. If only one wants a future, is the other willing to continue the relationship under these conditions?
2. *Understand one's motives and identifying feelings and emotions*. Each partner should make clear his or her feelings about the other and his or her reasons for wanting to continue or discontinue the relationship. The range of expressions can be from "I love you and want to marry you because I have never felt so right about a relationship before" to "I wish I loved you, but my feelings are more of friendship and I think it would only damage a great friendship to lead you on."
3. *Identify and explore alternative courses of action*. Breaking up now, continuing the relationship now with no further discussion to see what happens, or continuing the relationship with both parties knowing that there are different goals for the future are the alternative courses of action.
4. *Seek information that makes the short-term and long-term consequences clear for each choice*. Seeing a counselor who will help the partners assess their feelings about each other and the relationship, reading "relationship books" such as *Choices in Relationships* (Knox & Schacht, 2002), and exploring Internet sites such as rightmate.heartchoice.com, which focus on finding a compatible partner, will provide additional information for the partners.
5. *Weigh the positive and negative consequences for each alternative*.
   - *Breaking up now*—Positive consequence: getting the hurt over with now; Negative consequence: ending a relationship prematurely may be to end a relationship that might eventually flourish.
   - *Continue the relationship*—Positive consequence: The partners can continue to enjoy each other; Negative consequence: The partners are not making themselves available to new relationships that have a joint future.

6. *Select an alternative that has maximum positive consequences and minimal negative consequences*. The partners might decide that because their relationship will eventually end they will continue to see each other but make themselves open to seeing other people. Ideally, each partner would meet someone new and launch a new life as he or she slowly disengages from the current relationship. In reality, the more likely scenario is that the more involved person will have difficulty disengaging from the current relationship and finding a new partner with the attendant negative feelings. Hence, there is not always a solution that provides an immediate positive outcome for both parties. However, the long-term consequence of breaking up and moving on is that each partner can end up in a mutually valued relationship that has a future.
7. *Implement one's decision*. This step involves putting step 6 into action.

1-4b Important Skills for Decision Making

A variety of skills are helpful when making decisions. Information-gathering skills, such as reading and library or computer research, may be helpful in identifying alternative courses of action and projecting negative and positive consequences of various alternatives. Implementing one's decision may require skills in assertiveness and the ability to resist social pressure from peers or parents. It may also involve assertiveness in seeking guidance and social support.

Sometimes sexual choices are made by couples or groups, rather than by individuals. For example, a couple may be faced with the choice of whether to have a vasectomy, whether to seek sex therapy, or whether to take fertility drugs to become pregnant. A group, such as a state legislature, may be faced with the decision of whether to mandate sex education in the public schools, and if so, at what grade levels and with what curriculum. When decisions are made by couples or groups, additional decision-making skills are needed, including communication and listening skills that enable individuals to effectively convey and listen to each other's ideas and concerns. Negotiation and collaboration skills are also important for couple and group decision making.

Another decision-making skill is the ability to learn from past experience. We have all made decisions we regret. Making poor decisions is inevitable to some degree; it is part of growing up and part of life. To learn from our experiences, we might ask ourselves, "What could we have done differently?" and "What will we do differently in the future to avoid making a similar mistake?" Many of our students report that making sexual decisions when they have drunk too much alcohol increases the risk of unintended pregnancy and HIV or other sexually transmitted diseases. Moderating or reducing the level of drinking results in reducing the risks of such consequences.

We also can learn from the experiences of others, such as friends and family members. Evaluating the positive experiences that come with making good choices and the negative experiences that come with making poor choices is yet another way we can learn. Table 1-3 describes some of the best and worst choices reported by students in the authors' classes. As you read the table, think about what each student may have learned from his or her best and worst choices.

Walters (2001) teaches human sexuality and regularly conducts a class activity in which he invites students to write and submit a brief narrative of their best and worst sexual experiences. The narratives are shared in class (with safeguards to guarantee anonymity), and although students reported that they initially assumed the purpose of this class activity was entertainment, they began to observe prominent themes. Among the negative experiences, excessive alcohol intake associated with lower sexual performance and satisfaction, and consistent frequency of reports of sexual assault and coercion were noted. Frequently occurring positive experiences included expressing mutual love and adoration, giving and receiving physical pleasure. Box 1-3 looks at some of the experiences of **"hooking up."**

Hookup A sexual encounter (physical interaction that might or might not include intercourse), usually lasting just one night, between two people who are strangers or just briefly acquainted.

Box 1-3 Up Close

Factors Involved in "Hookups"

In trying to understand current collegiate sexual experiences, it may be helpful to look at the various factors associated with making sexual choices in regard to "hooking up." Paul, McManus, and Hayes (2000) examined the relative importance of social, relational, and individual psychological variables to see which differentiated between college students who engage in hookups (with intercourse and without) and those who do not.

A hookup was defined as a sexual encounter (physical interaction that might or might not include intercourse), usually lasting just one night, between two people who are strangers or just briefly acquainted. A random sample of undergraduate students living on campus completed questionnaires; 555 students participated. Almost all the students (98%) identified themselves as heterosexual. About one third were men and two thirds were women, with an overrepresentation of upperclassmen (35% juniors and 39% seniors).

Among the respondents, half reported having experienced at least one hookup that did not involve sexual intercourse; 30% reported having experienced a hookup that did include sexual intercourse; 22% reported never having hooked up. Included in the factors which discriminated between those who hooked up and those who did not were alcohol intoxication and ludus/storge love styles (game-playing and companionate love; see section 2-4a, "Love: Conceptions, Elements, and Styles," for a description of these styles).

Not surprisingly, another study found factors predictive of early sexual behavior of younger students. Using data collected through the National Longitudinal Study of Adolescent Health (1,372 students in grades 7 and 8, and 2,515 students in grades 9–12), Lynch (2002) found that the degree of family interaction/bonding and higher family economic status were related to less early sexual activity. For the younger students, self-esteem, and for the older students, academic achievement were related to delaying initiation of intercourse. For both age groups, substance use (especially drinking alcohol) was associated with sexual activity.

As investigators search to understand the complex issues influencing sexual activity, their findings can provide a clearer picture of the web of factors to which parents, educators, and service providers should attend. In addition, the research results can be informative to individuals who might apply such knowledge to their own decision making.

TABLE 1-3

Best and Worst Choices: Student Experiences

Best Choice	Worst Choice
Ending my relationship with someone I loved who was unfaithful to me.	Cheating on my partner: it wasn't worth it. The guilt has been almost unbearable.
Insisting on using a condom with a person I had just met. I later found out the person had an STD.	Cheating on my partner.
Forgiving my partner for cheating on me.	Being unfaithful to my partner.
Getting out of a relationship with someone who was married.	Getting into a relationship with someone who was married.
Waiting for more than a year to have sex in a relationship.	Getting drunk and having sex with people I didn't know.
Getting out of a sex- and drug-focused relationship.	Having unprotected sex on a one-night stand.
Getting out of a relationship with a partner who was jealous.	Trying to make my partner jealous.

1-5 SOCIAL CHANGES AND SEXUAL CHOICES

Whenever you make a sexual choice, you do so in the context of a changing society. For example, traditional family forms, virginity until marriage, and "till death do us part" marriages of your grandparents' generation have been replaced to some extent by alternative lifestyles (single-parent families, gay families), early sexual activity, and relatively high divorce rates. The cultural and social climates for choices are different for this generation. Some of the recent social changes that have affected human sexuality are discussed in sections 1-5a through 1-5h.

1-5a Sexuality on Television

A major social change affecting sexuality is the openness with which sex is treated on television.

NATIONAL DATA A team of researchers conducted a content analysis of 5,152 separate scenes from broadcast and cable television episodes in 1989–1999 and revealed that nearly two thirds (63%) consisted of sexual visual images ranging from nudity to simulated intercourse (Lichter, Lichter, & Amundson, 2001).

Popular television shows such as *Sex and the City* deal with explicit issues such as masturbation, orgasm, oral and anal sex. The drama series *Six Feet Under* has themes of homosexuality, homophobia, single parenting, infidelity, and swinging. Talk shows including those hosted by Dr. Phil, Oprah, and Jerry Springer feature programs on marital sexuality, acquaintance rape, infidelity, and transsexualism. MTV features specials in which college students are shown on spring break amid a frenzy of alcohol and sex. Music videos are often erotic; lyrics, too, contain sexual messages. In the national study of sex on television (Lichter et al., 2001), the authors commented:

> *...the most sex-oriented video was "Anywhere," with 37 sexual scenes (including lyrics as well as images) jammed into about three minutes of playing time, although only five were hard-core in nature. Providing a greater impression of sex-drenched material was LL Cool J's appropriately titled "Doin' It," which contained 27 sexual scenes, 11 of them hard-core. The leader in hard-core material was Jordan Knight's "Give It to You" with 14 hard-core images out of 15 overall (p. 3).*

Sex and the City reflects the new era of sexuality in our society—open and blatant.

Photofest

Televised sexuality has both positive and negative influences on sexual choices. On the positive side, reports on sexual abuse, date rape, and the "date rape drug" Rohypnol have helped to bring these abuses into public awareness. Media attention on HIV infection and other sexually transmitted diseases provides a valuable public educational service. Colleges and universities, billboards, subways, buses, and other public places often display educational posters with such messages as "Use condom sense" and "Against her will is against the law."

On the negative side, the media have been criticized for portraying women as sexual objects, depicting sexuality in violent contexts, and contributing to women's negative body images and self-concepts by portraying desirable women as only those who are young, thin, and beautiful. The media also may be criticized for exposing youth to sexually explicit images before they are old enough to make responsible sexual choices. Indeed, more than one half of the programming on prime-time television watched by teens has sexual content (Cope-Farrar & Kunkel, 2002). The Surgeon General noted "Rarely does media programming depict sexual behavior in the context of a long-term relationship, use of contraceptives, or the potentially negative consequences of sexual behavior" (Satcher, 2001).

1-5b Sexuality on the Internet

The Internet has been identified as "the next sexual revolution" (Cooper, Bois, Maheu, & Greenfield, 2001). For confirmation, log on to the Internet, where there are 100,000 web sites dedicated to sex (Carnes, 2001) and type in "sex" into any search engine. The Internet features erotic photos, videos, viewing sex acts "live," and directing a strip session "live." Individuals can exchange nude photos, have explicit sex dialogue, arrange to have "phone sex," meet in person, or find a prostitute. Individuals who "previously would never have ventured into a porn shop or ordered sex products through the mail now feel comfortable exploring explicit material from the privacy of their personal computers. Visits to pornography sites doubled in 2000, outpacing the rate of new Internet users and lavishing some sites with as many as 50 million hits" (Worden, 2001).

A major market is youth. Ninety percent of people ages 15–24 (or 28 million people) report having been online (Thomas, 2001). Almost 80% (77.4%) of 191 undergraduates (men more than women) reported having visited a sex site on their computer and 5% reported having given their credit card for membership to a sex site (Knox, Daniels, Sturdivant, & Zusman, 2001). Some become addicted to cybersex. A survey conducted by the Marital and Sexuality Center and MSNBC (2002) found that 6.5% of the male Internet population reported spending nearly six hours per week engaging in cybersex. Their motive was to relieve stress rather than to see sex online as entertainment or information.

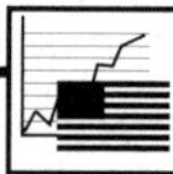

NATIONAL DATA Eighty-two percent of college students (men slightly more than women) report the use of a personal computer in the past 12 months (Bartlett, 2002).

INTERNATIONAL DATA Two thirds of 343 university students at a major Singapore university reported that they have been exposed to X-rated materials on the Internet (Wu & Koo, 2001).

Sex on the Internet has both positive and negative consequences and poses many ethical dilemmas. The advantages are educational, social, emotional, cognitive, and improved sexual health. As a sex education tool, the various search engines allow individuals to surf the Net for recent, accurate sex information. New information on the treatment of sexually transmitted diseases and sexual dysfunctions is available instantly and anonymously. Go Ask Alice is an online question-and-answer sex information resource sponsored by Columbia University. Alice fields questions on sex, relationships, drugs, and other topics. No question is taboo.

Socially, the Internet serves as a mechanism to connect individuals who want to meet others with similar interests (Benotsch, Kalichman, & Cage, 2002). Various mate matching or dating services provide an unlimited pool of individuals from which to choose, and participants may connect online immediately. This alternative for meeting others is particularly valuable for persons with limited time or mobility. The following reflects the experience of a divorced woman who met a new partner online:

> *I was 28, recently divorced from an eight-year marriage, and alone. I didn't want to complicate my life by getting involved with anyone at work and I didn't like the loud smoky bar routine. Alone one night, I turned on my computer, logged onto one of the commercial services, and went to one of the bulletin boards where a lot of people "hang out." I posted a note entitled, "Make me laugh." I thought this was innocuous enough as I did not want to appear desperate.*
>
> *To my surprise, I received over 50 responses. Most (85%) were from guys seeking cybersex, a few shared jokes, and still fewer just wanted to talk. Soon I was regularly sending notes to men in five different states. After several weeks I fell in love with one of them, arranged to meet him, and fell deeper in love. But he was recently divorced and didn't want to tie himself to one partner. I was heartbroken and alone again . . . but turned my computer back on.*
>
> *A man from Arizona began to pique my interest. Suddenly we began to e-mail each other nightly and share our histories, interests, values, and goals. Within a short time, I knew I had discovered my soul mate and fell even more deeply in love with this man than the previous cyber man. After a photo exchange, hours of phone conversations, and enormous phone bills (I mean $400 monthly phone bills), we met and discovered that we had found the love of our lives.*
>
> *Quickly we planned to meet each other's family and were married in six weeks. Although this sounds very impulsive, we discussed every imaginable issue and just felt that this was "right." Although we met six states away from each other via computer, we now live in our home and are rearing our twins born last month. Meeting "on-line" certainly worked for us. (Authors' files).*

Emotionally, the Internet may connect separated lovers. An end-of-the-day e-mail is one way some pair-bonded partners maintain their long-distance relationships. Others may be unhappy in their personal and interpersonal lives and may derive immense satisfaction from online love relationships.

Cognitively, the Internet may meet sexual fantasy needs. Individuals with similar sexual interests and fetishes may exchange photos and play out their sexual fantasies online. Safe sex is a benefit of Internet sex. Individuals can share sexual fantasies online with no risk of contracting sexually transmissible diseases.

But sexuality on the Internet has its disadvantages. A team of researchers (Mitchell, Finkelhor, & Wolak, 2001) analyzed data on a national random sample of 1,501 youth aged 10 through 17 years and found that almost one in five (19%) who used the Internet regularly were targets of unwanted sexual solicitation in the past year. These adolescents reported high levels of distress after these solicitation incidents (the solicitor attempted or made offline contact). Barron and Kimmel (2000) noted the nonconsensual sexual violence portrayed on Usenet (Internet newsgroups). And there is the concern of dependence on Net relationships and the potential for infidelity. Indeed, there is an Internet site set up by a "bored" housewife "for spouses to find discreet partners to have sex on the side." Schneider (2000) noted that the most pervasive of symptoms of cybersex was the partner's withdrawal from family and friends.

Because social, emotional, and sexual connections can be made quickly on the computer, people might abandon face-to-face relationships in reality. Indeed, they might become so socially isolated with their computer relationships that they neglect the development of their live interpersonal skills and relationships. One woman complained that "he's always in there on the computer and would rather be in chat rooms than in the room with me" (authors' files). Young et al. (2000) noted that the anonymity, convenience, and escape features of the Internet account for the impetus to use the computer to find a cybersex partner and that "electronic communication" can lead to marital discord, separation, and divorce. Schneider (2000) studied 91 women who had experienced serious adverse consequences from their partners' cybersex involvement even though in 60% of the cases the involvement did not lead to offline sex.

Think About It

Internet infidelity is also an issue about which some partners disagree. Does developing an online emotional relationship involving the exchange of sexual fantasies constitute being unfaithful to one's partner? Does such interaction degrade the value of faithfulness an individual has toward one's partner and relationship?

Just as individuals make personal choices about what they choose to access on the Internet, governments debate what should be on the menu (see Box 1-4).

1-5c Birth Control Availability

Love is a fourteen-letter word—Family Planning

—Planned Parenthood poster

Sexual choices have also been affected by the availability of birth control. In the past, even information about birth control was limited. In 1873, the **Comstock Act** was passed by Congress, prohibiting the mailing of "obscene matter," which included advertisements for methods of contraception. Anthony Comstock, the author of the bill, also influenced the passage of legislation in New York that made it illegal to provide verbal contraceptive information. Today, methods of birth control are widely available. You can place an order for condoms via the phone, through the mail, or over the Internet. Condoms and spermicides may be purchased at a number of stores in your community. More recent changes in birth control availability include the development of a female condom, the new one-month contraceptive shot, contraceptive patches, and the availability of postcoital contraception. They are discussed in detail in section 11-3, "Birth Control."

Comstock Act Law passed by Congress in 1873 prohibiting the mailing of obscene matter; this included advertisements for methods of contraception.

1-5d Divorce and Cohabitation

It is my fundamental belief that anyone has a right to divorce rather than stay in a loveless marriage.

—Kathleen Robertson, family law attorney

Both divorce and cohabitation affect sexual behavior.

National Data There are more than a million divorces each year (National Center for Health Statistics, 2002). About one fourth (24.1%) of first-year university students report that their parents are divorced (Bartlett, 2002).

Divorce is associated with a higher number of sexual partners. Indeed, divorced individuals are more likely to report having a higher number of sexual partners than individuals who are married.

National Data Twenty-six percent of the divorced compared to 4% of marrieds reported having between two and four sexual partners in the past 12 months (Michael, Gagnon, Laumann, & Kolata, 1994).

Box 1-4 Social Choices

Government Control of Sexual Content on the Internet

Should the government censor sexual content on the Internet? This question is the focus of an ongoing public debate that concerns protecting children from sexually explicit content on the Internet. One side of the issue is reflected in the Communications Decency Act, passed by Congress in 1996, which prohibited sending "indecent" messages over the Internet to people under age 18. But the Supreme Court rejected the law in 1997, citing that the law was too broadly worded and violated free-speech rights in that it restricted too much material that adults might want access to. A similar ruling in 2002 has resulted in no government crackdown, including on virtual child pornography. In support of not limiting sexual content on the Internet, the American Civil Liberties Union emphasized that governmental restrictions threaten material protected by the First Amendment, including sexually explicit poetry and material educating disabled persons on how to experience sexual pleasure.

Congress passed another law (Child Online Protection Act) in 1998, which makes it a crime to knowingly make available to people under age 17 any web materials that, based on "contemporary community standards," are designed to pander to prurient interests. The law requires commercial operators to verify that a user is an adult through credit card information and adult access codes. Businesses that break the law were subject to $50,000 fine and six months in jail. An inadvertent effect of the Act was to require public libraries to install Internet filters to block access to objectionable sites. A U.S. appeals court and panel of federal judges have struck down this law on the basis that it violates First Amendment rights.

Other governments have adopted restrictive Internet policies (Casanova, Solursh, Solursh, Roy, & Thigpen, 2001). In Singapore, the government requires Internet service providers to block access to certain web sites that contain pornography or inflame political, religious, or racial sensitivities. China's largest service provider blocks at least 100 sites, including Playboy. Germany is moving toward government control of the Internet (Newsbytes, 2001).

In the United States, parents, not the government, will be responsible for regulating children's use of the Internet. Software products, such as Net Nanny, Surfwatch, CYBERsitter, CyberPatrol, and Time's Up, are being marketed to help parents control what their children view on the Internet. These software programs allow parents to block unapproved web sites and categories (such as pornography), block transmission of personal data (such as address and telephone numbers), scan pages for sexual material before they are viewed, and track Internet usage. A more cumbersome solution is to require Internet users to provide passwords or identification numbers that would verify their ages before allowing access to certain web sites.

Another alternative is for parents to use the Internet with their children both to monitor what their children are viewing, and to teach their children values about what they believe is right and wrong on the Internet. Some parents believe that children must learn how to safely surf the Internet. One parent reported that the Internet is like a busy street, and just as you must teach your children how to safely cross in traffic, you must teach them how to avoid giving information to strangers on the Internet.

Cohabitation has also increased with more than 4 million unmarried households in the United States and about 60% of married couples reporting that they had cohabited before marriage (Stanley & Markman, 1997).

NATIONAL DATA Fifty-two percent of a Gallup Organization national random sample of adults, ages 18 and older, said that it was "morally acceptable" for an unmarried man and woman to live together (Gallup Organization Poll Analysis, 2001).

The acceptability of cohabitation varies greatly by culture. Twelve percent of first marriages in Italy, in contrast to 90% of first marriages in Sweden are preceded by cohabitation (Kierman, 2000).

Cohabitation, sexual values, and sexual behavior are related. In one study, a team of researchers (Knox, Cooper, & Zusman, 2001) found that college students open to living together were six times (12.7% vs. 2.6%) more likely to report that they have hedonistic sexual values than those opposed to living together. In addition, a nationwide survey of cohabitants revealed that they are less likely than spouses to be faithful to their partners (Treas & Giesen, 2000).

Think About It

Did increased social acceptance of sex outside marriage lead to increased rates of cohabitation? Or did increased rates of living together lead to increased social acceptance of sex outside marriage? Both changes have had their respective influences. Without the stigma and social disapproval previously associated with sex outside marriage and cohabitation, individuals are more likely to choose these options today than they were in previous generations.

1-5e Women in the Labor Force

With more than 74% of women in the current labor force (*Statistical Abstract of the United States: 2002*, Table 564; Table 5710), women are becoming increasingly financially independent from men. This has increased their opportunity to delay marriage (e.g., the woman does not "need" to marry for subsistence), to remain single (the woman is economically independent), and to divorce (e.g., the woman can afford to leave the marriage). Increased female workforce participation is also associated with the potential for sexual relationships with co-workers and incidents of sexual harassment at work. Finally, women's increased career commitment has affected childbearing choices—U.S. women are having fewer children and they are conceiving at later ages. Indeed, career women are now being admonished not to put off having children because their risk of infertility increases with age.

1-5f Social Movements

At least three social movements have influenced sexual choices: the sexual revolution, the women's movement, and the gay liberation movement. The **sexual revolution** created a cultural openness and approval for intercourse between unmarried individuals.

Sexual revolution Cultural openness of sexual issues and approval for intercourse between unmarried individuals.

NATIONAL DATA Fifty-three percent of a Gallup Organization national random sample of adults, ages 18 and older, said that sex between an unmarried man and woman was "morally acceptable" (Gallup Organization Poll Analysis, 2001).

Hence, the movement toward marriage changed from dating, love, and maybe intercourse with a spouse-to-be, then marriage and parenthood . . . to affection or love and sex with a number of partners, maybe living together, then marriage and children. And, acceptance of a child outside marriage has increased (e.g., actress Jodie Foster has had two children and has yet to name a father).

NATIONAL DATA Fifty-seven percent of a Gallup Organization national random sample of adults, ages 18 and older, said that it was "not morally wrong" for an unmarried couple to have a baby (Gallup Organization Poll Analysis, 2001).

Women's movement Social movement that supports the belief that women should have the right to make choices regarding their bodies and reproduction, thus advocating access to sex education, contraception, and abortion.

The **women's movement** has also influenced sexual choices. In the nineteenth century and earlier, few voices protested the subordinate status of women in U.S. society. The women's movement emerged to fight for equal rights and opportunities and against sexual exploitation. This movement supports the belief that women should have the right to make choices regarding their bodies and reproduction, thus advocating access to sex education, contraception, and abortion. The women's movement has sensitized women to their rights to equality in sexual interaction, such as initiating and terminating relationships, requiring respect from their partners, and expecting their partners to be attentive to their sexual needs.

Gay liberation movement Social movement that increased the visibility of gay, bisexual, and transgender people as viable lifestyles of sexual orientation and identity.

The **gay liberation movement** increased the visibility of gay, bisexual, and transgender people. Gay-, bisexual-, and transgender-oriented newspapers, magazines, and arts and entertainment guides in the United States reflect the viability of the various lifestyles as a sexual choice. For example, an increasing number of gays are also "coming out of the closet," such as former talk show host Rosie O'Donnell, actress Ellen DeGeneres, and Senator Barney Frank.

1-5g Fear of HIV and AIDS

One of the most significant social changes affecting sexuality has been the fear of contracting the human immunodeficiency virus (HIV) and acquired immune deficiency syndrome (AIDS). Although more than 900,000 people are living with HIV, an estimated 40,000 new HIV infections occur each year; almost 800,000 U.S. citizens are living with full-blown AIDS (Satcher, 2001). The threat of contracting HIV has put a new fear in sexual relationships—the fear that sexual activity may result in a potentially fatal disease. Concern over HIV and AIDS may affect numerous sexual choices, including the following:

- Should I have oral, vaginal, or anal intercourse?
- Should I have sex with a new partner?
- Should I engage in extra partner sex (sex outside a pair-bonded relationship)?
- Should I have multiple sex partners?
- Should I require HIV testing before having sex with a new partner?
- Should I require the use of a condom or dental dam during each act of sex?
- Should I continue a sexual relationship with a partner who has had sex outside the relationship?

Concern over HIV and AIDS does not, however, always result in cautious sexual behavior. Fewer than one in five reported using a condom at last intercourse with their "steady" partner (Anderson et al., 2000). In the context of a casual relationship, 62% of the adult respondents reported that they used a condom during their most recent intercourse (Anderson et al., 2000).

1-5h Reproductive and Medical Technology

Advances in reproductive technology include artificial insemination and test-tube fertilizations. These technologies allow infertile heterosexual couples, single heterosexual women, and lesbians to conceive through other than traditional sexual intercourse in traditional relationships. Cloning may someday provide another alternative in reproductive technology; however, recent advances in this field have come under heavy scrutiny (McGee, 2000; Friend, 2003) so that human cloning has been banned in the United States. Public opinion may, however, be reversed as infertile couples may argue that cloning may offer their only chance to bear a child. Gay rights advocates may also emphasize the value of cloning for same-sex couples.

> *It is absolutely inevitable that groups are going to try to clone a human being. But they are going to create a lot of dead and dying babies along the way.*
>
> *—Thomas Murray, bioethicist*

New medical technology has also created other choices (Severy & Spieler, 2000). Due to the development of prenatal testing such as ultrasound and amniocentesis, pregnant women face new choices: "Should I undergo prenatal testing?" and "If the tests reveal fetal abnormalities, should I continue the pregnancy?" Medical technology now allows men with erection difficulties to choose to have penile implants or to use medication (e.g., Viagra) that induces erection. An individual experiencing gender dysphoria (a condition in which one's gender identity does not match one's biological sex) may choose to undergo hormonal treatment and/or transsexual surgery to change his or her external sexual characteristics.

Many of the sexual choices that individuals face today are not the same as those our parents, grandparents, and great-grandparents confronted. For example, as discussed earlier, individuals in previous generations could not choose to use certain methods of birth control because they were either prohibited by law or had not yet been developed. HIV and AIDS did not influence sexual choices of earlier generations because these diseases were unknown until the 1980s. Likewise, the sexual choices faced by our children and the generations to come will reflect future social changes.

Think About It

How did each of the social changes identified here influence your sexual choices? For example, how has television's openness about sexuality influenced your sexual choices?

SUMMARY

This chapter emphasized the broad concept of sexuality, the theme of sexual choices, the many influences on our sexual choices, and recent social changes affecting sexuality in our society.

Elements of Human Sexuality

Human sexuality is a multifaceted concept consisting of thoughts, sexual self-concept, values, emotions, anatomy/physiology, reproduction, behaviors, relationships, and diversity. Although individuals and cultures may have differing views on the definition of sex, these elements are integral to the respective definitions.

Nature of Sexual Choices

We are continually making choices, many of which are difficult because they involve trade-offs, or disadvantages as well as advantages. Choices that result in irrevocable outcomes, such as becoming a parent or having an abortion, are among the most difficult ones individuals may face. However, we cannot avoid making choices because not to choose is, itself, a choice. For example, if we have oral, vaginal, or anal intercourse and have not decided to use a condom, we have made a decision to risk contracting and transmitting HIV and other sexually transmissible diseases. Other factors in regard to the nature of choices are that we can always choose a positive view (e.g., "my having contracted a sexually transmitted disease has taught me to use a condom in future sex") and some ambivalence and uncertainty are inherent in making most choices.

Influences on Sexual Choices

Although we like to think we make our own sexual decisions and have free will to do so, actually, we are strongly influenced by a number of factors when making sexual choices. These influences include emotional and cultural constraints, previous decisions, alcohol/drug use, peer/partner pressure, family factors, and our perception of locus of control.

Making Sexual Choices

Steps involved in making sexual choices include 1) clarifying values and goals; 2) understanding one's motives and identifying feelings and emotions; 3) identifying and exploring alternative courses of action; 4) seeking information that makes the short-term and long-term consequences clear for each choice; 5) weighing the positive and negative consequences for each alternative; 6) selecting an alternative that has maximum positive consequences and minimal negative consequences; and 7) implementing one's decision. These steps in conjunction with learning from our previous choices can help in making sexual decisions that have positive outcomes.

Social Changes and Sexual Choices

Numerous social changes impact sexual choices. They include sexuality on television (pervasiveness of sexuality in society but absence of pregnancy/STD prevention in sexual choices), sexuality on the Internet (more than 100,000 web sites), birth control availability (to separate love making from baby making), divorce/cohabitation (associated with higher number of sexual partners), more women in the labor force (associated with economic independence of women who are economically free of constraining relationships), social movements (sexual revolution expands options for individuals, women's liberation movement increases independence of women, gay liberation movement provides support and credibility for gay people), fear of HIV and AIDS (some increase in condom use), and reproductive and medical technology (provide help for infertile couples).

SUGGESTED WEBSITES

Note: These websites were functional when we went to press. Please access the online text for the most up-to-date URLs.

All About Sex
http://www.allaboutsex.org/

Ask Me Anything
http://www.SexEd.org/

Federal Health Portal
http://www.healthfinder.gov

Go Ask Alice
http://www.goaskalice.columbia.edu/

Positive Sexuality
http://www.positive.org/

Sexual Health Network
http://sexualhealth.com

Surgeon General Report to the Nation
http://www.surgeongeneral.gov

Sex Education Web Circle
http://www.sexuality.org/wc/

KEY TERMS

ambivalence (p. 10)
Comstock Act (p. 21)
determinism (p. 14)
external locus of control (p. 14)
free will (p. 14)
gay liberation movement (p. 24)
hookup (p. 16)
human sexuality (p. 2)
internal locus of control (p. 14)
libido (p. 7)
locus of control (p. 14)
lust (p. 7)
sex drive (p. 7)
sexual revolution (p. 23)
sexual self-concept (p. 3)
women's movement (p. 23)

CHAPTER QUIZ

1. Among the Sambia of the New Guinea Highlands, what are preadolescent males encouraged to do to ensure their heterosexuality and ability to impregnate their wives?
   a. have first intercourse by age 13
   b. perform fellatio on older unmarried males
   c. perform cunnilingus on older married females
   d. become circumcised by age 13
2. In a study cited in this chapter, students' attitudes on abortion, premarital sex, and oral sex were assessed both before and after the students took a human sexuality course. This study found that after taking the sexuality course, students' attitudes toward which of the following had changed?
   a. abortion
   b. premarital and oral sex
   c. both a and b
   d. neither a nor b
3. In a national sample of U.S. adults, researchers found that those in an ongoing love relationship were _______ likely to use a condom than those who had a partner that they were not seeing regularly.
   a. less
   b. more
4. In a study of more than 6,000 adolescent females, which of the following variables was NOT found to influence the age at which daughters began having sexual intercourse?
   a. family structure
   b. the relationship and interaction between mother and daughter
   c. the mothers' attitudes toward sex
   d. the mothers' discussion of sex
5. *Determinism* refers to the idea that our choices are largely determined by
   a. heredity and environment.
   b. free will.
6. A person with an internal locus of control believes that success and failures in life are
   a. determined by fate or chance.
   b. determined by other individuals.
   c. attributable to his or her own abilities and efforts.
   d. both a and b.
7. In a 2001 Gallup Organization national random sample of U.S. adults, what percentage said that it was "morally acceptable" for an unmarried man and woman to live together?
   a. more than 90%
   b. about half
   c. nearly one quarter
   d. less than 10%
8. In ____________, 90% of marriages are preceded by the partners living together.
   a. Mexico
   b. Sweden
   c. Italy
   d. United States
9. The high rate of U.S. women in the labor force is associated with each of the following EXCEPT
   a. older age at marriage.
   b. increased divorce rate.
   c. increased singlehood.
   d. women having more children.
10. The Comstock Act passed by Congress in 1873 did which of the following?
    a. prohibited mailing information about contraception
    b. prohibited women from using contraception
    c. required doctors to offer contraceptives to their married female patients
    d. required doctors to offer contraceptives to their unmarried female patients
11. What do the authors of your text refer to as the major "sex organ" of the human body?
    a. the skin
    b. the genitals
    c. the eyes
    d. the brain
12. Tattooing and body piercing are associated with a risk of being infected with Hepatitis B and Hepatitis C.
    a. True
    b. False
13. Recent research data have found that most U.S. college _______ agree that "If two people really like each other, it's all right for them to have sex even if they've known each other for only a very short time."
    a. women
    b. men
    c. both women and men
    d. neither a nor b
14. The word *libido* refers to which of the following?
    a. oral sex
    b. lacking sexual values
    c. craving for sexual gratification
    d. liking a person without feeling sexual attraction toward that person
15. What do the authors of your text mean when they say, "Choices involve trade-offs"?
    a. Sometimes it is better to let other people make choices for us.
    b. Choices involve disadvantages as well as advantages.
    c. When a choice is difficult to make, it might be best to avoid making any choice.
    d. In a love relationship, each partner should have a say in the choices that affect the couple.
16. In a study of 269 high school students cited in this chapter, students revealed the source of their sexual knowledge. Which of the following was most frequently identified as being a source of sexual knowledge among the high school students?
    a. friends
    b. parents
    c. books
    d. television

REFERENCES

Anderson, J. E., Wilson, R., Doll, L., Jones, T. S., & Baker, P. (2000). Condom use and HIV risk behaviors among U.S. adults: Data from a national survey. *Family Planning Perspectives, 31*, 24–28.

Bartlett, T. (2002, February). Freshman pay, mentally and physically, as they adjust to life in college: New survey provides more data on what happens during that crucial first year. *The Chronicle of Higher Education*, A35–A37.

Barron, M., & Kimmel, M. (2000). Sexual violence in three pornographic media: Toward a sociological explanation. *The Journal of Sex Research, 37*, 161–168.

Benotsch, E. G., Kalichman, S., & Cage, M. (2002). Men who have met sex partners via the Internet: Prevalence, predictors, and implications for HIV prevention. *Archives of Sexual Behavior, 31*, 177–183.

Birnbaum, G. E. (2003). The meaning of heterosexual intercourse among women with female orgasmic disorder. *Archives of Sexual Behavior, 32*, 61–71.

Bogart, L. M., Cecil, H., Wagstaff, D. A., Pinkerton, S. D., & Abramson, P. R. (2000). Is it "sex"?: College students' interpretations of sexual behavior terminology. *The Journal of Sex Research, 37*, 108–116.

Brantley, E. (2002). Poem, used by permission.

Carnes, P. J. (2001). Cybersex, courtship, and escalating arousal: Factors in addictive sexual desire. *Sexual Addiction & Compulsivity, 8*, 45–78.

Casanova, M. F., Solursh, D., Solursh, L., Roy, E., & Thigpen, L. (2001). The history of child pornography on the Internet. *Journal of Sex Education and Therapy, 25*, 245–251.

Cohen, A. B., & Tannenbaum, H. J. (2001). Lesbian and bisexual women's judgements of the attractiveness of different body types. *The Journal of Sex Research, 38*, 226–232.

Cooper, A., Boies, S., Maheu, M., & Greenfield, D. (2000). Sexuality and the Internet: The next sexual revolution. In L. T. Szuchman & F. Muscarella (Eds.), *Psychological perspectives on human sexuality* (pp. 519–545). New York: John Wiley & Sons.

Cope-Farrar, K., & Kunkel, S. (2002). Sexual messages in teens' favorite prime-time television programs. In J. D. Brown, J. R. Steele, & K. Walsh-Childers (Eds.), *Sexual teens, sexual media* (pp. 59–78). Mahwah, NJ: Lawrence Erlbaum.

Davis, E. C., & Friel, L. V. (2001). Adolescent sexuality: Disentangling the effects of family structure and family context. *Journal of Marriage and the Family, 63*, 669–681.

Durant, W. (1962) *The story of philosophy*. New York: Time Incorporated.

Feigenbaum, R., & Weinstein, E. (1995). College students' sexual attitudes and behaviors: Implications for *sexuality* education. *Journal of American College Health, 44*(3), 112–119.

Ferguson, S. J. (2001). *Making babies, making families*. Boston, MA: Beacon Press.

Fisher, H. (2001). Lust, attraction, attachment: Biology and evolution of the three primary emotion systems for mating, reproduction, and parenting. *Journal of Sex Education and Therapy, 25*, 96–104.

Friedman, R. C., & Downey, J. I. (2000). Psychoanalysis and sexual fantasies. *Archives of Sexual Behavior, 29*, 567–586.

Friend, T. (2003). The real face of cloning. *USA Today*, p. A1, et passim.

Gagnon, J. H., Giami, A., Michaels, S., & DeColomby, P. (2001). A comparative study of the couple in the social organization of sexuality in France and the United States. *The Journal of Sex Research, 38*, 24–34.

Gallup Organization Poll Analysis. (2001, May 24). Majority considers sex before marriage morally okay. www.gallup.com/poll/releases pr010524.asp

Golden, A. L. (2002). Letter from the editor: What do Americans hold dear? *Adolescent & Family Health, 2*, 97.

Goodson, P., McCormick, D., & Evans, A. (2001). Sex on the Internet: College students' emotional arousal when viewing sexually explicit materials on-line. *Journal of Sex Education and Therapy, 25*, 252–260.

Haavio-Mannila, E., & Purhonen, S. (2001). Slimness and self-rated sexual attractiveness: Comparisons of men and women in two cultures. *The Journal of Sex Research, 38*, 102–110.

Hanif, J., Frosh, A., Marnane, C., & Ghufoor, K. (2001). Lesson of the week: "High" ear piercing and the rising incidence of perichondritis of the pinna. *British Medical Journal, 322*, 906–907.

Herdt, G. (1981). *Guardians of the flutes: Idioms of masculinity*. New York: McGraw-Hill.

Herdt, G. (1989, June). Sexuality and masculine development up to middle adolescence among Sambia (Papua New Guinea). Paper presented at the annual meeting of the International Academy of Sex Research, Princeton, NJ.

Hicks, T. V., & Leitenberg, H. (2001). Sexual fantasies about one's partner versus someone else: Gender differences in incidence and frequency. *The Journal of Sex Research, 38*, 43–50.

Kierman, K. (2000). European perspectives on union formation. In L. J. Waite (Ed.), *The Ties That Bind* (pp. 40–58). New York: Aldine de Gruyter.

Knox, D., & Schacht, C. (2002). *Choices in relationships*. Belmont, CA: Wadsworth/Thomson Learning.

Knox, D., Cooper, C., & Zusman, M. E. (2001). Sexual values of college students. *College Student Journal, 35*, 24–27.

Knox, D., Daniels, V., Sturdivant, L., & Zusman, M. E. (2001). College student use of the Internet for mate selection. *College Student Journal, 35*, 158–160.

LaBrie, J. W., & Earleywine, M. (2000). Sexual risk behaviors and alcohol: Higher base rates revealed using the unmatched-count technique. *The Journal of Sex Research, 37*, 321–326.

Larsson, I., & Svedin, C. (2002). Sexual experiences in childhood: Young adults' recollections. *Archives of Sexual Behavior, 31*, 263–274.

Lichter, S. R., Lichter, L. S., & Amundson, D. R. (2001). Sexual imagery in popular entertainment. Center for Media and Publications. http://www.cmpa.com/archive/sexpopcult.htm

Lynch, C. O. (2002). Risk and protective factors associated with adolescent sexual activity. *Adolescent & Family Health, 2*, 99–107.

Mackay, J. L. (2001). Why have sex? *British Medical Journal, 322*, 623–625.

Marital and Sexuality Center and MSNBC Survey. (2002, January 8). 6.5% of male internet population are cybersex addicts. EuropeMedia.

McGee, G. (2000). Cloning, sex, and new kinds of families. *The Journal of Sex Research, 37*, 266–272.

McKenna, K. Y. A., Green, A. S., & Smith, P. A. (2001). Demarginalizing the sexual self. *The Journal of Sex Research*, 38, 302–311.

Michael, R. T. (2001). Private sex and public policy. In E. O. Laumann & R. T. Michael (Eds.), *Sex, love, and health in America: Private choices and public policies* (pp. 465–491). Chicago: The University of Chicago Press.

Michael, R. T., Gagnon, J. H., Laumann, E. O., & Kolata, G. (1994). *Sex in America: A Definitive Survey*. Boston: Little, Brown.

Mitchell, K. J., Finkelhor, D., & Wolak, J. (2001). Risk factors for and impact of online sexual solicitation of youth. *The Journal of the American Medical Association, 285*, 3011–3014.

Nahom, D. et al. (2001). Differences by gender and sexual experience in adolescent sexual behavior: Implications for education and HIV prevention. *Journal of School Health, 71*, 153–158.

National Center for Health Statistics. (2002). Births, marriages, divorces, and deaths: Provisional data for October 2001. *National Vital Statistics Report* 50, no. 11. Hyattsville, MD: Department of Health and Human Resources.

Newsbytes. (2001, August 31). Germans seek to centralize Internet content control. p. NWSBO1, 24300e.

Paul, E. L., McManus, B., & Hayes, A. (2000). "Hookups": Characteristics and correlates of college students' spontaneous and anonymous sexual experiences. *The Journal of Sex Research, 37*, 76–88.

Pinette, G. (2002). The dangers of body art and piercings: The medicine bundle. *Wind Speaker, 20*, 27.

Satcher, D. (U.S. Surgeon General). (2001, July 9). The Surgeon General's call to action to promote sexual health and responsible sexual behavior. U.S. Department of Health and Human Services, http://www.surgeongeneral.gov/library/sexualhealth/call.htm

Schneider, J. P. (2000). Effects of cybersex addiction on the family: Results of a survey. *Sexual Addiction and Compulsivity, 7*, 31–58.

Severy, L. J., & Spieler, J. (2000). New methods of family planning: Implications for intimate behavior. *The Journal of Sex Research, 37*, 258–265.

Starling, K. (2001, September 18). Out of the shadow. *The News and Observer*.

Stanley, S. M., & Markman, H. J. (1997). *Marriage in the 90s: A nationwide random phone survey*. Denver: PREP, Inc.

Statistical Abstract of the United States: 2002. (2002). 122nd ed. Washington, DC: U.S. Bureau of the Census.

Thomas, K. (2001, December 12). Survey shows many search for sex-related information. *USA Today*, p. D1.

Treas, J., & Giesen, D. (2000). Sexual infidelity among married and cohabiting Americans. *Journal of Marriage and the Family, 62*, 48–60.

Voss, J., & Kogan, L. (2001). Behavioral impact of a human sexuality course. *Journal of Sex Education and Therapy, 26*, 122–132.

Waite, L. J., & Joyner, K. (2001). Emotional and physical satisfaction with sex in married, cohabiting, and dating sexual unions: Do men and women differ? In E. O. Laumann & R. T. Michael (Eds.), *Sex, love, and health in America: Private choices and public policies* (pp. 239–269). Chicago: The University of Chicago Press.

Walters, A. S. (2001). They were the best of times and the worst of times: Students write about their sexual experiences. *Journal of Sex Education and Therapy, 26*, 115–121.

Weinberg, M. S., Lottes, I., & Shaver, F. M. (2000). Social correlates of permissive sexual attitudes: A test of Reis's hypotheses about Sweden and the United States. *The Journal of Sex Research, 37*, 44–52.

Wiederman, M. W. (2000). Women's body image self-consciousness during physical intimacy with a partner. *The Journal of Sex Research, 37*, 60–68.

Worden, S. (2001). E-trafficking. *Foreign Policy*, March, 92–97.

Wu, W., & Koo, S. H. (2001). Perceived effects of sexually explicit Internet content: The third-person effect in Singapore. *Journalism and Mass Communication Quarterly, 78*, 260–274.

Young, K. S., Griffin-Shelley, E., Cooper, A., O'Mara, J., & Buchanan, J. (2000). Online fidelity: A new dimension in couple relationships with implications for evaluation and treatment. *Sexual Addiction and Compulsivity, 7*, 59–74.

2

Values, Emotions, and Sexuality

Chapter Outline

The only sin in life is going against your own integrity.

—D. H. Lawrence

"...[T]o thine own self be true, and it must follow, as the night the day, thou canst not then be false to any man" wrote Shakespeare in *Hamlet* (act 1, scene 3). This adage is particularly true in regard to sexual values that affect our self-esteem, feelings about our partners, and our relationships. Consider the following situations that require a choice in sexual values.

Two people are drinking and dancing at a party. Although they just met only two hours ago, they feel a strong attraction to each other. Each is wondering how much sexual intimacy will be appropriate and whether they should go back to one of their apartments later that evening. How much sex and how soon in a new relationship are appropriate?

A couple is involved in a long-distance dating relationship and see each other only once a semester because they attend different universities. During their weekends apart throughout the semester, each feels lonely and vulnerable to spending time with someone else. Each has met someone new in their respective universities and is thinking about hanging out with them. Where do they draw the line about what is and what is not appropriate with others?

While one partner in a pair-bonded relationship was visiting a relative, the other had sex with a previous lover on a chance meeting. The individual felt guilty, confessed, and apologized, promising never to be unfaithful again. If this were your partner, how would you respond?

The preceding scenarios involve the issues of how much sex how soon, fidelity, and forgiveness. We are continually making sexual choices based on our sexual values. In this chapter we review alternative sexual values, their historical roots, and sources—how we developed our own sexual values. We also look at how emotions interact with values and pay particular attention to the concepts of love and emotions that are challenging to love and relationships. We begin by defining sexual values and looking at various alternative sexual values.

Think About It

Some of the studies we present in this chapter are based on samples limited to one university. As we will see in Chapter 3, "Sex Research and Theory," these samples are not representative of the larger population and may not be representative of other college student bodies. How do you hypothesize these data compare with student norms in your setting?

2-1 ALTERNATIVE SEXUAL VALUES

Sexual values Moral guidelines for making sexual choices.

Sexual values are moral guidelines for making sexual choices in nonmarital, marital, heterosexual, and homosexual relationships. Among the various sexual values are absolutism, relativism, and hedonism.

Think About It

Sexual values and sexual behavior may not always be consistent. How often (if ever) have you made a sexual decision that was not consistent with your sexual values? If so, what influenced you to do so (alcohol, peer influence)? How did you feel about your decision then and now (guilt, regret, indifference)?

2-1a Absolutism

Give me chastity and continence, but not quite yet.

—St. Augustine

Absolutism refers to a belief system that is based on the unconditional power and authority of religion, law, or tradition. Religion is a major source of absolutist sexual values in that many religions teach waiting until marriage to have sexual intercourse. An example is "True Love Waits," which is an international campaign designed to challenge teenagers and college students to remain sexually abstinent until marriage. Under this program, created and sponsored by the Baptist Sunday School Board, young people are asked to agree to the absolutist position and sign a commitment to the following: "Believing that true love waits, I make a commitment to God, myself, my family, my friends, my future mate, and my future children to be sexually abstinent from this day until the day I enter a biblical marriage relationship" (True Love Waits website, 2002, http://www.lifeway.com/tlw/tns_faq.asp).

Absolutism Belief system that is based on the unconditional power and authority of religion, law, or tradition.

In a broader sense, many religions take the position that marital intercourse is the only morally correct sexual behavior and that nonmarital, extramarital, and homosexual sex acts are sins against the self, God, and the community. Some religions also view masturbation, the use of contraception, the use of pornography, and abortion as sins. The federal government supports an absolutist position. Indeed, Congress has enacted a major new abstinence initiative (section 510 of Title V of the Social Security Act), projected to spend $87.5 million in federal, state, and local funds per year for five years with a focus on abstinence from sexual activity outside marriage (rather than solely emphasizing premarital abstinence for adolescents) (Sonfield and Gold, 2001).

Being an absolutist and not planning to have intercourse as an adolescent may have implications for the well-being of young people. A team of researchers (Whitaker, Miller, & Clark, 2000) studied a cross-sectional sample of 982 adolescents ages 14–16 and found that delayers (those who had not had intercourse and who rated their chance of having intercourse in the next 12 months as less than 50%) reported greater psychological health (e.g., greater self-esteem, less hopelessness) than anticipators (those who had not had intercourse but rated their chance of intercourse in the next 12 months as greater than 50%).

In regard to college students, 10% of 620 undergraduates at a southeastern university selected absolutism as their primary sexual value (Knox, Cooper, & Zusman, 2001). Demographic factors associated with absolutism among this university sample included being female (11.9%) rather than male (8.3%), being under age 19 (12.5%) rather than age 20 or older (6.5%), and not being emotionally involved (12.4%) rather than being emotionally involved (8.8%) (Knox et al., 2001). These percentages reflect the more conservative socialization of women, the liberalization of students' values as they move away from their family of origin (their parents), and the influence of love. Indeed, these data suggest that as persons become involved in a love relationship, they are more likely to question the idea of waiting until marriage to have intercourse and to view intercourse as acceptable.

CULTURAL DIVERSITY

In an effort to ascertain the importance of sexual values in mate selection in China, Zambia, Sweden, and the United States, two researchers asked college students in these countries: "How desirable is chastity in potential long-term mates or marriage partners?" Respondents were asked to indicate the degree to which they were concerned that their future spouse be a virgin on a scale from zero (irrelevant or unimportant) to three (indispensable). Chinese students were the most concerned (2.5 out of 3), and Swedish students were the least concerned (less than one half of 1). U.S. male students rated their concern at slightly less than 1, with U.S. women reporting a 0.5 level of concern (Buss & Schmitt, 1993).

Absolutist values are not specific to virginity. A considerable portion of our society is absolutist about fidelity in marriage—42 % of U.S. adults feel that extramarital sex is "morally wrong" (Gallup Organization Poll Analysis, 2001).

Asceticism Belief system based on the conviction that giving into carnal lust is wrong and that one must rise above the pursuit of sensual pleasure to live a life of self-discipline and self-denial.

Relativism Sexual value which emphasizes that sexual decisions should be made in the context of a particular situation.

A subcategory of absolutism is **asceticism**—a belief system that is based on the conviction that giving into carnal lust is wrong and that one must rise above the pursuit of sensual pleasure to live a life of self-discipline and self-denial. Asceticism is reflected in the sexual values of Catholic priests, monks, nuns, and other celibates.

2-1b Relativism

Relativism is a value system emphasizing that sexual decisions should be made in the context of a particular situation. Whereas an absolutist might feel that it is wrong for unmarried people to have intercourse, a relativist might feel that the moral correctness of sex outside marriage depends on the particular situation. For example, a relativist might feel that in some situations, sex between casual dating partners is wrong (such as when one individual pressures the other into having sex or lies in order to persuade the other to have sex). But in other cases—when there is no deception or coercion and the dating partners are practicing "safer sex"—intercourse between casual dating partners may be viewed as acceptable. Over three fourths (79%) of 620 undergraduates selected "relativism" as their primary sexual value, with women being more likely to be relativists than men (84.5% vs. 73%). In addition, persons who were involved in a love relationship were more likely than those who were casually dating (85.5% vs. 75.2%) to be relativists. Indeed, relativism was the predominant sexual value among college students in this study (Knox et al., 2001).

Sexual values and choices that are based on relativism often consider the degree of love, commitment, and relationship involvement as important factors. Table 2-1 reflects the sexual values of 620 undergraduates in both involved and casual relationships. The emotionally involved were significantly more likely to identify themselves as believing in relativism than those who reported they were in casual relationships. Similarly, "casual" daters were more than twice as likely as the "involved" to report being hedonistic.

CULTURAL DIVERSITY

Weinberg, Lottes, and Shaver (2000) compared sexual attitudes of undergraduates in America with those in Sweden and found the latter more permissive in their sexual values.

TABLE 2-1

Sexual Value by Level of Relationship

	Absolutism	Relativism	Hedonism
Involved	8.8% (26)	85.5% (272)	5.7% (18)
Casual	12.4% (37)	72.2% (223)	12.4% (37)

Source: Knox, D., Cooper, C., & Zusman, M. E. (2001). Sexual values of college students. *College Student Journal*, 35, 26. Used by permission.

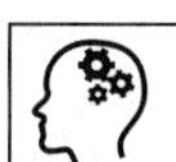

Think About It

An individual's sexual values may change across time. It is not uncommon that individuals are absolutist prior to involvement in an emotional relationship and become relativistic after they are involved. When the relationship ends, persons may become hedonistic for a brief time before becoming relativistic in a new relationship. How have your sexual values changed?

2-1c Hedonism

Hedonism is the sexual value that reflects a philosophy that the pursuit of pleasure and the avoidance of pain are the ultimate value and motivation for sexual behavior. The "playboy philosophy" emphasized by Hugh Hefner of *Playboy Magazine* is hedonistic—seek sexual pleasure.

Hedonism Sexual value which reflects a philosophy that the pursuit of pleasure and the avoidance of pain are the ultimate values and motivation for sexual behavior.

The hedonist's sexual values are reflected in the creed "If it feels good, do it." Hedonists are sensation seekers; they tend to pursue novel, exciting, and optimal levels of stimulation and arousal. Their goal is pleasure. More than one in five (22.3%) of 620 undergraduates selected "hedonism" as their primary sexual value. As noted in section 2-1b, persons who were dating casually were more likely than those who were involved in a love relationship (12.4% vs. 5.7%) to be hedonists. And, undergraduates who were willing to live together were six times more likely to have a hedonistic view of sexuality than those who were against cohabitation (12.7% vs. 2.6%). Finally, those who said that divorce was acceptable under certain conditions were much more likely to report hedonistic sexual values than those who would not divorce under any circumstances (32% vs. 7.2%) (Knox et al., 2001).

Clearly, hedonism is a liberal sexual value that casual daters, those open to cohabitation, and the divorced were more likely to support (Knox et al., 2001). Race may also be a factor, with Black men tending to report more positive views of recreational sex than non-Black. In contrast, Black women tended to be more conservative than White women and both White and Black men (Cubbins & Tanfer, 2000).

Previous researchers have found that the number of sexual partners of an individual is related to one's sexual values. Michael, Gagnon, Lauman, and Kolata (1994) found that those who reported having sex with two or more partners in the past 12 months were twice as likely to have a hedonistic (recreational) view of sex as individuals who reported having only one partner in the past year.

2-2 THE SEXUAL DOUBLE STANDARD

The **sexual double standard**—the view that encourages and accepts sexual expression of men more than women—is reflected in Table 2-2. Indeed, men were almost six times more hedonistic than women.

Sexual double standard One standard for women and another for men. An example of the double standard in U.S. society is that it is normative for men to have more sexual partners and women to have fewer partners.

Kimmel (2000) emphasized that the double standard continues to be reflected in today's sexual norms:

TABLE 2-2

Sexual Value by Sex of Respondent

	Hedonism	Absolutism	Relativism
Male Students	18.7% (43)	8.3% (19)	73.0% (168)
Female Students	3.6% (14)	11.9% (46)	84.5% (328)

Source: Knox, D., Cooper, C., & Zusman, M. E. (2001). Sexual values of college students. *College Student Journal*, 35, 24. Used by permission.

The double standard persists today—perhaps less in what we actually do, and more in the way we think about it. Men still stand to gain status and women to lose it from sexual experience: he's a stud who scores; she's a slut who "gives it up." Boys are taught to try to get sex; girls are taught strategies to foil the boys' attempts. "The whole game was to get a girl to give out," one man told sociologist Lillian Rubin. "You expected her to resist; she had to if she wasn't going to ruin her reputation. But you kept pushing." (p. 222)

Think About It

What choices would you make in the following situations?

- Your 17-year-old daughter tells you she wants to begin using birth control pills.
- While your partner is out of town, an old flame contacts you and suggests meeting for dinner.
- At a weekend outdoor concert, you meet someone to whom you are intensely attracted. It seems as though the interest is mutual (the person is coming on to you), but you find out that this person is married.
- You and your dating partner are celebrating your first anniversary by having dinner at your place. After dinner, you begin to kiss and drift into having sexual intercourse, but neither of you has a condom or any other form of birth control.

Based on your choices in these four situations, would you say that your sexual values reflect absolutism, relativism, hedonism, or a combination of these?

2-3 SOURCES OF SEXUAL VALUES

Various sources of sexual values include religion, the Victorians and science, the media, parents, and school-based sexuality education programs.

2-3a Religion

Religion is a major source of sexual values. Weinberg et al. (2000) compared undergraduates at an American and a Swedish university and found that the religiosity among Americans was higher and contributed to their more restrictive, negative views toward sexuality.

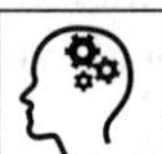

Think About It

The concern religion has with sexual expression is the sometimes insistence that there be a tie between sex and marital reproduction ("be fruitful and multiply"). An extreme example of this connection is the report of a Catholic bishop who refused to sanction the marriage of a man who was paraplegic because he would not be able to have sexual intercourse and father children (Mackay, 2001). To what degree has religion been an influence in your sexual values?

For some individuals, spirituality or religion serves as a basis for sexual values and decision making.

NATIONAL DATA Based on a national sample of 1,047 men and 1,285 women, those reporting affiliation with mainstream/conservative Protestantism or Catholicism were significantly more likely to be involved in monogamous relationships than those unaffiliated with organized religion (Laumann & Youm, 2001, p.125).

We live in a pluralistic society in which people have different sexual values. These values sometimes have their roots in religion. The Jewish and Christian influences have been the most prominent in the United States.

Jewish Heritage

Many of our values concerning sexuality can be traced to the laws and customs reflected in the Old Testament, written between 800 and 200 B.C. Examples of norms espoused include marriage is good, children are expected, and adultery is wrong. Homosexuality and **bestiality** (sex with animals) are also forbidden because they are nonprocreative.

Bestiality Sexual activity between a human being and an animal.

Spiritualistic dualism Term from early Christian doctrine whereby the body and spirit or mind were seen as being separate from each other.

Christian Heritage

While Judaism is based on the teachings of Moses in the Old Testament, Christianity emphasizes teachings in the New Testament. One idea is **spiritualistic dualism** whereby the body and spirit or mind are seen as being at odds with each other. The body is "temporal, material, corruptible and corrupting," while the spirit is pure and responsible for delivering the body from sin (Nelson, 1983, p.122).

Early Christian interpretations of sexuality as evil led to the adoption of a reward-punishment model to control believers. People who controlled their sexual appetites were rewarded by the knowledge that they were like Christ, who was essentially asexual. Those who gave in to their lusts would be punished in Hell's fires after death. However, a way to avoid such threats was to confess one's sins to members of the clergy. Such confession helped the church monitor the sexual behavior of its members and ensure compliance (Bullough, 1987).

2-3b The Puritans

The Puritans who settled along the coast of New England in the seventeenth century were radical Protestants who had seceded from the Church of England. We can trace many of our sexual values to their beliefs and social norms. Tannahill (1982) noted that the forcefulness and power of the Puritans in imposing their ways on others and the fact that new immigrants were predominantly Protestant explain why the Puritans influenced several generations of later colonists. In fact, Tannahill suggested that the Puritan ethic has had a disproportionate influence in the history of the United States. "Senators and Congressmen today, struggling (whatever the state of their faith and/or marital relationships) to project an image of dedicated family men, at work, at rest, at church, at play, owe this particular electoral hazard to the early New England settlers who wove the public demonstration of family solidarity into the American ethos" (p. 330).

The Puritans wanted their members to get married and stay married. Religious values (avoiding temptation), social values (being a member of a close-knit community), and economic values (working hard for material reward) helped to emphasize the importance of the marital relationship. The Puritan woman had little choice of an adult role other than wife and mother. Only in marriage could she achieve status in the community. Men and women were taught that their best chance for survival was to find a spouse to satisfy their needs for clothing, food, companionship, and sex.

The Puritans approved of sex only within marriage. They viewed sex as a passion to conquer or control and marriage as the only safe place for its expression. Rigid codes of dress helped to discourage sexual thoughts.

Any discussion of sex among the Puritans would not be complete without reference to **bundling,** also called **tarrying.** Not unique to the Puritans, bundling was a courtship custom in which the would-be groom slept in the prospective bride's bed in her parents' home. But there were rules to restrict sexual contact. Both partners were fully clothed, and a wooden bar was placed between them. In addition, the young woman might be encased in a long bag up to her armpits, her clothes might be sewn together at strategic points, and her parents might be sleeping in the same room.

Bundling A courtship custom among the Puritans in which the would-be groom slept in the prospective bride's bed (both fully clothed) in her parents' home. See also **tarrying.**

Tarrying A courtship custom among the Puritans in which the would-be groom slept in the prospective bride's bed (both fully clothed) in her parents' home. See also **bundling.**

The justifications for the bundling were convenience and economics. Aside from meeting at church, bundling was one of the few opportunities a couple had to get together to talk and learn about each other. Because daylight hours were consumed by heavy work demands, night became a time for courtship. But how did the bed become the courtship arena? New England winters were cold. Firewood, oil for lamps, and candles were in short supply. By talking in bed, the young couple could come to know each other without wasting valuable sources of energy.

Although bundling flourished in the middle of the eighteenth century, it provoked a great deal of controversy. "Jonathan Edwards attacked it from the pulpit, and other ministers, who had allowed it to go unnoticed, joined in its suppression" (Calhoun, 1960, p. 71). By about 1800, the custom had virtually disappeared.

2-3c Victorian Era and Science

The Victorian era (which took its name from England's Queen Alexandria Victoria, who reigned from 1837 to 1901) is popularly viewed as a time of prudery and propriety in sexual behavior. However, there was a great disparity between expressed middle-class morality and actual practices. In his study of this era, Wendell Johnson (1979) wrote

> *[W]hat were the Victorians actually doing? One might reply "Just about everything." Free love, adultery, male homosexuality and (in spite of the Queen's disbelief) lesbianism, nymphetism, sadism, and masochism, exhibitionism—the Victorians practiced them all . . . the number of whores per acre in mid-Victorian London and the consumption of pornography . . . would put today's Times Square to shame. (p.11)*

The official view of sexuality during the Victorian era was that sexual behavior and the discussion of it should be suppressed. There was also the emergence of "female types." There were "good" women and "bad" women in Victorian society. The latter were prostitutes or women who practiced no social graces in expressing their sexuality. Women who were not prostitutes but who did enjoy sexual feelings were in conflict. Some felt degraded, even insane. "If I love sex, I must be like a prostitute" was an inescapable conclusion. Some women even had clitoridectomies (surgical removal of the clitoris) performed to eliminate the "cause" of their sexual feelings.

Tannahill (1982) traced how the Victorian reincarnation of courtly love, which cast women in the role of untouchable moral guardians, fueled "an explosive increase in prostitution, an epidemic spread of venereal disease, and a morbid taste for masochism" (p. 347). The subsequent attempts of women to "set society to rights" was the foundation of their struggle for suffrage. In the twentieth century, the dissemination of scientific ideologies and discoveries, the industrial revolution, and economic reality presented a challenge to the artificial ideal of the Victorian family. The rise of scientific approaches is described next.

Beyond the Victorian influence, science has also influenced the way we think about sexuality. Several early twentieth century scientists were instrumental in shifting society's ideas about sex from a sacred to a scientific perspective, including Sigmund Freud (1885–1939), who described stages of psychosexual development in terms of the erogenous zones (areas of the body that can bring pleasure). Personality formation was shaped by one's negotiation of predictable developmental crises, such as the Oedipal conflict with its castration anxiety and the Electra complex with its penis envy. Even those who advocate psychoanalytic theory, however, allow that "it is difficult to prove Freudian contentions empirically. Much of the difficulty here lies in the fact that we are dealing in the realm of fantasy and infant fantasy to boot!" (Cameron & Rychlak, 1985, p. 47). Nevertheless, this did not prevent Freud's ideas from being widely disseminated and influential in our thinking about sex roles and sexual expectations.

Freud's work has been especially criticized for his pronouncements regarding the sexuality of women. "A large volume of empirical evidence has been accumulated to indicate that virtually all of Freud's inspired guesses about sexuality were wrong. . . . Yet we continue to see couples applying for sex therapy with concerns that reflect this Freudian view of female sexuality" (LoPiccolo, 1983, p. 52). Freud's views of male sexuality, judging that any sexual behavior other than penile penetration of the vagina implied arrested sexual development, were simply reflecting traditional Jewish attitudes, according to sexuality educator Sol Gordon. "'Infantile,' 'immature,' 'personality defect' is just name calling and the substitution of Freudian pseudoscientific language for the prohibitions of the Talmud" (LoPiccolo, 1983, p. 52).

2-3d Television and Media

In section 1-5a, "Sexuality on Television," we noted that sexuality is a major theme of television in the United States. However, as a source of sexual values and responsible treatments on contraception, condom usage, abstinence, or consequences of sexual behavior, it is woefully inadequate. Indeed, the television viewer learns that sex is romantic and exciting but learns nothing about discussing the need for contraception or HIV and STD protection. With few exceptions (*Sex and the City* has featured condom usage in a sexual encounter), viewers are inundated with role models who engage in casual sex without protection.

NATIONAL DATA Of 248 broadcast and television episodes involving 3,228 scenes showing sexual activity in 1989–1999, including 135 scenes of simulated on-screen sexual intercourse, only eight pregnancies and no case of sexually transmitted diseases resulted (Lichter, Lichter, & Amundson, 2001).

The potential impact of viewing these images is heightened by the sheer amount of exposure to them. It has been estimated that adolescents will have spent 15,000 hours watching television by the time they graduate from high school, in contrast to 12,000 hours in the classroom. Exposure to media sex is related to an increased perception of the frequency of sexual activity and serves as a powerful influence on the sexual attitudes, values, and beliefs of adolescents. Not surprisingly, television has been hypothesized to "function as a kind of 'super-peer,' normalizing these behaviors, and thus, encouraging them among teenagers" (Bar-on et al., 2001, p. 191). Music videos often include sexually suggestive images; 75% of concept videos (depicting a story) were observed to include sexual imagery in one content analysis (Bar-on et al., 2001). A study of single, Black females (ages 14–18) served in a Family Medicine Clinic revealed that girls who had viewed X-rated movies were twice as likely to have multiple sex partners, 2.2 times as likely to have not used contraception in the past six months, and 1.7 times more likely to test positive for chlamydia (Wingood et al., 2001).

On the positive side of media's use, television has been helpful in some communities to promote use of family-planning clinics. Trial advertising on local radio and television, and national cable television, has been positively received, with few viewer complaints (Bar-on et al., 2001). In a study that assessed AIDS knowledge among Arab-Americans living in the Detroit area, television was reported as the major AIDS information source (for 51% of telephone survey respondents), far outstripping other information sources, including friends (11%), school (6%), or newspapers (4%) (Kulwicki & Cass, 1996).

The Committee on Public Education of the American Pediatric Association has called for pediatricians to discuss the use of sexual images in the media (including portrayals of unsafe sex) with adolescent patients and their families. Additional recommendations include encouraging the broadcast industry to promote abstinence from sexual intercourse for teens, as well as encouraging adolescents and adults who are already sexually active to use condoms to prevent STDs and pregnancy. Finally, they have urged the creation of a national task force to be convened to study the issue of how media's sexual content impacts the knowledge and behavior of youth, plan research, and present recommendations to Congress, the broadcast industry, and the American people (Bar-on et al., 2001).

2-3e Family Members

Parents influence their children's sexual knowledge and values by what they teach—and don't teach—their children about sexuality. Parents continuously send signals about sexuality through their verbal and nonverbal behavior toward each other and their children. It is impossible to not communicate (teach), and parents are persistent models.

This father sent his son to Oral Roberts University, where absolutist sexual values are encouraged.

Traditionally, parents have been inadequate sources of sexual information for their children. Troth and Peterson (2000) studied 237 Australian university students aged 16–19 and found that neither fathers nor mothers engaged in any substantial amount of education or communication on the topic of safe sex. However, among those adolescents whose parents did engage in such education/communication, the youth were much more likely to have safe sex discussions with their partners and to use condoms.

Parental reluctance to talk to their children about sex is often based on their own insecurity about their level of sexual knowledge, as well as the fear that telling their children about sex will promote sexual activity. Many parents also feel that their children will learn about sex and birth control from other sources (such as school-based sex education programs), so the parents feel little need to talk about it. When parents and adolescents were interviewed about their conversations about sex, Fitzharris and Werner-Wilson (2000) found that the parents reported general discomfort about such conversations and adolescents fear bringing up the subject for fear of being judged or lectured to.

However, when/if children are perceived as being exposed to particular risks, their parents may push past their discomfort. Mothers who worried their teens might be exposed to HIV or who thought their youth had tried alcohol or other drugs were more likely to speak to them about sexual intercourse and contraception. Maternal concern about their adolescents' exposure to HIV was related to Latino mothers and their adolescents spending more time talking about sexual topics in videotaped interviews. When the mothers believed their teens had experience with substance use, they were more likely to discuss sexual topics at home (Romo, Lefkowitz, Sigman, & Au, 2001). Miller (2002) noted that parent-child closeness or connectedness, and parental supervision or regulation of children, in combination with parents' values against teen intercourse (or unprotected intercourse), decrease the risk of adolescent pregnancy.

2-3f Peers

Friendship and dating patterns have also been found to influence initiation of sexual activity. Using data from the National Longitudinal Survey of Youth (NLSY), researchers found that youth who reported as preteens that most of their friends were in higher grades (in contrast to those whose close friends were mostly in the same or lower grades) were almost twice as likely to become sexually experienced as young teens (between ages 13 and 16). "Going steady" was a better predictor of sexual debut than "frequent dating." One finding that surprised the researchers was that a small group of adolescents (65 out of the 1,678 studied) fit in the category "not going steady and almost never dating," yet they were more likely to experience sexual initiation at an early age. So, although casual dating, followed by steady dating, and then by sexual activity is a normative relationship path, it is not followed by all youth.

2-3g School Sex Education Programs

Sex education in the public school system is usually taught as part of another subject, such as health education, home economics, biology, or physical education. Because each state, rather than the federal government, is responsible for sex education in the public school system, there is considerable variation among the states in terms of the sex education they offer. Somers and Gleason (2001) evaluated the comparative contribution that multiple sources of education about sexual topics (family, peers, media, school, and professionals) made on teen sexual knowledge, attitudes, and behavior and found that, in general, teens tended to get less of their sex education from schools and more of their sex education from nonsibling family.

When schools provide sex education, it is usually abstinence education. Specifically, under Title V, Section 510, of the Social Security Act, the federal government funds states that offer abstinence promotion programs meeting the following eight-point definition of abstinence education (Sonfield & Gold, 2001). Sex education in the public school system

1. has as its exclusive purpose, teaching the social, psychological, and health gains to be realized by abstaining from sexual activity;
2. teaches abstinence from sexual activity outside marriage as the expected standard for all school-age children;
3. teaches that abstinence from sexual activity is the only certain way to avoid out-of-wedlock pregnancy, STDs, and other associated health problems;
4. teaches that a mutually faithful monogamous relationship in the context of marriage is the expected standard of human sexual activity;
5. teaches that sexual activity outside the context of marriage is likely to have harmful psychological and physical effects;
6. teaches that bearing children out-of-wedlock is likely to have harmful consequences for the child, the child's parents, and society;
7. teaches young people how to reject sexual advances and how alcohol and drug use increases vulnerability to sexual advances;
8. teaches the importance of attaining self-sufficiency before engaging in sexual activity.

Sonfield and Gold (2001) noted large discrepancies in the degree to which each state provided the expected eight-point program. The debate on sex education in the public school system continues (see Box 2-1).

Think About It

Which influence on your sexual values has been most profound, that of religion, science, the media, your parents, peers, or teachers? How have these various influences affected your sexual knowledge and values?

2-4 EMOTIONS: LOVE AND SEXUAL VALUES

Love is an emotion that influences one's sexual values. We noted earlier that persons involved in a relationship are more relativistic in their sexual values than those who are casually dating. But what is love? Ask individuals to identify the characteristics of love and you will hear "caring," "commitment," "trust," "companionship," "affection," "happiness," and "security." The most notable characteristic of love is diversity—people have different conceptions of love, attribute different elements to it, and express it in different styles.

2-4a Love: Conceptions, Elements, and Styles

There is only one happiness in life, to love and be loved.

—George Sand

One way to conceptualize love is on a continuum from romanticism to realism. Romantics believe in love at first sight, one true love, and love conquers all. Undergraduates most likely to agree with these beliefs are freshmen and sophomores (Knox, Schacht, & Zusman, 1999). Men are also more likely to be romantics in that they fall in love quicker (and fall out of love as quickly) (Kimmell, 2000).

Realists disagree with all the above beliefs of the romantic. Realists believe that love takes time to develop, that there are numerous people with whom one may fall in love, and love does not conquer all. Junior and senior undergraduates are more likely to be realists (Knox, Schacht, et al., 1999). The Love Attitudes Scale (see Box 2-2) provides a way for you to assess where you fall on the continuum from romanticism to realism.

Robert Sternberg (1986) identified several states of love on the basis of the presence or absence of three elements: intimacy, passion, and commitment. Sternberg defined these three elements of his "triangular theory of love" as follows:

- *Intimacy:* Emotional connectedness or bondedness
- *Passion:* Romantic feelings and physical sexual desire
- *Commitment:* Desire to maintain the relationship

Box 2-1 Social Choices

Content of Sex Education in the Public Schools?

Sexuality education was introduced in the American public school system in the late nineteenth century with the goal of combating STDs and instilling sexual morality. "The strong emphasis on abstinence-only sexuality education has been the most common approach and has become formalized over the past 20 years" (Elia, 2000, p. 123). The Federal Government (Welfare Reform Act of 1996) supports sex education in the public school system that is focused on abstinence education and has appropriated $50 million a year administered by the Maternal and Child Health Bureau and its state analogues. States have to contribute three "matching" dollars for every four federal dollars they receive. The combined federal and state funding can be used for various purposes such as media campaigns, programs in public schools, or programs outside public schools. To be eligible for this funding, programs must focus exclusively on "teaching the social, psychological, and health gains to be realized by abstaining from sexual activity" (Sonfield & Gold, 2001, p. 170). Programs that emphasize abstinence but also discuss contraception and other means of protection are not eligible.

Some parents and national organizations fear that teaching youth about safe sex and contraception actually encourages "immoral" premarital sexual promiscuity in the young. The concern reflects a fear that education about sexuality will lead people to experiment (Selverstone, 2000). The data suggest otherwise. Sather and Zinn (2002) compared the values and attitudes of two groups of seventh and eighth grade adolescents toward premarital sexual activity. One group received state-funded, abstinence-only education; the other group did not receive that education. Abstinence-only education did not significantly change adolescents' values and attitudes about premarital sexual activity, nor their intentions to engage in premarital sexual activity. The majority of both the treatment and control group subjects expressed disagreement with the statement: "It is okay for people my age to have sexual intercourse," and they did not intend to have sexual intercourse while an unmarried teenager.

In contrast to the belief that sex education should be restrictive, focused on biomedical/hygienic aspects, and promote abstinence is the belief that it should be "broad based covering the biological, ethical, psychological, sociocultural, and spiritual dimensions of sexuality" (Elia, 2000, p. 123). Wiley (2002) argues that presenting abstinence-only information may harm secondary students by not providing them with potential life-saving information. The substantial protection provided by condoms against certain sexually transmitted diseases, including human immunodeficiency virus (HIV) represents scientifically valid information that should be provided to students.

Numerous organizations favor comprehensive sexuality education. Among them are the American Medical Association, American Psychological Association, American Public Health Association, Child Welfare League of America, National Association of County and City Health Officials, National Council on Family Relations, National School Boards Association, Office of Family Ministries and Human Sexuality of the National Council of Churches, United States Conference of Mayors, and YWCA of the U.S.A. According to Berne and Huberman (1996), the World Health Organization reviewed 35 controlled studies of sex education programs in the United States and Europe and found that in no case did students who participated in the programs initiate intercourse at an earlier age than students in the control groups (exposed to no programs). Schools are the public institution with the greatest potential for reaching most young people. If we do not support sex education, how will we ensure that adolescents receive accurate information about sexuality, develop responsible decision-making skills, and have the guidance and support to explore and affirm their own values?

Public education must also be realistic. Young and Goldfarb (2000) note that abstinence education imposes a value or standard to which the vast majority of adults in the United States have not adhered—and simply do not support. Given that young adolescents are sexually active, it may be prudent to provide broad-based sex education classes to encourage protected sex.

Innovative suggestions in delivering sex education to youth include providing a comprehensive sex-related information and behavioral skills learning format via the Internet to help avoid sex-related problems and enhancing sexual well-being (Barak & Fisher, 2001). In addition, sex education in whatever format is most effective if it promotes sex-positive information and views rather than "fear and morality-based messages" (Bay-Cheng, 2001, p. 249).

According to Sternberg (1986), various types of love can be described on the basis of the three elements he identified:

1. *Nonlove:* Absence of all three components
2. *Liking:* Intimacy without passion or commitment
3. *Infatuation:* Passion without intimacy or commitment
4. *Romantic love:* Intimacy and passion without commitment
5. *Companionate love:* Intimacy and commitment without passion
6. *Fatuous love:* Passion and commitment without intimacy
7. *Empty love:* Commitment without passion or intimacy
8. *Consummate love:* Combination of intimacy, passion, and commitment

Box 2-2 Self-Assessment

INTERACTIVE BOX

The Love Attitudes Scale

This scale is designed to assess the degree to which you are romantic or realistic in your attitudes toward love. There are no right or wrong answers.

Directions: After reading each sentence carefully, circle the number that best represents the degree to which you agree or disagree with the sentence.

1—Strongly agree 2—Mildly agree 3—Undecided 4—Mildly disagree 5—Strongly disagree

	SA	MA	U	MD	SD
1. Love doesn't make sense. It just is.	1	2	3	4	5
2. When you fall "head over heels" in love, it's sure to be the real thing.	1	2	3	4	5
3. To be in love with someone you would like to marry but can't is a tragedy.	1	2	3	4	5
4. When love hits, you know it.	1	2	3	4	5
5. Common interests are really unimportant; as long as each of you is truly in love, you will adjust.	1	2	3	4	5
6. It doesn't matter if you marry after you have known your partner for only a short time as long as you know you are in love.	1	2	3	4	5
7. If you are going to love a person, you will "know" after a short time.	1	2	3	4	5
8. As long as two people love each other, the educational differences they have really do not matter.	1	2	3	4	5
9. You can love someone even though you do not like any of that person's friends.	1	2	3	4	5
10. When you are in love, you are usually in a daze.	1	2	3	4	5
11. Love "at first sight" is often the deepest and most enduring type of love.	1	2	3	4	5
12. When you are in love, it really does not matter what your partner does because you will love him or her anyway.	1	2	3	4	5
13. As long as you really love a person, you will be able to solve the problems you have with the person.	1	2	3	4	5
14. Usually you can really love and be happy with only one or two people in the world.	1	2	3	4	5
15. Regardless of other factors, if you truly love another person, that is a good enough reason to marry that person.	1	2	3	4	5
16. It is necessary to be in love with the one you marry to be happy.	1	2	3	4	5
17. Love is more of a feeling than a relationship.	1	2	3	4	5
18. People should not get married unless they are in love.	1	2	3	4	5
19. Most people truly love only once during their lives.	1	2	3	4	5
20. Somewhere there is an ideal mate for most people.	1	2	3	4	5
21. In most cases, you will "know it" when you meet the right partner.	1	2	3	4	5
22. Jealousy usually varies directly with love; that is, the more you are in love, the greater your tendency to become jealous will be.	1	2	3	4	5
23. When you are in love, you are motivated by what you feel rather than by what you think.	1	2	3	4	5
24. Love is best described as an exciting rather than a calm thing.	1	2	3	4	5
25. Most divorces probably result from falling out of love rather than failing to adjust.	1	2	3	4	5
26. When you are in love, your judgment is usually not too clear.	1	2	3	4	5
27. Love often comes only once in a lifetime.	1	2	3	4	5
28. Love is often a violent and uncontrollable emotion.	1	2	3	4	5
29. When selecting a marriage partner, differences in social class and religion are of small importance compared with love.	1	2	3	4	5
30. No matter what anyone says, love cannot be understood.	1	2	3	4	5

Scoring: Add the numbers you circled. 1 (strongly agree) is the most romantic response and 5 (strongly disagree) is the most realistic response. The lower your total score (30 is the lowest possible score), the more romantic your attitudes toward love. The higher your total score (150 is the highest possible score), the more realistic your attitudes toward love. A score of 90 places you at the midpoint between being an extreme romantic and an extreme realist. Both men and women undergraduates typically score above 90, with men scoring closer to 90 than women.

Source: Knox, D. (1969). Conceptions of love at three developmental levels. Dissertation, Florida State University. Contact Dr. Knox at davidknox@prodigy.net for permission to use this scale.

Each of these types of love has some variation in reality. For example, some level of commitment is felt between romantic lovers (romantic love), and some level of passion is felt between companionate lovers (companionate love). However, the predominant focus of romantic love is passion, and the predominant quality of companionate love is commitment.

Individuals bring different love triangles to the table of love. One lover may bring a predominance of passion with some intimacy but no commitment (romantic love), whereas the other person brings commitment but no passion or intimacy (empty love). The triangular theory of love allows lovers to see the degree to which they are matched in terms of the three basic elements of passion, intimacy, and commitment.

Hendrick and Hendrick (1992) described and studied another schema for looking at types of love relationships or orientations toward love (based on the theory of Canadian sociologist John Alan Lee). Although a person may show characteristics of more than one love style, people are often characterized as exhibiting one of six different love styles:

- *Eros:* Passionate love, not limited to physical passion
- *Ludus:* Game-playing love—for mutual enjoyment without serious intent
- *Storge:* Friendship; companionate love
- *Pragma:* Pragmatic and practical love
- *Mania:* Manic, jealous, obsessive love
- *Agape:* Selfless, idealistic love

Hendrick and Hendrick (1992) offered weather analogies to depict the six love styles: Eros lovers, they suggested, get hit by a bolt of lightning. Ludic lovers like rainstorms but don't like getting wet. Storgic lovers like to stay inside during the lightning and thunder but will go outside in soft, gentle rain showers. Pragma lovers will always have an umbrella in case of rain, Mania lovers don't mind getting wet, and Agape lovers will give their umbrella to their partner.

Montgomery and Sorell (1997) observed that love styles associated with the lowest relationship satisfaction are Ludus and Mania styles. Conversely, Eros and Agape love styles are associated with the highest relationship satisfaction. We await research on the relationship between love style and sexual satisfaction, although we might predict greater sexual satisfaction with Eros and Storge.

In a study of "hookups" between college students, certain love styles were characteristic of students who hooked up. Distinguishing features of those who had noncoital hookups were a ludic love style and high concern for personal safety. These individuals may have been participating in collegiate cultural expectations by engaging in "playful" sexual exploration, but refraining from intercourse out of their personal safety concern. As mentioned in Box 1-3, "Up Close: Factors Involved in 'Hookups,'" those who engaged in coital hookups were also characterized by ludic love styles, along with symptoms of alcohol intoxication. The researchers (Paul, McManus, & Hayes, 2000) worried that the combination of ludic orientation (motivated by the thrill of the game) and alcohol intoxication could be a precursor to sexual experiences that are forced or unwanted by a partner.

Interestingly, a sex difference was found with the love style of agape (altruistic love). Women who experienced coital hookups scored higher on the agape score than men. Did the women view having intercourse as an altruistic act (something they owed the men, or should do even if they didn't want to)? Or, the researchers speculated, even if the women didn't feel this way at the time of the hookup, this could be an after-the-fact explanation (or rationalization) of their sexual behavior, given the sexual double standard. It is unclear which comes first—particular love styles may drive individuals toward hookups, and hookup experiences may contribute to the formation of "anti-emotional-intimacy" love styles. Finally, it may be that one's approach to romantic and casual sexual relationships differs. Paul et al. suggest that it would be interesting to assess love styles within various types of relationships.

CULTURAL DIVERSITY 

The connection between love styles, marital satisfaction, and acculturation was studied in Mexican American and Anglo American couples (Contreras, Hendrick, & Hendrick, 1996). For all groups, passionate love scores best predicted marital satisfaction. Hispanic-oriented participants were more pragmatic and less idealistic about love and sex than bicultural Hispanic couples and Anglo Americans. Some theorists have argued that passionate love is an American phenomenon because of our emphasis on individualism, but studies from Europe, Russia, Japan, China, and the Pacific Islands confirm that men and women in a variety of cultures are as romantic as Americans (Hatfield & Rapson, 1996).

The level of emotional involvement in a relationship influences the level of sexual engagement, with men requiring less involvement than women. Carroll, Volk, and Hyde (1985) found that although the majority of men and women listed feeling loved or needed as the most important part of sexual behavior, fewer men (8%) compared to women (45%) reported that being emotionally involved was "always" required for having sexual intercourse. In this study of 249 students randomly selected from Dennison University, 84% of the men had engaged in intercourse without emotional involvement, whereas only 42% of the women had done so. However, when Sprecher and Regan (1996) questioned college men and women who had not had sexual intercourse about the reason for their virginity, not being in love, or in a long enough relationship, was the most frequent response from both sexes. A team of researchers (Browning, Hatfield, Kessler, & Levine, 2000) studied 191 undergraduates and found that love was still the primary motive for engaging in sexual behavior.

2-4b Love and Sex

Whether lovers are homosexual or heterosexual, there are similarities and differences between love and sex. We will compare these concepts now.

Similarities Between Love and Sex. In general, love and sex are more similar than they are different. These similarities include the following:

1. Both love and sex represent intense feelings. To be involved in a love relationship is one of the most exciting experiences an individual ever has. To know that another person loves us engenders feelings of happiness and joy. "No one ever really loved me until now," remarked one man, "and because of this love I have a very good feeling inside."

   Sex has the same capability to generate intense excitement and happiness. Although sex is more than orgasm, the latter is the epitome of intense pleasure.
2. Both love and sex involve physiological changes. When a person is in an intense love relationship, his or her brain produces phenylethylamine, a chemical correlate of amphetamine, which may result in a giddy feeling similar to an amphetamine high (Liebowitz, 1983). When the love affair breaks up, the person seems to crash and go through withdrawal because there is less phenylethylamine in his or her system. Some heartbroken lovers reach for chocolate, which contains phenylethylamine.

   Further support for the idea that love has a physiological component has been suggested by Money (1980), who studied patients who had undergone brain surgery or suffered from a pituitary deficiency. Although they were able to experience various emotions, passionate love was not one of them.

   The physiological changes the body experiences during sexual excitement have been well documented by researchers (Meston & Frohlich, 2000) including Masters and Johnson (1966) in their observations of more than 10,000 orgasms. Such changes include increased heart rate, blood pressure, and breathing.

3. Both love and sex have a cognitive component. To experience the maximum pleasure from both love and sex, the person must label or interpret what is happening in positive terms. For love to develop, each person in the relationship must define his or her meetings, glances, talks, and the like as enjoyable. The significance of labeling is illustrated by the experience of two women who dated the same man. Although they spent similar evenings, the first woman said, " I love him—he's great," but the other woman said, "He's a jerk."

   Positive labeling is also important in sex. Each person's touch, kiss, caress, and body type are different; sexual pleasure depends on labeling sexual interaction with that person as enjoyable. "I can't stand the way he French kisses" and "I love they way he French kisses" are two interpretations of kissing the same person. But only one of these interpretations will make the event pleasurable.
4. Both love and sex may be expressed in various ways. The expression of love may include words ("I love you"), gifts (flowers or candy), behaviors (being on time, a surprise phone call or visit, washing the partner's car), and touch (holding hands, tickling). Similarly, sex as well as love may be expressed through a glance, embracing, kissing, fondling, and intercourse. Many couples use sexual activity as their way of communicating the feelings of love and passion (Regan, 2000).
5. The need for love and sex increases with deprivation. The more we get, the less we feel we need; the less we get, the more we feel we need. The all-consuming passion of Romeo and Juliet, perhaps the most celebrated love story of all time, undoubtedly was fed by their enforced separation.

   Deprivation has the same effect on the need for sex. Statements of people who have been separated from their lover for several weeks may be similar to "I'm horny as a mountain goat," "We're going to spend the weekend in bed," and "The second thing we're going to do when we get together is take a drive out in the country."

Differences Between Love and Sex. There are several differences between love and sex. These include the following:

1. Love is crucial for human happiness; sex is important but not crucial. After analyzing the data from a study of more than 100,000 people about what makes them happy, one researcher concluded:

   Many people are unhappy with their sex lives, and many think this is an important lack, but almost no one seems to think that sex alone will bring happiness. Romance and love were often listed as crucial missing ingredients, but not sex; it was simply not mentioned. (Freeman, 1978, p. 56)
2. Love is pervasive, whereas sex tends to be localized. Love is felt all over, but sexual feeling is most often associated with various body parts (lips, breasts, or genitals). People do not say of love as they do of sex, "It feels good here."
3. Love tends to be more selective than sex. The standards people have for a love partner are generally higher than those they have for a sex partner. Expressions like "I'll take anything wearing pants," "Just show me a room full of skirts," and "I wouldn't kick him out of bed" reflect the desire to have sex with someone—anyone. Love wants the person rather than a person.

   The standards for a love partner may also be different from those for a sexual partner. For example, some people form relationships with others to meet emotional intimacy needs that are not met by their sexual partners. A sexual component need not be a part of the love relationship they have with these people.

2-4c Personal Choices: Sex With or Without Love?

Most sexual encounters occur on a continuum from love involvement to no love involvement. Opinions vary with regard to whether an emotional relationship is a worthy prerequisite for sexual involvement.

Sex is good and beautiful when both parties want it, but when one person wants sex only, that's bad. I love sex, but I like to feel that the man cares about me. I can't handle the type of sexual relationship where one night I spend the night with him and the next night he spends the night with someone else. I feel like I am being used. There are still a few women around like me who need the commitment before sex. (authors' files)

The two most important comments about their first intercourse experience made by the 292 undergraduate respondents in the Thomsen and Chang (2000) study were that they wished they had waited and they wished they had been in a committed (love) relationship. Few wait until marriage, as only 17% of adult women report that they had their first intercourse with the man they eventually married (Raley, 2000).

Other people feel that love is not necessary for sexual expression. "Some of the best sex I've had," remarked one person, "was with people I was not in love with." The ideal that sex with love is wholesome and sex without love is exploitative may be an untenable position. For example, two strangers can meet, share each other sexually, have a deep mutual admiration for each other's sensuous qualities, and then go their separate ways. Such an encounter is not necessarily an example of sexual exploitation. Rather, it may be an example of two individuals who have a preference for independence and singlehood rather than emotional involvement, commitment, and marriage. Given the risk of contracting STDs and HIV, we suggest that sex with numerous anonymous partners may have fatal consequences.

Each person in a sexual encounter will undoubtedly experience different degrees of love feelings, and the experience of each may differ across time. One woman reported that the first time she had intercourse with her future husband was shortly after they had met in a bar. She described their first sexual encounter as "raw naked sex" with no emotional feelings. But as they continued to see each other over a period of months, an emotional relationship developed, and "sex took on a love meaning for us."

Sex with love can also drift into sex without love. One man said he had been deeply in love with his wife, but that they had gradually drifted apart. Sex between them was no longer sex with love. Similarly, some women report being in relationships with men who feign love but actually use them for sex. Both love and sex can be viewed on a continuum. Love feelings can range from nonexistent to intense, and relationships can range from limited sexual interaction to intense interaction. Hence, rarely are sexual encounters completely with or without love; rather, they will include varying degrees of emotional involvement. Also, rarely are romantic love relationships completely with or without sex. Rather, they display varying degrees of sexual expression. Where on the continuum one chooses to be—at what degree of emotional and sexual involvement—will vary from person to person and from time to time.

The relationship between passion and intimacy was examined by social psychologists Baumeister and Bratslavsky (1999), who hypothesized that passion is related, not to intimacy itself, but to changes in intimacy level. When intimacy (caring, concern, and understanding) is increasing, a strong sense of passion is created (as when a relationship is new). When intimacy is stable (whether at a high or low level), passion declines. This implies that passion will be higher in the discovery phase of a relationship as one learns about the partner and they share experiences. After a couple has developed a high degree of intimacy, generating passion will become increasingly difficult.

♦

2-5 EMOTIONS: CHALLENGES TO LOVE AND RELATIONSHIPS

Some of the hardest work of my life has been moving thru jealousy.

—Paxus of Twin Oaks Community

Sometimes love is associated with distressing emotions, or is challenged by the complexities involved in attempting to establish and maintain intimate relationships. For example, in sections 2-5 through 2-5d we discuss jealousy and guilt, as well as manifestations of what Regan (2000) refers to as "love gone bad," or the "darker" aspects of love relationships: unrequited love and obsession.

2-5a Jealousy

Jealousy An emotional response to a perceived or real threat to an important or valued relationship.

Jealousy can be defined as an emotional response to a perceived or real threat to an important or valued relationship. People who feel jealous feel excluded or "left out" (Pines & Friedman, 1998). Although jealousy does not occur in all cultures (Cassidy & Lee, 1989), it does occur in our society and among both heterosexuals and homosexuals. Thirteen percent of 620 university students reported that jealousy was the most frequent problem that they encountered in their current or most recent relationship (Knox, Hatfield, & Zusman, 1998).

Pines and Friedman (1998) found no gender differences in likelihood, frequency, duration, or intensity of jealousy. Harris (2002) also found that men and women, regardless of sexual orientation, are more concerned about a mate's emotional infidelity than a mate's sexual infidelity.

Jealousy can be triggered by external or internal factors.

External factors refer to behaviors the partner engages in that are interpreted as (a) an emotional and/or sexual interest in someone (or something) else or (b) a lack of emotional and/or sexual interest in the primary partner.

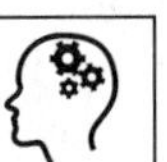

Think About It

Buss (2000) emphasized that "Jealousy is an adaptive emotion, forged over millions of years, symbiotic with long-term love. It evolved as a primary defense against threats of infidelity and abandonment" (p. 56). Persons become jealous when they fear replacement. To what degree do you predict you would feel jealous in a context where you observed your partner enjoying someone else who would like to have a relationship with your partner?

Jealousy may also exist even when there is no external behavior that indicates the partner is involved or interested in another relationship. Internal causes of jealousy refer to characteristics of individuals that predispose them to jealous feelings, independent of their partner's behavior. Examples include being mistrustful, having low self-esteem, being highly involved in and dependent on the relationship, and having no perceived alternative partners available (Pines, 1992). These internal causes of jealousy are explained as follows:

1. *Mistrust*. If an individual has been deceived or cheated on in a previous relationship, that individual may learn to be mistrustful in subsequent relationships. Such mistrust may manifest itself in jealousy.
2. *Low self-esteem*. Individuals who have low self-esteem tend to be jealous because they lack a sense of self-worth and hence find it difficult to believe anyone can value and love them. Feelings of worthlessness may contribute to suspicions that someone else is valued more.
3. *Being involved and dependent*. In general, individuals who are more involved in the relationship than their partner or who are more dependent on the relationship than their partner are prone to jealousy (Radecki-Bush, Bush, & Jennings, 1988). The person who is more involved in or dependent on the relationship not only is more likely to experience jealousy but also may intentionally induce jealousy in the partner. Such attempts to induce jealousy may involve flirting, exaggerating, or discussing an attraction to someone else, and spending time with others. According to White (1980), individuals may try to make their partner jealous as a way of testing the relationship (e.g., to see whether the partner still cares) and/or increasing specific rewards (e.g., to get more attention or affection). White found that women, especially those who thought they were more involved in the relationship than their partners, were more likely to induce jealousy in a relationship than men.

4. *Lack of perceived alternatives.* Individuals who have no alternative person or who feel inadequate in attracting others may be particularly vulnerable to jealousy. They feel that if they do not keep the person they have, they will be alone.
5. *Insecurity.* Individuals who feel insecure about the relationship with their partner may experience higher levels of jealousy (Attridge, Berscheid, & Sprecher, 1998).

Jealousy can have both desirable and undesirable consequences.

Desirable Outcomes of Jealousy

Jealousy may be functional if it occurs at a low level and results in open and honest discussion about the relationship. Not only may jealousy keep the partner aware that he or she is cared for (the implied message is "I love you and don't want to lose you to someone else"), but also the partner may learn that the development of other romantic and sexual relationships is unacceptable. One wife said:

> *When I started spending extra time with this guy at the office my husband got jealous and told me he thought I was getting in over my head and asked me to cut back on the relationship because it was "tearing him up." I felt he really loved me when he told me this and I chose to stop having lunch with the guy at work. (authors' files)*

According to Buss (2000), the evoking of jealousy also has the positive functions of assessing the partner's commitment and of alerting the partner that one could leave for greener mating pastures. Hence, one partner may deliberately invoke jealousy to solidify commitment and ward off being taken for granted. In addition, sexual passion may be reignited if one partner perceives that another would take his or her love object away. That "people want what others want" is an adage that may underlie the evocation of jealousy.

Sometimes the reaction to the jealousy of one's partner encourages further jealous behavior. Suppose John accuses Mary of being interested in someone else, and Mary denies the accusation and responds by saying "I love you" and by being very affectionate. From a behavioral or social learning perspective, if this pattern continues, Mary will teach John to continue being jealous. When John acts jealous, good things happen to him—Mary showers him with love and physical affection. Inadvertently, Mary may be reinforcing John for exhibiting jealous behavior.

To break the cycle, Mary should tell John of her love for him and be affectionate when he is not exhibiting jealous behavior. When he does act jealous, she might say she feels bad when he accuses her of something she isn't doing and ask him to stop. If he does not stop, she might terminate the interaction until John can be around her and not act jealous.

Undesirable Outcomes of Jealousy

Shakespeare referred to jealousy as the "green-eyed monster," suggesting that jealousy sometimes has undesirable outcomes for relationships. Three researchers (Barnett, Martinez, & Bluestein, 1995) confirmed the link between jealousy and marital dissatisfaction. Jealousy that stems from low self-esteem may also cause the partner of the jealous person to leave the relationship. Walsh (1991) explained:

> *An individual with feelings of negative self-worth . . . is continually imagining that no one could really be faithful to such an undeserving soul. If a person feels this way about him or herself, that atmosphere of insecurity, possessiveness, and accusations . . . makes it more probable that the mate will eventually come to share the self-evaluation and go forth to seek someone more deserving of his or her love. If such an event does occur, it merely seems to vindicate what we've known all along—we're no good.*

Relationships that continue when jealousy becomes entrenched may also hurt the partner of the jealous person. Peretti and Pudowski (1997) studied jealousy in 95 undergraduate men and 95 undergraduate women who were involved with a dating partner. The effects that the jealous partners had on the person they were dating included feelings of loss of affection, rejection, anxiety, and low self-esteem.

Jealousy may also result in the jealous partner's trying to control what the partner does and whom the partner sees. Stets (1995) studied 509 people in dating relationships (95%

were never-married) and observed that control was more common among non-White males who had low trust and high conflict with their partners. Stets also found that younger males were more prone to control—that older males had "more alternative identities that serve as the basis of their self esteem" (p. 498).

2-5b Guilt

Guilt may also come from sexual values in that persons who go against their values may feel guilty.

Sexual guilt Personal emotional reaction to engaging in sexual behavior that violates personal sexual values.

Sexual guilt is the feeling that results from the violation of one's own sexual values. Guilt may result when one goes against what one thinks he or she should not do ("I should not have gotten drunk and had intercourse"—one student referred to this as the "walk of shame" the next morning) or does not behave consistent with the way one thinks one should ("I should have been faithful").

A team of researchers (Weinberg, Lottes, & Shaver, 1995) examined guilt feelings reported by women and men in reference to their first and most recent intercourse experience: 75% of U.S. women, compared to 44% of U.S. men, felt guilty after their first intercourse experience. However, when asked about their most recent intercourse experience, 31% of the women and 44% of the men reported feeling guilty afterward. The lower percentage of women reporting guilt in their most recent intercourse experience may reflect a more stable emotional relationship context, which is the condition needed for cultural approval for female sexual expression.

Absolutist religious sexual values are associated with sexual guilt. One study found that women who frequently attended religious services were more likely to feel guilty about masturbation (Davidson, Darling, & Norton, 1995). Table 2-3 reflects the average level of guilt on a four-point continuum (from 1 to 4—with the higher the number, the higher the guilt) for various sexual situations reported by 249 undergraduate university students. You might compare your answers with theirs.

In some cases, sexual guilt may interfere with a person's sexual well-being. For example, some women feel guilty about experiencing sexual pleasure because they have been taught that "sex is bad" and "good women do not enjoy sex." In this situation, sexual guilt may interfere with a woman's ability to become sexually aroused and experience orgasm, even within a loving and committed relationship. One woman in the authors' classes said, "I never felt sex was OK, not even after I was married. I think my Catholic background and prudish parents did me in."

2-5c Unrequited Love

Although experiencing love, especially passionate love, can feel joyous, when love is unrequited, it can result in negative emotions. Baumeister, Wotman, and Stillwell (1993) solicited autobiographical accounts from those who had experienced being rejected and those who had rejected a suitor. Both the rejected lovers and the rejectors experienced distress. Those who were rejected reported decreases in self-esteem, as well as preoccupation with and longing for the person to whom they were attracted. Those who rejected someone's attention, while possibly feeling flattered by the interest of the person, were mainly annoyed, uncomfortable, resentful, and guilty for voicing rejection.

Suggestions for recovering from romantic rebuff include bolstering one's self-esteem by reviewing one's positive qualities and focusing on pleasing current or past relationships. Those who feel badly for hurting the feelings of an individual whose overtures they have rejected may want to review their reasons for their decision, to justify the decision to themselves (Regan, 2000). Orimoto and her colleagues interviewed students from a variety of ethnic backgrounds at the University of Hawaii to assess how they coped with breakups. While women were more likely to assess the problems and try to understand what happened, on the whole, men and women used similar coping strategies: trying to play things down and avoid reminders, using cognitive restructuring techniques to put the loss in perspective, and using distracting activities and self-improvement efforts (Hatfield & Rapson, 1996).

TABLE 2-3

Contexts Conducive to Sexual Guilt

How Guilty Would You Feel If	Average Score
1. You have intercourse with someone 18 years older than you. Both of you are unmarried.	2.04
2. You decide not to tell the person you are about to marry any information concerning your previous affectional relationship because you believe it will have no bearing on your marriage.	2.18
3. The person you are about to marry learns of a previous sexual affair with another person you did not particularly care for prior to your present relationship.	2.29
4. You reveal to an associate that a person who had invited you to dinner was gay and there were to be no other guests.	2.48
5. Your mother discovers that you, at age 16, are having intercourse with a member of the other sex.	2.76
6. You concealed from the person you are about to marry that you had earlier contracted and were cured of gonorrhea.	2.88
7. Your parents learn of your sexual relationship with someone of another race, and you know they disapprove.	3.03
8. As a student, you are in love with a teacher who is fired because your sexual relationship has been brought to the attention of the instructor's dean.	3.51
9. You are in a committed relationship with a person, yet you had intercourse with someone else.	3.52
10. Your fiancé/fiancée learns that you had a sexual encounter with your fiancé's/fiancée's best friend while your fiancé/fiancée was away visiting his/her grandmother.	3.66

Scoring: 1= No guilt; 2 = Little guilt; 3 = Moderate guilt; 4 = Considerable guilt

Source: Adapted from the original data collected for "Sexual guilt among college students," by Knox, D., Walters, L. H., & Walters, J. (1991). Sexual guilt among college students. *College Student Journal*, 25, 432–433.

2-5d Obsession

In the name of love, people have stalked the beloved, shot the beloved, and killed themselves in reaction to rejected "love." Symbolic interactionists note that the concept of romantic love has been so constructed as to be "used as an excuse for irresponsible, unpredictable behavior" (Winton, 1995, p. 141). Although most instances of unrequited love are resolved adequately, **obsessive relational intrusion (ORI)** has come to be recognized in various forms. ORI may be pursued by a stranger or an acquaintance who repeatedly invades one's physical or symbolic privacy in his or her attempts to have an intimate relationship (Cupach & Spitzberg, 1998). Activities may include sending unwanted letters, calls, gifts, and repeated requests for dates. **Stalking** is an extreme form of ORI and may involve following or watching a victim, property damage, threats, home invasion, or threats of physical harm. ORI can cause great emotional distress and impair the recipient's social and work activities.

Obsessive relational intrusion (ORI) Behavior that may be pursued by a stranger or an acquaintance who repeatedly invades one's physical or symbolic privacy in his or her attempts to have an intimate relationship.

Stalking An extreme form of obsessive relational intrusion and may involve following or watching a victim, property damage, threats, home invasion, or threats of physical harm.

Although various coping strategies have been identified, additional research is needed on how to manage unwanted attention (Regan, 2000). A survey (Spitzberg & Cupach, 1998) of young adults identified five general coping categories:

1. Making a direct statement to the person ("I am not interested in dating you, my feelings about you will not change, and I know that you will respect my decision and direct your attention elsewhere" Regan, 2000, p. 266).
2. Seeking protection through formal channels (police involvement, restraining order)
3. Avoiding the perpetrator (ignoring, avoiding the person)
4. Retaliating
5. Using informal coping methods (using telephone caller identification; seeking advice of others)

Direct statements and actions that unequivocally communicate disinterest are probably the most effective types of intervention.

2-6 ATTRACTION AND MATE SELECTION

The attraction of two people to each other is influenced by cultural, sociological, and psychological factors. In sections 2-6a through 2-6c we examine these factors.

2-6a Cultural Factors in Mate Selection

Endogamy The cultural expectation that one selects a marriage partner within one's own social group, such as race, religion, and social class.

Individuals are not free to marry whomever they please. Rather, their culture and society influence their choices. Two forms of cultural pressure operative in mate selection are endogamy and exogamy. **Endogamy** is the cultural expectation to select a marriage partner within one's own social group, such as race, religion, and social class. Endogamous pressures involve social approval and disapproval to encourage one to select a partner within one's own group. The pressure toward an endogamous mate choice is especially strong when race is concerned. Killian (1997) studied 20 Black-White married couples who reported that public reaction to their relationship was often negative. Almost all the respondents had experienced stares, disapproving expressions, and harassment at the work site. The effect of such relentless disapproval is reflected in the percentage of individuals who marry someone of the same race. Love may be blind, but it knows the color of one's partner.

Think About It

These endogamous pressures are not operative on all people at the same level or may not work at all. Heaton and Jacobson (2000) also found that military service and college attendance were associated with meeting and marrying someone outside one's own racial group. Why do you think these factors are associated with greater acceptance of interracial dating?

Exogamy The cultural expectation to marry outside one's own family group.

In contrast to endogamy, **exogamy** is the cultural expectation to marry outside one's own family group. Incest taboos are universal. In no society are children permitted to marry the parent of the other sex. In the United States, siblings and (in some states) first cousins are also prohibited from marrying each other. The reason for such restrictions is fear of genetic defects in children whose parents are too closely related.

When cultural factors have identified the general pool of eligibles for one's partner, individual mate choice becomes more operative. However, even when individuals feel that they are making their own choices, social influences are still operative.

2-6b Sociological Forces in Mate Selection

In addition to cultural factors there are various sociological forces that influence the choice of one's partner.

Homogamy

Homogamy theory Theory of mate selection that individuals are attracted to and become involved with those who are similar in such characteristics as age, race, religion, and social class.

Whereas endogamy is a concept that refers to cultural pressure, homogamy refers to individual initiative toward sameness. The **homogamy theory** of mate selection states that we tend to be attracted to and become involved with those who are similar to ourselves in such characteristics as age, race, religion, and social class.

Some data suggest that homogamy is more important in selecting a mate than choosing a date (Knox, Zusman, & Nieves, 1997). Two hundred seventy-eight undergraduates were asked to reveal the degree to which it was important to them to (a) date and (b) marry partners who had similar characteristics (age, education, occupation, values, etc.) on a 10-point continuum from 0 (not important) to 10 (very important). The respondents averaged 7.4 per item when asked about the importance of a future mate (in contrast to a mean of 6.8, reflecting importance of similarity in a dating partner).

Women were significantly more likely than men to prefer a mate with similar characteristics. Both women and men believed that happier and more durable relationships result when the partners are homogamous. Other research confirms their belief (Houts, Robins, & Huston 1996; Michael et al., 1994). Some of the homogamous factors operative in mate selection include the following.

1. *Race*. Racial homogamy operates strongly in selecting a living-together and marital partner (with greater homogamy for marital partners) (Blackwell & Lichter, 2000).

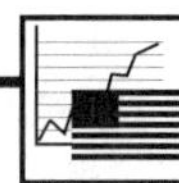

NATIONAL DATA Of the more than 56 million married couples in the United States, more than 95% consist of spouses who have the same racial background (*Statistical Abstract of the United States: 2002*, Table 47).

Some evidence suggests that openness among college students to dating/involvement with those across racial lines may be increasing. In a study of 620 university students (Knox, Zusman, Buffington, & Hemphill, 2000), almost half (49.6%) of the respondents reported that they were open to involvement in an interracial relationship. Almost a quarter (24.2%) said that they had dated someone of another race. Although there were no significant differences in sex (women vs. men) or university rank (freshman, sophomore, junior, senior) between those who were open to interracial involvements and those who were not, there were significant differences in regard to race, cohabitation experience, previous interracial dating experience, and openness to cohabit.

2. *Age*. When a friend gets you a date, you assume the person will be close to your age. Your peers are not likely to approve of your becoming involved with someone twice your age.

NATIONAL DATA The median ages of first-married females and males are 24.5 and 26.7, respectively (Saluter, 1996).

3. *Education*. Educational homogamy also operates strongly in selecting a living-together and marital partner (with greater homogamy for marital partners) (Blackwell & Lichter, 2000). Not only does college provide an opportunity to meet, date, live together, and marry another college student, but it also increases one's chance that only college-educated partners become acceptable as a potential cohabitant or spouse. The very pursuit of education becomes a value to be shared. However, Lewis and Oppenheimer (2000) observed that when persons of similar education are not available, women are particularly likely to marry someone with less education. And the older the woman, the more likely she is to marry a partner with less education.
4. *Social Class*. You have been reared in a particular social class that reflects your parents' occupations, incomes, and educations as well as your residence, language, and values. The social class in which you were reared will influence how comfortable you feel with a partner. "I never knew what a finger bowl was," recalled one man, "until I ate dinner with my girlfriend in her parents' Manhattan apartment. I knew then that while her lifestyle was exciting, I was more comfortable with paper napkins and potato chips. We stopped dating." Indeed, women who have high incomes may either be less attractive as partners or have less need for a husband. Greenstein (1992) noted in a national sample of 2,375 never-married women that high-income women were less likely to marry.

   The **mating gradient** refers to the tendency for husbands to be more advanced than their wives with regard to age, education, and occupational success. Two researchers assessed the expectations of 131 single female and 103 male college

Mating gradient The tendency for husbands to be more advanced than their wives with regard to age, education, and occupational success.

students and found that most women expected their husbands to be "superior in intelligence, ability, success, income, and education. Less than 10% of the women in this sample expected to exceed their marriage partner on any of the variables measured" (Ganong & Coleman, 1992, p. 61).

As a result of the mating gradient, some high-status women remain single. Upper-class women typically receive approval from their parents and peers only if they marry someone of equal status. Highly educated women, rather than drop their standards, may decide to remain unmarried. Conversely, those who improve their own educational and economic opportunities "improve the likelihood of marrying a man of means." This finding is based on a national sample of 1,711 women in their first marriages (Lichter, Anderson, & Hayward 1995, p. 429).

5. *Physical Appearance*. In general, people tend to become involved with those who are similar in physical attractiveness. However, a partner's attractiveness may be a more important consideration for men than for women. In the study of homogamous preferences in mate selection, men and women rated physical appearance an average of 7.7 and 6.8 (out of 10) in importance, respectively (Knox et al., 1997). Subramanian (1997) interviewed 3,000 individuals in 21 cities and found that single men ranked physical attractiveness as the most important quality in selecting a mate.

   Physical appearance and capacity are not the focus of some individuals. After Mitchell Tepper became physically challenged and dependent on a wheelchair, he wondered whether he could find a partner who would look beyond his chair. To his surprise, he met Cheryl, whom he later married and with whom he had a child. Mitch says "that contrary to popular belief . . . there are people in this world who care for more than physical qualities when they are looking for an intimate connection. There are people who are attracted to a myriad of other qualities or virtues that have nothing to do with physical appearance or physical ability. These qualities include but are not limited to intelligence, personality, humor, deep reflective thought, creativity, kindness, goodness, integrity, and spirit" (Tepper & Tepper, 1996).
6. *Marital Status*. The never-married tend to select as marriage partners the never-married, the divorced tend to select the divorced, and the widowed tend to select the widowed. Similar marital status may be more important to women than to men. In the study of homogamous preferences in mate selection, women and men rated similarity of marital status an average of 7.2 and 6.3 (out of 10) in importance, respectively (Knox et al., 1997).
7. *Religion*. Religion is not just a creed, thought, experience, or affiliation and it may impact individuals in various ways (Brodsky, 2000). More than 83% of all first-year college students reported that they had attended a religious service in the past year (Bartlett, 2002). Booth, Johnson, Branaman, and Sica (1995) found that religiosity is also related to marital happiness in that it may be associated with a common activity such as attending church.
8. *Love Story Homogamy*. Sternberg (2000) identified 25 potential love stories that individuals bring into a relationship and that "story compatibility" is associated with happy, fulfilling, and enduring relationships. These stories include
   a. *Gardening Story*. Relationships are seen as needing attention and nurturing to thrive.
   b. *Humor Story*. Being able to laugh at one's self and the relationship and not taking things too seriously are the conditions of a successful relationship.
   c. *Travel Story*. Relationships are like a shared journey that is both exciting and challenging.
   d. *Business Story*. Successful relationships depend on the partners assuming certain roles that mesh well.
   e. *Fantasy Story*. The partners believe that theirs is a perfect mate and match and that they have found each other.

   An example of a mismatch is the business and fantasy stories. Partners adopting the business story assume that all will be well if only each person will play his or her respective role. Meanwhile, partners adopting the fantasy story believe that everything will be okay and, if it isn't, the reason is that the partners were not meant for each other.

9. *Personality*. Partners who select others with similar personalities report high subjective well-being (Arrindell & Luteijn, 2000). Conservatives, liberals, risk takers, etc., tend to select each other. And their doing so has positive consequences for themselves and their relationship.

2-6c Psychological Factors in Mate Selection

Psychologists have focused on complementary needs, exchanges, parental characteristics, and personality types with regard to mate selection.

Complementary-Needs Theory

"In spite of the women's movement and a lot of assertive friends, I am a shy and dependent person," remarked a transfer student. "My need for dependency is met by Warren, who is the dominant, protective type." The tendency for a submissive person to become involved with a dominant person (one who likes to control the behavior of others) is an example of attraction based on complementary needs.

Complementary-needs theory states that we tend to select mates whose needs are opposite and complementary to our own needs. Partners can also be drawn to each other on the basis of nurturance versus receptivity. These complementary needs suggest that one person likes to give and take care of another, while the other likes to be the benefactor of such care. Other examples of complementary needs may involve responsibility versus irresponsibility, peacemaker versus troublemaker, and disorder versus order. The idea that mate selection is based on complementary needs was suggested by Winch (1955), who noted that needs can be complementary if they are different (for example, dominant and submissive) or if the partners have the same need at different levels of intensity. As an example of the latter, two individuals may have a complementary relationship when they both want to do advanced graduate study but do not both have a need to get a Ph.D. The partners will complement each other if one is comfortable with his or her level of aspiration as represented by a master's degree but still approves of the other's commitment to earn a Ph.D.

Complementary-needs theory Theory of mate selection which states that one tends to select mates whose needs are opposite and complementary to one's own needs.

Winch's theory of complementary needs, commonly referred to as "opposites attract," is based on the observation of 25 undergraduate married couples at Northwestern University. The findings have been criticized by other researchers who have not been able to replicate Winch's study (Saint, 1994). Two researchers said, "It would now appear that Winch's findings may have been an artifact of either his methodology or his sample of married people" (Meyer & Pepper, 1977).

Three questions can be raised about the theory of complementary needs:

1. Couldn't personality needs be met just as easily outside the couple's relationship as through mate selection? For example, couldn't a person who has the need to be dominant find such fulfillment in a job that involved an authoritative role, such as being a supervisor?
2. What is a complementary need as opposed to a similar value? For example, is desire to achieve at different levels a complementary need or a shared value?
3. Don't people change as they age? Could a dependent person grow and develop self-confidence so that he or she might no longer need to be involved with a dominant person? Indeed, the person might no longer enjoy interacting with a dominant person.

Think About It

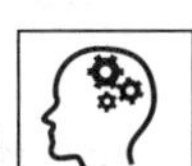

Skowron (2000) studied differences and couple discord and found that greater the differences among spouses in a relationship, the greater their marital distress. To what degree do you feel being similar or different from a partner affects relationship happiness?

Exchange Theory

Exchange theory Theory of mate selection which holds that partners select each other on the basis of who offers the greatest rewards at the lowest cost.

Exchange theory emphasizes that mate selection is based on assessing who offers the greatest rewards at the lowest cost. Five concepts help to explain the exchange process in mate selection:

1. Rewards are the behaviors (your partner looking at you with the eyes of love), words (saying "I love you"), resources (being beautiful or handsome; having a car, condo, and money), and services (cooking for you, typing for you) your partner provides for you that you value and that influence you to continue the relationship.
2. Costs are the unpleasant aspects of a relationship. A woman identified the costs associated with being involved with her partner: "He abuses drugs, doesn't have a job, and lives nine hours away." The costs her partner associated with being involved with this woman included "she nags me," "she doesn't like sex," and "she wants her mother to live with us if we marry."
3. Profit occurs when the rewards exceed the costs. Unless the couple referred to in concept #2 derive a profit from staying together, they are likely to end their relationship.
4. Loss occurs when the costs exceed the rewards.
5. No other person who offers a higher profit is currently available.

Most people have definite ideas about what they are looking for in a mate. The currency used in the marriage market consists of the socially valued characteristics of the persons involved, such as age, physical characteristics, and economic status. In our free-choice system of mate selection, we typically get as much in return for our social attributes as we can.

Many men advertising in the personals section of a local newspaper want a young, slim, attractive woman. That means that such a woman has her pick of partners. Any man she chooses must have some attribute of his own that she highly values (Michael et al., 1994). Subramanian (1997) reported data from more than 3,000 interviews in 21 cities and found that very attractive women believed that they were entitled to and expected an economically successful partner. Raley and Bratter (2000) analyzed data from a national sample of single women who were asked to indicate on a seven-point continuum (7 = most likely, 1= least likely), how likely they would be to marry someone who earned more money. The average score of the women was 5.87, suggesting a high likelihood that they would ensure that their marriage partner earned more money. The likelihood they gave of marrying someone who "cannot hold a steady job" was 1.7.

When you identify a person who offers you a good exchange for what you have to offer, other bargains are made about the conditions of your continued relationship. Waller and Hill (1951) observed that the person who has the least interest in continuing the relationship can control the relationship. This **principle of least interest** is illustrated by the woman who said, "He wants to date me more than I want to date him, so we end up going where I want to go and doing what I want to do." In this case, the woman trades her company for the man's acquiescence to her choices.

Principle of least interest The person who has the least interest in a relationship controls the relationship.

Parental Characteristics

Whereas the complementary needs and exchange theories of mate selection are relatively recent, Freud suggested that the choice of a love object in adulthood represents a shift in libidinal energy from the first love objects—the parents. Role theory and modeling theory emphasize that a son or daughter models after the parent of the same sex by selecting a partner similar to the one the parent selected. This means that a man looks for a wife who has similar characteristics to those of his mother and that a woman looks for a husband who is very similar to her father.

Desired Personality Characteristics for a Potential Mate

In an impressive cross-cultural study, Buss and colleagues asked more than 10,000 men and women from 37 countries, located on six continents and five islands, to identify the personality characteristics they most desired in a potential mate. The preferences for the top four characteristics identified by both men and women were identical: mutual attraction (love), dependable character, emotional stability/maturity, and pleasing disposition (Buss et al., 1990). One of the differences between men and women was men's greater emphasis on good looks and women's greater importance placed on ambition/economic potential.

Recently, Buss, Shackelford, Kirkpatrick, and Larsen (2001) examined factors influencing mate preferences among college students across the past half century (1939–1996). They found that during this time frame students increasingly rated the importance of mutual attraction and love. Although the earlier-mentioned sex differences persisted, the researchers observed some shift in men's values becoming more similar to those of women (putting more importance on a potential mate's financial prospect and less importance on domestic skills). This may reflect a trend toward a more common evaluation standard used by men and women. The characteristics of dependable character, emotional stability, and pleasing disposition remained important, and having a similar political background appeared irrelevant.

Finally, it is also apparent that although persons seeking partners consider particular characteristics ideal, they are willing to weigh the relative importance of those attributes. They also take into account constraints on their choices and are willing to compromise, as shown in the classic study by Pennebaker et al. (1979). When patrons at nightclubs near a college campus were approached at 9:00 P.M., 10:00 P.M., and midnight, they were asked to rate the attractiveness of men and women in the bars. As bar closing time approached, the ratings of attractiveness markedly increased for opposite-sex (not same-sex) individuals. The researchers interpreted this change as evidence of shifting criteria in response to selection pressure. In addition, researchers have discovered that partner selection varies for different types of relationships. Physical appearance seems more important in selecting casual sex partners, while long-term partners are chosen more for their positive social skills and emotional warmth (Regan, 2000).

SUMMARY

Sexual expression occurs on the basis of our values and emotions. This chapter emphasized how values and emotions influence sexual behavior.

Alternative Sexual Values

Sexual values are moral guidelines for making sexual choices in nonmarital, marital, heterosexual, and homosexual relationships. Among the various sexual values are absolutism (a belief system that is based on the unconditional power and authority of religion, law, or tradition), relativism (sexual decisions should be made in the context of a particular situation), and hedonism (the pursuit of pleasure and the avoidance of pain are the ultimate value and motivation for sexual behavior). Relativism is the predominant sexual value of university students.

The Sexual Double Standard

The sexual double standard in our society encourages men to have more sexual partners and women to have fewer partners. The standard still persists even in today's society.

Sources of Sexual Values

Many contemporary sexual values (such as the beliefs that masturbation, adultery, and homosexuality are wrong) have their roots in Jewish and Christian religious influences that emphasize sexuality within marriage. The Victorian era is known for its prudery and propriety about sexual behavior. Whereas private sexual behavior included "just about everything," the public norms emphasized sex only within marriage, suppression of talking about sex, and the labeling of "good" and "bad" women in reference to their sexual behavior. Scientific ideologies shifted the view of sex from the sacred to the scientific, whereby sexuality was dissected and explained.

Television, family members, peers, and sex education programs in public schools continue to be important sources of sexual values. Television exposure to sexuality can be faulted because it emphasizes romance and excitement but does not promote responsible pregnancy and STD prevention. Parents typically promote various sexual values, but as sources of sexual information, they are often inadequate. Parents' reluctance to talk to their children about sex is often based on their own insecurity about their level of sexual knowledge, as well as the fear that telling their children about sex will promote sexual activity. Teachers are variable sources of sex information and values because each state, rather than the federal government, is responsible for sex education in the public school system. Local school boards may also influence the content, with some programs emphasizing "value-free" sex education focusing on the biology of sex and reproduction. Other programs emphasize absolutist sexual values and urge "abstinence only." There continues to be a great debate about whether we, as a nation, should support sex education in public schools.

Emotions: Love and Sexual Values

Love and guilt are two emotions that interact with sexual values. Regarding love, women are more likely to require love as a context for sexual involvement. Hedonists feel that love is irrelevant when selecting a sexual partner.

Sternberg's triangular theory of love identifies types of love based on the presence or absence of three elements: intimacy, passion, and commitment. Another typology of love was developed by Lee to describe various love styles: ludus, storge, pragma, mania, and agape.

Sex and love have both similarities (both involve intense feelings, physiological changes, need increases with deprivation) and differences (love is crucial to human happiness, but sex is not; love requires the person, whereas sex wants a person).

Emotions: Challenges to Love and Relationships

Jealously results from feeling that one's love relationship with another is being threatened. Feelings of jealousy may ignite from both external and internal sources. Jealousy has both positive (establishes parameters) and negative (partner may feel unjustly accused and terminate relationship) consequences.

Sexual guilt is the feeling that results from the violation of one's own sexual values. Guilt may result when one goes against what one thinks he or she should not do ("I should not have gotten drunk and had intercourse"—one student referred to this as the "walk of shame" the next morning) or does not behave consistent with the way one thinks one should ("I should have been faithful").

Women report feeling more guilty than men after their first sexual intercourse but less guilty than men over their most recent sexual intercourse. The lower percentage of women reporting guilt in their most recent intercourse experience may reflect a more stable emotional relationship context, which is the condition needed for cultural approval for female sexual expression. Absolutist religious sexual values are associated with sexual guilt.

Unrequited love has been described as difficult for the would-be suitor, as well as for the person who rejects unwanted attention.

Obsessive relational intrusion and stalking involve unwanted pursuit and invasion of the target person's privacy. The victim's social and work-related activities may be curtailed as a result. Direct communication of disinterest may be helpful in managing such unwanted attention.

Attraction and Mate Selection

Individuals are attracted to each other in reference to cultural (endogamy, exogamy), sociological (homogamy), and psychological factors (complementary needs, exchange theory).

SUGGESTED WEBSITES

Note: These websites were functional when we went to press. Please access the online text for the most up-to-date URLs.

Alan Guttmacher Institute
http://www.agi-usa.org/

Abstinence Education—Pro
http://www.abstinence.net/
http://abstinenceedu.com/

Abstinence Education—Con
http://www.ncac.org/issues/abonlypresskit.html

American School Health Association
http://www.ashaweb.org/

Ecpat International
http://www.ecpat.net/eng/index.asp

Sexual Education
http://www/siecus.org
http://www.itsyoursexlife.com
http://www.sxetc.org/
http://www.qualitylife.org/

KEY TERMS

absolutism (p. 33)
asceticism (p. 34)
bestiality (p. 37)
bundling (p. 37)
complementary-needs theory (p. 55)
endogamy (p. 52)
exchange theory (p. 56)
exogamy (p. 52)
hedonism (p. 35)
homogamy theory (p. 52)
jealousy (p. 48)
mating gradient (p. 53)
obsessive relational intrusion (p. 51)
principle of least interest (p. 56)
relativism (p. 34)
sexual double standard (p. 35)
sexual guilt (p. 50)
sexual values (p. 32)
spiritualistic dualism (p. 37)
stalking (p. 51)
tarrying (p. 37)

CHAPTER QUIZ

1. Which of the following value systems emphasizes that sexual decisions should be made in the context of a particular situation?
- **a.** hedonism
- **b.** absolutism
- **c.** relativism
- **d.** asceticism

2. Which of the following sexual values is associated with a higher likelihood of having more than one sexual partner in the past year?
- **a.** hedonism
- **b.** relativism
- **c.** absolutism
- **d.** asceticism

3. In a case mentioned in your text, why did a Catholic bishop refuse to sanction the marriage of a man who was paraplegic?
- **a.** The man was not Catholic.
- **b.** The bishop believed that the man would not be able to have intercourse and father children.
- **c.** The man wanted to marry another man.
- **d.** The bishop believed that the man's motivation for marrying was to have a caregiver, rather than a soulmate.

4. An analysis of 248 television episodes involving 3,228 scenes showing sexual activity found which of the following?
- **a.** No episodes portrayed a character getting a sexually transmitted disease
- **b.** Five episodes portrayed a character getting infected with HIV.
- **c.** Sixty-two episodes portrayed a character getting infected with either HIV, syphilis, human papilloma virus, chlamydia, or herpes.
- **d.** Three episodes portrayed a character who died from AIDS and 14 episodes portrayed a character who became infected with either HIV or herpes.

5. The federal government supports school sex education programs that
- **a.** emphasize relativistic sexual values.
- **b.** provide students with access to contraception.
- **c.** emphasize practicing "safe sex" by using condoms.
- **d.** emphasize abstinence.

6. According to Robert Sternberg's (1986) "triangular theory of love," various types of love can be described on the basis of three elements. Which of the following is NOT one of the three elements of love, according to Sternberg's theory?
- **a.** passion
- **b.** compatibility
- **c.** commitment
- **d.** intimacy

7. According to Robert Sternberg's triangular theory of love, what kind of love involves the presence of all three elements of love?
   a. fatuous love
   b. romantic love
   c. consummate love
   d. companionate love
8. Which of the following love styles are associated with the lowest relationship satisfaction?
   a. eros and ludus
   b. mania and agape
   c. storge and pragma
   d. ludus and mania
9. When a person is in an intense love relationship, his or her brain produces phenylethylamine, a chemical that is similar to which of the following?
   a. amphetamines
   b. opiates
   c. hallucinogenics
   d. sedatives
10. Most women in the United States report that the man they had their first intercourse experience with is the man they eventually married.
   a. True
   b. False
11. According to research cited in your text, there are ________ gender differences in likelihood, frequency, duration, and intensity of jealousy.
   a. significant
   b. no
12. Mistrust, low self-esteem, and insecurity are examples of __________ causes of jealousy.
   a. internal
   b. external
13. Research cited in your text examined guilt feelings reported by women and men in reference to their first intercourse experience. This research found that ____________ reported feeling guilty after their first intercourse experience.
   a. more than half of both women and men
   b. less than one quarter of both women and men
   c. more than half of the women and less than half of the men
   d. more than half of the men and less than half of the women
14. Which of the following theories of mate selection states that we tend to be attracted to and become involved with those who are similar to ourselves in such characteristics as age, race, religion, and social class?
   a. complementary needs
   b. principle of least interest
   c. exchange theory
   d. homogamy
15. According to complementary-needs theory, a person who needs to nurture others is likely to select a mate who
   a. needs to be nurtured.
   b. also likes to nurture others.
   c. can nurture himself or herself.
   d. does not want to be nurtured.
16. In a cross-cultural study, researchers asked women and men in 37 countries to identify personality characteristics they most desired in a potential mate. Which of the following personality traits was NOT identified by the women and men in this study as a trait they most desired in a potential mate?
   a. dependable character
   b. economic ambition
   c. emotional maturity
   d. pleasing disposition

REFERENCES

Arrindell, W. A. & Luteijn, F. (2000). Similarity between intimate partners for personality traits as related to individual levels of satisfactions with life. *Personality and Individual Differences, 28*, 629–637.

Attridge, M., Berscheid, E., & Sprecher, S. (1998). Dependence and insecurity in romantic relationships: Development and validation of two companion scales. *Personal Relationships, 5*, 31–58.

Barak, A., & Fisher, W. A. (2001). Toward an Internet-driven, theoretically-based, innovative approach to sex education. *The Journal of Sex Research, 38*, 324–332.

Barnett, O. W., Martinez, T. E., & Bluestein, B. W. (1995). Jealousy and romantic attachment in maritally violent and nonviolent men. *Journal of Interpersonal Violence, 10*, 473–478.

Bar-on, M. E., Broughton, D. D., Buttross, S., Corrigan, S., Gedissman, A., Gonzalez de Rivas et al. (2001). Sexuality, contraception, and the media. *Pediatrics, 107*, 191–194.

Bartlett, T. (2002, February). Freshman pay, mentally and physically, as they adjust to life in college: New survey provides more data on what happens during that crucial first year. *The Chronicle of Higher Education*, A35–A37.

Baumeister, R. F., & Bratslavsky, E. (1999). Passion, intimacy, and time: Passionate love as a function of change in intimacy. *Personality & Social Psychology Review, 3*, 49–67.

Baumeister, R. R., Wotman, S. R., & Stillwell, A. M. (1993). Unrequited love: On heartbreak, anger, guilt, scriptlessness, and humiliation. *Journal of Personality and Social Psychology, 64*, 377–394.

Bay-Cheng, L. Y. (2001). SexEd.com: Values and norms in web-based sexuality education. *The Journal of Sex Research, 38*, 241–251.

Berne, L., & Huberman, B. (1996). Sexuality education works: Here's proof. *The Education Digest, 61* (6), 25–30.

Blackwell, D. L., & Lichter, D. T. (2000). Mate selection among married and cohabiting couples. *Journal of Family Issues, 21*, 275–302.

Booth, A., Johnson, D. R., Branaman, A., & Sica, A. (1995). Belief and behavior: Does religion matter in today's marriage? *Journal of Marriage and the Family, 57*, 661–671.

Brodsky, A. E. (2000). The role of religion in the lives of resilient, urban, African-American, single mothers. *Journal of Marriage and the Family, 55*, 338–355.

Browning, J. R., Hatfield, E., Kessler, D., & Levine, T. (2000). Sexual motives, gender, and sexual behavior. *Archives of Sexual Behavior, 29*, 135–154.

Bullough, V. L. (1987). A historical approach. In J. H. Greer & W. T. O'Donohue (Eds.), *Theories of human sexuality* (pp. 49–63). New York: Plenum Press.

Buss, D. M. (2000, May/June). Prescription for passion. *Psychology Today*. 54–61.

Buss, D. M. et al. (1990). International preferences in selecting mates: A study of 37 cultures. *Journal of Cross-Cultural Psychology, 21*(4), 5–47.

Buss, D. M., & Schmitt, D. P. (1993). Sexual strategies theory: An evolutionary perspective on human mating. *Psychological Review, 100*, 204–232.

Buss, D. M., Shackelford, T. K., Kirkpatrick, L. A., & Larsen, R. J. (2001). A half century of mate preferences: The cultural evolution of values. *Journal of Marriage and Family*, 63, 491–503.

Calhoun, A. (1960). *A Social History of the American Family*. New York: Barnes and Noble.

Cameron, N., & Rychlak, J. E. (1985). *Personality development and psychopathology* (2nd ed.). Boston: Houghton Mifflin.

Carroll, J. L., Volk, K. D., & Hyde, J. S. (1985). Differences between males and females in motives for engaging in sexual intercourse. *Archives of Sexual Behavior, 14*, 131–139.

Cassidy, M. L., & Lee, G. (1989). The study of polyandry: A critique and syntheses. *Journal of Comparative Family Studies, 20*, 1–11.

Contreras, R., Hendrick, S. S., & Hendrick, C. (1996). Perspectives on marital love and satisfaction in Mexican American and Anglo-American couples. *Journal of Counseling & Development, 74*, 408–415.

Cubbins, L. A., & Tanfer, K. (2000) The influence of gender on sex: A study of men's and women's self-reported high-risk sex behavior. *Archives of Sexual Behavior, 29*, 229–256.

Cupach, W. R., & Spitzberg, B. H. (1998). Obsessive relational intrusion and stalking. In B. H. Spitzberg & W. R. Cupach, (Eds.), *The dark side of close relationships* (pp. 233–263). Mahway, NJ: Erlbaum.

Davidson, K. J., Darling, C., & Norton, L. (1995). Religiosity and the sexuality of women: Sexual behavior and sexual satisfaction revisited. *The Journal of Sex Research, 32*, 235–243.

Devlin, P. (1965). *The enforcement of morals*. New York: Oxford University Press.

Elia, J. P. (2000). Democratic sexuality education: A departure from sexual ideologies and traditional schooling. *Journal of Sex Education and Therapy, 25*, 122–129.

Evanston, M. E., Broughton, D. D., Buttross, S., Corrigan, S., Gedissman, A., GonzAlez de Rivas et al. (2001). Sexuality, contraception, and the media. *Pediatrics, 107*, 191–194.

Fitzharris, J. L., & Werner-Wilson, R. J. (2000, November). Talking to adolescents about sex: Dilemmas and recommendations. Paper presented at the Annual Conference of the National Council on Family Relations, Minneapolis, MN.

Freeman, J. L. (1978). *Happy people*. New York: Harcourt Brace Jovanovich.

Gallup Organization Poll Analysis. (2001, May 24). Majority considers sex before marriage morally okay. www.gallup.com/poll/releases pr010524.asp

Ganong, L. W., & Coleman, M. (1992). Gender differences in expectations of self and future partner. *Journal of Family Issues, 13*, 55–64.

Greenstein, T. N. (1992). Delaying marriage: Women's work experience and marital timing. Paper presented at the 54th Annual Conference of the National Council on Family Relations, Orlando, FL.

Harris, C. R. (2002). Sexual and romantic jealousy in heterosexual and homosexual adults. *Psychological Science, 13*, 7–11.

Hatfield, E., & Rapson, R. L. (1996). *Love and sex: Cross-cultural perspectives*. Boston: Allyn & Bacon.

Heaton, T. B., & Jacobson, C. K. (2000). Intergroup marriage: An examination of opportunity structures. *Sociological Inquiry, 70*, 30–41.

Hendrick, S. S., & Hendrick, C. (1992). *Romantic love*. Newbury Park, CA: Sage.

Houts, R. M., Robins, E., & Huston, T. L. (1996). Compatibility and the development of premarital relationships. *Journal of Marriage and the Family*, 58, 7–20.

Johnson, W. S. (1979). *Living in sin: The Victorian sexual revolution*. Chicago: Nelson-Hall.

Killian, K. D. (1997). What's the difference: Negotiating race, class and gender in interracial relationships. Paper presented at the Annual Conference of the National Council on Family Relations, Crystal City, VA.

Kimmel, M. S. (2000). *The gendered society*. New York: Oxford University Press.

Knox, D. (1969). Conceptions of love at three developmental levels. Dissertation, Florida State University.

Knox, D., Cooper, C., & Zusman, M. E. (2001). Sexual values of college students. *College Student Journal, 35*, 24–27.

Knox, D., Hatfield, S., & Zusman, M. E. (1998). College student discussion of relationship problems. *College Student Journal, 32*, 19–21.

Knox, D., Schacht, C., & Zusman, M. E. (1999). Love relationships among college students. *College Student Journal, 33*, 149–151.

Knox, D., Walters, L. H., & Walters, J. (1991). Sexual guilt among college students. *College Student Journal, 25*, 432–433.

Knox, D., Zusman, M. E., Buffington, C., & Hemphill, G. (2000). Interracial dating attitudes among college students. *College Student Journal, 34*, 69–71.

Knox, D., Zusman, M. E., & Nieves, W. (1997). College students' homogamous preferences for a date and a mate. *College Student Journal, 31*, 445–448.

Kulwicki, A., & Cass, P. S. (1996). Arab-American knowledge, attitudes, and beliefs about AIDS. In B. Aswad & B. Bilge (Eds.), *Family & gender among American Muslims* (pp. 208–222). Philadelphia: Temple University Press.

Laumann, E. O., & Youm, Y. (2001). Sexual expression in America. In E. O. Laumann & R. T. Michael (Eds.), *Sex, love, and health in America* (pp. 109–147). Chicago: The University of Chicago Press.

Lewis, S. K., & Oppenheimer, V. K. (2000). Educational assortive mating across marriage markets: Non-Hispanic Whites in the United States. *Demography, 37*, 29–40.

Lichter, D. T., Anderson, R. N., & Hayward, M. D. (1995). Marriage markets and marital choice. *Journal of Family Issues, 16*, 412–431.

Lichter, S. R., Lichter, L. S., & Amundson, D. R. (2001). Sexual imagery in popular entertainment. Center for Media and Publications. http://www.cmpa.com/archive/sexpopcult.htm

Liebowitz, M. (1983). *The chemistry of love*. Boston: Little, Brown.

LoPiccolo, J. (1983). The prevention of sexual problems in men. In G. Albee, S. Gordon, & H. Leitenberg (Eds.), *Promoting sexual responsibility and preventing sexual problems* (pp. 39–65). Hanover, NH: University Press of New England.

Mackay, J. L. (2001). Why have sex? *British Medical Journal, 322*, 623–625.

Masters, W. H., & Johnson, V. E. (1966). *Human sexual response*. Boston, MA: Little, Brown.

Meston, C. M., & Frohlich, P. (2000). The neurobiology of sexual function. *Archives of General Psychiatry, 57*, 1012–1030.

Meyer, J. P., & Pepper, S. (1977). Need compatibility and marital adjustment in young married couples. *Journal of Personality and Social Psychology, 35*, 331–342.

Michael, R. T., Gagnon, J. H., Laumann, E. O., & Kolata, G. (1994). *Sex in America: A definitive survey*. Boston: Little, Brown.

Miller, B. C. (2002). Family influences on adolescent sexual and contraceptive behavior. *The Journal of Sex Research, 39*, 22–27.

Money, J. (1980). *Love and lovesickness: The science of sex, gender difference, and pair bonding*. Baltimore: Johns Hopkins University Press.

Montgomery, M. J., & Sorell, G. T. (1997). Differences in love attitudes across family life stages. *Family Relations, 46*, 55–61.

Nelson, J. B. (1983). Religious dimensions of sexual health. In G. W. Albee, S. Gordon, and H. Leitenberg (Eds.), *Promoting sexual responsibility and preventing sexual problems*. Hanover, NH: University Press of New England, 121–132.

Paul, E. L., McManus, B., and Hayes, A. (2000). "Hookups": Characteristics and correlates of college students' spontaneous and anonymous sexual experiences. *The Journal of Sex Research, 37*, 76–88.

Pennebaker, J. W., Dwyer, M. A., Caulkins, R. S., Litowitz, D. L., Ackreman, P. L., Anderson, D. B., et al. (1979). Don't the girls get prettier at closing time: A country and western application to psychology. *Personality and Social Psychology Bulletin, 5*, 122–125

Peretti, P. O., & Pudowski, B. C. (1997). Influence of jealousy on male and female college daters. *Social Behavior and Personality, 25*, 155–160.

Pines, A. M. (1992) *Romantic jealousy: Understanding and conquering the shadow of love*. New York: St. Martin's.

Pines, A. M., & Friedman, A. (1998). Gender differences in romantic jealousy. *Journal of Social Psychology, 138*, 54–71.

Radecki-Bush, C. R., Bush, J. P., & Jennings, J. (1988). Effects of jealousy threats on relationship perceptions and emotions. *Journal of Social and Personal Relationships*, 5, 285–303.

Raley, K., & Bratter, J. (2000). Not even if you were the last man on earth. *American Demographics*. February, 11–12.

Raley, R. K. (2000). Recent trends and differentials in marriage and cohabitation: The United States. In L. J. Waite (Ed.), *The ties that bind* (pp. 19–39). New York: Aldine de Gruyter.

Regan, P. (2000). Love relationships. In L. T. Szuchman & F. Muscarella (Eds.), *Psychological perspectives on human sexuality* (pp. 232–282). New York: Wiley.

Romo, L. F., Lefkowitz, E. S., Sigman, M., & Au, T. K. (2001). Determinants of mother–adolescent communication about sex in Latino families. *Adolescent & Family Health, 2*, 72–82.

Saint, D. J. (1994). Complementarity in marital relationships. *Journal of Social Psychology, 134*, 701–704.

Saluter, A. F. (1996). Marital status and living arrangements. March 1994. U.S. Bureau of the Census, Current Populations Reports, Series P20484. Washington, DC: U.S. Government Printing Office.

Sather, L., & Zinn, K. (2002). Effects of abstinence-only education on adolescent attitudes and values concerning premarital sexual intercourse. *Family and Community Health, 25*, 15–20.

Selverstone, R. (2000). On governance, psychology, education and sexuality. *Journal of Sex Education and Therapy, 25*, 114–121.

Skowron, E. A. (2000). The role of differentiation of self in marital adjustment. *Journal of Counseling Psychology, 47*, 229–237.

Snyder, D. K., & Regts, J. M. (1990). Personality correlates of marital dissatisfaction: A comparison of psychiatric, maritally distressed, and nonclinic samples. *Journal of Sex and Marital Therapy, 90*, 34–43.

Somers, C. L., & Gleason, J. H. (2001). Does source of sex education predict adolescents' sexual knowledge, attitudes and behaviors? *Education, 121*, 674–682.

Sonfield, A., & Gold, R. B. (2001). States' implementation of the section 510 abstinence education program, FY 1999. *Family Planning Perspectives, 33*, 166–171.

Spitzberg, B. H., & Cupach, W. R. (Eds.). (1998). *The dark side of close relationships*. Mahway, NJ: Erlbaum.

Sprecher, S., & Regan, P. C. (1996). College virgins: How men and women perceive their sexual status. *The Journal of Sex Research, 33*, 3–5.

Statistical Abstract of the United States: 2002. (2002). 122nd ed. Washington, DC: U.S. Bureau of the Census.

Sternberg, R. J. (1986). A triangular theory of love. *Psychological Review, 93*, 119–135.

Sternberg, R. J. (2000, July/August,). What's your love story? *Psychology Today*, 52–59.

Stets, J. E. (1995). Modeling control in relationships. *Journal of Marriage and the Family*, *57*, 489–501.

Subramanian, S. (1997, August). Economic considerations in mate selection criteria. Paper presented at the Annual Convention of the American Psychological Association, Chicago, IL.

Tannahill, R. (1982). *Sex in history*. New York: Stein and Day.

Tepper, M., & Tepper, C. (1996). Finding the Right Mate. Sexual Health Network.

Thomsen, D., & Chang, I. J. (2000, November). Predictors of satisfaction with first intercourse: A new perspective for sexuality education. Poster presentation at the 62nd Annual Conference for the National Council on Family Relations, Minneapolis, MN.

Troth, A., & Peterson, C. C. (2000). Factors predicting safe-sex talk and condom use in early sexual relationships. *Health Communication*, *12*, 195–218.

Waller, W., & Hill, R. (1951). *The family: A dynamic interpretation*. New York: Holt, Rinehart and Winston.

Walsh, A. (1991). *The science of love: Understanding love and its effects on mind and body*. Buffalo, NY: Prometheus.

Weinberg, M. S., Lottes, I. L., & Shaver, F. M. (1995). Swedish or American heterosexual college youth: Who is more permissive? *Archives of Sexual Behavior*, *24*, 409–437.

Weinberg, M. S., Lottes, I., & Shaver, F. M. (2000). Sociocultural correlates of permissive sexual attitudes: A test of Reiss's hypothesis about Sweden and the United States. *The Journal of Sex Research*, 37, 44–52.

Whitaker, D. J., Miller, K. S., & Clark, L. F. (2000). Reconceptualizing adolescent sexual behavior: Beyond did they or didn't they? *Family Planning Perspectives*, *32*, 111–121.

White, G. L. (1980). Inducing jealousy: A power perspective. *Personality and Social Psychology Bulletin*, 6, 222–227.

Wiley, D. C. (2002). The ethics of abstinence-only and abstinence-plus sexuality education. *The Journal of School Health*, *72*, 164–168.

Winch, R. F. (1955). The theory of complementary needs in mate selection. Final results on the test of the general hypothesis. *American Sociological Review*, *20*, 552–555.

Wingood, G. M., DiClemente, R. J., Harrington, K., Davies, S., Hook, III, E. W., & Kim Oh, M. (2002). Exposure to X-rated movies and adolescents' sexual and contraceptive-related attitudes and behaviors. *Pediatrics*, *107*, 1116–1119.

Winton, C. A. (1995). *Frameworks for studying families*. Guilford, CT: Dushkin Publishing Co.

Young, M., & Goldfarb, E. S. (2000). The problematic (a) –(h) in abstinence education. *Journal of Sex Education and Therapy*, *25*, 156–161.

3

Sex Research and Theory

Chapter Outline

Not everything that can be counted counts, and not everything that counts can be counted.

—*Albert Einstein*

Students taking courses in human sexuality are often kidded about being in such classes. Their peers may tease and ask them questions like "Does the class have a lab?" Biologists, psychologists, sociologists, health-care professionals, and others who study human sexuality in their occupational fields may also be subjected to ridicule or smirks. Nevertheless, the study of human sexuality is a serious endeavor. "Studies of all aspects of sex are legitimate, and a professional interest in sex is not prurient but as worthy as any other academic, scientific, or clinical interest" (Diamond, 2000, p. 390).

There is direct public benefit for research in human sexuality. For example, Mitchell, Finkelhor, and Wolak (2001) conducted a telephone survey of a random sample of 1,501 youth aged 10–17 who were regular Internet users and concluded that almost one in five (19%) were targets of unwanted sexual solicitation in the past year. Increased parental monitoring of Internet use by children and the development of social policies/criminal penalties for perpetrators can result from such research.

Human sexuality research involves gathering empirical data *and* using theory to make sense out of the data, although not necessarily in that order. Thus, theory and research are both parts of the scientific process. Theory and empirical research are linked through two forms of reasoning: deductive and inductive.

Deductive research Sequence of research starting with a specific theory, generating a specific expectation or hypothesis based on that theory, and then gathering data that will either support or refute the theory.

Inductive research Sequence of research that begins with specific empirical data, which are then used to formulate a theory to explain the data.

Empirical evidence Data that can be observed, measured, and quantified.

Deductive research involves starting with a specific theory, generating a specific expectation or hypothesis based on that theory, and then gathering data that will either support or refute the theory. For example, researchers might hypothesize that men might move a new acquaintance faster toward sex than women would do in the same situation, and ask university students to complete a questionnaire on dating scripts and sequencing. Alternatively, researchers might engage in **inductive research** that begins with specific data, which are then used to formulate (induce) an explanation (or theory) to explain the data (see Figure 3-1). In this case, researchers might have a data set which shows that men are more aggressive sexually and hypothesize that such aggressiveness is biologically and socially induced. In this chapter, after summarizing basic theories of sexuality, we describe how researchers conduct scientific studies of sexuality. First, however, we review the interdisciplinary nature of the study of sexology.

3-1 OVERVIEW OF SCIENTIFIC RESEARCH

Scientific research involves methods of collecting and analyzing **empirical evidence**, or data that can be observed. What makes scientific knowledge different from other sources

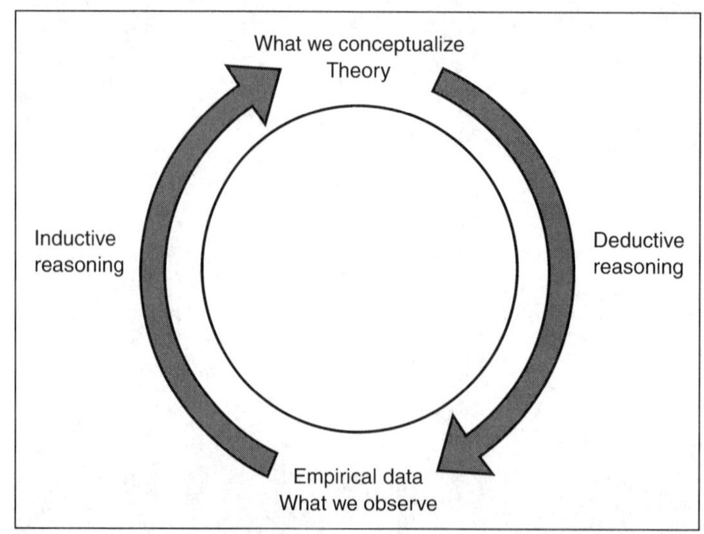

FIGURE 3-1
Links Between Theory and Research: Deductive and Inductive Reasoning

of knowledge, such as common sense (e.g., "living together before marriage means people get to know each other better and results in happier marriages"), intuition ("it just feels like this would be the case"), tradition ("Icelanders have always lived together before marriage and it seems to work"), and authority (religion does not support cohabitation), is the fact that scientific knowledge is supported by observable or empirical evidence (research shows a *higher* divorce rate if couples live together before marriage). Furthermore, researchers are expected to publish not only their findings, but also the methods they used to arrive at their findings. In this way, other researchers and academicians can replicate, scrutinize, and critically examine the research and its findings.

Think About It

How much of your knowledge about human sexuality is based on each of the various sources of knowledge: common sense, intuition, tradition, authority, and scientific research?

3-2 THE INTERDISCIPLINARY NATURE OF SEXOLOGY

Although there are numerous opportunities to study human sexuality, there are no departments in any fully accredited university where one can pursue a doctorate in sexology (Diamond, 2000). Sex researchers represent a broad range of disciplines. The study of sexuality is an interdisciplinary field that incorporates a number of different professions, including psychology, medicine, sociology, family studies, public health, social work, counseling and therapy, history, and education. Basically, the study of sexuality can be divided into three broad approaches: biosexology, psychosexology, and sociosexology.

Biosexology is the study of the biological aspects of sexuality. Studies in this field focus on such topics as the physiological and endocrinological aspects of sexual development and sexual response, the biological processes involved in sexually transmitted diseases, the role of evolution and genetics in our sexual development, the physiology of reproduction, and the development of new contraceptives. Biosexology is also concerned with the effects of drugs, medications, disease, and exercise on sexuality.

Biosexology Study of the biological aspects of sexuality.

Psychosexology involves the study of how psychological processes influence and are influenced by sexual development and behavior. For example, how do emotions and motivations affect sexual performance, the use of contraception, and safe sex practices? What psychological processes are involved in the development of sexual aggression and other forms of sexual deviance? How do various sexual and reproductive experiences (such as pregnancy, rape, infertility, sexual dysfunction, and acquiring a sexually transmitted disease) affect the emotional state of the individual?

Psychosexology Area of sexology focused on how psychological processes influence and are influenced by sexual development and behavior.

Sociosexology is concerned with how social and cultural forces influence and are influenced by sexual attitudes, beliefs, and behaviors. For example, how are culture, age, race, ethnicity, socioeconomic status, and gender related to attitudes, beliefs, and behaviors regarding masturbation, homosexuality, abortion, nonmarital sexual relationships, and HIV infection? Sociosexology is also concerned with how social policy and social institutions (marriage, religion, economics, law and politics, and the health-care system) influence and are influenced by human sexuality. Finally, this approach examines how sexual processes affect and are affected by intimate relationships.

Sociosexology Aspect of sexology that is concerned with how social and cultural forces influence and are influenced by sexual attitudes, beliefs, and behaviors.

In a presidential address to the International Academy of Sex Research, Milton Diamond (2000) emphasized "the need to establish sexology firmly and unequivocally as a fully fledged field of study" (p. 389). He suggested that,

> *[Sexology] is not to be a branch of biology or medicine or sociology or psychology or any other discipline. Yes, professionals of those areas may have a professional interest in sex, but those trained and training in sexology will be individuals aware and knowledgeable of the relevant factors in each of those other fields so that they can integrate, evaluate, produce, and otherwise further the overall subject. (Diamond, 2000, p. 389)*

Sexology A unique discipline that identifies important questions related to sexuality issues and finding/integrating answers from biology, psychology, and sociology based on scientific methods of investigation.

Hence, **sexology** may be thought of as a unique discipline that identifies important questions related to sexuality issues and finding/integrating answers from biology, psychology, and sociology based on scientific methods of investigation.

Think About It

In the sexuality education you received from parents, peers, and school programs, which category of sex information received the most emphasis: biosexology, psychosexology, or sociosexology?

3-3 THEORIES OF SEXUALITY

Theory A set of ideas designed to answer a question or explain a particular phenomenon.

A **theory** is a set of ideas designed to answer a question or to explain a particular phenomenon (e.g., Why does one person rape another or why do some men like to dress up in women's clothes?). In sections 3-3a through 3-3c, we review various theoretical perspectives and their applications to human sexuality.

3-3a Biological Theories

Physiological theories Theories that describe and explain how physiological processes affect and are affected by sexual behavior.

Biological theories of sexuality include both physiological theories and evolutionary theories. **Physiological theories** of sexuality describe and explain how physiological processes affect and are affected by sexual behavior. Cardiovascular, respiratory, neurological, and endocrinological functioning, as well as genetic factors, are all involved in sexual processes and behaviors. For example, what physiological processes are involved in sexual desire, arousal, lubrication, erection, and orgasm? How do various drugs and medications affect sexual functioning? How do various hormones affect sexuality? To what degree are behavioral differences between women and men attributable to their different genetic and hormonal make-ups? What role do hormones and genetics play in sexual orientation?

Evolutionary theories Theory that explains human sexual behavior and sexual anatomy on the basis of human evolution. (See also **sociobiological theories.**)

Sociobiological theories Framework that explains human sexual behavior and sexual anatomy as functional for human evolution. (See also **evolutionary theories.**)

Natural selection The belief that individuals who have genetic traits that are adaptive for survival are more likely to survive and pass on their genetic traits to their offspring.

Evolutionary or **sociobiological theories** of sexuality explain human sexual behavior on the basis of human evolution. According to evolutionary theories of sexuality, sexual behaviors and traits evolve through the process of natural selection (Barash, 1977). Through **natural selection,** individuals who have genetic traits that are adaptive for survival and reproduction are more likely to survive and pass on their genetic traits to their offspring. A male's sperm is viewed as representing little investment. Although a degree of paternal and partner commitment may improve a male's reproductive fitness, the male's best strategy to have offspring is to have many copulations. In contrast, a female's investment in not only contributing an egg, but in carrying a pregnancy to term, is a significantly greater investment. Internal fertilization, gestation, and lactation all increase the female's investment in her offspring (Daly & Wilson, 1983). It is in her sociobiological interest to discriminate among potential partners and mate with a partner who provides resources for supporting the development of the offspring. Dixson, Halliwell, East, Wignarajah, and Anderson (2003) reported that women rated as most attractive men with mesomorphic (muscular) features as opposed to men who were thin or heavily built.

As sociobiologists have pointed out, observing that a trait has evolved as a product of natural selection, or is "natural," does not mean that the trait is good or moral (Alcock, 2001). It means only that the trait is correlated with success in gene propagation. Alcock (p. 193) warns against the "naturalistic fallacy" that could hypothetically be used in defending a rapist by saying "my evolved genes made me do it." However, he suggests that evolutionary data could be used in the development of a high school rape prevention program! His proposed course would advise young men that their genetic heritage could make them more likely to develop a sexual psychology that "can lead some men today to engage in a spectrum of coercive activities . . . our now partially educated young men would be informed that they need not permit their evolved psyches, which are after all working on behalf of their genes, to lead them into actions that could cause others such unhappiness" (pp. 212–213). He would explain that the extreme distress of rape victims is also naturally selected to keep a woman's social partner from abandoning her. Young men and women, with a more accurate knowledge of human nature, could choose to behave adaptively in interpersonal or social, instead of evolutionary, terms.

3-3b Psychological Theories

Biological theories do not account for the influence of personality, learning, thoughts, and emotions on human sexuality. These aspects of sexuality are explained by psychological theories, including psychoanalytic theories, learning theories, and cognitive/affective theories.

Psychoanalytic Theories

Psychoanalytic theory, originally developed by Sigmund Freud (1856–1939), emphasizes the role of unconscious processes in our lives. This theory dominated the early views on the nature of human sexuality. A basic knowledge of Freud's ideas about personality structure is important for understanding his theories of sexuality.

Psychoanalytic theory Freud's theory that emphasizes the role of unconscious processes in one's life.

Freud believed that each person's personality consists of the id, ego, and superego. The **id** refers to instinctive biological drives, such as the need for sex, food, and water. Freud saw human sexuality as a biological force that drove individuals toward the satisfaction of sexual needs and desires. Indeed, one of Freud's most important contributions was his belief that infants and children are sexual beings who possess a positive sexual drive that is biologically wired into their systems.

Id Freud's term that refers to instinctive biological drives, such as the need for sex, food, and water.

Another part of the personality, the **ego**, deals with objective reality as the individual figures out how to obtain the desires of the id. The ego also must be realistic about social expectations. Whereas the id is self-centered and uninhibited, the ego is that part of the person's personality that inhibits the id in order to conform to social expectations. While the id operates on the "pleasure principle," the ego operates on the "reality principle." The ego ensures that individuals do not attempt to fulfill every need and desire whenever they occur. Freud would see rape as a failure of the ego to function properly.

Ego Freud's term for that part of an individual's psyche that deals with objective reality.

The **superego** is the conscience, which functions by guiding the individual to do what is morally right and good. It is the superego that creates feelings of guilt when the ego fails to inhibit the id, and the person engages in socially unacceptable behavior.

Superego Freud's term for the conscience, which functions by guiding the individual to do what is morally right and good.

Freud emphasized that personality develops in stages. When we successfully complete one stage, we are able to develop to the next stage. If we fail to successfully complete any given stage, we become fixated or stuck in that stage. Psychoanalysis untangles the repressed feelings created by a fixation at an earlier stage so that mature sexuality may emerge. The four basic psychosocial stages Freud identified are the oral, anal, phallic, and genital stages (see Table 3-1). Latency is not a stage, but a period of time when psychosexual development is dormant or on hold.

Although Freud developed his theories during an era of sexual repression, he proposed that libido (the sex drive) was the most important of human instincts. While his libido theory was an important contribution, Freud has been criticized as overemphasizing sexual motivation for behavior.

Some clinicians and theorists, initially attracted to psychoanalytic interpretations of human behavior, later extended Freud's work (Anna Freud, Erikson, and other ego-analysts). They, along with more culturally oriented writers, such as Karen Horney (1885–1952), recognized the importance of childhood personality development, but they believed that social, rather than sexual, factors were dominant in personality formation. They felt that the need to emerge from the helpless controlled state of an infant to that of an independent, autonomous individual was the driving force of the individual. Sex played a minor role in the drive for independence.

For example, Erikson (1902–1994) believed that individuals progress through a series of stages as they develop, but unlike Freud, he felt that the states were psychosocial, not

TABLE 3-1

Freud's Four Stages of Psychosocial Development

Stage	Age	Characteristics
Oral	womb to 18 months	Pleasures are derived primarily from meeting oral needs of sucking, licking, and chewing. Pleasure principle dominates, and id focuses on meeting pleasure needs.
Anal	1 to 3 years	Pleasures shift to anal needs and are derived from retention and elimination of urine and feces. Pleasure principle and id are still dominant mechanisms.
Phallic	3 to 6 years	Pleasures shift to stimulation of genitals. Girls discover they have no penis. Masturbation may be practiced, and ego negotiates with id and superego for social control of sexual impulses. Oedipus and Electra complexes develop during this period.
(Latency)	6 years to puberty	Repression of sexual urges.
Genital	Adolescence	Shift away from immature masturbation to appropriate peer-sex interaction.

psychosexual. He believed that central developmental tasks did not involve seeking oral, anal, and genital pleasures but rather establishing basic trust with people. Also, Erikson felt that personality formation did not end in adolescence, but was a lifelong process (most contemporary psychologists agree).

In contrast to Freud's psychoanalytic view of sexuality, other psychological theories explain human sexual attitudes and behaviors as learned. Learning theories include classical conditioning theory, operant learning theory, and social learning theory.

Classical Conditioning Theory

Classical conditioning Behavior modification technique whereby an unconditioned stimulus and a neutral stimulus are linked to elicit a desired response.

Classical conditioning is a process whereby a stimulus and a response that are not originally linked become linked. Ivan Pavlov (1849–1936), a Russian physician, observed that the presence of food caused dogs to salivate. Because salivation is a natural reflex to the presence of food, we call food an *unconditioned stimulus*. However, if Pavlov rang a bell and then gave the dogs food, the dogs soon learned that the bell meant that food was forthcoming, and they would salivate at the sound of the bell. Hence, the bell became a *conditioned stimulus* because it had become associated with the food and was now capable of producing the same response as the food (an unconditioned stimulus).

Sexual fetishes can be explained on the basis of classical conditioning. A fetish is a previously neutral stimulus that becomes a conditioned stimulus for erotic feelings. For example, some people have a feather, foot, or leather fetish, and they respond to these stimuli in erotic ways. But there is nothing about a feather that would serve to elicit erotic feelings unless the feather has been associated with erotic feelings in the past.

How might a person become conditioned to respond to a feather as an erotic stimulus? Perhaps the person may have masturbated and picked up a feather and rubbed it on his or her genitals. Or the person may have observed a stripper in person or on a video who used a feather as part of the erotic dance. In either case, the feather would become a conditioned stimulus and would elicit erotic feelings in the same way the masturbation and stripper did as an unconditioned stimulus.

Operant Learning Theory

Operant learning theory An explanation of human behavior which emphasizes that the consequences of a behavior influence whether or not that behavior will occur in the future.

Reinforcement A consequence that maintains or increases a behavior.

Operant learning theory, largely developed by B. F. Skinner (1904–1990), emphasizes that the consequences of a behavior influence whether or not that behavior will occur in the future. Consequences that follow a behavior may maintain or increase the behavior, or may decrease or terminate it. A consequence that maintains or increases a behavior is known as **reinforcement.** A consequence that decreases or terminates a behavior is known as **punishment.** A partner who has been reinforced for initiating sexual behavior is likely to do so again. A partner who has been punished for initiating sexual behavior is less likely to do so in the future.

Punishment A consequence that decreases or terminates a behavior.

Social Learning Theory

Another learning-based approach to understanding human sexuality is social learning theory, which is largely based on the work of Albert Bandura. **Social learning theory** emphasizes the process of learning through observation and imitation. Observational learning occurs through observing a model who demonstrates attitudes and behavior. For example, we may imitate the sexual attitudes and behaviors that we observe in our parents, peers, and in the media. The television industry's adoption of a program ratings system stems from concern about the sexual behaviors and values children learn through observing sexuality on television. Indeed, a report from the Federal Trade Commission accused the movie and video game industries of emphasizing sex and violent content in their products (Seiler, 2000).

Social learning theory Framework that emphasizes the process of learning through observation and imitation.

Cognitive/Affective Theories

Cognitive/affective theories of sexuality emphasize the role of thought processes and emotions in sexual behavior. The importance of cognitions in human life was recognized nearly 2,000 years ago by Epictetus, a philosopher who said, "Man is disturbed not by things but by the view that he takes of them." Aaron Beck and Albert Ellis, both cognitive therapists, emphasize that maladaptive or irrational thoughts may result in sexual problems. Thoughts such as "I should always have an orgasm" or "Always be interested in sex" may result in unnecessary frustration. Through cognitive therapy (which is based on cognitive theory), these cognitions may be examined.

Cognitive/affective theories As related to sexuality, these theories emphasize the role of thought processes and emotions in sexual behavior.

Emotions are related to cognitions. As the preceding example illustrates, changing the person's cognitions will affect the way a person feels about his or her sexuality. Affective theories of sexuality emphasize the fact that emotions (such as love, jealousy, fear, anxiety, embarrassment, and frustration) may precede sexual expression, may be a component of sexual expression, and/or may be a consequence of sexual activity.

Theoretical models from social psychology that are often used in helping public health practitioners design health-promoting interventions (e.g., condom use) are the *Theories of Reasoned Action (TRA)* and *Planned Behavior*. In Fishbein and Ajzen's (1975) original model, they asserted that one's intention to perform a behavior is a good predictor of actual behavior. Intentions are influenced by one's *attitude* toward the behavior and the social pressure one perceives to perform or not perform the behavior (*subjective norm*). This model was useful in predicting behaviors under the person's control. Later Ajzen proposed the Theory of Planned Behavior to extend the model to nonvolitional behaviors by adding the concept of *perceived behavioral control* (White, Terry, & Hoag, 1994). Use of the TRA was proposed as a framework for understanding and changing AIDS-related behaviors (Fishbein & Middlestadt, 1989).

These models, along with another from social psychology, Triandis' Theory of Interpersonal Behavior, and the Health Belief Model from public health have been employed in the study of safer sex behaviors, especially condom use, in the AIDS era. The models have been broadly applied, used to study university students in the United States (Wulfert & Wan, 1995), Australian university students (White et al., 1994), low-income African American and Hispanic youth (Norris & Ford, 1995), adult clients of a sexually transmitted disease clinic (Morrison, Gillmore, & Baker, 1995), and Latin American, Caribbean and South Asian immigrants to and residents of Canada (Godin et al., 1996).

3-3c Sociological Theories

Sociological theories of human sexuality explain how society and social groups affect and are affected by sexual attitudes and behaviors. The various sociological theoretical perspectives on human sexuality include symbolic interaction, structural-functional, conflict, feminist, and systems theories.

Symbolic Interaction Theory

Symbolic interaction theory Sociological theory that focuses on how meanings, labels, and definitions learned through interaction affect one's attitudes, self-concept, and behavior.

Symbolic interaction theory, developed by Max Weber (1864–1920), George Simmel (1858–1918), and Charles Horton Cooley (1864–1929), focuses on how meanings, labels, and definitions learned through interaction affect our attitudes, self-concept, and behavior. For example, our definitions of what are appropriate and inappropriate sexual behaviors are learned through our relationships with others. Sexual self-concepts, including body image and perception of one's self as an emotional and sexual partner, are also influenced by interactions with others.

According to the symbolic interaction view of sexuality, humans respond to their definitions of situations rather than to objective situations themselves. For example, your response to seeing a woman breast-feeding her infant in public is influenced by your definition of the event: Do you see a mother engaging in a natural, nurturing behavior? Or do you define the event as an inappropriate or even offensive display of public nudity? When you encounter a male college student who has not experienced sexual intercourse, do you view him as a person with high moral standards or as a "weirdo" or "nerd"?

Our definitions of situations and behaviors are largely influenced by family, religion, peers, school, media, and the larger societies in which we live. Consider the following examples:

- In Kenya, the secretary-general of the Kenya Episcopal Conference said that the government's decision to import 300 million condoms to fight HIV/AIDS implies that the government sanctions promiscuity (Donovan, 2001). The Kenyan government defines condom use as an appropriate and important behavior to prevent transmission of HIV; religious officials define condom use as promoting promiscuity and adultery, which undermine love within families and "destroy the dignity of sex in the human person" (quoted in Donovan, 2001, p. 9).
- In many developing countries where religion prohibits or discourages birth control, contraceptives, and abortion, women learn through interaction with others that deliberate control of fertility is defined as socially unacceptable. When some women learn new, positive definitions of fertility control, they become role models and influence other women's attitudes and behaviors regarding contraceptive use.
- In the United States, female breasts are defined as an erotic, sexual part of the female body; women can be arrested for exposing their naked breasts in public. Other societies attach no sexual significance to female breasts. In these societies, female breasts are exposed in public and the sight or touch of a woman's breast (to a heterosexual man) will not produce an erection or physiological response because no sexual meaning is attached to them.

Social scripts Shared interpretations that have three functions: to define situations, name actors, and plot behaviors.

An important component of symbolic interaction theory is the concept of **social scripts,** developed by John Gagnon (now a professor emeritus at Stoneybrook University). Social scripts are shared interpretations and have three functions: to define situations, name actors, and plot behaviors. For example the social script operative in prostitution is to define the situation (sex for money), name actors (prostitute and "john" or client), and plot behaviors (prostitute will perform sexual behaviors requested by client).

Think About It

In general, women and men learn different social scripts in regard to sexuality, with women more likely to define a situation or encounter at a bar or party where alcohol is flowing as having the potential for emotional involvement, the actors being those of potential romantic companions, and the behaviors, those of escalating romance. In contrast, men are more likely to define the situation at a bar or party as one devoid of an emotional future, the actors as two strangers who will remain so, and the behaviors whatever the woman will allow sexually. How do you account for these different interpretations or scripts?

Structural-Functional Theory

Structural-functional theory, developed by Talcott Parsons (1902–1979) and Robert Merton (1910–), views society as a system of interrelated parts that influence each other and work together to achieve social stability. The various parts of society include family, religion, government, economics, and education. Structural-functional theory suggests that social behavior may be either functional or dysfunctional. Functional behavior is behavior that contributes to social stability; dysfunctional behavior disrupts social stability. The institution of marriage, which is based on the emotional and sexual bonding of individuals, may be viewed as functional for society because it provides a structure in which children are born and socialized to be productive members of society. Hence, there is great social approval for sex within marriage; children created by a married couple are cared for by the parents and not by welfare, as is more common of children born to single parents. Similarly, extramarital sex is viewed as dysfunctional because it is associated with divorce, which can disrupt the care and socialization of children.

Structural-functional theory Framework that views society as a system of interrelated parts that influence each other and work together to achieve social stability.

Structural-functional theory also focuses on how parts of society influence each other and how changes in one area of society produce or necessitate changes in another. For example, some religious leaders denounce education programs that offer condoms to students. Similarly, the educational system in a society affects the birth rate in that society—low educational attainment of women is associated with high birth rates. Hence, reducing population growth in developing countries requires increasing the educational attainment of women in these countries. The economic institution in the United States, which includes more women in the workforce today than in previous generations, has influenced the government to establish laws concerning sexual harassment and family leave.

Conflict Theory

Whereas structural-functional theory views society as composed of different parts working together, **conflict theory,** developed by Karl Marx (1818–1883) and Ralf Dahrendorf (1929–), views society as composed of different parts competing for power and resources. For example, antiabortionist groups are in conflict with pro-choice groups; gay rights advocates are in conflict with groups who oppose gay rights; insurance companies are in conflict with consumers about whether contraceptives should be covered in health insurance plans.

Conflict theory Sociological theory that views society as consisting of different parts competing for power and resources.

Conflict theory explains social patterns by looking at which groups control and benefit from a particular social action or meaning. For example, cultural portrayals of healthy sexuality that emphasize physiological functioning of the genitals (rather than relationship factors such as intimacy) benefit the medical and pharmaceutical industries that profit from medical treatments and drugs designed to enhance genital performance. Political actions and decisions related to sexual issues may also be understood by looking at which groups benefit from such actions or decisions. For example, Congressional support for federal funding of stem cell research (which involves using embryonic cell tissue from aborted fetuses) may be related to the profit motive. Members of Congress who advocated expanding federal funding for stem cell research received more than $4 million in campaign contributions from pharmaceutical and biotechnology companies—industries that could benefit from billions of dollars in sales from stem cell research. Senator Orrin Hatch (R-UT), one of the strongest advocates of broader stem cell research, has received more than $300,000 in pharmaceutical-industry contributions, followed by Senator Arlen Specter (R-PA), who received more than $200,000 (*The Washington Spectator,* 2001).

Feminist Theories

Feminist theories overlap with conflict theory; they explain social patterns by examining which groups have the power and resources to meet their needs. *Feminist theory* specifically focuses on the imbalance of power and resources between women and men, and how these imbalances affect sexuality, studies in sexuality, and sexual health-care delivery. For example, the male-dominated medical profession promotes a "medical model" of sexuality that focuses on the physiological functioning of the genitals. For

Feminist theories Perspectives that analyze discrepancies in equality between men and women, and how these imbalances affect sexuality, studies in sexuality, and sexual health-care delivery.

Box 3-1 Self-Assessment

INTERACTIVE BOX

Attitudes Toward Feminism Scale

Following are statements on a variety of issues. Left of each statement is a place for indicating how much you agree or disagree. Please respond as you personally feel and use the following letter code for your answers.

A—Strongly Agree B—Agree C—Disagree D—Strongly Disagree

___ 1. It is naturally proper for parents to keep a daughter under closer control than a son.
___ 2. A man has the right to insist that his wife accept his view as to what can or cannot be afforded.
___ 3. There should be no distinction made between woman's work and man's work.
___ 4. Women should not be expected to subordinate their careers to home duties to any greater extent than men.
___ 5. There are no natural differences between men and women in sensitivity and emotionality.
___ 6. A wife should make every effort to minimize irritation and inconvenience to her husband.
___ 7. A woman should gracefully accept chivalrous attentions from men.
___ 8. A woman generally needs male protection and guidance.
___ 9. Married women should resist enslavement by domestic obligations.
___ 10. The unmarried mother is more immoral and irresponsible than the unmarried father.
___ 11. Married women should not work if their husbands are able to support them.
___ 12. A husband has the right to expect that his wife will want to bear children.
___ 13. Women should freely compete with men in every sphere of economic activity.
___ 14. There should be a single standard in matters relating to sexual behavior for both men and women.
___ 15. The father and mother should have equal authority and responsibility for discipline and guidance of the children.
___ 16. Regardless of sex, there should be equal pay for equal work.
___ 17. Only the very exceptional woman is qualified to enter politics.
___ 18. Women should be given equal opportunities with men for all vocational and professional training.
___ 19. The husband should be regarded as the legal representative of the family group in all matters of law.
___ 20. Husbands and wives should share in all household tasks if both are employed an equal number of hours outside the home.
___ 21. There is no particular reason why a girl standing in a crowded bus should expect a man to offer her his seat.
___ 22. Wifely submission is an outmoded virtue.
___ 23. The leadership of a community should be largely in the hands of men.
___ 24. Women who seek a career are ignoring a more enriching life of devotion to husband and children.
___ 25. It is ridiculous for a woman to run a locomotive and for a man to darn socks.
___ 26. Greater leniency should be adopted towards women convicted of crime than towards male offenders.
___ 27. Women should take a less active role in courtship than men.

example, the American Psychiatric Association's *Diagnostic and Statistical Manual* ascribes equal numbers of sexual problems to men and to women, which, according to Tiefer (2001), implies that the sexual concerns of women and men are equally represented.

But men and women do not have equal political sexual power or often personal sexual power. Women's legacy of political and economic subordination is reflected in incomplete health care (limited access to abortion and poor insurance coverage for contraception); greater social pressure to marry and frequent trading of sex for socioeconomic advantages; greater burdens in homecare, child care, and eldercare that limit energy for sex and other pursuits of the self; limits in nonmarital sexual opportunities because of dangers to reputation and the threat of sexual violence; and loss of personal sexual power as a result of child sexual abuse, poor self-esteem, depression, and other problems not uncommon in women's lives (Tiefer, 2001).

A feminist analysis suggests that these social patterns are due to the power imbalance between men and women, and the fact that men primarily make and enforce the laws. Feminist analysis also suggests that rape and sexual assault may be viewed as an abuse of

___ 28. Contemporary social problems are crying out for increased participation in their solution by women.
___ 29. There is no good reason why women should take the name of their husbands upon marriage.
___ 30. Men are naturally more aggressive and achievement-oriented than women.
___ 31. The modern wife has no more obligation to keep her figure than her husband to keep down his waistline.
___ 32. It is humiliating for a woman to have to ask her husband for money.
___ 33. There are many words and phrases which are unfit for a woman's lips.
___ 34. Legal restrictions in industry should be the same for both sexes.
___ 35. Women are more likely than men to be devious in obtaining their needs.
___ 36. A woman should not expect to go to the same places or to have quite the same freedom of action as a man.
___ 37. Women are generally too nervous and high-strung to make good surgeons.
___ 38. It is insulting to women to have the "obey" clause in the marriage vows.
___ 39. It is foolish to regard scrubbing floors as more proper for women than mowing the lawn.
___ 40. Women should not submit to sexual slavery in marriage.
___ 41. A woman earning as much as her male date should share equally in the cost of their common recreation.
___ 42. Women should recognize their intellectual limitations as compared with men.

Scoring: Score your answers as follows: A = +2, B = +1, C = –1, D = –2. Because half the items were phrased in a pro-feminist and half in an antifeminist direction, you will need to reverse the scores (+2 becomes –2, etc.) for the following items: 1, 2, 6, 7, 8, 10, 11, 12, 17, 19, 23, 24, 25, 26, 27, 30, 33, 35, 36, 37, and 42. Now sum your scores for all the items. Scores may range from +84 to –84.

Interpreting your score: The higher your score, the higher your agreement with feminist (Lott used the term "women's liberation") statements. You may be interested in comparing your score, or that of your classmates, with those obtained by Lott (1973) from undergraduate students at the University of Rhode Island. The sample was composed of 109 men and 133 women in an introductory psychology class, and 47 additional older women who were participating in a special Continuing Education for Women (CEW) program. Based on information presented by Lott (1973), the following mean scores were calculated: Men = 13.07, Women = 24.30, and Continuing Education Women = 30.67.

In 1985, Biaggio, Mohan, and Baldwin administered Lott's questionnaire to 76 students from a University of Idaho introductory psychology class and 63 community members randomly selected from the local phone directory. Although they did not present the scores of their respondents, they reported they did not find differences between men and women. Unlike Lott's students, in Biaggio et al.'s sample, women were not more pro-liberation than men. Biaggio et al. (1985, p. 61) stated, "It seems that some of the tenets of feminism have taken hold and earned broader acceptance. These data also point to an intersex convergence of attitudes, with men's and women's attitudes toward liberation and child rearing being less disparate now than during the period of Lott's study." It would be interesting to determine if there are differences in scores between members of each sex in your class.

References

Biaggio, M. K., Mohan, P. J., & Baldwin, C. (1985). Relationships among attitudes toward children, women's liberation, and personality characteristics, *Sex Roles, 12,* 47–62.

Lott, B. E. (1973). Who wants the children? Some relationships among attitudes toward children, parents, and the liberation of women. *American Psychologist, 28,* 573–582.

Source: Reproduced by permission of Dr. Bernice Lott, Department of Psychology, University of Rhode Island, Kingston, RI.

power that some men engage in as an attempt to intimidate women. (Up until the mid-90s, husbands could legally rape their wives in some states.) Liberal feminists emphasize educational and legal remedies for discrimination and unequal treatment of women. Radical feminists believe that it will take more revolutionary changes in institutions and social organizations before political, economic, and social conditions become more equitable.

Socialist feminist theory is critical of **patriarchy**—a system of social organization in which the father is the head of the family and family descent is traced through the male line (meaning that wives and children take the last name of the husband and father). Patriarchy involves the connotation that women and children are the property of their fathers and/or husbands. Cultural attitudes toward women and children as property may contribute to some cases of abuse (including sexual abuse) of women and children.

Patriarchy A system of social organization in which the father is the head of the family and family descent is traced through the male line.

Finally, multicultural feminists emphasize the diversity among women of different classes and races. For example, women with low incomes, African American women, and Latino women may experience different forms of oppression that must be addressed.

The Self-Assessment in Box 3-1 allows you to assess your attitudes toward feminism.

Think About It

Prior to the 1980s, most sex research was conducted by men who focused on "female sexual pleasure as a way to make men happy and families secure" (Ericksen, 1999, p. 12). But, with the increase in the number of women conducting sex research, the "focus began shifting to female pleasure as a woman's concern" (p. 12). As a woman, what aspects of human sexuality do you feel have not been sufficiently researched?

As a man, if you adopted a feminist perspective, how might this affect the way you would frame research questions?

Systems Theory

Systems theory Theoretical framework that emphasizes the interpersonal and relationship aspects of sexuality.

Systems theory, developed by Murray Bowen (1913–1990), emphasizes the interpersonal and relationship aspects of sexuality. One application of systems theory is in the area of sexual dysfunctions. For example, whereas a biological view of low sexual desire emphasizes the role of hormones or medications and a psychological view might emphasize negative cognitions and emotions regarding sexual arousal, a systems perspective views low sexual desire as a product of the interaction between two partners. Negative and conflictual interaction between partners can affect their interests in having sex with one another.

Table 3-2 presents different theoretical explanations for various sexuality observations.

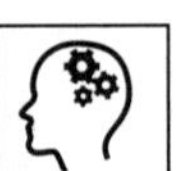

Think About It

To what degree do you think that the different theoretical explanations for human sexuality are necessarily incompatible? Or can biological, psychological, and sociological theories each contribute unique insights to our understanding of various aspects of sexuality?

3-4 ECLECTIC VIEW OF HUMAN SEXUALITY

Eclectic view View that recognizes the contribution of multiple perspectives to the understanding of sexuality.

Whereas some scholars who study human sexuality focus on one theoretical approach, others propose an **eclectic view** that recognizes the contributions that multiple perspectives make to our understanding of sexuality. In the words of sex researcher John Bancroft (1999), "we cannot expect to understand human sexuality unless we consider both biology and culture . . . and the interface between them as it affects the individual, the dyad, and the group" (p. 226).

For example, sexuality of the aging can be understood only in terms of biological, psychological, and social aspects of the aging process. Is decreased libido a function of decreased testosterone/progesterone or one's altered self-concept ("I am no longer sexually attractive") or asexual cultural expectations of sexuality among the elderly?

Other influences on sexuality in aging women include the following psychosocial and cultural variables:

1. Availability of a sexual partner who is interested in and capable of engaging in sexual activity. Older women are frequently widowed or divorced, and if they do have a partner, the partner may not be interested in sex or may have erection difficulties.
2. Socioeconomic status and level of education. Education may lead to greater freedom from cultural inhibitions and sexual stereotypes.
3. Cultural views and stereotypes of aging women. In some societies (e.g., China) older women are accorded higher status, and postmenopausal sexuality is characterized by openness and playfulness. The United States, on the other hand, has traditionally devalued older women and stereotyped them as being asexual.

TABLE 3-2

Sexuality Observations and Theoretical Explanations

Observation	Theory
1. Men are more sexually aggressive than women.	*Operant Learning* Men have been reinforced for being sexually aggressive. Women have been punished for being sexually aggressive. *Social Script* Our society scripts men to be more aggressive and women to be more passive sexually. Each sex learns through interactions with parents, peers, and partners that this is normative behavior. *Physiological* Men have large amounts of androgen and women have larger amounts of progesterone, which accounts for male aggressiveness and female passivity.
2. Pornography is consumed primarily by men.	*Operant Learning* Men derive erotic pleasure (reinforcement) from pornography. *Social Script* Men script each other to regard pornography as desired entertainment. Men swap pornography, which reflects a norm regarding pornography among males. Women rarely discuss pornography with each other. *Evolutionary* Men are biologically wired to become erect in response to visual sexual stimuli.
3. Men in most societies are allowed to have a number of sexual partners.	*Structural-Functional* In many societies, women outnumber men. Polygyny potentially provides a mate for every woman. *Conflict Theory* Social, political, and economic power of men provides the context for men to exploit women sexually by making rules in favor of polygyny. *Evolutionary* Men are biologically wired for variety; women for monogamy. These respective wirings produce reproductive success for the respective sexes.
4. Women and men tend to report lower levels of sexual desire in their elderly years.	*Social Script* Aging women and men learn social scripts that teach them that elderly persons are not expected to be sexual. *Systems* Elderly persons are often not in a relationship that elicits sexual desire. *Biological* Hormonal changes in the elderly account for decreased or absent sexual desire (physiological). There is no reproductive advantage for elderly women to be sexually active; there is minimal reproductive advantage for elderly men to be sexually active (evolutionary).
5. Extradyadic relationships, including marital infidelity, are common.	*Operant Learning* Immediate interpersonal reinforcement for extradyadic sex is stronger than delayed punishment for infidelity. *Biological* Humans (especially men) are biologically wired to be sexually receptive to numerous partners. *Structural Functional* Infidelity reflects the weakening of the family institution. *Systems* Emotional and sexual interactions between couples are failing to meet the needs of one or both partners.

Think About It

Why is it important to look at a sexual phenomenon or problem from different theoretical perspectives? Choose an aspect of your own sexuality or sexual experience and think about how you might view it from an eclectic theoretical perspective.

3-5 CONDUCTING SEX RESEARCH: A STEP-BY-STEP PROCESS

Conducting sex research, like all scientific research, involves following basic steps in the scientific process. These steps include identifying a research question, reviewing the literature, formulating a hypothesis and operationalizing variables, collecting data, and analyzing and interpreting the results.

3-5a Identifying a Research Question

A researcher's interest in a particular research question may be based on a personal life experience, or it may involve concern about certain human or social problems. Some researchers are hired by the government, by industry, or by some other organization to conduct research and investigate questions that are of interest to the organization.

Alfred C. Kinsey (1894–1956) and his colleagues conducted the first large survey study of human sexuality, the results of which they published in *Sexual Behavior in the Human Male* (1948) and *Sexual Behavior in the Human Female* (1953). His research questions were quite broad: "to discover what people do sexually, and what factors account for differences in sexual behavior among individuals, and among various segments of the population" (Kinsey, Pomeroy, & Martin, 1948, p.1). The project began with various questions about the frequency of and the motivations for certain beliefs and behaviors. Issues studied included such things as nonmarital and marital intercourse, attitudes toward sexuality, and how social factors such as education and income affect sexual behavior. Many research studies seek to answer more specific questions. For example, a recent study at the University of Vermont investigated whether women with histories of childhood sexual abuse would be less likely to have experienced subsequent sexual abuse if their parents were warm and caring (Jankowski, Leitenberg, Henning, & Coffey, 2002). (It turned out that parental caring did not alter the revictimization effect; even if they rated their parents high on parental caring, women who experienced childhood sexual abuse were twice as likely to experience sexual assault in late adolescence/adulthood compared to women without sexual abuse histories.)

Alfred C. Kinsey made the scientific collection of data on sexual behavior respectable.

@ Bettmann/CORBIS

Not all questions that concern us can be answered through scientific research. Questions involving values, religion, morality, and philosophical issues often fall outside the domain of science. For example, scientific research cannot answer the question of whether abortion is right or wrong. Scientific research can, however, reveal information that may help us make or evaluate our own moral or value choices. For example, researchers can investigate the psychological, social, physical, and economic consequences of various sexual decisions. Regarding abortion, researchers can identify the psychological consequences of aborting a child, rearing a child as a single parent, placing a child with an adoptive family, or rearing a child with the father.

The framing of research questions may also be affected by the social and political context of the times. Research topics and approaches that may be acceptable at one point in time may not meet current sensitivities and standards of a later time. For example, Green (2003) noted that when he applied for National Institute of Mental Health (NIMH) funds to do a follow-up study on "tomboys" and "non-tomboys" he had conducted 20 years earlier, "At our site, we were scolded by a psychiatrist who said that calling a girl a 'tomboy' was like calling a Black person a 'nigger.' So there was no systematic follow-up" (p.1). To gain approval and funding for research on sexuality-related topics, researchers may need to be especially aware of and contend with public perceptions of topics and "political correctness." They may also need to reassess language or assumptions that might be experienced by research participants or consumers as pejorative.

3-5b Reviewing the Literature

Numerous journals publish research on human sexuality, including *The Journal of Sex Research*, *Archives of Sexual Behavior*, *Journal of Homosexuality*, *Electronic Journal of Human Sexuality*, *Family Planning Perspectives*, *Psychology of Human Sexuality*, and many others. Reviewing the literature enables researchers to discover what other researchers have already learned about a topic, provides researchers with ideas about new research questions, and suggests ways to conduct research.

Students and researchers often find it helpful to locate review articles, which summarize, organize, integrate, and evaluate previously published material. Review articles are useful in conveying the current state of research, identifying gaps and inconsistencies, and recommending next steps in solving problems. Theoretical articles may trace the development of theory, critique theoretical approaches, or propose new theories (American Psychological Association, 2001).

3-5c Formulating a Hypothesis and Operationalizing Variables

To answer their research questions, researchers must transform their questions into testable hypotheses. A **hypothesis** is a tentative or educated guess designed to test a theory. Hypotheses involve predictions about the relationship between two or more variables (e.g., alcohol and condom use). A **variable** is any measurable event or characteristic that varies or is subject to change. There are two types of variables. The **dependent variable** is the variable that is measured to assess what, if any, effect the independent variable has on it. The **independent variable** is the variable that is presumed to cause or influence the dependent variable. Following is an example of a sex research hypothesis and the variables involved:

Hypothesis A tentative and testable proposal or an educated guess about the outcome of a research study.

Variable Any measurable event or characteristic that varies or is subject to change.

Dependent variable Variable that is measured to assess what, if any, effect the independent variable has on it.

Independent variable The variable that is presumed to cause or influence the dependent variable.

Hypothesis: High alcohol consumption is associated with lower condom use.

Independent Variable: alcohol consumption

Dependent Variable: condom use

Because human sexual behavior and attitudes are complex and influenced by many factors, researchers often assess the effects of several independent variables on one or more dependent variables. For example, Lee (2001) conducted research to assess how several independent variables (including adolescent living outside the home, single-parent status, family dysfunction, mother's education, and mother's childbearing in adolescence) affected adolescent pregnancy and childbearing. The researcher found that all these variables were positively associated with the probability of an adolescent bearing a child.

Some variables, such as age, gender, and educational attainment are easy to measure—the researcher simply asks the respondents to indicate their age, gender, and highest level of education achieved. However, researchers must carefully consider how they will **operationalize** variables (develop an **operational definition** or working definition) such as sexual satisfaction, rape, sexual desire, pornography, sexual orientation, and many others because there are many possible ways to measure these variables. For example, researchers studying premature ejaculation have used widely different definitions of it (Rowland, Cooper, & Schneider, 2001). Box 3-2 details ways in which researcher bias may distort research outcomes.

Operationalize Defining how a variable will be measured.

Operational definition Working definition; how a variable is defined in a particular study.

Box 3-2 Up Close

Researcher Bias

Although one of the goals of scientific studies is to gather data objectively, it may be impossible for researchers to be totally objective. McGraw, Zvonkovic, and Walker (2000) emphasized that research on marriages and families is inherently political in content and method. Researchers are human and have values, attitudes, and beliefs that may influence their research methods and findings. It may be important to know what the researcher's bias is in order to evaluate that researcher's findings. For example, a researcher who does not support abortion rights may conduct research that focuses only on the negative effects of abortion. Occasionally, researchers are not just biased but outright deceptive to keep the funding flowing (Pound, 2000).

Even the most conscientious scientists, however, are not without bias. Alfred Kinsey, a biologist, published two editions of a popular introductory biology text and workbook, and a general text on biology methods. He was an international expert on the gall wasp; some North American gall wasp species bear his name. His approach to science was taxonomy (classifying and describing the variations within and across species). But as his biographer Gathorne-Hardy (2000) noted, Kinsey's intellectual bias was therefore toward toleration. "Although Kinsey prided himself as an objective scientist, it was his very attempt to establish a taxonomy of sexual behaviors—treating all activities as more or less within the range of human behavior—that got him into trouble" (Bullough, 1999, p. 130). In trying to find all the variations in human sexual behaviors and validate sexual variety, he pursued unusual sexualities and was criticized for not realizing the distortion this brought to accurately representing the population (Ericksen, 1998). While one of Kinsey's biographers (Jones, 1997) suggested that Kinsey's interest in validating sexual variation was due to his attempts to come to grips with his own "private demons" (speculated sadomasochistic interests and increasing bisexual activity as he aged), other historians (Ericksen, 1998; Gathorne-Hardy, 2000; Bullough, 1998a, 1999) emphasized that Kinsey's motivation was to allow the scientific data to speak for itself and liberate America from Victorian repression. Some of the methodological criticisms of Kinsey's work and how contemporary researchers have addressed those issues are included in sections 3-6a through 3-6g, which describe the research process.

Finally, another source of potential bias occurs when researchers present an interpretation of what other researchers have done. Two layers of bias may be operative here: (a) when the original data were collected and interpreted and (b) when the second researcher read the study of the original researcher and made his or her own interpretation. Much of this text is based on the text authors' representations of someone else's study. As a consumer, you should be alert to the potential bias in reading such secondary sources. To help control for this bias, we have provided references to the original source for your own reading.

Think About It

Considering your personal, academic, or professional interests, what research question about sexuality would you be interested in investigating? Based on your research question, what hypothesis could you formulate and how might you operationalize your independent and dependent variables?

Science has a face, a house, and a price; it is important to ask who is doing science, in what institutional context, and at what cost. Understanding such things can give us insight into why scientific tools are sharp for certain types of problems and dull for others.

—*Robert Proctor, Cancer Wars*

3-6 METHODS OF DATA COLLECTION

After identifying a research question, reviewing the literature, formulating a hypothesis, and operationalizing variables, researchers collect data. Methods of data collection include experimental research, survey research, field research, direct laboratory observations, case studies, and historical research.

3-6a Experimental Research

Experimental research involves manipulating the independent variable to determine how it affects the dependent variable. In conducting an experiment, the researcher recruits participants and randomly assigns them either to an experimental group or a control group. After measuring the dependent variable in both groups, the researcher exposes participants in the experimental group to the independent variable (also known as the experimental treatment). Then the researcher measures the dependent variable in both groups again and compares the experimental group with the control group. Any differences between the groups may be due to the experimental treatment.

Experimental research Research methodology that involves manipulating the independent variable to determine how it affects the dependent variable.

For example, a team of researchers wanted to assess the effects of Vardenafil (independent variable or experimental treatment) on the ability to create and maintain an erection (dependent variable) in men with erectile dysfunction (Stark et al., 2001). After randomly assigning the 580 men to either the experimental group (the group that was to take the medication) or the control group (the group getting the placebo), the researchers found that 80% of the men on the 20 mg dose reported improved erections compared to 30% on placebo. The researchers concluded that Vardenafil is significantly associated with improved erectile functioning.

The major strength of the experimental method is that it provides information on causal relationships; that is, it shows how one variable affects another. A primary weakness is that experiments are often conducted on small samples, usually in artificial laboratory settings. For this reason, the findings may not be generalizable to other people in natural settings.

3-6b Survey Research

Survey research involves eliciting information from respondents using questions. An important part of survey research is selecting a **sample,** or a portion of the population in which the researcher is interested. Ideally, samples are representative of the population being studied. A **representative sample** allows the researcher to assume that responses obtained from the sample are similar to those that would be obtained from the larger population. Thus, the information obtained from a representative sample can be generalized to the larger population. For example, Laumann and Michael (2001) participated in crafting The National Health and Social Life Survey based on a representative sample of U.S. adults. The results of their survey, published in the book *Sex, Love, and Health in America,* may be generalized to the rest of the U.S. adult population that did not participate in the survey.

Survey research Research that involves eliciting information from respondents using questions.

Sample A portion of the population that the researcher studies and attempts to make inferences about the whole population.

Representative sample A sample the researcher studies that is representative of the population from which it is taken.

Although Kinsey is credited with having "legitimated the sex survey in American academia" (Ericksen, 1998), criticism of his research has especially focused on his sampling method. The large number of interviews of people from the Mid-West, especially Indiana, and the inclusion of special groups (homosexuals and prisoners), are factors that challenge the generalizability of Kinsey's results to the larger population of U.S. adults. Kinsey argued that, because of the enormity of his sample, randomization was not necessary. His goal was to conduct 100,000 interviews. Although this ambitious goal was not realized, by the time of his death Kinsey had interviewed 8,000 persons himself, and his staff another 10,000 (Bullough, 1998a). Kinsey believed that random sampling would not produce a satisfactory sample because too many people would refuse to participate and the extremes in the population would be missed. He sought to avoid this by approaching groups and obtaining interviews from every member of the group. He was most persuasive in obtaining these 100% groups (the YMCAs in a number of cities, state penal farms and prisons, an orphanage, the Nicodemus rural Black community, etc.), and they constituted a quarter of his sample (Gathorne-Hardy, 2000).

Most sex research studies are self-report studies that are not based on representative samples. For example, Areton's (2002) study on the sexual satisfaction of 112 obese women was based on respondents who replied to announcements on the World Wide Web, in magazine articles, and on bulletin boards. The modified "snowball" approach was initiated in which volunteers agreed to recruit additional participants.

As Boles (1998) noted, it is especially difficult to obtain a representative sample of "hidden" populations, such as prostitutes or illicit drug users. If she wanted to study attitudes toward abortion of students at a given university, she could obtain a list of all students registered for the semester and randomly select a sample (with each member of the population having an equal probability of being selected). But in studying prostitutes, there is no comprehensive list from which to draw. She identified centers of male prostitution and used those locales to distribute condoms and engage hustlers in conversation. Using the "snowball" technique, she asked respondents to refer her to friends who might participate. However, those hustlers willing to talk with her may or may not be representative of the entire group of male prostitutes on the streets. Samples based on Internet samples are also not representative because these surveys typically attract mostly male respondents with an average age under 25 years (Mackay, 2001).

Popular books on sexuality are often based on nonrepresentative samples. *Sex on Campus* by Elliott and Brantly (1997) was hyped in the media as "the naked truth about the real sex lives of college students." But only 1 in 10 of the 20,000 college students who were mailed a 151-item questionnaire for this study returned the questionnaire. Thus, we know nothing about the sexual attitudes and behaviors of the 90% who did not return the questionnaire.

Students who volunteer for sexuality research have been shown to be more likely to have had sexual intercourse, performed oral sex, score higher on sexual esteem and sexual sensation seeking, and report sexual attitudes that are less traditional than nonvolunteers (Wiederman, 1999). Wiederman cautioned that if such volunteers are not even representative of college students, then the validity of sexuality research may be particularly suspect, given that in his review of reports of sexuality research published since 1971, one half have been based on college student participants. Other researchers have emphasized that the availability of norms on populations other than college students is limited (Meyers & Shurts, 2002).

Obtaining a representative sample of a group may be very difficult, especially given the challenges of accessing hard-to-reach populations and participation biases as a result of nonresponse and volunteerism (Catania, 1999). The size of a sample is not a guarantee of its representativeness. Catania offered the example of a large study of more than 7,000 gay and bisexual male patients in San Francisco clinics which predicted future HIV trends that were 40% too high. On the other hand, a smaller probability-based sample obtained in the San Francisco Men's Health Study resulted in more accurate predictions. Notwithstanding these sample issues, there are several kinds of survey research.

Interview survey research
Type of research in which trained interviewers ask respondents a series of questions and either take written notes or tape-record the respondents' answers. Interviews may be conducted over the telephone or face-to-face.

1. *Interviews*. After selecting a sample, survey researchers either interview people or ask them to complete written questionnaires. In **interview survey research,** trained interviewers ask respondents a series of questions and either take written notes or tape-record the respondents' answers. Interviews may be conducted over the telephone or face-to-face. The Kinsey data were based on face-to-face interviews (thousands of which he personally conducted). Kinsey and his colleagues memorized the questions and coded the answers on a single sheet of paper divided into 287 little squares as the interviewee talked. This technique provided complete confidentiality because the codes were incomprehensible to all but Kinsey and his very few researchers (Gathorne-Hardy, 2000).

   One advantage of interview survey research is that it enables the researcher to clarify questions for the respondent and follow up on answers to particular questions. Face-to-face interviews provide a method of surveying individuals who do not have a telephone or mailing address. For example, some AIDS-related research attempts to assess high-risk behaviors among street youth and intravenous drug users, both high-risk groups for HIV infection. These groups may not have a telephone or address due to their transient lifestyle. However, these groups may be accessible if the researcher locates their hangouts and conducts face-to-face interviews.

A major disadvantage of interview research is the lack of privacy and anonymity. Respondents may feel embarrassed or threatened when asked to answer questions about sexual attitudes and behaviors. As a result, some respondents may choose not to participate and those who do may conceal or alter information to give socially desirable answers to interviewers' questions (such as "No, I have never had intercourse with someone other than my spouse during my marriage" or "Yes, I use condoms each time I have sex"). Other disadvantages of interview survey research are the time and expense. The average length of the personal interviews of 4,990 adult men and women reported on by Cubbins and Tanfer (2000) was 80 minutes. The average cost of the interviews in the Michael, Gagnon, Laumann, and Kolata (1994) study was $450 (which included the interviewer training, transportation to the respondents' homes, and computer data entry). Telephone interviews (Mitchell et al., 2001) are less time-consuming and cost less money, but they usually yield less information.

Although face-to-face interviews are often conducted one on one, sometimes they are held in a small group, called a **focus group.** Advantages of focus group research include the minimal expense of time and money and the fact that it allows participants to interact and raise new issues for the researcher to investigate. A disadvantage is the limited sample size, which means that the data from focus groups may not be representative of the larger research population.

Focus group Interviews conducted in a small group typically focused on one subject.

2. *Questionnaires*. Instead of conducting face-to face or phone interviews, researchers may develop questionnaires that they either mail, give to a sample of respondents, or post on a web site and invite respondents to answer. This latter use of the Internet has been identified as the "new frontier for the collection of sexuality data" (Mustanski, 2001, p. 299). Such questionnaire surveys also provide large quantities of data that can be analyzed relatively inexpensively as compared to face-to-face or telephone surveys, which typically yield less data yet take a great deal of time to complete. Francome and Freeman (2000) analyzed data from a questionnaire they mailed to 702 general practice physicians. Originally, they had mailed 1,000 questionnaires, making their response rate 71%.

Because researchers do not ask respondents to write their names on questionnaires, questionnaire research provides privacy and anonymity to the research participants. This reduces the likelihood that respondents will provide answers that are intentionally inaccurate or distorted. However, respondents may have difficulty accurately recalling information. To improve the accuracy of recall for interview and questionnaire respondents, the "daily diary" method of daily data collection is sometimes used. Gillmore et al. (2001) asked a sample of 177 university students to keep a daily diary for eight weeks on their sexual and health-related behaviors.

A major problem with self-report data is the accuracy of the data. In studies of adolescents Udry (1998) reported on the results of an honesty question on a self-administered questionnaire. "When we interviewed you a year ago, we asked you whether you had ever had sexual intercourse. What did you tell us? Was that true?" (Udry, 1998, p. 58). From 5 to 20% (varying by sex and race) admitted they lied during previous interviews. Many were incorrect in remembering their previous answers. Inconsistencies were not always due to dishonesty. One student explained, "Last year I told you I had had intercourse, because I thought I had. But now I know that I hadn't at that time because since then I *have* had intercourse" (p. 58).

One study investigated the discrepant reports of numbers of sexual partners given by men and women. Investigators (Brown & Sinclair, 1999) wondered if men's reports of two to four times as many opposite-sex partners as women was a result of male exaggeration or women's underreporting. They found that men and women used different strategies in estimating the number of sexual partners in their lifetime. Men's strategy of using rough approximations was associated with larger reports than the women's strategy of enumeration ("counted all the names I remembered").

When sexual information is sensitive or potentially stigmatizing, obtaining accurate information may be especially hard. For example, given the social pressure to avoid behaviors that increase risk to HIV exposure, it may be difficult for people to say they perform such behaviors. Seventy-five male couples in which one partner was HIV-positive and one was HIV-negative (also referred to as serodiscordant) were interviewed by well-trained male interviewers (Carballo-Dieguez, Remien, Dolezal, & Wagner, 1999). The members of the couple were interviewed separately, and then together, regarding their sexual behavior over the preceding year. Although a year is a long period for obtaining accurate recall, this length of time was used to obtain information that might vary seasonally due to summer travel. When the couple's individual reports of behavior were discrepant, the interviewer followed up in the joint interview to understand the differences. Overall, the partners' accounts were consistent, and the reports were viewed as reliable. When there were discrepancies, the main reasons were the following:

- Poor recall of infrequent events
- Inaccuracy in limiting reports to events within the specified time range
- Different views in what constitutes sex (in spite of specific definitions in the assessment)
- Technical differences ("We don't use condoms for foreplay but [we use them] when one is about to come")
- Lack of agreement about what took place

The major disadvantage of mail questionnaires is that obtaining an adequate response rate is difficult. Many people do not want to take the time or make the effort to complete a questionnaire, and others may not be able to read or understand the questions. Typically, only 20 to 40% of individuals in a sample complete and return a mail questionnaire. Indeed, the response rate of 71% in the Francome and Freeman study is quite good. A low response rate is problematic because nonrespondents (those people who do not respond to the survey) are usually different from those people who do respond. Also, because respondents do not constitute a representative sample, the researcher may not be able to generalize the research findings to the larger population.

Studies on sexuality and relationships are commonly found in popular magazines such as *Cosmopolitan*, *Playboy*, and *Redbook* and on the Internet. Sometimes these magazines or web sites conduct their own research by asking readers/visitors to complete questionnaires and mail them to magazine editors or take a survey online. The survey results are published in subsequent issues of such magazines or on the web site. "Cosmo's Sex Survey" (Mackenzie & Goins, 2001) provided data on more than 6,000 women who took *Cosmopolitan*'s online survey in regard to what women do, desire, and are "dying to do" (p. 165). The research weakness of the survey is that it revealed information from only a very select group of women—those who had logged on to *Cosmopolitan*'s web site. Women who don't go to *Cosmopolitan*'s web site and who don't take online surveys were not represented.

The results of magazine and Internet surveys should be viewed with caution because the data are not based on representative samples. Other problems with magazine and Internet surveys include the inadequacy of some questions, the methods of analysis, and the inherent bias of the publication or web site, which wants to reflect a positive image of its readership and visitors, entertain them, and sell magazines. Indeed, *Cosmopolitan*'s subsequent "Juiciest Sex Survey Ever" (O'Rourke, 2002) provides *no* information on their sample other than "more than 7000 men." The demographic characteristics of these respondents, how they were selected to be surveyed, and the nature of the data-collection process are not discussed.

3. *New Technologies for Research*. A new method for conducting survey research is asking respondents to provide answers to a computer that "talks." Romer et al. (1997) found that respondents rated computer interviews about sexual issues more favorably than face-to-face interviews and that the former were reliable. Respondents reported the privacy of computers as a major advantage. As the Internet is more broadly used, there will be more opportunity for its use to conduct sex research. Although the Internet may be useful in recruiting research participants who could not easily be accessed locally, Internet-recruited participants are more likely to be male, younger, wealthier, and better educated (especially in computer and technical skills) than participants recruited through more traditional methods (Binik, Mah, & Kiesler, 1999). Ethical concerns include privacy and protection of information about participants, the use of electronic advertising and unsolicited e-mail, the ways informed consent (and parental consent) can be verified, and the ways data will be stored and transmitted. Binik et al. made recommendations for Internet research safeguards, including that researchers should not promise anonymity that they cannot guarantee.

3-6c Personal Choices: Participating in Sex Research as a Subject?

As a student at a college or university, you may be asked to complete a questionnaire or participate in an interview as part of a sex research project being conducted by a professor or graduate student. Before deciding whether to participate in the study, you may want to be sure that the research follows established ethical guidelines for research with human participants. These guidelines include being informed by the researcher(s) about the nature and purpose of the study, being protected from physical or psychological harm, being guaranteed anonymity and confidentiality, and having the option to choose not to participate (or to discontinue participation) without penalty.

Individuals who participate in sexuality research benefit the larger society. The sexual information they share with researchers, which is later disseminated in professional journals, may enable all of us to make more informed sexual and relationship choices. But beware. The son (college student) of one of the authors was asked to participate in a sexually transmitted disease study. He was told that he would be infected with the STD and then given an antidote to the STD and that he would be offered $200 for his time. Even if the antidote worked flawlessly, he was not told of the fact that in the future he would need to check on subsequent health and insurance forms that he had had a sexually transmitted disease. He declined involvement. This research project was atypical. Most research includes making the proposed participant aware of potential harm.

3-6d Field Research

Field research involves observing and studying social behaviors in settings in which they occur naturally. Two types of field research are participant observation and nonparticipant observation. In **participant observation** research, the researcher participates in the phenomenon being studied to obtain an insider's perspective of the people and/or behavior being observed. Mason-Schrock (1996) studied transsexuals by attending support groups over a 15-month period and going to the group's annual party. Other sex researchers have studied "body piercing parties" (Myers, 1992), swinging (Bartell, 1970), nudist clubs/resorts (Schroer, 2001), strip clubs (Petersen & Dressel, 1982), and homosexuality in public restrooms (Humphreys, 1970) as participants. In the latter study, the researcher acted in the role of "lookout."

In **nonparticipant observation** research, the investigators observe the phenomenon being studied but do not actively participate in the group or the activity. For example, a researcher could study nude beaches and strip clubs as an observer without being a nudist or a stripper. The primary advantage of field research is that it yields detailed descriptive information about the behaviors, values, emotions, and norms of those being studied. A disadvantage of field research is that the individuals being studied may alter their behaviors if they know they are being observed. If researchers do not let the individuals know they are being studied, the researchers may be violating ethical codes of research conduct. Another potential problem with field research is that the researchers' observations are subjective and may be biased. In addition, because field research is usually based on small samples, the findings may not be generalizable.

Field research Method of data collection that involves observing and studying social behaviors in settings in which they occur naturally.

Participant observation Type of research in which the researcher participates in the phenomenon being studied to obtain an insider's perspective of the people and/or behavior being observed.

Nonparticipant observation Type of research in which the investigators observe the phenomenon being studied but do not actively participate in the group or the activity.

3-6e Direct Laboratory Observation

Direct laboratory observation In human sexuality research, actually observing individuals engage in sexual behavior. Masters and Johnson as well as Alfred C. Kinsey observed individuals and couples engaging in sexual behavior.

William Masters (1915–2001) and Virginia Johnson (1925–), of the Masters and Johnson Institute in Saint Louis, conducted **direct laboratory observation** through a one-way mirror of 694 individuals who engaged in a variety of sexual behaviors. They published their research (conducted over a 12-year period) in the nationwide best-seller, *Human Sexual Response* (1966). One problem with laboratory observation research is the use of volunteers. Are those who volunteer to participate in such research similar to those who do not? Some research suggests they are not. Not only are research volunteers more likely to be women (Senn & Desmarais, 2001), they are more likely to be sexually experienced, more interested in sexual variety, and less guilty about sex than nonvolunteers (Bogaert, 1996; Strassberg & Lowe, 1995). However, when investigators tried to recruit research participants for physically invasive laboratory procedures, men were more likely to volunteer. In a study using the penile plethysmograph (flexible piece of rubber tubing placed around the penis to measure the circumference of the penis) or the vaginal photoplethysmograph (tampon-shaped instrument inserted into the vagina to measure the amount of blood flow), women were much more likely to decline (Palud, Gaither, Hegstad, Rowan, & Devitt, 1999). Thus, volunteer samples may not be representative of the group from which they are recruited, and caution should be used in making generalizations based on the findings.

3-6f Case Studies

Case study A research method that involves conducting an in-depth, detailed analysis of an individual, group, relationship, or event.

A **case study** is a research approach that involves conducting an in-depth, detailed analysis of an individual, group, relationship, or event. Data obtained in a case study may come from interviews, observations, or analysis of records (medical, educational, and legal). Like field research, case studies yield detailed qualitative or descriptive information about the experiences of individuals. For example, Palmer and Bor (2001) used a multiple case study approach to investigate the range of issues and problems that confronted 10 gay male couples in which one of the partners was HIV-infected . During interviews with the couples in this study, the researchers asked questions about the following topics: 1) What information, services, and interventions did the serodiscordant couples find useful, if any, in providing practical and emotional support for their relationship? 2) How do serodiscordant couples consider and negotiate long-term planning for themselves? 3) How does the reality of serodiscordance affect their sexual relationship? and 4) How does the use of drug therapies affect day-to-day functioning for the couple? The researchers used the qualitative case study method because the sample group was small and the data required were intimate, detailed, and complex.

Case studies are valuable in providing detailed qualitative information about the experiences of individuals and groups. The main disadvantage of the case study method is that findings based on a small sample size (in some cases a sample size of one) are not necessarily generalizable.

3-6g Historical Research

Historical research involves investigating sexuality and sexual issues through the study of historical documents. Data sources used in conducting historical research include newspapers, magazines, letters, literature (such as novels and poetry), diaries, medical texts and popular health manuals, court records, hospital records, prison records, and official (government) statistics on such topics as birth rates, arrest and conviction rates, sexually transmittable diseases (STDs), and nonmarital pregnancies.

Historical sexuality research provides information about the changing nature of sexual behavior, norms, social control, and socially constructed meanings of sexuality. In an analysis of sexuality in U.S. life from colonial times to the present, D'Emilio and Freedman (1988) traced changes in sexual themes from a reproductive emphasis in the

Box 3-3 Social Choices

Public Funding for Sex Research?

In *The Surgeon General's Call to Action to Promote Sexual Health and Responsible Sexual Behavior* (2001), former U.S. Surgeon General David Satcher suggested that the United States should increase investment in research related to sexual health. Satcher argued that expanding the sex research base is important for providing a foundation of knowledge that can be used to promote sexual health and responsible sexual behavior. Janet Hyde (2001) also emphasized that "the need for sex research, in combination with sex education and sex therapy, is desperate, because sexual ignorance causes far too much harm in our society" (p. 100). In addition to the dearth of sex research in the United States, there are no institutes or specialists in most other countries, and there is no central depository of global sex information (Mackay, 2001).

Although many taxpayers and politicians value sex research and support public funding for sex research studies, others object to sexuality research and oppose funding it with tax dollars. Researchers who conducted The National Health and Social Life Survey (Laumann & Michael, 2001), a national survey on American sexual behavior, sought government funding for the project on the premise that the data would be helpful in understanding and solving social problems such as transmission of HIV and other STDs and teenage pregnancy. But the Senate refused funding because it feared public opposition to funding sex research with tax dollars. Senator Jesse Helms (R-NC) introduced an amendment to a National Institute of Health bill that specifically prohibited the government from paying for such a study. The amendment passed by a vote of 66 to 34. To conduct The National Health and Social Life Survey study, researchers solicited funds from the private sector.

References

Laumann, E. O. & Michael, R. T. (Eds.) (2001). *Sex, love, and health in America: Private choices and public policies*. Chicago: The University of Chicago Press.

Satcher, D. (2001). *The surgeon general's call to action to promote sexual health and responsible sexual behavior*. U.S. Dept. of Health and Human Services. www.surgeongeneral.gov/library/sexualhealth/call.htm

eighteenth century, to a focus on gender relations in the nineteenth century, to a concern for eroticism in the twentieth century.

Noted sexual historian Vern L. Bullough was awarded the Distinguished Achievement Award by the Society for the Scientific Study of Sex for his studies over the past half-century. He observed that interpretations of historical data "vary with those doing the interpreting, and the same facts can be reinterpreted or ignored by others" and that these differences may be influenced by whether the writer is an "insider" or "outsider" to the focus of the study (Bullough, 1998b, p. 13). For example, Bullough noted his disagreement with the historian John Boswell's conclusion of a friendly attitude toward homosexuality of the medieval Christian Church. However, Bullough allows that this interpretation could be influenced by Boswell's background (a gay man and Catholic convert who hoped to impact existing Catholic policy regarding homosexuality) in contrast to his own (a humanist and a heterosexual). On the other hand, Bullough also mentioned a critique of his discussion of homosexuality in Hinduism, which one writer found too positive. In reflecting on his work Bullough concludes, "In short, the history of sexuality can be fascinating, and I would urge others to study it, to challenge and correct me, or perhaps even to reaffirm what I have found" (p. 13).

Although the cost of a research study varies with the nature of the research question, the method of research used, and the number of participants, research is usually expensive. Who pays for sex research? Funding may come from private organizations and corporations, universities, or government agencies. Box 3-3 discusses whether taxpayers should pay for sex research.

Think About It

Earlier you were asked to formulate a sex research question and hypothesis based on your personal, academic, or professional interests. Which method of research would you select to answer your research question? What are the advantages and disadvantages of using the method you selected?

3-7 LEVELS OF DATA ANALYSIS

After collecting data on a research question, researchers analyze the data to test their hypotheses. There are three levels of data analysis: description, correlation, and causation.

3-7a Description

Descriptive research Qualitative or quantitative research that describes sexual processes, behaviors, and attitudes, as well as the people who experience them.

The goal of many sexuality research studies is to describe sexual processes, behaviors, and attitudes, as well as the people who experience them. **Descriptive research** may be qualitative or quantitative. Qualitative descriptions are verbal narratives that describe details and nuances of sexual phenomena. Quantitative descriptions of sexuality are numerical representations of sexual phenomena. Quantitative descriptive data analysis may involve computing the following: means (averages), frequencies, mode (the most frequently occurring observation in the data), median (the middle data point; half of the data points are above and half are below the median), and range (a measure of dispersion, comprising the highest and lowest values of a variable in a set of observations).

Descriptive research findings should be interpreted with caution. For example, research on gender differences in the meaning of sexual intimacy reveals that women view such intimacy as "any kind of sexual activity with one person with whom there is mutual emotional involvement." In contrast, men defined sexual intimacy as "sexual activity of any kind—particularly sexual intercourse and oral sex" (Knox, Sturdivant, & Zusman, 2001). Does this mean that women never emphasize sexual behaviors and men never emphasize emotional closeness? Of course not! What these findings mean is that men generally tend to emphasize physical acts and women tend to emphasize emotional closeness. As you read the research findings in this text, remember that they are generalizations, not absolute truths.

3-7b Correlation

Correlation Statistical index that represents the degree of relationship between two variables.

Positive correlation Relationship between two variables that exists when both variables change in the same direction.

Negative correlation Relationship between two variables that change in opposite directions.

Curvilinear correlation Relationship that exists when two variables vary in both the same and opposite directions.

Researchers are often interested in the relationships among variables. Remember that a variable is simply a measurable item or characteristic that is subject to change. **Correlation** refers to a relationship among two or more variables. Correlational research may answer such questions as "What is the relationship between sex and attitudes toward masturbation?" "What factors are associated with engaging in high-risk sexual behavior (such as the failure to use condoms)?" and "What is the relationship between homonegativity and religion?"

If there is a correlation or relationship between two variables, then a change in one variable is associated with a change in the other variable. A **positive correlation** exists when both variables change in the same direction. For example, in general, the greater the number of sexual partners a person has, the greater the chances are of contracting a sexually transmitted disease. As variable A (number of sexual partners) increases, variable B (chances of contracting an STD) also increases. Therefore, we may say that there is a positive correlation between the number of sexual partners and contracting STDs. Similarly, we might say that as the number of sexual partners decreases, the chance of contracting STDs decreases. Notice that in both cases, the variables change in the same direction.

A **negative correlation** exists when two variables change in opposite directions. For example, there is a negative correlation between condom use and contracting STDs. This means that as condom use increases, the chance of contracting STDs decreases.

Students often make the mistake of thinking that if two variables decrease, the correlation is negative. To avoid making this error, remember that in a positive correlation, it does not matter whether the variables increase or decrease, as long as they change in the same direction.

Sometimes the relationship between variables is curvilinear. A **curvilinear correlation** exists when two variables vary in both the same and opposite directions. For exam-

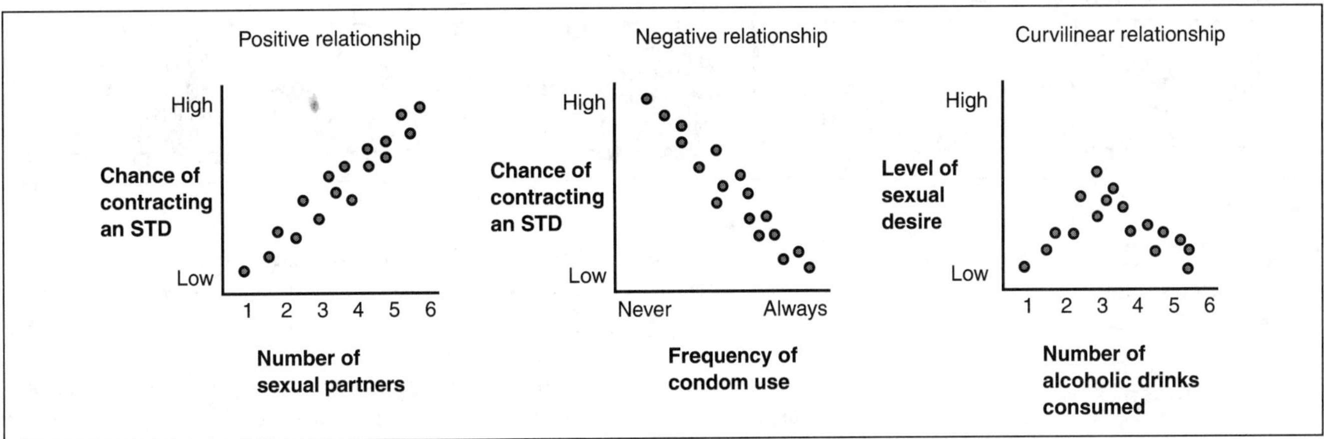

FIGURE 3-2
Graphs Depicting Positive, Negative, and Curvilinear Relationships

ple, suppose that if you have one alcoholic beverage, your desire for sex increases. With two drinks, your sexual desire increases more, and three drinks raise your interest even higher. So far, there is a positive correlation between alcohol consumption (variable A) and sexual desire (variable B); as one variable increases, the other also increases. But suppose after four drinks, you start feeling sleepy, dizzy, or nauseous, and your interest in sex decreases. After five drinks, you are either vomiting or semiconscious, and sex is of no interest to you. There is now a negative correlation between alcohol consumption and sexual desire; as alcohol consumption increases, sexual interest decreases. Figure 3-2 illustrates how positive, negative, and curvilinear correlations look when they are plotted on a graph.

A fourth type of correlation is called a spurious correlation. A **spurious correlation** exists when two variables appear to be related but only because they are both related to a third variable. When the third variable is controlled through a statistical method in which a variable is held constant, the apparent relationship between the dependent and independent variables disappears. For example, suppose a researcher finds that the more religiously devout you are, the more likely you are to contract a sexually transmitted disease. How can that be? Is there something about being religiously devout that, in and of itself, leads to STDs? The explanation is that religiously devout unmarried individuals are less likely to plan intercourse, and therefore, when they do have intercourse, they often are not prepared in terms of having a condom with them. Therefore, the correlation between religious devoutness and STDs is spurious. These variables appear to be related only because they are both related to a third variable (in this case, condom use).

Spurious correlation Pattern that exists when two variables appear to be related but only because they are both related to a third variable.

3-7c Causation

If data analysis reveals that two variables are correlated, we know only that a change in one variable is associated with a change in the other variable. We cannot assume, however, that a change in one variable causes a change in the other variable unless our data collection and analysis are specifically designed to assess causation. The research method that best allows us to assess causal relationships is the experimental method.

To demonstrate causality, three conditions must be met. First, the research must demonstrate that variable A is correlated with variable B. In other words, a change in variable A must be associated with a change in variable B. Second, the researcher must demonstrate that the presumed cause (variable A) occurs or changes prior to the presumed effect (variable B). In other words, the cause must precede the effect. For example, suppose a researcher finds that a negative correlation exists between marital conflict and frequency of marital intercourse (as marital conflict increases, frequency of marital intercourse decreases). To demonstrate that marital conflict causes the frequency of marital

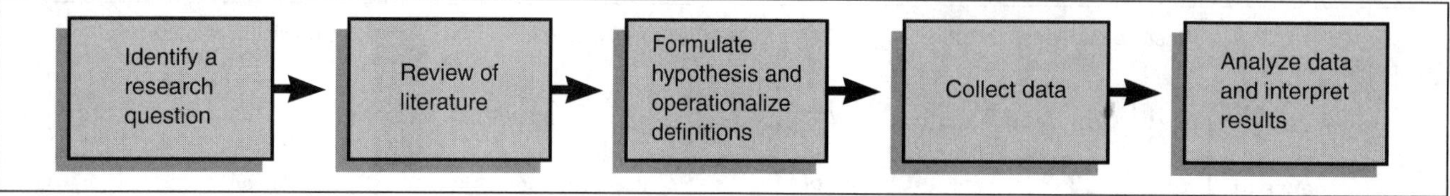

FIGURE 3-3
Steps of Conducting a Research Project

intercourse to decrease, the researcher must show that the marital conflict preceded the decrease in marital intercourse. Otherwise, the researcher cannot be sure whether marital conflict causes a decrease in marital intercourse or a decrease in marital intercourse causes marital conflict.

Third, the researcher must demonstrate that the observed correlation is nonspurious. A nonspurious correlation is a relationship between two variables that cannot be explained by a third variable. A nonspurious correlation suggests that an inherent causal link exists between the two variables. As we saw earlier, the correlation between religious devoutness and sexually transmitted diseases is spurious because a third variable—condom use—explains the correlation. Another example is available from a recent study that investigated the relationship between sexual assault history and current social support. A meta-analysis (technique to summarize results across studies) was used to examine data from six general population studies (Golding, Wilsnack, & Cooper, 2002). The researchers found that compared to persons without sexual assault history, those who have been assaulted report lower levels of social support. They were less likely to be married; have contact with friends and relatives; and receive social support from friends, relatives, and their spouse. The findings applied to men and women, whether European American, African American, or Latino. Because the sexual assaults occurred in the past, and the reported social support was current, it seems reasonable to speculate that the assault interfered with obtaining support. However, the researchers noted that the possibility cannot be ruled out that a third variable, perhaps poor social skills, increased both the sexual assault risk as well as the risk for low social support. Figure 3-3 summarizes the steps involved in conducting a research project.

3-8 INTERPRETATION AND DISCUSSION

Following analysis of the data, the researcher is in a position to evaluate and interpret the results and their implications. The researcher may qualify the results, draw inferences from them, assess the theoretical implications, and discuss possible applications (American Psychological Association, 2001).

The fiftieth anniversary of the publication of Kinsey et al. (1948) *Sexual Behavior in the Human Male* provided a perspective for reflecting on the impact of Kinsey's work on the scientific study of sexuality (DeLamater, 1998). Such an occasion provided a time to reflect on the changed atmosphere for sexual research in this day and age. What has been the impact of Kinsey? "He blazed a trail for future sex researchers" (Bullough, 1998a, p. 131). He provided data that challenged the prevailing view of women as asexual. His work opened discussion of sexual topics, making sex "an almost respectable topic of conversation" (Ericksen, 1999, p. 139). Gathorne-Hardy (2000, p. 448), Kinsey's most recent biographer, suggests that Kinsey and his team were one of the most important factors "enabling homosexuals to win a measure of tolerance."

As he responded to 40,000 to 50,000 letters, lectured, and published books whose contents were reported, Kinsey imparted information to the masses. He provided relief to many with his information "—that masturbating was harmless, that homosexuality and homosexual acts were common, that vaginal orgasm was rubbish, that wanting a lot or having very little sex was normal" (Gathorne-Hardy, 2000, p. 446). However, critics observed that researchers do more than merely record facts. Publishing results of sexuality surveys may accomplish more than simply reporting on trends; it may help shape them. Ericksen (1999) urged social scientists to look at our role in creating knowledge.

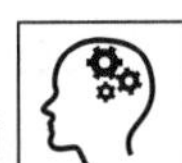

Think About It

Do you agree with Ericksen's statement that talking about sex and asking questions about sex make people more comfortable with sex and its variety?

SUMMARY

Research and theory provide ways of discovering and explaining new information about human sexuality. They are the bedrock of sexology as a discipline. Scientific research involves methods of collecting and analyzing empirical evidence, and is supported by observable evidence.

Overview of Scientific Research

Scientific research involves methods of collecting and analyzing empirical evidence, or data that can be observed. Scientific knowledge is different from common sense, intuition, tradition, and authority in that it is supported by observable evidence.

The Interdisciplinary Nature of Sex Research

Sexology, the scientific study of sexuality, is an interdisciplinary field that incorporates various fields including psychology, medicine, sociology, family studies, public health, social work, therapy, history, and education. Sexology can be divided into three broad disciplinary approaches: biosexology, psychosexology, and sociosexology. Biosexology is the study of the biological aspects of sexuality, such as the physiological and endocrinological aspects of sexual development and sexual response; the role of evolution and genetics in sexual development; the physiology of reproduction; the development of new contraceptives; and the effects of drugs, medications, disease, and exercise on sexuality.

Psychosexology involves the study of how psychological processes, such as emotions, cognitions, and personality, influence and are influenced by sexual development and behavior. Sociosexology is concerned with how social and cultural forces influence and are influenced by sexual attitudes, beliefs, and behaviors. HIV and AIDS research is a continuing aspect of study for the three disciplines.

Theories of Sexuality

Biological, psychological, and sociological theories each contribute unique insights to our understanding of various aspects of sexuality. Biological theories include physiological and evolutionary theories. Psychological theories include psychoanalytic, classical conditioning, operant learning, social learning, and cognitive/affective theories. Sociological theories include symbolic interaction, structural-functional, conflict, feminist, and systems theories.

Eclectic View of Human Sexuality

Many aspects of human sexuality are best explained by using an eclectic theoretical approach that considers biological, psychological, and sociological explanations. For example, for a diabetic man with erection difficulties, physiological explanations would involve pelvic vascular changes attributable to diabetes; psychological explanations would focus on the anxiety that might trigger such difficulty; and sociological explanations would focus on the relationship with his partner and the fact that his family physician may disapprove of his interest in sex "at his age." Biological treatments might involve the diabetic man quitting smoking (to improve vascular circulation); psychological treatment may involve changing cognitions so that erection is not viewed as essential to sexual pleasure; and sociological treatment may involve changing cultural views regarding sexuality among aging persons and incorporating sex therapy into health-care insurance plans.

Conducting Sex Research: A Step-By-Step Process

Unlike casual observations of sexuality, scientific sex research is conducted according to a systematic process. After identifying a research question, a researcher reviews the literature on the subject, formulates a hypothesis, operationalizes the research variables, and collects data using one of several scientific methods of data collection.

Methods of Data Collection

Experimental research, survey research, field research, direct laboratory observation, case studies, and historical research each have advantages and disadvantages. The major strength of the experimental method is that it provides information on causal relationships; that is, it shows how one variable affects another. A primary weakness of this method is that experiments are often conducted on small samples in artificial laboratory settings, so the findings may not be generalized to other people in natural settings.

An advantage of interview survey research is that it enables the researcher to clarify questions for the respondent and pursue answers to particular questions. Face-to-face interviews can be conducted with individuals who do not have a telephone or mailing address. A major disadvantage of interview research is lack of privacy and anonymity, which often causes some respondents to choose not to participate, to conceal, or to alter information.

Questionnaire survey research provides privacy and anonymity to the research participants, which reduces the likelihood that they will provide answers that are intentionally inaccurate or distorted. Questionnaire surveys are also less expensive and time-consuming than face-to face or telephone surveys. The major disadvantage of mail questionnaires is that it is difficult to obtain adequate response rates.

An advantage of field research is that it yields detailed descriptive information about the behaviors, values, emotions, and norms of those being studied. A disadvantage of field research is that the individuals being studied may alter their behaviors if they know they are being observed. Also, the researcher's observations and interpretations may be biased, and the findings may not be generalizable.

Masters and Johnson conducted direct laboratory observation through a one-way mirror of the sexual response patterns in women and men. One disadvantage of such research is that volunteers who participate in such research are not representative of the larger population. Like field research, case studies yield detailed descriptive information about the experiences of individuals. The case study method also allows rare cases of sexual phenomena to be investigated. The main disadvantage of the case study method is that findings based on a single case are not generalizable.

Historical research involves investigating sexuality and sexual issues through the study of historical documents. Historical research provides information on how sexual behavior, attitudes, and norms have changed with time.

Levels of Data Analysis

Levels of data analysis include description (qualitative or quantitative), correlation (positive, negative, curvilinear, or spurious), and causation. Determining causation is difficult because human experiences are influenced by so many factors that it is almost impossible to isolate one factor to assess its effects.

Interpretation and Discussion

Finally, following data analysis, the researcher evaluates and interprets the results and their implications. The researcher may qualify the results, draw inferences from them, assess the theoretical implications, and discuss possible applications.

SUGGESTED WEBSITES

Note: These websites were functional when we went to press. Please access the online text for the most up-to-date URLs.

Electronic Journal of Human Sexuality
http://www.ejhs.org/

Human Sexuality Research Collection
http://rmc.library.cornell.edu/HSC/faq/hscfaq.htm

Journal of Human Sexuality
http://www.leaderu.com/jhs/

Journal of Psychology and Human Sexuality
http://www.nisso.nl/Tijdschr/jopahs.htm

The Journal of Sex Research
http://www.ssc.wisc.edu/ssss/jsr.htm

Kinsey Institute
http://www.indiana.edu/~kinsey/

Psychological Research on the Net
http://psych.hanover.edu/APS/exponnet.html

Psychology Tests and Measurements
http://dir.yahoo.com/social_Science/Psychology/Research/Tests_and_Experiments/

Sexnet
sexnet@listserv.acns.nwu.edu

Sexuality
http://ethology.intercult.su.se/ethology/research/sexuality.html

Society for the Scientific Study of Sex
http://www.sexscience.org

Sexuality Research Fellowships
http://www.ssrc.org/fellowships/sexuality/

KEY TERMS

biosexology (p. 67)
case study (p. 86)
classical conditioning (p. 70)
cognitive/affective theories (p. 71)
conflict theory (p. 73)
correlation (p. 88)
curvilinear correlation (p. 88)
deductive research (p. 66)
dependent variable (p. 79)
descriptive research (p. 88)
direct laboratory observation (p. 86)
eclectic view (p. 76)
ego (p. 69)
empirical evidence (p. 66)
evolutionary theories (p. 68)
experimental research (p. 81)
feminist theories (p. 73)
field research (p. 85)
focus group (p. 83)
hypothesis (p. 79)
id (p. 69)
independent variable (p. 79)
inductive research (p. 66)
interview survey research (p. 82)
natural selection (p. 68)
negative correlation (p. 88)
nonparticipant observation (p. 85)
operant learning theory (p. 70)
operational definition (p. 79)
operationalize (p. 79)
participant observation (p. 85)
patriarchy (p. 75)
physiological theories (p. 68)
positive correlation (p. 88)
psychoanalytic theory (p. 69)
psychosexology (p. 67)
punishment (p. 71)
reinforcement (p. 70)
representative sample (p. 81)
sample (p. 81)
sexology (p. 68)
social learning theory (p. 71)
social scripts (p. 72)
sociobiological theories (p. 68)
sociosexology (p. 67)
spurious correlation (p. 89)
structural-functional theory (p. 73)
superego (p. 69)
survey research (p. 81)
symbolic interaction theory (p. 72)
systems theory (p. 76)
theory (p. 68)
variable (p. 79)

CHAPTER QUIZ

1. Which of the following source of knowledge relies on empirical evidence?
   a. science
   b. intuition
   c. tradition
   d. common sense
2. How many U.S. universities offer a doctorate degree in sexology?
   a. none
   b. 3
   c. 32
   d. 132
3. Which of the following is NOT one of Freud's four basic psychosexual stages of development?
   a. oral
   b. anal
   c. manual
   d. phallic
4. According to ___________ theory, a partner who has been reinforced for initiating sexual behavior is likely to do so again. A partner who has been punished for initiating sexual behavior is less likely to do so in the future.
   a. classical conditioning
   b. social learning
   c. psychoanalytic
   d. operant learning
5. According to _________ theory, cultural portrayals of healthy sexuality that emphasize physiological functioning of the genitals (rather than relationship factors such as intimacy) benefit the medical and pharmaceutical industries that profit from medical treatments and drugs designed to enhance genital performance.
   a. feminist
   b. conflict
   c. cognitive/affective
   d. sociobiological
6. Socialist feminist theory ______________ patriarchy.
   a. is supportive of
   b. is critical of
7. In a research study that assesses the effect of alcohol consumption on condom use, condom use is the __________ variable.
   a. dependent variable
   b. independent variable
   c. experimental variable
   d. control variable
8. Which type of research involves manipulating the independent variable to determine how it affects the dependent variable?
   a. experimental research
   b. survey research
   c. field research
   d. case studies
9. Which of the following are more likely to have had sexual intercourse, performed oral sex, score higher on sexual esteem and sexual sensation seeking, and report less traditional sexual attitudes?
   a. students who volunteer to participate in sexuality research
   b. students who do not volunteer to participate in sexuality research
10. The major disadvantage of ___________ is that it is difficult to obtain an adequate response rate.
   a. case studies
   b. interview research
   c. experimental research
   d. mail questionnaires
11. What type of research is conducted in focus groups?
   a. field research
   b. interview research
   c. experimental research
   d. participant observation research
12. Two types of __________ research are participant observation research and nonparticipant observation research.
   a. field
   b. survey
   c. experimental
   d. historical
13. The primary disadvantage of the case study method is that
   a. participants risk being harmed.
   b. the results are not generalizable.
   c. there is a low response rate.
   d. it is a very costly method of research.
14. Consider the statement "As the number of sexual partners decreases, the chance of contracting STDs decreases." This is an example of a ___________ correlation.
   a. positive
   b. negative
   c. curvilinear
15. A ___________ correlation exists when two variables appear to be related but only because they are both related to a third variable.
   a. spurious
   b. nonspurious
   c. valid
   d. reliable
16. Which research method best allows us to assess causal relationships?
   a. survey research
   b. historical research
   c. case studies
   d. experimental research

REFERENCES

Alcock, J. (2001). *The triumph of sociobiology*. Oxford: Oxford University Press.

American Psychological Association. (2001). *Publication manual of the American Psychological Association (5th ed.)*. Washington, DC: Author.

Areton, L. W. (2002, January 15). Factors in the sexual satisfaction of obese women in relationships. *Electronic Journal of Human Sexuality, 5*, http://www.ejhs.org/volume5/Areton/TOC.htm

Bancroft, J. (1999). Sexual science in the 21st century: Where are we going? A personal note. *The Journal of Sex Research, 36*, 226–229.

Barash, D. P. (1977). *Sociobiology and behavior*. New York: Elsevier.

Bartell, D. (1970). Group sex among the mid-Americans. *The Journal of Sex Research, 6*, 113–130.

Biaggio, M. K., Mohan, P. J., & Baldwin, C. (1985). Relationships among attitudes toward children, women's liberation, and personality characteristics. *Sex Roles, 12*, 47–62.

Binik, Y. M., Mah, K., & Kiesler, S. (1999). Ethical issues in conducting sex research on the Internet. *The Journal of Sex Research, 36*, 82–90.

Bogaert, A. E. (1996). Volunteer bias in human sexuality research: Evidence for both sexuality and personality differences in males. *Archives of Sexual Behavior, 25*, 125–140.

Boles, J. (1998). My life in prostitution. In G. G. Brannigan, E. R. Allgeier, & A. R. Allgeier (Eds.). *The sex scientists* (pp. 185–200). New York: Longman.

Brown, N. R., & Sinclair, R. C. (1999). Estimating number of lifetime sexual partners: Men and women do it differently. *The Journal of Sex Research, 36*, 292–297.

Bullough, V. L. (1998a). Alfred Kinsey and the Kinsey report: Historical overview and lasting contributions. *The Journal of Sex Research, 35*, 127–131.

Bullough, V. L. (1998b). History, the historian, and sex. In G. G. Brannigan, E. R. Allgeier, & A. R. Allgeier (Eds.). *The sex scientists* (pp. 1–14). New York: Longman.

Bullough, V. L. (1999). Kinsey: A different view. *The Journal of Sex Research, 36*, 309–311.

Carballo-Dieguez, A., Remien, R. H., Dolezal, C., & Wagner, G. (1999). Reliability of sexual behavior self-reports in male couples of discordant HIV status. *The Journal of Sex Research, 36*, 152–158.

Catania, J. A. (1999). A comment on advancing the frontiers of sexological methods. *The Journal of Sex Research, 36*, 1–2.

Cubbins, L. A., & Tanfer, K. (2000). The influence of gender on sex: A study of men's and women's self-reported high-risk sex behavior. *Archives of Sexual Behavior, 29*, 229–256.

Daly, M., & Wilson, M. (1983). *Sex, evolution, and behavior (Second Edition)*. Boston: Willard Grant Press.

Delamater, J. D. (1998). Introduction to special articles. *The Journal of Sex Research, 35*, 126.

D'Emilio, J., & Freedman, E. B. (1988). *Intimate matters: A social history of sexuality in America*. New York: Harper and Row.

Diamond, M. (2000). The field of sex research: Responsibility to ourselves and to society. *Archives of Sexual Behavior, 29*, 389–395.

Dixson, A. F., Halliwell, G., East, R., Wignarajah, P., & Anderson, M. J. (2003). Masculine somatotype and hirsuteness as determinants of sexual attractiveness to women. *Archives of Sexual Behavior, 32*, 29–39.

Donovan, G. (2001, July 7). Kenyan church official criticizes condom imports. *National Catholic Reporter, 37*(35), 9.

Elliott, L., & Brantley, C. (1997). *Sex on campus: The naked truth about the real sex lives of college students*. New York: Random House.

Ericksen, J. A. (1998). With enough cases, why do you need statistics? Revisiting Kinsey's methodology. *The Journal of Sex Research, 35*, 132–140.

Ericksen, J. A. (with Steffen, S. A.) (1999). *Kiss and tell: Surveying sex in the twentieth century*. Cambridge, MA: Harvard University Press.

Fishbein, M., & Ajzen, I. (1975). *Belief, attitude, intention and behavior: An introduction to theory and research*. Reading, MA: Addison-Wesley.

Fishbein, M., & Middlestadt, S. E. (1989). Using the Theory of Reasoned Action as a framework for understanding and changing AIDS-related behaviors. In V. M. Mays, G. W. Albee, & S. S. Schneider (Eds.) *Primary prevention of AIDS: Psychological approaches*. Newbury Park, CA: Sage.

Francome, C., & Freeman, E. (2000). British general practitioners' attitudes toward abortion. *Family Planning Perspectives, 32*, 189–191.

Gathorne-Hardy, J. (2000). *Sex the measure of all things: A life of Alfred C. Kinsey*. Bloomington and Indianapolis: Indiana University Press.

Gillmore, M. R., Gaylord, J., Hartway, J., Hoppe, M. J., Morrison, D. M., Leigh, B. C., & Rainey, D. T. (2001). Daily data collection of sexual and other health-related behaviors. *The Journal of Sex Research, 38*, 35–42.

Godin, G., Maticka-Tyndale, E., Adrien, A., Manson-Singer, S., Willms, D., & Cappon, P. (1996). Cross-cultural testing of three social cognitive theories: An application to condom use. *Journal of Applied Social Psychology, 26*, 1556–1586.

Golding, J. M., Wilsnack, S. C., & Cooper, M. L. (2002). Sexual assault history and social support: Six general population studies. *Journal of Traumatic Stress, 15*, 187–197.

Green, R. (2003). The "T" word. *Archives of Sexual Behavior, 32*, 1.

Gupta, G. R. (2001). Gender, sexuality, and HIV/AIDS: The what, the why and the how. *SIECUS Report, 29*(5), 6–12.

Humphreys, L. (1970). *Tearoom trade: Impersonal sex in public places*. Chicago: Aldine.

Hyde, J. S. (2001). The next decade of sexual science: Synergy from advances in related sciences. *The Journal of Sex Research, 38*, 97–101.

Jankowski, M. K., Leitenberg, H., Henning, K., & Coffey, P. (2002). Parental caring as a possible buffer against sexual revictimization in young adult survivors of child sexual abuse. *Journal of Traumatic Stress, 15*, 235–244.

Jones, J. H. (1997). *Alfred C. Kinsey: A public/private life*. New York: W. W. Norton.

Kinsey, A. C., Pomeroy, W. B., & Martin, C. E. (1948). *Sexual behavior in the human male*. Philadelphia: Saunders.

Kinsey, A. C., Pomeroy, W. B., Martin, C. E., & Gebhard, P. H. (1953). *Sexual behavior in the human female*. Philadelphia: Saunders.

Knox, D., Sturdivant, L., & Zusman, M. E. (2001). College student attitudes toward sexual involvement. *College Student Journal, 35*, 241–243.

Laumann, E. O., & Michael, R. T. (Eds.) (2001). *Sex, love, and health in America: Private choices and public policies*. Chicago: The University of Chicago Press.

Lee, M. C. (2001). Family and adolescent childbearing. *Journal of Adolescent Health, 28*, 307–312.

Lott, B. E. (1973). Who wants the children? Some relationships among attitudes toward children, parents, and the liberation of women. *American Psychologist, 28*, 573–582.

Mackay, J. (2001). Global sex: Sexuality and sexual practices around the world. *Sexual and Relationship Therapy, 16*, 71–82.

Mackenzie, J., & Goins, L. (2001, August). Cosmo's sex survey. *Cosmopolitan Magazine*, 165 et passim.

Mason-Schrock, D. (1996). Transsexuals' narrative construction of the 'True Self.' *Social Psychology Quarterly, 59*, 176–192.

Masters, W. H., & Johnson, V. E. (1966). *Human sexual response*. Boston: Little, Brown.

Meyers, J. F., & Shurts, W. M. (2002) Measuring positive emotionality: A review of instruments assessing love. *Measurement and Evaluation in Counseling and Development, 34*, 238–254.

McGraw, A., Zvonkovic, M., & Walker, A. J. (2000). Studying postmodern families: A feminist analysis of ethical tensions in work and family research. *Journal of Marriage and the Family, 62*, 68–77.

Michael, R. T , Gagnon, J. H., Laumann, E. O., & Kolata, G. (1994). *Sex in America: A definitive survey*. Boston: Little, Brown.

Mitchell, K. J., Finkelhor, D., & Wolak, J. (2001). Risk factors for and impact of online sexual solicitation of youth. *The Journal of the American Medical Association, 285*, 3011–3014.

Morrison, D. M., Gillmore, M. R., & Baker, S. A. (1995). Determinants of condom use among high-risk heterosexual adults: A test of the theory of reasoned action. *Journal of Applied Social Psychology, 25*, 651–676.

Mustanski, B. S. (2001). Getting wired: Exploiting the Internet for the collection of valid sexuality data. *The Journal of Sex Research, 38*, 293–301.

Myers, J. (1992). Nonmainstream body modification: Genital piercing, branding, burning and cutting. *Journal of Contemporary Ethnography, 21*, 267–306.

Norris, A. E., & Ford, K. (1995). Condom use by low-income African American and Hispanic youth with a well-known partner: Integrating the Health Belief Model, Theory of Reasoned Action, and the Construct Accessibility Model. *Journal of Applied Social Psychology, 25*, 1801–1830.

O'Rourke, T. (2002, August). Our juiciest sex survey ever. *Cosmopolitan Magazine*, 189–191.

Palmer, R., & Bor, R. (2001). The challenges to intimacy and sexual relationships for gay men in HIV serodiscordant relationships: A pilot study. *Journal of Marital and Family Therapy, 27*, 419–431.

Palud, J. J., Gaither, G. A., Hegstad, H. J., Rowan, L., & Devitt, M. K. (1999). Volunteer bias in human psychophysiological sexual arousal research: To whom do our research results apply? *The Journal of Sex Research, 36*, 171–179.

Petersen, D. M., & Dressel, P. L. (1982). Equal time for women: Social notes on the male strip show. *Urban Life, 11*, 185–208.

Pound, E. T. (2000, July 13). University ordered to correct problems. *USA Today*, p. 3A

Romer, D., Hornik, R., Stanton, B., Black, M., Li, X., Ricardo, I., & Feigelman, S. (1997). "Talking" computers: A reliable and private method to conduct interviews on sensitive topics with children. *The Journal of Sex Research, 34*, 3–9.

Rowland, D. L., Cooper, S. E., & Schneider, M. (2001). Defining premature ejaculation for experimental and clinical investigations. *Archives of Sexual Behavior, 30*, 235–253.

Satcher, D. (2001). The Surgeon General's Call to Action to Promote Sexual Health and Responsible Sexual Behavior. U.S. Dept. of Health and Human Services. www.surgeongeneral.gov/library/sexualhealth/call.htm

Schroer, S. E. (2001). Completely immersed and totally exposed: Sexuality in social nudism. Paper, Society for the Study of Social Problems.

Seiler, A. (2000, September 14). Entertainment marketing to children blasted. *USA Today*, p. 4A.

Senn, C. Y., & Desmarais, S. (2001). Are our recruitment practices for sex studies working across gender? The effect of topic and gender of recruiter on participation rates of university men and women. *The Journal of Sex Research, 38*, 111–117.

Stark, S., Sachse, R., & Liedl, T., et al. (2001). Vardenafil increases penile rigidity and tumescence in men with erectile dysfunction after a single oral dose. *European Urology*, 181–190.

Strassberg, D. S., & Lowe, K. (1995). Volunteer bias in sexuality research. *Archives of Sexual Behavior, 24*, 369–382.

Tiefer, L. (2001). A new view of women's sexual problems: Why new? Why now? *The Journal of Sex Research, 28*, 89–96.

Udry, J. R. (1998). Doing sex research on adolescents. In G. G. Brannigan, E. R. Allgeier, & A. R. Allgeier (Eds.). *The sex scientists* (pp. 49–60). New York: Longman.

The Washington Spectator. (2001, October 1). *27*(18), 4.

Wiederman, M. W. (1999). Volunteer bias in sexuality research using college student participants. *The Journal of Sex Research, 36*, 59–66.

White, K. M., Terry, D. J., & Hoag, M. A. (1994). Safer sex behavior: The role of attitudes, norms, and control factors. *Journal of Applied Social Psychology, 24*, 2164–2192.

Wulfert, E., & Wan, C. K. (1995). Safer sex intentions and condom use viewed from a Health Belief, Reasoned Action, and Social Cognitive perspective. *The Journal of Sex Research, 32*, 299–311.

4

Anatomy, Physiology, and Sexual Response

Chapter Outline

4-1 Female External Anatomy and Physiology
- 4-1a Mons Veneris
- 4-1b Labia
- 4-1c Clitoris
- 4-1d Vaginal Opening
- 4-1e Urethral Opening
- 4-1f The Female Breasts
- 4-1g Personal Choices: Breast Self-Examination and Mammogram

4-2 Female Internal Anatomy and Physiology
- 4-2a Vagina
- 4-2b The "G Spot"
- 4-2c Uterus
- 4-2d Personal Choices: Pap Smear Test and Pelvic Exam
- 4-2e Fallopian Tubes
- 4-2f Ovaries
- 4-2g Menstruation

4-3 Male External Anatomy and Physiology
- 4-3a Penis
- 4-3b Scrotum

4-4 Male Internal Anatomy and Physiology
- 4-4a Testes
- 4-4b Personal Choices: Timing of Testicular Self-Exam
- 4-4c Duct System
- 4-4d Seminal Vesicles and Prostate Gland
- 4-4e Personal Choices: Timing of Prostate Rectal Exam

4-5 Models of Sexual Response
- 4-5a Masters and Johnson's Four-Stage Model of Sexual Response
- 4-5b Helen Kaplan's Three-Stage Model of Sexual Response
- 4-5c Basson's Contemporary Model of Sexual Response
- 4-5d Personal Choices: Engaging in Sexual Behavior When Desire Is Low

4-6 Hormones and Sexual Response

4-7 Pheromones, Aphrodisiacs, and Sexual Response

Summary

Suggested Websites

Key Terms

Chapter Quiz

References

In the culture in which we live, it is the custom to be least informed upon that subject concerning which every individual should know most—namely, the structure and function of his/her own body.

—Ashley Montagu, anthropologist

A visit to any recreation/exercise/athletic center will provide ample evidence of America's obsession with the human body. Persons climb on Stairmasters and jog on treadmills until they are drenched with sweat with the goal of feeling good and looking great. Although we have emphasized that human sexuality is a broader concept than anatomy, knowledge of sexual anatomy and physiology is important in making choices in sexuality (e.g., see sections 4-1g, 4-2d, 4-4b, 4-4e, and 4-5d).

Sexual anatomy Term referring to internal and external genitals. (Also called *sex organs*.)

Sexual physiology The vascular, hormonal, and central nervous system processes involved in genital functioning.

If we think of the human body as a special type of machine, anatomy refers to the machine's parts, and physiology refers to how the parts work. Technically, anatomy is the study of body structure, and physiology is the study of bodily functions. **Sexual anatomy** refers to internal and external genitals, which are also called *sex organs*. **Sexual physiology** refers to the vascular, hormonal, and central nervous system processes involved in genital functioning. Sexual sensations involve the whole body—not just the sex organs. Furthermore, what happens above the neck—in the brain—largely influences sexual functioning.

Before detailing the respective anatomy of women and men, we examine the issue of nudism (see Box 4-1). This topic is relevant here because feeling comfortable about one's anatomy is important for sexual functioning. Nudists are stereotyped as "swinging perverts" who parade their anatomy "shamelessly." But what is the reality of nudists and nudism?

4-1 FEMALE EXTERNAL ANATOMY AND PHYSIOLOGY

Whoever called it necking was a poor judge of anatomy.

—Groucho Marx

Despite living in a culture that seems sexually obsessed, some women do not know the correct scientific names for their genitalia. Little girls are often not taught names for their external genital parts, but vague reference may be made to, "down there."

Think About It

Why is it that young girls may not be taught any anatomical terms for their "private" parts? How many share the experience related by novelist Alice Walker, who described how her grandmother taught her girls to bathe: "Wash down as far as possible, then wash up as far as possible, then wash possible" (Walker, 1988, p. 58)?

Vulva The external female genitalia.

The external female genitalia are collectively known as the **vulva** (VUL-vuh) (source of pronunciation guides, Applegate & Overton, 1994), which is a Latin term meaning "covering." External sex organs of the female include the mons veneris, labia, clitoris, urethral opening, and vaginal opening (see Figure 4-1). Female genitalia differ in size, shape, and color, resulting in considerable variability in appearance (see Figure 4-2).

Think About It

Two researchers (Braun & Kitzinger, 2001) reported on the identification of 317 different female genital slang terms and 351 male genital slang terms by 156 women and 125 men. How do you account for the large number of slang terms?

Box 4-1 Up Close

Nudists—Clothed When Practical, Nude When Possible

Cheri Alexander is a nudist. She is one of more than 50,000 members of the American Association for Nude Recreation (also known as AANR) that emphasizes the importance of body acceptance. She is also the founder of Travelites, one of 350 nudist clubs throughout America. She shared her experience with nudism in an interview. "Our members are from infancy to 90 and represent all body types and occupations. We are not swingers or sex freaks; we just enjoy clothing optional contexts, and getting together with others who share the exhilaration one feels when free of constricting clothes."

"I became a nudist during a vacation at a resort in the Caribbean when I took a day side trip to a clothing optional beach. I was the last one to take off my swimsuit and the last one to put my swimsuit back on at the end of the day. I never knew the freedom of being without clothes until I tried it."

"As executive director of Travelites and a member of AANR, The Naturist Society, and the National Nudist Council, I get over 100 emails daily from persons seeking information about our organizations. They soon discover we are monogamous, family people who feel most relaxed when we are nude. One of the most frequent questions asked is 'what about men having erections'? In my 34 years as a nudist, there have been only a couple of occasions at which this was an issue. In most cases, since nude recreation is a NON SEXUAL CONTEXT, men simply do not get erections. In one instance, a man was asleep by the pool and got an erection; someone simply tapped him on the shoulder, and he rolled over. In the other instance, a man was behaving inappropriately, and was asked to leave the nudist park."

Another question is about feeling anxious the first time one tries nudism. "At my club and several others, we do not require people disrobe immediately; we want them to feel comfortable. What usually happens is that individuals simply wrap up in a towel and slowly disrobe as their comfort level increases. Once they discover that others are looking at their eyes and not staring at or concerned about their bodies, they get relaxed."

"Body acceptance is what we are all about. Buying expensive clothes, putting on makeup and perfume are all ways of covering up the body. We feel one's birthday suit is natural and normal and seek contexts where we can be free." Sociologist Sandra Schroer (2001) reported on her participant observation research at various nudist clubs/resorts that nudists embrace the idea that sexuality is one way to express the freedom of being fully human.

"Sometimes we are asked about exposing children to nudity. Children are natural nudists and enjoy the freedom of not being concerned with clothes. At our nudist recreation centers, children are nude routinely since this is the norm. We as nudists are also 'family' and are very protective of our own and others to ensure that adults always act appropriately with our children." Weinberg (1965) observed that "sexual interests are very adequately controlled in nudist camps. Research on children reared in nudist contexts reflect that they have very healthy self-concepts since they have not been taught to be 'shameful' of their bodies." Hill (1996) reported that there are about 30 million nudists worldwide and that "contrary to academic and popular opinions, the advantages of being a naturist include being socially well-adjusted, having happier and longer marriages, experiencing lower incidence of sexual/child/spousal abuse, and rejecting all forms of pornography and body objectification."

References

Hill, T. L. (1996). The problem with non-nudists. *Society*, *20*, 23–25.

Schroer, S. E. (2001, August 18–22). Completely immersed and totally exposed: Sexuality in social nudism. Paper presented at the annual meeting of the Society for the Study of Social Problems, Anaheim, CA.

Weinberg, M. S. (1965). Sexual modesty, social meanings, and the nudist camp. *Social Problems*, *12*, 311–318.

4-1a Mons Veneris

The soft cushion of fatty tissue that lies over the pubic symphysis (joint between the left and right public bones) is called the **mons veneris** (mahns vuhNAIR-ihs), which is Latin for "mound of Venus" (Venus being the goddess of love).

The mons acts as a cushion to protect the pubic region during intercourse. Because this area is filled with many nerve endings, women often find gentle stimulation of this area to be highly pleasurable. Also known as the mons pubis, this area becomes covered with hair during puberty. The evolutionary function of this hair may be to trap and concentrate pelvic odors (for attracting a mate), and to serve as a visual cue to showcase the genital area (Angier, 1999).

Mons veneris The soft cushion of fatty tissue that lies over the pubic symphysis (joint between the left and right public bones).

4-1b Labia

The **labia majora** (LAY-be-uh mih-JOR-uh), or "major lips," are two elongated folds of fatty tissue that extend from the mons veneris to the **perineum** (PEHR-ih-NEE-um)—the area

Labia majora ("major lips") Two elongated folds of fatty tissue that extend from the mons veneris to the perineum.

Perineum The area of skin between the opening of the vagina and the anus.

FIGURE 4-1
External Female Genitalia

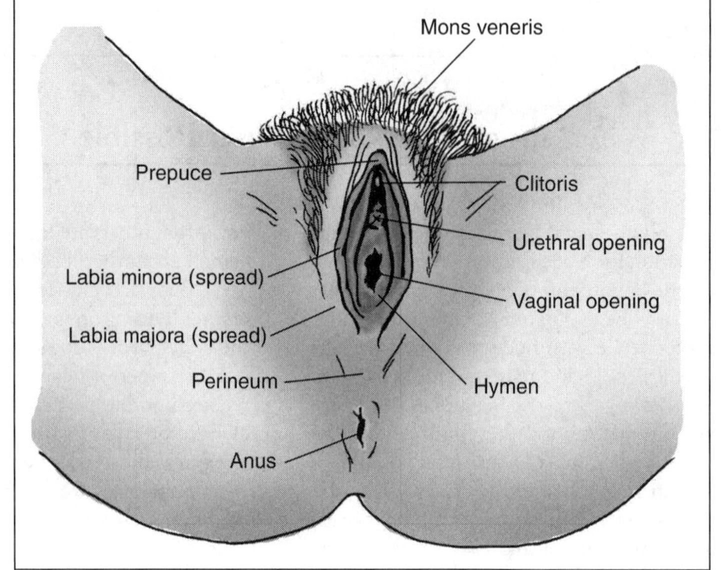

FIGURE 4-2
Variations in the Vulva

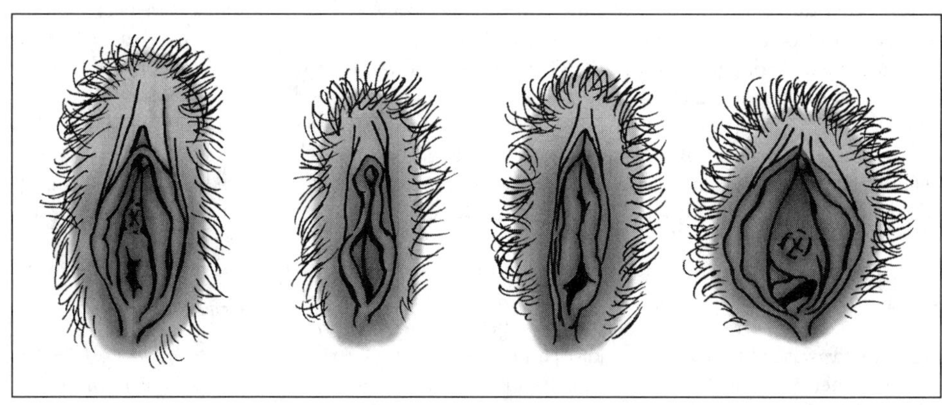

of skin between the opening of the vagina and the anus. The outer sides of these labia may be covered with hair, whereas the inner sides are smooth, and supplied with oil and sweat glands. Located between the labia majora lie two hairless, flat folds of skin called the **labia minora** (mih-NOR-uh), or "little lips," (also called the nymphae) that enfold the urethral and vaginal openings. The labia minora join at the top to form the prepuce, or hood, of the clitoris. It is not uncommon for the labia minora to protrude beyond the labia majora; the nymphae vary considerably in size from woman to woman.

Labia minora ("little lips") Two smaller elongated folds of fatty tissue that enfold the urethral and vaginal openings.

The labia minora have numerous nerve endings, making them very sensitive to tactile stimulation. They also have a rich supply of blood vessels; during sexual stimulation, the labia minora become engorged with blood, causing them to swell and change color. With prolonged stimulation, the inner surfaces of the labia minora receive a small amount of mucous secretion from the small **Bartholin's** (BAR-toe-linz) **glands,** which are located at the base of the minor lips. This does not significantly contribute to vaginal lubrication, however, and the main function of these glands remains unknown.

Bartholin's glands Located at the base of the minor lips of the female genitalia, they secrete a small amount of mucous to the inner surfaces of the labia minora.

The labia (and entire vulval area) sweats. The vulval area also secretes a blend of oils, fats, waxes, cholesterol, and cellular debris called sebum, which gives the pelvis a slippery feel. It serves a waterproofing function to repel urine, menstrual blood, and bacteria (Angier, 1999).

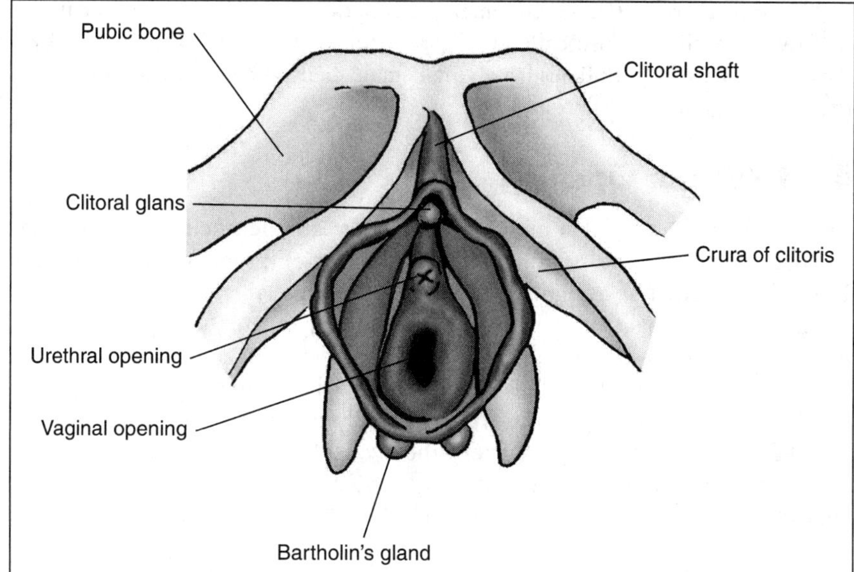

FIGURE 4-3
Anatomy of the Clitoris

4-1c Clitoris

The most sensitive organ of the female genitalia is the **clitoris** (KLIH-ter-iss)—a sensory organ located at the top of the labia minora (see Figure 4-3) and is equipped with 8,000 nerve fibers. The word *clitoris* is derived from the Greek, but there is debate about its origin. Suggestions include derivations from the verb *kleitoriazein* (to titillate lasciviously, to seek pleasure) and the Greek word for key (the key to female sexuality?) (Angier, 1999). The clitoris is extremely sensitive to touch, pressure, and temperature and is unique in that it is an organ whose only known function is to provide sexual sensations and erotic pleasure. In a sexually unaroused woman, the only visible part of the clitoris is the glans—a small external knob of tissue located just below the clitoral hood. The size of the clitoral glans, about 1/4 inch in diameter and 1/4 to 1 inch in length, is not related to the subjective experience of pleasure. The shaft of the clitoris, which is hidden from view by the clitoral hood, divides into two much larger structures called crura (Kroo-ra), which are attached to the pubic bone.

Clitoris Sensory organ located at the top of the labia minora of the female genitalia.

Think About It

Although the *clitoris* is the organ with some of the same tissue as the *penis*, the term is typically not used as the female counterpart to the penis. Rather, the term *vagina* is typically thought of by college students as the counterpart to the *penis* (Ogletree & Ginsburg, 2000). How do you account for this focus on the vagina?

The clitoris develops embryologically from the same tissue as the penis and has twice the number of nerve endings. The body of the clitoris consists of a spongy tissue that fills with blood during sexual arousal. This results in a doubling or tripling of its original size; it becomes swollen and springy, but not rigid. As with the penis, stimulation of any part of the female body may result in engorgement or swelling of the clitoris. However, describing the clitoris as a "miniature penis" is incorrect because the clitoris does not have a reproductive or urinary function. With sufficient sexual arousal, the glans of the clitoris disappears beneath the clitoral hood.

In some cultures female circumcision is performed and involves cutting the fold of skin over the clitoris, also called a clitoridectomy. We discuss this in detail in Box 9-3, "Social Choices: U.S. Policies Involving Female Genital Operations" (sometimes referred to as female genital mutilation).

4-1d Vaginal Opening

Vestibule The smooth tissue surrounding a woman's urethral opening.

Introitus The vaginal opening.

The area between the labia minora, called the **vestibule,** includes the urethral opening and the vaginal opening, or **introitus** (in-TRO-ih-tus) (pronunciation guide from Davies, 1998). The vaginal opening, like the anus, is surrounded by a ring of sphincter muscles. Although the vaginal opening can expand to accommodate the passage of a baby at childbirth, these muscles can involuntarily contract under conditions of tension, making it difficult to insert an object (such as a tampon) into the vagina.

Hymen A thin mucous membrane that may partially cover the vaginal opening.

The vaginal opening is sometimes partially covered by a thin mucous membrane called the **hymen.** Throughout history, the hymen has been regarded as proof of virginity. A newlywed woman who was found to be without a hymen was often returned to her parents, disgraced by exile, or even tortured or killed.

CULTURAL DIVERSITY 

It has been a common practice in many societies to display a bloody bedsheet after the wedding night as proof of the bride's virginity. In Japan and other countries, sexually experienced women sometimes have plastic surgeons reconstruct their hymens before marriage.

The hymen is, however, a poor indicator of virginity. Some women are born without hymens or with incomplete hymens. For other women, hymens are accidentally ruptured by vigorous physical activity or by insertion of a tampon. In some women, the hymen stretches during sexual intercourse without tearing. Most doctors cannot determine whether a woman is a virgin by simply examining her vaginal opening.

4-1e Urethral Opening

Urethra Short tube that connects the bladder with the urethral opening.

Above the vaginal opening but below the clitoris is the urethral opening, which allows urine to pass from the body. A short tube called the **urethra** connects the bladder (where urine collects) with the urethral opening. Small glands called Skene's glands—developed from the same embryonic tissue as the male prostate gland—are located just inside the urethral opening.

Cystitis A bladder inflammation.

Because of the shorter length of the female urethra and its close proximity to the anus, women are more susceptible than men to **cystitis,** or bladder inflammation. The most common symptom is frequent urination accompanied by burning sensations. Women (and men) with these symptoms should see a health-care practitioner. A common cause of cystitis is the transmission of bacteria that live in the intestines to the urethral opening. Women can avoid cystitis by cleansing themselves from the vulva toward the anus after a bowel movement and by avoiding vaginal intercourse after anal intercourse (unless a new condom is used).

4-1f The Female Breasts

The female breasts are designed to provide milk for infants and young children (see Box 4-2 for a discussion of public breast-feeding). Anthropologist Sarah Blaffer Hrdy has written that *mammae* (Latin for breasts) comes from the cry "mama," from children of various linguistic groups, appealing to be nursed at the breast (Angier, 1999). However, the breasts are not considered part of the reproductive system, and their development is con-

Box 4-2 Social Choices

Breast-Feeding in Public?

Although it is not against the law to breast-feed in public in any state, nursing mothers often experience harassment, intimidation, and discrimination for breast-feeding in public. Nursing mothers have been asked either to stop breast-feeding or to leave public places, including restaurants, malls, libraries, parks, bus stations, pools, movie theaters, hotel lobbies, department stores, and even doctors' offices.

As of 2001, 35 states have laws removing criminal penalties for breast-feeding and protecting the woman's right to breast-feed in public. Nevada, specifically, has enacted a law that sets forth the importance of breast-feeding and clarifies that women have a right to breast-feed their children in public, even if there is exposure of the breast. It also clarifies that breast-feeding is not an indecent or criminal act.

Several states have enacted legislation dealing with other breast-feeding issues. For example, Idaho and Iowa have enacted legislation allowing breast-feeding mothers to be exempted from jury duty. Florida and Texas have created worksite breast-feeding support policies for all state employees. These policies address such issues as work schedule flexibility and accessible locations and privacy for pumping breast milk or nursing. Texas encourages businesses to create supportive worksite breast-feeding policies by allowing businesses that develop such policies to use the designation "mother-friendly" in their promotional materials (Baldwin & Friedman, 2002).

Studies show that breast-feeding has significant benefits for both mother and infant. Breast-fed children have lower rates of death, meningitis, childhood leukemia and other cancers, diabetes, respiratory illness, bacterial and viral infections, ear infections, allergies, obesity, and developmental delays. Women who breast-feed have a lower risk for breast and ovarian cancers. About 60% of all new mothers in the United States try to breast-feed, but many quit after a short time. One reason they quit is that they feel discomfort from people who give disapproving looks, no matter how discreet they try to be in public.

As the legal system continues to recognize and encourage breast-feeding, a message is sent to the public at large that breast-feeding is an important issue—one that has an impact on our lives and the futures of our children. But society's views and taboos are not easily changed. Legislation that recognizes the importance of breast-feeding is just one step toward helping our society become more supportive of breast-feeding. A major victory was reflected in the legislation that President Bill Clinton signed into law in 1999 which made breast-feeding legal on all federal property where a woman and her child have a right to be. Under the law, it is now illegal to ask women who are nursing their infant children to move from federal property.

Perhaps such public policy and educational efforts will help reach the Healthy People 2000/2010 National Health Objectives to increase to at least 75% the proportion of mothers who breast-feed early in the post-partum period. The Objectives also include goals encouraging mothers to continue breast-feeding as their babies grow. Public education may be especially important in reaching the goal to increase to at least 50% the proportion of mothers who continue until their babies are 6 months old and to at least 25% the proportion who continue breast-feeding at 12 months (American Academy of Pediatrics, 2002).

---

sidered to be a secondary sex characteristic like pubic hair. **Secondary sex characteristics** are those that differentiate males and females that are not linked to reproduction. Female breasts begin to develop during puberty in response to increasing levels of estrogen. This hormone has a similar effect if injected in males.

Secondary sex characteristics Characteristics that differentiate males and females that are not linked to reproduction (e.g., beard in men, high voice in women).

Think About It

Although female breasts are regarded as having considerable erotic value in the United States, male breasts are not without erotic notice. For example, there are no flabby chested Chippendale dancers! Why do you think this is true?

Each adult female breast consists of 15 to 20 mammary, or milk-producing, glands, that are connected to the nipple by separate ducts (see Figure 4-4). The soft consistency and the size of the breasts are due to fatty tissues that loosely pack between the glands. Breasts vary in size and shape; it is common for a woman to have one breast that is slightly larger than the other.

FIGURE 4-4
Internal and External Anatomy of the Female Breast

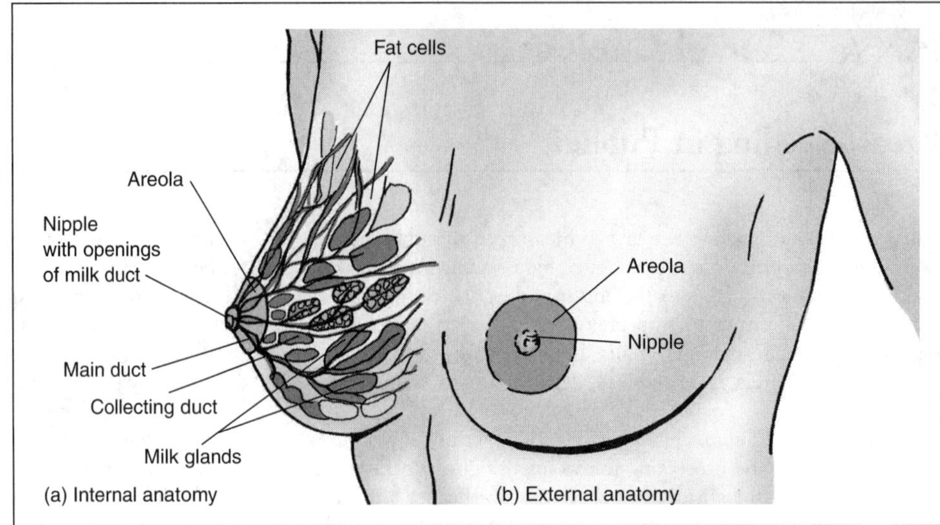

Cultural Diversity

Breast size varies depending on the continent. In the United Kingdom, the average bra size in 1997 was 36B, and in 1999 it was 36C. Data from Asia showed an average bra size of 34A in the 1980s and 34C in the 1990s (Mackay, 2000).

Areola Darkened ring around the nipple that keeps the nipples lubricated by secretions of oil during breast-feeding.

The nipples are made up of smooth muscle fibers with numerous nerve endings, making them sensitive to touch. The nipples are kept lubricated during breast-feeding by secretions of oil from the **areola** (EHR-ree-OH-luh), the darkened area around the nipple. This area becomes permanently darker after pregnancy. There is no relation between the size or shape of breasts and their sensitivity. Many women enjoy having their breasts stimulated; however, others derive no particular pleasure from such stimulation.

Think About It

During your childhood and adolescence, what, when, and how did you learn about external female sexual anatomy? Does your experience differ from the way you want your children to learn?

4-1g Personal Choices: Breast Self Examination and Mammogram

Breast cancer is the most common cancer in women. The National Cancer Institute (NCI) estimates that about 1 in 8 women in the United States (approximately 12.8 percent) will develop breast cancer in her lifetime (National Cancer Institute, 2001, http://cis.nci.nih.gov/fact/5_6.htm). A woman with breast cancer is much more likely to survive if the cancer is detected and treated early, before it develops to an advanced stage and spreads to other parts of the body.

Most breast lumps are discovered by women themselves. Although the majority of breast lumps are not cancerous, the American Cancer Society recommends that all women ages 20 and older examine their breasts each month (preferably after menstruation) to feel for unusual lumps and look for any changes in the contour of each breast, such as swelling, dimpling of skin, or changes in the nipple. Any of these observations, as

Observe:
Examine the breasts in the mirror, from both the front and side view. Place the arms in the three positions indicated in the diagram to observe different angles of the breasts. Take notice of any changes in the breast size, shape, or direction of growth, puckering or dimpling of the skin (including the nipple area), lumps, redness, or discharge.

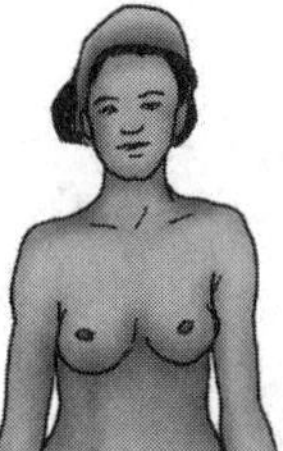

1. Arms down beside body.

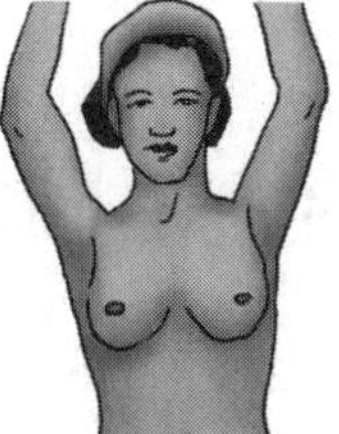

2. Arms lifted overhead.

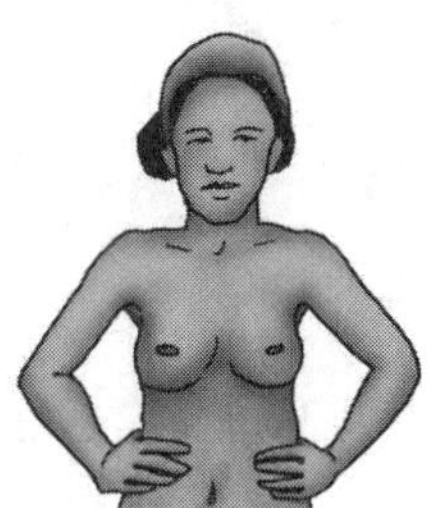

3. Hands on hips, pressing chest muscles forward.

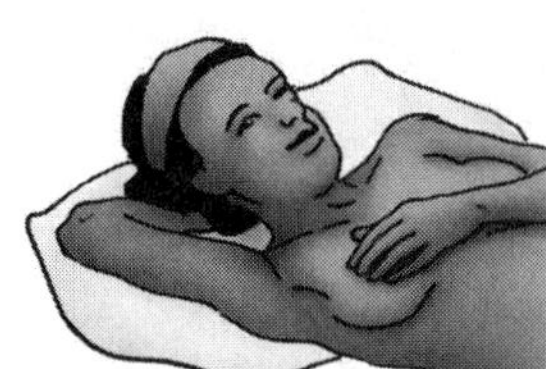

Self Examination:
Lying on your back with a pillow beneath your shoulder, place your arm behind your head. Put the three middle fingers of your free hand together, and use the pads of the fingers to press into the breast tissue, feeling for lumps or changes in the breast area.

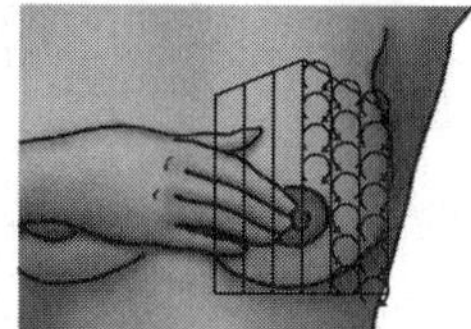

Think of each breast area as a grid that reaches from the top of the shoulder to the bra line vertically, and from the center of the chest to the center of the armpit horizontally. Check each breast area at least twice, using light to deep pressure to check the outer and inner tissue. Press into the breast tissue and move the fingers in small rotating motions covering the entire grid.

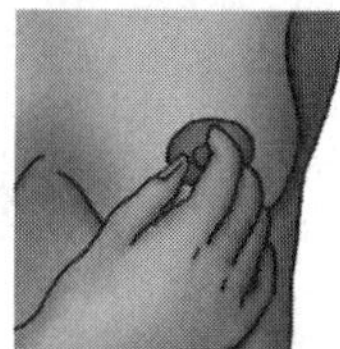

Check for any bleeding or discharge from the nipple by gently squeezing it. See a health-care provider immediately if you notice any changes in the breast.

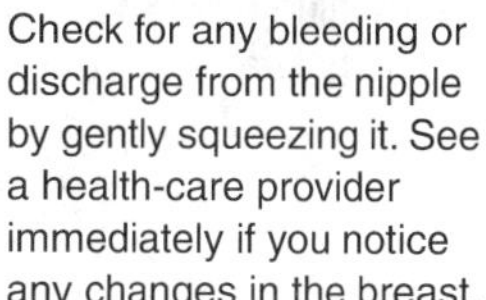

FIGURE 4-5
Breast Self-Exam

The best time to examine your breasts is after your menstrual period every month.

(Appreciation is expressed to Beth Cradle, MAEd, CHES, a health education specialist in human sexuality, at East Carolina University for providing the text.)

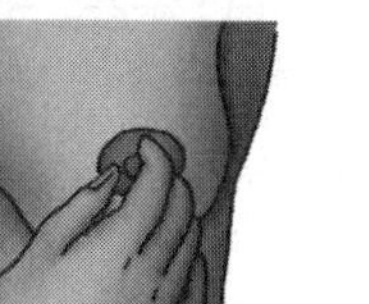

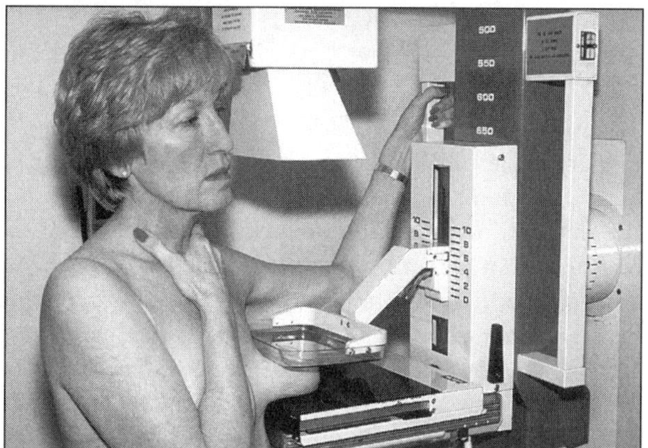

This woman is getting a mammogram.

© Susan Van Etten / PhotoEdit

well as discharge that results from gently squeezing each nipple, should be reported to a doctor immediately. Figure 4-5 illustrates how to perform a breast self-exam.

Some breast tumors are too small to feel during a physical breast examination. A **mammogram** is a low-dose X-ray technique used by a radiologist to detect small tumors inside the breast. If a lump or nodule is found, a breast biopsy is taken, which involves removing breast tissue for examination under the microscope. The American Cancer Society issued new guidelines that include the recommendation that all women should have a mammogram every year beginning at age 40. Although mammograms are safe, it is important to ensure that one is receiving a low-dose mammogram and that the facility performing the mammogram is certified by the American College of Radiology.

Mammogram A low-dose X-ray technique used by a radiologist to detect small tumors inside the breast.

FIGURE 4-6
Female Reproductive Anatomy

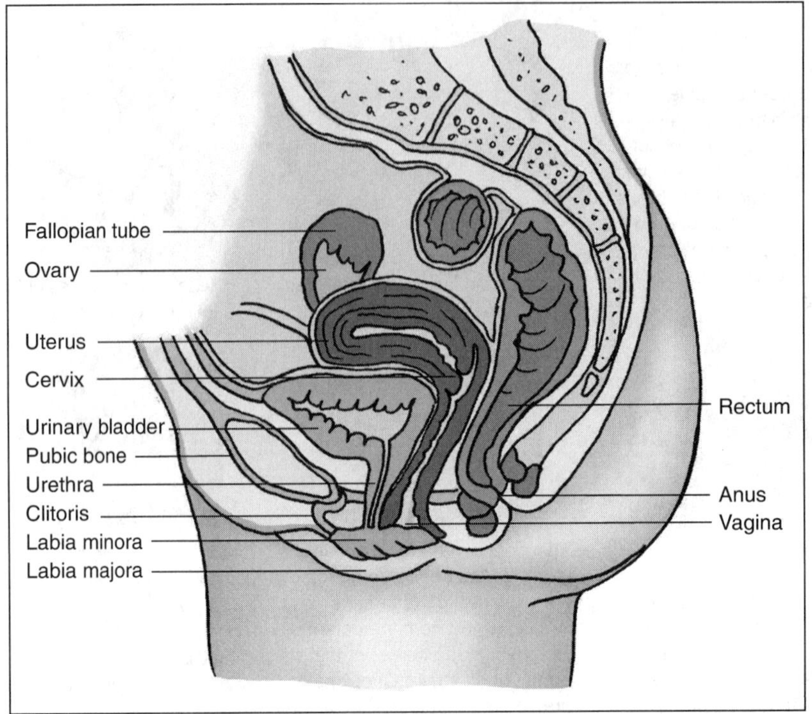

4-2 FEMALE INTERNAL ANATOMY AND PHYSIOLOGY

The internal sex organs of the female include the vagina, uterus, and paired fallopian tubes and ovaries (see Figure 4-6).

4-2a Vagina

Vagina A 3- to 5-inch long muscular tube that extends from the vulva to the cervix of the uterus.

Cervix The narrower portion of the uterus, which projects into the vagina.

The word *vagina* is derived from a Latin word meaning *sheath*. The **vagina** is a 3- to 5-inch long muscular tube that extends from the vulva to the **cervix** of the uterus. The vagina is located behind the bladder and in front of the rectum and points at a 45° angle toward the small of the back. The walls of the vagina are normally collapsed; thus, the vagina is really a potential space rather than an actual one. The walls of the vagina have a soft, pliable, mucosal surface similar to that of the mouth. During sexual arousal, the vaginal walls become engorged with blood, and the consequent pressure causes the mucous lining to secrete drops of fluid.

The vagina functions as a passageway for menstrual flow and as the birth canal, as well as an organ for sexual intercourse. The vagina can expand by as much as 2 inches in length and diameter during intercourse. Angier (1999, p. 51) observed, "Built of skin, muscle, and fibrous tissue, it is the most obliging of passageways, one that will stretch to accommodate travelers of any conceivable dimension, whether they are coming (penises, speculums) or going (infants)."

Some people erroneously believe that the vagina is a dirty part of the body. In fact, the vagina is a self-cleansing organ. The bacteria that are found naturally in the vagina help to destroy other potentially harmful bacteria. In addition, secretions from the vaginal walls help maintain the vagina's normally acidic environment. The use of feminine hygiene sprays, as well as douching, can cause irritation, allergic reactions, and vaginal infection by altering the natural, normal chemical balance of the vagina.

If a woman is experiencing a strong and unpleasant vaginal odor, she may have an infection and should seek medical evaluation. Some women seem more susceptible to

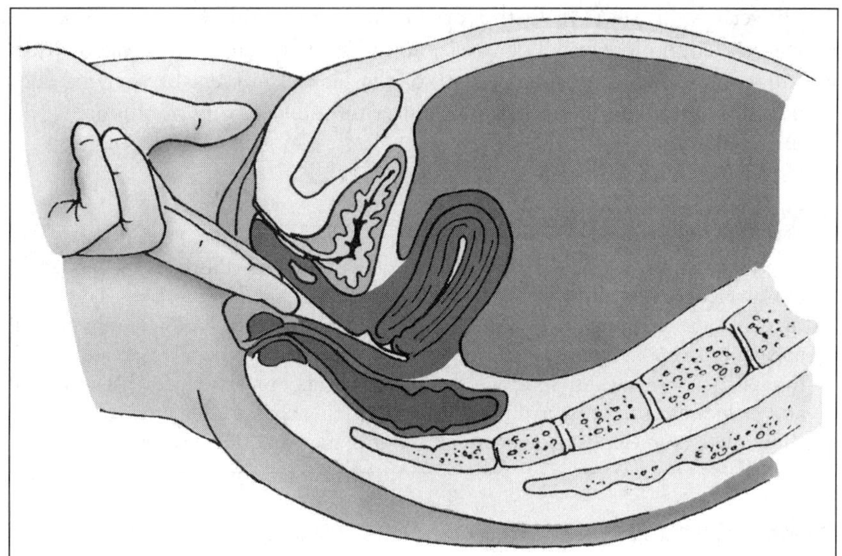

FIGURE 4-7
Location of the Grafenberg Spot

imbalances in vaginal flora and are more susceptible to vaginosis and yeast infection. In addition, being exposed to the semen of multiple partners can also upset the vaginal balance, and vaginosis can increase a woman's susceptibility to gonorrhea, syphilis, and HIV infection (Angier, 1999).

The lower third of the vagina is surrounded by the muscles of the pelvic floor, including the **pubococcygeus** (pyoo-boh-kahk-SIH-jee-us, or PC) and the levator ani. These muscles can influence sexual functioning, in that if they are too tense, vaginal entry may be difficult or impossible. On the other hand, some degree of muscle tone is probably desirable. Some sex therapists have advocated performing **Kegel exercises** (voluntarily contracting the PC muscle, as though stopping the flow of urine after beginning to urinate, several times at several sessions per day). Beji, Yalcin, and Erkan (2002) found that pelvic floor rehabilitation, including the use of Kegel exercises, improved sexual desire, performance during coitus, and achievement of orgasm in their study of 30 urogynecological clinic patients.

Pubococcygeus Muscle surrounding the opening to the vagina that can influence sexual functioning, in that if it is too tense, vaginal entry may be difficult or impossible.

Kegel exercises Voluntarily contracting the PC muscle, as though stopping the flow of urine after beginning to urinate, several times at several sessions per day.

G spot An alleged highly sensitive area on the front wall of the vagina 1 to 2 inches into the vaginal canal. (Also called the *Grafenberg spot*.)

4-2b The "G Spot"

In 1950, German gynecologist Ernst Grafenberg reported that he found a highly sensitive area on the anterior wall of the vagina 1 to 2 inches into the vaginal canal . This area, named the "*Grafenberg spot*" or "**G spot**," swells during stimulation (see Figure 4-7). Birch and Ruberg (2000) detailed how a woman might go about locating her G spot with the assistance of a partner:

> *...[L]ie on your back and have your partner, with palm up, insert a finger or two (if comfortable with two) into your vagina. He should not thrust, but rather should curl his finger(s) up, pressing up into the vaginal wall behind your pubic bone. Instruct him with regard to pressure and movement, which most typically is the "come here" finger motions you would use in summoning someone to you. If your first sensation appears to be that of needing to urinate, ignore that, as it should quickly subside. (p. 13)*

The existence of the G spot is controversial. Hines (2001) reviewed the literature on the G spot and concluded:

> *The evidence is far too weak to support the reality of the G-spot. Specifically, anecdotal observations and case studies made on the basis of a tiny number of subjects are not supported by subsequent anatomic and biochemical studies. (p. 359)*

Beverly Whipple (1999), the former President of the American Association of Sex Educators, Counselors and Therapists, and G spot researcher, suggested, "It may be that not all women have this distinct area, or the lack of universality may be due to the different methods of stimulating or different criteria for identifying this area" (p. 2).

Think About It

According to Tavris (1992, p. 230), the story of the G spot illustrates the tendency of sexologists to "reduce sexuality to its component muscles, tissues, arteries, nerve endings, and 'magic spots.'" Although the notion of finding and pushing the right button for physical bliss may be appealing, sexual response is more complex, as Tavris points out: "The reason, as Grafenberg, himself, acknowledged so long ago, is that sex occurs in many places, beginning in the brain and including, but not limited to, various interesting anatomical parts" (p. 241). Why do you think there is an emphasis on anatomical rather than emotional sexuality?

4-2c Uterus

Uterus The womb; a hollow, muscular organ in which a fertilized egg may implant and develop.

The **uterus** (YOO-ter-us), or womb, resembles a small, inverted pear. In women who have not given birth, it measures about 3 inches long and 3 inches wide at the top. It is here in the uterus that a fertilized ovum implants and develops into a fetus. No other organ is capable of expanding as much as the uterus does during pregnancy. Held in the pelvic cavity by ligaments, the uterus is generally perpendicular to the vagina. However, 1 in every 10 women has a uterus that tilts backward. Although this poses no serious problems, it may cause discomfort with some positions during intercourse.

Fundus The broad, rounded part of the uterus.

Cervix The narrower portion of the uterus, which projects into the vagina.

The broad, rounded part of the uterus is the **fundus,** and the narrower portion, which projects into the vagina, is the **cervix.** The cervix feels like a small, slippery bump (like the end of one's nose) at the top of the vagina. The opening of the cervix (through which semen and menstrual flow both pass) is normally the diameter of a pencil, but at childbirth, it dilates to about 4 inches to allow the passage of the baby. Secretory glands located in the cervical canal produce mucus that differs in consistency at different stages of the menstrual cycle.

4-2d Personal Choices: Pap Smear Test and Pelvic Exam

Pap smear test Procedure in which surface cells are scraped from the vaginal walls and cervix and examined under a microscope to detect the presence of cancer.

About 13,000 new cases of cervical cancer are detected each year, with about 5,000 women dying from this disease (National Cancer Institute, 2001; http://rex.nci.nih.gov/massmedia/backgrounders/cervical.html). A **Pap smear test** is valuable in the detection of cervical cancer and is recommended annually for young women who are (or have been) sexually active. Named after Dr. Papanicolaou, who originated the technique, a small sample of cells is swabbed from the cervix, transferred to a slide, and examined under a microscope. Women who smoke, have first intercourse at an early age, have specific strains of human papillomavirus (the virus that causes genital warts), have multiple sex partners, or have partners who have had multiple sex partners are at an increased risk for cervical cancer. Cervical cancer is almost 100% curable when detected and treated early.

Although use of the Papanicolaou (Pap) smear has significantly decreased the rate of cervical cancer, there is still much work to be done. Cytologic screening has served to identify those women who need further diagnostic testing to determine the absence or presence of disease associated with human papillomavirus (HPV) infection. Whether the conventional Pap smear is the best test to identify those women at greatest risk for lower genital neoplasia is the subject of intense debate (Apgar, 2001). Indeed, even when women have the test, they may not know the meaning of such tests. In a study of 1,027 women, only half understood that a normal Pap smear meant they had a low risk of cervical cancer (Marteau, Senior, & Sasieni, 2001).

♦

Cancer of the uterine corpus (or body) and ovary are more common than cancer of the cervix. However, the Pap smear test is not effective in detecting these types of cancers. A thorough annual pelvic examination performed by a health-care practitioner is recommended for early detection of these cancers.

4-2e Fallopian Tubes

The **Fallopian** (fuh-LOE-pee-en) **tubes,** or oviducts, extend about 4 inches laterally from either side of the uterus to the ovaries. It is in the Fallopian tubes that fertilization normally occurs. The tubes transport the ovum, or egg, from an ovary to the uterus, but the tubes do not make direct contact with the ovaries. The funnel-shaped ovarian end of the tubes, or infundibulums (IN-fun-DIH-byoo-lumz), are close to the ovaries and have fingerlike projections called fimbriae (FIM-bree-ay), which are thought to aid in picking up eggs from the abdominal cavity.

Fallopian tubes Oviducts, or tubes, that extend about 4 inches laterally from either side of the uterus to the ovaries and that transport the ovum from an ovary to the uterus.

Passage of an egg through one of the tubes each month, which takes about 3 days, is aided by the sweeping motion of hairlike structures, or cilia, on the inside of the tube. Occasionally, a fertilized egg becomes implanted in a site other than the uterus, resulting in an **ectopic pregnancy.** The most common type of ectopic pregnancy occurs within a Fallopian tube and poses a serious health threat to the woman unless surgically removed.

Ectopic pregnancy Condition in which a fertilized egg becomes implanted in a site other than the uterus.

Tying off the Fallopian tubes so that egg and sperm (long cells with a thin, motile tail) cannot meet is a common type of female sterilization. The tubes can also be blocked by inflammation; serious infections can result in permanent scarring and even sterility.

4-2f Ovaries

The **ovaries** (OH-ver-reez), which are attached by ligaments on both sides of the uterus, are the female gonads—comparable to the testes in the male. These two almond-shaped structures have two functions: producing ova and producing the female hormones estrogen and progesterone. At birth, the ovaries combined have about 2 million immature ova, each contained within a thin capsule to form a follicle. Some of the follicles begin to mature at puberty, but only about 400–500 mature ova will be released in a woman's lifetime.

Ovaries Female gonads, attached by ligaments on both sides of the uterus, that have the following two functions: producing ova and producing the female hormones estrogen and progesterone.

4-2g Menstruation

When girls reach the ages of 12 or 13 years, a part of the brain called the hypothalamus signals the pituitary gland at the base of the brain to begin releasing **follicle-stimulating hormone** (FSH) into the bloodstream. It is not known what causes the pituitary gland to release FSH at this time, but the hormone stimulates a follicle to develop and release a mature egg from the ovary. If the egg is fertilized, it will implant itself in the endometrium of the uterus, which has become thick and engorged with blood vessels in preparation for implantation. If the egg is not fertilized, the thickened tissue of the uterus is sloughed off. This flow of blood, mucus, and dead tissue (about 2–3 ounces worth) is called **menstruation,** or **menses,** from the Latin *mensis* (or *month*). The time of first menstruation is called **menarche.** Except during pregnancy, this process will repeat itself at monthly intervals until menopause. The average menstrual cycle is 28 days, but this varies from cycle to cycle and woman to woman. Some cycles range anywhere from 22 to 35 days.

Follicle-stimulating hormone Hormone responsible for the release of an egg from the ovary.

Menstruation/menses The sloughing off of blood, mucus, and lining of the uterus.

Menarche First menstruation.

Phases of the Menstrual Cycle

The menstrual cycle can be divided into four phases: preovulatory (follicular), ovulatory, postovulatory (luteal), and menstrual. In the preovulatory phase, a signal is sent from the hypothalamus for the release of FSH from the pituitary gland, stimulating the growth of about 20 follicles in one ovary. On about day 10, one follicle continues to grow and secretes increasing amounts of estrogen. This causes growth of the endometrium in the uterus along with an increase in the cervical mucus, providing a hospitable environment for sperm. Estrogen also signals the pituitary gland to stop any further release of FSH and to begin secreting luteinizing hormone (LH). When the levels of estrogen reach a critical point, there is a surge in blood levels of LH, followed by ovulation within 36 hours.

Box 4-3 Self-Assessment

Menstrual Attitude Questionnaire (MAQ)

The following scale measures attitudes and expectations toward menstruation. To complete the Menstrual Attitude Questionnaire rate each statement on a 7-point scale (disagree strongly = 1, agree strongly = 7). Men can also complete the questionnaire by substituting the word women in items using the first person. For example, instead of "Menstruation is something I just have to put up with," revise the item to read "Menstruation is something women just have to put up with."

Subscale 1

___ 1. A woman's performance in sports is not affected negatively by menstruation.*
___ 2. Women are more tired than usual when they are menstruating.
___ 3. I expect extra consideration from my friends when I am menstruating.
___ 4. The physiological effects of menstruation are normally no greater than other usual fluctuations in physical state.*
___ 5. Menstruation can adversely affect my performance in sports.
___ 6. I feel as fit during menstruation as I do any other time of the month.*
___ 7. I don't allow the fact that I'm menstruating to interfere with my usual activities.*
___ 8. Avoiding certain activities during menstruation is often very wise.
___ 9. I am more easily upset during my premenstrual or menstrual periods than at other times of the month.
___ 10. I don't believe my menstrual period affects how well I do on intellectual tasks.*
___ 11. I realize that I cannot expect as much of myself during menstruation, compared to the rest of the month.
___ 12. Women just have to accept the fact that they may not perform as well when they are menstruating.

Subscale 2

___ 1. Menstruation is something I just have to put up with.
___ 2. In some ways, I enjoy my menstrual periods.*
___ 3. Men have a real advantage in not having the monthly interruption of a menstrual period.
___ 4. I hope it will be possible someday to get a menstrual period over within a few minutes.
___ 5. The only thing menstruation is good for is to let me know I'm not pregnant.
___ 6. Menstruation provides a way for me to keep in touch with my body.*

Subscale 3

___ 1. Menstruation is a recurring affirmation of womanhood.
___ 2. Menstruation allows women to be more aware of their bodies.
___ 3. Menstruation provides a way for me to keep in touch with my body.
___ 4. Menstruation is an obvious example of the rhythmicity that pervades all of life.
___ 5. The recurrent monthly flow of menstruation is an external indication of a woman's general good health.

During ovulation, the follicle moves to the periphery of the ovary and expels the ovum into the abdominal cavity. Ovulation occurs about 14 days before the start of menstruation, regardless of cycle length.

In the postovulatory phase, the empty follicular sac (now called the corpus luteum, meaning yellow body) secretes hormones causing the endometrium to thicken further, building up nutrients. The breasts are also stimulated and may swell or become tender. If the egg is fertilized and implants in the uterine wall, the lining of the uterus is maintained during pregnancy by continuous secretions of hormones from the ovary. If fertilization does not occur, 10 days after ovulation the corpus luteum disintegrates, the levels of the hormones maintaining the endometrium decrease, and menstruation begins. During menstruation, which lasts from 2 to 8 days, the endometrial matter is sloughed off.

Attitudes Toward Menstruation

In many societies throughout history, menstruating women were thought to have special powers or to be unclean. They have been blamed for such phenomena as crop failure and dogs going mad. They also have been feared as sources of contamination for their sexual partners.

Subscale 4

___ 1. I can tell my period is approaching because of breast tenderness, backache, cramps, or other physical signs.
___ 2. I have learned to anticipate my menstrual period by the mood changes that precede it.
___ 3. My own moods are not influenced in any major way by the phase of my menstrual cycle.*
___ 4. I am more easily upset during my premenstrual or menstrual periods than at other times of the month.
___ 5. Most women show a weight gain just before or during menstruation.

Subscale 5

___ 1. Others should not be critical of a woman who is easily upset before or during her menstrual period.*
___ 2. Cramps are bothersome only if one pays attention to them.
___ 3. A woman who attributes her irritability to her approaching menstrual period is neurotic.
___ 4. I barely notice the minor physiological effects of my menstrual periods.
___ 5. Women who complain of menstrual distress are just using that as an excuse.
___ 6. Premenstrual tension/irritability is all in a woman's head.
___ 7. Most women make too much of the minor physiological effects of menstruation.

Scoring: A mean is computed for each subscale by dividing the sum of items by the number of items in each factor (reversing the scoring of items where necessary). An * indicates items for reverse scoring. (For example, a rating of 1 is changed to 7, 2 is changed to 6, 3 is changed to 5.)

Interpretation: A higher score indicates stronger endorsement of the concept measured by each subscale. Following is a summary of data obtained from four different samples. You may want to compare your scores with these groups.

Psychometric Information: Brooks-Gunn and Ruble (1980) investigated the reliability and internal consistency of the factors. They reported high Cronbach's alpha coefficients ranging from 0.90 to 0.97 for each factor (presented here as subscales) across two samples. There was high congruence between the same factors across the two samples.

Source: Brooks-Gunn, J. & Ruble, D. N. (1980). Menstrual attitude questionnaire (MAQ). *Psychosomatic Medicine*, 42, 505–507. Reprinted with the permission of the authors and Lippincott, Williams & Wilkins.

Summary Statistics for the Menstrual Attitude Questionnaire

	Sample							
Factor Scores	College Women (N = 191)		College Women (N = 154)		College Men (N = 82)		Adolescent Girls (N = 72)	
	mean	SD	mean	SD	mean	SD	mean	SD
1. Menstruating as a debilitating event.	3.39	1.09	3.61	0.98	4.45	0.73	3.75	1.28
2. Menstruation as a bothersome event.	4.18	1.26	4.65	1.09	4.13	0.93	3.99	1.54
3. Menstruation as a natural event.	4.64	1.09	4.51	1.04	4.55	0.93	4.62	0.84
4. Anticipation and prediction of the onset of menstruation.	3.79	1.16	4.98	1.11	5.04	0.74	3.85	1.34
5. Denial of any effect of menstruation.	2.73	0.96	3.17	1.05	2.83	0.79	3.12	1.08

CULTURAL DIVERSITY 

Chinese men believe that having sex with a menstruating woman causes illness because it disrupts the balance of Yang (male) and Yin (female) energy (Tang, Siu, Lai, & Chung, 1996). In India, some believe that men who touch menstruating women must be decontaminated and purified by a priest (Ullrich, 1977). However, at times menstrual blood has been thought to contain therapeutic elements, and has been used by Moroccans in dressing for sores and wounds, and in the West to treat gout, goiter, worms, and menstrual disorders (Angier, 1999).

You can explore your own attitudes about menstruation by completing the Menstrual Attitude Questionnaire in Box 4-3.

So I am perfectly happy if all the women in the world wish to say, "I have this thing called Premenstrual Syndrome" as long as they recognize that Harry has "testosterone swings" or "Excessive Testosterone Syndrome." Just give me equality.

—Carol Tavris

Problems of the Menstrual Cycle

Oligomenorrhea Irregular monthly periods.

Various problems have been associated with the menstrual cycle. Although most adolescent girls have regular monthly periods, irregularity, or **oligomenorrhea,** is not unusual. The interval between periods may be highly variable. A missed period may or may not indicate pregnancy. Issues such as anxiety, overwork, relationship problems with her partner, or fear of being pregnant can cause a woman to miss her period, as can intense training for competitive athletics. Some women have periods only once a year. If the menstrual cycle has not stabilized by age 17, a gynecologist should be consulted. Spotting or bleeding between periods also indicates the need for a checkup.

Amenorrhea Absence of menstruation for 3 or more months when a woman is not pregnant, menopausal, or breast-feeding.

Menorrhagia Excessive or prolonged menstruation.

Dysmenorrhea Painful menstruation.

Amenorrhea is the absence of menstruation for 3 or more months when a woman is not pregnant, menopausal, or breast-feeding. Pituitary or ovarian tumors or metabolic diseases are possible causes of amenorrhea; hence, a physician should be consulted. Excessive or prolonged menstruation, or **menorrhagia,** may suggest other problems. These include possible uterine infection and tumors.

Some women experience painful menstruation, or **dysmenorrhea,** symptoms of which can include spasmodic pelvic cramping and bloating, headaches, and backaches. In addition, they may feel tense, irritable, nauseated, and depressed. As the result of the hormone changes, some women retain excess body fluids and experience painful swelling of the breasts (mastalgia) during menstruation. Dysmenorrhea is caused by prostaglandins, chemicals in the menstrual flow that cause spasms of the uterus, and can be relieved by prostaglandin inhibitors. Masters and Johnson (1966) reported that orgasms provided relief from painful menstruation by speeding up the menstrual flow, thus eliminating the prostaglandins. Some women who experience dysmenorrhea report less intense symptoms after taking birth control pills, which contain estrogen and progesterone and disrupt the normal hormonal changes of the menstrual cycle. During ovulation, some women complain of lower abdominal pains, referred to as *mittelschmerz* (or middle pain).

Endometriosis The growth of endometrial tissue outside the uterus (in the Fallopian tubes or abdominal cavity), which may cause pain.

Premenstrual syndrome (PMS) Physical and psychological symptoms caused by hormonal changes from the time of ovulation to the beginning of, and sometimes during, menstruation.

Painful menstruation can also be caused by endometrial tissue growing outside the uterus (in the Fallopian tubes or abdominal cavity, for example). This condition is known as **endometriosis.** These tissues deteriorate during menstruation, just as the lining of the uterus normally does, and a painful infection can result when the tissue cannot be expelled. Treatment ranges from aspirin to surgery.

Finally, some women experience **premenstrual syndrome (PMS)**—physical and psychological symptoms caused by hormonal changes from the time of ovulation to the beginning of, and sometimes during, menstruation. Fifty-one percent of 83 Icelandic women, aged 20–40 years, using and not using oral contraceptives (OCs) diagnosed themselves as having premenstrual syndrome (Sveindottir & Backstrom, 2000).

More than 150 symptoms are associated with PMS, including tension, irritability, mood swings, lethargy, migraines, acne, backaches, joint pain, weight gain (due to increased appetite and water retention), and breast tenderness. Dietary treatment for PMS involves eliminating caffeine, sugar, salt, and alcohol from the diet; eating several small meals or snacks every 2 to 4 hours; and taking vitamin B_6. Some women find various methods of stress reduction helpful, such as meditation, yoga, aerobic exercise, and afternoon naps. Physicians may prescribe diuretics to relieve the increased water retention, and antidepressant medication, such as Paxil, Prozac or Zoloft, to relieve emotional PMS symptoms. Some antidepressants, however, have negative side effects, including reduced orgasmic capacity.

Premenstrual dysphoric disorder (PMDD) A proposed diagnostic category, indicating a more severe form of PMS, which interferes with the work, social activities, and relationships of the woman.

Premenstrual dysphoric disorder (PMDD) is a proposed diagnostic category, indicating a more severe form of PMS that interferes with the work, social activities, and relationships of the woman. Between 2 and 6% of 83 women aged 20–40 had symptoms warranting classification as PMDD (Sveindottir & Backstrom, 2000). According to the *Diagnostic and Statistical Manual of Mental Disorders (DSM-IV-TR*; American Psychiatric Association, 2000), which includes PMDD in an Appendix under the category of diagnoses needing further study, the essential features of PMDD are symptoms such as markedly depressed mood, marked anxiety, marked affective lability (mood swings), and decreased interest in activities. The duration of the symptoms must have occurred most months for the previous 12 months.

Negative mood, especially irritability and anger, most often prompt women to seek treatment (Endicott, Amsterdam, Eriksson, Frank, Freeman et al., 1999). Treatment studies indicate that up to 70% of women with PMDD respond to selective serotonin reuptake inhibitors (SSRIs), such as Prozac, Sertraline, etc. (Steiner, 2000). The decision to place PMDD in the *DSM-IV-TR* Appendix has sparked controversy. Critics have questioned whether PMDD should be categorized with the other mood disorders, and others have questioned why it would be considered a mental disorder rather than a clinical condition with a wide range of symptoms.

Think About It

Carol Tavris, a social psychologist and writer on women's issues, noted that "biomedical researchers have taken a set of bodily changes that are normal to women over the menstrual cycle, packaged them into a 'Premenstrual Syndrome,' and sold them back to women as a disorder, a problem that needs treatment . . ." (1992, p. 133). Who might profit from defining women's severe menstrual cycle symptoms as a "disorder"? Does the PMDD diagnosis lead to stigmatizing consequences for women, or is it helpful in establishing a distinct clinical entity that can benefit from treatment?

4-3 MALE EXTERNAL ANATOMY AND PHYSIOLOGY

Male external sexual and reproductive anatomy includes the penis and the scrotum. Like the vulva, male genitalia differ in appearance, and no single example can be labeled "normal" (see Figure 4-8).

4-3a Penis

The **penis** (PEE-nis) is the primary male sex organ, which, in the unaroused state, is soft and hangs between the legs.

Penis The primary male external sex organ, which, in the unaroused state, is soft and hangs between the legs.

NATIONAL DATA In Kinsey's study of penis length among White college men, 95.2% reported that their erect penis measured between 5 and 7.75 inches (Gebhard & Johnson, 1979).

When sexually stimulated, the penis enlarges, hardens, and becomes erect, enabling penetration. The penis not only functions reproductively (depositing sperm in the female's vagina) and sexually, but also contains the passageway from the bladder to eliminate urine.

NATIONAL DATA Based on a sample of 2,770 men who measured their flaccid and erect penises from base to tip, the shorter the flaccid penis, the more it grew when erect. The average short penis grew by 85% or more, to 5.8 inches. Long penises grew only 47%, to 6.5 inches (Jamison & Gebhard, 1988).

Does penis size matter? The answer depends on whom you ask. Males are socialized to believe that "the bigger the better," and think that potential partners would prefer a longer, thicker penis. The plethora of advertisements targeted to men to "increase your penis size now" testify to this male concern for a larger penis. However, sex therapist and educator, Bernie Zilbergeld (1992, p. 85) suggests that when men are unhappy with

FIGURE 4-8
Variations in External Male Genitalia

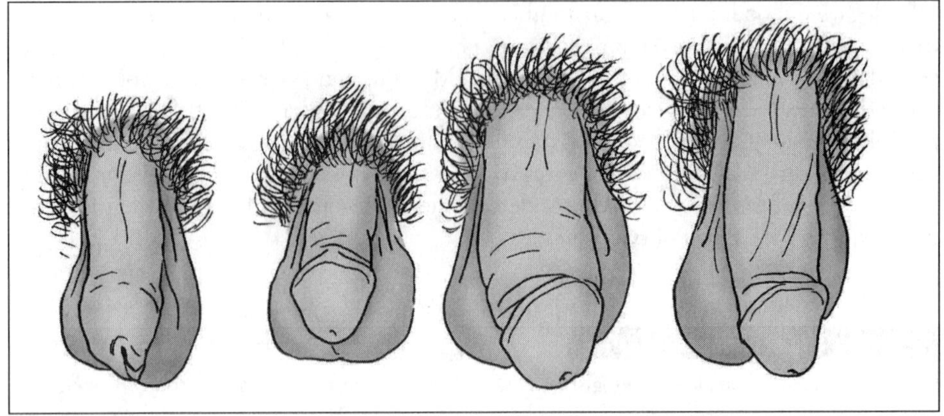

penis size, it is because of having learned to have unrealistic expectations. "Having repeatedly read and heard about gargantuan, hard-as-steel ramrods, our own real penises don't seem like much."

Rather than assuming that women prefer their male partner to have a large penis, Zilbergeld questioned a number of women about size preference. Although a few said they like very large penises, the vast majority did not. One 37-year-old woman said, "The penises in my fantasies are always very large and thick, but in real life a large penis can be hard to take. I'm much more orgasmic with an average-size penis; a large one is distracting" (p. 88). When Zilbergeld pressed the women to talk about smaller-than-average penises, several of the women said that they knew men who had such penises and were terrific lovers, particularly skilled at touching, kissing, and caressing. He heard, "It's the man that counts, not the size of his penis," and was told "The old adage, 'It's not the meat but the motion' most definitely applies" (p. 88). The size and shape of one's penis, he concluded, is not what makes one a good lover.

Glans The small rounded body of tissue on the head of the penis that can swell and harden.

Corona Raised rim on the glans of the penis that is especially sensitive to touch.

Frenulum The thin strip of skin on the underside of the head of the penis, which connects the glans with the shaft.

The visible, free-hanging portion of the penis consists of the body, or shaft, and the smooth, rounded **glans** (meaning small, rounded body or tissue that can swell and harden) at the tip. Like the glans of the female clitoris, the glans of the penis has numerous nerve endings. The penis is especially sensitive to touch on the raised rim, or **corona,** and on the **frenulum,** the thin strip of skin on the underside, which connects the glans with the body. The body of the penis is not nearly as sensitive as the glans. The urethral opening, or meatus, through which urine is expelled from the body, is normally located at the tip of the glans. Occasionally, the urethral opening is located at the side of the glans, an anatomical deviation that may prevent depositing the sperm at the cervical opening; this can be surgically corrected.

Unlike the penises of some other mammalian species, the human penis has no bone. Nor is the penis a muscle that the man can contract to cause erections. In cross-section, the penis can be seen to consist of three parallel cylinders of tissue containing many cavities: two corpora cavernosa (cavernous bodies) and a corpus spongiosum (spongy body) through which the urethra passes (see Figure 4-9). Each is bound in its own fibrous sheath. The spongy body can be felt on the underside when the penis is erect. The penis has numerous blood vessels, and when it is stimulated, the arteries dilate and blood enters faster than it can leave, as venous outflow is reduced. The cavities of the cavernous and spongy bodies fill with blood, and pressure against the fibrous membranes causes the penis to become erect. Like the clitoris, the penis is attached to the pubic bone by the inner tips of the cavernous bodies, called crura.

The root of the penis consists of the crura and the inner end of the spongy body, which is expanded to form the bulb. Two muscles surround the root of the penis and aid in ejaculation and urination. Voluntary and involuntary contractions of these muscles result in a slight jerking of the erect penis.

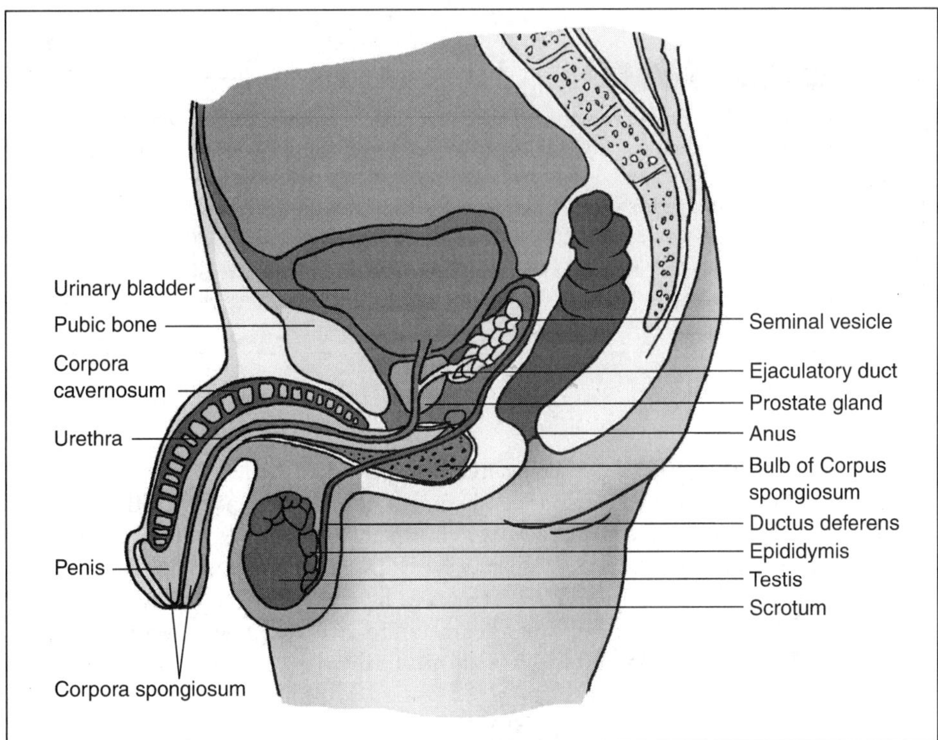

FIGURE 4-9
Male Reproductive Anatomy, Side View

The glans of the penis is actually the expanded front end of the spongy body. The skin of the penis, which is extremely loose to enable expansion during erection, folds over most of the glans. This foreskin, or prepuce, is fixed at the border between the glans and body of the penis. Small glands beneath the foreskin secrete small amounts of oils that have no known physiological function. These oily secretions can become mixed with sweat and bacteria to form smegma, a cheesy substance similar to that which can build up under the clitoral hood in women.

Circumcision is a surgical procedure in which the foreskin of the penis is pulled forward and cut off. Circumcision is a religious rite for members of the Jewish and Moslem faiths.

Circumcision Surgical procedure in which the foreskin of the penis is pulled forward and cut off. (Also known as *male genital mutilation*.)

CULTURAL DIVERSITY

In some societies, circumcision is often performed very crudely and without anesthesia as a puberty rite to symbolize the passage into manhood.

In the United States, when the procedure is done, it is generally performed within the first few days after birth. The primary reasons for performing circumcision today are to maintain tradition and to promote hygiene. Boys who are not circumcised are more likely to experience urinary tract infections within their first year. Although there are possible medical benefits of newborn male circumcision, the American Academy of Pediatrics (AAP) has asserted that the data are not strong enough to recommend that the procedure be routinely administered. The AAP policy states that in addition to medical factors, it is reasonable for parents making a decision about circumcision for their infants to consider cultural, religious, and ethnic traditions (AAP, 1999). The AAP reports data that in 1995 64% of male infants were circumcised in the United States, although exact figures are unknown. They estimate that $150–$270 million is spent annually to circumcise 1.2 million newborn boys in the United States.

Think About It

In the North Carolina State Legislature 2001 Session, there was debate over whether circumcision of newborns should be included in the state's Medicaid coverage. Initially, legislators said that because the procedure is not medically necessary, parents should pay the cost out of pocket. However, after protests that this decision set up a class distinction (it would be obvious in the locker room who came from a poor family), the House voted to add the funding back to the budget. "That cut will be restored, if you'll pardon the description," said State Representative David Redwine (Bonner, 2001). Do you think taxpayers should fund a procedure that is typically done for cultural rather than health reasons?

4-3b Scrotum

Scrotum The sac located below the penis that contains the testicles.

The **scrotum** (SKROH-tum) is the sac located below the penis that contains the testicles. Beneath the skin is a thin layer of muscle fibers that contract when it is cold, helping to draw the testicles closer to the body. In hot environments, the muscle fibers relax, and the testicles are suspended further away from the body. Sweat is produced by the numerous glands in the skin of the scrotum. These responses help regulate the temperature of the testicles. Sperm can be produced only at a temperature several degrees lower than normal body temperature, and any variation can result in sterility.

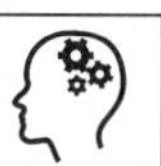

Think About It

Unlike female genitals, which are somewhat hidden from view and not handled during urination, male external genitalia are easily visible and are handled during urination. How might these differences between female and male genitalia affect the sexual knowledge, attitudes, and behaviors of women and men?

4-4 MALE INTERNAL ANATOMY AND PHYSIOLOGY

The male internal organs include the testicles (where sperm is produced), a duct system to transport the sperm out of the body, the seminal vesicles, and the prostate gland (see Figure 4-10).

4-4a Testes

Testes Male gonads that develop from the same embryonic tissue as the female gonads (the ovaries) and produce spermatozoa and male hormones. (Also called *testicles*.)

The paired **testes,** or *testicles*, are the male gonads that develop from the same embryonic tissue as the female gonads (the ovaries). The translation of the Latin *testes* is *witness*. In biblical times, it was the custom when giving witness to hold the testicles of the person to whom one was making an oath (hence, *testifying*). The Romans adopted this custom, except that they held their own testes while testifying. In essence, a man's word was literally as good as his testes.

The two oval-shaped testicles are suspended in the scrotum by the spermatic cord and enclosed within a fibrous sheath. It is normal for the left testicle to hang lower than the right one in right-handed men, and the reverse is true in left-handed men. However, the two testicles should be about the same size, and if one is noticeably larger, a physician should be consulted. The testes are very sensitive to pressure; some men find gentle touching of the scrotum to be sexually arousing, whereas others find this type of stimulation unpleasant.

The function of the testes is to produce spermatozoa and male hormones. Billions of sperm are produced each month in the seminiferous tubules, and the male hormone testosterone is produced in the interstitial or Leydig's cells that are located between the seminiferous tubules (see Figure 4-11).

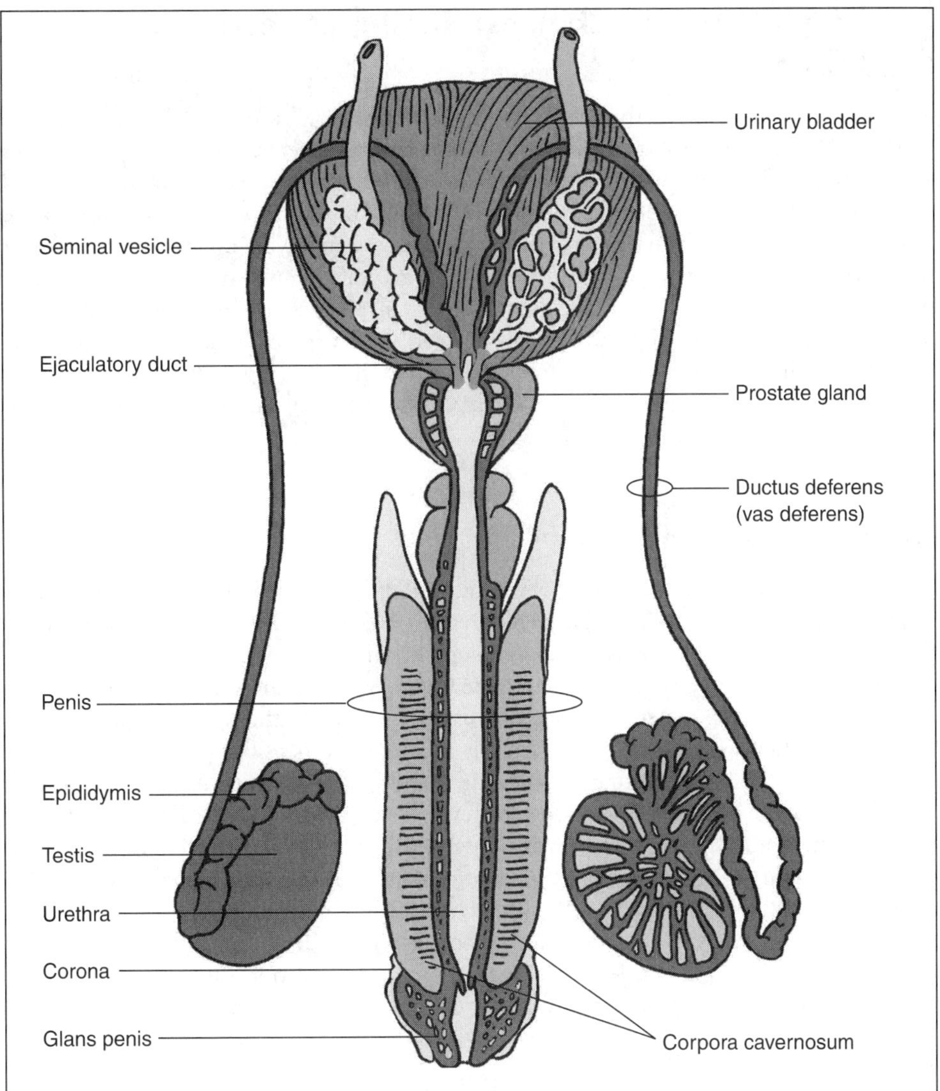

FIGURE 4-10
Male Internal Reproductive System, Posterior View

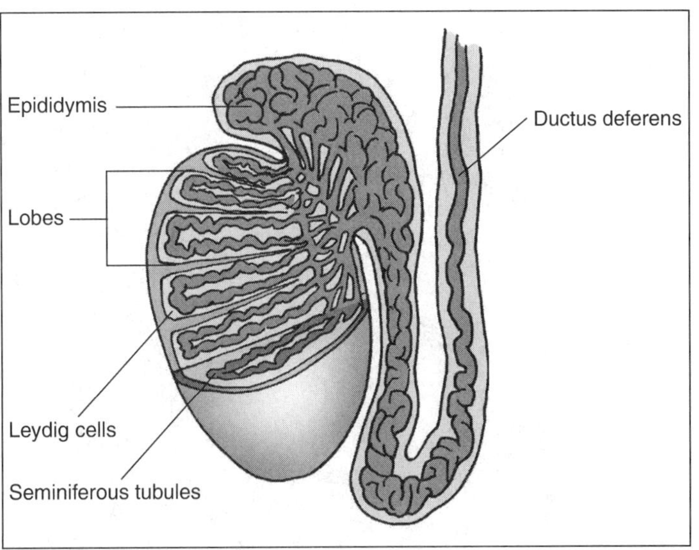

FIGURE 4-11
Cross-Section of Testicle

4-4b Personal Choices: Timing of Testicular Self-Exam

Testicular cancer is one of the least common cancers but also one of the most curable (Elliott, 2002). However, it is the most common form of cancer in young men (ages 15–35) (Alan Guttmacher Institute, 2002). Nevertheless, the key is early diagnosis and treatment. Most cases are discovered by the men or their partners. Cyclist Lance Armstrong and Magic Johnson, who had testicular cancer, have emphasized the need for self-exams. The most frequently occurring symptoms are a lump or nodule on a testicle or swelling of the testicles. The cure rate for testicular cancer is high, especially when detected at an early stage. The American Cancer Society recommends that all men perform a monthly testicular self-examination in addition to having a physician conduct a testicular examination during regular checkups. Figure 4-12 illustrates the proper method for performing a testicular self-examination.

♦

4-4c Duct System

Seminiferous tubules Part of the spermatic duct system, located within the testicles.

Epididymis Part of the spermatic duct system, connecting the testicles with the vas deferens.

Vas deferens Tube from the ejaculatory ducts to the testes that transport sperm.

The several hundred **seminiferous** (SEH-mih-NIH-fer-uhs) **tubules** come together to form a tube in each testicle called the **epididymis** (EH-pih-DID-ih-muss), the first part of the duct system that transports sperm. The epididymis, which can be felt on the top of each testicle, is a C-shaped, highly convoluted tube, which if uncoiled would measure 20 feet in length. The sperm spend from 2 to 6 weeks traveling through the epididymis as they mature; they are reabsorbed by the body if ejaculation does not occur.

The sperm leave the scrotum through the second part of the duct system, the **vas deferens** (VASS-DEH-fer-enz), or ductus deferens. These 14- to 16-inch-long paired ducts transport the sperm from the epididymis up and over the bladder to the prostate gland, where the sperm mix with seminal fluid to form semen. One form of male sterilization, vasectomy, involves cutting and tying off each vas deferens.

The final portion of the duct system is about 8 inches long and is divided into prostatic, membranous, and penile portions. In the prostatic portion, the previously paired duct system joins together to form the final common pathway. The male urethra trans-

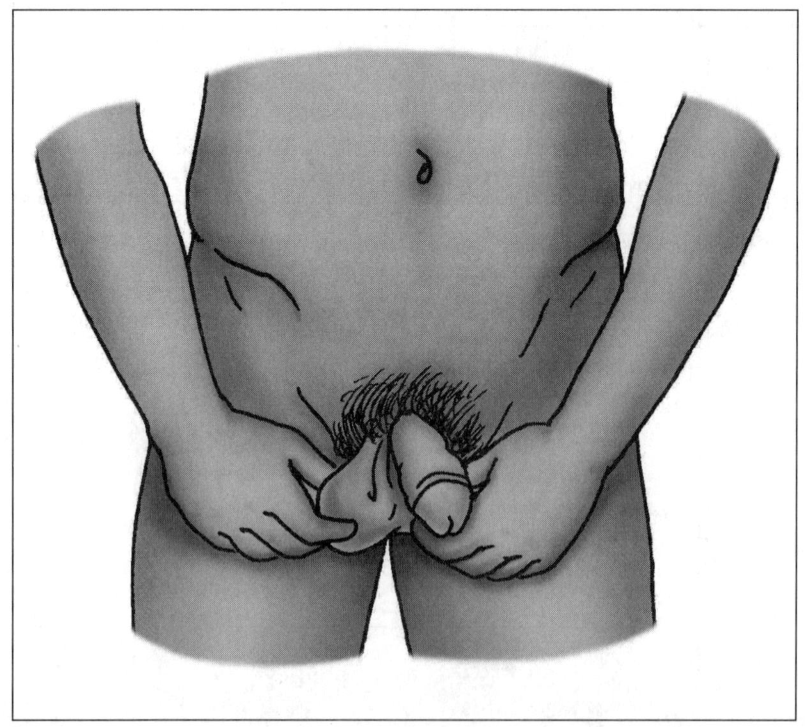

FIGURE 4-12
Method for Testicular Self-Examination, as Recommended by the American Cancer Society

After showering or bathing, check the scrotum visually for unusual swelling. Examine each testicle separately by rolling the testicle between the thumb and the first two fingers of both hands. Check for lumps, thickened tissue, swelling, or a change in size or consistency of the testicle once a month. Feel the epididymis, a cord-like structure, on the top and back of each testicle. Don't interpret this as an abnormality. Make an appointment with a health-care provider if any lumps or other abnormalities are found.

ports urine from the bladder, as well as semen. The urethral sphincter muscles surround the membranous portion of the urethra, enabling voluntary control of urination. The penile portion of the urethra runs through the corpus spongiosum, and the urethral opening is at the top of the glans. As in women, transmission of bacteria to the urethral opening can result in inflammation of the urethra (urethritis) and bladder. The most common symptoms are frequent urination accompanied by a burning sensation and discharge. Men should consult a health-care practitioner if these symptoms appear.

4-4d Seminal Vesicles and Prostate Gland

The **seminal vesicles** resemble two small sacs about 2 inches in length located behind the bladder. They are mistakenly called vesicles because it was once believed that they were storage areas for semen. The seminal vesicles, however, secrete their own fluids that mix with sperm and fluids from the prostate gland. Substances secreted from the seminal vesicles include fructose (a sweet fluid replenisher) and prostaglandins (which stimulate contractility of smooth muscles). Sperm that reach the ejaculatory duct as a result of both muscular contractions of the epididymis and ductus deferens and the sweeping motion of hair-like cilia on their inner walls are made active by fructose. Prostaglandins induce contractions of the uterus, possibly aiding movement of the sperm within the female.

Seminal vesicles Two small glands about 2 inches in length, located behind the bladder in the male, which secrete fluids that mix with sperm to become semen.

Much of the seminal fluid comes from the **prostate gland** (see Figure 4-10), a chestnut-sized structure located below the bladder and in front of the rectum. In the prostate, the ejaculatory ducts join the initial portion of the urethra from the bladder to form a single common passageway for urine and semen. The prostate enlarges at puberty as the result of increasing hormone levels. As the man ages, in some cases it becomes larger and constricts the urethra, interfering with urination. Treatments involve doing nothing, taking medication, receiving radiation, or surgically removing it. The prostate is also a common site of infection, resulting in an inflamed condition called prostatitis. Major symptoms are painful ejaculation or defecation, a condition easily treated with antibiotics. Some men develop prostate cancer, the most common type of male cancer; the risk of the male getting prostate cancer increases with age. All men should have their prostate checked annually, a procedure in which the physician inserts a finger into the rectum and palpates the prostate to check for any abnormalities.

Prostate gland A chestnut-sized structure in the male located below the bladder and in front of the rectum that produces much of the seminal fluid.

Think About It

Do you think that most young adults know more about the internal reproductive systems of women or of men? Why?

4-4e Personal Choices: Timing of Prostate Rectal Exam

The most common type of nonskin cancer in U.S. men is prostate cancer. More than 80% of all prostate cancers are diagnosed in men over the age of 65. The most common procedure for detecting prostate cancer is a digital rectal exam. The health-care professional inserts a gloved, lubricated finger into the rectal canal and then rotates the finger to see if the size of the prostate is normal and to check for any unusual lumps in the rectum.

The American Cancer Society recommends that every man aged 40 and older should have a digital rectal exam as part of his regular annual physical checkup. In addition, men who are over 50 should also have an annual prostatic specific antigen (PSA) test, which can provide additional information about the early presence of a cancerous growth. Because of the frequency of "false positives," however, a prostate biopsy is normally advised by the physician if the patient has a positive PSA result along with a family history of prostate cancer. The survival rate for prostate cancer is "relatively good" (Merrill & Morris,

2002). Although many men contract this disease, the majority do not die as a result of it. In 2000 an estimated 180,400 new cases and 31,900 deaths were expected (Alan Guttmacher Institute, 2002).

4-5 MODELS OF SEXUAL RESPONSE

Various sexologists have described patterns or stages of human sexual response. In sections 4-5a through 4-5d, we look at three primary models.

4-5a Masters and Johnson's Four-Stage Model of Sexual Response

William Masters and Virginia Johnson (1966) were the first sexologists to propose a four-stage model describing sexual response or the sequence of sexual events. Their model focused on four stages of genital response: excitement, plateau, orgasm, and resolution.

Excitement phase Phase of sexual response cycle whereby increasing arousal is manifested by increases in heart rate, blood pressure, respiration, overall muscle tension, and vasocongestion.

Vasocongestion Increased blood flow to the genital region.

Tumescence A swelling or enlargement of an organ, as caused by increased blood flow to the genitals.

Plateau phase Second phase of Masters and Johnson's model of the sexual response cycle, which involves the continuation of sexual arousal, including myotonia (muscle contractions), hyperventilation (heavy breathing), tachycardia (heart rate increase), and blood pressure elevation.

Myotonia Muscle contractions.

Hyperventilation Abnormally heavy breathing, resulting in loss of carbon dioxide from the blood, sometimes resulting in lowered blood pressure and fainting.

Tachycardia Increased heart rate.

Excitement Phase

During the **excitement phase,** individuals become sexually aroused in response to hormonal, tactile, auditory, visual, olfactory, cognitive, and relationship stimuli. For both women and men, the excitement phase of sexual response is characterized by peripheral arousal (increases in heart rate, blood pressure, respiration, and overall muscle tension) and genital arousal (**vasocongestion,** or increased blood flow to the genital region). In men, increased blood flow to the penis causes erection, or **tumescence;** in women, vasocongestion results in vaginal lubrication and engorgement of external genitals (labia majora, labia minora, and clitoris). During sexual excitement, the labia turn a darker color, and the upper two thirds of the vagina expands in width and depth.

Physiological signs of sexual excitement are not always linked to feeling sexually aroused. Men can feel aroused without becoming erect, and women can feel aroused without becoming lubricated. Conversely, men can have erections without feeling sexually aroused, and women can become lubricated without feeling aroused. For example, a man can have an erection as a response to fear, anger, exercise, or REM sleep. Women can become lubricated as a response to nervousness, excitement, or fear. Nevertheless, erection on the part of the man and lubrication on the part of the woman are usually indicative of sexual arousal. The source of the vaginal lubrication in women is the moisture from the small blood vessels that lie in the vaginal walls. This moisture is forced through the walls as the vaginal tissues engorge and produce a "sweating" of the vaginal barrel. Individual droplets merge to form a glistening coating of the vagina.

Plateau Phase

After reaching a high level of sexual arousal, women and men enter the **plateau phase** of the sexual response cycle. In women, the lower third of the vagina constricts and the upper two thirds expands, presumably to form a pool to catch the semen. At the same time, the clitoris withdraws behind the clitoral hood, providing insulation for the extremely sensitive glans of the clitoris. Direct clitoral stimulation at this time may be painful or unpleasant because the glans has a tremendous number of nerve endings concentrated in a small area. Even though the clitoris is under the hood, it continues to respond to stimulation of the area surrounding it.

During the plateau phase, the penis increases slightly in diameter, and the size of the testes increases considerably—from 50 to 100%. In some men, the head (glans) of the penis turns a deeper color. Other changes occur in both women and men: **myotonia** (muscle contractions), **hyperventilation** (heavy breathing), **tachycardia** (heart rate increase), and blood pressure elevation. Also, some women and men experience a "sex flush" that looks like a measles rash on parts of the chest, neck, face, and forehead. This flush sometimes suggests a high level of sexual excitement or tension.

Cognitive factors are also important in the maintenance of the plateau phase. Individuals in this stage must continue to define what is happening to them in erotic terms. Without such labeling, there will be a return to prearousal levels of physiological indicators.

Orgasm Phase

Orgasm is the climax of sexual excitement and is experienced as a release of tension involving intense pleasure. Physiologically, in both women and men, orgasm involves an increase in respiration, heart rate, and blood pressure. Although everyone is different, as is each person's experience of orgasm, researchers have provided some information on the various experiences of women and men:

Orgasm The climax of sexual excitement, experienced as a release of tension involving intense pleasure.

1. *Female orgasm*. Physiologically, the orgasmic experience for women involves simultaneous rhythmic contractions of the uterus, the outer third of the vagina, and the rectal sphincter. These contractions begin at 0.8-second intervals and then diminish in intensity, duration, and regularity. A mild orgasm may have only 3 to 5 contractions, whereas an intense orgasm may have 10 to 15 contractions. Waite and Joyner (2001) noted that both the woman and her partner rate their emotional satisfaction of their sexual relationship higher when the woman has frequent orgasms.

   Although there has been considerable debate on "clitoral versus vaginal" orgasm, Masters and Johnson (1966) stated that clitoral stimulation (either direct or indirect) is necessary for orgasm. They identified only one type of orgasm, refuting the categories of clitoral and vaginal orgasm.

   Subsequently, Singer (1973) suggested that there are two basic variations in female orgasmic experiences: vulval orgasms and uterine orgasms. **Vulval orgasms** (also known as **clitoral orgasms**) result primarily from manual stimulation of the clitoris and are characterized by spastic contractions of the outer third of the vagina. In contrast, **uterine orgasms** are caused by deep intravaginal stimulation and involve contractions in the uterus as well as vagina. **Blended orgasms** are those in which women experience both vulval contractions and deep uterine enjoyment. While women report varying degrees of emotional fulfillment with different types of orgasm, some women define orgasm in yet another way: 40% of 1,171 women reported that they experienced an "ejaculation" at the moment of orgasm (Darling, Davidson, & Conway-Welch, 1990). Some women report the ejaculate does not smell or stain like urine and is slightly milky; the amount is about half a teaspoon and rarely noticeable.
2. *Male orgasm*. Male orgasm and ejaculation are not one and the same process, although in most men the two occur simultaneously. Orgasm refers specifically to the pleasurable, rhythmic muscular contractions in the pelvic region and the release of sexual tension. Ejaculation refers to the release of semen that usually accompanies orgasm. Orgasm without ejaculation is not uncommon in boys before puberty. It also can occur if the prostate is diseased or as a side effect of some medications. Ejaculation without orgasm is less common but can occur in some cases of neurological illness (Brackett, Bloch, & Abae, 1994).

   Ejaculation in men occurs in two stages. In the first stage, there is a buildup of fluid from the prostate, seminal vesicles, and vas deferens in the prostatic urethra (the area behind the base of the penis and above the testes). When this pool of semen collects, the man enters a stage of ejaculatory inevitability; he knows he is going to ejaculate and cannot control or stop the process. The external appearance of semen does not occur until several seconds after the man experiences ejaculatory inevitability due to the distance the semen must travel through the urethra.

   In the second stage, the penile muscles contract two to three times at 0.8-second intervals, propelling the semen from the penis. The contractions may then continue at longer intervals. The more time that has passed since the last ejaculation, the greater the number of contractions, and the greater the volume of ejaculate and sperm count.

Vulval orgasm Type of orgasm that results primarily from manual stimulation of the clitoris and is characterized by contractions of the outer third of the vagina. (See also **clitoral orgasm**.)

Clitoral orgasm See **vulval orgasm.**

Uterine orgasm In contrast to a "clitoral" orgasm, an orgasm caused by deep intravaginal stimulation and involving contractions in the uterus as well as vagina.

Blended orgasm Type of orgasm whereby the woman experiences both vulval contractions and deep uterine enjoyment.

The subjective experience of orgasm in men begins with the sensation of deep warmth or pressure that accompanies ejaculatory inevitability, followed by intensely pleasurable contractions involving the genitals, perineum (the area between the anus and the scrotum), rectum, and anal sphincter. The process of semen traveling through the urethra may be experienced as a warm rush of fluid or a shooting sensation.

Resolution Phase

Resolution phase Final phase of Masters and Johnson's model of the sexual response cycle that describes the body's return to its pre-excitement condition.

After orgasm, the **resolution phase** of the sexual response cycle begins, which involves the body's return to its pre-excitement condition. In women, the vagina begins to shorten in both width and length, and the clitoris returns to its normal anatomic position. In men, there is usually (though not always) a loss of erection, and the testes decrease in size and descend into the scrotum. In both women and men, breathing, heart rate, and blood pressure return to normal. A thin layer of perspiration may appear over the entire body.

In the resolution phase, individuals may prefer to avoid additional genital stimulation. "My clitoris feels very sensitive—almost burns—and I don't want it touched after I orgasm." This statement characterizes the feelings of some women. Other women say their clitoris tickles when touched after orgasm. A man often wants to lie still and avoid stimulation of the head of the penis. When sexual arousal does not result in orgasm, resolution still takes place, but more gradually. Some women and men experience an unpleasant sensation of sexual tension or fullness in the genital area due to prolonged vasocongestion in the absence of orgasm.

Summary of Masters and Johnson's Different Sexual Response Cycles of Women and Men

Although the subjective experience of orgasm may be similar for women and men, there are distinct differences in the patterns of sexual response:

1. *Alternative cycles in women.* Masters and Johnson (1966) stated that a woman may experience the sexual response cycle in one of three ways. When there is sufficient and continuous stimulation, the most usual pattern is a progression from excitement through plateau to orgasm to resolution, passing through all phases and returning to none of these stages for a second time. Experientially, the woman gets excited, enjoys a climax, and cuddles in her partner's arms after one orgasm. If she is masturbating, she relaxes and savors the experience.

   In another pattern (again, assuming sufficient and continuous stimulation), the woman goes from excitement to plateau to orgasm to another or several orgasms and then to resolution. The interval between orgasms varies; in some cases, it is only a few seconds. In effect, the woman gets excited, climbs through the plateau phase, and bounces from orgasm to orgasm while briefly reaching the plateau phase between orgasms. In a study (Darling, Davidson, & Jennings, 1991) of 805 professional nurses, 48% of the respondents reported that they had experienced "multiple orgasm" at least once (43% usually did so). The number of orgasms reported during a multiorgasmic experience ranged from 2 to 20. Forty percent reported that each successive orgasm was stronger, 16% said they were weaker, and 9% reported no difference.

   Still another pattern of female sexual response is to move through the sequence of phases of the sexual response cycle but skip the orgasm phase. The woman gets excited and climbs to the plateau phase but does not have an orgasm. Insufficient stimulation, distraction, or lack of interest in the partner (if one is involved) are some of the reasons for not reaching orgasm. The woman moves from the plateau phase directly to the resolution phase.
2. *Alternative cycles in men.* Men typically progress through the sexual response cycle in a somewhat different pattern. When sexual excitement begins, there is usually only one pattern—excitement through plateau to orgasm. (It is recognized that, for a variety of physiological and psychological reasons, the male may plateau but not have an orgasm.) Following orgasm, most men experience a longer **refractory period** than

Refractory period Stage in the sexual response cycle after orgasm when the person cannot be sexually aroused.

women, during which the person cannot be sexually aroused. During the refractory period, the penis usually becomes flaccid, and further stimulation (particularly on the glans of the penis) is not immediately desired. However, some men remain erect after orgasm and desire continued stimulation.

The desire and ability to have another erection and begin stimulation depends on the man's age, fatigue, and the amount of alcohol or other drugs in his system. In general, the older, exhausted, alcohol-intoxicated individual will be less interested in renewed sexual stimulation than the younger, rested, sober man. The time of the refractory period varies. As noted previously, some men maintain an erection after orgasm and skip the refractory period to have another orgasm.

When the sexual response cycles of women and men are compared, three differences are noticeable:

1. Whereas men usually climax once (some men report multiple orgasms whereby they have an orgasm but do not ejaculate), women's responses are more variable. They may have an orgasm once, more than once, or not at all.
2. When the woman does experience more than one climax, she may be capable of doing so throughout her life span, although this may vary, depending on the type of orgasm. In contrast, the man usually needs a longer refractory period before he is capable of additional orgasms, especially as he ages (Bancroft, 1989).
3. Orgasm in men is never accompanied by urination, whereas this may occur in women. In a sample of 281 women, 32% reported that they expelled urine during orgasm "occasionally" (Darling et al., 1990, p. 41).

Although the Masters and Johnson model is the most widely presented model of human sexual response, it has been criticized on several counts. First, the idea of a four-stage process is arbitrary and imprecise. Second, instead of being titled "The" Sexual Response Cycle, perhaps "A" Sexual Response Model might be more accurate. Whereas Masters and Johnson and Kaplan reported only one reflex pathway in sexual responding, Perry and Whipple described a second reflex pathway that might account for the ability of some women who experience the vulval, uterine, or blended orgasms as described by Singer (Whipple, 1999). Third, the Masters and Johnson model virtually ignores cognitive and emotional states and focuses almost exclusively on objective physiological measures (Basson, 2001a). The measurement of the physiological changes (primarily changes in the genitals) may be taken to represent one aspect of sexuality only. Their model of sexual response de-emphasizes the emotional, spiritual, and intimacy aspects of sexuality and sexual interaction.

4-5b Helen Kaplan's Three-Stage Model of Sexual Response

In an effort to emphasize the motivational and psychological aspects of human sexual response, Helen Kaplan (1979) proposed a three-stage model consisting of desire, excitement, and orgasm. The first stage, sexual desire involves feeling "horny," sexy, or interested in sex; this stage may be accompanied by genital sensations. Kaplan's excitement and orgasm phases are very similar to those of Masters and Johnson; both models focus on vasocongestion and genital contractions in these two phases. However, Kaplan focused more attention on the motivational and psychological aspects of sexual response. The primary criticism of Kaplan's model is her suggestion that desire is a necessary prerequisite for excitement. However, desire is not necessary for arousal or orgasm to occur.

4-5c Basson's Contemporary Model of Sexual Response

Rosemary Basson (2001a; 2001b) emphasizes that psychological factors, as well as biological factors, affect the processing of sexual stimuli. She suggests that the beginning of

TABLE 4-1

Models of Human Sexual Response

Researchers	Stages				
Masters & Johnson (1966)		Arousal (vasocongestion resulting in lubrication and swelling)	Plateau	Orgasm	Resolution
Kaplan (1979)	Desire	Arousal		Orgasm	
Bancroft (1989)	Sexual appetite	Central arousal and peripheral arousal	Genital response		
Reed (Stayton, 1992)	Seduction	Sensations		Surrender reflex	Reflection
Everaerd, Laan, Both, & van der Velde (2000)		Appraisal of sexual stimuli	Genital responding and subjective arousal	Orgasm and subjective experience	
Basson (2001b)	Sexuality neutral or spontaneous sexual desire	Sexual arousal	Sexual desire and arousal	Emotional and physical satisfaction	

sexual response for many women is emotional intimacy, which may begin with sexual neutrality and an openness to sexual involvement that leads to sexual stimulation, then sexual arousal. So, for many women, it is not sexual desire that is the beginning point of sexual response, but a willingness to be receptive to sexual stimuli. Their desire to share a physical pleasure may be more for the sake of sharing than for satisfying sexual hunger. Men sometimes also experience intimacy-based desire, but more often than women, experience "spontaneous" desire (probably largely biologically based).

Whipple (1999) emphasized that healthy sexuality begins with acceptance of self and a focus on the process, rather just the goals, of sexual interaction. She said people should be encouraged to enjoy the variety of ways they can achieve sexual pleasure, instead of establishing specific goals (finding the G spot, experiencing female ejaculation). Your textbook authors suggest that her advice, which follows, applies to men as well:

> *Whatever the final outcome in terms of neural pathways and neurotransmitters involved in sexual response, it is important for you to be aware of the variety of sexual responses that women report and that have been documented in the laboratory. It is also important that women be aware of what is pleasurable to them, acknowledge this to themselves and then communicate what they find pleasurable to their partners. (Whipple, 1999, p. 15)*

Table 4-1 summarizes frequently cited models of human sexual response. The most extensively studied aspects of sexual response have been genital responses and peripheral arousal, such as increases in heart rate, blood pressure, breath rate, skin temperature, etc. (Bancroft, 1989). However, investigators are increasingly attending to cognitive and emotional variables, and their impact on perception of sensory stimuli, arousal, and sexual satisfaction. (Note the attempts to integrate the physiological, cognitive, and emotional components of sexual response in the table.)

4-5d Personal Choices: Engaging in Sexual Behavior When Desire Is Low

It is not unusual when one partner wants to engage in sex and the other does not. Basson (2001a) noted that as many as 30 to 40% of women in nonclinical samples report that they have low sexual desire. Should the partner who has low sex interest or desire agree to participate anyway?

Basson (2001a) reports that women need not expect of themselves to "automatically" be interested in sex but to be receptive to sexual stimulation, which they may then label in positive, sexual terms. Such labeling may result in enjoyment, which may lead to continuation of the stimulation and sexual involvement. Indeed, aside from pleasing the partner, a potential positive outcome from choosing to engage in sexual behavior independent of desire is that the individual may experience desire following involvement in sexual behavior. Cognitive behavior therapists conceptualize this phenomenon as "acting oneself into a new way of feeling rather than feeling oneself into a new way of acting." Rather than wait for the feelings of sexual desire to occur before engaging in sexual behavior, the person acts as though there is feeling, only to discover that the feeling sometimes follows. An old French saying reflects this phenomenon: *"L'appetit vient avec mangent,"* which translates into "The appetite comes with eating."

We are not suggesting that an individual who lacks sexual desire should routinely be open to sexual stimulation with his or her partner or comply with the partner's wishes. Individuals should respect their own feelings and preferences and should not feel coerced into engaging in sexual behavior when they do not want to do so. Nevertheless, recognizing the benefits of a positive sexual relationship with one's partner implies an openness to move toward greater enjoyment.

4-6 HORMONES AND SEXUAL RESPONSE

Hormones are chemical messengers that typically travel from cell to cell via the bloodstream. The hypothalamus and pituitary gland near the center of the brain regulate the endocrine system's secretion of hormones into the bloodstream (see Figure 4-13). The reproductive hormones (estrogens, progesterone, and androgens) are mainly produced in the gonads. They influence reproductive development through organizing and activating effects. Organizing effects include anatomical differentiation (the development of male or female genitals) and some differentiation of brain structure. At puberty, they

Hormone Chemical messenger that travels from cell to cell via the bloodstream.

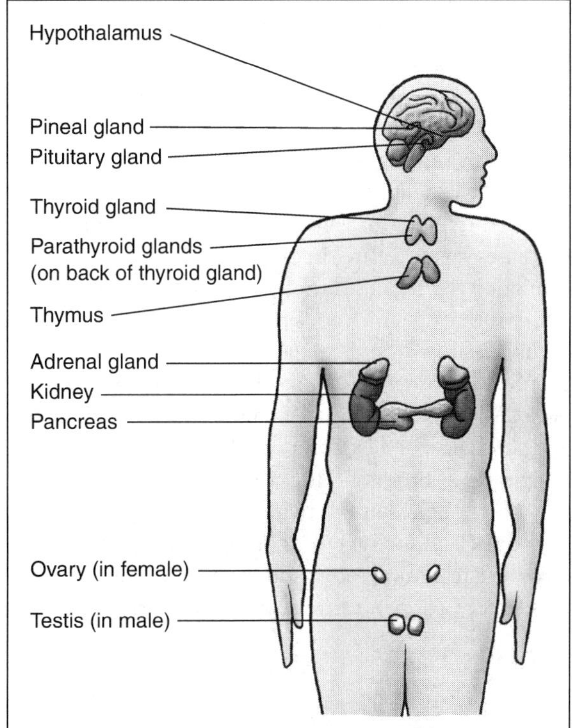

FIGURE 4-13
Endocrine System

Endocrine glands produce and release chemical regulators called hormones that affect sexual functioning.

lead to the development of secondary sex characteristics. Activating effects include influences on behavior and affective states. For example, researchers have studied the role of reproductive hormones and their possible influence on adolescent aggression and behavior problems, adolescent sexuality, the menstrual cycle, and related mood changes.

Endocrine factors relevant to sexual response are androgens, estrogens, progesterone, prolactin, oxytocin, cortisol, pheromones (Meston & Frohlich, 2000). Researchers do not agree on a direct link between hormones in the bloodstream and sex drive (Guzick & Hoeger, 2000; Galyer, Conaglen, Hare, & Conaglen, 1999). Indeed, a team of researchers who conducted a longitudinal study of 182 women not only found weak evidence for androgen levels and sexual desire, but they also found an unanticipated association—high androgen levels associated with lower levels of sexual desire (Dennerstein, Dudley, Hopper, & Burger, 1997). The state of the art conclusion on the relationship between hormones and sexual desire is that social (one's partner/peers), psychological (sexual self-concept/previous positive sexual experiences), and cultural (is it okay to be sexual?) factors may be far more important than hormonal levels.

Think About It

What are the implications of viewing sexual interest as a product of hormones versus social, psychological, and cultural influences? How would the respective views affect the way in which individuals and their partners conceptualize the absence of sex interest on the part of one or both partners?

4-7 PHEROMONES, APHRODISIACS, AND SEXUAL RESPONSE

Pheromones Chemicals secreted by an animal (or person) that influence the behavior or development of others of that species.

Pheromones are substances secreted from glands in the anus, urinary outlet, breasts, and mouth. Although there is evidence of pheromone-induced sex attraction or behavior in other animal species, most of the research on pheromones and sexuality in humans has been centered on female reproductive cycle influences (Meston & Frohlich, 2000). McClintock (1971) demonstrated menstrual synchrony on women living together.

One study (double-blind, placebo-controlled) on pheromones and human sexual behavior was conducted by Cutler, Friedmann, and McCoy (1998), who found that men exposed to a synthesized human male pheromone reported higher levels of sexual intercourse, sleeping with a romantic partner, and petting/affection/kissing. The authors interpreted this finding as evidence for male pheromones increasing the sexual attractiveness of men to women.

Aphrodisiac Any food, drink, drug, scent, or device that arouses and increases sexual desire.

The term **aphrodisiac** refers to any food, drink, drug, scent, or device that arouses and increases sexual desire; in other words, "it gets you in the mood and may prolong the pleasure once you're there" (Schwartz, 2001). One of the more prevalent myths of human sexuality is that specific foods have this effect. In reality, no food reliably increases a person's sexual desire. Where sexual interest does increase, it is often a result of a self-fulfilling prophecy. If a person thinks a substance will have a desire-inducing effect, it sometimes does. Allende (1999) makes this point in her exploration of the relationship between food and sensual/sexual experience. Her book, *Aphrodite: A Memoir of the Senses*, even includes recipes for aphrodisiac dishes from many cultures.

Nevertheless, folklore about aphrodisiacs has a long history, from the Chinese belief in the sex-enhancing power of a ground-up rhinoceros horn (the origin of the word *horny*) to beliefs regarding foods and other substances, such as oysters, crabs, tomatoes, eggs, carrots, celery, pepper, turtle soup, paprika, nutmeg, ginger, and saffron.

Coffee (with caffeine) has been confirmed as having a positive effect on maintaining sexual involvement. Diokno, Brown, and Herzog (1990) observed that at least one cup of coffee per day is significantly associated with a higher prevalence of sexual activity in women (age 60 and over) and with a higher potency rate in men (age 60 and over). Otherwise, Young (1990) emphasized that good mental health, an interesting and interested partner, and continuity of sexual function "form the soundest base for sustained sexual capability" (p. 122).

Damiana is the primary agent identified in the literature as being a sexual stimulant/aphrodisiac for women (Schwartz, 2001). Damiana has been used as a sexual stimulant for men, but its positive effects for women have been noted by Watson and Hynes (1993) in the book on *Love Potions: A Guide to Aphrodisia and Sexual Pleasures*. Similarly, **yohimbe** (sometimes sold under the trade name of Yokon) appears most frequently in the literature as a sexual stimulant for men. However, both are lacking in animal and human studies to empirically verify their alleged aphrodisiac qualities.

Damiana The primary agent identified in the literature as being a sexual stimulant/ aphrodisiac for women.

Yohimbe Substance alleged to be a sexual stimulant for men. (Sometimes sold under the trade name of Yokon.)

Muira puama Considered an aphrodisiac for men. (Also known as *erection root*.)

Muira puama, also known as *erection root*, has also emerged in discussions of aphrodisiacs for men. It is "believed to provide one of the most effective natural therapeutic approaches for achieving and maintaining quality sexual performance in men" (Schwartz, 2001). Ginseng, widely used as a stimulant in China, is also thought of as an aphrodisiac. More recently, Viagra is sometimes thought of as an aphrodisiac. However, Viagra does not work without physical stimulation and, therefore, does not technically qualify as an aphrodisiac.

SUMMARY

This chapter examined the basics of female and male internal and external sexual anatomy. We also reviewed some models for human sexual response, as well as the effect of hormones on sexual desire.

Female External Anatomy and Physiology

Female external sexual anatomy includes the mons veneris, labia, clitoris, vaginal opening, and urethral opening. The clitoris is the most sensitive part of a woman's sexual anatomy. Even though the female breasts provide the important function of nourishing offspring, they are secondary sex characteristics and are not considered part of the female reproductive anatomy.

Female Internal Anatomy and Physiology

The vagina, pubococcygeus muscle, uterus, Fallopian tubes, and ovaries comprise the internal sexual anatomy of the female. Fertilization of the female egg, or ovum, usually occurs in the Fallopian tubes. Around the ages of 12 or 13 years, the hypothalamus in females signals the pituitary gland to begin releasing follicle-stimulating hormone (FSH) into the bloodstream. This hormone stimulates a follicle to develop and release a mature egg from the ovary. If the egg is fertilized, it will normally implant itself in the endometrium of the uterus, which will be thick and engorged with blood vessels in preparation for implantation. If the egg is not fertilized, the thickened tissue of the uterus is shed. This flow of blood, mucus, and tissue is called menstruation.

Male External Anatomy and Physiology

The penis and scrotum make up the external anatomy of the male. Penile erection is caused by dilation of the numerous blood vessels within the penis, which results in blood entering the penis faster than it can leave. The trapped blood within the penis creates pressure and results in penile erection.

Male Internal Anatomy and Physiology

The testes, duct system, seminal vesicles, and prostate gland make up the internal sexual anatomy of the male. Sperm are produced in the testes. Semen is the mixture of sperm and seminal fluid. Most seminal fluid comes from the prostate gland, but a small amount is also secreted by two Cowper's, or bulbourethral, glands that are located below the prostate gland.

Models of Sexual Response

The Masters and Johnson's model of sexual response involves four phases: excitement, plateau, orgasm, and resolution. Their cycle has been criticized in that it is biologically and genitally focused. In contrast, Helen Kaplan proposed a three-stage model consisting of desire, excitement, and orgasm. Kaplan focused more attention on the motivational and psychological aspects of sexual response. The primary criticism of Kaplan's model is her suggestion that desire is a necessary prerequisite for excitement.

Rosemary Basson emphasized that the floor of sexual response for many women is emotional intimacy whereby they are open to sexual involvement that leads to sexual stimuli and then sexual arousal. Basson notes that previous models of sexual response (particularly for women) are absent, addressing the fact that the beginning point for many women is not sexual desire but an emotional openness for sexual involvement.

Hormones and Sexual Response

Researchers disagree on the link between hormones in the bloodstream and sexual desire. The best evidence to date seems to suggest that social (one's partner/peers), psychological (sexual self-concept/previous positive sexual experiences), and cultural (is it okay to be sexual?) factors may be far more important than hormonal levels.

Pheromones, Aphrodisiacs, and Sexual Response

Pheromones are substances secreted from glands in the anus, urinary outlet, breasts, and mouth. Although there is evidence of pheromone-induced sex attraction or behavior in other animal species, most of the research on pheromones and sexuality in humans has been centered on female menstrual synchrony of women living in close proximity. The term *aphrodisiac* refers to any substance that increases sexual desire. No food reliably increases a person's sexual desire. However, coffee (with caffeine) seems to have a positive effect on maintaining sexual involvement in persons over 60. Other compounds associated with having aphrodisiac qualities include damiana, yohimbe, muira puama, and ginseng. Systematic empirical data to support alleged sexual properties are lacking.

SUGGESTED WEBSITES

Note: These websites were functional when we went to press. Please access the online text for the most up-to-date URLs.

Advocating Circumcision Today
http://www.act-now.org

American Association for Nude Recreation
http://www.aanr.com

American Cancer Society
http://www.cancer.org

Breast-feeding
http://www.breastfeeding.com/
http://www.lalecheleague.org

Circumcision Resource Center
http://www.circumcision.org
http://wwww.mothersagainstcircumcision.org

Nudism
www.netnude.com/Travelites

Human Anatomy and Physiology Society
http://www.lionden.com/haps.htm

KEY TERMS

amenorrhea (p. 114)
aphrodisiac (p. 128)
areola (p. 106)
Bartholin's glands (p. 102)
blended orgasm (p. 123)
cervix (p. 108)
circumcision (p. 117)
clitoral orgasm (p. 123)
clitoris (p. 103)
corona (p. 116)
cystitis (p. 104)
damiana (p. 129)
dysmenorrhea (p. 114)
ectopic pregnancy (p. 111)
endometriosis (p. 114)
epididymis (p. 120)
excitement phase (p. 122)
Fallopian tubes (p. 111)
follicle-stimulating hormone (p. 111)
frenulum (p. 116)
fundus (p. 110)
G spot (p. 109)
glans (p. 116)
hormone (p. 127)
hymen (p. 104)
hyperventilation (p. 122)
introitus (p. 104)
Kegel exercises (p. 109)
labia majora (p. 101)
labia minora (p. 102)
mammogram (p. 107)
menarche (p. 111)
menorrhagia (p. 114)
menstruation/menses (p. 111)
mons veneris (p. 101)
muira puama (p. 129)
myotonia (p. 122)
oligomenorrhea (p. 114)
orgasm (p. 123)
ovaries (p. 111)
Pap smear test (p. 110)
penis (p. 115)
perineum (p. 101)
pheromones (p. 128)
plateau phase (p. 122)
premenstrual dysphoric disorder (PMDD) (p. 114)
premenstrual syndrome (PMS) (p. 114)
prostate gland (p. 121)
pubococcygeus (p. 109)
refractory period (p. 124)
resolution phase (p. 124)
scrotum (p. 118)
secondary sex characteristics (p. 105)
seminal vesicles (p. 121)
seminiferous tubules (p. 120)
sexual anatomy (p. 100)
sexual physiology (p. 100)
tachycardia (p. 122)
testes (p. 118)
tumescence (p. 122)
urethra (p. 104)
uterine orgasm (p. 123)
uterus (p. 110)
vagina (p. 108)
vas deferens (p. 120)
vasocongestion (p. 122)
vestibule (p. 104)
vulva (p. 100)
vulval orgasm (p. 123)
yohimbe (p. 129)

CHAPTER QUIZ

1. If we think of the human body as a special type of machine, __________ refers to the machine's parts, and __________ refers to how the parts work.
 a. physiology, anatomy
 b. anatomy, physiology

2. To attend a nudist recreation facility in the United States, you must be at least 18 years old; children are not allowed in nudist recreation facilities or clubs.
 a. True
 b. False

3. The __________ female genitalia are collectively known as the vulva.
 a. external
 b. internal

4. What is the most sensitive organ of the female genitalia?
 a. labia majora
 b. vagina
 c. labia minora
 d. clitoris

5. The presence of a hymen is __________ indicator of virginity.
 a. a reliable and accurate
 b. a poor and unreliable

6. Kegal exercises are recommended for which of the following?
 a. increasing breast size
 b. increasing penis rigidity
 c. toning the pubococcygeus muscle
 d. preventing sagging of the testicles

7. Where is the G spot located?
 a. in between the anus and the vagina
 b. in between the testicles and the anus
 c. on the posterior wall of the vagina, just beneath the cervix
 d. on the anterior wall of the vagina 1 to 2 inches into the vaginal canal

8. A Pap smear test is used to detect which of the following?
 a. cervical cancer
 b. breast cancer
 c. ectopic pregnancy
 d. the time of the month when a woman is most likely to become pregnant

9. The most common type of ectopic pregnancy is
 a. within a Fallopian tube and poses a serious health threat to the woman.
 b. outside the Fallopian tube and is not a serious health threat to the woman.

10. Ovulation occurs about __________ menstruation, regardless of cycle length.
 a. 24 hours before the start of
 b. 24 hours after the start of
 c. 7 days after the start of
 d. 14 days before the start of

11. Which of the following individuals experiences dysmenorrhea?
    a. Jack, who refuses to have sexual relations with his wife when she is menstruating because he has an irrational fear of coming into contact with menstrual blood.
    b. Elizabeth, who has not had a menstrual period since she was 19 (she is now 23).
    c. Ronald, who experiences a monthly cycle during which he has mood swings and other symptoms similar to premenstrual syndrome.
    d. Renee, who has severe cramping during her menstrual period such that she is unable to go to classes.
12. In the United States, ____________ than half of male infants are circumcised.
    a. fewer
    b. more
13. The testicles are part of the male ____________ anatomy and physiology.
    a. internal
    b. external
14. Singer (1973) suggested that there are two basic variations in female orgasmic experiences: ____________ orgasms and ____________ orgasms.
    a. self-induced; partner-induced
    b. brief; extended
    c. vulval; uterine
    d. voluntary; involuntary
15. The primary criticism of Kaplan's model is her suggestion that
    a. desire is a necessary prerequisite for excitement.
    b. emotions are not emphasized.
    c. her research did not include men.
    d. she provided no data for her assertions.
16. According to your text, which of the following foods is considered an aphrodisiac?
    a. oysters, salmon, and tuna
    b. chocolate and honey
    c. walnuts and asparagus
    d. none of the above

REFERENCES

Alan Guttmacher Institute. (2002). In their own right: Addressing the sexual and reproductive health needs of American men. New York: Author.

Allende, I. (1999). *Aphrodite: A memoir of the senses*. New York: Harper Collins.

American Academy of Pediatrics. (1999). New AAP circumcision policy released. Retrieved September 1, 2002, http://www.aap.org/advocacy/archives/marcircum.htm

American Academy of Pediatrics. (2002). Chapter breastfeeding coordinators. Retrieved September 1, 2002, http://:www.aap.org/adv ocacy/bf/brchapcoord.htm

American Psychiatric Association. (2000). *Diagnostic and statistical manual of mental disorders* (4th ed.), text revision. Washington, DC: Author.

Angier, N. (1999). *Woman: An intimate geography*. New York: Anchor.

Apgar, B. S. (2001). New tests for cervical cancer screening (liquid-based cytology and HPV DNA testing). *American Family Physician, 64*, 729–735.

Applegate, A., & Overton, V. (1994). *The elements of medical terminology*. Albany, NY: Delmar Publishers.

Baldwin, E. N., & Friedman, K. A. (2002). A current summary of breastfeeding legislation in the U.S. Retrieved September 1, 2002, http://www.lalecheleague.org/Law/Bills8a.html

Bancroft, J. H. (1989). *Human sexuality and its problems* (2nd ed.). New York: Churchill Livingston.

Basson, R. (2001a). Are the complexities of women's sexual function reflected in the new consensus definitions of dysfunction? *Journal of Sex and Marital Therapy, 27*, 105–112.

Basson, R. (2001b). Human sex-response cycles. *Journal of Sex and Marital Therapy, 27*, 33–43.

Beji, N. K., Yalcin, O., & Erkan, H. A. (2002) . The effect of pelvic floor training on sexual function. *Nursing Standard, 16*, 33–36.

Birch, R. W., & Ruberg, C. L. (2000). *Pathways to pleasure: A woman's guide to orgasm*. Howard, OH: PEC Publishing.

Bonner, L. (2001, November 17). Medicaid benefit restored. *News & Observer*, p. A3.

Brackett, N. L., Bloch, W. E., & Abae, M. (1994). Neurological anatomy and physiology of sexual function. In C. Singer & W. J. Weiner (Eds.), *Sexual dysfunction: A neuro-medical approach* (pp. 1–42). Armonk, NY: Furura.

Braun, V., & Kitzinger, C. (2001). "Snatch," "hole," or "honey-pot"? Semantic categories and the problem of nonspecificity in female genital slang. *The Journal of Sex Research, 38*, 146–158.

Brooks-Gunn, J., & Ruble, D. N. (1980). Menstrual attitude questionnaire (MAQ). *Psychosomatic Medicine, 42*, 505–507.

Cutler, W. B., Friedmann, E., & McCoy, N. L. (1998). Pheromonal influences on sociosexual behavior in men. *Archives of Sexual Behavior, 27*, 1–13.

Darling, C. A., Davidson, J. K., Sr., & Conway-Welch, C. (1990). Female ejaculation: Perceived origins, the Grafenberg spot/area, and sexual responsiveness. *Archives of Sexual Behavior, 19*, 29–47.

Darling, C. A., Davidson, J. K., Sr., & Jennings, D. A. (1991). The female sexual response revisited: Understanding the multiorgasmic experience in women. *Archives of Sexual Behavior, 20*, 527–540.

Davies, J. (1998). *Essentials of medical terminology*. Albany, NY: Delmar Publishers.

Dennerstein, L., Dudley, E. C., Hopper, J. L., & Burger, H. (1997). Sexuality, hormones and the menopause transition. *Maturitas, 26*, 83–93.

Diokno, A. C., Brown, M. B., & Herzog, A. R. (1990). Sexual functioning in the elderly. *Archives of Internal Medicine, 150*, 197–200.

Elliott, V. S. (2002). Many men exhibit health care avoidance: Physicians, public health officials look for ways to increase men's involvement in medical care and improve health indicators. *American Medical News, 45*, 1–3.

Endicott, J., Amsterdam, J., Eriksson, E., Frank, E., Freeman, E., et al. (1999). Is premenstrual dysphoric disorder a distinct clinical entity? *Journal of Women's Health & Gender-Based Medicine, 8*, 663–679.

Everaerd, W., Laan, E. T. M., Both, S., & van der Velde, J. (2000). Female sexuality. In L. T. Szuchman & F. Muscarella (Eds.), *Psychological perspectives on human sexuality* (pp. 101–146). New York: Wiley.

Everaerd, W., Laan, E. T. M., & Spiering, M. (2000). Male sexuality. In L. T. Szuchman & F. Muscarella (Eds.), *Psychological perspectives on human sexuality* (pp. 60–100). New York: Wiley.

Galyer, K. T., Conaglen, H. M., Hare, A., & Conaglen, J. V. (1999). The effect of gynecological surgery on sexual desire. *Journal of Sex and Marital Therapy, 25*, 81–88.

Gebhard, P. H., & Johnson, A. B. (1979). *The Kinsey data.* Philadelphia: Saunders.

Guzick, D. S., & Hoeger, K. (2000). Sex, hormones, and hysterectomies. *The New England Journal of Medicine online*, 343 (10).

Hill, T. L. (1996). The problem with non-nudists. *Society, 20*, 23–25.

Hines, T. M. (2001). The G-spot: A modern gynecologic myth. *American Journal of Obstetrics & Gynecology, 185*, 359–362.

Jamison, P. L., & Gebhard, P. H. (1988). Penis size increase between flaccid and erect states: An analysis of the Kinsey data. *Journal of Sexuality Research*, 24, 177–183.

Kaplan, H. (1979). *Disorders of sexual desire.* New York: Brunner/Mazel.

Mackay, J. (2000). *The Penguin atlas of human sexual behavior.* New York: Penguin.

Marteau, T. M., Senior, V., & Sasieni, P. (2001). Women's understanding of a "normal smear test result": experimental questionnaire based study. *British Medical Journal, 322*, 526–532.

Masters, W. H., & Johnson, V. E. (1966). *Human sexual response.* Boston: Little, Brown.

McClintock, M. K. (1971). Menstrual synchrony and suppression. *Nature, 229*, 244–245.

Merrill, R. M., & Morris, M. K. (2002). Prevalence-corrected prostate cancer incidence rates and trends. *American Journal of Epidemiology, 155*, 148–152.

Meston, C. M., & Frohlich, P. F. (2000). The neurobiology of sexual function. *Archives of General Psychiatry, 57*, 1012–1030.

National Cancer Institute. (2001). Cancer Facts. http://cis.nci.nih.gov/fact/5_6.htm

Ogletree, S. M., & Ginsburg, H. J. (2000). Kept under the hood: Neglect of the clitoris in common vernacular. *Sex Roles, 43*, 917–926.

Schroer, S. E. (2001, August 18–22). Completely immersed and totally exposed: Sexuality in social nudism. Paper presented at the annual meeting of the Society for the Study of Social Problems, Anaheim, CA.

Schwartz, D. A. (2001). Have I got an herb for you. *Chemical Innovation, 31*, 24–29.

Singer, I. (1973). *The goals of human sexuality.* New York: Norton.

Stayton, W. R. (1992). A theology of sexual pleasure. *SIECUS Report, 20* (4), 9–15.

Steiner, M. (2000). Recognition of premenstrual dysphoric disorder and its treatment. *Lancet, 356*, 1126–1127.

Sveindottir, H., & Backstrom, T. (2000). Prevalence of menstrual cycle symptom cyclicity and premenstrual dysphoric disorder in a random sample of women using and not using oral contraceptives. *Acta Obstetricia et Gynecologica Scandinavica, 79*, 405–413.

Tang, C. S., Siu, B. N., Lai, E. D., & Chung, T. K. H. (1996). Heterosexual Chinese women's sexual adjustment after gynecologic cancer. *The Journal of Sex Research, 33*, 189–195.

Tavris, C. (1992). *The mismeasure of woman.* New York: Simon & Schuster.

Ullrich, H. E. (1977). Caste differences between Brahmin and non-Brahmin women in a South Indian village. In A. Schlegel (Ed.), *Sexual stratification: A cross-cultural view* (pp. 94–108). New York: Columbia University Press.

Waite, L. J., & Joyner, K. (2001). Emotional and physical satisfaction with sex in married, cohabiting, and dating sexual unions: Do men and women differ? In E. O. Laumann & R. T. Michael (Eds.), *Sex, love, and health in America: Private choices and public policies* (pp. 239–269). Chicago: The University of Chicago Press.

Walker, A. (1988). *Living by the word.* San Diego: Harcourt Brace.

Watson, C., & Hynes, A. (1993). *Love potions: A guide to aphrodisia and sexual pleasures.* Los Angeles: J. P. Tarcher.

Weinberg, M. S. (1965). Sexual modesty, social meanings, and the nudist camp. *Social Problems, 12*, 311–318.

Whipple, B. (1999). Beyond the G spot: Recent research findings in women's sexuality. *Contemporary Sexuality*, 33(11–12), 1, 2, 4.

Young, W. R. (1990). Changes in sexual functioning during the aging process. In F. J. Bianoco & R. Hernandez Serrano (Eds.), *Sexology: An independent field* (pp. 121–128). New York: Elsevier Science.

Zilbergeld, B. (1992). *The new male sexuality.* New York: Bantam.

5

Gender Diversity in Sexuality

Chapter Outline

Nowhere in our intimate lives is there greater expression of gender differences than in our sexual relationships.

—Michael S. Kimmel, The Gendered Society

"I love men, even though they're lyin', cheatin' scumbags" said Gwyneth Paltrow, Academy Award winning actress in a *USA Today* interview. Her words reflect the feelings one sex sometimes has about the other in regard to fidelity and the perception that the sexes are fundamentally different (e.g., *Men Are from Mars; Women Are from Venus*). But in reality, boys and girls, men and women, are rarely, if ever, "opposites" (Lippa, 2002). In this chapter, we discuss gender differences in sexuality.

5-1 TERMINOLOGY

In common usage, the terms *sex* and *gender* are often used interchangeably. To psychologists, sociologists, health educators, sexologists, and sex therapists, however, these terms are not synonymous. After clarifying the distinction between *sex* and *gender*, we discuss other relevant terminology, including *gender identity*, *gender role*, *sexual identity*, and *gender role ideology*.

5-1a Sex

Sex Term that refers to the biological distinction between being female and being male, usually categorized on the basis of the reproductive organs and genetic makeup.

Primary sex characteristics Those characteristics that differentiate women and men, such as external genitalia (vulva and penis), gonads (ovaries and testes), sex chromosomes (XX and XY), and hormones (estrogen, progesterone, and testosterone).

Secondary sex characteristics Characteristics that differentiate males and females that are not linked to reproduction (e.g., beard in men, high voice in women).

Sex refers to the biological distinction between being female and being male. The **primary sex characteristics** that differentiate women and men include external genitalia (vulva and penis), gonads (ovaries and testes), sex chromosomes (XX and XY), and hormones (estrogen, progesterone, and testosterone). **Secondary sex characteristics** include the larger breasts of women and the deeper voice and presence of a beard in men.

Even though we commonly think of biological sex as consisting of two dichotomous categories (female and male), current views suggest that biological sex exists on a continuum. This view is supported by the existence of individuals with mixed or ambiguous genitals (hermaphrodites and pseudohermaphrodites, or intersexed individuals—discussed in section 5-2d on hormonal abnormalities). Indeed, some males produce fewer male hormones (androgens) than some females, just as some females produce fewer female hormones (estrogens) than some males (see Figure 5-1). In fact, biologist Anne Fausto-Sterling (1998) suggested that at least five sexes should be recognized: male, female, hermaphrodites (*herms*), female pseudohermaphrodites (*ferms*), and male pseudohermaphrodites (*merms*). Fausto-Sterling notes that the frequency of intersexuality has been suggested as 4% of births. If this percent is accurate, Fausto-Sterling (p. 222) points out to her students at Brown University that in their student body of about 6,000, about 240 students on their campus might be intersexuals—"surely enough to form a minority caucus of some kind."

5-1b Gender

I don't think boys in general watch the emotional world of relationships as closely as girls do. Girls track that world all day long, like watching the weather.

—Carol Gilligan

Gender The social and psychological characteristics associated with being female or male.

Gender refers to the social and psychological characteristics associated with being female or male. Characteristics typically associated with the female gender include being gentle, emotional, and cooperative; characteristics typically associated with the male gender include being aggressive, rational, and competitive. In popular usage, gender is dichotomized as an either/or concept (feminine or masculine), but gender may also be viewed as existing along a continuum of femininity and masculinity.

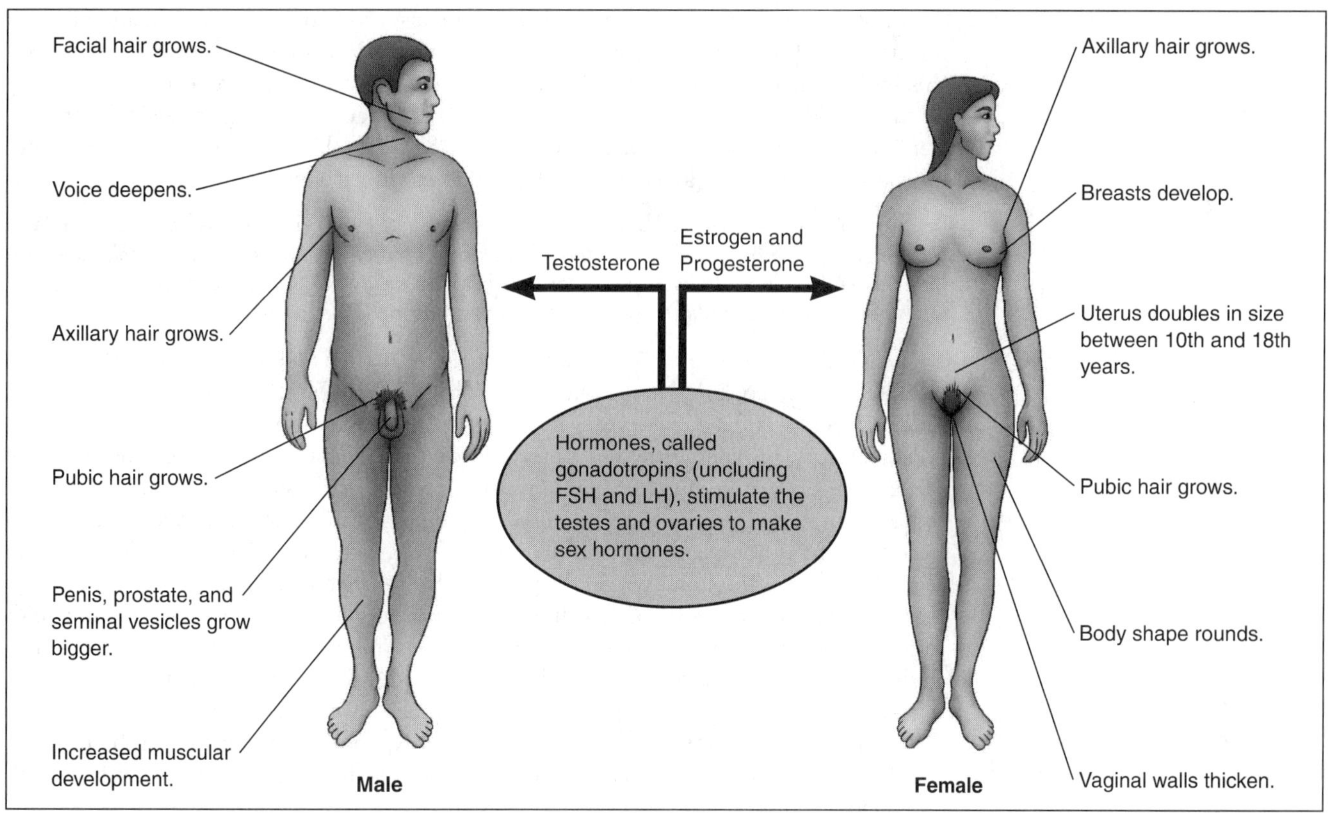

FIGURE 5-1
Effects of Hormones on Sexual Development during Puberty

The body's endocrine system produces hormones that trigger body changes in males and females.

Think About It

In spite of the presumed changes gender role relationships are undergoing, little change may have occurred in dating relationships. Researchers Laner and Ventrone (2000) found that dating interacting/scripts continue to be traditional, with the man asking out the woman, deciding on plans, and the woman waiting to be picked up, introducing the male to her family, and eating lightly at dinner. In regard to the latter, one woman in the authors' classes said, "I always order a salad on the first date. It is only after we've been dating that I ask if we can go to a buffet where I'll feel comfortable stuffing myself." Why do you think dating gender roles continue to reflect traditional scripts?

There is an ongoing controversy about whether gender differences are innate as opposed to learned or socially determined (Miller & Costello, 2001). Just as sexual orientation may be best explained as an interaction of biological and social/psychological variables, gender differences may also be seen as a consequence of both biological and social/psychological influences.

Whereas some researchers emphasize the role of social influences, others emphasize a biological imperative as the basis of gender role behavior. As evidence for the former, John Money, psychologist and former director of the now defunct Gender Identity Clinic at Johns Hopkins Medical School, encouraged the parents of a boy (Bruce) to rear him as a girl (Brenda) because of a botched circumcision that rendered the infant without a penis. Money argued that social mirrors dictate one's gender identity, so if the parents treated the child as a girl (name, dress, toys, etc.), the child would adopt the role of a girl and later that of a woman. The child was castrated and sex reassignment began.

But the experiment failed miserably. At the age of 14, the child was finally informed of his medical history and made the decision (after much distress and struggle) to reclaim his life as a male. He chose the biblical name David because "It reminded me of the guy with the odds stacked against him, the guy who was facing up to a giant eight feet tall. It reminded me of courage" (Colapinto, 2000, p. 182). David Reimer (who now speaks publicly about his life) was asked why he did not accept being a female rather than fighting it:

> *His answer was simple. Doing so did not feel right. He wanted to please his parents and placate the physicians so he often went along with their decisions, but the conflict between his feelings and theirs was mentally devastating and would have led to suicide if he had been forced to continue. (Diamond & Sigmundson, 1997, p. 301)*

Indeed, David did attempt suicide. Today he is married and the adoptive father of two children. In the book *As Nature Made Him: The Boy Who Was Raised as a Girl* (Colapinto, 2000), David worked with a writer to tell his story. In addition to revealing his poignant personal story, his courageous decision to make it public has also shed light on scientific debate on the "nature/nurture" question. In the past, David's situation was used as a textbook example of how "nurture" is the more important influence in gender identity, if a reassignment is done early enough. However, Dr. Milton Diamond, who followed up on David's case, met him and wrote a paper with Keith Sigmundson (who had been one of David's psychiatrists) in 1994, revealing the discrepant outcome. Their paper (Diamond & Sigmundson, 1997) was published three years later and asserted that while nurture may influence a person's degree of masculinity or femininity, nature is the stronger force in forming one's gender identity and sexual orientation. Given the genetic influences on the brain and nervous system and prenatal hormonal exposure, they emphasized the neurobiological basis of one's sex and cautioned against early surgical intervention for infants with ambiguous genitals.

To help avoid future cases of David Reimer's dilemma, The Intersex Society of North America has formed a nationwide, Internet-linked support group that seeks to end nonconsensual surgery for intersex persons and increase public awareness and tolerance of intersexual conditions (Miller, 2000).

5-1c Gender Identity

Gender identity The psychological state of viewing one's self as a girl or a boy, and later as a woman or a man.

Gender dysphoria A condition in which one's gender identity does not match one's biological sex.

Gender identity is the psychological state of viewing one's self as a girl or a boy, and later as a woman or a man. Such identity is largely learned and is a reflection of society's conceptions of femininity and masculinity. Some individuals experience **gender dysphoria,** a condition in which one's gender identity does not match one's biological sex (see the discussion of transsexualism in section 5-1d).

Think About It

For many years, gender dysphoria and transsexualism were viewed as "conditions" that were "cured" by sex reassignment surgery. However, a new paradigm has emerged that recognizes a category of individuals who transcend the gender dichotomy. These individuals, referred to as transgenderists, live in a gender role that does not match their biological sex. How do you account for the increased societal acceptance of transgenderists?

5-1d Transgendered

Cross-dresser A broad term for an individual who may dress or present himself or herself in the gender of the other sex. (See also **transvestites.**)

The term *transgendered* refers to individuals of one biological sex (female or male) who express behavior not typically assigned to their gender. **Cross-dresser** is a broad term for individuals who may dress or present themselves in the gender of the other sex. Some cross-dressers are heterosexual adult males who enjoy dressing and presenting themselves as women. Less commonly, cross-dressers may also be women who dress as men and present themselves as men. Some cross-dressers are bisexual or homosexual. Another term for cross-dresser is **transvestite,** although the latter term is commonly associated with homosexual men who dress provocatively as women to attract men—sometimes as sexual customers. Cross-dressers may also dress in the gender of the other for their own sexual excitement.

Transvestites A broad term for individuals who may dress or present themselves in the gender of the other sex. A more pejorative term than cross-dresser. (See also **cross-dresser.**)

Transsexuals Persons with the biological/anatomical sex of one gender (e.g., male) but the self-concept of the other sex (e.g., female).

Transsexuals are persons with the biological/anatomical sex of one gender (e.g., male) but the self-concept of the other sex (e.g., female). They experience extreme gender dysphoria, or unhappiness with their biological sex. "I am a woman trapped in a man's body" reflects the feelings of the male-to-female transsexual, who may take hormones to develop breasts and reduce facial hair, and may have sexual reassignment surgery to artificially construct a vagina. This person lives full-time as a woman.

The female-to-male transsexual is one who is a biological/anatomical female but who feels "I am a man trapped in a female's body." This person may take male hormones to grow facial hair and deepen her voice and may have surgery to create an artificial penis. This person lives full-time as a man.

Cole, O'Boyle, Emory, and Meyer (1997) studied 435 transsexuals (318 male to female; 117 female to male) to assess the presence of major psychopathology. They concluded, "gender dyspohric individuals appear to be relatively 'normal' in terms of an absence of diagnosable, comorbid psychiatric problems" (p. 21). About 7 to 10% of the group did have identifiable psychiatric problems, but this is consistent with the general population (p. 21). Although transsexuals are as psychologically "normal" as the rest of us, there is considerable prejudice against them adopting and/or rearing children.

INTERNATIONAL DATA A national sample of 668 Swedish adults revealed that 41% were opposed to transsexuals adopting and rearing children. Men and older age individuals held more restrictive views (Landen & Innala, 2000).

Although some studies have been conducted on the effects of sexual reassignment surgery, the research methodology has not been strong. Persons requesting sexual reassignment surgery are unwilling to participate in studies that use random assignment to surgical, psychotherapy, or waiting-list comparison groups. However, reviews of studies have indicated that postoperative adjustment is more favorable when the person (prior to surgery) was reasonably mentally and emotionally stable, successfully lived in the desired role (with convincing appearance and behavior) for at least a year, understood the limitations and consequences of surgery, and had psychological services. Surgical adequacy was also important. However, the research has been mainly medically centered; attention to self-understanding and learning more about the psychological functioning and cognitive style of transsexuals is recommended (Midence & Hargreaves, 1997).

There is an important distinction between transvestites and transsexuals. Transvestites dress in the clothing of the other gender. They may experience erotic stimulation from wearing clothing of the other sex that is often a prelude to heterosexual sexual activity. But they retain their identity as a male or female consistent with their respective genitals and are not typically interested in sex reassignment surgery. Hence, a male transvestite has a penis and enjoys dressing up as a woman but wants to keep his penis. "I like my plumbing," said one heterosexual cross-dresser who spoke in the authors' classes. A male transsexual has a penis but dresses as a woman because he sees himself as a woman and wants to have his genitals changed so that he can become anatomically female. Because the transsexual sees himself as a woman, he is likely to be attracted to men, although some male-to-female transsexuals identify as lesbians.

Individuals need not take hormones or have surgery to be regarded as transsexuals. The distinguishing variable is living full-time in the role of the gender opposite one's

Transgenderist An individual who lives in a gender role that does not match his or her biological sex but who does not surgically alter his or her genitalia (as does a transsexual).

biological sex. A man or woman who presents himself or herself full-time as a woman or man is a transsexual by definition. Some transsexuals prefer the term **transgenderist,** which means an individual who lives in a gender role that does not match his or her biological sex but who has no desire to surgically alter his or her genitalia (as does a transsexual). Examples are a genetic male who prefers to live as a female but does not want surgery or a genetic female who wants to live as a male but does not want surgery. Another variation is the she/male who looks like a woman and has the breasts of a woman yet has the genitalia and reproductive system of a male.

Doctor and Fleming (2001) reported data on 455 transvestites and 61 male-to-female transsexuals (all biological males) with the goal of identifying the components of transgenderism in these two transgenderist populations. The researchers identified five variables that were helpful in describing individual differences, experiences, and expression: self-identity, role, sexual arousal, androallure (the interest a transgendered person has in sexual involvement with a male), and pleasure. They did not find a single overarching variable for transgenderists, but many. For all five factors, there was some overlap, ranging from a low on the identity factor of only 6% (only 6% of the transvestites described feelings of very intense feminine gender identity, overlapping with the scale scores of most transsexuals), to a high of 46% for the androallure factor (46% of transvestites reported being attracted to a man, overlapping with the scale scores of most transsexuals).

5-1e Gender Role

Gender role The social norms that dictate appropriate female and male behavior.

Gender roles are the social norms that dictate what is socially regarded as appropriate female and male behavior. All societies have expectations of how boys and girls, men and women "should" behave. Gender roles influence women and men in virtually every sphere of life, including family and occupation. For example, traditional gender roles have influenced women to be housekeepers. In a random phone survey of 947 individuals in relationships, women reported doing more housework than men (Stanley & Markman, 1997). Women have also been socialized to enter "female" occupations such as elementary school teacher, day-care worker, and nurse. (See section 5-1f on pursuing a nontraditional occupational role.)

The term *sex roles* is often confused with and used interchangeably with the term *gender roles*. However, whereas gender roles are socially defined and can be enacted by either women or men, **sex roles** are defined by biological constraints and can be enacted by members of one biological sex only—wet nurse, sperm donor, child bearer.

Sex roles Roles filled by women or men that are defined by biological constraints and can be enacted by members of one biological sex only—wet nurse, sperm donor, child bearer.

5-1f Personal Choices: Pursue a Nontraditional Occupational Role?

There are few jobs that actually require a penis or a vagina. All other jobs should be open to everybody.

—Gloria Steinem, feminist

Women and men often choose occupations that are consistent with traditional gender role expectations. But there are personal and social advantages to choosing nontraditional occupational roles. On the individual level, women and men can make career choices on the basis of their personal talents and interests, rather than on the basis of arbitrary social restrictions regarding who can and cannot have a particular job or career. Because traditional male occupations are generally higher paying than traditional female occupations, women who make nontraditional career choices can gain access to higher paying and higher status jobs. In contrast, men who enter traditional female occupations, such as nursing and elementary school teaching, can develop their capacity for nurturing. Men are also likely to be promoted to supervisors and administrators in traditional female professions.

Lack of acceptance may be a disadvantage of entering a nontraditional role. Women in traditional all-male military careers or schooling (such as Citadel cadets) have reported undue harassment. In the field of nursing, male nurses are in the minority. Just under 5% of registered nurses in the United States in 1998 were men (Meadus, 2000). Men in the nursing profession battle the assumption that they cannot be as caring or compassionate as women. Some say they are viewed with suspicion and penalized for violating gender roles. The American Assembly for Men in Nursing is an organization developed to provide a framework to discuss issues that affect men as nurses.

On the societal level, an increase in nontraditional career choices reduces **occupational sex segregation,** thereby contributing to social equality between women and men. In addition, women and men who enter nontraditional occupations may contribute greatly to the field they enter. For example, traditional male-dominated occupations, such as politics, science and technology, and medicine, may benefit greatly from increased involvement of women in these fields. Similarly, the field of public school teaching, which is currently a female-dominated occupation, has not provided enough male role models for children. Additionally, when men enter a profession, broad-based salary increases tend to occur.

Occupational sex segregation The tendency for women and men to pursue different occupations.

Choosing nontraditional occupations may also help to eliminate gender stereotypes. Women are stereotyped as being nurturing in part because of their service-oriented jobs, whereas men are believed to be more technically proficient and more competent decision makers because of the kinds of jobs they hold. Women as airline pilots and men as day-care workers help to crack the stereotypes.

5-1g Sexual Identity

Sexual identity refers to a number of factors, including one's biological sex, gender identity, gender role, and sexual orientation. One's biological sex (also referred to as *natal sex*) refers to being male or female; gender identity, to seeing one's self as a woman or man; gender role, as the occupation of social/cultural roles defined as those appropriate for women or men; and sexual orientation, as heterosexual, homosexual, or bisexual. Individuals may have a clear sexual identity of being a heterosexual male who functions in "male" roles. Alternatively, one's sexual identity may be seen as a cluster of several variables such as a biological male with the gender identity of a woman but the gender role of a man and a bisexual sexual orientation.

Sexual identity Composite term that refers to factors including one's biological sex, gender identity, gender role, and sexual orientation.

One's sexual identity may also be in flux. Judith Verkerke, a Dutch transgender person, described her fluctuating identity as follows:

> *I developed from being unclear about my gender to being a boy, to a gay man, feminine gay man, to transvestite, and finally transsexual. . . . During my transition I became a lesbian. After a feminine period, I am now a masculine woman. . . . I experience my gender as flexible. . . . I sometimes feel a gay man, sometimes a hetero-man, a femme, a butch, to name a few. (Bockting, 1999, p. 5)*

5-1h Gender Role Ideology

Gender role ideology refers to the socially prescribed role relationships between women and men in any given society. These role relationship norms become important because they have implications for one's control of the sexual agenda. Wolff, Blanc, and Gage (2000) studied women in Uganda and noted that, because men have more relationship power there, they are more likely to control the timing and conditions (condoms) of sex. In the United States, gender role ideology has perpetuated and reflected male dominance in social (the double standard), economic (two thirds of poor adults are women; more than 95% of corporate executives are male), and political (85% of elected officeholders are male) spheres (Rhode, 1997).

Gender role ideology Socially prescribed role relationships between women and men in any given society.

CULTURAL DIVERSITY

The Human Development Report (1997) concludes, "no society treats its women as well as its men" (p. 39). Some of the practices particularly impacting women's health include female infanticide, female genital operations, prostitution, and prohibitions against birth control and abortion.

Think About It

Whereas traditional heterosexual relationships have reflected male dominance, homosexual relationships tend to be more equal, with greater gender role flexibility. When gender role ideology in homosexual relationships is assessed, lesbian relationships are more egalitarian and flexible than gay male relationships (Green, Bettinger, & Zacks, 1996). How do you explain these differences?

5-2 BIOLOGICAL BEGINNINGS

The distinction between the female and the male sexes begins at the moment of fertilization when the man's sperm and the woman's egg unite to form a zygote. Both chromosomal and hormonal factors contribute to the development of the zygote.

5-2a Chromosomes

Chromosomes Threadlike structures of DNA within the cell nucleus that carry the genes and transmit hereditary information.

Chromosomes are threadlike structures located within the nucleus of every cell in a person's body. Each cell contains 23 pairs of chromosomes, a total of 46 chromosomes per cell. Chromosomes contain genes, the basic units of heredity, which determine not only such physical characteristics as eye color, hair color, and body type, but also predispositions for such characteristics as baldness, color blindness, and hemophilia. One of these 23 pairs of chromosomes is referred to as *sex chromosomes* because they determine whether an individual will be female or male. There are two types of sex chromosomes, called X and Y. Normally, females have two X chromosomes, whereas males have one X and one Y chromosome.

When the egg and sperm meet in the Fallopian tube, each contains only half the normal number of chromosomes (one from each of the 23 pairs). The union of sperm and egg results in a single cell called a *zygote*, which has the normal 46 chromosomes. The egg will always have an X chromosome, but the sperm will have either an X or Y chromosome. Because the sex chromosome in the egg is always X (the female chromosome), the sex chromosome in the sperm will determine the sex of a child. If the sperm contains an X chromosome, the match with the female chromosome will be XX, and the child will be genetically female. If the sperm contains a Y chromosome (the male chromosome), the match with the female chromosome will be XY, and the child will be genetically male.

The fact that chromosomes control the biological sex of a child has enabled some parents to select the sex of their offspring. Whether or not this choice should be an option is discussed in Box 5-1.

Think About It

In addition to chromosomal differences, some research suggests that the brains of women and men are different. For example, the corpus callosum, the bundle of fibers that connects the left and right hemispheres of the brain, is proportionally larger in women than in men (Witelson, 1995), which may help to explain great skill in multitasking and earlier speech development in girls. To what degree do you feel that differences men and women evidence is a result of "brain" differences versus "socialization" differences?

Box 5-1 Social Choices

Selecting the Sex of One's Unborn Child?

Through modern reproductive technology, couples are now able to decide the sex of the child they wish to have. Although the practice is highly controversial, **prenatal sex selection** (also referred to as *sex preselection*) may be achieved through prenatal diagnosis (**amniocentesis** or chorionic villi sampling) and abortion. Amniocentesis (which is best performed in the 16th or 17th week of pregnancy) involves inserting a needle into the pregnant woman's uterus to withdraw fluid, which is then analyzed to see if the cells carry XX (female) or XY (male) chromosomes. Chorionic villi sampling (CVS) can be used to detect fetal sex as early as 8 weeks' gestation. Depending on the position of the fetus, ultrasound may reveal the fetus' genital area, but it is not considered a reliable test to determine the sex of the fetus. Using one or more of the various tests, if the fetus is the biological sex that is desired by the parents, it may be allowed to develop. Otherwise, the fetus may be aborted. Such a decision is not widely practiced (in the United States) by either physicians or parents but does occur.

Selecting the sex of one's child through prenatal sex selection is highly controversial. The strongest argument for prenatal sex selection is that it can prevent the birth of an infant with a serious and fatal sex-linked genetic disease. Another argument is that aborting a fetus of the "undesired sex" is less objectionable than killing the infant after it is born. The practice of female infanticide—the killing of female infants by drowning, strangling, or exposure—has been well-documented in Eastern countries, including China and India. This practice occurs because of the cultural value that is placed on having male children. In China, India, and many other Eastern countries, boys are seen as an asset because they provide labor in the fields and take care of elderly parents. Girls are considered economic liabilities because they require a dowry and then leave the family to care for their husbands and children. In India, amniocentesis clinics advertise with slogans like, "Better 500 rupees now than 500,000 later," referring to the contrasting costs of abortion now or a dowry at a later date. While less adamant, many couples in Western countries also want a "balanced" family—one that includes a child of each sex. Sex selection technology allows parents to achieve this balance.

Opposition to prenatal sex selection is strongest when abortion is used. Not only does abortion for sex selection outrage individuals who are against abortion for any reason, but it also offends many individuals who support women's right to choose abortion for other reasons. Many pro-choice individuals view abortion for the purpose of sex selection as morally unjustifiable and are concerned that using abortion for sex selection may generate so much public opposition that the freedom to choose abortion when there are strong moral reasons to do so may be jeopardized.

A more common alternative to prenatal sex selection is **preconceptual sex selection,** also called **family balancing;** this alternative involves selecting the sex of a child before it is conceived. One method separates sperm carrying the X and Y chromosomes. Genetics and IVF Institute in Fairfax, Virginia, offers an average of 88% chance of having a girl and a 73% chance of having a boy (based on data from the company's web site http://www.microsort.net/ in 2002). The company uses MicroSort technology, which sorts the X-bearing spermatozoa. This sperm sorting technique is based on the fact that the X chromosome has greater mass than the Y chromosome because of its higher total DNA content. Sperm are sorted by DNA analysis with fluorescence in situ hybridisation (FISH), and the sperm are then separated by flow cytometric separation according to whether they bear X or Y chromosomes (Mayor, 2001). Using artificial insemination, the woman's egg is then fertilized with the sperm carrying the chromosome of the desired sex. Some researchers have questioned whether the MicroSort procedure might change the nature of the DNA and give a long-term risk of damage to the children born (Mayor, 2001).

Preconceptual methods of sex selection, which do not involve abortion, are less objectionable than prenatal sex selection. However, the widespread acceptance of preconceptual methods of sex selection could have serious social consequences. For instance, the cultural preference for male children would influence couples who want only one child to select a male child, thereby creating an imbalance in the sex ratio. In Eastern countries (where female infanticide and abortion of female fetuses occur on a large scale), the sex ratio is already unbalanced. For example, the reported sex ratio at birth in China is very close to 106 males per 100 females (Junhong, 2001).

Although the majority of U.S. adults oppose sex selection through abortion, preconceptual sex selection could gain widespread acceptance. When such acceptance occurs, will other variables become issues, such as eye and hair color, height, weight, and skin color?

In May 2001, the ethics group of the Center for Human Reproduction published a policy that took a step toward revising its prohibition on nonmedical sex selection using the sperm separation technique. This technique is effective about 90% of the time when selecting girls and slightly lower for selecting boys. However, when couples undergo in vitro fertilization, specialists can be almost 100% accurate in identifying female or male embryos through genetic testing. The question has been raised that if the less certain sperm separation technique may be used, why not the more certain technique? A preliminary letter from the chairman of the ethics group suggested that given the May decision, "'a program might ethically offer pre implantation genetic diagnoses' for gender variety in a family" if a physician had "good reason to think that the couple is fully informed about the risks of the procedure, and are counseled about having unrealistic expectations about the behavior of children of the preferred gender" (Ethicist, 2001, p. A2). The letter was not a ruling by the entire ethics committee, but the organization's stand discouraging sex selection is likely to be reviewed in the near future.

Prenatal sex selection The selection of the sex of a child before the child is born.

Amniocentesis Prenatal test in which a needle is inserted (usually in the 16th or 17th week of pregnancy) into the pregnant woman's uterus to withdraw fluid, which is analyzed to see if the cells carry XX (female) or XY (male) chromosomes, and to identify chromosomal defects.

Preconceptual sex selection The selection of the sex of a child before it is conceived. (See also **family balancing.**)

Family balancing Act of selecting the sex of a child before it is conceived for a "balanced" (one boy, one girl) family. One method separates sperm carrying the X and Y chromosomes.

5-2b Chromosomal Abnormalities

As we have seen, normal development in males and females requires that the correct number of chromosomes be present in the developing fetus. Chromosomal abnormalities may result in atypical sexual development of the fetus. For every sex chromosome from the mother (X), there must be a corresponding sex chromosome from the father (X or Y) for normal sexual development to occur. Abnormalities result when there are too many or too few sex chromosomes. Either the father or the mother may contribute an abnormal sex chromosome (Miller, 2000).

NATIONAL DATA Abnormal sex chromosome combinations occur in an estimated 1 out of 300–400 live births (Miller, 2000).

Klinefelter's syndrome Condition that occurs in males and results from the presence of an extra X sex chromosome (XXY), resulting in abnormal testicular development, infertility, low interest in sex (low libido), and, in some cases, mental retardation.

Turner's syndrome Condition that occurs in females and results from the absense of an X chromosome (XO), resulting in a short webbed neck, absense of pubic and axillary hair, and very small ovaries.

Two of the most common of these abnormalities are **Klinefelter's syndrome** and Turner's syndrome. Klinefelter's syndrome occurs in males and results from the presence of an extra X sex chromosome (XXY). The result is abnormal testicular development, infertility, low interest in sex (low libido), and, in some cases, mental retardation. Males with an extra X chromosome often experience language deficits, neuromaturational lag, academic difficulties, and psychological distress. Common characteristics also include abnormally long legs and lack of a deep voice and beard.

Turner's syndrome occurs in females and results from the absence of an X chromosome (XO). It is characterized by abnormal ovarian development, failure to menstruate, infertility, and the lack of secondary sexual characteristics (such as minimal breast development). Turner's syndrome is also associated with short stature and a predisposition to heart and kidney defects. Treatment for Turner's syndrome includes hormone replacement therapy to develop secondary sexual characteristics and the use of a biosynthetic human growth hormone to promote growth. Such treatment directs girls with Turner's syndrome toward normal female development.

5-2c Hormones

Hormones are also important in the development of the fetus. Male and female embryos are indistinguishable from one another during the first several weeks of intrauterine life. In both males and females, two primitive gonads and two paired duct systems form about the 5th or 6th week of development. While the reproductive system of the male (epididymis, vas deferens, ejaculatory duct) develops from the Wolffian ducts and the female reproductive system (Fallopian tubes, uterus, vagina) from the Mullerian ducts, both ducts are present in the developing embryo at this stage (see Figure 5-2).

If the embryo is genetically a male (XY), a chemical substance controlled by the Y chromosome (H-Y antigen) stimulates the primitive gonads to develop into testes. The testes, in turn, begin secreting the male hormone testosterone, which stimulates the development of the male reproductive and external sexual organs. The testes also secrete a second substance, called Mullerian duct-inhibiting substance, which causes the potential female ducts to degenerate or become blind tubules. Thus, development of male anatomical structures depends on the presence of male hormones at a critical stage of development.

The development of a female requires that no additional testosterone be present. Without the controlling substance from the Y chromosome, the primitive gonads will develop into ovaries and the Mullerian duct system into Fallopian tubes, uterus, and vagina; and without testosterone, the Wolffian duct system will degenerate or become blind tubules. Animal studies have shown that if the primitive gonads are removed prior to differentiation into testes or ovaries, the organism will always develop anatomically into a female, regardless of genetic composition.

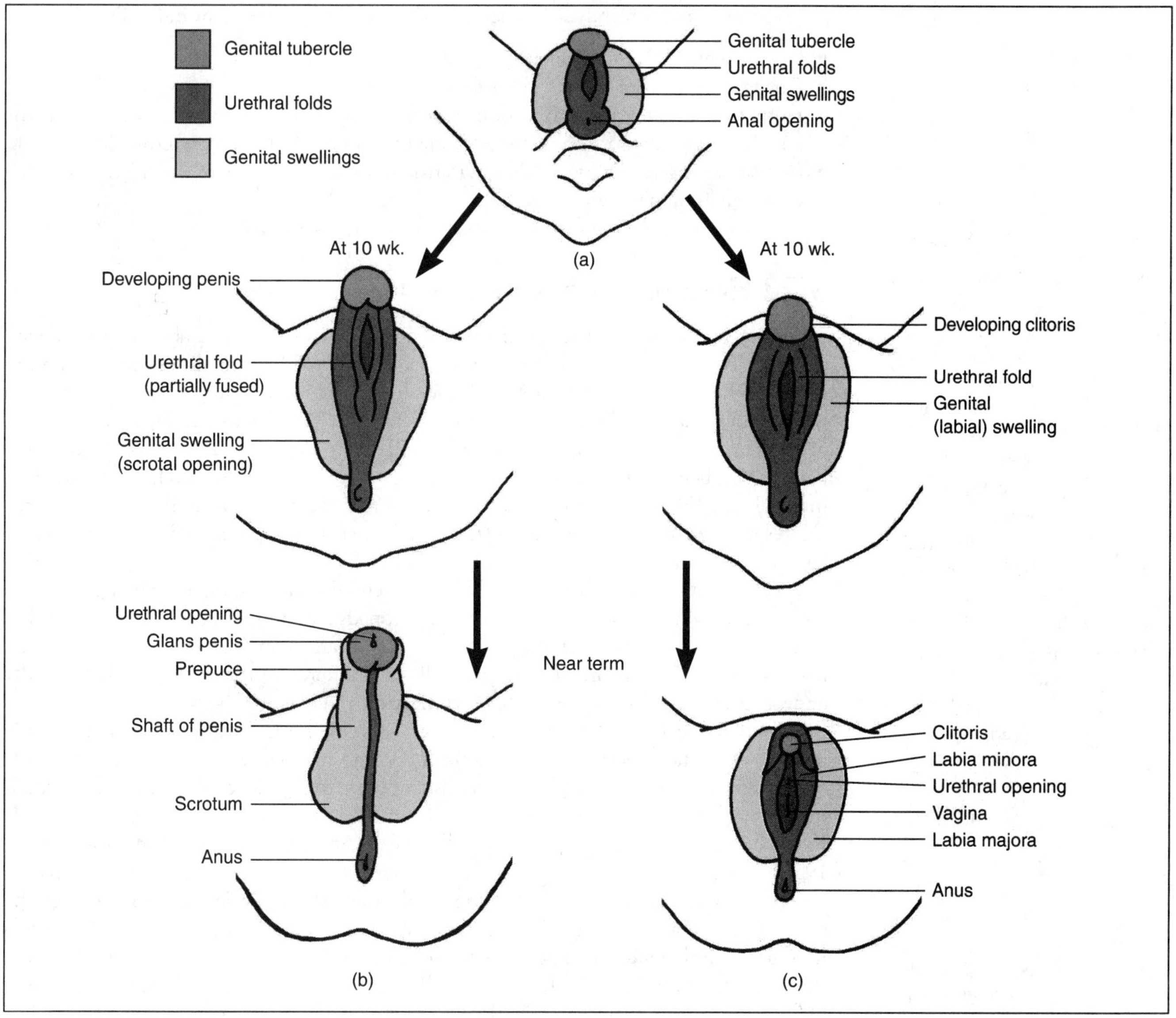

FIGURE 5-2
Sexual Differentiation of External Genitalia

(a) Undifferentiated stage (7 weeks). (b) Male development. (c) Female development.

Although the infant's gonads (testes and ovaries) produce the sex hormones (testosterone and estrogen), these hormones are regulated by the pituitary gland, which is located at the base of the brain about 2 inches behind the eyes. The pituitary releases hormones into the blood that determine the amount of testosterone released by the testes and the amounts of estrogen and progesterone released by the ovaries. Production of sex hormones in males is relatively constant; production of female hormones is cyclic. Does this mean the pituitary glands of males and females are different? In animal studies in which the pituitaries of male organisms have been transplanted into female organisms (and vice versa), the production of sex hormones remains cyclic in females and constant in males. The release of pituitary hormones, as it turns out, is controlled by additional hormones (also called releasing factors) from the hypothalamus, a part of the brain just above the pituitary. It is the hypothalamus that differs in males and females in both the connections between cells and the size of various groups of cells. The presence of testosterone before birth not only stimulates the development of the male reproductive system, but also apparently stimulates the development of a male hypothalamus. A female hypothalamus develops in the absence of testosterone.

To summarize, several factors determine the biological sex of an individual:

- *Chromosomes:* XX for female; XY for male
- *Gonads:* Ovaries for female; testes for male
- *Hormones:* Greater proportion of estrogen and progesterone than testosterone in the female; greater proportion of testosterone than estrogen and progesterone in the male
- *Internal sex organs:* Fallopian tubes, uterus, and vagina for female; epididymis, vas deferens, and seminal vesicles for male
- *External genitals:* Vulva for female; penis and scrotum for male

Hermaphroditism A rare condition in which individuals are born with both ovarian and testicular tissue. These individuals, called hermaphrodites, may have one ovary and one testicle, feminine breasts, and a vaginal opening beneath the penis.

Pseudohermaphroditism A condition in which an individual is born with gonads matching the sex chromosomes, but genitals resembling those of the other sex.

Fetally androgynized females Individuals with a condition caused by excessive androgen, whereby the clitoris greatly enlarges and the labia majora fuses together to resemble a scrotum, resulting in genitals that resemble those of a male.

Congenital Adrenal Hyperplasia (CAH) Malfunction that causes the adrenal glands of the XX fetus to produce excessive amounts of androgens, which results in androgenital syndrome.

Androgenital syndrome Genetic defect that causes the adrenal glands of the XX fetus to produce excessive amounts of androgens.

Female pseudohermaphrodites Individuals with androgenital syndrome who are genetically female.

Testicular feminization syndrome (TFS) Disorder that involves the lack of development of male genitals in the body of a person who is genetically male (a person who has XY chromosomes). The genitals of the infant look like a female but the infant is biologically a male. (See also **androgen-insensitivity syndrome.**)

5-2d Hormonal Abnormalities

Too much or too little of the wrong kind of hormone can also cause abnormal sex development. Two conditions that may result from hormonal abnormalities are hermaphroditism and pseudohermaphroditism. **Hermaphroditism** is an extremely rare condition in which individuals are born with both ovarian and testicular tissue. These individuals, called hermaphrodites, may have one ovary and one testicle, feminine breasts, and a vaginal opening beneath the penis. They are generally genetic females (XX), and while their internal reproductive systems are usually mixed and incomplete as well, many hermaphrodites menstruate. Hermaphrodites traditionally may have been reared as either males or females, depending largely on their appearance.

More common than hermaphroditism is **pseudohermaphroditism,** which refers to a condition in which an individual is born with gonads matching the sex chromosomes, but genitals resembling those of the other sex. There are numerous causes of pseudohermaphroditism. Two syndromes that we will discuss here are those that result in **fetally androgynized females** and **testicular feminization syndrome** in boys.

You will recall that for the female fetus to develop normally, it must avoid unusually high doses of androgen ("male" hormones). Androgens, however, are produced not only by the testes, but also by the adrenal glands. Exposure to high levels of androgen can result from a malfunction of the mother's adrenal glands or from the mother's ingestion of synthetic hormones (such as progestin) that have an androgen effect on the fetus. (In the 1950s, progestin was often prescribed for pregnant women to prevent premature delivery.)

Sometimes a genetic defect **(Congenital Adrenal Hyperplasia, CAH)** causes the adrenal glands of the XX fetus to produce excessive amounts of androgens, which results in **androgenital syndrome.** Excessive androgen causes the clitoris to greatly enlarge and the labia majora to fuse together to resemble a scrotum, resulting in genitals that resemble those of a male. Because individuals with this syndrome are genetically female, they are referred to as **female pseudohermaphrodites.** When such conditions as CAH are not recognized at birth, genetically female infants whose genitals appear to be male are usually reared as males. During adolescence, the male-reared female may notice lack of facial hair growth, failure of the voice to deepen, and enlargement of the breasts. Chromosomal tests would reveal the XX genetic makeup of the individual, at which point it is usually recommended that the individual retain his male gender identity and have surgery to remove female internal organs (ovaries and uterus). In addition, hormone therapy is provided to deepen the voice, produce facial hair growth, and minimize breast growth.

When CAH is recognized early, hormonal and surgical treatments result in a more typically feminine appearance. Although the term *androgenital syndrome* emphasizes the genital appearance, early exposure to androgens in girls has a masculinizing effect in other ways as well. Although girls with CAH have a female gender identity, studies suggest they engage in more male-typical play (rough-and-tumble play, sports, and playing with boys' toys) and may dislike girl-typical activities. Most girls with CAH grow up to be heterosexual, but more report lesbian or bisexual attraction compared to women without CAH (Lippa, 2002).

Another hormonal fetal abnormality that results in pseudohermaphroditism—**testicular feminization syndrome (TFS)**—involves the lack of development of male genitals in the body of a person who is genetically male (a person who has XY chromosomes).

In TFS, also known as **androgen-insensitivity syndrome (AIS),** the external tissues of the fetus fail to turn into male genitals. Even though normal amounts of androgen are produced, the tissues do not respond to the male hormones, and female external genitals are formed (labia, clitoris, and vaginal opening). The production of Mullerian duct-inhibiting substance is not impaired, so the Fallopian tubes and uterus do not develop, and the vagina is quite short. Hence, while the newborn infant has the external genital appearance of a female (and is therefore reared as a female), the infant has testes embedded in the abdomen. These individuals are called **male pseudohermaphrodites.**

Parents are usually unaware of this hormonal abnormality until they realize at mid-adolescence that their daughter has not menstruated. She cannot do so because she has no uterus. Surgery can remove the testes and increase the depth of the vagina. Androgen-insensitive XY individuals think of themselves as females (despite the fact that genetically they are males), and they often marry men (Lippa, 2002).

Some individuals with XY chromosomes also have a defective gene that creates problems with an enzyme involved in testosterone metabolism **(reductase-deficient males).** While these individual are prenatally exposed to testosterone, they are assumed to experience masculinization of their brains, but their genitals at birth look feminine or ambiguous. They are often reared as girls. But at puberty, with its androgen surge, their genitals masculinize. After puberty many of these individuals change from "female" to "male."

When infants are born with ambiguous genitals, they are neither clearly male nor female. These infants are called **intersexed infants.** When ambiguous genitals are detected at birth, parents and physicians face the decision of assigning either the male or female gender to the intersexed infant.

As noted earlier, in the past, infants with ambiguous genitals were reared in the gender most closely approximating the appearance of a particular sex. For example, if the infant's genitals were more similar to those of a female's, then it was assigned a female gender, regardless of its chromosomal makeup. Or, if there was a surgical mishap—during circumcision, for example—the genitals were reconstructed, and the "male" was reared as a "female." The practice of assigning sex on the basis of external appearance was based on the assumption that the environment was more important in determining a person's gender than one's biological sex. The long-term follow-up of reassigned infants (as discussed at the beginning of this section) challenged this thinking so that children may be more likely now to be reared in their biological (chromosomal) sex.

Androgen-insensitivity syndrome (AIS) Disorder caused by gene mutation in encoding androgen, resulting in feminization of external genitals and body type of XY individuals. (See also **testicular feminization syndrome.**)

Male pseudohermaphrodites Individuals who have the external genital appearance of a female (and are therefore reared as female) but whose testes are embedded in the abdomen.

Reductase-deficient males Individuals with XY chromosomes who also have a defective gene that creates problems with an enzyme involved in testosterone metabolism.

Intersexed infants Infants who are born with ambiguous genitals that are neither clearly male nor female.

Think About It

Zucker (1999) examined both sides of the differentiation issue and pointed out that there are examples in the literature in which reassignment of a boy as a girl has been successful and cases in which it has been a failure. In section 5-6c, we refer to gender postmodernism whereby, rather than forcing intersexed and transgender people into one gender category of "male" or "female," these individuals should be accepted as they are, absent any stigma. Should our society be open to more categories of gender expression?

5-3 THEORIES OF GENDER ROLE DEVELOPMENT

A number of theories attempt to explain why women and men exhibit different characteristics and behaviors. In sections 5-3a through 5-3e we examine the major theories of gender role development.

5-3a Sociobiology

Sociobiology emphasizes that social behavior has a biological basis in terms of being functional in human evolution. Theodosius Dobzhansky, the eminent biologist, noted that "Nothing in biology makes sense except in the light of evolution" (cited in

Sociobiology Framework in which social behavior is viewed as having a biological basis in terms of being functional in human evolution. (See also **sociobiological theories.**)

Thornhill & Palmer, 2000). In effect, given an appreciation of evolution by natural selection (certain behaviors occurred that contributed to the survival of the animal and its offspring), we can look at social behaviors as having an evolutionary survival function. Joseph (2000) emphasized that the differences between women and men (women nurture children; men hunt/kill animals for food) were functional for survival. Women stayed in the nest or gathered food nearby, while men could go afar to find food. Such a conceptualization focuses on the division of labor between women and men as functional for the survival of the species.

Although there is little agreement (even among sociologists) on the merits of sociobiology (Alcock, 2001; Miller & Costello, 2001), the theory emphasizes that biological differences (such as hormonal and chromosomal differences) between men and women account for the social and psychological differences in female and male characteristics, behaviors, and roles. For example, testosterone is a male hormone associated with aggression; progesterone is a female hormone associated with nurturance. Such hormonal differences are used to help explain that men have more sexual partners than women, that men are more likely to engage in casual sex, and that men are the perpetrators of most acts of sexual coercion as well as sexual harassment. However, critics of sociobiology point out that a particular dose of a particular hormone does not translate into a specific behavior (Miller & Costello, 2001).

In mate selection, heterosexual men tend to seek and mate with women who are youthful and attractive. These characteristics are associated with fertility, health, and lifetime reproductive potential for women. Alcock (2001) notes that

> *unwrinkled, unblemished skin is far more likely to be possessed by young, healthy women than by older (less fertile) or less healthy (less fertile) women. Are young, healthy women more likely to become pregnant and sustain a pregnancy successfully than older or less healthy women? The answer is yes. Is there any species of animal on earth in which males are more likely to mate with infertile females than with fertile ones, if given the opportunity to choose between the two? The answer is obvious. (p. 137)*

Similarly, women tend to select and mate with men whom they deem will provide the maximum parental investment in their offspring. The term **parental investment** refers to any investment by a parent that increases the offspring's chance of surviving and thus increases reproductive success. Parental investments require time and energy. Women have a great deal of parental investment in their offspring (9 months' gestation, taking care of dependent offspring) and tend to mate with men who have high status, economic resources, and a willingness to share economic resources.

Parental investment Any investment by a parent that increases the offspring's chance of surviving and thus increases reproductive success.

CULTURAL DIVERSITY 

David Buss (1989) found that the pattern of men seeking physically attractive young women and women seeking economically ambitious men was true in 37 groups of women and men in 33 different societies.

The sociobiological explanation for mate selection is extremely controversial. Critics argue that women may show concern for the earning capacity of a potential mate because women have been systematically denied access to similar economic resources, and selecting a mate with these resources is one of their remaining options. In addition, it is argued that both women and men, when selecting a mate, think more about their partners as companions than as future parents of their offspring. Finally, the sociobiological perspective fails to acknowledge the degree to which social and psychological factors influence our behavior. For example, Miller and Costello (2001) emphasized that biological determinists should "familiarize themselves with the sociological research on the cultural construction of gender" (p. 597).

5-3b Identification Theory

Although researchers do not agree on the merits of Freud's theories, Freud was one of the first researchers to study gender role acquisition. He suggested that children acquire the characteristics and behaviors of their same-sex parent through a process of identification. Boys identify with their fathers, and girls identify with their mothers. Freud (1925/1974, 1933/1965) said that children identify with the same-gender parent out of fear. Freud felt this fear could be one of two kinds: fear of loss of love or fear of retaliation. Fear of loss of love, which results in both girls and boys identifying with their mother, is caused by their deep dependence on her for love and nurturance. Fearful that she may withdraw her love, young children try to become like her to please her and to ensure the continuance of her love.

According to Freud, at about age 4, the child's identification with the mother begins to change, but in different ways for boys than for girls. Boys experience what Freud called the **Oedipal complex.** Based on the legend of the Greek youth Oedipus, who unknowingly killed his father and married his mother, the Oedipal complex involves the young boy's awakening sexual feelings for his mother as he becomes aware he has a penis and his mother does not. He unconsciously feels that if his father knew of the intense love feelings he has for his mother, the father would castrate him (which may be what happened to his mother, because she has no penis). The boy resolves the Oedipal struggle—feeling love for his father but wanting to kill him because he is a competitor for his mother's love—by becoming like his father by identifying with him. In this way, the boy can keep his penis and take pride in being like his father. According to Freud, the successful resolution of this Oedipal situation marks the beginning of a boy's appropriate gender role acquisition.

Oedipal complex Freud's term based on the legend of the Greek youth Oedipus, who unknowingly killed his father and married his mother; the Oedipal complex involves the young boy's awakening sexual feelings for his mother as he becomes aware he has a penis and his mother does not.

The **Electra complex** is based on the Greek myth in which Electra assists her brother in killing their mother and her lover to avenge their father's death. In Freudian terms, the Electra complex refers to unconscious sexual feelings a daughter develops for her father. These feelings develop when 3- to 6-year-old girls become aware that they do not have a penis. Freud believed that girls blame their mothers for cutting off their penis or causing it to be severed and that they develop "penis envy" and wish that they had a penis. To retaliate, girls take their love away from their mothers and begin to focus on their fathers as love objects. Girls feel that they can be fulfilled by being impregnated by their fathers who will give them a baby to substitute for the penis they do not have. To become impregnated by their fathers, girls recognize that they must be more like their mother. So they identify again with the mother. A modern interpretation of penis envy is that women do not desire to have a penis, but rather, they desire the economic and social advantages that men have (Chafetz, 1988).

Electra complex In psychoanalysis this term refers to a daughter's (unconscious) sexual desire for her father; the term refers to the Greek myth in which Electra assists her brother in killing their mother and her lover to avenge their father's death.

5-3c Social Learning Theory

Derived from the school of behavioral psychology, social learning theory emphasizes the role of reward and punishment in explaining how a child learns gender role behavior. For example, two young brothers enjoyed playing "lady." Each of them would put on a dress, wear high-heeled shoes, and carry a pocketbook. Their father came home early one day and angrily demanded they "take those clothes off and never put them on again." "Those things are for women," he said. The boys were punished for playing "lady" but rewarded with their father's approval for playing "cowboys," with plastic guns and "Bang! You're dead!" dialogue.

Reward and punishment alone are not sufficient to account for the way in which children learn gender roles. Direct instruction ("girls wear dresses," "men walk on the outside when walking with a woman") is another way children learn through social interaction with others. In addition, many of society's gender rules are learned through modeling. In modeling, the child observes another's behavior and imitates that behavior. Gender role models include parents, peers, siblings, and characters portrayed in the media.

The impact of modeling on the development of gender role behavior is controversial. For example, a modeling perspective implies that children will tend to imitate the parent of the same sex, but children are usually reared mainly by women in all cultures. Yet this persistent female model does not seem to interfere with the male's development of the behavior that is considered appropriate for his gender. One explanation suggests that boys learn early that our society generally grants boys and men more status and privileges than girls and women; therefore, they devalue the feminine and emphasize the masculine aspects of themselves.

CULTURAL DIVERSITY 

The fact that gender roles differ across societies provides evidence that gender roles are learned. Lippa and Tan (2001) studied gender roles among a sample of Asian American, Hispanic American, and White American individuals and found that those from more traditional, gender-polarized cultures (Asians and Hispanics) tended to show larger differences between women and men in those societies.

5-3d Cognitive-Developmental Theory

The cognitive-developmental theory of gender role acquisition reflects a blend of biological and social learning views. According to this theory, the biological readiness (in terms of the cognitive development of the child) influences how the child responds to gender cues in the environment (Kohlberg, 1966, 1976). For example, gender discrimination (the ability to identify social and psychological characteristics associated with being female and male) begins at about age 30 months. At that age, toddlers are able to assign a "boy's toy" to a boy and a "girl's toy" to a girl (Etaugh & Duits, 1990). However, at this age, children do not view gender as a permanent characteristic. Thus, while young children may define people who wear long hair as girls and those who never wear dresses as boys, they also believe they can change their gender by altering their hair or changing clothes.

Not until age 6 or 7 does the child view gender as permanent (Kohlberg, 1966, 1969). In Kohlberg's view, this cognitive understanding is not a result of social learning. Rather, it involves the development of a specific mental ability to grasp the idea that certain basic characteristics of people do not change. When children learn the concept of gender permanence, they seek to become competent and proper members of their gender group. For example, a child standing on the edge of a school playground may observe one group of children jumping rope while another group is playing football. That child's gender identity as either a girl or a boy connects with the observed "gender appropriate" behavior, and she or he joins one of the two groups. Once in the group, the child seeks to develop the behaviors that are socially defined as appropriate for her or his gender.

5-3e Gender Schema Theory

Gender schema theory
A network of associations with the concepts of male and female (or masculinity and femininity) that organize and guide perception.

Gender schema theory, a more recently developed theory of gender role acquisition, combines aspects of cognitive-developmental theory and social learning theory. The term *schema* refers to a "network of associations that organizes and guides an individual's perception" (Bem, 1983, p. 603). A gender schema is a network of associations with the concepts of male and female (or masculinity and femininity) that organizes and guides perception.

Consistent with social learning theory, the male and female associations that comprise the content of gender schemas are learned through interaction with the social environment. The gender schema then influences how an individual processes information by structuring and organizing perception. A gender schema influences how incoming information, including information about the self, is evaluated with regard to gender norms. This aspect of gender schema theory, which emphasizes the role of cognitive frameworks in processing information, reflects cognitive-developmental theory.

Gender schema theory suggests that people follow gender schemas to different degrees and in different ways. Some people, for example, organize many of their thoughts, perceptions, and evaluations around concepts of male and female, masculine and feminine. These people, whom we might describe as highly sex-typed, rely heavily on gender stereotypes and symbols to understand the social world. They see a wide variety of human characteristics, behaviors, roles, and jobs as decidedly masculine or feminine and evaluate themselves and others according to how well they conform to gender norms and stereotypes.

Other people follow gender schemas less closely or not at all. This does not necessarily mean that they lack what the highly sex-typed person might regard as appropriate masculine or feminine characteristics. Gender may simply not be the central means by which they organize their perceptions of themselves and the social world. Whereas the highly sex-typed person might immediately understand words such as *pink, nurturant, blushing, librarian*, and *curved* as "feminine," these words might not have any immediate gender connotation to the person with no gender schema (Sapiro, 1990, p. 88).

5-4 AGENTS OF GENDER ROLE SOCIALIZATION

Three of the four theories discussed in section 5-3 emphasize that gender roles are learned through interaction with the environment. Indeed, although biology may provide a basis for some roles (being 7'5" is helpful for a basketball player), cultural influences in the form of various socialization agents (parents, peers, teachers, religion, and the media) shape the individual toward various gender roles. These powerful influences in large part dictate what a person thinks, feels, and does in his or her role as a woman or a man.

5-4a Parents

The family is a gendered institution with female and male roles highly structured by gender. Lorber (2001) noted that parents "create a gendered world for their newborns by naming, birth announcements, and dress" (p. 23). Parents may also relate differently to their children on the basis of gender. Lindsey and Mize (2001) observed videotapes of parent-child play behavior of 33 preschool children (18 boys, 29 European American, middle- and upper-middle-class families) and observed that during the physical play session, father-son dyads engaged in more physical play than did father-daughter dyads.

Actual family structure of the parental unit is also influential in the development of a child's gender role behaviors and attitudes. Leve and Fagot (1997) compared 67 two-parent households, 32 single-mother households, and 13 single-father households and found that single-parent households and mothers provided less traditional gender role socialization than two-parent households and fathers. Their findings were confirmed by Wright and Young (1998), who observed that children from father-headed families have more traditional gender-related attitudes than those from mother-headed families.

This father is about to take his son fishing—an activity traditionally associated with males.

Think About It

In his study of adolescent boys, Pollack (2001) notes, "America's boys are crying out for a new gender revolution that does for them what the last forty years of feminism has tried to do for girls and women" (p. 18). This new revolution will depend on fathers who teach their sons that feelings and relationships are important. How equipped do you feel today's fathers are to provide these new models for their sons?

5-4b Peers

Although parents are usually the first socializing agents that influence a child's gender role development, peers become increasingly important during the school years. The gender role messages from adolescent peers call for traditional traits. For adolescent boys this usually means being nonemotional, except for expressing anger. Pollack (2001) recalls the words of a 16-year-old:

> *The pressure to be manly has always been there. Life would probably be easier if I didn't have to be that way. . . . At times it stops me from being able to show how I feel, especially around my guy friends. (p. 267)*

Whereas males are encouraged to restrict their emotional expression, female adolescents are under tremendous pressure to be physically attractive, popular, and achievement oriented. The latter may be traditional (cheerleading) or nontraditional (sports or academics). Adolescent females are sometimes in great conflict in that high academic success may be viewed as being less than feminine. Nahom et al. (2001) also noted that adolescent females (when compared to adolescent males) in their national sample were significantly more likely to report pressure to engage in sexual intercourse.

Peer disapproval for failure to conform to traditional gender stereotypes is reflected in the terms *sissy* and *tomboy*. These terms are used pejoratively to refer to children who exhibit behaviors stereotypically associated with the other gender.

5-4c Teachers

Teachers are important influences on gender role development. Whereas teachers in the past may have perpetuated traditional gender roles in the classroom (Renzetti & Curran, 1999), teachers today are becoming more gender neutral in the way they relate to students (Garrahy, 2001). And, the degree to which schools perpetuate traditional gender role views may be related to the status of the school. Tay and Gibbons (1998) studied 246 adolescents aged 12–15 attending four Singaporean secondary schools and found that students attending very elite schools were the least traditional and most egalitarian in their gender role ideologies.

5-4d Religion

Traditional and conservative interpretations of the Bible reflect the patriarchal nature of family roles. The following passage reflects this bias:

> *Wives be subject to your husband, as to the Lord. . . . Husbands, love your wives, even as Christ also loved the church. (Ephesians 5:22–25) (See also Colossians 3:18–19)*

Although the Bible has been interpreted in both sexist and nonsexist terms, male dominance is indisputable in the hierarchy of religious organizations, where power and status have been accorded mostly to men. Until recently, only men could be priests, ministers, and rabbis. In addition, the Catholic Church does not have female clergy, and men dominate the top positions in the U.S. dioceses.

Male bias is also reflected in terminology used to refer to God in Jewish, Christian, and Islamic religions. For example, God is traditionally referred to as "He," "Father," "Lord," and "King." Two researchers observed that individuals who attend religious services frequently are more likely to have traditional gender role ideologies than individuals who do not attend church frequently (Willetts-Bloom & Nock, 1994).

Think About It 

In response to an interest in removing sexist language from religious works, hymns are being rewritten. The 1865 hymn "Rejoice, You Pure in Heart" no longer speaks of "strong men and maidens meek" but speaks of "strong souls and spirits meek." And "The Father, Son, and Holy Ghost" has been changed to "Praise God the Spirit, Holy Fire." How aware do you feel persons who sing hymns are of the sex bias of the words? Why?

5-4e Media

Media, such as movies, television, magazines, newspapers, books, and music, both reflect and shape gender roles. Media images of women and men typically conform to traditional gender stereotypes, and media portrayals depicting the exploitation, victimization, and sexual objectification of women are common. *Sex and the City*, produced by HBO, projects "Mr. Big" (the on-and-off-again love interest of Carrie) as cool and in control, while Carrie and her three girlfriends (Miranda, Samantha, and Charlotte) are continually frazzled about their relationships with men.

Even popular self-help books give advice to both genders to behave consistent with traditional gender socialization. Zimmerman, Holm, and Haddock (2000) conducted a content analysis of the four best-selling self-help books (including *Men Are from Mars, Women Are from Venus*, a 7 million-copy seller) and found that women are encouraged to define themselves in relationship to their male partners. Furthermore, readers were told that female independence and assertiveness might jeopardize relationships with their partners. The theme of what's important in life for women is also reflected in the best-seller *See Jane Date* by Melissa Senate (2001). This Harlequin romance novel targets young female readers.

5-5 EFFECTS OF GENDER ROLES ON RELATIONSHIPS AND SEXUALITY

Gender role socialization influences virtually every sphere of life, including self-concept, educational achievement, occupation, income, and health. Women and men learn their gender roles from the society and culture in which they are socialized. In sections 5-5a through 5-5d we look at gender roles in other societies as well as some racial/ethnic differences. We also look at the effects of traditional gender role socialization for women and men in U.S. society.

5-5a Gender Roles in Other Societies

Because gender roles are largely influenced by culture, it is clear that individuals reared in different societies typically display the gender role patterns of those societies. This section discusses how gender roles differ in the following contrasting countries/continents: China, Sweden, Japan, and Africa.

Gender Roles in China

Gender roles in traditional China were very unequal. "Being female was not highly valued. . . female infanticide was common. . .girls were sold to become servants, prostitutes, or concubines. . . marriage was seen as the 'purchase' of a woman. Traditional customs kept women segregated, uneducated, dependent, and subservient" (Engel, 1982). Due to industrialization and urbanization, gender roles are in flux.

Regarding gender role ideology, Chinese women today at Taiwan University express a preference for Chinese men who are "true gentlemen," well versed in Confucian tradition, which includes poetry, books, rituals, and music. A team of researchers examined the sex role attitudes of 665 Chinese college students and concluded, "it is likely that the ideal man in Chinese society has never been the 'macho type' as in the United States" (Chia et al., 1995, p. 28). It is also possible that Chinese women "have suffered so much under the past tyranny of men that they react very strongly against the masculine, dominant type" (p. 28).

Pimentel (2000) found that among urban Chinese couples, those spouses who evidenced an egalitarian outlook and who shared household responsibilities and decision making reported higher levels of marital happiness. And this was true of both women and men.

Gender Roles in Sweden

The Swedish government is strongly concerned with equality between women and men. In 1974 Sweden became the first country in the world to introduce a system that enables mothers and fathers to share parental leave (paid by the government) from their jobs in any way they choose. Furthermore, Swedish law states that employers may not penalize the career of a working parent because he or she has used parental rights. By encouraging fathers to participate more in child rearing, the government aims to provide more opportunities for women to pursue other roles. Women hold about a quarter of the seats in the Swedish Parliament. However, few Swedish women are in high-status positions in business, and governmental efforts to reduce gender inequality are weak compared with the power of tradition. Nevertheless, a comparison of Swedish and U.S. students revealed greater acceptance of gender egalitarianism (Weinberg, Lottes, & Shaver, 2000).

Gender Roles in Japan

In a study comparing 728 Japanese and 608 American families, Japanese husbands were more likely than American husbands to want wives to be responsible for housework, child discipline, and financial management. Japanese wives were more likely than American wives to want husbands to be responsible for recreation planning, employment outside the home, and maintaining relationships with relatives. Indeed, Japanese, compared with Americans, have or prefer more traditional or sex-typed divisions of labor and are less prone to idealize sharing of family tasks and responsibilities (Engel & Kimmons, 1992; Engel, 1982).

However, like families everywhere in the industrialized world, Japanese families are changing. Not only are more Japanese women participating in the workforce, fathers are permitted to take paid leave after the birth of their child. But tradition is strong as fathers fear that taking off because of their family "that they would miss the opportunity for promotion, that they might be forced to take a pay cut, or that they would be transferred overseas and thus separated from their families" (Ishii-Kuntz, 2000, p. 16).

Gender Roles in Africa

As with all gender roles in all societies, African gender roles are in flux. In the past, the kinship system superseded the husband-wife relationship so that in matrilineal systems the wife gave more attention to her mother's family, just as in patrilineal systems the opposite prevailed—the husband gave his energy/attention to his father's family. Even today, "the attachment between the spouses with its potentially high emotional involvement has to compete in the individual's sentimental life with wider attachments to other kin" (Aborampah, 1999, p. 135).

This muted intensity of the husband-wife relationship is also affected by polygynous marriages, which can be found in nearly all African societies (p. 130). In addition, the husband and wife typically reside in separate living quarters. The fact that the respective spouses also have different work roles and do not eat their meals together (the men eat with other men and the wives with their children and extended kin) further weakens the marital tie. Women are very disadvantaged economically because property and capital are passed down through various lineages largely controlled by men.

Meredith Kennedy (2000) has lived in Africa and makes the following observations of African gender roles:

> *The roles of men and women in most African societies tend to be very separate and proscribed, with most authority and power in the men's domain. For instance, Maasai wives of East Africa do not travel much, since when a husband comes home he expects to find his wife (or wives) waiting for him with a gourd of sour milk. If she is not, he has the right to beat her when she shows up. As attempts are made to soften these boundaries and equalize the roles, the impacts are very visible and cause a lot of reverberations throughout these communal societies. Many African women who believe in and desire better lives will not call themselves "feminists" for fear of social censure. Change for people whose lives are based on tradition and "fitting in" can be very traumatic.*

5-5b Racial/Ethnic Differences in the United States

Gender roles are also influenced by race and ethnicity.

African American Role Relationships

African American marriages are influenced by strong ties to one's parents and the larger kinship system. And, in many cases, the mother-child relationship seems to take precedence over the wife-husband relationship. "The consanguineal bond is often stronger than the marriage relationship. Marriages may end but blood ties last forever" (McAdoo, 1998, p. 370).

African American women have always been strong and independent. Forced to take charge of the family because of the father's absence as a result of separation during slavery or his lack of job opportunities in a White racist society, the African American woman has always worked outside the home. "The dominant cultural norm of women remaining in the home while men worked outside the home was never a practical reality for African-American families" (Greene, 1995, p. 31). Because African American women have historically had incomes and power in the marital relationship, it is not surprising that both husbands and wives are supportive of feminist ideology (Hunter & Sellers, 1998).

Mexican American Role Relationships

Hispanics are the fastest-growing segment of the U.S. population. Great variability exists among Mexican American marriages. What is true in one relationship may not be true in another, and the same relationship may not resemble itself at two different points in time. Nevertheless, some "typical" characteristics of Mexican American relationships are detailed here:

1. *Male dominance*. Although role relationships between women and men are changing in all segments of society, traditional role relationships between the Mexican American sexes are characterized by male domination. "Male dominance is the designation of the father as the head of the household, the major decision maker, and the absolute power holder in the Mexican-American family. In his absence, this power position reverts to the oldest son. All members of the household are expected to carry out the orders of the male head" (Becerra, 1998, p. 159).
2. *Female submissiveness*. The complement to the male authority figure in the Mexican American marriage is the submissive female partner. Traditionally, the Latina is subservient to her husband and devotes her time totally to the roles of homemaker and mother. As more wives begin to work outside the home, the nature of the Mexican American husband-wife relationship is becoming more egalitarian in terms of joint decision making and joint child rearing (Vega, 1991).

5-5c Traditional Socialization Effects on Women

> *Men are always hurrying heedlessly past the emotional nuances of a story in order to reach its point. Women prefer to linger over the state of their feelings, to risk everything they have in order to experience the romantically heightened moment.*
>
> —*Greta Garbo*

Traditional female gender role socialization affects women in various ways and to different degrees (as follows). The sexuality and relationships of some women may be more or less influenced by traditional gender role socialization, depending in part on whether the woman accepts or rejects traditional gender roles.

Body Image

The participation of young children in beauty pageants brings into cultural focus the degree to which even very young girls are socialized to emphasize beauty and appearance. For women of beauty, it can be a curse. Cybill Shepherd observed,

I always knew that the power I gleaned from beauty dwarfed any other kind of achievement. No matter how hard I worked, I was credited only with the one thing that was effortless. The looks I was born with meant that I never lacked sexual partners but also meant that I could rarely discern who really cared about me. (Shepherd, 2000, p. 11)

In contrast, the effect for many women who do not match the cultural ideal is to have a negative body image. In a survey of body image, 56% of women, in contrast to 43% of men, reported dissatisfaction with their body (Garner, 1997). Women who felt unattractive reported that negative feelings about their body had a negative effect on their desire for sex (Garner, 1997). Women are also more likely than men to have eating disorders and to report going on diets. In regard to the latter, 96% of college women in a nonrandom sample reported dieting, in contrast to 59% of college men (Elliott & Brantley, 1997). In the United States we spend $33 billion annually on diets, $30 billion on cosmetics, and $1.5 billion on cosmetic surgery (80–90% of the purchasers are women) (Rhode, 1997). Greta Garbo, the actress and beauty of film in the 1920s–1930s, noted the futility of maintaining a youthful body. She said in her later years, "After my bath each day I examined my naked body in the mirror, and every day I noticed new wrinkles. So I underwent massages, dieted, and performed strenuous gymnastics to hold off old age. But I was not successful" (Gronowicz, 1990, p. 423) .

CULTURAL DIVERSITY 

Dissatisfaction with one's body image is not unique to American women. In their study of 305 Chinese college students, Tang, Lai, Phil, and Chung (1997) found that women were significantly more likely to have negative body images than men. They also found that having a better body image was related to being more sexually active.

Sexual Thoughts/Desire

Women report thinking about sex less often than men. Nineteen percent of women, in contrast to 54% of men, in a national sample reported thinking about sex "every day" or "several times a day" (Michael, Gagnon, Laumann, & Kolata, 1994). Women are also less likely to have sexual fantasies (Hsu et al., 1994) and be interested in watching erotica (Purnine, Carey, & Jorgensen, 1994). In effect, it is more socially acceptable for men in our society to express interest in sex, to fantasize about it, and to watch erotica. In terms of desire, 2.6% of a national sample of women, in contrast to 11.9% of men, reported that their first sex (if wanted) was based on the desire for physical pleasure (Mahay, Lauman, & Michaels, 2001).

Masturbation

Women are less likely to report masturbation than men. Among Americans aged 18–59, about 40% of women and 60% of men reported having masturbated in the previous 12 months (Michael et al., 1994). Traditional female socialization has taught women that it is "dirty" to touch themselves "down there."

CULTURAL DIVERSITY 

Tang et al. (1997) reported that twice as many Chinese college men reported having masturbated than college women (44 vs. 21%).

Perception of Genitals

Women have more negative perceptions of their own and their partners' genitals than men (Reinholtz & Muehlenhard, 1995).

Love and Sexuality

In a national sample of interviews with 1,669 women and 3,321 men, 27% of the women, in contrast to 47% of the men, reported ever having had casual sex (Cubbins & Tanfer, 2000). Women are more likely than men to require love as the context for sexual expression, to be absolutist in sexual values, and not to be hedonistic (Knox, Cooper, & Zusman, 2001). Indeed, a team of researchers (Browning, Hatfield, Kessler & Levine, 2001) analyzed the sexual motives of 256 undergraduates and found that "the 'Love motive' was endorsed more and the 'Pleasure motive' endorsed less by women than men" (p. 148).

Sexual Guilt

Women, when compared to men, report more sexual guilt over masturbation (Davidson & Moore, 1994) and first intercourse (Sprecher, Barbee, & Schwartz, 1995). One source of this guilt is religion, which acts as a mechanism of social control. That women have greater exposure to religion was documented by Cubbins and Tanfer (2000) who found that 44.3% of 1,669 women, in contrast to 36.4% of 3,321 men, in their national sample reported attending church one or more times a month.

Orgasm

Women are less likely than men to experience orgasm. This is particularly true at first intercourse. Seven percent of women, in contrast to 79% of men, reported orgasm during their first intercourse experience (Sprecher et al., 1995). Lower orgasmic frequency is not only related to sexual technique (less contact with the clitoris), but also to traditional female role socialization that discourages women from seeking sexual pleasure.

Age of Partners

Women are more likely than men to be sexually involved with partners older than themselves. Traditional cultural norms suggest that it is more acceptable for women to date and marry men who are older than it is for men to date and marry women who are older.

Sometimes the age discrepancy between the woman and her partner is dramatic. Some celebrities are a substantial number of years older than their spouses, including Tony Randall, who is 50 years older; Tony Bennett, who is 40 years older; and Johnny Carson, who is 26 years older. Women report that financial security, maturity, and dependability are the primary advantages of involvement with an older man (Knox, Britton, & Crisp, 1997).

Number of Partners

Women report having fewer sexual partners than men. In a national sample of interviews with 1,669 women, the mean total number of partners with whom they reported having had vaginal intercourse was 6.7; the mean total number of partners reported by 3,321 men was 13.6 (Cubbins & Tanfer, 2000). When the number of sexual partners in the past 12 months is the variable under consideration, 5.1% of men in a national sample compared to 1.7% of women in a national sample had five or more sexual partners (Laumann & Michael, 2001). Traditional female role socialization teaches women to limit the number of sexual partners so they will not be perceived as being "loose" or immoral.

CULTURAL DIVERSITY

In many traditional societies reflecting the Islamic faith, women are expected to have only one sexual partner (their husband) during their lifetime.

Economic Dependency

Although women are more economically independent today than in previous generations, many women are still dependent on their husband's income. Therefore, some women may stay with a male partner out of economic need. Although women earn slightly more than half of all bachelor's and master's degrees, they earn fewer advanced degrees beyond the master's degree than do men. For the year 2000, women earned 44% of the Ph.D.s (National Opinion Research Center, 2001). Even when women and men have equivalent academic degrees, women still earn about two thirds of what men earn. For example, the average earnings of a 25- to 34-year-old male and female college-educated person working full-time are $59,482 and $42,330, respectively (*Statistical Abstract of the United States: 2002*, Table 666). However, in lesbian couples, the extent to which financial resources affect the balance of power in the relationship is unclear; studies have yielded mixed results (Patterson, 2000).

Initiation of Relationships

As noted earlier, recent data confirm that traditional dating scripts are still operative, with women tending to wait for the man to initiate a relationship (Laner & Ventrone, 2000). Women have not been socialized to be aggressive in pursuing a new relationship. After an interaction has occurred, the woman may be aggressive in escalating the relationship.

Resentment and Anger in Sexual Relationships

Women who are socialized to accept that they are solely responsible for taking care of their aging parents, their young children, and their husbands are likely to experience role overload. Ross and Van Willigen (1996) noted that women report higher levels of anger than men because of the inequities in child care and household responsibilities. Both role overload and a perception of inequities may result in feelings of anger and resentment toward the partner and impact her sexual feelings or responsiveness to him.

Nonegalitarian Relationships

Egalitarian relationships Relationships in which the partners relate to each other as equals.

Egalitarian relationships are those in which partners relate to each other as equals. Although most women might be happier in relationships that are egalitarian, many tolerate nonegalitarian relationships because they have been influenced by traditional gender role socialization that is based on the idea that husbands are dominant in the family. Many women defer to their husbands or male partners because they have been taught to view men as more competent. Women also may resign themselves to inequality in order to avoid conflict.

5-5d Traditional Socialization Effects on Men

Men tend to be human doings rather than human beings.

—Warren Farrell, father's rights advocate

Men are also affected by their socialization in the following ways:

Less Emotional Intimacy

In general, men are socialized to restrict emotional experience and expression. Men are less emotional than women because traditional male socialization teaches that being emotional is not "manly"; it is a sign of weakness. One of Pollack's (2001) adolescent interviewees noted, "It [crying] comes off as physically weak. You just don't amount to much as a guy if you cry in front of others. When I get upset about things, I usually just go to my room and isolate myself" (p. 7). In addition, men are taught to believe that task accomplishment is an important goal and that emotional control is one general strategy for facilitating that goal. Men who restrict their emotional experience and expression limit their opportunity to discover the rewards of emotional intimacy.

Performance Anxiety

Birch (2000) emphasized that men are concerned about their sexual performance. Two researchers compared 119 men and 56 women on an array of sexual concerns and found that men were significantly more concerned about sexual performance than women (Cowden & Koch, 1995). Given that men are socialized to be concerned about penis size (Lee, 1996) and being positively perceived in the bedroom, this finding is not surprising.

Restriction of Potential Partners

Heterosexual men who focus on cultural definitions of female beauty overlook potential partners who may be compatible emotional and sexual life companions. In section 5-3a on sociobiology, we also noted that heterosexual men also tend to seek younger women. Indeed, Silverthorne and Quinsey (2000) asked 192 adults to express their age preferences for a preferred partner. Both heterosexual (and homosexual) men preferred younger partners. Focusing on younger women eliminates a large pool of potential partners closer to the men's ages.

Sexual Aggression and Coercion

Men are more likely than women to engage in sexually aggressive and coercive behavior. Hence, women are more likely than men to be victims of sexual aggression and coercion. Twenty-two percent of adult women in a national sample, in contrast to 2% of the men, reported being forced to do something sexual at some time in their lives (Michael et al., 1994). Women who were raped during a date identified the primary reason for the rape as sexual satisfaction: "He just wanted to get laid" (Lloyd & Emery, 2000, p. 96).

Purchase of Sex

Men are more likely than women to buy erotic material, purchase sexual services (such as phone sex), and view sex sites on the Internet. Forty-one percent of adult men and 16% of adult women in a national sample reported spending money on erotic material (X-rated videos, sex magazines, sex phone numbers, etc.) in the past 12 months (Michael et al., 1994). Among 191 undergraduates, men were significantly more likely to visit an Internet sex site than women (Knox, Daniels, Sturdivant & Zusman, 2001).

Lack of Domestic Skills

Men have traditionally learned that their role in the family is to be the primary breadwinner and that women take care of the children, prepare food, and perform household chores. Lack of domestic participation among men may create unhappiness in their partners, who feel unfairly burdened with household and child care responsibilities.

Although sometimes people assume that in same-sex couples one partner plays the "male" role and the other partner the "female" role, a number of research studies have shown that this is rarely the arrangement. Lesbian and gay couples are more likely to share domestic tasks equally; this is also the pattern for gay or lesbian couples raising children. (Patterson, 2000).

Involvement in Group Sex

Thirteen percent of a national sample of men ages 18–59 (in contrast to 1% of women the same age) reported that group sex was "very" appealing to them (Laumann & Michael, 2001). In terms of actual behavior, 13% of men and 10% of women in a nonrandom sample of 2,000 college students reported having engaged in a threesome (Elliott & Brantley, 1997). A much lower percentage (2%) of group sex was reported by a sample of 191 undergraduates studied by Browning et al. (2000).

5-5e Sexual Double Standard

Men are more likely than women to believe in the sexual double standard. By completing the Sexual Double Standard Scale in Box 5-2, you can measure the degree to which you have identical or different sexual standards for women and men.

In effect, traditional gender role socialization may have negative outcomes for the sexuality and intimate relationships of women and men. In an address to the XIII International AIDS Conference in Durban, South Africa in July of 2000, Dr. Geet Gupta identified ways that researchers from around the world have found that unequal gender balance in heterosexual relationships increases the risk of vulnerability to HIV. As women's sexual autonomy is curtailed, their risk is increased in the following ways. A culture of silence that dictates that "good" women are sexually ignorant keeps them uninformed about risk reduction. An emphasis on virginity may make girls afraid to seek information, fearing they will be thought to be sexually active. If sexually active, they may be

Box 5-2 Self-Assessment

INTERACTIVE BOX

Sexual Double Standard Scale

Rank each statement according to the following scale:

0—Disagree strongly 1—Disagree mildly 2—Agree mildly 3—Agree strongly

___ 1. It's worse for a woman to sleep around than it is for a man.
___ 2. It's best for a guy to lose his virginity before he's out of his teens.
___ 3. It's OK for a woman to have more than one sexual relationship at the same time.
___ 4. It is just as important for a man to be a virgin when he marries as it is for a woman.
___ 5. I approve of a 16-year-old girl's having sex just as much as a 16-year-old boy's having sex.
___ 6. I kind of admire a girl who has had sex with a lot of guys.
___ 7. I kind of feel sorry for a 21-year-old woman who is still a virgin.
___ 8. A woman's having casual sex is just as acceptable to me as a man's having casual sex.
___ 9. It's okay for a man to have sex with a woman with whom he is not in love.
___ 10. I kind of admire a guy who has had sex with a lot of girls.
___ 11. A woman who initiates sex is too aggressive.
___ 12. It's okay for a man to have more than one sexual relationship at the same time.
___ 13. I question the character of a woman who has had a lot of sexual partners.
___ 14. I admire a man who is a virgin when he gets married.
___ 15. A man should be more sexually experienced than his wife.
___ 16. A girl who has sex on the first date is "easy."
___ 17. I kind of feel sorry for a 21-year-old man who is still a virgin.
___ 18. I question the character of a guy who has had a lot of sexual partners.
___ 19. Women are naturally more monogamous (inclined to stick with one partner) than are men.
___ 20. A man should be sexually experienced when he gets married.
___ 21. A guy who has sex on the first date is "easy."
___ 22. It's okay for a woman to have sex with a man she is not in love with.
___ 23. A woman should be sexually experienced when she gets married.
___ 24. It's best for a girl to lose her virginity before she's out of her teens.
___ 25. I admire a woman who is a virgin when she gets married.
___ 26. A man who initiates sex is too aggressive.

Scoring: The scoring involves adding the scores of three items, reverse scoring three items, and adding difference scores between other items, as listed:

Total = #1 + #15 + #19 + (3 – #4) + (3 – #5) + (3 – #8) + (#2 – #24) + (#12 – #3) + (#10 – #6) + (#17 – #7) + (#9 – #22) + (#11 – #26) + (#13 – #18) + (#25 – #14) + (#16 – #21) + (#20 – #23).

Interpreting your score: A score of 0 indicates identical sexual standards for women and men. Scores greater than 0 reflect more restrictive standards for women than for men; the highest possible score is 48. Scores less than 0 reflect more restrictive standards for men than for women; the lowest possible score is –30. In a study of students from Texas A&M University, the men's mean score was 13.15 (n = 255), and the women's mean was 11.99 (n = 461) (Muehlenhard & Quackenbush, 1988). (When used in a research study, the title would not be at the top of the scale!) When asked to rate their partner's acceptance of the sexual double standard, female students rated their partners as more accepting of it than the women rated themselves. In fact, the women believed that men

reluctant to seek treatment for sexually transmitted diseases. Virgins in high prevalence countries may be especially at risk of rape due to false beliefs that sex with a virgin can cleanse a man who is infected. To preserve virginity, girls may engage in risky behaviors such as anal sex. Economic dependency increases the risk of engaging in sexual behavior for pay and of not leaving a dangerous relationship. Finally, violence against women is a factor in several ways, including making it risky for a woman to negotiate condom use or discuss fidelity with her partner (Gupta, 2001).

The greater power of men and increased sexual freedom increase their risk to HIV exposure as well. The expectation that men will be knowledgeable and experienced in sex decreases their likelihood of seeking information and increases their engaging in experiences to prove their manhood. The belief that it is essential to men's nature to seek many partners may interfere with fidelity. Masculine norms that prescribe sexual domination of women increase homonegativity and increase denial and secrecy regarding having sex with men. Socialization to deny vulnerability and to engage in risk-taking also increases the danger of potential infection. A national survey of 15- to 19-year-old men in the

adhere to the double standard even more than the men reported (Muehlenhard & McCoy, 1991).

Source: Muehlenhard, C. L., & Quackenbush, D. M. (1998). Sexual Double Standard Scale. In C. M. Davis, W. L. Yarber, R. Bauserman, G. Schreer, & S. L. Davis (Eds.), *Handbook of sexuality-related measures* (pp. 186–188). Thousand Oaks, CA: Sage. Reprinted by permission of the authors.

Reliability and validity: Muehlenhard and Quackenbush (cited in Muehlenhard & McCoy, 1991) reported a coefficient alpha of 0.726 for women's reports of their own acceptance of the sexual double standard and 0.817 for their ratings of their partners' beliefs. Correlations of the measure with other variables (traditional gender roles, erotophobia-erotophilia, self-monitoring) have been in the predicted directions.

In their study of 403 female general psychology students at the University of Kansas, Muehlenhard and McCoy (1991) examined the relationship between women's acceptance of the double standard (and their rating of their partners' acceptance) with the women's willingness to acknowledge their desire for sexual intercourse. The women were asked if they had ever been in the following situation:

> You were with a guy you'd *never* had sexual intercourse with before. He wanted to engage in sexual intercourse and you wanted to also, but for some reason you indicated that you didn't want to, although *you had every intention to and were willing to engage in sexual intercourse*. In other words, you indicated "no" and meant "yes." (p. 451)

They were also presented with a scenario in which they had wanted to engage in intercourse and "made it clear to the guy that you wanted to have sexual intercourse" (p. 452) and were asked if they had ever been in that situation. The women completed the Sexual Double Standard Scale (self and inferences about partner), the Attitudes Toward Women Scale, the Sexual Opinion Survey, and the Self-Monitoring Scale. Of these five variables, only the women's beliefs about their partner's acceptance of the double standard predicted whether the women had ever said "no" when they meant "yes" (scripted refusal) or said "yes" and meant "yes" (open acknowledgment). The researchers found that "women who had offered scripted refusals were more likely to believe that their partners accepted the sexual double standard than women who had openly acknowledged their desire for sexual intercourse" (p. 457).

Muehlenhard and McCoy observed that the sexual double standard puts women in a double bind. If they are open about their sexual desires, they risk being negatively labeled. So, is the safest (for one's reputation) course of action to be reluctant to acknowledge wanting to have sex? Muehlenhard and McCoy suggested that the sexual double standard could be decreased by pointing out its unfairness to both men and women. Men may feel pressured to push for sex whether or not they desire it (and whether or not they have a willing partner).

The majority of women had never engaged in scripted refusal (and those who had, reported doing so infrequently). Muehlenhard and McCoy emphasized that men should always take a "no" at face value. This may be even better advice in view of recent information obtained by Muehlenhard and her colleagues. Although these researchers thought the scenario for scripted refusal was clearly indicating a situation in which the woman wanted to have sex, more recent examples from women asked to describe the situation reflect *ambivalence* about having sex more than *willingness*. The situations that were described often indicated that the respondents had misinterpreted the researchers' questions. The number of respondents who engaged in "token resistance" (as evaluated by trained raters)—only 2 to 14% of women and 2 to 10% of men—was much smaller than the 35% indicated in previous studies (Rodgers & Muehlenhard, 1992). Therefore, despite the sexual double standard and stereotypes about women offering token resistance to intercourse, for the vast majority of men and women "no" really does mean "NO!"

References

Muehlenhard, C. L., & McCoy, M. (1991). Double standard/double bind: The sexual double standard and women's communication about sex. *Psychology of Women Quarterly, 15*, 447–461.

Muehlenhard, C. L., & Quackenbush, D. M. (1988). Can the Sexual Double Standard Put Women at Risk for Sexually Transmitted Disease? The Role of the Double Standard in Condom Use Among Women. From a paper presented at an annual Society for the Scientific Study of Sexuality (SSSS) meeting in San Francisco.

Rogers, C., & Muehlenhard, C. L. (1992). Token resistance: *New perspectives on an old stereotype*. Unpublished manuscript.

United States found greater reported substance use, violence, and unsafe sexual practices among young men who subscribed to traditional view of manhood (Gupta, 2001).

To combat these barriers of gender and sexual inequality, Gupta recommended beginning with recognition and public discussion of how the HIV epidemic is fueled by power imbalance in gender and sexuality. Dr. Gupta questioned the use of a macho image to sell condoms and recommended the importance of male role models who behave in gender-equitable ways. Empowering women can be done without disempowering men, and in accordance with the values of multiculturalism and diversity. The address ended with an urgent charge:

> *Gender roles that disempower women and give men a false sense of power are killing our young and our women and men in their most productive years. This must change. (Gupta, 2001, p.11)*

Individuals should be aware of the potential effects of their socialization and make deliberate choices to their benefit.

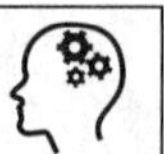

Think About It

How has your own gender socialization influenced your vulnerability to risky sexual choices or outcomes?

5-6 ANDROGYNY, GENDER ROLE TRANSCENDENCE, AND GENDER POSTMODERNISM

The perception of and tolerance for diversity of gender are changing. In sections 5-6a through 5-6c, we look at a wider range of behavior than traditional stereotypical roles of men and women.

5-6a Androgyny

Androgyny Having traits stereotypically associated with both masculinity and femininity.

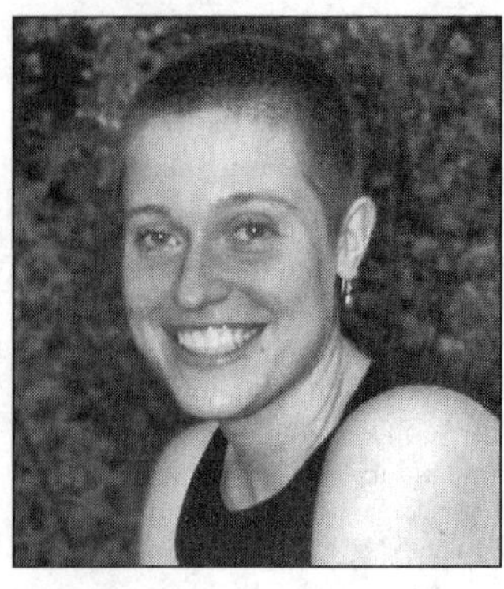

This woman shaved her head and said, "People aren't sure what I am until they get up close."

Androgyny refers to a blend of traits that are stereotypically associated with masculinity and femininity. Androgyny may also imply flexibility of traits; for example, an androgynous individual may be emotional in one situation, logical in another, assertive in another, and so forth. Ward (2001) classified 311 (159 male and 152 female) undergraduates at the National University of Singapore as androgynous (33.8% men and 16.0% women), feminine (11.0% men and 39.6% women), masculine (35.7% men and 13.9% women), and undifferentiated (19.5% men and 30.6% women). For men, masculinity and androgyny were associated with self-acceptance and psychological well-being. For women, masculinity and androgyny were associated with self-acceptance only. Neither masculinity nor androgyny was associated with psychological well-being. Stake (2000) analyzed data on interviews of 106 males and 197 females at a commuter college and found that the capacity to respond androgynously (not be rigid but be both instrumental as well as expressive) when coping skills were required was associated with positive mental health benefits.

Ward (2001) noted the problems with previous research on androgyny, specifically, the presumed relatively greater desirability of the masculine versus feminine traits. Feminine traits were, on the whole, evaluated as less desirable than masculine qualities. Some researchers suggested this bias was a cultural bias of male dominance.

5-6b Gender Role Transcendence

Gender role transcendence The abandonment of gender schema, or becoming "gender aschematic" so that personality traits, social and occupational roles, and other aspects of an individual's life become divorced from gender categories.

As noted earlier, we tend to impose a gender-based classification system on the world. Thus, we associate many aspects of our world, including colors, foods, social and occupational roles, and personality traits, with either masculinity or femininity. The concept of **gender role transcendence** involves abandoning gender schema or becoming "gender aschematic" (Bem, 1983) so that personality traits, social and occupational roles, and other aspects of our life become divorced from gender categories.

One way to transcend gender roles is to be reared that way because gender schema develop at an early age. For example, parents can attempt to foster non-sex-typed functioning in their children by encouraging emotional expression and independence in both boys and girls. Parents can also de-emphasize the importance of gender in children's lives with respect to choosing clothes, toys, colors, and activities. Even though many individuals may move toward gender role transcendence as they reach and pass middle age, few if any individuals completely reach this stage. As long as gender stereotypes and gender inequalities are ingrained in our social and cultural ideologies and institutions, gender role transcendence will remain unrealized.

5-6c Gender Postmodernism

Monro (2000) predicted a new era of **gender postmodernism** whereby there would be a dissolution of male and female categories as currently conceptualized in Western capitalist society. In essence, people would no longer be categorized as male or female but be recognized as capable of many identities. . . "a third-sex" (p. 37). A new conceptualization of "trans" people would call for new social structures "based on the principles of equality, diversity and the right to self determination" (p. 42). No longer would our society reflect transphobia but embrace pluralization "as an indication of social evolution, allowing greater choice and means of self-expression concerning gender" (p. 42).

Gender postmodernism A state where there is a dissolution of male and female categories as currently conceptualized in Western capitalist society.

However, Miller (2000) emphasized that a movement away from a dimorphic sex classification is not likely to take hold because "the predominant worldview revolves around the existence of two sexes. The first thing parents want to hear from the obstetrician after birth is 'it's a boy' or 'it's a girl.' Legally, every adult is either male or female. Although it might be a bit dramatic to drop the two-sex model, the existence of individuals who fall outside the two current gender identities deserves some thought" (p. 152).

American psychology has been preoccupied with the study of sex differences; theorists have alternately offered ideas and research support for maximizing or minimizing the differences. Rather than persist in debating whether these differences exist, or how great they are, those taking postmodern positions are likely to be asking different questions:

> *What does gender mean? How is the very concept of gender socially constructed? What does gender do? How does it operate—as a construct rather than as a trait—to structure identities and social relations? What functions does it serve? For whom? (Bohan, 2002, p.78)*

Kessler (1990, p. 131), a psychology professor and scholar in gender studies, suggested, "We need to consider different possibilities about how to manage intersexuality, including the possibility of not managing it at all." She suggested that it might be useful to avoid using the terms *hermaphrodite* or *intersex* altogether because they are so emotionally loaded. She notes that people are capable of accepting genital variation. Even maintaining the two gender system, being more accepting of such variation can weaken the force of genital appearance in labeling gender and soften the power of gender to define lives.

Think About It

The transgender movement can liberate our society from seeing gender as either male or female and transcend the "us versus them" paradigm. Leslie Feinberg recommends seeing gender not as "two poles with a raging void in between" but a circle that has "room in it for each person to explore and move on that circle throughout their lives" (Bockting, 1999, p. 7). Which demographic groups do you think will be more accepting of this new paradigm?

SUMMARY

Women and men have different biological makeups and socializations that influence differences in their sexuality.

Terminology

Sex refers to the biological distinction between females and males, whereas *gender* refers to the social and psychological characteristics often associated with being female or male. For example, characteristics typically associated with the female gender include being gentle, emotional, and cooperative; characteristics associated with the male gender include being aggressive, rational, and competitive. Other terminology related to sex and gender include *gender identity* (psychological view of one's self as a man or a woman), *transgendered* (broad term describing persons of one biological sex displaying behavior typically associated with the other sex), *gender role* (behavior associated with being defined as male or female), *sexual identity* (broad term including one's being a man or woman and one's sexual orientation), and *gender role ideology* (the role relationship between women and men).

Biological Beginnings

The biological sex of an individual is determined by chromosomes (XX for female; XY for male), gonads (ovaries for female; testes for male), hormones (greater proportion of estrogen and progesterone than testosterone in the female; greater proportion of testosterone than estrogen and progesterone in the male), internal sex organs (Fallopian tubes, uterus, and vagina for female; epididymis, vas deferens, and seminal vesicles for male) and external genitals (vulva for female; penis and scrotum for male).

Theories of Gender Role Development

Sociobiology emphasizes biological sources of social behavior, such as sexual aggression on the part of males due to higher levels of testosterone. Identification theory focuses on the influence of the same-sex parent when children are learning gender roles. Social learning theory discusses how children are rewarded and punished for expressing various gender role behaviors. Cognitive-developmental theorists are concerned with the developmental ages at which children are capable of learning social roles. Gender schema theory combines the cognitive-developmental theory and the social learning theory to form a more recent view of development. Specifically, gender schema influences how an individual processes information by structuring and organizing perception. Persons using a highly sex-typed schema see a wide variety of human characteristics, behavior, roles, and jobs as decidedly masculine or feminine and evaluate themselves and others according to how well they conform to gender norms and stereotypes.

Agents of Socialization

Parents, peers, teachers and educational materials, religion, and the media project and encourage traditional gender roles for women and men. The cumulative effect is the perpetuation of gender stereotypes. Each agent of socialization reinforces gender roles that are learned from other agents of socialization, thereby creating a gender role system that is deeply embedded in our culture.

Effects of Gender Role Socialization on Relationships and Sexuality

Traditional gender socialization as a woman is associated (compared to that of socialization as a man) with negative body image, fewer sexual thoughts, lower masturbation frequency, negative perception of genitals, preference for love as context of sex, lower frequency of orgasm, older partners, fewer partners, economic dependence on men, low frequency of initiating relationships, resentment/anger in sexual relationships, and greater likelihood of involvement in nonegalitarian relationships. Traditional gender socialization as a man is associated (compared to that of socialization as a woman) with less emotional intimacy, performance anxiety, restriction of potential partners, sexual aggression and coercion, purchase of sex, lack of domestic skills, involvement in group sex, and sexual double standard.

Androgyny, Gender Role Transcendence, and Gender Postmodernism

Androgyny refers to a blend of traits that are stereotypically associated with masculinity and femininity. Androgyny may also imply flexibility of traits; for example, an androgynous individual may be emotional in one situation, logical in another, assertive in another, and so forth. Gender role transcendence involves abandoning gender schema so that personality traits, social and occupational roles, and other aspects of life are not viewed as "masculine" or "feminine." Gender postmodernism predicts a new era in which people are no longer characterized as male or female but will be recognized as capable of many identities.

SUGGESTED WEBSITES

Note: These websites were functional when we went to press. Please access the online text for the most up-to-date URLs.

American Assembly for Men in Nursing
http://www.aamn.org

At-home Dad Newsletter
http://www.athomedad.net

Genetics and IVF Institute
http://www.givf.com/

Transgender Forum
http://www.tgforum.com

Tri-Ess: Society for the Second Self
http://www.tri-ess.com/

Female-to-Male Transsexuals
http://www.ftm-intl.org/

Why Men Are?
http://www.whymenare.com

KEY TERMS

amniocentesis (p. 143)
androgen-insensitivity syndrome (AIS) (p. 147)
androgenital syndrome (p. 196)
androgyny (p. 162)
chromosomes (p. 142)
Congenital Adrenal Hyperplasia (CAH) (p. 146)
cross-dresser (p. 138)
egalitarian relationships (p. 158)
Electra complex (p. 149)
family balancing (p. 143)
female pseudohermaphrodites (p. 146)
fetally androgynized females (p. 146)
gender (p. 136)
gender dysphoria (p. 138)
gender identity (p. 138)
gender postmodernism (p. 163)
gender roles (p. 140)
gender role ideology (p. 141)
gender role transcendence (p. 162)
gender schema theory (p. 150)
hermaphroditism (p. 146)
intersexed infants (p. 147)
Klinefelter's syndrome (p. 144)
male pseudohermaphrodites (p. 147)
occupational sex segregation (p. 141)
Oedipal complex (p. 149)
parental investment (p. 148)
preconceptual sex selection (p. 143)
prenatal sex selection (p. 143)
primary sex characteristics (p. 136)
pseudohermaphroditism (p. 146)
reductase-deficient males (p. 147)
secondary sex characteristics (p. 136)
sex (p. 136)
sex roles (p. 140)
sexual identity (p. 141)
sociobiology (p. 147)
testicular feminization syndrome (TFS) (p. 146)
transgenderist (p. 140)
transsexuals (p. 139)
transvestites (p. 139)
Turner's syndrome (p. 144)

CHAPTER QUIZ

1. The words *sex* and *gender* __________ the same thing.
   a. mean
   b. do not mean

2. According to biologist Anne Fausto-Sterling (1998), how many sexes are there?
   a. one
   b. two
   c. five
   d. an infinite number

3. To be classified as a transsexual, a person must have surgery and/or take hormones.
   a. True
   b. False

4. Which of the following individuals is most likely to think, "I am a woman trapped in a man's body"?
   a. Carl, a transvestite
   b. David, a transsexual
   c. Henry, a gay man
   d. Paul, a cross-dresser

5. Which of the following is a sex role?
   a. sperm donor
   b. baseball player
   c. auto mechanic
   d. construction worker

6. Although the stereotypical image of a nurse is a woman, in 1998, nearly half of nurses in the United States were men.
   a. True
   b. False
7. According to the *Human Development Report* (1997), ________ treat(s) women as well as men.
   a. most European societies
   b. Asian societies
   c. many tribal African societies
   d. no society
8. Compared to females, males have a greater proportion of which of the following?
   a. testosterone
   b. estrogen
   c. progesterone
   d. all the above
9. How does the boy resolve the Oedipal complex?
   a. by losing his virginity
   b. by becoming emotionally distant from his father
   c. by identifying with his father and becoming like him
   d. by repressing his sexual urges
10. Which of the following theories of gender role development emphasizes reward and punishment?
    a. social learning theory
    b. cognitive-developmental theory
    c. identification theory
    d. gender schema theory
11. According to Kohlberg, at what age does a child view gender as permanent?
    a. about 12 to 18 months
    b. 3 to 4 years old
    c. 6 or 7 years old
    d. at puberty
12. The Catholic Church has the most female clergy of any religion.
    a. True
    b. False
13. In a survey of body image (Garner, 1997), more than half of the ____________ reported dissatisfaction with their body.
    a. women
    b. men
    c. women and men
    d. none of the above
14. According to research based on a national sample (Michael et al., 1994), women think about sex
    a. as often as men do.
    b. more often than men do.
    c. less often than men do.
15. Egalitarian relationships are those
    a. that are based on traditional gender roles.
    b. that involve two people of the same sex.
    c. in which partners take turns being dominant in the relationship.
    d. in which partners relate to each other as equals.
16. Men are more likely than women to do which of the following?
    a. buy erotic material
    b. purchase sexual services (such as phone sex)
    c. view sex sites on the Internet.
    d. all the above

REFERENCES

Aborampah, O. (1999). Systems of kinship and marriage in Africa: Continuities and change. In S. L. Browning & R. R. Miller (Eds.), *Till death do us part: A multicultural anthology on marriage* (pp. 123–128). Stamford, CT: JAI Press.

Alcock, J. (2001). *The triumph of sociobiology*. New York: Oxford University Press.

Becerra, R. M. (1998). The Mexican American family. In C. H. Mindel, R. W. Habenstein, & R. Wright (Eds.), *Ethnic families in America: Patterns and variations* (4th ed.) (pp. 141–159). Upper Saddle River, NJ: Prentice-Hall.

Bem, S. (1983). Gender schema theory and its implications for child development: Raising genderaschematic children in a gender-schematic society. *Signs*, 8, 596–616.

Birch, R. W. (2000). *Sex and the aging male*. Howard, Ohio: PEC Publishing Company.

Bockting, W. O. (1999). From construction to context: Gender through the eyes of the transgendered. *SIECUS Report, 28*, 3–7.

Bohan, J. S. (2002). Sex differences and/in the self: Classic themes, feminist variations, postmodern challenges. *Psychology of Women Quarterly*, 26, 74–88.

Browning, J. R., Hatfield, E., Kessler, D., & Levine, T. (2001). Sexual motives, gender, and sexual behavior. *Archives of Sexual Behavior*, 29, 135–152.

Buss, D. M. (1989). Sex differences in human mate preferences: Evolutionary hypotheses tested in 37 cultures. *Behavioral and Brain Sciences, 12*, 1–13.

Chafetz, J. S. (1988). *Feminist sociology: An overview of contemporary theories*. Itasca, IL: E. E. Peacock.

Chia, R. C., Allred, L., Hall, C., Wuensch, K., Cheng, B., Ren, J. J., & Janousk, J. (1995, July). Cross-cultural comparisons in attitude toward women. Paper presented at the International Council of Psychologists, Taipei, Taiwan.

Colapinto, J. (2000). *As nature made him: The boy who was raised as a girl*. New York: Harper Collins.

Cole, C. M., O'Boyle, M., Emory, L. E., & Meyer, W. J. (1997). Comorbidity of gender dysphoria and other major psychiatric diagnoses. *Archives of Sexual Behavior*, 26, 13–26.

Cowden, C. R., & Koch, P. B. (1995). Attitudes related to sexual concerns: Gender and orientation comparisons. *Journal of Sex Education and Therapy*, *21*, 78–87.

Cubbins, L. A., & Tanfer, K. (2000). The influence of gender on sex: A study of men's and women's self-reported high-risk sex behavior. *Archives of Sexual Behavior, 29,* 229–256.

Davidson, J. K., & Moore, N. B. (1994). Masturbation and premarital sexual intercourse among college women: Making choices for sexual fulfillment. *Journal of Sex and Marital Therapy, 20,* 178–199.

Diamond, M., & Sigmundson, H. K. (1997). Sex reassignment at birth. *Archives of Pediatric Adolescent Medicine, 151,* 298–304.

Doctor, R. F., & Fleming, J. S. (2001). Measures of transgender behavior. *Archives of Sexual Behavior, 30,* 255–267.

Elliott, L., & Brantley, C. (1997). *Sex on campus: The naked truth about the real sex lives of college students.* New York: Random House.

Engel, J. W. (1982). Changes in male-female relationships and family life in People's Republic of China. Research Series 014. College of Tropical Agriculture and Human Resources, University of Hawaii.

Engel, J. W., & Kimmons, L. (1992). Division of labor in Japanese and American families. Paper presented at the 54th Annual Conference of the National Council on Family Relations, Orlando, FL.

Etaugh, C., & Duits, T. (1990). Development of gender discrimination: Role of stereotypic and counterstereotypic gender cues. *Sex Roles, 23,* 215–222.

Ethicist: Choosing baby's gender from embryos is OK. (2001, September 29). *The Daily Reflector,* Greenville, NC.

Fausto-Sterling, A. (1998). The five sexes: Why male and female are not enough. In B. M. Clinchy & J. K. Norem (Eds.), *The gender and psychology reader* (pp. 221–227). NY: New York University Press.

Freud, S. (1965). New introductory lectures in psychoanalysis (J. Strachey, Ed. and Trans.). New York: W. W. Norton. (Original work published in 1933).

Freud, S. (1974). Some psychological consequences of an anatomical distinction between the sexes. In J. Strouse (Ed.), *Women and analysis.* New York: Grossman. (Original work published in 1925).

Garner, D. M. (1997, February). The 1997 Body Image Survey results. *Psychology Today,* 30.

Garrahy, D. A. (2001). Three third-grade teachers' gender-related beliefs and behavior. *The Elementary School Journal, 102,* 81–98.

Green, R. J., Bettinger, M., & Zacks, E. (1996). Are lesbian couples fused and gay male couples disengaged? In J. Laird & R. J. Green (Eds.), *Lesbians and gays in couples and families* (pp. 185–230). San Francisco: Jossey-Bass.

Greene, B. (1995). African American families. *Phi Kappa Phi Journal, 75,* 29–32.

Gronowicz, A. (1990). *Garbo: Her story.* New York: Simon and Schuster.

Gupta, G. R. (2001). Gender, sexuality, and HIV/AIDS: The what, the why, and the how. *SIECUS Report, 29*(5), 6–12.

Hunter, A. G., & Sellers, S. L. (1998). Feminist attitudes among African American women and men. *Gender and Society, 12,* 81–99.

Hsu, B., Kling, A., Kessler, C., Knape, K., Diefenbach, E., & Elias, J. E. (1994). Gender differences in sexual fantasy and behavior in a college population: A ten-year replication. *Journal of Sex and Marital Therapy, 20,* 103–118.

Human Development Report. (1997). United Nations Development Programme. New York: Oxford University Press.

Ishii-Kuntz, M. (2000). Change and continuity in the Japanese family. *National Council on Family Relations Report,* No. 45.

Joseph, R. (2000). The evolution of sex differences in language, sexuality, and visual-spatial skills. *Archives of Sexual Behavior, 29,* 35–66.

Junhong, C. (2001). Prenatal sex determination and sex-selective abortion in rural central China. *Population and Development Review, 27,* 259–267.

Kennedy, M. (2000). Gender roles in Africa. Presentation, Department of Sociology, East Carolina University, Fall.

Kessler, S. J. (1990). *Lessons from the intersexed.* New Brunswick, NJ: Rutgers University Press.

Knox, D., Britton, T., & Crisp, B. (1997). Age discrepant relationships reported by university faculty and their students. *College Student Journal, 31,* 290–292.

Knox, D., Cooper, C., & Zusman, M. E. (2001). Sexual values of college students. *College Student Journal, 35,* 24–27.

Knox, D., Daniels, V., Sturdivant, L., & Zusman, M. E. (2001). College student use of the Internet for mate selection. *College Student Journal, 35,* 158–160.

Knox, D., Sturdivant, L., & Zusman, M. E. (2001). College student attitudes toward sexual intimacy. *College Student Journal, 35,* 241–243.

Kohlberg, L. (1966). A cognitive-developmental analysis of children's sex-role concepts and attitudes. In E. E. Maccoby (Ed.), *The development of sex differences* (pp. 82–172). Stanford, CA: Stanford University Press.

Kohlberg, L. (1969). State and sequence: The cognitive-developmental approach to socialization. In D. A. Goslin (Ed.), *Handbook of socialization theory and research* (pp. 347–480). Chicago: Rand McNally.

Kohlberg, L. (1976). Moral stages and moralization: The cognitive-developmental approach. In T. Lickona (Ed.), *Moral development and behavior* (pp. 31–53). New York: Holt, Rinehart, & Winston.

Landen, M., & Innala, S. (2000). Attitudes toward transsexualism in a Swedish national survey. *Archives of Sexual Behavior, 29,* 375–378.

Laner, M., & Ventrone, N. A. (2000). Dating scripts revisited. *Journal of Family Issues, 21,* 488–500.

Laumann, E. O., & Michael, R. T. (2001). Setting the scene. In E. O. Laumann & R. T. Michael (Eds.), *Sex, love, and health in America: Private choices and public policies* (pp. 1–37). Chicago: The University of Chicago Press.

Lee, P. A. (1996). Survey report: Concept of penis size. *Journal of Sex and Marital Therapy, 22,* 131–135.

Leve, L. D., & Fagot, B. I. (1997). Gender-role socialization and discipline processes in one and two parent families. *Sex Roles, 36,* 1–21.

Lindsey, E. W., & Mize, J. (2001). Contextual differences in parent-child play: Implications for children's gender role development. *Sex Roles: A Journal of Research, 44*, 155–176.

Lippa, R. A. (2002). *Gender, nature, and nurture*. Mahwah, NJ: Lawrence Erlbaum.

Lippa, R. A., & Tan, F. D. (2001). Does culture moderate the relationship between sexual orientation and gender-related personality traits? *Cross-Cultural Research, 35*, 65–87.

Lloyd, S. A., & Emery, B. C. (2000). *The dark side of courtship: Physical and sexual aggression*. Thousand Oaks, CA: Sage.

Lorber, J. (2001). "Night to his day": The social construction of gender. In T. E. Cohen (Ed.), *Men and masculinity: a text reader* (pp. 19–28). Belmont, CA: Wadsworth.

Mahay, J., Laumann, E. O., & Michaels, S. (2001). Race, gender, and class in sexual scripts. In E. O. Laumann & R. T. Michael (Eds.), *Sex, love, and health in America: Private choices and public policies* (pp. 197–238). Chicago: The University of Chicago Press.

Mayor, S. (2001). Specialists question effectiveness of sex selection technique. *British Medical Journal, 323*, 67–81.

McAdoo, H. P. (1998). African-American families. In C. H. Mindel, R. W. Habenstein, & R. Wright, Jr. (Eds.), *Ethnic families in America: Patterns and variations*. Upper Saddle River, NJ: Prentice-Hall, 361–381.

Meadus, R. J. (2000). Men in nursing: Barriers to recruitment. *Nursing Forum, 35*(3), 5.

Michael, R. T., Gagnon, J. H., Laumann, E. O., & Kolata, G. (1994). *Sex in America: A definitive survey*. Boston: Little, Brown.

Midence, K., & Hargreaves, I. (1997). Psychosocial adjustment in male-to-female transsexuals: An overview of the research evidence. *Journal of Psychology, 131*, 602–615.

Miller, E. M., & Costello, C. Y. (2001) The limits of biological determinism. *American Sociological Review, 66*, 592–598.

Miller, S. (2000). When sexual development goes awry. *The World & I, 15*, 148–155.

Monro, S. (2000). Theorizing transgender diversity: Towards a social model of health. *Sexual and Relationship Therapy, 15*, 33–42.

Muehlenhard, C. L., & McCoy, M. (1991). Double standard/double bind: The sexual double standard and women's communication about sex. *Psychology of Women Quarterly, 15*, 447–461.

Muehlenhard, C. L., & Quackenbush, D. M. (1988). Can the sexual double standard put women at risk for sexually transmitted disease? The role of the double standard in condom use among women. Paper, presented at the Society for the Scientific Study of Sexuality (SSSS), San Francisco, CA.

Muehelendard, C. L., & Quackenbush, D. M. (1998). Sexual Double Standard Scale. In C. M. Davis, W. L. Yarber, R. Bauserman, G. Schreer, & S. L. Davis (Eds.), *Handbook of sexuality-related measures* (pp. 186–188). Thousand Oaks, CA: Sage.

Nahom, D., Wells, E., Gillmore, M. R., Hoppe, M., Morrison, D. M., Archibald, M., Murowchick, E., Wilsdon, A., & Graham, L. (2001). Differences by gender and sexual experience in adolescent sexual behavior: Implications for education and HIV prevention. *Journal of School Health, 71*, 153–158.

National Opinion Research Center at the University of Chicago. (2001). *Summary Report 2000: Doctorate recipients from United States Universities*, Chicago, IL.

Patterson, C. J. (2000). Family relationships of lesbians and gay men. *Journal of Marriage and the Family, 62*, 1052–1070.

Pimentel, E. E. (2000). Just how do I love thee? Marital relations in urban China. *Journal of Marriage and the Family, 62*, 32–47.

Pollack, W. S. (with Shuster, T.) (2001). *Real boys' voices*. New York: Penguin Books.

Purnine, D. M., Carey, M. P., & Jorgensen, R. S. (1994). Gender differences regarding preferences for specific heterosexual practices. *Journal of Sex and Marital Therapy, 20*, 271–287.

Reinholtz, R. K., & Muehlenhard, C. L. (1995). Genital perceptions and sexual activity in a college population. *The Journal of Sex Research, 32*, 155–165.

Renzetti, C. M., & Curran, D. J. (1999). *Women, men, and society* (4th ed.). Boston: Allyn and Bacon.

Rhode, D. L. (1997). *Speaking of sex: The denial of gender inequality*. Cambridge, MA: Harvard University Press.

Richards, K. (1997). What is a transgenderist? In B. Bullough, V. Bullough, & J. Elias (Eds.), *Gender blending* (pp. 503–504). Amherst, NY: Prometheus Books.

Rogers, C., & Muehlenhard, C. L. (1992). *Token resistance: New perspectives on an old stereotype*. Unpublished manuscript.

Ross, C. E., & Van Willigen, M. (1996). Gender, parenthood, and anger. *Journal of Marriage and the Family, 58*, 572–582.

Sapiro, V. (1990). *Women in American society* (2nd ed.). Mountain View, CA: Mayfield.

Schrof, J. M. (1998, September). Remove the mystery of sorting sperm. *U.S. News and World Report*, 68.

Senate, M. (2001). *See Jane date*. New York: Red Dress, Inc.

Shepherd, C. (with Ball, A. L.) (2000). *Cybill disobedience*. New York: Harper Collins.

Silverthorne, Z. A., & Quinsey, V. L. (2000). Sexual partner age preference of homosexual and heterosexual men and women. *Archives of Sexual Behavior, 29*, 67–76.

Sprecher, S., Barbee, A., & Schwartz, P. (1995). 'Was it good for you, too?' Gender differences in first sexual intercourse experiences. *The Journal of Sex Research, 32*, 3–15.

Stake, J. E. (2000). When situations call for instrumentality and expressiveness: Resource appraisal, coping strategy choice, and adjustment. *Sex Roles, 42*, 865–885.

Stanley, S. M., & Markman, H. J. (1997). *Marriage in the 90s: A nationwide random phone survey*. Denver: PREP, Inc.

Statistical Abstract of the United States: 2002. (2002). 122nd ed. Washington, DC: U.S. Bureau of the Census.

Tang, C. S., Lai, E. D., Phil, M., & Chung, T. K. H. (1997). Assessment of sexual functioning for Chinese college students. *Archives of Sexual Behavior, 26,* 79–90.

Tay, L. S., & Gibbons, J. L. (1998). Attitudes toward gender roles among adolescents in Singapore. *Cross-Cultural Research, 32,* 257–258.

Thornhill, R., & Palmer, C. T. (2000). *A natural history of rape: Biological bases of sexual coercion.* Cambridge, MA: MIT Press.

Vega, W. A. (1991). Hispanic families in the 1980s: A decade of research. In A. Booth (Ed.) *Contemporary families* (pp. 297–306). Minneapolis, MN: National Council on Family Relations.

Ward, C. A. (2001). Models and measurements of psychological androgyny: A cross-cultural extension of theory and research. *Sex Roles: A Journal of Research, 43,* 529–552.

Weinberg, M. S., Lottes, I., & Shaver, F. M. (2000). Sociocultural correlates of permissive sexual attitudes: A test of Reiss's hypothesis about Sweden and the United States. *The Journal of Sex Research, 37,* 44–52.

Willetts-Bloom, M. C., & Nock, S. L. (1994). The influence of maternal employment on gender role attitudes of men and women. *Sex Roles, 30,* 371–389.

Witelson, S. F. (1995). Neuroanatomical bases of hemispheric functional specialization in the human brain: Possible developmental factors. In F. L. Kitterle (Ed.), *Hemispheric communication: Mechanisms and models* (pp. 61–84). Mahwah, NJ: Erlbaum.

Wolff, B., Blanc, A. K., & Gage, A. J. (2000). Who decides? Women's status and negotiation of sex in Uganda. *Culture, Health & Sexuality, 2,* 303–322.

Wright, D. W., & Young, R. (1998). The effects of family structure and maternal employment on the development of gender-related attitudes among men and women. *Journal of Family Issues, 19,* 300–314.

Zimmerman, T. S., Holm, K. E., & Haddock, S. A. (2000, November). *A decade of advice for women and men in best-selling self-help literature.* Poster session presented at 62nd Annual Meeting of the National Council on Family Relations, Minneapolis MN.

Zucker, K. J. (1999). Intersexuality and gender identity differentiation. *Annual Review of Sex Research.* Mount Vernon, VA: Society for the Scientific Study of Sex.

6

Sexual Orientation Diversity

Chapter Outline

I know what it feels like to try to blend in so that everybody will think that you are OK and they won't hurt you.

—Ellen DeGeneres, comedian, actress

Following the tragedy of September 11, 2001, the partners of gay and lesbian individuals were deemed eligible for the same Crime Victims Board benefits as surviving spouses. The executive order signed by New York Governor George Pataki included gay partners as family members, and their relationships were defined as family. The American Red Cross also took the position that families "come in different forms," which included persons who had been living together as domestic partners. For gays and lesbians to be included in the definition of family is increasingly common but remains an issue that fuels heated debate. In this chapter, we review definitions and conceptions of heterosexuality, homosexuality, and bisexuality. We will also examine theories of homosexuality, characteristics of homosexual and bisexual relationships, and the causes and consequences of homonegativity/homophobia.

Think About It

Although the terms *sexual preference* and *sexual orientation* are often used interchangeably, many sexuality researchers and academicians (including the authors of this text) prefer to use the term *sexual orientation.* The former term implies one is consciously choosing to whom one will be attracted. The latter term suggests that one's sexual orientation (whether heterosexual or homosexual) is innate (as is handedness) or may be influenced by multiple factors. What is your feeling about using the respective terms, and what meaning does each have for you?

Sexual orientation The classification of individuals as heterosexual, bisexual, or homosexual based on their emotional, cognitive, and sexual attractions as well as their self-identity and lifestyle.

Heterosexuality Sexual orientation whereby the predominance of emotional and sexual attraction is to persons of the other sex.

Homosexuality Sexual orientation that involves the predominance of emotional and sexual attractions to persons of the same sex.

Bisexuality The emotional and sexual attraction to members of both sexes.

LesBiGays A term that collectively refers to lesbians, gays, and bisexuals.

Transgendered Term that refers to individuals who express some characteristics other than their assigned gender, which is usually based on their biological sex (male or female).

Transgendered individuals Persons who do not fit neatly into either the male or female category, or their behavior is not congruent with the norms and expectations of their sex.

6-1 TERMS OF SEXUAL ORIENTATION

Sexual orientation refers to the classification of individuals as heterosexual, bisexual, or homosexual based on their emotional and sexual attractions, relationships, self-identity, and lifestyle. **Heterosexuality** refers to the predominance of emotional and sexual attraction to persons of the other sex. **Homosexuality** refers to the predominance of emotional and sexual attractions to persons of the same sex, and **bisexuality** is the emotional and sexual attraction to members of both sexes. Lesbians, gays, and bisexuals, sometimes referred to collectively as **LesBiGays,** are considered to be part of a larger population referred to as the **transgendered** community. **Transgendered individuals** include persons who do not fit neatly into either the male or female category, or their behavior is not congruent with the norms and expectations of their sex in the society in which they live (Bullough, 2000). Transgendered individuals include homosexuals, bisexuals, cross-dressers, and transsexuals. Because much of the current literature on the treatment and political agendas of the LesBiGay population includes other members of the transgendered community, the term *LGBT* has emerged; this term refers collectively to lesbians, gays, bisexuals, and transgendered individuals.

6-2 CONCEPTUAL MODELS OF SEXUAL ORIENTATION

The four models of sexual orientation are the dichotomous model, in which people are either heterosexual or homosexual; the unidimensional continuum model, in which sexual orientation is viewed on a continuum; the multidimensional model, which views sexuality as a function of degrees of various components such as emotions, behaviors, and cognitions; and the LesBiGay/Transgender affirmative model, which has an emphasis on diversity and gender issues.

6-2a Dichotomous Model

The **dichotomous model** (also referred to as the "either-or" model of sexuality) prevails not only in views on sexual orientation, but also in cultural understandings of biological sex (male vs. female) and gender (masculine vs. feminine). This model has been criticized by Kinsey Institute researchers who emphasized that "dichotomous categories such as heterosexual and homosexual fail to reflect adequately the complex realities of sexual orientation and human sexuality in general" (Sanders, Reinisch, & McWhirter, 1990, p. xx). The major criticism of the dichotomous model of sexual orientation is that it ignores the existence of bisexuality. As Firestein (1996) noted, it assumes that individuals who exhibit bisexual feelings and behavior are really either homosexual or heterosexual and are denying their true sexual orientation or trying to avoid the stigma that might come with a homosexual label. It also implies that heterosexual and homosexual populations are discrete, nonoverlapping, and unchanging.

Dichotomous model (also referred to as the "either-or" model of sexuality) Way of conceptualizing sexual orientation that prevails not only in views on sexual orientation, but also in cultural understandings of biological sex (male vs. female) and gender (masculine vs. feminine).

6-2b Unidimensional Continuum Model

In early research on sexual behavior, Kinsey and his colleagues (1948, 1953) found that a substantial proportion of respondents reported having had same-sex sexual experiences. Yet, very few of the individuals in Kinsey's research reported exclusive homosexual behavior. These data led Kinsey to conclude that, contrary to the commonly held dichotomous model of sexual orientation, most people are not exclusively heterosexual or homosexual. Rather, Kinsey suggested a **unidimensional continuum model** of sexual orientation. Kinsey and his colleagues (1953) developed the Heterosexual-Homosexual Rating Scale to assess where on the continuum of sexual orientation an individual is located (see Figure 6-1). The "Kinsey scale" was originally a unidimensional measure that assessed sexual orientation by assessing lifetime erotic attractions and sexual behavior.

Unidimensional continuum model Identification of one's sexual orientation on a scale from 0 (exclusively heterosexual) to 6 (exclusively homosexual) suggesting that most people are not on the extremes but somewhere in between.

Unlike the dichotomous model, the unidimensional continuum model recognized that the heterosexual and homosexual orientations are not mutually exclusive and that an individual's sexual orientation may have both heterosexual and homosexual elements. However, this model, as represented by the Heterosexual-Homosexual Rating Scale, is criticized for assuming that an individual's sexual behavior and feelings are synchronous (Paul, 1996). Although Bell and Weinberg (1978) later used separate Kinsey scale continua to measure sexual experiences and sexual feelings, these measures of sexual orientation still did not consider the social context of such behavior or the self-identity of the individual. Thus, the unidimensional continuum model fails to incorporate some important aspects of sexuality, such as self-identity, lifestyle, and social group preference. Although Kinsey's model had a tremendous impact on subsequent sexuality research and contributed to the emergence of the multidimensional model of sexual orientation, Firestein (1996) believes that the dichotomous model of sexual orientation continues to prevail in U.S. culture.

6-2c Multidimensional Model

Since Kinsey's early sexual research, our understanding of sexual orientation has become more complex and multidimensional. The **multidimensional model** of sexual orientation suggests that orientation consists of various independent components (including emotional and social preferences, behavior, self-identification, sexual attraction, fantasy, and lifestyle) and that these components may change over time. The "multidimensional model of sexual orientation has evolved out of the need to more accurately represent the diverse factors involved in the development and expression of human sexuality" (Fox, 1996, p. 9).

Multidimensional model Way of conceptualizing sexual orientation which suggests that a person's orientation consists of various independent components (including emotional feelings, lifestyle, self-identification, sexual attraction, fantasy, and behavior) and that these components may change over time.

For example, the Klein Sexual Orientation Grid (Klein, 1990) includes seven scales measuring distinct dimensions of sexual orientation: sexual behavior, sexual fantasies, erotic attraction, emotional preference, social group preference, self-identification, and lifestyle

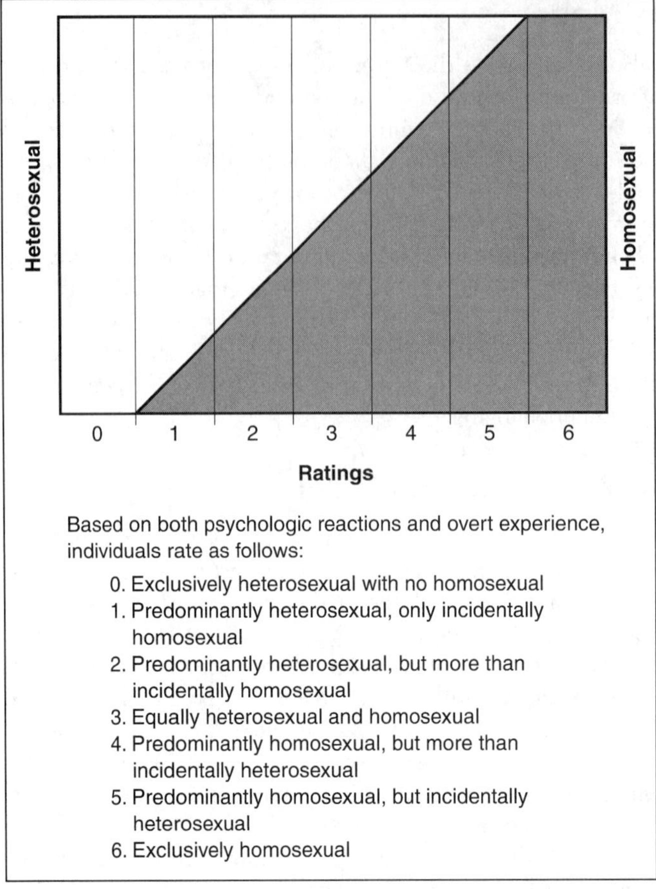

FIGURE 6-1
The Heterosexual-Homosexual Rating Scale

Source: Kinsey, A. C., Pomeroy, W. B., Martin, C. E., & Gebhard, P. H. (1953). *Sexual behavior in the human female* (p. 470, Figure 93). Philadelphia: W. B. Saunders. Reproduced by permission of The Kinsey Institute for Research in Sex, Gender, and Reproduction, Inc.

preference. Individuals rate themselves on a 7-point heterosexual-bisexual-homosexual scale for each variable for past, present, and ideal time frames, yielding a total of 21 self-ratings. An individual's satisfaction with these dimensions is measured by the present versus ideal ratings.

Perhaps the most important contribution of the multidimensional model is its incorporation of self-identity as a central element of sexual orientation. As sexuality researchers began to include self-identity as a variable in their studies, they found that attractions and sexual behavior are not always consistent with one's sexual self-identity. For example, in a study of 52 men who labeled themselves as heterosexual, almost one quarter reported that they had had sex with both women and men in the past two years; only 6% had sex exclusively with men (Doll et al., 1992). Thus, adult homosexual or bisexual attractions or behaviors do not necessarily imply a homosexual or bisexual self-identity. Also, prior homosexual, bisexual, or heterosexual experiences are not required to label one's self as homosexual. In sum, the multidimensional model of sexual orientation has broadened the construct of sexual orientation and its assessment to include self-identity; social and relationship aspects of sexual behavior; and temporal changes in sexual attractions, behaviors, and identity.

LesBiGay/Transgender affirmative model Way of conceptualizing sexual orientation that incorporates the insights of the multidimensional model but also affirms variations in sexual diversity and identity, and differences in the way individuals experience and express gender.

6-2d LesBiGay/Transgender Affirmative Model

The **LesBiGay/Transgender affirmative model** of sexual orientation incorporates the insights of the multidimensional model, but also affirms variations in sexual diversity and identity, and differences in the way individuals experience and express gender. Sexual self-identification involves both choice and constraint. Hence, individuals don't just define themselves as gay or straight but recognize that in addition to their sexual orientation, there are other issues of gender. Also, there is recognition that the definitions are culturally constructed. Esterberg (1997) explains that "people do not select freely from a menu of identities; rather, cultural ideals and social institutions shape the identities that may be chosen. For those who experience same-sex desire in the United States today, it is difficult to resist a lesbian, gay, or bisexual identity" (p. 26).

In this model, traditional notions of what constitutes psychological maturity and health among bisexual, gay, and lesbian individuals are challenged. Firestein (1996) suggests that "imitating the 1950s-style nuclear family, with the substitution of gender-role equality for the gender-role inequality present in most heterosexual relationships, still offers a far too narrow model for what constitutes optimal relational functioning" (p. 282). Rather than base standards of the mental health on the dominant culture's heterosexual norms, the LesBiGay/Transgender affirmative model recognizes "the appropriateness and value of diverse choices, such as the choice not to be partnered, to have loving relationships with more than one person at the same time, to parent singly or as part of a community of single and partnered parents, [and] to relate to individuals who are alternatively gendered or not defined in their gender" (Firestein, 1996, p. 282). Indeed, this is the most controversial of all the models.

Finally, this model "challenges us to examine. . . the similarities and differences between different sex and same-sex desire as these exist across individuals and also within the same individual" (Firestein, 1996, p. 282). "As we recognize the existence of same- and other-sex desires within the same person, the distance between heterosexuals and homosexuals is narrowed, and eventually closed. Ultimately, there is the recognition that no meaningful line can be drawn that distinguishes all heterosexually oriented individuals from all homosexually oriented individuals" (Firestein, 1996, p. 283). Firestein suggests that this realization may undermine discrimination, which is based on the ability to differentiate "us" from "them."

6-3 PREVALENCE OF HOMOSEXUALITY, HETEROSEXUALITY, AND BISEXUALITY

The prevalence of homosexuality, heterosexuality, and bisexuality is difficult to determine. Due to embarrassment, a desire for privacy, or fear of social disapproval, many individuals are not willing to answer questions about their sexuality honestly (Smith & Gates, 2001). Indeed, a team of researchers (Black, Gates, Sanders, & Taylor, 2000) estimated that only about one third of gay men and lesbian couples reported themselves as such in the latest census.

Estimates of the prevalence of sexual orientations also vary due to differences in the way researchers define and measure homosexuality, bisexuality, and heterosexuality.

Definitional problems also arise due to the considerable overlap between people with different sexual orientation self-identities and the fact that sexual attractions, behavior, and self-identity may or may not change over time. A team of researchers noted that women are able to move between heterosexual, lesbian, and bisexual patterns many times in adulthood (Peplau, Spalding, Conley, & Veniegas, 2000). And, in a study of 56 bisexuals, over time, there was a movement toward sexual activity with just one sex (although there was stability of the bisexual identity) (Weinberg, Williams, & Pryor, 2001). Nevertheless, research data have yielded rough estimates of prevalence rates of homosexuals and couple households.

NATIONAL DATA It is estimated that there are more than 10 million (10,456,405) gay and lesbian individuals in the United States, which represents between 4% and 5% of the total U.S. population age 18 and over (200 million) (Smith & Gates, 2001). According to the 2000 U.S. Census, 601,209 gay and lesbian families were reported, which comprise 304,148 gay male families and 297,061 lesbian families. The human rights campaign estimates that these 2000 census figures on gay and lesbian families represent a 62% undercount due to antigay sentiment (Smith & Gates, 2001).

INTERNATIONAL DATA A team of researchers found that 3.2% of British men compared to 1.7% of U.S. men and 1.3 % of British women compared to 2.8% of U.S. women reported any same gender partners since age 18 (Michael et al., 2001).

6-4 THEORIES OF SEXUAL ORIENTATION

One of the prevailing questions raised regarding homosexuality centers on its origin or "cause." Gay people are often irritated by the fact that heterosexual people seem overly concerned about finding "the cause" of homosexuality. However, the same question is rarely asked about heterosexuality because it is assumed that this sexual orientation is normal and needs no explanation. Questions about the cause of homosexuality imply that something is "wrong" with homosexuality.

Nevertheless, considerable research has been conducted on the origin of homosexuality and whether its basis is derived from nature (genetic, hormonal, innate) or nurture (learned through social experiences/cultural influences). Most researchers agree that an interaction of biological (nature) and social/cultural (environmental) forces is involved in the development of one's sexual orientation.

Before the end of the nineteenth century, most efforts to understand homosexuality were based on religious thinking. Scientific theories on the development of sexual orientation and homosexuality can be organized into those emphasizing biological and those emphasizing environmental factors. Theories focusing on biological factors include genetic, perinatal hormonal, and postpubertal hormonal. Environmental theories emphasize the following: parent and child interaction, sexual interaction, and gender role (Ellis, 1996).

6-4a Biological Explanations

Biological explanations on the development of sexual orientation usually focus on genetic or hormonal differences between heterosexuals and homosexuals. A discussion of three biological explorations for sexual orientation follows.

Genetic Theories

Is sexual orientation an inborn trait that is transmitted genetically, like eye color? There does seem to be a genetic influence, although unlike eye color, a single gene has not been confirmed. Miller (2000) noted that sexual orientation is a "polygenetic trait that is influenced by a number of genes" (p. 1). Previous research by Bailey and Pillard (1991) provided support of a genetic basis for sexual orientation. In their study of 56 gay men who were twins or had adoptive brothers, 52% of the identical twins, 22% of the fraternal twins, and 11% of adoptive brothers were homosexual. This finding "provided some support for the view that sexual orientation is influenced by constitutional factors. . . and emphasizes the necessity of considering causal factors arising within the individual, and not just his psychosocial environment" (p. 1095). A team of researchers (Dawood, Pillard, Horvath, Revelle, & Bailey, 2000) studied 37 gay male sibling pairs and suggested that genetic biological etiology was operative. Further support for a genetic influence toward homosexuality has been provided by Cantor, Blanchard, Paterson, and Bogaert (2002) who noted that men with older homosexual brothers are more likely to be homosexual themselves. ". . . [R]oughly one gay man in 7 owes his sexual orientation to the fraternal birth order effect" (p. 63).

Research on female twins also concludes that if one twin is gay, there is an increased chance that the other is also gay (Bailey, Pillard, Neale, & Agyei, 1993). However, other research on twins provides no evidence of a genetic basis for homosexuality (King & McDonald, 1992). Still other research on twins notes that genetic factors are mediated by childhood gender nonconformity (Bem, 2000). Children exposed to social contexts that allow for variation in gender role variation may feel greater freedom to vary the expression of one's sexual orientation.

Some evidence has also been presented that a homosexual orientation among men is related to the presence of a gene on the X chromosome inherited from the mother. In one study, two thirds of the gay siblings shared a distinctive pattern along a segment of their X chromosome. "Scientists say the possibility is remote that this genetic pattern would appear by chance" (Park, 1995, p. 95). Turner (1995) also presented evidence that male homosexuality has a genetic basis in the gene at the *Xq28* region. Still other research suggests that male homosexual and heterosexual brains reveal some differences (Reite, Sheeder, Richardson, & Teale, 1995). These differences, however, may be due to the effects of environmental and psychosocial factors on the brain (Swaab, Gooren, & Hofman, 1995).

Bogaert, Friesen, and Klentrou (2002) also suggested a biological predisposition to sexual orientation in that homosexual men report an earlier age of puberty (e.g., age of first pubic hair) than heterosexual men. "Thus, perhaps gay/bisexual men score, on average, in the female-typical direction on a variety of characteristics, including age of puberty, because relevant structures in the nervous system (e.g. sites in the anterior hypothalamus) have been feminized or demasculinized relative to heterosexual men" (p. 78).

Finally, LeVay (1991) suggested a biological component of homosexuality as a result of scanning the brains of 41 cadavers (19 homosexual men, 16 heterosexual men, and 6 heterosexual women). He found that the portion of the brain thought to be involved in the regulation of sexual activity (the third interstitial nucleus of the anterior hypothalamus known as INAH 3) was half the size in homosexual men as in heterosexual men. LeVay's research is controversial and raises more questions than it answers; for example, does that brain structure produce sexual orientation, or were the differences a result of adult behavior? LeVay (1994, p. 108) observed the complexities of biological factors (genes, level of sex steroids before birth, brain structure) and environmental events, and concluded, "I do not know—nor does anyone else—what makes a person gay, bisexual, or straight. I do believe, however, that the answer to this question will eventually be found by doing biological research in laboratories and not by simply talking about the topic, which is the way most people have studied it up to now."

Think About It

Given the possibility that there are "homosexual genes," parents may be able to select the sexual orientation for their children. Bailey (2001) has argued that it would be "morally acceptable" for parents to select for heterosexuality on the premise that such control is consistent with the value of parents having the freedom to rear the sort of children they wish and that such a selection is likely to benefit both parents and children. What is your opinion of Bailey's view?

Perinatal Hormonal Theories

In his discussion of prenatal influences on sexual orientation, Diamond (1995) discussed the effects of the maturation of the testes or ovaries and their release (or lack) of hormones. These hormones affect the structural development of the genitalia and other structures. At the gross and microscopic levels, they also organize the developing nervous system and influence sex-linked behaviors (biasing the individual toward male- or female-typical behaviors). Reviews of this process in nonhuman mammals (Kelly, 1991) and of the effects of paranatal administration of hormones during critical periods of development (Haug, Whalen, Aron, & Olsen, 1993) confirm the feminizing and masculinizing, as well as defeminizing and demasculinizing features. Research in the Netherlands (Bakker, Ophemert, & Slob, 1993) has shown that, in contrast to control animals, rats treated with hormones during a critical prenatal or neonatal period either preferred same-sex partners as adults or had no preference between male or female partners. The earlier the hormonal treatment was started after birth, the rats remained more "bisexual."

Ellis and Ames (1987) concluded that hormonal and neurological factors operating prior to birth, between the second and fifth month of gestation, are the "main determinants of sexual orientation" (p. 235). Fetal exposure to such hormones as testosterone is believed to impact the developing neural pathways of the brain. Money (1987) suggested that sexual orientation is programmed into the brain during critical prenatal periods and early childhood. The work of Ellis, Ames, Peckham, and Burke (1988) suggests that prenatal stress in pregnant women is linked with homosexuality in their sons. While the methodology relying on mothers' recollections of their pregnancy has been challenged, and further study is needed to refute or confirm this line of thinking, "the door seems open to this influence" (Diamond, 1995).

Postpubertal Hormonal Theories

Endocrinology (the study of hormones) research to determine whether the levels of sex hormones of gay men and lesbians resemble the other sex has yielded mixed results (Ellis, 1996). Although some studies of circulating testosterone levels in men have found slightly lower levels in gay men, most studies have not found significant differences. About half of the studies of women have found no differences; the other half have found higher levels of testosterone in lesbians (although the levels are still well below the normal level for men). Ellis concluded that the connection between postpubertal sex hormone levels and homosexuality is complex and is probably applicable only to some subgroups of gay men and lesbians.

Banks and Gartrell (1995) also reviewed the studies on sex hormones and the development of sexual orientation and concluded, "Overall, the data do not support a causal connection between hormones and human sexual orientation" (p. 248). They cited methodological problems as well as the questionability of generalizing animal studies to humans. Moreover, Fausto-Sterling (1995) emphasized the need to understand how physiological influences on the brain are affected by experience. Gooren (1995) concluded his review of homosexuality and hormones with the following:

> *If I were asked whether there is a biology of homosexuality, my answer would be yes. It is, however, a biology that allows multifarious expressions of sexuality. It is not true that biology causes people to have certain sexual encounters. It is more likely that other levels of human existence shape sexual expression. (p. 245)*

The belief in biological determinism of sexual orientation among homosexuals is strong. In a national study of homosexual men, 90% believe that they were born with their homosexual orientation; only 4% believe that environmental factors are the sole cause (Lever, 1994). Although the general public believes that homosexuality is more of a choice, acceptance of a biological explanation is increasing. In a Gallup poll conducted in 2001, half of those who were surveyed endorsed a genetic over an environmental explanation. This is in contrast to a 1977 Gallup poll, in which an environmental cause was endorsed four times more than a genetic one (Dahir, 2001).

6-4b Social/Cultural Explanations

According to social/cultural explanations for sexual orientation, while adrenal androgens provide the fuel for the sex drive (around age 10), they do not provide the direction or sexual orientation that is determined by sociocultural forces such as one's peer group, parents, and mass media (Hyde, 2000). Because these forces encourage heterosexuality, unique environmental influences help account for homosexuality. Sociocultural theories of homosexuality suggest that parent-child interaction, sexual experiences, and adoption of sex roles and self-labels are especially influential.

Parent-Child Interaction Theories

Freud's psychoanalytic theory has been described as one of the first scientific explanations of homosexuality (Ellis, 1996). His theories suggested that the relationship individuals have with their parents may predispose them toward heterosexuality or homosexuality.

Whereas heterosexual men identified closely with their fathers and had more distant relationships with their mothers, homosexual men had close emotional relationships with their mothers and were distant with their fathers (Freud had little to say about the development of sexual orientation of women).

The presumed script for the development of a homosexual male follows: The overprotective mother seeks to establish a binding emotional relationship with her son. But this closeness also elicits strong sexual feelings on the part of the son toward the mother, which are punished by her and blocked by the society through the incest taboo. The son is fearful of expressing sexual feelings for his mother. He generalizes this fear to other women; with the result that they are no longer viewed as potential sexual partners.

The son's distant relationship with his father prevents identification with a male role model. For example, the relationship between playwright Tennessee Williams and his father was one of mutual rejection—the father was contemptuous of his "sissy" son, and Williams was hostile to his father because of his father's arrogance.

Freud's theory of male homosexuality is not supported by the scientific community. First, it does not resolve the question "Is the absent or distant father relationship a result or a cause of the child's homosexuality?" Second, sons with overprotective mothers and rejecting fathers also grow up to be heterosexual, just as those with moderate mothering and warm fathering grow up to be homosexual. Third, two sons growing up in the same type of family may have different sexual orientations. A study of family backgrounds of 979 homosexual and 477 heterosexual people confirmed that parent-child relationships as the "cause" for homosexuality is highly questionable and highly suspect (Bell, Weinberg, & Hammersmith, 1981). The researchers concluded that the relationship individuals have with their parents "cannot be said to predict much about sexual orientation" (p. 62). It may be that some maternal protection and parental rejection are reactions to effeminate behaviors of "pre-gay" male children (Ellis, 1996).

Sexual Interaction Theories

Sexual interaction theories propose that such factors as availability of sexual partners, early sexual experiences, imprinting, and sexual reinforcement influence subsequent sexual orientation. Because homosexuality is more prevalent among men than women, shortages of women and an emphasis on chastity of women have been hypothesized to be conducive to male homosexuality (Ellis, 1996). The degree to which early sexual experiences have been negative or positive has been hypothesized as influencing sexual orientation. Having pleasurable same-sex experiences would be likely to increase the probability of a homosexual orientation. By the same token, early sexual experiences that are either unsuccessful or traumatic have been suspected as causing fear of heterosexual activity. One lesbian in the authors' classes explained her attraction to women as a result of being turned off to men—that her uncle molested her regularly and often for four years. However, one study that compared sexual histories of lesbian and heterosexual women found no difference in the incidence of traumatic experiences with men (Brannock & Chapman, 1990).

Think About It

Although previous research on the relationship between early childhood sexual molestation experiences on later sexual orientation has been lacking, Tomeo, Templer, Anderson, and Kotler (2001) conducted research on 942 nonclinical adult participants and found that gay men and lesbian women reported a significantly higher rate of childhood molestation than did heterosexual men and women. Forty-six percent of the homosexual men, in contrast to 7% of the heterosexual men, reported homosexual molestation. Twenty-two percent of lesbian women, in contrast to 1% of heterosexual women, reported homosexual molestation. How might these percentages be explained?

Sex-Role Theories

Sex-role theories include self-labeling theory and inappropriate (or nontraditional) sex-role training. How people perceive themselves and the reactions of others to their sex-role behavior are important in a child's development. The self-labeling theory is supported by research showing that gay men, when compared to heterosexual men, were more likely to dislike athletics and to have played with dolls (Strong, Devendra, & Randall, 2000). In a study comparing the recalled childhood experiences of heterosexual and lesbian women, lesbian women were much more likely to have imagined themselves as male characters, to have a preference for boys' games, and to have considered themselves tomboys as children (Phillips & Over, 1995). According to labeling theorists, "through a process of socialization, lesbians and gays incorporate ideas about what it means to be lesbian or gay into their own identities. The labeling of an individual's acts as homosexual—both by other lesbians and gays and by the straight world—and the stigmatization of that identity, over time, lead to the adoption of a homosexual identity" (Esterberg, 1997, p. 20). Although labeling theory is useful in emphasizing the fact that the labels "homosexual" and "heterosexual" are socially constructed categories, "it does not appear that individuals become lesbian or gay simply by a process of labeling by others" (Esterberg, 1997, p. 21).

The Exotic Becomes Erotic (EBE) theory provides an explanation of the development of sexual orientation that combines biological and environmental components (Bem, 1996). Bem suggests that a child's biological inheritance influences temperament (including characteristics such as aggressiveness and activity level), which predisposes him or her to prefer some activities more than others. Gender-conforming children (who enjoy sex-typical activities) will feel different from peers of the other sex and perceive them as dissimilar and exotic. Likewise, gender-nonconforming children (who enjoy atypical activities for their sex) will perceive same-sex peers as unfamiliar and exotic. These feelings result in autonomic arousal, which is transformed into erotic or romantic attraction. Bem observes that as natives of a gender-polarizing culture, we have learned to view the world through the lens of gender. He also notes that culture influences the way biological and behavioral scientists think about sexual orientation.

Think About It

Increases in biologically based explanations for sexual orientation may be related to approval of gay lifestyle issues. In the 2001 Gallup poll mentioned in section 6-4a, (which noted an increase in endorsement of a biological explanation), when asked if homosexuality is an "acceptable alternative lifestyle," 52% of respondents agreed that it is (an increase from 1977 when 38% agreed). In addition, 54% agreed that "homosexual relations between consenting adults should be legal," in contrast to 43% in 1977 (Dahir, 2001). Why do you feel biologically based explanations of sexual orientation may be related to greater acceptance?

6-5 GAY AND BISEXUAL IDENTITY DEVELOPMENT

Gay and bisexual identity development is usually a gradual process that progresses through various stages.

6-5a Stages of Development

In a review of six theories of gay identity development, Sophie (1985/1986) synthesized four essential stages of identity development:

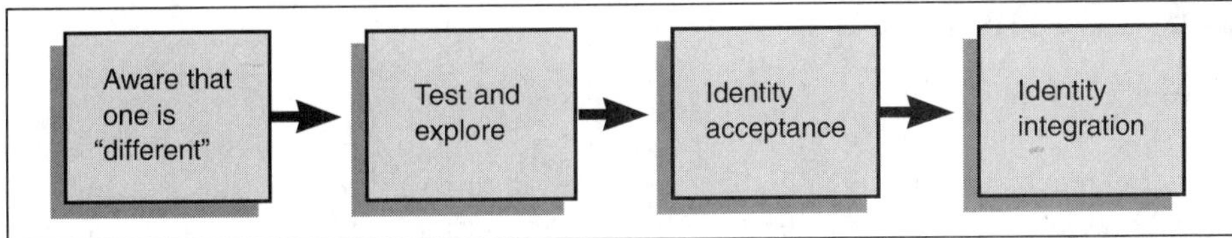

FIGURE 6-2
Synthesized Model of Gay Identity Development

This model is based on the theory development and research of Sophie (1985/1986) and Troiden (1989). Although not all gay or lesbian individuals follow this sequence, the model is helpful in showing commonly reported stages of gay identity development.

- *Stage 1: First awareness or realization that one is "different."* This awareness often begins before puberty. Girls and boys may feel different in their lack of interest in the other sex. An awareness of being different from others may also involve a vague feeling of not fitting in with one's peers, without knowing why.
- *Stage 2: Test and exploration.* At this stage, which often occurs in the teenage years, individuals may suspect they are homosexual but may not be sure. This stage involves exploring one's feelings and attractions, as well as initiating limited contact with other nonheterosexual individuals.
- *Stage 3: Identity acceptance.* In this stage, individuals come to define themselves as homosexual or bisexual. For women, developing a homosexual identity often occurs after developing an emotionally intimate, loving same-sex relationship. One woman declared, "It never occurred to me that I might be a lesbian until I met this woman, fell in love, and thought, 'Oh! That's why I didn't like kissing the guys!'" (quoted in Esterberg, 1997, p. 31). For men, identity acceptance often occurs after having an initial same-sex sexual experience. Troiden (1989) reported that gay men arrive at homosexual self-definitions between the ages of 19 and 21, whereas women arrive at homosexual self-definitions between the ages of 21 and 23. Bisexual self-identification typically occurs at later ages due to the difficulties bisexual women and men have in arriving at an identity that is not affirmed in either the heterosexual or the homosexual community.
- *Stage 4: Identity integration.* The final stage of developing a gay or bisexual identity involves developing pride in and commitment to one's sexual orientation. This stage also involves disclosing one's sexual orientation to others. Figure 6-2 summarizes the stages involved in developing a gay identity.

Not all homosexual and bisexual individuals go through identity development stages in an orderly, predictable fashion. In a study of 76 lesbian or bisexual female youths and 80 gay or bisexual male youths (age range, 14–21), the pattern of psychosexual development was first to become aware of attractions to those of the same sex, then to consider a homosexual or bisexual identity, and finally to feel certain about a gay or bisexual identity (Rosario, Meyer-Bahlburg, Exner, Gwadz, & Keller, 1996). Peacock (2000) noted how difficult it is to assimilate being gay into one's life pattern and that the absence of role models to do so makes the assimilation difficult.

Think About It

Savin-Williams and Diamond (2000) noted a considerable gap in first-time same-sex attractions and first disclosure—10 years for both sexes, with the initial attraction being experienced around age 8 to 9 (Hyde, 2000, also emphasized an upsurge in adrenal androgens around age 10). Men typically pursued same-sex activity first and then labeled themselves afterward, whereas for women the labeling came first. Why do you think there is such a long interval between initial same-sex attractions and disclosure?

Stage identity models might be criticized on the basis of their small samples, their narrow focus on sexuality, and their lack of attention to the larger sociohistorical context. A more comprehensive model of identity development would put sexual identity into a context that includes other important facets of identity, such as gender, race, and class.

6-6 COMING OUT

Gay and bisexual identity development also occurs through the process of "coming out." The issue of "coming out" received nationwide attention in 1997 with the disclosure of Ellen DeGeneres's character on the hit television show *Ellen* that she is a lesbian. GLAAD (Gay and Lesbian Alliance Against Defamation) gave her an award for the program, emphasizing the importance of such content on television for the gay rights movement. Indeed, there are many recurring gay and lesbian characters on prime-time television (including main characters in the shows *Will & Grace* and *Six Feet Under*). Rosie O'Donnell is among the more recent celebrities to make known her gay sexual orientation.

Coming out (A shortened form of "coming out of the closet") Refers to the sequence of defining one's self as homosexual in sexual orientation and disclosing one's self-identification to others.

The term **coming out** (a shortened form of "coming out of the closet") refers to the sequence of defining one's self as homosexual in sexual orientation and disclosing one's self-identification to others. Coming out helps to solidify commitment to a homosexual or bisexual identity. Most individuals/couples are very slow to make public their homosexuality. We have noted that gay and lesbian couples were most likely undercounted in the most recent U.S. census. In addition, of 400,000 same-sex couples in California, only about 7,600 have registered their partnerships with the state (Musbach, 2001a).

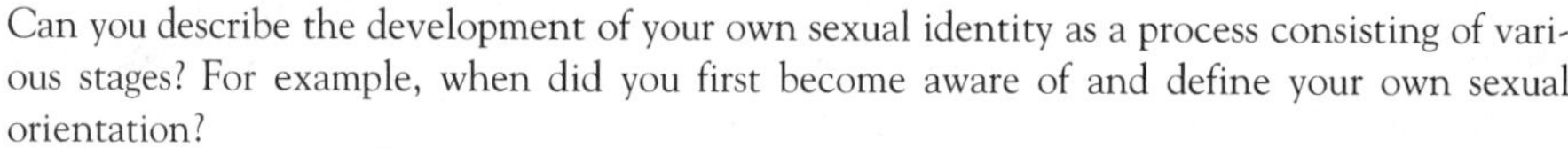

Think About It

Can you describe the development of your own sexual identity as a process consisting of various stages? For example, when did you first become aware of and define your own sexual orientation?

6-6a Coming Out to One's Self

Defining one's self as a homosexual and coming out to one's self can be a frightening and confusing experience. Flowers and Buston (2001) conducted interviews with 21 gay men who reported that feeling "different," "alienated," "isolated," and "living a lie" were common feelings on their way to identity formation.

The experience of women coming out to themselves is also difficult. At age 12, Kate had her first crush on a girl. Throughout her teenage years, Kate struggled against her attractions to women. At age 18, she experienced her first passionate kiss with another woman: "My reaction to that first encounter...was to get up out of bed, brush my teeth vigorously, walk back to bed, and say, 'I'm not that kind of girl': And the next night I was that kind of girl all over again" (Esterberg, 1997).

Collins (2000) noted that the process of accepting one's bisexual identity follows a predictable pattern including questioning/confusion, refusal/suppression, infusion/exploration, and resolution/acceptance. Progression through these stages may take years with relapses at each stage.

Coming out to others involves disclosing one's homosexual or bisexual identity to parents and other family members, friends and peers, employers, partners or spouses, and children. In coming out, some homosexual and bisexual individuals do not directly reveal their sexual orientation to others. Rather, they make no effort to hide their orientation from others. Parents and siblings are often the most difficult persons to come out to.

6-6b Coming Out to Parents and Siblings

Coming out to one's parents is a major decision. Before deciding to tell one's family that one is homosexual, it is recommended that the person feel personally secure with his or her homosexuality, have a support group of friends who are also secure and who have experienced coming out to their parents, and have a relatively good relationship with his or her parents. Coming out may occur in a letter, an e-mail, over the phone, or in person. The following recommendations (for coming out to one's parents) are made by a 21-year-old lesbian college student who came out to her parents in a letter (authors' files):

1. Avoid speaking from a defensive point of view. Too often, gay people are forced to defend their lifestyle as if it is wrong. If you approach your parents with the view that your homosexuality is a positive aspect of your personality, you will have a better chance of evoking a positive response from them.
2. Avoid talking about your current relationship. Homosexuality is often labeled as a phase rather than a permanent facet of one's life. Your parents may feel, as mine did, that your current partner is the cause of your lifestyle. Thus, when your relationship ends (so they hope), so will your homosexuality. Deal with the subject as it affects you as an individual.
3. Try to maintain a constant flow of positive reinforcement toward your parents. Reiterate your love for them as you would like them to do to you.
4. Be confident in your views and outlook on homosexuality. Before you begin to explain your position to anyone else, you must have it clear in your own mind.

Although the majority of families are neither totally rejecting nor totally accepting (Beeler & DiProva, 1999), parents must often grieve (which may take 5 years) and obtain accurate information about gay lifestyles. However, "a complete acceptance of a gay son or lesbian daughter's sexual orientation may be impossible for most parents" (LaSala, 2000). In effect, there are post disclosure changes such as "talking about coming out," engaging in conflict, and asking questions of self and others. Gays also look for support beyond the family and build a wider community (Oswald, 2000).

6-6c Personal Choices: Disclosing One's Homosexuality to Parents

Deciding to tell or not tell one's parents of one's homosexuality is very difficult. Evans and Broido (2000) found that the decision to come out to one's parents is related to the perceived risks/reactions of doing so. Not to come out is to hide one's true self from parents and to feel alienated, afraid, and alone. To tell them is to risk rejection and disapproval. Some parents of homosexuals suspect that their children are gay, even before they are told. Of 402 parents of gay and lesbian children, 26% stated that they suspected their offspring's homosexuality (Robinson, Walters, & Skeen, 1989). In general, youths are more likely to come out to mothers than to fathers (Cohen & Savin-Williams, 1996). Parents may be told face to face, through an intermediary (a sibling, another relative, or a counselor), or in a letter. There is probably no best way to disclose to parents.

6-6d Personal Choices: Would You Accept or Reject a Gay Son or Daughter?

Whereas young adults are confronted with the decision to tell their parents they are gay, parents are confronted with the decision of accepting or rejecting the homosexuality of their offspring. It is helpful to keep in mind that, just as homosexuals live in an antihomosexual society that encourages a negative self-concept (and are, therefore, victims of social forces that influence them), parents live in the same society, which encourages rejection of homosexuals (and are, therefore, also influenced by negative social forces). If parents want to maintain the relationship with their children, they must decide to override society's antigay bias. One parent said:

> *I can't say that I like it. In fact, I am sad that my child is homosexual. But I can't let that come between us and have decided to make it clear that I still love Chris to the fullest.*

Some parents are unwilling to accept their child's homosexuality:

I'm not the kind to put up with such behavior. I told my kid that what he was doing was wrong and that I wouldn't tolerate it. I haven't seen my son in four years. I'm sad about that but I'd be more sad having a faggot in my house.

Some parents who have rejected their offspring because of their homosexuality have regretted doing so because they missed the relationship with their offspring more than they hated the fact that they were gay. Alternatives available to parents include the following:

1. Outright rejection and attempts to force the child to change.
2. Continuing the relationship with the child but denying the child's lifestyle. "We never talk about it," said one parent, "but he is always welcome here and brings his lovers, too. I'd rather have my son as a homo than have no son at all."
3. Complete acceptance. The child's lifestyle is openly acknowledged and supported. The parents may become members of PFLAG (Parents and Friends of Lesbians and Gays). Most parents need time to accept their child's homosexuality. Parental acceptance and support are important for a person's sense of self-worth—no matter what his or her sexual orientation may be. Parental support may be particularly important for gay individuals because it may provide a buffer against the difficulties of living in a heterosexist society.

One parent who became aware that her son was gay said:

I had my suspicions, but when he told me he was gay I cried anyway. It was over the phone and I think this was more difficult because I couldn't hug him. At the time I think the tears shed were more for me and the dreams I was losing than for him and the prejudice and battles he would have to endure.

I found an organization called PFLAG—Parents and Friends of Lesbians and Gays—to be a lifesaver to both my husband and myself. It's a support group mostly of parents but it is also attended by siblings, friends, and gays themselves. They meet once a month and make you feel safe there to share your feelings and concerns about being a parent of a gay. They say when the child comes out of the closet, the parent goes in and there is some truth to that. They have a speaker and group discussions and also work toward changing legislation that is anti-gay. PFLAG also helped us to realize that it wasn't anything we said or did that made our son gay—it is how he was born. Needless to say, we love our son just as much now as before we knew. (authors' files)

Homosexual individuals usually disclose their sexual orientation to their siblings before they tell their parents. The reactions of siblings influence whether and when parents are told. Sibling reactions are often similar to those of parents. However, unlike parents, siblings do not experience guilt or self-blame (Strommen, 1989).

6-6e Coming Out to a Heterosexual Partner or Spouse and Children

Gay and bisexual people become involved in heterosexual relationships and marriages for reasons similar to heterosexuals—genuine love for a spouse, desire for children in a socially approved context, family pressure to marry, the desire to live a socially approved heterosexual lifestyle, and belief that marriage is the only way to achieve a happy adult life. In a probability sample of gay and bisexual men, 42% reported that they were currently married (Harry, 1990). Other researchers estimate that 20% of gay men are married (Strommen, 1989). Some individuals do not realize that they are gay or bisexual until after they are married.

Many homosexuals and bisexuals in heterosexual relationships do not disclose their sexual identity to their partners out of fear that their partners will reject them and that

These gay men and their children reflect the diversity of family life. Both men were involved in heterosexual marriages and now enjoy their children as pair-bonded gay dads.

there may be legal consequences (getting custody of the children would be jeopardized). The immediate and long-term consequences for coming out to one's partner vary widely from couple to couple. Some who disclose are able to work though the event. Buxton (2001) analyzed survey responses of 56 self-identified bisexual husbands and 51 heterosexual wives of bisexual men who maintained their marriage after disclosure. Honest communication, peer support, therapy, and "taking time" were identified as factors associated with positive coping. In addition, the couples were able to deconstruct not only traditional concepts of marriage but dichotomous views of sexual orientation.

There are about a half million gay dads in the United States (Knox, 2000). Dr. Jerry Bigner, himself a gay dad, provided several suggestions for coming out to one's children, including becoming comfortable with one's own gayness before coming out to one's children, discussing it with one's children when they are young before they find out from someone external to the family, ensuring one's child that "you won't be gay just because your dad is gay," and helping them with what they tell their friends (be selective) (Knox, 2000).

6-7 HOMOSEXUAL AND BISEXUAL RELATIONSHIPS

A team of researchers (Peplau, Veniegas, & Campbell, 1996) reviewed the literature on gay and bisexual relationships and concluded that while there are many similarities in the relationship experiences of same-sex and different-sex couples, "That which most clearly distinguishes same-sex from heterosexual couples is the social context of their lives. Whereas heterosexuals enjoy many social and institutional supports for their relationships, gay and lesbian couples are the object of prejudice and discrimination" (p. 268). Such a hostile social/psychological environment may lend itself to the development of a higher incidence of psychiatric disorders.

Sandfort, de Graaf, Bijl, and Schnabel (2001) analyzed interview data in a representative sample of the Dutch population (7,076 Dutch adults aged 18–64, 2.8% of men and 1.4% of women reported having had same-sex partners) and compared the differences between heterosexually and homosexually active subjects for the presence of 12-month prevalence of mood, anxiety, and substance use disorders as defined by the American Psychiatric Association's *Diagnostic and Statistical Manual of Mental Disorders*, or *DSM-III-R* (1987). They found that psychiatric disorders were more prevalent among homosexually active people compared with heterosexually active people. Homosexual men had a higher 12-month prevalence of mood disorders and anxiety disorders than heterosexual men. Homosexual women had a higher 12-month prevalence of substance use disorders than heterosexual women. More homosexual than heterosexual persons had 2 or more disorders during their lifetimes. The authors concluded that people with same-sex sexual behavior are at greater risk for psychiatric disorders.

6-7a Gay Male Relationships

A common stereotype of gay men is that they do not seek monogamous long-term relationships. Dreher (2002, p. 14) observed that "public sex is back. . . . The Internet is making this possible. Finding out where orgies are being held in your city on any given day is as easy as checking the Dow." Nevertheless, most gay men prefer long-term relationships.

National Data In a national survey of homosexual men, 71% reported that they preferred long-term monogamous relationships to other arrangements (Lever, 1994).

When sex outside the homosexual relationship does occur, it is usually infrequent and not emotionally involving (Green, Bettinger, & Zacks, 1996). Edmund White (1994) described the typical long-term gay couple:

> *If all goes well, two gay men will meet through sex, become lovers, weather the storms of jealousy and diminution of lust, develop shared interests (a hobby, a business, a house, a circle), and end up with a long-term. . . camaraderie that is not as disinterested as friendship or as seismic as passion. . . . Younger couples feel that this sort of relationship, when it happens to them, is incomplete, a compromise, and they break up in order to find total fulfillment (i.e. tireless passion) elsewhere. But older gay couples stay together, cultivate their mild, reasonable love, and defend it against the ever-present danger of the sexual allure exercised by a newcomer. . . . They may have. . . regular extracurricular sex partners or even beaux, but. . . with an eye attuned to nuance. . . at a certain point will intervene to banish a potential rival. (p. 164)*

Think About It

An increasing number of gay men are finding each other via the Internet. One third of a sample of 609 gay men reported that they had used the Internet to meet a sex partner (Benotsch, Kalichman, & Cage, 2002). These same respondents also reported higher numbers of partners and higher rates of sexual risk behaviors, including unprotected and receptive intercourse, than men who had not used the Internet. Why do you think a higher percentage of homosexuals than heterosexuals might use the Internet?

Another common stereotype is that gay men do not develop close, intimate relationships with their partners. A team of researchers (Green et al., 1996) compared 50 gay male couples with 218 married couples and found the former almost twice as likely to report the highest levels of cohesiveness (closeness) in their relationships. Gay male couples also report having more flexibility in their roles than heterosexual couples, and their

These gay men have been in a monogamous relationship for 20 years.

level of relationship satisfaction is roughly similar to heterosexual couples. Contrary to stereotypical beliefs, same-sex couples (male or female) do not typically adopt "husband" and "wife" roles (Peplau et al., 1996).

One unique aspect of gay male relationships in the United States involves coping with the high rate of HIV and AIDS. Many gay men have lost a love partner to this disease; some have experienced multiple losses. Those still in relationships with partners who are HIV positive experience profound changes such as developing a sense of urgency to "speed up" their relationship because they may not have much time left together (Palmer & Bor, 2001).

6-7b Lesbian Relationships

My lesbianism is an act of Christian charity. All those women out there praying for a man, and I'm giving them my share.

—Rita Mae Brown

Like many heterosexual women, most gay women value stable monogamous relationships that are emotionally as well as sexually satisfying. Transitory sexual encounters among gay women do occur, but they are the exception, not the rule. In a study of long-term gay relationships, 5 years was the average length of the relationship of 706 lesbian couples; 18% reported that they had been together 11 or more years. Ninety-one percent reported that they were sexually monogamous ("National Survey Results," 1990). The majority (57%) of the women in these lesbian relationships noted that they wore a ring to symbolize their commitment to each other. Some (19%) acknowledged their relationship with a ceremony. Most had met through friends or at work. Only 4% had met at a bar.

Women in our society, gay and "straight," are taught that sexual expression "should" occur in the context of emotional or romantic involvement. Ninety-three percent of 94 gay women in one study said their first homosexual experience was emotional; physical expression came later (Corbett & Morgan, 1983). Hence, for gay women, the formula is love first; for gay men, sex first—just as for their "straight" counterparts. Indeed, a joke in the lesbian community is that the second date of a lesbian couple involves getting a U-Haul together so that they can move in and "nest" together.

When lesbians engage in extra-partner sexual relations (sex external to the dyad), they (like heterosexual women) are likely to have emotional affairs rather than just sexual encounters. Nonmonogamy among lesbian couples is also likely to be related to dissatisfaction with the primary relationship. In addition, both lesbians and gay men are more likely than heterosexual couples to be open with their partners about their extra-partner activity (Nichols, 1987).

Kurdek (1995) reviewed the literature on lesbian and gay couples and concluded, "The most striking finding regarding the factors linked to relationship satisfaction is that they seem to be the same for lesbian couples, gay couples, and heterosexual couples." These factors include having equal power and control, being emotionally expressive, perceiving many attractions and few alternatives to the relationship, placing a high value on attachment, and sharing decision making. Also, as is true with heterosexual couples, relationship satisfaction among gay couples largely depends on the emotional intimacy of the partners (Deenen, Gijiis, & Van Naerssen, 1994).

Green et al. (1996) compared 52 lesbian couples with 50 gay male couples and 218 heterosexual married couples. They found that the lesbian couples were the most cohesive (closest), the most flexible in terms of their roles, and the most satisfied in their relationships.

6-7c Bisexual Relationships

Bisexuality is one of the least understood aspects of sexual orientation. So strong is the tendency to dichotomize sexual orientation that many people simply do not believe it exists.

—Margaret Nichols

Contrary to the common myth that bisexuals are, by definition, nonmonogamous, some bisexuals prefer monogamous relationships (especially considering the widespread concern about HIV). In one study, 16.4% of bisexuals reported being in monogamous relationships with no desire to stray (Rust, 1996). In the same study, lesbians and gay men were more likely than bisexual women and men to report that they were in monogamous relationships. Further, the study revealed that 29.5% of bisexual women and 15.4% of bisexual men reported that they would like to have a lifetime committed relationship, compared to 46.7% of lesbians and 75.9% of gay men (the high rate of desire for monogamy among gay men might be a response to the fear of HIV) (Rust, 1996).

Monogamous bisexual women and men may find that erotic attractions can be satisfied through fantasy and affectional needs through nonsexual friendships (Paul, 1996). Even in a monogamous relationship, "the partner of the bisexual person may feel that a bisexual person's decision to continue to identify as bisexual...is somehow a withholding of full commitment to the relationship. The bisexual person may be perceived as holding onto the possibility of other relationships by maintaining a bisexual identity and, therefore, not fully committed to the relationship" (Ochs, 1996, p. 234). However, this perception overlooks the fact that one's identity is separate from one's choices about relationship involvement or monogamy. Ochs (1996) noted that "a heterosexual's ability to establish and maintain a committed relationship with one person is not assumed to falter, even though the person retains a sexual identity as 'heterosexual' and may even admit to feeling attractions to other people despite her or his committed status" (p. 453).

In relationships in which one or more partners is bisexual, some couples attempt an "open" relationship that allows for extradyadic involvements. However, it is important for such couples to discuss and establish a mutually satisfactory set of ground rules. These ground rules should "recognize the acceptable limits of both partners, be readily subject to revision and renegotiation, and provide guidelines that are as explicit as possible with regard to that which is and is not acceptable in outside relationships" (Paul, 1996, p. 453).

6-8 SEXUAL ORIENTATION AND HIV INFECTION

Most worldwide HIV infection occurs through heterosexual transmission (Centers for Disease Control and Prevention, 2000). However, in the United States, HIV infection remains the most threatening STD for male homosexuals and bisexuals. Men who have sex with men account for more cases of AIDS in the United States than persons in any other transmission category (Centers for Disease Control and Prevention, 2000).

Huber and Kleinplatz (2002) examined the degree to which men who had sex with men in public bath houses and parks were more likely to self-identify as being heterosexuals or homosexuals. The researchers thought that heterosexual males as compared to homosexual males sought anonymous sex in these contexts. However, the data revealed no significant differences in the self-identified sexual orientation.

Women who have sex exclusively with other women have a much lower rate of HIV infection than men (both gay and "straight") and women who have sex with men. However, "female-to-female transmission of HIV can occur through exposure to cervical and vaginal secretions of an HIV-infected woman. The amount of shedding from these secretions likely increases the risk of HIV exposure" (Centers for Disease Control and Prevention, 2000). In addition, lesbians and bisexual women may also be at risk for HIV if they have sex with high-risk male partners (bisexuals) and inject drugs.

Think About It

Same-sex couples face many obstacles and struggles that heterosexual couples do not. However, Ochs (1996) points out that same-sex relationships also offer benefits, such as freedom from unwanted pregnancy, the absence of scripted gender roles, and the comfort and ease of being with someone with a more similar social conditioning. To what degree do you feel homosexuals value these advantages?

6-9 HETEROSEXUALITY, HOMONEGATIVITY, AND HOMOPHOBIA

Attitudes toward same-sex sexual behavior and relationships vary across cultures and across historical time periods. Today, most countries throughout the world, including the United States, are predominantly heterosexist. **Heterosexism** is the belief, stated or implied, that heterosexuality is superior (e.g., morally, socially, emotionally, and behaviorally) to homosexuality (Roffman, 2000). It involves the systematic degradation and stigmatization of any nonheterosexual form of behavior, identity, or relationship. Heterosexism involves the belief that heterosexuality is superior to homosexuality and results in prejudice and discrimination against homosexuals and bisexuals. Heterosexism assumes that all people are or should be heterosexual. Heterosexism is so pervasive that public space is controlled and heterosexualized in the sense that most tourism choices are assumed to be heterosexual. Indeed, gay individuals going on vacation often look for specific "gay friendly" towns (e.g., Key West, San Francisco), tourist spots, and bed/breakfast establishments (Pritchard, Morgan, Sedgley, Khan, & Jenkins, 2000).

Heterosexism The belief, stated or implied, that heterosexuality is superior (e.g., morally, socially, emotionally, and behaviorally) to homosexuality.

Before reading further, you may wish to complete the self-assessment in Box 6-1.

6-9a Homonegativity and Homophobia

SIECUS, the Sex Information and Education Council of the United States, affirms the sexual orientation of all persons. "Individuals have a right to accept, acknowledge, and live in accordance with their sexual orientation, be they bisexual, heterosexual, gay, or lesbian" (SIECUS, 2000). Nevertheless, negative attitudes toward homosexuality are reflected in the high percentage of the U.S. population that disapproves of homosexuality.

NATIONAL DATA Seventy-one percent of white men and 63 percent of white women report that "homosexual activity" is wrong (Michael, 2001).

Other countries also do not approve of homosexuality.

INTERNATIONAL DATA Homosexuality is illegal in about 50 countries; 8 countries have the death penalty for homosexuality—Afghanistan, Iran, Mauritania, Pakistan, Saudi Arabia, Sudan, United Arab Emirates, and Yemen (Mackay, 2001).

As long as the antigay campaigners continue to spread the message of ignorance and hate, our nation will remain a hostile, dangerous and sometimes deadly place for us, our friends and millions of America's gay and lesbian citizens.

—Eric Marcus

Homonegativity, the construct that refers to antigay responses, is multidimensional and includes negative feelings (fear, disgust, anger), thoughts (homosexuals are HIV carriers), and behavior (homosexuals deserve a beating). The affective component, **homophobia,** refers to emotional responses toward and aversion to homosexuals. Homophobia may be cultural (e.g., cultural stereotypes that lesbian/gay individuals are inherently bad, evil, immoral, abnormal, perverted, unhealthy, dangerous, sick, contagious, and/or predatory), social (dread fear that one will be perceived by others as gay), or psychological (irrational fear of lesbian/gay individuals and phobic reaction to them—a psychological defense mechanism against the fear that they themselves are gay) (Roffman, 2000).

Homonegativity Construct that refers to antigay responses including negative feelings (fear, disgust, anger), thoughts, and behavior.

Homophobia Negative emotional responses toward and aversion to homosexuals.

Box 6-1 Self Assessment

The Self-Report of Behavior Scale (Revised)

This questionnaire is designed to examine which of the following statements most closely describes your behavior during past encounters with people you thought were homosexuals. Rate each of the following self-statements as honestly as possible by choosing the frequency that best describes your behavior.

A—Never B—Rarely C—Occasionally D–Frequently E—Always

___ 1. I have spread negative talk about someone because I suspected that he or she was gay.
___ 2. I have participated in playing jokes on someone because I suspected that he or she was gay.
___ 3. I have changed roommates and/or rooms because I suspected my roommate to be gay.
___ 4. I have warned people whom I thought were gay and who were a little too friendly with me to keep away from me.
___ 5. I have attended anti-gay protests.
___ 6. I have been rude to someone because I thought that he or she was gay.
___ 7. I have changed seat locations because I suspected the person sitting next to me to be gay.
___ 8. I have had to force myself to stop from hitting someone because he or she was gay and very near me.
___ 9. When someone I thought to be gay has walked towards me as if to start a conversation, I have deliberately changed directions and walked away to avoid him or her.
___ 10. I have stared at a gay person in such a manner as to convey to him or her my disapproval of his or her being too close to me.
___ 11. I have been with a group in which one (or more) person(s) yelled insulting comments to a gay person or group of gay people.
___ 12. I have changed my normal behavior in a restroom because a person I believed to be gay was in there at the same time.
___ 13. When a gay person has "checked" me out, I have verbally threatened him or her.
___ 14. I have participated in damaging someone's property because he or she was gay.
___ 15. I have physically hit or pushed someone I thought was gay because he or she brushed his or her body against me when passing by.
___ 16. Within the past few months, I have told a joke that made fun of gay people.
___ 17. I have gotten into a physical fight with a gay person because I thought he or she had been making moves on me.
___ 18. I have refused to work on school and/or work projects with a partner I thought was gay.
___ 19. I have written graffiti about gay people or homosexuality.
___ 20. When a gay person has been near me, I have moved away to put more distance between us.

Scoring: The SBS-R is scored by totaling the number of points endorsed on all items (Never = 1; Rarely = 2; Occasionally = 3; Frequently = 4; Always = 5), yielding a range from 20–100 total points.

Comparison data: The SBS was originally developed by Sunita Patel (1989) in her thesis research in her clinical psychology master's program. College men (from a university campus and from a military base) were the original participants (Patel, Long, McCammon, & Wuensch, 1995). The scale was revised by Shartra Sylivant (1992), who used it with a coed high school student population, and by Tristan Roderick (1994), who involved college students to assess its psychometric properties. The scale was found to have high internal consistency. Two factors were identified, a passive avoidance toward homosexuals, and active or aggressive reactions.

In Roderick's study (Roderick, McCammon, Long, & Allred, 1998) the mean score for 182 college women was 24.76. The mean score for 84 men was significantly higher, at 31.60. A similar sex difference, although higher (more negative) scores were found in Sylivant's high school sample (with a mean of 33.74 for the young women, and 44.40 for the young men).

The following table provides detail for the scores of the college students in Roderick's sample (from a mid-sized state university in the southeast):

	N	Mean	Standard Deviation
Women	182	24.76	7.68
Men	84	31.60	10.36
Total	266	26.91	9.16

References

Patel, S. (1989). *Homophobia: Personality, emotional, and behavioral correlates*. Unpublished Master's Thesis, East Carolina University, Greenville, NC.

Patel, S., Long, T. E., McCammon, S. L., & Wuensch, K. L. (1995). Personality and emotional correlates of self reported antigay behaviors. *Journal of Interpersonal Violence, 10*, 354–366.

Roderick, T. (1994). *Homonegativity: An analysis of the SBS-R*. Unpublished Master's Thesis, East Carolina University, Greenville, NC.

Roderick, T., McCammon, S. L., Long, T. E., & Allred, L. J. (1998). Behavioral aspects of homonegativity. *Journal of Homosexuality, 36*, 79–88.

Sylivant, S. (1992). *The cognitive, affective, and behavioral components of adolescent homonegativity*. Unpublished Master's Thesis. East Carolina University, Greenville, NC.

Source: The SBS-R is reprinted by the permission of the students and faculty who participated in its development: Patel, S., McCammon, S. L., Long, T. E., Allred, L. J., Wuensch, K., Roderick, T., & Sylivant, S.

Think About It

Lesbians, gay men, and bisexuals identified "mistakes" heterosexuals make when trying to appear nonprejudiced (Conley, Calhoun, Evett, & Devine, 2001). They included

1. "I know someone who is gay." ("Who cares?" homosexuals think. They know gay people too!)
2. "Gays are really nice and have steady jobs." ("Like we wouldn't?" homosexuals think.)
3. "Will you take me to a gay bar?" (Like "Can we go to the zoo and see all the animals?")

How often have you observed these "mistakes"?

Homophobia is learned early, beginning in primary school (Plummer, 2001). Homophobia is not necessarily a clinical phobia (that is, one involving a compelling desire to avoid the feared object in spite of recognizing that the fear is unreasonable) but may involve distress that spreads from the original source to related objects or situations. For example, homophobics often feel discomfort not only with homosexuals, but also with traits or behaviors they associate with gay men or lesbians (such as effeminate behavior in men). Homophobics are also often reluctant to express affection toward someone of the same sex for fear of being labeled gay.

Demographic characteristics associated with homonegativity include being less educated, being "born again" or being an evangelical Christian, being a right-wing authoritarian, being African American or Hispanic, and being male. Indeed, traditional male role socialization burdens men with the expectation that they display traditional masculine heterosexual traits or else be regarded as feminine and socially unacceptable. Theodore and Basow (2000) studied homophobia in a group of college-aged men and found that the more the men believed that having traditionally prescribed masculine traits was important, but did not see themselves as measuring up, the more homophobic they were.

University men feel differently about lesbians and gay men. In a study of heterosexual college students, Louderback and Whitley (1997) replicated previous research showing that heterosexual women and men hold similar attitudes toward lesbians, but men are more negative toward gay men. The researchers explained that heterosexual men attribute a high erotic value to lesbianism and that this erotic value lessens their negative view of lesbians. The erotic value placed on lesbianism most likely stems from female-female sexual themes in erotic materials marketed to heterosexual men. Lance (2002) used contact theory to suggest that more tolerant attitudes toward lesbians can be engendered through classroom exposure. He invites presentations by lesbians in his human sexuality class and encourages dialogue via written questions which serve to "open up interaction" and reduce homophobia.

Think About It

Some college students are open to friendships with gays. Forty percent of 2,925 first-year students at the University of Maryland reported that they might like to have a lesbian or gay friend (Mohr & Sedlacek, 2000). What do you feel the attitude toward friendships with gay individuals is on your campus?

There are several sources for homonegativity and homophobia in the United States:

1. *Religion*. Although some religious groups (such as the Quakers) accept homosexuality, many religions teach that homosexuality is sinful and prohibited by God. "God made Adam and Eve, not Adam and Steve" is a phrase commonly cited by individuals whose homophobia is rooted in religion. The Roman Catholic Church rejects all homosexual expression (just as it rejects all sex outside marriage) and resists any attempt to validate or sanction the homosexual orientation. The Catholic Church regards homosexuality as a "disorder," a "condition." Homosexuality is not sinful;

Box 6-2 Social Choices

Should Same-Sex Marriage Be Legal?

In 2000, Vermont became the first state to legalize "civil unions" for same-sex couples. As of this writing, Vermont is the only state to legalize same-sex civil unions. While not equal to marriage in that other states do not recognize civil unions, the benefits include joint property rights, inheritance rights, shared health-care benefits, hospital visitation rights, and immunity from being compelled to testify against a partner. In Vermont, gay couples may obtain a civil union license (not a marriage license) for $20 from the town clerk and have the union certified by a judge or member of the clergy. In case of a breakup of the civil union, the couple would have to go through family court to obtain a legal dissolution. Holly Puterbauch, 54, and Lois Farnham, 55, were among the three same-sex couples who sued Vermont for the right to marry after being denied a marriage license, and who subsequently obtained a civil union.

As noted, the one difference between civil unions and traditional marriage unions is that the former may be recognized only in the state of Vermont. Hence, the civil union of a Vermont gay couple (unlike the marriage of a heterosexual couple) may not be recognized when they cross state lines. At least 36 states have banned gay marriages and Congress has passed the **Defense of Marriage Act** denying federal recognition of homosexual marriage and allowing states to ignore same-sex marriages licensed elsewhere. Although Hawaii recognizes same-sex relationships and provides some benefits to same-sex partners, Vermont most closely *approximates* legitimizing gay marriage (gay MARRIAGES are still illegal everywhere in the United States).

Most Americans support the traditional idea that marriage is a legal heterosexual relationship and oppose the legalization of same-sex marriages. Two thirds of adults in the United States oppose gay marriages (Michand, 2001). Those who view homosexuality as unnatural and against our country's moral standards do not want their children to learn that homosexuality is an accepted, "normal" lifestyle. Indeed, the most common argument against same-sex marriage is that it subverts the stability and integrity of the heterosexual family.

High school students tend to be supportive of gay marriages. Two thirds of a national sample of high school students agreed that gay marriages should be legal (Michand, 2001). Female and male college students differ in their support for gay marriages. Nearly two thirds (65.2%) of female university students and almost half (48.8%) of male university students agree or strongly agree that same-sex couples should have the right to legal marital status (American Council on Education and University of California, 2001).

Advocates of same-sex marriage argue that permitting such marriages might encourage many lesbians and gays to live within long-term, committed relationships. Hartinger (1994) suggests that "the result would be more people living more conventional lifestyles.... It's actually a conservative move, not a liberal one" (p. 239). Permitting gay marriage would, advocates argue, benefit not only homosexuals but the larger society as well. Marriage encourages monogamy. "In the wake of AIDS, encouraging gay monogamy is simply rational public health policy" (p. 239). The acceptance of same-sex marriages would also help to "eliminate heterosexism and homophobia by elevating homosexuality to the level of acceptability" (Bolte, 2001, p. 40).

The fear that children would be damaged by gay marriage is also debated. Patterson (2001) noted that not only do most children who are reared by gay parents have a heterosexual orientation as an

same-sex sexual behavior is the culprit and gay Catholics are encouraged to be abstinent. Some fundamentalist churches regard AIDS as God's punishment for homosexuality. Plugge-Foust (2001, p. 240) found that "conservative Christian religious ideology was the best predictor of homophobia."

On the other hand, some religious organizations reach out to gay members and sanction gay unions. Indeed, the General Assembly of the Presbyterian Church (USA) voted in 2000 that its ministers may conduct religious "holy union" ceremonies for same-sex couples as long as the ceremonies were not regarded as marriages (Commissioners' Resolution 00–13, 2000; Homosexuals in the Church, 2002). And, Rabbi Yoel Kahn (1997) made the following plea at a conference for American rabbis:

> *Deep, heartfelt yearning for companionship and intimacy is not an abomination before God. God does not want us to send the gays and lesbians among us into exile—either cut off from the Jewish community or into internal exile, living a lie for a lifetime. I believe that the time has come, I believe that God summons us to affirm the proper and rightful place of the homosexual Jew—and her or his family—in the synagogue and in the Jewish people.*

2. *Marital and procreative bias*. Many societies have traditionally condoned sex only when it occurs in a marital context that provides for the possibility of reproducing and rearing children. Although laws prohibiting homosexuals from marrying have been chal-

adult but that the "home environments provided by lesbian and gay parents are just as likely as those provided by heterosexual parents to enable psychosocial growth among family members" (p. 283).

In sum, advocates suggest that gay marriage would strengthen, not weaken, the family. Indeed, individuals in lesbian pair-bonded relationships report more satisfaction than heterosexual couples. Green et al. (1996) found that individuals in gay male relationships report slightly less satisfaction than heterosexual married couples but decidedly more than divorced individuals. However, a comparison between groups of homosexuals, bisexuals, and heterosexuals found little evidence that the dimension of sexual orientation is related to quality of life (sense of well-being/happiness), lifestyle (smoking/drinking), or health indicators (exercise) (Horowitz, Weis, & Laflin, 2001).

Cross culturally, Denmark, Sweden, and Iceland legally recognize same-sex marriages. But same-sex marriages and other-sex marriages may be treated differently. In the former, their marriages will not be recognized abroad and the nonbiological spouse may not automatically be granted full parental rights unless he or she adopts the child. Even adoption within the United States is problematic. A state appeals court in Los Angeles struck down a provision allowing one gay partner to adopt a child of the other (Perry, 2001). Norway, Greenland, France, Portugal, and the Netherlands legally recognize same-sex gay and lesbian partnerships but stop short of recognizing same-sex marriage.

Although Canada provides support for same-sex relationships in the form of spousal support, adoption, pension entitlement, and medical decision making, marriage is defined as a union between a man and a woman. Almost half (48%) of Canadians favor same-sex marriage (43% oppose it). Pollster Michael Marzolina collected national data on Canadian public opinion and reported, "The writing is on the wall for this issue...legalization of same sex marriage is inevitable" (Fife, 2002, p. A1).

In her interview study of 90 lesbians and gay men about their relationships and their perspectives on the marriage debate, Stiers (1999) documented that some respondents felt that they should not be pursuing this type of "mainstream" acceptance. However, others were adamant in arguing that legal rights to marry and parent are essential to obtaining full equality.

References

American Council on Education and University of California. (2001). The American freshman: National norms for fall, 2001. Los Angeles: Higher Education Research Institute. U.C.L.A. Graduate School of Education and Information Studies.

Bolte, A. (2001). Do wedding dresses come in lavender? The prospects and implications of same-sex marriage. In J. M. Lehmann (Ed.), *The gay & lesbian marriage & family reader* (pp. 25–46). Lincoln, NB: Gordian Knot Books.

Fife, R. (2002, July 25). Liberals find split on gay unions. *National Post*, A1

Green, R. J., Bettinger, M., & Zacks, E. (1996). Are lesbian couples fused and gay male couples disengaged? In J. Laird & R. J. Green (Eds.), *Lesbians and gays in couples and families* (pp. 185–230). San Francisco: Jossey Bass.

Hartinger, B. (1994). A case for gay marriage: In support of loving and monogamous relationships. In Robert T. Francoeur (Ed.), *Taking sides: Clashing views on controversial issues in human sexuality* (pp. 236–241). Guilford, CT: Dushkin.

Horowitz, S. M., Weis, D. L., & Laflin, M. T. (2001). Differences between sexual orientation behavior groups and social background, quality of life, and health behaviors. *The Journal of Sex Research, 38*, 205–218.

Michand, C. (2001). Survey: Students hold mostly pro-gay views. http://www.hrc.org/familynet

Patterson, C. J. (2001). Family relationships of lesbians and gay men. In R. M. Milardo (Ed.), *Understanding families into the new millennium: A decade in review* (pp. 271–288). Minneapolis, MN: National Council on Family Relations.

Perry, T. (2001, October 27). State appeals court voids gay adoption procedure. *Los Angeles Times*.

Stiers, G. A. (1999). *From this day forward: Commitment, marriage, and family in lesbian and gay relationships*. New York: St. Martin's Press.

Defense of Marriage Act Legislative act that denies federal recognition of homosexual marriage and allows states to ignore same-sex marriages licensed elsewhere.

---

lenged in the courts (see Box 6-2), and homosexuals may get a **civil union** license (in Vermont), they are denied a marriage license in all states. Finnis (2001) argued that homosexuality is thought to lead to the collapse of marriage as a civic institution and would harm children by subjecting them to nonmarital environments. As of 2002, 36 states have passed specific antimarriage laws targeting same-sex couples.

Civil union Legally recognized status between two gay individuals that approximates but does not equal marriage. Vermont permits civil unions.

3. *Concern about HIV and AIDS*. Although most cases of HIV and AIDS worldwide are attributed to heterosexual transmission, the rates of HIV and AIDS in the United States are much higher among gay and bisexual men than among other groups. Because of this, many people in the United States associate HIV and AIDS with homosexuality and bisexuality. Lesbians, incidentally, have a very low risk for sexually transmitted HIV—a lower risk than heterosexual women.

4. *Rigid gender roles*. Antigay sentiments also stem from rigid gender roles. Johnstone (2000) noted how cultural definitions of gay male and black male roles do not allow for an individual to be both. Similarly, lesbians are perceived as "stepping out of line" by relinquishing traditional female sexual and economic dependence on men. Both gay men and lesbians are often viewed as betrayers of their gender who must be punished. Louderback and Whitley (1997) confirmed previous research which found that individuals with traditional sex-role attitudes tend to hold more negative attitudes toward homosexuality. The researchers explained that men tend to hold more negative attitudes toward homosexuality than women because men tend to have more traditional attitudes toward the social roles of women and men in such areas as employment and household management.

5. *Psychiatric labeling*. Prior to 1973, the American Psychiatric Association defined homosexuality as a mental disorder. When the third edition of the *Diagnostic and Statistical Manual of Mental Disorders*, or *DSM-III*, (1980) was published, homosexuality was no longer included as a disorder. However, the *DSM-IV-TR* noted that "persistent and marked distress over one's sexual orientation" (formerly referred to as "ego-dystonic homosexuality") is listed as a "sexual disorder not otherwise specified" (American Psychiatric Association, 2000, p. 582). Hence, homosexuality itself is not regarded as a psychiatric disorder, but persistent and marked distress over being homosexual is a concern that warrants the label.

   There is controversy over "conversion" and "reparative" therapies that strive to help homosexual and bisexual people become heterosexual, or resume practicing heterosexuality. Some religious organizations sponsor ex-gay ministries, which claim to "cure" homosexuals and transform them into heterosexuals through prayer and other forms of "therapy." The American Psychological Association, American Psychiatric Association, American Academy of Pediatrics, and the American Medical Association agree that sexual orientation cannot be changed and that efforts to change sexual orientation do not work and may, in fact, be harmful (Human Rights Campaign, 2000). In addition, at least 13 ministries of one reparative therapy group, Exodus, have closed because their directors reverted to homosexuality (Fone, 2000). One of the students in the authors' classes attended Exodus and noted that "it was a place to cruise...nobody gets cured there."

6. *Myths and negative stereotypes*. Homonegativity may also stem from some of the unsupported beliefs and negative stereotypes regarding homosexuality. For example, many people believe that gays are child molesters, even though the ratio of heterosexual to homosexual child molesters is approximately 11:1 (Moser, 1992). Further, lesbians are stereotyped as women who want to be (or at least look and act like) men, whereas gay men are stereotyped as men who want to be (or at least look and act like) women. In reality, the gay population is as diverse as the heterosexual population not only in appearance, but also in social class, educational achievement, occupational status, race, ethnicity, and personality.

Attitudes toward homosexuals are becoming more tolerant. Altemeyer (2001) analyzed cross-sectional data on the attitudes of Canadian university students and their parents over a 14-year period and found increasing acceptance. Major causes for the increased tolerance was increased contact with persons known to be homosexual and evidence for the biological origins of sexual orientation.

6-9b Discrimination Against Homosexuals

Discrimination Behavior that involves treating categories of individuals unequally.

A negative attitude toward homosexuals is predictive of antigay behavior (Burn, 2000). Behavioral homonegativity involves **discrimination**, or behavior that involves treating categories of individuals unequally. Discrimination against lesbians and gays can occur at the individual level. Verbal pejoratives directed at gays in high school are particularly frequent and aggressive (Thurlow, 2001). In a national sample of gay adolescents, 12% reported threats in school (Russell, Franz, & Driscoll, 2001). Proactive staff development programs on heterosexism and homophobia to combat school antigay comments and violence are crucial (Allen, 2000; Robinson & Ferfolja, 2001).

Such verbal assaults and/or discrimination may continue in college. In a study of 484 young community college students, 94% acknowledged having engaged in antigay name-calling behavior (Franklin, 2000). In another study of 655 first-year undergraduates at a southeastern university, 70% said that they had "heard peers make insensitive or disparaging remarks" about a person's sexual orientation (Mather, 2000). Twenty-nine percent of the men and 17% of the women in this study reported that they would feel discomfort interacting with students who had a same-sex orientation (Mather, 2000).

Discrimination also occurs in the workplace. Although the Employment Nondiscrimination Act (ENDA) was reintroduced in 2001 (and has been every 2 years since 1974) to extend federal employment discrimination protection to include sexual orientation, only 12 states and the District of Columbia prohibit workplace discrimination based on sexual orientation. As of August 2002, the bill had not passed.

The most severe form of behavioral homonegativity is antigay violence, in which gay men and lesbians are physically attacked, injured, tortured, and even killed because of their sexual orientation (Bartle, 2000). Sexual orientation hate crimes are the third largest category of hate crimes, comprising 16.3% of all hate crimes (race = 53.6%; religion = 18.2%). Although the overall Crime Index has shown a decrease in crime, hate crimes have continued to increase (Johnson, 2001).

The most vicious form of hate crime is murder. Matthew Shepard was a 21-year-old gay college student at the University of Wyoming. Homophobics Russell Henderson and Aaron McKinney beat and lashed him to a split-rail fence because of his sexual orientation (they now face the death penalty for their crime). One third of 2,322 users of Gay.com and PlanetOut.com Internet sites reported that they had experienced an "antigay attack," including physical violence, verbal abuse, or destruction of personal property. Seventy percent felt that current laws did not protect them (Musbach, 2001b).

Ten percent of Franklin's (2000) young college students reported having engaged in antigay violent behavior. Studies investigating motives and correlates of negative behaviors against gays and lesbians have identified high adherence to traditional masculine roles, homophobia, and personality characteristics of impulsivity and social maladjustment (Patel, Long, McCammon, & Wuensch, 1995; Roderick, McCammon, Long, & Allred, 1998).

CULTURAL DIVERSITY

Discrimination of same-sex behavior also occurs at the legal level. A global overview of laws that criminalize sexual behavior between consenting adults indicates that such behavior is illegal in 85 countries (Sodomy Fact Sheet: A Global Overview, 2000). In 52 of these countries, laws criminalizing same-sex sexual behavior apply to both female and male homosexuality. Legal penalties include the death penalty in countries such as Sudan, Pakistan, and Somalia. For example, a Somali lesbian couple were sentenced to death for "exercising unnatural behavior" ("Jail, Death Sentences in Africa," 2001). Although executions in this region are performed by firing squads, religious tradition dictates that those convicted of homosexuality should either have a wall pushed onto them or be thrown off a roof or other high place.

Finally, lesbians and gay men are also discriminated against in family matters. Although between 6 and 14 million children are being reared by gay men and lesbians (Duran-Aydintug & Causey, 2001), there is the belief that homosexuals should not rear children. Two grounds are typically used: First, per se, which "presumes the parent to be unfit merely based on the existence of same-sex orientation. Lesbian mothers are thought to be 'unfit parents, emotionally unstable, or unable to assume a maternal role'" (Erera & Fredriksen, 2001, p. 88).

The second ground is the nexus approach, which is used to deny custody to homosexual parents on the basis of their being a negative influence on the sexual development of the child, the social stigmatization of the children who is being parented by homosexual parents, and the potential sexual molestation of children by homosexual parents (Duran-Aydintug & Causey, 2001). Although the effect of having homosexual parents on a child's sexual development is still being debated (Stacey & Biblarz, 2001), public concern remains. Social stigmatization is a fact of life (but biracial children are also stigmatized). Cases of documented sexual abuse by homosexual parents of their children are virtually "nonexistent" (Duran-Aydintug & Causey, 2001).

Think About It

Judges are given enormous latitude to rule against homosexual parents (Duran-Aydintug & Causey, 2001). The second author of this text served as an expert witness in a trial whereby a lesbian mother petitioned the court for custody of her children in a divorce from her husband. She was denied custody. The lawyer defending the lesbian mother said, "No judge in this town can keep his job if he gives a child to a gay parent." What is the political climate in your area for supporting the rights of gay individuals to rear children?

In many states, children can legally be taken out of the home of a lesbian mother or a gay father, even though research studies show that the children of lesbian mothers are just as likely to be well adjusted as those of straight mothers (no data have been reported yet on children of gay fathers) (Patterson, 2001). Gay and lesbian couples have also been denied the option of being legally married in the United States. Without legal marital status, gay couples are denied many benefits and rights that are granted to married couples. Box 6-2 discusses the controversy over granting homosexual couples the right to be legally married.

6-9c Biphobia

Biphobia Fearful, negative, discriminatory reactions toward bisexuals.

Just as the term *homophobia* is used to refer to negative attitudes and emotional responses and discriminatory behavior toward gay men and lesbians, **biphobia** refers to similar reactions and discrimination toward bisexuals. Eliason (2001) noted that bisexual men are viewed more negatively than bisexual women, gay men, or lesbians. Bisexuals are thought to be really homosexuals afraid to acknowledge their real identity or homosexuals maintaining heterosexual relationships to avoid rejection by the heterosexual mainstream. In addition, bisexual individuals are sometimes viewed as heterosexuals who are looking for exotic sexual experiences. Bisexuals may experience double discrimination in that they are accepted by neither the heterosexual nor homosexual community.

Gay women seem to exhibit greater levels of biphobia than do gay men. The reason is that many lesbian women associate their identity with a political stance against sexism and patriarchy. Some lesbians view heterosexual and bisexual women who "sleep with the enemy" as traitors to the feminist movement. One bisexual woman currently in a relationship with a man explains:

> *I have to be in the closet around straight people because they don't like that I like girls.... In the same way I've got to be kind of in the closet around lesbians because they're really quite put off by this man.... I can get shot down from both sides. It's a weird sensation. (quoted in Esterberg, 1997, p. 147)*

SUMMARY

Gay, lesbian, and bisexual individuals and their concerns are receiving increased visibility in our society. This chapter defines terms, models, prevalence, relationships, and homonegativity/homophobia.

Terms of Sexual Orientation

Sexual orientation refers to the classification of individuals as heterosexual, bisexual, or homosexual based on their emotional and sexual attractions, relationships, self-identity, and lifestyle. Heterosexuality refers to the predominance of emotional and sexual attraction to persons of the other sex; homosexuality, to persons of the same sex; bisexuality, to both sexes. LesBiGays is generic term for lesbians, gays, and bisexuals. Transgendered individuals do not fit neatly into either the male or female category, or their behavior is not congruent with the norms and expectations of their sex in the society in which they live. Examples of transgendered individuals include homosexuals, bisexuals, cross-dressers, and transsexuals.

Conceptual Models of Sexual Orientation

The four models of sexual orientation are the dichotomous model (people are either heterosexual or homosexual), the unidimensional continuum model (sexual orientation is viewed on a continuum from heterosexuality to homosexuality), the multidimensional model (sexuality involves the factors of emotions, behaviors, and cognitions), and the LesBiGay/Transgender affirmative model (uses insights from previous models and emphasizes available cultural menus).

Prevalence of Homosexuality, Heterosexuality, and Bisexuality

The prevalence of homosexuality, heterosexuality, and bisexuality is difficult to determine. This is due to fear of social disapproval and changing sexual attractions, behaviors, and identities over time. It is estimated that only one third of gay men and lesbian couples reported themselves as such in the latest census. Nevertheless, available data suggest that about 10 million individuals or 4 to 5 percent of the U.S. population are gay.

Theories of Sexual Orientation

Basic theories of sexual orientation are biological (genetic, chromosomal, hormonal) and social/cultural (parent-child interactions, early sexual experiences). Most researchers agree that an interaction of biological and social/cultural forces is involved in the development of one's sexual orientation.

Gay and Bisexual Identity Development

The development of a gay or bisexual identity involves four stages: awareness or realization that one is "different," test and exploration, identity acceptance, and identity integration.

Coming Out

"Coming out" refers to the recognition of a homosexual or bisexual orientation to one's self, parents, siblings, heterosexual partner or spouse and children, friends, and employers. The reactions are unpredictable. Coming out is especially difficult for bisexuals because both heterosexuals and homosexuals may reject them.

Homosexual and Bisexual Relationships

Homosexual, bisexual, and heterosexual relationships are more similar than different. However, unlike heterosexual couples (who receive social support for long-term relationships), same-sex couples receive little social support. Lack of social support contributes to the difficulty some same-sex couples have in maintaining committed relationships. Gay male relationships are stereotyped as short-term, and lacking closeness and intimacy. In reality, most gay men prefer long-term, close relationships. Lesbians value monogamous, emotionally and sexually satisfying relationships. Some bisexuals prefer monogamous relationships; others prefer "open" relationships that permit emotional and sexual involvement with more than one partner.

Sexual Orientation and HIV Infection

Most HIV infection occurs worldwide through heterosexual transmission; in the United States, through male-to-male transmission. Women who have sex exclusively with other women have a much lower rate of HIV infection than men (both gay and "straight") and women who have sex with men. However, lesbians and bisexual women may also be at risk for HIV if they have sex with high-risk male partners (bisexuals) and inject drugs.

Heterosexuality, Homonegativity, and Homophobia

Heterosexism is the belief that heterosexuality is superior (e.g., morally, socially, emotionally, and behaviorally) to homosexuality and involves the systematic degradation and stigmatization of any nonheterosexual form of behavior, identity, or relationship. Homonegativity includes negative feelings (fear, disgust, anger), thoughts (homosexuals are HIV carriers), and behavior (homosexuals deserve a beating). Homophobia refers to emotional responses toward and aversion to homosexuals. Homophobia may be cultural (stereotypes include that lesbian/gay individuals are inherently bad, evil, immoral, abnormal, perverted, unhealthy, dangerous, sick, contagious, and/or predatory), social (dread fear that one will be perceived by others as gay), or psychological (irrational fear of lesbian/gay individuals and phobic reaction to them).

SUGGESTED WEBSITES

Note: These websites were functional when we went to press. Please access the online text for the most up-to-date URLs.

Human Rights Campaign
http://www.hrc.org/familynet/newsstand.asp

Lesbian and Gay Community Centers
http://www.gaycenter.org/natctr

Major Gay Internet Sites
http://www.gay.com
http://www.planetout.com

Parents, Families, and Friends of Lesbians and Gays
http://www.pflag.org

Whosoever (a gay/lesbian online magazine for Christians)
http://www.whosoever.org/

KEY TERMS

biphobia (p. 196)
bisexuality (p. 172)
civil union (p. 193)
coming out (p. 182)
Defense of Marriage Act (p. 193)
dichotomous model (p. 173)
discrimination (p. 194)
heterosexism (p. 189)
heterosexuality (p. 172)
homonegativity (p. 189)
homophobia (p. 189)
homosexuality (p. 172)
LesBiGays (p. 172)
LesBiGay/Transgender affirmative model (p. 174)
multidimensional model (p. 173)
sexual orientation (p. 172)
transgendered (p. 172)
transgendered individuals (p. 172)
unidimensional continuum model (p. 173)

CHAPTER QUIZ

1. Lesbians, gay men, and bisexual individuals __________ part of the population known as "transgendered."
   a. are
   b. are not
2. Which model of sexual orientation does not recognize bisexuality?
   a. unidimensional continuum model
   b. multidimensional model
   c. dichotomous model
   d. LesBiGay/Transgender affirmative model
3. Kinsey's Homosexual-Heterosexual Rating Scale reflects which model of sexual orientation?
   a. unidimensional continuum model
   b. multidimensional model
   c. dichotomous model
   d. LesBiGay/Transgender affirmative model
4. The most important contribution of the multidimensional model of sexual orientation is its emphasis on
   a. self-identity.
   b. behavior.
   c. heredity.
   d. cognitions.

5. According to data cited in your text, about 4% to 5% of the U.S. adult population is lesbian or gay.
   a. True
   b. False

6. Between 1977 and 2001, the belief that homosexuality is caused by biological factors
   a. decreased.
   b. increased.

7. Based on 2001 Gallup poll data, more than half of U.S. adults agree that
   a. homosexuality is an "acceptable alternative lifestyle."
   b. "homosexual relations between consenting adults should be legal."
   c. both a and b.
   d. neither a nor b.

8. According to your text, gay youths are more likely to come out to which parent?
   a. mothers
   b. fathers

9. After reviewing the literature on gay and bisexual relationships, a team of researchers (Peplau et al., 1996) concluded that there are many similarities in the relationship experiences of same-sex and different-sex couples. What, according to these researchers, most distinguished same-sex from heterosexual couples?
   a. Same-sex couples tend to have lower levels of relationship satisfaction.
   b. Heterosexual couples tend to place a higher value on relationship commitment.
   c. Same-sex couples experience prejudice and discrimination.
   d. Heterosexual couples do a better job of rearing children.

10. All of the following are true EXCEPT
   a. Altemeyer's (2001) study of Canadian university students and parents over a 14-year period found increased intolerance.
   b. The general public tends to believe that a person chooses to be homosexual (rather than is "born that way").
   c. Acceptance of a biological explanation for homosexuality is increasing.
   d. The belief in biological determinism of sexual orientation among homosexuals is strong.

11. According to Freud, which of the following sets of relationships is conducive to a male becoming homosexual?
   a a close relationship with his father and a distant relationship with his mother
   b. early homosexual relationships with peers and a close relationship with his father
   c. early homosexual relationships with peers and a close relationship with his mother
   d. a close relationship with his mother and a distant relationship with his father

12. In a study of 402 parents of gay and lesbian children, _______ said that they already suspected that their child was homosexual.
   a. fewer than one half
   b. most (nearly 90%)

13. The theory that provides an explanation of the development of sexual orientation that combines biological and environmental components is known as
   a. PTT (Polygenetic Trait Theory)
   b. EBE—Exotic Becomes Erotic
   c. KHS—Kinsey's Homosexual Scale
   d. YESO—Yang's Explanation of Sexual Orientation

14. A national probability sample of gay and bisexual men revealed that _________ of gay and bisexual men are married.
   a. between 1 and 2%
   b. about 10%
   c. nearly one fourth
   d. more than 40%

15. According to a national survey of homosexual men, most reported that they preferred
   a. long-term monogamous relationships.
   b. long-term relationships with more than one man.
   c. short-term monogamous relationships.
   d. short-term relationships with more than one man.

16. In a study of 52 lesbian couples, 50 gay male couples, and 218 heterosexual couples, which couples reported the highest degree of cohesiveness (closeness) AND role flexibility?
   a. lesbian couples
   b. gay male couples
   c. heterosexual couples
   d. There were no differences between lesbian, gay, and heterosexual couples on these variables.

17. Worldwide most HIV infection occurs through
   a. homosexual transmission.
   b. heterosexual transmission.
   c. needle-sharing.
   d. blood transfusions.

18. Demographic characteristics associated with homonegativity include all the following EXCEPT
   a. being male.
   b. being an evangelical Christian.
   c. being a college graduate
   d. being African American or Hispanic.

19. What is the only state that has legalized "civil unions" between same-sex partners?
   a. Nevada
   b. New Hampshire
   c. Vermont
   d. California

REFERENCES

Allen, D. L. (2000, May). A case study of perspectives of gay and lesbian teachers: Overcoming heterosexism and homophobia in the school community. *Dissertation Abstracts International—The Humanities and Social Sciences, 60*, 3959–A.

Altemeyer, B. (2001). Changes in attitudes toward homosexuals. *Journal of Homosexuality, 42*, 63–75.

American Council on Education and University of California. (2001). The American freshman: National norms for fall, 2001. Los Angeles: Higher Education Research Institute. U.C.L.A. Graduate School of Education and Information Studies.

American Psychiatric Association. (1980). *Diagnostic and statistical manual of mental disorders* (3rd ed.). Washington, DC: Author.

American Psychiatric Association. (1987). *Diagnostic and statistical manual of mental disorders, R* (3rd ed., rev.). Washington, DC: Author.

American Psychiatric Association. (2000). *Diagnostic and statistical manual of mental disorders*, (4th ed., rev.). Washington, DC: Author.

Bailey, J. M. (2001). Parental selection of children's sexual orientation. *Archives of Sexual Behavior, 30*, 423–437.

Bailey, J. M., & Pillard, R. C. (1991). A genetic study of male sexual orientation. *Archives of General Psychiatry, 48*, 1089–1096.

Bailey, J. M., Pillard, R. C., Neale, M. C., & Agyei, Y. (1993). Heritable factors influence sexual orientation in women. *Archives of General Psychiatry, 50*, 217–223.

Bakker, J., Ophemert, J. V., & Slob, A. K. (1993). Organization of partner preference and sexual behavior and its nocturnal rhythmicity in male rats. *Behavioral Neuroscience, 107*, 1049–1058.

Banks, A., & Gartrell, N. K. (1995). Hormones and sexual orientation: A questionable link. *Journal of Homosexuality, 28*, 247–268.

Bartle, E. F. (2000). Lesbians and hate crimes. *Journal of Poverty, 4*, 23–43.

Beeler, J., & DiProva, V. (1999). Family adjustment following disclosure of homosexuality by a member: Themes discerned in narrative accounts. *Journal of Marital and Family Therapy, 25*, 443–459.

Bell, A. P., & Weinberg, M. S. (1978). *Homosexualities: A study of diversity among men and women*. New York: Simon and Schuster.

Bell, A. P., Weinberg, M. S., & Hammersmith, S. K. (1981). *Sexual preference: Its development in men and women: Statistical appendix*. Bloomington: Indiana University Press.

Bem, D. J. (1996). Exotic becomes erotic: A developmental theory of sexual orientation. *Psychological Review, 103*, 320–335.

Bem, D. J. (2000). Exotic becomes erotic: Interpreting the biological correlates of sexual orientation. *Archives of Sexual Behavior, 29*, 531–548.

Benari, A. (1995). The discovery that an offspring is gay: Parents', gay men's, and lesbians' perspectives. *Journal of Homosexuality, 30*, 89–112.

Benotsch, E. G., Kalichman, S., & Cage, M. (2002). Men who have met sex partners via the Internet: Prevalence, predictors, and implications for HIV prevention. *Archives of Sexual Behavior, 31*, 177–183.

Black, D., Gates, G., Sanders, S., & Taylor L. (2000). Demographics of the gay and lesbian population in the United States: Evidence from available systematic data sources. *Demography, 37*, 139–154.

Bogaert, A. F., Friesen, C., & Klentrou, P. (2002). Age of puberty and sexual orientation in a national probability sample. *Archives of Sexual Behavior, 31*, 73–82.

Bolte, A. (2001). Do wedding dresses come in lavender? The prospects and implications of same-sex marriage. In J. M. Lehmann (Ed.), *The gay & lesbian marriage & family reader* (pp. 25–46). Lincoln, NE: Gordian Knot Books.

Brannock, J. C., & Chapman, B. E. (1990). Negative sexual experiences with men among heterosexual women and lesbians. *Journal of Homosexuality, 19*, 105–110.

Bullough, V. L. (2000, July–September). Transgenderism and the concept of gender. *The International Journal of Transgenderism*. *www.symposion.com*

Burn, S. M. (2000). Heterosexuals' use of 'fag' and 'queer' to deride one another: A contributor to heterosexism and stigma. *Journal of Homosexuality, 40* (2), 1–11.

Buxton, A. P. (2001). Writing our own script: How bisexual men and their heterosexual wives maintained their marriages after disclosure. *Journal of Bisexuality, 1*, 155–189.

Cantor, J. M., Blanchard, R., Paterson, A. D., & Bogaert, A. F. (2002). How many gay men owe their sexual orientation to fraternal birth order? *Archives of Sexual Behavior, 31*, 63–71.

Centers for Disease Control and Prevention (2000). http://www.cdc.gov/hiv/stats/exposure.htm

Cohen, K. M., & Savin-Williams, R. C. (1996). Developmental perspectives on coming out to self and others. In R. C. Savin-Williams & K. M. Cohen (Eds.), *The lives of lesbians, gays, and bisexuals: From children to adults* (pp. 113–151). Fort Worth, TX: Harcourt Brace.

Collins, J. R. (2000). Biracial-Bisexual individuals: Identity coming of age. *International Journal of Sexuality and Gender Studies, 3*, 221–253.

Commissioners' Resolution 00–13. Concerning support of civil unions for same-gender couples. Retrieved September 12, 2002, http://horeb.pcusa.org/ga212/commissioner/0013.htm

Conley, T. D., Calhoun, C., Evett, S. R., & Devine, P. G. (2001). Mistakes that heterosexual people make when trying to appear non-prejudiced: The view from LGB people. *Journal of Homosexuality, 42*, 21–43.

Corbett, S. L., & Morgan, K. D. (1983). The process of lesbian identification. *Free Inquiry in Creative Sociology, 11*, 81–83.

Dahir, M. (2001, July 17). Why are we gay? *The Advocate, 842*, 30–39.

Dawood, K., Pillard, R. C., Horvath, C., Revelle, W., & Bailey, J. M. (2000). Familial aspects of male homosexuality. *Archives of Sexual Behavior, 29*, 155–163.

Deenen, A. A., Gijiis, L., & Van Naerssen, A. X. (1994). Intimacy and sexuality in gay male couples. *Archives of Sexual Behavior, 23*, 421–431.

Diamond, M. (1995). Biological aspects of sexual orientation and identity. In L. Diamont & R. D. McAnulty (Eds.), *The psychology of sexual orientation, behavior, and identity: A handbook* (pp. 45–80). Westport, CT: Greenwood Press.

Doll, L. S., Petersen, L. R., White, C. R., Johnson, E. S., Ward J. W., & the Blood Donor Study Group. (1992). Homosexuality and nonhomosexuality identified men: A behavioral comparison. *The Journal of Sex Research, 29*, 1–14.

Dreher, R. (2002). Beds, bathhouses, and beyond: The return of public sex. *National Review, 54*, 14.

Duran-Aydintug, C., & Causey, K. A. (2001). Child custody determination: Implications for lesbian mothers. In J. M. Lehmann (Ed.), *The gay & lesbian marriage & family reader* (pp. 47–64). Lincoln, NE: Gordian Knot Books.

Eliason, M. (2001). Bi-negativity: The stigma facing bisexual men. *Journal of Bisexuality, 1*, 137–154.

Ellis, L. (1996). Theories of homosexuality. In R. C. Savin-Williams & K. M. Cohen (Eds.), *The lives of lesbians, gays, and bisexuals: Children to adults* (pp. 11–34). Fort Worth, TX: Harcourt Brace.

Ellis, L., & Ames, M. A. (1987). Neurohormonal functioning and sexual orientation: A theory of homosexuality-heterosexuality. *Psychological Bulletin, 101*, 233–258.

Ellis, L., Ames, M. A., Peckham, W., & Burke, D. (1988). Sexual orientation of human offspring may be altered by severe maternal stress during pregnancy. *The Journal of Sex Research, 25*, 152–157.

Erera, P. I., & Fredriksen, K. (2001). Lesbian stepfamilies: A unique family structure. In J. M. Lehmann (Ed.), *The gay & lesbian marriage & family reader* (pp. 80–94). Lincoln, NE: Gordian Knot Books.

Esterberg, K. (1997). *Lesbian and bisexual identities: Constructing communities, constructing selves*. Philadelphia: Temple University Press.

Evans, N. J., & Broido, E. M. (2000). Coming out in college residence halls: Negotiation, meaning making, challenges, supports. *Journal of College Student Development, 40*, 658–668.

Fausto-Sterling, A. (1995). Animal models for the development of human sexuality: A critical evaluation. *Journal of Homosexuality, 28*, 217–236.

Fife, R. (2002, July 25). Liberals find split on gay unions. *National Post*, A1

Finnis, J. (2001). Virtue and the Constitution of the United States. *Fordham Law Review, 69*, 1595–1602.

Firestein, B. A. (1996). Bisexuality as paradigm shift: Transforming our disciplines. In B. A. Firestein (Ed.), *Bisexuality: The psychology and politics of an invisible minority* (pp. 263–291). Thousand Oaks, CA: Sage.

Flowers, P., & Buston, K. (2001). "I was terrified of being different": Exploring gay men's accounts of growing-up in a heterosexist society. *Journal of Adolescence, 24*, 51–65.

Fone, B. (2000). *Homophobia: A history*. New York: Henry Holt and Company.

Fox, R. C. (1996). Bisexuality in perspective: A review of theory and research. In B. A. Firestein (Ed.), *Bisexuality: The psychology and politics of an invisible minority* (pp. 3–50). Thousand Oaks, CA: Sage.

Franklin, K. (2000). Antigay behaviors among young adults: Prevalence, patterns, and motivations. *Journal of Interpersonal Violence, 15*, 339–362.

Gooren, L. J. G. (1995). Biomedical concepts of homosexuality: Folk belief in a white coat. *Journal of Homosexuality, 28*, 237–246.

Green, R. J., Bettinger, M., & Zacks, E. (1996). Are lesbian couples fused and gay male couples disengaged? In J. Laird & R. J. Green (Eds.), *Lesbians and gays in couples and families* (pp. 185–230). San Francisco: Jossey Bass.

Harry, J. (1990). A probability sample of gay males. *Journal of Homosexuality*, 19, 89–104.

Hartinger, B. (1994). A case for gay marriage: In support of loving and monogamous relationships. In Robert T. Francoeur (Ed.), *Taking sides: Clashing views on controversial issues in human sexuality* (pp. 236–241). Guilford, CT: Dushkin.

Haug, M., Whalen, R. E., Aron, C., & Olsen, K. (Eds.). (1993). *The development of sex differences and similarities in behavior*. Dordrecht: Kluwer Academic Publishers.

Homosexuals in the church. (2002). Retrieved September 12, 2002, http://www.pcusa.org/101/101-homosexual.htm

Horowitz, S. M., Weis, D. L., & Laflin, M. T. (2001). Differences between sexual orientation behavior groups and social background, quality of life, and health behaviors. *The Journal of Sex Research, 38*, 205–218.

Huber, J. D., & Kleinplatz, P. J. (2002). Sexual orientation identification of men who have sex with men in public settings in Canada. *Journal of Homosexuality, 42*(3), 1–20.

Human Rights Campaign. (2000). *Feeling free: Personal Stories: How love and self-acceptance saved us from 'Ex-Gay" Ministries*. Washington, DC: Human Rights Campaign Foundation.

Hyde, J. S. (2000). Becoming a heterosexual adult: The experiences of young women. *Journal of Social Issues, 56*, 283–296.

Jail, death sentences in Africa. (2001, February 21). PlanetOut.com, http://www.planetout.com/news/articleprint.html

Johnson, P. (2001, October 25). Hate crimes increase in the United States. PlanetOut.com

Johnstone, R. (2000). Sexual and ethnic scripts in the context of African American culture. *Alternate Routes, 16*, 5–8.

Kahn, Y. H. (1997). The Kedushah of homosexual relationships. In A. Sullivan (Ed.), *Same sex marriage: Pro and con* (pp. 71–77). New York: Vintage Books.

Kelly, D. D. (1991). Sexual differentiation of the nervous system. In E. R. Kandel, J. H. Schwartz, & T. M. Jessell (Eds.), *Principles of neuroscience* (pp. 959–973). Norwalk, CT: Appleton & Lange.

King, M., & McDonald, E. (1992). Homosexuals who are twins. A study of 46 probands. *British Journal of Psychiatry, 160*, 407–409.

Kinsey, A. C., Pomeroy, W. B., & Martin, C. E. (1948). *Sexual behavior in the human male*. Philadelphia: Saunders.

Kinsey, A. C., Pomeroy, W. B., Martin, C. E., & Gebhard, P. H. (1953). *Sexual behavior in the human female*. Philadelphia: Saunders.

Klein, F. (1990). The need to view sexual orientation as a multivariable dynamic process: A theoretical perspective. In D. P. McWhirter, S. A. Sanders, & J. M. Reinisch (Eds.), *Homosexuality/heterosexuality: Concepts of sexual orientation* (pp. 277–282). New York: Oxford University Press.

Knox, D. (2000). *Divorced dad's survival book*. Reading, MA: Perseus Publishing Co.

Kurdek, L. A. (1995). Lesbian and gay couples. In A. R. D'Augelli & C. J. Patterson (Eds.), *Lesbian, gay, and bisexual identities over the lifespan: Psychological perspectives* (pp. 243–261). New York: Oxford University Press.

Lance, L. M. (2002). Heterosexism and homophobia among college students. *College Student Journal, 36*, 411–415.

LaSala, M. (2000). Lesbians, gay men, and their parents: Family therapy for the coming-out crisis. *Family Process, 39*, 67–81.

LeVay, S. (1991) News and comment. *Science, 253*, 956–957.

LeVay, S. (1994). *The sexual brain*. Cambridge, MA: MIT Press.

Lever, J. (1994, August 23). The 1994 *Advocate* survey of sexuality and relationships: The men. *The Advocate*, 16–24.

Louderback, L. A., & Whitley, B. E. (1997). Perceived erotic value of homosexuality and sex-role attitudes as mediators of sex differences in heterosexual college students' attitudes toward lesbians and gay men. *The Journal of Sex Research, 34*, 175–182.

Mackay, J. (2001). Global sex: Sexuality and sexual practices around the world. *Sexual and Relationship Therapy, 16*, 71–82.

Mather, P. C. (2000). Diversity at East Carolina University, *Student Perspectives*, Fall.

Michael, R. T. (2001). Private sex and public policy. In E. O. Laumann & R. T. Michael (Eds.), *Sex, love, and health in America: Private choices and public policies* (pp. 465–491). Chicago: The University of Chicago Press.

Michael, R. T., Wadsworth, J., Feinleib, J. A., Johnson, A. M., Laumann, E. O., & Wellings, K. (2001). Private sexual behavior, public opinion, and public health policy related to sexually transmitted diseases: A U.S.–British comparison. In E. O. Laumann & R. T. Michael (Eds.), *Sex, love, and health in America: Private choices and public policies* (pp. 439–453). Chicago: The University of Chicago Press.

Michand, C. (2001). Survey: Students hold mostly pro-gay views. http://www.hrc.org/familynet

Miller, E. M. (2000). Homosexuality, birth order, and evolution: Toward an equilibrium reproductive economics of homosexuality. *Archives of Sexual Behavior, 29*, 1–34.

Mohr, J. J., & Sedlacek, W. E. (2000). Perceived barriers to friendship with lesbians and gay men among university students. *Journal of College Student Development, 41*, 70–80.

Money, J. (1987). Sin, sickness, or status? Homosexual gender identity and psychoneuroendocrinology. *American Psychologist, 42*, 384–399.

Moser, C. (1992). Lust, lack of desire, and paraphilias: Some thoughts and possible connections. *Journal of Sex and Marital Therapy, 18*, 65–69.

Musbach, T. (2001a, October 15.). Governor signs California partners law. PlanetOut.com

Musbach, T. (2001b, September 27). Survey: 33 percent endure anti-gay abuse. PlanetOut.com

National survey results of gay couples in long-lasting relationships. (1990, May/June). *Partners: Newsletter of Gay and Lesbian Couples* (pp. 1–16). (Available from Stevie Bryant & Demian, Box 9685, Seattle, WA 98109).

Nichols, M. (1987). Lesbian sexuality: Issues and developing theory. In Boston Lesbian Psychologies (Eds.), *Lesbian psychologies: Explorations and challenges* (pp. 97–125). Chicago: University of Illinois Press.

Ochs, R. (1996). Biphobia: It goes more than two ways. In B. A. Firestein (Ed.), *Bisexuality: The psychology and politics of an invisible minority* (pp. 217–239). Thousand Oaks, CA: Sage.

Oswald, R. F. (2000). Family and friendship relationships after young women come out as bisexual or lesbian. *Journal of Homosexuality, 38*, 65–83.

Palmer, R., & Bor, R. (2001). The challenges to intimacy and sexual relationships for gay men in HIV serodiscordant relationships: A pilot study. *Journal of Marital and Family Therapy, 27*(4), 419–431

Park, A. (1995, November 13). New evidence of a "gay gene." *Time*, 95.

Patel, S. (1989). *Homophobia: Personality, emotional, and behavioral correlates*. Unpublished Master's Thesis, East Carolina University, Greenville, NC.

Patel, S., Long, T. E., McCammon, S. L., & Wuensch, K. L. (1995). Personality and emotional correlates of self reported antigay behaviors. *Journal of Interpersonal Violence, 10*, 354–366.

Patterson, C. J. (1996). Lesbian and gay parents and their children. In R. C. Savin-Williams & K. M. Cohen (Eds.), *The lives of lesbians, gays, and bisexuals: From children to adults* (pp. 274–304). Fort Worth, TX: Harcourt Brace.

Patterson, C. J. (2001). Family relationships of lesbians and gay men. In R. M. Milardo (Ed.), *Understanding families into the new millennium: A decade in review* (pp. 271–288). Minneapolis, MN: National Council on Family Relations.

Paul, J. P. (1996). Bisexuality: Exploring/exploding the boundaries. In R. C. Savin-Williams & K. M. Cohen (Eds.), *The lives of lesbians, gays, and bisexuals: From children to adults* (pp. 436–461). Fort Worth, TX: Harcourt Brace.

Peacock, J. R. (2000). Gay male adult development: Some stage issues of an older cohort. *Journal of Homosexuality, 40*, 13–29.

Peplau, L. A., Spalding, L. R., Conley, T. D., & Veniegas, R. C. (2000). The development of sexual orientation in women. *Annual Review of Sex Research, 10*, 70–99.

Peplau, L. A., Veniegas, R. C., & Campbell, S. N. (1996). Gay and lesbian relationships. In R. C. Savin-Williams & K. M. Cohen (Eds.), *The lives of lesbians, gays, and bisexuals: From children to adults* (pp. 250–273). Fort Worth, TX: Harcourt Brace.

Perry, T. (2001, October 27). State appeals court voids gay adoption procedure. *Los Angeles Times.*

Phillips, G., & Over, R. (1995). Differences between heterosexual, bisexual, and lesbian women in recalled childhood experiences. *Archives of Sexual Behavior, 24*, 1–20.

Plugge-Foust, C. (2001). Homophobia, irrationality, and Christian ideology: Does a relationship exist? *Journal of Sex Education and Therapy, 25*, 240–244.

Plummer, D. C. (2001). The quest for modern manhood: Masculine stereotypes, peer culture and the social significance of homophobia. *Journal of Adolescence, 24*, 15–23.

Pritchard, A., Morgan, N. J., Sedgley, D., Khan, E., & Jenkins, A. (2000). Sexuality and holiday choices: Conversations with gay and lesbian tourists. *Leisure Studies, 19*, 267–282.

Reite, M., Sheeder, J., Richardson, D., & Teale, P. (1995). Cerebral laterality in homosexual males: Preliminary communication using magnetoencephalography. *Archives of Sexual Behavior, 24*, 585–593.

Robinson, B. E., Walters, L. H., & Skeen, P. (1989). Response of parents to learning that their child is homosexual and concern over AIDS: A national study. *Journal of Homosexuality, 18*, 59–80.

Robinson, K. H., & Ferfolja, T. (2001). What are we doing this for? Dealing with lesbian and gay issues in teacher education. *British Journal of Sociology of Education, 22*, 121–133.

Roderick, T. (1994). *Homonegativity: An analysis of the SBS-R.* Unpublished Master's Thesis, East Carolina University, Greenville, NC.

Roderick, T., McCammon, S. L., Long, T. E., & Allred, L. J. (1998). Behavioral aspects of homonegativity. *Journal of Homosexuality, 36*, 79–88.

Roffman, D. M. (2000). A model for helping schools address policy options regarding gay and lesbian youth. *Journal of Sex Education and Therapy, 25*, 130–136.

Rosario, M., Meyer-Bahlburg, H. E. L., Exner, T. M., Gwadz, M., & Keller, A. M. (1996). The psychosexual development of urban, lesbian, and bisexual youths. *The Journal of Sex Research, 33*, 113–126.

Russell, S. T., Franz, B. T., & Driscoll, A. K. (2001). Same-sex romantic attraction and experience of violence in adolescence. *American Journal of Public Health, 91*, 903–906.

Rust, P. (1996). Monogamy and polyamory: Relationship issues for bisexuals. In B. A. Firestein (Ed.), *Bisexuality: The psychology and politics of an invisible minority* (pp. 127–148). Thousand Oaks, CA: Sage.

Sanders, S. A., Reinisch, J. M., & McWhirter, D. P. (1990). An overview. In D. P. McWhirter, S. A. Sanders, & J. M. Reinisch (Eds.), *Homosexuality/heterosexuality: Concepts of sexual orientation* (pp. xix–xxviii). New York: Oxford.

Sandfort, T. G. M., de Graaf, R., Bijl, R. V., & Schnabel, P. (2001). Same-sex sexual behavior and psychiatric disorders: Findings from the Netherlands Mental Health Survey and Incidence Study. *Archives of General Psychiatry, 58*, 85–91.

Savin-Williams, R. C., & Diamond, L. M. (2000). Sexual identity trajectories among sexual-minority youths: Gender comparisons. *Archives of Sexual Behavior, 29*, 607–627.

SIECUS (Sexuality Information and Education Council of the United States). (2000). Fact sheets: Sexual orientation and identity. 130 West 42nd Street, Suite 350, New York, NY 10036.

Smith, D. M., & Gates, G. J. (2001, August 22). Gay and lesbian families in the United States: Same-sex unmarried partner households: Preliminary Analysis of 2000 U.S. Census Data, A Human Rights Campaign Report, www.hrc.org

Sodomy Fact Sheet: A Global Overview. (2000). The International Gay and Lesbian Human Rights Commission. 1350 Mission Street, San Francisco, CA 94103.

Sophie, J. (1985/1986). A critical examination of stage theories of lesbian identity development. *Journal of Homosexuality, 12*, 39–51.

Stacey, J., & Biblarz, T. J. (2001). Does the sexual orientation of parents matter? *American Sociological Review, 66*, 159–183.

Stiers, G. A. (1999). *From this day forward: Commitment, marriage, and family in lesbian and gay relationships*. New York: St. Martin's Press.

Strommen, E. E. (1989). You're a what? Family member reactions to the disclosure of homosexuality. *Journal of Homosexuality, 18*, 37–58.

Strong, S. M., Devendra, S., & Randall, P. K. (2000). Childhood gender nonconformity and body dissatisfaction in gay and heterosexual men. *Sex Roles, 43*, 427–439.

Swaab, D. E, Gooren, L. J. G., & Hofman, M. A. (1995). Brain research, gender, and sexual orientation. *The Journal of Sex Research*, *28*, 238–302.

Sylivant, S. (1992). *The cognitive, affective, and behavioral components of adolescent homonegativity*. Unpublished Master's Thesis. East Carolina University, Greenville, NC.

Theodore, P. S., & Basow, S. A. (2000). Heterosexual masculinity and homophobia: A reaction to the self? *Journal of Homosexuality*, *40*, 31–48.

Thurlow, C. (2001). Naming the "Outsider Within": Homophobic pejoratives and the verbal abuse of lesbian, gay and bisexual high-school pupils. *Journal of Adolescence*, *24*, 25–38.

Tomeo, M. E., Templer, D. L., Anderson, S., & Kotler, D. (2001). Comparative data of childhood and adolescent molestation in heterosexual and homosexual persons. *Archives of Sexual Behavior*, *30*, 535–541.

Troiden, R. R. (1989). The formation of homosexual identities. *Journal of Homosexuality*, *17*, 43–73.

Turner, W. J. (1995). Homosexuality, type 1: An Xq28 phenomenon. *Archives of Sexual Behavior*, *24*, 109–134.

Weinberg, G. (1973). *Society and the healthy homosexual*. New York: Anchor Books.

Weinberg, M. S., Williams, C. J., & Pryor, D. W. (2001). Bisexuals at midlife: Commitment, salience, and identity. *Journal of Contemporary Ethnography*, *30*, 180–208.

White, E. (1994). Sexual culture. In D. Bergman (Ed.), *The burning library: Essays by Edmund White* (pp. 157–167). New York: Knopf.

7

Individual and Interpersonal Sexual Behaviors

Chapter Outline

Masturbation—it's sex with someone I love.

—*Woody Allen*

The secret of a good sexual relationship is making love WITH your partner, not TO your partner.

—*Dianna Lowe, Kenneth Lowe*

What constitutes "sexual behavior" depends, in part, on intention and perception. For example, eating an ice-cream cone could be considered a "sexual behavior" if it is done with a sexual intention, or perceived as such by someone else. Indeed, virtually *any* behavior *could* be a sexual behavior, if it is intended or perceived as sexual. However, even behaviors that are widely viewed as sexual do not necessarily meet a person's criteria for what constitutes "having sex." For example, when a guidance counselor told female students that being forced to perform oral sex on a man was a form of rape, the students disagreed because, in their view, fellatio "is not really sex" (Remez, 2000). Indeed, a study of 223 undergraduates found that only 44% considered oral-genital stimulation as "sex," whereas 97% considered vaginal intercourse and 93% considered anal intercourse as "sex" (Bogart, Cecil, Wagstaff, Pinkerton, & Abramson, 2000).

This chapter focuses on behaviors that are commonly recognized as sexual, including masturbation, sexual cognitions/fantasies, touching, kissing, breast stimulation, manual and oral-genital stimulation, anal stimulation/anal intercourse, and vaginal intercourse. Although masturbation and fantasizing about sex can and do occur in interpersonal contexts, we focus on these as individual, rather than interpersonal, behaviors. Our discussion of interpersonal sexuality focuses on touching, kissing, breast/penile/clitoral/anal stimulation, as well as vaginal and anal intercourse.

7-1 EROTOPHILIA AND EROTOPHOBIA

For many individuals, sexual behavior—both individual and interpersonal—generally involves pleasure and enjoyment. But for other individuals, how anyone could actually *enjoy* masturbation/oral sex/intercourse, etc., is a mystery because *they* certainly don't find these behaviors to be pleasurable. The range of feelings toward sexual behavior can be conceptualized according to a continuum known as the *erotophilic-erotophobic continuum*.

The propensity to have positive emotional responses to sexuality is referred to as **erotophilia.** Individuals who are erotophilic tend to enjoy sex; find it pleasurable; and seek sexual partners, contexts, and experiences. The tendency to have negative emotional responses to sexuality is known as **erotophobia.** Individuals who are erotophobic tend to feel uncomfortable about sex, and try to avoid sexual partners, contexts, and experiences. Compared to erotophilic individuals, erotophobic individuals have more difficulty learning or talking about sexuality and may be less likely to acquire or to use contraception (Fisher, 1988). Although erotophobic individuals are less likely than erotophilic individuals to be sexually active, those who do engage in sexual relations have a higher risk of pregnancy and HIV/STD transmission because they feel uncomfortable discussing or using contraception or condoms.

Erotophilia The propensity to have very positive views of and emotional responses to sexuality.

Erotophobia The propensity to have very negative views of and emotional responses to sexuality.

Various factors influence whether a person is more erotophilic or erotophobic. Erotophobia is associated with having parents who were strict in their attitudes toward sex (Fisher, Byrne, White, & Kelley, 1988). Learning that sex is "bad" or "dirty," having traumatic sexual experiences, and having a negative self-concept and body image can also contribute to erotophobia. In contrast, learning that sex is "healthy" and "natural," having positive sexual experiences, and having a positive self-concept and body image can contribute to erotophilia.

As you read this chapter, notice your reactions: Do you find that reading about sexual behaviors is interesting and enjoyable? Or, does the material make you feel uncomfortable, anxious, or disgusted? Your reaction reflects where you fall on the erotophilic/erotophobic continuum, which you can assess in Box 7-1.

Box 7-1 Self-Assessment

Revised Sexual Opinion Survey

Please respond to each item as honestly as you can. There are no right or wrong answers. Place an X in the space on the scale that describes your feelings about each statement.

1. I think it would be very entertaining to look at erotica (sexually explicit books, movies, etc.).

   Strongly agree ___ ___ ___ ___ ___ ___ ___ Strongly disagree
2. Erotica (sexually explicit books, movies, etc.) is obviously filthy and people should not try to describe it as anything else.

   Strongly agree ___ ___ ___ ___ ___ ___ ___ Strongly disagree
3. Swimming in the nude with a member of the opposite sex would be an exciting experience.

   Strongly agree ___ ___ ___ ___ ___ ___ ___ Strongly disagree
4. Masturbation can be an exciting experience.

   Strongly agree ___ ___ ___ ___ ___ ___ ___ Strongly disagree
5. If I found out that a close friend of mine was a homosexual it would annoy me.

   Strongly agree ___ ___ ___ ___ ___ ___ ___ Strongly disagree
6. If people thought I was interested in oral sex, I would be embarrassed.

   Strongly agree ___ ___ ___ ___ ___ ___ ___ Strongly disagree
7. Engaging in group sex is an entertaining idea.

   Strongly agree ___ ___ ___ ___ ___ ___ ___ Strongly disagree
8. I personally find that thinking about engaging in sexual intercourse is arousing.

   Strongly agree ___ ___ ___ ___ ___ ___ ___ Strongly disagree
9. Seeing an erotic (sexually explicit) movie would be sexually arousing to me.

   Strongly agree ___ ___ ___ ___ ___ ___ ___ Strongly disagree
10. Thoughts that I may have homosexual tendencies would not worry me at all.

    Strongly agree ___ ___ ___ ___ ___ ___ ___ Strongly disagree
11. The idea of my being physically attracted to members of the same sex is not depressing.

    Strongly agree ___ ___ ___ ___ ___ ___ ___ Strongly disagree
12. Almost all erotic (sexually explicit) material is nauseating.

    Strongly agree ___ ___ ___ ___ ___ ___ ___ Strongly disagree
13. It would be emotionally upsetting to me to see someone exposing himself publicly.

    Strongly agree ___ ___ ___ ___ ___ ___ ___ Strongly disagree
14. Watching a stripper of the opposite sex would not be very exciting.

    Strongly agree ___ ___ ___ ___ ___ ___ ___ Strongly disagree
15. I would not enjoy seeing an erotic (sexually explicit) movie.

    Strongly agree ___ ___ ___ ___ ___ ___ ___ Strongly disagree
16. When I think about seeing pictures showing someone of the same sex as myself masturbating it nauseates me.

    Strongly agree ___ ___ ___ ___ ___ ___ ___ Strongly disagree
17. The thought of engaging in unusual sex practices is highly arousing.

    Strongly agree ___ ___ ___ ___ ___ ___ ___ Strongly disagree
18. Manipulating my genitals would probably be an arousing experience.

    Strongly agree ___ ___ ___ ___ ___ ___ ___ Strongly disagree
19. I do not enjoy daydreaming about sexual matters.

    Strongly agree ___ ___ ___ ___ ___ ___ ___ Strongly disagree
20. I am not curious about explicit erotica (sexually explicit books, movies, etc.).

    Strongly agree ___ ___ ___ ___ ___ ___ ___ Strongly disagree
21. The thought of having long-term sexual relations with more than one sex partner is not disgusting to me.

    Strongly agree ___ ___ ___ ___ ___ ___ ___ Strongly disagree

Scoring: Score responses from 1 = "Strongly agree" to 7 = "Strongly disagree". Add scores from Items 2, 5, 6, 12, 13, 14, 15, 16, 19, and 20. Subtract from this total the sum of Items 1, 3, 4, 7, 8, 9, 10, 11, 17, 18, and 21. Add 67 to this quantity.

Interpreting Your Score: The Sexual Opinion Survey (SOS) measures erotophobia/erotophilia, a personality dimension reflecting negative or positive emotional reaction to sexual cues. The possible scores range from 0 (most erotophobic) to 126 (most erotophilic). You may want to compare your score with those of a group of Canadian undergraduate students who completed this revised version of the SOS in a human sexuality course. The mean score of the men was 77.81 (n = 107, SD = 15.16). For women, the mean score was 67.11 (n = 216, SD = 18.59). The difference between the men and the women was statistically significant (t = 0.05) (Fisher, 1988).

Source: Used with the permission of *The Journal of Sex Research*, from "Sexual Opinion Survey" (including scoring and replacement items) by W. A. Fisher, D. Byrne, L. A. White, and K. Kelly. Vol. 25, #1 126–127, 1988. Permission conveyed through Copyright Clearance Center, Inc.

In general, men tend to be more erotophilic than women (Fisher, 1988). One study, for example, found that men were significantly more likely than women to agree strongly with the following statements: "I would prefer to have sex every day," "I would enjoy having sex outdoors," and "Swimming in the nude with my partner would be a turn-on" (Purnine, Carey, & Jorgensen, 1994). Before discussing specific sexual behaviors, we explore concepts related to the absence of or limitations on sexual behavior: virginity, chastity, celibacy, and abstinence.

7-2 VIRGINITY, CHASTITY, CELIBACY, AND ABSTINENCE

Virginity Refers to not having experienced sexual intercourse.

Virginity refers to not having experienced sexual intercourse. Virgins—individuals who have not experienced sexual intercourse—may or may not have experienced other forms of sexual interaction, such as manual or oral-genital stimulation. Undergraduates in one study (Sprecher & Regan, 1996) identified the following reasons for being a virgin:

- *Relationship concerns:* Not sufficiently in love or not in relationship long enough
- *Fear:* Worry about HIV and other sexually transmitted diseases, as well as pregnancy
- *Personal values/beliefs:* Belief or value that nonmarital intercourse is wrong
- *Self-concept issues:* Feeling shy, unattractive, undesirable

Interestingly, the women and men in this study who based their choice to be a virgin on their personal values or beliefs tended to have a more positive view of being a virgin compared to those whose decision to be a virgin was based on relationship factors, fear, or self-concept issues.

It is not uncommon for nonvirgins to regret the way in which they "lost" their virginity. In a study of first intercourse experiences of 292 undergraduates, the two most frequent comments made by the respondents about their first intercourse experience were that they wished they had been older at first intercourse and that they had been in a committed relationship (Thomsen & Chang, 2000). Those who reported the highest level of satisfaction with the experience expected the event to occur (they were not drunk and just "let it happen"), were in love with their partner, discussed and used condoms/birth control, and experienced orgasm.

Chastity The state of not having had sexual intercourse; also implies moral purity or virtuousness in both thought and conduct.

The term **chastity** also refers to not having had sexual intercourse, but "chastity" also implies moral purity or virtuousness in both thought and conduct. Individuals who practice chastity probably abstain not only from intercourse, but also from all sexual behaviors.

CULTURAL DIVERSITY 

From a cross-cultural perspective, anthropologist Gregersen (1983) noted that in most human societies, a chaste life (one without sexual intercourse) is viewed as "abnormal, intolerable, or dangerous" (p. 289). He observed that chastity was not prized among hunting and gathering groups and did not appear as a culturally defined virtue until about the fifth century B.C. with the development of Buddhist and Jain monks in India. During this time of overpopulation and limited food resources, chastity meant fewer children and more food for existing inhabitants.

Celibacy The condition of refraining from sexual intercourse, especially by reason of religious vows; also used to refer to being unmarried.

Celibacy often refers to the condition of being unmarried, especially by reason of religious vows, and also implies refraining from having sexual intercourse, although a person who practices celibacy is not necessarily a virgin. The official position of the contemporary Catholic Church maintains that priests, nuns, and monks are expected to be celibate in order that they might have the maximum time, freedom, and energy for the work of the church. Father Patrick Gaddy, an ordained priest in the Catholic Church, explains his choice to lead a celibate life:

Celibacy is a form of love in which, instead of focusing your love on one person, you learn to focus on a whole community. And for a priest, that means learning to share his love with the whole community in which he lives. A priest must learn to love the community with the same power that a young man would try to bring to his bride or give to his family. That is the key to being fulfilled as a celibate. (Skeen, 1991, p. 70)

Reported cases of child sexual abuse perpetrated by some Catholic priests has raised questions about the celibacy requirement for Catholic clergy: Is requiring celibacy realistic? Has the celibacy requirement contributed to the child sexual abuse perpetrated by the clergy? (However, it is not celibacy that causes sexual abuse of children; contributing factors will be discussed in Box 17-2, "Up Close: Pedophiles in the Catholic Church.") As the public grapples with these questions, the Pope has continued to affirm the expectation of celibacy for Catholic clergy.

The more commonly used term today that refers to refraining from having sexual intercourse is **abstinence.** Like celibacy, the practice of abstinence does not necessarily mean that the person is a virgin; a person who has experienced sexual intercourse can subsequently practice abstinence. For some individuals, abstinence means refraining from sexual intercourse, but not from other forms of sexual interaction. For other individuals, abstinence means refraining from not only sexual intercourse, but from other sexual behaviors as well. Abstinence can be voluntary or involuntary, and can last for short or extended periods of time.

Abstinence The condition of having refrained from having sexual intercourse.

NATIONAL DATA Fourteen percent of adult U.S. men and 10% of adult U.S. women reported not having had any sexual activity involving genital contact in the past 12 months (Michael, Gagnon, Laumann, & Kolata, 1994).

7-2a Voluntary Abstinence

Voluntary abstinence can be motivated by a number of reasons, including the desire to avoid sexually transmitted diseases and the desire to avoid pregnancy. Some individuals practice abstinence in order to better focus their energy on personal, academic, or professional development without the distractions of sexual involvements. Other individuals are voluntarily abstinent because they lack interest or sexual desire or may find sex to be aversive, for example, in cases where sexual activity triggers negative emotions associated with prior sexual abuse. For some gay and lesbian individuals who do not accept their sexual orientation, abstinence may be a way to avoid dealing with the stigma of living a homosexual lifestyle. Some couples choose to abstain from sexual intercourse as a way to enhance their enjoyment of the nonsexual aspects of their relationship. The practice of abstinence can also be related to cultural or religious beliefs and customs. For example, during the Muslim observation of Ramadan, in addition to fasting, during daylight hours believers abstain from sexual intercourse and even passionate kissing (Gregersen, 1983).

Voluntary abstinence Foregoing sexual intercourse for a period of time by choice.

There are also a variety of reproductive and medical reasons for practicing short periods of abstinence. As we discuss in section 11-3c, "Natural Family Planning Methods," women using the natural family planning method (or "calendar method") abstain from sexual intercourse during the time of month they are most likely to conceive. Some men are abstinent to increase the chance of impregnating their partners because research findings suggest that the longer the time interval between ejaculations, the more volume and concentration of sperm are present in the semen (Sauer, Zeffer, Buster, & Sokol, 1988). Medical conditions that can warrant short periods of abstinence include genital infections and pregnancy complications. In addition, a period of abstinence from sexual intercourse is recommended for women after having an abortion and after childbirth. For individuals dealing with "sexual addiction," abstinence is often a part of the treatment plan. Like the alcoholic who must abstain from using alcohol to maintain sobriety, the "sex addict" must become completely "sex sober" for a period of at least 6 months to gain control of the addiction (Carnes, 2001).

7-2b Involuntary Abstinence

Involuntary abstinence Not engaging in sexual intercourse for a period of time due to lack of a partner or restricted access to a partner.

Sexual celibacy The state of not having sexual intercourse or activity.

One of the most common reasons for **involuntary abstinence** is the lack of a sexual partner. This situation is common to many of us at different times in our lives. We may be between relationships, separated, divorced, or widowed, or we may be in a marriage or relationship in which our partner is unwilling to have sexual relations. Involuntary abstinence may also be induced by separation of partners due to military deployment, work-related travel, being in a long-distance relationship, or prison. Hospital, nursing, and retirement homes are also contexts of involuntary **sexual celibacy** (see Box 7-2).

Experiencing involuntary abstinence over a long period of time can be a very difficult emotional experience, as conveyed in the following excerpt (Donnelly, Burgess, Anderson, Davis, & Dillard, 2001):

> *My lack of any sex has had some very serious effects upon me. Obviously, I could get a prostitute any time, but I haven't done that. It would be no different than glorified masturbation. It is the fact that no woman has ever wanted to be sexual with me (as far as I can tell, even considered sex with me) that I find so painful. It makes me feel sexually worthless. And the fact that no woman has loved me or cared for me enough to have sex with me is tremendously damaging to my self-esteem. It makes me feel like a freak, an unloved person who is not worth anything to anyone. (p. 160)*

7-3 AUTOEROTIC BEHAVIOR

> *The guilt, fear, anxiety, and repulsion that surrounds masturbation is astounding, especially when one realizes not only how pervasive it is among human beings, but how beneficial, pleasurable, and relaxing an experience it can be.*
>
> *—Lonnie Garfield Barbach*

Masturbation A natural, common, and nonharmful means of sexual self-pleasuring that is engaged in by individuals of all ages, sexual orientations, and levels of functioning. (See also **autoerotic behavior.**)

Autoerotic behavior Natural, nonharmful means of sexual self-pleasuring that individuals of all ages and sexual orientations engage in. (See also **masturbation.**)

More commonly called **masturbation, autoerotic behavior** is "a natural, common, and nonharmful means of sexual self pleasuring that is engaged in by individuals of all ages, sexual orientations, and levels of functioning" (SIECUS, 1996). Masturbation has been referred to as "having sex with the only person whose sexual history you can trust completely." Other terms for masturbation include *self-pleasuring*, *solo sex*, and *sex without a partner*.

Several older, more pejorative terms for masturbation are *self-pollution*, *self-abuse*, *solitary vice*, *sin against nature*, *voluntary pollution*, and *onanism*. The negative connotations associated with these terms are a result of various accounts and myths that originated in religion, medicine, and traditional psychotherapy. Traditionally, parents have also transmitted a negative view of masturbation to their children. Due to traditional negative attitudes toward masturbation, shame, guilt, and anxiety continue to be common feelings associated with masturbation in our society.

NATIONAL DATA About half of the men and women who reported having masturbated said that they felt guilty (Michael et al.,1994, p. 166).

Despite current knowledge that suggests that negative views of masturbation are based largely on myths (see Table 7-1), social disapproval of masturbation persists. During the World AIDS Day Conference at the United Nations in December 1994, former Surgeon General Joycelyn Elders spoke to an audience of 200 members about the spread of STDs. After her presentation, a psychologist in the audience asked if she would consider promoting masturbation to discourage school-age children from engaging in riskier forms of sexual activity. Elders replied that masturbation "is something that is a part of human sexuality and . . . that perhaps should be taught" ("The Politics of Masturbation," 1994, p. 1714). Partly due to the public and political taboo of discussing—let alone advocating—masturbation, President Clinton asked for and received Elders's resignation. Why did Elders's comments about masturbation send shock waves through the U.S. conservative population? One reason is that historically, masturbation has been viewed as being both the cause and result of sin and sickness.

Box 7-2 Social Choices

Institutional Restrictions on Sexual Expression?

Hospitals are notorious for encouraging or enforcing abstinence. It is assumed that if you are in the hospital, you should have no sexual experience of any kind. There is no discussion of sexual activity, no privacy for masturbation (the nurse or physician can walk in at any time), and no accommodations for engaging in sexual relations with one's partner.

Nursing homes also institutionalize abstinence. Some nursing homes (believing that the elderly are sexless) do not even allow spouses to occupy the same room. Sexual expression among nursing home residents may also be infrequent due to chronic illness, the lack of willing partners, and a loss of interest. Some of these factors are related to the physiological effect of aging on sexual interest and behavior; other factors are under the control of physicians and staff. Barriers to sexual activity among nursing home residents may be removed by educating staff about sexuality in the elderly, providing privacy ("do not disturb" signs, closed doors, private rooms designated for intimacy), allowing conjugal visits or home visits, changing medications that may impair sexual function, and providing information and counseling about sexuality to interested residents.

TABLE 7-1

Myths and Truths About Masturbation

Myths	Truths
Masturbation causes insanity, headaches, epilepsy, acne, blindness, nosebleeds, "masturbator's heart," tenderness of the breasts, warts, nymphomania, undesirable odor, and hair on the palms.	There is no evidence that masturbation impairs physical or mental health.
Masturbation is an abnormal, unnatural behavior.	Masturbation is a normal function.
Masturbation is immature.	Masturbation is an effective way to experience sexual pleasure.
Masturbation is practiced mostly by simple-minded people.	Many people masturbate throughout their lives. Many sexually active people with available partners masturbate for additional gratification.
Masturbation is a substitute for intercourse.	Intercourse and masturbation can be viewed as complementary sexual experiences, not necessarily as mutually exclusive.
Masturbation is antisocial.	Masturbation can be an effective way to learn about your own sexual responses so you can communicate them to a partner. Masturbation can also occur during sexual interaction with one's partner.

7-3a Historical Origins of Negative Attitudes Toward Masturbation

There is extensive documentation of the historical origins of negative attitudes toward masturbation. According to the literature on this subject, the roots of negative views of masturbation lie in religion, medicine, and traditional psychotherapy.

Religion and Masturbation

A number of religious traditions have associated masturbation with evil or sin. St. Augustine and other early Christians believed that sexual fantasies (which often accompany masturbation) were caused by demons that led their victims down a hellish path of sin. Medieval Jewish and Christian leaders believed that ejaculated semen would breed devils (Allen, 2000). Those who are guilty of masturbating could still be "saved" by prayer, abstinence, holy water, and absolution.

Negative religious views toward masturbation stemmed from the belief that any non-procreative sexual act (i.e., any sex act that cannot lead to pregnancy and reproduction) is morally wrong. Traditional religious doctrines also disapprove of other forms of non-procreative sex, such as oral sex, anal intercourse, homosexual sex, and coitus interruptus. But as Allen (2000) explains, "masturbation inspired a special fear in the . . . Catholic Church, since it represented a purely physical act of sex, unredeemed by even the possibility of procreation—and also since it could be performed even by monks in the isolation of their cells" (p. 82).

Some religious groups have adopted more accepting views of masturbation. For example, a curriculum developed for Presbyterian Youth asserts that masturbation could be bad if it was used as a way to avoid relationships with other people or was done out of fear of becoming involved with someone else (Bartosch et al., 1989). However, masturbation could be a good choice if practiced by those who were not married or those whose spouses were not available for sexual relations due to absence, disability, or illness. This curriculum states that masturbation is a normal part of growing up.

Cultural Diversity

In ancient Chinese religious thought, life was viewed as a balance between the forces of yin and yang. Sex represented this harmonious balance; the essence of sexual **yang** was the male's semen and the essence of sexual **yin** was the woman's vaginal fluids. Female masturbation was virtually ignored because vaginal fluids (yin) were thought to be inexhaustible. However, semen (yang) was viewed as precious, and masturbation was regarded as a waste of vital yang essence (Bullough, 1976; Tannahill, 1982).

Yang In Chinese thought, the male force that was viewed as active.

Yin In Chinese thought, the female force that was seen as passive.

Medicine, Psychotherapy, and Masturbation

Semen-conservation doctrine From early Ayurvedic teachings in India, the belief that general good health in both sexes depended on conserving the life-giving power of "vital fluids" (semen and vaginal fluids).

The **semen-conservation doctrine** (from early Ayurvedic teachings in India) held that general good health in both sexes depended on conserving the life-giving power of "vital fluids" (Money, Prakasam, & Joshi, 1991). These fluids, which include both semen and vaginal fluids, were believed to be important for intelligence and memory and derived from good nutrition. Wastage or depletion of semen (regarded as more important) was discouraged because it might result in loss of resistance to all illnesses and in a decrease in well-being. The second-century physician Aretaeus the Cappadocian, for example, warned against men losing too much semen, "For it is the semen . . . which makes us to be men, hot, well braced in limbs, hairy, well voiced, spirited, strong to think and to act" (quoted in Allen, 2000, p. 83).

Early medicine's negative view of masturbation can also be traced to the fact that for centuries, physicians did not clearly distinguish between masturbation and the sexually transmitted disease gonorrhea (which, in Greek, means "flow of seed"). One of the symptoms of gonorrhea in men is the discharge of thick pus from the penis. The failure to differentiate between semen ejaculated during masturbation (or released during spontaneous nocturnal emissions) and the penile discharge associated with gonorrhea led physicians to lump gonorrhea and masturbation into one single pathology until the twentieth century (Allen, 2000). "Additionally, for a medical profession that was increasingly able to recognize problems it could not yet cure, self-abuse [masturbation] was an easy culprit to link with all kinds of diseases nobody could otherwise explain" (Allen, 2000, p. 86).

When Samuel Tissot, a highly respected Swiss doctor (he was physician to a Pope), published a book on the diseases produced by masturbation (Tissot, 1758/1766), he added medical credibility to the view that masturbation was harmful. Tissot presented graphic and gruesome case studies depicting the horrific effects of masturbation. Tissot provided drawings of those affected by masturbation, one of which portrays a man who had been reduced by masturbation to

> *A being that less resembled a living creature than a corpse. . . . A watery, palish blood issued from his nose; slaver constantly flowed from his mouth. Having diarrhea, he voided his excrement in bed without knowing it. He had a continual flux of semen. . . . The disorder of his mind was equal to that of his body. . . . (cited in Allen, 2000, p.88)*

By the mid-nineteenth century, Tissot's admonitions against masturbation had made their way into medical textbooks, journals, and books for parents.

Adding to the medical bias against masturbation was Reverend Sylvester Graham, who claimed that masturbation resulted in the loss of fluids that were vital to the body. In 1834, Graham wrote that losing an ounce of semen was equal to the loss of several ounces of blood. Graham believed that every time a man ejaculated, he ran the risk of contracting a disease of the nervous system. Among his solutions were Graham crackers, which would help prevent the development of carnal lust that resulted from eating carnivorous flesh (Graham, 1848). John Harvey Kellogg, MD, had similar beliefs to Graham and suggested his own cure—corn flakes. Kellogg's Corn Flakes were originally developed as a food to extinguish sexual desire and curb masturbation desires.

In the early twentieth century, psychotherapy joined medicine and religion to convince people of the negative effects of masturbation. In 1893, Sigmund Freud claimed that masturbation caused neurasthenia, a widely diagnosed psychosomatic illness characterized by weakness and nervousness (Allen, 2000). Freud, and other psychotherapists who followed his teachings, viewed masturbation as an infantile form of sexual gratification. People who masturbated "to excess" could fixate on themselves as a sexual object and would not be able to relate to others in a sexually mature way. The message was clear: If you want to be a good sexual partner in marriage, don't masturbate; if you do masturbate, don't do it too often.

The result of religious, medical, and therapeutic professions denigrating masturbation was devastating for individuals who succumbed to temptation, causing unnecessary shame, anxiety, fear, and guilt. The burden of these feelings was particularly heavy because there was no one with whom to share the guilt. In the case of a premarital pregnancy, responsibility could be shared. But with masturbation, the "crime" had been committed alone.

The perceived dangers of masturbation warranted extreme measures to deter children and adults from engaging in this behavior. Physicians recommended mechanical restraints (such as strait jackets and chastity belts), tying children's hands and feet at night, and circumcision as preventive measures (Allen, 2000). Because women who masturbated "could become obsessed with sex and thus unfit for their proper role in society," horseback riding, bicycling, and even using pedal-operated sewing machines ("which could stimulate working women until they became sexually sick") were to be avoided (Allen, 2000, p. 96). If preventive measures did not work, masturbators were often locked up in asylums, treated with drugs (such as sedatives and poisons), or subjected to a range of interventions designed to prevent masturbation by stimulating the genitals in painful ways, preventing genital sensation, or deadening it. These physician-prescribed interventions included putting ice on the genitals; blistering and scalding the penis, vulva, inner thighs, or perineum; inserting electrodes into the rectum and urethra; cauterizing the clitoris by anointing it with pure carbolic acid; circumcising the penis; and surgically removing the clitoris, ovaries, and testicles.

Attitudes toward masturbation began to change in the mid-twentieth century, after research by Kinsey and his colleagues revealed that 92% of the men in their sample reported having masturbated (Kinsey, Pomeroy, & Martin, 1948). Yet the researchers found no evidence of the dire consequences that had been earlier predicted for those who masturbate. These findings presented a major challenge to the prevailing medical views of masturbation as harmful. But in spite of Kinsey's evidence suggesting that masturbation was not physically, emotionally, or socially debilitating, physicians continued to convey to their patients negative attitudes toward masturbation. More recently, physicians' attitudes toward masturbation have become more positive, in part, due to the inclusion of human sexuality courses in medical school curricula. Indeed, masturbation is commonly prescribed as a treatment by sex therapists for women (see section 15-5a, "Female Orgasmic Disorder").

Today, medical concerns about adverse health effects of masturbation are limited to special cases in which masturbation can result in physical harm. One of these special cases is the practice of restricting the flow of blood to the brain by constricting one's neck with a rope or belt during masturbation. This dangerous practice, designed to intensify orgasm, can result in *autoerotic asphyxiation*—accidental death by strangulation.

Other types of harmful (or potentially harmful) masturbation behavior include using objects that can harm the genitalia (such as sharp objects) and masturbating excessively to the point of creating abrasions and open sores on the genitalia that can lead to infection. Such harmful masturbatory behavior is not typical among the general population and is more of a concern for caregivers of individuals with mental retardation (see also Box 18-1, "Social Choices: Caregiver Response to Masturbation by Mentally Retarded?").

Think About It 

How have you learned to view masturbation? What, or who, has influenced your views on masturbation?

7-3b Social and Psychological Correlates of Masturbation

Survey research reveals that reported frequency of masturbation tends to be associated with several factors: sex, race and ethnicity, education, and religion. Keep in mind, however, that survey data tell us more about what people *say* they do than what they *actually* do.

Think About It 

Obtaining research data on masturbation is difficult because many individuals, especially adolescents, are not comfortable reporting honest information about their masturbatory behavior (Halpern, Udry, & Campbell, 2000). How would you feel about revealing information about your masturbatory behavior to a researcher? Would you be willing to participate in a research study that required you to provide information on your masturbatory behavior? Would you be more willing to reveal accurate, honest information in an anonymous survey versus a face-to-face interview?

Sex

Men are more likely to report having masturbated than women.

National Data Among U.S. adults ages 18–59, about 60% of men and 40% of women report having masturbated in the year preceding the survey (Michael et al.,1994).

Rates for ever having masturbated are higher. In a sample of 280 undergraduates, 81% of the men and 45% of the women reported ever having masturbated (Leitenberg, Detzer, & Srebnik, 1993). The average age at which they first masturbated was 12.75 and 13.45 for men and women, respectively. Most (more than 80%) learned to masturbate through self-exploration.

CULTURAL DIVERSITY

Higher rates of masturbation among men, compared to women, have also been found in other countries. In a study of more than 20,000 Japanese high school and university students, 98% of the men and 39% of the women reported having masturbated (Hatano, 1991). A study of masturbation among a sample of 305 Chinese college students also revealed a higher rate among men, with twice as many men reported having masturbated as women (43.8% and 21.4%, respectively) (Tang, Lai, Phil, & Chung, 1997).

Explanations for higher rates of masturbation among men include greater genital availability, greater physical need to release periodic seminal buildup, traditional male social scripts that emphasize pleasure aspects of sexuality independent of relationship factors, and greater social support for sexual expression among men than women. In spite of the high percentage of men who masturbate, some men never choose to masturbate. Kinsey et al. (1948) suggested that a low sex drive, dependency on nocturnal emissions, and the regular availability of a sexual partner might account for this. Another explanation may be that men who do not masturbate have strong religious beliefs against masturbation.

Race and Ethnicity

Reported masturbatory behavior varies by race and ethnicity.

NATIONAL DATA Among White, Black, and Hispanic men, 28%, 17%, and 24%, respectively, report masturbating once a week. Among White, Black, and Hispanic women, 7%, 11%, and 5% report masturbating once a week (Laumann, Gagnon, Michael, & Michaels, 1994).

Notice that the rates for White men are higher than for Black men but the rates for Black women are higher than for White women. Possible explanations for the lower rates of masturbation among Black men (compared to White men) include (a) the Black male subculture teaches Black men that masturbation is an admission of not being able to find a sexual partner and (b) Black men have more frequent interpersonal sexual relations, which may lower the need to masturbate. The higher rate of reported masturbation among Black women compared to White women may be due to the shortage of available Black men—a factor that also helps to explain the high rate of singlehood among Black women (Kiecolt & Fossett, 1997). Black women with no regular partner in their lives may find sexual enjoyment through masturbation.

Education and Religion

Individuals with higher levels of education are more likely to report having masturbated in the past year than are individuals with lower levels of education. In a national sample of adults, among those with less than a high school education, more than half of the men and more than three quarters of the women reported that they did not masturbate in the past year (Michael et al., 1994). Among those with advanced degrees, only 1 out of 5 men and 6 out of 10 women reported that they did not masturbate (Michael et al., 1994).

Persons who attend religious services and regard themselves as devout are also less likely to report having masturbated than those who do not attend religious services or who do not regard themselves as devout (Kinsey et al., 1948; Kinsey, Pomeroy, Martin, & Gebhard, 1953). This correlation is not surprising in view of the traditional negative attitude of religion toward masturbation.

Think About It

Data on the relationship between educational attainment and reported masturbatory behavior do not resolve the following question: Do individuals with lower educational attainment have lower levels of masturbatory behavior, or are they less willing to report such behavior due to embarrassment, guilt, or shame? Similarly, do individuals who attend religious services and view themselves as devout have lower levels of masturbatory behavior, or are they less willing to report this behavior? What do you think?

7-3c Masturbation in Relationships

It is sometimes assumed that people who are married, cohabiting, or in established sexual relationships do not masturbate because they have a sexual partner. This assumption is inaccurate because individuals with partners report high rates of masturbatory behavior.

National Data Eighty-five percent of men and 45% of women who were living with a partner reported that they had masturbated in the past year (Michael et al., 1994).

People in marriages or other coupled relationships masturbate for many of the same reasons that single people do. Masturbation provides a unique pleasurable experience, it can relieve stress and tension, and can help a person relax and fall asleep. Masturbation also provides a way for partners to experience sexual pleasure when they are not sexually available to each other due to travel, work, hospitalization, military duty, or imprisonment. Some coupled individuals masturbate because their sexual relationship with their partner is unfulfilling or because they desire sexual pleasure at times that their partner is not interested in sexual activity. When one partner lacks the interest in or ability to participate in sexual activity due to illness or disability, the other partner can find sexual release and pleasure through masturbation. Some couples masturbate during the later stages of pregnancy when intercourse is uncomfortable or not desired.

Masturbation can have positive effects on a relationship. Masturbation can be incorporated into interpersonal sexual activity to increase enjoyment and variety. For example, a woman can stimulate her clitoral area with her fingers or with a vibrator while her partner penetrates her or stimulates her in other ways. Or, a man can masturbate while his partner provides anal penetration or stimulates him in other ways. For some couples, watching each other masturbate can be a turn-on that adds another erotic dimension to the couple's sex life. Couples can also masturbate while interacting on the phone or online.

Women who masturbate are better able to teach their partners how to pleasure them, so they may achieve higher levels of sexual satisfaction in their relationships. Their partners may also derive satisfaction from being able to provide them with pleasure. Finally, masturbation may help some spouses remain faithful by providing a means of experiencing sexual pleasure when the partner is not available, able, and/or interested in sexual activity.

Masturbation can also be problematic in relationships. When a partner's masturbation occurs during interaction with a phone-sex worker or cybersex partner, the other partner might understandably view this as a form of infidelity and feel jealousy and anger. More commonly, adults in couple relationships who masturbate do so alone, although they may fantasize about other people and/or view sexually explicit photos or videos. For some couples, solo masturbation is something the partners talk about with each other and accept as normal, healthy sexual behavior. For other couples, one or both partners may masturbate secretly, hiding it from the other partner. In this case, if one partner accidentally discovers that his or her partner masturbates and has done so regularly in secrecy, he or she may feel angry and hurt not about the masturbation, but about the fact that the partner had not been honest about it. Another potential problem involving masturbation in relationships is that some individuals can interpret their partner's masturbation as evidence that they are not desirable and/or are not satisfying the partner sexually. This interpretation can cause feelings of inadequacy and rejection.

Whereas some people have negative reactions to their partner viewing sexually explicit media while masturbating, other people have neutral or even positive reactions. In one study, 488 college students were asked to indicate their reactions to two hypothetical situations in which they returned from being out of town and found that their partner had, in one scenario, masturbated and, in the other scenario, had viewed sexually explicit materials (Clark & Wiederman, 2000). The women and men in this study generally did not react negatively to partner solitary masturbation or the viewing of sexually explicit materials, although women indicated more negative feelings about a partner's masturbation behavior than did men. For both men and women, a partner's viewing of sexually explicit materials was rated more negatively than a partner's masturbation. The researchers suggested that because the hypothetical scenarios involved the respondent being out of town, it is likely that the respondent would prefer his or partner to masturbate rather than seek sexual satisfaction from someone outside the relationship. The researchers also explained that, "If we had asked individuals to imagine that their partner was masturbating while they themselves were available and willing to engage in sexual activity, this scenario might lead the respondent to feel rejected or sexually inadequate" (p. 139).

In conclusion, individuals in coupled relationships who masturbate can do so during sexual interaction with their partner, by themselves, with someone outside the relationship (e.g., phone-sex workers or another lover), with or without viewing sexually explicit materials, and with or without the other partner's knowledge. Whether masturbation has positive or negative effects on the couple's relationship depends on the type of situation in which the masturbation occurs, as well as the values and interpretations each partner has of the behavior.

Think About It

How would you feel if you found out that your partner masturbates but hid knowledge of doing so from you? How would you respond if your partner expressed a negative reaction to your masturbating?

7-3d Masturbation in Groups

Also known as *social masturbation*, group masturbation involves three or more individuals masturbating together. Although statistical data on the practice of group masturbation are lacking, one researcher reported that a substantial number of heterosexual and homosexual men had participated in group masturbation as boys (Cornog, 2001). The slang term *circle jerk* refers to a boys' game in which a group of boys form a circle, take out their penises, and masturbate to see who can ejaculate the fastest and who can propel their ejaculate most accurately into the center of a chalk circle on a floor. Variations of the circle jerk include the boys stimulating each other or watching just one boy, the performer, masturbating to ejaculation. Girls, who have a lower incidence and frequency of masturbation, are more likely to masturbate in pairs, rather than in groups of three or more.

One adult version of group masturbation occurs in organized clubs, sometimes referred to as *jack-off* or *JO* clubs. There are more than 40 organized masturbation clubs found in large cities throughout the world (Cornog, 2001). For example, the New York Jacks is a male masturbation club begun in the 1980s. These clubs are similar to other clubs in that they may have membership cards, newsletters, theme parties, weekend retreats, and charity fund-raisers. In addition to organized masturbation clubs, there are probably many more small, informal, less public masturbation groups (Cornog, 2001).

Although gay men are probably more likely than lesbians and heterosexuals to participate in group masturbation, this type of group sexual activity is spreading to women and heterosexuals. In the last couple of decades, some clubs have organized mixed-gender group masturbation parties, sometimes referred to as *Jack and Jill Off* or *JJO*.

7-3e Personal Choices: Is Masturbation for Me? The Pros and Cons of Masturbation

The fact that a particular act is unpleasant or bad does not make it a disease; nor does the fact that it is pleasant or good make it a treatment.

—Thomas Szasz

Some individuals feel very uncomfortable about masturbating, especially when their religious beliefs prohibit masturbation. Deciding whether or not to masturbate is a very personal decision, and opting not to masturbate is just as legitimate a choice as the decision to masturbate. Nevertheless, it may be helpful to consider the pros and cons of masturbation in making one's own choices regarding this form of sexual behavior.

Pros of Masturbation

1. *Self-knowledge*. Masturbation can provide immediate feedback about what one enjoys. Self-knowledge about what feels good enables a person to know what he or she finds pleasurable, and to teach a partner how to provide pleasure.
2. *Increased body comfort*. Masturbation can increase an individual's comfort with her or his own body. Individuals who are comfortable with their bodies are more confident and less anxious during sexual interactions, resulting in more overall sexual satisfaction with one's partner (Buker, 2002). Not all individuals (particularly women) are comfortable when they begin masturbating, but comfort often develops with repeated experiences. Masturbation may also increase an individual's physical, as well as psychological, body comfort. Students in the authors' classes report that they masturbate to relieve tension, to get to sleep, and to help abate menstrual cramps.
3. *Orgasm more likely*. In a study of 292 undergraduates, prior experience with masturbation was the strongest single predictor of orgasm and emotional satisfaction with first intercourse (Thomsen & Chang, 2000).
4. *Pressure taken off partner*. Inevitably, partners in a relationship will vary in their desire for having interpersonal sex. During such times, the partner wanting more sex may feel frustrated, and the partner wanting less sex may feel guilty for not wanting to accommodate the partner. Masturbation might provide an alternative means of sexual satisfaction for the partner wanting more partner sex while taking the pressure off the other partner. The result may be less interpersonal stress for both people.
5. *No partner necessary*. In one study (Darling, Davidson, & Cox, 1991) the most frequently reported reason women gave for masturbating was that a partner was not available. Choosing to masturbate provides a way to enjoy a sexual experience or an orgasm when no partner may be available.
6. *Avoids risk of disease transmission or pregnancy*. When masturbation is enjoyed as a solo activity, there is no risk of transmitting or acquiring a sexually transmitted disease, nor is there any risk of pregnancy. However, when masturbation is enjoyed with another person in the context of an interpersonal sexual experience, the partners must be careful to avoid contact with each other's bodily fluids to avoid STD transmission and/or pregnancy.
7. *Unique, pleasurable experience*. Masturbation is a unique sexual experience, different from intercourse, manual/oral stimulation of the genitals, and other sexual behaviors. Some people who have interpersonal sex on a regular basis with their partners may also enjoy masturbation because they regard masturbation as a unique experience that partner sex cannot duplicate.

8. *Helpful in maintaining sexual fidelity.* For individuals in coupled relationships, masturbation can help the partners remain "faithful" when they are away from each other for extended periods of time, or can help partners who are unable to be sexually active due to illness or disability.
9. *Useful in treatment of sexual dysfunctions.* Sex therapists routinely recommend masturbation to women who report never having experienced orgasm as a means of learning the place(s), pressure, and rhythm of clitoral/genital stimulation that leads to orgasm. Women who know how to pleasure themselves to orgasm are better able to teach their partners how to do so. As noted earlier, women who masturbate to orgasm are more likely to report orgasm during intercourse.

Cons of Masturbation

1. *Feeling of being abnormal.* Some people feel they are abnormal because they masturbate "too frequently" or in unusual ways. Although masturbation that is consistently used to avoid the complexities of involvement in an intimate relationship may be symptomatic of a larger interpersonal deficit, frequent masturbation per se is not regarded as a problem and a person who masturbates "frequently" is not abnormal.

   Masturbating in unusual ways can be viewed as creative or simply "different" without the negative implication of "abnormal." One student in the authors' classes reported feeling abnormal because she could experience orgasm by contracting her abdomen muscles. Another student reported that he wondered if he was "normal" because he masturbated to a particular piece of classical music and tried to time his orgasm to the climax of the music. In section 7-3a, we mentioned special cases in which masturbation was harmful, such as the practice of constricting the neck during masturbation, which can lead to autoerotic asphyxiation, and the use of sharp objects during masturbation, which can cause injury to the genitalia. Aside from such examples, masturbatory behaviors that are not harmful need not elicit concern about "abnormality."
2. *Strengthened attraction to inappropriate stimuli.* Masturbation to an inappropriate stimulus or to fantasies of an inappropriate stimulus may strengthen erotic feelings toward that stimulus. For example, adults who masturbate while fantasizing about sexual interactions with children are strengthening their erotic responses to children. Repeated rehearsal of such sexual fantasies and masturbatory behavior contributes to sexual abuse of children (Maletzky, 1991).

♦

7-3f Personal Choices: Use a Vibrator?

Vibrators, which are made in many sizes, shapes, and styles, are only one type of sex toy that some individuals use during masturbation and/or lovemaking with their partners. You might think about the following considerations in choosing whether or not to use a vibrator.

Using a vibrator can provide sexual pleasure and orgasm, especially for women who may have difficulty achieving orgasm through other means of stimulation. Sex pioneer Virginia Johnson warned, however, that if a woman uses intense mechanical stimulation over a long period of time, she might lose her appreciation of the various stages of arousal and diminish her ultimate joy (Masters & Johnson, 1976). In other words, because the vibrator will usually produce an orgasm quickly, it may short-circuit erotic fantasies, slow buildup, and eventual release so that some of the emotional and cognitive aspects of orgasm are lost. Of course, these admonitions are also appropriate to men.

Vibrators can also add another pleasurable dimension to interpersonal sexual activity. For example, during lovemaking, a woman may stimulate her clitoris with a vibrator while her partner penetrates her vagina, kisses her, and/or caresses her. Whereas some partners are in favor of using a vibrator, others may be threatened by its use. One man, who said that his fiancée had gotten "hooked" on her vibrator, stated "I think she prefers it to me." It may be helpful for both partners to openly discuss their feelings regarding the use of a vibrator in their relationship. Jenn Buker (2002), founder of Girlzniteout, which specializes in mail order erotic toys, said "I tell my partner flat out, I need clitoral stimulation with a vibrator to have an orgasm, but it doesn't diminish my love for him or my enjoyment in intercourse."

♦

7-4 SEXUAL FANTASIES, SEXUAL COGNITIONS, AND SEXUAL DREAMS

Sexual fantasies Cognitions, or thoughts and/or images, that are sexual in nature.

Sexual fantasies are cognitions, or thoughts and/or images, that are sexual in nature. It is commonly assumed that engaging in sexual fantasy is a pleasant and enjoyable experience that is engaged in deliberately. Indeed, sex therapists routinely encourage individuals who have difficulty experiencing arousal and orgasm to use sexual fantasies to increase arousal and facilitate orgasm.

But sexual fantasies and the arousal they can produce are not always experienced as enjoyable. Some individuals experience negative reactions to their sexual fantasies, including guilt, embarrassment, and anxiety. In addition, sexual fantasies are not always deliberate and under the control of the individual. Sexual fantasies can occur not only unintentionally, but against one's will. For example, Mickey, the main character in the HBO television series *Mind of the Married Man*, loves his wife and feels guilty about having sexual fantasies involving women. Mickey sincerely tries not to have sexual thoughts about other women, but his efforts consistently fail as sexual thoughts and images occur against his will.

Sexual cognition A wide range of thoughts, images, and fantasies, including fleeting sexual thoughts or images, elaborate and ongoing sexual fantasies, sexual thoughts and fantasies that are engaged in deliberately, and sexual thoughts that are experienced as intrusive.

To avoid the connotation that sexual thoughts and images are inherently deliberate and pleasurable, Renaud and Byers (2001) suggest using the term **sexual cognition** to capture a wide range of thoughts, images, and fantasies, including the following: (a) fleeting sexual thoughts or images; (b) elaborate and ongoing sexual fantasies; (c) sexual thoughts and fantasies that are engaged in deliberately; and (d) sexual thoughts that are experienced as intrusive. Intrusive sexual cognitions are those that are experienced as bothersome, such as when a persistent sexual image or thought interferes with concentration on work.

Sexual cognitions are commonly experienced by both women and men, often during masturbation and interpersonal sexual interaction, although they can occur in just about any nonsexual situation as well, such as while driving a vehicle, sitting in a lecture hall, shopping for groceries, and folding laundry. As noted earlier, reactions to sexual cognitions can be positive, negative, or both simultaneously. In *Mind of the Married Man*, Mickey has both positive and negative reactions to his sexual thoughts involving other women—he enjoys the eroticism, but is burdened with guilt, troubled by his inability to control his thoughts, and conflicted about whether to share his sexual thoughts about other women with his wife.

In a study of 292 heterosexual undergraduates, participants were asked to select from a list of 56 sexual cognitions the sexual thought they had experienced as most positive, as well as the sexual thought they had experienced as most negative (Renaud & Byers, 2001). The sexual cognitions most commonly selected as the most positive were having intercourse with a loved partner (31.3%), kissing passionately (19%), having intercourse with someone I know but have not had sex with (9.8%), and making love out of doors in a romantic setting (8.2%). The sexual cognitions most commonly selected as the most negative were having incestuous sexual relations (10.5%), being embarrassed by failure of sexual performance (10.2%), engaging in sexual activity contrary to my sexual orientation (6.6%), and being sexually victimized (6.6%). This study found that a higher frequency of positive sexual cognitions was related to better sexual adjustment, including more masturbation experience and greater sexual satisfaction, for women and men. However, the frequency of negative sexual cognitions was not related to sexual maladjustment.

The content of sexual cognitions varies from individual to individual and in the same person over time. Nevertheless, patterns of differences between the sexual fantasies of women and men have been observed, as discussed in section 7-4a.

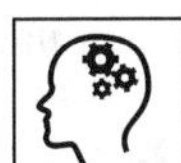

Think About It

Individuals may fantasize about events they do not actually want to occur. For example, women who have fantasies of being overpowered and forced to have sexual relations do not want to be raped in reality. Why do you think people fantasize about sexual experiences they do not actually want to have?

7-4a Sex Differences in Sexual Fantasy and Cognition

Both women and men experience sexual cognitions, but men report fantasizing more frequently than women (Jones & Barlow, 1990). Other sex differences in sexual cognitions reported in research literature include the following (Ellis & Symons, 1990; Leitenberg & Henning, 1995):

- The number of different people in one's fantasized sexual encounters is higher for men than for women. For example, 32% of men and only 8% of women reported having had fantasized a sexual encounter with more than 1,000 different people (Ellis & Symons, 1990).
- Men more than women imagine doing something sexual to their partner, whereas women more than men imagine something sexual being done to them.
- Men tend to have more explicit and visual imagery in their fantasies, whereas women tend to have more emotional and romantic imagery. In one study, 81% of the men compared with 43% of the women said that during sexual fantasy, they typically focused on visual images; 57% of women and 19% of men said that during sexual fantasy, they typically focused on emotional feelings (Ellis & Symons, 1990).
- Men are more likely than women to fantasize about having sex with multiple partners at the same time.
- Women are more likely than men to have fantasies in which they are submissive and are forced or overpowered.
- Men are more likely than women to have fantasies in which they are dominant over their partner.

7-4b Sexual Dreams

Virtually all men and about 70% of women have sexual dreams (Reinisch, 1990). Sexual dreams can result in arousal and orgasm in both women and men. About half of women who have sexual dreams report having experienced an orgasm during sleep (Reinisch, 1990). Among men ages 21–25, 70% reported experiencing a **nocturnal emission**—an ejaculation that results from an erotic dream (also known as a **wet dream**) (Kinsey et al., 1948). The frequency of wet dreams varies considerably. In Kinsey's study, some men in their teens reported having up to 12 wet dreams a week, whereas others reported having only a few in a year. The erections that men commonly have during sleep, called **nocturnal penile tumescence,** occur independently of sexual dreams.

Nocturnal emission An ejaculation that results from an erotic dream. (See also **wet dream.**)

Wet dream See **nocturnal emission.**

Nocturnal penile tumescence Erections that men commonly have during sleep.

Cultural Diversity

In a study of 964 men in India who presented themselves to a clinic for sexual dysfunctions, 71% of the men reported that "nocturnal emission" was their sexual problem of greatest concern. They felt that the loss of semen could lead to loss of virility and manhood (Verma, Khaitan, & Singh, 1998).

As is true of all types of sexual cognitions, sexual dreams are not necessarily pleasant and enjoyable, but can also be troubling and even frightening. For example, survivors of sexual abuse often have dreams in which they relive the sexual victimization, after which they wake up in a state of terror.

7-4c Personal Choices: Share Your Sexual Fantasies/Cognitions/Dreams with Your Partner?

Sharing one's sexual cognitions and dreams with a partner can be an enjoyable experience and added dimension to a couple's sexual intimacy. The respondents in Rubin's 1991 study (who were all under the age of 35) reported that they enjoyed sharing their sexual fantasies. One respondent noted, "It's very exciting to tell our fantasies to each other while we're making love" (p. 186).

Other people view sexual cognitions and dreams as private experiences rather than as experiences to be shared. Some people feel comfortable and enjoy sharing sexual cognitions and dreams with their partner when the cognition or dream involves the partner and no one else. But sexual cognitions and dreams often involve prior lovers and people other than the primary partner. In a sample of 349 university students, 98% of the men and 80% of the women reported having sexual fantasies about someone other than the primary partner in the past two months (Hicks & Leitenberg, 2001). When people experience sexual cognitions and dreams that involve prior lovers or anyone other than the primary partner, they often choose not to share their experience with their partner due to discomfort; guilt; concern about hurting the partner's feelings; and fear of the partner's disapproval, jealousy, or anger.

In deciding whether to share your sexual fantasies and dreams with your partner, you might consider discussing the issue with your partner. Find out what his or her thoughts and feelings are regarding having and sharing sexual cognitions and dreams that do and do not involve other people. Sharing sexual cognitions and dreams is not necessarily essential for intimacy and relationship satisfaction. But viewing sexual cognitions and dreams, including those involving others, as normal and inevitable and openly sharing them without guilt or fear signify a high level of trust and confidence in one's self, one's partner, and the relationship and can deepen the intimacy between the partners.

7-5 INTERPERSONAL SEXUAL BEHAVIORS

Most adult sexual behavior occurs in the context of a relationship. In sections 7-5a through 7-5i, we discuss a variety of interpersonal sexual behaviors from touching to anal intercourse.

7-5a Touching

Our skin contains about 900,000 sensory receptors (Montagu & Matson, 1979); it is a primary mechanism for experiencing pleasure. Many people regard touching as the most significant aspect of sex. The 3,000 women in Hite's (1977) study stated repeatedly that touching, holding, caressing, being close to, lying next to, and pressing bodies together were more important to them than intercourse or orgasm. For many, such physical closeness gave a feeling of emotional closeness that is satisfying whether or not intercourse or orgasm follows.

Heterosexual women commonly complain that they do not get enough touching from their partners and that men engage in foreplay only as a means of priming them for intercourse. Some say that just as some women fake orgasm, men fake foreplay. For most women, affectionate touching is an end in and of itself. In contrast, in a study of 7,000 men, the majority said that physical affection should always lead to intercourse and orgasm (Hite, 1981).

7-5b Kissing

When writing a letter to a loved one, we sometimes write a row of XXXs to represent kisses. This custom stems from the Middle Ages, when there were so many illiterate people that a cross (X) was acceptable as a signature on a legal document. The cross (X) stood for "St. Andrew's mark," and people vowed to be honest by writing a cross that represented his sacred name. To pledge their sincere honesty, people would kiss their signature. Thus, in time, the X became associated with the kiss (Ackerman, 1990, p.113).

There are different types of kissing. In one style of kissing, the partners gently touch their lips together for a short time with their mouths closed. In another, there is considerable pressure and movement for a prolonged time when the closed mouths meet. In still another, the partners kiss with their mouths open, using gentle or light pressure and variations in tongue movement. Kinsey referred to the latter as *deep kissing* (also known as *soul kissing, tongue kissing,* or *French kissing*).

Desmond Morris, a noted zoologist with an interest in the behavior of humans, suggested that mouth kissing had its origins in mother-infant interactions of early human history:

> *In early human societies, before commercial baby food was invented, mothers weaned their children by chewing up their food and then passing it into the infantile mouth by lip-to-lip contact—which naturally involved a considerable amount of tonguing and mutual mouth-pressure. This almost bird-like system of parental care seems strange and alien to us today, but our species probably practiced it for a million years or more, and adult erotic kissing today is almost certainly a Relic Gesture stemming from these origins. . . . Whether it has been handed down to us from generation to generation . . . or whether we have an inborn predisposition towards it, we cannot say. But, whichever is the case, it looks rather as though, with the deep kissing and tonguing of modern lovers, we are back again at the infantile mouth-feeding stage of the far-distant past. . . . If the young lovers exploring each other's mouths with their tongues feel the ancient comfort of parental mouth-feeding, this may help them to increase their mutual trust and thereby their pair bonding. (quoted in Ackerman, 1990, p.112)*

7-5c Breast Stimulation

In U.S. society, the female breasts are charged with eroticism. A billion-dollar pornographic industry encourages viewing women's breasts in erotic terms. Adult magazines feature women with naked breasts in seductive, erotic poses.

Although not all women derive erotic pleasure from breast stimulation, many women experience extreme pleasure and arousal in having their breasts stroked and/or sucked, and some report orgasm from nipple manipulation alone. Women may or may not manually stimulate their own breasts, either as an activity by itself, or during masturbation or lovemaking. Many women experience changes in their breast sensitivity during the month. For example, breasts often become swollen and tender prior to a woman's monthly menstrual period. For some women, breast tenderness increases enjoyment of breast stimulation; for others, it decreases enjoyment.

Male breasts have the same potential for erotic stimulation as female breasts. Stimulating the male's nipples can produce pleasure and arousal.

7-5d Penile Stimulation (Manual/Oral)

A man's partner may stimulate his penis manually or orally as a precursor to or substitute for intercourse (vaginal or anal).

Manual Stimulation

As noted, touching and rubbing the penis manually (which may occur mutually) provide pleasure to the man and may be pursued as a pleasure in itself or as a prelude to fellatio, vaginal intercourse, or anal intercourse. Manual stimulation may be continued to ejaculation or blend into oral sex or intercourse. A vibrator or personal lubrication product or saliva is sometimes used to enhance pleasure.

Oral Stimulation—Fellatio

Fellatio Oral stimulation of the man's genitals.

Oral stimulation of the man's genitals is known as **fellatio,** which comes from the Latin *fellare*, meaning "to suck." Fellatio may be a precursor to or substitute for intercourse (vaginal or anal).

NATIONAL DATA In a national sample, 81% of White men, 66% of Black men, and 65% of Hispanic men reported ever having received fellatio (Mahay, Laumann, & Michaels, 2001). Of White, Black, and Hispanic men receiving fellatio, 82%, 55%, and 68%, respectively, reported the experience as "appealing" (Mahay et al., 2001). In the same study, 75% of White women, 56% of Hispanic women, and 34% of Black women reported ever having provided fellatio for a male partner. Of White, Black, and Hispanic women providing fellatio, 55%, 25%, and 46%, respectively, regarded the experience as "appealing" (Mahay et al., 2001).

Although fellatio most often involves sucking the penis, fellatio may also include licking the shaft, glans, frenulum, and scrotum. The partner's hands also may caress the scrotum and perineum during fellatio. If fellatio results in orgasm, the semen may be swallowed without harm (in the absence of HIV infection) if the partner desires to do so. However, to reduce risk of HIV and other STD transmission, the penis should be covered with a condom during fellatio.

Some couples engage in oral sex simultaneously, whereby each partner is a giver and a receiver at the same time. The term 69 has been used to describe the positions of two partners engaging in mutual oral-genital stimulation (see Figure 7-1).

Fellatio can be used as a means of avoiding intercourse for moral reasons (to preserve virginity), to avoid pregnancy, and/or to avoid transmitting STDs. A primary motivation for fellatio is pleasure. Many men as well as women experience physical pleasure and satisfaction from receiving and/or giving fellatio. As is true with all sexual behaviors, positive interpretations of the experience contribute to the pleasure and satisfaction. For example, both the giver and the receiver of oral sex can view this behavior as an expression of love and intimacy. According to the laws of 15 states (in July 2002), oral sex was not an expression of love and intimacy, but rather a criminal act. Figure 7-2 shows the sodomy laws for each state at that time. However, in the June 2003 decision of the Supreme Court, striking down the Texas sodomy law, apparently invalidates the sodomy law of other states as well.

NATIONAL DATA As of July 2002, 15 states had sodomy laws that prohibit oral sex, as well as anal intercourse (National Gay and Lesbian Task Force, 2002). In 4 of these states, sodomy laws apply only to same-sex partners. In 11 states, sodomy laws apply to both same- and opposite-sex partners. (National Gay and Lesbian Task Force, 2002).

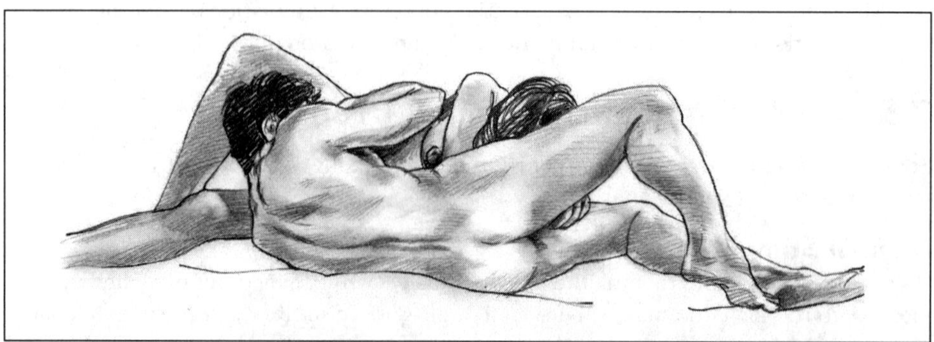

FIGURE 7-1
Simultaneous Oral-Genital Stimulation

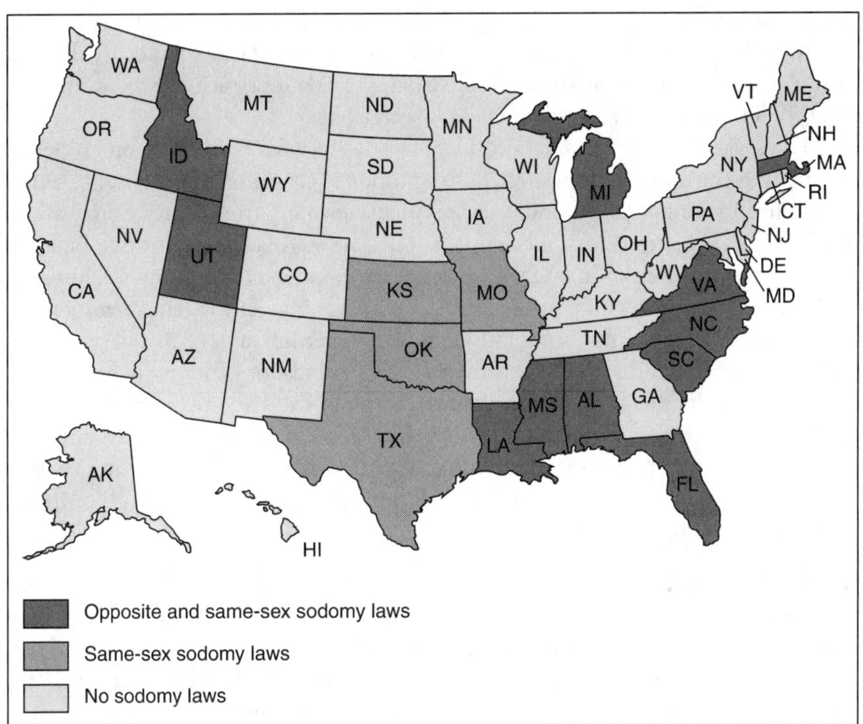

FIGURE 7-2
Sodomy Laws in the United States, July 2003

Source: National Gay and Lesbian Task Force, Washington, DC (202-393-5177)

Adolescent health professionals have observed that today's adolescents tend to regard oral sex as much less intimate and serious than vaginal intercourse (Remez, 2000). Interviews with high school juniors and seniors revealed that while intercourse is reserved for a special partner, oral sex requires few emotional ties.

Some men enjoy fellatio because it gives them a feeling of dominance. A common theme in pornographic media involves a man forcing his partner to perform fellatio. In this context, the act implies sexual submission, which may give the male an ego boost. This may also explain why some partners do not find giving fellatio appealing. However, the person providing fellatio can also feel dominant in that he or she is in a more active role than the more passive recipient. A sexuality educator at The Park School in Baltimore, Deborah Roffman, explained that "middle-school girls sometimes look at oral sex as an absolute bargain—you don't get pregnant, they think you don't get diseases, you're still a virgin and you're in control since it's something that they can do to boys (whereas sex is almost always described as something boys do to girls)" (quoted in Remez, 2000, p. 299). But this sense of control is illusory if the girl is pressured into performing fellatio "to make boys happy," or using it as a way to gain popularity, or doing it when alcohol is involved (Remez, 2000).

7-5e Clitoral Stimulation (Manual/Oral)

"Please take me clitorally" is the message most women would like their lovers to act on (Hite, 1977). Again and again, the women in Hite's study said that their partners spent too little time during lovemaking (sometimes none at all) stimulating their clitoris and that they needed such stimulation to derive maximum pleasure from the sexual experience. The clitoris may be stimulated by the fingers and hands, mouth, penis, and other body parts, as well as by sex toys, such as vibrators.

Manual Clitoral Stimulation

Manual stimulation of a woman's clitoris can provide pleasure and produce sexual arousal. Manual stimulation may be continued to orgasm or blend into oral sex or intercourse. A vibrator is sometimes used to enhance pleasure. It is important for the woman's clitoral area to be lubricated during stimulation; otherwise, stimulation can cause discomfort and pain. Personal lubricant products or saliva can provide lubrication if the woman is not sufficiently lubricated from her own vaginal secretions.

The styles of clitoral stimulation women desire vary. Some women enjoy their partner rubbing the mons veneris area, putting indirect pressure on the clitoris. Others prefer direct clitoral contact, with one or more fingers stroking the clitoris. Some women enjoy insertion of a dildo or one or more fingers into the vagina, with gentle or rapid thrusting, at the same time they stimulate the clitoris. A woman may also stimulate her own clitoris during lovemaking with a partner. Lesbian partners may enjoy **tribadism,** a form of intimacy in which two women stimulate each others' genital area (vulva, mons area, clitoris) with their own vulval area or with their fingers, hands, or other body parts such as their knee or thigh. In effect, they may rub each other at the same time, creating mutual pleasure; orgasm may or may not result. It is helpful for women to instruct their partners, verbally and through demonstration, in how and where they enjoy clitoral stimulation. Affectionate touch prior to genital stimulation, often enhances feelings of intimacy and arousal (see Figure 7-3).

Tribadism A form of intimacy in which two women stimulate each others' genital area (vulva, mons area, clitoris) with their own vulval area or with their fingers, hands, or other body parts such as their knee or thigh.

Oral Clitoral Stimulation

Cunnilingus, translated from the Latin, means "he who licks the vulva." Specifically, cunnilingus involves the stimulation of the clitoris, labia, and vaginal opening of the woman by her partner's tongue and lips. The technique many women enjoy is gentle teasing by the tongue, with stronger, more rhythmic sucking or tongue stroking movements when orgasm approaches. While the partner's mouth is caressing and licking the clitoral shaft and glans, some women prefer additional stimulation by a dildo, finger, or vibrator in the vagina or anus.

Cunnilingus Stimulation of the clitoris, labia, and vaginal opening of the woman by her partner's tongue and lips.

NATIONAL DATA White women reported the highest percentage of ever having received cunnilingus (79%), Black women the lowest percentage (49%), and Hispanic women between the White and Black percentages (62%) (Mahay et al., 2001). Of the White, Black, and Hispanic women who have received cunnilingus, 65%, 40%, and 63% reported that it was "appealing" (Mahay et al., 2001).

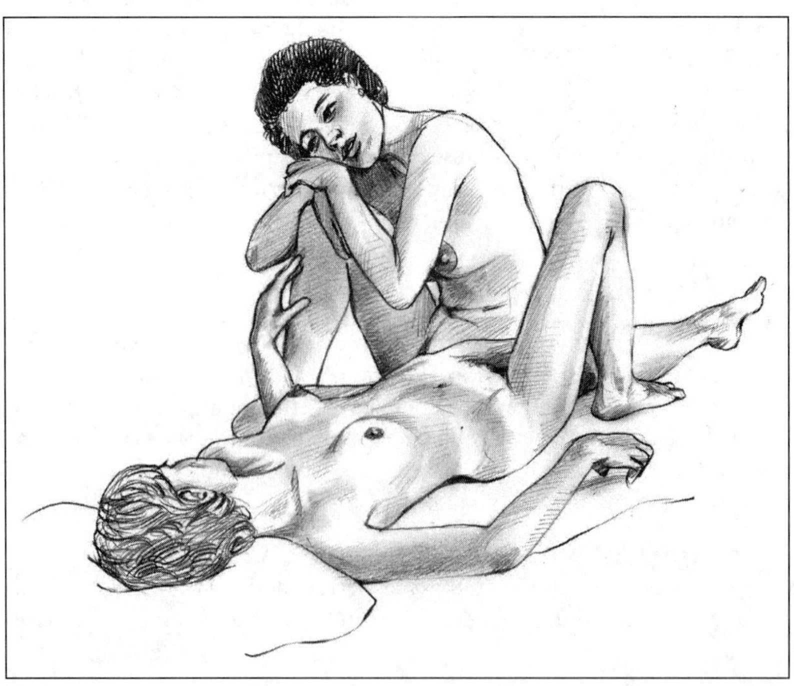

FIGURE 7-3
Affectionate Touch Enhances Feelings of Intimacy and Arousal

NATIONAL DATA White men reported the highest percentage of ever having performed cunnilingus (82%), Black men the lowest percentage (51%), and Hispanic men between the White and Black percentages (65%). Of the White, Black, and Hispanic men, 77%, 42%, and 54% reported that providing cunnilingus for their partners was "appealing" (Mahay et al., 2001).

To reduce risk of STD transmission, partners should use a **dental dam,** which is a thin piece of latex that covers the vulva during cunnilingus. In states that have sodomy laws prohibiting cunnilingus, dental dams are not available in local pharmacies or other stores because it is illegal for stores to sell them. However, a latex condom that is cut into a flat piece may act as a substitute for a dental dam. In addition, Saran Wrap—a brand of household plastic wrap—is the only plastic wrap that has been approved for use as a dental dam (B. Credle, personal communication, October 1, 2002). Dental dams can also be purchased over the Internet.

Dental dam Thin piece of latex that covers the vulva during cunnilingus.

Penile-Clitoral Stimulation

In addition to stimulating the clitoral area by hand and mouth, some heterosexual women rub their partner's penis across and around their clitoris. Such stimulation may or may not be followed by penetration. If the man is not wearing a condom, penile-clitoral stimulation carries a risk of causing pregnancy. If the man ejaculates near the woman's vaginal opening during penile-clitoral stimulation, or even if he just emits a small amount of preejaculatory fluid (which contains sperm), pregnancy is possible.

7-5f Anal Stimulation

Some people enjoy the sensation of a lover's finger in their anal opening and gently rotating and/or moving in and out. Others may prefer the insertion of a dildo or vibrator beyond the anal opening and short anal canal into the larger rectum. Many men, including heterosexuals, prefer this form of penetration (Morin, 2002).

Another form of anal stimulation called **fisting** involves the insertion of several fingers or an entire closed fist and forearm (typically lubricated with a non-petroleum-based lubricant) into a partner's rectum and sometimes the lower colon. Care during insertion is particularly important, that it not be abrupt or forceful, to avoid damage to the rectum, colon, and anal sphincter. Although anyone can perform or receive fisting, this activity is usually associated with male homosexual activity. Lesbians may also use a form of fisting that involves insertion into the vulva or vagina.

Fisting The insertion of several fingers or an entire closed fist and forearm (typically lubricated with a non-petroleum-based lubricant) into a partner's rectum and sometimes the lower colon.

Some partners enjoy oral-anal stimulation or **analingus** (also referred to as **rimming**) which involves the licking of and/or insertion of the tongue into the partner's anus. The idea of this form of sexual activity is disgusting to some people, and others avoid it due to health concerns. For protection, a latex barrier (or Saran Wrap) should be used during analingus.

Analingus Involves the licking of and/or insertion of the tongue into the partner's anus. (See also **rimming.**)

Rimming See **analingus.**

7-5g Vaginal Intercourse

Sexual intercourse, or **coitus,** refers to the sexual union of a man's penis and a woman's vagina (see Figure 7-4). A statewide survey of more than 4,000 adolescent females found that 45% reported having had intercourse by age 16. The earlier the age at first intercourse, the greater the risk of experiencing a premarital pregnancy (Leitenberg & Saltzman, 2000). In a sample of college students at four southern colleges, 83% reported having had vaginal intercourse (Kelley, Synovitz, Carlson, & Schuster, 2001). Individuals who have had intercourse report more social pressure to engage in intercourse than those who have never had intercourse (Nahom et al., 2001).

Sexual intercourse The sexual union of a man's penis and a woman's vagina. (See also **coitus.**)

Coitus The sexual union of a man's penis and a woman's vagina. (See also **sexual intercourse.**)

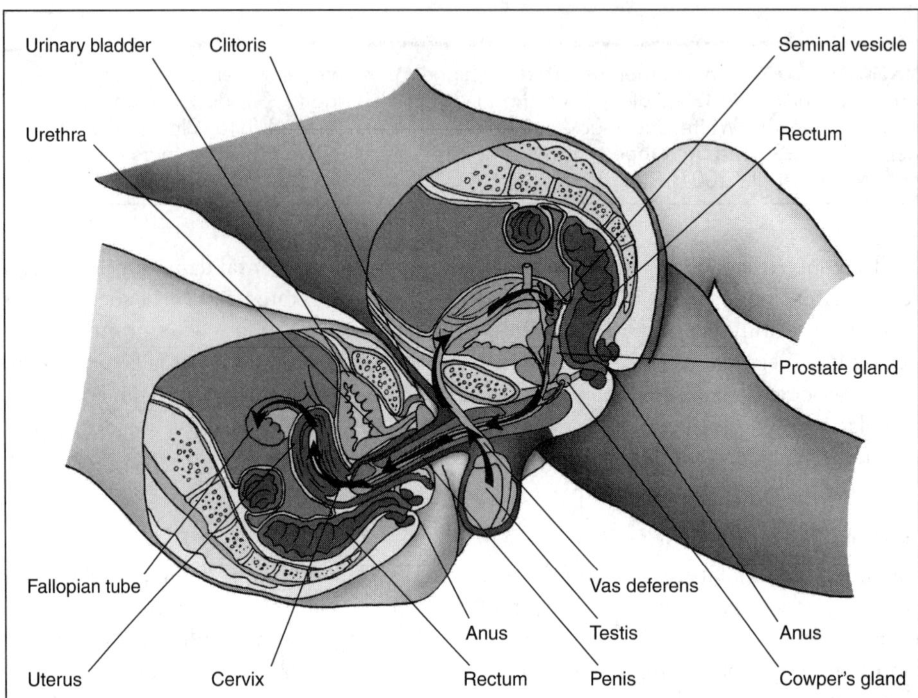

FIGURE 7-4
Sexual Intercourse

The arrows indicate the path of sperm after ejaculation as they travel to the fallopian tube, where fertilization is most likely to occur.

Positions for Intercourse

The world's earliest known and most detailed sex manuals were produced by the Chinese and typically included "introductory remarks on the cosmic significance of the sexual encounter" (Tannahill, 1982, p.169), foreplay recommendations, and techniques and positions for intercourse (illustrated for bedside reference). Many of these positions were poetically named and acrobatically described, such as Dragon in Flight, Tiger in the Forest, Swinging Monkey, Cicadas Mating, and Flying Through the Clouds (Humana & Wu, 1984). Following is a classification of positions for coitus (inserting a penis into a vagina) known to occur in different world cultures. The intercourse positions are classified based on general posture (lying, sitting, standing), position vis-à-vis partner (facing each other, rear entry), and dominance (man or woman on top, side by side) (Gregersen, 1983).

1. *Man-on-Top Position*. The man-on-top position is the most frequently reported position used during intercourse (see Figure 7-5). This position is also referred to as the "missionary position" because the Polynesians observed that the British missionaries had intercourse with the man on top. The woman reclines on her back, bends her knees, and spreads her legs. The man positions himself between her legs, supporting himself on his elbows and knees. The man or woman may guide his penis into her vagina. This position permits maximum male thrusting and facilitates eye contact, kissing, and caressing. Some partners may prefer to be on top or on bottom as an expression of their feelings about gender, dominance, and submission.

   Some women experience pain from the deep penetration. Closing her legs after penetration can reduce this pain. For some women, the man-above position makes clitoral contact and orgasm difficult, although many women find ways of moving their hips and/or positioning their body to achieve clitoral stimulation and/or orgasm. The woman's clitoris may also be stimulated by either the man's or the woman's hand or finger during man-on-top intercourse. For some men, the muscle tension produced by supporting their weight and active thrusting hastens ejaculation, which may be problematic for both the woman and the man.

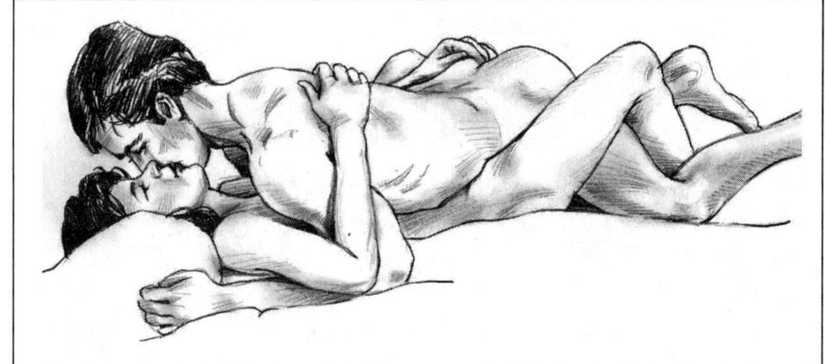

FIGURE 7-5
Man-on-Top Position

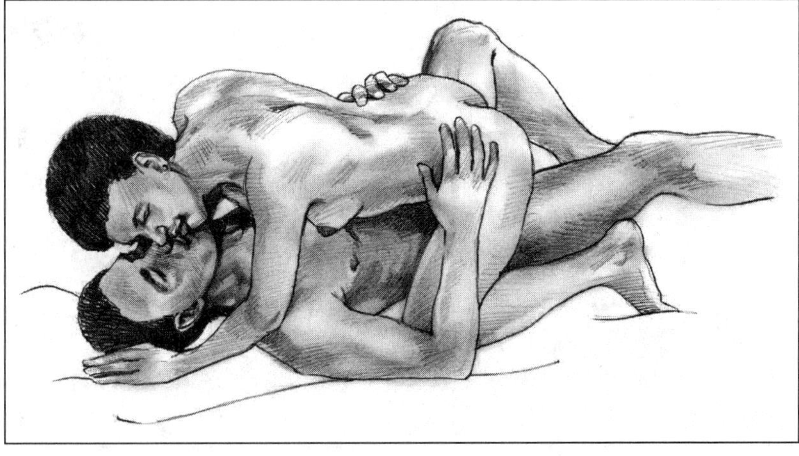

FIGURE 7-6
Woman-on-Top Position

A variation of the man-on-top position involves the woman lying on her back, with the man squatting or kneeling between the woman's spread legs. This is often referred to as the "Oceanic position," because it has been described in Pacific cultures. Body contact can be full and intimate, or minimal.

2. *Woman-on-Top Position*. In the woman-on-top position, the woman may either lie lengthwise, so that her legs are between her partner's, or kneel on top with her knees on either side of him (see Figure 7-6). The primary advantage of this position is that it provides the woman with more control so that she can move in ways that provide her with maximum pleasure. Many women report that this position is more likely to lead to orgasm than the man-on-top position. In this position, partners can also touch each other (or themselves), kiss, and maintain eye contact.

   Some women report drawbacks to the woman-above position. Some feel too shy in this position and do not enjoy "being on display." Others complain that the penis keeps falling out because the woman may lift too high before the downward stroke on the penis.

   For both women and men, being on the bottom position during intercourse is easier, and requires less energy and exertion, whereas being on the top position during intercourse is more work. Some partners' preferences for being on the bottom or the top depend on how tired or energetic they feel.

3. *Side-by-Side Position*. A relaxing position for both partners is the side-by-side position (see Figure 7-7). The partners lie on their sides, facing each other. The top legs are lifted and positioned to accommodate easy entry of the penis. Neither partner bears the strain of "doing all the work," and the partners have relative freedom to move their body as they wish to achieve the desired place of contact and rhythm of movement.

FIGURE 7-7
Side-by-Side Position

FIGURE 7-8
Rear Entry During Pregnancy

This position may be preferred in the latter months of pregnancy. Gregersen (1983) noted that this position is reported in a number of African societies, and suggested that it might well be called the "African position."

4. *Rear-Entry Position.* There are several ways to achieve a rear-entry intercourse position. The woman may lie on her side with her back to her partner (see Figure 7-8). She may also support herself on her knees and hands or forearms and elbows (see Figure 7-9), or she may lie on her stomach and tilt her buttocks upward while the man enters her vagina from behind. In another rear-entry variation, the man may lie on his back and the woman may kneel or squat above him with her back toward her partner.

   Many of the rear-entry intercourse positions permit the man or the woman to manually stimulate her breasts or clitoris or caress her legs and buttocks. Many women are unable to achieve orgasm using the rear-entry position. Although some women enjoy the deep penetration that results from rear-entry intercourse, others find it painful. Other disadvantages of rear-entry intercourse include a tendency for the penis to slip out and the loss of face-to-face contact. Sometimes the stigma of bestiality accompanies this position, and it is often described with animal names, as in the Chinese "Leaping Tiger," the Marquesan "horse intercourse," and the American term "doggie position" or "doggie style."

5. *Sitting Position.* In the sitting position, the man sits on a chair or the edge of the bed with his partner sitting across his thighs (see Figure 7-10). She can lower herself onto his erect penis or insert his penis after she is sitting. She may be facing him, or her back may be turned to him. The face-to-face sitting position involves maximum freedom to stimulate the breasts (manually or orally), to kiss, and to hug. It may allow the man to delay ejaculating because it doesn't involve pelvic thrusting. Chinese erotic art often depicts coitus in a sitting position, but this is not prominent in other cultures.

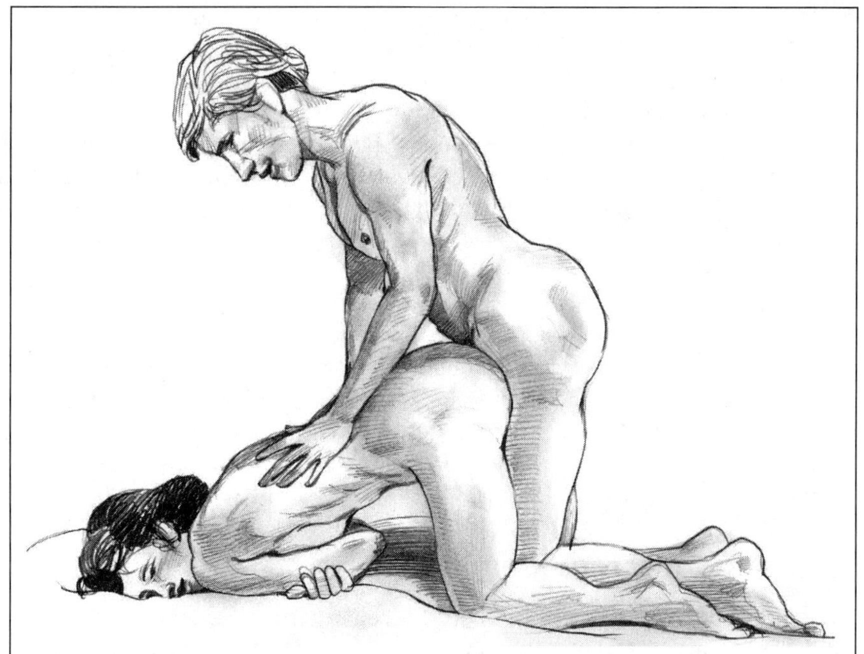

FIGURE 7-9
Rear Entry, Kneeling

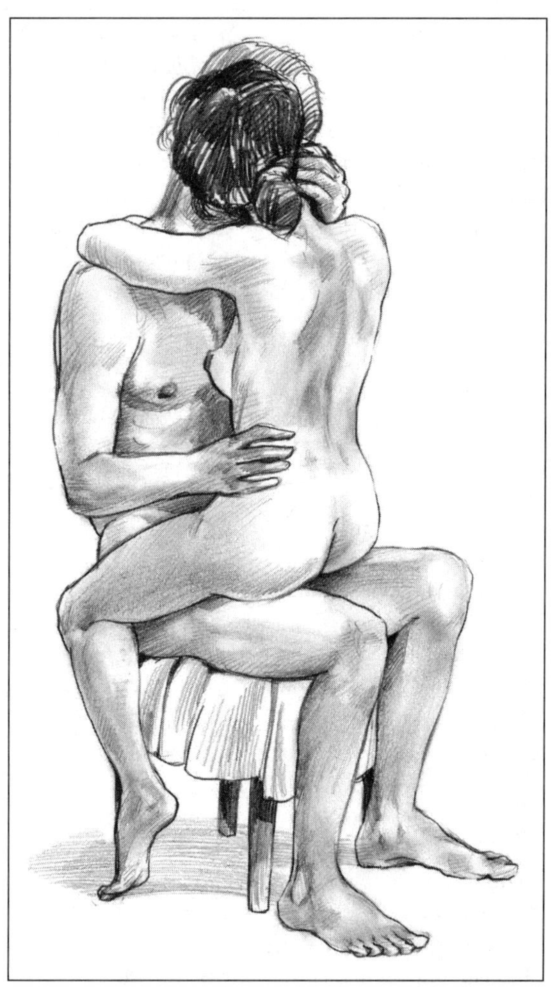

FIGURE 7-10
Sitting Position

6. *Standing Position*. In the standing position, the woman raises one leg, or the man picks hers up and places her onto his erect penis. She puts her legs around his waist and her arms around his neck while he is holding her. Both must be well coordinated and in good physical condition for this position.

   An easier variation of the standing position is for the man to stand while the woman sits or reclines on a raised surface (a high bed, a table, or a chair). The woman's legs are spread, and the man inserts his penis into her vagina while standing between her legs. In most cultures of the world, standing positions are associated with brief (often illicit) encounters.
7. *Variations*. There are innumerable variations to the basic positions described here. For example, in the man-above position, the woman's legs may be closed or open, bent or straight, over his shoulders or around his neck. The woman may be on her back or raised on her elbows. The partners may face each other or be head-to-toe. Couples can choose different positions to add variety to their lovemaking and to provide different types of stimulation and pleasure. Sexual intercourse positions may also vary according to pregnancy and health issues.

7-5h Anal Intercourse

Anal intercourse, whereby a male inserts his penis into his partner's anus, is the least practiced form of anal sex (the more common anal sex techniques include stimulation of the anus with the fingers, hand, or mouth) (Morin, 2002). Twenty-three percent of a random sample of nonvirginal undergraduate university students reported that they had engaged in anal intercourse (Baldwin & Baldwin, 2000). Those most likely to report having had anal intercourse were erotophilic, younger at first vaginal intercourse, and less effective contraception users.

Anal intercourse is one form (not the primary form) of sexual expression enjoyed by some homosexual males. Partners differ in their preference for and comfort in being the active or passive partner. Both partners may have orgasm during anal penetration—the active partner due to stimulation of the penis and the passive partner due to the fact that the partner's penis in his rectum exerts pressure on his prostate gland, which may trigger orgasm.

National Data There are racial and ethnic differences in the frequency of anal intercourse, with 31% of Hispanic men reporting ever having engaged in anal intercourse compared to 26% of non-Hispanic White men and 23% of Black men. Less than 4% of all these racial groups reported engaging in anal intercourse the last time they were involved in a sexual event (Mahay et al., 2001).

For couples who enjoy anal intercourse, or who want to try it, care and patience during insertion are critical to avoiding rectal tearing and pain. It is important for the receiving partner to be in control of the timing and depth of penetration. It is best for the receiving partner to be relaxed, specifically for his or her anal sphincter muscles to be relaxed, and for insertion to be slow and gradual. Using a lubricant is recommended for easing entry into the anus and minimizing discomfort. Two valuable resources for information on anal sex are *Anal Pleasure: A Guide for Men and Women* (Morin, 1998) and *The New Vibrations Guide to Sex* (Winks & Semans, 1997).

Anal intercourse is the sexual behavior associated with the highest risk of HIV infection—a fact not known by many undergraduates who practice anal intercourse (Baldwin & Baldwin, 2000). The person receiving anal intercourse is at higher risk than the man who inserts his penis into his partner's rectum. The reason is that anal intercourse often tears the rectum, allowing HIV-infected semen to come in contact with the bloodstream. In addition, the first few inches of the anus provide darkness, warmth, and moisture in the mucous membranes, which is a prime host for transmitting HIV. Couples who engage in anal intercourse should always use a condom to protect against transmission of HIV and other STDs. The use of water-based lubrication products, such as KY Jelly, may also enable the penis to enter the partner's rectum more easily and, thus, minimize tearing of the rectal tissue. If vaginal intercourse or oral contact with the penis follows anal intercourse, the penis should first be thoroughly washed.

Another risk associated with anal intercourse (as well as with manual or oral stimulation of the anus) is cystitis (bladder infection). Cystitis may result from bacteria from the anal region being spread to the urethral opening. Symptoms of cystitis may include a persistent urge to urinate, pain during urination, and fever. Cystitis is treated with antibiotics; if left untreated, a serious kidney infection could develop. Women are much more prone to developing cystitis than men. To reduce risk of cystitis, use a condom, clean the anal area before engaging in anal stimulation, urinate immediately after sex, and clean the anal and genital area after sex. Also, after a penis, mouth, or finger has come in contact with the anal area, avoid contact with the vagina and clitoris until the penis, mouth, or finger has been washed thoroughly.

CULTURAL DIVERSITY 

Telephone interviews with 852 randomly chosen persons in Denmark and Sweden revealed "the increasing practice of anal intercourse, particularly among women with many partners" suggesting that "this practice deserves attention, since it may erroneously be considered a safe sexual activity" (Jaeger et al., 2000, p. 91).

7-5i Personal Choices: Considerations for Becoming Sexually Active with a New Partner

Issues to consider in deciding whether to become sexually active with a new partner (for both heterosexuals and homosexuals) include personal consequences, partner consequences, relationship consequences, contraception and pregnancy, and HIV and other STDs.

Personal Consequences

In deciding whether to become sexually active with a partner, it may be helpful to try to predict how you might feel about yourself after you become sexually involved with this person. The effect that sexual involvement will have on you personally will be influenced by your personal and religious values, and the emotional involvement with your partner. Is sexual involvement consistent with your values? If not, you are likely to have feelings of guilt and regret. Does your emotional involvement, commitment, and relationship stability with your partner meet your standards for a sexual relationship? As the following excerpts reflect, the standards people have for entering a sexual relationship vary (the following excerpts were written by students in the authors' classes):

> *I believe that when a person falls in love with another, it is OK to have sex with that person. This should be thought about carefully, so as not to regret including sex too early in the relationship. I do not think sex should be a one-night thing, a one-week thing, or a one-month thing. You should grow to love and care for the person very much before giving your body to another. These feelings should be felt by both partners; if this is not the case, then you are not in love and you are not 'making love.'*

Those who are not in love and have sex in a casual context sometimes feel bad about their decision:

> *I viewed sex as a new toy—something to try as frequently as possible. I did my share of sleeping around, and all it did for me was to give me a total loss of self-respect and a bad reputation. Besides, sometimes your partner talks. I have heard rumors that I had sex with people I never did.*

Some students reported positive consequences of casual sex:

> *We met one night at a mutual friend's party. We liked each other immediately. We talked, sipped some wine, and ended up spending the night together. Though we never saw each other again, I have very positive memories of the encounter.*

Partner Consequences

Because a basic moral principle is to do no harm to others, it may be important to consider the effect of sexual involvement on your partner. Whereas sex with a new partner may be a pleasurable experience with positive consequences for you, your partner may react differently. What are your partner's feelings about sex in your relationship and her or his ability to handle the experience? What meaning (or lack of it) will he or she attribute to sex with you and what are the potential outcomes in terms of guilt and regret?

One woman reported that she had made a mistake in having sex with a friend. "To me," she said, "it was just a friendship and I knew that there was no romantic future. For my partner, it was different . . . the partner fell in love and wanted us to be lovers. The ending was bad and I learned I should have been more sensitive to how the partner would react."

Relationship Consequences

In deciding whether to become sexually active with a partner, think about how sexual involvement might affect the overall relationship. One study of 163 unmarried undergraduates found that 63% reported "no change" and 30% reported an "improved relationship" after they became sexually involved (Knox & Brigman, 1996). Another study investigated the effect of various levels of sexual intimacy (from kissing to intercourse) on relationship commitment and found that "the milder, but more affectionate behaviors of holding hands and kissing seemed to be more important indicators of couples' commitment than the more 'intense' behaviors of fondling and sexual intercourse" (Rostosky, Welsh, Kawaguchi, & Galliher, 1999, p. 331).

Contraception and Pregnancy

For heterosexuals, a potential consequence of intercourse is pregnancy. After a heterosexual couple decides to have intercourse, another decision must be made about what contraceptive method(s) to use for preventing pregnancy (assuming the couple does not want pregnancy to occur). You might also consider that the effectiveness of most contraceptive methods is less than 100%, so using a contraceptive method does not guarantee that pregnancy will not occur. Because the decision to have heterosexual intercourse means deciding to allow for the possibility of pregnancy, ask yourself: What would I do and how would I feel if I (or my partner) got pregnant? How would a pregnancy affect my life, my partner's life, and our relationship? These are important questions to ask in considering whether to have heterosexual intercourse. Most people think pregnancy won't happen to them, but it may come as a surprise. One woman recalled:

> *It was the first time I had had intercourse, so I didn't really think I'd get pregnant. But I did. And when I told him I was pregnant, he told me he didn't have any money and couldn't help me pay for the abortion. He really wanted nothing to do with me after that. (authors' files)*

HIV and Other Sexually Transmitted Diseases

Deciding whether to become sexually active with a partner also involves deciding whether to risk acquiring or transmitting sexually transmitted disease. Individuals who know that they have a sexually transmitted disease are advised to share this information with their prospective partner BEFORE sexual activity occurs. Exactly when and how to disclose one's sexual health status to a partner can be a difficult but important decision to face.

To minimize risk of acquiring or transmitting an STD, other choices are involved, such as choosing to avoid certain high-risk behaviors (e.g., anal intercourse) and choosing to use latex or polyurethane condoms (and dental dams for oral sex). Although this is good advice, only a third of undergraduates in one sample reported that they always used a condom during the past month (Civic, 2000). The most frequently cited reason for not using a condom was that one partner was on oral contraception.

If your partner has had many previous sexual partners and/or is a current or past intravenous drug user, or partner of an intravenous drug user, he or she is at higher risk of having a sexually transmitted disease. Keep in mind that, in one study, lying about the number of previous partners was reported as the most frequent lie new partners tell each other (Knox, Schacht, Holt, & Turner, 1993). It is also possible for a partner to be infected with an STD and not realize it.

The Influence of Alcohol/Other Drugs on Choices

A final issue concerning the decision to have sex involves being aware of the influence of alcohol and other drugs on such a decision. Seventy-eight percent of 210 college students reported that they had made one or more decisions while drinking that they later regretted. Seventy percent reported that they were less likely to use condoms when they had consumed alcohol (Poulson, Eppler, Satterwhite, Wuensch, & Bass, 1998).

Alternatives

Outercourse is a generic term that refers to any form of sexual intimacy that does not involve sexual intercourse. Examples typically include hugging, kissing, and mutual masturbation. Outercourse provides a way to experience sexual enjoyment without the risk of pregnancy and, for some individuals, may be more consistent with one's sexual values and less likely to result in guilt or regret.

Outercourse Activities that do not involve exposing a partner to blood, semen, or vaginal secretions. Outercourse includes hugging, cuddling, masturbating, fantasizing, massaging, and rubbing each other's body with clothes on.

Some individuals may include oral sex, analingus, and anal intercourse as forms of outercourse. However, although these alternatives involve no risk of pregnancy, they do incur risk of STD transmission.

SUMMARY

Sexuality differs in the same individual and couples across time, and between individuals and couples. In this chapter, we have examined the range of individual and interpersonal sexual behaviors and fantasies.

Erotophilia and Erotophobia

The range of feelings toward sexual behavior can be conceptualized according to a continuum known as the "erotophilic-erotophobic continuum." The propensity to have positive emotional responses to sexuality is referred to as erotophilia. The tendency to have negative emotional responses to sexuality is known as erotophobia. Individuals who are erotophobic tend to feel uncomfortable about sex and try to avoid sexual partners, contexts, and experiences. Although erotophobic individuals are less likely to be sexually active, those who do engage in sexual relations have a higher risk of pregnancy and HIV or STD transmission because they feel uncomfortable discussing or using contraception or condoms.

Virginity, Chastity, Celibacy, and Abstinence

Virginity refers to not having experienced sexual intercourse. Virgins—individuals who have not experienced sexual intercourse—may or may not have experienced other forms of sexual interaction, such as manual or oral-genital stimulation. The term *chastity* also refers to not having had sexual intercourse, but it also implies moral purity or virtuousness in both thought and conduct. Individuals who practice chastity probably abstain not only from intercourse, but also from all sexual behaviors. Celibacy may refer to the condition of being unmarried, especially by reason of religious vows, and also implies refraining from having sexual intercourse, although a person who practices celibacy is not necessarily a virgin. The more commonly used term today that refers to refraining from having sexual intercourse is *abstinence*. Like celibacy, the practice of abstinence does not necessarily mean that the person is a virgin; a person who has experienced sexual intercourse can subsequently practice abstinence. For some individuals, abstinence means refraining from sexual intercourse, but not from other forms of sexual interaction. For other individuals, abstinence means refraining from not only sexual intercourse, but from other sexual behaviors as well. Abstinence can be voluntary or involuntary, and can last for short or extended periods of time. Sometimes being abstinent is forced by institutional structure such as a nursing or retirement home.

Autoerotic Behavior

Autoerotic behavior, commonly known as masturbation, involves touching and stimulating one's self to achieve sexual pleasure and/or orgasm. Due to traditional negative attitudes toward masturbation that originated in religion, medicine, and traditional psychotherapy, shame, guilt, and anxiety continue to be common feelings associated with masturbation in our society. Most health-care professionals today agree that masturbation is a normal and healthy sexual behavior. Masturbation behavior varies by sex, race/ethnicity, and religion. Partnered individuals as well as singles engage in masturbation as a solo activity or with a partner. The effects of masturbation on relationships can be positive or negative and largely depend on the situation in which the behavior occurs and the values and interpretations of each partner. Masturbation also occurs in groups, and organized masturbation clubs can be found in large cities throughout the world.

Sexual Fantasies, Sexual Cognitions, and Sexual Dreams

Sexual fantasies are cognitions, or thoughts and/or images, that are sexual in nature. It is commonly assumed that engaging in sexual fantasy is a pleasant and enjoyable experience that is engaged in deliberately. But some individuals experience negative reactions to their sexual fantasies, including guilt, embarrassment, and anxiety. In addition, sexual fantasies are not always deliberate and under the control of the individual. The term *sexual cognitions* captures a wide range of thoughts, images, and fantasies, including (a) fleeting sexual thoughts or images; (b) elaborate and ongoing sexual fantasies; (c) sexual thoughts and fantasies that are engaged in deliberately; and (d) sexual thoughts that are experienced as intrusive. Sexual cognitions can be pleasant and enjoyable or unpleasant and troubling. Gender differences in sexual cognitions have been observed and are discussed in the chapter. Sexual dreams can result in arousal and orgasm in both women and men.

Interpersonal Sexual Behaviors

Most adult sexual behavior occurs in the context of a relationship. These behaviors include touching, kissing, breast stimulation, penile stimulation (manual/oral), clitoral stimulation (manual/oral), anal stimulation, vaginal intercourse, and anal intercourse. There are many variations of these sexual behaviors, many of which can be enjoyed by homosexual male couples, lesbian couples, and heterosexual couples. In deciding whether or not to become sexually active with a person, individuals might consider the consequences for one's self, one's partner, and the relationship; contraception and pregnancy issues; the need for protecting against transmission of HIV/STDs; and the influence of alcohol/drugs on making this decision.

SUGGESTED WEBSITES

Note: These websites were functional when we went to press. Please access the online text for the most up-to-date URLs.

Betty Dodson Online
http://www.bettydodson.com/

Body Health: A Multimedia AIDS and HIV Information Resource
http://www.thebody.com

The Kinsey Institute
http://www.indiana.edu/~kinsey/history.html

Masturbation
http://mypleasure.com/

Marriage Project
http://marriage.rutgers.edu

Oral Sex
http://oralcaress.com/sexuality.htm

Sex Information
http://www.sex-help.info

Society for Human Sexuality
http://www.sexuality.org

The Safer Sex Page
http://www.safersex.org/

KEY TERMS

abstinence (p. 209)
analingus (p. 227)
autoerotic behavior (p. 210)
celibacy (p. 208)
chastity (p. 208)
coitus (p. 227)
cunnilingus (p. 226)
dental dam (p. 227)
erotophilia (p. 206)
erotophobia (p. 206)
fellatio (p. 224)
fisting (p. 227)
involuntary abstinence (p. 210)
masturbation (p. 210)
nocturnal emission (p. 221)
nocturnal penile tumescence (p. 221)
outercourse (p. 235)
rimming (p. 227)
semen-conservation doctrine (p. 212)
sexual celibacy (p. 210)
sexual cognition (p. 220)
sexual fantasies (p. 220)
sexual intercourse (p. 227)
tribadism (p. 226)
virginity (p. 208)
voluntary abstinence (p. 209)
wet dream (p. 221)
yang (p. 212)
yin (p. 212)

CHAPTER QUIZ

1. Erotophilia and erotophobia refer to which of the following?
   a. types of sexual dysfunctions
   b. forms of masturbation
   c. positive or negative emotional responses to sexuality
   d. legal terms that distinguish between consensual and nonconsensual sex

2. In a study of first intercourse experiences of 292 undergraduates, which of the following was one of the two most frequent comments made by the respondents about their first intercourse experience?
   a. It was a good thing they had consumed alcohol before the experience; otherwise, they would have been too afraid.
   b. They could not believe they had waited so long to lose their virginity.
   c. They don't understand why losing one's virginity is such a big deal in our society.
   d. They wished they had been in a committed relationship.

3. When a male is abstinent, what happens to his sperm?
   a. It leaks out of the penis without awareness.
   b. It increases in volume and concentration.
   c. It is absorbed into the body and the body eventually ceases to make it.
   d. It loses its motility.

4. During the World AIDS Day Conference at the United Nations in December 1994, former Surgeon General Joycelyn Elders spoke about the spread of STDs. After her presentation, a psychologist in the audience asked whether she would consider promoting masturbation to discourage school-age children from engaging in riskier forms of sexual activity. Elders replied that masturbation "is something that is a part of human sexuality and . . . . that perhaps should be taught" ("The Politics of Masturbation," 1994, p. 1714). After Elders's presentation, what happened?
   a. President Clinton asked for and received Elders's resignation.
   b. Elders received an award from President Clinton for her contributions to the battle against HIV/AIDS.
   c. She received a standing ovation.
   d. Both b and c.

5. Kellogg's Corn Flakes were designed to
   a. curb masturbation by reducing carnal lusts.
   b. increase a person's libido by eating natural grains.
   c. ensure the normal development of secondary sex characteristics in adolescents.
   d. increase fertility among women and men.

6. Based on data presented in your text, who has the higher rate of reported masturbation: women or men?
   a. women
   b. men
7. Most people who masturbate are single and do not have a steady partner. Masturbation rarely occurs among women and men who have a steady partner.
   a. True
   b. False
8. What do sex therapists routinely recommend to women who report never having experienced orgasm?
   a. Try a different partner.
   b. Take Viagra.
   c. Masturbate.
   d. Find a good psychotherapist.
9. Sexual fantasies are ____________ enjoyable and pleasurable.
   a. not always
   b. always
10. To avoid the connotation that sexual thoughts and images are inherently deliberate and pleasurable, Renaud and Byers (2001) suggest using which of the following terms?
   a. sexual cognitions
   b. spontaneous sexual imaginings
   c. cognitive sexual sublimation
   d. mindful sexuality
11. According to your text, which of the following statements is true?
   a. The reported frequency of sexual fantasizing is equal for women and men.
   b. Women report fantasizing more frequently than men.
   c. Men report fantasizing more frequently than women.
12. It is possible for ____________ to experience orgasm during sleep while having a sexual dream.
   a. women
   b. men
   c. both women and men
   d. none of the above
13. In some states, ____________ is against the law.
   a. breast-feeding
   b. masturbation
   c. oral sex (fellatio and cunnilingus)
   d. none of the above
14. Who is most likely to participate in tribadism?
   a. children
   b. people living in rural Africa
   c. single men
   d. lesbians
15. Dragon in Flight, Tiger in the Forest, Swinging Monkey, Cicadas Mating, and Flying Through the Clouds refer to which of the following?
   a. intercourse positions identified in ancient Chinese sex manuals
   b. ancient Chinese courtship dances in which women seduced men
   c. ancient Chinese courtship dances in which men seduced women
   d. popular alcoholic drinks that, in the Chinese culture, are believed to increase sexual desire and arousal
16. What is outercourse?
   a. any form of sexual intimacy that does not involve intercourse
   b. sexual intercourse that takes place in an outdoor setting
   c. the practice of a man withdrawing his penis from his partner's vagina or anus before ejaculation occurs
   d. having sexual intercourse with someone other than one's primary partner

REFERENCES

Ackerman, D. (1990). *A natural history of the senses*. New York: Random House.

Allen, P. L. (2000). *The wages of sin: Sex and disease, past and present*. Chicago: University of Chicago Press.

Baldwin, J. I., & Baldwin, J. D. (2000). Heterosexual anal intercourse: An understudied, high-risk sexual behavior. *Archives of Sexual Behavior, 29*, 357–374.

Bartosch, J., Berry, W., Maodush-Pitzer, D., Hunter-Geboy, C., Thompson, P. M., & Woodard, L. (1989). *God's gift of sexuality: A study for young people in the reformed tradition in the Presbyterian church (USA) and reformed church in America*. Louisville, KY: Presbyterian Publishing House.

Bogart, L. M., Cecil, H., Wagstaff, D. A., Pinkerton, S. D., & Abramson, P. R. (2000). Is it "sex"?: College students' interpretations of sexual behavior terminology. *The Journal of Sex Research, 37*, 108–116.

Buker, J. (2002, Fall). Masturbation. Presentation, Sociology of Human Sexuality, East Carolina University, Greenville, NC.

Bullough, V. L. (1976). Sexual variance in society and history. New York: Wiley.

Carnes, P. J. (2001). Cybersex, courtship, and escalating arousal: Factors in addictive sexual desire. *Sexual Addiction & Compulsivity, 8*, 45–78.

Civic, D. (2000). College students' reasons for nonuse of condoms within dating relationships. *Journal of Sex and Marital Therapy, 26*, 95–105.

Clark, C. A., & Wiederman, M. W. (2000). Gender and reactions to a hypothetical relationship partner's masturbation and use of sexually explicit media. *The Journal of Sex Research, 37*, 133–142.

Cornog, M. (2001). Group masturbation among young and old: A summary with questions. *Journal of Sex Education and Therapy, 26*, 340–346.

Darling, C. A., Davidson, J. K., Sr., & Cox, R. P. (1991). Female sexual response and the timing of partner orgasm. *Journal of Sex and Marital Therapy, 17,* 3–21.

Donnelly, D., Burgess, E., Anderson, S., Davis, R., & Dillard, J. (2001). Involuntary celibacy: A life course analysis. *The Journal of Sex Research, 38,* 159–169.

Elliott, L., & Brantley, C. (1997). *Sex on campus: The naked truth about the real sex lives of college students.* New York: Random House.

Ellis, B. J., & Symons, D. (1990). Sex differences in sexual fantasy: An evolutionary psychological approach. *The Journal of Sex Research, 27,* 527–555.

Fisher, W. A. (1988). The sexual opinion survey. In C. M. Davis, W. L. Yarber, & S. L. Davis (Eds.), *Sexuality related measures: A compendium* (pp. 34–38). Lake Mills, IA: Graphic.

Fisher, W. A., Byrne, D., White, L. A., & Kelley, K. (1988). Erotophobia-erotophilia as a dimension of personality. *The Journal of Sex Research, 25,* 123–151.

Friedman, R. C., & Downey, J. I. (2000). Psychoanalysis and sexual fantasies. *Archives of Sexual Behavior, 29,* 567–586.

Graham, S. (1848). *Lecture to young men on chastity, intended also for the serious consideration of parents and guardians* (10th ed.). Boston: C. H. Price.

Gregersen, E. (1983). *Sexual practices: The story of human sexuality.* New York: Franklin Watts.

Halpern, C. J. T., Udry, J. R., & Campbell, B. (2000). Adolescent males' willingness to report masturbation. *The Journal of Sex Research, 37,* 327–332.

Hatano, Y. (1991). Changes in the sexual activities of Japanese youth. *Journal of Sex Education and Therapy, 17,* 1–14.

Hicks, T. V., & Leitenberg, H. (2001). Sexual fantasies about one's partner versus someone else: Gender differences in incidence and frequency. *The Journal of Sex Research, 38,* 43–50.

Hite, S. (1977). *The Hite report: A nationwide study of female sexuality.* New York: Dell.

Hite, S. (1981). *The Hite report on male sexuality.* New York: Knopf.

Humana, C., & Wu, N. (1984). *Chinese sex secrets: A look behind the screen.* New York: Gallery Books.

Jaeger, A. B., Gramkow, A., Sorensen, P., Melbye, M., Adami, H., Glimelius, B., et al. (2000). Correlates of heterosexual behavior among 23–87 year olds in Denmark and Sweden, 1992–1998. *Archives of Sexual Behavior, 29,* 91–106.

Jones, J. C., & Barlow, D. H. (1990). Self-reported frequency of sexual urges, fantasies, and masturbatory fantasies in heterosexual males and females. *Archives of Sexual Behavior, 19,* 269–279.

Kelley, R. M., Synovitz, L., Carlson, G., & Schuster, A. L. (2001). Sexual behaviors of college students attending four universities in a southern state. *Research Quarterly for Exercise Sport, 72,* 31–42.

Kiecolt, K. J., & Fossett, M. A. (1997). Mate availability and marriage among African-Americans. *African-American Perspectives, 3,* 12–18.

Kinsey, A. C., Pomeroy, W. B., & Martin, C. E. (1948). *Sexual behavior in the human male.* Philadelphia: Saunders.

Kinsey, A. C., Pomeroy, W. B., Martin, C. E., & Gebhard, P. H. (1953). *Sexual behavior in the human female.* Philadelphia: Saunders.

Knox, D., & Brigman, B. (1996). University students' reactions to intercourse. *College Student Journal, 30,* 547–548.

Knox, D., Schacht, C., Holt, J., & Turner, J. (1993) Sexual lies among university students. *College Student Journal, 27,* 269–272.

Laumann, E. O., Gagnon, J. H., Michael, R. T., & Michaels, S. (1994). *The social organization of sexuality: Sexual practices in the United States.* Chicago: The University of Chicago Press.

Leitenberg, H., & Henning, K. (1995). Sexual fantasy. *Psychological Bulletin, 117,* 469–496.

Leitenberg, H., & Saltzman, H. (2000). A statewide survey of age at first intercourse for adolescent females and age of their male partners: Relation to other risk behaviors and statutory rape implications. *Archives of Sexual Behavior, 29,* 203–215.

Leitenberg, H., Detzer, M. J., & Srebnik, D. (1993). Gender differences in masturbation and the relation of masturbation experience in preadolescence and/or early adolescence to sexual behavior and sexual adjustment in young adulthood. *Archives of Sexual Behavior, 22,* 87–98.

Mahay, J., Laumann, E. O., & Michaels, S. (2001). Race, gender, and class in sexual scripts. In E. O. Laumann & R. T. Michael (Eds.), *Sex, love, and health in America: Private choices and public policies* (pp. 197–238). Chicago: University of Chicago Press.

Maletzky, B. M. (1991). *Treating the sexual offender.* Newbury Park, NJ: Sage.

Masters, V. H., & Johnson, V. E. (1976). *The pleasure bond.* New York: Bantam.

Michael, R. T., Gagnon, J. H., Laumann, E. O., & Kolata, G. (1994). *Sex in America: A definitive survey.* Boston: Little, Brown.

Money, J., Prakasam, K. S., & Joshi, V. N. (1991). Semen conservation doctrine from ancient Ayurvedic to modern sexological theory. *American Journal of Psychotherapy, 45,* 9–13.

Montagu, A., & Matson, E. (1979). *The human connection.* New York: McGraw-Hill.

Morin, J. (1998). *Anal pleasure* (3rd ed.). San Francisco, CA: Down There Press.

Morin, J. (2002). Ten rules of anal sex. http://www.sexuality.org/l/incoming/analrule.html

Nahom, D., Wells, E., Gillmore, M. R., Hoppe, M., Morrison, D. M., Archibald, M., et al. (2001). Differences by gender and sexual experience in adolescent sexual behavior: Implications for education and HIV prevention. *Journal of School Health, 71,* 153–158.

National Gay and Lesbian Task Force. (2002, October 14). www.ngltf.org

The politics of masturbation. (1994). *The Lancet, 344,* 1714–1715.

Poulson, R. L., Eppler, M. A., Satterwhite, T. N., Wuensch, K. L., & Bass, L. A. (1998). Alcohol consumption, strength of religious beliefs, and risky sexual behavior in college students. *Journal of American College Health, 46,* 227–234.

Purnine, D. M., Carey, M. P., & Jorgensen, R. S. (1994). Gender differences regarding preferences for specific heterosexual practices. *Journal of Sex and Marital Therapy, 20,* 271–287.

Reinisch, J. M. (1990). The Kinsey Institute new report on sex. New York: St. Martin's Press.

Remez, L. (2000). Oral sex among adolescents: Is it sex or is it abstinence? *Family Planning Perspectives, 32,* 298.

Renaud, C. A., & Byers, E. S. (2001). Positive and negative sexual cognitions, subjective experience and relationships to sexual adjustment. *The Journal of Sex Research, 38*(3), 252–263.

Rostosky, S. S., Welsh, D., Kawaguchi, M. C., & Galliher, R. V. (1999). Commitment and sexual behaviors in adolescent dating relationships. In J. M. Adams & W. H. Jones (Eds.), *Handbook of interpersonal commitment and relationship stability* (pp. 323–328). New York: Academic/Plenum Publishers.

Rubin, L. B. (1991). *Erotic wars: What happened to the sexual revolution?* New York: Harper Perennial.

Sauer, M. V., Zeffer, K. B., Buster, J. E., & Sokol, R. Z. (1988). The effect of abstinence on sperm motility in normal men. *American Journal of Obstetrics and Gynecology, 158,* 604–607.

Sexuality Information and Education Council of the United States (SIECUS). (1996). SIECUS positions on human sexuality, sexual health, and sexuality education and information, 1995–1996. *SIECUS Report, 24*(3), 21–23.

Skeen, D. (1991). *Different sexual worlds: Contemporary case studies of sexuality.* Lexington, MA: Lexington Books.

Sprecher, S., & Regan, P. C. (1996). College virgins: How men and women perceive their sexual status. *The Journal of Sex Research, 33,* 3–15.

Tang, C. S., Lai, E. D., Phil, M., & Chung, T. K. H. (1997). Assessment of sexual functioning for Chinese college students. *Archives of Sexual Behavior, 26,* 79–90.

Tannahill, E. (1982). *Sex in history.* New York: Scarborough.

Thomsen, D., & Chang, I. J. (2000, November). Predictors of satisfaction with first intercourse: A new perspective for sexuality education. Poster presentation at the 62nd Annual Conference for the National Council on Family Relations, Minneapolis, MN.

Tissot, S. A. (1766). *Onania, or a treatise upon the disorders produced by masturbation* (A. Hume, Trans.). London: J. Pridden. (Original work published 1758).

Verma, K. K., Khaitan, B. K., & Singh, O. P. (1998). The frequency of sexual dysfunctions in patients attending a sex therapy clinic in North India. *Archives of Sexual Behavior, 27,* 309–315.

Winks, C., & Semans, A. (1997). *The new vibrations guide to sex* (2nd ed.). San Francisco, CA: Cleis Press.

Sexuality Across the Life Span

Chapter Outline

In youth we learn, in age we understand.

—*Marie Ebner von Eschenbach*

The typical baseball game is sectioned off into nine innings or stages, with each being unique and having an effect on the next inning or stage. So it is with sexual choices. A person's sexuality depends on the inning or stage the person is in, on whether that person is a child, an adolescent, an adult, or a senior citizen. At each life stage, an individual may experience different interests, activities, and capacities. In this chapter, we examine sexuality across the life span and look at some of the choices individuals face at different stages in their lives.

8-1 SEXUALITY IN INFANCY AND CHILDHOOD

A life-cycle view of sexuality emphasizes that early experiences are important influences in subsequent sexual development.

8-1a Infancy

In regard to sexuality development, just as infants are born with digestive and respiratory systems, they also are born with a sexual response system that has already begun to function. Ultrasound on the pregnant woman has been used to document fetal erection of the penis. Such an erection confirms that, with the exception of the reproductive system (which will be delayed until puberty), all the human body systems begin functioning prenatally (Calderone, 1991). Indeed, almost immediately after birth, boys often have erections and girls may have clitoral erections or vaginal lubrication.

Infancy The first year of life following birth.

As noted, the sexual response system functions prior to birth, and sexual behavior occurs in infancy. **Infancy** is defined as the first year of life following birth. Psychoanalytic theorists discuss infant sexuality in terms of two concepts: autoerotism and object love (Widlocher, 2002). *Autoerotism* refers to self-pleasuring from an organ or body part per se. This definition would include an infant gaining pleasure from sucking.

Honig (2000) noted that infants and young children exhibit sexual behaviors earlier than previously indicated by early childhood educators. Because sexual pleasure is an unconditioned positive stimulus, infants are capable of learning associations via classical conditioning processes. Both boys and girls in the nursery have been observed engaging in genital play (boys begin this behavior at about 6 months of age; girls, at about 11 months). Obvious masturbation has been observed in boys at about 15–16 months. Girls tend to stimulate themselves less directly by rocking or through thigh pressure. Both boys and girls have been observed masturbating to the point of orgasm as early as 6 months of age (Bancroft, 1989).

Because infants may learn to associate sexual pleasure with a particular cloth bunny—hence the beginning of a fetish—or they may learn the positive or negative emotions associated with their bodies, it is important for parents not to overreact. Parents who slap their infants for touching their own body parts and label such behaviors as "dirty" may teach their children to associate anxiety and guilt with sexuality. It is crucial to keep in mind that for babies to find pleasure in touching their bodies is developmentally normal. Sexuality educator Dr. Mary Calderone observed that parental attempts to suppress a child's sexuality could have a long-lasting negative impact. "They [parents] should be instructed that they are not simply bringing up their child, but someone's future husband or wife, and a possible parent of their own grandchild. Do they really want to pass on to the next generation the damaging chain of negative sexual conditionings that they themselves have undoubtedly experienced?" (Calderone, 1991, p.110). However, although parents should be careful to teach children that it is okay to touch themselves, there are societal restrictions such as when (in private). There are also restrictions about touching others (with their consent) and the need for an awareness of consequences (physical, personal, and interpersonal). Hence, responsible sexuality is not just about protecting one's self-esteem.

Although we can assume that touching the genitals results in pleasurable feelings, it is unlikely that infants attach sexual meaning to these experiences in the ways that adults do. It is also important to keep in mind that even though infants are capable of sexual responsiveness, they are not experiencing arousal in the same sense as a young adult. Pedophiles who claim that the child "wanted it" may not be mindful that infants and young children have not learned the social scripting of arousal and sexuality that comes as the child gets older and moves toward reproductive age, maturity, and relationships.

Object relations theory holds that our early relationships establish images or representations of ourselves and others that influence our future relationships. This process is involved in attachment, which involves an infant forming a mental representation of a person (e.g., loving parent) in the immediate environment and interacting with this person to obtain a response, "ultimately to be loved by the other" (Widlocher, 2002, p. 13). Infancy is an important time in that parents who show physical affection and provide emotional bonding for their infant create a context of security and trust that are valuable for later intimate relationships. The effect of early separations of infants from their families, as studied by child psychiatrist Bowlby, revealed negative effects on their later personality and functioning when the infants matured. Not only separation, but also more subtle attachment difficulties are hypothesized to impact future relationships and personality development.

Object relations theory Psychodynamic theory in which early relationships with people or things (objects of an infant's drive for satisfaction) establish the blueprint for future relationships.

A graphologist who analyzed Alfred Kinsey's handwriting advanced an interpretation of Kinsey's personality in which she seemed to hypothesize impaired attachment. Renna Nezos said that the renowned sex researcher lacked "close physical nurturing as a baby and child" and that this "left him emotionally stunted, longing to attract people to him and seeking fame as a substitute for love" (Gathorne-Hardy, 2000, p. 459). However, this interpretation does not fit with what is known about his childhood. His mother was described as "a gentle woman of great sweetness" (p. 4) who likely served as a devoted nurse to young Kinsey, who was ill most of his first 10 years with measles, chicken pox, rickets, rheumatic fever, and typhoid.

8-1b Childhood

Childhood extends from age 2 to age 12 and involves physical, cognitive, social, and sexual development. Larsson and Svedin (2002) studied childhood sexual behavior through the recollections of 269 high school students (mean age 18.6). Sixty-one percent of the boys and 67% of the girls reported having had mutual sexual experiences such as talking about sex or looking at pornographic material when they were 6–10 years of age. A slightly larger proportion (76% of the boys and 74% of the girls) had had experiences during the 11–12 age period (including showing genitals, touching genitals of another child, etc.). Boys shared their experiences with a girl in 57.3% of the cases, with another boy in 11.4%, and 33.3% of the boys had childhood sexual experiences with both sexes. For the girls the sexual experiences were more equally distributed, with 29.1% reporting only same-sex experiences, whereas 30.9% had played with only boys, and a total of 40% had sexual experiences with both sexes. In 7.6% of the cases there was an age difference of more than 2 years between the participating children.

Childhood Developmental time frame that extends from age 2 to age 12 and involves physical, cognitive, social, and sexual development.

The most common feelings connected to sexual activities together with other children were excitement, feeling silly/giggly, pleasant body sensations, feeling good/fine, and appreciation of the event as natural. Thirteen percent reported coercive experiences in which they had been tricked, bribed, threatened, or physically forced into participation. Some children, 8.2%, had coerced another child into participation in sexual activities. The majority thought of their childhood experiences as normal. Gender differences were evident, with girls reporting more coercion, guilt, and less masturbation (36% vs. 62% for boys). The authors concluded that some kind of coercive sexual experience appears to be part of growing up for quite a few children.

Herdt and McClintock (2000) noted that sexual attraction emerges "after the advent of adrenal puberty, typically precipitating the development of stable and memorable sexual attraction by the age of 10 across cultures" (p. 601). Hence, before children reach adolescence, their hormones are active.

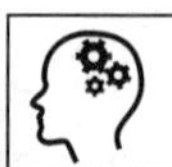

Think About It

A favorite game among preschool children is "doctor." This game, which may be played between boys, between girls, or between boys and girls, involves one child assuming the role of patient and the other the role of doctor. The patient undresses, and the doctor examines the patient both visually and by touching his or her body, including the genitals. Some parents, believing such exploration is wrong, punish their children for playing "doctor." Alternatively, parents might respond by saying something nonpunitive, such as "It is interesting to find out how other people's bodies look, isn't it?" However, developmental psychologists suggest that parents should be concerned, and should intervene, if one child is unwilling or coerced into playing doctor, if the children are not the same age (within a couple of years), or if the activity is potentially harmful, such as inserting objects into themselves or each other. In such situations, parents might say something like "Your body is wonderful and it is natural that you are interested in your own body. But it is your body, and only you should touch yourself in private places." What reactions do you recall your parents making to your early sexual behavior?

8-1c Parent-Child Communication About Sexuality

Sexual debut One's first sexual intercourse.

Recent studies suggest that parent-child sexual communication is most effective when it is initiated prior to an adolescent's beginning to have sexual intercourse (**sexual debut**) (Hutchinson, 2002; Miller, Levin, Whitaker, & Xu, 1998). The groundwork for establishing positive communication about sexual topics can be initiated when one's children are toddlers or preschool-age. This foundation includes parental encouragement of the child's pride in his or her body, acceptance of the young child's self-exploration, and sharing of family values and norms related to sexuality. Parents of school-age children might take advantage of teaching opportunities in daily living (commenting on television programs or song lyrics), being approachable, and initiating content (not waiting for a child to ask questions). Parents can reminisce about their experiences at their child's age and ask the child about his or her concerns (Hutchinson, 2002). Organizations that offer resources to equip parents for such teaching include the Sex Information and Education Council of the United States, or SIECUS (which provides tips for parents and offers an annotated bibliography), the SIECUS Family Communication Clearinghouse (which offers information about interventions to increase parent-child communication about sexuality), and Planned Parenthood (which distributes a kit for parents that includes a video, parent's guide, and activity workbook for 10- to 14-year-olds).

8-1d Personal Choices: Exposing Children to Parental Nudity?

Some parents are concerned about the effects parental nudity may have on their children. "Will it traumatize my children or affect their sexual development negatively if I allow them to see me nude?" parents ask. Others are concerned that they may have already damaged their children, who have walked in on the parents and observed them having intercourse. (This is known as the "primal scene.") To what degree should parents be concerned about these issues?

Research suggests that there is no cause for alarm. A team of researchers (Okami, Abramson, & Pendleton, 1998) studied 200 male and 200 female children in an 18-year longitudinal study on early childhood exposure to parental nudity and concluded that pervasive beliefs in the harmfulness of parental nudity are exaggerated.

8-2 SEXUALITY IN ADOLESCENCE

Adolescence is a time when one becomes increasingly aware of one's own and others' sexuality.

Adolescence is a time of excitement, adventure, and confusion.

8-2a Adolescence

Adolescence is defined as the developmental period in which youth move from childhood to adulthood. Although impacted by historical and cultural context, in the United States and most cultures today, adolescence typically begins between the ages of 10 and 13 and ends between the ages of 18 and 22. Early adolescence (middle school or junior high school ages) includes the time of most pubertal change. In late adolescence (the mid to late teen years) identity exploration, dating, and career exploration are often more pronounced than in early adolescence (Santrock, 2003). Numerous changes occur during adolescence. The most noticeable are the physical changes.

Adolescence
The developmental period in which youth move from childhood to adulthood.

8-2b Physical Changes

The adolescent's body undergoes rapid physiological and anatomical change. The term **puberty** comes from the Latin *pubescere*, which means to be covered with hair. Pubic hair and axillary (underarm) hair in young girls and pubic, axillary, and facial hair in young boys are evidence that the hypothalamus is triggering the pituitary gland to release gonadotropins into the bloodstream. These are hormones that cause the testes in the male to increase testosterone production and the ovaries in the female to increase estrogen production.

Puberty Developmental stage in which a youth achieves reproductive capacity.

CULTURAL DIVERSITY 

Schalet (2000) studied a sample of U.S. and Dutch parents of adolescents and observed that the former view adolescent sexuality as biologically driven, which causes disruption for the teenager and family. In contrast, Dutch parents view the sexuality of teens as "normal" in the context of their love relationships and emphasize the importance of responsible "safe sex." The result is that U.S. parents exclude talking about sexuality from conversation, whereas Dutch parents embrace it.

Further physical changes in adolescence include the development of secondary sex characteristics, such as breasts in the female and a deepened voice in the male. A growth spurt also ensues, with girls preceding boys by about 2 years. The growth spurt is characterized by girls becoming taller than boys their age. Genitals of the respective sexes also enlarge (the penis and testes in the male and the labia in the female). Internally, the prostate gland and seminal vesicles begin to function to make it possible for the young adolescent male to ejaculate. (Sperm is present in the ejaculate at about age 14.) First ejaculation usually occurs around age 13 or 14, but the timing is variable.

Girls experience their own internal changes. The uterus, cervix, and vaginal walls respond to hormone changes to produce the first menstruation, or *menarche*. This usually occurs between the ages of 12 and 13, but the timing is highly variable. A study of more than 17,000 girls seen in U.S. pediatric offices suggests that early puberty may be more common than previously realized (Herman-Giddens et al., 1997). A small number (3% of African Americans and 1% of Whites) of girls as young as 3 years of age had breast or pubic hair development. The average age for breast development was 8.9 for African American girls and 10 for White girls, with similar ages for the development of pubic hair. Menstruation occurred at ages 12.2 and 12.9, respectively.

A team of researchers (Duncan, Ritter, Dornbusch, Gross, & Carlsmith, 1990) examined the relationship between pubertal timing and body image and found that early maturation in males is associated with being rated as more popular, relaxed, good-natured, and poised. However, data on girls have been inconsistent; some studies show that early maturing girls enjoy greater prestige and self-confidence, whereas others show that they are more self-conscious and less popular. Girls who mature early are more likely to smoke and drink, have older friends, and seek independence from parents. They are also at greater risk of eating disorders and depression (Sarigiani & Petersen, 2000). However, maturational timing is not the only factor that influences social development and adjustment. Some researchers have questioned whether the impact of puberty's effects have been exaggerated, and note that puberty occurs within varying biological, cognitive, and socioemotional contexts (Santrock, 2003).

Adolescents are particularly concerned about the degree to which their bodies match the cultural image and are unhappy about it when it does not. Girls are more likely to be dissatisfied with their body image than boys. Among female adolescents ages 13–19, 54% report being dissatisfied with their bodies; 41% of male adolescents the same age are dissatisfied (Garner, 1997).

8-2c Psychological Changes

In addition to physical changes, psychological changes also occur in adolescence. Psychological changes include moving from a state of childish dependence to a state of relative independence, resolving sexual identity issues, and feeling secure that one is normal. An example of adolescent ambivalence about growing up is the adolescent female who has a bottle of blow bubbles and a bottle of perfume on her bedroom dresser. Adolescents often want the freedom of adults but still have the dependence of children.

Think About It

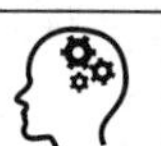

Resolving sexual identity issues requires becoming comfortable with one's sexual orientation. There are an estimated 2.9 million gay or lesbian adolescents in the United States (Bailey & Phariss, 1996). They have been described as an "invisible" minority within the schools that is just beginning to be acknowledged (Bailey & Phariss, 1996). Adolescents are already concerned about "fitting in"; being homosexual may add to the burden adolescents feel when they discover that they are not part of the heterosexual mainstream.

As psychologist William S. Pollack traveled across the country talking with boys, he found that it was complicated for the boys with whom he spoke to accept gay friends and gay feelings in themselves. A boy he calls Bradley, 17, from a suburb in the Northeast said, "The friend that I spend the most time with, Peter, doesn't know I'm gay. I don't want the friendship we have now to change. We're great friends and we go to the movies, and I'm worried that if I were to tell him, it would change everything. It's probably an irrational fear—he is not homophobic. But I worry." (Pollack, 2000, p. 291). What have been your reactions to the knowledge that a friend is gay?

8-2d New Sexual Behaviors

In addition to physical and psychological changes, adolescence is a time of discovering one's sexuality with others. Adolescents report a typical progression of increasingly intimate sexual behaviors; kissing occurs prior to petting, which is followed by intercourse or oral sex (Feldman, Turner, & Araujo, 1999). A team of researchers conducted a 7-year longitudinal study to assess the intentions and behaviors of 1,173 students from the third through the tenth grades (ages 9 through 15) (Nahom et al., 2001). The higher the grade, the more likely the teen intended to have sex, with boys being more likely to have such intentions than girls. By the tenth grade, 40% of the boys and 44% of the girls reported having had sexual intercourse. The percentages increase as adolescents moved through the teen years.

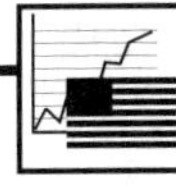

NATIONAL DATA Fifty-five percent of a national sample of unmarried 15- to 19-year-old males reported having had vaginal intercourse; the corresponding percentage for adolescent females was 49% (Althaus, 2001).

CULTURAL DIVERSITY

Joyner and Laumann (2001) in their nationwide study of teen sexuality noted that "Being foreign born [particularly in Japan/China] decreases the likelihood of teen sex. An important question is whether this variable influences the costs and benefits that individuals associate with having sex or simply their opportunity to have it" (p. 67).

In the United States the average age at first intercourse in adolescence is related to race and gender, with African American men reporting intercourse shortly after age 15 and African American women around age 17. In inner-city urban areas very early initiation of intercourse has been reported; in a study in Baltimore 81% of 14-year-old Black youth reported they had already engaged in intercourse (Clark, Zabin, & Hardy, 1984). White men and women have intercourse at the average age of 17 (Michael, Gagnon, Laumann, & Kolata, 1994). Latino adolescents begin intercourse at an average age of 16.5, and Asian American teens average age 18 (Feldman et al., 1999). A national study found that among male and female adolescents, greater parental education, living in a two-parent family, and White race were independently associated with never having had sexual intercourse (Santelli, Lowry, Brener, & Robin, 2000).

Most adolescents select as their first sexual intercourse partner someone who is of the same race or ethnicity in that 78% of 8,024 adolescents reported that their relationships were with someone of the same race or ethnicity (Ford, Sohn, & Lepkowski, 2001). Condom use has been found to be influenced by the racial and ethnic similarity to the partner—the more similar the partners were to each other in terms of race or ethnicity, the more likely the adolescent reported condom use (Ford et al., 2001).

Think About It

The predominant reasons women reported they had their first wanted (in contrast to being forced) sexual intercourse were "affection for partner" (48%) and "curiosity/readiness for sex" (24%). The predominant reasons men reported they had first wanted sexual intercourse were "curiosity/readiness for sex" (51%) and "affection" (25%). Twelve percent of the men reported "physical pleasure" as their primary motivation (Michael et al., 1994). If you have experienced intercourse, what were your motivations the first time?

First intercourse experiences are often characterized by anxiety, pain, fear, and awkwardness. The following is a description of a first intercourse experience of a student from the authors' classes:

> *I was 15 and my partner was 16. I had two fears. The first was my fear of getting her pregnant the first time. The second was of "parking" in dark and desolate areas. Therefore, once we decided to have intercourse, we spent a boring evening waiting for my parents to go to sleep so we could move to the station wagon in the driveway.*
>
> *After near hyperventilation in an attempt to fog the windows (to prevent others from seeing in), we commenced to prepare for the long-awaited event. In recognition of my first fear, I wore four prophylactics. She, out of fear, was not lubricating well, and needless to say, I couldn't feel anything through four layers of latex.*
>
> *We were able to climax, which I attribute solely to sheer emotional excitement, yet both of us were later able to admit that the experience was disappointing. We knew it could only get better.*

In her book about initial intercourse experiences of 150 women, *The First Time*, Karen Bouris (1994) found that fewer than 20% described positive first intercourse experiences that included conscious choice, good communication with their partner, and being ready physically and emotionally. Based on her interviews with adolescent girls, psychiatrist Lynn Ponton (2000) identified multiple meanings that being sexually active may have to adolescents besides physical pleasure or passion: confirmation that she/he is lovable, indicator of adult status, status in one's peer group, relief from boredom, escape from pressures of life, an expected part of her/his current relationship, a weapon or conquest. Ponton offers suggestions of what NOT to do: (a) rush prematurely into intercourse, (b) trade it as a commodity (e.g., for status, popularity, affection), or (c) give in to pressures in a relationship.

Investigators have studied the relationships between sexual experience and other social, psychological, and behavioral variables. In one recent study (Whitaker, Miller, & Clark, 2000), interview data were collected from 907 high school students in Alabama, New York, and Puerto Rico. The researchers compared four groups of teenagers—those who did not intend to initiate sexual intercourse in the next year (delayers), those who did anticipate having intercourse (anticipators), those who had one sexual partner, and those with two or more partners. A steady linear trend across the four categories showed that compared to delayers, those closer to having sex and those with one or more partners reported more use of alcohol and marijuana; lower self-esteem and more hopelessness; riskier peer behaviors; and looser ties to family, school, and church. In an earlier study, adolescents who had their first sexual experience before age 14 were more likely to use controlled substances, have mothers who were sexually active as teens, and have mothers who worked extensively (Mott et al., 1996). Condom use during first intercourse reported by male and female adolescents is similar.

NATIONAL DATA Sixty-nine percent of a national sample of unmarried 15- to 19-year-old males reported that they used a condom the first time they had intercourse. Seventy percent of the unmarried 15- to 19-year-old females reported condom use by their partners (Althaus, 2001).

To summarize, most adolescents ages 10–14 in the United States have not had sexual intercourse. By age 15 only 22% of girls and 27% of boys report having had intercourse, but by age 19 the percentages reveal that 77% of girls and 85% of boys say they have had sexual intercourse (Alan Guttmacher Institute, 1999). Whitaker et al. (2000) identified two main implications for health educators and those who provide care for youth and their families. First, educational and service interventions should be targeted to specific groups based on gender, ethnicity, or age to make preventive messages and services more

Box 8-1 Social Choices

Are Adolescents Competent to Make Abortion Decisions?

Approximately 80% of the 900,000 teen pregnancies reported annually in the United States are unintended (Miller & Coyl, 2000). In most states, parental consent must be obtained before medical services can be delivered to minors (adolescents under the age of 18). However, in many states, an exception is made for services related to sensitive health-care concerns, such as sexuality, substance abuse, and mental health. Health professionals recognize that minors may be reluctant to seek health care if they are required to tell their parents or obtain parental consent.

An adolescent's capacity to independently make decisions regarding abortion has been the focus of legislation in many states. As of July 31, 2001, 42 states have laws on the books requiring parental consent or notification prior to a minor's abortion. In 31 states, a judicial or other bypass procedure is available, in which a judge can rule to bypass the parental involvement if the minor is judged sufficiently mature to give her own consent, or if it is judged that parental notification is not in her best interests (www.plannedparenthood.org/LIBRARY/ABORTION/StateLaws.html).

Legislation that restricts adolescents' access to abortion is based on the assumption that adolescents are not as mature as adults and are less likely to make sound decisions when they are faced with an unintended pregnancy. A number of psychologists have challenged this assumption. For example, Lewis (1987) reported several studies affirming that minors with low self-perceived competence and high conflict regarding the pregnancy decision were more likely to involve their parents in the abortion decision. In another study, 75 young women who were seeking a pregnancy test completed an audiotaped interview that was scored on four criteria of legal competence. All the adolescents who considered abortion appeared as competent as legal adults. Only adolescents who were age 15 or younger who did not consider abortion appeared less competent (Ambuel & Rappaport, 1992). Lewis (1987) cited another study revealing that although high school students generate fewer alternative solutions to hypothetical stories than college students, the high school students were better able to generate potential consequences. Lewis argued that minors may be as competent as adults in reasoning about decisions, but the social circumstances in which they function may limit their ability to implement their reasoning.

As policymakers continue to struggle with the issue of adolescent access to abortion, they may choose either to consider or to ignore Lewis's (1987) conclusion: "At present, psychological research gives no basis for restrictions on minors' privacy in decision making on the ground of competence alone" (p. 87). Indeed, adolescents seem to be capable of making decisions on this issue for themselves.

References

Ambuel, B., & Rappaport, J. (1992). Developmental trends in adolescents' psychological and legal competence to consent to abortion. *Law and Human Behavior, 16*(2), 129–154.

Miller, B. C., & Coyl, D. D. (2000). Adolescent pregnancy and childbearing in relation to infant adoption in the United States. *Adoption Quarterly, 4*, 3–25.

Lewis, C. C. (1987). Minors' competence to consent to abortion. *American Psychologist, 42*, 84–88.

relevant and effective. Second, interventions and messages should address the social and psychological context in which sexual behaviors occur.

In Box 8-1, we address the issue of whether adolescents are competent to make independent choices concerning abortion.

8-3 SEXUALITY IN EARLY ADULTHOOD

Most individuals move into adulthood (age 21) as never-marrieds and most (95% of both sexes) eventually marry (*Statistical Abstract of the United States: 2002*, Table 46). Not all relationships are heterosexual or marriage-focused. Sexuality among adults also occurs among homosexuals in casual dating or committed relationships.

8-3a Sexuality Among the Never-Married and Not-Cohabitating

One of the basic choices during young adulthood is whether to remain single. Although more than 95% of both women and men marry by age 75 (*Statistical Abstract of the United States: 2002*, Table 48), due to education and career concerns, an increasing percentage of young adults are remaining single longer. And while they are single, most elect to have sexual intercourse.

TABLE 8-1

The Case for Singlehood

Benefits of Singlehood	Limitations of Marriage
Freedom to do as one wishes	Restrictions from spouse or children
Responsible for one's self only	Responsible for spouse and children
Close friends of both sexes	Pressure to avoid other close-sex friendships
Spontaneous lifestyle	Routine, predictable sex/lifestyle
Feeling of self-sufficiency	Potential to feel dependent
Freedom to spend money as one wishes	Expenditures influenced by needs of spouse and children
Freedom to move as career dictates	Restrictions on career mobility
No control/influence from spouse	Potential to be controlled/influenced by spouse
No emotional or financial stress caused by divorce	Possibility of divorce

NATIONAL DATA Only 12% of the never-married and not-cohabiting report that they have had no sexual partners since age 18 (Michael et al., 1994).

While most marry in their mid-20s (and have intercourse until they do), some delay marriage even longer (Gloria Steinem, ardent feminist and founder of Ms. *Magazine*, married when she was 66). Table 8-1 reflects the benefits of singlehood and the limitations of marriage.

The primary advantage of remaining single is independence and control over one's life. When a decision has been made to involve another person in one's life, it follows that one's choices become vulnerable to the influence of the other. The person who chooses to remain single may view such restrictions on freedom as something to avoid. Freedom to have sex with a number of partners is another perceived advantage of remaining single.

NATIONAL DATA Nine percent of the never-married and not-cohabitating reported having had five or more sexual partners in the previous 12 months; this percentage compares to 1% of marrieds and 5% of cohabitants who reported the same number of sexual partners (Michael et al., 1994).

Think About It

The more partners a person reports having sex with in the past 12 months, the less satisfied the person reports his or her sex life to be. Of adults reporting between two and four partners in the past 12 months, 22.4% reported being "unhappy" with their sex life; in contrast, of adults who reported having one sex partner in the past 12 months, 9.4% reported being "unhappy" with their sex life (Laumann & Michael, 2001, p. 18). Why do you think persons with more partners within the same time period report less happiness with their sex life?

However, compared to individuals who are married or living together, never-married singles report having intercourse less frequently.

NATIONAL DATA Based on data from the 1992 National Health and Social Life Survey, the number of times a national sample of singles reported having sex per month was 4.45 compared to 4.79 for marrieds and 6.72 for cohabitants (Waite & Joyner, 2001).

The never-married may also be particularly vulnerable to engaging in high-risk sexual behavior with multiple partners. The self-assessment in Box 8-2 allows you to determine the degree to which you engage in behavior that involves a high risk for HIV infection.

8-3b Sexuality Among Cohabitants

Cohabitation is defined as two heterosexual adults involved in an emotional and sexual relationship sharing a common residence for at least 4 nights a week for 3 months. Cohabitation has become a stage in the "getting to know you" process as couples move toward increasing levels of commitment (Raley, 2000). Indeed, almost 60% of U.S. women who married in the 1990s reported that they had lived with someone before they married (Bachrach, Hindin, & Thomson, 2000).

Cohabitation A living situation in which two heterosexual adults involved in an emotional and sexual relationship share a common residence for four nights a week for three months.

NATIONAL DATA Ninety-five percent of cohabitants report that they have had between one and four sex partners in the past 12 months (75% report only one partner) (Michael et al., 1994).

There are various types of living-together relationships. Some of these categories follow:

- *Adventurers*—New partners who have an affectionate relationship and want to live together because they enjoy each other. They are focused on the here and now, not the future of the relationship.
- *Testers*—Couples involved in a good relationship who want to assess whether staying together and having a future together would be right for them.
- *Engaged*—Couples in love and planning to marry.
- *Career seekers*—Couples who enjoy each other for now but are on respective career paths that will probably separate them eventually.
- *Money savers*—Couples who live together primarily out of economic convenience. They are open to the possibility of a future together but regard such a possibility as unlikely.
- *Young couples*—Some young couples who feel that they are not developmentally ready to take on the social expectations of marriage as an institution. They are most likely in their teens and want to wait until they are older to marry. In the meantime, they enjoy living together.
- *Alternative avoiders*—Couples who don't like the idea of living alone, dating an endless (and meaningless?) array of partners, or getting married. They feel a real relationship is a commitment of the heart, not a legal document. Living together is their best alternative.

Most cohabitants regard themselves as committed to each other (Jamieson et al., 2002). They typically have intercourse more frequently than those who are single but not living together, and their satisfaction is higher than other never-marrieds; however, their emotional and physical satisfaction is less than spouses (Waite & Joyner, 2001).

Box 8-2 Self-Assessment

Student Sexual Risks Scale

The following self-assessment allows you to evaluate the degree to which you may be at risk for engaging in behavior that exposes you to HIV. Safer sex means sexual activity that reduces the risk of transmitting the AIDS virus. Using condoms is an example of safer sex. Unsafe, risky, or unprotected sex refers to sex without a condom, or to other sexual activity that might increase the risk of AIDS virus transmission. For each of the following items, check the response that best characterizes your option.

A—Agree U—Undecided D—Disagree

1. If my partner wanted me to have unprotected sex, I would probably give in.
   A ______ U ______ D ______
2. The proper use of a condom could enhance sexual pleasure.
   A ______ U ______ D ______
3. I may have had sex with someone who was at risk for HIV/AIDS.
   A ______ U ______ D ______
4. If I were going to have sex, I would take precautions to reduce my risk of HIV/AIDS.
   A ______ U ______ D ______
5. Condoms ruin the natural sex act.
   A ______ U ______ D ______
6. When I think that one of my friends might have sex on a date, I ask him/her if he/she has a condom.
   A ______ U ______ D ______
7. I am at risk for HIV/AIDS.
   A ______ U ______ D ______
8. I would try to use a condom when I had sex.
   A ______ U ______ D ______
9. Condoms interfere with romance.
   A ______ U ______ D ______
10. My friends talk a lot about safer sex.
    A ______ U ______ D ______
11. If my partner wanted me to participate in risky sex and I said that we needed to be safer, we would still probably end up having unsafe sex.
    A ______ U ______ D ______
12. Generally, I am in favor of using condoms.
    A ______ U ______ D ______
13. I would avoid using condoms if at all possible.
    A ______ U ______ D ______
14. If a friend knew that I might have sex on a date, he/she would ask me whether I was carrying a condom.
    A ______ U ______ D ______
15. There is a possibility that I have HIV/AIDS.
    A ______ U ______ D ______
16. If I had a date, I would probably not drink alcohol or use drugs.
    A ______ U ______ D ______
17. Safer sex reduces the mental pleasure of sex.
    A ______ U ______ D ______
18. If I thought that one of my friends had sex on a date, I would ask him/her if he/she used a condom.
    A ______ U ______ D ______
19. The idea of using a condom doesn't appeal to me.
    A ______ U ______ D ______
20. Safer sex is a habit for me.
    A ______ U ______ D ______
21. If a friend knew that I had sex on a date, he/she wouldn't care whether I had used a condom or not.
    A ______ U ______ D ______
22. If my partner wanted me to participate in risky sex and I suggested a lower-risk alternative, we would have the safer sex instead.
    A ______ U ______ D ______
23. The sensory aspects (smell, touch, etc.) of condoms make them unpleasant.
    A ______ U ______ D ______
24. I intend to follow "safer sex" guidelines within the next year.
    A ______ U ______ D ______

CULTURAL DIVERSITY 

A couple's race influences their intention to get pregnant while living together. In a sample of women who became pregnant while cohabiting, Hispanic women were 77% more likely and Black women were 69% more likely than White women to report that the pregnancy was intended (Manning, 2001).

25. With condoms, you can't really give yourself over to your partner.

A ____ U ____ D ____

26. I am determined to practice safer sex.

A ____ U ____ D ____

27. If my partner wanted me to have unprotected sex and I made some excuse to use a condom, we would still end up having unprotected sex.

A ____ U ____ D ____

28. If I had sex and I told my friends that I did not use condoms, they would be angry or disappointed.

A ____ U ____ D ____

29. I think safer sex would get boring fast.

A ____ U ____ D ____

30. My sexual experiences do not put me at risk for HIV/AIDS.

A ____ U ____ D ____

31. Condoms are irritating.

A ____ U ____ D ____

32. My friends and I encourage each other before dates to practice safer sex.

A ____ U ____ D ____

33. When I socialize, I usually drink alcohol or use drugs.

A ____ U ____ D ____

34. If I were going to have sex in the next year, I would use condoms.

A ____ U ____ D ____

35. If a sexual partner didn't want to use condoms, we would have sex without using condoms.

A ____ U ____ D ____

36. People can get the same pleasure from safer sex as from unprotected sex.

A ____ U ____ D ____

37. Using condoms interrupts sex play.

A ____ U ____ D ____

38. It is a hassle to use condoms.

A ____ U ____ D ____

(To be read after completing the scale)

Scoring: Begin by giving yourself eighty points. Subtract one point for every undecided response. Subtract two points every time that you disagreed with odd-numbered items or with item number 38. Subtract two points every time you agreed with even-numbered items 2 through 36.

Interpreting Your Score: Research shows that students who make higher scores on the SSRS are more likely to engage in risky sexual activities, such as having multiple sex partners and failing to consistently use condoms during sex. In contrast, students who practice safer sex tend to endorse more positive attitudes toward safer sex, and tend to have peer networks that encourage safer sexual practices. These students usually plan on making sexual activity safer, and they feel confident in their ability to negotiate safer sex even when a dating partner may press for riskier sex. Students who practice safer sex often refrain from using alcohol or drugs, which may impede negotiation of safer sex, and often report having engaged in lower-risk activities in the past. How do you measure up?

(Below 15) Lower Risk
(Of 200 students surveyed by DeHart and Birkimer [1997], 16% were in this category.) Congratulations! Your score on the SSRS indicates that, relative to other students, your thoughts and behaviors are more supportive of safer sex. Is there any room for improvement in your score? If so, you may want to examine items for which you lost points and try to build safer sexual strengths in those areas. You can help protect others from HIV by educating your peers about making sexual activity safer.

(15 to 37) Average Risk
(Of 200 students surveyed by DeHart and Birkimer, 68% were in this category.) Your score on the SSRS is about average in comparison with those of other college students. Though you don't fall into the higher-risk category, be aware that "average" people can get HIV, too. In fact, a recent study indicated that the rate of HIV among college students is ten times that in the general heterosexual population. Thus, you may want to enhance your sexual safety by figuring out where you lost points and work toward safer sexual strengths in those areas.

(38 and above) Higher Risk
(Of 200 students surveyed by DeHart and Birkimer, 16% were in this category.) Relative to other students, your score on the SSRS indicates that your thoughts and behaviors are less supportive of safer sex. Such high scores tend to be associated with greater HIV-risk behavior. Rather than simply giving in to riskier attitudes and behaviors, you may want to empower yourself and reduce your risk by critically examining areas for improvement. On which items did you lose points? Think about how you can strengthen your sexual safety in these areas. Reading more about safer sex can help, and sometimes colleges and health clinics offer courses or workshops on safer sex. You can get more information about resources in your area by contacting the CDC's HIV/AIDS Information Line at 1-800-342-2437.

Source: DeHart, D. D., & Birkimer, J. C. (1997). The Student Sexual Risks Scale (modification of SRS for popular use; facilitates student self-administration, scoring, and normative interpretation). Developed for this text by Dana D. DeHart, College of Social Work at the University of South Carolina; and John C. Birkimer, University of Louisville. Used by permission of Dana DeHart and John C. Birkimer.

8-3c Sexuality Among the Married

Marital sex is less of a negotiation and an adventure and more of a routine.

—Randall Collins and Scott Coltrane, sociologists

In spite of the perceived benefits of singlehood or living together, marriage remains the lifestyle chosen by most Americans, with more than 95% of both women and men eventually marrying by age 75 (*Statistical Abstract of the United States: 2002*, Table 48). About

Most Americans choose marriage, and many married couples enjoy a satisfying sex life.
Royalty-Free/CORBIS

5 million individuals marry each year (National Center for Health Statistics, 2002). Marital sex is characterized by its social legitimacy, declining frequency, and its superiority in terms of physical and emotional satisfaction.

Social Legitimacy

In our society, marital intercourse is the most legitimate form of sexual behavior. Homosexual, premarital, and extramarital intercourse does not enjoy as high a level of social approval as does marital sex. It is not only okay to have intercourse when married, it is expected. People assume that married couples make love and that something is wrong if they do not.

National Data The number of times a national sample of married adults reported having sex per month was 4.79 (Waite & Joyner, 2001).

Declining Frequency

Sexual intercourse often occurs more than once a week, particularly among relatively young married couples. A sample of 261 wives were interviewed 12 months after the birth of their baby and noted that they had had intercourse about six times (5.82) in the past 30 days (Hyde, DeLamater, & Durik, 2001). However, this frequency of six times a month declines as the age of the spouses increases.

Satiation Psychological term that refers to the repeated exposure to a stimulus which results in the loss of ability of that stimulus to reinforce.

Reasons for declining frequency are related to the demands of employment, the care of children, and satiation. Psychologists use the term **satiation** to mean that repeated exposure to a stimulus results in the loss of its ability to reinforce. For example, the first time you listen to a new CD, you derive considerable enjoyment and satisfaction from it. You may play it over and over during the first few days. But after a week or so, listening to the same music is no longer new and does not give you the same level of enjoyment that it first did. So it is with intercourse. The thousandth time that a person has intercourse with the same partner is not as new and exciting as the first few times.

Some spouses do not have intercourse at all. One percent of husbands and 3% of wives in a nationwide study of sexuality reported that they had not had intercourse in the past 12 months (Michael et al., 1994, p. 116). Health, age, sexual orientation, stress, depression, and conflict were some of the reasons given for not having intercourse with one's spouse. Such an arrangement may be accompanied by either limited or extensive affection.

Emotional and Physical Satisfaction

Despite declining frequency, marital sex remains a satisfying experience. On a scale from one (not at all satisfying) to four (extremely satisfying), 3.8 was the average score reported by a sample of 261 wives (Hyde et al., 2001). The husbands of the wives estimated the satisfaction of their wives at 3.6. Contrary to the popular belief that unattached singles have the best sex, it is the married and pair-bonded adults who enjoy the most satisfying sexual relationships. In a national sample, 88% of married people said they received great physical pleasure from their sexual lives, and almost 85% said they received great emotional satisfaction (Michael et al., 1994). Married women are particularly likely to report emotional satisfaction with sex (Waite & Joyner, 2001). Individuals least likely to report being physically and emotionally pleased in their sexual relationships are those who are not married, not living with anyone, and not in a stable relationship with one person (Michael et al., 1994).

Full-time employment on the part of the wife does not have a negative effect on either the frequency or the satisfaction of a couple's sexual relationship. Hyde et al. (2001) compared the sexual relationships of homemakers with wage-earner wives and found no differences. The more important factor in a couple's sexual relationship was the degree to which the spouses valued their partners and relationship.

8-3d Sexuality Among the Divorced

Nothing grows again, more easily than love.

—*Seneca, Roman philosopher*

Between 40% and 50% of individuals who marry will eventually divorce. Of the more than 2 million who divorce each year, the meanings of intercourse for the separated or divorced vary. For many, intercourse is a way to reestablish, indeed repair, their crippled self-esteem. Questions like "Am I desirable?" "Will anyone want a retread?" and "Am I capable of loving again?" loom in the minds of the divorced women and men. One way some persons seek to connect with others and to feel wanted is through sex. Being held by another in a sexual embrace may be interpreted by the individual as providing some evidence that one is desirable. "I felt that as long as someone was having sex with me, I wasn't dead and I did matter," said one recently divorced woman (authors' files).

Whereas some divorced people use sex to mend their self-esteem, others use it to test their sexual adequacy. The divorced person may have been told by the former spouse that he or she was an inept lover. One man said his wife used to make fun of him because he was occasionally impotent. Intercourse with a new partner who did not belittle him reassured him of his sexual adequacy, and his impotence ceased to be a problem. A woman described how her husband would sneer at her body and say no man would ever want her because she was so fat. After the divorce, she found a man who thought she was attractive and who did not consider her weight to be a problem. Other divorced men and women say that things their spouses did not like, their new partners view as turn-ons (e.g., one wife said her former husband thought she was too aggressive but her new partner loved this quality). The result is a renewed sense of sexual desirability.

Beyond these motives for sexual interactions, many divorced people simply enjoy the sexual freedom their divorced status offers. Freed from the guilt that spouses who have extramarital intercourse may experience, the divorced are free to experiment with different partners.

National Data Forty-four percent of divorced cohabiting individuals report having from 5 to 10 sexual partners since age 18 as compared to 19% of marrieds (Michael et al., 1994).

The divorced may go through predictable stages of sexual expression. The initial impact of the separation is usually accompanied by a period of emotional pain. During this time, the divorced may turn to sex for intimacy to soothe some of the pain. This stage of looking for intimacy through intercourse overlaps with the divorced person's feeling a renewed sense of freedom to explore a wider range of sexual partners and behaviors than marriage provided. "I was a virgin at marriage and was married for 12 years. I've never had sex with anyone but my spouse, so I'm curious to know what other people are like sexually," one divorced person said.

Divorced women are often perceived as more sexually experienced than single women. Apt and Hurlbert (1995) assessed the perceptions men had of a photograph of a woman who was identified either as being single or as being divorced. When the woman was identified as being divorced, she was perceived as having greater "sexual experience" and "sexual knowledge" and as being more "sexually assertive" and "promiscuous."

Because divorced people are usually in their 30s, they may not be as sensitized to the danger of contracting HIV as persons in their 20s. Yet HIV is not a disease limited to the young. In the United States, 64% of male HIV diagnoses are among men aged 30 and older; 53% of female HIV diagnoses are among women aged 30 and older (Centers for Disease Control and Prevention, 2000). Divorced persons who resume dating and participate in sexual intimacy may need to switch from contraceptive methods that were adequate for a monogamous married couple to such methods as condom use, which offer STD risk reduction.

8-3e Sexuality in the Middle Years

Age, like sexuality, is largely socially defined. Cultural definitions of "old" and "young" vary from society to society, from time to time, and from person to person. For example, the older a person is, the less likely it is that he or she will define a particular age as old. A child of 12 thinks that 18 is "old" just as an 18-year-old thinks that 40 is ancient. Forty-year-olds think that 50 is "still young." With an average life expectancy of 20 years in ancient Greece or Rome, a person was old at the age of 18; a person was old at 30 in medieval Europe; and in 1850, a person was old at the age of 40 in the United States.

Middle age Time in a person's life that begins when the last child leaves home and continues until retirement or the death of either spouse; defined by the U.S. Census Bureau as age 45.

Middle age is commonly thought to occur between the ages of 40 and 60. Family life specialists define middle age as beginning when the last child leaves home and continuing until retirement or the death of either spouse. Middle age is a time of transition for women, men, and their sexuality. In general, beginning at age 50, there appears to be a gradual continuous decline in sexual interest and activity. Some of this decline is a function of normal aging, and some may be related to age-related disease processes. A major change in the sexuality of women is the experience of going through menopause. For men, sexual changes are associated with a decrease in testosterone.

8-3f Women and Menopause

Menopause The permanent cessation of menstruation that occurs in middle age.

Menopause is a primary physical event for middle-aged women. Defined as the permanent cessation of menstruation, menopause is caused by the gradual decline of estrogen produced by the ovaries. It occurs around age 50 for most women but may begin much earlier or later. Signs that the woman may be nearing menopause include decreased menstrual flow and a less predictable cycle. After 12 months with no period, the woman is said to be through menopause. During this time, a woman who does not want to risk a pregnancy should use some form of contraception. Women with irregular periods may remain at risk for pregnancy for up to 24 months following their last menstrual period.

Think About It

Guillemin (2000) noted the importance of conceptualizing menopause not as a simple biological event but one that is the product of biological, social, and psychological determinants. Indeed, she suggests that women's bodies are not just sites of biological processes but that they are constructed by social factors that become targets of technologies—the "technologies of menopause." What examples can you identify of the social construction of menopause?

Although the term **climacteric** is often used synonymously with menopause, it refers to changes that both men and women experience. The term *menopause* refers only to the time when the menstrual flow permanently stops, whereas *climacteric* refers to the whole process of hormonal change induced by the ovaries or testes, pituitary gland, and hypothalamus. Reactions to such hormonal changes may include hot flashes, in which the woman feels a sudden rush of heat from the waist up. Hot flashes are often accompanied by an increased reddening of the skin surface and a drenching perspiration. Other symptoms may include heart palpitations, dizziness, irritability, headaches, backache, and weight gain.

Climacteric Term often used synonymously with menopause, refers to changes that both men and women experience at midlife.

For most women, the symptoms associated with decreasing levels of estrogen will stop within one year of their final period. Some women find estrogen replacement therapy (ERT) or hormone replacement therapy (HRT)—estrogen plus progestin—helpful to control hot flashes, night sweats, and vaginal dryness. Indeed, Finley, Gregg, Solomon, and Gay (2001) studied 428 women 50–70 years of age and noted that physician encouragement was associated with actual use of HRT. Other factors associated with use included having had a hysterectomy, higher income, younger age, and regular adherence to cervical cancer screening.

About 40% of menopausal women in the late 1990s took HRT (Carney et al., 2000). However, with new data from the Women's Health Initiative study, which found that long-term use of combined estrogen plus progestin (HRT) increases a woman's risk for breast cancer, heart attack, stroke, and blood clots (Women's Health Initiative Investigators, 2002), this percentage is likely to drop considerably. The 5-year study on 16,608 post-menopausal women ages 50–79 found a higher incidence of heart disease in the HRT group (164 cases) than in the placebo group (122 cases) (Women's Health Initiative Investigators, 2002). So, while it is clear that women should not plan on HRT use to protect them against cardiovascular disease, many women take HRT for other reasons. The study investigators noted that the risks were not as high for women who took HRT no longer than 2 to 5 years to control such symptoms as hot flashes and night sweats. Women with a history of breast cancer or heart disease are typically advised against taking HRT. Any woman considering using either estrogen or HRT for treatment of menopausal symptoms is encouraged to review her individual health history and medical goals with her health-care provider. The study is available online on the web site of *The Journal of the American Medical Association* (www.jama.com, click on "Past Issues," then on "July 17, 2002").

Although studies have documented the incidence of depression and anxiety in women during mid-life, research that blames its incidence on menopause has been criticized for being based on samples of women seeking medical help. The effect of hormonal alterations on mood has not been clearly delineated. However, the mood changes that are reported by some women during menopause may be due to a combination of factors, including hormonal changes, normal aging processes, dietary and lifestyle habits, social and psychological transitions, and cultural beliefs and expectations.

CULTURAL DIVERSITY 

A cross-cultural look at menopause suggests that a woman's reaction to this phase of her life may be related to the society in which she lives. For example, among Chinese women, fewer menopausal symptoms have been observed. Whereas 70–85% of North American women experience hot flashes, only 18% of factory workers in Hong Kong are affected by them (Tang, 1994). Researchers have suggested that this may be true because older women in China are highly respected, as are older people generally.

8-3g Men and the Decrease in Testosterone

Some researchers suggest that men go through their own menopause because there is also a drop in sex hormones similar to that in women. But the drop in testosterone is highly variable. In some men, the level can drop so low that men may experience depression, anxiety, hot flashes, decreased libido, difficulty achieving/maintaining an erection, and diminished memory. But other men experience no profound drop, and those who do may or may not respond to hormonal intervention (Gould, Petty, & Jacobs, 2000).

Birch (2000) summarized the effect of testosterone on male sexual desire:

> *Often the blood of men with low sex drive is tested by their physicians for natural testosterone, and for some men the level of this hormone is found to be low, but not in all cases. Conversely, some men with high sexual drive are found to have high levels of testosterone, but not all strongly driven men do. Clearly the influence of blood chemistry on the brain is somehow related to sexual desire, but this human sexual yearning is far more complicated than just being the result of testosterone. (p. 13)*

Indeed, the changes most men experience as they age occur over a long period of time, and the depression and anxiety seem to be as much related to their life situation (for example, lack of career success) as to hormonal alterations. A middle-aged man who is not successful in his career is often forced to recognize that he will never achieve what he had hoped but instead will carry his unfulfilled dreams to the grave. This knowledge may be coupled with his awareness of diminishing sexual vigor. For the man who has been taught that masculinity is measured by career success and sexual prowess, middle age may be particularly difficult.

8-4 EXTRADYADIC SEXUAL INVOLVEMENT

Extradyadic sexual involvement Sexual relationship that occurs outside the couple, as when an individual of a dyad (couple) becomes sexually involved with someone other than the partner or mate.

Extramarital Attraction of a spouse to someone other than one's mate.

The term **extradyadic sexual involvement** refers to sexual involvement with someone other than the primary partner or person with whom one is involved in an emotional and sexual relationship. Whereas the term **extramarital** refers to the attraction of a spouse to someone other than the mate, *extradyadic* refers to all pair-bonded individuals who are attracted to someone other than the partner.

Extradyadic sexual involvements (external to the dyad—a two-person relationship) may occur at any point in the life cycle (from late adolescence through the later years) and between individuals of any sexual orientation. Individuals who are involved with one partner sometimes find themselves emotionally and sexually attracted to others. It is a myth that people in stable love relationships are no longer attracted to others. Indeed, because of the reality of such potential attraction, partners in a relationship can benefit from addressing this issue.

NATIONAL DATA In a study of 1,717 adults (aged 18–59) who had been married only once, 16% reported ever having engaged in extramarital sex (Olenick, 2000). In contrast, 23% of husbands and 12% of wives in a national sample reported having had sex outside the marriage (Wiederman, 1977).

In a national sample of 2,010 adults who had been in a cohabiting or marital relationship in the 12 months prior to the survey, 5% reported unfaithful behavior during the period (Olenick, 2000). Similarly, 4% of husbands and 2% of wives reported intercourse outside their marriage in the past 12 months (Wiederman, 1997).

Postnatal abstinence The abstaining from sexual intercourse after the baby is born.

Factors associated with extradyadic involvement are thinking about sex several times a day, having a high number of previous sex partners, being male, being Black, and having been part of a couple for a long time. Disapproving of sexual infidelity and sharing social networks with one's partner were associated with reduced odds of ever having been unfaithful (Olenick, 2000). Abstaining from intercourse after the baby is born **(postnatal abstinence)** is also associated with the husband seeking extramarital partners (Ali & Cleland, 2001).

CULTURAL DIVERSITY 

Postnatal abstinence, also referred to as *postparturm abstinence*, is a custom found in some West African countries. The practice is based on the belief that the sperm will poison the mother's breast milk and thereby harm the nursing infant. The mean length of postnatal abstinence is 14.8 months (Ali & Cleland, 2001).

Most persons involved in a cohabiting or married relationship expect their partners to be faithful.

NATIONAL DATA Of 2,010 adults, 94% of cohabitants expect their partners to be faithful and 95% believe their partners expect fidelity; 98% of spouses expect their partners to be faithful and 99% believe their partners expect fidelity (Olenick, 2000).

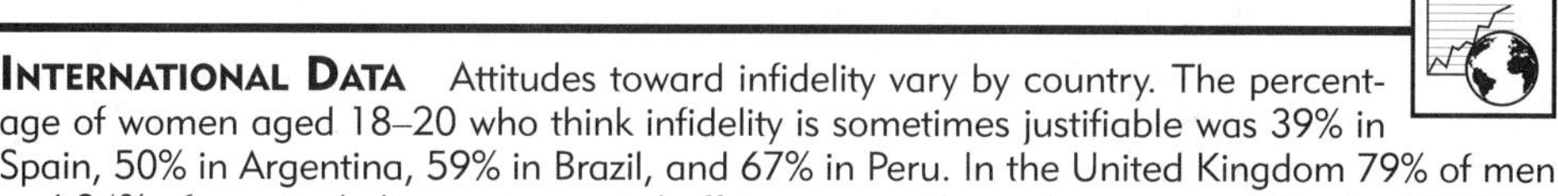

INTERNATIONAL DATA Attitudes toward infidelity vary by country. The percentage of women aged 18–20 who think infidelity is sometimes justifiable was 39% in Spain, 50% in Argentina, 59% in Brazil, and 67% in Peru. In the United Kingdom 79% of men and 84% of women believe extramarital affairs are mostly or always wrong (Mackay, 2000).

8-4a Types of Extradyadic Sexual Involvements

Extradyadic encounters include brief sexual encounters, romantic affairs, open marriages, and swinging.

Brief Sexual Encounters

Extradyadic involvements that are brief and involve little to no emotional investment are referred to as brief sexual encounters. The lyrics to the song "Strangers in the Night" describe two people exchanging glances who end up having sex that same night. Although the partners may see each other again, more often than not, their sexual encounter is a one-time experience. Sexual involvements with prostitutes or gigolos are also examples of brief sexual encounters.

Romantic Affairs

Intense reciprocal emotional feelings characterize many romantic affairs. The affair between Francesca Johnson and Robert Kincaid, as personified in the novel and movie *The Bridges of Madison County*, depicted a romantic affair. One condition of such love affairs is restriction. The "Bridges" couple was restricted by marriage and children (hers) and by time (he would be with her only 4 days). Such limited access makes the time that romantic lovers spend together very special. In addition, the lover in a romantic affair is not associated with the struggles of marriage—paying bills, caring for children, washing dishes, cleaning house, mowing the lawn—and experiences the affair from a more romantic perspective. Section 8-4b considers the effects of extramarital affairs on marriage relationships.

Open Marriages

Open marriages are those in which the spouses regard their own relationship as primary but agree that each will have sexual relationships with others. Unlike affairs, extramarital sex in open marriages involves no dishonesty because each spouse is aware of the partner's having sex with someone else. The concept of open marriage may also apply to cohabiting couples. Partners in open marriages usually have "rules" such as always making each other aware (beforehand) of when, where, and with whom extradyadic sex is to occur; not seeing the same person more than once or twice; not kissing on the mouth; and always having sex with each other before going to bed at night.

Open marriage A marriage in which the spouses regard their own relationship as primary but agree that each will have sexual relationships with others.

When 35 couples in sexually open marriages were compared with 35 married couples who did not have sexually open marriages, the open-marriage couples reported greater satisfaction with their marital sexual relationship. The researchers (Wheeler & Kilmann, 1983) commented that for some couples engaging in recreational sexual activities with outside partners apparently does not interfere with each member's perception of a positive marital sexual relationship; for these couples, it may be that their marital sexual relationship is enhanced by agreed-on sexual contact with outside partners. This may not be the case for couple members who engage in covert extramarital sexual relationships, often as an "escape" from a dysfunctional marital relationship (p. 304).

Although a motivation for becoming involved in an open marriage is to enhance the couple's sexual and marital relationship, most of these relationships do not last. Even the originators of the concept of open marriage, Nena and George O'Neill, have since divorced. Because most individuals in our society are socialized to emphasize fidelity as important in marriage, including others sexually (even with the knowledge and approval of the mate) in one's marriage may become problematic for one's self, one's partner, and one's marriage.

Swinging

Swinging Agreement between the partners of one marriage or committed relationship that they will have sexual relations with the partners of another relationship. (Also referred to as *comarital sex.*)

One form of an open marriage is **swinging,** also referred to as *comarital sex*, whereby the partners of one marriage or committed relationship have sexual relations with the partners of another relationship, generally at the same time. Swingers may be "open" in the sense that each person in the pair-bonded couple has sex with a new partner in the same room or "closed" in that the individuals will split off and go to separate bedrooms with the new partners (Gould, 1999). Swinging involves mutual consent between the partners for extradyadic sexual activity and is touted for its "honesty" because each partner knows of the other's sexual involvement outside the dyad.

A swing club is one place swingers meet to have sex with others outside the marriage. Jenks (2001) reviewed *The Lifestyle: A look at the erotic rites of swingers* by Terry Gould (1999). Though not a swinger, Gould is a journalist who interviewed and visited some of the 300 swing clubs in more than 24 countries. At these clubs, pair-bonded partners meet others and may or may not have sex (various definitions apply) while adhering to three basic rules: (a) showing consideration to one's spouse, (b) not touching a new person unless invited to do so, and (c) using a condom consistent with the wishes of the woman. The demographic profile of swingers suggests that a large proportion have graduate degrees, vote Republican, and identify with one of the three major religions in U.S. culture.

Robert McGinley is the guru of the modern swinging movement. He is founder of the North American Swing Club Association, which holds an annual Lifestyles convention that is attended by thousands. Proponents of swinging point to its honesty, openness of communication between the partners, and direct confrontation of the issue of jealousy. Detractors of swinging regard it as deviant, immoral, and antimarriage.

Polyamory

Polyamory A relationship of more than three individuals in a pair-bonded relationship (some of the individuals may be married to each other) who have an emotional, sexual, and parenting relationship.

Computer affair Emotionally intense relationship between individuals whose primary method of communication is the computer. The relationship may escalate to phone calls, meetings, and sexual behavior.

This term **polyamory** refers to more than three individuals in a pair-bonded relationship (some of the individuals may be married to each other) who have an emotional, sexual, and parenting relationship. An example is a married couple who have a child. The husband also has a male lover, and a second woman enjoys an emotional/physical relationship with all members of the group and helps parent the child.

Computer affairs

Becoming more common today is the computer affair. A **computer affair** may be defined as an emotionally intense relationship between individuals whose primary method of communication is the computer. The relationship may escalate to phone calls, meetings, and sexual behavior

Although legally, adultery does not exist unless two persons have physical sex, an online computer affair can be just as disruptive to a marriage or a couple's relationship. Computer friendships may move to feelings of intimacy; involve secrecy (one's partner does not know the level of involvement); include sexual tension (even though there is no overt sex); and take time, attention, energy, or affection away from one's partner. Finkenauer and Hazam (2000) noted that just the perception that one's partner is keeping a secret (e.g., having an affair) is strongly associated with marital unhappiness.

Young, Griffin-Shelley, Cooper, O'Mara, and Buchanan (2002) noted that anonymity, convenience, and escape account for the impetus to use the computer to find a cybersex partner and that "electronic communication" can lead to marital discord, separation, and divorce. Schneider (2000) studied 91 women who had experienced serious adverse consequences from their partner's cybersex involvement and found that in 60%

of the cases the cybersex did not include offline sex. The respondents also reported that in 68% of the cases one or both spouses had lost interest in relational sex and that the cyber-affair was as emotionally painful as an offline affair.

8-4b Personal Choices: Consequences of Extradyadic Sex

The majority of spouses do not have the inclination (our society/culture encourages marital fidelity), opportunity (an available partner), or context (out of town or away from the spouse) for extradyadic sex. Indeed, the overwhelming majority of spouses are faithful most of the time. Only 5% of spouses and cohabitants in a national sample reported an extradyadic sexual encounter in the past 12 months (Olenick, 2000). In this section, we look at the consequences of deciding to move away from and to move toward involvement in extradyadic sex.

Potential Negative Outcomes of Extradyadic Sex

Spouses who engage in sex with someone else risk permanent emotional damage to the partner and the relationship. Although knowledge of the act of one's spouse being emotional/physical with another is a painful sense of betrayal, it is the act of being deceived that may compound the pain. As a result, the partner may develop a deep sense of distrust, which often lingers in the relationship long after the affair is over.

Another reason having an affair hurts the partner and the relationship is that it shifts the decision-making process from a couple focus to an individual focus. Choosing to engage in sex with someone other than the primary partner is a decision based on what the individual wants (individualism), not on what the couple wants (familism).

In addition to feeling betrayed, deceived, and devalued as potential outcomes of an affair, another danger is the development of a pattern of having affairs. "Once you've had an affair and gotten away with it, it's easier the second time," said one spouse. "And the third time, you don't give it a thought." Increasingly, the spouse looks outside the existing relationship for sex and companionship.

Engaging in extradyadic sex may also result in the termination of the primary relationship. In a study of the reasons college students end relationships, "another person" was a factor involved in the majority of endings (Knox, Gibson, Zusman, & Gallmeier, 1997). Even though a relationship may not end, it may be permanently wounded by a lingering feeling of mistrust that has invaded the relationship.

If the partner finds out the spouse wants a divorce because of involvement with someone new, the "adulterer" may also pay an economic price. In some states, adultery is grounds for alimony.

Another potential danger in having extradyadic sex is the potential to contract a sexually transmitted infection. The HIV epidemic has increased the concern over this possibility. Spouses who engage in extradyadic sex may not only contract a sexually transmitted infection, but may also transmit the infection to their partners (and potentially their unborn offspring). In some cases, extradyadic sex may be deadly.

Finally, spouses who engage in extradyadic sex relationships risk the possibility of their partner finding out and going into a jealous rage. Jealousy may result in violence and even the death of the unfaithful spouse or the lover involved. Another possible tragic outcome of extramarital relationships is that a spouse who "cheats" or has been "cheated on" becomes depressed and commits suicide.

Partners who decide to avoid extradyadic encounters might focus on the small choices that lead to a sexual encounter. Because extradyadic sex occurs in an identifiable sequence of behaviors (e.g., eye contact, flirting, sex references, touching, etc.) and contexts (e.g., away from spouse, presence of alcohol/drugs, etc.), the person can choose to avoid them. Avoiding intimate conversations and drinking with someone to whom you are attracted helps ensure that a sexual encounter will not occur. Not to make these choices ("not to decide is to decide") is to increase the chance that extradyadic sex will occur.

Potential Positive Outcomes of Extradyadic Sex

Some spouses who have had an affair do not regret doing so. One woman known to the authors said that while her husband constantly criticized her, the man with whom she had had the extramarital relationship "needed me and made me feel loved and important again." This woman eventually divorced her husband and said that she never regretted moving from an emotionally dead and abusive relationship to one in which she was loved and nurtured. In this case, the extramarital affair served as a bridge out of the marriage.

For some spouses who have an affair and stay married, the marriage may benefit. Some partners become more sensitive to the problems in their marriage. "For us," one spouse said, "the affair helped us to look at our marriage, to know that we were in trouble, and to seek help." Couples need not view the discovery of an affair as the end of their marriage; to the contrary, it can be a new beginning.

Another positive effect of a partner's discovering an affair is that the partner may become more sensitive to the needs of the spouse and more motivated to satisfy them. The partner may realize that if the spouse is not satisfied at home, he or she will go elsewhere. One husband said his wife had an affair because he was too busy with his work and did not spend enough time with her. Her affair taught him that she had alternatives—other men who would love her emotionally and sexually. To ensure that he did not lose her, he cut back on his work hours and spent more time with his wife.

8-4c Motivations for Extradyadic Sexual Encounters

Partners involved in committed relationships report a number of reasons why they become involved in extradyadic sexual relationships. Some of these reasons are discussed here.

Variety, Novelty, and Excitement

Extradyadic sexual involvement may be motivated by the desire for variety, novelty, and excitement. One of the characteristics of sex in long-term committed relationships is the tendency for it to become routine. Early in a relationship, the partners seemingly cannot have sex often enough. But with constant availability, the partners may achieve a level of satisfaction, and the attractiveness and excitement of sex with the primary partner seem to wane. The **Coolidge effect** is a term used to describe this waning of sexual excitement and the effect of novelty and variety on sexual arousal:

Coolidge effect The effect of novelty and variety on sexual arousal; when a novel partner is available, a sexually satiated male regains capacity for arousal.

> *One day President and Mrs. Coolidge were visiting a government farm. Soon after their arrival, they were taken off on separate tours. When Mrs. Coolidge passed the chicken pens, she paused to ask the man in charge if the rooster copulated more than once each day. "Dozens of times," was the reply. "Please tell that to the President," Mrs. Coolidge requested. When the President passed the pens and was told about the rooster, he asked, "Same hen every time?" "Oh no, Mr. President, a different one each time." The President nodded slowly, and then said, "Tell that to Mrs. Coolidge." (Bermant, 1976, pp. 76–77)*

The Coolidge effect illustrates the effect of novelty and variety on the copulation behaviors of roosters, not humans. Varying levels of sexual novelty and variety may, indeed, be important for achieving sexual satisfaction for many individuals. However, unlike roosters, humans need not have multiple sexual partners to experience novelty and variety. Rather, humans may create sexual novelty and variety within a monogamous relationship by having sex in novel contexts (e.g., bed and breakfasts) and different places, exploring different intercourse positions, engaging in a variety of noncoital petting behaviors, wearing a variety of erotic clothing, watching erotic films, and utilizing sexual fantasies.

Friendship

Extradyadic sexual involvements may develop from friendships. Friendships that develop into extradyadic sexual relationships often begin in the workplace. Co-workers share the same world 8 to 10 hours a day and, over a period of time, may develop good feelings for each other that eventually lead to a sexual relationship. Most people have the skill of establishing a nonsexual relationship with a close and intimate friend, but others have difficulty drawing the line.

Relationship Dissatisfaction

It is commonly believed that people who have affairs are not happy in their marriage, but persons in both stable and happy marriages may have extramarital sex. Nevertheless, one source of relationship dissatisfaction is an unfulfilling sexual relationship. Some people engage in extradyadic sex because their partner is not interested in sex. Others may go outside the relationship because their partners will not engage in the sexual behaviors they want and enjoy. The unwillingness of the spouse to engage in oral sex, anal intercourse, or a variety of sexual positions sometimes results in the other partner looking elsewhere for a more cooperative sexual partner.

Revenge

Some extradyadic sexual involvements are acts of revenge against one's partner for engaging in extradyadic sexual activity. When partners find out that their mate has had or is having an affair, they are often hurt and angry. One response to these feelings is to have an affair to get even with the unfaithful partner. However, the revenge motive can also be operative for reasons other than the partner having outside sex. "My husband called me fat and pitiful but my lover called me beautiful and wonderful," said one wife.

Involvement in Homosexual Relationship

Some individuals in heterosexual committed relationships engage in extradyadic sex because they feel an attraction to same-sex individuals. Some gay individuals marry as a way of denying their homosexuality or creating a social pretense that they are heterosexual. These individuals are likely to feel unfulfilled in their marriage and may seek involvement in an extramarital homosexual relationship. Other individuals may marry and discover after their marriage that they are attracted to same-sex partners. Such individuals may feel that they have been homosexual or bisexual all along. Others may feel that their sexual orientation has changed from heterosexual to homosexual or bisexual. Still others may be unsure of their sexual orientation and want to explore a homosexual relationship. Finally, there are others who feel that they are predominantly heterosexual but wish to experience homosexual sex for variety. Of course, same-sex committed partners may be bisexual and seek heterosexual extradyadic partners.

Aging

A frequent motive for intercourse outside marriage is the desire to re-experience the world of youth. Our society promotes the idea that it is good to be young and bad to be old. Sexual attractiveness is equated with youth, and having an affair may confirm to an older partner that he or she is still sexually desirable. Also, people may try to recapture the love, excitement, adventure, and romance associated with youth by having an affair.

One writer (Gordon, 1988) interviewed men who had left their wives for a younger woman. The men tended to report that they were attracted not by the physical beauty of their new partners, but by their youthful attitudes—the openness, innocence, unscarred emotions. They also emphasized the uncritical love they felt from their younger partner. Gordon labeled these men as having "Jennifer Fever"—they had developed a pattern of denying the aging process by seeking a youthful partner to create the illusion that they were not getting older. Gordon suggested the term "Jennifer" because she found that the name of the younger woman was often Jennifer. Gordon further warned that these men would seek another "Jennifer" as the current one aged.

Absence from Partner

One factor that predisposes a person to an extradyadic sexual encounter is prolonged separation from the partner. Some spouses whose partners are away for military service report that the loneliness can become intense and that they become vulnerable to an affair. Partners in commuter relationships may also be vulnerable to extradyadic sexual relationships.

Think About It

The spouse who chooses to have an affair is often judged as being unfaithful to the vows of the marriage, as being deceitful to the partner, and as inflicting enormous pain on the partner (and children). What is often not considered is that when an affair is defined in terms of giving emotional energy, time, and economic resources to something or someone outside the primary relationship, other types of "affairs" may be equally devastating to one's partner and relationship. Spouses who choose to devote their lives to their careers, parents, friends, or recreational interests may deprive the partner of significant amounts of emotional energy, time, and money and create a context in which the partner may choose to become involved with a person who provides more attention and interest. What relationships are you aware of in which a spouse felt neglected by the partner who was focused on someone or something external to the marriage?

8-5 SEXUALITY IN THE LATER YEARS

We do not stop playing because we grow old, we grow old because we stop playing.
—Anonymous

There are misconceptions of sexuality in the later years. A survey of young adult (age less than 30) college students in psychology courses revealed their current and projected attitudes of the elderly at age 70 in regard to sexuality (Floyd & Weiss, 2001). Contrary to what is actually more likely to occur as men and women age, male respondents reported more strongly than female respondents that they anticipated not having a partner available. In reality, women are much more likely to be without a partner in the later years.

NATIONAL DATA Ten percent of the adult population consists of widowed women as compared to 2.2% of widowed men (*Statistical Abstract of the United States: 2002*, Table 46). Most women become widows; 66% are widows by age 75 (*Statistical Abstract of the United States: 2002*, Table 48).

Birch (2000) emphasized the reality of sexuality for the aging couple:

Unfortunately, an aging couple can no longer depend on the same wild, spontaneous sex they had experienced in their youth. The everyday pressures and responsibilities of mature adulthood alone could hamper spontaneity, but matters are made worse by an aging body in an aging relationship. It is one of those regrettable realities of life that an aging couple is not likely to be suddenly swept away by simultaneous intense lust! (p. 85)

There are different categories and definitions of being "old." Three groups of the elderly are the "young-old" (ages 65–74), the "old-old" (75–84), and those 85 and beyond. Chronological age is only one index of age. Other indices of aging are physiological (hearing capacity diminishes with age), cultural (the Masai elderly in East Africa are respected and revered), sociological (the occupation of roles such as grandparent and Medicare patient reserved for the elderly), and psychological (one's self-concept may become more negative as the elderly may feel devalued in a youth culture).

CULTURAL DIVERSITY 

Sexuality of the elderly is influenced by culture. For example, Chinese American women (at all ages) are taught (by traditional Chinese culture) to feel that being curious, concerned, and knowledgeable about their own bodies is inappropriate (Zeiss & Kasl-Godley, 2001).

This happily married couple of 50 years says that humor in a relationship is important for intimacy.

8-5a Sexuality of Elderly Men

Sexual functioning changes with age (Zeiss & Kasl-Godley, 2001). Specific physiological changes that occur in elderly men during the sexual response cycle follow:

- *Excitement Phase*—As men age, it takes them longer to get an erection. Whereas the young man may get an erection within 10 seconds, elderly men may take several minutes (10 to 30). During this time, they usually need intense stimulation (manual or oral). Unaware that the greater delay in becoming erect is a normal consequence of aging, men who experience this for the first time may panic and be unable to get an erection.
- *Plateau Phase*—The erection may be less rigid than when the man was younger, and there is usually a longer delay before ejaculation. This latter change is usually regarded as an advantage of aging by both the man and his partner.
- *Orgasm Phase*—Orgasm in the elderly man is usually less intense, with fewer contractions and less fluid expelled.
- *Resolution Phase*—The elderly man loses his erection rather quickly after ejaculation. The refractory period is also increased. Whereas the young man needs only a short time after ejaculation to get an erection, the elderly man may need considerably longer.

Significant declines in male sexuality are influenced by the absence of good health (Zeiss & Kasl-Godley, 2001). For example, "after a stroke, many men are unable to obtain or maintain erections, or they may not have the strength and mobility to continue engaging in sexual intercourse" (p. 20). In addition, the elderly who are institutionalized (e.g., in a nursing home) may have few opportunities for sexual interaction due to restrictive policies. Researchers Spector and Fremeth (1996) studied 40 elders (mean age, 82.5) in long-term care institutions and found that sexual activity was infrequent.

Although genital activity may decline, the need for psychological/physical intimacy continues. Bullard-Poe, Powell, and Mulligan (1994) studied 45 men, ages 44–99, in a nursing home. Social, nonsexual-physical, intellectual, emotional, and sexual-physical intimacy were rated in that order as most important to the residents. These findings were true whether the men were married or not. Indeed, although capacity may decrease as well as actual behavior, social, emotional, and intellectual intimacy needs continue. Schlesinger (1996) stated that the main reason elderly men do not have intercourse is "fear of impotency and the ensuing self devaluation" (p. 121). Hugh Hefner, now in his 70s, suggests a way for elderly men to avoid such fear; he hails Viagra as the world's greatest legal drug.

8-5b Sexuality of Elderly Women

Elderly women also experience a variety of physiological changes during the sexual response cycle:

- *Excitement Phase*—Vaginal lubrication takes several minutes or longer, as opposed to 10 to 30 seconds in youth. Both the length and the width of the vagina decrease. Considerable decreased lubrication and vaginal size may be associated with pain during intercourse.
- *Plateau Phase*—Little change occurs as the woman ages. During this phase, the vaginal orgasmic platform is formed, and the uterus elevates.
- *Orgasm Phase*—Elderly women continue to experience and enjoy orgasm. Of women aged 60 to 91, those reporting their frequency of orgasm now as opposed to when they were younger, 65% said "unchanged," 20% said "increased," and 14% said "decreased" (Starr & Weiner, 1981).
- *Resolution Phase*—Defined as a return to the pre-excitement state, the resolution phase of the sexual response phase happens more quickly in elderly than in younger women. Clitoral retraction and orgasmic platform disappear quickly after orgasm.

Gelfand (2000) summarized the changes in sexuality among elderly women as the result of decreasing levels of estrogen and testosterone, with concomitant effects on decreased libido, sensitivity, and response.

One of the few studies on the sexuality of elderly women and men was by Bretschneider and McCoy (1988), who reported data on 102 White women and 100 White men ranging in age from 80 to 102. Some of the findings follow:

- Thirty-eight percent of the women and 66% of the men reported that sex was currently important to them.
- Thirty percent of the women and 62% of the men reported they had sexual intercourse sometimes.
- Of those with sexual partners, 64% of the women and 82% of the men said that they were at least mildly happy with their partners as lovers.
- Forty percent of the women and 72% of the men reported that they currently masturbated.
- Touching and caressing without sexual intercourse were the most frequently engaged-in behaviors by women (64%) and by men (82%).

These findings suggest that declines in sexual enjoyment and frequency are greater for women in the later years than for men. Other studies confirm that sexual frequency decreases with age (Meston, 1997).

NATIONAL DATA Ninety-five percent of women and 55% of men over the age of 80 report not having had sex with anyone in the past 12 months. The higher percentage of abstinent women is caused by the absence of a male partner (Michael et al., 1994).

Although changes in physical activity occur with aging, the need for emotional intimacy continues. A woman in her 80s commented on the changes in sexuality in old age and the feelings of passion that endure:

> *The longing to belong with somebody, to love somebody, to have somebody, and to feel the touch of somebody near us remain equally young, fresh and intact as always. The need for love and intimacy does not change as we get older. Even when our physical capacity for sex wanes slightly, we still have overwhelming feelings of desire, passion and love. As a person in her eighties, I remind everyone of the importance of feeling—with your heart, body and mind. My feelings won't disappear when I turn ninety just as they didn't evaporate when I turned eighty or seventy or sixty. (Reti,1995, p. 215)*

Think About It

How is the sexuality of aging women and men affected by cultural stereotypes and expectations? How might a generation of today's young women, who have grown up in a sexually open and permissive era, differ when they become elderly (in terms of their sexuality) from elderly women of today who were reared in a more conservative, restrictive era?

SUMMARY

Sexuality changes throughout one's life span.

Sexuality in Infancy and Childhood

Infants are born with a sexual response system that begins to function early in life. At birth, some boys are born with erections, and some girls are born with a vaginal discharge equivalent to lubricating fluid. Early emotional bonding experiences are important for the development of intimate physical and emotional relationships as an adult.

Children often experiment with their own bodies as sources of physical pleasure and also show an interest in the bodies of other children. Some parents are careful not to punish their children for normal sexual exploration because doing so teaches children that sex is "bad." Research suggests that children who are exposed to parental nudity, the "family bed," or the "primal scene" do not suffer negative consequences.

Sexuality in Adolescence

Adolescents experience considerable physical and psychological changes. They are concerned about their bodies matching the cultural ideal. They are also making sexual choices about first intercourse, preventing pregnancy and STDs, and abortion.

Sexuality in Early Adulthood

Never-married young adults who live alone and those who live with someone report different sexual lives. Those who are unattached report having less frequent sex but report more partners than those who are living with someone. However, those who cohabit report a higher quality of sexual experience, similar to those who are married.

Marital sex is the most socially legitimate, physically pleasurable, and emotionally satisfying sex that people report. Divorced individuals report more sexual partners than never-marrieds or marrieds.

Divorced women are stereotyped as having greater sexual experience and sexual knowledge and being more sexually assertive and promiscuous. Divorced people may be more vulnerable to contracting STDs because they are less sensitized to the danger of contracting HIV than never-married individuals in their 20s.

Sexuality is affected by the aging process. Women experience menopause around age 50, and some experience hot flashes, irritability, and headaches. Hormone replacement therapy may relieve menopausal symptoms but should not be taken to prevent cardiovascular disease. Men in the middle years experience decreasing levels of testosterone, which results in more difficulty in getting and maintaining an erection and a greater amount of time between erections.

Extradyadic Sexual Involvements

The term *extradyadic* includes sexual involvement with someone other than the person with whom one is involved in an emotional and sexual relationship. The different types of extradyadic relationships include. brief sexual encounters, romantic affairs, open marriages, swinging, polyamorous relationships, and computer affairs.

Motivations for extradyadic sexual involvements include variety, novelty, excitement, friendship, relationship dissatisfaction, revenge, desire for a homosexual relationship, aging, and absence from partner. Although there are exceptions, the relationship consequences of extramarital sex are usually negative. Rebuilding the lost trust is a major challenge.

Sexuality in the Later Years

As individuals age, sexual capacity, interest, and activity tend to decrease. In men, physiological changes include problems with achieving and maintaining erections, and less intense orgasms occur. In women, physiological changes include less vaginal lubrication. However, many elderly women and men value the emotional intimacy associated with sexual expression. Although genital expression may decrease, the need for touch and love do not.

SUGGESTED WEBSITES

Note: These websites were functional when we went to press. Please access the online text for the most up-to-date URLs.

Aging and Sexuality
http://www.sex-and-aging.info

Childhood Sexuality
http://www.cfoc.org/teenagesexuality.htm

Marriage
http://www.bettermarriages.org/

Parent-Child Communication About Sex
http://www.siecus.org
http://www.familiesaretalking.org
http://www.plannedparenthood.org/

Polyamory
http://lovemore.com/

Rutgers University Sex Site
http://www.sxect.org

Teenage Sexuality
http://www.itsyoursexlife.org
http://iwannaknow.org
http://www.sxetc.org
http://www.teengrowth.com

KEY TERMS

adolescence (p. 245)
childhood (p. 243)
climacteric (p. 257)
cohabitation (p. 251)
computer affair (p. 260)
Coolidge effect (p. 262)
extradyadic sexual involvement (p. 258)
extramarital (p. 258)
infancy (p. 242)
menopause (p. 256)
middle age (p. 256)
object relations theory (p. 243)
open marriage (p. 259)
polyamory (p. 260)
postnatal abstinence (p. 258)
puberty (p. 245)
satiation (p. 254)
sexual debut (p. 244)
swinging (p. 260)

CHAPTER QUIZ

1. Both boys and girls have been observed masturbating to orgasm as early as
  a. 7 years.
  b. 4 years.
  c. 2 years.
  d. 6 months.

2. Herdt and McClintock (2000) noted that stable and memorable sexual attraction occurs by what age?
  a. 6
  b. 10
  c. 13
  d. 16

3. The term *puberty* comes from the Latin *pubescere*, which means
  a. to be covered with hair.
  b. in a confused state.
  c. to be in a dangerous situation.
  d. being in between two places.

4. The term *menarche* refers to which of the following?
  a. an individual who is biologically both male and female
  b. a woman who is over 50 and who has never had sexual intercourse
  c. first menstruation
  d. cessation of menstruation

5. By age 19, most ___________ in the United States report having had sexual intercourse.
   a. girls
   b. boys
   c. both a and b
   d. neither a nor b

6. According to data presented in your text, the more partners a person reports having sex with in the past 12 months, the ________ satisfied the person reports his or her sex life to be.
   a. more
   b. less

7. Based on national data, on average, which of the following individuals reports having sex most frequently?
   a. couples living together but not married
   b. single adults
   c. married couples

8. Among U.S. women who married in the 1990s, more than half reported that they had lived with someone before they married.
   a. True
   b. False

9. According to data from a national sample, most married people said they ___________ their sex lives.
   a. were frustrated with
   b. were bored by
   c. received great emotional satisfaction, but only occasional physical pleasure from
   d. received great emotional satisfaction and great physical pleasure from

10. A woman is considered to be through menopause when
   a. she has her 50th birthday.
   b. she misses her first menstrual period after age 50.
   c. she has had 3 irregular menstrual periods in a row.
   d. she has had no menstrual period for 12 months.

11. Data from the Women's Health Initiative study found that long-term use of hormone replacement therapy (combined estrogen plus progestin) ___________ a woman's risk for breast cancer, heart attack, stroke, and blood clots.
   a. increases
   b. decreases

12. The concept of an open marriage refers to a marriage
   a. characterized by open communication.
   b. in which the partners have flexible rather than traditional roles.
   c. in which spouses agree to allow each one to have sexual relationships with others.
   d. in which spouses agree to re-evaluate their marriage each year, rather than assume they will stay together "until death do us part."

13. As men age, the time it takes to achieve an erection
   a. increases.
   b. decreases.

14. In a study of women aged 60–91, more than half described their frequency of orgasm now compared to when they were younger as
   a. increased.
   b. decreased.
   c. unchanged.

15. In a study on the sexuality of elderly women and men ranging in age from 80 to 102, Bretschneider and McCoy (1988) found that most of the ___________ reported that sex was currently important to them.
   a. women
   b. men
   c. both a and b
   d. neither a nor b

16. In a study on the sexuality of elderly women and men ranging in age from 80 to 102, Bretschneider and McCoy (1988) found that most of the ___________ reported that they currently masturbated.
   a. women
   b. men
   c. both a and b
   d. neither a nor b

REFERENCES

Alan Guttmacher Institute. (1999). *Teen sex and pregnancy.* Retrieved March 6, 2003, from www.guttmacher.org/pubs.fb_teen_sex.html

Ali, M. M., & Cleland, J. G. (2001). The link between postnatal abstinence and extramarital sex in Cote d'Ivoire. *Studies in Family Planning, 32,* 214–225.

Althaus, F. (2001). Levels of sexual experience among U.S. teenagers have declined for the first time in three decades. *Family Planning Perspectives, 33,* 180–181.

Ambuel, B., & Rappaport, J. (1992). Developmental trends in adolescents' psychological and legal competence to consent to abortion. *Law and Human Behavior, 16*(2), 129–154.

Andre, T., Frevert, R. L., & Schuchmann, D. (1989). From whom have college students learned about sex? *Youth and Society, 20,* 241–268.

Apt, C., & Hurlbert, D. E. (1995). Male cognitive schemata in the sexual perceptions associated with the marital status of women. *Journal of Sex Education and Therapy, 21,* 1–10.

Bachrach, C. M., Hindin, J., & Thomson, E. (2000). The changing shape of ties that bind: An overview and synthesis. In L. J. Waite (Ed.), *The ties that bind* (pp. 3–16). New York: Aldine de Gruyter.

Bailey, N. J., & Phariss, T. (1996). Breaking through the wall of silence: Gay, lesbian, and bisexual issues for middle level educators. *Middle School Journal, 27,* 38–46.

Bancroft, J. (1989). *Human sexuality and its problems* (2nd ed.). Edinburgh: Churchill Livingstone.

Bermant, G. (1976). Sexual behavior: Hard times with the Coolidge effect. In M. H. Siegel & H. P. Zeigler (Eds.), *Psychological research: The inside story*. New York: Harper and Row.

Birch, R. W. (2000). *Sex and the aging male*. Howard, OH: PEC Publishing Co.

Bouris, K. (1994). *The first time*. Berkeley, CA: Conari Press.

Bretschneider, J. G., & McCoy, N. L. (1988). Sexual interest and behavior in healthy 80 to 102 year olds. *Archives of Sexual Behavior, 17*, 109–129.

Bullard-Poe, L., Powell, C., & Mulligan, T. (1994). The importance of intimacy to men living in a nursing home. *Archives of Sexual Behavior, 23*, 231–236.

Calderone, M. S. (1991). Fetal erection and its message to us. In M. A. Watson (Ed.), *Readings in sexology* (2nd ed.) (pp. 108–111). Dubuque, IA: Kendall/Hunt.

Carney, P. A., Goodrich, M. E., O'Mahony, D. M., Tosteson, A. N., Eliassen, M. S., Poplack, S. P., et al. (2000). Mammography in New Hampshire: Characteristics of the women and the exams they receive. *Journal of Community Health, 25*, 183–198.

Centers for Disease Control and Prevention (2000). *HIV/AIDS Surveillance Report, 12*, 3–43.

Chapin, J. R. (2000). Adolescent sex and mass media: A developmental approach. *Adolescence, 35*, 799–811.

Clark, S. D., Zabin, L. S., & Hardy, J. B. (1984). Sex, contraception, and parenthood: Experience and attitudes among urban black young men. *Family Planning Perspectives, 16*, 77–82.

DeHart, D. D., & Birkimer, J. C. (1997). The Student Sexual Risks Scale. Columbia, SC & Louisville, KY: University of South Carolina, College of Social Work; & University of Louisville.

Duncan, E. D., Ritter, P. L., Dornbusch, S. M., Gross, R. T., & Carlsmith, J. M. (1990). The effects of pubertal timing on body image, school behavior, and deviance. In R. E. Muuss (Ed.), *Adolescent behavior and society* (pp. 51–56). New York: McGraw-Hill.

Feldman, S. S., Turner, R., & Araujo, K. (1999). Interpersonal context as an influence on sexual timetables of youths: Gender and ethnic effects. *Journal of Research on Adolescence, 9*, 25–52.

Finkenauer, C., & Hazam, H. (2000). Disclosure and secrecy in marriage: Do both contribute to marital satisfaction? *Journal of Social and Personal Relationships, 17*, 245–263.

Finley, C., Gregg, E. W., Solomon, L., & Gay, E. (2001). Disparities in hormone replacement therapy use by socioeconomic status in a primary care population. *Journal of Community Health, 26*, 39–50.

Floyd, M., & Weiss, L. (2001). Sex and aging: A survey of young adults. *Journal of Sex Education and Therapy, 26*, 133–139.

Ford, K., Sohn, W., & Lepkowski, J. (2001). Characteristics of adolescents' sexual partners and their association with use of condoms and other contraceptive methods. *Family Planning Perspectives, 33*, 100–105.

Garner, D. M. (1997). The 1997 Body Image Survey results. *Psychology Today, 30*, 31.

Gathorne-Hardy, J. (2000). *Sex the measure of all things: A life of Alfred C. Kinsey*. Bloomington and Indianapolis: Indiana University Press.

Gelfand, M. M. (2000). Sexuality among older women. *Journal of Women's Health and Gender-Based Medicine, 9*, 15–20.

Gordon, B. (1988). *Jennifer fever*. New York: Harper and Row.

Gould, D. C., Petty, R., & Jacobs, H. S. (2000). The male menopause—does it exist? *British Medical Journal, 320*, 858–861.

Gould, T. (1999). *The lifestyle: A look at the erotic rites of swingers*. Buffalo, NY: Firefly Books.

Guillemin, M. (2000). Blood, bone, women and HRT: Co-constructions in the menopause clinic. *Australian Feminist Studies, 15*, 191–203.

Hatfield, E., & Rapson, R. L. (1996). *Love and sex: Cross-cultural perspectives*. Boston: Allyn and Bacon.

Herdt, G., & McClintock, M. (2000). The magical age of 10. *Archives of Sexual Behavior, 29*, 587–606.

Herman-Giddens, M. E., Slora, E. J., Wasserman, R. C., Bourdony, C. J., Bhapkar, M. V., Koch, G. G., et al. (1997). Secondary sexual characteristics and menses in young girls seen in office practice: A study from the pediatric research in office settings network. *Pediatrics, 99*, 505–512.

Honig, A. S. (2000). Psychosexual development in infants and young children: Implications for caregivers. *Young Children, 55*, 70–77.

Hutchinson, M. K. (2002). The influence of sexual risk communication between parents and daughters on sexual risk behaviors. *Family Relations, 51*, 238–247.

Hyde, J. S., DeLamater, J. D., Durik, A. M. (2001). Sexuality and the dual-earner couple, Part II: Beyond the baby years. *The Journal of Sex Research, 38*, 10–23.

Jamieson, L., Anderson, M., McCrone, D., Bechhofer, F., Stewart, R., & Li, Y. (2002). Cohabitation and commitment: Partnership plans of young men and women. *The Sociological Review, 50*, 356–377.

Jenks, R. (2001). To swing or not to swing! *The Journal of Sex Research, 38*, 171–174.

Joyner, K., & Laumann, E. O. (2001). Teenage sex and the sexual revolution. In E. O. Laumann & R. T. Michael (Eds.), *Sex, love, and health in America: Private choices and public policies* (pp. 41–71). Chicago: The University of Chicago Press.

Knox, D, Gibson, L., Zusman, M. E., & Gallmeier, C. (1997). Why college students end relationships. *College Student Journal, 31*, 449–452.

Larsson, I., & Svedin, C. (2002). Sexual experiences in childhood: Young adult's recollections. *Archives of Sexual Behavior, 31*, 263–274.

Laumann, E. O., & Michael, R. T. (2001). Setting the scene. In E. O. Laumann & R. T. Michael (Eds.), *Sex, love, and health in America: Private choices and public policies* (pp. 1–37). Chicago: The University of Chicago Press.

Laumann, E. O., & Youm, Y. (2001). Sexual expression in America. In E. O. Laumann & R. T. Michael (Eds.), *Sex, love, and health in America: Private choices and public policies* (pp. 109–147). Chicago: The University of Chicago Press.

Lewis, C. C. (1987). Minors' competence to consent to abortion. *American Psychologist, 42*, 84–88.

Mackay, J. (2000). *The Penguin atlas of human sexual behavior*. New York: Penguin.

Manning, W. D. (2001). Childbearing in cohabiting unions: Racial and ethnic differences. *Family Planning Perspectives, 33*, 217–223.

Meston, C. M. (1977). Aging and sexuality. *Western Journal of Medicine, 67*, 285–291.

Metz, M. E., & Seifert, M. H., Jr. (1990). Men's expectations of physicians in sexual health concerns. *Journal of Sex and Marital Therapy, 16*, 79–88.

Michael, R. T, Gagnon, J. H., Laumann, E. O., & Kolata, G. (1994). *Sex in America: A definitive survey*. Boston: Little, Brown.

Miller, B. C., & Coyl, D. D. (2000). Adolescent pregnancy and childbearing in relation to infant adoption in the United States. *Adoption Quarterly, 4*, 3–25.

Miller, K., Levin, M., Whitaker, D., & Xu, X. (1998). Patterns of condom use among adolescents: The impact of mother-adolescent communication. *American Journal of Public Health, 88*, 1542–1544.

Mott, E. L., Fondell, M. M., Hu, P. N., Kowaleski Jones, L., & Menaghan, E. G. (1996). The determinants of first sex by age 14 in a high-risk adolescent population. *Family Planning Perspectives, 28*, 13–18.

Nahom, D., Wells, E., Gillmore, M. R., Hoppe, M., Morrison, D. M., Archibald, M., et al. (2001). Differences by gender and sexual experience in adolescent sexual behavior: Implications for education and HIV prevention. *Journal of School Health, 71*, 153–158.

National Center for Health Statistics. (2002, June 26). Births, marriages, divorces, and deaths: Provisional data for October 2001. *National Vital Statistics Report, 50* (11). Hyattsville, MD: Author.

Okami, P., Abramson, P. R., & Pendleton, L. (1998). Early childhood exposure to parental nudity and scenes of parental sexuality ("primal scenes"): An 18-year longitudinal study of outcome. *Archives of Sexual Behavior, 27*, 361–384.

Olenick, I. (2000). Odds of spousal infidelity are influenced by social and demographic factors. *Family Planning Perspectives, 32*, 148–155.

Pollack, W. S. (with Shuster, T.). (2000). *Real boys' voices*. New York: Penguin.

Ponton, L. (2000). *The sex lives of teenagers*. New York: Plume.

Raley, R. K. (2000). Recent trends and differentials in marriage and cohabitation: The United States. In L. J. Waite (Ed.), *The ties that bind* (pp. 19–38). New York: Aldine de Gruyter.

Reti, L. (1995). Golden age and love: An insider's report. In R. Neugebauer-Visano (Ed.), *Seniors and sexuality: Experiencing intimacy in later life* (pp. 215–216). Toronto: Canadian Scholars Press.

Rodgers, J. L., & Rowe, D. C. (1990). Adolescent sexual activity and mildly deviant behavior. *Journal of Family Issues, 11*, 274–293.

Santelli, J. S., Lowry, R., Brener, N., & Robin, L. (2000). The association of sexual behaviors with socioeconomic status, family structure, and race/ethnicity among US adolescents. *American Journal of Public Health, 90*, 1582–1588.

Santrock, J. W. (2003). *Adolescence* (9th ed.). Boston: McGraw-Hill.

Sarigiani, P. A., & Petersen, A. C. (2000). Adolescence: Puberty and biological maturation. In A. Kazdin (Ed.), *Encyclopedia of psychology*. Washington, DC, & New York: American Psychological Association and Oxford University Press.

Schalet, A. T. (2000). Raging hormones, regulated love: Adolescent sexuality and the constitution of the modern individual in the United States and the Netherlands. *Body & Society, 6*, 75–105.

Schlesinger, B. (1996). The sexless years or sex rediscovered. *Journal of Gerontological Social Work, 26*, 117–131.

Schneider, J. P. (2000). Effects of cybersex addiction on the family: Results of a survey. *Sexual Addiction and Compulsivity, 7*, 31–58.

Spector, I. P., & Fremeth, S. M. (1996). Sexual behaviors and attitudes of geriatric residents in long-term care facilities. *Journal of Sex and Marital Therapy, 22*, 235–246.

Starr, B., & Weiner, M. (1981). *The Starr-Weiner report on sex and sexuality in the mature years*. New York: Stein and Day.

Statistical Abstract of the United States: 2002. (2002). 122nd ed. Washington, DC: U.S. Bureau of the Census.

Tang, G. W. (1994). The climacteric of Chinese factory workers. *Maturitas, 19*(3), 177–182.

Waite, L. J., & Joyner, K. (2001). Emotional and physical satisfaction with sex in married, cohabiting, and dating sexual unions: Do men and women differ? In E. O. Laumann & R. T. Michael, (Eds.), *Sex, love, and health in America: Private choices and public policies* (pp. 239–269). Chicago: The University of Chicago Press.

Wheeler, J., & Kilmann, P. R. (1983). Comarital sexual behavior: Individual and relationship variables. *Archives of Sexual Behavior, 12*, 295–306.

Whitaker, D. J., Miller, K. S., & Clark, L. F. (2000). Reconceptualizing adolescent sexual behavior: Beyond did they or didn't they? *Family Planning Perspectives, 32*, 111–117.

Widlocher, D. (2002). *Infantile sexuality and attachment*. New York: Other Press.

Wiederman, M. W. (1997). Extramarital sex: Prevalence and correlates in a national survey. *The Journal of Sex Research, 34*, 167–174.

Women's Health Initiative Investigators. (2002). Risks and benefits of estrogen plus progestin in healthy postmenopausal women: Principal results from the Women's Health Initiative randomized controlled trial. *Journal of the American Medical Association, 288*, 321–333.

Young, K. S., Griffin-Shelley, E., Cooper, A., O'Mara, J., & Buchanan, J. (2002). Online fidelity: A new dimension in couple relationships with implications for evaluation and treatment. *Sexual Addiction and Compulsivity, 7*, 59–74.

Zeiss, A. M., & Kasl-Godley, J. (2001). Sexuality in older adults' relationships. *Generations, 25*, 18–25.

9

Cultural Diversity in Sexuality

Chapter Outline

While human biology is the ultimate basis for our sexual behavior, culture and society are the most important influences on how individuals experience and express their sexuality.

—*J. Patrick Gray and Linda Wolfe, anthropologists*

Suppose that as a 7- to 15-year-old-boy, you learned that fellating older males was necessary for you to be able to become a man, develop your own sperm, and become capable of fertilizing a woman. Or suppose that as a preadolescent girl, you learned that one of the ways to get God (Allah) to approve of you was to submit to having your clitoris cut off. Sambian boys (in New Guinea) are expected to engage in fellatio, and Muslim girls (in some parts of the Middle East) are expected to participate in a clitoridectomy in response to cultural beliefs and values (Elliston, 1995). As these examples illustrate, the cultural context in which a person is reared dictates what sexual behavior the person may engage in and the attitude that person is expected to have toward the behavior.

After discussing cross-cultural research in human sexuality, we examine the issue of what is "normal" sexual behavior and review how sexual behaviors are viewed differently in different cultures. We emphasize that sexual choices are often influenced by cultural contexts and social forces.

9-1 ETHNOGRAPHY AND ETHNOLOGY

Each culture envelops sex with a different environment of ideas, beliefs, values, and regulations, and no two are identical.

—*William H. Davenport*

Early studies (pre-1920s) of human sexuality in non-European cultures largely consisted of unsystematic observations and anecdotal reports from a variety of sources, including missionaries, government officials, and travelers. Despite the fact that these early observations were unreliable, they nonetheless suggested that many aspects of human sexuality were shaped by culture.

In the 1920s, anthropologist Bronislaw Malinowski published *Sex and Repression in Savage Society* (1927), which compared psychosexual development in the Trobriand culture with the segment of European society that Freud had studied. In 1929, Malinowski published *Sexual Life of Savages in North-Western Melanesia,* which described sexuality in that culture. These two landmark studies led to the development of two types of cross-cultural research in human sexuality: ethnography and ethnology.

Ethnography The descriptive study of cultures or subcultures.

Ethnography refers to the descriptive study of cultures or subcultures. Ethnographic studies of sexuality describe the sexual patterns of behavior and beliefs in various cultures or subcultures. To investigate human sexuality in other cultures, researchers often use field research methods whereby they collect data by interviewing members of a certain community. In his early ethnographic study of sexuality in the Trobriand Islands, Malinowski (1929) described various aspects of sexual behavior among the natives:

> *(As told by a native) when we go on a lovemaking expedition we . . . walk, we arrive at a large tree, we sit down; we search each other's heads and consume the lice, we tell the woman that we want to copulate. (p. 336)*
>
> *The more usual position . . . is for the man to squat in front of the woman and, with his hands resting on the ground, to move towards her or, taking hold of her legs, to pull her towards him. When the sexual organs are close to each other the insertion takes place. . . . The woman may stretch her legs and place them directly on the man's hips, with his arms outside of them, but a far more usual position is with her legs embracing the man's arms, and resting on the elbow. (pp. 336–337)*
>
> *Another element of lovemaking . . . [is] . . . the biting off of eyelashes. As far as I could judge from descriptions and demonstrations, a lover will tenderly or passionately bend over his mistress's eyes and bite off the tip of her eyelashes. . . . I was never quite able to grasp either the mechanism or the sensuous value of this caress. (p. 334)*

Ethnology refers to the comparative study of two or more cultures or subcultures. Ethnological studies of sexuality compare the sexual patterns of behavior and beliefs of two or more cultures or subcultures. In an early ethnological study, Malinowski (1927) offered the following comparison of sexuality in Melanesia and European society:

Ethnology The comparative study of two or more cultures or subcultures.

> *In fact, it might be said that for [Melanesian] children the categories of decent-indecent, pure-impure, do not exist. . . . In Melanesia there is no taboo on sex in general. . . . When we consider that these children run about naked, that their excretory functions are treated openly and naturally, that there is no general taboo on bodily parts or on nakedness in general; when we further consider that small children at the age of three and four are beginning to be aware of . . . genital sexuality, and of the fact that this will be their pleasure quite soon . . . we can see that social factors rather than biological explain the difference between the two societies. (pp. 54–55)*

Researchers conducting ethnographic or ethnological studies on human sexuality must contend with several problems. First, the researcher must either be fluent in the language of the culture being studied or must have a translator or interpreter. Also, researchers often rely on informants—persons who live in the culture being studied—as a source of data. Because some sexual behavior occurs in private, informants are able to give reliable reports only of their own experiences and observations, which are limited and biased. Informants may also provide inaccurate information to make a good impression on the researcher and present themselves in a way they feel is socially desirable.

Another problem with cross-cultural research is the inherent bias of the researcher, who typically formulates research questions operative in his or her own culture. Hence, a researcher from the United States studying multiple wives among the Masai in South Africa may focus on patterns of jealousy where none exists and not explore socialization patterns of women and men for polygyny.

Still another problem in doing cross-cultural research stems from the fact that every culture is composed of different cultures or subpopulations. In studying the same culture, one ethnographer may focus on people of a particular gender, social class, age, occupation, or sexual orientation, whereas another ethnographer may focus on a different group. Formulating a description of an entire culture based on the observation of one particular subset of the population is misleading. In an edited book of cross-cultural studies, Cecil (1996) explains that women's lives are often ignored in cross-cultural studies because ethnographers have restricted access to women informants. An exception to this omission is one anthropologist's story of the life of a !Kung woman; see Box 9-1.

Finally, culture is not static but changes over time. Ethnographic or ethnological research conducted years ago may not accurately reflect current cultural practices and beliefs. For example, Margaret Mead (1928) described adolescent Samoan females as sexually relaxed, carefree, and free of psychological conflict. But Freeman (1983) studied young women in the same culture years later and described them as aggressive, impulsive, and sexually hung up. The differences between Mead's and Freeman's observations could reflect the cultural changes that occurred in Samoan culture over a 50-year period.

9-2 WHAT IS "NORMAL" SEXUAL BEHAVIOR?

People of all cultures are born into the world without values or beliefs about what is "normal." Through family, school, peers, media, religion, and government, we learn what our culture defines as normal sexual behavior. With no standard of comparison and no knowledge of alternatives, children accept the things their society teaches them. For example, most U.S. children learn that they must wear clothes. Unless they have been reared by nudists (who take their children to family nudist retreats), they will feel that nudism is "not normal." Otherwise, they may well adopt the norm of most nudists—"clothed when practical, nude when possible."

Box 9-1 Up Close

Marjorie Shostak Talks with Nisa

In an ethnographic field study, Harvard anthropologist Marjorie Shostak (1983) spent 20 months among the !Kung San in the Kalahari Desert of southern Africa. She spoke extensively with women over several years, including 50-year-old Nisa, to learn about their lives as members of a people whose traditional means of subsistence was gathering and hunting. Nisa told the story of her remarkable life, which included her accounts of saving a baby brother from infanticide, being married at age 12, separating, divorcing, remarrying, being widowed, bearing four children (although none survived), and foraging for food in a harsh desert environment.

When Nisa complained of an uncomfortable itch in her genitals, Shostak inquired about what she meant. Nisa playfully explained, "You really *don't* know things, do you? The itch is desire, desire for a man. Let me teach you, because you are still a child." Laughing and pointing she continued, "These are your genitals. If a man doesn't take them, they itch and itch and itch! They become aroused and cry out for a man. It's only when he takes them that the itch goes away" (p. 367).

As an anthropologist, Shostak (p. 349) framed her interviews with Nisa and the other women with the fairly neutral request, "Teach me what it is to be a !Kung woman." However, as she reviewed the tapes of her interviews, she was struck by how often sexual topics were discussed. Was this an accurate representation of !Kung culture, or had Nisa been presenting what she thought an anthropologist might be interested in hearing? Shostak (p. 350) said that another anthropologist had told her that in their funny (and frequently scathing) character portrayals, the !Kung had depicted Shostak "as someone who ran up to women, looked them straight in the eye, and said, 'Did you screw your husband last night?'" But across the months of living with the !Kung and participating in the flow of talk, work, and movement of the village, Shostak concluded that in most respects Nisa was a typical !Kung woman.

Shostak was appreciative of the gift Nisa gave her—a view into the complex and quickly passing world of the !Kung. She concluded that the reason the !Kung shared their world with her was that they so valued human ties.

9-2a Criteria Used to Define "Normal" Sexual Behavior

Cultures use various criteria to define what is normal. These criteria include prevalence, moral correctness, naturalness, and adaptiveness/comfort.

Prevalence

We tend to assume that if most people engage in a sexual behavior, it is normal.

National Data Seventy-three percent of adult U.S. women report having received oral sex (Michael, Gagnon, Laumann, & Kolata, 1994).

Given that almost three fourths of U.S. women report receiving cunnilingus at some time in their lives, we tend to think of this sexual behavior as normal. Conversely, sexual behaviors that rarely occur are sometimes considered not normal. Because only 20% of U.S. women report that the last time they had sex, their partner performed cunnilingus on them (Michael et al., 1994), we tend to think that the woman's experiencing cunnilingus every time she has sex is not normal.

Statistical model of normality A way to conceptualize prevalence; better known as the *normal curve*. This statistical presentation of the prevalence of a phenomenon reveals the distribution in a large population.

Another way to conceptualize prevalence is via the **statistical model of normality,** better known as the *normal curve*. This statistical presentation of the prevalence of a phenomenon reveals the distribution in a large population. For example, when a national sample of men and women identified the duration of their last sexual event, 13% reported that it lasted less than 15 minutes, 70% reported that it lasted 15–60 minutes, and 17% reported that it lasted 60 or more minutes. This is a "normal" curve distribution that shows the majority have sex between 15–60 minutes with smaller percentages under 15 minutes and more than an hour (Laumann & Michael, 2001, p. 17).

CULTURAL DIVERSITY 

Prevalence rates also vary by culture. For example, rates of various sexual behaviors (intercourse, masturbation, and oral sex) of Chinese college students are lower than those of U.S. students (Tang, Lai, Phil, & Chung, 1997).

Moral Correctness

Sexual behaviors are also considered normal if they are viewed as morally correct. According to many religions (e.g., Islam), penile-vaginal intercourse between husband and wife is the only morally correct form of sexual behavior. Other forms of sexual expression, including oral sex, masturbation, anal sex, and sex between persons not married and between persons of the same sex, are considered abnormal because they are viewed as immoral. One of the reasons some homosexuals seek the approval of the church is that religion is such a powerful gatekeeper of definitions of sexual normality.

Naturalness

Sexual behaviors also are viewed as natural or unnatural, depending on whether they result in procreation. Because masturbation, homosexuality, oral sex, and anal sex do not result in pregnancy and childbearing, these acts are sometimes viewed as unnatural (and, by implication, abnormal). Sometimes people judge a behavior as natural if it occurs in the natural world (in the animal kingdom) or is biologically determined. People often ask if "homosexual" behavior occurs in animals, implying that if so, the behaviors of gays and lesbians are more "natural" and acceptable.

CULTURAL DIVERSITY 

Although "naturalness" may be judged on whether a behavior follows "nature," Gregersen (1983, p. 10) observed that cultures do not always agree on what is natural. He described the views of the Kagaba Indians of Colombia, who unlike many groups in the world, do not believe that children born of incestuous relations will be more likely to be deformed. However, they do believe that if a man's rhythm is thrown off during sexual intercourse, he, his partner, and his children might be harmed.

Adaptiveness/comfort

Sexual behaviors are usually considered "normal" if they are adaptive, comfortable, and have positive outcomes for the participants. Sexual behavior that causes physical or emotional harm or suffering or that interferes with one's functioning may be considered abnormal. An example of sexual behavior considered abnormal is sex with children, which is typically associated with negative outcomes for both adult and child. Of course, the determination of what constitutes adequate functioning is subjective and is influenced by social and cultural norms. Some societies encourage and permit adults having sex with children.

Think About It 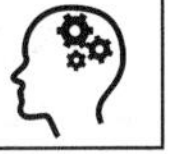

Which of the four criteria used to define what is "normal" sexual behavior carries the most weight in your own personal view?

9-2b Historical Variations in Definitions of "Normal" Sexual Behavior

Within the same culture, sexual behaviors may be labeled as normal in one historical time and abnormal in another. For example, although kissing in public is acceptable normal behavior today (be alert to public couple kissing on your campus), in the American colonial era, kissing in public was considered unacceptable and punishable by being "lodged in the stocks" in public. During this era, unmarried persons who were discovered to have engaged in intercourse were viewed as individuals who had succumbed to the temptations of the flesh. After they were discovered, they had to make a public confession and were also subject to fines and a public lashing. Public kissing in Taiwan and in Mainland China today is not illegal, but it is frowned upon—there is social disapproval for kissing one's beloved in public.

9-3 ETHNOCENTRISM VERSUS CULTURAL RELATIVISM

Ethnocentrism and cultural relativism are central concepts in understanding human sexuality from a cross-cultural perspective.

9-3a Ethnocentrism

Ethnocentrism Judging other cultures according to the standards of one's own culture and viewing one's own culture as superior.

Members of every society learn to view the cultural norms of their own social group as appropriate and the norms of other cultures as strange. The combination of judging other cultures according to the standards of one's own culture and viewing one's own culture as superior is called **ethnocentrism.** Most people are ethnocentric in that they assume that their cultural norms, beliefs, and values are natural, universal, and correct and that other cultures are strange or wrong. Researchers' observations and interpretations may be biased by their own cultural backgrounds and values. For example, clitoridectomy is abhorred in American society, with its individualism, feminism, and respect for personhood. But among some Africans and Muslims, the practice is viewed through their cultural eyes as appropriate and routine.

9-3b Cultural Relativism

Any effort to educate and promote healthy sexuality must take into consideration the practices of the culture in which the individual has been socialized.

—Barbara Rynerson

Cultural relativism Understanding other cultures according to the standards of the culture in which the behaviors and beliefs exist.

An alternative to viewing others' sexual behavior and beliefs as inferior and abnormal is to view them as different and as "normal" according to the standards of the culture in which the behaviors and beliefs exist. This perspective on cultural differences, known as **cultural relativism,** involves understanding other cultures according to their own standards. Those who adopt the principle of cultural relativism view the beliefs and practices of another culture according to the values and standards of that culture.

Think About It

Topless beaches are common in France. How might an American visitor to France who were to adopt a culturally relativistic view of topless French women view such behavior?

In her *Abnormal Psychology* textbook, Nolen-Hoeksema (2001) gives the example of one man kissing another man as a behavior considered normal in some cultures but not in others. She observes that the maladaptiveness criterion for abnormality is influenced by one's culture and gender. Based on culture and gender, people may be more or less likely to engage in certain behaviors, as well more or less willing to admit to performing the behaviors.

9-3c Personal Choices: Is a Cultural-Relativistic Perspective Amoral?

Cultural relativism has been criticized as being an amoral perspective that accepts and tolerates all forms of cultural practices and beliefs. However, a cultural-relativistic view of human sexuality *does not* imply that all cultural variations in sexuality must be accepted; it merely means that sexual behaviors and beliefs are viewed from the perspective of the cultures that practice the behavior and hold the beliefs. The sexual choices you make do affect you as an individual and do affect your relationship with your partner.

According to U.S. cultural values and standards, some sexual practices and beliefs are viewed as "wrong" because they endanger the health and well-being of individuals. For example, most Americans view female infanticide and female genital operations (discussed in section 9-4j) as "wrong." Most Americans would question the belief that "intercourse helps young girls to mature" (which, among the Lepcha people of India, means that by the age of 12, most Lepcha girls are engaging in regular intercourse). Viewing such practices and beliefs from a cultural-relativistic perspective involves trying to understand why some cultures accept and promote these practices and beliefs and why these beliefs and practices are important to the people in these cultures. Understanding sexual practices and beliefs according to the perspective of other cultures does not mean that one must abandon one's own moral judgment.

Think About It

Do you think that cultural relativism is advocated equally in traditional societies and modern societies? To what degree might the claim that "cultural relativism is a better perspective than ethnocentrism" itself be an ethnocentric view?

9-4 CULTURAL VARIATIONS IN SEXUALITY

Culture refers to the meanings and ways of living that characterize a society. Three central elements of culture include beliefs, values, and norms.

9-4a Central Elements of Culture

Beliefs refer to definitions and explanations about what a person accepts to be true. We "believe" that men think about sex and are more driven to have sex than women. Cultural beliefs also influence sexual behaviors. The common belief among some U.S. men that, when a woman says "no," she really means "yes" or "maybe" contributes to some men coercing women to have sex with them. The belief that HIV/AIDS is a homosexual disease may result in heterosexuals not using condoms. Values, another central element of culture, are standards regarding what is good and bad, right and wrong, or desirable and undesirable. Individuals' personal values are greatly influenced by societal values.

Beliefs Mental acceptance of definitions and explanations about what is true.

NATIONAL DATA A survey of first-year students at two- and four-year universities in the United States revealed that their top two values were "being well-off financially" and "raising a family," respectively (American Council of Education & University of California, 2001).

Norms are socially defined rules of behavior. Norms serve as guidelines for our behavior and our expectations of the behavior of others. Sociologists have identified three types of norms: folkways, laws, and mores. **Folkways** refer to the customs and traditions of society. Most U.S. women, for example, wear bras to support their breasts. Although there is

Norms Socially defined rules of behavior.

Folkways Customs and traditions of society.

Laws Norms that are formalized and backed by political authority.

Mores Norms that have a moral basis.

no law requiring women to wear bras, most do so because it is expected of them; it is part of the cultural folkways of U.S. society. **Laws** are norms that are formalized and backed by political authority. Virtually every society has laws concerning sexual behavior. **Mores** are norms that have a moral basis. Mores reflect a sense of what is moral and immoral. Mores may also be laws. For example, child sexual abuse is a violation of the law and a violation of our mores because we view such behavior as immoral. Some behaviors may violate mores but may be legally permitted. For example, among some segments of society, intercourse before marriage is considered immoral and therefore a violation of mores; however, sex before marriage between consenting adults is not illegal.

One of the norms of U.S. society is the expectation that persons marry someone of a similar race. This norm is pervasive in that more than 95% of U.S. adults marry someone of the same race (*Statistical Abstract of the United States: 2002*, Table 47). The self-assessment in Box 9-2 enables you to assess the degree to which this norm affects your views toward interracial dating.

This interracial married couple is rare. Only about one half of one percent of all married couples in the United States consist of interracial spouses in which one is White and the other is Black.

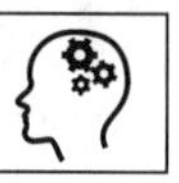

Think About It

Norms regarding interracial involvements are changing. In a study of 620 undergraduate university students, half reported that they were open to involvement in an interracial relationship (Knox, Zusman, Buffington, & Hemphill, 2000). To what degree are you open to an interracial relationship?

9-4b Western and Eastern Conceptions of Sexuality

Cross-cultural variations are also evident in how an individual views sexuality and its importance in the individual's life. Western conceptions of sexuality tend to focus on sexual performance, orgasm, and physical satisfaction. In contrast, some Eastern cultures view sexuality as a vehicle for spiritual development and personal transformation. Tantric sex, described in Hindu and Buddhist Tantric scriptures, reflects the essence of Asian sexuality. The Sanskrit term *T'antra* means *integration*, suggesting full involvement of the natural human drives in the pursuit of a fully realized existence. One technique in Tantric practice is to be still and motionless during intercourse so as not to have an orgasm. The purpose of such an exercise is to intensify sexual-spiritual energy.

Chinese sexuality is based primarily on Confucian and Taoist traditions. According to Confucian sexual philosophy, which emphasizes procreation and social order, sex for pleasure and sex outside marriage are prohibited for both men and women. The Taoist tradition, on the other hand, focuses on the balance between yin and yang, personal health, and longevity. Semen is valued as a source of vitality, and men need to preserve it by avoiding ejaculation during intercourse. Masturbation and excessive sexual activities are viewed as causes of men's illnesses because they lead to excessive waste of semen (Tang et al., 1997, p. 80).

9-4c Permissive and Repressive Cultural Contexts

The sexual beliefs, values, and norms of the Mangaians and the inhabitants of Inis Beag represent two extremes on the continuum of sexual permissiveness and sexual repressiveness.

Mangaians

Anthropologist Donald Marshall (1971) studied the sexual patterns of the Mangaians of Mangaia (southern Polynesian Islands) and observed the extreme sexual openness with which its members are reared. Adult Mangaians copulated in the same room with all kin. Their doing so was not regarded as particularly significant because household members (including children) were busy with work or play. Masturbation by both sexes at 7–10 years of age was advocated and practiced (Marshall, 1971).

Box 9-2 Self-Assessment

INTERACTIVE BOX

Attitudes Toward Interracial Dating Scale

Interracial dating and marrying is the dating or marrying of two people from different races. Individuals throughout the U.S. tend to differ in terms of how they view such relationships. The purpose of this survey is to gain a better understanding of what people think and feel about interracial relationships. In this survey, there are no right or wrong answers; we are interested in your honest reactions and opinions. Please read each statement carefully, and respond by using the following scale:

Strongly Disagree 1 2 3 4 5 6 7 Strongly Agree

___ 1. I believe that interracial couples date outside their race to get attention.
___ 2. I feel that interracial couples have little in common.
___ 3. When I see an interracial couple I find myself evaluating them negatively.
___ 4. People date outside their own race because they feel inferior.
___ 5. Dating interracially shows a lack of respect for one's own race.
___ 6. I would be upset with a family member who dated outside his/her race.
___ 7. I would be upset with a close friend who dated outside his/her race.
___ 8. I feel uneasy around an interracial couple.
___ 9. People of different races should associate together only in non-dating settings.
___ 10. I am offended when I see an interracial couple.
___ 11. Interracial couples are more likely to have low self-esteem.
___ 12. Interracial dating interferes with my fundamental beliefs.
___ 13. People should date only within their race.
___ 14. I dislike seeing interracial couples together.
___ 15. I would not pursue a relationship with someone of a different race regardless of my feelings for him or her.
___ 16. Interracial dating interferes with my concept of cultural identity.
___ 17. I support dating between people with the same skin color, but not with a different skin color.
___ 18. I can imagine myself in a long-term relationship with someone of another race.
___ 19. As long as the people involved love each other, I do not have a problem with interracial dating.
___ 20. I think interracial dating is a good thing.

Scoring: Having placed a number representing the continuum from one to 7 in each of the 20 spaces on the left, reverse score items 18, 19, and 20. For example if you selected 7 for item 18, replace it with a one, if you selected 1, replace it with a 7 etc. Next, add your scores and divide by 20. Possible scores range from 1 to 7 with 1 representing the most positive attitudes toward interracial dating and 7 representing the most negative attitudes toward interracial dating.

Norms: The norming sample was based upon 113 male and 200 female students attending Valdosta State University in Valdosta, Georgia. All participants were U.S. citizens and received no compensation for their participation. The average age of the participants completing the Attitudes toward Interracial Dating Scale was 23.02 years (*SD* = 5.09) and ranged in age from 18–50. The ethnic composition of the sample was 62.9% White, 32.6% Black, 1% Asian, 0.6% Hispanic, and 2.2% classified themselves as "Other." The classification of the sample was 9.3% Freshman, 16.3% Sophomore, 29.1% Junior, 37.1% Senior, and 2.9% were Graduate students. The average score on the Interracial Dating Scale (IRDS) was 2.88 (*SD* = 1.48) and ranged from 1.00 to 6.60 suggesting very positive views of interracial dating. Men scored an average of 2.96; women 2.84. There were no significant differences between women and men. Reliability—internal consistency—of the scale was .96.

Source: "The Attitudes Toward Interracial Dating Scale," 2002, by Mark Whatley, Ph.D. Department of Psychology, Valdosta State University, Valdosta, Georgia 31698. Used by permission. Other uses of this scale by written permission of Dr. Whatley only. His e-mail is mwhatley@valdosta.edu.

Beyond early exposure to parental intercourse and masturbation, childhood sex play with the same or other sex individuals was encouraged. Premarital sex was also encouraged, with no stigma for the experienced bride or groom. In marriage, partners were expected to mutually enjoy sex, and orgasm was a goal for both wife and husband. Extramarital sex also was tolerated.

A major theme of sexuality among the Mangaians was participation on the part of the woman. She was to be sexually active beginning in childhood, to be orgasmic, and to be an active participant. Sexual passivity was viewed as deviant. In addition, affectional feelings usually followed, rather than preceded, sexual behavior with others in adult relationships.

Inhabitants of Inis Beag

In contrast to the sexual openness of the Mangaians is the restrictive society of Inis Beag. John Messenger (1971/1993) studied every member (350) of the small agrarian Irish island community (which he called "Inis Beag" to protect its identity) from 1958 to 1966. From birth, members were segregated by sex in the family, church, and school. Men bonded with men and women with women. Marriage was for economic and reproductive reasons only, with women marrying around age 25 and men around age 36. This latter age for men was necessary because they had to own land before they could ask a woman to marry them.

Unlike the Mangaian women who were taught to be assertive and to enjoy sex, women of Inis Beag were taught to be sexually passive and to endure the sexual advances of men. Female orgasm was not in the vocabulary of the islanders, and nudity was avoided. Even though the economic livelihood of the community depended on the men catching fish from canoes, they could not swim because they were embarrassed to be without clothing and thus had never learned. Even bathing was to be done in absolute privacy.

Male masturbation seemed to be common, but premarital coitus was unknown. Marital copulation was limited; it was initiated by the husband, was performed using only the male-superior position, and took place without the underclothes being removed. Because sex was rarely discussed, sexual myths permeated the community. Women believed that menopause caused insanity, and men believed that sex debilitated them. Hence, they would avoid sex the night before a strenuous event. Messenger viewed this sexual Puritanism as one of the most important reasons for the dwindling population of Inis Beag.

As the comparison between the Mangaians and the inhabitants of Inis Beag illustrates, sexual beliefs, values, and norms vary widely. Other examples of cultural variations in sexuality follow.

9-4d Age at First Sexual Intercourse

Age at first intercourse is partly determined by cultural norms. Among a national sample of U.S. adults, the age at first intercourse was 17.5 (Michael et al., 1994). The mean age at first intercourse among 1,659 undergraduates at a large Midwestern university was 16.5, with no significant differences between women and men (Sprecher, Barbee, & Schwartz, 1995). In contrast, Japanese youth report having first intercourse around age 21 (Hatano, 1991). A major factor affecting the expression of sexual behavior among Japanese youth is the emphasis in the culture on academic preparation.

The tight pressure of university entrance examinations (admission to which university of which rank) is often considered to be the decisive factor for the whole life of a Japanese student; senior high school students are particularly suppressed in their heterosexual behaviors in lieu of the preparatory studies. Based on the same logic, parents, and perhaps classroom teachers too, are eager to require that the children concentrate only on schoolwork; therefore, they definitely discourage the sexual activity of the children (pp. 12–13). Sprecher and Hatfield (1996) noted that after Japanese students go to college, they evidence more sexual freedom.

Chinese college students report having first intercourse later than U.S. college students but earlier than Japanese students. Tang et al. (1997) collected data on 305 Chinese students. The age at first intercourse was 17.14 and 18.13 for men and women, respectively. But only 11% of the respondents reported that they had had intercourse, even though their average age was 20.1. Tang et al. (1997) suggested that preoccupation with academic preparation, strong preference for emotional commitment, and living with parents (only 20% of college students live in a college dorm) accounted for lower rates of early premarital experience.

9-4e Premarital Sex

Wide variations in sexual values exist in different societies with regard to premarital and extramarital intercourse. A team of researchers (Meston, Trapnell, & Gorzalka, 1996) compared the petting and intercourse behaviors as well as the number of previous partners and "one-night stands" of 356 Asian and 346 American undergraduate students and found that on all measures, the Asian students reported lower frequencies. In general, Asian cultures promote more conservative sexual values and have greater restrictions on the access of young men and women to each other.

Premarital sexual behavior may be punished in one society, tolerated in a second, and rewarded in a third. In the Gilbert Islands (in the South Pacific close to Somoa), virginity until marriage is an exalted sexual value, and violations are not tolerated. Premarital couples who are discovered to have had intercourse before the wedding have been put to death. Our society tolerates premarital intercourse, particularly if the partners are "in love." In contrast, the Marquesans on Juku Hiva Island in Eastern Polynesia encouraged premarital sexual exploration (homosexual and heterosexual) in both men and women at an early age (10). To ensure proper sexual instruction, young men have their first intercourse with a woman in her 30s or 40s, and young women have intercourse with elder tribal leaders.

Most societies communicate disapproval to the woman who has premarital intercourse by shunning her and making it difficult for her to marry (her reputation is ruined). In some societies, women who have had premarital sex also risk divorce. In traditional China,

> *Newlyweds were expected to wear a special white suit or sleep on a special cloth, which provided visible evidence of "deflowering" and loss of virginity. In the morning after consummation, the bloodstained evidence was produced for inspection by the groom's mother. . . . Virginity of the bride (but not the groom) was an implied condition of the marriage contract. Failure to provide proof of virginity could result in dismissal, divorce, or reclamation of the bride-price. (Engel, 1982, p.8)*

9-4f Positions and Frequency of Intercourse

Although sexual intercourse is a universal act, its expression is influenced by culture. Societies have different beliefs, values, and norms about intercourse positions and frequency. Although the preferred coital position in most cultures is face-to-face with the woman lying on her back, due to crowded sleeping arrangements in many cultures, some couples adopt the side position because they feel it is less conspicuous.

The frequency of intercourse also varies with the culture. In the United States, couples have intercourse, on average, two times a week (Michael et al., 1994). But among the Basonge in the Sasai province of Zaire, couples (even in their 50s and 60s) report that they have intercourse every night (Merriam, 1972). In contrast, a man of the Cayapa Indians of Ecuador may go for several years without having intercourse. Their term for intercourse, *medio trabajo*, means "a little work" (Altschuler, 1972).

9-4g Extramarital Sex

Most societies have prohibitions against extramarital sex.

INTERNATIONAL DATA Three quarters of 58 societies have prohibitions for both men and women against extramarital intercourse (Frayser, 1985).

The rules of marriage in some societies permit extramarital partners. For example, traditionally, the wife of an Aleut husband was expected to have sex with a houseguest as a symbol of hospitality. And, in the traditional Chinese family, wealthy men were allowed to have concubines or second wives as a way of "expanding the family, particularly for the upper classes" (Engel, 1982, p. 9).

> *Concubinage also served as a safety valve in the traditional Chinese family. It provided some relief from the very carefully prescribed behaviors for men's roles in the family. The concubine was often chosen by the fellow himself on the basis of personal attraction and romance, in contrast to the mate-selection process in the arranged marriage. . . . As one might expect, it was not uncommon for jealousy to arise among the wives and concubines in a household. (p. 9)*

Among the Masai (200,000 of whom live in Arusha, Tanzania, East Africa), a Masai man coming back from a long journey in the forest herding cows/goats/sheep can put a spear outside the house of another man's wife to alert the husband that he is inside having sex with his wife. Seeing the spear, the husband does not bother the visitor because to do so would be impolite (interview with Shaaban Mgonja, Masai guide, Arusha, Tanzania, East Africa, January 24, 2001).

Cross-culturally, the double standard seems evident with regard to who is allowed to have sex with someone other than one's spouse. In her study of 58 societies, Frayser (1985) reported that no society gave women the option to have affairs while denying it to men.

Hatfield and Rapson (1996) summarized studies of extramarital sexual activity and concluded that in Western countries, two changes have occurred. First, the sexual double standard seems to be eroding, and there is greater similarity in men's and women's experimentation with extramarital sex. Second, in contrast to the past, extramarital relations are occurring earlier, more frequently, and with more partners.

Patriarchy A system of social organization in which the father is the head of the family and family descent is traced through the male line.

In most countries, the sexuality (both premarital and extramarital) of women has been controlled by men. **Patriarchy** is a term that originally referred to the supremacy of a father over his family. Patriarchal authority allowed fathers to prohibit premarital sexual behavior of their daughters so as to ensure their marriageability. Anthropologists have observed that even societies that describe women as sexually pure and passive go to great lengths to prevent them from being unchaste. Because most of the world's cultures trace descent through the male line, the purpose of this effort is probably to ensure that paternity of children and their status as heirs are undisputed (Hrdy, 1981, 1993).

Individuals who ignore the rules prohibiting extramarital intercourse are punished. Forms of punishment include the lover paying a fine to the woman's husband and brother, the lover submitting to a public beating by the husband, the wife submitting to a private beating by the husband, temporary public ostracism, and death. A Kenuzi husband (in Egypt) is allowed to kill his wife if he even suspects her of infidelity. According to the Islamic faith, the penalty for a person caught committing adultery (four witnesses are necessary) is public stoning (the person is buried at the waist and stoned). Adultery may be punished by death in Iran, Pakistan, Saudi Arabia, and Yemen (Mackay, 2000).

9-4h Incest

Incest is disapproved of in most societies. Anthropologist Claude Levi-Strauss (1969/1993) hypothesized that the incest prohibition grew out of the need for social alliance. The social function of incest was to ensure that women married outside the close family group so as to create a connection with another family or clan in order to create new resources. Levi-Strauss saw prohibiting incest not so much as a rule proscribing marriage with one's mother, sister, or daughter, but as a rule that the mother, sister, or daughter marry outside the family unit so as to make connections or create alliances with others.

Cultures differ in how they define incest and punish infractions (Davenport, 1987). In some cultures, certain cousins are permitted and even encouraged to have sexual relations, but marriage between them is forbidden. The incest taboo is extended only to primary relatives (parents, offspring, siblings) in some cultures; in others, incest is prohibited among all traceable relatives. The Dahomey of West Africa and the Incas of Peru have viewed sex between siblings as natural and desirable, excluding sex between parents and children (Stephens, 1982).

Social sanctions against those who commit incest range "from ridicule to threats of supernatural punishment to the partners being put to death" (Gray & Wolfe, 1992, p. 645). Frayser (1985) described a variety of sanctions that are applied to those who violate the incest taboo. The Cayapa Indians of Ecuador have been known to suspend violators over a table covered with candles and roast them to death. The ancient Incas also imposed death for violation of the incest taboo.

In some cultures, the sanctions for violating the incest taboo are less severe. Punishment may be as mild as temporary verbal disapproval. For example, the Havasupai Indians of the Grand Canyon merely reprimand offenders verbally. Moderate punishment may involve temporary body damage (such as whipping) or ostracism for a limited period of time.

It has been generally assumed that the incest taboo was universal. However, historical records show that in a number of societies, royalty were encouraged to marry (and, therefore, be incestuous with) a family member, especially a sibling. Furthermore, "in some societies there are no obvious incest taboos in the sense of rules (and sanctioned rules especially) against it, only a notion that no one would commit incest anyway" (Brown, 1991, p. 119).

9-4i Homosexuality

Societies differ in terms of how they regard homosexuality. Among the people of East Bay, a village in Melanesia, homosexuality is tolerated only in males. Prior to marriage, young men engage in mutual masturbation and anal intercourse. Many married men are bisexual (Shepherd, 1987). Among the Araucanians (in South America) lesbian activities are common among young girls in the spring. However, these acts are typically viewed as an indicator that the girls are ready to marry—boys (Gregersen, 1983).

Batak males (in northern Sumatra) engage in homosexual relations before marriage. At puberty, Batak boys leave their parents' home and sleep in a home with 12 to 15 boys. In this group, each boy is initiated into homosexual practices. After marriage, the majority of Batak men cease homosexual activity (Money & Ehrhardt, 1973).

In Hungary, homosexuality in women or men is punishable by up to 5 years in prison (Drakulic, 1990). Homosexuals in the former Soviet Union kept their sexual orientation hidden for fear of government reprisal. However, there is evidence that in many countries of the world (such as France, Canada, and Hong Kong), people hold more accepting attitudes toward homosexuality (Hatfield & Rapson, 1996).

Not only do societies differ in their acceptance or nonacceptance of homosexuality, but they also differ in how or whether they categorize sexual orientation. For example, Dr. Terry Tafoya, a psychologist who is also a Taos Pueblo and Warm Springs Indian, observed, "for many Native Americans, there was never the rigid classification typical of Western polarity that divides the world into straight and gay. Determination of an individual's identity on the basis of sexual behavior makes no conceptual sense to many American Indians" (Tafoya, 1989, p. 288). Tafoya noted (p. 287) that at least 135 tribes have particular terms for persons "who are not exactly male or female," some of whose characteristics would match Western society's concepts of gay or lesbian.

One such term, **berdache,** has often been used by anthropologists in describing individuals who crossed gender lines. In a review of historical records of American berdaches, Trexler (2002) found that they were most often biological males who were dressed and trained to act like girls and women, although some girls who acted like boys were noted. They were most often selected by their parents as infants or children for this role, to serve familial or community functions. Usually, children whose gender was modified were the third or fourth child in the family, in which all the children were of one sex, and the father lacked a son to hunt with him, or the mother had no daughter to learn domestic or nurturing skills. The main characteristics were dressing and assuming the labor of the opposite sex. In some communities the young men who were berdaches served as sexual partners for the community braves, thus protecting the marriageable girls from violation.

Berdache A native American term often used by anthropologists in describing individuals who cross gender lines.

Terry Tafoya, Ph.D. is a Taos Pueblo and Warm Springs Indian. He co-founded the National Native American AIDS Prevention Center.

Photo courtesy of Terry Tafoya

Two-spirit men Term for traditional Native American men who have both masculine and feminine traits; although they may participate in same-sex intimacy, they are less likely to identify themselves using such terms as homosexual, gay, or berdache.

Female genital operations See **female genital mutilation.**

Female genital mutilation (FGM) The various practices of cutting or amputating some or all of the female external genitalia—the prepuce or hood of the clitoris, the glans and shaft of the clitoris, the labia minora (small genital lips), and the labia majora (large genital lips). (See also **female genital operations.**)

While changing the original sex to the opposite gender was usually done at a young age, in the Plains nations this often took place at puberty. It often involved some process of obtaining supernatural approval, as dreaming or seeing a vision involving a buffalo or the moon (both associated with womanhood).

In contemporary Native American cultures, religious beliefs recognize both people and gods who are not completely male or female. According to Tafoya and Wirth (1996), today's traditional Native American men who participate in same-sex intimacy are less likely to identify themselves using such terms as homosexual, gay, or berdache, and are more likely to describe themselves as **two-spirit men.** However, he noted that more urbanized Indian people may identify as gay or bisexual. And, influenced by Western-influenced homophobic thinking, in some tribal groups in which the berdaches were once accepted, there is now stigma, resulting in the living of "double lives," different on the reservation and off (Tafoya, 1989).

9-4j Female Genital Operations

Although piercing genitals and/or nipples for the purpose of sexual pleasure (among other reasons; see Box 1-2, "Up Close: Body Piercing") is currently in vogue in the United States, cutting off parts of the genitals is viewed with some horror. But such cutting occurs routinely in some other cultures, and has for 2,000 years (Epstein, Graham, & Rimsza, 2001). **Female genital operations,** sometimes referred to as **female genital mutilation** (FGM) or *female genital cutting,* refer to the various practices of cutting or amputating some or all of the female external genitalia: the prepuce or hood of the clitoris, the glans and shaft of the clitoris, the labia minora (small genital lips), and the labia majora (large genital lips). Female genital mutilation can take several forms, the most common being type II—excision of the clitoris with partial or total excision of the labia minora. The most severe form is type III, which involves the cutting off of the clitoris and some or all of the labia minora and an infibulation in which the labia majora are stitched together (leaving a tiny hole for the passage of menses and urine). An estimated 175 million women of all ages have undergone some form of female genital operation (Bosch, 2001). The practice occurs at all social levels in at least 28 African countries, as well as on the Arab Peninsula, and in a few regions of Asia (Lightfoot-Klein, Chase, Hammond, & Goldman, 2000).

Typically, traditional village women perform the cutting, without anesthesia to dull the pain and without sterile cutting instruments. Health complications from genital operations, including infection, hemorrhage, and chronic pelvic inflammatory disease, are not uncommon. No exact statistics are available on the fatalities, but Lightfoot-Klein estimates that in the Sudan, where the procedures are extreme, medical estimates of fatalities ranged from 10–30% (Lightfoot-Klein et al., 2000). In addition, women who undergo this ritual are deprived of experiencing sexual pleasure and are often left with painful scars. In the Sudan the operations are performed on girls "in the 5–7 year age range; the girls, however, may be older or younger, since it is common to circumcise two or three sisters at the same time. These occasions are ones of celebration with new dresses, bracelets, and gifts for the girls" (Gruenbaum, 2001, p. 481).

The reasons for the ritual of female genital cutting vary greatly by region and ethnic group. In many cultures that practice female genital operations, the ritual serves as an initiation into womanhood. In other cultures, the practice helps ensure a girl's virginity before marriage and fidelity afterward—hence, a "morality prevention" (Dandash, Refaat, & Eyada, 2001). Because women in the cultures that practice female genital cutting are economically dependent on men, parents insist on the rite so their daughters are marriageable. In Egypt, mothers most likely to have their daughters circumcised were illiterate, living in rural areas, over 40 years of age, and married before they themselves were 20 (Dandash et al., 2001). Other meanings of female genital cutting include honoring one's family and perpetuating a custom approved by the ancestors, carrying out a rite of passage, and enhancing a woman's ability to reproduce (Leonard, 2000). In Lightfoot-Klein's interview with more than 400 respondents, the most common reason given in support of the procedures was "It is custom" (Lightfoot-Klein et al., 2000, p. 446). Various researchers have interpreted female genital operations from psychoanalytic (shifting of the erogenous zone from the clitoris to the vagina), feminist (reflects patriarchal control of women), and human rights (form of child abuse) perspectives (Leonard, 2000).

The practice of female genital operations has become a public issue in the United States. We examine this issue in Box 9-3.

9-4k Male Genital Operations

The most familiar form of **male genital mutilation** is circumcision, which involves the surgical removal of the foreskin, usually during infancy. Circumcision was performed by the Egyptians as early as 4000 B.C. Male circumcision occurs in cultures that share the Judeo-Christian-Islamic tradition and among the aborigines of Australia and in sub-Saharan Africa. Although the majority of the world's men are genitally intact (not circumcised), the United States is the last developed nation to continue circumcising the majority of infants for nontherapeutic and nonreligious reasons. Infant circumcision rates in the United States fluctuate at around 60%, whereas in Canada they are less than 25%, in Australia less than 10%, and in Britain less than 1% (Lightfoot-Klein et al., 2000).

Male genital mutilation See **circumcision.**

Some cultures practice male circumcision for various reasons, including religious, aesthetic, hygienic, and sociological. To Jewish people, circumcision symbolizes Abraham's covenant with God. In some cultures, male circumcision has a sociological function in that it testifies that "the circumcised individual has undergone rituals and ordeals that establish maturity or it is an enhancement of masculinity" (Davenport, 1987, p. 207). As discussed in section 4-3a, "Penis," in the United States, male circumcision is practiced primarily for social conformity.

Think About It 

Given the lack of evidence for hygienic necessity for male circumcision, why do you think Americans have such dramatically different attitudes toward male and female genital surgeries?

Another form of male genital mutilation that occurs in parts of Australia is **penile supraincision,** which involves making a longitudinal slit through the dorsal of the foreskin. Among Mangaian youths, this practice occurs around age 13 to denote the onset of adolescence. After having received the proper sexual training (on style, timing, and position) by an older woman from the community, the male is supraincised, which certifies that he is ready for sexual intercourse.

Penile supraincision A longitudinal slit through the dorsal (top) of the foreskin.

Another form of male genital mutilation occurs among some of the inland Dayak peoples of Borneo. A few Dayak men voluntarily undergo a transverse perforation of the penis through which a wooden pin is inserted. A small knob is attached to each protruding end of the pin. The Dayak people believe that these knobs increase the woman's sexual pleasure during intercourse. This form of genital mutilation is quite painful and provides "an opportunity to display fortitude, hence it signals something about the courage, virility, and stoicism of those who suffer the operation" (Davenport, 1987, p. 208).

9-4l Expression of Gender Roles

Sex-differentiated roles (those identified as specific to women and to men) vary from culture to culture. Although women are typically scripted as nurturing caretakers and men as aggressive hunters or fighters, in many societies the social structures and traditions may vary. Gender role expectations may be flexible, or the punishment for violating them may be harsh. For example, Haddad and Smith (1996) described Islamic values about dating among American Muslim families. Girls are not allowed unchaperoned dating; and when

Box 9-3 Social Choices

U.S. Policies Involving Female Genital Operations

Although female genital operations occur primarily in African and some Middle Eastern and Asian countries, the practice also occurs in the United States among immigrant families who bring their cultural traditions with them. Each year, about 7,000 immigrants to the United States (from countries that practice various forms of female genital operations) undergo the procedure either in the United States or during a visit to their homeland. The practice has become visible due to the increasing number of physicians involved in international assistance and travel (Bosch, 2001).

In July 2001, the European Parliament Women's Rights Committee adopted a report to condemn all forms of female genital mutilation, describing it as a "serious violation of human rights and an act of violence against women which directly affects their integrity as people" (Bosch, 2001, p. 1178). In addition to causing many organic and psychosexual complications (trauma at the time of the operation may affect comfort during intercourse), mutilation might have a substantial role in facilitating HIV transmission if one instrument is used on several girls (Epstein et al., 2001).

In the mid-1990s, the U.S. Congress passed a federal law essentially banning female genital operations as practiced for ritualistic behavior (some cutting may be necessary for intersexed individuals; see the discussion in section 5-2d, "Hormonal Abnormalities"). This law also directs federal authorities to inform new immigrants from countries where the operation is practiced that parents who arrange for the genital cutting of their female children in the United States (as well as people who perform the cutting) may face up to 5 years in prison. France, the United Kingdom, Sweden, and the Netherlands have already outlawed the practice; in France, immigrant families have been prosecuted for violating the ban. Such cases are usually reported to the police by doctors, who detect the practice while examining female patients.

Some U.S. health-care providers fear that the ban on female genital operations will not eliminate the practice, but rather will result in African parents withholding medical care for their daughters in order to avoid detection and prosecution. After African mothers repeatedly requested that their daughters have genital operations in the hospital, physicians at a Seattle hospital proposed offering a largely symbolic form of the ritual, in which they would nick the tip of a girl's clitoris, with her consent, under a local anesthetic. No tissue would be removed.

Another policy issue concerning female genital operations involves giving asylum to refugee women who come to the United States to avoid genital cutting. In 1994, 17-year-old Fauziya Kasinga fled from her home in Togo to escape having her genitals cut. After escaping to the United States, Kasinga turned herself in to immigration officials, asking for asylum. To win asylum, refugees must show that, because of their race, nationality, religion, politics, or membership in a particular social group, they have either been persecuted or have a "well-founded fear" of persecution. Kasinga's claim for asylum was denied by a judge with the Executive Office for Immigration Review. While awaiting an appeal of the decision, Kasinga was held in prison for more than a year, part of which she spent in a maximum security wing with serious criminals. When asked what she would do if her appeal were denied, Kasinga replied, "I'd prefer to stay in jail rather than go back and face what would be done" (McCarthy, 1996).

---

a young man visits her with family present, it should be for the purpose of pursuing marriage. When girls violate these rules, they may be ostracized by their families; in some documented cases in Dearborn, Michigan, and Milwaukee, Wisconsin, Arab girls who engaged in premarital sexual relationships were killed (Haddad & Smith, 1996).

Cainkar (1996) interviewed Palestinian women who noted there were greater freedoms allowed for Palestinian men and boys. "From the time they are born, girls are looked at differently. Boys act superior and they grow up that way. The girls should be shy and obedient" (p. 48). However, although the Palestinian women see American women as having more social freedom than they have, they are reluctant to trade places with American women. "The freedom has many dark sides," said one woman (p. 49). They see American women as often mistreated or abandoned by their husbands, and less respected by men.

In contrast to such firmly etched roles, women in American Indian cultures have had more flexibility. Although tribes vary, many have shared egalitarian relationships between men and women, and in some they have had broad latitude in gender role and lifestyle (LaFromboise, Heyle, & Ozer, 1999). For example, alternative female roles in Plains tribes include Cheyenne women horse-riders and "warrior women" of the Apache, Crow, Cheyenne, Blackfeet, and Pawnee tribes. Girls who were interested in traditional male tasks, or who refused female tasks, could participate in puberty initiation ceremonies for boys in Kaska families. Today many Indian women identify positions of authority and leadership as extensions of their care-taking role and are attempting to integrate traditional and contemporary demands within their culture.

In the summer of 1996, the Board of Immigration Appeals granted political asylum to Kasinga, recognizing female genital operations as a form of persecution against women. This ruling set a binding precedent for all U.S. immigration judges.

Finally, some U.S. policies attempt to discourage female genital operations in the countries that practice this ritual. For example, the federal ban on the operation requires U.S. representatives to the World Bank and other international financial institutions to oppose loans to countries that have not carried out educational programs to prevent it. However, Western governments' efforts to eradicate female genital operations in Africa or Asia are often perceived by members of these societies as cultural imperialism that these countries have endured historically. James and Robertson (2002) have identified many of the errors made by Western society in trying to reduce genital cutting—reducing Africa's 54 countries and hundreds of cultures to "one uncivilized place," focusing on African women in terms of their genitals, and emphasizing only the most severe form of cutting (infibulation, which removes the clitoris and the labia minora).

Changing a country's deeply held beliefs and values concerning this practice cannot be achieved by denigration. More effective approaches to discouraging the practice include the following (James & Robertson, 2002):

1. Respect the beliefs and values of countries that practice female genital operations. Calling the practice "genital mutilation" or "a barbaric practice" and referring to it as a form of "child abuse" and "torture" convey disregard for the beliefs and values of the cultures where it is practiced. In essence, we might adopt a culturally relativistic point of view (without moral acceptance of the practice). However, Kennedy (2002) traveled extensively in Africa and emphasized that the term *female circumcision* should not be used as the equivalent of female genital operations in general, or infibulation (stitching together of the labia majora so as to leave a tiny hole for menses and urine), specifically. Female genital operations, she noted, are not equivalent to the removal of foreskin.
2. Remember that the practice is "arranged and paid for by loving parents who deeply believe that the surgeries are for their daughters' welfare. Parents fear...that leaving their daughters uncircumcised will make them unmarriageable. Parents worry about their daughters during the procedures and care for their wounds afterward to help them recover . . . Parents who do this are not monsters, but are ordinary, decent, caring persons" (Lane & Rubinstein, 1996, p.38).
3. Finally, it is important to be culturally sensitive to the meaning of being a woman. Indeed, genital cutting is mixed up with how a woman sees herself, so Westerner's are cutting into her identity when attempting to alter long-held historical practices.

References

Bosch, X. (2001). Female genital mutilation in developed countries. *The Lancet*, 358, 1177–1179.

Epstein, D., Graham, P., & Rimsza, M. (2001). Medical complications of female genital mutilation. *Journal of American College Health*, 49, 275–286.

Gruenbaum, E. (2001). The movement against clitoridectomy and infibulation in Sudan: Public health policy and the Women's Movement. In C. B. Brettell (Ed.), *Gender in cross-cultural perspective* (pp. 480–492). Upper Saddle River, NJ: Prentice-Hall.

James, S. M., & Robertson, C. C. (Eds.). (2002). *Genital cutting and transnational sisterhood: Disputing U.S. polemics*. Urbana, IL: University of Illinois Press.

Kennedy, M. (2002, January). Presentation on infibulation. Department of Sociology, East Carolina University.

Lane, S. D. & Rubinstein R. A. (1996). Judging the other: Responding to traditional female genital surgeries. *Hastings Center Report*, 26 (3, 31-40).

McCarthy, S. (1996, July/August). Fleeing mutilation, fighting for asylum. *Ms.*, 12–16.

Rigid concepts for manhood seem to occur in societies in which there is considerable competition for resources (Wade & Tavris, 1999). One theory suggests that, in exchange for men being willing to take risks, society gives them power, prestige, and women. The characteristics associated with masculinity, however, are not universal because emotional expressiveness varies by culture. In many cultures in the Middle East and South America, men are permitted to be emotionally expressive, whereas in many Asian cultures they are expected to be in control of their emotions. In the United States, Pollack (2000) described the "Boy Code," which tells boys that they should rarely, if ever, convey emotions other than anger.

Think About It

What sexual beliefs and practices that are viewed as "normal" in the United States might be viewed as strange or abnormal to someone from another culture? What sexual values, beliefs, or norms that characterize other societies would you want to incorporate into U.S. culture? Why?

9-5 APPLICATIONS OF CULTURAL STUDY

The study of cultural variations related to sexual behavior is valuable in its own right because it reveals the breadth and commonalities of human experience. In addition, becoming familiar with cultural variations in sexuality-related issues provides information helpful to health-care providers and educators. Cultural sensitivity and cultural competence among health-care providers permit individualized and appropriate care to patients. More relevant and effective educational curricula and interventions can be designed with knowledge of the cultural contexts in which they will be applied.

9-5a Culturally Competent Health Care

An example of the lack of cultural knowledge impacting medical care is provided by Lightfoot-Klein et al. (2000) with an anecdote about Aswatif, a Somalian woman about to give birth in a hospital in the United States. Recently her family had come to the United States, where her husband is a graduate student. Aswatif's friends helped her pack her small bag to take to the hospital. Her friend Selva, who had already had a baby in a U.S. hospital, joked with Aswatif, "Don't forget to tell them all about your car accident!" (p. 440). Aswatif has not been in an accident, but her friend knows the question likely to come from a nurse, midwife, or physician who examines Aswatif and is not familiar with female genital mutilation. When the five-inch scar from her mons veneris to her reduced vaginal opening and perfectly smooth pudendum are revealed, it is almost certain Aswatif will be asked, "What happened to you? Were you in a car accident?" (p. 441). Although the friends laugh about this possibility, it is likely that Aswatif feels anxious about whether the health practitioner will be knowledgeable about her physical condition or understand the demands for propriety toward women in her culture.

9-5b Culturally Relevant Educational Programs

In this chapter we have reviewed variations in sex-related behaviors of different countries or nationalities. In addition to the cultural variations of countries, races, and ethnicities, other social settings and contexts can create cultures as well: social class, history, economic status, and gender. However, for each person within a demographic group (ethnic heritage, socioeconomic class), there may be many variations on the underlying cultural themes. For example, a working-class African American man may live in a multicultural Spanish-speaking neighborhood (Michal-Johnson & Bowen, 1992). The degree to which people maintain affiliation with their cultural communities is influential in determining the cultural norms that influence them. Discovering which cultural aspects are salient is particularly important in designing educational curricula and intervention programs to promote healthy decision making or behavior change.

For example, in developing an educational campaign for a group or giving educational counsel to an individual, it is helpful to first understand what life is like for that person or group and how they see the world and how they see the issue at hand. Despite the fact that individual African Americans were infected with HIV in the early 1980s, the significance of the disease and the need for preventive efforts were not widely recognized in the larger African American community (Michal-Johnson & Bowen, 1992). This slow acceptance of HIV risks has been explained within the context of historical and cultural experiences within the Black community. Dalton (1989) identified such factors as the sense that African Americans were blamed for the disease coming to America, suspicion and mistrust among the Black community when Whites suddenly expressed interest in them, and feelings of resentment at being dictated to. One implication of this cultural experience is that educational programs should consider how information is delivered and by whom; many Blacks and Latinos are more likely to pay careful attention to a prevention message that comes from a person of color than from a White, middle-class, male authority figure (De La Cancela, 1989).

In the development of population-level educational campaigns and interventions, sometimes generic educational materials are used, as in the HIV/AIDS educational pamphlet mailed to homes in the United States by former Surgeon General C. Everett Koop (Michal-Johnson & Bowen, 1992). However, for reaching particular groups,

culture-specific materials, which take into consideration the "primary cultural attitudes, values, beliefs, and practices of diverse members of a community" (p. 150) are used designing messages. For example, HIV/AIDS educational materials may need to be tailored to particular groups to make them meaningful. Tafoya gives the illustration of the Native American two-spirit man. Educational materials designed for gay or bisexual men may not seem relevant to him because he considers himself a member of a "third gender" (Tafoya, 1989, p. 287). Therefore, Tafoya recommended that AIDS prevention efforts should include not only gay and lesbian Native Americans, but also Indians who would not identify themselves as gay.

Culture-specific Of or relating to primary cultural attitudes, values, beliefs, and practices of diverse members of a community.

Finally, other examples of culture-specific intervention and educational programs may be viewed on the web site of the Centers for Disease Control and Prevention. A summary is now available of The AIDS Evaluation of Street Outreach Projects (AESOP). The investigators discovered that many factors can influence the delivery of services to street populations and should be considered in program evaluations: weather, police activity, law changes, riots, and special events that spark relocation. For example, after the death of cultural icon Jerry Garcia of the Grateful Dead, many youthful Deadheads left the San Francisco street scene (Greenberg & Newman, 1999). Knowledge of such aspects of youth street culture are important for interpreting data on service provision and program results; otherwise, it would be difficult to understand whether outreach programs were reaching those in need of service and the reasons for fluctuations in service rates.

Even though campaigns may be well-intentioned, developers are cautioned that findings will be short-sighted if culture is not incorporated as a basic underlying principle. Although identifying relevant cultural factors may be time-consuming, overlooking the cultural dynamics of a particular group may yield inaccurate findings or decreased effectiveness (Michal-Johnson & Bowen, 1992).

SUMMARY

The debate continues about the degree to which human sexual expression is biologically or culturally driven. In this chapter, we have emphasized the importance of the latter.

Ethnography and Ethnology

Ethnography is the description of behavior in a society or culture; ethnology is the comparison of patterns between cultures. It is important for ethnographers and ethnologists to understand the language and symbols for sexuality that are used in the culture they are studying. They must also be aware that sexual behavior is often private and informants are usually reporting what they know in their own life or subculture.

What Is "Normal" Sexual Behavior?

Cultures use various criteria to define what is "normal." Most sexual behaviors that occur frequently are consistent with the values of the prevailing religious and moral values, result (or can potentially result) in procreation, and have no negative consequences for its participants are regarded as normal.

Ethnocentrism Versus Cultural Relativism

Ethnocentrism involves judging other cultures according to the standards of one's own culture and viewing one's own culture as superior. Most people are ethnocentric in that they assume that their cultural norms, beliefs, and values are natural, universal, and correct and that other cultures are strange or wrong. Cultural relativism involves viewing sexual behavior and beliefs of others as different, and as "normal" according to the standards of the culture in which the behaviors and beliefs exist. This perspective on cultural differences involves understanding other cultures according to their own standards. Those who adopt the principle of cultural relativism view the beliefs and practices of another culture according to the values and standards of that culture. A cultural-relativistic view of human sexuality does not, however, imply that all cultural variations in sexuality must be accepted; it merely means that sexual behaviors and beliefs are viewed from the perspective of the cultures that practice the behavior and hold the beliefs.

Cultural Variation in Sexuality

Beliefs, values, and norms are three elements of culture that underlie cultural variations in human sexuality. Cultures exist on a continuum from being sexually permissive (Mangaians) to being sexually repressive (inhabitants of Inis Beag). Cultures also have different beliefs, values, and norms concerning age at first intercourse, premarital sex, homosexuality, incest, extramarital sex, role conceptions of sexuality, and male and female genital operations.

More than 28 countries, most of them in Africa, practice female genital operations that involve cutting off the clitoris and small genital lips and stitching together the large genital lips. The practice is arranged by parents who deeply believe that the surgery ensures marriageability and is, therefore, in the best interest of their daughter. Because immigrants from countries that practice female genital operations have immigrated to the United States, U.S. policies have restricted such operations within its borders.

Applications of Cultural Study

Aspects of cultural study are not limited to variables of nationality, race, and ethnicity. Culture is also shaped by such factors as social class, socioeconomic status, gender, and historical period. Being knowledgeable about patients' cultures allows health-care providers to give individualized care. Culture-specific educational programs, designed with consideration of a particular group's cultural norms, may be more effective with some groups than more general curricula or interventions.

SUGGESTED WEBSITES

Note: These websites were functional when we went to press. Please access the online text for the most up-to-date URLs.

Center for Sex Research
http://www.csun.edu/~sr2022/

Centers for Disease Control and Prevention
http://www.cdc.gov/

Foundation for the Advancement of Sexual Equity
http://www.faseweb.org/

Society for Human Sexuality
http://www.sexuality.org/

Terry Tafoya, Ph.D.
http://www.tamanawit.com

KEY TERMS

beliefs (p. 279)
berdache (p. 285)
cultural relativism (p. 278)
culture-specific (p. 291)
ethnocentrism (p. 278)
ethnography (p. 274)
ethnology (p. 275)
female genital mutilation (p. 286)
female genital operations (p. 286)
folkways (p. 279)
laws (p. 280)
male genital mutilation (p. 287)
mores (p. 280)
norms (p. 279)
patriarchy (p. 284)
penile supraincision (p. 287)
statistical model of normality (p. 276)
two-spirit men (p. 286)

CHAPTER QUIZ

1. Malinowski's comparison of sexuality in Melanesia and European society is an example of which of the following?
   a. ethnography
   b. ethnology
2. The "itch" Nisa (the 50-year-old !Kung San woman of the Kalahari) referred to was
   a. the desire to have children.
   b. the desire for a man.
   c. the desire to be free of patriarchal control.
   d. a sexually transmitted disease.
3. According to your text's discussion of criteria used to define "normal" sexual behavior, it is normal for U.S. women to have experienced cunnilingus because
   a. it feels good.
   b. this behavior is found among many animals.
   c. most U.S. women report having experienced cunnilingus.
   d. the behavior has been recorded in ancient sex manuals.
4. According to your text, most people _______ ethnocentric.
   a. are
   b. are not
5. The term *cultural* ____________ refers to a perspective on cultural differences that involves understanding the beliefs and practices of other cultures according to the values and standards of that culture.
   a. *relativism*
   b. *standardization*
   c. *evaluation*
   d. *neutrality*
6. What are *folkways*?
   a. attempts to mimic a cultural practice from one society in a different society
   b. myths that are passed from generation to generation
   c. ways in which people commonly violate laws
   d. the custom and traditions of society
7. By comparing the Mangaians and the inhabitants of Inis Beag, we can conclude that the sexual beliefs, values, and norms
   a. vary widely across societies.
   b. are largely similar across societies.
8. According to a national sample of U.S. adults, the average age at first intercourse is
   a. 14.5.
   b. 16.
   c. 17.5.
   d. 19.
9. In the United States, couples have intercourse on average
   a. once a week.
   b. once a month.
   c. twice a month.
   d. twice a week.
10. Traditionally, what would happen to an Aleut wife if she had sex with a houseguest?
    a. She would be expected to give the child to the houseguest.
    b. She would be abandoned and left to die.
    c. Her husband would divorce her.
    d. none of the above.
11. Among the Masai in Arusha, Tanzania (East Africa), what does it mean if a husband sees a spear outside his wife's house?
    a. His wife has her menstrual period.
    b. His wife is having sex with another man.
    c. His wife is having sex with another woman.
    d. His wife is divorcing him.
12. In some countries, adultery many be punished by death.
    a. True
    b. False
13. Incest is ____________ in most societies.
    a. tolerated but not encouraged
    b. encouraged
    c. prohibited
    d. ignored
14. In countries where female genital operations (or female genital mutilation) are performed, who typically performs the operations?
    a. the woman's husband
    b. the woman's father
    c. the local doctor
    d. women in the village
15. The majority of the world's men ____________ circumcised.
    a. are
    b. are not
16. In the United States, boys who follow the "Boy Code" (as defined by Pollack, 2000) rarely display emotions, other than
    a. anger.
    b. fear.
    c. joy.
    d. sadness.

REFERENCES

Altschuler, M. (1972). Cayapa personality and sexual motivation. In D. S. Marshall & R. C. Suggs (Eds.), *Human sexual behavior* (pp. 38–58). Englewood Cliffs, NJ: Prentice-Hall.

American Council on Education and University of California. (2001). The American freshman: National norms for fall, 2001. Los Angeles: Los Angeles Higher Education Research Institute. U.C.L.A. Graduate School of Education and Information Studies.

Bosch, X. (2001). Female genital mutilation in developed countries. *The Lancet, 358,* 1177–1179.

Brown, D. E. (1991). *Human universals*. Philadelphia: Temple University Press.

Cainkar, L. (1996). Immigrant Palestinian women evaluate their lives. In B. C. Aswad & B. Bilge (Eds.), *Family & gender among American Muslims: Issues facing Middle Eastern immigrants and their descendants* (pp. 41–58). Philadelphia: Temple.

Cecil, R. (1996). Introduction: An insignificant event? Literary and anthropological perspectives on pregnancy loss. In R. Cecil (Ed.), *The anthropology of pregnancy loss: Comparative studies in miscarriage, stillbirth, and neonatal death* (pp. 1–14). Herndon, VA: Berg.

Dalton, H. L. (1989). AIDS in blackface. *Daedelus, 118,* 205–227.

Dandash, K. F., Refaat, A. H., & Eyada, M. (2001). Female genital mutilation: A descriptive study. *Journal of Sex and Marital Therapy, 27,* 453–458.

Davenport, W. H. (1977). Sex in cross-cultural perspective. In E. A. Beach (Ed.), *Human sexuality in four perspectives* (pp. 115–163). Baltimore: Johns Hopkins University Press.

Davenport, W. H. (1987). An anthropological approach. In J. H. Geer & W. T. O'Donohue (Eds.), *Theories of human sexuality* (pp. 197–236). New York: Plenum Press.

De La Cancela, V. (1989). Minority AIDS prevention: Moving beyond cultural perspectives towards sociopolitical empowerment. *AIDS Education and Prevention, 1,* 141–153.

Drakulic, S. (1990, July/August). In their own words: Women of Eastern Europe. *Ms.*, 36–47.

Dugger, C. W. (1996, October 5). Genital ritual is unyielding in Africa. *New York Times*, pp. 1, 6.

Dugger, C. W. (1996, October 12). New law bans genital cutting in the United States. *New York Times*, pp. 1, 28.

Elliston, D. A. (1995). Erotic anthropology: "Ritualized homosexuality" in Melanesia and beyond. *American Anthropologist, 22,* 848–867.

Engel, J. W. (1982). *Changes in male female relationships and family life in People's Republic of China* (research series 014). College of Tropical Agriculture and Human Resources, University of Hawaii.

Epstein, D., Graham, P., & Rimsza, M. (2001). Medical complications of female genital mutilation. *Journal of American College Health,* 49, 275–286.

Frayser, S. G. (1985). *Varieties of sexual experience*. New Haven, CT: Human Relations Area Files Press.

Freeman, D. (1983). *Margaret Mead and Samoa: The making and unmaking of an anthropological myth*. Cambridge, MA: Harvard University Press.

Gagnon, J. H., Giami, A., Michaels, S., & Colomby, P. (2001). A comparative study of the couple in the social organization of sexuality in France and the United States. *The Journal of Sex Research,* 38, 24–34.

Gray, J. P., & Wolfe, L. D. (1992). An anthropological look at human sexuality. In W. H. Masters, V. E. Johnson, & R. C. Kolodny (Eds.), *Human sexuality* (4th ed.). LaPorte, IN: HarperCollins.

Greenberg, J. B., & Neuman, M. S. (1999). *The AIDS evaluation of street outreach projects (AESOP): What we have learned from the AIDS evaluation of street outreach projects: A summary document*. Retrieved September 22, 2002, from National Center for HIV, STD and TB Prevention, Centers for Disease Control and Prevention Web site: www.cdc.gov/nchstp/dstd/Research/aesop.pdf

Gregersen, E. (1983). *Sexual practices: The story of human sexuality*. New York: Franklin Watts.

Gruenbaum, E. (2001). The movement against clitoridectomy and infibulation in Sudan: Public health policy and the Women's Movement. In C. B. Brettell (Ed.) (with C. F. Sargent), *Gender in cross-cultural perspective* (pp. 480–492). Upper Saddle River, NJ: Prentice-Hall.

Haddad, Y. Y., & Smith, J. I. (1996). Islamic values among American Muslims. In B. C. Aswad & B. Bilge (Eds.), *Family & gender among American Muslims: Issues facing Middle Eastern immigrants and their descendants* (pp. 19–40). Philadelphia: Temple.

Hatano, Y. (1991). Changes in sexual activities of Japanese youth. *Journal of Sex Education and Therapy, 17,* 1–14.

Hatfield, E., & Rapson, R. L. (1996). *Love and sex: Cross-cultural perspectives*. Boston: Allyn and Bacon.

Herdt, G. (1991). Commentary on status of sex research: Cross-cultural implications of sexual development. *Journal of Psychology and Human Sexuality, 4,* 5–12.

Hrdy, S. (1993). A disputed legacy. In D. N. Suggs & A. W. Miracle (Eds.), *Culture and sexuality* (pp. 19–37). Pacific Grove, CA: Brooks/Cole. (Original work published 1981).

Hrdy, S. B. (1981). *The woman that never evolved*. Cambridge, MA: Harvard University Press.

James, S. M., & Robertson, C. C. (Eds.). (2002). *Genital cutting and transnational sisterhood: Disputing U.S. polemics*. Urbana, IL: University of Illinois Press.

Kennedy, M. (2002, January). Presentation on infibulation. Department of Sociology, East Carolina University.

Knox, D., Zusman, M. E., Buffington, C., & Hemphill, G. (2000). Interracial dating attitudes among college students. *College Student Journal, 34,* 69–71.

LaFromboise, T. D., Heyle, A. M., & Ozer, E. J. (1999). Changing and diverse roles of women in American Indian cultures. In L. A. Peplau, S. C. DeBro, R. C. Veniegas, & P. L. Taylor (Eds.), *Gender, culture, and ethnicity: Current research about women and men* (pp. 48–61). Mountain View, CA: Mayfield.

Lane, S. D. & Rubinstein R. A. (1996). Judging the other: Responding to traditional female genital surgeries. *Hastings Center Report, 26* (3, 31-40).

Laumann, E. O., & Michael, R. T. (2001). Introduction: Setting the scene. In E. O. Laumann & R. T. Michael (Eds.), *Sex, love, and health in America: Private choices and public policies* (pp. 1–37). Chicago: The University of Chicago Press.

Leonard, L. (2000). Interpreting female genital cutting: Moving beyond the impasse. *Annual Review of Sex Research, 11*, 158–191.

Levi-Strauss, C. (1993). The incest prohibition. In D. N. Suggs & A. W. Miracle (Eds.), *Culture and sexuality* (pp. 229–236). Pacific Grove, CA: Brooks/Cole. (Original work published 1969).

Lightfoot-Klein, H., Chase, C., Hammond, T., & Goldman, R. (2000). Genital surgery on children below the age of consent. In L. T. Szuchman & F. Muscarella (Eds.), *Psychological perspectives on human sexuality* (pp. 440–479). New York: John Wiley & Sons.

Mackay, J. (2000). *The Penguin atlas of human sexual behavior.* New York: Penguin.

Malinowski, B. (1927). *Sex and repression in savage society.* New York: Harcourt, Brace.

Malinowski, B. (1929). *Sexual life of savages in north-western Melanesia.* New York: Halcyon House.

Marshall, D. S. (1971). Sexual behavior on Mangaia. In D. S. Marshall & R. C. Suggs (Eds.), *Human sexual behavior: Variations in the ethnographic spectrum* (pp. 103–162). New York: Basic Books.

McCarthy, S. (1996, July/August). Fleeing mutilation, fighting for asylum. *Ms.*, 12–16.

Mead, M. (1928). *Coming of age in Samoa.* Middlesex: Penguin Books.

Merriam, A. P. (1972). Aspects of sexual behavior among the Bala (Basongye). In D. S. Marshall & R. C. Suggs (Eds.), *Human sexual behavior* (pp. 71–102). Englewood Cliffs, NJ: Prentice-Hall.

Messenger, J. C. (1993). Sex and repression in an Irish folk community. In D. N. Suggs & A. W. Miracle (Eds.), *Culture and sexuality* (pp. 240–261). Pacific Grove, CA: Brooks/Cole. (Original work published 1971).

Meston, C. M., Trapnell, P. D., & Gorzalka, B. B. (1996). Ethnic and gender differences in sexuality: Variations in sexual behavior between Asian and non-Asian university students. *Archives of Sexual Behavior, 25*, 33–41.

Michael, R. T, Gagnon, J. H., Laumann, E. O., & Kolata, G. (1994). *Sex in America: A definitive survey.* Boston: Little, Brown.

Michal-Johnson, P., & Bowen, S. P. (1992). The place of culture in HIV education. In T. Edgar, M. A. Fitzpatrick, & V. S. Freimuth (Eds.), *AIDS: A communication perspective* (pp. 147–172). Hillsdale, NJ: Lawrence Erlbaum.

Money, J., & Ehrhardt, A. A. (1973). *Man and woman, boy and girl.* Baltimore: Johns Hopkins University Press.

Nolen-Hoeksema, S. (2001). *Abnormal psychology* (2nd ed.). Boston: McGraw-Hill.

Pollack, W. S. (with Shuster, T.). (2000). *Real boys' voices.* New York: Penguin.

Shepherd, G. (1987). Rank, gender, and homosexuality: Mombasa as a key to understanding sexual options. In P. Caplan (Ed.), *The social construction of sexuality.* New York: Tavistock.

Shostak, M. (1983). *Nisa: The life and words of a !Kung woman.* New York: Vintage.

Sprecher, S., & Hatfield, E. (1996). Premarital sexual standards among U.S. college students: Comparison with Russian and Japanese students. *Archives of Sexual Behavior, 25*, 261–288.

Sprecher, S., Barbee, A., & Schwartz, P. (1995). Was it good for you, too? Gender differences in first sexual intercourse experiences. *The Journal of Sex Research, 32*, 3–15.

Statistical Abstract of the United States: 2002. (2002). 122nd ed. Washington, DC: U.S. Bureau of the Census.

Stephens, W. N. (1982). *The family in cross-cultural perspective.* Washington, DC: University Press of America.

Tafoya, T. (1989). Pulling coyote's tale: Native American sexuality and AIDS. In V. M. Mays, G. W. Albee, & S. F. Schneider (Eds.), *Primary prevention of AIDS: Psychological approaches* (pp. 280–289). Newbury Park, CA: Sage.

Tafoya, T., & Wirth, D. A. (1996). Native American two-spirit men. In J. F. Longres (Ed.), *Men of color: A context for service to homosexually active men* (pp. 51–67). New York: Haworth.

Tang, C. S., Lai, E. D., Phil, M., & Chung, T. K. H. (1997). Assessment of sexual functioning for Chinese college students. *Archives of Sexual Behavior, 26*, 79–90.

Trexler, R. C. (2002). Making the American berdache: Choice or constraint? *Journal of Social History, 35*, 613–638.

Wade, C., & Tavris, C. (1999). Gender and culture. In L. A. Peplau, S. C. DeBro, R. C. Veniegas, & P. L. Taylor (Eds.), *Gender, culture, and ethnicity: Current research about women and men* (pp. 15–22). Mountain View, CA: Mayfield.

Whatley, M. (2002). The attitudes toward interracial dating scale. Valdosta, GA: Valdosta State University, Department of Psychology.

10

Partner Communication and Sexuality

Chapter Outline

My wife said I don't listen to her—at least I think that's what she said.
—Laurence J. Peter, humorist

"You can't screw a relationship together" is a profound statement psychologist Dr. Robert Birch sometimes uses to emphasize the importance of communicating about relationship issues as a prerequisite for a good sexual relationship. And when the foundation of a good relationship is built, it is equally as important to communicate clearly about one's sexual desires and preferences. The following examples illustrate the need for communicating about sexuality:

> *Mary is involved in an emotional and sexual relationship with Tom. Cunnilingus is the only way she can experience an orgasm, but she is reluctant to talk to Tom about her need. She has a dilemma: If she tells Tom, she risks his disapproval and his rejection of doing what she asks. If she does not tell Tom about her need, she risks growing resentful and feeling dissatisfied in their sexual relationship.*

> *Bob has drifted into a flirtatious relationship with a woman in his office. He is emotionally and sexually attracted to her. He knows she feels the same. Bob is also in love with Karen and is committed to her emotionally and sexually. Should he tell Karen about his attraction to the woman at work? Should he disclose that he has dreamed about her? That he has sexual fantasies about her? How open should he be?*

> *Carol and her husband, Dean, get into frequent arguments. Their pattern is that, after arguing, they "cool off" by not talking to each other for a few hours. Then Dean usually approaches Carol for sex as a way to "make up." Carol always wants to talk about their conflict and resolve it before having sex, but she is afraid that if she rejects Dean's sexual advances, he will become angry again. What should she do?*

Communication The exchange of messages between two or more people.

The individuals in these scenarios would probably ask themselves two questions: "What should I say?" and "How should I say it?" These two questions reflect the awareness that **communication** involves both information and the process of exchanging information between individuals. The information, or messages exchanged between individuals, is referred to as the *content* of the communication. The way in which the information is delivered, received, and responded to is referred to as the *process* of communication.

In this chapter, we discuss the importance of communication in achieving intimacy, relationship, and sexual satisfaction; review some principles of effective communication; discuss honesty in relationships; and examine how conflicts in relationships can be resolved. Our premise is that good communication patterns are associated with relationship and sexual satisfaction.

10-1 INTIMACY, RELATIONSHIP, AND SEXUAL SATISFACTION

It's more important to be right with each other than it is to be right.
—Fraley and Marilyn Bost, married 27 years

Intimacy The emotional closeness and bond between two individuals.

Most U.S. adults value being in an intimate love relationship. Although we commonly use and hear the term *sexual intimacy*, not all sexual encounters are intimate. Likewise, not all intimate relationships are sexual. **Intimacy** refers to the emotional closeness and bond between two individuals. Although two newly acquainted individuals may experience strong feelings of passion toward one another, intimacy develops over time as they disclose their views, values, histories, goals, fears, dislikes, and preferences to each other. This process of self-disclosure, or communicating personal information to another person, is a major factor that influences a couple's level of intimacy. Disclosing personal information is not only essential for the development of an intimate love relationship, but it is also important for maintaining intimacy with one's partner over time. Women are significantly more likely than men to disclose (Gallmeier, Zusman, Knox, & Gibson, 1997), and the higher the level of disclosure, the more committed spouses report that they are to each other (Patford, 2000).

Cultural Diversity 

Individuals in Japan are taught that quick self-disclosure in social relationships is inappropriate. They are much less likely to disclose information about themselves than are individuals socialized in the United States (Nakanishi, 1986).

In addition to disclosure as a mechanism to achieve and maintain intimacy, communication is also important for relationship and sexual satisfaction. In a study of 53 women and 34 men married or cohabiting an average of 13 years, the researchers found that the greater the satisfaction with communication in general, the greater the reported sexual satisfaction (MacNeil & Byers, 1997).

Finally, a number of longitudinal studies of couples reveal that communication problems and poor handling of marital conflicts are effective predictors of future marital distress or divorce (Gottman, 1994; Stanley & Markman, 1995). Over time, destructive interactional patterns undermine couples' happiness "through the active erosion of love, sexual attraction, friendship, trust, and commitment" (Stanley & Markman, 1995, p. 392). Good communication requires an understanding and use of basic principles. After looking at various theories on communication, we identify some basic principles of communication.

Think About It 

Can individuals who are not sexually involved with one another have an intimate relationship? Can individuals who are sexually involved with one another have a relationship that is not intimate? How can individuals avoid confusing "relationship intimacy" with "sexual intimacy"?

10-2 COMMUNICATION THEORY

Because communication involves interaction in social contexts, we examine various theoretical frameworks for relationship communication. Models of communication come from the fields of mathematics, psychology, and sociology; they focus on various aspects of the communication process (Bitner, 1988). Three that seem especially relevant to communication between couples include identity formation theories, social learning theory, and social exchange theory.

10-2a Identity Formation Theory

One reason that interpersonal communication is so important, according to such theorists as George Herbert Mead and Erik Erikson, is that our self-identity develops largely as a result of social interaction (Giffin & Patton, 1976). We learn about ourselves from the responses others make to us; their communications give us cues about how important, capable, or inadequate we are. Cooley (1964) coined the term **looking glass self** to describe the idea that the image people have of themselves is a reflection of what other people tell them about themselves. Reflections from others that are inconsistent or contradictory with one's self-image may cause tension or anxiety. Communication to

Looking glass self The idea that the image people have of themselves is a reflection of what other people tell them about themselves

request clarification or explanation may help to reduce the discomfort. At times discrepancies in feedback may be due to differing perspectives. For example, would your participating in a sexual hook-up be adventurous or immoral? Giffin and Patton (1976, p. 57) suggested, "...you will need to employ interpersonal communication for further evaluation of your own self-image as it is reflected by those in whom you have the greatest confidence."

So, although one can gain a clearer picture of self through interpersonal communication, it is important that these images are accurately perceived and honestly reflected back (Giffin & Patton, 1976). According to Giffin and Patton, this is best accomplished through a combination of offering self-disclosure and obtaining feedback from trusted, honest people. However, their recommendations for how to accomplish this focus on abstract concepts (self-actualization) rather than specific behaviors. Recommendations for how to make optimal use of the communication process to improve relationships are available in the social learning theory and social exchange models.

10-2b Social Learning Theory

Couple communication is often specified as the verbal behavior of partners, which may be assessed and modified according to the same operant principles as those guiding other behaviors. Verbal behavior is influenced by its consequences; stimuli following verbal behavior can increase or diminish the future rate of response, depending on whether the behavior is reinforced or punished. For example, if a person expresses an opinion and the partner says "good," "mm-hm," "neat," or "correct," this is likely to be a verbal reinforcer. However, if the partner says, "you're wrong," "uh-uh," or "you're crazy," this is likely to be punishing. However, as Thomas (1977) observed, neither the content of a statement nor the intent of the speaker determines whether a behavior is actually reinforcing or punishing; this is determined by observing the result. For example, in a lively political discussion, if a partner says "I disagree," this may encourage the respondent to elaborate on his or her opinion.

Verbal statements may be discriminative or serve as cues for other types of responses. For example, a partner may say, "I am going upstairs to take a shower" (in other words, "I am getting cleaned up to prepare for intimacy"). A discriminative stimulus may also be used to cue that a behavior will not lead to reinforcement, as when the partner replies, "I am not in the mood."

Tracking verbal behaviors may be quite complex; the speakers may shift rapidly, and the contingencies for verbalizations may be different with each interchange. Therefore, careful analysis may be needed to determine the antecedent-consequent relationships for interactions (Thomas, 1977).

10-2c Social Exchange Theory

Social exchange theorists combine behavioral psychology and economic theory (Galvin & Brommel, 1982). Exchange theorists suggest that the interaction between partners can be described as a ratio of rewards to costs. For example, two strangers who meet with the possibility of hooking up will continue to interact only if each has a high ratio of rewards at little cost. *Rewards* are positive outcomes of the interaction—each smiles at the other, says nice things, touches the other gently and nondemandingly, etc. *Costs* refer to negative outcomes of the interaction, such as receiving criticism or feeling regret, which make the interaction painful. As long as the rewards outweigh the costs (and there is a profit for the interaction), the relationship will continue. When the costs are higher than the rewards (and there is a loss for the interaction), the relationship will stop. In long-term relationships, a person may forgo immediate rewards in anticipation of long-term gain. Although this idea doesn't sound romantic, sociological theorists observe that even love relationships are established and continued on the basis of reciprocity—exchanged benefits and costs.

Social learning theory and social exchange theory have provided the conceptual basis for a number of interventions to enhance couples' communication and prevent marital distress. Rather than focus on personality dimensions that do not seem very amenable to change, therapists and educators have drawn from behavioral marital therapy principles to develop programs to help couples change negative communication patterns. Many of the concepts included in their curricula are summarized in section 10-3.

10-3 PRINCIPLES OF EFFECTIVE COMMUNICATION IN INTIMATE RELATIONSHIPS

As important as communication is for developing and sustaining fulfilling and enduring relationships, U.S. adults receive little training or education in the art of communication. In sections 10-3a through 10-3k, we review some of the principles common to intimate, sexual relationships.

10-3a Initiate Discussion of Important Issues

Effective communication means addressing important issues. Failure to bring up a nagging recurring relationship issue may translate into the issue never being addressed (recall our earlier discussion in section 1-2a, "Not to Decide Is to Decide"). In a study of 203 undergraduates, women were significantly more likely than men to initiate discussions of a problem in their relationships (Knox, Hatfield, & Zusman, 1998). However, Samp and Solomon (2001) noted that communicating a problem behavior to a partner was least likely if the partner was perceived as not being committed to the relationship.

With the potential risk for HIV and sexually transmitted diseases (STDs), talking about condom use with a sexual partner is an important topic. But only a third of 210 undergraduates reported consistent use of a condom in the past month (Civic, 2000). Those most likely to discuss previous sexual partner issues in assessing the need for a condom were more likely to be in a committed relationship and to not have been drinking (Moore & Davidson, 2000). Sometimes bringing up a discussion about condom use results in one partner trying to persuade the other not to use a condom. In a sample of 954 university students, 15% of the women and almost 17% of the men admitted trying to talk their partners out of using a condom. Forty-one percent of the women and 30% of the men reported that a partner had tried to dissuade them from using a condom (Oncale & King, 2001). In another study, respondents reported using a series of both verbal (suggesting, demanding) and nonverbal (actually putting the condom on, withholding sex until the condom was on) strategies to get their partner to use a condom (Bird, Harvey, & Beckman, 2001).

Having conversations about condom use is important! According to a meta-analysis of 26 studies (involving 5,511 participants), those who talked about condoms prior to having sex were more likely than nontalkers to use condoms. If such a conversation occurred, there was a 38% increase in the probability of condom use (Allen, Emmers-Sommer, & Crowell, 2002).

Think About It

Sometimes partners do not initiate discussion of a particular issue because they fear disapproval from the partner for doing so. But not to initiate such a discussion may result in resentment that will impact the partner even more. To what degree do you feel comfortable bringing up important topics that you feel will make you or your partner uncomfortable?

Another obstacle to discussing important issues is fear of rejection. Box 10-1 examines issues related to disclosing one's sexual health history to one's partner.

Box 10-1 Social Choices

Consequences for Revealing Having an STD

Individuals often struggle over whether, or how, to tell a partner about their sexual health condition or history. If a person in a committed relationship becomes infected with an STD, that individual, or his or her partner, may have been unfaithful and had sex with someone outside the relationship. Thus, disclosure about an STD may also mean confessing one's own infidelity or confronting one's partner about his or her possible infidelity. (However, the infection may have occurred prior to the current relationship but was undetected.)

For women in abusive relationships, telling their partner that they have an STD often involves fear that their partner will react violently. Individuals who are infected with an STD and who are beginning a new relationship face a different set of concerns. Will their new partner view them negatively? Will they want to continue the relationship or end the relationship abruptly?

Examples of what individuals who had herpes disclosed and the actual reactions by the partner follow:

In one case an individual told five partners in an upfront manner on the first date. Trying to make it a little funny, he said,

> "I guess I should tell you something. . . . Before you fall madly in love with me and we run away to Las Vegas and get married . . . I have Herpes." In every case, five out of five, the first date was the last!

Trying another approach, the individual with herpes waited until later in the relationship when he felt the time was right for intimacy:

> Second verse almost the same as the first. Four out of five never saw me again.

Another person had a more positive experience:

> We began kissing madly, and eventually I felt I must tell him I have herpes. After I got the words out he looked at me with delight and said, "Does that mean you're planning to sleep with me? That's marvelous!" ("Treatment Update," 1997, pp. 3–4)

Although telling a partner about having an STD may be difficult and embarrassing, avoiding disclosure or lying about having an STD represents a serious ethical violation. Even if a condom is used (e.g., "I won't tell, I'll just use a condom"), they do not provide 100% protection, so the partner has a right to have the information of the presence of an STD so that he or she can make a decision about taking a risk.

The responsibility to inform a partner that one has an STD—before having sex with that partner—is a moral one. But there are also legal reasons for disclosing one's sexual health condition to a partner. If you have an STD and you do not tell your partner, you may be liable for damages if you transmit the disease to your partner. In more than half the states, transmission of a communicable disease, including many STDs, is considered a crime. According to the North Dakota Century Code

> . . . if the procedures of the previous section have been exhausted, and a person believed to be infected with HIV continues to engage in behavior that presents an imminent danger to the public health, a court may issue other orders, including an order to take the person into custody, for a period not to exceed 90 days and place the person in a facility designated or approved by the state health officer. (American Civil Liberties Union, 1998)

Some states and cities have **partner notification laws** that require health-care providers to advise all persons with serious sexually transmitted diseases about the importance of informing their sex or needle-sharing partner (or partners). Partner notification laws may also require health-care providers to either notify any partners the infected person names or forward the information about partners to the Department of Health, where public health officers notify the partner (or partners) that he or she has been exposed to an STD and schedule an STD testing appointment. The privacy of the infected individual is protected by not revealing his or her name to the partner being notified of potential infection. In cases where the infected person refuses to identify partners, standard partner notification laws require doctors to undertake notification without cooperation, if they know whom the partner or spouse is. Although there is some public support for partner notification laws, the American Civil Liberties Union is against such laws . . . "Scientific research shows that partner notification that is not voluntary or that is linked to HIV surveillance through name reporting will not work" (http://www.aclu.org/issues/aids/hiv_partner.html#I).

Before ending this section, let's examine how the partner being told of an STD might respond. One of the underlying causes for the spread of STDs among college-aged students is the fear that telling a potential partner will result not only in personal rejection, but "the whole university knowing." To express appreciation for the honesty of the disclosure, to show compassion, and to guarantee confidentiality would be a welcome response to the disclosing party. One coed disclosed to a partner that she had an STD. She said of his response, "He held me, told me he knew it was hard for me to tell him, and that we would get through this. He was wonderful and we are still together."

Partner notification laws A set of laws that require health-care providers to advise all persons with serious sexually transmitted diseases about the importance of informing their sex or needle-sharing partner (or partners).

10-3b Choose Good Timing

The phrase "timing is everything" can be applied to interpersonal communication. In general, it is best to discuss important or difficult issues when partners are alone together in private with no distractions, both partners have ample time to talk, and both partners are rested and sober. Avoid discussing important issues when you or your partner are tired or under unusual stress. If one partner (or both) is very upset, it may be best to wait awhile until things have "cooled off" before discussing an issue. If you are not sure whether the timing is right, you can always ask your partner by saying something like (assuming the topic is the future of the relationship) "Can we talk about where this relationship is going?" "Is this a good time for you to talk?" Likewise, if your partner brings up an issue and it is not a good time for you to discuss the matter, suggest a specific alternative time to have the discussion. Good timing in communication also means that information should be communicated at a time that allows the receiver to make an informed response. For example, discussions about sexual issues, such as pregnancy prevention, STD protection, and monogamy, should occur *before* partners engage in sexual activity.

Regardless of what these individuals have said, what is their nonverbal message to each other?

10-3c Give Congruent Messages

The process of communication involves both verbal and nonverbal messages. **Verbal messages** are the words individuals say to each other. **Nonverbal messages** include facial expressions, gestures, bodily contact, and tone of voice. What happens when verbal and nonverbal messages do not match? For example, suppose Lashanda and Brian are giving feedback about the last time they had sex. Lashanda says to Brian, "It was good"; yet she has a sullen facial expression and tone of voice and does not make eye contact. Lashanda's verbal and nonverbal messages are not congruent—they do not match. When this happens, the other partner typically gives more weight to the nonverbal message (L'Abate & Bagarozzi, 1993). In this scenario, Brian would probably give more weight to the nonverbal message, thus believing that Lashanda did not enjoy their most recent sexual experience. He might also feel that she was not being honest with him.

Verbal messages Words individuals say to each other.

Nonverbal messages Type of communication in which facial expressions, gestures, bodily contact, and tone of voice predominate.

Think About It

Krahe and Kolpin (2000) noted the importance of being clear about one's wishes and emphasized the need to avoid two main forms of ambiguous communication: token resistance (saying "no" when you mean "yes") and compliance (saying "yes" when you mean "no"). Failure to be clear leaves one vulnerable to sexual aggression. To what degree are you aware of having used these forms of ambiguous communication?

Of course, individuals are not always direct in communicating issues to each other. Hickman and Muehlenhard (1999) surveyed 214 female and 210 male undergraduates to assess how they signaled their consent to have sexual intercourse. While "not resisting" was the most frequent method of consent, women were more likely than men to use indirect verbal signals (e.g., asking whether the other person had a condom). Men, in contrast, were more likely than women to use indirect nonverbal signals (e.g., touching, kissing, or caressing the other person).

The self-assessment in Box 10-2 assesses the verbal and nonverbal ways in which partners communicate interest in sexual interactions.

10-3d Minimize Criticism; Maximize Compliments

Research on marital interaction has consistently shown that one brutal "zinger" can erase 20 acts of kindness (Notarius & Markman, 1994). Because intimate partners are capable of hurting each other so deeply, it is important not to criticize your partner. Calling a partner "fat," "stupid," or a "lousy lover" can devastate him or her.

Box 10-2 Self-Assessment

The Sexual Signaling Behaviors Inventory

When you think your partner can be persuaded to have sex though he or she has not yet become aware of your desire, what do you usually do? Check all items that apply.

_______ A. ask directly
_______ B. use some code words with which (s)he is familiar
_______ C. use more eye contact
_______ D. use touching (snuggling, kissing, etc.)
_______ E. change appearance or clothing
_______ F. remove clothing
_______ G. change tone of voice
_______ H. make indirect talk of sex
_______ I. do more favors for the other
_______ J. set mood atmosphere (music, lighting, etc.)
_______ K. share a drink
_______ L. tease
_______ M. look at sexual material
_______ N. play games such as chase or light "roughhousing"
_______ O. make compliments ("I love you," "You're nice")
_______ P. use some force
_______ Q. use "suggestive" body movements or postures
_______ R. allow hands to wander
_______ S. lie down
_______ T. other (describe ___________)

This scale was developed by Dr. Clinton Jesser (1978), a sociology professor who was interested in determining how college students communicate to their heterosexual partners when they want coitus (sexual intercourse). He wondered whether women would use more indirect signals than men and whether men would evaluate women's indirect communication as more desirable. He surveyed 153 students at a large Midwestern university and examined the responses of the 50 men (90%) and 75 women (71%) in the sample who were coitally experienced. The most frequently reported signals were "use touching (snuggling, kissing, etc.)" and "allow hands to wander," which were both endorsed by more than 70% of the men and the women. The next most frequent item was "ask directly," which was reported by 58% of the women and 56% of the men. Although there was essentially no difference in the reports of men and women who said they ask directly, women were more likely to report using eye contact, changing their appearance or clothing, and changing their tone of voice. The women who used the direct approach (42 of the 75) were no more likely to be rebuffed than those using an indirect approach. No formal checks of the reliability or validity of this measure have been made, although Dr. Jesser noted that more women report being direct than are perceived by men as being direct. Dr. Jesser (1998) suggested that the Sexual Signaling Behaviors Inventory could be used with gay and lesbian participants.

Reference

Jesser, C. J. (1998). The sexual signaling behaviors inventory. In C. M. Davis, W. L. Yarber, R. Bauserman, G. Schreer, & S. L. Davis (Eds.), *Sexuality Related Measures* (pp. 423–424). Thousand Oaks, CA: Sage.

Self-fulfilling prophecy Behaving in such a way as to make expectations come true. For example, caustic accusations to a partner for infidelity may actually drive the partner to be unfaithful.

Conversely, complimenting your partner and making positive remarks can enhance the relationship. Not only are sincere compliments and positive remarks good to hear, they can create a **self-fulfilling prophecy** effect. A partner who is often told that he or she is an attentive and affectionate lover is more likely to behave accordingly to make these expectations come true than a partner who receives no feedback or negative feedback.

Gottman, Coan, Carrere, and Swanson (1998) studied 130 newlywed couples to examine marital communication patterns that are predictive of marital satisfaction. He found that high positive-to-negative effect predicted satisfaction among stable couples. In fact, Gottman and his colleagues have conducted longitudinal studies with more than 2,000 married couples. They have found that, on the average, happy couples have five times as many positive interactions and expressions as negatives. This 5-to-1 rate of positives to negatives is "the magic ratio" according to Gottman (1994, p. 56). He compares this ratio to the pH of soil, the balance between acidity and alkalinity, that is essential for fertility. Likewise, a relationship must be balanced by a great deal more positivity than negativity for love to be nourished.

In Gottman's research, he has also found four negative qualities that sabotage attempts for partner communication and that emerged as the strongest predictors of divorce: criticism, contempt, defensiveness, and stonewalling (Gottman, 1994). These qualities are so potentially destructive to a relationship that he calls them "the Four Horsemen of the Apocalypse." Criticism involves an attack on the partner's personality or character (rather than a specific behavior). Contempt involves an intention to insult a partner and may involve psychological abuse. Examples include hostile humor, name-calling, and insults. Defensiveness (denying responsibility, making excuses) tends to escalate conflicts. Most symptomatic of relationship disaster is stonewalling, or shutting a partner out. "The Stonewaller just removes himself by turning into a stone wall" (p. 94).

Making positive statements is particularly important during the beginning and end of a discussion. In psychology, the term **primacy/recency effect** refers to the tendency of individuals to remember best what occurs first and last in a sequence. After discussing a difficult issue, partners may be more likely to come away with a positive feeling about the interaction if it begins and ends with positive comments. For example, suppose your partner tries a new sexual intercourse position with you that you find unpleasant. You might tell your partner, "I didn't enjoy that; please don't do it again." Or, you could say, "I am glad that you feel comfortable enough with me to try new things, but that position was a bit uncomfortable and painful for me. I'd rather be on top. Being able to tell you what I like and don't like is one of the things I like most about our relationship."

Primacy/recency effect
The tendency of individuals to remember best what occurs first and last in a sequence.

Suppose you are so upset with your partner about an issue that you begin a discussion by blurting out a negative comment. You can still end the conversation on a positive note by saying something positive like "Thank you for listening to my anger and allowing me to vent." Or, if your partner begins a discussion with a negative remark, such as "Our sex life is so boring, you never want to try anything new," you can respond with a positive comment, such as "Thank you for telling me about your frustration with our sex life. It is important for me to know how you feel."

10-3e Communicate Feelings

NATIONAL DATA Based on a survey of 1,003 men and women ages 20–29 for the National Marriage Project, 80% of women feel that a husband who can communicate about his deepest feelings is more desirable than one who makes a good living (Whitehead & Popenoe, 2001).

In intimate relationships, it is important to communicate feelings as well as thoughts. This advice sounds simple, but many people are not in touch with their feelings, or they confuse feelings with thoughts. If you listen to yourself and to others, you will hear people communicating thoughts, but these thoughts are often labeled as feelings. For example, the statement "I feel that we should be tested for STDs" is communicating an idea, not an emotion. Feelings include sadness, fear, anger, joy, excitement, guilt, boredom, anxiety, frustration, and depression. "We should be tested for STDs" is not an emotion. The statement "I am afraid to have sex with you because we have not been tested for STDs" is expressing a feeling—fear.

To communicate emotions, a person must first recognize and label, or describe, the emotions. Unfortunately, many people learn to hide and repress unpleasant feelings. Before you can communicate your emotions to a partner, you must first get in touch with your feelings and give yourself permission to feel them and talk about them. Attempts to cover up or minimize unpleasant feelings may be made with the best intentions; however, repressing your emotions or interrupting the emotions of your partner often serves to prolong the emotional state rather than to resolve it.

10-3f Tell Your Partner What You Want

In a relationship, it is important for partners to decide what they want from each other, to tell each other in clear behavioral terms what they want and do so in a positive, rather

TABLE 10-1

Rephrasing Complaints into Requests

Complaints	Requests
I don't like to make love when you are sweaty and dirty.	Please take a shower before we make love. Or, I'll guarantee better sex if you shower first.
Don't rub so hard.	Please rub more softly . . . like this.
I don't want you to stay up so late at night.	How about coming to bed at 10:30 and let me know how I can make it worth doing so?
Leave me alone; I'm trying to get ready for work!	We can have some long, slow sex after a glass of wine tonight.
Whenever I ask you to massage me, you end up wanting to have sex with me.	Half the time, it would be nice for you to massage me without expecting sex.

TABLE 10-2

Examples of Vague and Specific Communication

Vague	Specific
I want more foreplay.	I would like for us to kiss and gently rub each other more than we do now. I mean, maybe for 15 minutes or so.
I'd like us to try something new.	I'd like us to use a vibrator—I hear the Rabbit is a real buzz.
Let's spice up our sex life with a video sometime.	Let's rent an adult video Saturday night.

than negative, way. Rather than complain about what you don't want, it is helpful to make requests for, or statements about, what you do want. Table 10-1 provides examples of how complaints can be reframed into requests.

One common error people make when communicating is not being specific enough about what they want. When you tell your partner what you want, make sure you communicate clearly and precisely. Table 10-2 presents examples of vague and specific communication.

10-3g Make Statements Instead of Asking Questions

When partners are uncomfortable or unwilling to express their feelings and wants, they may put their statements in the form of questions. For example, partners who have difficulty expressing what they want may ask the question "Do you think we should see a sex therapist?" instead of making the statement "I would like for us to see a sex therapist."

Transforming statements into questions allows partners to mask or hide their true feelings, thoughts, and desires and thus interferes with the development and maintenance of relationship intimacy. Begin listening to your questions and those of your partner and try to discern which questions are really statements that are masking feelings, wants, or both. When you catch yourself or your partner doing this, rephrase the question into a statement. And remember the rule: Ask a question only when you don't know something that you need to know.

Open-ended question A broad question designed to elicit a great deal of information.

Closed-ended question Type of question that yields little information and can be answered in one word.

10-3h Ask Open-Ended Questions

When you want information from your partner, asking open-ended questions is helpful. An **open-ended question** is a broad question designed to elicit a lot of information. In contrast, a **closed-ended question** can be answered in one word. Open-ended questions are useful in finding out your partner's feelings, thoughts, and desires. Table 10-3 provides examples of open- and closed-ended questions.

TABLE 10-3

Open-Ended and Closed-Ended Questions

Open-Ended Question	Closed-Ended Questions
What are your thoughts about condom use?	Do you have a condom?
What can I do to please you sexually?	Would you like oral sex?
Do you want to have children? How many?	Tell me your thoughts about having children.
Do you want to try a rear-entry position? Have sex in the rocking chair? Blindfold me?	How do you feel about trying something new?
Do you believe in abortion?	What are your views on abortion?

One way to use open-ended questions in a sexual relationship is to follow the **touch-and-ask-rule,** whereby each touch and caress is accompanied by the question "How does that feel?" The partner then gives feedback. By using this rule, a couple can learn a lot about how to please each other. Guiding and moving the partner's hand or body are also ways of giving feedback.

Touch-and-ask rule Sexual technique whereby each touch and caress is accompanied by the question "How does that feel?" to be followed by feedback from the partner.

Reflective listening Communication technique in which one person restates the meaning of what his or her partner has said in a conversation.

10-3i Use Reflective Listening

The first duty of love is to listen.

—Paul Tillich, theologian

One of the most important communication skills is the art of **reflective listening,** or restating the meaning of what your partner has said to you in a conversation. When you use reflective listening, your partner is more likely to feel that you are truly listening and that you understand his or her feelings, thoughts, and desires. In practicing reflective listening, it is important to repeat both the ideas or thoughts expressed by your partner, as well as the emotions that your partner has conveyed. For example, suppose that after you have made love, your partner says, "Next time, can we spend a little more time on foreplay?" You might respond by reflecting back your partner's message: "It sounds like you are feeling frustrated because you didn't get enough foreplay, and in the future, you would like us to have more foreplay before we have intercourse." Another example of a reflective statement you could use is this example: "You feel frustrated that we didn't take more time to be loving and affectionate before having sex. It sounds like having more foreplay is important to you."

Using the technique of reflective listening is particularly difficult when one partner blames or criticizes the other. When people are blamed or criticized, they typically respond by withdrawing from the interaction, attacking back (through blaming or criticizing the other person), or defending or explaining themselves. Each of these responses may produce further conflict and frustration. Alternatively, instead of withdrawing, attacking back, or defending and explaining, the listener can simply reflect back what the partner has said. At some point in the discussion, the criticized partner may and should express his or her thoughts, feelings, and views on the situation. But it is best to first acknowledge the other person's feelings and thoughts through reflective listening. In Table 10-4, we present an example of a critical or accusatory remark, followed by four types of possible responses. Compare the reflective listening response with the other three responses.

This couple is using the reflective listening technique to improve their communication.

10-3j Use "I" Statements

"I" statements focus on the feelings and thoughts of the communicator without making a judgment on others. Because "I" statements are a clear and nonthreatening way of expressing what you want and how you feel, they are likely to result in a positive change in the listener's behavior.

"I" statements Statements that focus on the feelings and thoughts of the communicator without making a judgment on what the other person says or does.

TABLE 10-4

Four Responses to a Critical or Accusatory Remark

Critical or Accusatory Remark
"You told me you had never slept with anyone before. You lied to me."
Four Possible Responses
1. Withdraw from the interaction: "I can't handle this; I'm out of here."
2. Attack back: "Well, you didn't tell me you had herpes. That's lying too, you know!"
3. Defend or explain: "Being a virgin seemed so important to you; I didn't want to disappoint you. I didn't mean to hurt you."
4. Reflective listening: "You are angry at me for telling you I hadn't slept with anyone when I really had. You wish that I had been truthful with you."

"You" statements
In communication theory, those statements that blame or criticize the listener and often result in increasing negative feelings and behavior in the relationship

In contrast, **"you" statements** blame or criticize the listener and often result in increasing negative feelings and behavior in the relationship. For example, suppose you are angry at your partner for being late. Rather than say, "You are always late and irresponsible" (which is a "you" statement), you might respond with, "I get upset when you are late and would feel better if you called me when you will be delayed." The latter focuses on your feelings and a desirable future behavior rather than blaming the partner for being late.

Applying the communication principles presented in this chapter to everyday interactions can enhance both individual and relationship well-being and increase your sexual satisfaction with your partner. The principles and techniques are fairly simple, but just because using them is simple doesn't mean it is easy. To apply effective communication techniques, you must first abandon old patterns of communication. Replacing old communication patterns with new ones is not an easy task, but most couples report that the effort is worthwhile.

If you are interested in an additional resource for relationship enhancement, examples are the PREPARE Program, to prepare for marriage; the ENRICH program, to enrich your marriage (Olson & Olson, 2000); and the Prevention and Relationship Enhancement Program, or PREP (Markman, Renick, Floyd, Stanley, & Clements, 1993; Stanley & Markman, 1995; Stanley et al., 2001). Many marriage and family therapists and clergy have been trained to use these and other relationship-building curricula.

10-3k Personal Choices: What to Do When Your Partner Will Not Communicate

Loneliness is never more cruel than when it is felt in close proximity with someone who has ceased to communicate.

—Germaine Greer, writer

One of the most frustrating experiences in relationships occurs when one partner wants and tries to communicate, but the other partner will not. Of course, partners always communicate—not communicating is a way of communicating. But what if your partner will not respond to something you say? You might try the following (Duncan & Rock, 1993).

1. Change your strategy. Rather than trying to coax your partner into talking, become less available for conversation and stop trying to initiate or maintain discussion. Keep it short if a discussion does start. This strategy removes the pressure on the partner to talk and shifts the power in the relationship.
2. Interpret silence in a positive way, such as "We are so close we don't always have to be talking," or "I feel good when you're quiet because I know that it means everything is all right between us." This negates any power your partner might be expressing through silence.
3. Focus less on the relationship and more on satisfying yourself. When you do things for yourself, you need less from others in the way of attention and assurance.

♦

10-4 HONESTY AND DISHONESTY IN INTERPERSONAL COMMUNICATION

The secret of a successful marriage is no secrets.

—Bernice Hoskinson, married 50 years

Although most people agree that honesty in relationships is important, dishonesty is rampant. Lying in adolescence to parents is commonplace. Two hundred eighty-one undergraduates at a large Southeastern university completed an anonymous 26-item questionnaire about the degree to which they deceived their parents during high school. Only 5% of the respondents reported that they had never lied to their parents about "where I was." "Who I was with," "my alcohol use," and "my sexual behavior" were additional topics about which they had lied the most (Knox, Zusman, McGinty, & Gescheidler, 2001).

10-4a Forms of Dishonesty and Deception

Dishonesty and deception take various forms. In addition to telling an outright lie, people may exaggerate the truth, pretend, or conceal the truth. They may put up a good front, be two-faced, or tell a partial truth. People also engage in self-deception when they deny or fail to acknowledge their own thoughts, feelings, values, beliefs, priorities, goals, and desires.

Another form of dishonesty occurs when people withhold information or are silent about particular issues. Lerner (1993) comments on the difference between lying and withholding information:

> *In contrast to how we react to stated lies, we are slower to pass negative judgment on what is withheld. After all, no one can tell "the whole truth" all the time. . . . Deception through silence or withholding may be excused, and even praised: "My daughter is lucky I never told her about her father," "The doctor was kind enough to spare her the truth about her illness." (pp. 12–13)*

10-4b Privacy Versus Secrecy and Deception

In virtually every relationship, partners have not shared with each other details about themselves or their past. Sometimes partners do not share their feelings and concerns with each other. But when is withholding information about yourself an act of privacy, and when is it an act of secrecy or deception? When we withhold private information, we are creating or responding to boundaries between ourselves and other people. There may be no harm done in maintaining aspects of ourselves as "private" and not to be disclosed to others. Indeed, it is healthy to have and maintain boundaries between the self and others. However, the more intimate the relationship, the greater our desire is to share our most personal and private selves with our partner—and the greater the emotional consequences of not sharing.

We often withhold information or keep secrets in our intimate relationships because we fear disapproval from our partner and want to avoid conflict in the relationship. In intimate relationships, however, keeping secrets can block opportunities for healing, resolution, self-acceptance, and deeper intimacy between partners. Taylor (1997) suggested in the book *Love Affairs* that deception in intimate relationships is a form of infidelity:

> *Any betrayal is an infidelity, even the slightest and most commonplace deception. Someone who withholds from a spouse knowledge of personal finances, of associates, of how time away from home is spent, or anything whatever that would be of interest to the other, is being faithless. Equally to the point, such infidelity can be far worse than sexual inconstancy. (p. 10)*

10-4c Extent of Dishonesty Among College Students

Lying in relationships among college students is not uncommon. In one study, 77 college students kept diaries of their daily social interactions and reported telling two lies a day (DePaulo, Kirkendol, Lashy, Wyer, & Epstein, 1996). Participants said they did not regard their lies as serious and did not plan them or worry about being caught. In another study, 137 students reported 21 lies they had told to a current or past partner. The most frequently told lie, reported by 31% of the respondents, was "the number of previous sex partners" (Knox, Schacht, Hold, & Turner, 1993).

NATIONAL DATA Fifteen percent of a national sample of men infected with an STD had had sex while they were infected. Fifteen percent did not inform their partners of their infection before having intercourse (Payn, Tanfer, Billy, & Grady, 1997).

10-4d Personal Choices: Is Honesty Always the Best Policy?

Good communication often implies open communication, but how much honesty is good for a relationship? Some individuals believe that relationships can be functional only when a certain amount of illusion is maintained. Not to be told that you are overweight, not the best of lovers, and have bad manners allows you to maintain the illusion that your partner never thinks of your weight (particularly when you eat the second bag of potato chips), sexual inadequacy, or manners. You are happier and your relationship is not hampered by your partner's honesty.

Being open yourself may also be used against you. Suppose you tell your partner of all your previous partners or sexual relationships because you want an "open and honest relationship with nothing between us," but you discover that your partner uses the information against you? Was your honesty worth the disclosure?

Disclosing an extramarital affair requires special consideration; spouses might carefully consider the consequences before disclosing. Pepper Schwartz cautions spouses (particularly women) to think twice before confessing. "According to my research, only confess if you want to end your marriage, or if the relationship is so bad that you are willing to risk ending it in order to help it" (quoted by Van Matre, 1992, p. d-8). Some couples, however, may find that the disclosure of an affair by one partner forces them to examine problems in their relationship, seek marriage therapy, or both. In such cases, disclosure may ultimately result in bringing the couple closer together in an emotional sense.

Most individuals are careful about what they say to each other and, in some cases, deliberately withhold information for fear of negative outcomes. But some information should not be withheld from the partner, including previous marriages and children, a sexual orientation different from what the partner expects, alcohol or other drug addiction, a sexually transmitted disease (such as HIV or genital herpes), and any known physical disabilities (such as sterility). Disclosures of this nature include anything that would have a significant impact on the relationship.

Some individuals wait until after the marriage to disclose. One example is a cross-dresser who, fearing his wife's disapproval, did not disclose his proclivity until years after the marriage. Indeed, he never disclosed, but she found his bra and panties and confronted him. Although she was ultimately able to accept his desire to cross-dress (and they would shop together), his lack of disclosure was a definite risk. In another case a cross-dresser who had not told his wife during courtship divorced him. Although they had been married 16 years, had four children, and she viewed him as a good provider, good father, and faithful husband (he had never had sex outside their marriage), she regarded his deception across the years as unforgivable. (She found out because he had forgotten to remove his earrings one day after he had been cross-dressing.)

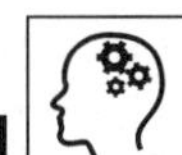

Think About It

To what degree have you been open with your partner, and to what degree do you feel your partner has been open with you? Make the case for and against being completely open with one's partner.

10-5 RESOLVING CONFLICT IN RELATIONSHIPS

It's not the differences between partners that cause problems but how the differences are handled when they arise.

—Clifford Notarius and Howard Markman, marriage therapists

Being able to resolve conflict is an essential skill for relationship survival, maintenance, and satisfaction. Of 343 university students surveyed, more than half (56%) reported having a very troublesome relationship within the past 5 years. Of those who had a troubled relationship, most (69%) reported talking to the partner in an attempt to resolve the problem; 19% avoided discussing the problem, and 18% avoided the partner (Levitt, Silver, & Franco, 1996). Knox et al. (1998) studied 203 undergraduates and identified the most to least difficult relationship problems to discuss were (in that order) the future of the relationship, ex-partners, sex, and jealousy .

Howard Markman (developer of the PREP curriculum mentioned in section 10-3j) is head of the Center for Marital and Family Studies at the University of Denver. He and his colleagues have been studying 150 couples at yearly intervals (beginning before marriage) to determine those factors most responsible for marital success. They have found that communication skills that reflect the ability to handle conflict and disagreement are the single biggest predictor of marital success over time (Markman, Stanley, & Blumberg, 1994). According to Markman et al.,

> *Remember: it's not how much you love one another, how good your sex life is, or what problems you have with money that best predicts the future quality of your marriage. . . . The key is for you to develop constructive tactics and ground rules for handling the conflicts and disagreements that are inevitable in any significant relationship. (p. 6)*

There is also merit in developing and using conflict negotiation skills before problems develop. Not only are individuals more willing to work on issues when things are going well, but they have not developed negative patterns of response that are difficult to change. In sections 10-5a through 10-5f, we review principles and techniques that are helpful in resolving interpersonal conflict.

10-5a Approach Communication from a Premise of Respect/Negotiation

Partners who care about each other and their relationship can best achieve their relationship goals by approaching communication on a particular issue or topic from a premise of respect and negotiation. Each partner must regard the other as an equal and acknowledge that each partner's perspective and view deserve respect. Neither partner is to denigrate the partner or dictate an outcome. Rather, the goal of a discussion is for each to have a positive feeling about the outcome rather than have one's position accepted. As one spouse said, "It is better for us to be right with each other than to be right in getting your way." This context of respect and negotiation implies that emotionally and/or abusive relationships do not lend themselves to productive discussion and conflict resolution.

10-5b Address Any Recurring Issues

Some couples are uncomfortable confronting their partner to talk about issues that plague them. They fear that such confrontation will further weaken their relationship. Pam is jealous that Mark spends more time with other people at parties than with her. "When we go someplace together," she blurts out, "he drops me to disappear with someone else for two hours." Her jealousy is spreading to other areas of their relationship. "When we are walking down the street and he turns his head to look at another woman, I get furious." If Pam and Mark don't discuss her feelings about Mark's behavior, their relationship may deteriorate as a result of a negative response cycle: He looks at another woman, she gets angry, he gets angry at her getting angry and finds that he is even more attracted to other women, she gets angrier because he escalates his looking at other women, and so on.

To bring the matter up, Pam might say, "I feel jealous when you spend more time with other women at parties than with me. I need some help in dealing with these feelings." By expressing her concern in this way, she has identified the problem from her perspective and asked for her partner's cooperation in handling it (she did not attack but invited her partner's help in dealing with an issue).

10-5c Focus on What You Want (Rather Than What You Don't Want)

Dealing with conflict is more likely to result in resolution if the partners focus on what they want rather than what they don't want. For example, rather than tell Mark she doesn't want him to spend so much time with other women at parties, Pam might tell him that she wants him to spend more time with her at parties. "I'd feel better if we go together and stay together," she said. "We don't need to be joined at the hip, and we will certainly want to talk with others, but the bulk of our time there should be spent with each other."

10-5d Find Out Your Partner's Point of View

We often assume that we know what our partner thinks and why our partner does things. Sometimes we are wrong. Rather than assume how our partner thinks and feels about a particular issue, we might ask our partner open-ended questions in an effort to get him or her to tell us thoughts and feelings about a particular situation. Pam's words to Mark might be "What is it like for you when we go to parties?" "How do you feel about my jealousy?"

After your partner has shared his or her thoughts about an issue with you, it is important for you to summarize your partner's perspective in a nonjudgmental way. After Mark has told Pam how he feels about their being at parties together, she can summarize his perspective by saying, "You feel that I cling to you more than I should, and you would like me to let you wander around without feeling like you're making me angry." (She may not agree with his view, but she knows exactly what it is—and Mark knows that she knows.)

10-5e Generate Win-Win Solutions to the Conflict

Win-win solution Outcome of an interpersonal conflict whereby both people feel satisfied with the agreement or resolution.

A **win-win solution** is one in which both people involved in a conflict feel satisfied with the agreement or resolution to the conflict. It is imperative to look for win-win solutions to conflicts. Solutions in which one person wins and the other person loses involve one person not getting his or her needs met. As a result, the person who "loses" may develop feelings of resentment, anger, hurt, and hostility toward the winner and may even look for ways to get even. In this way, the winner is also a loser. In intimate relationships, one winner really means two losers.

Brainstorming Problem-solving strategy of suggesting as many alternatives as possible without evaluating them.

Generating win-win solutions to interpersonal conflicts often requires brainstorming. The technique of **brainstorming** involves suggesting as many alternatives as possible without evaluating them. Brainstorming is crucial to conflict resolution because it shifts the partners' focus from criticizing each other's perspective to working together to develop alternative solutions. Any solution may be an acceptable one as long as the solution is one of mutual agreement.

Think About It

The ability to negotiate conflict may improve across time. Mackey and O'Brien (1999) interviewed 60 wives and 60 husbands over three time periods of marriage (beginning, childrearing, empty-nest) and found that the ability of spouses to negotiate conflict improved across time. By the empty-nest phase, about three quarters of husbands and wives reported engaging in mutual decision making. To what degree are the relationships in which you are involved win-win relationships?

10-5f Evaluate and Select a Solution

After a number of solutions are generated, each solution should be evaluated and the best one selected. In evaluating solutions to conflicts, it may be helpful to ask the following questions:

- Does the solution satisfy both individuals—is it a win-win solution?
- Is the solution specific? Does the solution specify exactly who is to do what, how, and when?
- Is the solution realistic? Can both parties realistically follow through with what they have agreed to do?
- Does the solution prevent the problem from recurring?
- Does the solution specify what is to happen if the problem recurs?

Greeff and De Bruyne (2000) studied several styles of conflict and noted that the "collaborating" style was associated with the highest level of marital and spousal satisfaction. This style was characterized by each partner saying how he or she felt about a situation and cooperating to find a win-win solution. Styles that were not helpful were the "competing" (each partner tried to force his or her answer on the other—a win-lose approach) and "avoiding" (the partners would simply avoid addressing the issue and hope that it would go away) styles. This pattern of avoidance was used most frequently by depressed spouses who did not have the energy to engage their partners. Figure 10-1 summarizes the steps to take in resolving conflicts.

Think About It

Identify the last conflict you had with your partner and note which steps you took (or skipped) in an attempt to resolve the issue. Such conflict resolution becomes relevant to sexuality in that anger outside the bedroom can affect feelings of intimacy and behavior in the bedroom.

10-6 GENDER DIFFERENCES IN COMMUNICATION

Sociolinguistic scholar and author of 17 books, Deborah Tannen (1990, p. 42) stated, "Male-female conversation is cross-cultural communication." By this she meant that men and women are socialized in different same-sex cultures, and when they talk to the other sex, they are talking to a member of another culture. Tannen also found that men and women differ in public and private speaking; she explained the differences using the terms "report talk" and "rapport-talk." Men generally approach communication, even in private situations, like public speaking or giving a report. They see talk as for information. In contrast, women generally engage in "rapport-talk," using talk for interaction and establishing connections. McGinty, Knox, and Zusman (2003) also noted that women are more attentive than are men to nonverbal messages in communication, and that the more

FIGURE 10-1
Steps for Resolving Conflict

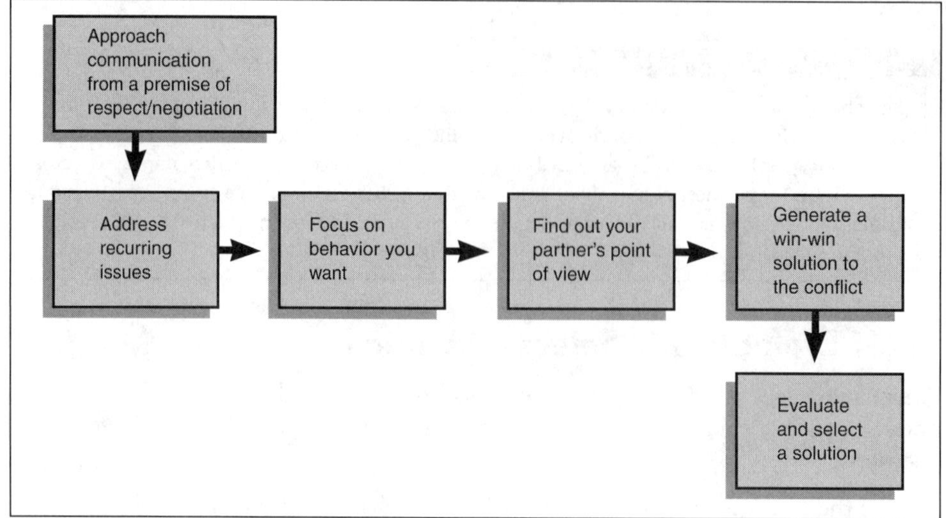

involved they are with the partner, the more attentive they become. Sillars, Roberts, Leonard, and Dun (2000) compared the communication behaviors of women and men and observed that women are more other-directed and relationship-sensitive than men.

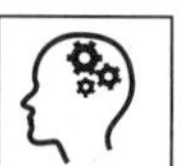

Think About It

Observe women and men in a group talking, and you might notice that men tend to speak more often and at a higher volume than women. Are these differences due to gender or status? In other words, are the differences due to being a woman or a man, or to the fact that in many societies women are of lower status and men of higher status (e.g., politically, economically, socially, etc.)?

Tannen (1990) proposes that the difference between men's and women's styles contributes to misunderstandings:

> *Understanding style differences for what they are takes the sting out of them. Believing that "you're not interested in me," "you don't care about me as much as I care about you," or "you want to take away my freedom" feels awful. Believing that "you have a different way of showing you're listening" or "showing you care" allows for no-fault negotiation: You can ask for or make adjustments without casting or taking blame. (p. 298)*

Tannen suggests that understanding gender differences in conversational style can help bridge communication gaps and go a long way in opening lines of communication. However, Tannen's views have been criticized by feminists who assert that differences between women and men in conversation, known as "conversational troubles," arise not from misunderstandings due to cultural differences but from "instances of conflict between subjects positioned not just differently but unequally" (Cameron, 1998, p. 946).

Another possible explanation for the differences in men's and women's communicating about emotionally laden content may stem from biological factors. In Gottman's (1994) research, when men and women's heart rates were monitored as they discussed major conflict areas, the men's heart rates quickly rose to a fast rate and took a longer time to recover. Gottman hypothesized that men are more biologically reactive to stress and therefore protect themselves by withdrawing. And, given socialization pressures to suppress a show of feelings, Gottman says it is not surprising that 85% of stonewallers are men. Likewise, Markman et al. (1994) found that women (when in a physically safe relationship) were more likely to use verbal skills than avoidance in handling conflicts. Aside from a reluctance to discuss conflictual issues, men also seem less willing to discuss sexual issues than women. In a study of Midwestern university students, 33% of women and 75% of men "never did ask" partners about their past sexual history (Stebleton & Rothenberger, 1993). A review of 18 studies examining men's and women's willingness to engage in safer sexual communication showed that women were more likely to initiate such discussions. Educational interventions to reduce risk of HIV exposure need to take such interpersonal communication dynamics into consideration.

10-7 INTERNET COMMUNICATION

> *The Internet is a virtual store open 24 hours a day . . . with millions of users on-line, someone who knows how to navigate the World Wide Web can, at any moment, find a kindred spirit with a similar sexual interest or desire.*
>
> *—Al Cooper, Sylvain Boies, Marlene Maheu, David Greenfield*

Although we mostly think of communication as being between two people face-to-face, increasingly communication is occurring over the Internet. Cooper, Boies, Maheu, and Greenfield (2000) report that an estimated 15 million people go online every day and spend an average of 9.8 hours a week. Although some of this time is devoted to visiting some of the 200 million web pages available, the computer is also being used to communicate with others for information (e.g., travel), commerce (eBay), friendship, romance, mate selection, and sex. Sex has been identified as the most frequently searched topic on the Internet. The purposes of these searches may include a vast range of intents: finding educational materials or therapists; shopping for, purchasing, or selling sexuality related goods or material for entertainment/masturbatory use offline; seeking partners for brief or long-term relationships; engaging in mutual erotic dialog (**cybersex**); exploring gender and identity roles by changing gender or creating new personas; and seeking targets for sex-related Internet crime (cyber-stalking, pedophilic "grooming" of children; Griffiths, 2001).

Cybersex The exchange of mutual erotic dialog via computer.

10-7a College Student Use of the Internet

One hundred ninety-one college students reported their motivations for logging onto the Internet (Knox, Daniels, Sturdivant, & Zusman, 2001). Friendship, not romance or a mate, was the goal reported by 40% of the respondents. One in six (59%) reported that he or she was successful in meeting someone online and a quarter (25.7%) of them became friends. Aside from "social reasons" for using the Internet, conducting research/doing academic work was the primary reason 53% of the students gave for logging on. Although more than three quarters (77%) had visited a sex site (men more than women), less than 3% reported seeking a cybersex partner.

10-7b Positive Effects of the Internet on Communication

The Internet affects communication in a number of positive ways, including making communication easier, shifting through a number of partners quickly, increasing one's potential for more open disclosure, and keeping people connected who are separated by great distances. Almost half (49.2%) of the students in the Internet college student survey noted that they "felt less shy on the Internet than in face-to-face interaction" (Knox et al., 2001). E-mails allow one to "think" about what he or she is going to say and provide time to select the right words. Indeed, some people may feel so anxious about personal face-to-face interaction that they avoid it completely. The lower anxiety about interaction via the Internet may allow some relationships to develop that would not otherwise.

Dating is time-consuming and expensive. A person can log on to one of the many dating services (e.g., Rightmate.heartchoice.com), sift through hundreds of thousands of individuals to identify those with basic desired characteristics (e.g., race, age, education, religion, smoking preference, sexual orientation, sexual preference, etc.), and come up with photos and e-mail addresses of persons he or she wants to pursue. All of this can happen within 20 minutes.

After one has identified someone with the desired background characteristics, there is a common basis to be disclosing about one's own life. A major effect of such quick disclosure to others is the quick trip to feelings of intimacy expressed in "I felt I could share anything"; this phenomenon is known as "pseudo-intimacy" (Cooper et al., 2001). The authors know a couple who disclosed quickly to each other and escalated their relationship from e-mailing to phone calls to actually meeting within 24 hours.

The rapid exchange of communication messages via e-mail also helps to bridge the distance in long-distance relationships where separation is caused by career (job in another town), education (college in another town), or family responsibilities (caring for a parent in another town). Some couples separated by long distances spend their evenings e-mailing each other. Such frequent contact helps to nurture the relationship and reduces the negative effect of being separated on the relationship.

Another positive effect of the Internet on communication is to make connections between people who have unique interests or experiences. Persons who have been raped, have sexually transmitted diseases (herpes, HPV, AIDS), are paraplegic, or have particular fetishes may find others on the Internet who share these experiences/predilections and communicate with them. Without such an Internet connection, one may feel isolated and "abnormal."

Still another positive effect of communication on the Internet is being able to try out a new identity online. A person who experiences feelings of being attracted to same-sex individuals may interact with homosexuals online to experience how such interaction feels without the attendant anxiety of doing so in person. Cross-dressers, transsexuals, etc., may also try out new identities.

10-7c Negative Effects of the Internet on Communication

Internet communication also has negative consequences on communication. They include neglect of one's current available relationships for "cyberspace" relationships, social isolation, deception, and compulsive use of the Internet for cybersex. Regarding neglect, one spouse noted that the partner is "always" on the computer at night checking e-mail and "I feel jealous and abandoned. Hey—I'm in the house—shut that thing off and talk to me."

Social isolation is encouraged by the computer because e-mail interaction can replace face-to-face interaction with others. Theoretically, a person can have numerous online relationships with others, never meet anyone face-to-face, and never feel interpersonally "connected." Meanwhile, the social skills for meeting and/or interacting with others are not being developed.

Deception is another downside of Internet communication. Four in 10 of the college students in the Internet study (Knox et al., 2001) reported that they had been deceptive about what they said via e-mail. Women were more deceptive than men (43% vs. 35%). Age, weight, appearance, marital status, and gender were among the issues the respondents reporting lying about.

Finally, the Internet is sometimes used for compulsive expression of unconventional sex practices, including "preoccupation with pornography, multiple affairs, sex with several or anonymous partners" (Cooper, Scherer, Boies, & Gordon, 1999). The Triple-A Engine (access, affordability, and anonymity features of the Internet) lends itself to such compulsive unconventional use for 8.5% of respondents. Such compulsive behavior typically has negative consequences for pair-bonded partners of these Internet users who may feel betrayed and replaced.

An additional "model" has been proposed to identify factors that facilitate developing and maintaining sexual or emotional relationships on the Internet—ACE (anonymity, convenience, escape; Young, 1999). In his review of studies addressing the implications of Internet sex activities, Griffiths (2001) noted the frequently repeated claim that the easy availability of online sex may promote people who would normally not engage in sexual experimentation to be drawn into it. However, he observes the limitations of the empirical research on this topic. If anyone has ever been curious about the broad range of sexual behaviors, cybersex may provide a private, safe, and anonymous way to explore these fantasies. But, Griffiths (2001) concludes, based on the few studies available and anecdotal reports from therapists, Internet sex addiction does appear to exist for a minority of individuals. "Even if other researchers fail to acknowledge the existence of Internet sex addiction as a bona fide addiction, the limited empirical evidence appears to indicate that sex on the Internet is associated with serious, negative consequences for some users (albeit a small minority)" (p. 341).

SUMMARY

This chapter focused on the value of good communication to intimacy, relationship, and sexual satisfaction; sociological theories of communication; the principles of effective communication; the issue of honesty in relationships; conflict resolution in relationships through generating win-win solutions; the differences in the way men and women approach and execute communication; and communication via the Internet.

Intimacy, Relationship, and Sexual Satisfaction

Good communication and self-disclosure are important factors in creating and maintaining intimacy, relationship, and sexual satisfaction. Disclosing personal information is associated with increased intimacy and sexual satisfaction. Women and those in committed relationships are more likely to disclose than men and those in casual relationships.

Communication Theory

Because communication involves interaction in social contexts, theories including identity formation (communication skills are a product of interaction with others), social learning (verbal interaction is a consequence of communication), and social exchange (people continue to interact or don't in reference to rewards/costs ratio) may be used to help understand communication between partners.

Principles of Effective Communication in Intimate Relationships

Effective communication in intimate relationships is based on understanding and using various communication principles. They include initiating discussions about important issues, giving congruent messages, minimizing negative remarks and maximizing positive remarks, expressing feelings, practicing reflective listening, and using "I" messages.

Honesty and Dishonesty in Interpersonal Communication

Most individuals value honesty in their relationships. Honest communication is associated with trust and intimacy. Despite the importance of honesty in relationships, deception occurs frequently in interpersonal relationships. All but 5% of a sample of college students reported having lied to their parents during adolescence.

Lying is not uncommon in college student relationships. Partners sometimes lie to each other about previous sexual relationships, how they feel about each other, and how they experience each other sexually. In one study, 77 college students kept diaries of their daily social interactions and reported telling two lies a day.

Telling lies is not the only form of dishonesty. People exaggerate, minimize, tell partial truths, pretend, and engage in self-deception. A partner may withhold information or keep secrets to protect the other partner, preserve the relationship, or both. However, the more intimate the relationship, the greater our desire to share our most personal and private selves with our partner, and the greater the emotional consequences of not sharing. In intimate relationships, keeping secrets can block opportunities for healing, resolution, self-acceptance, and deeper intimacy between partners. However, being honest on all occasions on all issues may not be the best policy.

Resolving Conflict in Relationships

Having a plan to communicate about conflicts is essential. Such a plan includes approaching a discussion from the point of view of respect for the partner and a willingness to negotiate an outcome rather than dictate a solution, addressing recurring issues rather than suppressing them, focusing on what you want (rather than what you don't want), finding out your partner's point of view, generating win-win solutions to conflict, and evaluating and selecting a solution.

Gender Differences in Communication

Deborah Tannen observed that men and women are socialized in different same-sex cultures, and when they talk to the other sex, they are talking to a member of another culture. Men approach communication, even in private situations, like public speaking or giving a report. They see talk as for information. In contrast, women engage in "rapport-talk," using talk to interact and establish connections. Deborah Tannen's work (including 17 books) has been prolific and not without controversy. She has been criticized as being not scientific and oblivious to feminist views of communication.

Internet Communication

An estimated 15 million people go online every day and spend an average of 9.8 hours a week. The computer is used to communicate with others for information (e.g., travel), commerce (eBay), friendship, romance, mate selection, and sex. Friendship, not romance or a mate, was the goal reported by 40% of the respondents.

The Internet affects communication in a number of positive ways, including making communication easier, shifting through a number of partners quickly, increasing one's potential for more open disclosure, and keeping people connected who are separated by great distances.

The negative effects of communication on the Internet include neglect of one's current available relationships for "cyberspace" relationships, social isolation, deception, and compulsive use of the Internet for cybersex.

SUGGESTED WEBSITES

Note: These websites were functional when we went to press. Please access the online text for the most up-to-date URLs.

American Association for Marriage and Family Therapy
http://aamft.org

Assessment of Online Sexual Behavior
http://www.onlinesexaddict.com/osaq.html
http://www.sexhelp.com (versions for heterosexual men, gay men, or women)

Association of Couples for Marriage Enrichment
http://marriageenrichment.com

Communication Resources
http://communication.ucsd.edu/resources/commlinks.html

Cybersex Addiction
www.netaddiction.com
www.sex-centre.com
www.cyberwidows.com

Gottman Institute
http://www.gottman.com/

Marriage Encounter
http://www.wwme.org/

KEY TERMS

brainstorming (p. 312)
closed-ended question (p. 306)
communication (p. 298)
cybersex (p. 315)
"I" statements (p. 307)
intimacy (p. 298)
looking glass self (p. 299)
nonverbal messages (p. 303)
open-ended question (p. 306)
partner notification laws (p. 302)
primacy/recency effect (p. 305)
reflective listening (p. 307)
self-fulfilling prophecy (p. 304)
touch-and-ask rule (p. 307)
verbal messages (p. 303)
win-win solution (p. 312)
"you" statements (p. 308)

CHAPTER QUIZ

1. According to your text, *intimacy* refers to which of the following?
   a. emotional closeness and bond between two people
   b. the level of commitment in a relationship
   c. the degree to which partners are open to a variety of physical and sexual behaviors with each other
   d. mutual passion
2. According to ___________ theory, the interaction between partners can be described as a ratio of rewards to costs.
   a. social exchange
   b. social learning
   c. identity formation
3. According to a meta-analysis of 26 studies, those who talked about condoms prior to having sex were ___________ nontalkers to use condoms.
   a. equally likely as
   b. more likely than
   c. less likely than
4. Suppose Karen tells her partner, Jim, that she doesn't mind if he goes to a strip bar with his friends, but as she tells him this, she looks down and has a sullen expression on her face. According to your text, Jim is likely to give more weight to Karen's ___________ communication.
   a. verbal
   b. nonverbal
5. Research by Notarius and Markman (1994) on marital interaction has consistently shown that one brutal "zinger" can erase ___________ of kindness by the same person.
   a. 1 act
   b. 2 acts
   c. 10 acts
   d. 20 acts
6. Gottman (1994) identified four negative qualities that are strong predictors of divorce. They include each of the following EXCEPT
   a. criticism.
   b. stonewalling.
   c. defensiveness.
   d. impatience.
7. Based on a survey of 1,003 women and men ages 20–29, most of the women (80%) reported feeling that a husband who can communicate about his deepest feelings is ___________ one who makes a good living.
   a. just as important as
   b. more desirable than
   c. not as desirable as
8. An "open-ended question" is a question that
   a. cannot be answered.
   b. the person asking the question already knows the answer to.
   c. can be answered in one word.
   d. is designed to elicit a lot of information.
9. Which of the following is an example of reflective listening in response to the statement, "I'm not in love with you"?
   a. "It's early in our relationship . . . give it time and maybe love will grow."
   b. "I appreciate your being up front with me."
   c. "You don't love me."
   d. "I don't love you either."
10. The authors of your text recommend using ___________ statements.
    a. "I"
    b. "You"
11. In a study cited in your text, 137 students reported 21 lies they had told to a current or past partner. What was the most frequently told lie?
    a. whether the person had ever been in love
    b. what kinds of grades the person makes in his or her classes
    c. the number of previous sex partners the person has had
    d. how much the person weighs
12. Pepper Schwartz advises wives who have had an affair to do which of the following?
    a. Be open and honest because your husband will eventually find out. It is better for your husband to find out from you than from someone else.
    b. Confess because your husband has probably also had an affair, and your confession will help reduce his guilt over his own infidelity.
    c. Confess only if you want to end your marriage, or if the marriage is so bad that you are willing to risk ending it in order to help it.
13. Howard Markman and his colleagues found that the greatest single predictor of marital success is
    a. communication and conflict resolution skills.
    b. having a lot in common and few issues to argue about.
    c. having parents who are still married.
    d. length of time partners knew each other before getting married.
14. According to Greeff and De Bruyne (2000), this style of conflict resolution is associated with the highest level of marital and spousal satisfaction.
    a. competing
    b. compromise
    c. collaborating
    d. avoiding
15. Deborah Tannen (1990) explained gender differences in communication by using the terms "___________ talk" to describe male communication and "___________ talk" to describe female communication.
    a. future-focused; present-focused
    b. I; you
    c. report; rapport
    d. mind; matter
16. Research on the phenomenon of Internet sex addiction suggests that
    a. up to 50% of those who use the Internet for sexual purposes become addicted to this use.
    b. a minority of individuals who use the Internet for sexual purposes can be described as addicted to Internet sex.
    c. Internet sex is a concept discussed in the popular media, but it has not been substantiated by studies or case reports.

REFERENCES

Allen, M., Emmers-Sommer, T. M., & Crowell, T. L. (2002). Couples negotiating safer sex behaviors: A meta-analysis of the impact of conversation and gender. In M. Allen, R. W. Preiss, B. M. Gayle, & N. A. Burrell (Eds.), *Interpersonal communication research: Advances through meta-analysis* (pp. 263–279). Mahwah, NJ: Lawrence Erlbaum.

American Civil Liberties Union. (1998, March). HIV partner notification: Why coercion won't work. An American Civil Liberties Union Report. http://www.aclu.org/issues/aids/hiv_partner.html#I

Bird, S. T., Harvey, S. M., & Beckman, L. (2001). Getting your partner to use condoms: Interviews with men and women at risk of HIV/STDs. *The Journal of Sex Research, 38,* 233–242.

Bitner, J. R. (1988). *Fundamentals of communication* (2nd ed.). Englewood Cliffs, NJ: Prentice-Hall.

Cameron, D. (1998). Gender, language and discourse: A review. *Signs, 23,* 945–951.

Civic, D. (2000). College students' reasons for nonuse of a condom within dating relationships. *Journal of Sex and Marital Therapy, 26,* 95–105.

Cooley, C. H. (1964). *Human nature and the social order.* New York: Schocken.

Cooper, A., Boies, S., Maheu, M., & Greenfield, D. (2001). Sexuality and the Internet: The next sexual revolution. In L. T. Szuchman & F. Muscarella (Eds.), *Psychological perspectives on human sexuality* (pp. 519–545). New York: John Wiley & Sons.

Cooper, A., Scherer, C., Boies, S. C., & Gordon, B. (1999). Sexuality on the Internet: From sexual exploration to pathological expression. *Professional Psychology: Research and Practice, 30,* 154–164.

DePaulo, B. M., Kirkendol, S. E., Kashy, D. A., Wyer, M. M., & Epstein, J. A. (1996). Lying in everyday life. *Journal of Personality and Social Psychology, 70,* 979–997.

Duncan, B. L., & Rock, J. W. (1993). Saving relationships: The power of the unpredictable. *Psychology Today, 26,* 46–51, 86, 95.

Gallmeier, C. P., Zusman, M. E., Knox, D., & Gibson, L. (1997). Can we talk? Gender differences in disclosure patterns and expectations. *Free Inquiry in Creative Sociology, 25,* 129–225.

Galvin, K. M., & Brommel, B. J. (1982). *Family communication: Cohesion and change.* Glenview, IL: Scott, Foresman & Co.

Giffin, K., & Patton, B. R. (1976). *Fundamentals of interpersonal communication* (2nd ed.). New York: Harper & Row.

Gottman, J. (with Silver, N.). (1994). *Why marriages succeed or fail . . . And how you can make yours last.* New York: Simon & Schuster.

Gottman, J. M., Coan, J., Carrere, S., & Swanson, C. (1998). Predicting marital happiness and stability from newlywed interactions. *Journal of Marriage and the Family, 60,* 5–22.

Greeff, A. P., & De Bruyne, T. (2000). Conflict management style and marital satisfaction. *Journal of Sex and Marital Satisfaction, 26,* 321–334.

Griffiths, M. (2001). Sex on the Internet: Observations and implications for Internet sex addiction. *The Journal of Sex Research, 38,* 333–342.

Hickman, S. E., & Muehlenhard, C. L. (1999). "By the semi-mystical appearance of a condom": How young women and men communicate sexual consent in heterosexual situations. *The Journal of Sex Research, 36,* 258–272.

Jesser, C. J. (1978). The sexual signaling behaviors inventory. *The Journal of Sex Research, 14,* 118–128.

Jesser, C. J. (1998). The sexual signaling behaviors inventory. In C. M. Davis, W. L. Yarber, R. Bauserman, G. Schreer, & S. L. Davis (Eds.), *Sexuality Related Measures* (pp. 423–424). Thousand Oaks, CA: Sage.

Knox, D., Daniels, V., Sturdivant, L., & Zusman, M. E. (2001). College student use of the Internet for mate selection. *College Student Journal, 35,* 158–160.

Knox, D., Hatfield, S., & Zusman, M. E. (1998). College student discussion of relationship problems. *College Student Journal, 32,* 19–21.

Knox, D., Schacht, C., Holt, J., & Turner, J. (1993). Sexual lies among university students. *College Student Journal, 27,* 269–272.

Knox, D., Zusman, M. E., McGinty, K., & Gescheidler, J. (2001). Deception of parents during adolescence. *Journal of Adolescence, 36,* 611–614.

Krahe, B., & Kolpin, F. (2000). Ambiguous communication of sexual intentions as a risk marker of sexual aggression. *Sex Roles, 42,* 313–337.

L'Abate, L., & Bagarozzi, D. A. (1993). *Sourcebook of marriage and family interaction.* New York: Brunner/ Mazel.

Lerner, H. G. (1993). *The dance of deception: Pretending and truth-telling in women's lives.* New York: HarperCollins.

Levitt, M. J., Silver, M. E., & Franco, N. (1996). Troublesome relationships: A part of human experience. *Journal of Social and Personal Relationships, 13,* 523–536.

Mackey, R. A., & O'Brien, B. A. (1999). Adaptation in lasting marriages. *Families in Society: The Journal of Contemporary Human Services, 80,* 587–596.

MacNeil, S., & Byers, E. S. (1997). The relationships between sexual problems, communication, and sexual satisfaction. *The Canadian Journal of Human Sexuality, 6,* 277–284.

Marchand, J. F., & Hock, E. (2000). Avoidance and attacking conflict resolution strategies among married couples: Relationship to depressive symptoms and marital satisfaction. *Family Relations, 49,* 201–206.

Markman, H. J., Renick, M. J., Floyd, F. J., Stanley, S. M., & Clements, M. (1993). Preventing marital distress through communication and conflict management training: A 4- and 5-year follow-up. *Journal of Consulting and Clinical Psychology, 61,* 70–77.

Markman, H., Stanley, S., & Blumberg, S. L. (1994). *Fighting for your marriage: Positive steps for preventing divorce and preserving a lasting love.* San Francisco: Jossey-Bass.

McGinty, K., Knox, D., & Zusman, M. E. (2003). Nonverbal and verbal communication in 'involved' and 'casual' relationships among college students. *College Student Journal, 37*, 68–71.

Moore, N. B., & Davidson, J. K., Jr. (2000). Communicating with new sex partners: College women and questions that make a difference. *Journal of Sex and Marital Therapy, 26*, 215–230.

Nakanishi, M. (1986). Perceptions of self-disclosure in initial interaction: A Japanese sample. *Human Communication Research, 13*, 167–190.

Notarius, C., & Markman, H. (1994). *We can work it out. Making sense of marital conflict*. New York: Putnam.

Olson, D. H., & Olson, A. K. (2000). *Empowering couples: Building on your strengths* (2nd ed.). Minneapolis, MN: Life Innovations, Inc.

Oncale, R. M., & King, B. M. (2001). Comparison of men's and women's attempts to dissuade sexual partners from the couple using condoms. *Archives of Sexual Behavior, 30*, 379–391.

Patford, J. L. (2000). Partners and cross-sex friends: A preliminary study of the way marital and de facto partnerships affect verbal intimacy with cross-sex friends. *Journal of Family Studies*, 6, 106–119.

Payn, B., Tanfer, K., Billy, J. O. G., & Grady, W. R. (1997). Men's behavior change following infection with a sexually transmitted disease. *Family Planning Perspectives, 29*, 152–157.

Samp, J. A., & Solomon, D. H. (2001). Coping with problematic events in dating relationships: The influence of dependence power on severity appraisals and decisions to communicate. *Western Journal of Communication*, 65, 138–151.

Sillars, A., Roberts, L. J., Leonard, K. E., & Dun, T. (2000). Cognition during marital conflict: The relationship of thought and talk. *Journal of Social and Personal Relationships, 17*, 479–503.

Stanley, S. M., & Markman, H. J. (1995). Strengthening marriages and preventing divorce. *Family Relations, 44*, 392–401.

Stanley, S. M., Markman, H. J., Prado, L. M., Olmos-Gallo, P. A., Tonelli, L., St. Peters, M., et al. (2001). Community-based premarital prevention: Clergy and lay leaders on the front lines. *Family Relations*, 50, 67–76.

Stebleton, M., & Rothenberger, J. (1993). Truth or consequences: Dishonesty in dating and HIV/AIDS-related issues in college population. *Journal of American College Health, 42*, 51–54.

Sullivan, E. (2001). *The concise book of lying*. New York: Farrar, Straus & Giroux.

Tannen, D. (1990). *You just don't understand: Women and men in conversation*. New York: Ballentine.

Taylor, R. (1997). *Love affairs: Marriage and infidelity*. Amherst, NY: Prometheus Books.

Thomas, E. J. (1977). *Marital communication and decision making: Analysis, assessment, and change*. New York: The Free Press.

Treatment Update. (1997, Summer). *The Helper*, 19(2), 3–4.

Van Matre, L. (1992, August 28). Honesty can be worst policy in affair. *The Daily Reflector*, p. d–8.

Whitehead, B. D., & Popenoe, D. (2001). Singles seek soul mates for marriage. The Gallup Organization, Poll Analysis. http://www.gallup.com/poll/releasexs/pr010627b.asp

Young, K. (1999, August). *Cyber-disorders: The mental illness concern for the millennium*. Paper presented at the 108th Annual Meeting of the American Psychological Association, Boston, MA.

Planning Children and Birth Control

Chapter Outline

Cross-cultural research shows that children everywhere are valued mainly for psychological reasons.

—James Walters and Linda Walters
past presidents, National Council on Family Relations

Love is a fourteen letter word—Family Planning.

—Planned Parenthood poster

In a survey conducted by the American Council on Education and the University of California (Bartlett, 2002) female and male undergraduates in a national sample of first-year college students at more than 50 four-year institutions respectively ranked "raising a family" as their first and second most important goal in life (men ranked being financially secure first). Indeed, between 90% and 95% of women and men attempt to have children (Daniluk, 2001). Although many people consider becoming a parent to be one of the most rewarding experiences in life, it also brings lifestyle changes, economic concerns, and other challenges. Shifting the focus from an adult marriage to a child-centered family focus is one of the major developmental tasks of adulthood.

Family planning has benefits for both the mother and the child. Having several children at short intervals increases the chances of premature birth, infectious disease, and death of the mother or the baby. Parents can minimize such risks by planning fewer children with longer intervals in between. Women who plan their pregnancies can also modify their behaviors and seek preconception care from a health-care practitioner to maximize their chances of having healthy pregnancies and babies. For example, women planning pregnancies can make sure they eat properly and avoid alcohol and other substances that could harm developing fetuses.

Couples may also benefit from family planning by pacing the financial demands of parenthood. Having children 4 years apart helps to avoid having more than one child in day care or college at the same time.

Conscientious family planning will help to reduce the number of surprise pregnancies. Even with the availability of various contraceptive methods, many women experience unintended pregnancies. Of the 6 million pregnancies to all U.S. women each year, one half are unplanned (Burkman, 2002). The percentage of unplanned pregnancies to women with low incomes is even higher. In one study of 250 low-income women who had experienced 839 pregnancies, 57% reported that their pregnancies were unintended (Zabin, Huggins, Emerson, & Cullins, 2000).

Sexually active teenagers are the most vulnerable. "More than 17% of teenage women are estimated to have become pregnant during their first nonmarital teenage sexual relationship" (Zavodny, 2001). Although teen pregnancy rates have declined in the United States, this country still has the highest rates of teen pregnancy, birth, and abortion among the fully industrialized countries. Four in 10 teen girls become pregnant at least once prior to age 20. Delaying pregnancies until a young woman is in her 20s results in many health, educational, and social benefits. Children born to teen mothers are at greater risk of infant mortality and low birth weight, are at greater risk of growing up in poverty and in single parent homes, suffer higher rates of abuse and neglect, and perform more poorly in school (National Campaign to Prevent Teen Pregnancy, 2002).

Population growth (adding 1 billion people every 14 years), fueled by unplanned pregnancies, is placing enormous pressure on the environment. As the human population grows, meeting human needs and improving quality of life become increasingly difficult. Challenges include access to food and fresh water, access to health care, decreases in diversity of plants and animals, and increases in global emission of carbon dioxide, or "greenhouse gas," causing global warming and weather pattern disruption ("Population and the Environment," 2002). (For related information, see The Demographic Facts of Life at www.populationconnection/org/Reports-Publications.)

In this chapter, we encourage you to consider three basic questions:

- Do you want to have children?
- How many?
- What form of birth control will you use to influence the number and timing of pregnancies?

11-1 DO YOU WANT TO HAVE CHILDREN?

In the United States, children are an expected part of one's adult life. In sections 11-1a through 11-1d, we examine the social influences that motivate individuals to want children. We also discuss the difficulties associated with parenthood.

11-1a Social Influences Motivating Individuals to Have Children

Our society tends to encourage childbearing, an attitude known as **pronatalism.** Our family, friends, religions, government, and schools help us develop positive attitudes toward parenthood. Cultural observances also function to reinforce these attitudes.

Pronatalism Social bias in favor of having children.

Family

Our experience of being reared in families encourages us to have families of our own. Our parents are our models. If they married, we marry. If a young woman has her first pregnancy when she is a teen, her daughter is more likely to begin childbearing as a teenager. Some parents exert a much more active influence. "I'm 73 and don't have much time. Will I ever see a grandchild?" asked the mother of an only child. Other remarks parents have made include "If you don't hurry up, your younger sister is going to have a baby before you do," "We're setting up a trust fund for your brother's child, and we'll do the same for yours," "Did you know that Bryan and Melinda (the adult child's contemporaries) just had a daughter?" "I think you'll regret not having children when you're old," and "Don't you want a son to carry on your name?"

Friends

Our friends who have children influence us to do likewise. After sharing an enjoyable weekend with friends who had a little girl, one husband wrote to the host and hostess, "Lucy and I are always affected by Karen—she is such a good child to have around. We haven't made up our minds yet, but our desire to have a child of our own always increases after we leave your home." This couple became parents 16 months later.

Religion

Religion may be a powerful influence on the decision to have children. Roman Catholics are taught that having children is the basic purpose of marriage and gives meaning to the union. Although many Catholics use contraception and reject their church's emphasis on procreation, some internalize the church's message. One Catholic woman said, "My body was made by God, and I should use it to produce children for Him. Other people may not understand it, but that's how I feel." Judaism also has a strong family orientation. Women who elect not to have children are more likely to report no religious affiliation (Kaufman, 2000).

Government

The tax structures imposed by our federal and state governments support parenthood. Married couples without children pay higher taxes than couples with children, although the reduction in taxes is not sufficient to offset the cost of rearing a child and is not large enough to be a primary inducement to have children.

Cultural Observances

Our society reaffirms its approval of parents every year by identifying special days for Mom and Dad. Each year on Mother's Day and Father's Day (and now Grandparents' Day), parenthood is celebrated across the nation with cards, gifts, and embraces. There is no cultural counterpart (such as Childfree Day) for people who choose not to have children.

Antinatalism Social attitude that is anti or against children.

Think About It

Aspects of our society reflect **antinatalism** (against children). Indeed, there is a continuous fight to get corporations to implement or enforce any family policies (from family leaves to flex time to on-site day care). Profit and money—not children—are priorities. In addition, although people are generally tolerant of their own children, they often exhibit antinatalistic behavior in reference to the children of others. Notice the unwillingness of some individuals to sit next to a child on an airplane. What other examples illustrate an antinatalistic view?

11-1b Individual Motivations for Having Children

Individual motivations, as well as social influences, play important roles in making the decision to have children. Some of these motivations are conscious, such as the desire for love and companionship with one's own offspring and the desire to be personally fulfilled by having a child. Other motivations are more difficult to perceive—having a child as an attempt to recapture childhood and youth, for example.

Cultural Diversity

In premodern societies (before industrialization and urbanization) spouses tried to have as many children as possible because children were an economic asset. At an early age, children worked as farm hands or in other jobs for wages that they gave to their parents. Children were also expected to take care of their parents when the parents were old.

In China and Korea, the eldest son is expected to take care of his aging parents by earning money for them and by marrying and bringing his wife into their home to physically care for them. Her parents need their own son and daughter-in-law for old-age insurance. Beyond their economic value and old-age insurance, children were regarded as a symbol of virility for the man, a source of prestige for the woman, and a sign of good fortune for the couple. In modern societies, large numbers of children are economic liabilities rather than assets.

Think About It

How much of the decision to have children do you feel is biologically driven, socially structured/influenced, or a consequence of individual personality preference? How much of the desire for children is conscious and deliberate, and how much is a result of people's tendency to drift from one stage of life (marriage to parenthood) to the next?

11-1c Lifestyle Changes and Economic Costs of Parenthood

Although there are numerous potential positive outcomes for becoming a parent, there are also drawbacks. Every parent knows that parenthood involves difficulties as well as joys. Some of the difficulties associated with parenthood are discussed next.

Lifestyle Changes

Becoming a parent often involves changes in lifestyle. Daily living routines become focused around the needs of the children. Living arrangements change to provide space for another person in the household. Some parents change their work schedule to allow them to be home more. Food shopping and menus change to accommodate the appetites of children. A major lifestyle change is the loss of freedom of activity and flexibility in one's personal schedule.

Lifestyle changes are particularly dramatic for women. The time and effort required to be pregnant and rear children often compete with the time and energy needed to finish one's education. Hofferth, Reid, and Mott (2001) observed that early childbearing has a significant negative impact on years of completed schooling. Teenage mothers have about 2 fewer years of education than do women who delay their first birth until age 30.

Building a career is also negatively impacted by the birth of children. Parents learn quickly it is difficult to both be an involved on-the-spot parent and climb the career ladder. The careers of women may suffer most.

Financial Costs

Meeting the financial obligations of parenthood is difficult for many parents. New parents are often shocked at the relentless expenses. The annual cost of a child less than 2 years old for middle income parents ($39,100 to $65,800)—which includes housing, food, transportation, clothing, health care, and child care—is $9,030. For a 15- to 17-year-old the cost is $10,140 (*Statistical Abstract of the United States: 2002,* Table 647). These costs do not include the wages lost when a parent drops out of the workforce to provide child care.

Because of lifestyle and economic considerations, some women put off having a child until they are older. How old is too old? Should the government intervene? We address these concerns in Box 11-1.

When a person decides to have a child, the timing becomes important. The use of reproductive technology allows couples to delay having children. However, the ability to become pregnant decreases with age, so couples should take care when deciding how long to wait. Some wait too long only to discover that they cannot become pregnant.

11-1d Personal Choices: Choices Resulting from New Reproductive Technologies

The development of various reproductive technologies has created a new range of choices with regard to family planning. Examples of such choices are presented in the following paragraphs.

Example One

A young woman who wants to delay pregnancy and childrearing until after she has established herself professionally in a career may, in her youth, have her healthy eggs extracted, frozen, and artificially inseminated later when she is in her 40s or 50s. Doing so would reduce some of the risks associated with birth defects in women who elect to have children during middle age. Alternatively, a middle-aged woman may want to use an egg from a younger woman and have it fertilized with her partner's sperm and artificially inseminated.

What are the disadvantages of delaying pregnancy through the use of reproductive technologies? Risk to the fetus and risk to the mother are the predominant problems. Although some of the risks to the fetus can be avoided by using a "young" egg ("old" eggs are much more likely to be defective), the middle-aged pregnant woman is much more likely to be diabetic, be overweight, and have high blood pressure, which may also affect the fetus negatively.

In addition, what are the implications for the child who will have two elderly parents who may die before her or his graduation from high school?

Example Two

Couples who have genetic histories that include sickle-cell anemia or cystic fibrosis may have such defects tested for in several embryos and implant only those without the defects. But if embryos can be destroyed because of a genetic defect, can sex of the child also be used as a basis for discarding the embryo?

Box 11-1 Social Choices

How Old Is Too Old to Be a Parent?

Actor Tony Randall had a child at the age of 77, and Senator Strom Thurmond was in his 80s when he became a father. Situations like these are becoming more common, and questions are now being asked about the appropriateness of elderly individuals becoming parents. Should social policies on this issue be developed?

There are advantages and disadvantages of having a child as an elderly parent. The primary developmental advantage for the child of retirement-aged parents is the attention the parents can devote to their offspring. Not distracted by their career, these parents have more time to nurture, play with, and teach their children. And, although they may have less energy, their experience and knowledge are doubtless better. Indeed the "biological disadvantage is to a degree balanced by social advantage" (Stein & Susser, 2000, p. 1682)

The primary disadvantage of having a child in the later years is that the parents are likely to die before, or early in, the child's adult life. When Tony Randall's daughter, Julie, begins college, her dad will be 95. The daughter of James Dickey, the Southern writer, lamented the fact that her late father (to whom she was born when he was in his 50s) would not be present at her graduation or wedding.

There are also medical concerns for both the mother and the baby during pregnancy in later life. They include an increased risk of **morbidity** (chronic illness and disease) and **mortality** (death) for the mother. These risks are typically a function of chronic disorders that go along with aging, such as diabetes, hypertension, and cardiac disease. Stillbirths, miscarriage, ectopic pregnancies, multiple births, and congenital malformations are also higher in women with advancing age (Stein & Susser, 2000). However, prenatal testing can identify some potential problems such as the risk of Down's syndrome, and any chromosome abnormality and negative neonatal outcomes are not inevitable (Bianco et al., 1996). Based on a review of the studies on pregnancy and childbirth in women over 35, Cunningham et al. (1997, p. 577) noted:

> Women should realistically appraise the risks of pregnancy later in life, but should not necessarily fear delaying childbirth. Pregnancy after 35 is increasingly common in our society, and improved obstetrical care has made advanced maternal age compatible with successful pregnancy for the great majority of such women.

Because an older woman can usually have a healthy baby, government regulations on the age at which a woman can become pregnant are not likely. In addition, women might lie about their age, making governmental control difficult. Fearing that she would not be accepted into the University of Southern California's Program for Assisted Reproduction, Arceli Keh did not reveal her real age. She told them she was 50 (she was actually 63).

References

Bianco, A., Stone, J., Lynch, L., Lapinski R., Berkowitz, B., & Berkowitz, R. L. (1996). Pregnancy outcome at age 40 and older. *Obstetrics and Gynecology, 87,* 917–922.

Cunningham, F. G., MacDonald, P. C., Gant, N. F., Leveno, K. J., Gilstrap, L. C., Harkins, G. D. V., et al. (Eds.). (1997). *Williams Obstetrics* (20th ed.). Stamford, CT: Appleton and Lange.

Stein, Z., & Susser, M. (2000). The risks of having children in later life. *British Medical Journal, 320,* 1681–1683.

Morbidity Chronic illness and disease.

Mortality Death.

Finally, it is possible that the risks of assisted reproductive technology are not yet fully known. For example, about 20,000 children have been conceived with the help of intracytoplasmic sperm injection (injecting sperm into an egg). This process changes the timing of events of fertilization, with the DNA (carried in the head of the sperm) unraveling more slowly. Although obvious birth defects have not been apparent, there is speculation that sex chromosome abnormalities could become apparent when the children reach puberty (Newman, 2000).

11-2 HOW MANY CHILDREN DO YOU WANT?

People differ in terms of whether they want children and how many if they do.

11-2a None—The Childfree Alternative

Late-night TV talk show host Jay Leno and his wife, Mavis, are an example of a couple who have chosen not to have children. About 20% of individuals aged 65 or over report that they have never had children (Wu & Hart, 2002). Typical reasons individual couples give for not having children include the freedom to spend their time and money as they choose, to enjoy their partner without interference, to pursue their career, to avoid health problems associated with pregnancy, and to avoid passing on genetic disorders to a new generation (DeOllos & Kapinus, 2002).

The social pressure, particularly for women, to have children is enormous. "Motherhood is still considered to be a primary role for women and women who do not mother either biologically or socially are often stereotyped as either desperate or selfish" (Letherby, 2002, p. 7). Women today who want to remain childfree tend to have egalitarian gender role attitudes (Kaufman, 2000), to evidence greater interest in a career, and to value freedom from the constraints of having children. They also tend to be better educated, to live in urban areas, and to be less affiliated with religion (DeOllos & Kapinus, 2002). Childfree women have life satisfaction and mental health similar to women who have children (Wu & Hart, 2002).

How happy are the marriages of couples who elect to remain childfree compared with the marriages of couples who opt for having children? Though marital satisfaction declines across time for all couples whether or not they have children, children tend to lessen marital satisfaction by decreasing spousal time together, spousal interaction, and agreement over finances. Fifty-five percent of a sample of voluntarily childfree couples reported that their marriage was "very happy." Thirty-five percent reported that their marriage was "happy" (Foust, 1997). However, DeOllos and Kapinus (2002) reviewed the studies comparing marital satisfaction of childfree and parent couples and found contradictory results. Hence, the jury is still out on whether childfree and parent couples have happier marriages.

Another consequence of not having children is an increased risk of being in a residential care facility in one's old age (Wenger, Scott, & Patterson, 2000). Married childfree women are the most vulnerable because their spouses are likely to die before them. With no children to care for them and siblings likely having their own families, these women are likely to end up in a residential care facility.

Think About It

Is the childfree lifestyle for you? If you derive your primary satisfactions from interacting with adults and from your career, and if you require an atmosphere of freedom (including financial freedom) and privacy, perhaps the answer is yes. But if your desire for a child is at least equal to your desire for a satisfying adult relationship, career, and freedom, the answer may be no.

Although in sections 11-2b through 11-2e we discuss concepts of family size, it is important to acknowledge that not all people have a fixed goal for family size, and intentions often change over partners, events, and time periods. In fact, individual preferences such as "I want to have a child with this particular partner" may influence the timing of childbearing more than an absolute notion of ideal family size (Zabin et al., 2000).

11-2b One Child?

Chelsea, the daughter of Hillary and Bill Clinton, has given national attention to the one-child family. The number of children a couple chooses to have is influenced by the society in which the couple lives. In China, the one-child family is actively encouraged and has resulted in a drop in the country's birthrate. Although most only children are stereotyped as being spoiled, selfish, and lonely, data suggest that they are happy, bright, and socially skilled (Toman, 1993).

CULTURAL DIVERSITY 

One consequence of China's overpopulation and subsequent development of a one-child policy is the pressure on parents to have sons rather than daughters as their children. As noted in section 11-1b, sons are valued to take care of parents in their old age. These sons take care of their parents by marrying a woman who becomes responsible for taking care of their husband's elderly parents. Although daughters are often cherished as "little emperors" by Chinese adults, they do not function to care for their aging parents because they are expected to marry and to take care of their husband's parents.

11-2c Two Children?

Couples choose to have two children for several reasons. Some couples feel that a family is not complete without two children, and they want their firstborn to have a sibling and companion. Parents might have two children with the hope of having a child of each sex. Many mothers want a second child because they enjoyed their first child and want to repeat the experience. Others want to avoid having an only child because of the negative stereotypes associated with only children.

11-2d Three Children?

Couples are more likely to have a third child, and to do so quickly, if they already have two girls rather than two boys. They are least likely to bear a third child if they already have a boy and a girl (Jones, Tepperman, & Wilson, 1995).

Some individuals may want three children because they enjoy children and feel that "three is better than two." In some instances, a couple that has two children of the same sex may want to try one more time to have a child of the other sex.

Having a third child creates a "middle child." This child may sometimes feel neglected because parents of three children may focus more on the "baby" and the firstborn than on the child in between. However, an advantage to being a middle child is the chance to experience both a younger and an older sibling.

11-2e Four or More Children?

Larger families have complex interactional patterns and different values. The addition of each subsequent child dramatically increases the possible relationships in the family. For example, in the one-child family, 4 interpersonal relationships are possible: mother-father, mother-child, father-child, and father-mother-child. In a family of four, 11 relationships are possible; in a family of five, 26; and in a family of six, 57.

In addition to relationships, values change as families grow larger. Whereas members of a small family tend to value independence and personal development, large-family members necessarily value cooperation, harmony, and sharing. A parent of nine children said, "Meals around our house are a cooperative endeavor. One child prepares the drinks, another the bread, and still another sets the table. You have to develop cooperation, or nobody gets fed."

Each additional child also has a negative effect on the existing children by reducing the amount of parental time available. As each child is added to the unit, each child gets less time with the respective parents. The same is true of financial resources. Each additional child dilutes the financial resources available so that things such as educational materials, money for college, and a computer are less easily attained as the number of children in a family increases.

11-2f Personal Choices: Choose to Have a Child Without a Partner?

Although women have traditionally taken on parenthood after marriage, some have begun to consider having children even though they do not have steady partners. Indeed, 79% of a sample of 248 undergraduate university students reported that "it is perfectly OK for a woman to decide to have and to raise a child without a husband" (Knox, Sturdivant, Zusman, & Sandie, 2000, p. 585). As an aside, women and men in this sample disagreed over the importance of men in the development of children. Only about a quarter (26%) of women compared with almost half (48%) of the men agreed with the statement "men are better disciplinarians than women" (p. 586).

Some women who elect single motherhood are in their 30s, may not be interested in marriage, or have become tired of waiting for the "right" partner to come along. Jodi Foster, Academy Award® winning actress, has elected to have children without a husband. She now has two children and smiles when asked, "Who's the father?" The implication is that she has a right to her private life and that choosing to have a single-parent family is a viable option.

The stereotypical demographic profile of the single mother is no longer that of the young and poor woman who becomes a single parent because of carelessness, lack of judgment, or desire for a government stipend, but that of a mature woman who consciously chose single parenthood (Knox et al., 2000, p. 587).

An organization for women who want children and who may or may not marry is Single Mothers by Choice. The organization provides support for unmarried women who are contemplating having a child. The organization also has "thinkers' groups" for women who are uncertain about whether to have a child. Most women attending these groups decide not to have children after they have considered the various issues. Some of the problems faced by women who elect to rear children alone include the following:

1. *Satisfaction of the emotional and disciplinary needs of the child.* Perhaps the greatest challenge for single parents is satisfying the emotional needs of their children—alone. Children need love, which a parent may express in numerous ways—from giving hugs to helping with homework. But the single parent who is tired from working all day and who has no one else with whom to share parenting at night may be less able to meet the emotional needs of a child. Many single parents resolve this problem by getting help from their parents or extended family.
2. *Satisfaction of adult emotional needs.* Single parents have emotional needs of their own that children are often incapable of satisfying. The unmet need to share an emotional relationship with an adult can weigh heavily on the single parent. One single mother said, "I'm working two jobs, taking care of my kids, and trying to go to school. Plus my mother has cancer. Who am I going to talk to about that?" (authors' files).
3. *Satisfaction of adult sexual needs.* Some single parents regard their parental role as interfering with their sexual relationships. They may be concerned that their children will find out if they have a sexual encounter at home or be frustrated if they have to go away from home to enjoy a sexual relationship. Some choices with which they are confronted include "Do I wait until my children are asleep and then ask my lover to leave before morning?" "Do I openly acknowledge my lover's presence in my life to my children and ask them not to tell anybody?" "Suppose my kids get attached to my lover, who may not be a permanent part of our lives?"
4. *Lack of money.* Single-parent families, particularly those headed by women, report that money is always lacking.

NATIONAL DATA The median income for a female householder with no husband present is $28,126 (male householder with no wife present is $42,143), compared with $59,343 for two-parent households (*Statistical Abstract of the United States: 2002*, Table 654).

5. *Guardianship*. If the other parent is completely out of the child's life, the single parent needs to appoint a guardian to take care of her or his child in the event of her or his own death or disability.
6. *Prenatal care*. Single women who decide to have a child have poorer pregnancy outcomes than married women. In a Finnish study of 56,596 infants, those who were born to single mothers were more likely to be born prematurely, to have low birth weights, and to die shortly after birth than those born to married mothers (Manderbacka, Merilainen, Hemminki, Rahkonen, & Teperi, 1992). The researchers hypothesized that the reason for such findings may have been the lack of social support for the pregnancy or the working conditions of the mothers, which resulted in less prenatal care for their babies.
7. *Absence of a father*. Another consequence for children of single-parent mothers is that they often do not have the opportunity to develop an emotionally supportive relationship with their father. Knox et al. (2000) reported that children who grow up without fathers are more likely to drop out of school, be unemployed, abuse drugs, experience mental illness, and be a target of child sexual abuse. Conversely, those with fathers in their lives report higher life satisfaction, more stable marriages, and closer friendships. Sociologist David Popenoe observed that "fatherlessness is a major cause of the degenerating conditions of our young" (Peterson, 1995, 6d). Ansel Adams, the late great photographer, attributes his personal and life success to his father who steadfastly guided his development.

Though the risk of negative outcomes is higher for children in single-parent homes, most are happy and well adjusted. Benefits to single parents themselves include a sense of pride and self-esteem that result from being independent.

We have seen that individuals are subject to various social forces and influences in regard to whether to have children, and if so, how many. In section 11-3, we examine the various methods to control family size.

♦

11-3 BIRTH CONTROL

Since ancient times, men and women have practiced methods of birth control (Tone, 2001). An Egyptian medical papyrus (dated to 1850 B.C.) recommended use of suppositories made from crocodile dung or honey. In the fourth century B.C. Aristotle noted the practice of women coating their cervixes with olive oil before intercourse. Intra-vaginal plugs or tampons have been made of crushed root by women in preindustrial West Africa, bamboo tissue by Japanese women, and seaweed and algae by women of Easter Island. In early America (in addition to abstinence), methods included prolonged lactation, male withdrawal, suppositories, and douching solutions made from household substances. During the Depression, Lysol douche (although ineffective) was the best-selling contraceptive.

In sections 11-3a through 11-3f, we look at the various methods of contraception. All methods have one of three goals: to suppress ovulation, to prevent the male sperm from fertilizing the female egg, or to keep the fertilized egg from implanting in the uterus.

11-3a Hormonal Methods

Hormonal methods of contraception currently available to women include the "pill," Norplant®, Jadelle®, Depo-Provera®, Lunnelle®, NuvaRing®, and Ortho Evra®.

Oral Contraceptive Agents (Birth Control Pill)

The birth control pill is the most commonly used method of all the nonsurgical forms of contraception. Although 8% of women who take the pill still become pregnant in the first year of use (Ranjit, Bankile, Darroch, & Singh, 2001), it remains a desirable birth control option.

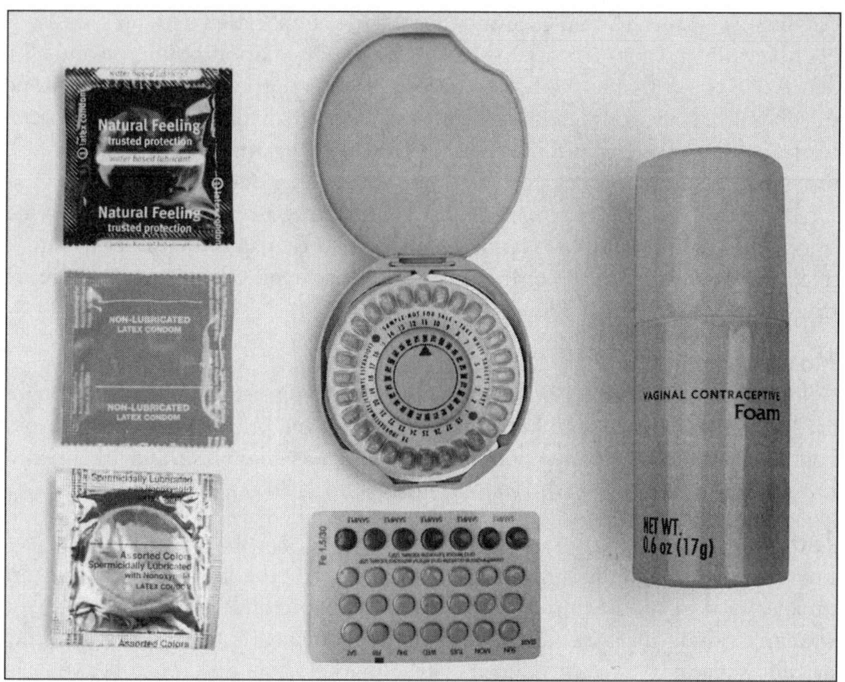

Many methods of birth control are available today.
Photo courtesy of Ben Lattin.

Oral contraceptives are available in basically two types: the combination pill, which contains varying levels of estrogen and progestin, and the minipill, which is progestin only. Combination pills work by raising the natural level of hormones in a woman's body, inhibiting ovulation, creating an environment where sperm cannot easily reach the egg, and hampering implantation of a fertilized egg.

The second type of birth control pill, the minipill, contains the same progesterone-like hormone found in the combination pill but does not contain estrogen. Progestin-only pills are taken every day with no hormone-free interval. Like the combination pill, the progestin in the minipill provides a hostile environment for sperm and does not allow implantation of a fertilized egg in the uterus, but unlike the combination pill, the minipill does not always inhibit ovulation. For this reason, the minipill is somewhat less effective than other types of birth control pills. The minipill has also been associated with a higher incidence of irregular bleeding.

Neither the combination pill nor the minipill should be taken unless prescribed by a health-care provider who has detailed information about the woman's previous medical history. Contraindications—reasons for not prescribing birth control pills—include hypertension, impaired liver function, known or suspected tumors that are estrogen-dependent, undiagnosed abnormal genital bleeding, pregnancy at the time of the examination, and a history of poor blood circulation or blood clotting. The major complications associated with taking oral contraceptives are blood clots and high blood pressure. Also, the risk of heart attack is increased for those who smoke or have other risk factors for heart disease. If they smoke, women over 35 should generally use other forms of contraception.

Although the long-term negative consequences of taking birth control pills are still the subject of research, short-term negative effects are experienced by 25% of all women who use them. These side effects include increased susceptibility to vaginal infections, nausea, slight weight gain, vaginal bleeding between periods, breast tenderness, headaches, and mood changes (some women become depressed and experience a loss of sexual desire). Women should also be aware of situations in which the pill is not effective, such as the first month of use, with certain prescription medications, and when pills are missed. On the positive side, pill use reduces the incidence of ectopic pregnancy and offers noncontraceptive benefits: reduced incidence of ovarian and endometrial cancers, pelvic inflammatory disease, anemia, and benign breast disease.

Finally, women should be aware that pill use is associated with an increased incidence of chlamydia and gonorrhea. One reason for the association of pill use and a higher incidence of STDs is that sexually active women who use the pill sometimes erroneously feel that because they are protected from becoming pregnant, they are also protected from contracting STDs. The pill provides no protection against STDs; the only methods that provide some protection against STDs are the male and female condoms.

Despite the widespread use of birth control pills, many women prefer a method that is longer-acting and does not require daily action. Research continues toward identifying safe, effective hormonal contraceptive delivery methods that are more convenient (Schwartz & Gabelnick, 2002).

Norplant® The first hormonal contraceptive implant system, using six flexible silicon capsules, inserted under the skin of a woman's upper arm.

Jadelle® A system of rod-shaped silicone implants that are inserted under the skin in the upper inner arm to provide time-release progestin into a woman's system for contraception.

Norplant®

A long-acting reversible hormonal contraceptive consisting of six thin flexible silicone capsules (34 mm in length) implanted under the skin of the upper arm, **Norplant,** which had been used in the United States for 10 years, was taken off the market permanently in the summer of 2002 (Wyeth Pharmaceuticals, Inc., 2002).

Jadelle®

Like Norplant, **Jadelle** is a system of rod-shaped silicone implants that are inserted under the skin in the upper inner arm which provide time-release progestin into a woman's system for contraception. This method has replaced Norplant, the first hormonal implant system introduced on the market. The difference between Jadelle and Norplant is that Jadelle consists of only two thin flexible silicone rods, whereas Norplant consists of six capsules, and Jadelle is inserted with a needle rather than through a minor surgical procedure. Jadelle was originally approved for 3 years of constant contraceptive protection, but in July 2002, the FDA extended approval for use for 5 years of pregnancy protection. Side effects are similar to those produced by Norplant, with the most common side effect that occurs being irregular menstrual bleeding (Jadelle® Implants, 2003, March 13). Population Council scientists are also developing a single rod implant containing Nestrone® (a synthetic progestin similar to the natural hormone progesterone). It may be used by lactating women and may protect against pregnancy for 2 years.

Depo-Provera® A synthetic compound similar to progesterone injected into the woman's arm or buttock that protects a woman against pregnancy for 3 months by preventing ovulation.

Depo-Provera®

Also known as "Depo" and "the shot," **Depo-Provera** is a synthetic compound similar to progesterone injected into the woman's arm or buttock that protects a woman against pregnancy for 3 months by preventing ovulation. It has been used by 30 million women worldwide since it was introduced in the late 1960s (although it was not approved for use in the United States until 1992).

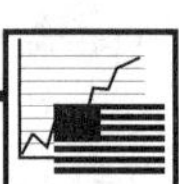

National Data The failure rate for the Depo-Provera shot the first 12 months of use is 2–3% (Fu, Darroch, Hass, & Ranjit, 2000).

Side effects of Depo-Provera include menstrual spotting, irregular bleeding, and some heavy bleeding the first few months of use, although 8 out of 10 women using Depo-Provera will eventually experience amenorrhea, or the absence of a menstrual period. Mood changes, headaches, dizziness, and fatigue have also been observed. Some women report a weight gain of 5–10 pounds. Also, after the injections are stopped, it takes an average of 18 months before the woman will become pregnant at the same rate as women who have not used Depo-Provera. Slightly less than 3% of U.S. women report using the injectable contraceptive. The reasons they cite include lack of knowledge, fear of side effects or health hazards, and satisfaction with their current contraceptive method (Tanfer, Wierzbicki, & Payne, 2000).

Lunelle® Once a Month Shot

(Warning: Pharmacia, the company that makes Lunelle, issued a recall in late 2002 because the product currently on the market may be sub-potent, which reduces the pregnancy prevention effectiveness rates.) At the time of this text's publication, no official information about the re-release of this product was available. **Lunelle** provides a one-month alternative to Depo-Provera. It is a hormonal injection that provides constant pregnancy protection for 28 days. Lunelle is beneficial for women who do not want to take a pill every day; those who experience the possibly stronger side effects of Depo-Provera; or those who must take a prescribed medication on a regular basis that interferes with hormonal absorption, a common problem for "pill" users. The disadvantage, however, is that the injection must be administered by a health-care provider once a month, which some women find to be inconvenient. Side effects are similar to that of oral contraceptives. Lunelle became available in the United States in 2000 but has been widely used in other countries for many years.

Lunelle® A hormonal method of contraception currently available; a 1-month injection must be administered by a physician.

Lunelle is an option for those who regularly take prescribed medications that have some interference with effectiveness rates (such as antibiotics or antidepressants), but not for people who take anticonvulsant medications. These types of drugs, commonly used by people suffering from epilepsy, may have some interaction on any hormonal methods of birth control because of the way they affect metabolism. St. John's wort, an herbal supplement, has also been found to reduce the effectiveness of most hormonal methods.

Vaginal Rings

NuvaRing®, which is a soft, flexible, and transparent ring approximately 2 inches in diameter that is worn inside the vagina, provides month-long pregnancy protection. Like oral contraceptives, NuvaRing is a highly effective contraceptive when used according to the labeling. Out of 100 women using NuvaRing for a year, one or two will become pregnant. This method is self-administered. NuvaRing is inserted into the vagina and is designed to release hormones that are absorbed by the woman's body for 3 weeks. The ring is then removed for a week, at which time the menstrual cycle will occur; afterward the ring is then replaced with a new ring. Side effects of NuvaRing are similar to that of the birth control pill (U.S. Food & Drug Administration, 1999). In a one-year study by the manufacturer, more than 2,000 women tested NuvaRing; 85% of the women were satisfied, and 95% would recommend it to others (Roumen, Apter, Mulders, & Dieben, 2001). In 2001 *Time* magazine recognized NuvaRing as one of the best health inventions of the year. NuvaRing became available in the United States in mid-2002.

NuvaRing® A soft, flexible, and transparent ring approximately 2 inches in diameter that is worn inside the vagina; it provides month-long pregnancy protection.

Transdermal Applications

Ortho Evra® is a contraceptive transdermal patch that delivers hormones to a woman's body through skin absorption. The contraceptive patch is worn for 3 weeks (anywhere on the body except the breasts) and is changed on a weekly basis. The fourth week is patch-free and the time when the menstrual cycle will occur (Mishell, 2002). Under no circumstances should more than 7 days lapse without wearing a patch (Zieman, 2002).

Ortho Evra® A contraceptive transdermal patch that delivers hormones to a woman's body through skin absorption. The contraceptive patch is worn for 3 weeks (anywhere on the body except the breasts) and is changed on a weekly basis.

Ortho Evra provides pregnancy protection and has side effects similar to the pill. Ortho Evra simply offers a different delivery method of the hormones needed to prevent pregnancy from occurring. However, a major advantage of the patch over the pill is higher compliance rates with the patch (Mishell, 2002). In clinical trials, the contraceptive patch was found to keep its adhesiveness even through showers, workouts, and water activities, such as swimming. Another transdermal delivery system under development is a contraceptive gel that can be applied to a woman's abdomen. Current efforts in the development of this Nestorone-containing gel yielded a product that women apply to the abdomen for contraceptive or hormone therapy. Because marketing studies in a number of locales have demonstrated that gels are more acceptable in some cultures and patches in others, both Nestorone gel and patch formulations are currently being investigated and developed (Population Council, 2003).

Male Hormonal Methods

Because of the dissatisfaction with the few contraceptive options available to men, research and development are occurring in this area. Several promising male products under development rely on MENT ™, a synthetic steroid that resembles testosterone. In contrast to testosterone, however, MENT does not have the effect of enlarging the prostate. A MENT implant and MENT transdermal gel and patch formulation are being developed for contraception and hormone therapy (Population Council Annual Report, 1999). When male hormonal methods do become available, men will need access to clinical screening, prescriptions, and monitoring similar to the follow-up of women who are taking the pill (Alan Guttmacher Institute, 2002).

11-3b Barrier Methods

The male and female condom, spermicides, diaphragm, and cervical cap are barrier methods of preventing pregnancy.

Male Condom

The condom is a thin sheath, made of latex, polyurethane, or natural membranes. Latex condoms, which can be used only with water-based lubricants, historically have been more popularly used. The polyurethane condom, however, which is thinner but just as durable as latex, is growing in popularity. Polyurethane condoms can be used with oil-based lubricants, are an option for people who have latex-sensitive allergies, block the HIV virus (87% effectiveness; Davis & Weller, 2000) and other sexually transmitted diseases, and allow for greater sensitivity during intercourse. Condoms made of natural membranes (sheep intestinal lining) are not recommended for any purpose other than pregnancy prevention because they are not effective in preventing transmission of HIV or other STDs. Never-married women and those who have been formerly married who are not in a stable relationship are the most likely to report condom use (Bankole, Darroch, & Singh, 2000).

NATIONAL DATA The failure rate for the male condom for the first 12 months of use is 14% (Ranjit et al., 2001).

The condom works by being rolled over and down the shaft of the erect penis before intercourse (see Figure 11-1). When the man ejaculates, sperm are caught inside the condom. When used in combination with a spermicidal lubricant that is placed inside the reservoir tip of the condom as well as a spermicidal or sperm-killing agent that the woman inserts inside her vagina, the condom is a highly effective contraceptive.

FIGURE 11-1
How to Put on a Condom

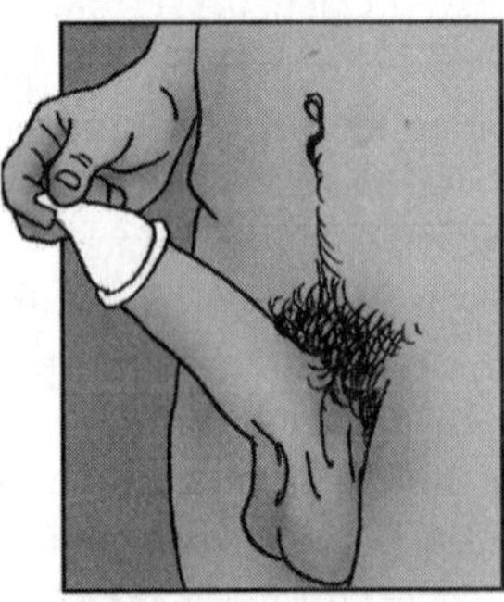

Place condom over head of the erect penis. If condom does not have reservoir tip, pinch the top of the condom to leave room for semen.

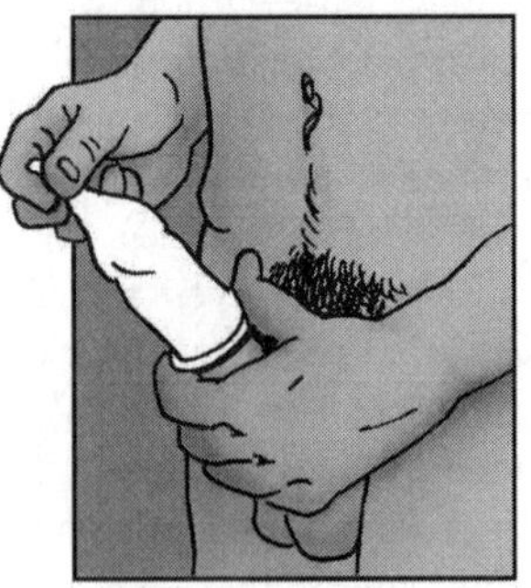

While holding the top, unroll the condom.

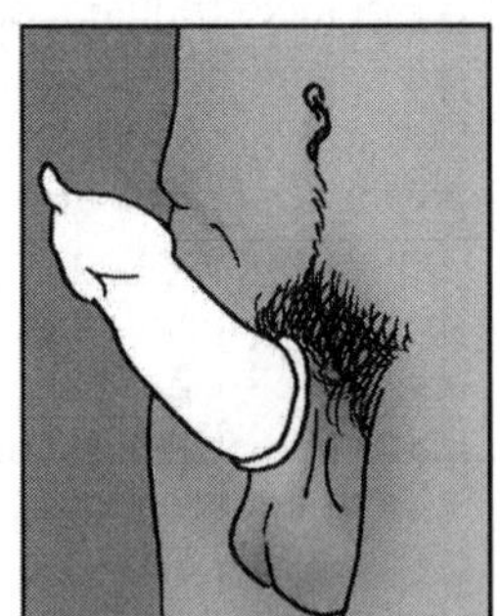

Continue unrolling the condom to the base of the penis.

Like any contraceptive, the condom is effective only when used properly. It should be placed on the penis early enough to avoid any seminal leakage into the vagina. In addition, polyurethane or latex condoms with a reservoir tip are preferable because they are less likely to break. (Even with a reservoir tip, air should be squeezed out of the tip of the condom as it is being placed on the penis to reduce the chance of breaking during ejaculation.) But such breakage does occur. (Tip: If the condom breaks, immediately insert a spermicide into the vagina to reduce the risk of pregnancy.) Finally, the penis should be withdrawn from the vagina immediately after ejaculation, before the man's penis returns to its flaccid state. If the penis is not withdrawn and the erection subsides, semen may leak from the base of the condom into the labia. Alternatively, when the erection subsides, the condom will come off when the man withdraws his penis if he does not hold onto the condom. Either way, the sperm will begin to travel up the vagina to the reproductive tract and fertilization may occur.

In addition to furnishing extra pregnancy protection, spermicides also provide lubrication, which permits easy entrance of the condom-covered penis into the vagina. If no spermicide is used and the condom is not of the prelubricated variety, a sterile lubricant (such as K-Y Jelly or Astroglide) may be needed. Vaseline or other kinds of petroleum jelly should not be used with condoms because vaginal infections and/or condom breakage may result.

Female Condom

The female condom resembles the male condom except that it fits in the woman's vagina to protect her from pregnancy, HIV infection, and other STDs. The **female condom** is a lubricated, polyurethane adaptation of the male version. It is about 6 inches long and has flexible rings at both ends. It is inserted like a diaphragm, with the inner ring fitting behind the pubic bone against the cervix; the outer ring remains outside the body and encircles the labial area (see Figure 11-2). Like the male version, the female condom is not reusable. Female condoms have been approved by the FDA and are being marketed under the brand names Femidom and Reality. The one-size-fits-all device is available without a prescription.

Female condom A lubricated, polyurethane adaptation of the male condom. It is about 6 inches long and has flexible rings at both ends—one inserted vaginally, which covers the cervix, and one external, which partially covers the labia.

The female condom is durable and may not tear as easily as latex male condoms. Some women may encounter some difficulty with first attempts to insert the female condom. A major advantage of the female condom is that, like the male counterpart, it helps protect against transmission of the HIV virus and other STDs, giving women an option for protection if their partner refuses to wear a condom. Placement may occur up to 8 hours before use, allowing greater spontaneity (Beksinska et al., 2001).

A number of studies that have been conducted internationally have found that women assess the female condom as acceptable and have high rates of trial use with positive reactions (Artz et al., 2000). Women who have had a sexually transmitted disease are more likely to use the female condom. Eighty-five percent of 895 women who attended an STD clinic reported that they had used the female condom during the past 6 months (Macaluso et al., 2000). If women have instruction and training in the use of the female

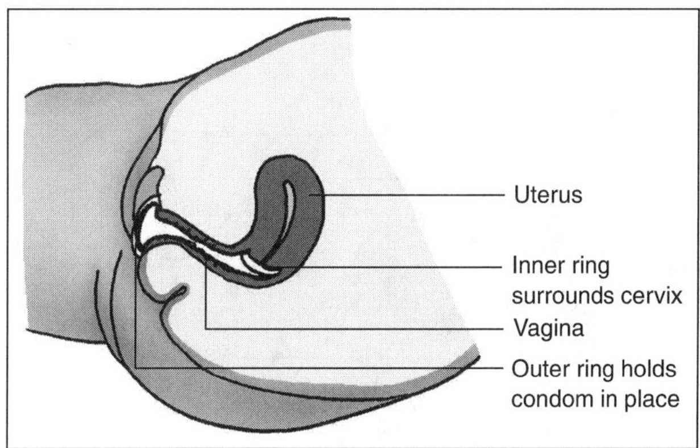

FIGURE 11-2
The Female Condom

The 6 inch-long sheath lines the vagina and is held in place by two plastic rings.

condom, including a chance to practice using the method, this increases its use. Women who had a chance to practice skills on a pelvic model were more likely to rate the method favorably, use it, and use it correctly. Although not a method completely under the woman's control, the female condom gives women more control than using the male condom (Van Devanter et al., 2002).

Vaginal Spermicides

Spermicide A chemical that kills sperm.

A **spermicide** is a chemical that kills sperm. Vaginal spermicides come in several forms, including foam, cream, jelly, film, and suppository. In the United States, the active agent in most spermicides is nonoxynol-9, which has previously been recommended for added STD protection. However, recent preliminary research in South African countries has shown that women who used nonoxynol-9 became infected with HIV at approximately a 50% higher rate than women who used a placebo gel (Van Damme, 2000). Spermicidal creams or gels should be used with a diaphragm. Spermicidal foams, creams, gels, suppositories, and films may be used alone or with a condom.

NATIONAL DATA The failure rate for spermicides for the first 12 months of use is 27% (Ranjit et al., 2001).

Spermicides must be applied before the penis enters the vagina (appropriate applicators are included when the product is purchased) no more than 20 minutes before intercourse (see Figure 11-3). Foam is effective immediately, but suppositories, creams, or jellies require a few minutes to allow the product to melt and spread inside the vagina (package instructions describe the exact time required). Each time intercourse is repeated, more spermicide must be applied. Spermicide must be left in place for at least 6–8 hours after intercourse; douching or rinsing the vagina should not be done during this period.

One advantage of using spermicides is that they are available without a prescription or medical examination. They also do not manipulate the woman's hormonal system and have few side effects. It was believed that a major noncontraceptive benefit of some spermicides is that they offer some protection against sexually transmitted diseases. However, 2002 guidelines for prevention and treatment of STDs from the Centers for Disease Control (CDC) suggest that spermicides are not recommended for STD/HIV protection. Furthermore, the CDC emphasizes that condoms lubricated with spermicides offer no more protection from STDs than other lubricated condoms, and spermicidally lubricated condoms may have a shorter shelf-life, cost more, and are associated with increased urinary tract infections in women (Centers for Disease Control and Prevention, 2002).

Contraceptive Sponge

The Today contraceptive sponge is a disk-shaped polyurethane device containing the spermicide nonoxynol-9. This small device, which has a 72–86% effectiveness rate, is

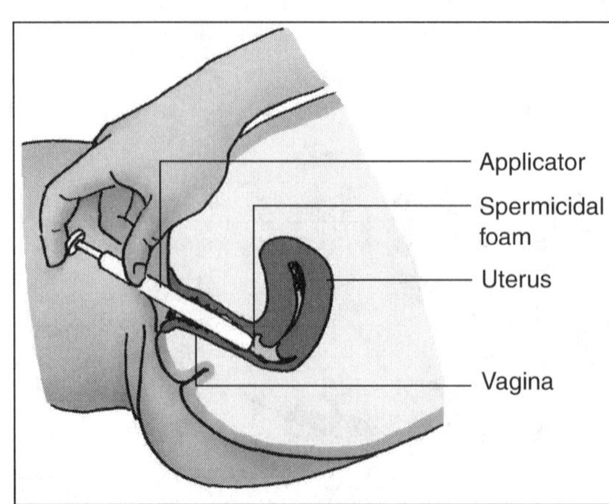

FIGURE 11-3
Vaginal Spermicides

Sperm-killing chemicals are available in the form of foams, jellies, creams, suppositories, and films.

dampened with water to activate the spermicide and then inserted into the vagina before intercourse begins. The sponge protects for repeated acts of intercourse for 24 hours without the need for supplying additional spermicide. It cannot be removed for at least 6 hours after intercourse, but it should not be left in place for more than 30 hours. Possible side effects that may occur with use include irritation, allergic reactions, or difficulty with removal, and the risk of Toxic Shock Syndrome, a rare but serious infection, is greater when the device is kept in place longer than recommended. The sponge provides no protection from sexually transmitted infections (Food & Drug Administration, 2002).

In July 1995, Whitehall-Robins Healthcare, the manufacturer of the sponge, made the voluntary decision to stop production of the contraceptive method after an FDA inspection of the plant disclosed bacterial contamination of the water used to make the Today Sponge, citing its unwillingness to finance equipment upgrades (McLearn, 1995). Allendale pharmaceuticals acquired the rights to reproduce the product in December 1998 and was set to release the already-approved method the following Fall. Due to requests by the FDA for packaging changes and additional safety testing, however, the sponge is still not currently available on the market (U.S. Food & Drug Administration, 2002) except in Canada, and no release date is set (Mendelsohn, 2002).

Intrauterine Device (IUD)

Although not technically a barrier method, the IUD is a structural device that prevents implantation. The **intrauterine device,** or IUD, is an object inserted into the uterus by a physician to prevent the fertilized egg from implanting on the uterine wall or to dislodge the fertilized egg if it has already implanted (see Figure 11-4). Two common IUDs sold in the United States are ParaGard Copper T 380A and the Progestasert Progesterone T. The Copper T is partly wrapped in copper and can remain in the uterus for 10 years. The Progesterone T contains a supply of progestin, which it continuously releases into the uterus in small amounts; after a year the supply runs out and a new IUD must be inserted. The Copper T has a lower failure rate than the Progesterone T. Recently, the FDA also approved an IUD called Mirena, widely used for years in Europe, for use in the United States. Mirena releases tiny amounts of the hormone levonorgestrel into the uterus and protects against pregnancy for 5 years.

Intrauterine device (IUD)
A device inserted into the uterus by a physician to prevent the fertilized egg from implanting on the uterine wall

Worldwide, the IUD is a popular method; 60% of women using IUDs continue their use after 2 years (Motamed, 2002). As a result of infertility and miscarriage associated with the Dalkon Shield IUD and subsequent lawsuits against its manufacturer by persons who were damaged by the device, use of all IUDs in the United States declined in the 1980s. However, other IUDs do not share the rates of pelvic inflammatory disease (PID) or resultant infertility associated with the Dalkon Shield. Nevertheless, other manufacturers voluntarily withdrew their IUDs from the U.S. market. In contrast to the 1% rate of use by women in the United States, the IUD accounts for 9–24% of all contraceptive

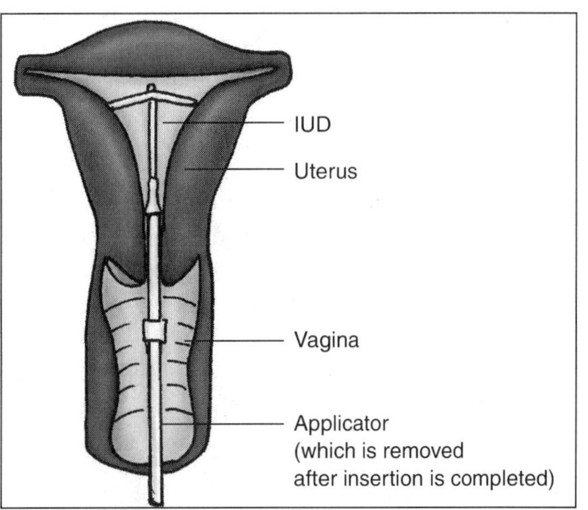

FIGURE 11-4
The IUD, as It Is Inserted by a Health-Care Practitioner

use in five European countries (Italy, Spain, Poland, Germany, and Denmark). The January 2001 re-introduction of the IUD in the United States and training of health-care providers in its proper screening, insertion, and follow-up care may prompt its revival in this country (Hubacher, 2002). The IUD is often an excellent choice for women who do not anticipate future pregnancies but do not wish to be sterilized or for women who are unable to use hormonal contraceptives, but not for women who have multiple sex partners.

NATIONAL DATA The failure rate for the IUD for the first 12 months of use is 3–4% (Ranjit et al., 2001).

Diaphragm

Diaphragm A shallow rubber dome attached to a flexible, circular steel spring, 2–4 inches in diameter, that can be inserted vaginally to cover the cervix and prevent sperm from entering the uterus.

Another barrier method of contraception is the **diaphragm**—a shallow rubber dome attached to a flexible, circular steel spring. Varying in diameter from 2–4 inches, the diaphragm covers the cervix and prevents sperm from moving beyond the vagina into the uterus. This device should always be used with a spermicidal jelly or cream.

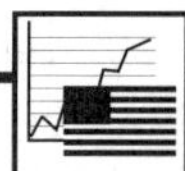

NATIONAL DATA The failure rate for the diaphragm for the first 12 months of use is 13% (Ranjit et al., 2001).

To obtain a diaphragm, a woman must have an internal pelvic examination by a health-care provider, who will select the appropriate size and instruct the woman on how to insert the diaphragm. The woman will be told to apply spermicidal cream or jelly on the inside of the diaphragm and around the rim before inserting it into the vagina (no more than 2 hours before intercourse). The diaphragm must also be left in place for 6–8 hours after intercourse to permit any lingering sperm to be killed by the spermicidal agent (see Figure 11-5).

After the birth of a child, a miscarriage, abdominal surgery, or the gain or loss of 10 pounds, a woman who uses a diaphragm should consult her physician or health-care practitioner to ensure a continued good fit. In any case, the diaphragm should be checked every 2 years for fit.

A major advantage of the diaphragm is that it does not interfere with the woman's hormonal system and has few, if any, side effects. Also, for those couples who feel that menstruation diminishes their capacity to enjoy intercourse, the diaphragm may be used to catch the menstrual flow for a brief time.

On the negative side, some women feel that use of the diaphragm with the spermicidal gel is messy and a nuisance, and it is possible that use of a spermicide may produce an allergic reaction. Furthermore, some partners feel that spermicides make oral-genital contact less enjoyable. Finally, if the diaphragm does not fit properly or is left in place too long (more than 24 hours), pregnancy or toxic shock syndrome can result.

Cervical Cap

Cervical cap A thimble-shaped contraceptive device made of rubber or polyethylene that fits tightly over the cervix and is held in place by suction.

The **cervical cap** is a thimble-shaped contraceptive device made of rubber or polyethylene that fits tightly over the cervix and is held in place by suction. Like the diaphragm, the cervical cap, which is used in conjunction with spermicidal cream or jelly, prevents sperm from entering the uterus. Cervical caps have been widely available in Europe for some time and were approved for marketing in the United States in 1988. The cervical cap cannot be used during menstruation because the suction cannot be maintained. The effectiveness, problems, risks, and advantages are similar to those of the diaphragm.

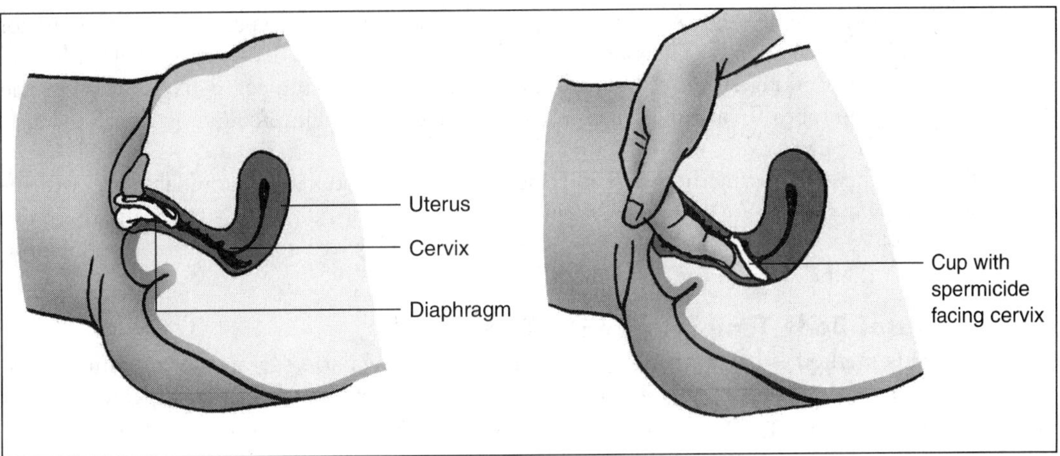

FIGURE 11-5
The Diaphragm

NATIONAL DATA The failure rate for the cervical cap for the first 12 months of use is 12% (Fu et al., 2000).

11-3c Natural Family Planning Methods

Also referred to as **periodic abstinence,** rhythm method, and fertility awareness, natural family planning involves refraining from sexual intercourse during the 1 to 2 weeks each month when the woman is thought to be fertile. Women who use periodic abstinence must know their time of ovulation and avoid intercourse just before, during, and immediately after that time. Calculating the fertile period involves three assumptions: (1) ovulation occurs on day 14 (plus or minus 2 days) before the onset of the next menstrual period; (2) sperm typically remain viable for 2–3 days; and (3) the ovum survives for 24 hours.

Periodic abstinence Refraining from sexual intercourse during the 1 to 2 weeks each month when the woman is thought to be fertile. (Also known as rhythm method, fertility awareness, and natural family planning.)

NATIONAL DATA The failure rate for periodic abstinence for the first 12 months of use is 23% (Ranjit et al., 2001).

The time period during which the woman is fertile can be predicted in four ways: the calendar method, the basal body temperature method, the cervical mucus method, and the hormone-in-urine method. These methods may be used not only to avoid pregnancy, but also to facilitate conception if the woman wants to become pregnant. We provide only basic instructions here for using periodic abstinence as a method of contraception. Individuals considering this method should consult with a trained health-care practitioner for more detailed instruction.

Calendar Method

The calendar method is the oldest and most widely practiced method of avoiding pregnancy through periodic abstinence. The calendar method allows women to calculate the onset and duration of their fertile period. When using the calendar method to predict when the egg is ready to be fertilized, the woman keeps a record of the length of her menstrual cycles for 8 months. The menstrual cycle is counted from day one of the menstrual period through the last day before the onset of the next period. She then calculates her fertile period by subtracting 18 days from the length of her shortest cycle and 11 days from the length of her longest cycle. The resulting figures indicate the range of her fertility period. It is during this time that the woman must abstain from intercourse if pregnancy is not desired.

For example, suppose that during an 8-month period, a woman had cycle lengths of 26, 32, 27, 30, 28, 27, 28, and 29 days. Subtracting 18 from her shortest cycle (26) and 11 from her longest cycle (32), she knows the days that the egg is likely to be in the Fallopian tubes. To avoid getting pregnant, she must avoid intercourse on days 8 through 21 of her cycle.

The calendar method of predicting the "safe" period may be unreliable for two reasons. First, the next month the woman may ovulate at a different time than any of the previous 8 months. Second, sperm life varies; they may live up to 5 days, long enough to meet the next egg in the Fallopian tubes.

Basal Body Temperature (BBT) Method

This method is based on determining the time of ovulation by measuring temperature changes that occur in the woman's body shortly after ovulation. The basal body temperature is the temperature of the body at rest on waking in the morning. To establish her BBT, the woman must take her temperature before she gets out of bed for 3 months. Shortly before, during, or right after ovulation, the woman's BBT usually rises about 0.4–0.8 degrees Fahrenheit. Some women notice a temperature drop about 12 to 24 hours before it begins to rise after ovulation. Intercourse must be avoided from the time the woman's temperature drops until her temperature has remained elevated for 3 consecutive days. Intercourse may be resumed on the night of the third day after the BBT has risen and remained elevated for 3 consecutive days. Advantages include being "natural" and avoiding chemicals. Disadvantages include the higher pregnancy rate for persons using this method.

Cervical Mucus Method

The cervical mucus method, also known as the *Billings method* of natural family planning, is based on observations of changes in the cervical mucus during the woman's monthly cycle. The woman may observe her cervical mucus by wiping herself with toilet paper.

The woman should abstain from intercourse during her menstrual period because the mucus is obscured by menstrual blood and cannot be observed, and ovulation can occur during menstruation. After menstruation ceases, intercourse is permitted on days when no mucus is present or thick mucus is present in small amounts. Intercourse should be avoided just prior to, during, and immediately after ovulation if pregnancy is not desired. Before ovulation, mucus is cloudy, yellow or white, and sticky. During ovulation, cervical mucus is thin, clear, slippery, and stretchy and resembles raw egg white. This phase is known as the *peak symptom*. During ovulation, some women experience ovulatory pain referred to as **mittelschmerz.** Such pain may include feelings of heaviness, abdominal swelling, rectal pain or discomfort, and lower abdominal pain or discomfort on either side. Mittelschmerz is useful for identifying ovulation but not for predicting it. Intercourse may resume 4 days after the disappearance of the peak symptom and continue until the next menses. During this time, cervical mucus may be either clear and watery, or cloudy and sticky, or there may be no mucus noticed at all.

Mittelschmerz Term used in reference to the pain experienced during ovulation.

Advantages of the cervical mucus method include that it requires the woman to become familiar with her reproductive system, and it can give early warning about some STDs (which can affect cervical mucus). However, the cervical mucus method requires the woman to distinguish between mucus and semen, spermicidal agents, lubrication, and infectious discharges. Also, the woman must not douche because she will wash away what she is trying to observe.

Hormone-in-Urine Method

A hormone (LH, luteinizing hormone) is released in increasing amounts in the ovulating woman 12 to 24 hours prior to ovulation. Women can purchase over-the-counter ovulation tests, such as First Response and Ovutime, that are designed to ascertain the surge of LH into the urine (signaling ovulation) so the couple will know to avoid intercourse to maximize the chance of preventing pregnancy. Some test kits involve the woman exposing a test stick during urination, whereas others involve collecting the urine in a small cup and placing the test stick in the cup. In practice, the woman conducts a number of urine tests over a period of days because each test kit comes supplied with five or six tests. Some women experience the LH hormone surge within a 10-hour span, so the woman may need to test herself more than once a day. Of course, this method can also be used to predict the best time to have intercourse to maximize chances of becoming pregnant.

11-3d Nonmethods: Withdrawal and Douching

Because withdrawal and douching are not effective in preventing pregnancy, we call them *nonmethods* of birth control (some may argue that *natural family planning methods* are also nonmethods because a high rate of pregnancies results). Also known as **coitus interruptus, withdrawal** is the practice whereby the man withdraws his penis from the vagina before he ejaculates. The advantages of coitus interruptus are that it requires no devices or chemicals, and it is always available. The disadvantages of withdrawal are that it does not provide protection from STDs, it may interrupt the sexual response cycle and diminish the pleasure for the couple, and it is very ineffective in preventing pregnancy.

Coitus interruptus The practice whereby the man withdraws his penis from the vagina before he ejaculates. (See also **withdrawal.**)

Withdrawal See **coitus interruptus.**

NATIONAL DATA The failure rate for withdrawal for the first 12 months of use is 24% (Ranjit et al., 2001).

Withdrawal is not a reliable form of contraception for two reasons. First, a man can unknowingly emit a small amount of pre-ejaculatory fluid, which may contain sperm. One drop can contain millions of sperm. In addition, the man may lack the self-control to withdraw his penis before ejaculation, or he may delay his withdrawal too long and inadvertently ejaculate some semen near the vaginal opening of his partner. Sperm deposited there can live in the moist labia and make their way up the vagina.

Although some women believe that douching is an effective form of contraception, it is not. Douching refers to rinsing or cleansing the vaginal canal. After intercourse, the woman fills a syringe with water, a variety of solutions that can be purchased over-the-counter, or a spermicidal agent and flushes (so she assumes) the sperm from her vagina. But in some cases, the fluid will actually force sperm up through the cervix. In other cases, a large number of sperm may already have passed through the cervix to the uterus, so the douche may do little good. Sperm may be found in the cervical mucus within 90 seconds after ejaculation.

In effect, douching does little to deter conception and may even encourage it. In addition, douching is associated with an increased risk for pelvic inflammatory disease and ectopic pregnancy.

11-3e Emergency Contraception

Also called **postcoital contraception, emergency contraception** refers to various types of morning-after pills that are used primarily in three circumstances: (1) when a woman has unprotected intercourse, (2) when a contraceptive method fails (such as condom breakage or slippage), and (3) when a woman is raped. Emergency contraception methods should be used only in emergencies—those times when unprotected intercourse has occurred, and medication can be taken within 72 hours of exposure. Planned Parenthood now makes emergency contraception available by phone. A person can call in, get a prescription, and begin taking the medication immediately, assuming she has access to a pharmacy that will fill the prescription.

Postcoital contraception See **emergency contraception.**

Emergency contraception Contraceptive administered within 72 hours following unprotected intercourse; referred to as the "morning-after pill." (See also **postcoital contraception.**)

Fear that emergency contraception is being used as a routine method of contraception is not supported by data. Of 235 women who had received emergency contraception, 70% were using the pill and 73% were using a condom prior to their need for emergency contraception (Harvey, Beckman, Sherman, & Petitti, 2000). A larger problem is the lack of awareness of emergency contraception. Some women are simply not aware that it exists.

Combined Estrogen-Progesterone

The most common morning-after pills are the combined estrogen-progesterone oral contraceptives routinely taken to prevent pregnancy. In higher doses, they serve to prevent ovulation, fertilization of the egg, or transportation of the egg to the uterus. They may also make the uterine lining inhospitable to implantation. Known as the *Yuzpe method* after the physician who proposed it, this method involves ingesting a certain number of tablets of combined estrogen-progesterone. *Emergency contraception must be taken within 72 hours of unprotected intercourse to be effective.* Common side effects of combined estrogen-progesterone emergency contraception pills (sold under the trade names Preven and Plan B) include nausea, vomiting, headaches, and breast tenderness, although some women also experience abdominal pain, headache, and dizziness. Side effects subside within a day or two after treatment is completed. The pregnancy rate is 1.2% if combined estrogen-progesterone is taken within 12 hours of unprotected intercourse, 2.3% if taken within 48 hours, and 4.9% if taken within 48–72 hours (Rosenfeld, 1997). Although the FDA has not yet approved the availability of the morning-after pill over-the-counter, the American Medical Association supports this action.

Postcoital IUD Insertion

Insertion of a copper IUD within 5–7 days after ovulation in a cycle when unprotected intercourse has occurred is very effective for preventing pregnancy. This option, however, is used much less frequently than hormonal treatment because women who need emergency contraception often are not appropriate IUD candidates.

Mifepristone (RU-486)

Mifepristone A synthetic steroid that effectively inhibits implantation of a fertilized egg by making the endometrium unsuitable for implantation. In effect, it aborts the fetus, and may be used within the first 7 weeks of pregnancy. (See also **RU-486.**)

RU-486 See **Mifepristone.**

Mifepristone, also known as **RU-486,** is a synthetic steroid that effectively inhibits implantation of a fertilized egg by making the endometrium unsuitable for implantation. The so-called *abortion pill*, recently approved by the FDA in the United States, is marketed under the name Mifeprex and can be given to induce abortion within 7 weeks of pregnancy. Side effects of RU-486 are usually severe and may include cramping, nausea, vomiting, and breast tenderness. The pregnancy rate associated with RU-486 is 1.6%, which suggests that RU-486 is an effective means of emergency contraception (Rosenfeld, 1997). More than 90% of U.S. women who tried RU-486 would recommend it to others and choose it over surgery again. Its use remains controversial.

Cultural Diversity 

A greater proportion of U.S. women report no contraceptive use at either the first or most recent intercourse (25% and 20%, respectively) than nonuse in France (11% and 12%, respectively), Great Britain (21% and 4%, respectively) and Sweden (22% and 7%, respectively) (Darroch, Singh, Frost, & The Study Team, 2001).

11-3f Effectiveness of Various Contraceptive Choices

In Table 11-1, we present data on the effectiveness of various contraceptive methods in preventing pregnancy and protecting against sexually transmitted diseases. Table 11-1 also describes the benefits, disadvantages, and costs of various methods of contraception. Also included in the chart is the obvious and most effective form of birth control: abstinence. Its cost is the lowest, it is 100% effective for pregnancy prevention, and it also eliminates the risk of HIV and STD infection from intercourse. Abstinence can be practiced for a week, a month, several years, until marriage, or until someone finds the "right" sexual partner.

Think About It 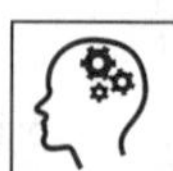

Individuals rarely use one method of birth control throughout their fertile years. Which methods seem most suitable for you, and why, for each stage of your life?

TABLE 11-1 Methods of Contraception and Sexually Transmitted Disease Protection*

Method	Pregnancy Protection[1]	STD Protection	Benefits	Disadvantages	Cost[2]
Oral contraceptive (The Pill)	95–99.5%	No	High effectiveness rate. 24-hour protection. Menstrual regulation.	Daily administration. Side effects possible. Medication interactions.	$10–42 per month
Norplant® (6 rod 5-year implant)	99.95%	No	High effectiveness rate. Long-term protection.	Local surgery to implant. Removal can be difficult. (*No longer available, but current users may continue.)	$500–700 per insertion
Jadelle® (2 rod 3–5 year implant)	99.95%	No	High effectiveness rate. Long-term protection.	Side effects possible. Menstrual changes.	$300–600 per insertion
Depo-Provera® (3-month injection)	99.7%	No	High effectiveness rate. Long-term protection.	Decreases body calcium. Side effects likely.	$45–75 per injection
Lunelle® (1-month injection)	99.7%	No	Same as oral contraceptives except use is monthly, not daily.	Injection must be administered by a physician.	$26–38 per injection
Ortho Evra® (Transdermal Patch)	98.5–99.9%	No	Same as oral contraceptives except use is weekly, not daily.	Patch changed weekly. Side effects possible.	$15–32 per month
NuvaRing® (Vaginal Ring)	99–99.9%	No	Same as oral contraceptives except use is monthly, not daily.	Must be comfortable with body for insertion.	$15–48 per month
Male Condom	86–97%	Yes	Few or no side effects. Easy to purchase and use.	Can interrupt spontaneity.	$2–10 a box
Female Condom	79–95%	Yes	Few or no side effects. Easy to purchase.	Decreased sensation. Insertion takes practice.	$4–10 a box
Spermicide	74–94%	No	Many forms to choose. Easy to purchase and use.	Can cause irritation. Can be messy.	$8–18 per box/tube/can
Diaphragm & Cervical Cap	80–94%	No	Few side effects. Can be inserted within 2 hours before intercourse.	Can be messy. Increased risk of vaginal/UTI infections.	$50 to $200 plus spermicide
Intrauterine Device (IUD)	97.4–99.2%	No	Little maintenance. Longer term protection.	Risk of PID increased. Chance of expulsion.	$150–300
Withdrawal	81–96%	No	Requires little planning. Always available.	Pre-ejaculatory fluid can contain sperm.	$0
Periodic Abstinence	75–91%	No	No side effects. Accepted in all religions/cultures.	Requires a lot of planning.	$0
Emergency Contraception	75%	No	Provides an option after intercourse has occurred.	Need ability to interpret fertility signs. Must be taken within 72 hours. Side effects likely.	$10–32
Abstinence	100%	Yes	No risk of pregnancy or STDs.	Partners both have to agree to abstain.	$0

[1]Percentages range from actual/typical use to perfect use rates.

[2]Costs may vary.

*This table was developed by Beth Credle, MAEd, CHES, a health education specialist in human sexuality, at East Carolina University. Ms. Credle also updated this chapter to provide state-of-the-art information as of February, 2003.

11-4 STERILIZATION

Sterilization Surgical procedure that permanently prevents reproduction.

Unlike the temporary and reversible methods of contraception discussed in section 11-3, **sterilization** is a permanent surgical procedure that prevents reproduction. Sterilization is the most prevalent method of contraception in the United States (Godecker, Thomson, & Bumpass, 2001). Sterilization may be a contraceptive method of choice when the woman should not have more children for health reasons or when individuals are certain about their desire to have no more children or to remain child-free. Most couples complete their intended childbearing in their late 20s or early 30s, leaving more than 15 years of continued risk of unwanted pregnancy. Because of the risk of pill use at older ages and the lower reliability of alternative birth control methods, sterilization has become the most popular method of contraception among married women who have completed their families.

Slightly more than half of all sterilizations are performed on women. In addition to men being fearful of a vasectomy (which they sometimes equate with castration and the removal of their manhood), women may be more open to sterilization—"I'm the one that ends up being pregnant and having the baby," said one woman. "So I want to make sure that I never get pregnant again."

11-4a Female Sterilization

Oophorectomy Surgical removal of the ovaries.

Hysterectomy Surgical removal of the uterus.

Salpingectomy Tubal ligation or "tying of the tubes" sterilization procedure whereby the woman's Fallopian tubes are cut out and the ends are tied, clamped, or cauterized so that eggs cannot pass down the Fallopian tubes to be fertilized.

Although a woman may be sterilized by removal of her ovaries (**oophorectomy**) or uterus (**hysterectomy**), these operations are not normally undertaken for the sole purpose of sterilization because the ovaries produce important hormones (as well as eggs) and because both procedures carry the risks of major surgery.

The usual procedures of female sterilization are the salpingectomy and a variant of it, the laparoscopy. **Salpingectomy,** also known as tubal ligation, or tying the tubes (see Figure 11-6), is often performed under a general anesthetic while the woman is in the hospital. Many women elect to have this procedure performed just after they have delivered a baby. An incision is made in the lower abdomen, just above the pubic line, and the Fallopian tubes are brought into view one at a time. A part of each tube is cut out, and the ends are tied, clamped, or cauterized (burned). The operation takes about 30 minutes. About 700,000 such procedures are performed annually with about half being performed postpartum and half being performed as interval procedures unrelated to the timing of the woman's pregnancy (Mackay, Kieke, Koonin, & Beattie, 2001).

Laparoscopy A tubal ligation performed with the use of a laparoscope.

A less expensive and quicker (about 15 minutes) form of salpingectomy, which is performed on an outpatient basis, is the **laparoscopy.** Often using local anesthesia, the surgeon inserts a small, lighted viewing instrument (laparoscope) through the woman's abdominal wall just below the navel through which the uterus and the Fallopian tubes can be seen. The

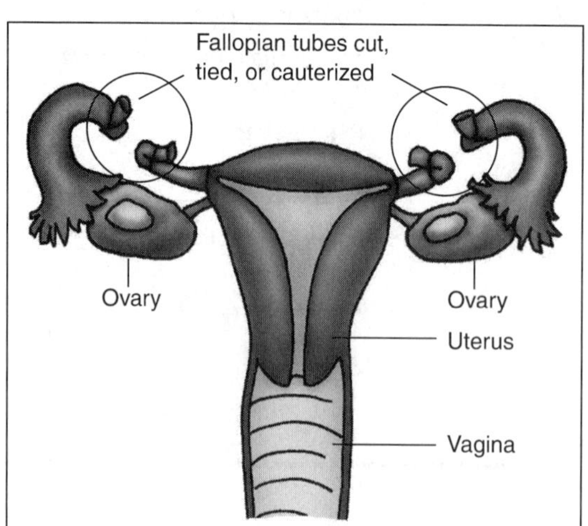

FIGURE 11-6
Female Sterilization: Tubal Sterilization

The Fallopian tubes are interrupted surgically—cut and tied or blocked—to prevent passage of the eggs from the ovaries to the uterus.

surgeon then makes another small incision in the lower abdomen and inserts a special pair of forceps that carry electricity to cauterize the tubes. The laparoscope and the forceps are then withdrawn, the small wounds are closed with a single stitch, and small bandages are placed over the closed incisions. (Laparoscopy is also known as "the band-aid operation.") As an alternative to reaching the Fallopian tubes through an opening below the navel, the surgeon may make a small incision in the back of the vaginal barrel (vaginal tubal ligation).

In late 2002, the FDA approved **Essure,** a permanent sterilization procedure that requires no cutting and only a local anesthetic in a half-hour procedure that blocks the Fallopian tubes. Women typically may return home within 45 minutes (and to work the next day). Essure is already available in Australia, Europe, Singapore, and Canada.

Essure A permanent sterilization procedure that requires no cutting and only a local anesthetic in a half-hour procedure that blocks the Fallopian tubes.

These procedures for female sterilization are more than 95% effective, but sometimes they have complications. In rare cases, a blood vessel in the abdomen is torn open during the sterilization and bleeds into the abdominal cavity. When this happens, another operation is necessary to find the bleeding vessel and tie it closed. Occasionally, injury occurs to the small or large intestine, which may cause nausea, vomiting, and loss of appetite. The fact that death may result, if only rarely, is a reminder that female sterilization is surgery and, like all surgery, involves some risks.

In addition, although some female sterilizations may be reversed, a woman should become sterilized only if she does not want to have a biological child. Hillis, Marchbanks, Ratlif Taylor, Peterson, et al. (2000) reported that women who were age 30 or younger at the time they were sterilized were twice as likely to report feelings of regret than women who were older than 30.

Another form of permanent birth control in development is the selective tubal occlusion procedure (STOP). It involves placing a metal coil into a woman's Fallopian tubes, causing tissue to form a "plug" that blocks egg passage. The method has been compared to a vasectomy in terms of cost, risk, and time away from work, but is not reversible ("New Contraception Option," 2000).

11-4b Male Sterilization

The **vasectomy** is the most frequent form of male sterilization. It is usually performed in the physician's office under a local anesthetic. In this operation the physician makes two small incisions, one on either side of the scrotum, so that a small portion of each vas deferens (the sperm-carrying ducts) can be cut out and tied closed (see Figure 11-7). Sperm are still produced in the testicles, but because there is no tube to the penis, they remain in the epididymis and eventually dissolve. The procedure takes about 15 minutes and costs about $800. The man can leave the physician's office within a short time. Men most likely to seek a vasectomy are in their 30s or older, have been married more than 8 years, and already have three children (Forste, Tanfer, & Tedrow, 1995).

Vasectomy A minor surgical procedure whereby the vas deferens are cut so as to prevent sperm from entering the penis.

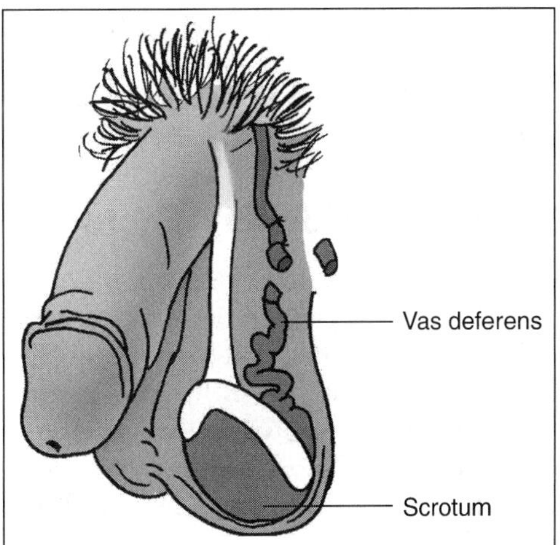

FIGURE 11-7
Male Sterilization: Vasectomy

A pair of incisions is made in the scrotum, and the vas deferens—the tubes connecting the testes and the urethra—are cut and tied off to prevent the passage of sperm to the urethra.

NATIONAL DATA Eleven percent of U.S. women report being married to or living with a man who has had a vasectomy (Godecker et al., 2001).

Because sperm do not disappear from the ejaculate immediately after a vasectomy (some remain in the vas deferens above the severed portion), a couple should use another method of contraception until the man has had about 20 ejaculations. The man is then asked to bring a sample of his ejaculate to the physician's office for examination under a microscope for a sperm count. In about 1% of the cases, the vas deferens grows back and the man becomes fertile again. In other cases, the man may have more than two tubes, which the physician was not aware of.

A vasectomy does not affect the man's desire for sex, ability to have an erection or an orgasm, amount of ejaculate (sperm comprise only a minute portion of the seminal fluid), or health. A recent study in New Zealand affirmed that despite earlier concerns, vasectomy (even after 25 years or more) does not increase the risk of prostate cancer (Cox, Sneyd, Paul, Delahunt, & Skegg, 2002). Although in some instances a vasectomy may be reversed, a man should get a vasectomy only if he does not want to have a biological child.

Reversible methods of blocking the vas deferens are being developed. In Asia, Indonesia, and Europe, clinical trials of Vasoc are underway; in these trials, a silicone plug is injected into the vas deferens. Another plug design (the "Shug"), using dual silicone plugs that are inserted surgically, is undergoing clinical trials ("Contraceptive Technologies," 2002).

11-5 FACTORS INFLUENCING CONTRACEPTIVE CHOICE AND USE

Despite the array of contraceptive choices that exist, of the 210 million pregnancies that occur throughout the world each year, 40% were not intended. "Successful prevention of unplanned pregnancies relies not only on access to available marketed products, but also on the products' acceptability and couples' willingness and ability to use them effectively" (Schwartz & Gabelnick, 2002, p. 310). In sections 11-5a through 11-5c we look at the factors involved in selecting a particular contraceptive procedure.

11-5a Psychological Constructs

Emotional responses to sexual topics (erotophobia/erotophilia) can impact individuals' behaviors of acquiring or using contraception. Embarrassment may be a factor—embarrassment toward discussing birth control with a partner, getting the pill, or buying condoms.

The measure in Box 11-2 was developed to assess the level of embarrassment ("psychological discomfort, self-consciousness, and feeling of being ill-at-ease") in college students regarding condom use. This self-assessment takes approximately 10 minutes to complete.

11-5b Relationship Factors

Relationship factors are an important influence in contraceptive use in that relationship dynamics and negotiation skills impact contraceptive use. A study of low-income women in family planning and STD clinics in Miami found that whether contraceptive decisions were made jointly or by one's partner impacted on condom use. Among women who reported that their partner made the contraception decision, 28% reported consistent or occasional condom use. When the woman made the decision herself, the use was 24%. In contrast, when the couple made the decision jointly, 41% used condoms (Soler et al., 2000).

Box 11-2 Self-Assessment

INTERACTIVE BOX

Self Assessment: Condom Embarrassment Scale (CES)

Strongly Disagree 1 2 3 4 5 Strongly Agree

___ 1. I am embarrassed or would be embarrassed about buying a condom from a drug store near campus.
___ 2. I am embarrassed or would be embarrassed about buying a condom from a drug store close to where my parents live.
___ 3. I am embarrassed or would be embarrassed about buying a condom from a place where I could be certain no one I know would see me.
___ 4. I am embarrassed or would be embarrassed about obtaining condoms from Student Health Services (Infirmary).
___ 5. I am embarrassed or would be embarrassed about obtaining condoms from a local health department.
___ 6. I am embarrassed or would be embarrassed about asking a pharmacist or drug store clerk where condoms are located in the store.
___ 7. I am embarrassed or would be embarrassed about asking a doctor or other health-care professional questions about condom use.
___ 8. I am embarrassed or would be embarrassed about stopping during foreplay and asking my partner to use a condom.
___ 9. I would be embarrassed if a new partner insisted that we use a condom.
___ 10. I am embarrassed or would be embarrassed to tell my partner during foreplay that I am not willing to have sexual intercourse unless we use a condom.
___ 11. I am embarrassed or would be embarrassed about being prepared and providing a condom during lovemaking if my partner didn't have one.
___ 12. I am embarrassed or would be embarrassed about carrying a condom around in my wallet/purse.
___ 13. I am embarrassed or would be embarrassed about talking to my partner about my thoughts and feelings about condom use.
___ 14. I am embarrassed or would be embarrassed if my partner watched me dispose of a condom after we had used it.
___ 15. (FEMALE:) I am embarrassed or would be embarrassed about watching my partner put on a condom.
___ (MALE:) I am embarrassed or would be embarrassed if my partner watched me put on a condom.
___ 16. (FEMALE:) I am embarrassed or would be embarrassed about helping my partner put on a condom.
___ (MALE:) I am embarrassed or would be embarrassed if my partner helped me put on a condom.
___ 17. (FEMALE:) I am embarrassed or would be embarrassed about watching my partner remove a condom.
___ (MALE:) I am embarrassed or would be embarrassed if my partner watched me remove a condom.
___ 18. (FEMALE:) I am embarrassed or would be embarrassed about helping my partner remove a condom.
___ (MALE:) I am embarrassed or would be embarrassed if my partner helped me remove a condom.

Scoring: After assigning a number to each item, add the scores. The possible range of scores is from 18 to 90, with 18 indicating the lowest embarrassment and 90 indicating the highest. Among the 256 college students in the original study using this assessment, the mean score on the CES was 44.88 (SD = 14.85). The mean score for women (46.54) was significantly higher than for men (41.81).

The developers of the CES found that its summed score was significantly correlated with the Sex Anxiety Inventory ($r = .39$). Women who scored higher on a test of STD/condom knowledge were less embarrassed about obtaining and using condoms ($r = -.35$). For the men, knowledge and embarrassment scores were not correlated. CES scores were related to various behaviors. Not surprisingly, those who have actually made a condom purchase reported less condom embarrassment than those who had not bought condoms. Respondents who were sexually active had lower embarrassment scores than students who were not sexually active.

Source: Scale used by permission of *American Journal of Health Education/American Association for Health Education*, which appeared in Vail-Smith, K., Durham, T. W., & Howard, H. A. (1992). A scale to measure embarrassment associated with condom use. *Journal of Health Education, 23*, 209–212.

(Note: The CES is also reprinted with permission of the authors, who encourage its use for research or educational purposes. The authors of the scale would appreciate receiving information about the results. Address correspondence to Karen Vail-Smith, Department of Health Education, East Carolina University, Greenville, NC 27858-4353; e-mail: vail-smithk@mail.ecu.edu.)

Cultural Diversity 

In the Soler et al. (2000) study, nearly all the Black (90%) and White (95%) women reported feeling extremely or somewhat comfortable talking with their partner about condoms, compared to 76% of Hispanic women.

Research results regarding the impact of relationship type (whether partners are acquaintances, exclusively dating, or engaged) are mixed. Some studies find that couples with strong emotional ties are more likely to discuss and practice contraception than couples in casual relationships. On the other hand, some studies have found men more likely to use condoms in casual relationships (especially for protection from STDs). More research is needed on couples' decision-making processes in contraception choice and use.

NATIONAL DATA According to analyses of the 1995 Survey of Family Growth, half (52%) of adolescents who had just met their sexual partner used no contraceptive method at first intercourse; among those who were going steady with their partner, 24% used no method (Manning, Longmore, & Giordano, 2000).

Although condom use has risen, even among nonmonogamous couples a minority use condoms. The question has been raised as to whether the availability of such coitus-independent methods as the pill has been a factor in the low use of condoms. Has the ability to separate contraception from sexual activity decreased the likelihood that people would gain competence and become comfortable in communicating about sex and integrating method use into coitus (Darroch, 2000)?

11-5c Accessibility of Contraceptives

An important factor in considering which contraception procedure to use is affordability. In the United States, even those who have health insurance find that coverage for contraceptives is often limited. A study of women (ages 25–34), conducted by the Women's Research and Education Institute, determined that for more than half of the women, their health plans exclude reversible contraceptives (such as the pill) from coverage. Insurance is more likely to cover sterilizations, which are obtained more by women with low incomes compared to women with more financial resources (Costello, Stone, & White, in press). A study of health insurance benefits in Washington state found that only 51% of the plans covered at least one contraceptive service or device, often requiring a higher-than-standard copayment (Kurth, Bielinski, Graap, Conniff, & Connell, 2001). If even those with "good insurance" have limited choice of sexual and reproductive health benefits, consider the limitations for those who have no choice but to pay out-of-pocket.

SUMMARY

The decision to become a parent is one of the most important an individual or couple will make. In this chapter we have reviewed the range of decisions from no children to several children and the various methods to ensure one's desired family size. Family planning is helpful in achieving one's family goals in terms of timing, number of children, and the interval between children. More than half of U.S. pregnancies are not planned.

Do You Want to Have Children?

Spouses, children, and society all benefit from family planning. The benefits include less health risk to mother and child, fewer unwanted children, decreased economic burden for the parents and society, and population control. The decision to become a parent is encouraged by family, friends, religions, government, and cultural observances. The reasons people give for having children include personal fulfillment and the desire for a close relationship with their offspring.

How Many Children Do You Want?

Some couples opt for a childfree lifestyle. Reasons women give for wanting to be childfree are more personal freedom, greater time and intimacy with their spouse, and career demands. Husbands are generally less committed than their wives to remaining childfree. Some of the factors in a couple's decision to have more than one child are the desire to repeat a good experience, the feeling that two children provide companionship for each other, and the desire to have a child of each sex.

Birth Control

Hormonal methods of contraception currently available to women include the "pill," Jadelle®, Depo-Provera®, Lunelle®, NuvaRing®, and Ortho Evra®. Barrier methods include the male and female condom, spermicides, diaphragm, and cervical cap. Natural family planning methods involve refraining from sexual intercourse during the 1 to 2 weeks each month when the woman is thought to be fertile. Nonmethods include withdrawal and douching.

Emergency contraception refers to various types of morning-after pills that are used when a woman has unprotected intercourse, when a contraceptive method fails (such as condom breakage or slippage), or when a woman is raped.

Sterilization

Sterilization is a surgical procedure that prevents fertilization, usually by blocking the passage of eggs or sperm through the Fallopian tubes or vas deferens, respectively. The procedure for female sterilization is called salpingectomy, or tubal ligation. Laparoscopy is a variation of tubal ligation. The most frequent form of male sterilization is vasectomy.

Factors Influencing Contraceptive Choice and Use

Psychological factors such as erotophilia/erotophobia, self-efficacy, and embarrassment can influence contraceptive use. Relationship type, relationship dynamics, and communication skills may also be factors influencing use. Access to contraceptives may be influenced by their cost and by insurance status and ability to pay.

SUGGESTED WEBSITES

Note: These websites were functional when we went to press. Please access the online text for the most up-to-date URLs.

Alan Guttmacher Institute
http://www.agi-usa.org

Association of Voluntary and Safe Contraception
http://www.avsc.org./avsc/

Kaiser Foundation
http://www.kaisernetwork.org/Daily_reports/rep_index.cfm?DR_ID=10171

National Right to Life
http://www.nrlc.org/

Planned Parenthood Federation of America
http://www.plannedparenthood.org

Population Council
http://www.popcouncil.org

Reproductive Freedom and Choice
http://www.naral.org/

Sexual Health Boutique
http://www.safedreams.com

KEY TERMS

antinatalism (p. 326)
cervical cap (p. 340)
coitus interruptus (p. 343)
diaphragm (p. 340)
Depo-Provera® (p. 334)
emergency contraception (p. 343)
Essure (p. 347)
female condom (p. 337)
hysterectomy (p. 346)
intrauterine device (p. 339)
Jadelle® (p. 334)
laparoscopy (p. 346)
Lunelle® (p. 335)
Mifepristone (p. 344)
Mittelschmerz (p.342)
morbidity (p. 328)
mortality (p. 328)
Norplant® (p. 334)
NuvaRing® (p. 335)
oophorectomy (p. 346)
Ortho Evra® (p. 335)
periodic abstinence (p. 341)
postcoital contraception (p. 343)
pronatalism (p. 325)
RU-486 (p. 344)
salpingectomy (p. 346)
spermicide (p. 338)
sterilization (p. 346)
vasectomy (p. 347)
withdrawal (p. 343)

CHAPTER QUIZ

1. *Pronatalism* refers to which of the following?
   a. competition among siblings for parental attention
   b. a social attitude that encourages childbearing
   c. the tendency for couples to want to have a male child as the firstborn
   d. the social attitude that encourages couples to limit their family size to one child
2. The annual cost per child by husband-wife middle income families for a child less than two years old is around
   a. $900.
   b. $1,200.
   c. $9,000.
   d. $19,000.
3. According to your text, which couple is most likely to have a third child?
   a. a couple who have two boys
   b. a couple who have two girls
   c. a couple who have one girl and one boy
   d. all the above are equally likely to have a third child
4. In a sample of 248 undergraduate university students, the majority reported that "it is _______________ for a woman to decide to have and to raise a child without a husband" (Knox et al., 2000).
   a. perfectly OK
   b. morally wrong
   c. unfair to the child
   d. both b and c
5. Which of the following is the most commonly used method of all the nonsurgical forms of contraception?
   a. the diaphragm
   b. the condom
   c. Depo-Provera®
   d. the birth control pill
6. One shot of Depo Provera® protects a woman from getting pregnant for which of the following time periods?
   a. 3 weeks
   b. 3 months
   c. 6 months
   d. 1 year
7. NuvaRing®, which is a contraceptive device worn inside the vagina, provides pregnancy protection for
   a. up to 6 hours.
   b. one act of intercourse.
   c. 1 month.
   d. 3 months.
8. Which of the following is NOT a barrier method of contraception?
   a. cervical cap
   b. transdermal patch
   c. condom
   d. diaphragm
9. After ejaculation, sperm typically remain viable (able to fertilize an ovum) for how long?
   a. 20 to 30 minutes, but may survive for up to 2 to 3 hours
   b. 2 to 3 hours, but may survive for up to 24 hours
   c. 24 hours, but may survive for up to 2 or 3 days
   d. 2 to 3 days, but may survive for up to 5 days
10. Which of the following is also known as coitus interruptus?
   a. withdrawal
   b. intrauterine device
   c. postcoital contraception
   d. sterilization
11. Emergency contraception must be taken within ___________ after unprotected intercourse.
   a. 24 hours
   b. 2 days
   c. 72 hours
   d. 1 week
12. Mifepristone (RU-486), which can be used to induce abortion, must be taken within ___________ of becoming pregnant.
   a. 3 days
   b. 2 weeks
   c. 7 weeks
   d. 3 months
13. Which of the following are LEAST LIKELY to report contraceptive use at either their first or most recent intercourse?
   a. Swedish women
   b. U.S. women
   c. British women
   d. French women
14. More than half of all sterilizations are performed on
   a. women.
   b. men.
15. In late 2002, the FDA approved Essure, which is a
   a. brand of female condom.
   b. permanent sterilization procedure.
   c. emergency contraceptive pill.
   d. spermicidal foam.
16. According to data cited in your text, which of the following women are least likely to report feeling extremely or somewhat comfortable talking with their partner about condoms?
   a. Black women
   b. Hispanic women
   c. White women

REFERENCES

Alan Guttmacher Institute. (2002). *In their own right: Addressing the sexual and reproductive health needs of American men*. New York: Author.

Artz, L., Macaluso, M., Brill, I., Kelaghan, J., Austin, H., Fleenor, M., et al. (2000). Effectiveness of an intervention promoting the female condom to patients at sexually transmitted disease clinics. *American Journal of Public Health, 90*, 237–244.

Bankole, A., Darroch, J. E., & Singh, S. (2000). Determinants of trends in condom use in the United States, 1988–1995. *Family Planning Perspectives, 31*, 264–271

Bartlett, T. (2002, February). Freshmen pay, mentally and physically, as they adjust to life in college. *The Chronicle of Higher Education*, A35–A37.

Beksinska, M. E., Rees, H. V., Dickson-Tetteh, K. E., Mqoqi, N., Kleinschmidt, I., & McIntyre, J. A. (2001). Structural integrity of the female condom after multiple uses, washing, drying, and relubrication. *Contraception, 63*, 33–36.

Bianco, A., Stone, J., Lynch, L., Lapinski R., Berkowitz, B., & Berkowitz, R. L. (1996). Pregnancy outcome at age 40 and older. *Obstetrics and Gynecology, 87*, 917–922.

Boyd, R. L. (1989). Minority status and childlessness. *Sociological Inquiry, 59*, 331–342.

Burkman, R. (2002, August). Rationale for new contraceptive methods. *The Female Patient*, 4–13.

Cates, W., Jr., & Stone, K. M. (1992). Family planning, sexually transmitted diseases and contraceptive choice: A literature update—Part I. *Family Planning Perspectives, 24*, 75–82.

Centers for Disease Control and Prevention. (2002). Sexually transmitted diseases treatment guidelines 2002. MMWR 2002; 51 (No. RR-6): [1-84].

Cohen, S. (1995, October 1). Suits cite unexpected Norplant side effects. *The Charlotte Observer*, p. 19a.

Contraceptive Technologies: How Much Choice Do We Really Have? (2002). Retrieved June 24, 2002, from www.populationconnection.org

Costello, C., Stone, A., & White, V. (in press). *The American woman 2003–2004. Daughters of revolution: Young women today*. New York: Palgrave.

Cox, B., Sneyd, M. J., Paul, C., Delahunt, B., & Skegg, D. C. (2002). Vasectomy and the risk of prostate cancer. *Journal of the American Medical Association, 287*, 3110–3115.

Cunningham, F. G., MacDonald, P. C., Gant, N. F., Leveno, K. J., Gilstrap, L. C., Harkins, G. D. V., et al. (Eds.). (1997). *Williams Obstetrics* (20th ed.). Stamford, CT: Appleton and Lange.

Daniluk, J. C. (2001). *The infertility survival guide*. Oakland, CA: New Harbinger.

Darroch, J. E. (2000). The pill and men's involvement in contraception. *Family Planning Perspectives, 32*, 90–91.

Darroch, J. E., Singh, S., Frost, J. J., & The Study Team. (2001). Differences in teenage pregnancy rates among five developed countries: The roles of sexual activity and contraceptive use. *Family Planning Perspectives, 33*, 244–250.

Davis, K. R., & Weller, S. C. (2000). The effectiveness of condoms in reducing heterosexual transmission of HIV. *Family Planning Perspectives, 31*, 272–279.

DeOllos, I. Y., & Kapinus, C. A. (2002). Aging childless individuals and couples: Suggestions for new directions in research. *Sociological Inquiry, 72*, 72–80.

Forste, R., Tanfer, K., & Tedrow, L. (1995). Sterilization among currently married men in the United States, 1991. *Family Planning Perspectives, 27*, 100–107.

Foust, A. (1997). An investigation of voluntary childlessness and the marital satisfaction of couples over the life cycle. Paper presented at the Annual Conference of the National Council on Family Relations, Crystal City, VA.

Fu, H., Darroch, J. E., Hass, T., & Ranjit, N. (2000). Contraceptive failure rates: New estimates from the 1995 National Survey of Family Growth. *Family Planning Perspectives, 31*, 56–63.

Godecker, A. L., Thomson, E., & Bumpass, L. L. (2001). Union status, marital history and female contraceptive sterilization in the United States. *Family Planning Perspectives, 33*, 35–41.

Harvey, S. M., Beckman, L. J., Sherman, C., & Petitti, D. (2000). Women's experience and satisfaction with emergency contraception. *Family Planning Perspectives, 31*, 237–247.

Hillis, S. D., Marchbanks, P. A., Ratlif Taylor, L., Peterson, H. B., & for the U.S. Collaborative Review of Sterilization Working Group. (2000). Poststerilization regret: Findings from the United States collaborative review of sterilization. *Obstetrics and Gynecology, 93*, 889–895.

Hofferth, S. L., Reid, L., & Mott, F. L. (2001). The effects of early childbearing on schooling over time. *Family Planning Perspectives, 33*, 259–267.

Hubacher, D. (2002). The checkered history and bright future of intrauterine contraception in the United States. *Perspectives on Sexual and Reproductive Health, 34*, 98–103.

Jones, C. L., Tepperman, L., & Wilson, S. J. (1995). *The futures of the family*. Englewood Cliffs, NJ: Prentice-Hall.

Kaufman, G. (2000). Do gender role attitudes matter? Family formation and dissolution among traditional and egalitarian men and women. *Journal of Family Studies, 21*, 128–144.

Knox, D., Sturdivant, L., Zusman, M. E., & Sandie, A. P. (2000). Single motherhood: College student views. *College Student Journal, 34*, 585–588.

Kurth, A., Bielinski, L., Graap, K., Conniff, J., & Connell, F. A. (2001). Reproductive and sexual health benefits in private health insurance plans in Washington state. *Family Planning Perspectives, 33*, 153–179.

Letherby, G. (2002). Childless and bereft?: Stereotypes and realities in relation to "voluntary" and "involuntary" childlessness and womanhood. *Sociological Inquiry, 72*, 7–20.

Macaluso, M., Demand, M., Artz, L., Fleenor, M., Robey, L., Kelaghan, J., et al. (2000). Female condom use among women at high risk of sexually transmitted disease. *Family Planning Perspectives, 32*, 138–144.

Mackay, A. P., Kieke, B. A., Jr., Koonin, L. M., & Beattie, K. (2001). Tubal sterilization in the United States: 1994–1996. *Family Planning Perspectives, 33,* 161–165.

Manderbacka, K. J., Merilainen, E., Hemminki, O., Rahkonen, O., & Teperi, J. (1992). Marital status as a predictor of perinatal outcome in Finland. *Journal of Marriage and the Family, 54,* 508–515.

Manning, W. D., Longmore, M. A., & Giordano, P. C. (2000). The relationship context of contraceptive use at first intercourse. *Family Planning Perspectives, 32,* 104–110.

McLearn, D. C. (1995, January 12). *U.S. Food and Drug Information Talk Papers* (T95-1). Washington, DC: U.S. Food & Drug Administration.

Mendelsohn, N. (2002). Women clamor for long-delayed return of the sponge. Retrieved March 19, 2003, from http://www.womensenews.org/article.cfm/dyn/aid/848/context/archive

Mishell, D. R. (2002, August). The transdermal contraceptive system. *The Female Patient,* 14–25.

Motamed, S. (2002). 100 million women can't be wrong: What most American women don't know about the IUD. Retrieved June 25, 2002, from www.plannedparenthood.org/articles/IUD/html

National Campaign to Prevent Teen Pregnancy. (2002). *Not just another single issue: Teen pregnancy prevention's link to other critical social issues.* Washington, DC: Author.

New Contraception Option May Soon Become Available. (2000). Population connection. Retrieved June 25, 2002, from www.populationconnection.org/Reports_Publications/Reports/report140.html

Newman, J. (April, 2000). How old is too old to have a baby? *Discover,* 60–67.

Peterson, K. S. (1995, March 30). Family advocates declare war on divorce. *USA Today,* p. 6D.

Population and the Environment. (2002). Retrieved June 24, 2002, from www.populationconnection.org

Population Council. (2003). Female contraceptive development. Retrieved February 10, 2003, from www.popcouncil.org/biomed/femalecontras.html

Population Council. (2003). Jadele® Implants. Retrieved March 13, 2002, from www.popcouncil.org/faqs/jadellefaq.html

Population Council Annual Report. (1999). Nestorone: A synthetic progestin that expands women's choices. Retrieved March 17, 2003, from http://www.popcouncil.org/about/ar99/nestorone.html

Ranjit, N., Bankole, A., Darroch, J. E., & Singh, S. (2001). Contraceptive failure in the first two years of use: Differences across socioeconomic subgroups. *Family Planning Perspectives, 33,* 19–27.

Rosenfeld, J. (1997). Postcoital contraception and abortion. In J. Rosenfeld (Ed.), *Women's health in primary care* (pp. 315–329). Baltimore: Williams & Wilkins.

Roumen, F., Apter, D., Mulders, T., & Dieben, T. (2001). Efficacy, tolerability and acceptability of a novel contraceptive vaginal ring releasing etonogestrel and ethinyl oestradiol. *Human Reproduction, 16,* 469–475.

Schwartz, J. L., & Gabelnick, H. L. (2002). Current contraceptive research. *Perspectives on Sexual and Reproductive Health, 34,* 310–316.

Soler, H., Quadagno, D., Sly, D. F., Riehman, K. S., Eberstein, W. W., & Harrison, D. F. (2000). Relationship dynamics, ethnicity and condom use among low-income women. *Family Planning Perspectives, 32,* 82–88.

Statistical Abstract of the United States: 2002. (2002). 122nd ed. Washington, DC: U.S. Bureau of the Census.

Stein, Z., & Susser, M. (2000). The risks of having children in later life. *British Medical Journal, 320,* 1681–1683.

Tanfer, K. S., Wierzbicki, S., & Payne, B. (2000). Why are US women not using long-acting contraceptives? *Family Planning Perspectives, 32,* 176–183.

Toman, W. (1993). *Family constellation: Its effects on personality and social behavior.* New York: Springer.

Tone, A. (2001). *Devices and desires: A history of contraceptives in America.* New York: Hill and Wang.

U.S. Food & Drug Administration. (1999, July–August). "Today" to return "tomorrow." Retrieved March 19, 2003, from http://www.fda.gov/fdac/departs/1999/499_upd.html

U.S. Food & Drug Administration. (2002). *Office of Public Affairs Birth Control Guide.* Washington, DC: Author.

Vail-Smith, K., Durham, T. W., & Howard, H. A. (1992). A scale to measure embarrassment associated with condom use. *Journal of Health Education, 23,* 209–212.

Van Damme, L. (2000, July 9–14). Advances in topical microbicides. Paper presented at the 13th International AIDS Conference, Durban, South Africa.

Van Devanter, N., Gonzales, V., Merzel, C., Parikh, N. S., Celantano, D., & Greenberg, J. (2002). *American Journal of Public Health, 92,* 109–115.

Wasson, H., & Ward, D. (2000, May 12). Cost of parenthood rising. *USA Today,* p. A1

Wenger, G. C., Scott, A., & Patterson, N. (2000). How important is parenthood? Childlessness and support in old age in England. *Aging and Society, 20,* 161–182.

Wu, Z., & Hart, R. (2002). The mental health of the childless elderly. *Sociological Inquiry, 72,* 21–42.

Wyeth Pharmaceuticals, Inc. (2002, July 26). Back-up contraception no longer required for women using Norplant system, news release. Madison, NJ: Author.

Zabin, L. S., Huggins, G. R., Emerson, M. R., & Cullins, V. E. (2000). Partner effects on a woman's intention to conceive: "Not with this partner." *Family Planning Perspectives, 32,* 39–45.

Zavodny, M. (2001). The effect of partners' characteristics on teenage pregnancy and its resolution. *Family Planning Perspectives, 33,* 192–199

Zieman, M. (2002, August). Managing patients using the transdermal contraceptive system. *The Female Patient,* 26–32.

12

Abortion and Adoption

Chapter Outline

Abortion—no one becomes pregnant in order to undergo this uncomfortable, expensive, and potentially dangerous and emotionally draining procedure.

—Robert T. Michael

Nicholas Perruche was a French child who was born deaf, partially blind, and with severe brain damage. He subsequently brought suit against the doctor who encouraged his mother (who had been exposed to German measles) to bring him to full term. The suit, which Perruche won, established the right of a child "not to be born" (Spriggs & Savulescu, 2002). Although the ruling has subsequently been overturned in the French courts, the Perruche case reflects the complexity of abortion issues.

The following passage reflects the experience of millions of U.S. women each year who are pregnant and don't want to be:

> *I was in shock. We had had intercourse only once and my periods were always regular. This was no time in my life to be pregnant/having a baby. But I wouldn't feel right about an abortion or letting someone else raise my baby. I was a wreck deciding what to do (authors' files).*

In this chapter, we discuss the alternatives to an unwanted or unintended pregnancy: aborting the child or planning for the child to be adopted. We discussed the option of having a child as a single parent in section 11-2f, "Personal Choices: Choose to Have a Child Without a Partner?" We now begin with the discussion on abortion.

12-1 ABORTION IN THE UNITED STATES

NATIONAL DATA Three million American women become pregnant each year without planning to do so (Seims, 2002). There are about 1.3 million abortions annually (*Statistical Abstract of the United States: 2002,* Table 83). Hence, about 40% of women who become pregnant unintentionally end up having an abortion.

Think About It

The available abortion numbers do not reflect reality because only about 35–50% of abortions that actually occur are reported (Michael, 2001). What are several reasons you believe individuals or agencies do not report abortions?

Abortion The deliberate termination of a pregnancy through chemical or surgical means. (See also **induced abortion.**)

Induced abortion See **abortion.**

Spontaneous abortion See **miscarriage.**

Miscarriage The unintended termination of a pregnancy. (See also **spontaneous abortion.**)

Abortion rate The number of abortions per 1,000 women aged 15–44.

Abortion ratio The number of abortions per 1,000 live births.

An **abortion** may be either an **induced abortion,** which is the deliberate termination of a pregnancy through chemical or surgical means, or a **spontaneous abortion (miscarriage)**, which is the unintended termination of a pregnancy. In this text, however, we use the term *abortion* to refer to induced abortion.

12-1a Incidence of Abortion

Table 12-1 reflects the abortion rates and ratios in the United States for selected years. **Abortion rate** refers to the number of abortions per 1,000 women aged 15–44; **abortion ratio** refers to the number of abortions per 1,000 live births.

Compared to 1990, the number of abortions per 1,000 women aged 15–44 and the number of abortions per 1,000 live births has dropped. Reasons for the decreasing number of abortions include a reduced rate of unintended pregnancies and more supportive attitudes toward women becoming single parents. In addition, part of the decline may be due to an increase in restrictive abortion policies, such as those requiring parental consent and mandatory waiting periods. A drop in Medicaid-financed abortions also lowers

TABLE 12-1

Abortion Rates and Ratios for Selected Years

Year	Rate (Number of abortions per 1,000 women aged 15–44)	Ratio (Number of abortions per 1,000 live births)
1990	27.4	389
1995	22.9	351
1997	22.2	340

Source: *Statistical Abstract of the United States*: 2002, Table 88.

the abortion rate by as much as 25%. "Thus, there is a growing body of evidence of price sensitivity on the part of lower-income women" (Michael, 2001, p. 380).

Abortion rates vary by country. Overall, women in developed and developing regions have similar abortion levels—39 procedures per 1,000 women and 34 per 1,000, respectively. Belgium, the Netherlands, Germany, and Switzerland have abortion rates below 10 per 1,000 women of reproductive age; in all other countries of Western Europe and in the United States and Canada, rates are 10–23 per 1,000. The United States exceeds European countries, Australia, and Canada in abortion rates (Miller & Hanks, 2002). Romania, Cuba, and Vietnam have the highest reported abortion rates in the world (78 –83 abortions per 1,000 women). Rates are also above 50 per 1,000 in Chile and Peru. Worldwide, the lifetime average is about 1 abortion per woman (Alan Guttmacher Institute, 1999).

12-1b Who Chooses to Have an Abortion and Why?

A study in New York City identified women obtaining an abortion as unmarried, young (particularly those under age 16), no religious affiliation, previous abortion, and White (Michael, 2001; Hollander, 2001). Because there are proportionately more White women than minorities in the United States, about half of all abortions are by White women. However, African American women are nearly three times as likely as White women to have an abortion, and Hispanic women are roughly two times as likely.

Nationally, however, the numbers of abortions to teens has decreased in recent years compared to other age groups, largely because of their use of long-acting (injectable) hormonal contraceptive methods, increased use of contraceptives at first intercourse, and decline in sexual activity (Finer & Henshaw, 2003). About 19% of abortions in 2000 and 2001 were obtained by teenagers (Jones, Darroch, & Henshaw, 2002). The majority of abortions (56%) during that time period were obtained by women in their 20s. The abortion rates for women older than their 20s decreases with age because older women are less fertile, may have selected sterilization, and are more likely to be married (Jones et al., 2002).

NATIONAL DATA More than 17% of teenage women are estimated to have become pregnant during their first nonmarital teenage sexual relationship. The most frequent outcome (62%) is a live birth (44% outside marriage; 18% in marriage), whereas 37% have an abortion (Zavondy, 2001) .

Ninety-two pregnant women who sought an abortion reported the following reasons for doing so (Barnett, Freudenberg, & Willie, 1992): fear that the children would cause difficulties with their training or work (46%); pressure from their partners to have an abortion (29%); or concern that their relationships with their partners were unstable (20%). Women also have abortions because of inadequate finances, the feeling they are not ready for the responsibility of having a child, and the perceived effect on existing children.

Abortions are also performed for health reasons, although this is not a frequent reason. Some women choose to abort after learning, through prenatal testing, that their fetus has a serious abnormality. Other women may choose to abort if their physician informs them that continuing the pregnancy would jeopardize their health or life. Only 3% of women in one study reported their reason for abortion was a possible fetal problem, and 3% because of their own health (Torres & Forrest, 1988). Abortions performed to protect the life or health of the woman are called **therapeutic abortions**. However, there is disagreement over the definition. Garrett, Baillie, and Garrett (2001) noted, "Some physicians argue that an abortion is therapeutic if it prevents or alleviates a serious physical or mental illness, or even if it alleviates temporary emotional upsets. In short, the health of the pregnant woman is given such a broad definition that a very large number of abortions can be classified as therapeutic" (p. 218). Abortions obtained because rape or incest caused the pregnancy were also infrequent (1%; Torres & Forrest, 1988).

Therapeutic abortion An abortion performed to protect the life or health of the woman.

Some women with multifetal pregnancies (a common outcome of the use of fertility drugs) may have a procedure called *transabdominal first trimester selective termination*. In this procedure, the lives of some fetuses are terminated to increase the chance of survival for the others or to minimize the health risks associated with multifetal pregnancy for the woman. For example, a woman carrying five fetuses may elect to abort three of them to minimize the health risks of the other two.

12-2 METHODS OF ABORTION

Prior to the availability of modern surgical techniques, abortion in the late eighteenth and early nineteenth centuries was performed by flushing the uterus with caustic substances (such as gunpowder, quinine, or oil of juniper) or by inserting sticks of silver nitrate into the cervix. In sections 12-2a through 12-2f, we look at modern-day methods of abortion. The procedure used to perform an abortion depends largely on the stage of the pregnancy, as measured from the first day of the last menstrual period.

12-2a Suction Curettage

Suction curettage Abortion procedure performed the first 6 to 8 weeks of pregnancy whereby a hollow plastic rod is inserted into the woman's uterus where the fetal tissue is evacuated. (See also **vacuum aspiration.**)

Vacuum aspiration See **suction curettage.**

Pregnancy may be terminated during the first 6 to 8 weeks through a procedure called **suction curettage,** also referred to as **vacuum aspiration.** After the administration of a local anesthetic (a general anesthetic may be used at the patient's request), a hollow plastic rod attached to a suction aspirator is inserted into the woman's uterus through the cervix. The device suctions the fetal tissue out of the uterus into a container. Following the suction procedure, the physician may explore the uterine cavity with a small metal instrument (curette) to ensure that all the tissue has been removed. The procedure, which takes about 10 to 20 minutes, can be performed on an outpatient basis in a clinic or a physician's office. Following this procedure, the patient usually experiences some bleeding and cramping, which is normal (see Figure 12-1).

12-2b Dilation and Suction

Dilation and suction (D&S) Abortion procedure during the first 12 weeks whereby the cervix is dilated before the suction procedure occurs.

Dilation and curettage (D&C) Abortion procedure whereby a physician uses a metal surgical instrument to scrape any remaining fetal tissue and placenta from the uterine walls after suctioning the contents of the uterus.

Dilation and suction (D&S), a method of abortion used during the first 12 weeks of pregnancy, is essentially the same as suction curettage, except that the cervix is dilated before the suction procedure. Cervical dilation may be achieved by inserting laminaria into the cervix the day before the abortion is performed. Laminaria are dried, sterile rods of compressed seaweed stems that, when inserted into the cervix, absorb moisture and increase in diameter, thereby dilating the cervix. Cervical dilation may also be achieved by using a metal device designed to dilate the cervix just prior to the abortion. After suctioning the contents of the uterus, a physician uses a metal surgical instrument to scrape any remaining fetal tissue and placenta from the uterine walls. (This method is also known as **dilation and curettage,** or **D&C.**) A local or general anesthetic may be used.

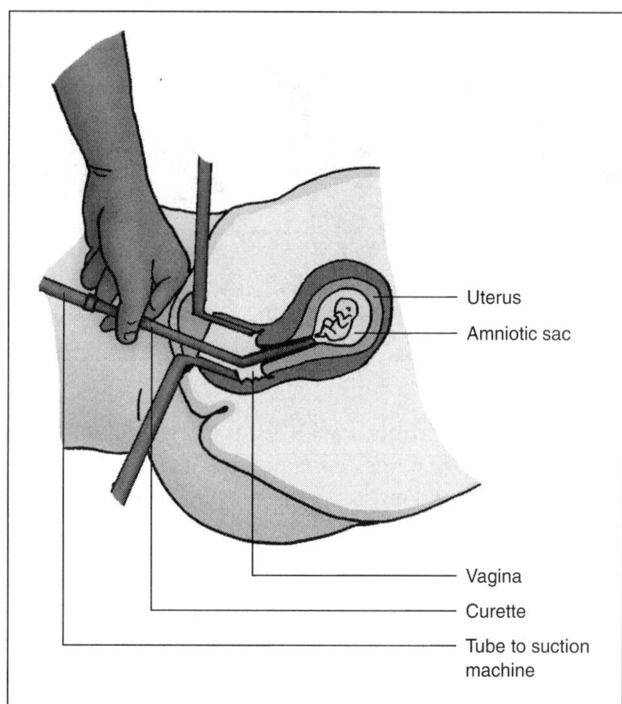

FIGURE 12-1
Suction Curettage
The contents of the uterus are removed with a suction machine. This method is most often used during the first 3 months of pregnancy.

12-2c Dilation and Evacuation

Dilation and evacuation (D&E), an abortion procedure used in the second trimester of pregnancy (13–24 weeks' gestation), involves dilating the cervix and dismembering the fetus inside the uterus so that the body parts can be more easily suctioned out. Extraction instruments called *ringed forceps* are also used to remove the fetal tissue. A local or general anesthetic may be used.

Dilation and evacuation (D&E) Abortion procedure during the second trimester (13 to 24 weeks' gestation) whereby the cervix is dilated and the fetal parts inside are dismembered so they can be suctioned out.

Intact dilation and extraction (D&X) Abortion procedure involving breech delivery of fetus, except for the head, partial evacuation of the brain, resulting in the vaginal delivery of a dead fetus. (See also **partial birth abortion.**)

12-2d Intact Dilation and Extraction

An alternative to D&E is a procedure called **intact dilation and extraction (D&X),** which results in the whole fetus being aborted. After dilating the cervix, a physician pulls the fetus down into the birth canal, feet first. Then, with the rest of the body delivered and the head still lodged against the cervix, the physician inserts an instrument to make an opening in the base of the skull, inserts a suction catheter into this hole, evacuates the contents, and removes the fetus. An advantage of this procedure, if the fetus is malformed, is that certain types of testing can be more easily performed on an intact fetus to assess the woman's chances for a normal pregnancy in the future.

Abortion opponents have labeled dilation and extraction abortions **partial birth abortions** because the limbs and torso are typically delivered before the fetus has died. When D&X abortions are performed, it is typically because the fetus has a serious defect, the woman's health is jeopardized by the pregnancy, or both. Abortions are rarely performed by dilation and extraction. Based on reports of abortion providers surveyed, it is estimated that only 0.17% of all abortions performed in 2000 were performed using this type of procedure (Finer & Henshaw, 2003).

Partial birth abortion Nonmedical term used by abortion opponents to describe abortions performed very late in pregnancy in which the terminated fetus is delivered. (See also **intact dilation and extraction.**)

12-2e Induced Abortions

Another abortion method used late in the second trimester involves inducing premature labor by injecting either saline or prostaglandins through the abdomen into the amniotic sac around the fetus. Prostaglandins may also be administered through vaginal suppositories. The injection or suppositories induce contractions that cause the cervix to dilate. An intravenous drip of oxytocin continues the labor contractions. The contractions are

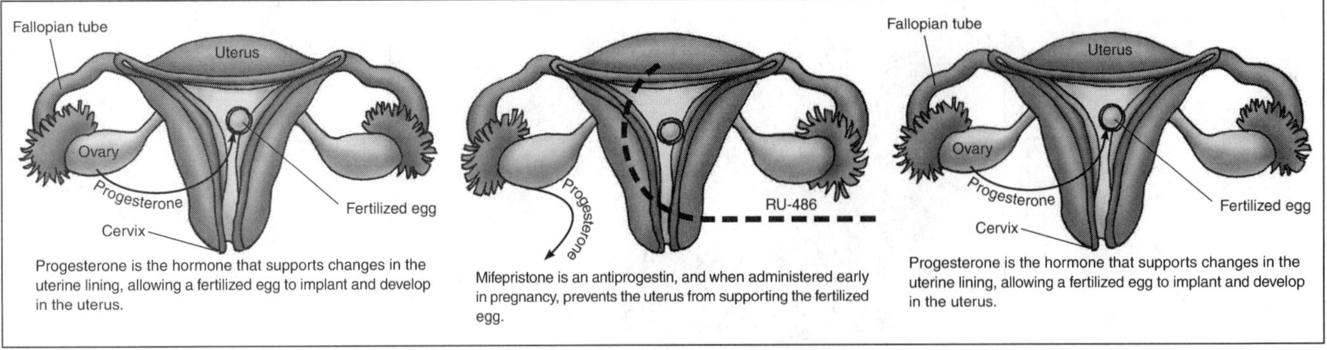

FIGURE 12-2
How Early Medical Abortion Works

INTERACTIVE FIGURE

painful and can continue for several hours until the woman expels the fetus and placenta. Painkillers and local anesthesia are used to ease the woman's discomfort. This procedure is major surgery and must be performed in a hospital.

12-2f Pharmaceutical Abortion

Also called **medical abortions, pharmaceutical abortions** involve the intentional termination of pregnancy through the use of pharmaceutical drugs. In 1997, the drug Mifepristone became available in the United States after being approved by the U.S. Food and Drug Administration (see Figure 12-2). This drug was originally known by its French name, **RU-486;** it is now sold as Mifeprex and is known as the "abortion pill." Actually use of the drug to induce abortion involves several steps. A physician determines the length of pregnancy to make sure the woman is less than 9 weeks' pregnant. (The permitted length of gestation varies; in France Mifepristone is approved for use up to 40 days since the onset of the last menstrual period, and up to 63 days in Great Britain and Sweden. Current FDA approval in the United States is for up to 49 days). Mifepristone is an antiprogestin, which interferes with the uterine development that would support implantation of the fertilized egg. Two days after the Mifepristone is administered, a prostaglandin (misoprostol) is administered, which causes stimulation of uterine contractions that help to dislodge and expel the embryo. A heavy menstrual flow follows. The woman makes a final visit to the physician to confirm that the abortion has been completed and to make sure the bleeding has stopped (Jones & Henshaw, 2002). When within 6 weeks of the last menstrual period, Mifeprix successfully aborts 96–98% of pregnancies (Rimensnyder, 2002).

Medical abortion The intentional termination of pregnancy through the use of pharmaceutical drugs. (See also **pharmaceutical abortion.**)

Pharmaceutical abortion See **medical abortion.**

RU-486 See **Mifepristone.**

When women are offered a choice of surgical or medical abortion, most choose the medical method. The primary reasons for preferring medical abortions include greater privacy and autonomy (it can be done at home), less invasiveness, and greater naturalness (Fielding, Edmunds, & Schaff, 2002; Harvey, Beckman, & Satre, 2001). Another advantage of selecting a medical abortion is that such drugs can be dispensed by a physician in the privacy of an office, which means women can avoid antiabortion forces that target abortion clinics. A decade of experience with Mifepristone in France, Great Britain, and Sweden has not shown that its availability has caused an increase in the number of abortions, but it has influenced their timing at earlier gestation. This experience suggests that the acceptance of Mifepristone in the United States will be slow and gradual but will have similar impact (Boonstra, 2002).

12-3 ABORTION LEGISLATION IN THE UNITED STATES

Roe v. Wade The 1973 Supreme Court decision declaring that during the first three months of pregnancy the decision to have an abortion would be between the woman and her physician.

One of the most controversial political issues in U.S. society is abortion legislation. After a brief look at the historical background of abortion legislation, we will discuss the landmark ***Roe v. Wade*** case and more recent legislative action regarding abortion in the United States.

12-3a Historical Background of Abortion Legislation

In the Colonial United States, abortion was neither prohibited nor uncommon. During this time, the states were governed by English common law, which permitted abortion until **quickening,** the time when the woman could feel movement of the fetus inside her (usually in the fourth or fifth month of pregnancy). Even if an abortion was performed after quickening, the woman was immune from prosecution.

Quickening The stage of pregnancy in which the woman can feel movement of the fetus inside her (usually in the fourth or fifth month of pregnancy).

The legal control of abortion by statute began in 1821. Because thousands of women had died taking medically prescribed poisons to induce abortions, Connecticut passed a law prohibiting the use of poisons to induce post-quickening abortions. This statute existed primarily to protect the lives of women. In 1828, New York enacted a law making abortion of an unquickened fetus a misdemeanor crime and abortion of a quickened fetus second-degree manslaughter, unless the abortion was necessary to preserve the woman's life.

In the mid-nineteenth century, the American Medical Association led the campaign to criminalize abortion. Their concerns were both economic and moral (Petchesky, 1990). Formally trained physicians competed economically with midwives, who assisted not only in births, but also in abortions. Moral concerns in the medical community over abortion resulted, in part from advances in the scientific understanding of human development as a continuous process. These concerns led physicians to question the relevance of the distinction between quickened and nonquickened fetuses.

The movement to ban abortion was also spurred by concern over the increasing number of married, White, middle-class Protestant women who were having abortions in the mid-nineteenth century. At the same time, immigrant and Catholic birthrates climbed. Medical professionals warned that "respectable women (white, middle-class Protestants) would be 'out-bred' by ignorant, lower-class aliens" (Petchesky, 1990, p. 82).

The medical profession opposed contraception, as well as abortion. Both contraception and abortion were associated with "obscenity, lewdness, sex, and worst of all, rebellious women" (Petchesky, 1990, p. 82) and were thus viewed as threats to traditional gender roles and conservative sexual values. Physicians condemned women who had abortions as "selfish" and criticized them for abandoning maternal and child-care duties.

Think About It

The competing values of the fetus and the mother in the abortion debate are socially constructed. "...[I]n the late 18th and early 19th centuries, the debates over the propriety of abortion apparently centered on the illicit sex that necessitated it as more abortions were performed on single women wishing to conceal the fact that they had been sexually active" (Michael, 2001, p. 378). To what degree do you feel the current abortion debate is political or religious?

By 1900, abortion was illegal in all U.S. jurisdictions. In most states, the sole legal reason an abortion could be performed was if continuation of the pregnancy threatened the life of the woman. Women who sought abortions for personal, social, or economic reasons were forced to seek more dangerous illegal abortions. In spite of the criminalization of abortion during this era, it is estimated that as many as one in three pregnancies was terminated by induced abortion (Rubin, 1987).

12-3b *Roe v. Wade*: A Landmark Decision

The twentieth century movement to legalize abortion was led by advocates of women's rights and family planning. But the abortion rights movement did not gain ground until 1973, when the U.S. Supreme Court ruled in the famous *Roe v. Wade* case that any restriction on abortions during the first trimester of pregnancy was unconstitutional. This ruling declared that during the first 3 months of pregnancy, the decision to have an abortion would be between the pregnant woman and her physician. In the second trimester (the fourth through the sixth months of pregnancy), the state might regulate the abortion procedure (by requiring that the abortion take place in a hospital, for example) so as to protect the woman's health. During the last trimester, the state would have an interest in protecting the viable fetus, so the state might restrict or prohibit abortion. In effect, the Supreme Court ruled that the fetus is a potential life and not a "person" until the third trimester. The *Roe v. Wade* decision was based on the right to privacy; government intrusion in the doctor-patient relationship and a woman's reproductive decisions were seen as violations of that right. The current abortion debate is a conflict between two fundamental values: the right of a fetus to live and the right of a woman to determine her own fate (Michael, 2001).

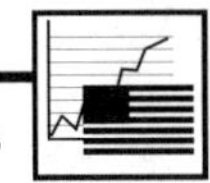

NATIONAL DATA Following the legalization of abortion in Roe v. Wade, birthrates declined by 5–8%, with the largest declines occurring among unmarried women, teenagers, and women older than 35 (Bitler & Zavodny, 2002).

12-3c Abortion Legislation Since *Roe v. Wade*

The votes [for a total ban] are not there. To stop all abortions will require significant change in the culture.

—Phyllis Schlafly,
founder of Eagle Forum, a conservative, pro-family organization

A number of abortion rulings and bills have been passed since the *Roe v. Wade* decision. Some of them are as follows:

1. *Planned Parenthood of Central Missouri v. Danforth* (1976). In the first post-Roe ruling, the Court overturned a law requiring a married woman to obtain her husband's consent for an abortion. This ruling stated that a woman's right to choose abortion is not subject to the veto of her partner in the pregnancy. The Court also stated that minors could not be blocked in obtaining an abortion by allowing their parents an absolute veto power.
2. (1976). The first of the Hyde amendments was passed, restricting Medicaid funding for abortions. In effect, abortion would not be available for women with limited resources.
3. *Bellotti v. Baird* (1979). The Court upheld a Massachusetts law requiring minors to notify both parents or obtain their consent for an abortion. However, the Court held that parental consent or notification does not infringe on a minor's rights if the minor can bypass the parents by obtaining a "judicial bypass." A minor may seek this judicial bypass from a judge, who will determine whether the minor is "mature" enough to make the abortion decision herself and whether abortion is in the minor's best interest. Some minors may seek such a bypass because they fear parental disapproval and want to avoid contributing to stress in the family.
4. *Rust v. Sullivan* (1991). The Supreme Court ruled that federally funded family planning clinics were prohibited from giving a woman any information about abortion. This prohibition (labeled by pro-choice advocates as the "gag rule") meant that when pregnant women attending these clinics asked for abortion information, they were told that the family planning clinic does not consider abortion an appropriate method of family planning.

Legislation and policy issues regarding the use of aborted fetal tissue for medical and research purposes are discussed in Box 12-1. In section 12-6, we discuss how restrictive abortion legislation affects the physical and psychological consequences of abortion.

Box 12-1 Social Choices

Using Aborted Fetuses for Medical Research?

Fetal tissue is uniquely suitable for medical research in that it is "nonspecific," meaning it can develop into any kind of tissue (such as muscle or organ) if it is transplanted into humans. In the treatment of diseases, fetal tissue takes over the function of damaged tissue. Fetal tissue has been used in the development of immunizations for polio and rubella. Fetal cells might also be implanted to help cure Parkinson's disease, diabetes, leukemia, Huntington's disease, Alzheimer's disease, and spinal cord damage. At least 155 other genetic disorders also could be corrected before birth through fetal tissue transplants (Begley, Hager, Glick, & Foote, 1996). In other words, while still developing in the womb, fetuses with certain genetic disorders can receive transplants from nondefective fetal tissue and subsequently develop into physically normal, healthy infants and children.

Despite the potential and actual benefits of using fetal tissue for medical and research purposes, many antiabortion activists oppose the "harvesting" of fetuses for such purposes. Abortion opponents argue that using fetal tissue for medical and research purposes would encourage abortion because many women would be swayed toward having an abortion if they knew the aborted fetus would be used to benefit society. Supporters of the scientific and medical use of fetal tissue argue that "whatever wrong might be involved in use of fetal tissue obtained from induced abortions is outweighed by the potential benefits to patients" (Strong, 1997, p. 185). The medical community and the general public have raised concerns over the commercialization of fetal tissue and the potential for using fetal tissue for medical and research purposes.

In response to ethical concerns about the medical and research use of fetal tissue, a National Institutes of Health ethics advisory panel recommended various guidelines for the scientific use of fetal tissue, including the following (Woodward, Hager, & Glick, 1996): abortion counselors should not discuss the donation of fetuses to science until after clients have decided to undergo an abortion so that the decision whether to abort or continue the pregnancy would not be influenced by the possible scientific benefit to others; women should not be coerced into providing fetal tissue for scientific or medical purposes; after a woman chooses to abort her fetus, she should not be allowed to designate the beneficiary of the aborted tissue (this guideline would prevent women from conceiving and aborting to provide fetal tissue for transplantation for an ailing relative or friend); physicians should not use riskier abortion methods or delay the abortion to obtain a better fetal specimen; and to prevent women and physicians from seeking abortions for profit, fetal tissue or organs could not be bought or sold. (However, fees could be paid to companies and third parties for the retrieval, preparation, and storage of fetal materials.) These guidelines have not yet been institutionalized, and no organized system is currently in place to distribute fetal tissue on a nonprofit, equitable basis.

Although the ban on using federal funds for fetal tissue research and medical transplantation has been lifted and fetal tissue is currently being used for these purposes, opposition to using fetal tissue has not subsided. The controversy over using aborted fetal tissue for medical and research purposes is likely to continue as long as abortion itself is controversial.

References

Begley, S., Hager, M., Glick, D., & Foote, J. (1996). Fetal tissue research will benefit medical science. In C. P. Cozic & J. Petrikin (Eds.), *The abortion controversy* (pp. 221–227). San Diego, CA: Greenhaven Press.

Strong, C. (1997). Fetal tissue research is ethical. In T. L. Roleff (Ed.), *Abortion: Opposing viewpoints* (pp. 184–189). San Diego, CA: Greenhaven Press.

Woodward, K. L., Hager, M., & Glick, D. (1996). The ethics of fetal tissue research and transplantation: An overview. In C. P. Cozic & J. Petrikin (Eds.), *The abortion controversy* (pp. 216–220). San Diego, CA: Greenhaven Press.

12-4 A CROSS-CULTURAL VIEW OF ABORTION

Due to the unavailability or expense of using contraceptive technology, many women throughout the world resort to abortion as a form of birth control. Abortion accounts for 10–20% of fertility regulation in Africa and 25% of fertility regulation in Latin America. In Central and Eastern European countries, 60% of all fertility regulation is estimated to be due to abortion (Miller & Rosenfield, 1996).

12-4a Abortion Policies Around the World

International Data The World Health Organization has calculated that approximately 50 million pregnancies are terminated by abortion each year (Baird, 2000).

Policies concerning abortion vary around the world. On one end of the continuum is the Kafir tribe in Central Asia, in which there is no taboo or restriction in regard to abortion. Women are free to choose to terminate their pregnancies. One reason for the Kafirs' approval of abortion is that childbirth in the tribe is associated with high rates of maternal mortality. Because birthing children may threaten the life of significant numbers of women in the community, women may be encouraged to abort, especially when they are viewed as too young, too sick, too old, or too small to bear children.

Abortion may also be encouraged by a tribe or society for other reasons, including practicality, economics, lineage, and honor. Abortion is practical in migratory societies, wherein women must control their pregnancies because they are limited in the number of children they can nurse and transport. Economic motivations become apparent when resources (such as food) are scarce; the number of children born to a group must be controlled. Abortion for reasons of lineage or honor is encouraged when a woman becomes impregnated in an adulterous relationship. To protect the lineage and honor of her family, she may have an abortion. Abortion also occurs when the fetus is thought to be a female. In this type of abortion, referred to as **sex-selective abortion,** females are either aborted or killed after birth (**female infanticide**).

Sex-selective abortion
An abortion that is performed because the fetus is thought to be a particular sex (usually female). (See also **female infanticide.**)

Female infanticide
The abortion or killing of females (in contrast to males) after the baby is born. (See also **sex-selective abortion.**)

INTERNATIONAL DATA Worldwide, between 60 and 100 million women and girls are "missing"—they have been aborted or killed (Watts & Zimmerman, 2002).

Although the Kafir tribe has an open policy on abortion, their policy is an exception. In most cultures, abortion is considered "wrong." Countries that do not permit abortion under any conditions include Brazil, Egypt, the Philippines, and Nepal. In Nepal, women who abort can be sentenced to 20 years in jail; whereas men who murder receive sentences of 10 years (Goodwin, 1997). Where abortion is allowed, preserving the mother's life is the primary reason.

12-4b Abortion and Women's Health: A Global View

Access to safe, legal abortion is restricted in many countries throughout the world. Many countries do not have the medical technology and facilities, nor the legal support, for providing women access to safe abortions. Unsafe abortion represents a serious threat to the health and lives of women throughout the world.

INTERNATIONAL DATA An estimated 100,000 to 200,000 women die each year as a result of complications of abortion (Baird, 2000).

Immediate negative consequences include hemorrhage, uterine perforation, cervical trauma, pelvic peritonitis, pelvic abscess, and jaundice. Long-term consequences of unsafe abortion include chronic pelvic pain, pelvic inflammatory disease (PID), tubal occlusion, infertility, and eventual hysterectomy.

12-5 ATTITUDES TOWARD ABORTION

Few issues in human sexuality are as controversial as abortion. Attitudes toward abortion range from fierce opposition to approval of abortion under certain circumstances (including rape and endangerment of a woman's life) to staunch support for legal and affordable access to abortion on request.

12-5a Private Attitudes Toward Abortion

Although the "nation is deeply divided over the issue of abortion" (Michael, 2001, p. 379), the majority of U.S. adults favor legal availability of abortion.

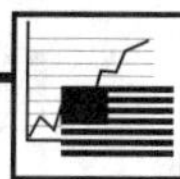

NATIONAL DATA Fifty-five percent of first-year college students agree that abortion should be legal (Bartlett, 2002)

Attitudes toward abortion vary according to the circumstances. For example, abortion is more likely to be viewed as an acceptable option if the mother's health is endangered by continuing the pregnancy, if a severe birth defect exists, or if the pregnancy is the result of rape or incest. Situational contexts which may generate less approval for an abortion include a woman's feeling that she could not afford a baby or her wanting an abortion when the father did not (Boggess & Bradner, 2000).

12-5b Advocacy Groups: Pro-Life, Pro-Choice, and Pro-Dialogue

A dichotomization of attitudes toward abortion is reflected in two opposing groups of abortion activists. Individuals and groups who oppose abortion are commonly referred to as "pro-life" or "antiabortion."

Pro-life

Pro-life groups advocate restrictive abortion policies or a complete ban on abortion. They essentially believe the following:

- The unborn fetus has a right to live and that right should be protected.
- Abortion is a violent and immoral solution to unintended pregnancy.
- The life of an unborn fetus is sacred and should be protected, even at the cost of individual difficulties for the pregnant woman.

Individuals who are over the age of 44, female, mothers of three or more children, married to white-collar workers, affiliated with a religion, and Catholic are most likely to be pro-life (Granberg, 1991; Begue, 2001).

Pro-choice

Pro-choice advocates support the legal availability of abortion for all women. They essentially believe the following:

- Freedom of choice is a central value.
- Those who must personally bear the burden of their moral choices ought to have the right to make these choices.
- Procreation choices must be free of governmental control.

In *Breaking the Abortion Deadlock: From Choice to Consent,* Dr. Eileen McDonagh (1996) argues that if a woman has the right to defend herself against a rapist, she also should be able to defend herself against the invasion of a fetus. Although abortion opponents argue that a woman doesn't have the right to terminate the life of a fetus, Dr. McDonagh argues that the fetus doesn't have the right to invade a woman's body. No laws, she says, besides those restricting abortion, allow a person to invade another's body.

People most likely to be pro-choice have the following characteristics: they are female, are mothers of one or two children, have some college education, are employed, and have annual income of more than $50,000. Although many self-proclaimed feminists

Abortion activists often protest in support of their views.

AP Photo/Joe Marquette

and women's organizations, such as the National Organization for Women (NOW), have been active in promoting abortion rights, not all feminists are pro-choice.

Contrary to common notion, however, not all religious groups oppose the legal availability of abortion. For example, Catholics for Free Choice, a pro-choice organization established 30 years ago, supports the right to legal abortion and promotes family planning. This organization disagrees with the notion that abortion is necessarily sinful in all circumstances.

Labeling the opposing groups in the abortion controversy is problematic. Some pro-choice advocates object to the use of the term *pro-life* when referring to their opponents because it implies that *pro-choice* advocates do not value life. They argue that restricting or banning legal abortion lessens the quality of life for women by forcing them to either bear unwanted children or to obtain an illegal and perhaps unsafe abortion. The quality of life for children born unwanted is also a concern of pro-choice advocates. Pro-choice advocates do not view abortion as desirable, but as a necessary evil, and they often combine their efforts to make and keep abortion available with efforts to reduce abortion by family planning and the use of effective contraception.

Some pro-choice advocates also object to the label *pro-abortion* because some who are pro-choice are personally opposed to abortion. Indeed, some individuals feel that they can be antiabortion and pro-choice at the same time.

We use the term *pro-dialogue advocates* to refer to those who seek to explore and focus on concerns that are common to both pro-life and pro-choice advocates. (We have borrowed the term from a group in Fargo, North Dakota.) In 1981, the first abortion clinic in North Dakota, established in the town of Fargo, became the center of fierce opposition between pro-life and pro-choice activists. A number of these activists formed a group called Pro-Dialogue, whose purpose was to bring members of both sides of the controversy together to find shared concerns. Anthropologist Faye Ginsburg, who went to Fargo to interview activists on both sides, quotes the minutes of the first meeting of Pro-Dialogue:

> *As we talked and listened that night, we discovered some very important common ground. We wished that women would not be faced with pregnancies that they couldn't afford, that at times they weren't ready for, by people they didn't love, or for any of the many reasons women have abortions. The common ground gave us something concrete . . . a goal we could work toward together. (Ginsburg, 1989, cited in Maloy and Patterson, 1992, p. 327).*

Think About It

Maloy and Patterson (1992) conducted 95 interviews with women and couples who have faced the dilemma of whether to give birth or have an abortion. The researchers commented that "each of their stories includes something the abortion debate has thus far avoided discussing—some element of ambiguity, complexity, uncertainty, loss, or respect for an opposing view" (p. 9). Although public discourse about abortion is dominated by two opposing views—one advocating the rights of the fetus, the other advocating the rights of women—Maloy and Patterson noted that the women and couples to whom they spoke rarely, if ever, mentioned rights:

> They did not base their actions on an explicit choice between the woman and the fetus. . . . In almost every case, the outcomes of these private dilemmas hung on practical and emotional matters—the quality of the connection between the woman and the man, the financial resources available, the number of other children a woman already had, the state of her self-esteem, the other important options that pregnancy might or might not foreclose. (p. 6)

To what degree do you feel women get abortions for theoretical versus practical reasons?

12-6 PHYSICAL AND PSYCHOLOGICAL EFFECTS OF ABORTION

Women who have experienced or are contemplating abortion may be concerned about the potential physical and psychological effects.

12-6a Physical Effects of Abortion

Legal abortions, performed under safe conditions, in such countries as the United States are "now so effective and safe that almost always it is safer for the woman to have an abortion than to continue with the pregnancy" (Baird, 2000, p. 251). The earlier in the pregnancy the abortion is performed, the safer it is.

Rates of Mortality and Complications

Mortality rates associated with legal abortion are very low (between 0.4 and 1 woman per 100,000 abortions). This risk is less than the risk of death from an injection of penicillin. Women are 10 times more likely to die from childbirth than from abortion. (The mortality rate of childbirth is 9.1 maternal deaths per 100,000 live births.) Of deaths caused by legal abortion, 23% are from infection, 23% are from embolism, 20% are from hemorrhage, and 16% are from anesthetic complications (Rosenfeld, 1997; Baird, 2000).

The complication rate of legal abortions is also low. According to the National Abortion Federation, among women obtaining abortions during the first 13 weeks of pregnancy, 97% have no complications or post abortion complaints, 2.5% have minor complications that can be handled at the physician's office or abortion clinic, and less than 0.5% require some additional surgical procedure and/or hospitalization (Miller, 1996).

Post abortion complications include the possibility of incomplete abortion, which occurs when the initial procedure misses the fetus and a repeat procedure must be done. Other possible complications include uterine infection; excessive bleeding; perforation or laceration of the uterus, bowel, or adjacent organs; and an adverse reaction to a medication or anesthetic. Post abortion information given to women includes to expect bleeding up to 2 weeks (usually not heavy) and to return to their health-care provider 30 days after the abortion to check that all is well (Baird, 2000).

Long-Term Effects

Vacuum aspiration abortions, comprising most U.S. abortions, do not increase the risks to future childbearing. However, late-term abortions do increase the risks of subsequent miscarriages, premature deliveries, and low birth-weight babies (Council on Scientific Affairs, American Medical Association, 1992; Baird, 2000).

Effects of Legal Restrictions on Physical Consequences

Some abortion restrictions are in the best interest of women. For example, laws mandating that abortions be performed by physicians provide women with assurance that their abortion providers have formal medical training. But other laws restricting abortion may compromise a woman's health because they may delay the abortion, thus threatening the woman's health (Baird, 2000). Each of these restrictions causes delays between the time a woman decides to seek an abortion and the time she actually undergoes the procedure. For example, in Mississippi a woman must receive, in person, information about the fetus and abortion alternatives, and then wait at least 24 hours before she may obtain an abortion. A study of the impact of this law found that it was associated with delays in obtaining an abortion. The mean gestational age of the fetus was lengthened by four days, increasing the rate of second-trimester abortion procedures—an increase of 7.5% of abortions to 11.5% (Joyce & Kaestner, 2000).

The most common abortion restrictions include parental and spousal notification laws, mandatory counseling and waiting periods, and limitations on public funding. State requirements of parental notification have modestly contributed to an increase in the proportion of White women heading single-parent families (Lichter, McLaughlin, & Ribar, 1998).

Analysis of the impact of Medicaid funding restrictions on abortions revealed that such state restrictions are associated with increased female-headed households among Black families. These analyses show that, in contrast to public policy interests in strengthening the traditional two-parent family, abortion restriction has had the opposite influence because unmarried women are increasingly choosing nonmarital births (Lichter et al., 1998).

12-6b Psychological Effects of Abortion

Hollander (2001) studied 442 women 2 years after they had had an abortion and found that 16% regretted their decision. This number was up from 11% one month after the abortion. However, 69% reported that they would make the same decision to abort if faced with the same situation. The predominant emotion in reference to the abortion was relief, rather than either positive or negative emotions. Although 20% met the criteria for clinical depression, only 1% experienced post-traumatic stress disorder. The researcher concluded "for most women, elective abortion . . . does not pose a risk to mental health" (p. 3). This finding is similar to the findings of a panel convened by the American Psychological Association, which reviewed the scientific literature on the mental health impact of abortion. For most women, a legal first trimester abortion does not create psychological hazards, and symptoms of distress are within normal bounds (Adler et al., 1992). Such a conclusion is not to deny that an abortion is a difficult experience for some women and may be associated with increased substance use (to the point of abuse) as a method of coping (Reardon & Ney, 2000).

Younger unmarried women who have not had a child tend to have more negative responses than older women who have already given birth. Women whose culture or religion prohibits abortion and women with less perceived support for their determination to obtain an abortion tend to experience more distress. Second trimester abortions, which may reflect greater conflict about the pregnancy and involve more distressing medical procedures, are associated with a higher likelihood of negative response. Nevertheless, "[a]lthough making the decision to terminate an unwanted pregnancy is difficult, available psychological evidence suggests that women tend to cope successfully and go on with their lives" (Adler et al., 1992, p. 1202).

Is There a "Postabortion Syndrome?"

Few would deny that abortion is a stressful experience. But what degree of psychological stress is involved has become a debated issue. Some opponents of abortion, who have been criticized as ignoring the well-being of the women (and focusing only on the interests of unborn fetuses), have changed their tactics by focusing on women's psychological well-being, claiming that women who undergo abortion experience a range of adverse psychological effects referred to as **post abortion syndrome (PAS).** The symptoms of PAS may include depression, anxiety, shame, helplessness, lowered self-esteem, flashbacks of the abortion, uncontrollable crying, alcohol or drug dependency, eating disorders, and relationship problems. The concept of post abortion syndrome has little to no validity in the scientific community. Much of the evidence of PAS is anecdotal and not supported by scientific studies. As noted earlier in this section, 1% of women who have had an abortion meet the criteria of post-traumatic stress disorder.

Post abortion syndrome (PAS) Term with no credibility in the scientific community, refers to symptoms following abortion such as depression, anxiety, shame, helplessness, lowered self-esteem, uncontrollable crying, alcohol or drug dependency, eating disorders, and relationship problems.

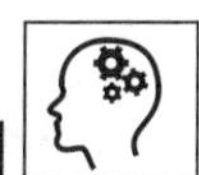

Think About It

Because abortion decisions typically result from troubled situations, such as lack of resources, relationship unhappiness or instability, sexual coercion, or fetal or maternal health problems, it is often difficult to distinguish the stress of the decision to end the pregnancy from the stress of the surrounding circumstances (Stotland, 1996). How might this knowledge be used to help a woman decide how to respond to an unintended pregnancy?

12-6c Personal Choices: Deciding Whether to Have an Abortion

Women who are faced with the question of whether to have an abortion may benefit by considering the following guidelines:

- Consider all the alternatives available to you, realizing that no alternative may be all good or all bad. As you consider each alternative, think about both the short- and long-term consequences of each course of action.
- Obtain information about each alternative course of action. Inform yourself about the medical, financial, and legal aspects of abortion, childbearing, parenting, and adoption.
- Talk with trusted family members, friends, or unbiased counselors. Talk with the man who participated in the pregnancy. If possible, also talk with women who have had abortions, as well as women who have kept and reared their babies or placed their babies in adoptive homes. If you feel that someone is pressuring you in your decision making, look for help elsewhere.
- Consider your own personal and moral commitments in life. Understand your own feelings, values, and beliefs concerning the fetus, and weigh those against the circumstances surrounding your pregnancy.

12-7 THE REAL CHALLENGE: REDUCING THE NEED FOR ABORTION

As long as women experience unintended and unwanted pregnancies, they will have abortions, regardless of the legal status and restrictions on abortion. Maloy and Patterson (1992, p. 328) suggest that "the real challenge . . . is how to prevent most unwanted pregnancies and how to deal more positively with the ones that occur." They offer the following suggestions for meeting this challenge:

1. Create laws and policies that demonstrate concern for both women and the value of developing life.
2. Support research for better male and female contraceptives. In addition, make contraceptives more accessible and affordable. Health-care reform might also include provisions to cover expenses related to contraceptives.

3. Encourage men to share the responsibility for birth control.
4. Promote greater sexual responsibility among men by establishing paternity and enforcing child support.
5. Involve schools, churches, community organizations, and pro-life and pro-choice groups in helping parents talk with their children about sex and sexual responsibility.
6. Provide education to children about the responsibilities of sexuality and parenthood.
7. Implement social policies and services to ease negative family experiences—such as divorce, neglect, abuse, and addiction—that are related to early sexual activity.
8. Encourage more teenage role models to counsel their peers against early sexual activity and birth control misuse.
9. Encourage popular media role models to convey the message that abstinence is okay.
10. Help women proceed with pregnancies they may want to continue through social policies such as subsidized housing, affordable and high-quality child care, job training, and perhaps a national health program.

CULTURAL DIVERSITY 

Sweden has set an example in combining liberal abortion laws with efforts to make abortion a last resort. The Swedish government provides generous maternal benefits, aggressively enforces child support rulings, mandates sex education, promotes available and affordable contraception, requires women seeking second-trimester abortions to meet with a social worker, and prohibits abortion if the fetus was likely to be viable (exceptions are made if the mother's health is endangered by the pregnancy).

12-8 ADOPTION PLACEMENT: AN ALTERNATIVE TO ABORTION

With the legalization of abortion, more unmarried pregnant women have chosen to end their pregnancies. Those choosing to carry their babies to term are more likely to keep them because there is more social acceptance for an unmarried woman to rear her baby in a single-parent home. Some of these women allow their babies to be adopted by another family. Adoption is the legal process in which a child's legal rights toward his or her biological parents are terminated and similar rights are created toward the child's adoptive parents.

NATIONAL DATA Less than 2% of pregnant unmarried women choose to place their babies for adoption (Lindsay, 1997). There are only approximately 100,000 adoptions annually in the United States (Simon & Roorda, 2000).

12-8a Who Makes Their Child Available for Adoption?

Teens who place their babies for adoption are young (16 rather than 19), attending school, have mothers themselves who are somewhat better educated, and have mothers who approve of placing the child for adoption (Donnelly & Voydanoff, 1996).

12-8b Barriers to Choosing the Adoption Option

The longer a woman delays making an adoption plan, the more likely she is to emotionally bond with her baby and the less likely she is to place her baby for adoption. In considering what is best for their child, young, unwed pregnant women may wonder about the psychological effects adoption will have on the child. It is a common belief that individuals who have been adopted experience a range of emotional problems in childhood and as adults. However, in a review of studies comparing adopted children and nonadopted children, Bartholet (1993) found no significant disadvantages of adoptive, as opposed to biological, parenting; in fact, some significant advantages were noticed. For example, one study comparing adults who were adopted as children with adults who had not been adopted found that those who had been adopted were more positive about life, perceived their adoptive parents to be more nurturing than the nonadopted adults did, and were more confident (Marquis & Detweiler, 1985).

One's racial background is another barrier to a teen placing her child for adoption. Indeed, "the most significant barrier to a young black mother's making an adoption decision is that relinquishing a newborn is not readily accepted within the black cultural milieu" (Yeost, 1995, p. 157). Children born to young, unwed African American mothers are often absorbed into the kinship system; they are informally adopted by the pregnant woman's mother, sister, aunt, or other family member. In the traditional African American kinship system, family boundaries are flexible and parenting is a shared and multigenerational responsibility.

Pregnant women and their partners sometimes view adoption as a process that involves "giving your child to strangers" and "never seeing your child again." However, as we discuss in section 12-8c, adoption plans now increasingly allow the birth parents to select the adoptive family and include open adoption terms that allow some ongoing contact between the birth family and the adoptive family.

Some proponents of "the adoption option" argue that unmarried pregnant women rarely choose adoption because they view alternatives to adoption—abortion or single parenting—as superior alternatives. Olasky (1997) suggests that "abortion seems to convey an immediate benefit: It makes the problem disappear . . ." (p. 44). Despite the decreased financial support to single parents due to welfare reform, single parenting is encouraged by public financial support and its social acceptability. "Adoption, on the other hand, is altruistic—life for a child and a gift to an often-childless couple—but it is also inconvenient and embarrassing, especially when compared to abortions done in secret. Teenagers generally ask not what they can do for others, but what others are thinking about them" (p. 44). Olasky (1997) reflects a segment of conservative America in his conclusion that "for adoption to flourish, the other alternatives [i.e., abortion and single-parenting] need to become shameful once again" (p. 44).

12-8c Policies and Processes in Adoption

Women wishing to relinquish their babies to adoptive parents may do so through formal or informal procedures. **Informal adoption,** most common in African American families, involves a woman placing her child with another caregiver, usually within the kinship system, without going through formal court procedures. **Formal adoption** involves a legal agreement consenting to adoption or relinquishing one's parental rights. About half of all adoptions are to one's relatives; half to persons unrelated to the mother (Simon & Roorda, 2000).

Informal adoption A type of adoption most common in African American families that involves a woman placing her child with another caregiver, usually within the kinship system, without going through formal court procedures.

Formal adoption A legal agreement consenting to adoption or relinquishing one's parental rights.

Although this chapter focuses on the adoption of infants born to women who do not want or cannot care for them, children of all ages may be adopted. For example, parents who abuse, neglect, or abandon their children or commit a felony may lose custody of their children. The state provides institutional or foster care unless (or until) an adoptive home is found. Children whose parents die may also be adopted. Stepparents may adopt their stepchildren, but the biological parent must first relinquish parent status. Even adults can be adopted by other adults! Adult adoptions may be done to make someone a legal relative—a strategy used by some gay couples.

State laws governing adoptions vary widely. In general, the birth parent (or parents) must sign a consent to the adoption or a relinquishment of parental rights, which is not legally binding prior to the birth of the baby. The consent or relinquishment may be revoked for a limited period of time after birth, allowing the birth parents to change their mind. The biological father of the child usually must be notified of the adoption plan, but the procedures for this notification vary from state to state.

These proud parents adopted this child from Guatemala through a private adoption agency.

The prospective adoptive parent (or parents) must file a petition to adopt. After the child is in the custody of the adoptive parents, the adoptive family undergoes a period of court supervision (usually 6 months to a year), after which the adoption is finalized.

Agency Versus Independent Adoption

Adoptions may be arranged by public or private agencies, or they may be arranged independently. A private adoption agency is supported by private funds and should be licensed or approved by the state in which it operates. A public agency is the local branch of a state social service agency.

Agency adoption A type of adoption in which birth parents release their child to the adoption agency, which then places the child with a carefully selected family.

Independent adoption An adoption arranged without an agency whereby the initial contact is made directly between a pregnant woman and adoptive parents or the pregnant woman and an attorney, depending on state law.

In **agency adoption,** birth parents release their child to the adoption agency, which then places the child with a carefully selected family. In an independent adoption (arranged without an agency), initial contact can be made directly between a pregnant woman and adoptive parents or the pregnant woman and an attorney, depending on state law. A few states do not permit independent adoptions, but most do.

In an **independent adoption,** adoptive parents customarily pay for the birth mother's medical and legal expenses. Some states also require the adoptive parents to pay for counseling for the birth mother before, and perhaps after, the adoption is final. In some states, the adoptive parents may also help with the birth mother's living or clothing expenses. It is illegal, however, for prospective adoptive parents to offer birth parents any type of payment or "gift" in order to adopt the child. According to law, birth mothers cannot release their child for adoption until after the delivery; therefore, money spent before delivery by prospective adoptive parents is a gamble. If the birth mother decides to keep her baby, she is not legally required to pay back the money the prospective adoptive parents spent on her medical and other bills. However, she, her partner, or her parents may voluntarily choose to repay the money.

Open Versus Closed Adoptions

Closed adoption Traditional adoption that involves confidentiality, secrecy, and sealed adoption records; after the child is adopted, the birth parents have no further contact with the child or the adoptive family.

The practice of adoption has changed in recent decades. In previous generations, unwed pregnant women were hidden and secluded in maternity homes or went to stay with distant relatives during the pregnancy. Nonmarital pregnancy was considered a shameful sin and a disgrace to the pregnant woman and her family. For nearly a century, the fact that a child was adopted was often hidden from friends, neighbors, and the adopted child. **Closed adoption,** which involved confidentiality, secrecy, and sealed adoption records, became the norm. After the child was born, the birth parents disappeared and had no further contact with the child or the adoptive family. Traditional, closed adoption procedures "gave birth parents no input into the future of their children. They were encouraged to trust the agency's judgment, accept the agency's rules, agree to sealed records that would preclude any further contact with the child, and get on with their lives" (Hochman & Huston, 1994, p. 3).

Today, open adoption is becoming more common. In an open adoption, birth parents and adoptive parents have some knowledge about each other, and the birth parents may even help choose the adoptive parents. Open adoptions can take many forms. Birth parents may choose an adoptive family for their child by reading resumes or descriptions of prospective adopters and looking at their photographs. Birth parents may also meet and interview prospective adopters. This may be the only contact between the two families, or the two families may agree to have ongoing contact throughout the child's life. Some birth mothers use the adoptive mother as their coach during labor and delivery.

An **open adoption** allows birth parents to have some control over the adoption process such as deciding who the birth parents are, having access to the child, etc. Birth parents and adoptive parents have the flexibility to create an adoption plan that suits their values and preferences. A typical open adoption involves two to four contacts between the adoptive family and the birth family annually. "In some open adoptions, the adoptive family considers the birth parents an important part of their extended family" (Lindsay, 1997, p. 22).

Open adoption Type of adoption that allows birth parents to have some control over the adoption process—selection of the adoptive parents, access to the child if desired, etc.

Birth Father's Rights

Years ago, an unmarried father's permission was not required if the pregnant woman made an adoption plan; only the birth mother's consent was required. Today, the father's consent, if he can be found, is usually required before an adoption can be finalized. If the father cannot be located, the court is petitioned to remove the rights of the absent or unknown father.

12-8d Psychological Reactions to Placing a Baby for Adoption

Birth mothers usually experience grief, loss, and emotional pain after placing their baby for adoption. In one study of women who placed their babies for adoption, the greater the feelings of guilt and shame regarding the decision to relinquish the child, the higher the levels of unresolved grief (De Simone, 1996). Women who believed that others coerced them into relinquishing their babies felt deep guilt, shame, and regret regarding their decision. Birth mothers who experienced lower levels of grief tended to be more satisfied with their current marital status and family composition (De Simone, 1996). In addition, "birth mothers who had personal achievements of which they felt especially proud since the relinquishment, i.e., raising a family, graduating from college or professional school, or having a career" had lower levels of grief (pp. 72–73). Finally, the study found that birth mothers who had gained information about their child since the placement had lower levels of grief.

Another reaction birth parents may have to placing their baby for adoption is anger—toward themselves, their partner (or other birth parent), their family, and the adoption system. Birth mothers may feel angry at themselves for getting pregnant or angry at the person who impregnated them. They may feel anger toward family members and professionals who may have pressured them to place their babies for adoption. They may be angry at "the system" for failing to provide them with the emotional or financial support that might have enabled them to keep and parent their baby. Birth mothers may even be angry at the individuals who adopt their child: They "may feel grateful to adopting parents but, at the same time, resent them for their ability to enjoy the child instead" (Donnelly & Voydanoff, 1996, p. 427).

Although some women regret their decision to relinquish their children, others, especially those who are not pressured into adoption, accept their decision as painful but necessary. As one birth mother stated, "I knew that something can hurt a lot and still be the right thing to do" (quoted in Olasky, 1995, p. 25).

Birth parents may cope with the emotional pain of relinquishing a child for adoption in a number of ways, including the following (Lindsay, 1997; Smith, 1995):

- Going to counseling
- Attending birth-parent support group meetings
- Writing down their feelings in a story or poem or in a journal
- Being on a panel that talks to pregnant teens about the experience of pregnancy and the decision to place a child for adoption
- Writing letters, even if they are not sent, to their child
- Holding a private ceremony each year on the child's birthday
- Searching for the child (if the adoption was confidential and closed)
- Reading books written for birth parents to help them resolve their grief over placing their child for adoption

12-8e Personal Choices: Deciding to Place One's Baby for Adoption

A woman experiencing an unintended or unwanted pregnancy who does not want to have an abortion must choose between parenting the child and placing the child for adoption. Teenagers and women faced with this situation get lots of conflicting advice. Friends and family often have different reactions, including "What do you mean, you'll keep the baby?" "You can't raise a baby by yourself," or "How could you think of giving your baby away?" When faced with the decision of keeping a baby versus placing it for adoption, a woman must first realize that her decision may not please everyone. Although being open to the advice of others is important, she must ultimately make the decision for herself based on her best assessment of what is good for her and her baby. Making a decision to please someone else, including family and friends, may result in future resentment and regret over the decision.

Making this type of life-altering decision is best made after considering the short- and long-term advantages and disadvantages of each option. In assessing each option, it is helpful to talk with other birth parents who have placed their babies for adoption, as well as women who have decided to parent their children under less than ideal circumstances (such as still being in school, being young, being single, and having few resources). Birth fathers, as well as birth mothers, play a role in deciding the fate of the child. If possible, both birth parents should be involved in the decision-making process.

Most women in this situation choose to keep their children. Before making the choice to do this, the woman might ask herself how parenting will affect her education, future occupation, dreams, goals, and current and future relationships. She might also investigate the types and amount of social and financial assistance she may receive from the birth father, parents and other family members, and the government. Will her own resources, along with the support she may receive, be enough to provide the kind of life she wants for herself and her child?

If the answers to these questions paint a questionable picture of the future, adoption offers an alternative with several potential advantages. In the words of one woman:

> *Adoption can give birth parents a chance to gain control over their lives. It can open up a future that might include pregnancy and parenting experiences for which they will be prepared. In the meantime, adoption enables them to provide their child with the kind of nurturing home that they are not now in a position to offer. (Bartholet, 1995, p. 56)*

Researchers have found that unmarried birth mothers who made adoption plans advanced further educationally, were more likely to be employed and have a higher income, were less likely to have a repeat out-of-wedlock pregnancy, were less likely to have an abortion if they did have a repeat out-of-wedlock pregnancy, were more likely to subsequently marry, and were less likely to receive public assistance than birth mothers who chose to parent their children born out of wedlock (National Council for Adoption, 1999). However, those who place their children for adoption are also more likely than those who keep their infants to regret their decision (Donnelly & Voydanoff, 1996). Such regret, however, may be short term; one study found that regret over the decision to place a child for adoption is most intense one year after the birth but lessens drastically by the end of the second year (Donnelly & Voydanoff, 1996). Finally, it is also important to recognize that "adoption, regardless of how positive the outcome, begins with a traumatic loss for those involved" (Watson, 1996, p. 526).

Think About It

In the past, the phrase "giving up for adoption" was commonly used. Today, the term "making an adoption plan" is preferred because this phrase implies that the birth parents are involved in the adoption process. How do you think women making their children available for adoption conceptualize the adoption process?

12-9 ADOPTION—THE NEW PARENTS' POINT OF VIEW

When you adopt, you don't just do it for yourself, you do it for the needs of the child.
—Rosie O'Donnell, former talk show host

Some would-be parents are interested in adopting a child. Their motives include wanting a child because of their inability to have a biological child (infertility), their desire to give an otherwise unwanted child a permanent loving home, or their desire to avoid contributing to overpopulation by having more biological children. Some couples may seek adoption for all these motives.

12-9a Who Chooses to Adopt a Child?

Whereas demographic characteristics of those who typically adopt are White, educated, and high income, increasingly, adoptees are being placed in nontraditional families including older, gay, and single individuals; it is recognized that these individuals may also be White, educated, and high income (Finley, 2000). Rosie O'Donnell represents the unmarried gay adoptive mother. She lives in Florida where state law (Mississippi and Utah have similar laws) prohibit gay and lesbian individuals and couples from adopting children. Regarding single parents in general, Haugaard, Palmer, and Wojslawowicz (1999) reviewed the research literature on adoption and suggested that there is no indication that adoptions by single parents are more problematic than adoptions by two parents. The adoption by newly remarried Liza Minelli (her fourth) and David Gest reflect further diversity of couples who adopt. Money and position may have had an influence in their being able to adopt a 3-year-old so soon after their wedding. Typically, couples who have been married at least 3 years (Minelli and Gest had been married 6 months when the adoption was approved) are preferable as adoptive parents.

Whether single or married, some individuals/couples seeking to adopt a child use the Internet. Examples of sites offering online information about adoption include www.adopt.org and www.adoption.com/photolisting. The National Adoption Center, in conjunction with the Department of Health and Human Services, plans to provide a national adoption online site for children who are waiting to be adopted.

12-9b Characteristics of Children Available for Adoption

Adoptees in the highest demand are infant, White, healthy children. Older, non-White children with health problems have been difficult to place. Indeed, there are more than 100,000 "special needs" children in need of an adoptive home (Ryan, 2000).

12-9c Same-Race Adoptions

In a study on transracial adoption attitudes of college students (using the Attitudes Toward Transracial Adoption Scale), 30 was the average score (possible range 15–105; with the lower the score, the more positive the attitude) of 188 undergraduates, reflecting overwhelmingly positive attitudes toward transracial adoption. Significant differences included that women, persons willing to adopt a child at all, interracially experienced daters, and those open to interracial dating were more willing to adopt transracially than men, persons rejecting adoption as an optional route to parenthood, persons with no previous interracial dating experience, and persons closed to interracial dating (Whatley, Jahangardi, Ross & Knox (in press).

A recent controversy surrounding adoption is whether it is beneficial for children to be adopted by parents of the same racial background (Hollingsworth, 2000). In regard to the adoption of African American children by same-race parents, the National Association of Black Social Workers (NABSW) passed a resolution against transracial adoptions, citing that such adoptions prevented Black children from developing a positive sense of themselves "that would be necessary to cope with racism and prejudice that would eventually occur" (Hollingsworth, 1997, p. 44). The counter argument is that healthy self-concepts, an appreciation for one's racial heritage, and coping with racism/prejudice can be learned in a variety of contexts.

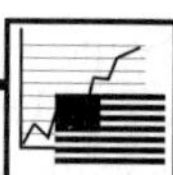

NATIONAL DATA Eight percent of adoptions are transracial; of these 1.2% involve a Black child adopted by a White family (Simon & Roorda, 2000).

The self-assessment in Box 12-2 addresses the issue of transracial adoption.

Legal restrictions on transracial adoptions have disappeared. The Adoption and Safe Families Act of 1996 prohibited the use of race "to delay or deny the placement of a child for adoption" (Simon & Roorda, 2000, p. 3). Social approval for transracial adoptions is increasing. Hollingsworth (2000) reported on a telephone survey of 916 individuals and found that 71% believed that race should not be a factor in who should be allowed to adopt. Data comparing children reared in transracial and same-race homes show few differences (Simon & Roorda, 2000).

One 26-year-old Black female was asked how she felt being reared by White parents and replied, "Again, they are my family and I love them, but I am black. I have to deal with my reality as a black woman" (Simon & Roorda, 2000, p. 41). The advice of a Black man reared in a White home to White parents considering a transracial adoption, "Make sure they have the influence of blacks in their lives; even if they have to go out and make friends with black families—it's a must" (p. 25). Indeed, Huh and Reid (2000) found that positive adjustment by adoptees was associated with participation in the cultural activities of the race of the parents who adopted them.

Box 12-2 Self-Assessment

Attitudes toward Transracial Adoption Scale

Transracial adoption is defined as the practice of parents adopting children of another race, for example, a White couple adopting a Korean or African American child. Please read each item carefully and consider what you believe about each statement. There are no right or wrong answers to any of these statements, so please give your honest reaction and opinion. After reading each statement, select the number which best reflects your answer using the following scale:

Strongly Disagree 1 2 3 4 5 6 7 Strongly Agree

___ 1. Transracial adoption can interfere with a child's well-being.
___ 2. Transracial adoption should not be allowed.
___ 3. I would never adopt a child of another race.
___ 4. I think that transracial adoption is unfair to the children.
___ 5. I believe that adopting parents should adopt a child within their own race.
___ 6. Only same race couples should be allowed to adopt.
___ 7. Biracial couples are not well prepared to raise children.
___ 8. Transracially adopted children need to choose one culture over another.
___ 9. Transracially adopted children feel as though they are not part of the family they live in.
___ 10. Transracial adoption should only occur between certain races.
___ 11. I am against transracial adoption.
___ 12. A person has to be desperate to adopt a child of another race.
___ 13. Children adopted by parents of a different race have more difficulty developing socially than children adopted by foster parents of the same race.
___ 14. Members of multiracial families do not get along well.
___ 15. Transracial adoption results in "cultural genocide."

Scoring: After assigning a number to each item, add the items. The lower the number (15 is the lowest number), the more positive one's view of transracial adoptions. The higher the number (105 is the highest number) the more negative one's view of transracial adoptions. The norming sample was based upon 34 male and 69 female students attending Valdosta State University. The average score on the Attitudes toward Transracial Adoption Scale was 2.27 (SD = 1.15) (suggesting a generally positive view of transracial adoption by the respondents) and ranged from 1.00 to 6.60. There was no significant difference between male participants' scores (M = 2.51, SD = 1.40) and female participants' scores (M = 2.15, SD = 0.99), $F(1, 101) = 2.28$, $p > .05$. There were no significant differences between ethnicities as well.

The average age of participants completing the Attitudes toward Transracial Adoption Scale was 22.22 years (SD = 4.23) and ranged in age from 18–48. The ethnic composition of the sample was 74.8% White, 20.4% Black, 1.9% Asian, 1.0% Hispanic, 1.0% American Indian, and one person did not indicate ethnicity. The classification of the sample was 15.5% Freshman, 6.8% Sophomore, 32.0% Junior, 42.7% Senior, and 2.9% were graduate students.

Source: "Attitudes toward Transracial Adoption Scale," 2003, by Mark Whatley, Ph.D., Department of Psychology, Valdosta State University, Valdosta, Georgia 31698. Used by permission. Other uses of this scale by written permission of Dr. Whatley only. His e-mail is mwhatley@valdosta.edu. Information on the reliability and validity of this scale is available from Dr. Whatley.

SUMMARY

Abortion in the United States

About 40% of women who experience an unintended pregnancy have an abortion. The United States leads European countries, Australia, and Canada in abortion rates.

Unmarried women, young women (particularly those under age 16), those reporting no religious affiliation, those who have previously had an abortion, and White women represent the largest percentage of women getting an abortion. Reasons for doing so include fear that the birth of a baby would cause difficulties with their training or work, pressure from their partners to have an abortion, or concern that their relationships with their partners were unstable. Some women also chose abortions when their pregnancies resulted from rape or from infidelity.

Methods of Abortion

Prior to the availability of modern surgical techniques, abortion in the late eighteenth and early nineteenth centuries was performed by flushing the uterus with caustic substances (such as gunpowder, quinine, or oil of juniper) or by inserting sticks of silver nitrate into the cervix. Abortions today are done by suction curettage (vacuum aspiration) during the first 6 to 8 weeks of pregnancy, dilation and suction during the first 12 weeks, dilation and evacuation from 13 to 24 weeks' gestation, and intact dilation and extraction, which results in the whole fetus being aborted (also known as "partial birth abortion").

An abortion may also be induced by injecting saline or prostaglandins through the abdomen into the amniotic sac around the fetus or through the use of the drug RU-486 (Mifepristone; sold as Mifeprex and known as "the abortion pill") if the woman is less than 9 weeks' pregnant.

Abortion Legislation in the United States

The legal control of abortion by statute began in 1821. Because thousands of women had died taking medically prescribed poisons to induce abortions, Connecticut passed a law prohibiting the use of poisons to induce post quickening abortions. In the mid-nineteenth century, the American Medical Association led the campaign to criminalize abortion. Their concerns were both economic and moral. Formally trained physicians competed economically with midwives, who assisted not only in births, but also in abortions. In the medical community moral concerns over abortion resulted, in part from advances in the scientific understanding of human development as a continuous process.

The abortion rights movement did not gain ground until 1973, when the U.S. Supreme Court ruled in the famous *Roe v. Wade* case that any restriction on abortions during the first trimester of pregnancy was unconstitutional. This ruling declared that during the first 3 months of pregnancy, the decision to have an abortion would be between the pregnant woman and her physician. In the second trimester (the fourth through the sixth month of pregnancy), the state might regulate the abortion procedure (by requiring that the abortion take place in a hospital, for example) so as to protect the woman's health. During the last trimester, the state would have an interest in protecting the viable fetus, so the state might restrict or prohibit abortion. In effect, the Supreme Court ruled that the fetus is a potential life and not a "person" until the third trimester.

A Cross-Cultural View of Abortion

Worldwide, about 50 million pregnancies are terminated by abortion. Policies concerning abortion vary around the world. On one end of the continuum is the Kafir tribe in Central Asia, in which there is no taboo or restriction in regard to abortion. Women are free to choose to terminate their pregnancies. However, the Kafir policy on abortion is an exception. In most cultures, abortion is considered wrong. Countries that do not permit abortion under any conditions include Brazil, Egypt, the Philippines, and Nepal. In Nepal, women who abort can be sentenced to 20 years in jail (whereas men who murder receive sentences of 10 years).

Attitudes Toward Abortion

The United States is deeply divided over the issue of abortion. Attitudes toward abortion range from fierce opposition to abortion under certain circumstances (including rape and endangerment of a woman's life) to staunch support for legal and affordable access to abortion on request. Abortion is more likely to be viewed as an acceptable option if the mother's health is endangered by continuing the pregnancy, if a severe birth defect exists, or if the pregnancy is the result of rape or incest. Although "pro-life" and "pro-choice" groups dominate public discourse on abortion, most people have views that are mixed. Pro-dialogue advocates attempt to bring both sides of the abortion controversy together to find a common ground and focus on reducing the need for abortion.

Physical and Psychological Effects of Abortion

Legal abortions, performed under safe conditions, are now safer than continuing the pregnancy. The earlier in the pregnancy the abortion is performed, the safer it is. Women are 10 times more likely to die from childbirth than from abortion.

Sixteen percent of 442 women regretted their abortion 2 years after the abortion. Almost 70% reported that they would make the same decision to abort if faced with the same situation. For most women, elective abortion does not pose a risk to mental health. The concept of post abortion syndrome has little to no validity in the scientific community.

Much of the evidence of PAS is anecdotal and not supported by scientific studies. One percent of women who had had an abortion meet the criteria for post traumatic stress disorder.

The Real Challenge: Reducing the Need for Abortion

Various social policies and strategies have been suggested to reduce the need for abortion by preventing most unwanted pregnancies and dealing more positively with the ones that occur.

Adoption: An Alternative to Abortion

About 2% of women experiencing an unwanted pregnancy place their children for adoption. Teens who place their babies for adoption are young (16 rather than 19), attending school, have mothers themselves who are somewhat better educated, and have mothers who approve of placing the children for adoption. The longer a woman delays making an adoption plan, the more likely she is to emotionally bond with her baby and the less likely she is to place her baby for an adoption.

Adoption: The New Parents' Point of View

Motives of parents who adopt a child include wanting a child because of their inability to have a biological child (infertility), their desire to give an otherwise unwanted child a permanent loving home, or their desire to avoid contributing to overpopulation by having more biological children. Whereas demographic characteristics of those who typically adopt are White, educated, and high income, increasingly, adoptees are being placed in nontraditional families including older, gay, and single individuals.

SUGGESTED WEBSITES

Note: These websites were functional when we went to press. Please access the online text for the most up-to-date URLs.

Abortion and Reproductive Rights
http://www.naral.org/

Abortion Clinics Online
http://www.gynpages.com/

Abortion Facts
http://www.abortionfacts.com/

Adopt an Angel
http://www.adoptanangel.org/

Adopt US Kids
http://www.adoptuskids.org

Adoption Web Ring
http://www.plumsite.com/adoptionring/

Children's Hope
http://www.childrenshope.com/

European Adoption Consultants
http://www.eaci.com/

International Adoption
http://travel.state.gov/adopt.html

National Adoption Clearinghouse Information
http://www.calib.com/naic/

National Adoption Center
http://www.adopt.org/

Pro Choice Resource Center
http://www.prochoiceresource.org/

Pro Life Resource Center
http://www.prolifeinfo.org/

KEY TERMS

abortion (p. 356)
abortion rate (p. 356)
abortion ratio (p. 356)
agency adoption (p. 372)
closed adoption (p. 372)
dilation and curettage (D&C) (p. 358)
dilation and evacuation (D&E) (p. 359)
dilation and suction (D&S) (p. 358)
female infanticide (p. 364)
formal adoption (p. 371)
independent adoption (p. 372)
induced abortion (p. 356)
informal adoption (p. 371)
intact dilation and extraction (D&X) (p. 359)
medical abortion (p. 360)
miscarriage (p. 356)
open adoption (p. 373)
partial birth abortions (p. 359)
pharmaceutical abortion (p. 360)
post abortion syndrome (PAS) (p. 369)
quickening (p. 361)
Roe v. Wade (p. 360)
RU-486 (p. 360)
sex-selective abortion (p. 364)
spontaneous abortion (p. 356)
suction curettage (p. 358)
therapeutic abortion (p. 358)
vacuum aspiration (p. 358)

CHAPTER QUIZ

1. Between 1990 and 1997, the U.S. abortion ____________ increased.
   a. rate
   b. ratio
   c. both a and b
   d. neither a nor b
2. Which of the following U.S. women have the lowest abortion rate?
   a. White women
   b. Hispanic women
   c. African American women
   d. Abortion rates among White, Hispanic, and African American women are roughly the same.
3. When a U.S. teenager gets pregnant, the most frequent outcome is
   a. an abortion.
   b. getting married and having the baby.
   c. having the baby outside marriage.
   d. miscarriage.
4. Abortions performed to protect the life or health of the woman are called
   a. medical abortions.
   b. justified abortions.
   c. therapeutic abortions.
   d. protective abortions.
5. Suction curettage (also known as vacuum aspiration)
   a. takes about 2 to 3 hours and must be done in a hospital.
   b. takes about 10 to 20 minutes and can be performed in a clinic or physician's office.
6. Which method of abortion is used in the second trimester of pregnancy (13 to 24 weeks' gestation)?
   a. suction curettage
   b. dilation and evacuation
   c. dilation and suction
   d. all the above
7. Which method of abortion has been labeled "partial birth abortion" by abortion opponents?
   a. dilation and evacuation
   b. dilation and suction
   c. dilation and extraction
   d. all the above
8. To terminate a pregnancy using RU-486, a woman must be less than ____________ weeks' pregnant.
   a. 3
   b. 6
   c. 9
   d. 12
9. When women are offered a choice of surgical or medical abortion, most choose the ____________ method.
   a. medical
   b. surgical
10. *Roe v. Wade* allowed women to get an abortion during the first ____________ of pregnancy and that the decision would be made between the woman and her ____________.
    a. 3 weeks; husband
    b. 3 weeks; physician
    c. 3 months; physician
    d. 3 months; husband
11. Aborted fetal tissue is valuable because it
    a. is disease resistant.
    b. is inexpensive and is widely available.
    c. can develop into any kind of tissue.
    d. can be used in the production of a variety of cosmetics and household products.
12. Some countries in the world do not permit abortion under any conditions.
    a. True
    b. False
13. The majority of first-year U.S. college students report that abortion ____________ be legal.
    a. should
    b. should not
14. All religious groups oppose abortion.
    a. True
    b. False
15. In a study of 442 women 2 years after they had had an abortion, the majority of the women regretted their decision to have the abortion.
    a. True
    b. False
16. According to data presented in your text, in the United States, ____________ of pregnant unmarried women choose to place their baby for adoption.
    a. about half
    b. the majority
    c. less than 2%

REFERENCES

Adler, N. E., David, H. P, Major, B. N., Roth, S. H., Russo, N. F., & Wyatt, G. E. (1992). Psychological factors in abortion: A review. *American Psychologist, 47*, 1194–1204.

Alan Guttmacher Institute. (1999). *Induced abortion worldwide: Facts in brief*. Retrieved March 22, 2003, from http//www.alanguttmacher.org/pubs/fb_0599.html

Baird, D. T. (2000). Therapeutic abortion. In A. Glasier & A. Gebbie (Eds.), *Family planning and reproductive healthcare* (pp. 249–262). London: Churchill Livingston.

Barnett, W., Freudenberg, N., & Willie, R. (1992). Partnership after induced abortion: A prospective controlled study. *Archives of Sexual Behavior, 21*, 443–455.

Bartholet, E. (1993). *Family bonds: Adoption and the politics of parenting*. New York: Houghton Mifflin.

Bartholet, E. (1995). Creating more adoption possibilities should be encouraged. In A. Harnack (Ed.), *Adoption: Opposing viewpoints* (pp. 55–62). San Diego, CA: Greenhaven Press.

Bartlett, T. (2002, February 1). Freshmen pay, mentally and physically as they adjust to college life. *Chronicle of Higher Education*, A35–A36.

Begley, S., Hager, M., Glick, D., & Foote, J. (1996). Fetal tissue research will benefit medical science. In C. P. Cozic & J. Petrikin (Eds.), *The abortion controversy* (pp. 221–227). San Diego, CA: Greenhaven Press.

Begue, L. (2001). Social judgement of abortion: A black-sheep effect in a Catholic sheepfold. *The Journal of Social Psychology, 141*, 640–650.

Bitler, M., & Zavodny, M. (2002). Did abortion legalization reduce the number of unwanted children? Evidence from adoptions. *Perspectives on Sexual and Reproductive Health, 34*, 25–33.

Boggess, S., & Bradner, C. (2000). Trends in adolescent males' abortion attitudes, 1988–1995: Differences by race and ethnicity. *Family Planning Perspectives, 32*, 118–123.

Boonstra, H. (2002). Mifepristone in the United States: Status and future. *The Guttmacher Report on Public Policy*, 5 (3). Retrieved on December 9, 2002, from www.guttmacher.org/pubs/journals/gro50304.html

Council on Scientific Affairs, American Medical Association. (1992). Council Report: Induced termination of pregnancy before and after *Roe v. Wade:* Trends in mortality and morbidity of women. *Journal of the American Medical Association*, 268, 3231–3239.

De Simone, M. (1996). Birth mother loss: Contributing factors to unresolved grief. *Clinical Social Work Journal, 24*(1), 65–76.

Donnelly, B. W., & Voydanoff, P. (1996). Parenting versus placing for adoption: Consequences for adolescent mothers. *Family Relations, 45*, 427–434.

Fielding, S. L., Edmunds, E., & Schaff, E. A. (2002). Having an abortion using Mifepristone and home misoprostol: A qualitative analysis of women's experiences. *Perspectives on Sexual and Reproductive Health, 34*, 34–40.

Finer, L. B., & Henshaw, S. K. (2003). Abortion incidence and services in the United States in 2000. *Perspectives on Sexual and Reproductive Health, 35*, 6–15.

Finley, G. E. (2000). Adoptive families: Dramatic changes across generations. *National Council on Family Relations, 45*, 6–7.

Garrett, T. M., Baillie, H. W., & Garrett, R. M. (2001). *Health care ethics* (4th ed.). Upper Saddle River, NJ: Prentice-Hall.

Goodwin, J. (1997). Prisoners of biology: In Nepal, there's no abortion debate, just a life sentence. *Utne Reader, 79*, 66–72.

Granberg, D. (1991). Conformity to religious norms regarding abortion. *Sociological Quarterly, 32*, 267–275.

Harvey, S. M., Beckman, L. J., & Satre, S. J. (2001). Choice of and satisfaction with methods of medical and surgical abortion among U.S. clinic patients. *Family Planning Perspectives, 33*, 212–223.

Haugaard, J. J., Palmer, M., & Wojslawowicz, J. C. (1999). Single-parent adoptions. *Adoption Quarterly, 2*, 65–74.

Henshaw, S. K. (1998). Abortion incidence and services in the United States, 1995–1996. *Family Planning Perspectives, 30*, 263–270, 287.

Hochman, G., & Huston, A. (1994). *Open adoption*. Rockville, MD: National Adoption Information Clearinghouse. Retrieved March 22, 2003, from http://www.calib.com/naic/pubs/f_openad.cfm

Hollander, D. (2001). After abortion, mixed mental health. *Family Planning Perspectives, 33*, 1–3.

Hollingsworth, L. D. (1997). Same race adoption among African Americans: A ten year empirical review. *African American Research Perspectives, 13*, 44–49.

Hollingsworth, L. D. (2000). Sociodemographic influences in the prediction of attitudes toward transracial adoption. *Families in Society, 81*, 92–100.

Huh, N. S., & Reid, W. J. (2000). Intercountry, transracial adoption, and ethnic identity: A Korean example. *International Social Work, 43*, 75–87.

Jones, R. K., Darroch, J. E., & Henshaw, S. K. (2002). Patterns in the socioeconomic characteristics of women obtaining abortions in 2000–2001. *Perspectives on Sexual and Reproductive Health, 34*, 226–235.

Jones, R. K., & Henshaw, S. K. (2002). Mifepristone for early medical abortion: Experiences in France, Great Britain and Sweden. *Perspectives on Sexual and Reproductive Health*, 34. Retrieved on December 9, 2002, from www.guttmacher.org/pubs/journals/3415402.html

Joyce, T., & Kaestner, R. (2000). The impact of Mississippi's mandatory delay law on the timing of abortion. *Family Planning Perspectives, 32*, 4–13.

Lichter, D. T., McLaughlin, D. K., & Ribar, D. C. (1998). State abortion policy, geographic access to abortion providers and changing family formation. *Family Planning Perspectives, 30*, 281–287.

Lindsay, J. W. (1997). *Pregnant? Adoption is an option*. Buena Park, CA: Morning Glory Press.

Maloy, K., & Patterson, M. (1992). *Birth or abortion? Private struggles in a political world*. New York: Plenum Press.

Marquis, K., & Detweiler, R. (1985). Does adopted mean different? An attributional analysis. *Journal of Personality and Social Psychology*, *48*, 1054–1066.

McDonagh, E. (1996). *Breaking the abortion deadlock: From choice to consent*. New York: Oxford University Press.

Michael, R. T. (2001). Abortion decisions in the United States. In E. O. Laumann & R. T. Michael (Eds.), *Sex, love, and health in America: Private choices and public policies* (pp. 377–438). Chicago: The University of Chicago Press.

Miller, D. H. (1996). Medical and psychological consequences of legal abortion in the United States. In R. L. Parrott & C. M. Condit (Eds.), *Evaluating women's health messages* (pp. 17–32). Thousand Oaks, CA: Sage.

Miller, K., & Rosenfield, A. (1996). Population and women's reproductive health: An international perspective. *Annual Review of Public Health*, *17*, 359–382.

Miller, V. S., & Hanks, R. B. (2002). Induced abortion: An ethical conundrum for counselors. *Journal of Counseling and Development*, *80*, 57–64.

National Council for Adoption. (1999). *Adoption factbook III*. Alexandria, VA: Author.

Olasky, M. (1995). Adoption is an act of compassion. In A. Harnack (Ed.), *Adoption: Opposing viewpoints* (pp. 24–30). San Diego, CA: Greenhaven Press.

Olasky, M. (1997). Forgotten choice. *National Review*, *49*(4), 43–45.

Petchesky, R. P. (1990). *Abortion and women's choice: The state, sexuality, and reproductive freedom* (rev. ed.). Northeastern Series in Feminist Theory. Boston: Northeastern University Press.

Reardon, D. C., & Ney, P. G. (2000). Abortion and subsequent substance abuse. *American Journal of Drug and Alcohol Abuse*, *26*, 61–73.

Rimensnyder, S. (2002). Weak choice. *Reason*, *33*, 14–19.

Rosenfeld, J. (1997). Postcoital contraception and abortion. In J. Rosenfeld (Ed.), *Women's health in primary care* (pp. 315–329). Media, PA: Williams & Wilkins.

Rubin, E. (1987). *Abortion, politics, and the courts:* Roe v Wade *and its aftermath* (2nd ed.). Westport, CT: Greenwood Press.

Ryan, S. D. (2000). Examining social workers' placement recommendations of children with gay and lesbian adoptive parents. *Families in Society: The Journal of Contemporary Human Services*, *81*, 517–526.

Seims, Sara. (2002, May 23). Alan Guttmacher Institute Letter.

Simon, R. J., & Roorda, R. M. (2000). *In their own voices: Transracial adoptees tell their stories*. New York: Columbia University Press.

Smith, D. (1995). *The impact of adoption on birth parents*. Adopt: Assistance Information Support. Retrieved March 22, 2003, from http://www adopting.org/impact.html#top

Spriggs, M., & Savulescu, J. (2002). The Perruche judgement and the "right not to be born." *Journal of Medical Ethics*, *28*, 63–65.

Statistical Abstract of the United States: 2002. (2002). 122nd ed. Washington, DC: U.S. Bureau of the Census.

Stotland, N. L. (1996). Conceptions and misconceptions: Decisions about pregnancy. *General Hospital Psychiatry*, *18*, 238–243.

Strong, C. (1997). Fetal tissue research is ethical. In T. L. Roleff (Ed.), *Abortion: Opposing viewpoints* (pp. 184–189). San Diego, CA: Greenhaven Press.

Torres, A., & Forrest, J. D. (1988). Why do women have abortions? *Family Planning Perspectives*, *20*, 169–176.

Watson, K. W. (1996). Family centered adoption practice. *Families in Society: The Journal of Contemporary Human Services*, *77*, 523–534.

Watts, C., & Zimmerman, C. (2002). Violence against women: Global scope and magnitude. *Lancet*, *359*, 1232–1236.

Whatley, M. (2003). Attitudes toward transracial adoption scale. Unpublished manuscript, Department of Psychology, Valdosta State University, Valdosta, GA.

Whatley, M., Jahangardi, J. N., Ross, R., & Knox, D. (in press) College student attitudes toward transracial adoption. *College Student Journal*.

Woodward, K. L., Hager, M., & Glick, D. (1996). The ethics of fetal tissue research and transplantation: An overview. In C. P. Cozic & J. Petrikin (Eds.), *The abortion controversy* (pp. 216–220). San Diego, CA: Greenhaven Press.

Yeost, C. (1995). Informal adoptions should be supported. In A. Harnack (Ed.), *Adoption: Opposing viewpoints* (pp. 154–164). San Diego, CA: Greenhaven Press.

Zavondy, M. (2001). The effect of partners' characteristics on teenage pregnancy and its resolution. *Family Planning Perspectives*, *33*, 192–199.

Pregnancy, Childbirth, and Transition to Parenthood

Chapter Outline

I do beseech you to direct your efforts more to preparing youth for the path and less to preparing the path for youth.

—*Judge Ben Lindsey, 1920s domestic judge*

Most married couples look forward to having children, assume pregnancy will occur naturally, and rarely consider that getting pregnant will be a problem. But for about 15% of couples, a pregnancy is not forthcoming and becomes a preoccupation that alters their self-concept, relationship, and finances. Even after pregnancy, the baby and subsequent parenting challenges change an individual's and couple's life forever. In this chapter, we address many of the choices and issues individuals and couples face in regard to getting pregnant and becoming parents through pregnancy. We begin with a discussion of fertilization and infertility.

13-1 FERTILIZATION AND PREGNANCY

Fertilization The union of a sperm and an egg resulting in a zygote. (See also **conception.**)

Fertilization takes place when a woman's egg, or ovum, unites with a man's sperm to produce a zygote, which begins the development of an embryo. This process may occur through sexual intercourse, artificial insemination, or in vitro fertilization.

At orgasm, the man ejaculates a thick white substance called *semen*, which contains about 300 million sperm. After the semen is deposited in or near the vagina, the sperm begin to travel up the vagina, through the opening of the cervix, up the uterus, and into the Fallopian tubes. If the woman has ovulated (released a mature egg from an ovary into a Fallopian tube) within 8 hours, or if she ovulates during the 2 or 3 days the sperm typically remain alive, a sperm may join and fertilize the egg.

Pregnancy State of carrying developing offspring within the woman's body.

Conception The point at which the egg and sperm are joined. (See also **fertilization.**)

Although popular usage does not differentiate between the terms *fertilization* and the *beginning of* ***pregnancy,*** *fertilization* or **conception** refers to the fusion of the egg and sperm, while *pregnancy* is not considered to begin until 5 to 7 days later, when the fertilized egg is implanted (typically in the uterine wall; Pinon, 2002). Hence, not all fertilizations result in a pregnancy. An estimated 30–40% of conceptuses are lost prior to or during implantation.

Because a woman is fertile for only a limited time each month, when is the best time to have intercourse to maximize the chance of pregnancy? In most healthy women, pregnancy results from having intercourse around the time of ovulation. The day of ovulation is the last day for fertilization to occur; a large study of fertility patterns found that most conceptions occur as a result of intercourse that took place 1, 2, or even up to 5 days prior to ovulation (Angier, 1999).

There are several ways to predict ovulation. Many women have breast tenderness, and some experience a "pinging" sensation in their abdomen at the time of ovulation.

As noted in section 11-3c, "Natural Family Planning Methods," a woman may also detect ovulation by recording her basal body temperature and examining her cervical mucus. After menstruation, the vagina in most women is without noticeable discharge because the mucus is thick. As the time of ovulation nears, the mucus thins to the consistency of egg white, which the woman may experience as increased vaginal discharge. If pregnancy is the goal, intercourse should occur during this time. In essence, the technology of the periodic abstinence method to avoid pregnancy (also discussed in section 11-3c) can be used to maximize the potential for pregnancy.

The position during intercourse may also be important for fertilization. To maximize the chance of fertilization, during intercourse, the woman should be on her back, and a pillow should be placed under her buttocks after receiving the sperm so that a pool of semen will collect near her cervix. She should remain in this position for about 30 minutes to allow the sperm to reach the Fallopian tubes.

13-2 INFERTILITY

Infertility is truly a bio-psycho-social condition.

—*Constance Shapiro*

Infertility is defined as the inability to achieve a pregnancy after at least 1 year of regular sexual relations without birth control, or the inability to carry a pregnancy to a live birth. Different types of infertility include the following:

Infertility The inability to achieve a pregnancy after at least 1 year of regular sexual relations without birth control, or the inability to carry a pregnancy to a live birth.

1. *Primary infertility*. The woman has never conceived even though she wants to and has had regular sexual relations for the past 12 months.
2. *Secondary infertility*. The woman has previously conceived but is currently unable to do so even though she wants to and has had regular sexual relations for the past 12 months.
3. *Pregnancy wastage*. The woman has been able to conceive but has been unable to produce a live birth.

NATIONAL DATA About 6 million American women and their partners cope with infertility (Hart, 2002). About 15% of couples have not conceived after a year of unprotected intercourse (Daniluk, 2001).

13-2a Causes of Infertility

Infertility problems may be attributed to the man (40%), the woman (40%), or both (20%). Some of the more common causes of infertility in men include low sperm production, poor sperm motility, effects of sexually transmitted diseases (such as chlamydia, gonorrhea, and syphilis), and interference with the passage of sperm through the genital ducts due to an enlarged prostate. The causes of infertility in women include blocked Fallopian tubes, endocrine imbalances that prevent ovulation, dysfunctional ovaries, chemically hostile cervical mucus that may kill sperm, and effects of sexually transmitted diseases (e.g., HPV, chlamydia). High or low body mass is also associated with a decreased probability of getting pregnant (Wang & Norman, 2000). Finally, environmental contaminants also have been the culprit in infertility. McGuinness, Buck, Mendola, Lowell, and Vena (2001) found that pregnant women who ate sport fish from Lake Ontario from 1991 to 1993 had a higher incidence of not being able to carry their baby to term.

13-2b Psychological Reactions to Infertility

Not being able to get pregnant may be a psychological crisis, a grief experience, or an economic burden. Van Den Akker (2001) observed of 105 infertile respondents that three fourths were "devastated by their in/subfertility diagnosis" (p. 152). Sixty-four percent of the women and 47% of the men said they could not be happy if they could never have a child. About a quarter of the infertile men and women sought an adoption. Others tried various forms of treatment to get pregnant but were shocked at how long the process took and how expensive it was. One of Daniluk's (2001) respondents noted,

> *We decided at the beginning that we would not spend our life savings on treatment—that we would stop before we got to in-vitro-fertilization. And then before we knew it, it was two years, three IVF attempts, and over $20,000 later—still no baby. (p. 130)*

Regarding the grief aspect of infertility, for some it was mixed with anger. Another of Daniluk's couples who were not able to conceive said,

> *I was angry . . . there isn't anything else in my life that I've worked that hard at really, that I didn't get . . . like I deserved to have succeeded. I didn't have the energy to do anything else, I just couldn't do it anymore. But I was really angry. It was like, this isn't the way it was suppose to end. (p. 131)*

Think About It

In what way is infertility similar to the death of a family member? How is it different?

The couple's sexual relationship also changes. Sex becomes programmed and in reference to the ovulation cycle. Making love may become a chore—an obligation, to do it again, to try once more.

In the United States the demand for infertility services increased during the 1980s and 1990s. Based on data from the 1995 National Survey of Family Growth, it is estimated that of the 6.7 million women who had fertility problems in 1995, 42% received some type of infertility services. The vast majority of these interventions were noninvasive treatments that could be considered "low technology" services. The most common services the women had ever received included advice (60%), diagnostic testing (50%), medical intervention to prevent miscarriage (44%), and ovulation-inducing drugs (35%) (Stephen & Chandra, 2000).

Those who seek fertility services tend to be older, have more education, and have a higher income. Although "high technology" infertility treatment is expensive and often fails, there is an array of reproductive technologies from which to choose. We explore each of them in section 13-3.

13-3 REPRODUCTIVE TECHNOLOGY

A number of technological innovations are available to assist women and couples in becoming pregnant. They include hormonal therapy, artificial insemination, ovum transfer, in vitro fertilization, gamete intrafallopian transfer, and zygote intrafallopian transfer.

13-3a Hormone Therapy

Drug therapies are often used to treat hormonal imbalances, induce ovulation, and correct problems in the luteal phase of the menstrual cycle. Frequently used drugs include Clomid, Pergonal, and human chorionic gonadotropin (HCG)—a hormone extracted from human placenta. These drugs stimulate the ovary to ripen and release an egg. Although they are fairly effective in stimulating ovulation, hyper-stimulation of the ovary can occur, which may result in permanent damage to the ovary.

Hormone therapy also increases the likelihood of ovulating multiple eggs, resulting in multiple births. The increase of triplets and higher-order multiple births over the past decade in the United States is largely attributed to the rise in use of ovulation-inducing drugs for treating infertility. The health of babies born with several siblings is compromised (low birth weight) and the strain on the parents is usually forthcoming. Garel and Blondel (1992) interviewed 12 mothers 1 year following their deliveries of triplets in a public hospital in Paris. The mothers reported strained marriages, social isolation, and difficulty giving adequate attention to three children at the same time. Eight of the mothers reported psychological difficulties, and three had been treated for depression. The researchers recommended that families with triplets should receive increased attention, counseling, and support through specialized clinics, clubs, or home visits. The mothers stated that prior to a much-wanted pregnancy, parents can hardly anticipate the risks and hardships involved with having multiple children.

Artificial insemination
The introduction of sperm into a woman's vagina or cervix by means of a syringe, rather than a penis. The sperm may be from a partner, a husband (AIH, artificial insemination by husband), or a donor (AID, artificial insemination by donor).

13-3b Artificial Insemination

When the sperm of the male partner are low in count or motility, sperm from several ejaculations may be pooled and placed directly into the cervix. This procedure is known as **artificial insemination** *by husband* (AIH).

When sperm from someone other than the woman's partner is used to fertilize a woman, the technique is referred to as *artificial insemination by donor* (AID). Lesbians who want to become pregnant may use sperm from a friend or from a sperm bank. (Some sperm banks cater exclusively to lesbians.) Regardless of the source of the sperm, it should be screened for genetic abnormalities/sexually transmitted diseases, quarantined for 180 days, and retested for HIV; also, the donor should be under 50 to diminish hazards related to aging. These precautions are not routinely taken—let the buyer beware!

Sometimes the male partner's sperm is mixed with a donor's sperm so that the couple has the psychological benefit of knowing that the male partner may be the biological father. However, the male partner's sperm is not mixed with the donor's sperm when the male partner is the carrier of a genetic disease, such as Tay-Sachs disease. Although achieving a pregnancy is the goal of would-be parents, they are concerned about whether and what to tell the child about the fact that he or she has an unknown donor father. An infertile woman who spoke in one of the authors' classes noted that she had had a daughter via donor sperm and was told by her physician not to tell the child. But the woman did so and reported that "it was a relief" to finally share the information, which was well received by the daughter.

13-3c Artificial Insemination of a Surrogate Mother

In some instances, artificial insemination does not help a woman get pregnant. (Her Fallopian tubes may be blocked, or her cervical mucus may be hostile to sperm.) The couple who still want a child and have decided against adoption may consider parenthood through a **surrogate mother** (also called a **contract mother**). There are two types of surrogate mothers. One is the contracted surrogate mother who supplies the egg, is impregnated with the male partner's sperm, carries the child to term, and gives the baby to the man and his partner. A second type is the surrogate mother who carries to term a baby to whom she is not genetically related. As with AID, the motivation of the prospective parents is to have a child who is genetically related to at least one of them. For the surrogate mother, the primary motivation is to help childless couples achieve their aspirations of parenthood and to make money. (The surrogate mother is usually paid about $10,000.)

Surrogate mother A woman who voluntarily agrees to be artificially inseminated, carry a baby to term, and give up the legal right to the baby at birth to a couple or individual desiring such a baby. The woman may also be implanted with a fertilized zygote from another sperm and egg so that she is not biologically related to the baby she carries to term. (See also **contract mother.**)

Contract mother See **surrogate mother.**

Legally, there are few guidelines for couples who engage a surrogate mother for procreative services. The surrogate can change her mind and decide to keep the child, as did a New Jersey surrogate mother in 1987. In what became known as the "Baby M Case," Mary Beth Whitehead decided she wanted to keep her baby, even though she had signed a contract to give up the baby to William Stern and his wife, Elizabeth, for $10,000. Whitehead turned down the fee and fled the state with the baby, who was found by private investigators and returned to the Sterns. Whitehead (1989) questioned the label applied to her of "surrogate mother," because she was the biological mother who provided the egg, carried the pregnancy to term, and gave birth. Initially, a judge upheld the surrogacy contract, severed Whitehead's parental rights, and presided over Elizabeth Stern's adoption of Baby M. A year later, the Supreme Court of New Jersey ruled surrogacy for hire was illegal because it resembled baby selling and re-established Whitehead's parental rights. (It gave her liberal visitation rights.) However, the court ruled that Richard Stern was the primary custodial parent.

In another case in 1991, surrogate mother Elvie Jordon changed her mind when she discovered that the couple to whom she had given her baby were getting divorced. Jordon filed suit to get custody of her 17-month-old daughter, Marissa, who was living with Bob Moschetta (the biological father and ex-husband of Cindy Moschetta). A California superior court justice ruled that Elvie Jordon and Bob Moschetta (the biological mother and father) would share joint legal and physical custody of Marissa. (Cindy Moschetta was found to have no legal rights and was given no visitation privileges.)

13-3d Ovum Transfer

Ovum transfer A procedure whereby sperm is placed into a surrogate woman. When the egg is fertilized, her uterus is flushed out, and the zygote is implanted into the otherwise infertile female partner.

Embryo transfer A procedure whereby a cyropreserved embryo (one's own or donated) is implanted into a woman who will carry the pregnancy to term.

Another alternative for the infertile couple is **ovum transfer.** A physician places the sperm of the male partner in a surrogate woman. After about 5 days, her uterus is flushed out (endometrial lavage), and the contents are analyzed under a microscope to identify the presence of a fertilized ovum. The fertilized ovum is then inserted into the uterus of the otherwise infertile partner. It is also possible for an embryo to be frozen (cryopreserved) and implanted at a later time (called **embryo transfer**).

Infertile couples who opt for ovum or embryo transfer may do so in order to have the baby biologically related to at least one of them (the father) or so the partner will have the experience of pregnancy and childbirth. As noted in section 13-3c for surrogate mothers, the surrogate woman in this procedure participates out of her desire to help an infertile couple or to make money.

13-3e In Vitro Fertilization

In vitro fertilization Procedure that involves removing the woman's ovum and placing it in a lab dish, fertilizing it with a partner's or donor's sperm, and inserting the fertilized egg into the woman's uterus. (Also known as **test tube fertilization.**)

Laparoscope A narrow, telescope-like medical instrument. One use involves inserting the instrument through an incision just below the woman's navel to view the Fallopian tubes and ovaries.

Cryopreservation Preservation by freezing, as when fertilized eggs are frozen for possible implantation at a later time.

About 2 million couples cannot have a baby because the woman's Fallopian tubes are blocked or damaged, preventing the passage of eggs to the uterus. In some cases, blocked tubes can be opened via laser surgery or by inflating a tiny balloon within the clogged passage. When these procedures are not successful (or when the woman decides to avoid invasive tests and exploratory surgery), **in vitro** (meaning "in glass") **fertilization,** also known as "test tube fertilization," is an alternative.

Using a **laparoscope** (a narrow, telescopelike instrument inserted through an incision just below the woman's navel to view the tubes and ovaries), the physician is able to see a mature egg as it is released from the woman's ovary. The time of release can be predicted accurately within 2 hours. When the egg emerges, the physician uses an aspirator to remove the egg, placing it in a small tube containing a stabilizing fluid. The egg is taken to the laboratory, put in a culture or petri dish, kept at a certain temperature-acidity level, and surrounded by sperm from the woman's partner (or donor). After one of these sperm fertilizes the egg, the egg divides and is implanted by the physician in the wall of the woman's uterus. Usually, several fertilized eggs are implanted in the hope that one will survive.

Occasionally, some fertilized eggs are frozen and implanted at a later time, if necessary. This procedure is known as **cryopreservation.** Separated or divorced couples may disagree over who owns the frozen embryos, and the legal system is still wrestling with the fate of their unused embryos, sperm, or ova in the event of a divorce or death of the parents.

13-3f Other Reproductive Technologies

Gamete intrafallopian transfer (GIFT) A procedure whereby a physician places an egg and sperm directly into the Fallopian tube.

Zygote intrafallopian transfer (ZIFT) Procedure that involves fertilizing an egg in a lab dish and placing the zygote or embryo directly into the Fallopian tube.

Microinjection Procedure whereby a physician injects sperm directly into an egg.

Partial zona drilling (PZD) Procedure that involves drilling tiny holes in the protective shell of the egg to increase the chance of it being fertilized.

A major problem with in vitro fertilization is that only about 15–20% of the fertilized eggs will implant in the uterine wall. To improve this implant percentage (to between 40 and 50%), physicians place the egg and sperm directly into the Fallopian tube, where they meet and fertilize. Then the fertilized egg travels down into the uterus and implants. Because the term for sperm and egg together is *gamete*, this procedure is called **gamete intrafallopian transfer,** or GIFT. **Zygote intrafallopian transfer,** or ZIFT, involves fertilizing the egg in a lab dish and placing the zygote or embryo directly into the Fallopian tube. ZIFT has a success rate similar to gamete intrafallopian transfer.

Some infertility cases are the result of sperm that lack motility. In those cases, a physician may inject sperm directly into the egg by means of **microinjection.**

Eggs most likely to implant on the uterine wall are those whose shells have been poked open. To enhance implantation, physicians isolate an egg and drill tiny holes in its protective shell. This procedure is known as **partial zona drilling (PZD).**

Infertile couples hoping to get pregnant through one of the more than 300 in vitro fertilization (IVF) clinics should make informed choices by asking questions such as "What is the center's pregnancy rate for women with similar diagnoses?" "What percentage of these women have a live birth?" "How many cycles are attempted per patient?" The

Box 13-1 Social Choices

Pursue Human Cloning Technology?

Dr. Panayiotis Zavos, of Lexington, Kentucky, told a House Government Reform subcommittee in May of 2002 that "2002 will be the year of the clones." The article by MSNBC News Services (http://www.msnbc.com/news/752767.asp#BODY) quoted Zavos as saying that he expected the pregnancy to occur outside the United States. In alluding to the location of the clinics where the cloning would occur, he said: one in "well I guess you could say it's Europe" and one "in between Greece and India." He declined to give further details but said he had lined up 12 suitable couples who had exhausted all other fertility options. Some are Americans, Zavos said, and five couples include at least one physician each. Human cloning is inevitable. Raelians, a group claiming that extraterrestrials landed on earth 25,000 years ago and cloned humans, say they cloned a human being in December 2002. They have provided no evidence for their claim.

Cloning first received worldwide attention in July 1996 when scientist Ian Wilmut of Scotland successfully cloned an adult sheep named Dolly. He did so by placing an udder cell from a 6-year-old sheep with an immature egg cell from another sheep and implanting the resulting embryo in a third sheep. This technological breakthrough prompted quick European action that resulted in a ban on human cloning. And, in the United States, the Human Cloning Prohibition Act of 2002 bans human cloning while allowing therapeutic and presumably research cloning. Reproductive cloning seems universally abhorred (Krauthammer, 2002).

The debate on therapeutic and research cloning continues. Although some individuals are prepared to endorse the cloning of the human embryo to be able to study and use its component parts, they want the proviso that the embryo be destroyed before it grows into a fetus or child. Others want to outlaw all cloning. President George W. Bush has made it clear that he opposes reproductive and therapeutic cloning and backs legislation introduced by Senator Sam Brownback (R-Kan.) to criminalize all cloning. Protests in Florida against the Brownback/Landrieu Bill 1899 emphasize the value of therapeutic cloning.

One argument in favor of developing human cloning technology is that it has medical value; it may potentially allow people to have "their own reserve of therapeutic cells that would increase their chance of being cured of various diseases, such as cancer, degenerative disorders and viral or inflammatory diseases" (Kahn, 1997, p. 119). Human cloning technology could also provide an alternative reproductive route for couples who are infertile and for couples in which one partner is at risk for transmitting a genetic disorder to any offspring. Cloning technology may also provide a means of reproduction for single individuals and gay and lesbian couples. (Depending on one's personal values and beliefs, this could be viewed as a benefit or a drawback.)

Arguments against human cloning are largely based on moral and ethical considerations. Critics of human cloning suggest that, whether used for medical therapeutic purposes or as a means of reproduction, human cloning is a threat to human dignity. Kahn (1997) suggests that "part of the individuality and dignity of a person probably lies in the uniqueness and unpredictability of his or her development" (p. 119). Cloned humans would be deprived of this individuality and dignity because they would be genetic carbon copies of other individuals. There is also concern that human cloning technology would be used by the "wrong people," such as oppressive dictators and fanatical terrorists, to reproduce and increase the members of their groups.

---

most successful reproductive technology programs report live birth rates of 20% (Rosenthal, 1997). Expressed another way, 80% of couples are not successful in having a baby. Daniluk (2001) reported the experiences of 65 infertile couples who had tried a myriad of procedures to get pregnant—60% were unsuccessful. (See Box 13-1.)

13-4 PRECONCEPTION CARE

Many women who plan their pregnancies want to enhance their health and well-being prior to conception to maximize their chance of having a healthy pregnancy and baby. **Preconception care** (also referred to as *preconception counseling*) includes risk assessment, interventions to reduce risk (such as treatment of infections and diseases and assistance with quitting smoking), and general health promotion (such as encouraging healthy eating, sleep, and exercise patterns; avoiding drugs; and eating a nutritional diet; Hall, 2000). The risk assessment component of preconception care includes screening before pregnancy for genetic risk factors that might affect the health of the woman or her child. An example would be testing women from certain ethnic groups to assess whether they are carriers of a genetic disease such as Tay-Sachs disease.

Preconception care Risk assessment, interventions to reduce risk (such as treatment of infections and diseases and assistance with quitting smoking), and general health promotion (such as encouraging healthy eating, sleep, and exercise patterns; avoiding drugs; and eating a nutritional diet) to help ensure the development of a healthy baby during pregnancy. (Also called *preconception counseling*.)

Box 13-2 Self-Assessment

Do You Need Preconception Counseling?

To determine whether you might benefit from preconception counseling, ask yourself the following questions:

1. Do you have a major medical problem, such as diabetes, asthma, anemia, or high blood pressure?
2. Do you know of any family members who have had a child with a birth defect or mental retardation?
3. Have you had a child with a birth defect or mental retardation?
4. Are you concerned about inherited diseases, such as Tay-Sachs disease, sickle cell anemia, hemophilia, or thalassemia?
5. Are you 35 years of age or older?
6. Do you smoke, drink alcohol, or take illegal drugs?
7. Do you take prescription or over-the-counter medications regularly?
8. Do you use birth control pills?
9. Do you have a cat?
10. Are you a strict vegetarian?
11. Are you dieting or fasting for any reason?
12. Do you run long distances or exercise strenuously?
13. Do you work with chemicals, toxic substances, radiation, or anesthesia?
14. Do you suspect that you or your partner may have a sexually transmitted disease?
15. Have you had German measles (rubella) or a German measles vaccination?
16. Have you ever had a miscarriage, ectopic pregnancy, stillbirth, or complicated pregnancy?
17. Have you recently traveled outside the United States?

If your answer to any of these questions is yes, you definitely should seek counseling from an obstetrician, nurse midwife, or family practitioner 3 to 6 months before you hope to conceive a child.

Source: From *Instructor's Guide for Hale's An Invitation to Health*, 7th ed., by Diane Hales.

Other examples of preconception care include immunizing nonpregnant women against rubella (live virus vaccines are contraindicated during pregnancy), diagnosing and controlling diabetes, advising the daily use of folate supplements to prevent neural tube (fetal brain and spine) defects, testing and counseling for HIV, identifying and treating substance abuse, and advising women to avoid any substances (such as medications) that could harm a fetus. The degree to which women alter their behavior during pregnancy is not known. However, Bussell and Marlow (2000) found that 9% of their sample of 31 mothers changed their diet in anticipation of getting pregnant.

Although all women can potentially benefit from preconception care, such care is particularly indicated for women who are at risk for pregnancy or childbirth complications. The self-assessment in Box 13-2 presents questions women can ask to determine whether they should seek preconception counseling.

13-5 PREGNANCY AND CHILDBIRTH

Immediately after the egg and sperm unite, typically in the Fallopian tube, the egg begins to divide and is pushed by hairlike cilia down the tube into the uterus, where it attaches itself to the inner wall. The placenta forms in the endometrium of the mother's uterus and its blood vessels. The placenta has been compared to a busy freight terminal (Nilsson & Hamberger, 1990) because nourishment is obtained from the mother's blood and the embryo discards its waste. The **umbilical cord** connects the developing fetus and the placenta; this flexible cord contains the two arteries and the vein that facilitate this exchange. Furnished with a rich supply of blood and nutrients, the developing organism is called an **embryo** for the first 8 weeks and a **fetus** thereafter (see Figure 13-1).

Umbilical cord Cord which connects the developing fetus and the placenta.

Embryo The developing organism from conception to the 8th week of pregnancy.

Fetus The developing organism from the 8th week of pregnancy forward.

Ectopic pregnancy Condition in which a fertilized egg becomes implanted in a site other than the uterus.

Detecting pregnancy as early as possible is important. Not only does early detection enable the woman to begin prenatal precautions and medical care during the most vulnerable stage of fetal development, it also allows women with an unintended pregnancy time to consider whether they want to have an abortion, which may then be performed when it is safest (early in pregnancy). Finally, early diagnosis may permit early detection of an **ectopic pregnancy.** Such a pregnancy involves the baby developing outside the

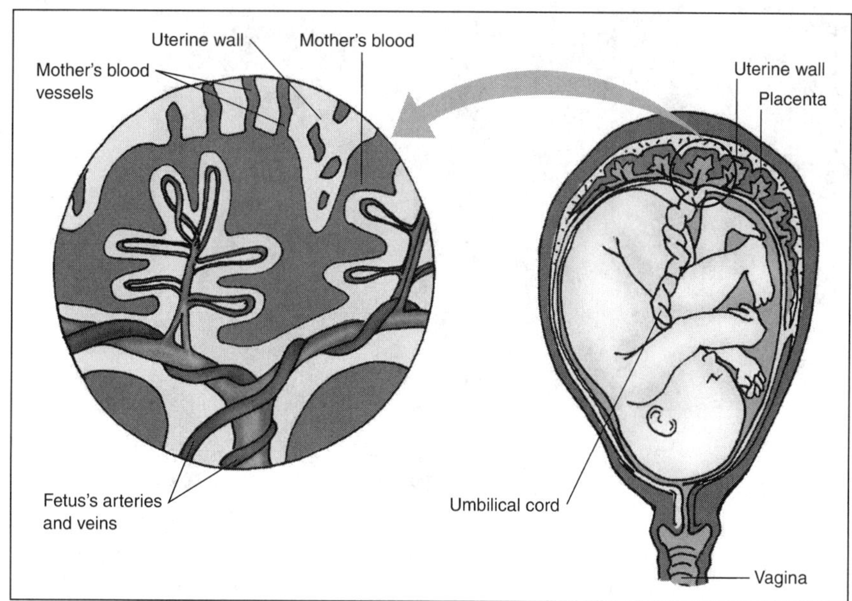

FIGURE 13-1
The Developing Embryo

uterus, such as in the cervix, abdominal area, or ovary. Most ectopic pregnancies occur in the Fallopian tube. The increase in tubal pregnancies in the past few years has been attributed to the rise in sexually transmitted diseases. Infection that results in the formation of scar tissue may interfere in the passage of the fertilized egg to the uterus. The pregnancy does not reach term because the growth of the fetus is too limited (Pinon, 2002).

An ectopic pregnancy is potentially dangerous because the tubal wall can be ruptured and cause severe bleeding that can be lethal to the mother (Pinon, 2002). Signs of such a pregnancy should be taken seriously. These signs include sudden intense pain in the lower abdomen, irregular bleeding, or dizziness that persists for more than a few seconds.

New treatments for ectopic pregnancy include microsurgery incisions that allow the physician to remove the embryo while leaving the reproductive system intact. In some cases, methotrexate may be prescribed to destroy the pregnancy-related tissue.

13-5a Pregnancy Testing

Signs of pregnancy may include a missed period, morning sickness, enlarged and tender breasts, frequent urination, and excessive fatigue. However, pregnancy is best confirmed by laboratory tests and a physical examination.

Several laboratory tests of pregnancy have a high degree of accuracy. All of them depend on the presence of a hormone produced by the developing embryo, human chorionic gonadotropin (HCG), which appears in the pregnant woman's urine. One procedure, formally known as the lutex agglutination inhibition immunologic slide test, detects HCG in about 2 1/2 hours and can reveal whether the woman is pregnant within 14 days after the first missed menstrual period. All commercially available pregnancy tests use the lutex agglutination principle and are reasonably reliable in providing information about the existence of a pregnancy. The most common error in the home pregnancy tests is that the woman takes the test too early in pregnancy and concludes that she is not pregnant when, in fact, she is (false negative).

HCG also appears in the bloodstream of the pregnant woman. A radioimmunoassay test, a laboratory examination of the blood, can determine whether the woman is pregnant within 8 days of conception. A new test, radioreceptorassay, also analyzes the blood and is 100% accurate on the first day after the first missed period. Pregnancy tests in which urine of the presumed pregnant woman is injected into a mouse, rabbit, or frog have been replaced by these tests.

Pregnancy is a time of shared anticipation.

The Image Bank/Getty Images

If the laboratory test indicates pregnancy, the physician usually conducts a pelvic examination to find out if the woman's uterus has enlarged or changed color. These changes take place around the sixth week of pregnancy.

13-5b Physical Changes During Pregnancy

Figure 13-2 shows the size of the fetus as it develops during pregnancy.

The usual course of a typical 266-day pregnancy is divided into trimesters, or 3-month periods, during which the woman may experience some discomfort due to physical changes (see Table 13-1). Women vary in the degree to which they experience these changes. Some may experience few or none of the related symptoms, whereas others may experience many of them.

13-5c Prenatal Care and Prenatal Testing

As noted in section 13-4, some women seek preconception care to help ensure a healthy pregnancy and baby. Others do not receive pregnancy-related health care until after they become pregnant. Like preconception care, prenatal care involves receiving adequate nutrition, achieving adequate weight gain, and avoiding harmful substances such as alcohol, nicotine, illegal drugs, some medications, and toxic chemicals in the workplace. Vitamin and mineral supplements are commonly recommended, especially iron and folate (or folic acid) supplements.

In general, exercise in pregnancy is beneficial. It reduces the incidence of muscle cramps, fatigue, and shortness of breath. It also reduces the increase in baseline maternal heart rate that occurs in pregnancy. Women who undertake regular exercise have a lower incidence of third- and fourth-degree vaginal tears. And children of exercising mothers have similar birth weights as children of sedentary mothers, and mental performance at age 5 is higher—this latter correlation may be due to the fact that active mothers may promote more interactive games/activities for their children than sedentary moms. If there are no specific obstetric or medical contraindications (such as anemia, hypertension, pain of any kind, fetal distress, heart palpitations, or vaginal or uterine bleeding), fit pregnant women can safely maintain the same level of fitness during pregnancy, although exercise schedules may have to be reduced (Maffulli & Bruno, 2002).

Fetal alcohol syndrome (FAS) The possible negative consequences (e.g., facial malformation, low birth weight) for the fetus and infant of the mother who drinks alcohol during pregnancy.

Pregnant women should eliminate their alcohol intake to avoid **fetal alcohol syndrome (FAS),** which refers to the possible negative consequences for the fetus and infant of the mother who drinks alcohol. Possible negative consequences for the developing infant include increased risk of low birth weight, growth retardation, facial malformations, and intellectual retardation. Avoiding alcohol intake during the early weeks of pregnancy (and before pregnancy if no reliable method of birth control is being used) is

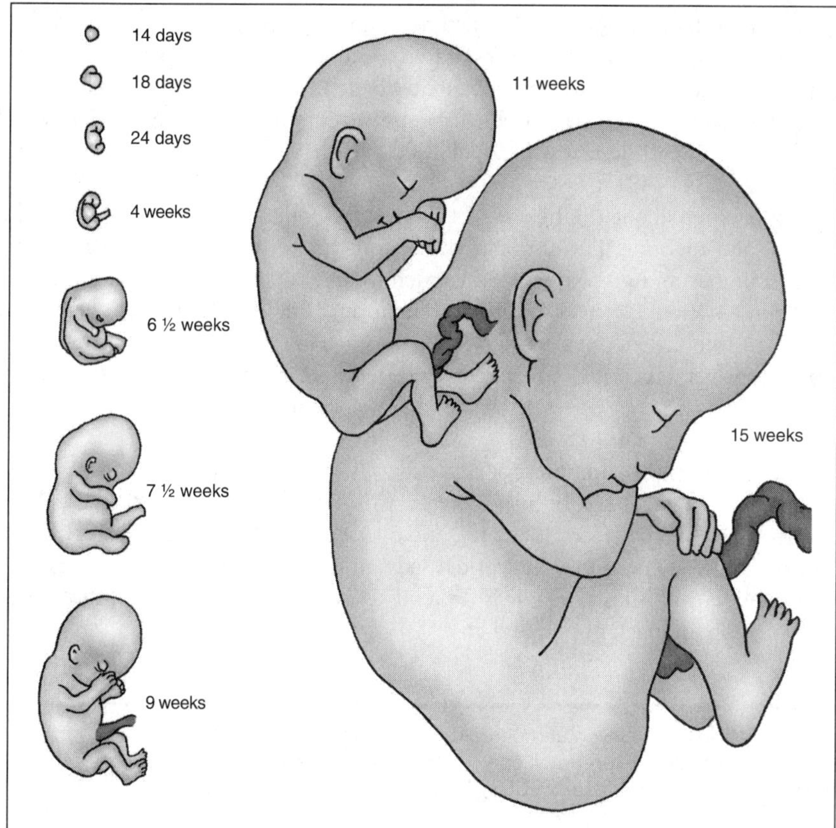

FIGURE 13-2
Growth of the Embryo and Fetus from 2 to 15 Weeks After Conception

TABLE 13-1
Side Effects of Pregnancy

	First Trimester Weeks 0–14	Second Trimester Weeks 15–26	Third Trimester Weeks 27–40
Nausea	X		
Vomiting	X		
Frequent urination	X		X
Leg cramps	X		
Vaginal discharge	X	X	X
Fatigue	X	X	X
Constipation	X	X	X
Swelling		X	X
Varicose veins		X	X
Backache		X	X
Heartburn		X	
Shortness of breath		X	

particularly critical, and alcohol consumed in the later months may impede organ growth and cognitive ability. According to the National Institute of Medicine, an estimated 20% of women who drink continue drinking while pregnant, resulting in about 1 infant in 1,000 being born with FAS (Pinon, 2002).

Smoking cigarettes during pregnancy is also associated with harm to the developing fetus. Negative consequences include lower birth-weight babies, premature babies, and higher fetal or infant deaths. "An estimated 100,000 spontaneous abortions, 5,000 congenital abnormalities, and 200,000 cases of IUGR [intrauterine growth retardation] are attributed to maternal smoking" (Pinon, 2002, p. 342). Paternal smoking may be equally hazardous. Tobacco smoke contains many mutagenic compounds that are easily absorbed into the blood and reach the testes. Paternal smoking is also associated with greater risk of perinatal mortality, lower birth weight, congenital malformation, and childhood cancers. "For example, the neonatal death rate for infants of smoking fathers was 17.2 per 1000 live births, while it was 11.9 per 1000 live births for infants of nonsmoking fathers" (Pinon, 2002, p. 342).

Concerned about the health of their babies, some pregnant women avoid not only alcohol and nicotine, but also caffeine and such over-the-counter drugs as aspirin and antihistamines and prescription drugs such as amphetamines and tranquilizers. Caffeine has been associated with IUGR and prematurity (Pinon, 2002). The placenta was once thought to be an effective barrier to the passage of many chemicals to the developing fetus. However, it is not as effective as once believed. The dose of a substance received by the fetus and the stage of gestation are more important in their effect than the dose experienced by the mother.

Illegal drugs (also nonprescription drugs), such as marijuana and cocaine, should also be avoided. Cocaine has been associated with preterm labor and delivery, lower birthweight babies, limb defects, lower IQ, and oversensitivity to stimulation. These "crack" or "cocaine" babies may enter the world disadvantaged; however, because their mothers may have used various substances, it is difficult to isolate the specific effects of cocaine from malnutrition and lack of prenatal care.

NATIONAL DATA Seventeen percent of U.S. women who delivered a live baby in 1999 did not receive prenatal care in the first trimester of pregnancy (*Statistical Abstract of the United States: 2001*, Table 80).

Prenatal care may also involve prenatal testing. Such tests range from screening measures routinely used in prenatal care to invasive prenatal diagnostic tests. The National Institutes of Health now recommend routine prenatal genetic screening for cystic fibrosis, the most common inherited disease, which affects about 25,000 infants annually.

Ultrasound scan Procedure whereby sound waves are used to project an image of the developing fetus on a video screen; used in prenatal testing.

An **ultrasound scan** involves looking at sound waves being intermittently beamed at the fetus, producing a detailed image on a video screen. This noninvasive test immediately provides pictures of the maternal and fetal outlines and inner organs. Although its long-term effects are still being studied, it appears to be one of the safest procedures for the amount of information it provides. Ultrasound allows the physician to determine the length of gestation (the age of the fetus) and assess the presence of structural abnormalities. Although ultrasound may reveal the fetus's genital area (depending on the position of the fetus), it is not considered a reliable test to determine the sex of the fetus.

Other prenatal tests are used to identify fetuses with chromosomal and biochemical defects. These procedures are usually offered to women who have a child with a birth defect, or some other risk factor (such as advanced maternal age, now defined at around 35 years of age). Their purpose is to detect defects early enough so that if the test is positive, the woman can either be prepared for the birth of a child with health problems or terminate the pregnancy. Their availability has provided to many people the confidence to initiate a pregnancy despite familial history of serious genetic disease or prior birth of affected children.

Amniocentesis Prenatal test in which a needle is inserted (usually in the 16th or 17th week of pregnancy) into the pregnant woman's uterus to withdraw fluid, which is analyzed to see if the cells carry XX (female) or XY (male) chromosomes, and to identify chromosomal defects.

Amniocentesis (which is best performed in the 16th or 17th week of pregnancy) involves inserting a slender needle through the abdomen into the amniotic sac and taking about 1 ounce of fluid (see Figure 13-3). Fetal cells, which are present in this amniotic fluid, are sent to a laboratory, where they are cultured (permitted to multiply in a special medium) and then analyzed for defects.

Amniocentesis involves some risk. In rare cases (about 0.5% of the time, or 1 in 200 cases), the fetus may be damaged by the needle, even though an ultrasound scan has been used to identify its position. Congenital orthopedic defects, such as clubfoot, and

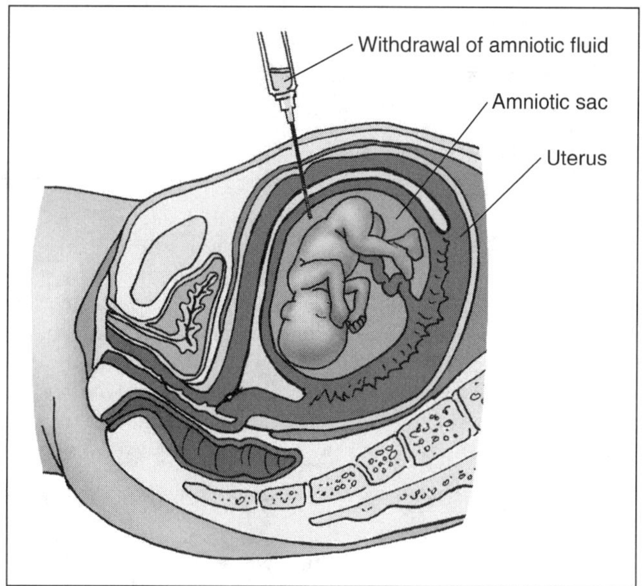

FIGURE 13-3
Amniocentesis

premature birth have been associated with amniocentesis. Also, if no specific abnormality is detected (as is the case 97.5% of the time), this does not guarantee that the baby will be normal and healthy. Cleft palate, cleft lip, and most heart defects are not detected by amniocentesis.

Unfortunately, after the amniocentesis procedure at 16 to 17 weeks of gestation, an additional 3 or 4 weeks is required for cell tissue culture. By this time, the woman may be 20 to 22 weeks pregnant; the pregnancy is publicly visible, and she has probably felt fetal movement. Terminating a pregnancy at this juncture may be quite traumatic. To terminate a pregnancy that has progressed to 20 or 22 weeks, a saline or prostaglandin (induced miscarriage) abortion procedure is frequently used, which involves the delivery of the fetus. (Other procedures for terminating pregnancy are discussed in section 12-2, "Methods of Abortion." See also Box 13-3.)

13-5d Miscarriage

A **miscarriage,** also known as **spontaneous abortion,** is the unintended loss of an embryo or fetus that occurs before the 20th week of pregnancy. Miscarriages occur in about 15–25% of all pregnancies; about 60% of early (less than 12 weeks) spontaneous abortions are associated with chromosomal abnormalities in the developing zygote, embryo, or fetus (Callahan, Caughey, & Heffner, 1998).

Miscarriage The unintended termination of a pregnancy. (See also **spontaneous abortion.**)

Spontaneous abortion See **miscarriage.**

Women who experience a miscarriage often feel intense grief. They may also feel guilt, anger, a sense of failure, and jealousy of other pregnant women or women with children. They may blame themselves for the miscarriage. Some feel that they are being punished for something they have done in the past—frequent, casual, anonymous premarital sex; an abortion; an extramarital affair. Others feel that they have failed not only as a woman or mother, but also in living up to the expectations of their partner, parents, and other children. (Women who have a miscarriage are often inappropriately urged to "try again" rather than focus on their grief.) Others are hurt or angry at the insensitivity of their friends who show little empathy for their feelings of sadness and emptiness at the loss of "their baby." Friends and family can be helpful by acknowledging the loss instead of attempting to minimize it.

On the other hand, if the pregnancy was unwanted, a woman who experiences a miscarriage may feel relief. Investigators in Western Cape, South Africa, who interviewed eight women from varying demographic backgrounds who had experienced miscarriage or stillbirth found that the women's experience varied, depending on the meaning the

Box 13-3 Social Choices

Criminal Prosecution for Fetal Abuse?

Should pregnant women who abuse alcohol, crack cocaine, and other drugs harmful to a fetus be prosecuted? Though more than 100,000 infants have been exposed to such drugs while they were developing in their mothers, the courts have been reluctant to prosecute. Arguments against such prosecution are based on the difficulty of defining when the fetus becomes a person whose rights have been violated; the lack of warning to women that drug abuse during pregnancy may be a prosecutable offense; the vagueness of what exactly constitutes "the crime"; and the fact that fetal abuse is a lifestyle issue. Regarding the latter, many women who take drugs during their pregnancy live in poverty, which means they often lack prenatal care and have nutritional deficiencies. Indeed, prenatal care, drug treatment, and general health services are least accessible for poor and minority women. An additional problem is that sending pregnant women to jail or prison for drug abuse interferes with their ability to receive treatment during pregnancy.

pregnancy held. If the pregnancy was wanted, it was not uncommon for physicians and family members to underestimate and dismiss the psychological investment women had in their unborn baby. Based on their interviews, Corbet-Owen and Kruger (2001) concluded that it is important for professionals and members of the support system to listen in a caring and sensitive way to try to understand the meanings and feelings surrounding a pregnancy loss.

13-5e Psychological Changes During Pregnancy

Affonso and Mayberry (1989) assessed the stresses of 221 women during and after pregnancy. Stress related to physical issues was the most frequently reported problem. "The total group identified fatigue, disturbed sleep, feeling physically restricted, and nausea or vomiting as the most common physical distresses" (p. 46). The second most frequently experienced stressor was associated "with 'weight gain' and feelings of being 'fat,' 'unattractive,' and 'distorted'" (Affonso & Mayberry, 1989, p. 48).

The third most frequently reported concern during pregnancy was for the "baby's welfare and dealing with changes relative to household arrangements and restrictions in physical activities, especially as the woman nears childbirth" (Affonso & Mayberry, 1989, p. 49). Some of the women reported that they were plagued by such frequent thoughts as "Something might happen to my baby," "Am I doing the right thing to protect my baby?" and "I shouldn't have done this because now I'm worried about how it affected my baby" (p. 49).

As women near the end of pregnancy, fears of pain, complications, and the threat of a cesarean section are high-intensity stressors. At the beginning of pregnancy, some women feel trapped. They feel they have begun a course of action from which they cannot easily withdraw (Engel, 1990).

The man also experiences his own set of feelings during pregnancy. Shapiro (1987) interviewed 227 expectant and recent fathers and noted several concerns:

1. *Queasiness*. Respondents in Shapiro's study reported that their greatest fear before birth was coping with the actual birth process. They were queasy about being in the midst of blood and bodily fluids and felt they would faint or get sick. Most did neither.
2. *Worry over increased responsibility*. More than 80% reported feeling that they were now the sole support for three people. Many took second jobs or worked longer hours.
3. *Uncertain paternity*. Half of the men feared that the child their partner was carrying was not their own. "For most of them, such fears were based less on any real concern that the wife had been unfaithful than on a general insecurity brought on by being part of something as monumental as the creation of life" (p. 39).

4. *Fear of the loss of spouse, the child, or both.* Some men feared that both the wife and baby might die during childbirth and that they would be alone. They also feared that the baby would be brain damaged or defective in some way.
5. *Fear of being replaced.* The words of one respondent reflect a common fear among expectant fathers—that of being replaced: The one thing that really scares me is that the best of our lives together will be gone as soon as the baby is born . . . in some ways, I'm feeling displaced. . . . (p. 42) Some of the men had affairs late in their wife's pregnancy. These men perceived their wives to be more focused on and bonded with the impending baby than with them. Because they missed the attention they had received from their wife prior to pregnancy, they sought to replace that attention with that of other women.

13-5f Sex During Pregnancy

Sexual desire, behavior, and satisfaction may change during pregnancy. Although massive hormonal changes take place in pregnancy, no evidence links these changes to reduced libido (Bitzer & Alder, 2001). Rather, the psychosocial changes are more likely to account for changes in sex desire:

> *Fears that sexual activity will harm, although unproved, are common not only in women but also in their partners. Increased emotional liability is common during pregnancy and can affect sexuality. Changes in body image in connection to somatic changes can have an effect on a woman's sense of attractiveness and familiarity with her body . . . husbands may see their wives as future mothers rather than as sex partners. (p. 51)*

In regard to sexual frequency, there is a decline across the three semesters of pregnancy. Dyspareunia (pain during intercourse) may be more common during pregnancy. However, "most women and couples adapt well to the alterations in sexuality caused by pregnancy" (Bitzer & Alder, 2001, p. 52). Pregnancy can either lead to a broadening and deepening of the individual's/couple's sex life or a marking point for "sexual problems, dysfunction, and difficulties" (p. 49). Differences in sexual desire, which may have existed prior to the pregnancy, seem to be critical in whether there are long-term negative effects of the pregnancy on the couple's sex life.

Are there conditions under which a pregnant woman should forgo intercourse and orgasmic activity? Yes. Women who are experiencing vaginal bleeding or abdominal pain, those whose amniotic membrane has ruptured, and those whose cervix has begun to efface or dilate after 24 weeks should abstain from sexual intercourse. Also, those with a history of premature delivery or a history of miscarriage should consult their physician or midwife about intercourse during pregnancy.

13-5g Labor

The beginning of labor signals the end of pregnancy. Labor occurs in three stages, and although there are great variations, it lasts an average of 13 hours for the woman having her first baby (she is referred to as **primigravida**) and about 8 hours if the woman has given birth before (**multigravida**). Figure 13-4 illustrates the various stages of labor.

Primigravida The condition of being pregnant for the first time.

Multigravida A woman who has experienced more than one pregnancy.

It is not known what causes the onset of labor, which is marked by uterine contractions. But there are distinctions between the contractions of true and preparatory (also known as Braxton Hicks contractions) labor. Table 13-2 illustrates the respective differences.

First Stage of Labor

Labor begins with regular uterine contractions, at 15- to 20-minute intervals, that last from 10 to 30 seconds. The first stage lasts for about 9 hours if it is the woman's first baby and about 5 hours in subsequent deliveries. During this first stage, the woman often has cramps and backache. The membranes of the amniotic sac may rupture, spilling the amniotic fluid.

FIGURE 13-4
Stages of Labor

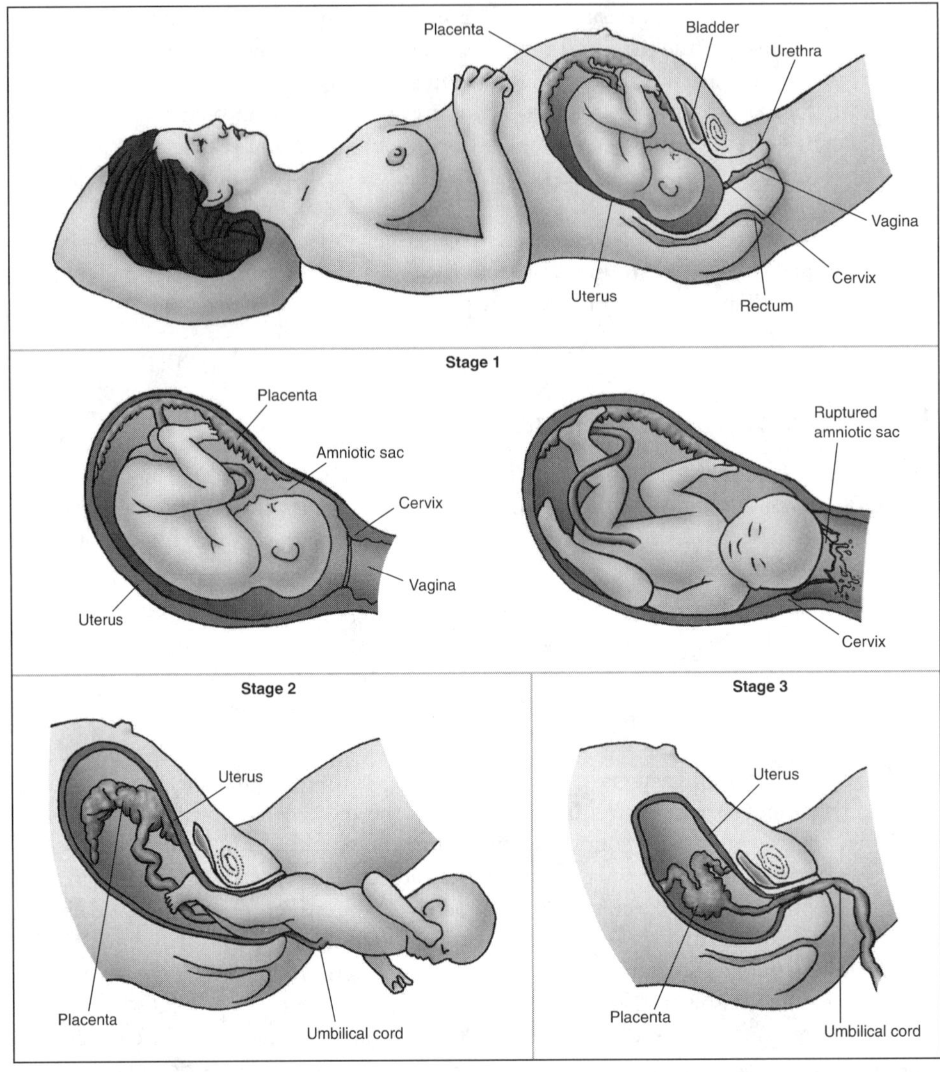

TABLE 13-2

Contractions Characteristic of True and Preparatory Labor

True Labor	Preparatory Labor
Occur at regular intervals	Occur at irregular intervals
Intervals gradually shorten	Intervals remain long
Intensity gradually increases	Intensity remains the same
Discomfort in back and abdomen	Discomfort chiefly in lower abdomen
Cervix dilates	Cervix does not dilate
Not affected by sedation	Usually relieved by sedation

Throughout the first stage, the uterine contractions become stronger, lasting for 30 to 45 seconds, and more frequent (every 3 to 5 minutes). These contractions result in effacement and dilation of the cervix. With effacement, the cervix flattens out and grows longer; with dilation, the cervical opening through which the baby will pass becomes larger. At the end of the first stage, the cervix is dilated 3 1/2 to 4 inches; contractions occur every 1 to 2 minutes and last up to a minute.

During the first stage, the baby is moving into position to be born. The fetal heart rate is monitored continually by stethoscope or ultrasound, and the woman's temperature and blood pressure are checked. She may experience leg cramps, nausea, or irritability during this first stage of labor.

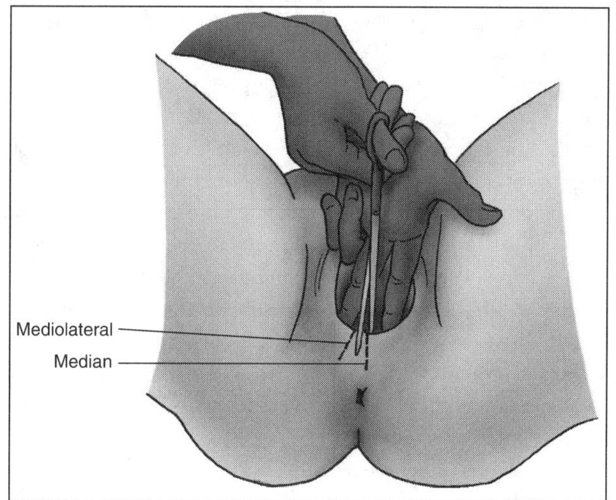

FIGURE 13-5
Alternative Episiotomy Sites

Second Stage of Labor

Also known as the *expulsive stage* of labor, the second stage begins when the cervix is completely dilated and ends when the baby is born. It lasts about 50 minutes if it is the woman's first baby and 20 minutes for subsequent births. Uterine contractions may last 1 1/2 minutes and be 1 to 2 minutes apart. These contractions move the baby further into the vaginal birth canal. The woman may help this process by pushing movements. The head of the baby emerges first, followed by the shoulders and trunk. Although most babies are born head first, some are born breech. In a **breech birth,** the baby's feet or buttocks come out of the vagina first. Breech deliveries are much more complicated.

Breech birth Delivery in which the baby's feet or buttocks come out of the vagina first.

Episiotomy Birthing procedure that involves cutting the perineum (the area between the vagina and the anus) to make a larger opening for the baby and to prevent uncontrolled tearing of the perineum.

To ease the birth, the physician may perform an **episiotomy,** which involves cutting the perineum (the area between the vagina and the anus) in one of two places to make a larger opening for the baby and to prevent uncontrolled tearing (see Figure 13-5).

Immediately after the baby is born, its nostrils are cleared of mucus using a small suction bulb. The umbilical cord is then clamped twice—about 1 and 2 inches from the infant's abdomen—and cut between the clamps. The baby is cleaned of placental matter and put in a temperature-controlled bassinet or held by the parents.

Third Stage of Labor

After the baby is born, the placenta, or afterbirth, is delivered. Usually within 5 minutes after the birth of the baby, the placenta separates itself from the uterine wall and is expelled from the vagina. If it does not disengage easily and by itself, the birth attendant will manually remove it. If an episiotomy was done, the physician will repair it by stitching up the incision after the placenta is delivered.

The time from 1 to 4 hours after delivery is regarded by some physicians as a fourth stage of labor. During this time, the mother's uterus relaxes and returns to a more normal state. Bleeding of the cervix, which results from the detachment of the placenta from the uterine wall, stops.

13-5h Cesarean Childbirth

Cesarean section, in which an incision is made in the woman's abdomen and the uterus and the baby is manually removed, occurs in 25% of U.S. births (Brink, 2002). During this procedure, the woman is put to sleep with general anesthesia or given a spinal injection, which enables her to remain awake and aware of the delivery.

Cesarean section A surgical incision made in the woman's abdomen and the uterus to deliver a fetus.

Cesarean deliveries are most often performed when there would be risk to the mother or baby in a normal delivery. For example, cesarean sections are indicated when the fetus is positioned abnormally, the head is too large for the mother's pelvis, labor is not progressing properly, there is fetal distress, the woman has an active STD or diabetes, or the woman develops toxemia during pregnancy. Additional reasons for cesarean deliveries include convenience for the physician, demand for perfect delivery outcomes and the threat of malpractice, decreased use of forceps, and an increase in the number of first pregnancies among older women. There is also evidence that vaginal deliveries are associated with incontinence and sagging pelvic organs years after the delivery. Recently, there has been a concern that rising rates of deliveries by cesarean are the result of a "generation of mothers unwilling to endure the pain and inconvenience of having a baby the old fashioned way. Accustomed to controlling every detail of their lives, these women are too impatient for the uncertain timing of labor and too pampered for hours of contractions" (Brink, 2002, p. 42).

Although cesareans are major surgery, the risk of death to the mother is low. When death occurs, it is usually the result of a pre-existing condition, such as severe toxemia or heart disease—not a result of the surgery itself. The cesarean section, or C-section, is regarded as one of the safest of all abdominal surgeries and holds the record for the fewest postoperative problems. Nevertheless, C-sections involve the risk of infection from surgery and longer recovery.

There has been considerable criticism of physicians who routinely perform cesarean surgery when it is not medically indicated. C-sections, both primary and repeat, are more likely to occur on Fridays. The implication is that C-sections are being performed in reference to the physician's social life rather than the best interests of the mother and baby (Brink, 2002).

Of course, giving birth always involves the issue of maternal and infant mortality. **Maternal mortality** refers to deaths that result from complications associated with pregnancy or childbirth. The major causes of maternal mortality include hemorrhage, unsafe induced abortion procedures, hypertension, obstructed labor, and infection.

Maternal mortality Deaths that result from complications associated with pregnancy or childbirth.

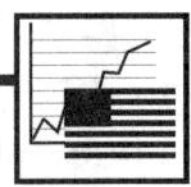

National Data Maternal deaths account for 9.9 deaths per 1,000 live births (*Statistical Abstract of the United States: 2002*, Table 98).

Infant mortality refers to deaths among infants under 1 year of age.

Infant mortality Deaths among infants under 1 year of age.

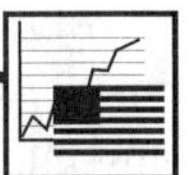

National Data There are 7.1 infant deaths per 1,000 births (*Statistical Abstract of the United States: 2002*, Table 98).

In the United States, both maternal and infant mortality rates vary by race, with minorities having significantly higher rates than Whites. This is due to the disproportionate numbers of minorities who live in poverty and lack access to affordable health care.

13-5i Personal Choices: Hospital or Home Birth?*

The American College of Obstetricians and Gynecologists views childbirth as a medical event that should take place in a hospital. Part of the reason that the medical profession does not advocate home births is the fear of something going wrong during a home birth. It is not always possible to identify which deliveries may become complicated. In addition, physicians are not routinely trained to perform out-of-hospital births.

Although more than 95% of all U.S. births do occur in the hospital, some expectant parents are concerned that traditional childbirth procedures are too impersonal, costly, and potentially dangerous. Those who opt for home births are primarily concerned about avoiding separation from the new infant, maintaining control over who can be present at the delivery, and avoiding what they view as an unnecessary medicalization of a "natural" process.

The midwife is most often asked to assist in home births. There are several different categories of midwives in the U.S., based on the educational path chosen. Lay midwives are usually apprentice trained and attend births only in the home. State laws vary on the licensing and regulation of lay midwives. Nurse midwives are nationally board certified and have usually completed a master's degree in nurse midwifery offered at various universities, including Georgetown, Emory, St. Louis, and Columbia, and most are members of the American College of Nurse Midwives. Nurse midwives are trained to assist couples in the birthing process in the home, birth center, or hospital settings. Nurse midwives are licensed in every state. Two organizations, Association for Childbirth at Home (ACAH) and Home Oriented Maternity Experience (HOME), help couples prepare for home births.

What is the relative safety of home versus hospital births? In a study designed to answer this question, researchers Murphy and Fullerton (1998) concluded that home birth "can be accomplished with good outcomes under the care of qualified practitioners and within a system that facilitates transfer to hospital care when necessary" (p. 461). However, two more recent studies in the state of Washington (Pang, Heffelfinger, Huang, Benedetti, & Weiss, 2002) and in British Columbia (Janssen et al., 2002) differed in their conclusions. Outcomes of planned home births in Washington from 1989–1996 were reviewed. The planned home births resulted in greater infant risks (neonatal deaths and lower scores of infant well-being) and maternal risks (prolonged labor and postpartum bleeding) than hospital births. In the British Columbia study, following regulation of midwifery, the birth outcomes from 2000–2001 were studied. Women who gave birth at home had fewer procedures during labor (epidural analgesia, induced labor, episiotomy). When complications occurred, they were more serious for mothers and babies delivered at home. There were no statistically significant differences in perinatal outcomes.

European studies comparing planned home births to hospital deliveries confirmed that home birth can be a safe choice for women with a low risk for obstetrical complications or poor perinatal outcomes (Remez, 1997). Factors associated with safe home births include low-risk pregnancies, a trained birth attendant, and quick access to adequate hospital services.

Rather than choose between having their baby in a hospital or at home, some prefer a birthing center, which is more likely to be available in larger metropolitan areas. Birthing centers provide a home-like environment for the woman and family to experience labor. The provider is more likely to be a certified nurse midwife with an obstetrician for backup in case of the need for transport. National data from the United States suggest that low-risk mothers who choose to have their babies in birthing centers are no more likely to have poor birth outcomes or to require a cesarean section than are low-risk women who give birth in the hospital (Rooks et al., 1989).

Midwifery is legal or not depending on the state. Table 13-3 provides a list of states and various legal statuses.

*Jan Salstrom, a certified nurse midwife, contributed to this section.

13-5j Childbirth Preparation

Several training programs, sometimes referred to as "methods" of childbirth, have been developed to enhance the experience of childbirth. Sometimes called "natural childbirth," the two most popular forms are the Dick-Read and Lamaze methods. In the Dick-Read method, education and a positive philosophy are used to reduce pain. The Lamaze (or psychoprophylactic) method is based on principles of Pavlovian conditioning applied to childbirth by Russian and European physicians. Although Lamaze classes differ, typically they involve six to eight classes held in the final trimester of pregnancy. Wideman and Singer (1984) identified five essential elements of Lamaze: (a) education about anatomy and physiology, (b) respiration techniques, (c) conditioned relaxation, (d) cognitive restructuring, and (e) social support. The educational information about uterine

TABLE 13-3

Direct Entry Midwifery by State Law[1]

Legally Prohibited	Effectively Prohibited	Statutory Provisions Unclear	Legal and Regulated	Legal and Unregulated
Delaware (2)	Alabama	Michigan	Alaska (2, 3)	Connecticut
Illinois (3)	Georgia	Nevada	Arizona	District of Columbia
Iowa	Kentucky	North Carolina (5)	Arkansas	Hawaii
Maryland	Minnesota	Ohio (3)	California	Idaho (2)
Nebraska (2)	Missouri (3)	Wisconsin	Colorado	Indiana
Oklahoma	New Jersey (4)		Florida	Kansas
South Dakota	Pennsylvania (4)		Louisiana	Maine
Virginia (7)			Montana	Massachusetts
West Virginia			New Hampshire (6)	Mississippi
			New Mexico	North Dakota
			New York	Tennessee
			Oregon	Utah
			Rhode Island	Vermont
			South Carolina	Wyoming
			Texas	
			Washington	

Notes:

1) Direct entry midwives enter the profession of midwifery without a nursing credential.
2) Exemption is allowed for serving traditional religious cultural communities.
3) Uncompensated midwifery care is permitted.
4) Statute does not require nursing credential, but regulations do.
5) Statute requires certification by ACC; regulations refer only to nurse midwives.
6) Compliance with regulations is voluntary.
7) Exemption is allowed for midwives with permits that were issued prior to 1977 and are currently maintained.
Source: Copyright American College of Nurse-Midwives

contractions, stages of labor, and the process of birth are designed to take away the "fear of the unknown." The conditioned relaxation involves learning to interpret the stimulus of a contraction as a signal to relax rather than tense up. Lamaze, a French obstetrician, modified the Russian methodology and added training on breathing techniques matched to each stage of labor. Lamaze also added the father as a "coach" to provide assistance and support to the mother in labor. In contemporary practice, if the father is not available, the coach may be a relative or close friend.

Although Lamaze doesn't abolish pain, studies show that this method does alleviate it and can help make childbirth a more positive experience. Of four studies reviewed by Wideman and Singer, three showed a positive correlation between Lamaze preparation and the mother's emotions (toward herself, the father, baby, pregnancy, labor, and delivery) and the father's sense of self-control. Women tended to recollect less pain and generally used less medication for pain (Wideman & Singer, 1984).

13-6 TRANSITION TO PARENTHOOD

Transition to parenthood refers to that period of time from the beginning of pregnancy through the first few months after the birth of the baby. The transition occurs for the mother, the father, and the couple. One factor associated with a more difficult transition is a premature and low birth-weight baby, which may incur an added financial strain on the couple. The cost of an uncomplicated birth is about $7,000 compared to $20,000 to $40,000 for a premature/low birth-weight baby (Barad & Witt, 2000).

13-6a Transition to Motherhood

Just say there is no other can take the place of mother.
—from the Civil War poem "Break the News to Mother"

Although pregnancy and childbirth are sometimes thought of as a painful ordeal, some women describe the experience as fantastic, joyful, and unsurpassed. A strong emotional bond between a mother and her baby usually develops early so that mother and infant resist separation. Sociobiologists suggest a biological basis for the attachment between a mother and her offspring. The mother alone carries the fetus in her body for 9 months, lactates to provide milk, and produces oxytocin—a hormone from the pituitary gland (produced during the expulsive stage of labor) that has been associated with the onset of maternal behavior in lower animals.

Postpartum Blues

Not all mothers feel joyous after childbirth. Emotional bonding may be temporarily impeded by a mild depression, characterized by irritability, crying, loss of appetite, and difficulty in sleeping. Some new mothers experience postpartum blues (also known as baby blues). These are temporary symptoms of shifting moods, frequent crying, irritability, and fatigue in the first few weeks after the baby is born. About 10% experience **postpartum depression**—a more severe reaction than baby blues (O'Hara & Swain, 1996). Postpartum depression is believed to be a result of the numerous physiological and psychological changes occurring during pregnancy, labor, and delivery. Although the woman may become depressed in the hospital, she more often experiences these feelings within the first month after returning home with her baby. Behaviors also associated with postpartum depression include eating high-fat diet, not exercising, and smoking (Gennaro & Fehder, 2000). Most women recover within a short time; some (about 5%) seek therapy to speed their recovery. Severe postpartum depression with psychotic features is rare, and resulting violence by new mothers against their newborns is even more rare (Nolen-Hoeksema, 1990). However, in some cases women who have committed infanticide as a result of postpartum psychosis have been judged not guilty by reason of insanity (Williamson, 1993).

Postpartum depression
A severe depressive reaction following the birth of one's baby.

To minimize baby blues and postpartum depression, one must recognize that having misgivings about the new infant is normal and appropriate. In addition, the woman who has negative feelings about her new role as mother should elicit help with the baby from her family so that she can continue to keep up her social contacts with friends.

One aspect of motherhood some women do not like is social isolation. Motherhood restricts the woman's social world by reducing both the number of people with whom she interacts and the time she spends interacting with those people (Munch, McPherson, & Smith-Lovin, 1997). Women accustomed to a great deal of social contact in their work may notice the change.

Choosing Priorities

For some women, motherhood is the ultimate fulfillment; for others, the ultimate frustration. For all women, it is a life-changing event (Lerner, 1997). Priorities must be established. When forced to choose between her job and family responsibilities (the babysitter does not show up, the child is sick or hurt, etc.), the employed woman and mother (unlike the man and father) generally prioritizes the role of mother over the role of employee. Women report higher levels of anger than men because of the inequities in child care and household responsibilities (Ross & Van Willigen, 1996). Nevertheless, most women, particularly mothers in their first marriage, report that motherhood is a profoundly happy time (Demo & Acock, 1996).

13-6b Transition to Fatherhood

The importance of the father in the lives of his children goes beyond his economic contribution (Knox & Leggett, 2000; Nelson, Hughes, Katz, & Searight, 2000; Popenoe,

1996). Children from intact homes or those in which fathers maintained an active involvement in their lives after divorce tend to

make good grades	be less involved in crime
have good health	have a strong work ethic
have durable marriages	have a strong moral conscience
have higher life satisfaction	have higher incomes as adults
have higher education levels	form close friendships
have stable jobs	have fewer premarital births
have lower child sex abuse	exhibit less anoretic symptomatology

In spite of the value of fathers for children, they typically do not have good role models showing how to be a good father. Duindam (1999) cited research which revealed that only 7% of 182 men viewed their father as a positive model for fatherhood (p. 54).

In recent years there has been a renewed cultural awareness of fatherhood (Coltrane, 2000). A coalition of Evangelical Christian organizations, fathers' rights groups, politicians, and family-value advocates have emphasized the importance of marriage, family, and fathers to the well-being of children. One such specific group is the male-oriented group Promise Keepers, which encourages men to recommit themselves to acting responsibly regarding their children. The fatherhood movement evolved out of a reaction to the trend in recent decades for divorce to become acceptable and fathers to be viewed as unnecessary (Horn, 1997).

13-6c Transition to Couplehood

Researchers disagree on the effect of children on a couple's marriage. Some research suggests that parenthood decreases marital happiness. Interview data from a probability sample of 3,407 White and African American adults in 21 cities revealed that those who were parents were less happy in their relationships than those who did not have children (Tucker, 1997). Cowan and Cowan (1992) followed 72 expectant couples and 24 child-free couples for 10 years. They noted a decrease in relationship satisfaction among parents as a result of unfulfilled expectations, different patterns of engagement in the role of parent, and different perceptions of their role as lovers/partners. Both partners were surprised that the baby did not bring them closer together. The husbands viewed themselves less in the role of parent than did the wives, and the wives viewed themselves less in the role of lover than did the husbands. Other researchers have found that parenthood is more satisfying to mothers than fathers and that the latter are more focused on marital happiness (Rogers & White, 1998).

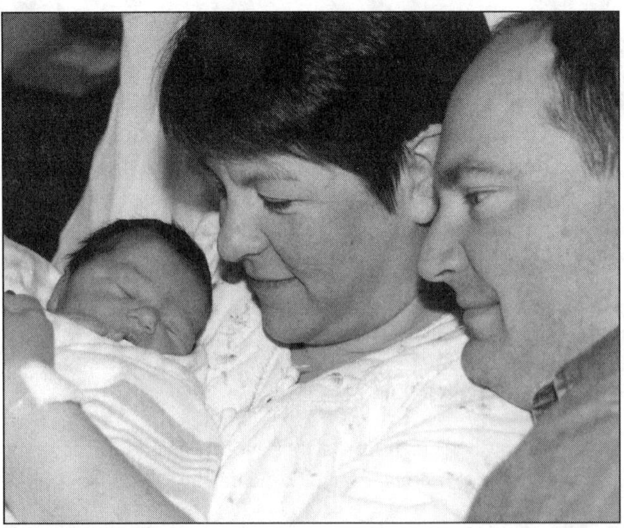

A baby changes the focus of spouses from each other to their infant.

Some research reveals that time, not children, is associated with a decrease in marital happiness. In a study comparing married couples who had children with those who did not, the researchers observed that, over time, the spouses in both groups reported declines in love feelings, marital satisfaction, activities together, and positive interactions. The parents were no less happy in their marriages than the childfree couples. The researchers concluded that "the transition to parenthood is not an inescapable detriment to marital quality" (MacDermid, Huston, & McHale, 1990).

SUMMARY

This chapter focused on various medical, social, and psychological issues concerning pregnancy, infertility, and reproductive technologies. It also discussed the transition to parenthood for women, men, and couples.

Fertilization and Conception

Pregnancy is preceded by fertilization (a woman's egg unites with a man's sperm) and begins when the fertilized egg implants on the uterine wall.

Infertility

Infertility, the inability to achieve a pregnancy after at least 1 year of regular sexual relations without birth control, affects 15–20% of U.S. married couples. Common causes of male infertility include low sperm production and poor semen motility. Causes of female infertility include blocked Fallopian tubes and impaired ovulation. The effects of some sexually transmitted diseases may result in infertility for both men and women.

Reproductive Technology

Reproductive technologies include hormone therapy, artificial insemination, artificial insemination of a surrogate mother, in vitro fertilization, and ovum transfer.

Preconception Care

Preconception care includes risk assessment, interventions to reduce risk, and general health promotion prior to becoming pregnant. Women who want to maximize their chance of having a healthy pregnancy and baby may seek preconception care.

Pregnancy and Childbirth

Early signs of pregnancy include lack of menstruation, nausea and vomiting (morning sickness), enlarged and tender breasts, frequent urination, and fatigue. Pregnancy is best confirmed by laboratory tests and a physical examination. In the early stages of pregnancy, some women experience leg cramps, constipation, backache, varicose veins, swelling, heartburn, increased vaginal discharge, and shortness of breath. Prenatal care helps to ensure a healthy pregnancy and healthy baby. Miscarriages, or spontaneous abortions, are not uncommon in early pregnancy. Labor occurs in three stages. About 25% of U.S. births are cesarean births in which an incision is made in the woman's abdomen and uterus and the baby is manually removed.

Transition to Parenthood

The transition to parenthood involves that period of time from the beginning of pregnancy through the first few months after the birth of the baby. The transition is usually more profound for the mother, due to the fact that her hormonal system is altered. New mothers also may experience postpartum depression, and are confronted with reordering their priorities. Most women tend to place family considerations above career considerations.

The active participation of fathers in the lives of their children is one of the greatest predictors of positive outcomes for children. Research findings regarding how children affect marital happiness are inconsistent.

SUGGESTED WEBSITES

Note: These websites were functional when we went to press. Please access the online text for the most up-to-date URLs.

American Society for Reproductive Medicine
http://www.asrm.com

Childbirth
http://www.childbirth.org/

Children—The Annie E. Casey Foundation
http://www.aecf.org/

Fatherhood Initiative
http://fatherhood.hhs.gov/index.shtml

Infertility—International Council on Infertility Information
http://www.inciid.org/

Infertility—American Infertility Association
http://www.americaninfertility.org/

Motherhood—Practical
http://www.practicalmotherhood.com/

Pregnancy.Org
http://www.pregnancy.org/

Reproductive Health
http://www.cdc.gov/nccdphp/drh/art.htm

Society for the Assisted Reproductive Technology Internet Website
http://www.sart.org/

KEY TERMS

amniocentesis (p. 394)
artificial insemination (p. 386)
breech birth (p. 399)
cesarean section (p. 399)
conception (p. 384)
contract mother (p. 387)
cryopreservation (p. 388)
ectopic pregnancy (p. 390)
embryo (p. 390)
embryo transfer (p.388)
episiotomy (p. 399)
fertilization (p. 384)
fetal alcohol syndrome (FAS) (p. 392)
fetus (p. 390)
gamete intrafallopian transfer (GIFT)(p. 388)
infant mortality (p. 400)
infertility (p. 385)
in vitro fertilization (p. 388)
laparoscope (p. 388)
maternal mortality (p. 400)
microinjection (p. 388)
miscarriage (p. 395)
multigravida (p. 397)
ovum transfer (p. 388)
partial zona drilling (PZD) (p. 388)
preconception care (p. 389)
postpartum depression (p. 403)
pregnancy (p. 384)
primigravida (p. 397)
spontaneous abortion (p. 395)
surrogate mother (p. 387)
ultrasound scan (p. 394)
umbilical cord (p. 390)
zygote intrafallopian transfer (ZIFT) (p. 388)

CHAPTER QUIZ

1. Fertilization and pregnancy are two terms that ____________ the same thing.
   a. mean
   b. do not mean

2. The best intercourse position for the woman to get pregnant is for the woman to be
   a. on top.
   b. on the bottom.
   c. on her side.
   d. on her hands (or elbows) and knees.

3. Infertility is defined as the inability to achieve a pregnancy after at least ____________ without birth control, or the inability to carry a pregnancy to a live birth.
   a. 10 intercourse experiences
   b. 50 intercourse experiences
   c. 6 months of sexual relations
   d. 1 year of sexual relations

4. According to your text, which of the following statements is true?
   a. Most infertility problems may be attributed to the man.
   b. Most infertility problems may be attributed to the woman.
   c. Most infertility problems may be attributed to both the man and the woman.
   d. Fertility problems are equally likely to be attributed to the man as they are to the woman.

5. Which of the following increases the likelihood of ovulating multiple eggs, resulting in multiple births?
   a. having intercourse more than once in a 24-hour period
   b. having intercourse more than once in a 3-day period
   c. hormone therapy for infertility
   d. having intercourse with multiple partners in a 3-day period

6. Ovum transfer involves a physician placing the sperm of the male partner in
   a. the uterus of his partner.
   b. the uterus of a the woman who will carry the pregnancy.
   c. a glass dish, to which his partner's egg is added.
7. Cryopreservation involves which of the following?
   a. a technique whereby men can increase their sperm count by practicing short-term abstinence
   b. preserving aborted fetal tissue for use in medical research or intervention
   c. medical intervention designed to increase the viability of multiple pregnancies
   d. freezing fertilized eggs for possible future implantation
8. The majority of eggs fertilized through in vitro fertilization implant on the uterine wall.
   a. True
   b. False
9. Partial zona drilling involves which of the following?
   a. a procedure designed to open blocked Fallopian tubes
   b. a prenatal testing procedure designed to detect a variety of fetal abnormalities
   c. a procedure that reverses a vasectomy
   d. a procedure whereby tiny holes are drilled into the shell of the egg
10. After the egg and sperm unite and attach to the uterine wall, the developing organism is called an *embryo* for the first ____________ and a *fetus* thereafter.
    a. 3 days
    b. 8 days
    c. 3 weeks
    d. 8 weeks
11. Ectopic pregnancies usually occur in
    a. the Fallopian tube.
    b. the uterus.
    c. a test tube.
    d. a surrogate.
12. What does the presence of human chorionic gonadotropin (HCG) in a woman's urine mean?
    a. The woman is going through menopause and cannot become pregnant.
    b. The woman is pregnant.
    c. The woman's developing fetus has a genetic abnormality.
    d. The woman should receive preconception counseling.
13. Although most women in developing countries do not receive any prenatal care, virtually all women in the United States who give birth receive prenatal care beginning in the first trimester.
    a. True
    b. False
14. Most early (less than 12 weeks) miscarriages are associated with which of the following?
    a. alcohol consumption of the pregnant woman
    b. chromosomal abnormalities in the developing zygote, embryo, or fetus
    c. physical violence (abuse) or trauma, such as a fall or car accident
    d. over-the-counter medication
15. For women having their first baby, labor lasts an average of
    a. 3 hours.
    b. 8 hours.
    c. 13 hours.
    d. 28 hours.
16. According to a study of 182 men, most of the men viewed their father as a positive model for fatherhood.
    a. True
    b. False

REFERENCES

Affonso, D. D., & Mayberry, L. J. (1989). Common stressors reported by a group of childbearing American women. In P. N. Stern (Ed.), *Pregnancy and parenting* (pp. 41–55). New York: Hemisphere.

Angier, N. (1999). *Woman: An intimate geography*. Boston: Houghton Mifflin.

Barad, D. H., & Witt, B. R. (2000). Choices: Biomedical ethics and women's health: Multiple pregnancies and assisted reproductive technologies. *Journal of Women's Health & Gender-based Medicine*, 9, 101–108.

Bitzer, J., & Alder, J. (2001). Sexuality during pregnancy and the postpartum period. *Journal of Sex Education and Therapy*, *25*, 49–58.

Brink, S. (2002, August 5). Too posh to push? *U. S. News and World Report*, 42–43.

Bussell, G., & Marlow, N. (2000). The dietary beliefs and attitudes of women who have had a low-birthweight baby: A retrospective preconception study. *Journal of Human Nutrition & Dietetics*, *13*, 20–40.

Callahan, T. L., Caughey, A. B., & Heffner, L. J. (1998). *Blueprints in obstetrics & gynecology*. Malden, MA: Blackwell Science, Inc.

Coltrane, S. (2000). Fatherhood and marriage in the 21st century. *Phi Kappa Phi Journal*, 80, 25–28.

Corbet-Owen, C., & Kruger, L. (2001). The health system and emotional care: Validating the many meanings of spontaneous pregnancy loss. *Families, Systems & Health*, *19*, 411–427.

Cowan, C. P., & Cowan, P. A. (1992, July/August). Is there love after baby? *Psychology Today*, *25*, 58 et passim.

Daniluk, J. C. (2001). 'If we had to do it over again . . .': Couples' reflections on their experiences of infertility treatments. *Family Journal*, 9, 122–134.

Demo, D. H., & Acock, A. C. (1996). Singlehood, marriage, and remarriage: The effects of family structure and family relationships on mother's well-being. *Journal of Family Issues*, *17*, 388–407.

Duindam, V. (1999). Men in the household: Caring fathers. In L. McKie, S. Bowlby, & S. Gregory (Eds.), *Gender, power, and the household* (pp. 43–59). London: MacMillan.

Engel, N. S. (1990). The maternity cycle and sexuality. In C. I. Fogel & D. Lauver (Eds.), *Sexual health promotion* (pp. 179–205). Philadelphia: W. B. Saunders.

Garel, M., & Blondel, B. (1992). Assessment at 1 year of the psychological consequences of having triplets. *Human Reproduction, 7*, 729–732.

Gennaro, S., & Fehder, W. (2000). Health behaviors in postpartum women. *Family Community Health, 22*, 16–26.

Hales, D. (1997). *Instructor's guide for Hale's an invitation to health* (7th ed.). Pacific Grove, CA:: Brooks/Cole Publishing Company.

Hall, R. T. (2000). Prevention of premature birth: Do pediatricians have a role? *Pediatrics, 105*, 1137–1141.

Hart, V. A. (2002). Infertility and the role of psychotherapy. *Issues in Mental Health Nursing, 23*, 31–42.

Horn, W. (1997). You've come a long way, daddy. *Policy Review, 84*, 24–31.

Janssen, P.A., Shoo, K. L., Ryan, E. M., Etches, D. J., Farquharson, D. F., Peacock, D., et al. (2002). Outcomes of planned home births versus planned hospital births after regulation of midwifery in British Columbia. *Canadian Medical Association Journal, 166*, 315–323.

Kahn, A. (1997). Clone mammals . . . Clone man? *Nature, 383*, 119.

Knox, D., & Leggett, K. (2000). *The divorced dad's survival book: How to stay connected with your kids*. Reading, MA: Perseus Books.

Krauthammer, C. (2002, April 29). Crossing lines—A secular argument against cloning. *The New Republic*, 20.

Lerner, H. (1997). *The mother dance*. New York: HarperCollins.

MacDermid, S. M., Huston, T. L., & McHale, S. M. (1990). Changes in marriage associated with the transition to parenthood: Individual differences as a function of sex-role attitudes and changes in the division of household labor. *Journal of Marriage and the Family, 52*, 475–486.

Maffulli, N., & Bruno, A. (2002). Exercise in pregnancy: How safe is it? Sports Medicine & Arthroscopy Review. *The Female Athlete, 10*, 15–22.

McGuinness, B. M., Buck, G. M., Mendola, P. S., Lowell, E., & Vena, J. E. (2001). Infecundity and consumption of polychlorinated biphenyl-contaminated fish. *Archives of Environmental Health, 56*, 250–254.

MSNBC News. (2002). Genie out of the bottle on cloning: Expert Kentucky doctor expects pregnancy in human cloning by year's end. Retrieved May 15, 2002, from MSNBC News Web site at http://www.msnbc.com/news/752767.asp#BODY

Munch, A., McPherson, J. M., & Smith-Lovin, L. (1997). Gender, children, and social contact: The effects of childrearing for men and women. *American Sociological Review, 62*, 509–520.

Murphy P. A., & Fullerton, J. (1998). Outcomes of intended home births in nurse-midwifery practice: A prospective descriptive study. *Obstetrics and Gynecology, 92*, 461–470.

Nelson, W. L., Hughes, H. M., Katz, B., & Searight, H. R. (2000). Anoretic eating attitudes and behaviors of male and female college students. *Adolescence, 34*, 621–633.

Nilsson, L., & Hamberger, L. (1990). *A child is born*. New York: Delacorte Press.

Nolen-Hoeksema, S. (1990). *Sex differences in depression*. Stanford, CA: Stanford University Press.

O'Hara, M. W., & Swain, A. M. (1996). Rates and risk of postpartum depression—a meta-analysis. *International Review of Psychiatry, 8*, 37–54.

Pang, J. W., Heffelfinger, J. D., Huang, G. J., Benedetti, T. J., & Weiss, N. S. (2002). Outcomes of planned home births in Washington State: 1989–1996. *Obstetrics and Gynecology, 100*, 253–259.

Pinon, R., Jr. (2002). *Biology of human reproduction*. Sausalito, CA: University Science Books.

Popenoe, D. (1996). *Life without father*. New York: Free Press.

Remez, L. (1997). Planned home birth can be as safe as hospital delivery for women with low-risk pregnancies. *Family Planning Perspectives, 29*, 141–143.

Rogers, S. J., & White, L. K. (1998). Satisfaction with parenting: The role of marital happiness, family structure, and parents' gender. *Journal of Marriage and the Family, 60*, 393–398.

Rooks, J. P, Weatherby, N. L., Ernst, E. K., Stapleton, S., Rosen, D., & Rosenfield, A. (1989). Outcomes of care in birth centers. *New England Journal of Medicine, 321*, 1804–1811.

Rosenthal, M. B. (1997). Infertility. In J. Rosenfeld (Ed.), *Women's health in primary care* (pp. 351–362). Baltimore, MD: Williams & Wilkins.

Ross, C. E., & Van Willigen, M. (1996). Gender, parenthood, and anger. *Journal of Marriage and the Family, 58*, 572–582.

Shapiro, J. L. (1987). The expectant father. *Psychology Today, 21*, 36–42.

Statistical Abstract of the United States: 2002. (2002). 122nd ed. Washington, DC: U.S. Bureau of the Census.

Stephen, E. H., & Chandra, A. (2000). Use of infertility services in the United States: 1995. *Family Planning Perspectives, 32*, 132–137.

Tucker, M. B. (1997, August). *Economic contributions to marital satisfaction and commitment*. Paper presented at the Annual Convention of the American Psychological Association, Chicago, IL.

Van Den Akker, O. B. A. (2001). Adoption in the age of reproductive technology. *Journal of Reproductive & Infant Psychology, 19*, 147–159.

Wang, J. X., & Norman, R. J. (2000). Body mass and probability of pregnancy during assisted reproduction treatment: Retrospective study. *British Medical Journal, 321*, 1320–1322.

Whitehead, M. (1989). *A mother's story: The truth about the Baby M case*. New York: St. Martin's Press.

Wideman, M. V., & Singer, J. E. (1984). The role of psychological mechanisms in preparation for childbirth. *American Psychologist, 39*, 1357–1371.

Williamson, G. L. (1993). Postpartum depression syndrome as a defense to criminal behavior. *Journal of Family Violence, 8*, 151–165.

Sexually Transmitted Diseases

Chapter Outline

Some students have a hard time understanding that the consequence of one unprotected sexual encounter may not be reversible.

—American College Health Association

Every semester, we ask a health educator from the university where we teach to talk with our classes about sexually transmitted diseases. Every semester, the health educator leads off with the same phrase—"One in four students at our university is estimated to contract a sexually transmitted disease during the four years they are here" (Credle, 2002). The message is clear. Human sexual interactions are not just about fun and pleasure but may have profound implications for health and well-being.

Sexually transmitted disease (STD) A disease caused by any of more than 25 infectious organisms that are transmitted primarily through sexual activity.

This chapter presents information about this life-impacting **sexually transmitted disease (STD)** issue. How widespread are the diseases? Who is at risk? What behaviors are associated with contracting STDs? What are the health, economic, and psychological consequences of STDs? What choices can you make to reduce your risk of acquiring an STD? What can society do to control and prevent the spread of STDs?

14-1 SEXUALLY TRANSMITTED DISEASES: AN OVERVIEW

"The term STD (sexually transmitted disease) denotes a disease caused by any of more than 25 infectious organisms that are transmitted primarily through sexual activity" (Pinon, 2002, p. 429). Person-to-person sexual contact is the main mode of infection, with vaginal and anal intercourse providing the most efficient transmission; the infections can also be transmitted orally. The association of STDs with "what is seen as illicit, illegal, or promiscuous sexual behavior" (Pinon, 2002, p. 427) is stigmatizing and makes discussion of these infections more emotionally charged than, say, tuberculosis. People often feel ashamed to be diagnosed with an STD. A medical reporter noted, "Sexual diseases have always been regarded more as a punishment for vice than the result of infection" (Berreby, 1989, p. 30). Hence, individuals are often reluctant to talk frankly about STDs and the steps that could be taken to treat and prevent them.

Think About It

What's in a name? STDs used to be referred to as *venereal diseases* (a term derived from the name for the Roman goddess of love, Venus). As that term became stigmatized, it was replaced with *STD.* Currently, some health educators use the term **sexually transmitted infection (STI)** to reduce some of the negative emotional reaction some people now associate with *STD.* In addition, not all STIs are diseases. Would you have a different reaction to learning you had acquired a sexually transmitted infection in contrast to a sexually transmitted disease? In this text we typically use the term *STD* because that is the terminology currently used by the Centers for Disease Control and the World Health Organization.

Sexually transmitted infection (STI) An infection transmitted primarily through sexual activity. A recent term sometimes used to avoid the negative connotations sometimes associated with *STD.*

Researchers estimate that only the common cold infects more people than STDs. However, it should not be surprising that infections spread through sexual contact are so common. "After all, people in all walks of life do have sex. It's as much a part of our biological make-up as eating and sleeping. And when we have sex, we sometimes pass a variety of common germs back and forth" (Ebel & Wald, 2002, p. 3).

14-1a Past Two Decades

During the past two decades, a great deal of knowledge has become available regarding sexually transmitted diseases. In the 1960s genital herpes simplex virus and human papillomavirus infections were recognized, and since 1980, eight new STDs have been identified (Pinon, 2002). The most well known among these is HIV/AIDS. In 1997, the Institute of Medicine dubbed the STDs "hidden epidemics" and warned of their tremendous threat to the health and economy of the United States (Eng & Butler, 1997). The threat of STDs to developing countries is even greater. Although the scientific and medical communities have studied these diseases, developed therapies, and offered ways of reducing their spread, only syphilis is even close to being eradicated in the United States. The other STDs continue, largely unabated.

14-1b Ignorance Abounds

Despite the fact that much information has been learned on STDs, many people remain largely ignorant of these diseases. The vulnerability of young people to infection is compounded by their lack of knowledge. For example, in Sub-Saharan Africa, half of teenage girls do not realize that a healthy-looking person can be infected with human immunodeficiency virus, or HIV (UNAIDS, 2002a).

INTERNATIONAL DATA According to UNICEF, in more than a dozen countries (including Bolivia, Botswana, the Dominican Republic, Uzbekistan, and Vietnam), more than half of young people ages 15–24 have never heard of AIDS or have serious misconceptions about its transmission. In Mozambique, 74% of young women and 62% of young men ages 15–19 do not know of a single method of HIV/AIDS prevention (UNAIDS, 2001).

Despite the fact that about one third of those living with HIV/AIDS are 15–24 years old (UNAIDS, 2001), most young adults have not been tested for HIV and other STDs. Many people are infected and do not even know it. Many STDs are **asymptomatic** (do not produce symptoms or signs), or yield symptoms so mild that medical care is not sought. People may be asymptomatic yet pass on the disease to others. Nine out of 10 men have heard of HIV, AIDS, gonorrhea, and syphilis, but they are less likely to know about genital warts, and only one in three knows that chlamydia can infect men (Alan Guttmacher Institute, 2002). Up to 85% of women and 50% of men who are infected with chlamydia have no symptoms. They may not be aware of the infection until years later when a significant health problem develops (e.g., liver cancer from hepatitis B, infertility from undiagnosed chlamydia or gonorrhea; Healthy People 2010, 2002).

Asymptomatic Producing no symptoms or signs, or as in some STDs, yielding symptoms so mild that medical care is not sought.

14-2 SEXUALLY TRANSMITTED DISEASES: A PANDEMIC

Sexually transmitted diseases represent a major individual and public health concern. It is estimated that in the United States, 15 million new sexually transmitted infections occur annually (Centers for Disease Control, 2001), and 400 million worldwide (Alan Guttmacher Institute, 2002). An overview of U.S. and global statistics on STDs reveals how widespread sexually transmitted diseases are. The consequences of STDs—their impact on physical health, economics, and psychological well-being—convey the seriousness of the STD pandemic (worldwide epidemic).

14-2a The Scope of the Problem: U.S. and Global Statistics on STDs

Sexually transmitted diseases are widespread in the United States and many other countries throughout the world.

TABLE 14-1

Incidence Rates of the Most Common STDs in the United States

STD	Annual Estimated Incidence
Human papillomavirus (HPV)	5.5 million
Trichomoniasis	5 million
Chlamydia	3 million
Herpes	1 million
Gonorrhea	650,000
Hepatitis B	120,000
Syphilis	70,000

Source: Centers for Disease Control. (2001). *Tracking the hidden epidemics: Trends in STDs in the United States 2000. Centers for Disease Control and Prevention.* Retrieved February 12, 2002, from www.cdc.gov/nchstp/od/news/RevBrochure1pdfmag.htm

U.S. Statistics on STDs

In the United States, at least one person in four will contract an STD at some point in his or her lifetime (SIECUS Fact Sheet, 1997). Table 14-1 presents the annual estimated incidence (new cases) of the most common STDs in the United States.

Global Statistics on STDs

Sexually transmitted diseases and their consequences represent major public health problems, especially for developing countries that lack resources for preventing and treating STDs. Six out of 10 women in many countries have an STD (1997 UNFPA Report, 1997). Current statistics on the AIDS pandemic reveal that 40 million of the world's people are infected with the virus, and HIV/AIDS is the fourth leading cause of death worldwide (UNAIDS, 2001). As Figure 14-1 illustrates, Africa has suffered the highest incidence of AIDS cases; in Sub-Saharan Africa HIV/AIDS is the leading cause of death.

Each day, more than a million people contract an STD (McKay, 2000). Although some of these diseases were not curable initially (syphilis and gonorrhea), effective treatments have been developed and refined so that, for people with access to diagnosis and the proper medication, many of the infections can be cured.

14-3 MODES OF TRANSMISSION, SYMPTOMS, AND TREATMENT FOR STDs

STDs can be classified based on the type of microorganism that causes the infection and by the type of disease produced. Some remain located at the site of infection, but others progress and affect body systems. In sections 14-3a through 14-3c, we provide an overview of the STDs based on the primary location of the infection (as organized in Callahan, Caughey, & Heffner, 1998) and by the type of microorganism causing the disease. The main agents responsible for STDs are bacteria, protozoa, and viruses. STDs caused by bacteria and protozoa can generally be cured through treatment with antibiotics. Treatment for viral STDs is palliative (may relieve symptoms or slow down the disease progression, but does not cure the disease). The course of viral infections may include latent periods (times with no outward symptoms), but the symptoms may reappear (Pinon, 2002).

14-3a Infections of the Lower Reproductive Tract

Infectious diseases that affect the external genitals may be ulcerative (causing skin lesions) or nonulcerative (commonly causing itching and pain).

Vulvitis

Candidiasis A vaginal yeast infection that tends to occur in women during pregnancy, when they are on oral contraceptives, or when they have poor resistance to disease.

The most common cause of vulvitis is **candidiasis,** also known as *monilia* and *yeast infection*. Candidiasis tends to occur in women during pregnancy, when they are on oral contraceptives, or when they have poor resistance to disease. Symptoms of candidiasis include vaginal irritation, itching, thick cottage-cheeselike discharge, and pain during intercourse. Treatment involves inserting antifungal suppositories or creams into the vagina. Antibiotics are not effective because candida are not bacteria. This type of infection can spread to a partner, so it is important for both the identified patient and the sexual partner to be treated.

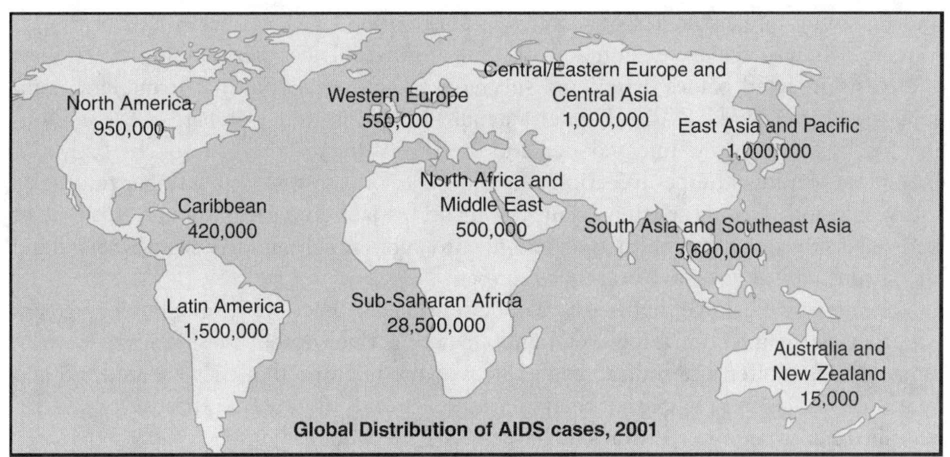

FIGURE 14-1
Global Distribution of AIDS Cases

Source: Data from *Weekly Epidemiological Record* of the World Health Organization and Joint United Nations Programme on HIV/AIDS (UNAIDS, 2002b). UNAIDS Report on the Global HIV/AIDS Epidemic. Geneva, Switzerland: Author.

Chancroid

Also known as *soft chancre,* chancroid is most common in tropical countries. In the United States, chancroid is predominantly seen among immigrants or U.S. citizens who travel to developing countries. This STD is more common among men. Chancroid is transmitted through either sexual contact with the chancroid ulcer or discharge from infected local lymph glands. Two to five days after exposure, a small papule forms at the site of contact. This lesion develops into an ulcer that exudes pus, bleeds easily, and is very painful. Local lymph glands enlarge, become inflamed, and may drip pus. The difference between a chancroid and a chancre is that the former is soft and painful. Chancroid is treated with antibiotics.

Chancroid STD characterized by a painful ulcer in the anal genital region. Less common in North America than in other tropical countries.

Pubic Lice and Scabies

Pubic lice, also called "crabs," attach themselves to the base of coarse pubic hair and suck blood from the victim. Their biting the skin to release the blood causes severe itching. Pubic lice are caught from an infected person, often through sexual contact, and also may be transmitted by contact with toilet seats, clothing, and bedding that harbor the creatures. Applications of lindane, sold under the brand name Kwell, usually kill the lice within 24 hours.

Pubic lice The crab louse (pediculosis) causes itching, and irritated skin, usually confined to the pubic hair.

Scabies results from a parasite, Sarcoptes scabiei, that penetrates the skin and lays eggs. The larvae of these eggs burrow tunnels under the skin and cause intense itching. Although genitals are a prime target for the mites, the groin, buttocks, breasts, and knees may also be infested with them. Because the itching is intense, scabies sufferers tend to scratch the affected area, which may result in bleeding and spreading the scabies. Treatment includes applying lindane (Kwell) or crotamiton (Eurax) and a thorough cleaning of self, clothing, and bedding.

Herpes

The term *herpes* refers to more than 50 related viruses (including the viruses that cause infectious mononucleosis, chickenpox, and shingles). One type of herpes virus is **herpes simplex virus type 2 (HSV-2),** also known as **genital herpes.** Another type of herpes, known as **herpes simplex virus type 1 (HSV-1),** is associated with fever blisters around the mouth (oral-facial lesions). **Oral herpes** is very commonplace and is usually a benign infection. Although researchers estimate that 66% of people over the age of 12 are infected with HSV-1, only about one third of those have had flare-ups with visible cold sores. Although the two types of HSV have sites of preference, HSV-1 also can infect the genitals, and HSV-2 can result in facial cold sores (Eble, 2002).

One in five Americans age 12 or older carries the genital herpes virus—a 30% increase since the late 1970s. About 90% of these individuals do not know they are infected (Fleming et al., 1997). The herpes virus is spread by direct skin-to-skin contact, such as kissing and oral, vaginal, or anal sex with an infected individual. Pregnant women can transmit the herpes virus to their newborn infants. Fortunately, this type of

Herpes simplex virus type 2 (HSV-2) See **genital herpes.**

Genital herpes A viral infection that may cause blistering, typically of the genitals; it may also infect the lips, mouth, and eyes. (See also **herpes simplex virus type 2.**)

Herpes simplex virus type 1 (HSV-1) A viral infection that may cause blistering, typically of the lips and mouth; it may also infect the genitals. (See also **oral herpes.**)

Oral herpes Sores of the lip and mouth, often caused by herpes simplex virus type I but can also be cause by herpes simplex virus type II.

transmission is rare, estimated as occurring in only 1 per 3,000 to 1 per 20,000 births. Of concern, when such transmission does occur, the consequences can be quite severe, with one in six infected babies dying, and survivors sometimes sustaining permanent brain damage (Ebel & Wald, 2002). Herpes may also be spread from one part of the body to another by touching the infected area and then touching another area of the body. For example, touching a herpes infection can allow the virus to spread to a finger that has a cut or abrasion. This most often occurs during an initial outbreak. Although this type of transmission is not common, it is a good idea to avoid touching HSV lesions and avoid biting your nails if you have oral-facial herpes.

Some people believe that herpes can be spread only when there are obvious signs or symptoms of the infection. However, herpes may be active without causing signs or symptoms. Herpes is often transmitted by people who are unaware that they are infected and by people who do not realize that their herpes infection is in its active phase. One woman described her experience contracting herpes:

> *I had contracted herpes from a partner who had a case of "unrecognized" herpes—never a severe or noticeable outbreak, never any past problems with this condition. Being a sexually cautious person—I was a virgin at the time—I was floored when my symptoms showed up, much to the surprise of my partner as well. ("Personal Perspectives," 1997, p. 4)*

When a person is first infected with herpes, symptoms usually appear within 2 weeks after exposure. The initial symptoms of oral herpes infection often include small pimples or blisters ("cold sores" or "fever blisters") on the mouth or face. Herpes may produce sores in the genital areas of women and men, and skin lesions may appear on the thigh or buttocks. These sores, resembling blisters or pimples, eventually crust over and scab. In the 2–4 weeks herpes sores need to heal, some people experience a second outbreak of lesions, and some will have flulike symptoms including fever, aches, and swollen glands. Primary infections may be treated with acyclovir.

After the symptoms of genital herpes subside (the sores dry up, scab over, and disappear, and the infected person feels well again), the virus settles in the nerve cells in the spinal column. HSV-2 causes repeated outbreaks in about one third of those who are infected. Stress, menstruation, sunburn, fatigue, and the presence of other infections seem to be related.

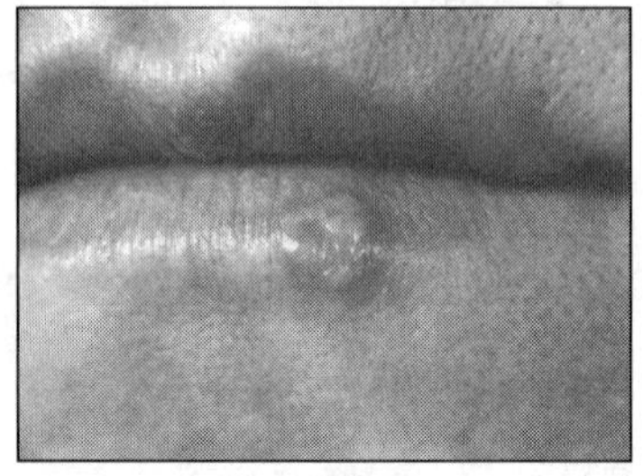

One symptom of lip herpes is an eruption of small, painful blisters or sores in the mouth area.

Library of Congress

Researchers are making progress toward developing vaccines to prevent herpes infection by boosting cellular immune response. A new type of herpes vaccine is now being tested in human clinical trials. A clinical trial is also underway to test a topical gel that appears promising in reducing symptoms (Ebel & Wald, 2002). Pregnant women with herpes outbreaks at the time of delivery can have cesarean deliveries to prevent exposure of newborns to the herpes virus. Scientific advances in research related to herpes are reported for lay readers in a quarterly journal, *The Helper*, published by the American Social Health Association (see the "Suggested Websites" section).

Human Papillomavirus or Genital Warts

Human papillomavirus (HPV) A sexually transmitted viral disease that may produce genital warts.

Genital warts See **human papillomavirus.**

There are more than 60 types of **human papillomavirus (HPV).** More than a dozen of them can cause warts (called **genital warts**) or more subtle signs of infection in the genital tract. HPV can be transmitted through vaginal or anal intercourse and through fellatio and cunnilingus. It is also possible for HPV to be transmitted from an infected pregnant woman to her infant.

HPV can remain inactive for months or years before any obvious signs of infection appear. Often, small to large warts or bumplike growths appear within 3 to 6 months after exposure. Warts may be pink or red and may appear in clusters or alone. In women, genital warts most commonly develop on the vulva, in the vagina, or on the cervix. They can also appear on or near the anus. In men, the warts appear most often on the penis, but can appear on the scrotum, the anus, or within the rectum. Although rare, HPV also can produce warts in areas of the mouths of both sexes.

Only one in three cases of HPV infection is symptomatic by the presence of warts; thus, many infected individuals remain undiagnosed and may unknowingly transmit the infection to others (Tobin, 1997). The seriousness of HPV is that three of its serotypes are

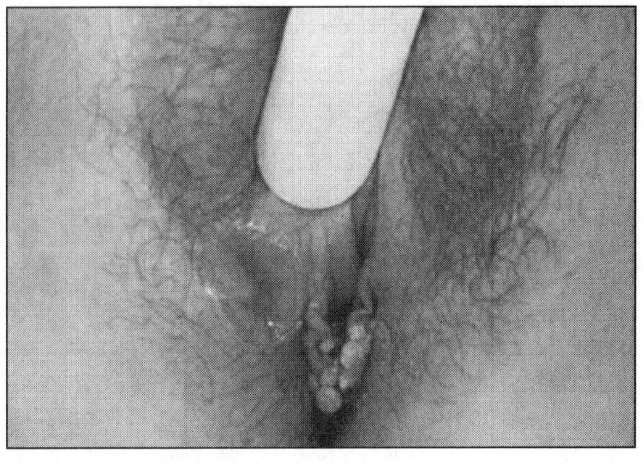

In some cases, HPV produces no visible symptoms. In other cases, HPV produces visible warts on the genital region.

Library of Congress

linked with cervical cancer. (A serologic assay, or serology, detects antibodies in the blood and diagnoses the type of infection a person has acquired.)

Health-care providers disagree about the efficacy of treating HPV when warts are not detectable. When the warts can be seen by visual inspection or by colposcope, however, various treatments may be recommended, depending on the number of warts and their location, the availability of equipment, the training of health-care providers, and the preferences of the patient. Treatment options for removing warts include cryotherapy (freezing), surgical removal, laser surgery, cauterization (burning), and topical application of chemicals such as podophyllin.

Treatment of warts destroys some infected cells, but not all of them. HPV is present in a wider area of skin other than just the precise wart location; therefore, recurrence of genital warts is not uncommon, even after treatment. Patients are advised to schedule follow-up visits with their health-care practitioners, check themselves regularly for visible warts, and talk with their sexual partners about using condoms to reduce the risk of transmitting the infection.

Molluscum Contagiosum

Molluscum contagiosum, also referred to as "water warts," is caused by a virus. It is transmitted through close contact with a person who is infected or through autoinoculation (spread from one location on one's body to another location). These small lesions can occur anywhere on the body besides the palms and soles of the feet. Although they generally resolve on their own, they can be treated chemically, with cryotherapy, or surgically removed.

Vaginitis

Vaginitis Infection of the vagina.

Three types of **vaginitis,** or vaginal infection, include trichomoniasis, candidiasis, and Gardnerella. Most women get vaginitis at some time in their lives, and many do not develop it from sexual contact. It can be caused by anything that upsets the balance of vaginal microflora, including illness, antibiotics, or overgrowth of one organism. It may be the result of bacteria from the rectum being transferred to the vagina. This can result from improper hygiene, or from anal intercourse or manipulation combined with vaginal intercourse or manipulation. Vaginal infection may also result from foreign objects, such as tampons and diaphragms, being left in the vagina too long.

Although some infected women show no symptoms, trichomoniasis is usually characterized by a foul-smelling, thin, frothy discharge that may be green, yellow, gray, or white and causes an irritating rash in the vulva and painful intercourse if left untreated. Antibiotics, such as metronidazole (Flagyl), are usually effective in treating trichomoniasis. When taking Flagyl, patients need to be aware of its Antabuse (nausea-inducing) effect when combined with alcohol. Because the partner may harbor trichomoniasis organisms without symptoms, both the woman and her sexual partner should be treated.

Gardnerella may not cause symptoms or may result in a profuse discharge and a "fishy" odor. This organism (bacterium) is quite common. Estimates of prevalence of bacterial vaginosis range from 5% in college students up to 60% in STD clinics. It may also be treated with Flagyl, and partners should be treated.

14-3b Cervical and Upper Reproductive Tract Infections

Chlamydia

Chlamydia A common sexually transmitted infection caused by the microorganism *chlamydia trachomatis*, often asymptomatic (therefore known as "the silent disease").

Chlamydia trachomatis (CT), also referred to simply as **chlamydia** (clah-MID-ee-uh), is a bacterium that can infect the genitals, eyes, and lungs. Chlamydia is the most common bacterial STD in the United States.

CT is easily transmitted directly from person to person through sexual contact. The microorganisms are found most often in the urethra of men; the cervix, uterus, and Fallopian tubes of women; and in the rectum of both women and men. CT infections can also occur indirectly (through contact with a towel containing bacteria, for example). Genital-to-eye transmission of the bacteria can also occur. If a person with a genital CT infection rubs his or her eye (or touches the eye of a partner) after touching his or her infected genitals, the bacteria can be transferred to the eye (and vice versa). In addition, an infant can get CT while passing through the cervix of its infected mother during delivery.

Chlamydia rarely shows obvious symptoms, which accounts for it being known as "the silent disease." As many as 40% of infected men and 80% of infected women experience no initial symptoms (Pinon, 2002). When men have symptoms, they may include pus from the penis, sores on the penis, sore testes, or a bloody stool. In women, symptoms may include low-back pain, pelvic pain, boils on the vaginal lips, or a bloody discharge. Symptoms in either sex may include sores on the tongue, sores on the fingers, low-grade fever, pain during urination, or frequent urge to urinate.

Chlamydia can be effectively treated with antibiotics, especially for early and uncomplicated infections. Left untreated, chlamydia can lead to pelvic inflammatory disease, sterility, arthritis, blindness, miscarriage, and premature birth. Chlamydia may co-occur with gonorrhea.

Gonorrhea

Gonorrhea A bacterial infection that is sexually transmitted. (Also known as "the clap," "the drip," "the whites," and "morning drop.")

Also known as "the clap," "the whites," "morning drop," and "the drip," **gonorrhea** is a bacterial infection. Individuals most often contract gonorrhea through sexual contact with someone who is carrying the gonococcus bacteria. Gonococci cannot live long outside the human body. Even though these bacteria can be cultured from a toilet seat, there are no documented cases of gonorrhea being transmitted in any way other than intimate physical contact. These bacteria thrive in warm, moist cavities, including the urinary tract, cervix, rectum, mouth, and throat. A pregnant woman can transmit gonorrhea during childbirth by causing an eye infection in the newborn.

Although some infected men show no signs, about two thirds of men exhibit symptoms between 3 and 8 days after exposure. They begin to discharge a thick, white pus from the penis and start to feel pain or discomfort during urination. They may also have swollen lymph glands in the groin. Women are more likely to show no signs of the infection (about 50% have no symptoms), but when they do, the symptoms may include a discharge from the vagina, along with a burning sensation (Pinon, 2002). Often, a woman becomes aware of gonorrhea only after she feels extreme discomfort, which is usually a result of the untreated infection traveling up into her uterus and Fallopian tubes. Infertility, ectopic pregnancy, spontaneous abortion, and premature delivery may result. Among men, symptoms may include painful urination and penile discharge, and painful defecation and rectal discharge. The major complication for men is epididymitis, which may be signaled by severe scrotal pain. This could result in abdominal pain, infertility, and erectile problems.

Gonorrhea is treated with antibiotics. A major problem with new cases of gonorrhea is that the emerging new strains of the bacteria are resistant to penicillin and tetracycline. Newer and more expensive antibiotics are required.

Nongonococcal Urethritis

Nongonococcal urethritis (NGU) An infection of the urethra—the tube that carries urine from the bladder.

Nongonococcal urethritis (NGU) is an infection of the urethra—the tube that carries urine from the bladder. NGU is caused by several different sexually transmitted organisms. The most common and most serious organism that causes NGU is chlamydia.

Organisms that cause nongonococcal urethritis are transmitted through sexual contact and from mother to newborn. Because individuals with NGU are often asymptomatic, they unknowingly transmit infection to their partners.

In men, symptoms of NGU include penile discharge, burning during urination, and burning or itching around the opening of the penis. Some men experience no symptoms or have symptoms so mild that they go unnoticed. In women, symptoms of NGU may include vaginal discharge, burning during urination, abdominal pain, bleeding between periods, and fever. Many infected women show no symptoms.

Once identified, NGU is treated with tetracycline or other antibiotics. Even when symptoms are mild or nonexistent, untreated NGU can cause damage to the reproductive organs and lead to infertility; result in miscarriages; and cause eye, ear, and lung infections in newborns.

Syphilis

Syphilis is a sexually transmitted disease caused by bacteria. In the late 1980s and early 1990s, syphilis rates in the United States increased dramatically, causing an increase in concern about this disease. Since 1990, the number of reported cases declined every year, until 2001, in which there was a slight increase. This increase occurred only among men, particularly among men who have sex with men (MSM). In the past few years, the rates of congenital syphilis have been reduced to half the previous rate. The Centers for Disease Control continues to have the goal of syphilis eradication by 2005 (as defined by 90% of counties being syphilis-free; Centers for Disease Control, 2002).

Syphilis A sexually transmitted (or congenital) disease caused by a spirochete (Treponema pallidum); if untreated, it can progress to a systemic infection through three stages and can be fatal.

Syphilis is transmitted through kissing or having genital contact with an infected individual. The spirochete bacteria enter the body through mucous membranes that line various body openings, such as the inside of the cheek, the vagina, and the urethra of the penis. Syphilis can also be transmitted from an infected pregnant woman to her unborn baby (congenital syphilis).

Syphilis progresses through identifiable stages. Each of these stages—primary, secondary, latent, and tertiary—involves different symptoms. In stage one (primary stage syphilis), a small sore or chancre appears at the site of infection between 10 and 90 days after exposure. The chancre, which appears on the tip of the man's penis, in the labia or cervix of the woman, or in either partner's mouth or rectum, neither hurts nor itches and, if left untreated, will disappear in 3 to 5 weeks. The disappearance leads infected people to believe that they are cured (this is one of the tricky aspects of syphilis). In reality, the disease is still present and doing great harm, even though there are no visible symptoms. Because the chancre is painless and often occurs internally in women, it is far more likely to remain undetected in women than in men.

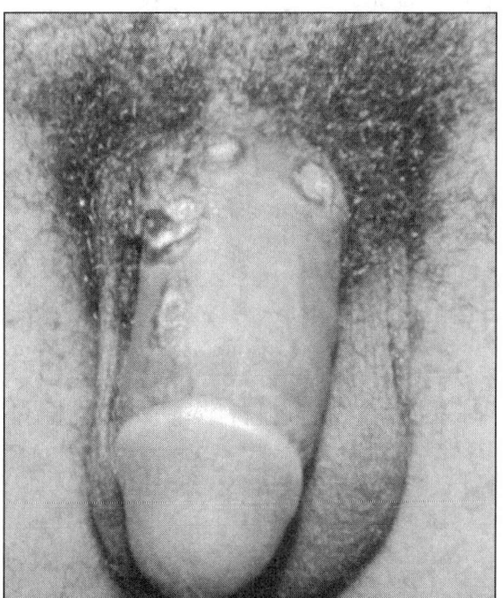

This is an example of a chancre of primary stage syphilis on a penis.

Library of Congress

Box 14-1 Self-Assessment

INTERACTIVE BOX

HIV Knowledge Questionnaire

The HIV-Knowledge Questionnaire (HIV-K-Q) measures one's knowledge about the consequences of HIV, and how it is transmitted and prevented. For each statement, please circle true (T), false (F), or I don't know (DK). If you don't know, please do not guess; instead, please circle DK.

T F DK 1. HIV and AIDS are the same thing.
T F DK 2. There is a cure for AIDS.
T F DK 3. A person can get HIV from a toilet seat.
T F DK 4. Coughing and sneezing DO NOT spread HIV.
T F DK 5. HIV can be spread by mosquitoes.
T F DK 6. AIDS is the cause of HIV.
T F DK 7. A person can get HIV by sharing a glass of water with someone who has HIV.
T F DK 8. HIV is killed by bleach.
T F DK 9. It is possible to get HIV when a person gets a tattoo.
T F DK 10. A pregnant woman with HIV can give the virus to her unborn baby.
T F DK 11. Pulling out the penis before a man climaxes or cums keeps a woman from getting HIV during sex.
T F DK 12. A woman can get HIV if she has anal sex with a man.
T F DK 13. Showering, or washing one's genitals or private parts, after sex keeps a person from getting HIV.
T F DK 14. Eating healthy foods can keep a person from getting HIV.
T F DK 15. All pregnant women infected with HIV will have babies born with AIDS.
T F DK 16. Using a latex condom or rubber can lower a person's chances of getting AIDS.
T F DK 17. A person with HIV can look and feel healthy.
T F DK 18. People who have been infected with HIV quickly show serious signs of being infected.
T F DK 19. A person can be infected with HIV for 5 years or more without getting AIDS.
T F DK 20. There is a vaccine that can stop adults from getting HIV.
T F DK 21. Some drugs have been made for the treatment of AIDS.
T F DK 22. Women are always tested for HIV during their Pap smears.
T F DK 23. A person cannot get HIV by having oral sex, mouth-to-penis, with a man who has HIV.
T F DK 24. A person can get HIV even if she or he has sex with another person only one other time.
T F DK 25. Using a lambskin condom or rubber is the best protection against HIV.
T F DK 26. People are likely to get HIV by deep kissing, putting their tongue in their partner's mouth, if their partner has HIV.

During the second stage (secondary stage syphilis), beginning from 2 to 12 weeks after the chancre has disappeared, other signs of syphilis may become evident, including a rash over the entire body or on the hands or feet. Syphilis has been called "the great imitator" because it mimics so many other diseases (mononucleosis, cancer, and psoriasis, for example). Welts and swelling of the lymph nodes can also occur, as well as fever, headaches, sore throat, and hair loss. Whatever the symptoms, they too will disappear without treatment, perhaps causing the person to again believe that nothing is wrong.

Following the secondary stage is the latency stage, during which there are no symptoms and the person is not infectious. However, the spirochetes are still in the body and can attack any organ at any time.

Tertiary syphilis is quite uncommon today, but this third stage can cause serious disability or even death. Heart disease, blindness, brain damage, loss of bowel and bladder control, difficulty in walking, and erectile dysfunction can result. Complications may not begin until 15 to 30 years after initial infection.

Treatment for syphilis is similar to that for gonorrhea. Penicillin or other antibiotics are effective. Infected persons treated in the early stages can be completely cured with no ill effects. If the syphilis has progressed into the tertiary stage, however, damage that has been done cannot be repaired.

Before reading further, you may want to assess your knowledge of HIV; see the self-assessment in Box 14-1.

T F DK 27. A person can get HIV by giving blood.

T F DK 28. A woman cannot get HIV is she has sex during her period.

T F DK 29. You can usually tell if someone has HIV by looking at them.

T F DK 30. There is a female condom that can help decrease a woman's chance of being infected with HIV.

T F DK 31. A natural skin condom works better against HIV than does a latex condom.

T F DK 32. A person will NOT get HIV if she or he is taking antibiotics.

T F DK 33. Having sex with more than one partner can increase a person's chance of being infected with HIV.

T F DK 34. Taking a test for HIV one week after having sex will tell a person if she or he has HIV.

T F DK 35. A person can get HIV by sitting in a hot tub or a swimming pool with a person who has HIV.

T F DK 36. A person can get HIV through contact with saliva, tears, sweat, or urine.

T F DK 37. A person can get HIV from the wetness of a woman's vagina.

T F DK 38. A person can get HIV if having oral sex, mouth on vagina, with a woman.

T F DK 39. If a person tests positive for HIV, then the test site will have to tell all of his, or her, partners.

T F DK 40. Using Vaseline or baby oil with condoms lowers the chance of getting HIV.

T F DK 41. Washing drug use equipment with cold water kills HIV.

T F DK 42. A woman can get HIV if she has vaginal sex with a man who has HIV.

T F DK 43. Athletes who share needles when using steroids can get HIV from the needles.

T F DK 44. Douching after sex will keep a woman from getting HIV.

T F DK 45. Taking vitamins keeps a person from getting HIV.

Scoring: Your score is obtained by summing the number of items you answered correctly. Score items answered *"I Don't Know"* as incorrect. The range of possible scores is 0–45. To make the score easier to interpret, compute your raw score into a percentage correct score (number correct divided by 45). The following items are TRUE: 4, 8, 9, 10, 12, 16, 17, 19, 21, 24, 30, 33, 37, 38, 42, 43. The other items are FALSE.

Comparison data: You may be interested in seeing how your score compares with the average scores among five separate samples who have responded to this questionnaire. As might be expected, HIV experts scored the highest (91%), followed by university students (82%), urban women (72%), primary care patients (69%), and community couples (52%). The investigators were surprised that the urban women and primary care groups were more knowledgeable than the community couples. They hypothesized that the community couples may feel less need to be informed on this topic, given the relatively lower rate of HIV infection in middle-income communities, and their likely assumption of sexual exclusivity in their relationship. All of the groups scored higher than what would be achieved by chance (33%).

Reference

Carey, M. P., Morrison-Beedy, D., & Johnson, B. T. (1998). The HIV-Knowledge Questionnaire. In C. M. Davis, Y. L. Yarber, R. Bauserman, G. Schreer, & S. L. Davis (Eds), *Handbook of Sexuality-Related Measures* (pp. 313–315). Thousand Oaks, CA: Sage.

14-3c Systemic Infections

When a friend tells you he or she has AIDS, the appropriate first reaction is an embrace, not a shudder.

—Mary Catherine Bateson, Richard Goldsby

Human Immunodeficiency Virus and Acquired Immunodeficiency Syndrome

Human immunodeficiency virus (HIV) attacks the white blood cells (T-lymphocytes) in human blood and causes **acquired immunodeficiency syndrome (AIDS).** AIDS is characterized by a breakdown of the body's immune system that makes individuals vulnerable to a variety of opportunistic diseases. Before 1993, a diagnosis of AIDS was made only when an HIV-infected individual developed one of more than 20 serious illnesses delineated by the Centers for Disease Control and Prevention (CDC), such as pneumocystis carinii pneumonia, pulmonary tuberculosis, cervical cancer, or Kaposi's sarcoma (a form of cancer). Since 1993, the definition of AIDS has been expanded to include anyone with HIV whose immune system is severely impaired, as indicated by a T-cell (or CD4 cell) count of less than 200 cells per cubic millimeter of blood. T-cell counts in healthy people not infected with HIV range from 800 to 1200 per cubic millimeter of blood.

Human immunodeficiency virus (HIV) A virus that attacks the immune system and may lead to AIDS.

Acquired immunodeficiency syndrome (AIDS) The last stage of HIV infection in which the immune system of a person's body is so weakened that it becomes vulnerable to disease and infection (opportunistic infections).

Transmission of HIV infection is influenced by the stage of the disease in the infected partner. HIV is more infectious in the early stages and again in the later stages, after AIDS symptoms have started to appear (Pinkerton & Abramson, 1997). The human immunodeficiency virus can be transmitted in various ways:

1. *Sexual contact*. HIV is found in several body fluids of infected individuals, including blood, semen, and possibly vaginal secretions. During sexual contact with an infected individual, the virus enters a person's bloodstream through the rectum, vagina, penis (the uncircumcised penis is at greater risk because of the greater retention of the partner's fluids), and the mouth during oral sex (especially when ejaculation occurs in the mouth). Saliva, sweat, and tears are not body fluids through which HIV is transmitted.
2. *Intravenous drug use*. Drug users who are infected with HIV can transmit the virus to other drug users with whom they share needles, syringes, and other drug-related implements.
3. *Blood transfusion*. HIV can be transmitted through HIV-infected blood or blood products. Currently, all blood donors are screened, and blood is not accepted from high-risk individuals. Blood that is accepted from donors is tested for the presence of HIV. However, prior to 1985, donor blood was not tested for HIV. Individuals who received blood or blood products prior to 1985 may have been infected with HIV.
4. *Mother-child transmission of HIV*. A pregnant woman infected with HIV can infect her unborn child. However, this risk is profoundly decreased if the mother receives anti-HIV treatment during pregnancy. According to the Women and Infant Transition Study, women on highly active antiretroviral therapy (HAART) regimens had a rate of infant transmission of 1.1%, whereas pregnant women taking zidovudine (AZT) alone had a rate of 7.7% (amfAR Global Link, 2003). HIV can be transmitted through breast-feeding. Although this risk can be reduced through formula feeding, this solution can be problematic in developing countries in which there are problems obtaining adequate supplies of formula and clean water.
5. *Organ or tissue transplants and donor semen*. Receiving transplant organs and tissues, as well as receiving semen for artificial insemination, could involve risk of contracting HIV if the donors have not been tested for HIV. Such testing is essential, and recipients should insist on knowing the HIV status of the organ, tissue, or semen donor.
6. *Occupational transmission of HIV*. Certain occupational workers regularly come into contact with human blood and are therefore susceptible to occupational transmission of HIV. Health-care workers (such as nurses and physicians), laboratory technicians, morgue technicians, rescue workers, dentists, police officers, prison guards, and other individuals who are likely to come into contact with bleeding individuals should use protection such as latex gloves before making physical contact with an injured or bleeding individual. Lay persons also should use latex gloves when coming into contact with another person's blood, and these gloves should be part of every first-aid kit.

HIV/AIDS is known as a spectrum illness: Although everyone infected with HIV has the same disease, he or she may have different symptoms at different stages. Some HIV-infected individuals display no symptoms at all for many years after exposure. Unless they are tested for HIV, many HIV-infected individuals don't know they are infected. When symptoms do appear, they may include swollen lymph glands, oral thrush (a white coating or spotting in the mouth), and memory problems. If full-blown AIDS develops, severe immune system breakdown can lead to the onset of illnesses such as pneumocystis carinii pneumonia, pulmonary tuberculosis, cervical cancer, and Kaposi's sarcoma.

Presently, there is no cure for HIV/AIDS and no vaccine to prevent infection. In the United States and other developed countries, treatments are available to inhibit HIV growth and to fight or prevent opportunistic diseases. These drugs do not cure HIV, but they do slow the progression of the disease and increase survival rates in patients. Two types of drugs are currently used to attack HIV enzymes. Reverse transcriptase inhibitors include abacavir, delavirdine, didanosine (ddI), efavirenz, lamivudine (3TC), nevirapine, stavudine (d4T), zalcitabine (ddC), and zidovudine (AZT). Protease inhibitors include amprenavir, indinavir, nelfinavir, ritonavir, and saquinavir. Physicians often prescribe these drugs to be taken in combination, referred to as "cocktail" therapy, or in a regimen known as **highly active antiretroviral therapy (HAART;** Facts About HIV/AIDS, 2002). HAART usually includes three drugs from at least two different classes.

Highly active antiretroviral therapy (HAART) A combination of drugs an HIV-infected person takes to treat the virus. (Also known as "cocktail therapy.")

Long-term nonprogressor (LTNP) An individual who has been affirmed as HIV-seropositive but has nevertheless retained a healthy immune system.

As a result of infected individuals' access to combination treatments including protease inhibitors, in Western countries the survival period after diagnosis has been extended. At the international AIDS Conference in 1994 a new category—**long-term nonprogressor (LTNP)**—was introduced. This term refers to those who have been affirmed as HIV-seropositive but have nevertheless retained a healthy immune system. At the most recent international AIDS Conference, it was estimated that 5% of people with HIV infection are LTNP, remaining healthy (not losing T-cells) for as long as 7 years without taking HIV medications. This implies that some people may possibly have an innate immunity to HIV ("Innate Immunity and Interferon," 2002).

Research is underway to develop drugs to prevent HIV from attaching to human immune cells (fusion inhibitors) and infecting them (entry inhibitors). Other research applications involve the use of postexposure prophylaxis (currently recommended by the CDC only for health-care professionals exposed through on-the-job accidents) and the development of microbicides to prevent infection during sexual contact. Available both in print and online, the American Foundation for AIDS Research (AmfAR) Global Link is a comprehensive guide to improved and experimental HIV/AIDS treatments and active clinical trials in North America and throughout the world (see www.amfar.org).

Treatment for HIV and AIDS also includes adopting lifestyle habits that promote well-being: a balanced diet, ample rest, regular exercise, and relaxation. It is also important for persons with HIV/AIDS to avoid stressors on the immune system, such as tobacco, recreational drugs, and other STDs. Establishing a supportive network of family and friends is also essential in managing the stress of having HIV/AIDS.

A newly identified psychological challenge for AIDS survivors is the "resurrection" of individuals who had expected to die from AIDS but now have a new opportunity for survival due to recent treatment developments. This phenomenon has been referred to as the **Lazarus Syndrome,** named after the biblical figure, Lazarus, who was raised from the dead by Christ. Care providers have found that having a chance for a "second life" can provoke anxiety; individuals in this situation may feel as if they are walking on eggshells, uncertain as to how long treatment effects may last (Demmer, 2000). They may feel survivor guilt because of friends or others who died before the treatment innovations were available, or because the treatments were not effective for them. In addition, support systems may be depleted, and financial pressures may be challenging as they face rebuilding family relations, social networks, and work possibilities.

Lazarus Syndrome Psychological challenge experienced by individuals who had expected to die from AIDS but now have a new opportunity for survival due to recent treatment developments.

Hepatitis B

Hepatitis B An inflammatory disease of the liver caused by a virus.

Hepatitis B is an inflammatory disease of the liver caused by a virus. Other forms of hepatitis viruses include types A, C, D, and E. Hepatitis B (HBV) is most often transmitted through vaginal, oral, or anal sexual contact with an infected individual. Infection may also occur from transfusions of contaminated blood or from sharing contaminated personal items, such as razors or needles (used for steroid injections, drug use, body piercing, or tattoos). Pregnant women may also transmit hepatitis B to their newborns.

The symptoms of hepatitis B infection, which take 2 to 6 months to appear, include skin rash, muscle and joint pain, fatigue, loss of appetite, nausea and vomiting, headache, fever, dark urine, jaundice, and liver enlargement and tenderness. There is no treatment to cure hepatitis B; people usually recover naturally and develop immunity to future infection. While the disease is running its course, health-care professionals recommend rest, a high-protein diet with lots of fluids, and the avoidance of alcohol and drugs that may stress the liver. As many as 10% of those infected with hepatitis B become carriers of the virus for several years or even their lifetime. Some hepatitis B infections lead to cirrhosis of the liver or liver cancer.

Currently, the only effective vaccine for prevention of an STD is the hepatitis B vaccine. The Centers for Disease Control and Prevention recommend that all adolescents and young adults receive a hepatitis B vaccination. The vaccine is given in the arm in three separate doses.

14-4 WHO IS AT RISK FOR STD INFECTION?

Various biological and behavioral factors are associated with an increased risk of acquiring an STD. The incidence of STDs is a result of three factors:

1. Exposure (the rate of sexual contacts between uninfected persons with infected individuals)
2. Transmission (the probability of an exposed person acquiring the infection)
3. Duration (the length of time an infected person is contagious and able to spread the disease (Healthy People 2010, 2002). Variables influencing exposure, transmission, and duration are discussed in sections 14-4a through 14-4i.

14-4a Number of Sex Partners

The more sexual partners an individual has, the higher the risk of being exposed to a sexually transmitted disease. Data from 9,882 sexually active women participating in the National Survey of Family Growth revealed that women with a history of having more than five lifetime sexual partners had a significantly increased risk of having a bacterial STD and pelvic inflammatory disease (PID). "Those who had more than five partners, compared to women with only one partner, were nine times more likely to report an infection history. Moreover, the number of sexual partners demonstrated a clear 'dose effect': As the number of sexual partners increased, so did the probability of reporting a bacterial STD" (Miller, Cain, Rogers, Gribble, & Turner, 1999, p. 8).

14-4b Relationship Status

People who were not married (never married, divorced, separated, or widowed) reported having more sexual partners in a year than those who were married (Finer, Darroch & Singh, 1999). Thus, being single is associated with a higher STD risk than being married or living with a partner. Having "multiple partners," was defined as having two or more sexual partners in the prior year, and was found to increase one's *direct* risk for STDs. One's *indirect* risk was increased if at least one of the person's *partners* had additional partners during that time.

NATIONAL DATA Among sexually active adults, 80–87% of women and 76% of men reported having one sexual partner in the prior year. About 10% had sex with two partners; 5–10% of women and 14% of men had three or more partners (Finer et al., 1999).

Young women are more likely to have multiple partners. Almost two thirds of unmarried women and adolescents and more than half of women aged 20–24 were at risk of STDs in the preceding year (Finer et al., 1999).

Married and cohabiting individuals are more likely to use condoms with secondary partners than with primary partners, thus placing their primary partners at risk for STDs. In the Finer et al. study (1999), women whose partners had other partners were less likely to have used condoms at last intercourse.

14-4c Age

In the United States, adolescents and young adults are the age group with the greatest risk of acquiring an STD. For example, rates of chlamydia and gonorrhea in women are highest among 15- to 19-year-olds (Centers for Disease Control, 1995). STD rates are high among adolescents and young adults because they are more likely to have multiple sexual partners, their partners may be at higher risk of being infected, and they may be more likely to engage in intercourse without using condoms. Young adolescent girls have an increased risk of HIV infection due, in part, to their minimal vaginal mucus production, which provides less of a barrier to HIV.

Young girls also have an increased presence of cervical ectopy, which increases their risk of acquiring HIV and chlamydia. **Cervical ectopy** refers to an outgrowth of membranous tissue from the cervix toward the vagina. This outgrowth of cervical tissue, common in adolescent girls, is more susceptible to some STDs than the more protective membranous tissue of the vagina (Hankins, 1996).

Cervical ectopy An outgrowth of membranous tissue from the cervix toward the vagina.

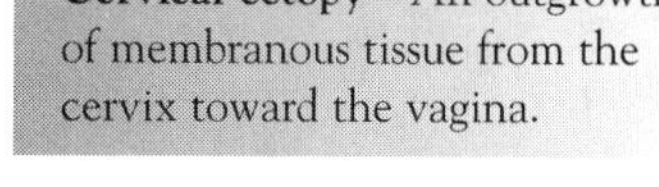

NATIONAL DATA Each year of age that women delayed beginning sexual intercourse reduced the odds of their contracting a bacterial STD by 6% (Miller et al., 1999).

A further problem with early initiation of sexual activity is that the partners of young teens are more likely to be part of a sexual network that includes infected people with untreated STDs. Furthermore, teens may be especially reluctant to seek medical services for STDs and may encounter difficulties in accessing services (Healthy People 2010, 2002).

14-4d Gender

The transmission of an STD (likelihood of acquiring the infection once exposed) is influenced by one's sex. Women are biologically more susceptible than men to becoming infected if exposed to STDs. A woman who has one act of unprotected intercourse with a man infected with gonorrhea has a 50–90% chance of contracting the disease. In contrast, a man who has one act of unprotected intercourse with a woman infected with gonorrhea has about a 20% chance of becoming infected. When exposed to chlamydia, approximately two thirds of women and one third of men are infected by a single encounter with a partner who is infected (Pinon, 2002). Likewise, male-to-female transmission of HIV is two to four times more efficient than female-to-male transmission (Hankins, 1996): This is due to the larger mucosal surface area exposed to the virus in women, the greater amount of virus present in semen as compared with vaginal secretions, and the shortness and location of the female urethra (shorter distance for infectious organisms to travel).

Although lesbians are not immune from HIV and other STD infections, women who have sexual relations only with women (and whose partners do likewise) have a substantially lower risk of acquiring STDs than heterosexual women. Studies investigating the risk of HIV transmission among lesbians suggest there is a small (although not yet quantified) risk associated with the most common female-to-female sexual practices (oral sex, manual stimulation). The main source of HIV infection among lesbians has been primarily related to injection drug use and secondarily to sex with HIV-infected men (Mays, Cochran, Pies, Chu, & Ehrhardt, 1996).

14-4e Substance Use

Current media campaigns warn of the dangers of combining alcohol and drugs with sex. Perhaps you have seen the warning "Get drunk, get high, get AIDS." Drinking alcohol or using drugs is associated with an increased risk of acquiring HIV and other STDs. At the community level, the introduction of new drugs can have a drastic influence on sexual behavior in high-risk sexual networks. Substance use increases the risk of STD transmission when it is associated with the exchange of sex for drugs, a greater number of anonymous sex partners, or decreases in use of barrier protection (e.g., condoms) and seeking medical care. For example, in the late 1980s the nationwide syphilis epidemic was fueled by increases in use of crack cocaine (Healthy People 2010, 2002).

At the individual level, substance use is associated with impaired judgment regarding sexual decisions. One study of more than 1,200 sexually active adolescents revealed that adolescents engaged in riskier sexual behaviors when they used alcohol or drugs (Cooper, Pierce, & Farmer Huselid, 1994). In a laboratory experiment involving 20 men, participants were randomly assigned to an experimental group who drank vodka and tonic to achieve a blood alcohol level of .08% or to a control group who drank only tonic (Gordon & Carey, 1996). All participants then completed a battery of tests related to condom use. Compared to the men who did not consume alcohol, those who consumed alcohol tended to report more negative attitudes toward condoms (they believed, for example, that condoms decrease pleasure or that discussing condom use with a partner is embarrassing) and lower self-efficacy regarding the initiation of condom use in sexual encounters. Using alcohol and other recreational drugs not only affects judgment and attitudes about sexual behavior, but it may also damage immune systems, making individuals more susceptible to infectious diseases in general.

In the United States, injection of illegal drugs is the risk behavior most frequently associated with heterosexual and perinatal transmission of HIV. The infection can be passed through the sharing of contaminated needles. An STD can be transmitted by a pregnant woman to her fetus prior to or during birth. The most dramatic increase in AIDS incidence has been among women, African Americans, and people infected heterosexually and through injection drug use.

In a review of trends in the HIV/AIDS epidemic, the Centers for Disease Control (1998) noted that without question, drug use fuels the spread of HIV/AIDS among the African American and Hispanic populations. This occurs through the direct result of injection drugs, transmission through sex with an infected partner, and sex in exchange for money or drugs. The highest prevalence rates among patients in drug treatment centers and among childbearing women have been detected in the South and along the East Coast.

14-4f Physical or Sexual Abuse

Women who have been sexually abused are almost twice as likely to test positive for STDs as women who do not have such histories. For those with histories of both physical and sexual abuse, the odds were tripled (Wingood, DiClemente, & Raj, 2000; Johnson & Hellerstedt, 2002). A history of sexual abuse increases the likelihood of a young woman beginning voluntary intercourse at an earlier age, an STD risk. Individuals who have been raped or sexually assaulted are also at risk for acquiring an STD because sexual coercion decreases the possibility of self-protection. Forced sexual activity is also more likely to result in vaginal or anal abrasions, thereby increasing susceptibility to HIV. Women who are physically abused (even if not through sexual violence) may engage in risky sexual behaviors out of fear and may be unable to negotiate use of condoms.

A study of youth who were involved in intensive psychiatric treatment found that those with a history of sexual abuse were three times more likely than nonabused peers to report inconsistent condom use. They were also more likely to have had STDs, less knowledge of HIV, and lower scores on the Condom Self-Efficacy Scale (Brown, Lourie, Zlotnich, & Cohn, 2000). Health service providers and those who work with youth should be aware that a history of sexual abuse may be an indicator of a particular need to educate and counsel regarding HIV risk-reduction skills.

14-4g Lower Socioeconomic and Minority Status

Rates of STDs are higher among populations that are economically disadvantaged. The reason is that individuals in lower socioeconomic conditions tend to lack health insurance, have inadequate access to health care, and receive inadequate education (including education related to STDs). Because racial and ethnic minorities are disproportionately represented among the poor, rates of STDs are higher among minority populations

(Healthy People 2010, 2002). For example, 77% of reported gonorrhea cases are among African Americans, a rate that is 31 times that for Whites. For Hispanic persons, the gonorrhea rates were almost three times the rate for Whites. The rate of syphilis has declined for all ethnic and racial groups, with the exception of American Indians and Alaska Natives. However, in 1997 about 82% of reported cases of primary and secondary syphilis were among African Americans. The rate of congenital syphilis showed a similar overrepresentation among minority populations.

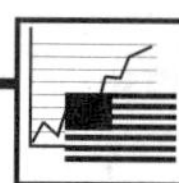

NATIONAL DATA The rate of congenital syphilis ranged from 113.5 per 100,000 live births to African Americans, to 34.6 per 100,000 live births to Hispanics, to 3.3 per 100,000 live births to Whites (Healthy People 2010, 2002).

Minority racial and ethnic groups are, on the average, younger, and (as noted earlier) youths have higher STD risks. Finally, minorities tend to live in concentrated areas of poverty; this "creates potential sex partner pools of high risk and high STD prevalence and perhaps reinforces risky behaviors" (Aral, 1996, p.14). Rates of HIV and other STDs are higher in urban areas than in rural areas. The reason is primarily that individuals with high-risk factors tend to be concentrated in urban areas. One of the reasons STDs remain "hidden" is that they disproportionately impact disenfranchised persons and vulnerable groups whose needs may not be apparent to more affluent society, such as sex workers, youth, persons in detention, and migrant workers (Healthy People 2010, 2002), and the poor in developing countries. People who live in poverty or on the margins of society are more likely to be part of social networks encouraging risky sexual behavior and less likely to seek or have access to health care.

14-4h High-Risk Sexual Behavior

The term *high-risk group* implies that certain traits determine who will become infected with an STD. Kerr (1990, p. 431) noted that "the concept of high-risk groups has led many persons to falsely believe that they are not susceptible to HIV infection since they do not fall into one of these groups." It is not the group one belongs to, but rather the behaviors one practices, that puts one at risk for STD infection. Anyone who engages in risky sexual behavior is susceptible to acquiring STDs. With some exceptions (such as sexual victimization and mother-child transmission), STDs result from people choosing to engage in behaviors that place them at risk. These choices, rather than people's group affiliation, most influence STD transmission.

Although worldwide most cases of HIV and AIDS are found among the heterosexual population, in the United States, HIV rates are highest among gay and bisexual men. AIDS incidence has remained the highest among men who have sex with men (MSM; Centers for Disease Control, 1998). This is due to the high rate of anal intercourse—a high-risk sexual behavior—among gay and bisexual men. In one sample of young MSM (ages 15–22), between 5% and 8% were HIV-infected. The disproportionate impact on minorities was observed, with a higher percentage of infection observed among African Americans (13%) and Hispanics (5%) than among Whites (4%; Centers for Disease Control, 1998).

Although improvements in condom use and limitations of number of partners had been seen among MSM, recent data suggest that unsafe sexual behavior among MSM may be increasing. For example, STD clinic data in 29 cities in the United States show a 5–13% increase in the proportion of gonorrhea cases attributed to sexual activity between men (Alan Guttmacher Institute, 2002). It is feared that some have interpreted modern treatment advances as encouragement to reduce caution and engage in risky behaviors. Table 14-2 presents various behaviors and their level of STD risk.

TABLE 14-2

Which Sexual Behaviors Are Most Risky?

Extremely High Risk	Moderate Risk
Unprotected anal and vaginal intercourse	Unprotected oral sex on a man or woman
Sharing needles (for drug use and body piercing)	Unprotected oral-anal contact (rimming)
Sharing devices that draw blood (such as whips)	Unprotected fisting or intercourse using one or more fingers
Sharing unprotected sex toys (such as dildos)	
Allowing body fluids to come in contact with broken skin and mucous membranes	

Low Risk	No Risk
Deep (French) kissing	Dry kissing
Anal and vaginal intercourse with a condom used correctly	Hugging and nongenital touching
Fisting or intercourse using one or more fingers protected by a finger cot* or latex glove	Massage
Oral-anal contact (rimming) with a dental dam**	Using vibrators or sex toys (not shared)
Oral sex on a man or woman using a condom or dental dam	Masturbation (alone or with partner)

*A *finger cot* is a mini-condom worn on the fingers for finger intercourse.
** A *dental dam* is a latex square used to cover the anus or vagina during oral sex. Household plastic wrap or a condom cut lengthwise can be used as a substitute for a dental dam.

14-4i Personal Choices: Being Tested for HIV and Other STDs

Many people do not get tested for HIV and other STDs because they believe they are not infected. Several STDs are asymptomatic; that is, they often do not produce symptoms. Thus, individuals may have an STD and not know it. Other individuals believe that if they are not in a "high-risk category," testing is not needed. Some individuals do not get tested because they fear the results may indicate they *are* infected. For this same reason, some individuals get tested but never follow up to get the results.

With HIV and other STDs, what you don't know can hurt you. The longer an STD goes undiagnosed and untreated, the more likely that it will produce serious health consequences, including sterility, cancer, and death. The sooner an infected individual is tested and diagnosed, the sooner that individual can begin treatment for the disease and begin to alter sexual or needle-sharing behavior, thereby reducing the risk of transmitting the disease to others. Early detection of HIV enables the infected individual to begin interventions that slow the growth of HIV and prevent opportunistic diseases. An HIV-infected individual whose disease is detected and treated in the early stages has a better prognosis for living longer with a higher quality of life than an individual whose HIV infection is detected during later stages. Early detection of other STDs can prevent or minimize the negative health effects they might otherwise produce. Because of the ulcerations caused by genital herpes, syphilis, and chancroid, and the inflammation caused by gonorrhea, chlamydia, and trichomoniasis, these infections facilitate transmission of HIV. Therefore, rapid diagnosis and treatment of these STDs may help prevent sexual transmission of HIV (Chernesky, 1997).

Getting tested for HIV and other STDs requires an investment of time, effort and, potentially, money. Getting tested also requires individuals to overcome any embarrassment and fear associated with discussing their sexual behaviors with health-care providers, having their genitals examined, and coping with the possibility of being told they have an STD.

Where do individuals go to get tested for HIV and other STDs, and what do the tests involve? STD testing is available at most local public health centers, STD clinics, family planning clinics, private health-care providers, hospitals, and university health centers. One can also get tested for HIV in the privacy of the home. One type of HIV test can be bought at pharmacies, college health centers, and public health clinics, or it can be ordered through the mail for a cost of around $50. The test involves pricking a finger, putting three drops of blood on a special card, and mailing the card to a laboratory. To obtain the results, one calls the company's toll-free number after 7 days and gives the personal identification number that was included with the test kit. HIV counselors are available to discuss the test results and give advice and information.

Some STD testing involves getting a sample of the person's blood or urine and testing it for the presence of a particular STD. Testing for chlamydia in women involves a health-care provider inserting a cotton swab inside the vagina to obtain a specimen that is then cultured. This swab procedure is done during a pelvic exam. For men, chlamydia testing involves a health-care provider inserting a cotton swab into the penis. Although a urine test has been developed to detect chlamydia, it is not commonly used because data on its credibility are lacking. A recently developed oral HIV test involves placing a specially treated pad between the lower cheek and gum for 2 minutes. The pad soaks up fluid that is then tested for HIV antibodies.

Finally, it is important to realize that testing, in and of itself, is not an STD prevention strategy. In one study of women who had been tested for HIV, many said that testing was a way to feel safe. However, they neglected to discuss whether they had been concurrently tested with their partner or if their partner was engaging in any risky behaviors. To feel confident in a negative HIV test result, one should have mutual testing with one's partner and then a month later undergo mutual testing again (Exner, Hoffman, Parikh, Leu, & Ehrhardt, 2002).

Think About It

We have just reviewed the reasons many individuals who engage in high-risk behavior for acquiring HIV and other STDs are nevertheless unlikely to seek testing for STDs. If you are sexually active, have you ever reasoned, "I could tell if someone is infected" or "It would be too embarrassing to be tested" or "I wouldn't want my partner to think I didn't trust him/her"?

♦

14-5 CONSEQUENCES OF SEXUALLY TRANSMITTED DISEASES

In the United States, most teenagers and adults today are aware that HIV and AIDS can cause serious health consequences. However, the emphasis on HIV/AIDS may be inadvertently overshadowing the seriousness of other STDs. In addition to health consequences, HIV and other STDs can cause psychological distress and can also place an economic burden on individuals and society.

14-5a Health Consequences

Untreated STDs can result in severe health consequences. Women are more likely than men to suffer serious health consequences from contracting STDs. Because women are less likely to produce symptoms, they are less likely to be diagnosed until severe problems develop.

INTERNATIONAL DATA HIV/AIDS is the fourth largest global cause of death. In 2001 the HIV/AIDS epidemic claimed nearly 3 million lives. AIDS has lowered life expectancy by 15 years in Sub-Saharan Africa, by 6 years in Haiti, and 4 years in Cambodia. It is projected that between 2000 and 2020, in the most-affected 45 countries, 68 million people will die earlier than they would have, due to AIDS (UNAIDS, 2002a).

Pelvic inflammatory disease (PID) Inflammation of the upper female reproductive system, possibly including the uterus, ovaries, fallopian tubes, and nearby structures; the most common serious complication of STDs, causing infertility in 20% of PID patients.

Untreated sexually transmitted diseases may cause infections of the cervix, uterus, and uterine tubes, or **pelvic inflammatory disease (PID).** This is a major health problem in women of reproductive age, often requiring hospitalization and surgery. PID is associated with complications such as infertility, ectopic pregnancy, and chronic abdominal pain. Chlamydia and gonorrhea are important causes of PID in women.

STDs are also associated with health problems for pregnant women and infants. Various STDs may be transmitted to the fetus, newborn, or infant through the placenta (congenital infection), during passage through the birth canal (perinatal infection), or after birth through breast-feeding or close contact. Health consequences include spontaneous abortion, stillbirth, and premature delivery.

For both women and men, STDs increase the level of susceptibility to HIV. Individuals with active genital herpes, syphilis, chancroid infection, chlamydia, gonorrhea, or trichomoniasis are three to five times more likely to contract HIV than noninfected individuals (SIECUS Fact Sheet, 1997). This is true partly because tissue inflammation, ulcerations, and open sores associated with STDs provide the HIV virus with entries into partners' bloodstreams.

The health consequences of HIV and AIDS have caused great alarm; AIDS causes more deaths than any other STD. The largest number of deaths related to STDs other than AIDS is caused by cervical and other cancers associated with the human papillomavirus and liver disease cancer caused by the hepatitis B virus (Committee on Prevention and Control of STDs, 1997). Untreated syphilis can cause serious damage to the cardiovascular and nervous systems and may also cause blindness and death.

In Asia and Africa, 2 million individuals each year are permanently blinded by chlamydial infections (Aral & Holmes, 1991). The rate of blindness due to chlamydia is much lower in the United States, due to the climate and the fact that medication is readily available to control the infection.

14-5b Economic Consequences

The economic costs of STDs place a burden on individuals and their families and drain the tax dollars that support public health insurance (such as Medicaid) and public health-care facilities.

In the United States $10 billion per year is spent on STDs other than AIDS (Pinon, 2002). Individuals with AIDS (and their families) are particularly hard hit by the financial costs associated with this disease. Medicines alone can cost more than $1,000 per month. A volunteer at a community AIDS support organization commented, "There are days when our clients must make a decision about whether they will eat that day or take their medicine" (B. Baker, personal communication, 1997).

Annual medication costs (at the beginning of 2000) of $10,000 to $12,000 are prohibitive to most families. Needless to say, the drug therapies "are out of reach of the 90 percent of the world's HIV-infected people, who live in developing countries" (Pinkerton & Abramson, 1997, p. 373). The number of very poor and destitute families is expected to rise. Many families have reduced expenditures for basic needs and sold their assets to attempt to pay for health care and funerals; many youth, especially girls, have been taken out of school to care for sick family members or to earn money (UNAIDS, 2001). A pilot project has been initiated by Medecins Sans Frontieres (in English, Doctors Without Borders) in three clinics in a suburb of Cape Town in South Africa. The program began by treating only a dozen people but plans to eventually treat 150 adults and 30 children to show that it is possible to provide AIDS drugs and successfully treat poor people in South Africa (Associated Press, 2002).

14-5c Psychological Consequences

Individuals who learn they are infected with a sexually transmitted disease often experience psychological consequences similar to those experienced with other life crises. These psychological reactions include shock, withdrawal from social interaction, anger (especially at the person who gave them the infection), fear, shame, and depression.

Telling one's partner (or a potential partner) that one has an STD can be very stressful. Individuals infected with an STD often encounter rejection. One woman with herpes stayed in an unhappy relationship for 7 years because "she felt that no one but the man who gave her herpes would ever want her" ("Winning the War in Your Mind," 1997, p. 1). (See Box 10-1, "Social Choices: Consequences for Revealing Having an STD," for a discussion about telling your partner about your sexual health status.)

Individuals with HIV and AIDS are prone to high levels of psychological distress. In a sample of 736 people with AIDS, more than 40% scored above a cutoff for significant depressive symptoms on a scale measuring depression (Fleishman & Fogel, 1994). The levels of psychological distress among individuals in this sample were lower in those who had high levels of social support from friends and family members.

The psychological effects of having an STD partly depend on the coping strategies used by the infected individual. In one study of individuals with AIDS, researchers identified three coping strategies individuals used after finding out they were infected with HIV (Fleishman & Fogel, 1994). These strategies include "avoidance coping," "positive coping," and "seeking social support" (see Table 14-3). Researchers found that individuals who used positive coping strategies experienced fewer depressive symptoms, whereas individuals who used avoidance coping or sought social support experienced greater depressive symptoms. Regarding the latter finding, researchers suggested that support seeking may be a response to, rather than a cause of, distress.

TABLE 14-3

Coping Strategies Used by Individuals After Learning They Are HIV Positive

Positive Coping Strategy	Avoidance Coping Strategy	Seeking Social Support Coping Strategy
1. Try to learn more about AIDS.	1. Try to push it out of your mind.	1. Ask friends or relatives for advice.
2. Tell yourself to accept it.	2. Think about better times in the past.	2. Seek sympathy and understanding from friends.
3. Think about people who are less fortunate than you.	3. Make yourself feel better by drinking or taking drugs.	
4. Look on the bright side.	4. Avoid being with people.	
5. Make plans for the future.	5. Go on as if nothing happened.	
	6. Keep your feelings to yourself.	
	7. Keep others from knowing how bad things are.	
	8. Let yourself feel so angry that you want to hit or smash something.	

Source: Fleishman, J. A., & Fogel, B. (1994). Coping and depressive symptoms among people with AIDS. *Health Psychology,* 13(2), 156–169.

Think About It

How might educational programs go about informing people of the potential seriousness of untreated STDs without fueling fear that is out of proportion?

14-6 PREVENTION AND CONTROL OF SEXUALLY TRANSMITTED DISEASES

Don't say, "It [AIDS] can't happen to me." It can.

—Garlin Lancaster, AIDS activist, now deceased

It is no exaggeration to say that prevention of STDs promotes sexual health, saves lives, and averts devastating social and economic costs to people and countries (SIECUS, 2002). If the AIDS epidemic is unchecked, 45 million new infections by 2010 are projected; however, swift implementation of a comprehensive set of interventions could reverse the course of this epidemic (Stover et al., 2002). Significant political and financial commitment will be required. Political commitment is needed to reduce barriers to implement preventive efforts, to reduce stigma so people will seek counseling, testing, and treatment. To effectively enhance prevention programs, and sustain these efforts until 2010, would cost about $27 billion. But, as Stover et al. (2002, p. 75) observed, "The costs of scaling up prevention programmes are large, but any delay will be even more costly."

Due to the serious health consequences of AIDS, STD prevention and control efforts in recent years have largely focused on preventing transmission of HIV. However, given the potentially serious health consequences of other STDs—including the increased susceptibility to HIV infection—prevention and control of all STDs are warranted.

Researchers have found that HIV-infected men who have another STD have a higher concentration of HIV in their semen compared to HIV-infected men who do not have a concurrent STD. In one study, the concentration of HIV in the semen of HIV-infected men was eight times higher in men who had another STD than in those who did not have a concurrent STD (Cohen et al., 1997). Thus, the risk of HIV transmission via semen is increased by concurrent infection with a sexually transmitted disease. Ulcerations, lesions, or sores caused by many sexually transmitted diseases provide a site for HIV to enter the bloodstream. Because STDs facilitate transmission of HIV, efforts to prevent, detect, and treat STDs may help reduce HIV transmission. It is estimated, for example, that treating or preventing 100 cases of syphilis among high-risk groups would prevent 1,200 HIV infections during a 10-year period (Committee on Prevention and Control of STDs, 1997).

Efforts to prevent and control STDs involve modifying high-risk behaviors, delivering public and private sexual health care, reducing the sharing of potentially infected needles, using computer technology, providing educational interventions, and initiating community development.

14-6a Modification of High-Risk Sexual Behavior

The most reliable ways to avoid getting a sexually transmitted disease are to reduce risky sexual contact and to avoid injecting illicit drugs. In a nationwide study of sex education teachers, abstinence was one of the most commonly cited goals of sex education (Forrest & Silverman, 1989). Yet, the majority of the U.S. population begins engaging in sexual intercourse during their teenage years. Abstinence from sexual intercourse does not mean that a person is immune from acquiring an STD. Even virgins are at risk for STDs. A study of more than 2,000 students in grades 9 through 12 found that 47% reported they were virgins (Schuster, Bell, & Kanouse, 1996). However, of those who were virgins, 9%, 10%, and 1% reported they had engaged in fellatio with ejaculation, cunnilingus, and anal sex, respectively. Most (86%) of those who engaged in fellatio reported that they never used a condom. The researchers noted that "although remaining a virgin all but eliminates the possibility of becoming pregnant, activities such as fellatio, cunnilingus, and anal intercourse can spread sexually transmitted diseases" (Schuster et al., 1996, p. 1570).

Individuals (including virgins) who are sexually active may reduce their risks of acquiring an STD by having sexual contact only with one partner who is not infected, who is monogamous, and who does not inject drugs. Rather than rush into sexual relationships, allow time to build trusting, caring, and honest relationships in which you can share your sexual histories. Physical intimacy and pleasure may be achieved by practicing outercourse—activities that do not involve exposing a partner to blood, semen, or vaginal secretions. Outercourse includes hugging, cuddling, masturbating, fantasizing, massaging, and rubbing body to body while clothed. Also, carefully inspect your partner's genitals before sexual contact, as well as your own. Although some STDs produce no visible signs, it is possible to see herpes blisters, chancres, genital warts, and rashes. If you notice anything unusual about your partner's genitals (or your own), abstain from sexual contact and seek a medical examination.

Showering or washing the genital area with soap and water both before and after sexual activity is also helpful in preventing infections. And finally, use of condoms and dental dams during vaginal and anal intercourse, fellatio, and cunnilingus is also important.

Studies have shown that consistent, correct condom use reduces the overall risk of acquiring and transmitting HIV and other STDs. However, condoms do not offer a 100% guarantee against the transmission of STDs for a variety of reasons. First, condoms are not always used consistently and correctly. Using a condom "most of the time" or "almost always" is not the same as using one every time a person engages in vaginal or anal intercourse or fellatio. It is also important to use a condom correctly (see Figure 11-1 and Table 14-4 on correct condom use). Even when used correctly, condom breakage and slippage may still occur.

TABLE 14-4

Correct Condom Use

1. Use only condoms that are made in the United States or Japan. Condoms that are made in other countries may not have been tested for effectiveness.
2. Check the expiration date of the condom. Do not use condoms that have passed the expiration date.
3. Store condoms in a cool, dry place. Do not keep condoms in wallet or car, where they can become hot, and do not keep them in the refrigerator.
4. Use only latex or polyurethane condoms for fellatio and vaginal or anal intercourse. Natural lamb-skin condoms are an ineffective barrier against HIV.
5. Use condoms with a reservoir tip, or pinch 1/2 inch at the tip of the condom to collect the semen.
6. Unroll the condom slowly and carefully onto the erect penis before the first contact of penis to vagina, anus, or mouth.
7. If the penis has a foreskin, put the condom on with the foreskin pushed back. When the shaft is covered, push the foreskin toward the top of the penis to allow the foreskin to move without breaking the condom.
8. Make sure there is no air trapped inside the condom. (If there is, it could cause breakage.) Have a spare condom available in case you find a tear or a hole in the one you are using.
9. Use only water-based lubricants, such as K-Y Jelly or other personal lubricants. Products containing oil, such as Vaseline, baby oil, and lotions, can destroy latex products.
10. Remove the penis from the partner immediately after ejaculation, before the penis loses its erection. Hold the condom securely on the base of the penis while withdrawing it from the partner, and be careful not to spill the contents.
11. Never reuse a condom.

NATIONAL DATA Data from the 1991 follow-up survey of the National Survey of Adolescent Males (NSAM) were collected from 1,676 young men aged 17–22. Of those men using condoms in the previous 12 months, 23% experienced at least one condom break. Of all condoms used, 2.5% broke (Lindberg, Sonenstein, Ku, & Levine, 1997).

The NSAM survey found that experience with condoms and knowledge about them seemed to reduce the risk of condom breakage. Unfortunately, only about half of the men who had used condoms reported having recent sex education. Because condom failure reduces confidence in the method, education about how to respond to breakage (insert spermicide into the vagina or wash the penis and vulva with soap and water, and seek postcoital contraception) and how to prevent it may encourage condom use (Lindberg et al., 1997).

Condoms may be less effective when used during anal intercourse than vaginal intercourse because condom breakage and slippage rates may be higher. In a review of the literature on condom slippage and breakage during anal intercourse, Silverman and Gross (1997) reported that in retrospective surveys, in which participants were asked to recall the number of condoms used during a particular period and the number that had failed during anal intercourse, rates of condom breakage ranged from 0.5% to 6% and slippage rates ranged from 3.8% to 5%. In prospective studies, in which participants were followed over a period of time to elicit condom use, slippage, and breakage experience, slippage rates ranged from 0% to 33% and breakage rates ranged from 0% to 32 %. Finally, condoms do not protect against all STDs because some STD infections, such as HPV and herpes, can occur on the testicles, around the anus, and in other areas that are not protected by the condom.

Research on condom use has identified a number of factors that influence whether an individual uses condoms. These factors include the following:

- Perceived susceptibility (the degree to which an individual feels he or she is at risk for contracting an STD)
- Perceived seriousness of STDs (the degree to which an individual views STDs as having severe or serious consequences)
- Belief that using condoms will reduce the risk of STDs
- Belief that the benefits of using condoms will outweigh any of the costs (inconvenience, decreased pleasure, expense, and so on)
- Sense of *self-efficacy* regarding condom use; that is, the person's belief that he or she has the skills and abilities necessary to use condoms in a variety of circumstances in the face of various obstacles, such as a reluctant or unwilling partner
- A person's intention to use condoms
- A person's perception of the degree to which social norms expect condom use

One of the more controversial STD prevention strategies involves making condoms available to high school students. Box 14-2 looks at this controversy.

Attitudes toward pregnancy prevention and use of other birth control methods also influence condom use. A study of nearly 2,900 high school students in Miami revealed that the more the students knew about HIV and AIDS, the less emphasis they placed on pregnancy prevention, and as the importance of pregnancy prevention decreased, so did the frequency of using condoms (Langer, Zimmerman, & Katz, 1997). Young men who were dating someone steadily and who felt pregnancy prevention was more important than AIDS prevention were the most likely to report they used condoms often. Female, Hispanic, and African American students were the most likely to put equal emphasis on pregnancy and AIDS prevention. A study of women served in 17 clinics in southeastern Texas found that most women who selected an injectable contraceptive did not use condoms to protect themselves from STD exposure (Sangi-Haghpeykar, Poindexter, & Bateman, 1997).

Box 14-2 Up Close

Factors Involved in "Hookups"

By the time they reach the 12th grade, the majority of U.S. students have engaged in sexual intercourse. Unprotected teenage sexual activity contributes to teenage pregnancy and the high rate of STDs among adolescents, who constitute one quarter of the 12 million new STD cases each year. School programs that provide condoms are designed to reduce teenage pregnancy and the spread of STDs by increasing condom use; they do so by reducing teenagers' embarrassment when buying condoms, eliminating the cost, and improving access. An evaluation of a small sample of students from Philadelphia high schools, nine of which implemented health resource drop-in centers (offering reproductive health information, condoms, and general health referrals), showed encouraging trends toward a decline in unprotected intercourse in schools making high use of the clinics (Furstenberg, Geitz, Teitler, & Weiss, 1997).

In a survey of 431 U.S. schools that have condom availability programs in place, nearly all offered condoms as part of a more comprehensive program involving other components such as counseling, sex education, or HIV education (Kirby & Brown, 1996). In 81% of the schools in this survey, either active or passive parental consent was required before a student could obtain a condom. Ten percent of schools required active consent, in which students obtained written parental consent to receive condoms. In the 71% of schools that required passive consent, the school sent notices home to parents indicating that they must sign the form or contact someone at the school only if they wished to withhold consent. After parental consent, the second most common requirement was counseling, which was mandatory in about half (49%) of the schools with condom availability programs. "During counseling, students are commonly informed that abstinence is the safest method of protection against STDs; they are also instructed about the proper methods of storing and using condoms" (Kirby & Brown, 1996, p. 199).

In most schools with condom availability programs, condoms are free of charge. Only 3% of schools with such programs make condoms available to students through vending machines, at a cost of about 25 cents per condom. In most condom availability programs, students must ask an adult (principal, teacher, counselor, nurse, or other) for condoms. Only 5% of the schools in the Kirby and Brown survey provided condoms in bowls or baskets.

Chances are, the high school you attended did not make condoms available to students. Only 2.2% of all public high schools and 0.3% of all high school districts in the United States make condoms available to students (Kirby & Brown, 1996). Why are these programs not widely implemented? Some parents are afraid that increased condom availability will encourage students to be more sexually active. However, evaluation of the Philadelphia school health resource centers found that condom availability did not increase the level of sexual activity among the students (Furstenberg et al., 1997). In some states, there are legal restrictions against such programs. Although many states require high schools to provide instruction in HIV or STD prevention, 19 states prohibit or restrict availability of (or in some cases, information about) contraceptives to students through school health and education programs (Committee on Prevention and Control of STDs, 1997). Segments of the population, as well as powerful conservative groups such as the Family Research Council and Focus on the Family, strongly oppose school condom availability on the premise that giving young people condoms might seem to condone their sexual activities or encourage promiscuity. Parents opposed to condom availability programs have filed suits against school districts, claiming that such programs usurped their parental rights. In 1993, a New York state appellate court ruled in favor of those opposed to New York City's school condom availability program, which was the first program in the nation to make condoms available without parental consent. The result was that the public schools implemented the program but allowed parents an "opt-out" option whereby they could send notification to the school if they did not want their children to have access to condoms. Less than 1% of parents of high school students in the New York City school system have chosen that option (Mahler, 1996). More recently, the Massachusetts supreme judicial court upheld a lower court ruling rejecting parents' claim that school condom availability programs violate their rights. The parents challenged the court's ruling, but the U.S. Supreme Court declined to review the case. In refusing to hear this case, "the Supreme Court has, for now, left resolution of these issues in the hands of the states" (Mahler, 1996, p. 77).

Parental opposition to school condom availability programs is in contrast to the recommendation of such organizations as The American School Health Association, the American College of Obstetricians and Gynecologists, the National Medical Association, and the National Institute of Medicine that condoms be made available to adolescents as part of comprehensive school health and STD prevention programs.

At present, it is uncertain whether the public will demand, or even allow, public schools to implement this recommendation throughout the United States. Giving teenagers condoms contradicts moral values that are against nonmarital sexual relations. However, as one school official responded, "This is not a matter of morality, it is a matter of life and death (Seligmann, Beachy, Gordon, McCormick, & Starr, 1991, p. 61).

References

Committee on Prevention and Control of STDs. (1997). The hidden epidemic: Confronting sexually transmitted diseases. SIECUS Report, 25(3), 4–14.

Furstenberg, F. F., Geitz, L. M., Teitler, J. O., & Weiss, C. C. (1997). Does condom availability make a difference? An evaluation of Philadelphia's health resource centers. *Family Planning Perspectives, 29,* 123–127.

Kirby, D. B., & Brown, N. L. (1996). Condom availability programs in U.S. schools. *Family Planning Perspectives, 28,* 196–202.

Mahler, K. (1996). Condom availability in the schools: Lessons from the courtroom. *Family Planning Perspectives, 28*(2), 75–77.

Seligmann, J., Beachy, L., Gordon, J., McCormick, J., & Starr, M. (1991, December 9). Condoms in the classroom. *Newsweek,* 61.

Numerous school, clinic, and community programs have been designed and implemented to prevent STDs by modifying high-risk sexual behaviors. HIV and STD prevention programs utilize a variety of instructional techniques, including group discussions, role-plays, lectures, videos, and peer counseling. Such programs typically provide education about sex, STDs, and contraception; encourage abstinence and responsible sexual decision making; teach behavioral skills in sexual communication and condom use; and provide condoms (Card et al., 1996).

14-6b Public and Private Sexual Health Services

Sexual health services, including STD screening, diagnostic testing, and treatment for STDs, are provided by public clinics, agencies, health centers, and private health-care providers. A screening test, or a test used for screening purposes, is one that is applied to someone with no symptoms or signs of the disease being assessed. If the person has either symptoms or signs of a particular STD, the test is not a screening test but a diagnostic test. In addition to screening, diagnostic testing, and STD treatment, sexual health services may perform the following functions:

- Identify persons who are unaware, misinformed, or in denial of their risks for HIV and other STDs and facilitate an accurate self-perception of risks
- Teach clients how to reduce their risks of acquiring or transmitting an STD
- Refer clients to resources providing psychosocial support to facilitate desired behavior changes
- Provide referrals to drug treatment services for clients whose substance abuse problems increase their STD risks
- Provide family planning information and referrals for women of childbearing ages who are infected or at high risk for contracting HIV or other STDs
- Provide referrals for any necessary medical and psychosocial services
- Communicate to clients the responsibility to notify sex and needle-sharing partners

Most public health departments, community health centers, and other agencies (such as Planned Parenthood) also provide condoms free of charge (Frost & Bolzan, 1997). Primary health-care providers (pediatricians, family physicians, nurse practitioners, and physician assistants), in both public and private settings, can play an important role in preventing STD transmission. However, many primary providers neglect to assess their clients' risk behaviors, screen for STDs, or provide counseling concerning safer sex. One study found that in a sample of more than 2,000 teenage females, only 57% of those who were sexually experienced had ever had a pelvic exam (Paperny, 1997). Despite the prevalence of chlamydia among adolescents, one study done in San Diego, California, revealed that less than half of primary health-care clinicians who provided adolescent health care routinely screened sexually active adolescent girls for chlamydia; less than 20% routinely screened sexually active boys (Gunn, Veinbergs, & Friedman, 1997). The researchers recommended that primary care providers expand routine chlamydia screening to all sexually active adolescents.

Cost is one barrier to STD services; in addition, many individuals do not have easy access to sexual health services. To improve accessibility, more STD prevention and control programs need to be delivered through alternative approaches, such as school health programs, peer teen outreach, and mobile clinics.

14-6c Syringe-Exchange Programs

Syringe-exchange programs Programs designed to reduce the transmission of HIV that is associated with drug injection by providing sterile syringes in exchange for used, potentially HIV-contaminated syringes.

Syringe-exchange programs are designed to reduce the transmission of HIV that is associated with drug injection by providing sterile syringes in exchange for used, potentially HIV-contaminated syringes. (Another method is to sterilize a shared needle with bleach after each use.) Other services that are sometimes provided by such programs include latex condom distribution, HIV testing and counseling, primary health-care services, and outreach efforts to reach subpopulations of intravenous drug users (such as youth, the homeless, or those who inject steroids).

Syringe-exchange programs are a major component of HIV-prevention strategies in most developed countries. In the United States, these programs are controversial. Advocates point to the importance of providing sterile needles for drug users to prevent HIV transmission. Critics, on the other hand, argue that syringe-exchange programs condone and promote drug use and have successfully lobbied for a federal ban that prohibits federal spending on syringe-exchange programs.

Despite the controversy over, and lack of federal support for, syringe-exchange programs, there has been a rapid growth of such programs. The majority of syringe-exchange programs (70%) operate in five states: California, New York, Washington, Connecticut, and Hawaii. In a 1995 survey of 60 syringe-exchange programs, 33 reported that they operated in a state in which such programs were legal (55%); the remaining 27 programs (45%) operated in a state in which they were illegal (Paone, Des Jarlais, Clark, & Shi, 1996). The legal status of a program affected the services it delivered. Programs that had legal status tended to have adequate supplies, funding for adequate disposal of biohazardous wastes, more operating hours, and formal arrangements with drug-treatment programs. The researchers strongly suggest expansion of syringe-exchange programs by lifting the ban on federal funding and repealing state laws that make them illegal.

14-6d Computer Technology: A Revolution in STD Intervention

Federal, state, and local governments each provide funding of public sexual health services at STD clinics and health departments. However, government downsizing, the economic crises faced by some large jurisdictions (including Los Angeles and the District of Columbia), and the increased need for sexual health services that accompanied the HIV/AIDS epidemic has left many public sexual health facilities short on staff and funds. In response to these cutbacks, clinics of the future are expected to implement computer technology that will perform a range of functions, including eliciting personal and confidential behavioral risk data from clients, gathering medical and social data, generating personalized scripts (including educational messages), referring patients to other providers, and providing specific risk-reducing behavioral information and material. "Implementing modern computer technology into the clinic setting can decrease the number of support staff, essentially do away with paper functions such as record keeping and laboratory surveillance, supplement behavioral risk assessments of clients, and deliver interventions such as counseling" (Conlon, 1997, p.13).

Computer technology in sexual health-care facilities may not only reduce the cost of providing such services (fewer staff are needed), but also may provide more reliable information about clients' symptoms, high-risk behaviors, and sexual histories. Traditionally, sexual health-care providers have obtained such sensitive information through face-to face interviews. But individuals, especially adolescents, are reluctant to divulge sexual and drug use information due to guilt, embarrassment, mistrust, and fear of disapproval. An interactive multimedia computer program called Youth Health Provider was designed to obtain a thorough behavioral and health history, identify problem areas and health needs, provide problem-specific health advice and local referrals, administer health education videos, and dispense specific printed take-home materials. Examples of questions asked by the Youth Health Provider computer program include "Does it burn or hurt when you urinate or pee lately?" and "Would you like to learn more about how not to get STDs?" The program also asks participants if they have any lumps or sores in, on, or around their genitals or have experienced any pus, drip, or discharge from their penises or vaginas. Of more than 4,000 teens ages 13–19 who used the Youth Health Provider program, 85% indicated they were totally honest in responding to the computer's questions, and 89% said they preferred the computer interview over a face-to-face interview or written questionnaire (Paperny, 1997).

Evaluation research on computer technology designed to reduce HIV/STD risk has shown promising results. One such series of interactive video programs, "The Choice Is Yours—Preventing HIV/STDs," was designed to provide the decision-making skills and information necessary to make competent decisions, and to teach the social skills needed to deal safely with sexual situations (Noell, Ary, & Duncan, 1997). Separate programs were developed for each of three races (Hispanic, African American, and White) at each of two age levels (middle school and high school). In a randomized experiment involving 827 students, those who participated in the video program showed significant changes in their believing that sex occurs as a result of decisions (versus "it just happens"), their believing that even a single incident of unprotected sex can result in an STD or pregnancy, their intentions and attitudes toward the use of condoms, and their self-efficacy in remaining abstinent.

In addition to "The Choice Is Yours" program, various interactive computer programs have been developed to help prevent transmission of HIV/STDs. "Life Challenge," developed by the New York State Department of Health, uses a time travel/adventure game format to provide information on STDs and allow participants to practice negotiating safe sex with a partner. Users record and play back their responses as they negotiate with their selected computerized partner about whether to have sex and whether to use a condom. An evaluation of the program found that users had significant gains in STD knowledge and self-efficacy scores (Thomas, Cahill, & Santilli, 1997).

The various programs, services, and technology designed to control and prevent sexually transmitted diseases require public support and funding. In an era of spending cutbacks, securing funds for STD prevention and control is an ongoing challenge. With this challenge comes the opportunity to reduce disease and death and the opportunity to improve the health and well-being of the U.S. population.

Think About It

Suppose you are responsible for deciding whether condoms should be available in the public school system your children are attending. What would you recommend and why? How would you respond to disagreements with your recommendation?

SUMMARY

As more individuals have more sex with more partners, the risk of contracting a sexually transmitted disease increases. The physical, psychological, and economic effects of STDs can be dramatic; thus, individual and social efforts to prevent and treat STDs are warranted.

Sexually Transmitted Diseases: An Overview

Sexually transmitted diseases are those caused by any of more than 25 infectious organisms that are transmitted primarily through sexual activity. Person-to-person sexual contact is the main mode of infection, with vaginal and anal intercourse providing the most efficient transmission; the infections can also be transmitted orally. In the past 20 years eight new STDs have been identified, the most well known of which is HIV/AIDS. STDs are known as "hidden epidemics" and are a threat to the health and economy of the United States.

Despite the fact that much information has been learned on STDs, many people remain largely ignorant of these diseases. The vulnerability of young people to infection is compounded by their lack of knowledge. For example, in Sub-Saharan Africa, half of teenage girls do not realized that a healthy-looking person can be infected with human immunodeficiency virus (HIV).

Sexually Transmitted Diseases: A Pandemic

Individuals in the United States have a one in four chance of contracting an STD. Globally, 60% of women have an STD. Each day, more than a million people contract an STD. Worldwide 40 million people have AIDS, with HIV/AIDS the fourth leading cause of death.

Modes of Transmission, Symptoms, and Treatment for STDs

The main agents responsible for STDs are bacteria, protozoa, and viruses. STDs caused by bacteria and protozoa can generally be cured through treatment with antibiotics. Treatment for viral STDs is palliative (may relieve symptoms or slow down the disease progression, but does not cure the disease).

Infections of the lower reproductive tract include vulvitis, chancroid, pubic lice, scabies, herpes, human papillomavirus (HPV), molluscum contagiosum, and vaginitis. Infections of the cervical and upper reproductive tract include chlamydia, gonorrhea, nongonococcal urethritis (NGU), and syphilis. Systemic infections include human immunodeficiency virus (HIV), which may lead to acquired immunodeficiency syndrome (AIDS).

STDs are transmitted through sexual contact, intravenous drug use, blood transfusion, mother-child transmission of HIV, organ or tissue transplants, donor semen, and occupational transmission of HIV. Treatment for HIV and AIDS includes taking drugs as well as adopting lifestyle habits that promote well-being: a balanced diet, ample rest, regular exercise, and relaxation.

Who Is at Risk for STD Infection?

Persons most at risk for an STD infection have a high number of sexual partners or have sex with those who have had a high number of sexual partners, are not married, are adolescents and young adults, are female, use drugs, have been physically/sexually abused, and are of lower socioeconomic and minority status. Individuals also likely to become infected engage in high-risk sexual behavior such as unprotected anal and vaginal intercourse and sharing needles.

Consequences of Sexually Transmitted Diseases

Consequences of contracting a sexually transmitted disease include damage to one's health (infections, infertility, ectopic pregnancy, chronic abdominal pain, blindness, and death), finances (annual costs for HIV treatment average $11,000), and mental health (shock, withdrawal from social interaction, anger, fear, shame, and depression).

Prevention and Control of Sexually Transmitted Diseases

Due to the serious health consequences of AIDS, STD prevention and control efforts in recent years have focused largely on preventing transmission of HIV. However, given the potentially serious health consequences of other STDs—including the increased susceptibility to HIV infection—prevention and control of all STDs are warranted. The most reliable ways to avoid getting a sexually transmitted disease are to reduce risky sexual contact and to avoid injecting illicit drugs.

Individuals (including virgins) who are sexually active may reduce their risks of acquiring an STD by having sexual contact with only one partner who is not infected, who is monogamous, and who does not inject drugs. Rather than rush into sexual relationships, allow time to build trusting, caring, and honest relationships in which you can share your sexual histories. Physical intimacy and pleasure may be achieved by practicing outercourse—activities that do not involve exposing a partner to blood, semen, or vaginal secretions. Outercourse includes hugging, cuddling, masturbating, fantasizing, massaging, and rubbing body to body while clothed. Also, carefully inspect your partner's genitals before sexual contact, as well as your own. Although some STDs produce no visible signs, it is possible to see herpes blisters, chancres, genital warts, and rashes. If you notice anything unusual about your partner's genitals (or your own), abstain from sexual contact and seek a medical examination.

SUGGESTED WEBSITES

Note: These websites were functional when we went to press. Please access the online text for the most up-to-date URLs.

American Social Health Association
http://www.ashastd.org

Centers for Disease Control
http://www.cdc.gov/

World Health Organization
http://www.who.int/health-topics/std.htm

HIV/AIDS

American Foundation for AIDS Research (amfAR)
http://www.amfar.org
(Note the HIV/AIDS Timeline: 1981–2000)

Joint United Nations Programme on HIV/AIDS
http://www.unaids.org

Medline on STDs
http://www.nlm.nih.gov/medlineplus/sexuallytransmitteddiseases.html

Prevention
http://www.cdc.gov/nchstp/dstd/dstdp.html

Sexual Library
http://www.sexuality.org

KEY TERMS

acquired immunodeficiency syndrome (AIDS) (p. 419)
asymptomatic (p. 411)
candidiasis (p. 412)
cervical ectopy (p. 423)
chancroid (p. 413)
chlamydia (p. 416)
genital herpes (p. 413)
genital warts (p. 414)
gonorrhea (p. 416)
hepatitis B (p. 421)
herpes simplex virus type 1 (HSV-1) (p. 413)
herpes simplex virus type 2 (HSV-2) (p. 413)
highly active antiretroviral therapy (HAART) (p. 421)
human immunodeficiency virus (HIV) (p. 419)
human papillomavirus (HPV) (p. 414)
Lazarus Syndrome (p. 421)
long-term nonprogressor (LTNP) (p. 421)
nongonococcal urethritis (NGU) (p. 416)
oral herpes (p. 413)
pelvic inflammatory disease (PID) (p. 428)
pubic lice (p. 413)
sexually transmitted disease (STD) (p. 410)
sexually transmitted infection (STI) (p. 410)
syringe-exchange programs (p. 434)
syphilis (p. 417)
vaginitis (p. 415)

CHAPTER QUIZ

1. Many STDs are asymptomatic, which means that
a. they do not produce symptoms or signs.
b. the symptoms get worse over time.
c. the symptoms get better over time.
d. the symptoms can be treated with medication.

2. In the United States, at least one person in ___________ will contract an STD at some point in his or her lifetime (SIECUS Fact Sheet, 1997).
a. 4
b. 10
c. 40
d. 100

3. In ___________, HIV/AIDS is the leading cause of death.
a. the United States
b. China
c. Sub-Saharan Africa
d. none of the above

4. Candidiasis, also known as monilia and yeast infection, ___________ be spread to a partner.
a. can
b. cannot

5. Most people who have genital herpes ___________ they are infected.
a. know
b. do not know

6. Which of the following STDs can cause genital warts?
a. herpes
b. chlamydia
c. syphilis
d. human papillomavirus

7. Which of the following is the most common bacterial STD in the United States?
a. Gardnerella
b. gonorrhea
c. chlamydia
d. syphilis

8. Although the symptoms of untreated chlamydia may cause discomfort, there are no serious effects of leaving chlamydia untreated.
a. True
b. False

9. Gonorrhea is treated with which of the following?
a. laser surgery
b. cortisone ointment
c. antibiotics
d. none of the above

10. Syphilis can be transmitted through which of the following?
a. kissing
b. genital contact
c. from an infected pregnant woman to her unborn baby
d. all the above

11. Which of the following STDs progresses through stages (primary, secondary, latent, and tertiary)?
   a. syphilis
   b. gonorrhea
   c. HIV/AIDS
   d. human papillomavirus

12. Which of the following BEST represents the current definition of AIDS?
   a. an HIV-infected person who has developed an opportunistic disease
   b. a person infected with HIV
   c. a person infected with HIV who has a high T-cell count (greater than 800)
   d. a person infected with HIV who has a low T-cell count (less than 200)

13. Some people with ___________ experience what has been referred to as the Lazarus Syndrome.
   a. syphilis
   b. herpes
   c. human papillomavirus
   d. AIDS

14. Rates of STDs are higher among populations that are economically
   a. advantaged.
   b. disadvantaged.

15. One type of HIV test can be bought at pharmacies, college health centers, and public health clinics, or it can be ordered through the mail for a cost of around $50. The test involves obtaining a sample of ___________ and mailing it to a laboratory.
   a. blood
   b. hair
   c. urine
   d. saliva

16. Most public high schools in the United States ___________ condoms available to students.
   a. make
   b. do not make

REFERENCES

Alan Guttmacher Institute. (2002). *In their own right: Addressing the sexual and reproductive health needs of American men*. New York: Author.

amfAR Global Link. (2003). *Preventing mother-to-child transmission highlights from Durban conference*. Retrieved March, 25, 2003, from http://www.amfar.org/cgibin/iowa/td/conf/record.html?record=25&page=4

Aral, S. O. (1996). The social context of syphilis persistence in the southeastern United States. *Sexually Transmitted Diseases, 23*(1), 9–15.

Aral, S. O., & Holmes, K. K. (1991). Sexually transmitted diseases in the AIDS era. *Scientific American, 264*, 62–69.

Associated Press. (2002, June 13). Group tries to show possibility of bringing AIDS drugs to poor. *The Daily Reflector*, Greenville, NC, p. A7.

Berreby, D. (1989, May). Contagious fortune: A less than cheery report about the sex disease in your future. MS, 30–32.

Brown, L. K., Lourie, K. J., Zlotnich, C., & Cohn, J. (2000). Impact of sexual abuse on the HIV-risk-related behavior of adolescents in intensive psychiatric treatment. *The American Journal of Psychiatry, 157*, 1413–1415.

Callahan, T. L., Caughey, A. B., & Heffner, L. J. (1998). *Blueprints in Obstetrics & Gynecology*. Oxford: Blackwell Science.

Card, J. J., Niego, S., Mallari, A., & Farrell, W. S. (1996). The program archive on sexuality health & adolescence: Promising "prevention programs in a box." *Family Planning Perspectives*, 28, 210–220.

Centers for Disease Control. (1995). *Summary of notifiable diseases, United States, 1995*. Washington, DC: U.S. Department of Health and Human Services.

Centers for Disease Control. (1998). *Trends in the HIV & AIDS epidemic*. Retrieved February 12, 2002, from http://www.cdc.gov/hiv/pubs

Centers for Disease Control. (2001). *Tracking the hidden epidemics: Trends in STDs in the United States 2000*. Retrieved February 12, 2002, from www.cdc.gov/nchstp/od/news/RevBrochure1pdfmag.htm

Centers for Disease Control. (2002, November 1). Overall syphilis rate rises for first time since 1990. Press Release. Retrieved March 26, 2003, from www.cdc.gov/od/oc/media/pressrel/r021101b.htm

Chernesky, M. A. (1997). How can industry, academia, public health authorities, and the sexually transmitted diseases diagnostics initiative work together to help control sexually transmitted diseases in developing countries? *Sexually Transmitted Diseases, 24*(2), 61–63.

Cohen, M. S., Hoffman, I. E., Royce, R. A., Kazembe, E., Dyer, J. R., Daly, C. C., et al. (1997). Reduction of concentration of HIV-1 in semen after treatment of urethritis: Implications for prevention of sexual transmission of HIV-1. *Lancet, 349*(9069), 1868–1873.

Committee on Prevention and Control of STDs. (1997). The hidden epidemic: Confronting sexually transmitted diseases. *SIECUS Report, 25*(3), 4–14.

Conlon, R. T. (1997). Introducing technology into the public STD clinic. *Health Education & Behavior, 24*(1), 12–19.

Cooper, M., Pierce, R. S., & Farmer Huselid, R. (1994). Substance use and sexual risk taking among black adolescents and white adolescents. *Health Psychology, 13*(3), 251–262.

Credle, B. (2002, November 4). Sexually transmitted infections. A presentation to "Courtship and Marriage" class at East Carolina University, Greenville, NC.

Demmer, C. (2000). Grief and survival in the era of HIV treatment advances. *Illness, Crisis & Loss*, 8, 5–16.

Ebel, C., & Wald, A. (2002). *Managing herpes: How to live and love with a chronic STD*. Research Triangle Park, NC: American Social Health Association.

Eng, T. R., & Butler, W. T. (Eds.). (1997). *The hidden epidemic: Confronting sexually transmitted diseases*. Institute of Medicine, Division of Health Promotion and Disease Prevention. Washington, DC: National Academy Press.

Exner, T. M., Hoffman, S., Parikh, K., Leu, C.-S., & Ehrhardt, A. A. (2002). HIV counseling and testing: Women's experiences and the perceived role of testing as a prevention strategy. *Perspectives on Sexual and Reproductive Health, 34*, 76–83.

Finer, L. B., Darroch, J. E., & Singh, S. (1999). Sexual partnership patterns as a behavioral risk factor for sexually transmitted diseases. *Family Planning Perspectives, 31*, 228–236.

Fleishman, J. A., & Fogel, B. (1994). Coping and depressive symptoms among people with AIDS. *Health Psychology, 13*(2), 156–169.

Fleming, D. T., McQuillan, G. M., Johnson, R. E., Nahmias, A. J., Aral, S. O., Lee, E. K., et al. (1997). Herpes simplex virus type 2 in the United States: 1976–1994. *New England Journal of Medicine, 333*(16), 1105–1111.

Forrest, J. D., & Silverman, J. (1989). What public school teachers teach about preventing pregnancy, AIDS and sexually transmitted diseases. *Family Planning Perspectives, 21*, 65–72.

Frost, J. J., & Bolzan, M. (1997). The provision of public sector services by family planning agencies in 1995. *Family Planning Perspectives, 29*(1), 6–14.

Furstenberg, F. F., Geitz, L. M., Teitler, J. O., & Weiss, C. C. (1997). Does condom availability make a difference? An evaluation of Philadelphia's health resource centers. *Family Planning Perspectives, 29*, 123–127.

Gordon, C. M., & Carey, M. P. (1996). Alcohol's effects on requisites for sexual risk reduction in men: An initial experimental investigation. *Health Psychology, 15*, 56–60.

Gorman, C. (1996, February 12). Battling the AIDS virus. *Time*, 62–65.

Gunn, R. A., Veinbergs, E., & Friedman, L. S. (1997). Notes from the field: Adolescent health care providers: Establishing a dialogue and assessing sexually transmitted disease prevention practices. *Sexually Transmitted Diseases, 24*(2), 90–93.

Hankins, C. (1996). Sexual transmission of HIV to women in industrialized countries. *World Health Statistics Quarterly, 49*, 106–112.

Healthy People 2010. (2002). *Sexually transmitted diseases*. Retrieved July 5, 2002, from http://web.health.gov/healthypeople/Document/HTML/Volume2/25STDs.htm

Helweg-Larsen, M., & Collins, B. E. (1994). The UCLA multidimensional condom attitudes scale: Documenting the complex determinants of condom use in college students. *Health Psychology, 13*(3), 224–237.

Innate immunity and interferon. (2002). *Basic research updates from Barcelona: Selected highlights from the XIV international AIDS conference*. Retrieved July 30, 2002, from www.amfar.org/cgibin/iowa/researchb/record.html?record=171

Johnson, P. J., & Hellerstedt, W. L. (2002). Current or past physical or sexual abuse as a risk marker for sexually transmitted disease in pregnant women. *Perspectives on Sexual and Reproductive Health, 34*, 62–67.

Kerr, D. L. (1990). AIDS SPEAK: Sensitive and accurate communication and the HIV epidemic. *Journal of School Health, 60*, 431–432.

Kirby, D. B., & Brown, N. L. (1996). Condom availability programs in U.S. schools. *Family Planning Perspectives, 28*, 196–202.

Langer, L. M., Zimmerman, R. S., & Katz, J. (1997). Which is more important to high school students: Preventing pregnancy or preventing AIDS? *Family Planning Perspectives, 29*, 67–69, 75.

Lindberg, A. D., Sonenstein, E. L., Ku, L., & Levine, G. (1997). Young men's experience with condom breakage. *Family Planning Perspectives, 29*, 128–131, 140.

Mahler, K. (1996). Condom availability in the schools: Lessons from the courtroom. *Family Planning Perspectives, 28*(2), 75–77.

Mays, V. M., Cochran, S. D., Pies, C., Chu, S. Y., & Ehrhardt, A. (1996). The risk of HIV infection for lesbians and other women who have sex with women: Implications for HIV research, prevention, policy, and services. *Women's Health: Research on Gender, Behavior, and Policy, 2*, 119–139.

McKay, J. (2000). *The Penguin atlas of human sexual behavior: Sexuality and sexual practice around the world*. New York: Penguin.

Michael, R. T., Gagnon, J. H., Laumann, E. O., & Kolata, G. (1994). *Sex in America: A definitive survey*. Boston: Little, Brown. (1994).

Miller, H. G., Cain, V. S., Rogers, S. M., Gribble, J. N., & Turner, C. F. (1999). Correlates of sexually transmitted bacterial infections among U.S. women in 1995. *Family Planning Perspectives, 31*, 4–9, 23.

1997 UNFPA Report—The Right to Choose: Reproductive Rights and Health. (1997). *Popline* (World Population News Service), *19*, 4–5.

Noell, J., Ary, D., & Duncan, T. (1997). Development and evaluation of a sexual decision-making and social skills program: "The Choice Is Yours—Preventing HIV/STDs." *Health Education & Behavior, 24*(1), 87–101.

Paone, D., Des Jarlais, D., Clark, J., & Shi, Q. (1996). Syringe exchange programs in the United States: Where are we now? *AIDS & Public Policy Journal, 11*(3), 144–147.

Paperny, D. M. N. (1997). Computerized health assessment and education for adolescent HIV and STD prevention in health care settings and schools. *Health Education & Behavior, 24*(1), 54–70.

Personal perspectives. (1997, Summer). *The Helper, 19*(2), 3–4,11.

Pinkerton, S. D., & Abramson, P. R. (1997). Condoms and the prevention of AIDS. *American Scientist, 85*, 364–373.

Pinon, R., Jr. (2002). *Biology of Human Reproduction*, Sausalito, CA: University Science Books.

Ross, M. W., & Schonnesson, L. N. (2000). HIV/AIDS and sexuality. In L. T. Szuchman & F. Muscarella (Eds.), *Psychological perspectives on human sexuality* (pp. 383–415). New York: Wiley.

Sangi-Haghpeykar, H., Poindexter, A. N., III, & Bateman, L. (1997). Consistency of condom use among users of injectable contraceptives. *Family Planning Perspectives, 29*, 67–69, 75.

Schuster, M. A., Bell, R. M., & Kanouse, D. E. (1996). The sexual practices of adolescent virgins: Genital sexual activities of high school students who have never had vaginal intercourse. *American Journal of Public Health, 86*, 1570–1576.

Seligmann, J., Beachy, L., Gordon, J., McCormick, J., & Starr, M. (1991, December 9). Condoms in the classroom. *Newsweek*, 61.

SIECUS. (2002). *Knowledge empowers–knowledge saves lives. Comprehensive sexuality education and HIV/AIDS*. Retrieved July 5, 2002, from www.siecus.org/media/press/hivaids factsheet.pdf

SIECUS Fact Sheet. (1997). Sexually transmitted diseases in the United States. *SIECUS Report, 25*(3), 22–24.

Silverman, B. G., & Gross, T. P. (1997). Use and effectiveness of condoms during anal intercourse. *Sexually Transmitted Diseases, 24*(1), 11–17.

Stover, J., Walker, N., Garnett, G. P., Salomon, J. A., Stanecki, K. A., Ghys, P., et al. (2002). Can we reverse the HIV/AIDS pandemic with an expanded response? *Lancet, 360*, 73–77.

Thomas, R., Cahill, J., & Santilli, L. (1997). Using an interactive computer game to increase skill and self efficacy regarding safer sex negotiation: Field results. *Health Education and Behavior, 24*, 71–86.

Tobin, M. (1997). Sexually transmitted diseases. In J. Rosenfeld (Ed.), *Women's Health in Primary Care* (pp. 383–397). Baltimore, MD: Williams & Wilkins.

UNAIDS. (December, 2001). *AIDS epidemic update. Joint United Nations Programme on HIV/AIDS (UNAIDS) and World Health Organization (WHO)*. Retrieved July 5, 2002, from http://www.UNAIDS.org/epidemic_update/report_dec01/index.html#full

UNAIDS. (2002a). *Focus: AIDS and young people*. Retrieved July 5, 2002, from http://www.unaids.org/barcelona/presskit/embargo.htm

UNAIDS. (2002b). *Weekly Epidemiological Record* of the World Health Organization and Joint United Nations Programme on HIV/AIDS UNAIDS Report on the Global HIV/AIDS Epidemic. Geneva, Switzerland: Author.

Wingood, G. M., DiClemente, R. J., & Raj, A. (2000). Adverse consequences of intimate partner abuse among women in non-urban domestic violence shelters. *American Journal of Preventive Medicine, 19*, 270–275.

Winning the war in your mind. (1997, Spring). *The Helper, 19*(1), 1, 5–7.

15

Sexual Dysfunctions and Sex Therapy

Chapter Outline

The obsessive focus on getting the genitals to perform properly, if not perfectly, results in the neglect of much of what makes sexual problems so complex—personally and theoretically. First on the list would be the relational aspects of sexual experience.

—Lenore Tiefer, psychologist

A common belief among clinicians who treat sexual dysfunctions is that when a couple's sex life is good, it is about 15% of the relationship, but when the sex is bad, it becomes a focus of the relationship. Psychiatrist Robert Sammons notes among the couples he sees, "the only thing that's important is that which is missing" (personal communication, 2002). So regardless of how well everything else is in a couple's relationship, for some couples a bad sex life spells gloom and doom. Although Sammons's statement may be an oversimplification of the complexity of relationships and an overstatement of the importance of sex in relationships, it emphasizes the association between sexual and relationship satisfaction. Because more than a third of both adult women and men report having had at least one sexual problem in the past 12 months (Laumann, Paik, & Rosen, 2001), detailed discussion of sexual dysfunctions seems warranted.

15-1 DEFINITIONS OF SEXUAL DYSFUNCTIONS

Sexual dysfunction An impairment or difficulty that affects sexual functioning or produces sexual pain.

A **sexual dysfunction** is an impairment or difficulty that affects sexual functioning or produces sexual pain.

NATIONAL DATA Based on data from the National Health and Social Life Survey, 31% of men and 43% of women reported having had at least one major sexual dysfunction in the past 12 months (Laumann et al., 2001, p. 369). However, it should be noted that these "dysfunctions" were not clinical diagnoses but reports of experiencing any of the listed sexual problems (lack of sexual desire, anxiety about sexual performance, lubrication problems, etc.) for 2 months or more during the previous year.

Medicalization of sexual dysfunctions The emphasis that sexual dysfunctions have a medical or biological basis rather than an emotional or relationship cause.

One way to discuss sexual dysfunctions is to do so in terms of the stages in which sexual problems occur across the sexual response cycle. But doing so emphasizes the physical processes within the genitals (the **medicalization of sexual dysfunctions**) rather than a person's or couple's overall emotional relationship and sexual satisfaction. Tiefer (2001a) refers to this as "downplaying the relational aspects of sexual experience" (p. 39). Throughout the discussion of each sexual dysfunction, it is important to keep in mind the cognitions and feelings of the individuals and their partners. From this point of view, a couple may be incapable of sexual intercourse due to one or more sexual dysfunctions, yet may still be happy with one another and their sexual relationship.

Concern about medicalization of male sexual functioning was raised in the 1980s (Bancroft 1982; Tiefer 1986), with discussion of medical causes for sexual problems and searches for medical treatments continuing in the 1990s (Tiefer, 1996). Erectile problems were being managed through penile implants and injections into the cavernosa of the penis, with the promise of oral medication on the horizon. Then, with the advance of sildenafil (Viagra, as discussed in section 15-4a), a "sexuopharmacological solution" was increasingly promoted to address the mechanics of erection, but the interpersonal context of sexual activity with a partner has been neglected. This trend has continued with a "focus on women's sexual problems with a similar medical paradigm emphasizing physical causes, physical aspects of sexual experience, and physiological assessments and treatments for women's sexual problems" (Tiefer, 2001b, p. 890). In this section we summarize recent developments in this area and critiques of this work, and include an alternative model that has been proposed for viewing women's sexual problems.

Sexual dysfunctions occur in both heterosexual and homosexual relationships. Whereas the former are assumed to be normative, gay, bisexual, or transsexual individuals

". . . must find a way to deal with negative cultural myths . . . to counter allegations that they are abnormal or immoral" (Hall, 2001, p. 280). In addition, lesbian and gay couples may be especially likely to encounter specific issues related to sexual dysfunction. Lesbians legitimize their status "by forming permanent partnerships which has implications when sexual problems arise . . . lovers do not part company when the high level of erotic arousal that fuels romantic twosomes fizzles. Instead they bond more closely, determined to overcome whatever obstacle is impeding the progress of their relationship" (p. 281). Although sex therapists must be attentive to nonsexual aspects of a dysfunction, such a focus for lesbian couples may be a prerequisite. Same-sex male couples may also bring unique issues to sex therapy. Although HIV status is not unique to same-sex couples, Carballo-Dieguez and Remien (2001) noted that as HIV illness progresses, "loss of sexual interest, erectile dysfunction, and endocrine abnormalities are likely to appear" (p. 302). The researchers also noted that the drugs taken to inhibit the disease may slow progress in sex therapy.

In this chapter, we will review sexual dysfunctions as they are classified in the *Diagnostic and Statistical Manual of Mental Disorders, Fourth Edition* (commonly referred to as *DSM-IV-TR*; American Psychiatric Association, 2000). Clinicians and researchers from many disciplines, including physicians, psychologists, social workers, nurses, and other health and mental health professionals, use this handbook. Although its title implies that mental disorders are distinct from physical disorders, there is much overlap between them, and the term *mental disorders* is used because an appropriate substitute has not been found. "A compelling literature documents that there is much 'physical' in 'mental' disorders and much 'mental' in 'physical' disorders" (American Psychiatric Association, 2000, p. xxx). This is certainly true in reference to sexual problems. Aside from the *DSM* implication that sexual problems are "mental" problems, another criticism, particularly in regard to female sexual problems, is that it tends to reflect a heterosexual, phallocentric model of sexual behavior, with intercourse being considered the gold standard or referent for many of the diagnoses (Leiblum, 2000, p.121). Although we have mentioned some criticisms of the *DSM-IV-TR*, it remains a very widely used resource and is the standard diagnostic reference among health and mental health professionals in the United States.

Think About It 

Sexual dysfunctions are not evenly distributed in our population but are more common among younger women and older men, among the unmarried than the married, and among persons reporting less than more education. Quality of life also seems to be associated with the absence of sexual dysfunctions. Women reporting low desire, arousal difficulties, and pain during sex tend to report low physical and emotional satisfaction/happiness. Men with erectile dysfunction and low desire also tend to report less happiness (Laumann et al., 2001). How important do you feel sexual satisfaction is to personal and relationship satisfaction?

A **sexual disorder** is diagnosed when a disturbance in sexual desire or the psychophysiological components of one's sexual response cycle cause significant distress and interpersonal difficulty. The types of dysfunction—organized according to the component of the response cycle affected—are summarized in Table 15-1. Although we will use the sexual response system to discuss sexual dysfunctions, our doing so is not without awareness of the liabilities (particularly in regard to women) of this classification. According to Tavris (2002):

> *Women's sexual lives diverge greatly, and their sexual needs, satisfactions, and problems do not fit neatly into categories of desire, arousal, orgasm or pain. Women differ in their values, approaches to sexuality, social and cultural backgrounds and current situations, and these do not fit well with a single approach to problems—that of dysfunction—or with one-size-fits-all approaches to treatment. (p. 227)*

Sexual disorder Diagnosis that a disturbance in sexual desire or the psychophysiological components of one's sexual response cycle cause significant distress and interpersonal difficulty.

TABLE 15-1

Types of Sexual Dysfunctions in Women and Men

Aspects of Sexuality Affected	Sexual Dysfunction	
	Women	Men
Sexual desire	Hypoactive sexual desire disorder Sexual aversion disorder	Hypoactive sexual desire disorder Sexual aversion disorder
Arousal	Female sexual arousal disorder	Male erectile disorder
Orgasm	Female orgasmic disorder	Male orgasmic disorder Premature ejaculation
Sexual pain	Dyspareunia Vaginismus	Dyspareunia

Lifelong dysfunction A sexual dysfunction that a person has always experienced; for example, a person may have always lacked sexual desire. (See also **primary dysfunction.**)

Primary dysfunction See **lifelong dysfunction.**

Acquired dysfunction Sexual dysfunction that a person is currently experiencing but has not always experienced. (See also **secondary dysfunction.**)

Secondary dysfunction See **acquired dysfunction.**

Situational dysfunction Sexual dysfunction that occurs with one partner or in one situation only.

Generalized dysfunction Sexual dysfunction that occurs with all partners, contexts, and settings.

According to the *DSM-IV-TR*, each of the dysfunctions identified in Table 15-1 may also be classified as being lifelong or acquired. A **lifelong dysfunction** (previously referred to as a **primary dysfunction**) is one that a person has always experienced; for example, a person may have always lacked sexual desire. An **acquired dysfunction,** or **secondary dysfunction,** is one that a person is currently experiencing but has not always experienced. One may also have a **situational dysfunction,** in that it occurs only with one partner or in one situation, or a **generalized dysfunction,** in that it occurs with all partners, contexts, and settings. Basic causes may be organic, psychogenic, mixed, or unknown.

There are alternatives to the *DSM-IV-TR* classification system. The World Health Organization International Classifications of Diseases-10 (ICD-10) categories of sexual dysfunction include such diagnoses as lack or loss of sexual desire, sexual aversion disorder, failure of genital response, orgasmic dysfunction, nonorganic vaginismus, nonorganic dyspareunia, and excessive sexual drive (Basson, Berman et al., 2001). This system also relies heavily on the Masters and Johnson/Kaplan models of the human sexual response cycle model. Both the *DSM-IV-TR* and the ICD-10 include criteria which recognize that the dysfunction causes distress to the person diagnosed. However, dissatisfaction with these classification systems has resulted in efforts to establish more consistent guidelines for clinical diagnosis and treatment plans.

The National Institutes of Health Consensus Development Conference on Impotence, which was convened in 1992, mainly reviewed physical aspects and organic causes for erectile dysfunction and diagnostic guidelines. With the advent of sildenafil, a more recent consensus panel has recommended a revised assessment and treatment model that includes educational interventions and a sequential treatment plan (The Process of Care Consensus Panel, 1999). On a parallel track, a multidisciplinary, international consensus development conference was convened to address the shortcomings of earlier classifications of female sexual dysfunction in 1998 (Basson, Berman et al., 2001). The American Foundation for Urologic Disease convened the first Consensus Development Panel of Female Sexual Dysfunction. The major classification categories of the ICD-10 and *DSM-IV-TR* were maintained, although the definitions of *hypoactive sexual desire* and *sexual arousal disorder* were broadened, and a new category of noncoital sexual pain disorder was added. The addition of a category of sexual satisfaction disorder was debated but not included.

The work of this group has sparked vigorous analysis. The financial interest of participants and strong influence of the pharmaceutical industry sponsors have been pointed out (Bancroft, Graham, & McCord, 2001; Tiefer, 2001b). Bancroft et al. (2001; from the Kinsey Institute for Research in Sex, Gender, and Reproduction) criticized the atheoretical approach taken by the group and suggested conceptualization of women's sexual problems at three levels:

1. The context, or sexual situation, which includes a woman's psychological response to the situation, and how prior experience as well as sociocultural and personality factors may influence her sexual attitudes and response
2. The connection between cognitive processing and physiological response
3. Physiological response, and her reaction to those responses, which may further amplify or inhibit her physiological response

Tiefer and The Working Group on A New View of Women's Sexual Problems (2001b) offered an alternative to medical-oriented classification schemes. The underpinnings of their categories included the recognition that men's and women's sexual responses are not equivalent ; the relational context of sexuality is important; and women vary widely in their sexual needs, satisfactions, and problems (which are not neatly categorized into desire, arousal, orgasm, and pain). The classification they offered defines sexual problems as "discontent or dissatisfaction with any emotional, physical, or relational aspect of sexual experience" (p. 95) that might arise in the following aspects: (a) sociocultural, political, or economic factors; (b) problems relating to partner and relationship; (c) psychological factors; and/or (d) medical factors.

15-2 CAUSES AND CONTRIBUTING FACTORS IN SEXUAL DYSFUNCTIONS

The numerous causes of sexual dysfunctions are described fully in sections 15-2a through 15-2f.

15-2a Organic Factors

Organic and neurophysiological factors are increasingly being considered as causes for sexual dysfunctions (Allard, 2002). Such factors include physical illness, disease, or disability and its treatment (such as surgery, medication, or chemotherapy). Deeks and McCabe (2001) noted that age was a good predictor of sexual frequency and satisfaction. They studied 304 women ages 35–65 and found that the younger the woman, the more satisfaction.

A physical condition (such as diabetes, arthritis, pituitary tumors, or vascular disease) or treatment may also interfere with physiological or anatomical mechanisms involved in sexual desire, arousal, or orgasm. Neurological conditions or diseases such as stroke, multiple sclerosis (MS), Parkinson's disease (PD), epilepsy, and tumors may alter the motor and sensory pathways, "thus affecting participation in and enjoyment of sexual encounters (Kalayjian & Morrell, 2001, p. 94). Ghizzani and Montomoli (2001) emphasized the interplay between anorexia nervosa (excessive weight loss) and its attendant hormonal effects, which may depress sexual desire.

The same organic/biological factors may affect both women and men. Indeed, hypertension and its treatment are associated with sexual dysfunction in both women (Burchardt et al., 2002) and men (Talakoub, Munarriz, Hoag, Gioia, & Goldstein, 2002). And, although diabetes has long been known to be associated with erectile dysfunction in men, some data suggest its deleterious effects in females. Erol et al. (2002) studied 72 young diabetic type II women and found that 77% reported lack of libido (interest in sex) and almost half (49%) reported orgasmic dysfunction. These percentages were significantly higher than a control group of 60 age-matched healthy women. Only 20% of the controls complained of reduced libido. Nevertheless, women who complain of sexual problems are more likely to be healthy than men (Talakoub et al., 2002).

Another common physical cause of sexual dysfunction is fatigue. Gilhooly, Ottenweller, Lange, Tiersky, and Natelson (2001) found that female sexual dysfunction was particularly related to chronic fatigue experienced by Gulf War veterans. For many people, the persistent demands of career, school, children, and domestic tasks leave little physical energy for sexual activity. Fatigue may affect the sexual desire and arousal phases of the sexual response cycle in both women and men.

To test this commonly assumed relationship between work and sex, a team of researchers (Hyde, DeLameter, & Durik, 2001) examined the effect of the wife's employment (whether part or full time) on the sexual relationship satisfaction of 261 couples and found no significant differences. More important was the significance of sex to the spouse and to the relationship than to the number of hours worked. The same was true for husbands: Their work involvement was unrelated to the couple's sexual functioning or satisfaction. Hence, two careers in one marriage do not have a negative effect on a couple's sexual relationship as long as sex is an independent important value.

Although we discuss drugs and sexuality in detail in section 18-9, "Alcohol, Other Drugs, and Sexuality," here we note that alcohol, marijuana, barbiturates, and amphetamines, as well as numerous medications used to treat various diseases and illnesses, affect sexuality and may cause or contribute to sexual dysfunction. Finally, sexual dysfunction often results from a combination of biological and psychosocial factors. For example, a woman may experience a lack of sexual desire because she is chronically fatigued (biological factor) from taking care of young children, a husband, and an aging mother-in-law who lives in the house. Compounding her fatigue is resentment (psychosocial factor) toward her husband for not sharing the child care and/or housework and not helping to care for his mother.

15-2b Sociocultural Factors

In addition to physical or biological factors, sociocultural factors may also cause or contribute to sexual dysfunction. They include restrictive upbringing and religious training. For example, in some families, parents may openly express negative attitudes toward sexuality by teaching their children that "sex is dirty." Some parents punish children and adolescents for engaging in masturbation or other sexual exploration. In many families, sex is never discussed with the children. Children who learn that sex is a taboo subject may come to regard sex as somehow wrong or shameful.

Some religions (Catholicism) teach that sex is only for procreation or that sexual relations are only appropriate if penile-vaginal and between husband and wife (Islam). Persons who depart from cultural scripts may internalize negative feelings about sexuality, and these feelings may interfere with their ability to experience sexual desire, arousal, and orgasm.

Traditionally, Japanese women have low expectations that they will have strong sex desire and do not define its absence as a problem (Kameya, 2001).

Another sociocultural factor that may contribute to sexual dysfunction is society's traditional gender role socialization. Women may be socialized to be sexually passive and to "please their man"; men may be taught to be sexually aggressive and to "be in control" of sexual situations. Women do indeed live in a different sociocultural world than men. Tavris (2002) noted:

> *Social, political, and economic conditions, including poverty and widespread and diverse forms of sexual violence, limit women's access to sexual health, pleasure, and satisfaction in most parts of the world. Women's social environments can prevent the expression of biological capacities, a reality ignored by a strictly physiological framing of sexual dysfunctions. (p. 226)*

Still another sociocultural factor contributing to sexual dysfunction is our society's emphasis on intercourse as "the" sexual act and on orgasm as necessary for satisfaction.

Nongenital sexual expressions and sexual experiences that do not result in orgasm are given little recognition. The result is enormous pressure on couples to engage in "the act" and for orgasm to result.

15-2c Psychological Factors

Numerous psychological factors play a role in sexual dysfunction.

1. *Child sexual abuse*. As noted in section 17-5, "Child Sexual Abuse," sexual abuse is not unusual.

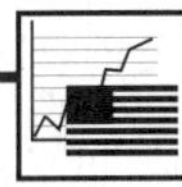

NATIONAL DATA About 25% of adult women and 12% of adult men report having had sexual contact with someone at least 5 years older than them when they were 14 years of age or younger (McDonald & Bradford, 2000)

Such early sexual trauma may significantly negatively impact one's sexual desire, arousal, and orgasm. Maltz (2001) noted:

> *Sexual abuse involves . . . a betrayal of human trust. . . . The years of secrecy, shame, emotional isolation, and feeling unloved and unprotected that often accompany abuse can damage the development of healthy self-esteem and lead to chronic depression, antisocial activity, and self-destructive behavior. . . . Victims may end up hating their bodies for their sexual drives and responses, erroneously believing that something about their sexuality caused the abuse to occur.* (p. 261)

2. *Anxiety*. Anxiety may be aroused by thoughts and fears about sexual performance or the ability to please the partner. Other sources of anxiety may result from fear of intimacy, concern about the partner's commitment to the relationship, fear of rejection, and uncertainty about the partner's intentions, or sexual expectations. Gindin and Resnicoff (2002) reported the treatment of 199 unconsummated marriages and noted that the underlying cause was "sexual anxiety, which shows up as coital phobias, vaginismus, dyspareunia, erectile dysfunction, and ultrapremature ejaculation" (p. 97).

   One specific type of anxiety related to sexual dysfunction is **performance anxiety,** which refers to excessive concern over adequate sexual performance. The woman or man becomes so anxious about having an orgasm or erection that anxiety interferes with both goals.

Performance anxiety Excessive concern over adequate sexual performance, which may result in sexual dysfunction.

3. *Fear*. Impairment in the desire, arousal, or orgasm phases of sexual response may result from fear of any of the following: unwanted pregnancy or sexually transmitted diseases (STDs), intimacy or commitment, physical pain, displeasing a partner, or losing self-control during sexual arousal or orgasm. Fear of "not measuring up" may also be operative (e.g., "I'm too fat and not a good lover"; authors' files).
4. *Guilt*. Guilt, which may be related to the enjoyment of sexual activity, choice of sexual partner (e.g., prostitute), participation in "forbidden" or "sinful" sexual activity, or involvement in an extradyadic sexual relationship, may also interfere with sexual functioning.
5. *Depression and low self-esteem*. Sexual dysfunction may result from depression, which is known to suppress sexual drive. Talakoub et al. (2002) studied 250 women with sexual dysfunction and noted that, although they were otherwise healthy, they "had high levels of personal distress and depression" (p. 234). Basson (2001a) noted that depression is the most common factor inhibiting sexual arousal. Related to depression is low self-esteem, which may cause an individual to feel unworthy of being loved or experiencing pleasure.
6. *Conflict concerning one's sexual orientation*. Because of the social stigma associated with being homosexual, some gay men and lesbians experience internal conflict about their sexual orientation. Some may deny their homosexuality and seek heterosexual relationships, only to find that sexual activity with other-sex individuals doesn't feel right for them.

Box 15-1 Social Choices

Consult a Physician or Psychologist for Sexual Dysfunction?

Although second opinions are often required for major surgery, no public policy protects individuals in regard to the treatment they receive for sexual dysfunctions. Indeed, as discussed earlier, some sex therapists feel that sex therapy is becoming too "medicalized." Tiefer (2001b) lamented that in her 13 years of working in medical center urology departments, she observed "the amount of time devoted to getting the penis hard and the vagina wet vastly outweighs the attention devoted to assessment or education about sexual motives, scripts, pleasure, power, emotionality, sensuality, communication, or connectedness" (p. 90). She repeatedly observed physicians and technicians complete extensive penis function workups with no knowledge of the sexual relationships of the penis owner!

In one urology department study, Tiefer and Melman (1983) found significant discrepancies in the problem descriptions given by most male patients and their female sex partners. Couples had often not even talked with each other about the problems. Talking to their medical care provider might be limited to reporting a cluster of symptoms or completing a checklist handed out by the receptionist. Tiefer (1996) found that "the more routinized the encounter or pressured the time frame . . . the more likely each patient's concern will acquire a medical label and workup. Third-party reimbursement constraints further promote this process" (p. 261). Although conversations about sexual concerns may be embarrassing and difficult (for the patient and the care provider), finding a care provider who does more than merely reaching for a prescription pad is worth the effort.

Certainly, there are physiological bases for sexual dysfunctions, and pharmacological treatment is indicated. But assessment of or education about relational issues such as sexual motives, scripts, power, and emotionality are equally important. Bean (2002) noted in regard to sexual problems presented by women, "Layers of history in the woman's past experiences, knowledge, social background, and physical traumas may conceal the true origin of the dysfunction" (p. 33). Hence, treatment for the sexual dysfunctions of both women and men must be tailored to the specific disorder, whether it be a result of psychological, neurological, vascular, or combined etiologies.

References

Bean, J. L. (2002). Expressions of female sexuality. *Journal of Sex and Marital Therapy*, 28, 29–38.

Tiefer, L. (1996). The medicalization of sexuality: Conceptual, normative, and professional issues. *Annual Review of Sex Research*, 7, 252–282.

Tiefer, L. (2001b) A new view of women's sexual problems: Why new? Why now? *The Journal of Sex Research*, 38, 89–96.

Tiefer, L., & Melman, A. (1983). Interview of wives: A necessary adjunct in the evaluation of impotence. *Sexuality and Disability*, 6, 167–175.

15-2d Relationship Factors

One partner's dysfunction is the other partner's distress.

—William Masters and Virginia Johnson

Sexual dysfunction and relationship conflict seldom exist in isolation. Marriage and sex therapists always focus on the relationship between the partners before addressing a specific sexual dysfunction (such as lack of orgasm or erectile dysfunction). The relationship/sexuality connection may be particularly strong in women. Basson (2002a) speculated on a number of reasons for sex with a partner, "enhancement of emotional closeness, bonding, commitment, desire to increase a sense of attractiveness and attraction to a partner, and desire to share physical sexual pleasure—for the sake of sharing more than for satisfying sexual hunger" (p. 34). Similarly, Tavris (2002) noted that relational aspects of sexuality "often lie at the root of sexual satisfactions and problems—for example, desires for intimacy, wishes to please a partner, or in some cases wishes to avoid offending, losing, or angering a partner" (p. 227). Greeff and Malherbe (2001) re-emphasized the importance of emotional intimacy and marital satisfaction. Whereas emotional intimacy was more important for women than men, it was associated with marital satisfaction for both spouses.

In some cases, relationship problems, such as anger, lack of trust, lack of intimacy, or lack of communication, can contribute to sexual dysfunctions. In other cases, sexual dysfunctions may contribute to relationship problems.

The fact that sexual dysfunctions may have a biological and psychogenic components raises questions about what the public should assume about treatment and how they should proceed when seeking treatment. Box 15-1 addresses the need to provide guidelines for patients and clients.

15-2e Cognitive Factors

"Sexual desire, arousal and satisfaction will only result if, in addition to sexual stimuli, there are psychosexual ingredients such as positive partner interaction, attitude, and skill" observed Delizonna, Wincze, Litz, Brown, and Barlow (2001, p. 29). They had asked 28 men without sexual dysfunction to reach a full erection during each of two conditions—using a vacuum device that creates an erection and by self-stimulating while watching an erotic video. Hence, although there was an erection in both cases, only one was accompanied by mental feelings of sexual arousal, which was evaluated as being more enjoyable. Basson (2001a) also emphasized the importance of the mind perceiving sexual stimuli in positive sexual terms.

In addition to cognitive involvement in the sexual process, what a person believes about sex may be related to sexual difficulties. Consider the following examples:

- A woman in her 50s believes the myth that women her age should not be interested in sex.
- A man in his 50s believes the myth that men his age are unable to achieve an erection that is satisfactory for intercourse.
- A heterosexual couple believes that the only appropriate way for the woman to have an orgasm is through sexual intercourse.
- A person believes that it is wrong to have sexual fantasies during lovemaking.

These are just a few examples of beliefs or myths that may interfere with sexual desire, arousal, or orgasm. Inadequate sex education can contribute to belief in such myths and to ignorance of sexual anatomy and physiology, which may also be related to sexual difficulties. For example, a woman who does not know where her clitoris is (or that it even exists) may have difficulty experiencing orgasm. The self-assessment in Box 15-2 is designed to assess your knowledge about sexuality.

15-2f Personal Choices: Individual or Conjoint Therapy?

Although only 10% of men and 20% of women who report experiencing sexual dysfunction seek medical help for their dysfunction (Laumann et al., 2001), should a person experiencing a sexual problem seek therapy alone (individual therapy) or with his or her partner (couple or conjoint therapy)? The answer depends on the person. Some people prefer to go alone. One woman said:

> *If I ask him to go to therapy with me, he'll think I'm more emotionally involved than I am. And since I don't want to encourage him, I'll just work out my problems without him. (authors' files)*

A person also might see a sex therapist alone if no partner is available, if the partner won't go, or if the person feels more comfortable discussing sex in the partner's absence. In addition, individual therapy might be the best treatment approach when the roots of the sexual conflicts are such that the person is unsure whether he or she wants to remain in the relationship or is involved in (or would like to be) an affair.

However, individuals also might want their partners to become involved in the therapy for several reasons, including the following: to work on the problem with someone, to share the experience, to prevent one partner from being identified as the "one with the problem," to explore relationship factors that may be contributing to the sexual problem, and to address the difficulties in dealing with the sexual problem. When 356 college students were asked to rate the acceptability and credibility of various marital therapy formats (conjoint, concurrent, group, and individual), the conjoint treatment format (when the therapist sees both partners together at the same time) was consistently rated as the most acceptable and credible (Wilson, Flammang, & Dehle, 1992).

Box 15-2 Self-Assessment

How Much Do You Know About Sexuality?

Take this true-false test to assess how much you know about sexuality.

T F 1. Sexual expression is purely natural, not a function of learning.
T F 2. Foreplay is for the woman; intercourse is for the man.
T F 3. Once a couple establishes a good sexual relationship, they don't need to set aside time for intimacy together.
T F 4. If you love each other and communicate, everything will go fine sexually.
T F 5. Sex and love are two sides of the same coin.
T F 6. Technique is more important than intimacy in achieving a satisfying sexual relationship.
T F 7. Casual sex is more exciting than intimate sex.
T F 8. If you have a good sexual relationship, you will have a fulfilling experience each time you have sex.
T F 9. After age 25 your sex drive dramatically decreases, and most people stop being sexual by 65.
T F 10. It is primarily the man's role to initiate sex.
T F 11. If one or both partners become aroused, intercourse must follow or there will be frustration.
T F 12. Men are more sexual than women.
T F 13. Having a "G" spot and multiple orgasms is a sign you are a sexually liberated woman.
T F 14. Since men don't have spontaneous erections after age 50, they are less able to have intercourse.
T F 15. When you lose sexual desire, the best remedy is to seek another partner.
T F 16. The most common female sexual problem is pain during intercourse.
T F 17. The most common male sexual problem is not having enough sex.
T F 18. Penis size is crucial for female sexual satisfaction.
T F 19. Oral/genital sex is an exciting but perverse sexual behavior.
T F 20. Simultaneous orgasms provide the most erotic pleasure.
T F 21. Married people do not masturbate.
T F 22. Using sexual fantasies during intercourse indicates dissatisfaction with your partner.
T F 23. Clitoral orgasms are far superior to vaginal orgasms.
T F 24. Male-on-top is the most natural position for intercourse.
T F 25. People of today are doing much better sexually than the previous generation.

Scoring and Interpretation: Add the number of trues you checked. This is the number of sex myths you believe. What you took was a sex-myth test, so all the answers are false. Don't be surprised if you believed several of these myths; the average person thinks nine of these statements are true. Even among college students taking a human sexual-behavior course, the average number of myths believed is seven (McCarthy & McCarthy, 1984)!

Source: From *Sexual Awareness: Enhancing Sexual Pleasure*, by B. McCarthy and E. McCarthy, 1984, pp. 13–14. Copyright 1984 by Carroll & Graf Publishers, Inc. Reprinted by permission of Avalon Publishers.

In a study of sexually nonresponsive women, researchers found that sex therapy for the woman alone was as effective as treating the couple in conjoint therapy (Whitehead, Mathews, & Ramage, 1987). However, the researchers also stated that conjoint therapy was "the treatment of choice" in that it had a more positive outcome for the woman's anxiety and for her perception of her partner (p. 204).

Another treatment alternative is to combine individual therapy with conjoint therapy. For example, one or both partners may receive individual therapy and, either concurrently or subsequently, also receive conjoint therapy. Such an arrangement requires a very skilled therapist who must remain "balanced" when working with the couple. This may become difficult if one partner is being seen alone in individual therapy. Some therapists resolve this dilemma by seeing both partners in individual therapy.

15-3 DESIRE-PHASE DYSFUNCTIONS

The *DSM-IV-TR* classifies two types of desire-phase dysfunctions: hypoactive sexual desire and sexual aversion. Although it is not a *DSM-IV-TR* category, hyperactive sexual desire disorder will also be discussed.

15-3a Hypoactive Sexual Desire Disorder

Loss of sexual desire has been considered the most difficult of all the sexual dysfunctions to treat.

—Marita McCabe, psychologist

Hypoactive sexual desire disorder is the persistent or recurrent deficiency (or absence) of sexual fantasies/thoughts and/or desire for, or receptivity to, sexual activity, which causes personal distress (Ferguson, 2002). Other terms used to refer to low interest in sex include *inhibited sexual desire*, *low sexual desire*, and *impaired sexual interest*. Like other sexual dysfunctions, hypoactive sexual desire may be lifelong, acquired, situational, or generalized.

Hypoactive sexual desire disorder The persistent or recurrent deficiency (or absence) of sexual fantasies/thoughts and /or desire for, or receptivity to, sexual activity, which causes personal distress.

National Data When a national sample of women were asked to identify their most frequent sexual problem, more than half (51%) identified lack of interest in sex (Dunn, Croft, & Hackett, 2000). Data from the National Health and Social Life Survey revealed that a third of women report lacking an interest in sex (Laumann et al., 2001).

Cultural Diversity

Lesbians in long-term relationships sometimes refer to the concept of the "lesbian death bed." This term refers to a dramatic, sustained drop-off in sexual frequency that is believed to occur in some long-term lesbian couples (Iasenza, 2001, p. 59). The belief is thought to have its origin in the fact that "there is no man in the relationship to ensure initiation of sexual activity" (p. 59). Although some therapists have observed that lesbian women may not have been socialized to initiate sex, there is also evidence that, compared to heterosexual women, lesbian women may be more sexually arousable, comfortable using erotic or arousing language, and more likely to report a higher level of satisfaction with the quality of their sexual relationship. Indeed, the "lesbian death bed" is a misnomer. In addition, that part of the definition that suggests a drop-off in frequency of sex in long-term relationships is equally true of heterosexual relationships.

Assessing whether or not someone has hypoactive sexual desire is problematic. First, there are no clear criteria for determining "abnormal" levels of sexual desire. Two people can vary greatly in the degree to which they experience sexual interest or desire, and each may feel comfortable with his or her level of desire. Furthermore, sexual desire predictably decreases over time. It is important not to interpret normal declines in sexual interest and activity as a sexual dysfunction.

Causes and Contributing Factors

Lack of interest in sex may be caused by one or more factors, including restrictive upbringing; relationship dissatisfaction; nonacceptance of one's sexual orientation; learning a passive sexual role; and physical factors such as stress, illness, drugs, and fatigue. In addition, abnormal hormonal states have been shown to be associated with low sexual desire. Guay and Jacobson (2002) studied 105 women who complained of low sexual desire and found that 70% had decreased levels of total testosterone. "This reinforces the theory that the problem of low libido lies within the adrenal gland, where DHEA-S (weaker androgen than testosterone) is produced" (p. 135). Talakoub et al. (2002) also found low androgen levels in women complaining of decreased sexual desire, arousal, and orgasm.

Treatment

Treatment for lack of interest in sex depends on the underlying causes of the problem. Some of the ways in which lack of sexual desire may be treated include the following:

1. *Improving relationship satisfaction*. As noted earlier, "treating the relationship before treating the sexual problem" is standard therapy with any sexual dysfunction, including lack of interest in sex. A common prerequisite for being interested in sex with a partner—particularly from the viewpoint of a woman—is "psychological intimacy"—to be in love and to feel comfortable and secure with her partner. Couple therapy that emphasizes a mutual loving relationship becomes the first goal of therapy. Indeed, Donahey and Miller (2001) noted that "relationship" issues contribute to 30% of the change effects seen in sex therapy (the largest effect was "extratherapeutic," accounting for 40%).
2. *Creating the conditions for satisfying sex*. Women who report low interest in sex may not have had a partner who created the stimulation, both physiological and psychological, which elicited her sexual feelings or desires. Lazarus (1989) noted that some women with dysfunctions were "simply having sexual intercourse with the wrong man!" (p. 91).

Sensate focus Treatment used in sex therapy developed by Masters and Johnson whereby the partners focus on pleasuring each other in nongenital ways.

3. *Practicing sensate focus*. **Sensate focus** is an exercise whereby the partners focus on pleasuring each other in nongenital ways. The exercises were developed by Masters and Johnson (1966) to treat various sexual dysfunctions. Couples who are not experiencing sexual dysfunction but who want to enhance their sexual relationship may also use sensate focus.

   In doing the sensate focus exercise, partners (in the privacy of their bedroom) remove their clothing and take turns touching, feeling, caressing, and exploring each other in ways intended to provide sensual pleasure. In the first phase of sensate focus, genital touching is not allowed. The person being touched should indicate whether he or she finds a particular touching behavior unpleasant, at which point the partner will stop or change what is being done.

   During the second phase of sensate focus, the person being touched is instructed to give positive as well as negative feedback (to indicate what is enjoyable as well as what is unpleasant). During the third phase, genital touching can be included, without the intention of producing orgasm. The goal of progressing through the three phases of sensate focus is to help the partners learn to give and receive pleasure by promoting trust and communication and reducing anxiety related to sexual performance.
4. *Viewing/reading erotic materials and invoking fantasy*. Levine (2002) noted that sexual desire can be brought about by viewing and reading about people having explicit enjoyable sex or reading about a romantic sequence between two appealing people or invoking a fantasy that has been reliably erotic in the past.
5. *Replacing hormones*. After assessing and treating the social/relationship conditions for hypoactive sexual desire (including low arousal and low orgasmic capacity), hormone assessment may be helpful. For some women, androgen replacement therapy has resulted in a significant increase in the domains of desire, arousal, lubrication, satisfaction, and orgasm (Munarriz et al., 2002, p. 165). Guay (2001) reported that 50–100 mg of oral DHEA per day restored sexual desire in 6 of 8 women who reported having a depressed libido.
6. *Changing medications (if possible) in cases in which medication interferes with sexual desire*. Hensley and Nurnberg (2002) found that selective serotonin reuptake inhibitors (SSRIs) such as Prozac or Paxil that are used to treat depression, anxiety, or premenstrual dysphoric disorder may interfere with interest, arousal, and performance. However, the gains in reducing depression via medication may be significant such that reduced depression may result in improving sexual functioning (Michelson, Schmidt, Lee, & Tepner, 2001). Careful monitoring of the effects of medication is indicated.
7. *Masturbating*. Masturbation may also be recommended on the premise that individuals may "act themselves into a new way of thinking quicker than they can think themselves into a new way of acting." Such masturbation may be helpful in the development of positive sexual feelings.

8. *Taking supplements*. ArginMax is a nutritional supplement containing extracts of ginseng, ginkgo, damiana leaf, and various vitamins and minerals. Of 77 women desiring to improve their sexual functioning, 34 received the supplements and 43 received a placebo. After 4 weeks almost three fourths (73.5%) of the experimental group, compared to 37.2% of the control group, reported increases in sexual desire, clitoral sensitivity, and frequency of orgasm. No significant side effects were noted (Ito, Trant, & Polan, 2001).
9. *Resting and relaxing*. Other treatments for lack of sexual desire include rest and relaxation. This treatment is indicated when the culprit is chronic fatigue syndrome (CFS), the symptoms of which are overwhelming fatigue, low-grade fever, and sore throat.
10. *Learning about alternate models of sexual response*. Some women have found it helpful to learn that not having "spontaneous" sexual desire can be "normal." Basson (2001b) taught clients who presented with complaints of low sexual desire that even if they did not spontaneously experience desire, they could move from a state of sexual "neutrality" to a willingness to be receptive to stimuli to feeling sexual pleasure and arousal. Motivational factors for sexual intimacy might include a desire for increased emotional closeness with the partner, increased bonding, and commitment.

15-3b Sexual Aversion Disorder

Another desire-phase disorder is sexual aversion, also known as *sexual phobia* and *sexual panic disorder*. **Sexual aversion disorder** is defined as the persistent or recurrent phobic aversion to and avoidance of sexual contact with a sexual partner. The individual reports anxiety, fear, or disgust when confronted with a sexual opportunity with a partner. Some individuals experience generalized revulsion to all sexual stimuli, including kissing and touching.

Sexual aversion disorder The persistent or recurrent phobic aversion to and avoidance of sexual contact with a sexual partner.

Causes and Contributing Factors

The immediate cause of sexual aversion is an intense fear of sex. Such fear may result from negative sexual attitudes acquired in childhood or from sexual trauma, such as rape or incest. Some cases of sexual aversion may be caused by fear of intimacy, intrapsychic conflicts, or hostility toward the other sex.

Treatment

Treatment for sexual aversion involves providing insight into the possible ways in which the negative attitudes toward sexual activity developed, increasing the communication skills of the partners, and practicing sensate focus. Understanding the origins of the sexual aversion may enable the individual to view change as possible. Through communication with the partner and sensate focus exercises, the individual may learn to associate more positive feelings with sexual behavior. When there is a trauma history, therapy for trauma symptoms or post-traumatic stress disorder may need to precede a focus on the sexual aversion.

15-3c Hyperactive Sexual Desire Disorder

On the other end of the continuum from hypoactive sexual desire disorder is **hyperactive sexual desire disorder.** Although the *DSM-IV-TR* (American Psychiatric Association, 2000) does not recognize the concept of "sex addiction," here we note that some individuals have a very high (hyperactive) sexual interest; they behave as though they are driven to sexual expression; and the pursuit of sex may have negative affects on the health, relationships, or career of the individual. Having repetitive extradyadic affairs, frequenting massage parlors, and hiring prostitutes may all be associated with hyperactive sexual desire.

Hyperactive sexual desire disorder Very high (hyperactive) sexual interest, which influences persons to behave as though they are driven to sexual expression and the pursuit of sex, which may have negative effects on the health, relationships, or career of the individual.

However, Klein (2002) notes that definitions of sexual activity, including hyperactive sexual desire, are socially constructed. "Things like the emphasis on victimhood. Things like the increasing medicalization and biological determinism in sexuality; the increasing legitimacy of religious concepts and solutions; the increasing political cloud of sex negativity. These form the discourse, the cultural context for anyone who's developing models of sexuality today" (http://www.ejhs.org/volume5/SexAddiction.htm). Hence, Klein cautions against definitions which suggest that too much sexual interest or sex is bad.

CULTURAL DIVERSITY 

Cultures differ in the ways they treat sexual dysfunctions. In China, men with erectile dysfunction are sometimes regarded as "suffering from deficiency of Yang elements in the kidney." Their treatment is to drink a solution prepared with water and several chemicals designed to benefit kidney function. They may also be given acupuncture therapy (Shikai, 1990, p. 198).

15-4 AROUSAL-PHASE DYSFUNCTIONS

Even though a person may have the desire for sexual engagement, he or she may have difficulty becoming sexually aroused.

15-4a Sexual Arousal Disorder

Problems of sexual arousal are characterized by failure of the physiological responses that normally occur during this phase and a lack of pleasurable sensations usually associated with sexual arousal. The two types of arousal phase disorders are female **sexual arousal disorder** and male erectile disorder.

Sexual arousal disorder See **female sexual arousal disorder.**

Female sexual arousal disorder The persistent or recurrent inability to attain or maintain sufficient sexual excitement or a lack of genital (lubrication/swelling) or other somatic responses. (See also **sexual arousal disorder**.)

Female Sexual Arousal Disorder

Female sexual arousal disorder may be defined as the persistent or recurrent inability to attain or maintain sufficient sexual excitement or a lack of genital (lubrication/swelling) or other somatic responses (Ferguson, 2002, p. 78). Like other sexual dysfunctions, female sexual arousal disorder may be lifelong, acquired, situational, or generalized.

Factors that may cause sexual arousal difficulties are similar to the factors associated with hypoactive sexual desire. Thus, relationship dissatisfaction, restrictive upbringing, and nonacceptance of one's sexual orientation may contribute to arousal difficulties. In addition, Basson (2002a) noted that women who do not become sexually aroused are not interpreting the external context and their genital engorgement as sexually exciting.

Female sexual arousal dysfunction may also result from estrogen deficiency; the most common cause of estrogen deficiency is menopause. Other biological factors that may be related to lack of sexual arousal in women include neurogenic disorders (such as multiple sclerosis) and some drugs (such as antihistamines and antihypertensives). Strong emotions, such as fear and anger, and stress may also interfere with sexual responsiveness.

Treatment for women who have difficulty experiencing sexual arousal is similar to the treatment for hypoactive sexual desire. New innovations include the "off label" use of sildenafil as the primary treatment (Perelman, 2002). Although sildenafil (e.g., Viagra) is becoming increasingly used to treat male erectile dysfunction, the positive consequences of its use in treating female sexual dysfunction are being studied. "Concerns about the medicalization of women's sexual health are understandable, yet the value of integrating pharmacotherapy and sex therapy will become progressively more apparent" (p. 203). Berman et al. (2001) reported the treatment of 48 women with complaints of sexual arousal disorder who took 100 mg of sildenafil. Baseline and follow-up data on these women revealed significant improvements in their arousal, desire, satisfaction, and experiencing orgasm. No significant adverse side effects of the medication were observed.

Erotic films may also be helpful in increasing arousal. Brotto and Gorzalka (2002) found in a sample of 71 women that exposure to erotic film had a significant and positive effect on sexual arousal as defined by genital responding. This film effect was true regardless of the woman's age or menopausal status.

Box 15-3 Up Close

Persistent Sexual Arousal Syndrome

The opposite of female sexual arousal disorder is **persistent sexual arousal syndrome (PSAS)** characterized by the woman's complaint of excessive and seemingly continuous arousal rather than of deficient or absent arousal. The term is not synonymous with *hypersexuality* because the former refers to physiological arousal in the absence of desire (Leiblum & Nathan, 2001). The phenomenon is new to the sex therapy community, but now that it has been identified, many gynecologists and sex therapists report having seen one or two such cases in their practice. "To date, no obvious hormonal, vascular, neurological, or psychological causes have been identified as underlying the symptoms of any of the patients" (p. 365). Although different treatments such as antidepressants, antiandrogens, birth control pills, hypnosis, and anesthetizing creams have been tried, none have proven widely effective.

Persistent sexual arousal syndrome (PSAS) Condition in which a woman experiences excessive and seemingly continuous arousal.

A team of researchers (Billups et al., 2001) observed that the use of Eros-CTD by 28 women complaining of sexual dysfunction was associated with increasing genital sensation, lubrication, arousal, orgasm, and satisfaction. Eros-CTD is a small battery-powered device that, when placed over the clitoris, and the pump activated, causes increased blood flow and engorgement. "No evidence of clitoral trauma, bruising, or irritation was observed during the final physical examination conducted on any of the patients in the study" (p. 441). This product is available in the United States only by prescription (an extreme medicalization of female sexuality).

Focus on the woman's partner is also indicated. As suggested earlier, the problem may not be the woman's inability to become aroused, but her partner's not providing the kind of stimulation required for arousal to occur. An insensitive, accusatory, selfish partner who does not nurture the love relationship with the partner and provide the time, type, and amount of stimulation she needs may be a more productive focus of the "woman's dysfunction." Although these reasons are real and significant, more often ignorance may be the major culprit in that the partner is unaware or has not been sufficiently socialized to be a good lover.

In Box 15-3, we note the phenomenon of persistent sexual arousal syndrome as it relates to women.

Male Erectile Disorder

The American Psychiatric Association defines **male erectile disorder** as a persistent or recurrent inability to attain, or to maintain until completion of sexual activity, an adequate erection. Like other sexual dysfunctions, erectile dysfunction may be lifelong, acquired, situational, or generalized. Occasional isolated episodes of the inability to attain or maintain an erection are not considered dysfunctional; they are regarded as normal occurrences.

Male erectile disorder A persistent or recurrent inability to attain, or to maintain until completion of sexual activity, an adequate erection.

NATIONAL DATA The most frequent sexual problem identified by men (48%) was erectile dysfunction (Dunn et al., 2000).

Most cases of erectile dysfunction are caused by physiological conditions including heavy smoking, alcohol or drug abuse, chronic disease (kidney or liver failure), pelvic surgery, blockage in the arteries, diabetes, and various medications. Erectile dysfunction is also related to age; the older the man, the more likely he is to report difficulty creating and maintaining an erection.

Psychiatric, emotional, and psychosocial problems may also interfere with erectile capacity. Examples include depression, fear (of unwanted pregnancy, intimacy, HIV, or other STDs), guilt, and relationship dissatisfaction. For example, the man who is having an extradyadic sexual relationship may feel guilty. This guilt may lead to difficulty in experiencing or maintaining an erection in sexual interaction with the primary partner or the extradyadic partner.

Anxiety may also inhibit the man's ability to create and maintain an erection. One source of anxiety is performance pressure, which may be self-imposed or imposed by a partner. In self-imposed performance anxiety, the man constantly "checks" (mentally or visually) to see that he is erect. Such self-monitoring (also referred to as **spectatoring**) creates anxiety because the man fears that he may not be erect. Partner-imposed performance pressure involves the partner's communicating that the man must get and stay erect to be regarded as a good lover. Such pressure usually increases the man's anxiety, thus ensuring no erection. Whether self or partner imposed, the anxiety associated with performance pressure results in a vicious cycle—anxiety, erectile difficulty, embarrassment, followed by anxiety, erectile difficulty, and so on.

Spectatoring Self-monitoring one's own sexual responses to the point that a sexual dysfunction may occur.

Performance anxiety may also be related to alcohol use. After consuming more than a few drinks, the man may initiate sex but may become anxious after failing to achieve an erection. (Too much alcohol will interfere with erection—in Shakespeare's words, "Drink—it provokes the desire, but it takes away the performance." *Macbeth*, act 2, scene 3.) Although alcohol may be responsible for his initial "failure," his erection difficulties may continue because of his anxiety.

This 70-year-old man says, "Hugh Hefner was right—Viagra is the world's greatest legal drug."

Men who require of themselves that they satisfy their partner with the use of only their penis are even more vulnerable to erectile failure. Men who are accustomed to satisfying their partner through cuddling, massage, oral sex, and/or digital stimulation feel they have various options for providing their partner pleasure. Hence, a flaccid penis is no cause for alarm—they just move to another option.

In regard to the treatment of male erectile disorder, "[b]oth the general public and medical community now prefer medical intervention first, and only if that is unsuccessful is psychological or sex therapy assessment and intervention considered. Viagra increases the blood flow to the stimulated penis and facilitates erection in the majority of males (70%), regardless of etiology" (McCarthy, 2001, p. 1). In the past 5 years, since Viagra was introduced by Phizer Pharmaceuticals, more than 20 million men have tried it, generating $1.7 billion in sales. For the 20–30% of men who aren't helped by Viagra, or for those who are bothered by its side effects (headaches, flushed face, blue tint to vision), two new drugs (Cialis and Levitra) have been approved in Europe and are being evaluated by the Food and Drug Administration (Kinzie, 2003).

Think About It

Because Viagra is assumed to be the fail-safe method of ensuring an erection, a man may panic if he discovers his erection is not forthcoming or is lost even though he has taken the "magic bullet." Sex therapists recommend it is imperative that the man or couple prepare for such occasions because erections are not always predictable. What is needed is a cognitive strategy that accepts occasional erectile problems. "This allows the man (and couple) to treat the experience as 'a lapse, not a relapse'" (McCarthy, 2001, p. 2). To what degree do you feel men are able to adopt this cognitive perception?

15-5 ORGASM-PHASE DYSFUNCTIONS

Orgasm-phase dysfunctions include female orgasmic disorder and male orgasmic disorder.

15-5a Female Orgasmic Disorder

NATIONAL DATA Between 4 and 7% of women report having unusual difficulty experiencing orgasm (Simons & Carey, 2001).

The essential feature of **female orgasmic disorder** is a persistent or recurrent difficulty, delay in, or absence of experiencing orgasm following sufficient stimulation and arousal. Because normal sexual excitement is typically considered to be sexual intercourse, the problem with labeling the lack of orgasm as a disorder rests on the fact that the majority of women are not capable of orgasm without additional stimulation. Black (2001) recommends the term **preorgasmia,** which implies that the woman will be able to achieve orgasm given sufficient context, stimulation, training, etc.

Female orgasmic disorder A persistent or recurrent difficulty, delay in, or absence of experiencing orgasm following sufficient stimulation and arousal.

Preorgasmia Condition which implies that the woman will be able to achieve orgasm given sufficient context, stimulation, or training.

Because women vary a great deal in the type or intensity of stimulation needed to trigger orgasm, a clinician making this diagnosis takes into consideration the woman's age, sexual experience, relationship with the partner, and whether the sexual stimulation is adequate. Lifelong orgasmic disorders are more common than acquired ones and are more often diagnosed in younger women than in older women (American Psychiatric Association, 2000).

Causes and Contributing Factors

Biological factors associated with orgasmic dysfunction can be related to fatigue, stress, alcohol, and some medications, such as antidepressants and antihypertensives. Diseases or tumors that affect the neurological system, diabetes, and radical pelvic surgery (for cancer, for example) may also impair a woman's ability to experience orgasm.

Psychosocial and cultural factors associated with orgasmic dysfunctions are similar to those related to lack of sexual desire. Causes of orgasm difficulties in women include a restrictive upbringing and learning a passive female sexual role. Guilt, shame, disgust, fear of intimacy, fear of losing control, ambivalence about commitment, and spectatoring may also interfere with the ability to experience orgasm. Other women may not achieve orgasm because of their belief in the myth that women are not supposed to enjoy sex. Experiencing a traumatic event, such as being raped, could interfere with orgasmic capacity.

Relationship factors, such as the lack of intimacy or emotional connection with the partner, are associated with preorgasmia. A team of researchers (Birnbaum, Glaubman, & Mikulincer, 2001) noted, "women seem to experience heterosexual intercourse as a direct reflection of the dyadic relationship as well as a sign of love they feel toward the partner, the love and esteem the partner feels toward them, and the emotional interdependence existing in the relationship" (p. 201).

For some women, the lack of information can result in orgasmic difficulties. (Some women do not know that clitoral stimulation is important for orgasm to occur, for example.) Some women might not achieve orgasm with their partners because they are ashamed and insecure about telling their partners what they want in terms of sexual stimulation.

Think About It

A woman who does not achieve orgasm because of lack of sufficient stimulation is not considered to have a sexual dysfunction. In one study, 64% of the women who did not experience orgasm during sexual intercourse said that the primary reason was lack of noncoital clitoral stimulation. The types of stimulation most effective in inducing orgasm were manual and oral stimulation and manipulation of the clitoral and vaginal area (Darling, Davidson, & Cox, 1991). To what degree do you feel women's partners view the woman's not having an orgasm as their not providing the necessary clitoral stimulation?

Treatment

Because the causes for orgasm difficulties vary, the treatment must be tailored to the particular woman. Treatment can include resting/relaxing, changing medication, or limiting alcohol consumption prior to sexual activity. Sensate focus exercises might help a woman explore her sexual feelings and increase her comfort with her partner. Treatment can also involve improving relationship satisfaction and teaching the woman how to communicate her sexual needs.

Masturbation is a widely used treatment for women with orgasm difficulties. LoPiccolo and Lobitz (1972) developed a nine-step program of masturbation for women with orgasm difficulties. The rationale behind masturbation as a therapeutic technique is that masturbation is the technique that is most likely to produce orgasm. Masturbation gives the individual complete control of the stimulation, provides direct feedback to the woman of the type of stimulation she enjoys, and eliminates the distraction of a partner. Kinsey, Pomeroy, Martin, and Gebhard (1953) reported that the average woman reached orgasm in 95% or more of her masturbatory attempts. In addition, the intense orgasm produced by masturbation leads to increased vascularity in the vagina, labia, and clitoris, which enhances the potential for future orgasms.

Vibrators are helpful in providing sufficient stimulation to induce orgasm. A number of different vibrators are available online (see http://www.girlzniteout.com/).

Not all therapists agree that masturbation is beneficial for the pair-bonded nonorgasmic woman. Schnarch (1991, 1993) suggests that masturbation focuses the individual on personal, individualistic happenings, when intimacy with the partner is the more appropriate focus:

> *The essence of sexual intimacy lies not in mastering specific sexual skills or reducing performance anxiety or having regular orgasms but in the ability to allow one's self to deeply know and to be deeply known by the partner. (Schnarch, 1993, p. 43)*

15-5b Male Orgasmic Disorder

Inhibited male orgasm
A persistent or recurrent delay in or absence of orgasm following a normal sexual excitement phase. (See also **retarded ejaculation** and **male orgasmic disorder.**)

Retarded ejaculation
See **inhibited male orgasm.**

Male orgasmic disorder
See **inhibited male orgasm.**

Difficulty experiencing orgasm also occurs in men. Also known as **inhibited male orgasm** and **retarded ejaculation, male orgasmic disorder** is defined as a persistent or recurrent delay in or absence of orgasm following a normal sexual excitement phase. The clinician making the judgment about male orgasmic disorder should take into account the man's age and whether the stimulation has been adequate in focus, intensity, and duration.

CULTURAL DIVERSITY 

The inability to achieve orgasm is viewed as a problem in modern Western society. But traditional Chinese Taoist philosophy views avoiding ejaculation during intercourse in positive terms because this vital source of energy needs to be preserved (Tang, Lai, Phil, & Chung, 1997).

Like other sexual dysfunctions, male orgasmic disorder may be lifelong, acquired, situational, or generalized. In most cases of inhibited male orgasm, the man is unable to reach orgasm during sexual intercourse but is able to reach orgasm through other means, such as masturbation. Orgasm difficulties are more common in elderly men.

Causes and Contributing Factors

Several medications may interfere with ejaculation, including some hormone-based medications, tranquilizers, barbiturates, antidepressants, and antihypertensives. Prozac and Paxil are particularly associated with retarded ejaculation. Injury or disease that impairs the neurological system may also interfere with orgasm in the male.

Psychosocial causes of male orgasmic disorder include anxiety, fear, spectatoring, and negative attitudes toward sexuality. For example, traumatic experiences or embarrassing ones, such as being discovered by parents while masturbating, can lead to fear, anxiety, and punishment associated with impending orgasm. Thus, the sensation of impending orgasm can become conditioned to produce the response of fear and anxiety, which inhibits orgasm. Some men are obsessed with trying to become aroused and pleasing their partners, which may lead to anxiety and spectatoring, which inhibits the ejaculatory reflex. Fear of pregnancy and guilt may also interfere with a man's ability to achieve orgasm and to ejaculate. Learning negative messages about genitals or sexual activities from one's parents or religious training may also lead to ejaculation difficulties.

Job/career difficulties or the presence of children in the household can also influence sexual performance. Men who have lost their jobs, are depressed about their economic future, or are anxious about kids knocking on the door may find that their sexual focus is affected.

Just as with many women, some men are unable to orgasm because of a lack of sufficient stimulation. Some heterosexual men may have developed a pattern of masturbation that involves vigorous stimulation; they then are unable to obtain sufficient stimulation from the vagina during coitus.

Treatment

Treatment for male orgasmic disorder may involve changing medications. More frequently, treatment focuses on the psychosocial origins of retarded ejaculation and may consist of exploring the negative attitudes and cognitions that interfere with ejaculation and re-educating to change such negative attitudes.

Treatment may also involve sensate focus exercises, which allow the couple to experience physical intimacy without putting pressure on the man to perform sexually. Eventually, the man's partner helps him ejaculate through oral or manual stimulation. Research on treating inhibited orgasm has focused mainly on men in heterosexual relationships. After the couple is confident that the man can be brought to orgasm orally or manually, the partner stimulates him to a high level of sexual excitement and, at the moment of orgasm, inserts his penis into her vagina so that he ejaculates inside her. After several sessions, the woman gradually reduces the amount of time she orally or manually manipulates her partner and increases the amount of time she stimulates him with her vagina (Masters & Johnson, 1970). Alternatively, the goal in treating male orgasmic disorder may be to enjoy sexual activities with a partner without the expectation that ejaculation must occur inside the vagina.

15-5c Premature Ejaculation

Also known as **rapid ejaculation, premature ejaculation** is defined as the persistent or recurrent onset of orgasm and ejaculation—with minimal sexual stimulation—before, on, or shortly after penetration. One quarter of a random sample of male university alumni defined themselves as having a problem with premature ejaculation (Grenier & Byers, 2001).

Rapid ejaculation
The persistent or recurrent onset of orgasm and ejaculation—with minimal sexual stimulation—before, on, or shortly after penetration. (See also **premature ejaculation.**)

Premature ejaculation
See **rapid ejaculation.**

National Data The second most frequent sexual problem identified by men (43%) was premature ejaculation (Dunn et al., 2000).

Psychologist Robert Birch (2000) disagrees with the use of the terms *rapid ejaculation* and *premature ejaculation* and emphasizes that there is no sexual dysfunction in the timing of a man's ejaculation—that men simply differ in their interval from beginning stimulation to ejaculation and that nature does not require the satisfaction of the partner as a prerequisite for procreation. Although there has been the absence of an agreed-upon definition, the latency, or time from vaginal penetration to ejaculation, is most often used as the operational definition (Rowland, Cooper, & Schneider, 2001). In one study 100% of the men with a latency of 1 minute considered themselves to have an "RE (rapid ejaculation) problem," as did 42% of the men with a latency of 2 minutes, and 32% of the men with a latency of 3 minutes (Grenier & Byers, 2001, p. 372). Definitions other than *latency* have included the level of control, concern, and satisfaction reported by men in regard to their latency to ejaculation. Some negative consequences of RE include a somewhat negative impact on the man's self concept, sexual pleasure, and sexual relationship. The overall relationship with the partner was not affected (Grenier & Byers, 2001).

Causes and Contributing Factors

Although there is disagreement about the cause of rapid ejaculation, biological causes are paramount in that some men may have a constitutionally hypersensitive sympathetic nervous system that predisposes them to rapid ejaculation (Slob, Verhulst, Gijs, Maksimovic, & Van Der Werff Ten Bosch, 2002). Psychosocial factors associated with premature ejaculation include early learning experiences such as the adolescent having to ejaculate quickly before being discovered.

Treatment

A procedure for treating premature ejaculation is the *squeeze technique*, developed by Masters and Johnson. The partner stimulates the man's penis manually until the man signals that he feels the urge to ejaculate. At the man's signal, the partner places the thumb on the underside of his penis and squeezes hard for 3 to 4 seconds. This pressure causes the man to lose his urge to ejaculate. After 30 seconds, the partner resumes stimulation, applying the squeeze technique again when the man signals. The important rule to remember is that the partner should apply the squeeze technique whenever the man gives the slightest hint of readiness to ejaculate. (The man can also use the squeeze technique during masturbation to teach himself to delay his ejaculation.)

Success of the squeeze technique is disputed. Whereas success rates of Masters and Johnson (1970) are often interpreted to be 98%, subsequent research has shown rates closer to 60%. And most of the gains are lost at follow-up. "Since it is not entirely clear why the intervention works in the first place, it is difficult to identify why the treatment gains were lost over time," observe Grenier and Byers (1995, p. 465).

Another technique used to delay ejaculation is known as the *pause technique*, also referred to as the *stop-start technique*. This technique involves the man's stopping penile stimulation (or signaling his partner to stop stimulation) at the point that he begins to feel the urge to ejaculate. After the period of pre-ejaculatory sensations subsides, stimulation resumes. This process may be repeated as often as desired by the partners.

Some medications have been associated with delaying ejaculation. Clomipramine, Prozac, and Paxil seem to be safe treatment options for patients with premature ejaculation.

Intracavernous injection (ICI) has also been suggested as a treatment for premature ejaculation. Indeed, Slob et al. (2002) reported a sample of men who ejaculated quickly but who, in 77% of the cases, became erect with ICI, resulting in an erection for 140 minutes. These results indicate the view that "the use of ICI at home could be a serious therapeutic option in men with rapid ejaculation" (p. 69).

15-6 SEXUAL PAIN—DYSFUNCTIONS

Two types of pain experienced in reference to sexual engagement are dyspareunia and vaginismus.

15-6a Dyspareunia

Dyspareunia The recurrent or persistent genital pain associated with intercourse or attempts at sexual intercourse.

Dyspareunia refers to the "recurrent or persistent genital pain associated with intercourse or attempts at sexual intercourse" (Basson, 2001c, p. 110). The pain may occur as soon as partial penile entry begins, during penile containment/movement, during thrusting, at ejaculation by the partner, or after intercourse and may be experienced by either women or men. The symptoms range from mild discomfort to sharp pain. Gordon (2002) reported on seven women who complained of clitoral pain.

Causes and Contributing Factors

Dyspareunia in women may be caused by biological factors, such as vaginal or pelvic infections or inflammations, and allergic reactions to deodorants, douches, and contraceptive devices.

Dyspareunia may also be caused by a lack of lubrication, a rigid hymen, tender scarring following an episiotomy, or an improperly positioned uterus or ovary. Although there was no common etiology for dyspareunia, "trauma was a common theme resulting from operations, vaginal delivery, back injuries and, in one case, a vibrator" (Gordon, 2002, p. 127).

In men, pain may be caused by inflammations of or lesions on the penis (often caused by herpes), **Peyronie's disease** (which causes a curving or bending of the penis during erection), and **urethritis** (inflammation of the urethra). Because dyspareunia is often a symptom of a medical problem, a health-care provider should be consulted.

Peyronie's disease Disease that causes a painful curving or bending in the penis during erection.

Urethritis Inflammation of the urethra.

Dyspareunia may also be caused by psychosocial factors, including guilt, anxiety, or unresolved feelings about a previous trauma, such as rape or childhood molestation. Religious and parental prohibitions against sexual activity and relationship conflicts may also result in dyspareunia.

Treatment

Dyspareunia that is caused by biological factors may be treated by evaluating the medical condition that is causing the coital pain. If medical or surgical procedures cannot resolve the pain, the person with dyspareunia may try different intercourse positions or other sexual activities that provide pleasure with no or minimal pain.

When dyspareunia is caused by psychosocial factors, treatment may involve re-education to replace negative attitudes toward sexual activity with positive ones. Individual therapy may help the person resolve feelings of guilt or anxiety associated with sexual activity. Couple therapy may be indicated to resolve relationship conflicts. Sensate focus exercises may help the individual relax and enjoy sexual contact.

15-6b Vaginismus

Vaginismus is the recurrent or persistent involuntary spasm of the musculature of the outer third of the vagina that interferes with vaginal penetration. Vaginismus may be lifelong or acquired. Lifelong vaginismus means that the vaginal muscles have always constricted to prevent penetration of any object, including tampons. Acquired vaginismus, the more usual variety, suggests that the vagina has permitted penetration in the past but currently constricts when penetration is imminent.

Vaginismus The recurrent or persistent involuntary spasm of the musculature of the outer third of the vagina that interferes with vaginal penetration.

Some researchers suggest alternative ways to conceptualize vaginismus. Ohkawa (2001) recommends as a replacement the term *female disorders of vaginal penetration*, which emphasizes the phobic and pain factors of the malady. Similarly, Basson (2001c) recommends the term *PRAVE* (phobic anxiety regarding vaginal entry) be used to describe women who have "minimal actual introital penile contact" (p. 109) due to extreme phobic reactions to intercourse.

Causes and Contributing Factors

In women who experience dyspareunia (which may be caused by biological or psychosocial factors), vaginismus may be a protective response to prevent pain. In other words, if a woman anticipates coital pain, she may involuntarily constrict her vagina to prevent painful intercourse.

Vaginismus may also be related to psychosocial factors, such as a restrictive parental and religious upbringing in which the woman learned to view intercourse as dirty and shameful. Other psychosocial factors include rape, incest, and childhood molestation.

Treatment

Treatment for vaginismus should begin with a gynecological examination to determine if an organic or physical problem is the cause. If the origin is psychological, the treatment may involve teaching the woman relaxation techniques. When relaxation is achieved, the woman is instructed to introduce her index finger into her vagina. The use of lubricants, such as K-Y Jelly, may be helpful. After the woman is able to insert one finger into her vagina, she is instructed to introduce two fingers into the vagina, and this exercise is repeated until she feels relaxed enough to contain the penis. Some therapists use graduated dilators. When the woman learns that she is capable of vaginal containment of the penis, she is usually able to have intercourse without difficulty. Therapy focusing on the woman's cognitions and perceptions about sex and sexuality with her particular partner may precede or accompany the finger exercise.

15-7 APPROACHES USED IN SEX THERAPY

Before becoming involved in any type of sex therapy, individuals should be careful in choosing a therapist. A basic concern is training. With rare exceptions, there are no laws preventing a person from advertising that she or he is a sex therapist. Anyone can legally open an office in most communities and offer sex therapy. Academic degrees, therapy experience under supervision, and exposure to other aspects of formal training in human sexuality are not legally required to market one's self as a sex therapist. California is the only state that exercises some legal restraint on sex therapy. To be licensed in California as a physician; psychologist; social worker; or marriage, family, or child counselor, a person must have had training in human sexuality.

To help upgrade the skills of those providing sex therapy, the American Association of Sex Educators, Counselors, and Therapists (AASECT) offers a Certified Sex Therapist certificate to applicants who have a minimum of a master's degree in a clinical field (psychology, social work, nursing, marriage therapy), have conducted sex therapy under supervision for a minimum of 100 hours, and have attended a 2-day workshop on human sexuality (sponsored by AASECT) to sort out their own attitudes and values about human sexuality. AASECT guidelines indicate that the therapist should have a basic understanding of sexual and reproductive anatomy and physiology, sexual development (biological and psychological), interpersonal relationships, gender-related issues, marital and family dynamics, sociocultural factors in sexual values and behavior, medical issues affecting sexuality (including pregnancy, STDs, drugs, illness and disability, contraception, and fertility), sex research, sexual abuse, and personality theories.

The therapists certified by AASECT are expected to conduct their practice in a manner that reflects the organization's Code of Ethics for Sex Therapists. Beyond being knowledgeable about treating sexual dysfunctions, being empathic, and being trained in communication and counseling skills, the certified sex therapist is expected to refrain from engaging in sexual activity with clients.

Therapists have different approaches and may sometimes use a combination of approaches (Pridal & LoPiccolo, 2000). Some of the approaches important in the development of sex therapy and contemporary treatment approaches are described in sections 15-7a through 15-7f.

15-7a Masters and Johnson's Approach

Masters and Johnson's approach to sex therapy was a key influence in the field of sex therapy. When the Masters and Johnson Institute in St. Louis began in 1964, couples went through an intensive 2-week sex therapy program. Treatment began with assessment procedures, including a physical examination and interviews with therapists who took medical and personal histories. On the third day, the therapists met with the couple to discuss their assessment of the nature, extent, and origin of the sexual problem to recommend treatment procedures and to answer any questions. All couples receiving treatment at the Masters and Johnson Institute were instructed to engage in sensate focus exercises (described in section 15-3a).

The essential elements of the early Masters and Johnson (1970) approach to resolving sexual dysfunctions are as follows:

1. Both partners in a marital or coupled unit are expected to participate in sex therapy.
2. A male and a female sex therapist provide the treatment for heterosexual couples; in this way, each patient has a same-sex role model.
3. Sexual dysfunctions are conceptualized as having been learned. Hence, much of sex therapy is devoted to sex education and information.

4. Performance anxiety, fear of failure, and excessive need to please the partner are regarded as underlying causes of sexual problems and are addressed in therapy.
5. Communication between the partners is regarded as critical to a good sexual relationship. Hence, enhancing communication between the sexual partners becomes a goal.
6. The specific resolution of a sexual dysfunction involves behavioral change that is accomplished through the assignment of progressive tasks and behavioral prescriptions.

15-7b Kaplan's Approach

The approach developed by the late Helen Kaplan (1974) of Cornell Medical Center does not have a rigid 2-week format, nor does it assume that therapy will continue indefinitely. The goal of this approach is to assist the partners in achieving their sexual goals in as short a time as possible. Sessions are usually held once or twice a week (with an occasional phone call during the week) while the partners continue to live at home. Although participation of both partners is seen as a crucial ingredient for successful sex therapy, Kaplan's approach does not require that sexual partners participate equally in the therapy program. For example, in the case of inhibited female orgasm, the therapist may spend most of the time working with the woman in individual sessions.

Like Masters and Johnson, Kaplan assigned behavioral "homework" tasks that are designed to help the individual or couple overcome a sexual dysfunction. However, she suggested that some individuals may not respond to behavioral interventions when the source of the sexual dysfunction is rooted in unconscious intrapsychic conflicts, deep-seated personality traits, or interpersonal dynamics. Thus, an important part of Kaplan's approach to sex therapy is insight therapy, through which the presumed deeper roots of sexual dysfunction are uncovered.

Kaplan also noted that sex therapy clients often resist treatment and that therapists must be aware of such resistance and help clients overcome it. In sex therapy, "resistance" refers to the client's unconscious opposition to or lack of cooperation in treatment: Resistance may involve clients' doing something to interfere with the resolution of their sexual problem. Examples of resistance include "forgetting" therapy appointments, "not finding time" to complete homework assignments, doing homework assignments incorrectly, or antagonizing the partner. For sex therapy to be effective, the sex therapist must diffuse any resistance on the part of the client. The therapist may diffuse resistance by confronting the client directly, exploring unconscious conflicts, or making use of dream material.

15-7c The PLISSIT Model Approach

Another well-known approach for treating sexual problems and dysfunctions is the PLISSIT model (Annon, 1976). The **PLISSIT model** outlines four treatment levels: permission, limited information, specific suggestions, and intensive therapy. The permission level of the PLISSIT model involves encouraging clients to discuss their sexual problems. The therapist may also assure clients that (in many cases) their thoughts, feelings, behaviors, and concerns are "normal," common, and understandable. The second level of the PLISSIT model involves giving the client limited information, such as educating the client about sexual response, sexual anatomy, or the effects of medications or alcohol on sexual functioning. This level of intervention also involves dispelling sexual myths. The third level of intervention involves specific suggestions. Examples of specific suggestions include instructing couples on how to do sensate focus exercises, instructing women on masturbation techniques, and instructing men and their partners on how to cope with premature ejaculation (such as using the squeeze technique). The fourth level of treatment involves intensive therapy. This level of intervention is used when the other three have not alleviated the sexual dysfunction or problem. Intensive therapy may consist of any of the other sex therapy approaches described in this chapter, such as Masters and Johnson's approach (or a variation of it) or Kaplan's approach (discussed in section 15-7e).

PLISSIT model Method of sex therapy that involves four treatment levels: permission, limited information, specific suggestions, and intensive therapy.

15-7d LoPiccolo's Approach

Building on the contributions of Masters and Johnson's system of sex therapy, and drawing from cognitive-behavioral therapy and systems theory, Joseph LoPiccolo (1992) offered a three-part theory he dubbed "postmodern." Although his comments focused on erectile failure, the three theoretical elements he described are applicable to understanding other categories of sexual dysfunction as well:

1. *Systems theory*. LoPiccolo recommended that in assessing sexual dysfunction, the therapist should carefully examine the effect of the dysfunction on the relationship between the partners. Although sexual problems may cause distress, they may also serve a purpose. Unlike Kaplan's approach, in which resistance is examined when standard therapies haven't worked, in LoPiccolo's framework, the therapist begins in the first session to prevent resistance. Clients may be asked to anticipate any possible negative effects on their marital relationship if the husband were to regain erectile functioning. "For example, might a husband feel more powerful and revert to a more authoritarian role with the wife if he became more 'potent' again? Might the wife find his sexual needs burdensome if the husband regained erectile function?" (p. 178).
2. *Integrated (physiological and psychological) planning*. Classifying people's dysfunctions as organic or psychogenic is often not useful, and may be harmful. As noted, both organic and psychogenic factors are operating. LoPiccolo suggested that even when organic etiology is clearly established, a thorough psychological evaluation is also indicated.
3. *Sexual behavior patterns*. Finally, as discussed in sections 15-7a through 15-7e on treatment of specific dysfunctions, it is important to examine the specific sexual behaviors of the couple. Are the behaviors used to cue sexual desire and arousal adequate? Does the couple need to reconsider the methods, sites, or philosophies of stimulation?

Some sex therapists (not necessarily identified with any approach) work with sex surrogates to help clients achieve their goals. Box 15-4 details this practice.

15-7e The Cognitive Therapy Approach

Cognitive sex therapy Treatment method emphasizing that negative thoughts and attitudes about sex interfere with sexual interest, pleasure, and performance.

Cognitive therapy emphasizes that negative thoughts and attitudes about sex interfere with sexual interest, pleasure, and performance. **Cognitive sex therapy** consists of exploring more positive ways of viewing sex and sexuality. For example, a person who has no interest in sex may believe that sex is shameful and sinful and that "good people" regard sex as disgusting. A sex therapist using a cognitive approach might encourage this person to examine the negative consequences of such thoughts and ask the person to consider a different vein of "self talk." When one consciously replaces the old, negative thoughts about sex with positive thoughts like "sex is great, an experience to share, and a fantastic feeling," sexual desire would have a better cognitive context in which to develop. Similarly, a sex therapist may help a couple who thinks masturbation is sinful and selfish to regard it as a means of discovering self-pleasure so as to enhance their sexual relationship.

Negative cognitions may also interfere with personal, partner, and relationship functioning. "I'm too fat and not sexually desirable," "My partner is cheating on me," and "We should never have gotten married" are examples of negative thoughts that will affect one's sexual responsiveness. Addressing these cognitions and replacing them with different thoughts ("My partner loves the way I am," "My partner loves/cares about me," and "We are on our eighth year of a great relationship") become the goal of therapy.

Negative attitudes and cognitions about sex often result from sexual trauma, such as rape and incest. One way to change these negative attitudes and cognitions is for the therapist to teach the individual to view himself or herself as a survivor, rather than a victim. In addition, the therapist can suggest that "living well is the best revenge" against the person who perpetrated the trauma.

Box 15-4 Up Close

Surrogate Partner Sex Therapy

More than 81 million of the U.S. adult (over age 18) population are not married. This number includes 48.2 million never married, 19.8 million divorced, and 13.7 million widowed (*Statistical Abstract of the United States: 2002*, Table 46). Although some of these individuals are involved in ongoing relationships, others who are not involved have limited opportunities for practicing sex therapy techniques (e.g., sensate focus). To overcome this problem, some sex therapists recommend a surrogate partner. **Surrogate sex partner therapy** involves a person with sexual difficulties becoming sexually involved with a trained individual (other than the primary therapist) for therapeutic purposes. The surrogate partner and the client perform the exercises recommended by the sex therapist. Although most surrogate partners are women, some are men.

The Riskin-Banker Sex Therapy Center (http://www.surrogatesextherapy.com/) is an example of a sex therapy center that offers a Surrogate Partner Sex Therapy Program. The program operates an "in-house" program in that both counseling and experiential sessions take place in the Center (in Orange County, California). The surrogate partners work closely with licensed, certified sex therapists. This team approach enables clients to receive the necessary psychological care, as well as address the critical behavioral components, in a secure, nonthreatening environment.

One organization for surrogates is the International Professional Surrogates Association, which requires 60+ hours of training with significant additional reading and writing/study required. Surrogates work closely with the therapist and only see the client with specific directives from the therapist who is working with the client.

Surrogate sex partner therapy Treatment method that involves a person with sexual difficulties becoming sexually involved with a trained individual (other than the primary therapist) for therapeutic purposes.

15-7f Cognitive Behavior Therapy Approaches

Because positive sexual fantasies are associated with positive affect, general physiological arousal, and sexual arousal (Renaud & Byers, 2001), cognitive behavior therapists encourage its use by asking the patient to deliberately identify arousing sexual fantasies. Cognitive therapy may also be combined with behavior therapy. McCabe (2001) reported data on cognitive behavioral therapy treatment of 95 men and 105 women complaining of sexual dysfunction:

> *The treatment program was ten-sessions and focused on enhancing communication between the partners, increasing sexual skills, and lowering sexual anxiety and performance anxiety. . . . Homework exercises comprised both cognitive and behavioral strategies and behavioral exercises to enhance communication between partners, as well as sensate focus exercises. (p. 265)*

Therapy was successful for 53.3% of the men, with greatest gains in treating premature ejaculation, erectile dysfunction, and retarded ejaculation. Treatment success for women was 44.4%, with greatest success in treating preorgasmia and sexual arousal disorder; least success occurred with women who experienced lack of sexual interest. These treatment gains must be viewed in the context of the patients having experienced the sexual dysfunctions for several years and who had had repeated failures at attempted sexual activity. Nevertheless, the respondents expressed lower levels of sexual dysfunction, more positive attitudes toward sex, and lower likelihood of viewing themselves as a sexual failure.

15-7g Effectiveness of Sex Therapy

Donahey and Miller (2001) reviewed the literature on the effectiveness of sex therapy and concluded, "aside from the occasional significant finding for a particular therapy, the critical mass of data revealed no differences in efficacy among the various treatments" (p. 221). They note that there are four common factors to all therapeutic approaches that have more to do with treatment outcome than specific strategies or techniques. These factors and their relative percentage contribution to outcome include the extratherapeutic (40%), relationship (30%), placebo/hope/expectancy (15%), and structure/model/technique (15%) (p. 222).

Notice that the largest common factor is the extratherapeutic. This refers to "any and all" aspects of the client and his or her environment that facilitates recovery, regardless of formal participation in therapy. Examples include a movie which the couple sees that alters their view of their relationship/problem, conversations with each other or others independent of therapy, and a job or life change that has a positive impact on the individual or relationship.

The second factor common to all approaches involves the relationship between the client(s) and the therapist. Strong rapport with the therapist is associated with empowering the therapist to influence the client(s) toward completing homework assignments and having positive expectancies of therapy.

Hope—and expecting a positive outcome—is the third factor. Evidence of a placebo effect comes from the Viagra literature, which shows that 10–30% of men who take a placebo pill they think is Viagra report significant erectile improvement (Donahey & Miller, 2001). Although the actual effects of a medication or procedure should not be overlooked, therapists who are alert to creating positive expectancies may inadvertently improve overall functioning.

The final common factor is the actual treatment strategy. Having a point of view that provides structure and focus for the therapeutic process is important to a positive outcome. "The particular orientation or technique is less important than the degree to which it helps the therapist develop and practice attitudes and behaviors consistent with the common curative factors" (p. 228). Hence, when the therapist communicates a specific treatment modality, this tends to have a positive effect.

Reports of sex therapy effectiveness are highly varied for several reasons. First, the degree to which sex therapy is effective in resolving sexual problems depends on the problem being treated. Some problems are easier to treat than others. In general, acquired problems are easier to treat than lifelong problems, and situational problems are easier to treat than generalized (or global) problems. Premature ejaculation and vaginismus are more likely to respond quickly to therapeutic intervention. Problems of sexual desire may be the most difficult to treat. Erectile dysfunction, inability to achieve orgasm, and hypoactive sexual desire require more time. Second, the presence of restrictive religious beliefs, severe depression, or paraphilias may work against sex therapy progress.

Sex therapy effectiveness rates may also vary because of the methodological problems in determining such rates. For example, who should decide whether treatment has failed or succeeded—the client or the therapist? What criteria should be used in determining success or failure? What if the client is successful in resolving sexual dysfunctions but is not successful in resolving related nonsexual issues, such as marital conflict, negative body image, and low self-esteem? What if the client is successful in resolving these related nonsexual issues but is still sexually dysfunctional? What criteria will be used to measure success and failure? Different answers to these questions will yield different results regarding reported success rates of sex therapy.

As we end this section on the treatment of sexual dysfunctions, it is important to point out that sex therapy has its downside. Indeed, rather than improving a person's sexuality and a couple's happiness, it can have negative outcomes. McCarthy (1995) noted some of the unwanted effects of sex therapy as

> *increased sexual self-consciousness, increased anticipatory and performance anxiety, an acute problem becoming a chronic sexual dysfunction, therapy resulting in the dissolution of what had been a marginally functional relationship, increased feelings of personal deficit, and vulnerability resulting from shared sexual secrets being used against the person, especially in divorce proceedings. (p. 36)*

Although the buyer should beware, couples who decide to seek sex therapy should see only a credentialed therapist. The American Association of Sex Educators, Counselors, and Therapists, P.O. Box 5488, Richmond, VA 23220-0488 (aasect.org) maintains a list of certified sex therapists throughout the country.

15-7h Personal Choices: See a Male-Female Team or an Individual Therapist?

For heterosexual couples, is it best to see one therapist or a male-female sex therapy team? Masters and Johnson recommend the latter for couple therapy, suggesting that the male client can better relate to a male therapist and a female client can better relate to a female therapist. A dual-sex team also provides a model for appropriate male-female interaction.

Although many sex therapists have adopted the dual-sex team approach, there is no evidence that such a team is more effective than individual male or female therapists (Clement & Schmidt, 1983; LoPiccolo, Heiman, Hogan, & Roberts, 1985). In addition, therapy with a dual-sex therapy team is likely to be more expensive than therapy with an individual therapist. Rather than how many therapists of what sex are in the therapy setting, the quality of the therapy seems to be the important variable.

It is clear that much remains to be learned about diagnosing and treating sexual dysfunctions, and helping men and women experience their potential for pleasure and enrichment through satisfying and meaningful sexual experience. As Tiefer asked (1996, p. 281), "But, hey, what else is a new millennium for?"

SUMMARY

Sex is typically not the focus of a couple's relationship unless there are sexual problems. In such cases, the couple may become overly focused on their sexual problems (reported by 31% of men and 43% of women in the past 12 months). The *DSM-IV-TR* has been the standard for classifying sexual dysfunctions. A conference in 1998 (Report of the International Consensus Development Conference on Female Sexual Dysfunction) revised the classifications, moving toward further "medicalization" of sexual dysfunctions. Some professionals are concerned that this focus does not emphasize what is important—the relational and contextual aspects of intimacy and have offered an alternative conceptualization.

Causes and Contributing Factors in Sexual Dysfunctions

A number of factors may cause or contribute to sexual dysfunctions. Biological factors include physical illness, disease, aging, and disability and its treatment (surgery, medication, chemotherapy). Chronic fatigue fostered by the relentless demands of career, school, children, and domestic tasks may leave little physical energy for sexual activity. Drugs, both legal and illegal, may also impair sexual functioning.

Sociocultural factors include negative upbringing (sex is dirty), negative religion (sex is sinful), and traditional gender role socialization (female passivity). Intrapsychic factors include anxiety, fear of intimacy, fear of rejection, and sexual abuse. Relationship factors include negative feelings and lack of trust toward one's partner. Finally, cognitive factors—such as the belief that one is too old to enjoy sex—will affect sexual functioning.

Desire-Phase Dysfunction

Hypoactive sexual desire (or little interest in sex) occurs in both women and men. Causes may be any or all of those mentioned in the preceding paragraphs, and treatment follows from the most likely culprits. In many cases, improving the relationship is an important prerequisite to increasing one's sexual desire.

Sexual aversion disorder involves anxiety, fear, or disgust when confronted with a sexual opportunity with a partner. Some individuals experience generalized revulsion to all sexual stimuli, including kissing and touching. Insight and cognitive therapies are usually the most helpful.

Arousal-Phase Dysfunctions

Sexual arousal dysfunction results in the individual's inability to attain, or to maintain until completion of the sexual activity, an adequate lubrication-swelling response in women, or erection in men. The condition may be lifelong, acquired, situational, or generalized. Treatment varies with the cause.

Orgasm-Phase Dysfunctions

Female orgasmic disorder, or difficulty with experiencing orgasm, can be lifelong, acquired, situational, or generalized. It is important to be aware that the cause may be inadequate stimulation provided through interaction with the partner, rather than a problem with the woman's response. Types of male orgasmic disorder include premature ejaculation and retarded ejaculation. Both psychosocial and biological factors are involved in each of these dysfunctions, and the treatments vary according to the cause.

Sexual Pain Dysfunctions

Dyspareunia refers to genital pain that may occur in both women and men before, during, or after intercourse. Vaginismus is recurrent or persistent involuntary contraction of the vagina when penetration is attempted. Recent researchers have recommended changing the name for this problem or conceptualizing it as a form of sexual aversion. These conditions may be lifelong, acquired, situational, or generalized. Treatment is directed by the psychological or biological cause.

Approaches Used in Sex Therapy

The various approaches used in sex therapy include the Masters and Johnson approach, Kaplan approach, PLISSIT model, LoPiccolo approach, cognitive therapy approach, and cognitive/behavioral therapy approaches. Some sex therapists feel that sex therapy is becoming too "medicalized." Specifically with regard to the treatment of erectile dysfunction, "comprehensive urology and impotence centers" have emerged to offer medical solutions to psychogenic problems. Other sex therapists feel that too much emphasis on anatomical functioning is misguided, and recommend paying more attention to contextual and relationship variables.

SUGGESTED WEBSITES

Note: These websites were functional when we went to press. Please access the online text for the most up-to-date URLs.

American Association for Marriage and Family Therapy
http://www.aamft.org/index_nm.asp

American Association of Sex Education, Counselors, and Therapists
http://www.aasect.org/

American Psychological Association
http://www.apa.org/

An Adult Sex Education Site
http://www.sex-help.info

Institute for Behavior Therapy
http://ifbt.com/

Medical Aspects of Human Sexuality
http://www.medicalsexuality.org/

National Association of Social Workers
http://www.naswdc.org/

Kinsey Institute
http://www.indiana.edu/~kinsey/index.html

Sex Therapy Online
http://www.sexology.org/

Sexual Health
http://www.sexualhealth.com/

Society for Sex Therapy and Research
http://www.sstarnet.org/

Surrogate Sex Therapy
http://www.surrogatesextherapy.com/

KEY TERMS

acquired dysfunction (p. 446)
cognitive sex therapy (p. 466)
dyspareunia (p. 462)
female orgasmic disorder (p. 459)
female sexual arousal disorder (p. 456)
generalized dysfunction (p. 446)
hyperactive sexual desire disorder (p. 455)
hypoactive sexual desire disorder (p. 453)
inhibited male orgasm (p. 460)
lifelong dysfunction (p. 446)
male erectile disorder (p. 457)
male orgasmic disorder (p. 460)
medicalization of sexual dysfunctions (p. 444)
performance anxiety (p. 449)
persistent sexual arousal syndrome (PSAS) (p. 455)
Peyronie's disease (p. 463)
PLISSIT model (p. 465)
premature ejaculation (p. 461)
preorgasmia (p. 459)
primary dysfunction (p. 446)
rapid ejaculation (p. 461)
retarded ejaculation (p. 460)
secondary dysfunction (p. 446)
sensate focus (p. 454)
sexual arousal disorder (p. 456)
sexual aversion disorder (p. 455)
sexual disorder (p. 445)
sexual dysfunction (p. 444)
situational dysfunction (p. 446)
spectatoring (p. 458)
surrogate sex partner therapy (p. 467)
urethritis (p. 463)
vaginismus (p. 463)

CHAPTER QUIZ

1. National U.S. data presented in your text reveal that 31% of men and 43% of women reported having at least one major sexual dysfunction in
   a. their lifetime.
   b. the past 5 years.
   c. the past week.
   d. the past year.

2. Sexual dysfunctions can be classified as being either lifelong, acquired, situational, or
   a. adaptive.
   b. generalized.
   c. regressive.
   d. progressive.

3. Anxiety that involves excessive concern over adequate sexual performance is known as
   a. sexual performance syndrome.
   b. performance anxiety.
   c. sexual performance obsession.
   d. performance neurosis.

4. Tiefer and her colleagues (2001b) developed a "New View of Women's Sexual Problems" whereby they defined women's sexual problems as "discontent or dissatisfaction with any emotional, physical or ____________ aspect of sexual experience."
   a. reproductive
   b. spiritual
   c. relational
   d. contraceptive

5. The majority of ____________ who report experiencing sexual dysfunction seek medical help for their dysfunction.
   a. women
   b. men
   c. both a and b
   d. neither a nor b

6. What is sensate focus?
   a. excessive concern with sexual performance
   b. an exercise in which partners focus on pleasuring each other in nongenital ways
   c. another term for "hyperactive sexual desire"
   d. the practice of fantasizing about pleasurable and erotic experiences

7. Female sexual arousal dysfunction may result from __________ associated with menopause.
   a. estrogen deficiency
   b. an excess of estrogen

8. Masturbation is ____________ orgasm difficulties.
   a. a widely used treatment for women with
   b. a common cause of female

9. The squeeze technique is used to treat which of the following sexual dysfunctions?
   a. female orgasmic disorder
   b. hypoactive sexual desire disorder
   c. erectile dysfunction
   d. premature ejaculation

10. Dyspareunia refers to which of the following?
   a. inability to ejaculate
   b. excessive vaginal lubrication
   c. excessive volume of semen in an ejaculation
   d. genital pain associated with intercourse

11. According to the *DSM-IV-TR*, what is vaginismus?
   a. recurrent or persistent involuntary spasm of the musculature of the outer third of the vagina
   b. recurrent or persistent vaginal infections that can be caused by either yeast or one of several bacteria
   c. recurrent or persistent pain in the vaginal area
   d. excessive vaginal lubrication

12. Academic degrees, therapy experience under supervision, and exposure to other aspects of formal training in human sexuality ____________ legally required to market one's self as a sex therapist.
   a. are
   b. are not

13. In the early Masters and Johnson's approach to sex therapy,
   a. only one person is involved in treatment (if the person has a partner, the partner can also receive treatment, but it must be from a different therapist).
   b. usually one person participates in treatment, but he or she has the option of involving a partner in the treatment sessions.
   c. both partners are expected to participate in treatment.
   d. usually both partners participate in treatment, but if one does not want to participate, therapy can involve just one person.

14. In the PLISSIT model approach to sex therapy, the *P* stands for which of the following?
a. pleasure
b. permission
c. participation
d. performance

15. Surrogate partner sex therapy __________ available in the United States.
a. is
b. is not

16. There __________ evidence that a placebo effect can result in improved erectile functioning.
a. is no
b. is

REFERENCES

Allard, J. (2002). Neurophysiology and pharmacology of female genital sexual response. *Journal of Sex and Marital Therapy, 28,* 101–121.

American Psychiatric Association. (2000). *Diagnostic and statistical manual of mental disorders* (4th ed.), text revision. Washington, DC: Author.

Annon, J. (1976). The PLISSIT model. *Journal of Sex Education and Therapy, 2,* 1–15.

Bancroft, J. (1982). Erectile impotence: Psyche or some? *International Journal of Andrology, 5,* 353–355.

Bancroft, J., Graham, C. A., & McCord, C. (2001). Conceptualizing women's sexual problems. *Journal of Sex and Marital Therapy, 27,* 95–103.

Basson, R. (2001a). Human sex-response cycles. *Journal of Sex and Marital Therapy, 27,* 33– 43 .

Basson, R. (2001b). Using a different model for female response to address women's problematic low sexual desire. *Journal of Sex and Marital Therapy, 27,* 395–403.

Basson, R. (2001c). Are the complexities of women's sexual function reflected in the new consensus definitions of dysfunction? *Journal of Sex and Marital Therapy, 27,* 105–112.

Basson, R. (2002a). A model of women's sexual arousal. *Journal of Sex and Marital Therapy, 28,* 1–10.

Basson, R. (2002b). Women's sexual desire—Disordered or misunderstood? *Journal of Sex and Marital Therapy, 28,* 17–28.

Basson, R., Berman, J., Burnett, A., Derogatis, L., Ferguson, D., Fourcroy, J., et al. (2001). Report of the International Consensus Development Conference on Female Sexual Dysfunction: Definitions and classifications. *Journal of Sex and Marital Therapy, 27,* 83–94.

Bean, J. L. (2002). Expressions of female sexuality. *Journal of Sex and Marital Therapy, 28,* 29–38.

Berman, J. R., Berman, L. A., Lin, H., Flaherty, E., Lahey, N., Goldstein, I., et al. (2001). Effect of sildenafil on subjective and physiologic parameters of the female sexual response in women with sexual arousal disorder. *Journal of Sex and Marital Therapy, 27,* 411–420.

Billups, K. L., Berman, L., Berman, J., Metz, M. E., Glennon, M. E., & Goldstein, I. (2001). A new non-pharmacological vacuum therapy for female sexual dysfunction. *Journal of Sex and Marital Therapy, 27,* 435–441.

Birch, R. W. (2000). *Sex and the aging male: Understanding and coping with change.* Howard, OH: PEC Publishing Co.

Birnbaum, G., Glaubman, H., & Mikulincer, M. (2001). Women's experience of heterosexual intercourse-scale construction, factor structure, and relations to orgasmic disorder. *The Journal of Sex Research, 38,* 191–204.

Black, J. (2001). Pertinent points. *Journal of Sex and Marital Therapy, 27,* 117–119.

Brotto, L. A., & Gorzalka, B. B. (2002). Genital and subjective sexual arousal in postmenopausal women: Influence of laboratory-induced hyperventilation. *Journal of Sex and Marital Therapy, 28,* 39–53.

Burchardt, M., Burchardt, T., Anastasiadis, A. G., Kiss, A. J., Baer, L., Pawar, R. V., et al. (2002). Sexual dysfunction is common and overlooked in female patients with hypertension. *Journal of Sex and Marital Therapy, 28,* 17–26.

Carballo-Dieguez, A., & Remien, R. (2001). Sex therapy with male couples of mixed- (serodiscordant-) HIV status. In P. J. Kleinplatz (Ed.), *New directions in sex therapy* (pp. 302–321). Philadelphia: Brunner-Routledge.

Clement, U., & Schmidt, G. (1983). The outcome of couple therapy for sexual dysfunctions using three different formats. *Journal of Sex and Marital Therapy, 9,* 67–78.

Darling, C. A., Davidson, J. K., & Cox, R. P. (1991). Female sexual response and the timing of partner orgasm. *Journal of Sex and Marital Therapy, 17,* 3–21.

Deeks, A. A., & McCabe, M. P. (2001). Sexual function and the menopausal woman: The importance of age and partner's sexual functioning. *The Journal of Sex Research, 38,* 219–225.

Delizonna, L. L., Wincze, J. P., Litz, B. T., Brown, T. A., & Barlow, D. H. (2001). A comparison of subjective and physiological measures of mechanically produced and erotically produced erections (Or, Is an erection an erection?). *Journal of Sex and Marital Therapy, 27,* 21–31.

Donahey, K. M., & Miller, S. D. (2001). Applying a common factors perspective to sex therapy. *Journal of Sex Education and Therapy, 25,* 221–230.

Dunn, K. M., Croft, P. R., & Hackett, G. I. (2000). Satisfaction in the sex life of a general population. *Journal of Sex and Marital Therapy, 26,* 141–152.

Erol, B., Tefekli, A., Ozbey, I., Salman, F., Dincag, N., Kadioglu, A., et al. (2002). Sexual dysfunction in Type II diabetic females: A comparative study. *Journal of Sex and Marital Therapy, 28*, 55–62.

Ferguson, D. M. (2002). Clinical trial development in female sexual dysfunction. *Journal of Sex and Marital Therapy, 28*, 77–83.

Ghizzani, A., & Montomoli, M. (2001). Anorexia nervosa and sexuality in women: A review. *Journal of Sex Education and Therapy, 25*, 80–88.

Gilhooly, P. E., Ottenweller, J. E., Lange, G., Tiersky, L., & Natelson, B. H. (2001). Chronic fatigue and sexual dysfunction in female Gulf War veterans. *Journal of Sex and Marital Therapy, 27*, 483–487.

Gindin, L. R., & Resnicoff, D. (2002). Unconsummated marriages: A separate and different clinical entity. *Journal of Sex and Marital Therapy, 28*, 85–99.

Gordon, A. S. (2002). Clitoral pain: The great unexplored pain in women. *Journal of Sex and Marital Therapy, 28*, 123–128.

Greeff, A. P., & Malherbe, H. L. (2001). Intimacy and marital satisfaction in spouses. *Journal of Sex and Marital Therapy, 27*, 247–257.

Grenier, G., & Byers, E. S. (1995). Rapid ejaculation: A review of conceptual, etiological, and treatment issues. *Archives of Sexual Behavior, 24*, 447–472.

Grenier, G., & Byers, E. S. (2001). Operationalizing premature or rapid ejaculation. *The Journal of Sex Research, 38*, 369–378.

Guay, A. T. (2001). Decreased testosterone in regularly menstruating women with decreased libido: A clinical observation. *Journal of Sex and Marital Therapy, 27*, 513–519.

Guay, A. T., & Jacobson, J. (2002). Decreased free testosterone and dehydroepiandrosterone-sulfate (DHEA-S) levels in women with decreased libido. *Journal of Sex and Marital Therapy, 28*, 129–142.

Hall, M. (2001). Beyond forever after: Narrative therapy with lesbian couples. In P. J. Kleinplatz (Ed.), *New directions in sex therapy* (pp. 279–301). Philadelphia: Brunner-Routledge.

Hensley, P. L., & Nurnberg, H. G. (2002). SSRI sexual dysfunction: A female perspective. *Journal of Sex and Marital Therapy, 28*, 143–153.

Hyde, J. S., DeLameter, J. D., & Durik, A. M. (2001). Sexuality and the dual-earner couple, Part II: Beyond the baby years. *The Journal of Sex Research, 38*, 10–22.

Iasenza, S. (2001). Lesbian sexuality post-Stonewall to post-modernism: Putting the 'Lesbian Death Bed' concept to bed. *Journal of Sex Education and Therapy, 25*, 59–69.

Ito, T. Y., Trant, A. S., & Polan, M. L. (2001). A double-blind placebo-controlled study of ArginMax, a nutritional supplement for enhancement of female sexual function. *Journal of Sex and Marital Therapy, 27*, 541–549.

Kalayjian, L. A., & Morrell, M. J. (2001). Female sexuality and neurological disease. *Journal of Sex Education and Therapy, 25*, 89–95.

Kameya, Y. (2001). How Japanese culture affects the sexual functions of normal females. *Journal of Sex and Marital Therapy, 27*, 151–152.

Kaplan, H. S. (1974). The classification of the female sexual dysfunctions. *Journal of Sex and Marital Therapy, 2*, 124–138.

Kinsey, A. C., Pomeroy, W. B., Martin, C. E., & Gebhard, P. H. (1953). *Sexual behavior in the human female*. Philadelphia: Saunders.

Kinzie, S. (2003, March 27). The Viagra revolution. *The News & Observer*, Raleigh, NC, p. E1, 3.

Klein, M. (2002). Sex addiction: A dangerous clinical concept. *Electronic Journal of Human Sexuality*, 5, Retrieved August 20, 2002, from http://www.ejhs.org/volume5/SexAddiction.htm

Laumann, E. O., Paik, A., & Rosen, R. C. (2001). Sexual dysfunction in the United States: Prevalence and predictors. In E. O. Laumann & R. T. Michael (Eds.), *Sex, love, and health in America: Private choices and public policies* (pp. 352–376). Chicago: University of Chicago Press.

Lazarus, A. A. (1989). Dyspareunia: A multimodal psychotherapeutic perspective. In S. R. Leiblum & R. C. Rosen (Eds.), *Principles and practice of sex therapy* (2nd ed., update for the 1990s, pp. 89–112). New York: Guilford Press.

Leiblum, S. R. (2000). Redefining female sexual response. *Contemporary OB/GYN, 45*, 120–126.

Leiblum, S. R., & Nathan, S. G. (2001). Persistent sexual arousal syndrome: A newly discovered pattern of female sexuality. *Journal of Sex and Marital Therapy, 27*, 365–380.

Levine, S. B. (2002). Reexploring the concept of sexual desire. *Journal of Sex and Marital Therapy, 28*, 39–51.

LoPiccolo, J. (1992). Postmodern sex therapy for erectile failure. In R. C. Rosen & S. R. Leiblum (Eds.), *Erectile disorders: Assessment and treatment* (pp. 171–197). New York: Guilford Press.

LoPiccolo, J., Heiman, J. R., Hogan, D. R., & Roberts, C. W. (1985). Effectiveness of single therapists versus cotherapy teams in sex therapy. *Journal of Consulting and Clinical Psychology, 53*, 287–294.

LoPiccolo, J., & Lobitz, C. (1972). The role of masturbation in the treatment of orgasmic dysfunction. *Archives of Sexual Behavior, 2*, 163–171.

Maltz, W. (2001). Sex therapy with survivors of sexual abuse. In P. J. Kleinplatz (Ed.), *New directions in sex therapy* (pp. 258–278). Philadelphia: Brunner-Routledge.

Masters, W. H., & Johnson, V. E. (1966). *Human sexual response*. Boston: Little, Brown.

Masters, W. H., & Johnson, V. E. (1970). *Human sexual inadequacy*. Boston: Little, Brown.

McCabe, M. P. (2001). Evaluation of a cognitive behavior therapy program for people with sexual dysfunction. *Journal of Sex and Marital Therapy, 27*, 259–271.

McCarthy, B. (1995). Learning from unsuccessful sex therapy patients. *Journal of Sex Therapy*, 21, 31–39.

McCarthy, B. (2001). Relapse prevention strategies and techniques with erectile dysfunction. *Journal of Sex and Marital Therapy, 27*, 1–18.

McCarthy, B., & McCarthy, E. (1984). How much do you know about sexuality? *Sexual awareness: Enhancing sexual pleasure* (pp. 13–14). New York: Carroll & Graf.

McDonald, J., & Bradford, W. (2000). The treatment of sexual deviation using a pharmacological approach. *The Journal of Sex Research, 37*, 248–257.

Michelson, D., Schmidt, M., Lee, J., & Tepner, R. (2001). Changes in sexual function during acute and six-month fluoxetine therapy: A prospective assessment. *Journal of Sex and Marital Therapy, 27*, 289–302.

Munarriz, R., Talakoub, L., Flaherty, E., Gioia, M., Hoag, L., Kim, N. N., et al. (2002). Androgen replacement therapy and dehydroepiandrosterone for androgen insufficiency and female sexual dysfunction: Androgen and questionnaire results. *Journal of Sex and Marital Therapy, 28*, 165–173.

Ohkawa, R. (2001). Vaginismus is better not included in sexual pain disorder. *Journal of Sex and Marital Therapy, 27*, 191–192.

Perelman, M. A. (2002). FSD partner issues: Expanding sex therapy with sildenafil. *Journal of Sex and Marital Therapy, 28*, 195–204.

Pridal, C. G., & LoPiccolo, J. (2000). Multielement treatment of desire disorders: Integration of cognitive, behavioral, and systemic therapy. In S. R. Leiblum, & R. C. Rosen (Eds.), *Principles and practice of sex therapy* (3rd ed., pp. 57–84). New York: Guilford.

The Process of Care Consensus Panel. (1999). The process of care model for evaluation and treatment of erectile dysfunction. *International Journal of Impotence Research, 11*, 59.

Renaud, C. A., & Byers, S. E. (2001). Positive and negative sexual cognitions: Subjective experience and relationships to sexual adjustment. *The Journal of Sex Research, 38*, 252–262.

Rowland, D. L., Cooper, S. E., & Schneider, M. (2001). Defining premature ejaculation for experimental and clinical investigations. *Archives of Sexual Behavior, 30*, 235–253.

Schnarch, D. (1991). *Constructing the sexual crucible: An integration of sexual and marital therapy.* New York: Norton.

Schnarch, D. (1993). Inside the sexual crucible. *Family Therapy Networker, 17*, 40–49.

Shikai, X. (1990). Treatment of impotence in traditional Chinese medicine. *Journal of Sex Education and Therapy, 16*, 198–200.

Simons, J. S., & Carey, M. P. (2001). Prevalence of sexual dysfunctions: Results from a decade of research. *Archives of Sexual Behavior, 30*, 177–219.

Slob, A. K., Verhulst, A. C. M., Gijs, L., Maksimovic, P. A., & Van Der Werff Ten Bosch, J. J. (2002). Intracavernous injection during diagnostic screening for erectile dysfunction; Five-year experience with over 600 patients. *Journal of Sex and Marital Therapy, 28*, 61–70.

Statistical Abstract of the United States: 2002. (2002). 122nd ed. Washington, DC: U.S. Bureau of the Census.

Talakoub, L., Munarriz, R., Hoag, L., Gioia, M. F. E., & Goldstein, I. (2002). Epidemiological characteristics of 250 women with sexual dysfunction who presented for initial evaluation. *Journal of Sex and Marital Therapy, 28* (suppl 1) 217–224.

Tang, C. S., Lai, E. D., Phil, M., & Chung, T. K. H. (1997). Assessment of sexual functioning for Chinese college students. *Archives of Sexual Behavior, 26*, 79–90.

Tavris, C. (2002). Beyond dysfunction: A new view of women's sexual problems. *Journal of Sex and Marital Therapy, 28*, 225–232.

Tiefer, L. (1986). In pursuit of the perfect penis: The medicalization of male sexuality. *American Behavioral Scientist, 29*, 579–599.

Tiefer, L. (1996). The medicalization of sexuality: Conceptual, normative, and professional issues. *Annual Review of Sex Research, 7*, 252–282.

Tiefer, L. (2001a). Feminist critique of sex therapy: Foregrounding the politics of sex. In P. J. Kleinplatz, (Ed.), *New directions in sex therapy* (pp. 29–49). Philadelphia: Brunner-Routledge.

Tiefer, L. (2001b). A new view of women's sexual problems: Why new? Why now? *The Journal of Sex Research, 38*, 89–96.

Tiefer, L., & Melman, A. (1983). Interview of wives: A necessary adjunct in the evaluation of impotence. *Sexuality and Disability, 6*, 167–175.

Whitehead, A., Mathews, A., & Ramage, M. (1987). The treatment of sexually unresponsive women: A comparative evaluation. *Behavior Research and Therapy, 25*, 195–205.

Wilson, G. L., Flammang, M. R., & Dehle, C. M. (1992). Therapeutic formats in the resolution of relationship dysfunction: An acceptability investigation. *Journal of Sex and Marital Therapy, 18*, 20–33.

16

Variant Sexual Behavior and the Commercialization of Sex

Chapter Outline

There is no absolute criterion by which to distinguish paraphilic behavior from normal behavior.

—Ratnin Dewaraja

♦ ♦ ♦

In section 9-2, "What Is 'Normal' Sexual Behavior?" we discussed the definition of "normal" sexual behavior and looked at how sexual behavior is expressed in various cultures. In this chapter we look at sexual behavior viewed as atypical or variant from the norm, or at least variant from what is commonly admitted as normative. We focus on paraphilias and controversies involved in the use of that term. We examine the terminology used for paraphilias identified in the *Diagnostic and Statistical Manual of Mental Disorders* (*DSM-IV-TR;* American Psychiatric Association, 2000), how they develop, and how they are treated if they become a problem for the individual and/or society. Because involvement in prostitution and pornography may be employed to address variant sexual interests, and social attempts are made to regulate them, we discuss these issues in this chapter.

16-1 VARIANT SEXUAL BEHAVIOR: DEFINITIONS AND OVERVIEW

Sex is a biological drive and can be disturbed both in intensity and direction.

—Linda Seligman

What are determined to be acceptable sexual interests vary over time and across cultures. Although some attributes are eroticized more commonly than others (e.g., feet more than hands), there is almost no attribute that has not been eroticized (Moser, 2001). Scientific views of what is acceptable have changed drastically over the past century. The examples of such behaviors as masturbation and oral-genital sexual contact demonstrate the changes in thinking because these behaviors are no longer regarded as causes or outcomes of mental illness. Nevertheless, scientists, medical professionals, religious leaders, lawmakers, and society's members all contribute to determinations about what sexual interests are viewed as normal or abnormal, and methods of social control are implemented to regulate their expression:

> *Simplistically, the general public finds some sexual interests acceptable (heterosexual coitus within marriage), some possibly acceptable (homosexual attraction), some odd (shoe fetishes), and some disgusting (pedophilia). . . . Since the dawn of civilization, every society has attempted to control the sexual behavior of its members. What is perceived as appropriate and normal sexual activity is socially relative, and society acts as an agent of control over aberrant sexual expression. (Moser, 2001, p. 92)*

Drawing the line between what is aberrant and what is acceptable involves subjective judgment, which often reflects the comfort zone of the person evaluating the behavior. "It has been said that compulsive masturbation is diagnosed when the patient has a higher masturbatory frequency than the person making the assessment. Promiscuity is identified as having more partners than the one stating the opinion" (Moser, 2001, p. 94). Does this mean that all sexual interests or behaviors are equally acceptable? No, some are clearly not acceptable and not to be condoned (i.e., an adult having sexual contact with a child). But the mental health field has been criticized for categorizing as pathological some practices that may not be dysfunctional or cause harm (except for their stigma) because they are distasteful to the professionals.

Paraphilia An overdependence on a culturally unacceptable or unusual stimulus for sexual arousal and satisfaction.

Lovemap A mental representation or template of one's idealized lover that develops early in the individual's life.

The term **paraphilia** was coined in 1924 but was popularized by John Money in the 1980s to describe a complication of lovemap development. Money (1986, p. xvi) described the **lovemap** as an individualized mental template that "depicts your idealized lover, and what, as a pair, you do together in the idealized, romantic, erotic, and sexualized relationship." The lovemap is part of one's mental imagery and fantasies, and may be translated into action. A paraphilia is a lovemap that has developed with distortions or displacements, which include the substitute image of the paraphilia (atypical sexual behavior or interest). The term *paraphilia* is derived from the words *para,* meaning "deviation," and *philia*, meaning "attracted." Hence, the *paraphiliac* is attracted to a stimulus that is regarded by the society as deviant. It is not unusual for a person to express more than one paraphilia.

Paraphilia was included as a category of mental health diagnosis with the *Diagnostic and Statistical Manual of Mental Disorders* (*DSM-III*; American Psychiatric Association, 1980) and subsequent editions. Although the inclusion of the paraphilia categories in the *DSM*, and even the use of the term *paraphilia*, has been criticized as "merely pathologizing practices that many psychiatrists find distasteful" (Moser, 2001, p. 91), nevertheless the *DSM* is the major resource used in the United States for categorization of mental health–related concerns, so will be summarized here. See Table 16-1 for the more common paraphilias.

The *DSM-IV-TR* (American Psychiatric Association, 2000) defines *paraphilia* as being aroused by certain objects or situations that are not typical and that may interfere with the capacity for reciprocal, affectionate sexual activity with a partner. For example, a person who has a high heel fetish may be unable to become aroused unless the partner wears 3-inch red high heel shoes. Although the partner may not mind wearing heels, feeling required to do so for the partner to become aroused may be problematic.

The essential elements of a paraphilia are recurrent, intense, sexually arousing fantasies, sexual urges, or behaviors generally involving the following:

1. Nonhuman objects (e.g., high heel fetish)
2. The suffering or humiliation of one's self or one's partner (not just simulated; e.g., sadism, masochism)
3. Children or other nonconsenting persons (pedophilia, exhibitionism, voyeurism, frotteurism)

All three of these criteria need not necessarily be involved for the label of paraphilia to apply. For example, the pedophile focuses on human subjects (which leaves out the first criterion), and the cross-dresser focuses on clothing, not people (which leaves out the third criterion). What all paraphilias do have in common is that the object being focused on becomes imbued with erotic value, and there is an intense yearning to experience the object. In some cases, the paraphilia is experienced as a compulsion that interferes with work and relationships. Using our example of the high heel fetish, the person may spend hours and a great deal of money collecting high heels and require the partner to strut around in them for show.

TABLE 16-1

The *DSM-IV-TR* Major Paraphilias

Paraphilia	Description
Exhibitionism	Exposing one's genitals to a stranger or having a recurrent urge to do so.
Frotteurism	Touching or rubbing a nonconsenting person in a sexual manner or having a recurrent urge to do so.
Pedophilia	Engaging in sexual behavior with a child or having a recurrent urge to do so.
Voyeurism	Watching a person who is either nude, undressing, or engaging in sexual behavior and is unaware that someone is watching, or having a recurrent urge to do so.
Fetishism	Becoming sexually aroused by actual or fantasized objects (such as leather, lingerie, or shoes).
Transvestic fetishism	Becoming sexually aroused by dressing in the clothes of the other sex.
Sexual sadism	Becoming sexually aroused by actual or fantasized infliction of pain, humiliation, or physical constraint on another.
Sexual masochism	Becoming sexually aroused by actual or fantasized inflicted pain, humiliation, or physical constraint by another.

Some paraphilic behaviors occur more frequently than others. A team of researchers (Abel et al., 1987) looked at the relative percentages of various paraphilic behaviors reported by a sample of nonincarcerated men with paraphilias. The most frequently reported paraphilic behavior was exhibitionism (about 25% of the respondents), followed by frotteurism (18%), nonincestual pedophilia (14%), and voyeurism (10%). The least reported paraphilia in this sample was sexual sadism (about 1%). However, because people are generally unwilling to report such behaviors, most of what we know about people who engage in paraphilic behaviors comes from those who have been caught engaging in illegal acts.

In fact, some paraphilias may be much more frequent than widely acknowledged. Keegan (2001) cited a Canadian study of erotic fantasies in men in which two thirds of men report heterosexual pedophilic fantasies, and one third reported rape fantasies. Although Keegan felt that these data are overestimates of the prevalence of mild pedophilia and sexual sadism, he suggested that even if they overestimate by a factor of 10, this would still reveal a level of pedophilia and sexual sadism at 6% and 3% of men (a higher prevalence than many psychiatric disorders).

Paraphilias vary in severity from disturbing fantasies (sometimes accompanied by masturbation) to sexual victimization, which may include murder (e.g., erotophonophilia—lust murder, in which the partner is killed as a means of atoning for sex with the individual, as in a serial killer who murders prostitutes after having sex with them). Although there are few classic profile characteristics (sexual orientation, ethnicity, socioeconomic background), paraphilias most often occur in men and are very rarely diagnosed in women (American Psychiatric Association, 2000). Among individuals seen clinically for the treatment of paraphilias, approximately half are married. Adolescents as well as adults report one or more paraphilias. In a sample of 485 males younger than 18 being evaluated for possible juvenile sex offenses, 10–30% reported involvement in exhibitionism, fetishism, frottage, voyeurism, obscene phone calls, and phone sex, with the average age of onset between 10 and 12 years (Zolondek, Abel, Northey, & Jordan, 2001).

Think About It

Sex-offending paraphilic behavior may go unnoticed for years. By the time it becomes visible to the police or court system, countless victims, sometimes numbering in the hundreds, may have been affected (Seligman, 2000). What paraphilic sexual behaviors have you encountered that have escaped legal detection?

Some people with a paraphilia may become so preoccupied with the object that they feel out of control. They experience uncontrollable urges, feel unable to stop themselves from pursuing the activity, and increase the frequency and intensity of their involvement. In other cases, the person may feel in control of the paraphilic impulses and carefully select the time and the place of the expression (Seligman, 2000).

The relationships of the person with a paraphilia may suffer if the partner becomes aware of the paraphilia. For example, wives are sometimes shocked by the discovery of their husbands dressing in women's clothes. In some cases the spouse may be asked to participate in the paraphilia—for example, the partner is asked to be the recipient of the sexual sadist's paraphilia or to dress up the partner in wet diapers (autonepiophilia).

Think About It

Some sexually variant behaviors are practiced by couples with the goal of enhancing physical excitement (e.g., sadism/masochism). These behaviors may be a part of mature sexual expression when they are mutually agreed to and pleasurable for both parties. However, intervention may be needed if the behavior becomes compulsive and distressing to the individual, or coercive. To what degree do you think sexual behaviors that result in pain should be of concern to the law?

16-1a Legal Versus Illegal Paraphilias

The definitions of paraphilias presented in this chapter, which are based on the *DSM-IV-TR* (American Psychiatric Association, 2000) developed by mental health professionals, do not necessarily meet legal or other nonmedical criteria for what constitutes mental disability. Paraphilias are legal or illegal depending on the degree to which the rights of others are affected. Formicophilia, olfactophilia, and klismaphilia do not infringe on the rights of others and are of little concern to the law. Voyeurism, exhibitionism, and pedophilia are examples of paraphilias that interfere with the rights of others and carry legal penalties. Voyeurism and exhibitionism are clinical terms; in the legal system, these criminal acts may be referred to as "secret peeping" and "indecent exposure." They are usually regarded as misdemeanors and are punishable by a fine. (Repeat offenses may involve mandatory outpatient treatment at a mental health facility.) Pedophilic acts are punishable by imprisonment. Legal charges may range from taking indecent liberties with a minor, to sodomy or rape. When people with paraphilias break the law, they are referred to as *sex offenders*. The majority of apprehended sex offenders are arrested for acts of exhibitionism, pedophilia, and voyeurism (American Psychiatric Association, 2000).

Laws regulating sexual behavior vary from state to state. Some states regard exhibitionism as a misdemeanor; others classify it as a felony. The penalty ranges from a fine to a prison term. If the exhibitionist is drunk or has mental retardation, police officers tend to regard this self-exposure differently from those who compulsively expose themselves and are repeatedly picked up for exhibitionism.

16-1b Personal Choices: Whose Business Is a Paraphilia?

Persons with a paraphilia normally do not seek treatment unless forced to do so. For example, a person with pedophilic interests seeks treatment in exchange for a reduced prison term. Whereas some paraphilias are illegal and harmful to one's self (such as autoerotic asphyxiation) or other people (such as erotophonophilia), other paraphilias may be viewed as not worthy of the guilt, depression, and social disapproval they engender. Examples of such paraphilias include acrotomophilia (amputee partner), autonepiophilia, and formicophilia (ants or other insects crawling on the body).

Individuals with paraphilias that are not harmful to themselves or others might choose to disregard society's negative label of their behavior. Such a choice, in combination with a positive view of themselves, may have productive consequences for them with no negative consequences for society. For example, cross-dressing is a paraphilia that may be enjoyable for the individual and of limited consequence to the partner (assuming the partner's knowledge and acceptance).

16-2 TYPES OF PARAPHILIAS

In sections 16-2a through 16-2j, we discuss the major types of paraphilias identified in the *DSM-IV-TR* (and listed in Table 16-1) and briefly identify a variety of others (American Psychiatric Association, 2000). We also discuss legal and illegal paraphilias (exception—we discuss pedophilia in section 17-5, "Child Sexual Abuse") and consider the question of whether rape is a paraphilia. The emphasis in diagnosis of these paraphilias should be on current, intense urges and fantasies; action on the urges is secondary and need not necessarily be present.

16-2a Exhibitionism

Exhibitionism involves an intense, recurrent sexual urge (over a period of at least 6 months), often accompanied by sexually arousing fantasies, to expose one's genitals to a stranger. The onset of exhibitionist urges usually occurs before age 18, although it can

Exhibitionism Paraphilia that involves an intense, recurrent sexual urge (over a period of at least 6 months), often accompanied by sexually arousing fantasies, to expose one's genitals to a stranger.

begin later. Few arrests are made in older age groups, which may suggest that the condition becomes less severe after age 40 (American Psychiatric Association, 2000).

Money (1986) provided an example of the extent to which the male exhibitionist feels driven to expose himself:

> *When the urge does come, it comes so strong that you really want to do it. It just blocks off everything that makes sense . . . everything else that could maybe stop you. . . . You want to do it so bad. . . . I was driving, and the urge just came out from nowhere to do it. . . . I must have passed up about ten or fifteen places where I could have done it, trying not to do it. . . . But it just kept tingling with me. Stop here! Stop there! Stop Here! Go ahead! You can do it! And the feeling that I had inside was one like, if I didn't do it, I'd be missing out on something very, very great. It just kept on going. I ended up driving halfway to Annapolis, trying not to do it, just passing up places. And it got so strong, I just had to do it. I just had to get out and do it. (p. 35)*

Exhibitionist individuals expose themselves to people they do not know for several reasons. Sexual excitement is a primary one. Hearing a victim yell and watching his or her horrified face is sexually stimulating for some individuals. Once sexually excited, the exhibitionist individual may masturbate to orgasm.

A male exhibitionist may expose himself to shock women. Exhibiting himself may be a way of directing anger and hostility toward women. Although the woman he exposes himself to has not injured him, other women may have belittled him (or he has perceived it that way); or he has recently been unable to have and maintain an erection, blames his lack of erection on women, and exposes himself as a way of getting back at them.

Some individuals expose themselves as a way of relieving stress. When the stress reaches a peak, individuals exhibit themselves, masturbate, and relieve the stress. Still others expose themselves with a sexually arousing fantasy in which the person observing them will become sexually aroused (American Psychiatric Association, 2000).

Some people have referred to exhibitionism, public masturbation, and voyeurism as "victimless crimes"; however, these behaviors can cause harm because victims may be distressed. A study of college women's experiences of exposure episodes (Cox, 1988) revealed that 42% of the women rated their experience as moderately to very severely distressing. Eleven percent said it affected their attitude toward men and/or sex, and 14% reported it affected their attitudes toward themselves as women.. Furthermore, Maletzky (1991) noted that, in a small minority of offenders, these offenses can predispose the offenders toward more aggressive acts, such as pedophilia and frotteurism.

If confronted by exhibitionism, we suggest that a victim remain calm and try not to appear shocked or alarmed. However, we recommend leaving the situation and immediately making a report to the local law enforcement agency (police, sheriff, or campus security). Law enforcement agencies may benefit from obtaining reports of "minor" offenses of exhibitionism and voyeurism. One reason is that although sex offenders have a preferred method of offending, if access to that method is unavailable or blocked, they may engage in a less preferred method. Langevin, Paitich, and Russon (1985) reported that all the voyeurs referred to their sex offender clinic had also committed other sexual offenses. Langevin and Lang (1987) cited two studies of exhibitionist men in which "20% of them had committed one or more violent assaults in the past" (p. 213). Information provided in reports to law enforcement agencies may be helpful in investigating other crimes. It is a myth that "nuisance" offenders have no propensity for violence (Hazelwood, Dietz, & Warren, 1992).

Frotteurism Paraphilia that involves recurring, intense, sexual urges (for at least 6 months), accompanied by fantasies of touching or rubbing, often with the genitals, against a nonconsenting person.

Toucheurism Paraphilia that involves actively using one's hands on the victim. Although the person may be distressed over the overwhelming urge to touch or rub against another, he also may act on those fantasies.

16-2b Frotteurism

A crowded bar, concert, or subway is the ideal environment for the frotteur. According to the *DSM-IV-TR* (American Psychiatric Association, 2000), **frotteurism** is the recurring, intense, sexual urge (that has lasted for at least 6 months; arousing fantasies may also be involved) that involves touching or rubbing, often with the genitals, against a nonconsenting person. **Toucheurism** involves actively using one's hands on the victim. Although the person may be distressed about the overwhelming urge to touch or rub against another, he also may act on those fantasies. The person usually chooses a crowded place for the activity. He presses against the sexually desired person while saying, "Excuse me," and then moves to another part of the crowd and presses against someone else. This behavior, known as *frottage*, usually goes unnoticed. But the feelings aroused by pressing against another may be used in a masturbatory fantasy later.

The person with frotteurism may also fantasize about having an exclusive and caring relationship with the person he touches or rubs. However, "he recognizes that to avoid possible prosecution, he must escape detection after touching his victim" (American Psychiatric Association, 2000). Frotteurism usually begins by adolescence, but most acts occur when the person is 15 to 25 years old, after which there is a decline in frequency.

16-2c Voyeurism

Voyeurism (also called **scopophilia**) involves recurrent, intense urges to look at unsuspecting people who are naked, undressing, or engaging in sexual behavior. To be diagnosed with voyeurism, the person must have had these urges for at least 6 months and either acted on or been distressed by them (American Psychiatric Association, 2000). The person who looks at magazines with nude photos or who watches erotic films is not necessarily classified as having voyeurism because the people posing in the magazines and films know that they are being watched. However, a voyeuristic person may look at nude people in magazines or in movies and fantasize that they do not know they are being looked at.

Voyeurism Paraphilia that involves recurrent, intense urges to look at unsuspecting people who are naked, undressing, or engaging in sexual behavior. (See also **scopophilia.**)

Scopophilia See **voyeurism.**

Voyeuristic persons (sometimes referred to as "Peeping Toms") spend a lot of time planning to peep and will risk a great deal to do so. They regard climbing over fences, hiding in bushes, and shivering in the cold as worth the trouble. Peeping is the stimulus for sexual excitement, which most often results in ejaculation through masturbation either during the peeping or later. The person's targets are usually female strangers. Although some voyeurs are married, they may not derive excitement from watching their wives or any familiar woman undress.

Voyeurism is usually regarded as a male disorder, typically occurring among young men. However, Hurlbert (1992) presented what he believed to be the first reported case study of an adult female voyeurist. The 26-year-old woman he described had a psychological diagnosis of schizoid personality disorder; she was very withdrawn and isolated from social contact. She felt sexual feelings and experienced orgasm only when self-stimulating during voyeuristic activities. She felt humiliated and remorseful over her sexual activities, yet dropped out of treatment, resigned to continue her life as a "loner."

16-2d Fetishism

Fetishism involves a pattern, of at least 6 months' duration, of deriving sexual arousal or sexual gratification from actual or fantasized inanimate objects. A diagnosis of fetishism requires that the person has either acted on such urges or has been disturbed by them. Gebhard (1976) suggested that fetishes are a "graded phenomenon":

Fetishism Paraphilia that involves a pattern, of at least 6 months' duration, of deriving sexual arousal or sexual gratification from actual or fantasized inanimate objects.

> *At one end of the range is slight preference; next is strong preference; next is the point where the fetish item is a necessity to sexual activity; and at the terminal end of the range the fetish item substitutes for a living sexual partner. . . . Statistical normality ends and fetishism begins somewhere at the level of strong preference. (pp. 157–158)*

When a fetish begins at the slight preference level, it may progress in its intensity from being a preference, to being a necessity, to being a symbolic substitute for a sexual partner. Gebhard (1976) suggested that fetishism is an illustration of what philosopher Alfred North Whitehead called "the fallacy of misplaced concreteness": The symbol is given all the power and reality of the actual thing, and the person responds to the symbol just as he or she would to the thing (p. 161). Figure 16-1 illustrates the stages in the development of a fetish.

FIGURE 16-1
Stages in the Development of a Fetish

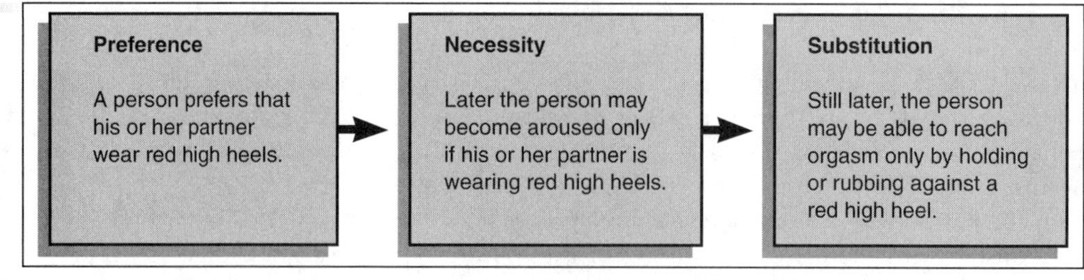

CULTURAL DIVERSITY

The powerful symbolic component of fetishes may account for the fact that fetishism is virtually nonexistent in preliterate cultures. Rather, "fetishism seems largely confined to literate people taught to be imaginative and to make extensive use of symbolism in verbal and written communication and hence in their thought processes" (Gebhard, 1976, p. 162).

Fetishes may be divided into two types: media and form (Gebhard, 1976). "A media fetish is one wherein the substance rather than the form of the object is the important aspect" (p. 159). For example, a person with a leather fetish responds to leather as an erotic stimulus whether the leather is in the form of a glove, shoe, or coat. "A form fetish is one wherein the form of the object is more important than the material of which it is constituted" (p. 159). For example, a person with a shoe fetish responds to shoes as an erotic stimulus no matter whether the shoes are made of plastic, leather, or cloth. The most common form of fetish objects are clothing items, including panties, stockings, lingerie, high-heeled shoes, and boots. Common media fetishes include leather, satin, and latex. Fetishes may also include sounds (a particular song, the clicking of a train on the tracks) and scents (perfume, incense). The Salience of Fetishism Scale in Box 16-1 is a way researchers in a study have assessed the degree to which subjects had a foot fetish. However, you can substitute most any word you choose (e.g., leather) to assess the degree to which you have alternative fetishes.

Sometimes a paraphilia involves both scent and texture, as in autonepiophilia (deriving sexual arousal or gratification from wearing wet diapers). One man explained:

> *I've had a fetish for wearing wet diapers and latex rubber panties, since being a bedwetter as a boy. . . . Over the years I have been in seven adult diaper clubs and correspond with some 250 to 300 men, who love diapers, too. . . . Marriage was unhappy for me. I could not permit myself to enjoy wearing wet diapers at home, except for a short time when I would fake loss of bladder control. (Money, 1988, p. 142)*

Transvestic fetishism Paraphilia that involves recurrent, intense, sexual urges and sexually arousing fantasies, of at least 6 months' duration, involving cross-dressing (e.g., a man dressing in a woman's clothes).

Cross-dressing Dressing in the clothes of the other gender, typically a man dressing in a woman's clothes.

16-2e Transvestic Fetishism (Cross-Dressing)

Transvestic fetishism (*DSM-IV-TR* terminology) involves recurrent, intense, sexual urges and sexually arousing fantasies (of at least 6 months' duration) while dressing in the clothes of the other gender, typically a man dressing in a woman's clothes. Although women regularly cross-dress in terms of wearing pants and a bow tie, there is little to no cultural disapproval for doing so. However, men who cross-dress are the subject of considerable disapproval.

The man who acts on his **cross-dressing** urges is usually distressed by doing so. His cross-dressing may range from occasional solitary episodes to immersion into a cross-dressing subculture. The *DSM-IV-TR* (American Psychiatric Association, 2000) identi-

Box 16-1 Self-Assessment

Salience of Fetishism Scale

The following questions were developed by researchers who were invited to do a study of an organization made up of homosexual and bisexual foot fetishists. This was not a clinical sample, but it involved a large voluntary organization, and the researchers felt that the data they gathered may have wider applicability to other fetishists besides their sample. You may be interested in reviewing the questions to determine the degree to which the fetish was central to the respondent's sex life.

1. Is foot play necessary for your sexual arousal?
2. Is foot fantasy necessary for your sexual arousal?
3. Is foot fantasy usually the main focus of your self-masturbation?
4. What was the frequency of masturbatory fantasies about feet during adolescence?
5. Are feet usually the main focus of your sexual activity with others?
6. How often do you self-masturbate without fantasizing about feet?
7. How often do you self-masturbate while fantasizing about feet?
8. Do you think you could stop fantasizing about feet if you wanted to?
9. Have you ever made a serious attempt to stop your interest in feet?
10. How often do you engage in sexual activity with another without foot play?
11. How often do you engage in sexual activity with another involving foot play?

Scoring and Interpretation: Since the variables used in the scales had different possible ranges, the researchers standardized the scores and made each variable range from 0 to 1. Then they summed the scores for each respondent. The results revealed that while there was a range of salience among the respondents, most clustered at the high end of the scale; 22% had the highest possible score on most of the variables. The salience of fetishism in the men's sex lives was not highly correlated to a measure of self-reported psychological problems. This showed that a man could report that fetishism was very important in his sex life but still have little in the way of psychological problems.

Source: Republished with the permission of The Society for the Scientific Study of Sex, from *The Journal of Sex Research* from "If the shoe fits . . .": Exploring male homosexual foot fetishism" by M. S. Weinberg, C. J. Williams, and C. Calhan, Vol. 32, 17–27, 1955. Scale from page 25. Permission conveyed through Copyright Clearance Center, Inc.

fies the sexual orientation of the man who cross-dresses as a heterosexual who may masturbate (at least initially) when dressed as a woman. However, over time, the sexual arousal motive for his cross-dressing diminishes. As he ages, his cross-dressing is more often motivated as a method of reducing anxiety, coping with depression, or creating a feeling of peace and calm.

Many men who cross-dress do not report motives of sexual excitement. When asked why they cross-dressed, men in one study offered such responses as "I don't know," "I need to express my femme side," "I like the way it makes me feel—more attractive, at ease, more fun," "to release my anima/my feminine side," "I am more comfortable—at peace with myself," and "I stopped trying to figure it out years ago" (Reynolds & Caron, 2000, pp. 71–72).

Think About It

Individuals may cross-dress for various reasons: They want to make a fashion statement, they want to express their androgyny, cross-dressing makes them feel congruent with their self-identity, they want to entertain, and they want to experience sexual arousal. To what degree do you think the motivation people attach to cross-dressing influences their evaluation of the cross-dresser?

Transvestite A broad term for individuals who may dress or present themselves in the gender of the other sex. A more pejorative term than *cross-dresser.*

Whereas the term *cross-dresser* typically refers to a heterosexual male who dresses in the clothes of a woman, the term **transvestites** more often refers to homosexual men who dress as women to attract men as sex partners or to perform before an audience as a "drag queen" for a drag show. Such a show typically involves dressing as a famous person (e.g., Barbra Streisand) and lip-synching songs.

Transsexuals are people who want to change their anatomy to be consistent with their self-concept gender. For example, a biological male who sees himself as a woman and who wants to have his penis/scrotum removed and a vagina constructed is a *male-to-female transsexual.* A biological female who sees herself as a man and wants to have a penis constructed to replace the vagina is a *female-to-male transsexual.* Men who cross-dress or wear the clothes of the other gender most often have no desire to have their anatomy altered.

NATIONAL DATA About 6% of the U.S. population consist of men who cross-dress; 1% of the U.S. population are categorized as transsexuals (Garber, 1992).

Although medical and mental health professionals attempt to diagnose transvestic syndromes, transvestites (TVs) and transsexuals (TSs) often resist such categorizations. "Needless to say, members of the TV-TS community do not think of themselves as 'patients,' nor do they particularly like the word 'transvestite,' which seems to imply a compulsive disorder; they prefer 'cross-dresser,' which suggests a choice of lifestyle" (Garber, 1992, p. 4).

As noted, most men who cross-dress are usually heterosexual. In a survey of Tri-Ess (a national cross-dressing organization) members, the majority of respondents (68%) said they were heterosexual; 10%, bisexual; 2%, homosexual; and 20% were celibate (not sexually active; Bullough & Bullough, 1997a). Sixty percent of cross-dressers in the Doctor and Prince (1977) survey also reported that they were heterosexual. Box 16-2 reveals the life of a cross-dressing spouse and parent.

Reynolds and Caron (2000) conducted a study to investigate how intimate relationships are impacted when heterosexual men cross-dress. In their nonrandom sample of 21 male heterosexual cross-dressers living in Maine and New Hampshire, most of the men were married to women who tolerated or accepted their activity. Of the 18 men who told their wives about their cross-dressing, 15 were still together. The later in a relationship the woman found out about her husband's activity, the more negative her attitude toward it. The main fear of the wives was that others would find out, or that it would harm their children. Most of the men said that they made concessions in limiting their cross-dress-

This happily married couple with two children is on a cruise with 50 other cross-dressers.

Box 16-2 Up Close

My Life as a Cross-Dressing Husband and Dad

by Anonymous

Being a cross-dresser can be very confusing and very frustrating. I told my "ex" about a month before we married, that I liked wearing women's clothing. I told her that I could quit and burned all of my clothing (called **purging**). How wrong I was! After about three months of being married, I told her that I needed to get some hosiery and panties to wear. She said that this would be OK, as long they were not lace. This progressed to the point that I needed to wear shoes and later boots. Over time, I escalated to 5-inch stiletto heels and, I began to wear women's pajamas, at night, because I liked the silky feel.

All of this progressed into my wearing various forms of lingerie which I only wore with my wife's consent and presence. While I always tried to be very respectful of my wife's wishes, I soon realized that I needed to cross-dress more often and with more intensity than she was comfortable with. When my two daughters were born, I had to be very discreet as to when I would dress as a woman. I remember many a night of getting up with my oldest daughter and rocking her to sleep while wearing hose, high heels, and lingerie, in our moonlit living room.

On several occasions, my "ex" told me that she wanted me to get rid of my things. She "wanted my things out of her house." So, I put my clothes in a box that I kept in a utility building. But I missed my cross-dressing, continued to do it, and became very sneaky about it. When my work week would end on Friday, I would rush home quickly, and dress for several hours before I picked up my daughters from kindergarten. Of course, I felt very guilty about my sneaking around.

When the girls were about 8 and 5, respectively, we bought a house. Again, my "ex" told me that she wanted me to get rid of my "things", she wanted them out of her house. I only became sneakier and sneakier. For example, I started hiding my shoes and hosiery under a dresser in the bedroom, so that when the family was gone, to let's say, the grocery store, I could quickly and easily slip into some of my things for a few moments of ecstatic relaxing bliss (which often included masturbating while I was dressed.) I knew that I would pay for this later when my wife would want to have sex and I couldn't perform. Also, several times, I would underestimate when they would return from the store and they would almost catch me while dressed. . . .

The older my girls got, the less time I had to dress. It finally got to the point, that the only time that I could dress, would be when the family would go out of town (to grandmother's house). I loved for them to be gone and was irritated by their return. Indeed, my daughters asked their mom if I was having an affair with another woman while they were gone. In essence, there was another woman, but this woman is the one who resided within me.

It is hard to explain the frustration of not being able to dress; it would lead to anger and anxiety. This anger reached its greatest height about two years before my wife and I ended our marriage. What caused this was that my "ex" demanded that I get rid of my feminine clothing. She actually insisted on one occasion that she accompany me to get rid of them. I finally did do it; I gave them to Goodwill so that I could get a tax break. I also went to see a psychiatrist who helped me realize that this was an important need, that cross-dressing was something that I was probably going to continue. My "ex" totally rejected this advice and we divorced.

Purging Act of throwing away or burning one's clothes as a desperate means of ending one's cross-dressing.

---

ing activities to make their relationship work. Half of the men said their partner had made efforts to try to understand the husband's interest by becoming more knowledgeable about cross-dressing.

Although the *DSM-IV-TR* defines transvestic fetishism as a heterosexual phenomenon, surveys of men who cross-dress find that not all the respondents are heterosexual. As noted earlier, Bullough and Bullough (1997a, 1997b) discovered that a notable portion of their survey respondents were bisexual, homosexual, or not sexually active with a partner. In studies of cross-dressing communities in Java, Thailand, the Philippines, Guatemala, Peru, and Brazil, the men who cross-dress often identify themselves as homosexual. Few have had sexual reassignment surgery, but some consider themselves preoperative transsexuals. The study of men from Maine and New Hampshire (Reynolds & Caron, 2000) found that despite the men's participation in a study of heterosexual cross-dressers, 6 of the 21 men described themselves "as possibly being on a continuum to transsexualism" (p. 76). Apparently, there is variation in the gender identity and sexual orientation of men who cross-dress.

Psychiatrists and psychologists are more likely now to try to understand cross-dressing using a broader approach than the historical focus on such explanations as influence of a strong mother figure, castration anxiety, and homosexual panic. However, Bullough and

Bullough (1997b, p. 2) note that an "illness model" is still used "to conceptualize all types of cross dressing." They observed that the continuing inclusion of *transvestism* in the *DSM* (despite removal of *homosexuality* in 1974) is a reflection of the fact that transvestism has not been studied as much as homosexuality. Furthermore, transvestites have not been "as politically astute as the gay-power movement in demanding that their diagnosis be removed from the DSM. Only recently has such an effort begun to be mounted in the cross-dressing community" (pp. 2–3).

16-2f Sexual Sadism

Sexual sadism Paraphilia characterized by recurrent, intense, sexual urges and sexually arousing fantasies, of at least 6 months' duration, involving acts that hurt or humiliate the sexual partner.

Sexual sadism and sexual masochism are two sides of the same coin in that they both involve associating psychological or physical suffering and humiliation with sexual arousal or pleasure. **Sexual sadism** is characterized by recurrent, intense, sexual urges and sexually arousing fantasies, of at least 6 months' duration, involving acts (real, not simulated) that hurt or humiliate the sexual partner. In some cases, sadistic people will have acted on these urges; when these sadistic acts are practiced with nonconsenting partners, the severity of the acts increases over time.

When the sadist and masochist get together, it is the sadist who enjoys inflicting the pain on the masochist. Such infliction of pain and social scripting ("Have you been a bad boy? Mommy must give you a good spanking.") normally occurs in the context of an explicit (and sometimes written) agreement between the parties as to the limits of what is acceptable (handcuffs, hot wax, whipping) and a "safe" word which alerts the sadist that the masochist wants to stop whatever is going on (and the sadist agrees to stop when the masochist says this word). Hence, sado/masochistic sexual behavior may be consensual.

The term *sadism* refers to the Marquis de Sade (1740–1814), French author, philosopher, and sadomasochist who described literally the experiences of people who enjoyed hurting and dominating their sexual partners. The cries and suffering of the sexual partner were the source of sadistic sexual excitement. Such suffering may be by consenting masochistic partners or by those who are forced to participate. Sadistic acts or fantasies may involve dominance (forcing the victim to crawl), restraint or bondage (tying the victim to a chair), spanking, whipping, beating, burning, shocking (with electricity), cutting, strangling, mutilating, or killing.

16-2g Sexual Masochism

Sexual masochism Paraphilia characterized by recurrent, intense, sexual urges and sexually arousing fantasies, of at least 6 months' duration, in which sexual arousal or gratification is obtained through enacting scripts that involve experiencing suffering and pain.

Sexual masochism is characterized by recurrent, intense, sexual urges and sexually arousing fantasies, of at least 6 months' duration, in which sexual arousal or gratification is obtained through enacting scripts that involve the person receiving the acts of the sadist so that he or she suffers pain and humiliation. Such pain may be physical or psychological and may involve being humiliated, beaten, bound, cut, bitten, spanked, choked, pricked, or shocked. Although pain may actually be experienced, the diagnosis of the paraphilia may involve only intense, recurrent urges and fantasies for at least 6 months. The person may have these fantasies while masturbating or while having sexual relations.

Think About It

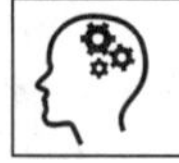

Green (2001) identified a court case in England regarding the right of consenting individuals to participate in "serious" sadomasochism. The trial was based on a 1987 videotape of 50 men having sadomasochistic encounters over a 10-year period. The video depicted scenes of "maltreatment of the genitalia, sometimes with hot wax, sandpaper, fish hooks, and needles plus ritualistic beatings, either with bare hand or implements including stinging nettles, spiked belts, and a cat-o-nine tails" (p. 543). Given that two consenting adults are involved in these activities, at what point do you think legal intervention would be appropriate, if at all?

Gebhard (1976) emphasized that it is not the pain per se that is sexually exciting to the masochistic person, but rather the enactment of the script that involves pain. In common masochistic scripts, "the masochist must allegedly have done something meriting punishment, there must be threats and suspense before the punishment is meted out. . . . Some masochists dislike the pain while it is being inflicted, but obtain gratification by anticipation of the pain or by thinking about it after it has ceased" (pp. 163–164).

16-2h Sadomasochistic Clubs and Subculture

A team of researchers (Santtila, Sandnabba, Alison, & Nordling, 2002) surveyed 22 women and 162 men who were members of two sadomasochistically oriented clubs and identified the 29 sexual behaviors they reported engaging in. Some categories, examples, and percents included receipt of pain (clothespins attached to nipples, 68%; spanking, 64%), humiliation (flagellation, 82%; verbal humiliation, 70%), and physical restraint (bondage, 88%; handcuffs, 73%). In general, less intense behaviors preceded more intense behaviors.

Sadistic and masochistic persons may use each other to act out their sexual scripts. A favorite pattern is bondage and discipline (B&D), also referred to as dominance and submission (D&S), where the sadist ties up (bondage) and whips (disciplines) the masochist. Often, the sadist will act out a scene by telling the masochist of a series of the latter's wrongdoings and the punishment to follow while the masochist screams for mercy. Both delight in the activity.

Some large cities have "clubs" that specialize in D&S (S&M). The "staff" consists of dominants (sadists), submissives (masochists), and "switch-hitters." Equipment may include a wide range of racks, cages, chains, wooden crosses, and whipping posts. Customers have been served by being bound, gagged, stretched, and beaten. Some partners exhibit mild forms of D&S in their relationship, as illustrated in the following example:

> *I like to be tied up and blindfolded. I can't tell what my partner is doing but, on occasion, he has used candles and dripped the hot wax on my body and my breasts. I like it when he orders me around and dominates me. It's not S and M but a step towards it. I, too, tie my boyfriend up and do as I want with him while he is totally submissive. I don't want whips and severe pain, even though we have used handcuffs and ropes; we love each other and know it's fun, and we're not trying to hurt each other. (authors' files)*

A less severe form of D&S involves mild spanking in which one partner will playfully spank the buttocks of the partner. The spanking is not regarded as painful by the giver or receiver. Comfort (1987) studied what he referred to as "so-called 'bondage' or the playing of 'restraint games'" and found that it occurred with surprising frequency, not only in fantasy, but also in couples' activities. While he said "the 'bondage' routine is a definite situational fetish for some individuals and a strong preference for others (of both sexes)," a high number of his informants "seemed to be incorporating it into a varied sexual repertoire as one more resource" (p. 13). While this type of "bondage" could be enacted in a sadomasochistic way, Comfort found that couples used it more as a sexual technique, a kind of foreplay, rather than as a compulsive fantasy or activity. In section 16-2f, we noted the use of "safe" words that couples use to ensure that their sex play is kept within mutually acceptable limits.

In their book reporting interviews with 100 participants and experts on D&S, Brame, Brame, and Jacobs (1993) stated

> *D&Sers make a real and absolute distinction between explicitly consensual acts between adult partners for their mutual pleasure and all acts of violence against unconsenting partners. Imposing any sexual activity on a reluctant partner is morally offensive; imposing it on an unwilling partner (or upon anyone who cannot give legal consent) is a criminal offense." (p. xi)*

Those interviewed in the Brame et al. book (1993, p. 5) present D&S as a controlled expression of adult sexuality that allows intense intimacy and sharing. They advance the credo of "Safe, Sane, and Consensual—de Sade would be disgusted." While some people enjoy D&S, as Comfort suggested, as an embellishment of erotic play, others find that the experience of sexual submission or dominance is the essential element of an erotic encounter. It has been more than 100 years since Krafft-Ebing first identified sadomasochism, categorized it as a pathology, and formed the basis for the current clinical diagnosis. However, contemporary dissemination about the D&S subculture is not being distributed by scientist or researchers, but by people involved in the subculture themselves. With the media explosion of publications, media talk shows, and computer bulletin boards, sexual minority communities have grown. Brame et al. observe that the anonymity and accessibility of online networks have promoted exchange of ideas previously too distressing to discuss freely. This is likely to offer confirmation to others with similar interests to discover that "a community of shared interest and sympathetic understanding exists" (Brame et al., 1993, p. 27).

16-2i Other Paraphilias

Although we have discussed the major paraphilias presented in the *DSM-IV-TR* (American Psychiatric Association, 2000), there are many others. Examples of other varieties are presented in Table 16-2.

Miletski (2001) studied zoophilia by asking 82 men and 11 women who had had sexual relationships with animals (defined as "any physical contact between a person and an animal that results in sexual pleasure for the human participant"; p. 86) to complete a 23-page, 350-item anonymous questionnaire. The most frequent animal sex partner for men was a male dog (90%), with the most frequent sexual behaviors those of masturbating the animal (64%), performing fellatio on the animal (42%), and submitting to anal intercourse by the animal (42%). The most frequent animal sex partner for women was the male dog (100%), with the most frequent sexual behaviors those of masturbating the animal (64%), having the animal perform cunnilingus on them (55%), having vaginal-penile intercourse with the animal (55%), and performing fellatio on the animal (45%). Zoophiles live a life of "secrecy fraught with fear of being outed, depression, low self-esteem, anger, stress, anxiety, shame, guilt, grieving the loss of animal sex partners, coming out, childhood abuse, wanting to be animals, and wanting to stop bestiality" (p. 89).

Many of the sexually variant acts listed in Table 16-2 are enacted in the context of power exchange between the participants that is the source of erotic excitement. Through submission, some people find escape from responsibility, trust in their partner, and a sexual delight in surrender. Through domination, some people enjoy the development of the emotional bond between dominant and submissive, the opportunity to cultivate imaginative abilities and playfulness, and the sense of control of one's partner (Brame et al., 1993). In addition to the acts listed in the table, other variant activities that may be done for erotic motives include tattooing, piercing, and scarification. Most of these activities are controversial and, in some jurisdictions, illegal, even when engaged in by consenting persons. However, learning about them can help explain part of the mystery and complexity of human sexual expression.

16-2j Is Rape a Paraphilia?

There is professional disagreement over whether rape should be classified as a paraphilia. Abel and Rouleau (1990) argued that rape is a paraphilia on the basis of clinical interviews with rapists who report having compulsive urges and fantasies to commit rape, feeling guilty afterward, and repeating the behavior. Persons with paraphilias characteristically experience compulsive urges and fantasies and guilt and also repeat the paraphilic behavior. In addition, the age of onset for interest in rape and the age of onset for other

TABLE 16-2

Other Paraphilias

Paraphilia	Description
Acrotomophilia	Deriving sexual arousal or gratification from engaging in sex with an amputee.
Apotomnophilia	Becoming sexually aroused by the thought of becoming an amputee.
Asphyxiophilia	Cutting off one's air supply to enhance orgasm.
Autonepiophilia	Deriving sexual arousal or gratification from wearing wet diapers.
Avoniepiphilia	Deriving sexual arousal by wearing diapers.
Coprophilia	Using feces for sexual arousal either by watching another defecate or by defecating on someone.
Ephebophilia	Engaging in sexual behavior with an adolescent or having a recurrent urge to do so.
Erotophonophilia	Committing lust murder, in which the partner is killed as a means of atoning for sex with the individual.
Formicophilia	Becoming sexually aroused by ants, bugs, or other small, crawling creatures.
Gerontophilia	Becoming sexually aroused by elderly individuals.
Klismaphilia	Becoming sexually aroused by receiving an enema.
Mysophilia	Deriving sexual excitement from filthy or soiled objects.
Narratophilia	Listening to "dirty talk" as a means of becoming sexually aroused. Phone sex companies depend on people with this paraphilia for their income.
Necrophilia	Deriving sexual arousal or gratification from sexual activity with a dead person (or a person acting the role of a corpse).
Nepiophilia	Becoming sexually aroused by babies.
Olfactophilia	Becoming sexually aroused by certain scents.
Partialism	Deriving sexual arousal or gratification from a specific nongenital body part (such as the foot).
Pictophilia	Becoming sexually aroused in reference to sexy photographs.
Raptophilia	Becoming sexually aroused by surprise attack and violent assault.
Scatalogia	Becoming sexually aroused by calling a stranger on the phone and either talking about sex or making sexual sounds (breathing heavily; also called telephonicophilia).
Somnophilia	Fondling a person who is sleeping so as to become sexually aroused. The person is often a stranger.
Urophilia	Using urine for sexual arousal either by watching someone urinate or by urinating on someone.
Zoophilia	Becoming aroused by sexual contact with animals (commonly known as bestiality).

paraphilias is similar. More than half of rapists report developing their interest in rape by age 21, the age by which other paraphilias often develop.

The *DSM-IV-TR* (American Psychiatric Association, 2000) does not list rape as a specific paraphilic disorder. Perhaps psychiatrists do not classify rape as a paraphilia because it is more violent and sexually aggressive than other paraphilias (except some expressions of sadomasochism). In addition, society may be reluctant to accept rape as a paraphilia because paraphilias are associated with less punishment than rape.

Think About It

Have you experienced a preference for a sexual stimulus that you feel borders on a compulsion? To what degree does such a proclivity affect you or your relationships? Are there any potential legal consequences for the movement of this preference into a compulsion?

16-3 THE ORIGINS OF PARAPHILIAS: THEORETICAL PERSPECTIVES

Various theoretical perspectives offer explanations for why paraphilias exist or why particular individuals develop paraphilias.

16-3a Psychoanalytic Theory

From a psychoanalytic perspective, paraphilias may be viewed as symptoms of unresolved subconscious conflicts. For example, an exhibitionistic man may frighten unsuspecting women by exposing himself to them as a way of rebelling against them. Such rebellion may stem from having a domineering mother or an unresolved Oedipal complex, which has left the person unable to engage in heterosexual intercourse. The urge to exhibit himself may be a subconscious symbolic substitute that compensates for the inability to have sexual relations with women.

Kline (1987) reviewed psychoanalytic conceptualization of paraphilias and empirical research designed to test these theories. He concluded that although the evidence was not sufficient to refute Freudian theories, it also did not offer objective support. He lamented that because psychoanalytic theories "have reached a low ebb" (p. 173), it is unlikely that high-quality research will put them to a scientific test.

16-3b Feminist Perspective

Paraphilias such as pedophilia and sexual sadism are, from a feminist perspective, expressions of aggression more than sexuality. The pedophile, sadist, and rapist express control and dominance through their paraphilic fantasies and behaviors.

The feminist perspective explains why there are many more men with paraphilia than women with paraphilia: Our culture has perpetuated traditional gender roles that emphasize male dominance, sexual aggression, and control. Some paraphilias may be motivated by expressing hostility and holding the momentary feeling of power over a victim (Bancroft, 1989). An example of the desire to dominate was provided in a description of advertising the sex scenes available on The Amateur Action bulletin board system. Typically, the online service received a lukewarm response to straightforward depictions of oral sex. However, when words such as *choke* or *choking* were used, the demand from consumers doubled (Elmer-Dewitt, 1995).

16-3c Learning Theory

Learning theorists emphasize that paraphilias are learned by means of both classical and operant conditioning. In 1966, Rachman demonstrated how a fetish can be learned through classical conditioning. Using an experimental design, Rachman paired women's boots with erotic slides of nude women. As a result, the participants began to experience erotic arousal at the sight of the boots alone.

Scarf, panty, and high-heeled shoe fetishes may be a result of classical conditioning. The person may have experienced sexual pleasure when in the presence of these objects, learned to associate these objects with the pleasure, and developed a preference for these objects during sex.

Operant conditioning may also account for the development of some paraphilias. For example, the exhibitionist may be reinforced by the startled response of a woman and seek conditions under which she will exhibit a startled response (exposing his penis). By exposing his penis, he causes her to yell, is reinforced, and wants to repeat the behavior with a new stranger. Orgasm may also be an operant conditioning reinforcer (Weinberg, Williams, & Calhan, 1995).

Similarly, paraphilias may result from negative reinforcement. *Negative reinforcement* is defined as the strengthening of a behavior associated with the removal of something aversive. A paraphilia may be established because the associated behaviors remove feelings of anxiety, sadness, loneliness, and anger. Hence, when the exhibitionist exhibits to a victim, he feels a temporary reprieve from feelings of anxiety, which are replaced by feelings of excitement.

16-3d Biological Theory

The degree to which biological variables are responsible for the development of paraphilias is controversial. Just as heterosexuality, homosexuality, and bisexuality may be based on biological predispositions, so may paraphilic tendencies. Some people may be biologically "wired" to respond erotically to atypical stimuli. Moser (1992) contended that paraphilias are strong sexual responses to an individualized, specific set of uncommon or inappropriate objects or potential partners and that these "lust" responses are "a basic aspect of sexual identity, set early in life, unchangeable by common sex therapy techniques and are not learned in a classical sense" (p. 66). Although he did not define the mechanisms for these presumably innate predilections, other investigators have proposed that there are neurochemical interactions during embryo development that influence cerebral organization (Flor-Henry, 1987).

16-3e Paraphilia as a Vandalized Lovemap

In section 16-1, John Money's (1986, 1988) term *lovemap* was used to describe a mental representation or template that develops early in the individual's life. It establishes, or at least influences, the type of sexual partner and activities that will arouse a person. Given the standard developmental hormones introduced into the developing fetus at the appropriate time and the traditional heterosexual socialization, people tend to be emotionally and sexually attracted to the other sex.

The critical years in the development of the lovemap are between ages 5 and 8 (Carnes, 2001). "Major erotosexual traumas during this period may disrupt the consolidation of the lovemap that would otherwise be taking place" (Money, 1986, p.19). Money provided examples of the social experiences that "vandalize" or disrupt traditional sexual-erotic development socialization and showed how these disruptions may contribute to the development of pedophilia.

For example, a pedophile may have been involved in a relationship with an older man and learned to repeat the age-discrepant sexual experience with a younger boy. "In adolescence and adulthood, they remain sexuoerotically boyish, and are paraphilically attracted only to juveniles of the same age as their own when they became a pedophile's partner" (Money, 1986, p. 21). Often, the experience itself will not be enough to trigger a pedophiliac lovemap. But in combination with a traumatic experience, such as grief over a loved one's death, the man may become particularly vulnerable. Hence, the feeling of having lost a significant other and the enjoyment of sexual pleasure in an age-discrepant context may bond one to that context for reasons related to emotional insecurity and physical pleasure.

Carnes (2001) provided another example of distortions in one's arousal template. "Consider the very successful scientist who told of a violent childhood. He can remember his father battering his mother so badly he could hear her body hit the wall in the next room. He would masturbate to comfort himself in his anxiety" (p. 49). In effect, arousal became associated with the trauma and drama of violence in a relationship.

16-3f Paraphilia as a Courtship Disorder

Some paraphilias may also be conceptualized as expressions of a common "underlying" disorder (Carnes, 2001). The disorder in this case is a distortion of "normal" courtship, which is assumed to consist of a series of phases in which progressively more intimate expressions of sexual behavior occur. An example is that courtship includes flirting and seducing the partner. This pattern may be twisted (and hence, a **courtship disorder**) so that the person flirts with the goal of seducing out of power and conquest, not intimacy. The person is "hooked on falling in love and winning the attention of the other" (p. 61). Similarly, "the rapist short circuits all stages and immediately attempts intercourse" (Langevin & Lang, 1987, p. 203).

Courtship disorder A distortion of the standard sequence of interpersonal events in courtship that lead to the development of an intimate relationship; used as a theory to explain rape, the rapist short-circuits the courtship stages and progresses immediately to intercourse.

Another byproduct of the courtship disorder is that the person with a paraphilia may have difficulty loving a person because of his preoccupation with the paraphilic object. The deficient ability to love and the inability to progress through the courtship sequence make it difficult to have a conventional sexual relationship.

16-4 TREATMENT OF PARAPHILIAS

The behavioral expression of some of the paraphilias we have discussed (such as exhibitionism and pedophilia) interferes with the rights of others. When people engaging in such behaviors come to the attention of the law, they are often required to enter a treatment program. Indeed, the U.S. Supreme Court has upheld the civil commitment of sexually violent predators for treatment as constitutional. In effect, these individuals may be legally kept in psychiatric hospitals or special facilities for the treatment of their sexual deviation prior to release. Whereas most people with paraphilias must be forced to address them, some individuals seek treatment voluntarily. Figure 16-2 presents the stages in the treatment of paraphilias.

After the existence of the paraphilia has become socially visible, treatment of the sex offender begins with a thorough assessment. This assessment involves collecting information regarding the offense of record, as well as a sexual, social, and psychiatric history. The therapist usually gathers the law enforcement report, victim statement, pre-sentence investigation, and summaries of previous placements and treatment. Interviews with the client and relevant other people are conducted, and psychological testing may be done. Assessment specific to sexual behaviors also includes a sex hormone profile, sexual interest questionnaires, and sexual orientation assessment (McDonald & Bradford, 2000). The Multiphasic Sex Inventory obtains reports of deviant behaviors, as well as indications of sexual knowledge and cognitive distortions. Its scales measuring child molestation and rape are the most well developed, although it does address other paraphilias. The polygraph is sometimes used to corroborate self-reports obtained in clinical interviews. Measurements of penile tumescence (changes in the volume and circumference of the penis) are also used to assess physiological arousal. The penile plethysmograph employs a sensor or transducer that measures and records changes in penis size in response to sexual stimuli (audiotapes or slides).

FIGURE 16-2
Stages in Treatment of Paraphilias

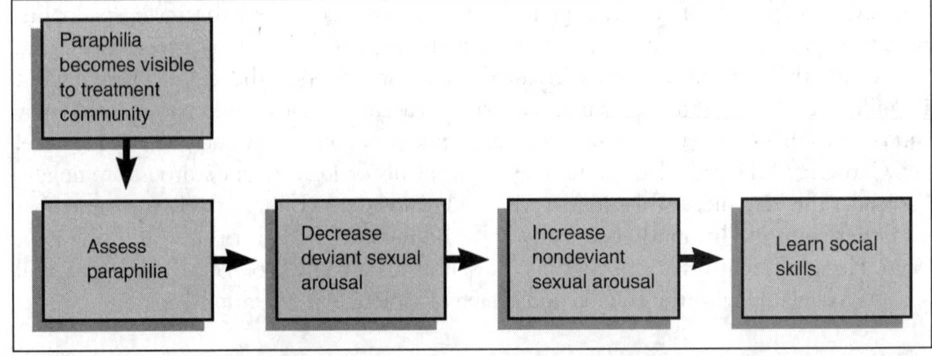

Models for treatment of paraphilias, particularly pedophilia, view sex as a biological drive that can be disturbed in both intensity and direction. After a thorough evaluation, treatment begins and is usually focused on decreasing deviant sexual arousal, increasing nondeviant sexual arousal, teaching social skills, changing faulty cognitions, resolving sexual dysfunctions, managing alcohol abuse, or a combination of these tasks. Although a range of procedures is used to treat paraphilias, the recidivism (the rate at which treated people return to the paraphilic behavior) is high (Feierman & Feierman, 2000).

16-4a Decreasing Deviant Sexual Arousal

Effective treatment of a paraphilia involves decreasing the deviant sexual arousal response, or the response to that which society regards as nonsexual stimuli. The therapeutic goal is for the person to no longer require the paraphilic target stimulus as a preferred or necessary condition of sexual arousal. Treatment that focuses on decreasing deviant sexual arousal may involve medications, aversive conditioning, and covert sensitization. In regard to the use of medications to control paraphilias, there is considerable social debate. This controversy is discussed in Box 16-3.

Aversive Conditioning

Deviant sexual arousal may also be decreased through **aversive conditioning.** Such conditioning involves pairing an aversive or unpleasant stimulus with the paraphilic stimulus to decrease the deviant sexual arousal and reduce the probability of engaging in the paraphilic behavior. One example of an aversive stimulus is an unpleasant smell. For the heterosexual male pedophile, this type of aversion therapy is carried out by having the patient listen to audio depictions of sexual activities with children or with adult women. After the taped narrative of sexual activity with the child is played, the therapist administers a noxious odor so that the patient associates this with the stimulus of the child. After removing the odor, the therapist changes the tape narrative to that of sexual activity with an adult woman. In this way, the patient associates relief from the noxious stimuli (and, consequently, a more pleasant feeling) with the stimulus of the adult woman.

Aversive conditioning A type of behavior therapy that involves pairing an aversive or unpleasant stimulus with a previously reinforcing stimulus; used in sex offender treatment to decrease deviant sexual arousal and reduce the probability of engaging in paraphilic behavior.

The therapist might also use emetic drugs (which induce vomiting or nausea). Because it is believed that a fetish results from learning to associate a particular object with sexual pleasure, the stimulus object may be reconditioned by associating an unpleasant experience with it. For example, the person might be given emetic drugs to induce vomiting when in the presence of the fetish object. These procedures are still being researched.

Covert Sensitization

Covert sensitization involves using negative thoughts as a way of developing negative feelings associated with a deviant sexual stimulus. For example, a therapist may induce negative thoughts by saying the following to the patient:

Covert sensitization Therapeutic technique that involves instructing the client to use negative thoughts as a way of developing negative feelings associated with a deviant sexual stimulus.

> *I want you to imagine going into the bedroom of your 7-year-old niece when her parents are in another part of the house. As you open the door, you see her asleep in her bed. But as you approach the bed, you begin to feel very nauseous and feel that you are going to throw up. You vomit and feel the particles in your mouth and the stench in your nostrils. You also think that if you act on your urges and are discovered, you will be shamed out of the family.*

This scenario is designed to associate negative feelings and thoughts with acting on a sexual urge to touch a child to reduce the probability that the patient will engage in this behavior. Covert sensitization may be used to apply negative imagined consequences for offending and positive consequences for imagining alternatives to offending.

16-4b Increasing Nondeviant Sexual Arousal

In treating individuals with paraphilias, it is important not only to decrease deviant sexual arousal, but also to increase nondeviant sexual arousal. Thus, treatment of paraphilias also involves increasing the level of sexual arousal the individual has in reference to culturally appropriate sexual stimuli. For example, the therapist would try to increase the

Box 16-3 Social Choices

Treating Paraphilic Sex Offenders with Hormones?

The use of hormones to quell the sexual lust of the paraphiliac sex offenders involves a consideration of the rights of society to be protected from harm versus the rights of an offender to avoid being given medication that may have unwanted side effects. The rights of society have been established by the Supreme Court, which views the protection of children from pedophiles as paramount. California, Georgia, Montana, and Florida offer chemical castration as a condition of parole for repeat sex offenders (Meisenkothen, 1999).

Because sex is seen as a biological drive, hormones and neurotransmitters are used to mediate the intensity and direction of that drive (McDonald & Bradford, 2001). Antiandrogen drugs such as Depo-Provera (medroxyprogesterone acetate, or MPA) lowers the blood level of testosterone and seems to have a direct pharmacologic effect on brain pathways that mediate sexual behavior. Alternatively, cyproterone acetate may be used. Either may have the effect of removing the paraphilic preoccupation but still allow the person to act on his sexual interest in his partner without dysfunction. In other cases, Depo-Provera may result in a complete shutdown of eroticism. Although these treatments are controversial, Depo-Provera and cyproterone acetate may be used to treat pedophiles, exhibitionists, pedophiles, voyeurs, and rapists. Lehne and Money (2000) reported on the 40-year follow-up of the first man ever to receive Depo-Provera treatment for control of sex-offending paraphilic behavior. After intermittent treatment and relapse, he has ceased illegal sexual activity. Instead of having sexual fantasies involving children, he now fantasizes himself being treated as an "adult baby" and has exchanged "infantilism" fantasy stories over the Internet.

More recently, selective serotonin reuptake inhibitors (SSRIs) such as fluoxetine (trade name Prozac) have been used to reduce an individual's sexually deviant fantasies, urges, masturbation, and sexual behavior. For severe cases, luteinizing hormone-releasing hormone agonists (LHRH agonists), which have the effect of pharmacological castration, may be used. These hormone and serotonin reuptake inhibitors, "[w]hen combined with cognitive behavioral treatment," may provide some reduction in the urge to express paraphilic behaviors. Chow and Choy (2002) also noted the positive effects of SSRI in the treatment of a female pedophile—reductions in pedophilic arousal, fantasies, and impulsivity. But there are also negative effects such as loss of capacity to orgasm.

In addition, LHRH agonist leuprolide acetate is a chemical compound that has been used in the treatment of paraphilias to successfully reduce sexually aggressive behavior as well as to reduce penile erection, ejaculation, masturbation, sexually deviant impulsiveness, and fantasies. "All men (11) reported a reduction in paraphilic activities during therapy" (Briken, Nika, & Berner, 2001, p. 50). Their disorders included sadism, pedophilia or sexual impulsive-control disorder.

A rarely used alternative to chemical castration is surgical castration, whereby repeat child molesters in Canada may agree to the surgery in exchange for reduced jail time. The procedure results in reducing the man's interest in sex, sexual arousal, and activity in that it helps to control sexually deviant compulsions. Quebec reported the castration of three pedophile males, the last of which occurred in 2000. Does castration work? Men who have had their testes surgically removed, either to treat disease or control sexual behavior, report various levels of continued sexual ability. But a 20-year study of 1,036 sex offenders showed that the 84% repeat offense rate dropped to 2.3% after castration (Smithson, 2000).

sexual urges of a pedophile to the stimulus of a consenting adult partner. The mechanisms for increasing nondeviant sexual arousal include masturbatory conditioning, exposure, and systematic desensitization.

Masturbatory conditioning involves associating the pleasure of orgasm with a nondeviant stimulus. In this way, the previously nonarousing nondeviant stimulus becomes a stimulus for arousal. The therapist instructs the client to fantasize about the paraphilic urge or behavior while masturbating. Then, as tension mounts and pleasure increases, the client is instructed to switch fantasies from the deviant stimulus (such as a child) to a nondeviant stimulus (such as a consenting adult).

Exposure involves introducing the individual to the nondeviant stimulus for increasingly longer periods of time, during which the individual has an opportunity to develop positive associations. For example, if the exhibitionist feels uncomfortable in the presence of adult women, the therapist might assign the patient to attend social functions with a male friend and to stand increasingly closer to women in social contexts. Such exposure may help to reduce the fear and anxiety associated with women and facilitate a greater willingness to engage in social interaction with women.

Systematic desensitization is another procedure to promote behaviors that are incompatible with offending behaviors. Where the client feels extreme anxiety in the presence of the nondeviant stimulus, systematic desensitization may be employed to reduce such anxiety. In systematic desensitization, the client imagines a series of scenes that involve the nondeviant sexual stimulus (such as an adult female) and then ranks these scenes according to the level of anxiety or discomfort they produce. Then, while the client is relaxed (the therapist will have taught the person how to relax using a progressive relaxation procedure), the therapist will present the various scenes from lowest to highest anxiety to the client. The client's being relaxed while fantasizing about the various encounters with women reduces the fear and anxiety associated with women. To ensure generalization, the therapist will ask the person to increase the level of real-life exposure to adult women using the exposure technique described in the preceding paragraph.

16-4c Personal Choices: Can People Control Their Paraphilias?

Therapists disagree about the degree to which persons with paraphilias can control the behavioral expression of their paraphilia. Whereas some feel that those with pedophilia, exhibitionism, and voyeurism are uncontrollably and compulsively driven to express their paraphilia (and will not be able to change these "lust" cues; Moser, 1992), others suggest that these persons can exercise conscious control over their paraphilic behavior.

Pedophilia, exhibitionism, and voyeurism may be conceptualized as requiring a series of choices leading to the expression of the paraphilic behavior. For example, a pedophile who fondles a young boy in the park on a summer afternoon is engaging in a behavior that was preceded by a number of choices leading to that behavior. These choices may have included taking off from work, looking at child pornography, drinking alcohol, going to the playground, buying candy, sitting on the bench where a young boy was also sitting, talking to the boy, offering the boy some candy, and so on. At any of these choice points, the pedophile may have chosen to engage in a behavior that was incompatible with child molestation. Each of these behaviors, when taken alone, is a relatively easier choice: The person might choose to stay at work, look at alternative magazines, and so forth.

Similarly, the exhibitionist who exposes himself in the library to a stranger may alternatively have chosen to masturbate at home, to avoid alcohol, and to go with a friend to a movie. Finally, the voyeur might choose to schedule time with others when he is particularly vulnerable to "peeping," to avoid walking on another person's property (where peeping often occurs), and to select alternative behaviors, such as going to a movie during prime "peeping time."

In addition to consciously exercising to choose behaviors to control one's paraphilia, one can also control one's level of arousal. Nagayama Hall (1991) studied 169 in-patient adult male sex offenders in terms of their sexual arousal. While listening to erotic tapes, 84% were able to inhibit being sexually aroused as a result of sheer conscious control. The investigator simply asked them to "stop yourself from being sexually aroused" (p. 363), and all but 16% were able to do so.

In addition to making deliberate choices that are incompatible with the expression of paraphilic behaviors, the person who is concerned about his sexual interest may choose to seek therapy to address such issues as self-esteem, guilt, anxiety, sexual dysfunctions, and lack of social skills. By confronting these issues and ensuring that they do not contribute to unwanted behavior, the person is taking deliberate control of his sexual expression.

♦

16-4d Learning Social Skills

In section 16-3f, we discussed courtship disorder as an underlying problem in the development of some paraphilias. People with paraphilias typically have low self-esteem, anxiety in social situations, and no skills in initiating and maintaining an intimate interpersonal relationship. Treatment of paraphilias often involves teaching the person how to initiate a conversation, empathize, listen, and keep a conversation going so that the person will be better able to develop a close emotional bond with an adult partner. Social skill training often takes place in a group therapy setting where group members may practice basic communication and interaction skills with each other.

16-4e Changing Faulty Cognitions

Some paraphilic behaviors are continued on the basis of faulty cognitions. For example, the exhibitionist may think that "women are really turned on by the sight of a naked penis and would enjoy someone exposing himself." The pedophile may believe that children profit from sexual experiences with adults as a form of sex education. The rapist may think that women "really mean 'yes' when they say 'no' and enjoy having forced sex."

Correcting these cognitive distortions often occurs in the context of group therapy. Group members challenge the irrational beliefs of each other and acknowledge their own irrational beliefs. Irrational beliefs are replaced with new beliefs: Women are disgusted by exhibitionists, children are harmed by adult sexual exploitation, and women abhor being raped.

16-4f Resolving Sexual Dysfunctions

Some paraphilias are continued because of sexual dysfunctions that prevent the paraphiliac individual from engaging in sexual behavior with a partner. For example, the exhibitionist and voyeur may feel unable to engage in sex with a partner due to erectile dysfunction. They may also suffer rapid ejaculation or retarded ejaculation and want to avoid exposure of these dysfunctions in a relationship. Unless these sexual dysfunctions are treated, the paraphiliac individual may continue to feel sexually inadequate and perceive no alternative for sexual gratification other than engaging in paraphilic behavior.

Think About It

Assume you were developing a treatment program for a man with pedophilia. How might you prioritize the various techniques discussed in this chapter in developing your treatment plan for this individual?

16-4g Sexual Addiction: A False Concept?

Sexual addiction Sometimes described as an intimacy disorder manifested by a compulsive cycle of preoccupation and ritualization of sexual behavior and despair.

Sexual addiction has been described as an intimacy disorder manifested by a compulsive cycle of preoccupation and ritualization of sexual behavior and despair (Adams & Robinson, 2001). Sexual thoughts or behaviors may negatively affect the self-concept, relationships, or work of an individual. The addiction model has been used to characterize the denial, loss of control, and pathological prioritization that can occur. The origin of the disorder is rooted in impaired early attachment experiences; sexual addiction becomes a way to compensate for early attachment failure. Treatment involves understanding the key elements that drive the compulsive disorder (Carnes, 2001) and learning to establish enduring and trusting intimate connections with others (Adams & Robinson, 2001). For example, Carnes (2001) noted that the sexually rejected spouse seeks sex with others compulsively to "even the score" and get back at the rejecting spouse who "deserves" the infidelity.

Although a journal about sexual addiction (*Sexual Addiction and Compulsivity*) is published quarterly and numerous self-help organizations are available, such as Sex Addicts Anonymous, Sexaholics Anonymous, Sexual Compulsives Anonymous, and Sex and Love Addicts Anonymous, the American Psychiatric Association (APA) no longer recognizes sexual addiction as a disorder. Wise and Schmidt (1996), reporting on the APA's review of the *DSM-III-R* (American Psychiatric Association, 1987) use of the concept, noted:

> *There is abundant clinical evidence of sexual activity that can be characterized as "excessive." However, the concept of sexual addiction is troublesome in that the term "addiction" has a specific meaning associated with physiological processes of withdrawal. In addition, there is no scientific database to support the concept of excessive sexual behavior as being in the realm of an addiction. Competing concepts of compulsivity or impulsive control disorders are intriguing possibilities but lack database support. The whole issue of excessive sexual behavior is worthy of scientific study, but the interests of research are not served by restricting the focus of these efforts to a process of addiction. (p. 1140)*

Nevertheless, Griffiths (2001) does use the term *sex addiction* in reference to *Internet addiction*. And, the American Psychiatric Association does recognize that "excessive sexual behavior" may occur in both women and men and that the clinical description of **nymphomania** (excessive sexual behavior in women) and **satyriasis** (excessive sexual behavior in men) may apply. However, how these concepts should be treated is an open question (Wise & Schmidt, 1996, p. 1141).

Nymphomania Excessive sexual desire or behavior in women.

Satyriasis Excessive sexual behavior in men.

16-5 COMMERCIALIZATION OF SEX

We have been discussing paraphilias as an example of variant sexual behavior. In sections 16-5b and 16-5c, we discuss two additional forms of sexual variations: prostitution and pornography. We discuss these under the rubric of the commercialization of sex because the sale of one's body for sexual service and the sale of photographs of nude bodies are commercial enterprises. Because some variant sexual behaviors are stigmatized, often people with those interests seek commercial sex workers to indulge their sexual interests. We begin with a discussion of the law and sexuality because both prostitution and pornography are subject to legal regulation.

16-5a Sex and the Law

An unending debate in U.S. society exists around the issue of private rights versus social morality. For example, should consenting adults be permitted to engage in any sexual behaviors they choose, or should the law define morally acceptable parameters?

John Stuart Mill (1859/1985) emphasized the rights of the individual by arguing that the only purpose of government should be to protect its citizens from harm by others. He also advocated

> *The liberty of the individual must be thus far limited; he must not make himself a nuisance to other people. But if he refrains from molesting others in what concerns them, and merely acts according to his own inclination and judgement in things which concern himself . . . he should be allowed, without molestation, to carry his opinions into practice at his own cost. (pp. 119–120)*

In contrast, Lord Devlin (1965) argued that no private morality should operate outside the concern of criminal law. He felt that the health of society was defined by its adherence to a binding moral code and recommended that legal definitions of morality be identified and enforced. A more recent version of legislating morality was reflected by the Meese Commission Report on pornography (*Attorney General's Commission on Pornography*; U.S. Department of Justice, 1986). The commission took the position that the protection of society's moral environment is a legitimate purpose of government and recommended more restrictive laws on pornography.

One of the ways society has achieved compromise and balance between the radically opposing views of private versus public morality has been to view certain sexual behaviors on a continuum of offensiveness and to assign relative penalties for engaging in them. For example, child sexual abuse and rape are regarded as severely offensive and are subject to strong social sanctions. However, frottage may go unrecognized in criminal statistics because such behavior is likely to be prosecuted under a more generalized category, such as assault.

The following are five categories of sexual acts according to criminal classification (MacNamara & Sagarin, 1977):

- *Category I*—Criminal acts that require enforcement to protect society. Rape and child molestation are examples.
- *Category II—Sexual acts with potential victimization*. Exhibitionism and voyeurism are examples. Although these behaviors themselves may not be regarded as morally severe, they may create harm to the victims, who deserve protection.
- *Category III—Sexual acts midway between those considered morally reprehensible and those creating victims*. Prostitution and adultery are examples. Both are said to reflect immorality, and both have the potential to produce victims (the prostitutes in the case of prostitution and the spouse or children of the adulterer).
- *Category IV—Sex acts between consenting adults, including homosexual behavior and behaviors within marriage*.
- *Category V*—Behaviors that do not involve sexual contact, but are either criminalized or considered to be sex crimes. Abortion (in countries where it is illegal) and the sale and distribution of child pornography are examples.

It is commonly assumed that most people have not committed criminal sexual acts. However, people often engage in sexual activities that may be considered criminal and are not apprehended by the law. In a sample of 60 undergraduate college men (who are often used as nonoffender controls in sex research), nearly two thirds reported having engaged in some form of sexual misconduct in the past. More than half (52%) had engaged in a sexual offense for which they could be arrested (Templeman & Stinnett, 1991). Some examples included voyeurism (42%), frottage (35%), obscene phone calls (8%), and coercive sex (8%; p.142). In spite of the relatively high incidence of having engaged in punishable sex offenses, only 2 of the 60 respondents (3%) had been arrested.

16-5b Prostitution

Prostitution The exchange of money, drugs, or goods for access to one's body for the purpose of the purchaser's pleasure or enjoyment.

Prostitution is defined as providing sexual behavior, enjoyment, and/or pleasure through the use of one's body in exchange for money, drugs, or other goods. Prostitution is also referred to as *sex work*. Money may be exchanged for various types of services, including lap dancing, stripping, modeling for sexual photos, or being a phone sex partner. Although prostitutes are typically thought of as adult women, worldwide about 1 million children (under the age of 18) are forced into the sex trade annually (Willis & Levy, 2002).

Studies on recruitment into prostitution have focused on the characteristics associated with women who end up as prostitutes. Van Brunschot and Brannigan (2002) studied the backgrounds of 42 female street prostitutes and compared them with 57 female undergraduates. Although childhood physical and sexual abuse was higher for the prostitutes than the undergraduates, the researchers observed that the primary background characteristics were that the prostitutes reported having had their first sexual experience at age 13 or younger (suggesting lack of parental supervision), did not feel emotionally close to their birth or foster parents, and sought emotional satisfaction through involvement with older men. As for child prostitutes, most of the 10 million worldwide are forced into prostitution to provide financial support for their family (Willis & Levy, 2002).

Prostitution is a controversial topic, with some individuals viewing it as a form of sexual abuse and exploitation and others viewing it as a legitimate activity that adults have the right to engage in. Proponents of the prostitution-as-abuse perspective argue that prostitutes are physically, morally, and economically exploited. Dangers of prostitution include murder, rape, beatings, robbery, psychological abuse, and emotional pain. Spiwak Rotlewicz (2001) reported that in a study of prostitutes in Colombia, South America, 70% of the women reported physical assault since entering prostitution; 68% reported that their lives had been threatened. Vulnerability to diseases—particularly AIDS—is a substantial risk. Of the children rescued from brothels in parts of southeast Asia, 50–90% are infected with HIV (Willis & Levy, 2002).

Most prostitutes are trapped and can't get out. Many are chemically dependent and trade sex for money to buy drugs. Through personal interviews with 43 streetwalking prostitutes, Dalla (2002) found that the women began prostituting to support an existing drug habit and went straight to the streets (the lowest status type of prostitution). Most of these women became regular drug users, and as their addictions became worse, they became more willing to accept lower payment (in money or crack) for their services. The prevalence of crack cocaine profoundly influenced the subculture—"Simply put, the tricks were getting cheaper and the violence more rampant and more severe" (p. 70). Street-level work is the most dangerous and least glamorous type of prostitution.

Alternatively, call girls (at the top of the prostitution hierarchy) are more likely to work in a relatively safe environment with regular clients and may run a lucrative business (Flowers, 1998). Many prostitutes say that their occupation is simply a way of earning an income in a recreation-oriented service industry (Anderson, 2002). They argue that they are abused by the courts and the police who harass them. These women note that prostitutes are more often women than men, and are more often arrested than the men they serve.

COYOTE, an acronym for Call Off Your Old Tired Ethics, was formed in San Francisco by an ex-prostitute, Margo St. James. COYOTE has promoted the idea of a prostitutes' union to change the public image of prostitutes and to fight the moral and legal discrimination to which they are subjected. Rather than viewing prostitution as the use of a woman's body by a man for his satisfaction, Zatz (1997) has suggested, "What's wrong with the description, 'Prostitution is about the use of a man's desire by a woman for her own profit'?" (p. 295)

Prostitution occurs worldwide. **Trafficking** (the use of force and deception to transfer victims into situations of extreme exploitation) has become an international industry. The latest technology in recruiting prostitutes is through the Internet (Worden, 2001). Traffickers use the Internet to entice women in developing countries with the hope of good jobs and lure them into a life of sexual servitude—in brothels, sold as mail order brides, or used as videoconference strippers.

Trafficking Related to prostitution, using force and deception to transfer persons into situations of extreme exploitation.

Think About It

Two researchers (Xantidis & McCabe, 2000) identified the characteristics of 66 male clients of prostitutes in Australia and noted no age, education, marital status, or occupational differences from men who did and did not seek sex with prostitutes. However, men who were clients were more likely to report a high need for novelty and variety in sexual encounters. Busch, Bell, Hotaling, and Monto (2002) studied 1,342 men who had been arrested for trying to hire a prostitute and found that patriarchal views of women and perceived entitlement to power and control were characteristics of the johns (clients).

INTERNATIONAL DATA It has been estimated that of the 700,000 to 2 million women and children globally trafficked in prostitution each year, 45,000 to 50,000 are trafficked to the United States. Of these, approximately 30,000 are from Southeast Asia, 10,000 from Latin America, 4,000 from the newly independent states and Eastern Europe, and 1,000 from other regions (Richard, 1999).

Over the past decade, analysis of prostitution has been transformed from conceptualization as a "victimless crime" to an examination of its sociopolitical reality (Davis, 1993). The prostitution industry and trafficking in persons (mostly girls and women, but including boys and men also) have been described as a violation of human rights and as a form of torture that is tolerated in many countries, and the notion of entering prostitution as a "choice" has been challenged. Jacqueline Boles (1998) noted that the prostitution scene has changed significantly since the late 1960s. At that time most prostitutes thought of themselves as "working girls" in sex work. Today, in many cases girls "work" out of desperation and may feel driven to obtain drugs or to escape poverty. She also observed that transvestite prostitution is more common today. In addition, in today's worldwide male and female prostitution trade, children are sold into sexual servitude for a lifetime:

> *Just as prostitution is not about individuals, {it} isn't about choice. Instead prostitution is about the absence of meaningful choices; about having alternative routes to survival cut off or being in a situation where you don't have options to begin with. Nothing demonstrates this more clearly than the fact that most women who enter "the profession" do so as children, at age sixteen or younger. It becomes clear that the majority of prostitutes are socialized into "sex work" in childhood and adolescence when consent is meaningless and choice an illusion. (Dorchen Leidholdt, Prostitution: A Violation of Human Rights. Yeshiva University, 1993, quoted by Spiwak Rotlewicz, 2001).*

In Box 16-4, we discuss the controversy over whether prostitution should be legalized or decriminalized.

16-5c Pornography and Erotica

Pornography Sexually explicit pictures, writing, or other images, usually pairing sex with power and violence.

Degrading pornography Sexually explicit material that degrades, debases, and dehumanizes people, typically women.

Violent pornography Sexually explicit visual images of sexual violence usually directed by men against women.

Erotica Sexually explicit material that is neither a degrading nor violent portrayal of consensual sexual activity.

The term **pornography**—derived from the words *porne* ("prostitute") and *graphein* ("to write")—originally meant "stories of prostitutes." **Degrading pornography** is sexually explicit material that degrades, debases, and dehumanizes people, generally women. **Violent pornography** is sexually explicit and endorses the utility and normativeness of sexual violence usually directed by men against women. There is debate over what is pornography and what is erotica. One viewpoint suggests that the perception of what is "pornographic" or what is "erotic" is subjective. Fisher and Barak (2001) identified **erotica** as sexually explicit material that is a neither degrading nor violent portrayal of consensual sexual activity.

Almost 700 million hard-core pornographic videos are rented annually in the United States. Hotel chains such as Sheraton, Hyatt, Hilton, and Holiday Inn report annual income from renting adult videos at almost $200 million a year (Bedard & Gertz, 2000).

A team of researchers (Goodson, McCormick, & Evans, 2001) found that 43.5% of 506 undergraduate students reported they had, at some time, accessed sexually explicit materials through the Internet. But they did so rarely. Only 2.9% said they accessed these materials "frequently." Male students were significantly more likely to have accessed the Internet for viewing sexually explicit materials than women. Nationally, the percentage of U.S. adult men and women who spend money on sexually explicit magazines or books is 16% versus 4%, on the purchase of X-rated videos is 23% versus 11%, and clubs with nude or seminude dancers is 23% versus 11% (Michael et al., 1994).

Obscenity Label for sexual material that meets three criteria: (a) the dominant theme of the material must appeal to a prurient interest in sex; (b) the material must be patently offensive to the community; and (c) the sexual material must have no redeeming social value.

Koukounas and McCabe (2001) presented erotic film segments to 30 men (mean age 29.5) who reported both sexual arousal and positive feelings in response to the visual images. Although some people enjoy viewing pornography or erotica, others view it as offensive and obscene. **Obscenity** has been legally defined by meeting three criteria. First, the dominant theme of the material must appeal to a prurient interest in sex. Such interest implies that the material is sexually arousing in a lewd way. Second, the material must be patently offensive to the community. In general, a community can dictate what its standards are regarding the sale, display, and distribution of sexual materials. Third, the sexual material must have no redeeming social value. If the material can be viewed as entertaining or educational (if it helps with the sexual communication of couples, for example), a case can be made for its social value. More recently, obscenity has been

Box 16-4 Social Choices

Legalization or Decriminalization of Prostitution?

Sex researchers, enforcement officials, politicians, and prostitutes continue to debate the issue of whether prostitution should be legalized or decriminalized in the United States. Arguments for the legalization of prostitution include that it would permit the taxation of the billions of currently untaxed dollars spent on prostitution, help control and regulate the criminal activity associated with prostitution, help prevent teenage prostitution, and help protect prostitutes against abuse by pimps and clients (by enabling prostitutes to report abuse without fear of being arrested). Furthermore, if prostitution were legal, public health regulations could require prostitutes to use condoms and have regular gynecological exams to ensure they are not infected with a sexually transmitted infection and to treat any diseases they may acquire. Just as restaurants must pass a health inspection and display a rating certificate, prostitutes could be required to obtain a similar certificate of health.

Prostitution has been legalized in some districts of Nevada and in other countries (including Germany, where prostitutes work in large dormitories and are checked regularly by a physician for sexually transmitted infections). Clients make their selection by observing the available women on closed-circuit television monitors. These bordellos are sometimes a safer and healthier environment for both prostitutes and clients than street prostitution. Ahmad (2001) has called for the decriminalization of prostitution in Asia. He notes that prostitutes who are punished for their behavior are less open about their profession and less likely to use and benefit from HIV preventative programs. Hence, the goal becomes reducing HIV transmission and other sexually transmitted infections rather than punishing prostitutes. Most of the prostitute rights organizations in the United States (e.g., the Association of Seattle Prostitutes, Friends and Lovers of Prostitutes) favor decriminalization (making no laws affecting its practice; Boles, 1998).

Some opponents of legalized prostitution feel that it is wrong to condone any type of sexual behavior that occurs outside a marital relationship. Other opponents feel that prostitution perpetuates the sexual objectification of women. For example, Women Hurt in Systems of Prostitution Engaged in Protest (WHISPER) do not advocate decriminalization or legalization. They believe that such actions would improve the lot of only the most educated and sophisticated prostitutes (Boles, 1998). Surprisingly, even some prostitutes oppose legalizing their trade. In Nevada, where prostitution is legalized, some prostitutes resent the legal conditions of their employment. Legal prostitutes cannot discriminate against certain customers by refusing to service them: They must service whoever comes in the door. They also feel that the law interferes with their private lives. For example, legal prostitutes can go to town only during certain hours and cannot appear in the company of a client in a restaurant. The stigmatization of the profession through fingerprinting and registration makes it difficult for prostitutes to leave the profession and enter another.

Although it is improbable that trafficking can be eliminated, developing economic alternatives in poor countries, strengthening the penalties and laws against traffickers, and improving assistance and protection for the victims may significantly reduce it. There is a great need for shelters and clinics to provide health and counseling services, and reintegration assistance when the trafficking victims return home (Richard, 1999).

---

defined as "sexually explicit visual, printed, or recorded material or a live performance that is found beyond a reasonable doubt to be material that is not protected under the First Amendment" (Bullis, 1995, pp. 13–14). A larger percentage of U.S. adults consider homosexual pornography unacceptable rather than heterosexual pornography (31% vs. 18%; Bedard & Gertz, 2000). College students who have less favorable attitudes toward pornography are more likely to be women, those affiliated with religious organizations, those who report less sexual behavior, and those who have never seen such materials (Lottes, Weinberg, & Weller, 1993).

The effects of pornography have been studied extensively. In 1967, the U.S. Commission on Obscenity and Pornography found no evidence that explicit sexual material played a significant role in causing individual or social harm. Rather, such material seemed to be sought for entertainment and educational purposes and seemed to enhance sexual communication. Further, the commission recommended that all federal, state, and local legislation prohibiting the sale, exhibition, and distribution of sexual material to adults be repealed. The U.S. Senate and President Nixon rejected the committee's recommendations.

To update the commission's findings, President Reagan established the Meese Commission on Pornography in 1985. This 11-person commission concluded that pornography is harmful to both individuals and society, and called for more stringent law enforcement regulation. Linz, Donnerstein, and Penrod (1987) examined the same data as did the commission and concluded, "we can find no consistent evidence for these specific conclusions" (p. 951). Critics of the Meese Commission argued that it was biased against pornography. Of the 11 members, 6 had previously gone on record prior to the conference as opposed to pornography because they believed it had harmful effects. For example, one of these was Dr. James Dodson, the president of Focus on the Family, a conservative organization.

In the summer of 1986, the Surgeon General's workshop on Pornography and Public Health was convened in Arlington, Virginia, with 19 specialists in the area of pornography. Conclusions about the workshop's presentations and discussions (Koop, 1987) follow:

1. Prolonged exposure to pornography results in people believing that less common sexual practices are more common than they are.
2. Pornography depicting sexual aggression as pleasurable to the victim increases the acceptance of the use of coercion in sexual relations. [Malamuth, Addison, and Koss (2000) suggest that exposure to frequent violent pornography and sexual aggression are reliably associated.]
3. Such acceptance may increase the chance of engaging in sexual aggression.
4. In laboratory studies measuring short-term effects, exposure to violent pornography increases punitive behavior toward women. In regard to this latter conclusion, Linz et al. (1987) noted, "what is conspicuously absent from the Surgeon General's summary is an endorsement of the view that exposure to sexually violent material leads to aggressive or assaultive behavior outside the confines of the laboratory" (p. 950). Fisher and Grenier (1994) failed to find consistent negative effects of violent pornography on men's fantasies, attitudes, and behaviors toward women. Like much sex research, the data are inconclusive.
5. Children who participate in the production of pornography experience adverse and enduring effects.

Kiddie porn See **chicken porn.**

Chicken porn Pornography depicting children involved in sexual activity (also referred to as **kiddie porn.**)

In regard to child pornography, also referred to as **kiddie porn** and **chicken porn,** there is a strong cultural value that views the use of children in sex films as immoral and abusive. These children do not have the option of free choice and are manipulated or forced into participation. The Sexual Exploitation of Children Act was enacted in 1997 and prohibits the use of a minor in the "making of pornography, the transport of a child across state lines, the taking of a pornographic picture of a minor, and the production and circulation of materials advertising child pornography. It also prohibits the transfer, sale, purchase, and receipt of minors when the purpose of such transfer, sale, purchase, or receipt is to use the child or youth in the production of child pornography. The transportation, importation, shipment, and receipt of child pornography by any interstate means, including by mail or computer, is also prohibited." Possession of child porn carries a 5-year prison sentence. Greater involvement involves stronger penalties. Owner Thomas Reedy of Landslide Operation was convicted on federal charges related to possessing and distributing child pornography and received 1,335 years in prison (Johnson, 2001).

Beyond child pornography, legislative attempts are being made to restrict the flow of sexually explicit material. The primary motive behind the Communications Decency Act of 1996 (which made it a crime—punishable by a $250,000 fine or up to 2 years in prison—for anyone to make "indecent" material available to children on the Internet) was to protect children from pornography. The courts are still trying to figure out how to protect children without censoring the content available to adults (Mauro, 1997). The U.S. Customs Service is the country's front line of defense to combat the illegal importation and proliferation of child pornography. See the "Suggested Websites" section for the Internet address to Victims of Pornography and Regulation of Pornography on the Internet (two antipornography organizations).

Although consistent proof of a causal link between sexually explicit material and "harm" is lacking, attacks against such material continue (Evans-DeCicco & Cowan, 2001). In fact, some sex researchers have found neutral to positive effects from exposure to sexually explicit material. In one study, more than 7,000 adults who had been exposed to sexually explicit materials in sex education seminars or workshops were asked about the effects of such exposure. Almost all the research participants reported experiencing these media as not harmful, and most reported positive responses to the explicit visual material (Rosser et al., 1995). This conclusion is not surprising, however, given that all the participants had volunteered to view the films.

Think About It

What would the absolutist, relativist, and hedonist say about prostitution and pornography, and what would they recommend as public policy?

SUMMARY

Most people have some preference for how, when, and with whom they experience sexual expression. Although a paraphilia involves a preference, it is usually experienced as a drive, and the preference is typically unusual.

Paraphilia: Definition and Overview

Paraphilias are an overdependence on a culturally unacceptable or unusual stimulus for sexual arousal and satisfaction. The most common paraphilias are exhibitionism and frotteurism. Most individuals who have a paraphilia have an average of three to four different types. Paraphilias may become the major sexual activity in a person's life and may interfere with the person's capacity for reciprocal, affectionate sexual interactions. Although there are few classic profile characteristics (sexual orientation, ethnicity, socioeconomic background), paraphilias most often occur in men and are very rarely diagnosed in women. Paraphilias are legal or illegal depending on the degree to which the rights of others are affected. The majority of apprehended sex offenders are arrested for acts of exhibitionism, pedophilia, and voyeurism.

Types of Paraphilias

The major paraphilias considered in this chapter are exhibitionism, frotteurism, voyeurism, fetishism, transvestic fetishism, sexual sadism, and sexual masochism. People who engage in exhibitionism, frotteurism, and voyeurism are usually not violent, but such acts should be reported to law enforcement officials.

The Origins of Paraphilias: Theoretical Perspectives

Theoretical explanations for paraphilias include psychoanalytic (unconscious processes), feminist (control, power, aggression), learning (classical/operant paradigms), biological (innate), and lovemap (biological predisposition plus unusual learning experiences) perspectives. Paraphilias may also be viewed as a courtship disorder whereby the individual has not learned the culturally acceptable social skills for emotional and sexual engagement.

Treatment of Paraphilias

Treatment of paraphilias involves decreasing deviant sexual arousal, increasing nondeviant sexual arousal, developing interpersonal social skills, changing faulty cognitions, and resolving sexual dysfunctions. The American Psychiatric Association's position on sexual addiction is that the concept is conceptually vague, with no empirical support. Specifically, the term *addiction* has a physiological meaning in reference to withdrawal, which has no counterpart in sexuality. The APA recommends abandoning the term.

Commercialization of Sex

Commercialization of sex includes prostitution and pornography. Whether they should be illegal continues to be debated. On the one hand are the rights of the individual to use his or her body as he or she pleases and to buy whatever sexually explicit materials are available. On the other hand both prostitution and pornography are argued to be exploitive of those involved in the industry and morally debasing for individuals and society as the consumer.

SUGGESTED WEBSITES

Note: These websites were functional when we went to press. Please access the online text for the most up-to-date URLs.

Prostitution
http://www.prostitutionresearch.com

Regulation of Pornography on the Internet
http://www.missingkids.com

Victims of Pornography
http://www.victimsofpornography.org/

Cross-Dressers—Heterosexual
http://www.tri-ess.com/

National Council on Sexual Addiction and Compulsivity
http://www.ncsac.org

Sexaholics Anonymous
http://www.sa.org/

Trafficking
http://hrw.org (Human Rights Watch: Click on "More Campaigns" and look for "Campaign Against the Trafficking of Women and Girls")

http://www.uri.edu (University of Rhode Island: Click on Arts & Sciences: Social Sciences: Women's Studies, Donna Hughes)

KEY TERMS

aversive conditioning (p. 493)
chicken porn (p. 502)
courtship disorder (p. 492)
covert sensitization (p. 493)
cross-dressing (p. 482)
degrading pornography (p. 500)
erotica (p. 500)
exhibitionism (p. 479)
fetishism (p. 481)
frotteurism (p. 480)
kiddie porn (p. 502)
lovemap (p. 476)
nymphomania (p. 497)
obscenity (p. 500)
paraphilia (p. 476)
pornography (p. 500)
prostitution (p. 498)
purging (p. 485)
satyriasis (p. 497)
scopophilia (p. 481)
sexual addiction (p. 496)
sexual masochism (p. 486)
sexual sadism (p. 486)
toucheurism (p. 480)
trafficking (p. 499)
transvestic fetishism (p. 482)
transvestites (p. 484)
violent pornography (p. 500)
voyeurism (p. 481)

CHAPTER QUIZ

1. In the word *paraphilia* the first part *para* means
- **a.** deviation.
- **b.** sexual.
- **c.** perverse.
- **d.** psychotic.

2. A team of researchers (Abel et al., 1987) looked at the relative percentages of various paraphilic behaviors reported by a sample of nonincarcerated men with paraphilias. The most frequently reported paraphilic behavior was
- **a.** voyeurism.
- **b.** exhibitionism.
- **c.** sexual sadism.
- **d.** nonincestual pedophilia.

3. The majority of apprehended sex offenders are arrested for acts of each of the following EXCEPT
- **a.** voyeurism.
- **b.** pedophilia.
- **c.** autonepiophilia.
- **d.** exhibitionism.

4. Exhibitionism involves an intense, recurrent sexual urge (over a period of at least ____________), often accompanied by sexually arousing fantasies, to expose one's genitals to a stranger.
- **a.** 6 weeks
- **b.** 6 months
- **c.** 1 year
- **d.** 6 years

5. Frotteurism is most likely to occur in which of the following places?
   a. a crowded subway
   b. a deserted beach
   c. one's bedroom
   d. one's automobile
6. Anyone who looks at magazines with nude photos or who watches erotic films can be classified as being a voyeur.
   a. True
   b. False
7. Fetishes can be divided into two types:
   a. harmful and playful
   b. internally focused and externally focused
   c. public and private
   d. media and form
8. A biological female who sees herself as a man and wants to have a penis constructed to replace the vagina is a
   a. homoerotic lesbian.
   b. female-to-male transsexual.
   c. transvestite.
   d. cross-dresser.
9. Which of the following involves sexual urges and fantasies that involve acts that hurt or humiliate the sexual partner?
   a. sexual sadism
   b. sexual masochism
10. Some large cities have "clubs" that specialize in sadomasochism (S&M). The "staff" consists of ___________ (sadists), ___________ (masochists), and "switch-hitters."
   a. spankers; spankees
   b. bosses; workers
   c. dominants; submissives
   d. bulldogs; poodles
11. Where would someone with klismaphilia most likely find the object that he or she needs for sexual arousal?
   a. a zoo
   b. a clothing store
   c. a hardware store
   d. a pharmacy
12. Which perspective views paraphilias such as pedophilia and sexual sadism as expressions of aggression more than sexuality?
   a. feminist
   b. psychoanalytic
   c. learning
   d. biological
13. In a sample of 60 undergraduate college men, more than half reported that they had engaged in a sexual offense for which they could be arrested (such as voyeurism, frottage, obscene phone calls, and coercive sex).
   a. True
   b. False
14. Prostitution has been legalized in some districts of
   a. Nevada.
   b. New York.
   c. Hawaii and California.
   d. none of the above.
15. Obscenity has been legally defined by meeting three criteria. First, the dominant theme of the material must appeal to a prurient interest in sex (i.e., the material is sexually arousing in a lewd way). Second, the material must be patently offensive to the community. Third, the sexual material must
   a. display nudity.
   b. display sexual acts.
   c. display aggression.
   d. have no redeeming social value.
16. The term *chicken porn* refers to which of the following?
   a. pornography involving animals
   b. "soft" porn (showing nudity but not explicit genitalia or sexual acts)
   c. child pornography
   d. lesbian pornography

REFERENCES

Abel, G. G., Becker, J. V., Mittelman, M. S., Cunningham-Rathner, J., Rouleau, J. L., & Murphy, W. D. (1987). Self-reported sex crimes of non-incarcerated paraphiliacs. *Journal of Interpersonal Violence, 2*, 3–25.

Abel, G. G., & Rouleau, J. L. (1990). The nature and extent of sexual assault. In W. L. Marshall, D. R. Laws, & H. E. Barbaree (Eds.), *Handbook of sexual assault* (pp. 9–21). New York: Plenum Press.

Adams, K. M., & Robinson, D. W. (2001). Shame reduction, affect regulation, and sexual boundary development: Essential building blocks of sexual addiction treatment. *Sexual Addiction and Compulsivity, 8*, 23–44.

Ahmad, K. (2001). Call for decriminalization of prostitution in Asia. *The Lancet, 358*, 643–655.

American Psychiatric Association. (1980). *Diagnostic and statistical manual of mental disorders* (3rd ed.). Washington, DC: Author.

American Psychiatric Association. (1987). *Diagnostic and statistical manual of mental disorders* (3rd ed., rev.). Washington, DC: Author.

American Psychiatric Association. (2000). *Diagnostic and statistical manual of mental disorders* (4th ed., text rev.). Washington, DC: Author.

Anderson, S. A. (2002). Prostitution and sexual autonomy: Making sense of the prohibition of prostitution. *Ethics, 112*, 748–782.

Bancroft, J. (1989). *Human sexuality and its problems* (2nd ed.). Edinburgh: Churchill Livingstone.

Bedard, L. E., & Gertz, M. G. (2000). Differences in community standards for the viewing of heterosexual and homosexual pornography. *International Journal of Public Opinion Research, 12*, 324–332.

Boles, J. (1998). My life in prostitution. In G. G. Brannigan, E. R. Allgeier, & A. R. Allgeier (Eds.), *The sex scientists* (pp. 185–200). New York: Longman.

Brame, G. G., Brame, W. D., & Jacobs, J. (1993). *Different loving: An exploration of the world of sexual dominance and submission.* New York: Villard.

Briken, P., Nika, E., & Berner, W. (2001). Treatment of paraphilia with luteinizing hormone-releasing hormone agonists. *Journal of Sex and Marital Therapy, 27,* 45–55.

Bullis, R. K. (1995). From gag rules to blindfolds: The Pornography Victims Compensation Act. *Journal of Sex Education and Therapy, 21,* 11–21.

Bullough, B., & Bullough, V. (1997a). Men who cross-dress: A survey. In B. Bullough, V. Bullough, & J. Elias (Eds.), *Gender blending* (pp. 174–188). Amherst, NY: Prometheus Books.

Bullough, B., & Bullough, V. (1997b). Are transvestites necessarily heterosexual? *Archives of Sexual Behavior, 26,* 1–12.

Busch, N. B., Bell, H., Hotaling, N., & Monto, M. A. (2002). Male customers of prostituted women: Exploring the perceptions of entitlement to power and control and implications for violent behavior toward women. *Violence Against Women,* 8, 1093–1113.

Carnes, P. J. (2001). Cybersex, courtship, and escalating arousal: Factors in addictive sexual desire. *Sexual Addiction and Compulsivity,* 8, 45–78.

Chow, E. W. C., & Choy, A. L. (2002). Clinical characteristics and treatment response to SSRI in a female pedophile. *Archives of Sexual Behavior, 31,* 211–215.

Comfort, A. (1987). Deviation and variation. In G. D. Wilson (Ed.), *Variant sexuality: Research and theory* (pp. 1–20). Baltimore, MD: Johns Hopkins University Press.

Cox, D. J. (1988). Incidence and nature of male genital exposure behavior as reported by college women. *The Journal of Sex Research, 24,* 227–233.

Dalla, R. L. (2002). Night moves: A qualitative investigation of street-level sex work. *Psychology of Women Quarterly, 26,* 63–73.

Davis, N. J. (1993). *Prostitution: An international handbook on trends, problems, and policies.* Westport, CT: Greenwood Press.

Devlin, P. (1965). *The enforcement of morals.* Oxford: Oxford University Press.

Doctor, R. F., & Prince, V. (1977). Transvestism: A survey of 1032 cross-dressers. *Archives of Sexual Behavior, 26,* 589–605.

Elmer-Dewitt, P. (1995, July 3). On a screen near you: Cyberporn. *Time, 146,* 38–45.

Evans-DeCicco, J. A., & Cowan, G. (2001). Attitudes toward pornography and the characteristics attributed to pornography actors. *Sex Roles, 41,* 351–363.

Feierman, J. R., & Feierman, L. A. (2000). Paraphilias. In L. T. Szuchman & F. Muscarella (Eds.), *Psychological perspectives on human sexuality.* New York: Wiley.

Fisher, W. A., & Barak, A. (2001). Internet pornography: A social psychological perspective on Internet sexuality. *The Journal of Sex Research,* 38, 312–323.

Fisher, W A., & Grenier, G. (1994). Violent pornography, anti-woman thoughts, and anti-woman acts: In search of reliable effects. *The Journal of Sex Research, 31,* 23–38.

Flor-Henry, P. (1987). Cerebral aspects of sexual deviation. In G. D. Wilson (Ed.), *Variant sexuality: Research and theory* (pp. 49–83). Baltimore, MD: John Hopkins University Press.

Flowers, R. B. (1998). *The prostitution of women and girls.* Jefferson, NC: McFarland & Company.

Garber, M. (1992). *Vested interests: Cross-dressing and cultural anxiety.* New York: HarperPerennial.

Gebhard, P. H. (1976). Fetishism and sadomasochism. In M. S. Weinberg (Ed.), *Sex research: Studies from the Kinsey Institute* (pp. 156–166). New York: Oxford University Press.

Goodson, P., McCormick, D., & Evans, A. (2001). Searching for sexually explicit materials on the Internet: An exploratory study of college students' behavior and attitudes. *Archives of Sexual Behavior,* 30, 101–109.

Green, R. (2001). (Serious) sadomasochism: A protected right of privacy? *Archives of Sexual Behavior, 30,* 543–550.

Griffiths, M. (2001). Sex on the Internet: Observations and implications for Internet sex addiction. *The Journal of Sex Research, 38,* 333–342.

Hazelwood, R. R., Dietz, R. E., & Warren, J. (1992). The criminal sexual sadist. *FBI Law Enforcement Bulletin, 61*(2), 12–20.

Hurlbert, D. F. (1992). Voyeurism in an adult female with schizoid personality: A case report. *Journal of Sex Education and Therapy, 18,* 17–21.

Johnson, K. (2001, August 9). 100 arrested in Net child porn ring. *USA Today,* p. 1A.

Keegan, J. M. W. (2001). The neurobiology, neuropharmacology, and pharmacological treatment of the paraphilias and compulsive sexual behavior. *Canadian Journal of Psychiatry,* 46, 26–33.

Kline, P. (1987). Sexual deviation: Psychoanalytic research and theory. In G. D. Wilson (Ed.), *Variant sexuality: Research and theory* (pp. 150–175). Baltimore, MD: Johns Hopkins University Press.

Koop, C. E. (1987). Report of the Surgeon General's Workshop on Pornography and Public Health. *American Psychologist, 42,* 944–945.

Koukounas, E., & McCabe, M. P. (2001). Sexual and emotional variables influencing sexual response to erotica: A psychophysiological investigation. *Archives of Sexual Behavior,* 30, 393–408.

Langevin, R., & Lang, R. A. (1987). The courtship disorders. In G. D. Wilson (Ed.), *Variant sexuality: Research and theory* (pp. 202–228). Baltimore, MD: Johns Hopkins University Press.

Langevin, R., Paitich, D. P., & Russon, A. E. (1985). Voyeurism: Does it predict sexual aggression or violence in general? In R. Langevin (Ed.), *Erotic preference, gender identity, and aggression in men* (pp. 77–98). Hillsdale, NY: Erlbaum.

Lehne, G. K., & Money, J. (2000). The first case of paraphilia treated with depo-provera: 40-year outcome. *Journal of Sex Education and Therapy, 25,* 213–220.

Linz, D., Donnerstein, E., & Penrod, S. (1987). The findings and recommendations of the Attorney General's Commission on Pornography: Do the psychological 'facts' fit the political fury? *American Psychologist, 42,* 946–953.

Lottes, I., Weinberg, M., & Weller, I. (1993). Reactions to pornography on a college campus: For or against? *Sex Roles, 29,* 69–89.

MacNamara, D., & Sagarin, E. (1977). *Sex, crime, and the law.* New York: Free Press.

Malamuth, N. M., Addison, T., & Koss, M. (2000). Pornography and sexual aggression: Are there three reliable effects and can we understand them? *Annual Review of Sex Research, 11,* 26–86.

Maletzky, B. M. (1991). *Treating the sexual offender.* Newbury Park, CA: Sage.

Mauro, T. (1997, March 18). Taming the Internet. *USA Today,* p. lA.

McDonald, J., & Bradford, W. (2000). The treatment of sexual deviation using a pharmacological approach. *The Journal of Sex Research, 37,* 248–257.

Meisenkothen, C. (1999). Chemical castration—Breaking the cycle of paraphiliac recidivism. *Social Justice, 26,* 139–140.

Michael, R. T., Gagnon, J. H., Laumann, E. O., & Kolata, G. (1994). *Sex in America: A definitive survey.* Boston: Little, Brown.

Miletski, H. (2001). Zoophilia—Implications for therapy. *Journal of Sex Education and Therapy, 26,* 85–89.

Mill, J. S. (1985). *On liberty.* New York: Penguin. (Original work published 1859).

Money, J. (1986). *Lovemaps: Clinical concepts of sexual/erotic health and pathology, paraphilia, and gender transposition in childhood, adolescence, and maturity.* New York. Irvington.

Money, J. (1988). *Gay, straight, and in-between.* New York: Oxford University Press.

Moser, C. (1992). Lust, lack of desire, and paraphilias. Some thoughts and possible connections. *Journal of Sex and Marital Therapy, 18,* 65–69.

Moser, C. (2001). Paraphilia: A critique of a confused concept. In P. J. Kleinplatz (Ed.), *New Directions in sex therapy: Innovations and alternatives* (pp. 91–108). New York: Brunner-Routledge.

Nagayama Hall, G. C. (1991). Sexual arousal as a function of physiological and cognitive variables in a sexual offender population. *Archives of Sexual Behavior, 20,* 359–369.

Rachman, S. (1966). Sexual fetishism: An experimental analogue. *Psychological Record, 16,* 293–296.

Reynolds, A. L., & Caron, S. L. (2000). How intimate relationships are impacted when heterosexual men crossdress. *Journal of Psychology and Human Sexuality, 12*(3), 63–77.

Richard, A. O. (1999). International trafficking in women to the United States: A contemporary manifestation of slavery and organized crime. Center for the Study of Intelligence. Retrieved January 2, 2002, from www.cia.gov/csi/monograph/women/trafficking.pdf

Rosser, B. R. S., Dwyer, M., Coleman, E., Miner, M., Metz, M., Robinson, B. E., et al. (1995). Using sexually explicit material in adult sex education: An eighteen-year comparative analysis. *Journal of Sex Education and Therapy, 21,* 117–128.

Santtila, P., Sandnabba, N. K., Alison, L., & Nordling, N. (2002). Investigating the underlying structure in sadomasochistically oriented behavior. *Archives of Sexual Behavior, 31,* 185–196.

Seligman, L. (2000). Assessment and treatment of paraphilias. *Journal of Counseling and Development, 78,* 107–113.

Smithson, C. (2000). One way out of jail. *Alberta Report, 27,* 32–38.

Spiwak Rotlewicz, F. (2001, December). *Prostitution: An accepted form of torture in Western society?* Presented at the 17th Annual Meeting of the International Society for Traumatic Stress Studies, New Orleans, LA.

Templeman, T. L., & Stinnett, R. D. (1991). Patterns of sexual arousal and history in a "normal" sample of young men. *Archives of Sexual Behavior, 20,* 137–150.

U.S. Department of Justice. (1986). *Attorney General's Commission on Pornography: Final Report.* Washington, DC: Author.

Van Brunschot, E. G., & Brannigan, A. (2002). Childhood treatment and subsequent conduct disorders: The case of female street prostitution. *International Journal of Law and Psychiatry, 25,* 219–234.

Weinberg, M. S., Williams, C. J., & Calhan, C. (1995). "If the shoe fits . . .": Exploring male homosexual foot fetishism. *The Journal of Sex Research, 32,* 17–27.

Willis, B. M., & Levy, B. S. (2002). Child prostitution: Global health burden, research needs, and interventions. *Lancet, 359,* 1417–1423.

Wise, T. N., & Schmidt, C. W. (1996). Paraphilias. In T. A. Widiger, A. J. Frances, H. A. Pincus, R. Ross, M. B. First, & W. Davis (Eds.), *DSM-IV sourcebook.* Washington, DC: American Psychiatric Association.

Worden, S. (2001). E-trafficing. *Foreign Policy, 123,* 92–97.

Xantidis, L., & McCabe, M. P. (2000). Personality characteristics of male clients of female commercial sex workers in Australia. *Archives of Sexual Behavior, 29,* 165–176.

Zatz, N. D. (1997). Sex work/sex act: Law, labor, and desire in constructions of prostitution. *Signs, 22,* 277–308.

Zolondek, S. C., Abel, G. G., Northey, W. F., & Jordan, A. D. (2001). The self-reported behaviors of juvenile sexual offenders. *Journal of Interpersonal Violence, 16,* 73–85.

17

Sexual Coercion

Chapter Outline

I was only nine years of age when I was raped by my 19-year-old cousin. He was the first of three family members to sexually molest me.

—*Oprah Winfrey, talk-show host*

Although we tend to think of sexual involvement as a series of voluntary, gentle, and intimate encounters, the data reveal that an alarming percentage of people are forced to have sex against their will. In this chapter we discuss the various forms of sexual coercion, its victims and perpetrators. At the outset we emphasize that forced sex occurs in dating, living together, and marriage/civil union contexts in both heterosexual and homosexual relationships.

17-1 SEXUAL COERCION: RAPE AND SEXUAL ASSAULT

Sexual coercion The use of force (actual or threatened) to engage a person in sexual acts against that person's will.

Sexual coercion involves using force (actual or threatened) to engage a person in sexual acts against that person's will. Although sexual coercion has existed for centuries, only in the past couple of decades have social scientists, medical and mental health professionals, and politicians acknowledged the prevalence and seriousness of sexually coercive acts. Professionals are also now trained to acknowledge that "blaming the victim is not appropriate, but rather that the survivor needs to be treated with dignity and respect" (Hotelling, 2001, p. 285).

17-1a Definitions of Rape

Forcible rape Sexual force involving three elements: vaginal, oral, or anal penetration; the use of force or threat of force; and nonconsent of the victim.

Statutory rape Sexual intercourse without use of force with a person below the legal age of consent.

Marital rape Forcible rape by one's spouse; marital rape is now illegal in all states.

Forced sex Acts of sex (or attempted sex) in which one party is nonconsenting, regardless of the age and sex of the offender and victim—whether or not the act meets criteria for what legally constitutes rape.

Rape Acts of sex (or attempted sex) in which one party is nonconsenting, regardless of the age and sex of the offender and victim.

One of the difficulties in studying rape and sexual assault is that these terms are variously defined in legal codes and research literature. Criminal law distinguishes between forcible rape and statutory rape. **Forcible rape** usually includes three elements: penetration of the vagina, mouth, or anus; force or threat of force; and nonconsent of the victim (Resnick, Kilpatrick, & Lipovsky, 1991). **Statutory rape** involves sexual intercourse without use of force with a person below the legal age of consent. **Marital rape,** now recognized in all states, is forcible rape by one's spouse.

Because legal definitions of rape are varied and restrictive, the term *forced sex* is more descriptive. In this section, we use the terms **forced sex** and **rape** interchangeably to refer to acts of sex (or attempted sex) in which one party is nonconsenting, regardless of the age and sex of the offender and victim—whether or not the act meets criteria for what legally constitutes rape. In an analysis of 1,076 patients seen for sexual assault in a Denver hospital, vaginal intercourse, oral assault, and anal penetration were involved in 83%, 25%, and 17% of the cases, respectively. In about a quarter (27%) of the cases, a weapon was used (Riggs, 2000).

17-1b Prevalence of Rape

NATIONAL DATA About one in five (22%) of U.S. women ages 18–59 reported that they had ever been forced sexually by a man (Laumann, Gagnon, Michael, & Michaels, 1994). The National Violence Against Women Survey revealed that 15% of women reported having been raped (Tjaden & Thoennes, 1998).

Data from college samples reveal higher percentages of forced sex. More than half (52%) of a sample of 383 undergraduate women reported that they had experienced unwanted sexual activity before the age of 18. Thirty-three percent reported some form of a sexual assault while in college (Kalof, 2000). Almost a fourth (23.2%) of 65 male undergraduates reported that they had experienced one or more unwanted sexual incidents (Felton, Gumm, & Pittenger, 2001). Ottens (2001) reviewed the literature on numerous samples and found that about half of college women and a quarter of college men reported having experienced some form of sexual victimization (rape, attempted rape, sexual coercion).

INTERNATIONAL DATA In nonindustrial societies, rape prevalence estimates of women are thought to occur from 43–90% (Rozee & Koss, 2000).

There are few defining characteristics of rape victims. However, women ages 18–39, with no religious affiliation, from the central city of the 100 largest cities in the United States, and White had a higher prevalence of being raped (Laumann et al., 1994). In regard to racial or ethnic background, Whites have the highest (23%) incidence and Hispanics (14%) the lowest, with Blacks (19%) having an intermediate reported incidence of being forced to have sex (Laumann et al., 1994). Sexual assaults on gay men, lesbians, and bisexuals, perpetrated either by strangers or by acquaintances, occur at rates similar to or higher than heterosexual counterparts (Tuel, 2001).

Think About It

Not all reported rapes actually happened. Kanin (1994) documented 45 disposed, false rape allegations in a small metropolitan community over a 9-year period. Women made the false rape charges for three reasons: to provide an alibi, for revenge, and for attention or sympathy. The penalty for false allegations may vary from a $2,000 fine to 6 months in jail. Damage to the reputation of the innocent person who is accused of rape can be enormous. Do you think the courts are more focused on punishing the rapist or protecting alleged rapists from being falsely accused?

Men are also raped. Men who are victims of such coercion by women report mostly that the method by which they are sexually coerced is psychological, such as verbal persuasion or the threat of love withdrawal. And they may fear telling others about the experience (Struckman-Johnson & Struckman-Johnson, 1994). Ottens (2001) reviewed the literature on numerous samples and found that a quarter of college men reported having experienced some form of sexual victimization (rape, attempted rape, sexual coercion). Michael Scarce (1997) provided male survivor accounts, mostly of men who identified themselves and their attackers as heterosexual. The testimonials in his book show that not only are men vulnerable to rape, but that antigay prejudice, intimidation, and humiliation keep men from reporting their experience to medical and law enforcement officials.

17-1c Characteristics of Men Who Rape

Men who rape tend to believe in **rape myths.** Also referred to as **rape-supportive beliefs,** rape myths refer to the attitudes and beliefs that are generally false but are widely and persistently held, and that serve to deny and justify male sexual aggression against women. Such rape myths include that women have an unconscious desire to be raped, that when a woman says "no" she really means "yes," that women who dress provocatively are really asking for sex, and that only strangers commit rape. The rape literature suggests that men are more accepting of rape myths than women and use such beliefs to justify their conviction that they did not actually commit a rape (Buddie & Miller, 2001).

Rape myths Generally false but widely held attitudes and beliefs that serve to justify male sexual aggression against women. (See also **rape-supportive beliefs.**)

Rape-supportive beliefs See **rape myths.**

In addition to believing in rape myths, men who rape may share these characteristics: They ignore personal space (e.g., hands all over you), abuse alcohol or other drugs (reduced judgment), sexualize conversations, are dominant/aggressive, have rigid gender roles, use threats in displays of anger, have a quick temper, and are impersonal/aloof emotionally (Rozee & Koss, 2000; Fouts & Knapp, 2001). Gordon (2002) also observed that undergraduate male rapists tend to have been involved in other delinquent acts and to have been subjected to violence in their family of origin. Most rapists are also likely to be known to the person they rape.

Acquaintances

Forty-six percent of a national sample of 204 women who reported that they had been forced to do something sexual revealed that they were in love with the person who forced sex on them, 22% knew the perpetrator well, and 19% said the perpetrator was an "acquaintance" (Laumann et al., 1994). Acquaintance rape also occurs in gay relationships. In a study of 29 men who were victims of sexual assault, half of the male/male assaults were acquaintance assaults (Stermac, Sheridan, Davidson, & Dunn, 1996).

Date rape Nonconsensual sex between people who are dating or on a date. (See also **acquaintance rape.**)

Acquaintance rape Nonconsensual sex between people who know each other, are dating, or on a date. (See also **date rape.**)

Date rape is the most typical form of **acquaintance rape;** it refers to nonconsensual sex between people who are dating or on a date. The following is the recollection of a woman who was raped by her boyfriend on a date:

> *Last spring, I met this guy and a relationship started which was great. One year later, he raped me. The term was almost over and we would not be able to spend much time together during the summer. Therefore, we planned to go out to eat and spend some time together.*
>
> *After dinner we drove to a park. I did not mind or suspect anything for we had done this many times. Then he asked me into the back seat. I got into the back seat with him because I trusted him and he said he wanted to be close to me as we talked. He began talking. He told me that he was tired of always pleasing me and not getting a reward. Therefore, he was going to "make love to me" whether I wanted to or not. I thought he was joking, so I asked him to stop playing. He told me he was serious, and after looking at him closely, I knew he was serious. I began to plead with him not to have sex with me. He did not listen. He began to tear my clothes off and confine me so that I could not move. All this time I was fighting him. At one time, I managed to open the door, but he threw me back into the seat, hit me, then he got on me and raped me. After he was satisfied, he stopped, told me to get dressed and stop crying. He said he was sorry it had to happen that way.*
>
> *He brought me back to the dorm and expected me to kiss him good night. He didn't think he had done anything wrong. Before this happened, I loved this man very much, but afterward I felt great hatred for him.*
>
> *My life has not been the same since that night. I do not trust men as I once did, nor do I feel completely comfortable when I'm with my present boyfriend. He wants to know why I back off when he tries to be intimate with me. However, right now I can't tell him, as he knows the guy who raped me. (authors' files)*

Date rapes most often occur in the context of alcohol or drugs. "Alcohol plays a dual role in men's expression of sexual violence. When self-administered, it may be believed to heighten sexuality; or it may be provided to women as a coercive tactic" (Marchell & Cummings, 2001, p. 33).

About half of the undergraduate respondents (45.4% of women; 57.1% men) in the Felton et al. (2001) study agreed that "drinking or using drugs" had gotten them into a sexual situation that they later regretted. Tyson (1997) assessed date rape expectations of 141 university students and found that both women and men predicted rape most often when the man was intoxicated and the woman was sober. The students predicted that rape was least likely when both the man and woman were sober.

Rohypnol (Also known as dulcitas, the "forget me drug") Drug used in date rape scenarios which causes profound and prolonged sedation, a feeling of well-being, and short-term memory loss.

GHB Gamma hydroxybutyrate, a date rape drug that may be fatal; it acts faster than Rohypnol to induce confusion, intense sleepiness, unconsciousness, and memory loss.

Two illegal drugs that have been associated with date rape cases are Rohypnol and gamma hydroxybutyrate (GHB). **Rohypnol** (also known as dulcitas, the "forget me drug") causes profound and prolonged sedation and short-term memory loss. It has 10 times the potency of Valium by weight and lasts for about 8 hours (Zorza, 2001). **GHB,** which is potentially fatal, acts faster than Rohypnol to induce confusion, intense sleepiness, unconsciousness, and memory loss. Although most symptoms last for 3–6 hours, the drowsiness may last for 3 days. Police in Los Angeles County routinely test date rape victims for both Rohypnol and GHB. Although both of these drugs may be used to incapacitate a woman, "alcohol can be considered the most widely used 'date rape drug'" (Marchell & Cummings, 2001, p. 33).

Husband

Nine percent of perpetrators of sexual coercion reported by the 204 women in the Laumann et al. (1994) study were the women's husbands. Marital rape may occur as part of a larger pattern of verbal and emotional abuse by the husband. Other data on marital rape suggest a range from 7–14% of rapes are perpetrated by husbands (Monson, Byrd, & Langhinrichsen-Rohling, 1996). Marital rapes have included not only vaginal intercourse, but also forced fellatio and anal intercourse. Historically, husbands could not be prosecuted for rape because the wife was the husband's property and "taking her sexually" was his right. Today, every state recognizes marital rape as a crime. Most wives are reluctant to press charges, but those who do are usually successful in seeing their husbands convicted. Russell (1991) reported that 88% of husbands who were reported to the police and arrested for rape were eventually convicted. One reason for such a high conviction rate is that such rapes are often particularly brutal or deviant.

Think About It

Because most rapes of adult women are perpetrated by men with whom the women were acquainted or romantically involved, rape is one of the most underreported violent crimes in the United States. More than 80% of rapes are not reported (Dunn, Vail-Smith, & Knight, 1999). What social changes do you feel can be made to increase the reporting of rape?

Strangers

Only 4% of perpetrators of sexual coercion reported by the 204 women in the Laumann et al. (1994) study were strangers. Rape by a stranger is known as **predatory rape** or **classic rape,** and may involve a weapon (a gun or knife). Rapes by strangers are taken more seriously by the courts, and prosecuted rapists who do not know their victims are more often convicted.

Predatory rape Rape by a stranger which may involve a weapon. (See also **classic rape.**)

Classic rape Rape by a stranger which may involve a weapon. See **predatory rape.**

Gang

Some rapes involve more than one perpetrator, and they may be either strangers or acquaintances. In an analysis of 1,076 patients seen for sexual assault in a Denver hospital, 20% reported that there was more than one assailant (Riggs, 2000). Watts and Zimmerman (2002) reported that gang rapes are not uncommon in South Africa, Papua New Guinea, and parts of the United States and are often associated with gang initiation, rites of passage, ethnic hatred, and racism.

Chris O'Sullivan (1991) studied acquaintance gang rapes on campus and found that men who would not rape alone may become rapists in the company of their sexually aggressive buddies. She also noted that athletes and fraternity men were more likely to be sexually aggressive and explained that, in gang rapes, there is often one leader of a closely knit group (athletic team, fraternity, or roommates) who instigates the rape. The other group members follow the leader. Participation in gang rape may be motivated by the quest for recreation, adventure, and acceptance by and camaraderie among the group members.

Three social-psychological factors help explain why group members who individually would not commit rape would do so in a group context. First, the group context allows members to diffuse responsibility for the gang rape by blaming others in the group. Second, a group context may produce a state of deindividuation, or "loss of self-awareness, including awareness of one's beliefs, attitudes, and self standards" (O'Sullivan, 1991, p. 148). Lastly, in a group setting, modeling of aggression occurs. Not only does watching group members rape a woman convey to other group members that this behavior is considered appropriate and fun, it also demonstrates techniques of how to force someone to have sex.

17-1d Women as Perpetrators

Whereas 90% of violent crimes (including forced sex) are perpetrated by men (O'Brien, 2001), women may also be perpetrators. Eighteen of the women in Russell and Oswald's (2001) study reported that they were perpetrators.

Recently, the problem of women-to-women sexual violence has been investigated. Girshick (2002) surveyed 91 women who described sexual violence perpetrated on them by women. In more than half the situations (56%), the perpetrator was a partner, lover, or girlfriend. In 7% of the situations, the perpetrator was a professional (therapist, teacher, doctor, supervisor), and only 2% were strangers. The pain and isolation of the victims were profound.

17-2 THEORIES OF RAPE

Various theories have been suggested in an attempt to explain why rape occurs.

17-2a Evolutionary and Biological Theories of Rape

Evolutionary and biological theories explain rape on the basis of anatomy, biologically based drives, and natural selection for reproductive success (Thornhill & Palmer, 2000). In addition to men being physically stronger than women, some biological theories of rape emphasize that rape results from a strong biological sex drive in men. This strong sex drive is explained in part by the high level of androgens and other sex hormones to which the male brain is exposed. Walsh, Isaacson, Rehman, and Hall (1997) also found higher levels of copper/zinc ratios (which play a role in the behavioral expression of violence) in assaultive males compared to controls.

Evolutionary (or sociobiological) theory suggests that males have a strong sex drive because natural selection favors males who copulate with numerous females. Males achieve reproductive success through copulating with as many females as possible; females achieve reproductive success through limiting their copulation behavior to males who are committed to help care for the female and her offspring.

Evolutionary/biological theories of rape have been criticized on the basis that societies differ in their rape rates (suggesting that such rates are due to social not biological influences), that insemination from rapes might yield a low pregnancy rate (so having many offspring would not result), that some women are very strong and can defend themselves, that the expression of testosterone is heavily influenced by social norms which dictate appropriate interpersonal sexual behavior, and that genetic determinism to rape simply does not exist. Indeed, evolutionary/biological theories would suggest that men are hormonally predisposed to rape; critics argue this is an exaggeration of biological influences.

17-2b Psychopathological Theory of Rape

According to the psychopathological theory of rape, rapists are viewed as having a mental disorder. Most people in the general population agree with this theory and think of rapists as being "crazy." Groth and Birnbaum (1979) developed a typology of rapes, each of which is based on some form of emotional or intrapsychic problem. Groth's typology includes the following: (a) anger rape, which results from the rapist's extreme anger (rape is viewed as the ultimate expression of anger toward another person); (b) power rape, which is motivated by the rapist's desire to sexually possess his victim (this need to possess is often based on the rapist's insecurity regarding his masculinity); and (c) sadistic rape, which involves elements of sexuality and aggression. (In sadistic rape, the offender derives sexual pleasure from inflicting intense pain and humiliation on his victim, who is usually a stranger.)

The psychopathological theory of rape may be criticized on the basis that the subject populations used for studies on rapists have been made up of incarcerated rapists. Also, not all rapists display the same symptomology or show marked deviation on standard psychological tests. Russell (1984) argued that "there is no denying that some rapists are mentally ill; the psychopathological model only becomes objectionable when it is used to apply to all or most rapists, as is done so often" (p. 148).

17-2c Feminist Theory of Rape

Feminist scholarship and activism have . . . led to a paradigmatic shift away from the notion of women as temptress of innocent man and toward the insistence on male responsibility for his actions in the perpetration of violence against women.

—*Patricia Rozee and Mary Koss*

The feminist theory of rape emphasizes the unequal distribution of power between men and women in society (Schuiteman, 2001). Proponents of this theory believe that men dominate women in the political and economic sphere, and that rape is an extension of the dominance, power, and control men exert over women. Hence, rape is viewed as an act of power and dominance, not an act of sex.

CULTURAL DIVERSITY 

Support for the view that rape is essentially a male response associated with the social inequality between the sexes is provided by data suggesting that the incidence and prevalence of rape in different societies vary by the degree of inequality between the women and men in those societies. In one study of 95 societies (Sanday, 1981), rape was either absent or rare in almost half (47%) of the cases. In these societies (the Ashanti of West Africa, for example), women tend to have equal status with men. "In 'rape free' societies women are treated with considerable respect, and prestige is attached to female reproductive and productive roles" (p. 16). Similarly, Lottes and Weinberg (1996) found lower rates of sexual coercion among Swedish students when compared to U.S. students. The researchers pointed out that women in Sweden have more institutional power and social benefits than women in the United States, which means there is greater equality between the sexes in Sweden.

Societies in which women are viewed as inferior to men tend to be more rape prone. Women in rape-prone societies are also viewed as property, implying that men may take them by violent means. Research that supports the feminist theory of rape is also provided by Frank (1991), who found that self-reported rapists placed greater emphasis on power and dominance in their relationships with women.

17-2d Social Learning Theory of Rape

The social learning theory of rape views rape as "behavior that males learn through the acquisition of social attitudes favorable to rape, and through the imitation of depictions of sexuality interlinked with aggression" (Ellis, 1989, p. 16). According to Ellis (1989), men learn aggressive behavior toward women, including rape behavior, through the following four interrelated processes. (See also Box 17-1.)

1. *The sex-violence linkage effect.* This process refers to the association of sexuality and violence. For example, many slasher and horror films, some pornography, and even some music videos depict sex and violence together, thus causing the viewer to form a link or association between sex and violence.
2. *The modeling effect.* This process involves imitating rape scenes and other acts of violence toward women that are seen in real life and in the mass media. Barron and Kimmel (2000) found that sexually violent content exists and increases as one moves from magazines to video to Usenet (Internet newsgroups).
3. *The desensitization effect.* This process involves becoming desensitized to the pain, fear, and humiliation of sexual aggression through repeated exposure to sexual aggression.
4. *The rape myth effect.* In this process, men learn to view women as "really wanting it" and to deny that their force constitutes rape.

Box 17-1 Self Assessment

Rape Supportive Attitude Scale

Indicate whether you *strongly disagree* (1), *disagree* (2), *are undecided or have no opinion* (3), *agree* (4), or *strongly agree* (5). The scale takes about 10 minutes to complete.

1—Strongly disagree 2—Disagree 3—Undecided 4—Agree 5—Strongly agree

___ 1. Being roughed up is sexually stimulating to many women.
___ 2. A man has some justification in forcing a female to have sex with him when she led him to believe she would go to bed with him.
___ 3. The degree of a woman's resistance should be the major factor in determining if a rape has occurred.
___ 4. The reason most rapists commit rape is for sex.
___ 5. If a girl engages in necking or petting and she lets things get out of hand, it is her fault if her partner forces sex on her.
___ 6. Many women falsely report that they have been raped because they are pregnant and want to protect their reputation.
___ 7. A man has some justification in forcing a woman to have sex with him if she allowed herself to be picked up.
___ 8. Sometimes the only way a man can get a cold woman turned on is to use force.
___ 9. A charge of rape two days after the act has occurred is probably not rape.
___ 10. A raped woman is a less desirable woman.
___ 11. A man is somewhat justified in forcing a woman to have sex with him if he has had sex with her in the past.
___ 12. In order to protect the male, it should be difficult to prove that a rape has occurred.
___ 13. Many times a woman will pretend she doesn't want to have intercourse because she doesn't want to seem loose, but she's really hoping the man will force her.
___ 14. A woman who is stuck-up and thinks she is too good to talk to guys deserves to be taught a lesson.
___ 15. One reason that women falsely report rape is that they frequently have a need to call attention to themselves.
___ 16. In a majority of rapes the victim is promiscuous or had a bad reputation.
___ 17. Many women have an unconscious wish to be raped, and may then unconsciously set up a situation in which they are likely to be attacked.
___ 18. Rape is the expression of an uncontrollable desire for sex.
___ 19. A man is somewhat justified in forcing a woman to have sex with him if they have dated for a long time.
___ 20. Rape of a woman by a man she knows can be defined as a "woman who changed her mind afterwards."

Scoring and Interpretation: All of the items are scored in the same direction. To determine your score for the scale add the responses (coded 1 through 5) to the 20 items. The higher the score, the more rape supportive or victim-callous attitudes are supported. This scale measures seven beliefs which have been found to promote rape, and also interfere with the recovery of rape survivors. The beliefs include: "(a) women enjoy sexual violence, (b) women are responsible for rape prevention, (c) sex rather than power is the primary motivation for rape, (d) rape happens only to certain kinds of women, (e) a woman is less desirable after she has been raped, (f) women falsely report many rape claims, and (g) rape is justified in some situations" (Lottes, 1998).

The Rape Supportive Attitude Scale was administered to college students, mostly single and in the 19- to 22-year-old age range, at schools in the northeastern United States (Lottes, 1991). In both studies the students took the scale in regularly scheduled classes. The scale items were randomly distributed within a 70-item questionnaire. The first sample included 98 men and 148 women from education, health, and sociology classes at two universities. Students from three universities comprised the second sample, which included 195 men and 195 women enrolled in business, engineering, English, education, history, mathematics, physics, political science, and sociology classes. Men scored significantly higher on the scale than women.

Reliability and Validity: The Cronbach alpha value for the first sample of students was .91, and .91 for the second sample as well. A single, dominant factor emerged from a principal components analysis of the data, which accounted for 37% of the variance. Men's scores on the Rape Supportive Attitude Scale were correlated with scores on the Hypermasculinity Inventory. For men and women scores on the Rape Supportive Attitude Scale were significantly correlated with measures of nonegalitarian gender role beliefs, traditional attitudes toward female sexuality, adversarial sexual beliefs, arousal to sexual violence, and nonacceptance of homosexuality.

Reference

Lottes, I. L. (1991). Belief systems: Sexuality and rape. *Journal of Psychology and Human Sexuality*, *4*, 37–59.

Source: From "Rape Supportive Attitudes Scale" by Ilsa L. Lottes in *Handbook of Sexuality-Related Measures*. Edited by C. M. Davis, W. L. Yarber, R. Bauserman, G. Schreer, and S. L. Davis (1998), p. 504. Reprinted by permission of Dr. Lottes.

17-3 CONSEQUENCES OF RAPE AND TREATMENT FOR RAPE SURVIVORS

Rape is a traumatic experience, and almost all rape survivors experience acute stress.

17-3a Helping Someone Who Has Been Raped

It sometimes happens that one's partner (girlfriend or spouse), relative, or friend is raped. How might one be of help to someone who has just been sexually assaulted? Creating a safe context whereby the person no longer feels under threat is paramount. This means staying with the person and maintaining close physical contact. Accepting the person's range and flood of emotions is also important; these emotions may vary from rage to passivity to sadness to guilt. Other issues include assessing the degree to which the person should or is willing to go to the hospital to rule out any medical concerns and/or to assess the person's willingness to contact a rape counselor and report the rape to the police. Indeed, today many rape crisis centers work closely with the police to provide both emotional help and specific direction in terms of how to go about finding and prosecuting the perpetrator. Recovery from the rape may also be facilitated by quick therapeutic involvement.

17-3b Consequences of Rape

An individual who has been raped has been traumatized. Initial reactions to rape include an acute period of disorganization, helplessness, vulnerability, and anger. The person may also blame himself or herself for the incident.

The most devastating aspect of rape may not be the genital contact, but rather the sense of cognitive and emotional violation. The woman who felt that her environment was safe and predictable, that other people were trustworthy, and that she was competent and autonomous may become someone who is fearful of her surroundings, suspicious of other people, and unsure of her ability to control her life.

Rape trauma syndrome was described by Burgess and Holstrom (1974) following a study of women who sought post-rape assistance through a hospital emergency department. This syndrome refers to the acute and long-term reorganization process that occurs as a result of forcible rape or attempted rape. The acute phase involves fear, anxiety, crying, and restlessness. Long-term reorganization may involve moving to another community and changing one's phone number. Nightmares, sexual dysfunctions, and phobias associated with the rape may also occur. Examples of the latter include fear of being alone, being in the dark, or touching a man's penis.

Rape trauma syndrome Acute and long-term reorganization process that occurs as a result of forcible rape or attempted rape.

A more contemporary description for rape after-effects (sequelae) is **post-traumatic stress disorder (PTSD),** a *Diagnostic and Statistical Manual of Mental Disorders* (*DSM-IV-TR;* American Psychiatric Association, 2000) diagnosis that characterizes a particular set of reactions to traumatic events, including military combat, natural disasters, or other events that invoke terror, helplessness, and fear of loss of life. It is also a reaction experienced by some rape victims. The rape survivor may have persistent episodes of re-experiencing the event, such as flashbacks, hallucinations, or nightmares. The survivor may attempt to avoid any stimuli associated with the trauma. This may involve efforts to avoid thoughts, feelings, or activities associated with the trauma; a restricted range of affect (such as the inability to have love feelings); feelings of detachment or estrangement from others; and the inability to recall aspects of the trauma. The person may also report symptoms of increased arousal, such as difficulty sleeping, increased irritability, and outbursts of anger. Rothbaum, Foa, Riggs, Murdock, and Walsh (1992) found that 94% of the women they assessed within the first 2 weeks of a rape experience had symptoms that met the diagnostic criteria for PTSD. (However, PTSD is not diagnosed unless the full symptom pattern is present for more than 1 month.) At 3 months after the rape, PTSD persisted for almost half (47%) of the women.

Post-traumatic stress disorder (PTSD) Mental health diagnostic category that characterizes a particular set of symptoms following traumatic events (including military combat, natural disasters, or other events that invoke terror, helplessness, and fear of loss of life), experienced by many rape victims.

Cultural Diversity 

Resnick et al. (1991) found that rape survivors are more likely than survivors of some other types of traumas to experience PTSD. What do you hypothesize to be the reasons for the higher PTSD rate among rape survivors?

In a longitudinal study of 1,399 youth (women and men)—both college students and noncollege youth—having been raped was associated with anger, social isolation, depressed mood, and lower self-esteem. The more violent the coercion, the more difficult the adjustment (Zweig, Barber, & Eccles, 1997). Gay men who have been sexually coerced are also more likely to report symptoms of dissociation, trauma-related anxiety, and borderline personality (Kalichman et al., 2001).

17-3c Treatment for Rape Survivors

Not all rape victims experience persistent symptoms of trauma. Research has confirmed a dose-response relationship, with those exposed to greater frequency, duration, and severity of trauma more likely to develop PTSD and depression (Acierno et al., 2001). Researchers who studied the association between adult rape, childhood sexual assault, and depression found that adults who experienced adult rape and sexual assault were not likely to experience persistent depression unless they had also experienced prior sexual abuse as a child (Cheasty, Clare, & Collins, 2002). Many survivors benefit from crisis counseling and/or longer therapy.

Crisis counseling may last from a few days to 2 or 3 months after the assault. The primary goals of crisis counseling include establishing a therapeutic relationship, encouraging emotional expression, and providing information about reporting rape to the police and symptoms the victim may experience. The therapist may also promote adjustment of immediate role responsibilities, which may take the form of encouraging the person to take time off from work or eliciting the support of others to provide a period for processing the rape experience.

Crisis counselors also discuss with the victim the importance of seeing a physician to take care of medical needs (care for physical injuries, testing for STDs and pregnancy) as well as to document the rape if the victim decides to take legal action. The latter is often a difficult choice for most rape victims because it makes their rape experience public and exposes them to questioning and interrogation by strangers.

Long-term therapy for rape may include a number of behavioral techniques, sexual therapy, exposure, and cognitive therapy. Exposure techniques may involve survivors retelling the traumatic event or writing a narrative to be used in treatment to reduce rape-related fears (Rauch, Hembree & Foa, 2001). The latter involves recognizing and eliminating dysfunctional thoughts. Cognitive therapy emphasizes reframing the rape experience from one of great horror to one in which the person has benefited—by learning to be more cautious, by recognizing one's vulnerability, and by appreciating the safety of one's close relationships. Cognitive therapy also encourages the person to increase the frequency of positive self-statements so as to enhance self-esteem. For example, persons who have been raped are encouraged to view themselves as survivors rather than as victims. Cognitive processing therapy (Resick & Schnicke, 1993) combines exposure therapy and cognitive restructuring; research studies have shown this approach is helpful in decreasing PTSD symptoms.

17-3d Treatment for the Rape Perpetrator

Data on reporting and conviction rates in Ohio are available. Of 92,490 rapes reported, less than 5% actually resulted in a conviction (Langan & Dawson, 1988). Koss (2000) examined partner violence and rape conviction rates against women and said that they were "miniscule." Data in two London police stations revealed a conviction rate of 8–10%

(Gregory & Lees, 1996). Sex offenders rarely seek treatment prior to any involvement with legal authorities and on their own volition. Most sex offenders in treatment are required to be there by legal authorities, and many therapists in outpatient programs refuse to take voluntary clients.

The timing of therapy is important. Unless therapy occurs when the offender is facing a court sentencing or as a condition of probation, the perpetrator usually denies the existence of a problem and has little motivation for treatment. Experienced clinicians typically request a court order before beginning treatment or recommend a period of inpatient treatment. This approach has proved to be important in keeping offenders in treatment, due to their denial and minimization of their offenses. It also helps reduce the "two-week cure" ("Thank you, doc. That was great. I learned a lot. No, I don't think I need therapy any more. Well, I'll never do that again. So long.") (Salter, 1988, p. 87). When well-meaning people allow offenders to seek voluntary therapy instead of reporting the offenders to legal authorities, they have no leverage to maintain the offenders' participation in treatment or to protect the safety of the community (Salter, 1988).

Therapeutic alternatives used in the treatment of sex offenders include providing group therapy, providing medications to reduce deviant sexual arousal (chemical castration discussed in Box 16-3, "Social Choices: Treating Paraphilic Sex Offenders with Hormones?"), and increasing arousal to appropriate stimuli. Still other modalities used in sex offender treatment programs include teaching relaxation and stress management, providing communication skills training, teaching impulse control, and dealing with the offender's own past sexual or physical abuse. Some treatment programs involve after-care treatment designed to assist the client when he is released from treatment. After-care treatment may include assisting the client in gaining further education or in securing employment.

17-4 PREVENTION OF RAPE

Rozee and Koss (2000) noted that rape prevention programs have had little effect on rape prevalence, which has remained at 15% for the past 25 years. Rape prevention programs that focus on teaching women to be cautious about being alone at night have had little effect on reducing prevalence rates. What may be more effective is to help women identify the signs of an impending rape and to take action to avoid or extricate herself. Alternatively, men need to be taught to look for signs of resistance by their partner and to stop.

17-4a A Program for Women: Teaching Women to Avoid Rape

Nurius and Norris (1996) have provided a conceptual model of AAA: Assess, Acknowledge, and Act.

- *Assess*. A man rejects a woman's firm "no" so that the woman assesses the situation as potentially dangerous and examines her isolation and potential for escape.
- *Acknowledge*. She defines the situation as one of impending rape, without which women are reluctant to act.
- *Act*. She tries to leave the situation by whatever means possible, yells for help, and becomes physically resistant in the form of pushing, biting, and kicking.

Think About It

A persistent myth that has prevented women from being forceful to extricate themselves from a rapist is that the more they resist (verbally and behaviorally), the more the rapist will beat and hurt them. The data confirm otherwise. Ullman and Knight (1991) found that more forceful resistance was related to less severe sexual abuse even when taking into account the level of offender aggression.

To what degree do you feel that the woman should or should not make a forceful attempt to resist?

17-4b A Program for Men: Teaching Men Not to Rape

Mirroring the AAA program for women, described in section 17-4a, is a similar one for men with AAA in which the letters refer to Ask, Acknowledge, and Act (Nurius & Norris, 1996).

- *Ask*. The man asks himself first if the woman is above the age of consent and second if she is under the influence of alcohol or other substances so that she is impaired in her consent.
- *Acknowledge*. If the answer to these questions is yes, the man acknowledges that asking for sex with this woman is inappropriate.
- *Act*. The man stops initiating sexual behavior.

Other aspects of teaching men not to rape are to alert them to rape myths. Foubert (2000) reported results of a rape-prevention program designed exclusively for men that included a reduction in male acceptance of rape myths. A long-term follow-up also revealed a reduction in the likelihood of future raping and in sexually coercive behavior. Preventing rape also involves men making new choices in regard to how they view having sex with a woman. Men must be educated that sex with an intoxicated or drugged partner can be considered sexual assault for which they can be prosecuted and imprisoned (Fouts & Knapp, 2001). Men who attend same-sex (all male) prevention groups have better treatment outcomes than those who are in mixed-sex prevention groups (Rozee & Koss, 2000)

17-5 CHILD SEXUAL ABUSE

An alarming percentage of adults report having been sexually abused as children.

NATIONAL DATA About 25% of adult women and 12% of adult men report having had sexual contact with someone at least 5 years older than them when they were 14 years of age or younger (McDonald & Bradford, 2000).

Of adult women who were molested in childhood by a man, 33% reported that they were age 6 or younger, with 40% reporting that they were between the ages of 7 and 10. Thirty percent of adult men who were molested by a man as a child were age 6 or younger; 46% were between the ages of 7 and 10. A "family friend" was the most likely perpetrator (Laumann et al., 1994). What is known about child sexual abuse is often provided directly in interviews. But the content disclosed may be influenced by the sex of the interviewer. Based on a study of 22 interviewers and 8,276 clients to assess sexual abuse, Dailey and Claus (2001) found that persons were more likely to disclose prior sexual abuse to female than to male interviewers.

NATIONAL DATA Data reported to the Administration for Children and Families indicated that in the year 2000 approximately 879,000 children were found to be maltreated. Of those children 63% were neglected, 19% were physically abused, 10% were sexually abused, and 8% were psychologically maltreated. Although rates of other types of maltreatment are similar for girls and boys, for sexual abuse there are 1.7 victims per 1,000 female children, compared to 0.4 victims per 1,000 male children (National Clearinghouse on Child Abuse and Neglect Information, 2002).

Think About It

Is there less child sexual abuse today than in the past? Data collected by the National Child Abuse and Neglect Data system show a decline in substantiated child sexual abuse cases in the United States over the 1990s—a decrease from 150,000 cases in 1992 to 92,000 in 1999 (Jones, Finkelhor, & Kopiec, 2001). Has the rate decreased or do variations in research design, reporting by citizens and professionals, and data collection practices explain the differences?

Cultural Diversity

Sex abuse is not unique to the United States. In a sample of 649 undergraduates at the University of the North, South Africa, 23% of the women and 22% of the men reported some form of sexual abuse (Madu, 2001). Actual behaviors included oral/anal/vaginal intercourse (9%), "sexual touching" (14%), and "kissing" (18%; Madu, 2001).

17-5a Theories of Child Sexual Abuse

Regardless of the rate, a number of theories have been suggested as to why child sexual abuse occurs.

Freudian Theory

Freudian theory maintains that humans are naturally capable of sexual arousal from a variety of stimuli, including children. For most people, cultural taboos and socialization act to repress any sexual interest that adults have in children.

Social Learning Theory

Social learning theory suggests that adults learn to regard children as sexual objects. Such learning may result from being exposed to child pornography or from being inadvertently sexually stimulated by contact with a child. For example, the grandfather who bounces his grandchild on his lap could have an erection while doing so and could learn to associate sexual feelings with the child. Or a brother hugging his sister may discover that her body feels good against his.

Male Sex Role Socialization

Male sex role socialization teaches men to be sexually aroused by sexual activities independent of the interpersonal context. Hence, some men find it easier to disregard that the sex they are enjoying is with a child. In addition, men are socialized to be attracted to partners who are smaller, younger, and less powerful than themselves. Finally, fathers are socialized to be the controlling parent in families and use their power to take what they want sexually from the children in the home.

History of Childhood Sexual Abuse

Some parents who sexually abuse their children were sexually abused themselves. In effect, they are modeling behavior they learned in the family of orientation.

17-5b Intrafamilial Child Sexual Abuse

Regardless of the rate or theory, the person who engages the child sexually is either inside the child's family (intrafamilial child sex abuse) or external to the family (extrafamilial child sex abuse).

Intrafamilial child sexual abuse The exploitative sexual contact or attempted or forced sex that occurs between related individuals when the victim is under the age of 18. (Also known as *incestuous child abuse*.)

Also referred to as *incestuous child abuse*, **intrafamilial child sexual abuse** refers to exploitative sexual contact or attempted or forced sex that occurs between relatives when the victim is under the age of 18. Sexual contact or attempted sexual contact includes intercourse, fondling of the breasts and genitals, and oral sex. "Relatives" in this instance include biologically related individuals, stepparents, and step siblings. More than half (53%) of a sample of 649 undergraduates who reported oral/anal/vaginal sexual abuse identified family or extended family members as the perpetrators (Madu, 2001). In a Swedish study of 496 cases of sex crimes against children, 72% of the perpetrators were known to the child, with the most severe offenses taking place within the family (Carlstedt, Forsman, & Soderstrom, 2001). Other researchers have observed that in 80% of the cases of child sexual abuse, the perpetrator is a relative (parent/stepparent, brother, uncle) or family friend of the child (McDonald & Bradford, 2000).

Think About It

Legal scholars continue to debate what constitutes taking advantage of a child sexually. Should sexual relations of and with persons under a certain age be criminalized even if the person consents? Should sexual relations with minors within a relationship of authority be criminalized? Should criminal proceedings be instituted automatically or upon complaint only? (Graupner, 2000).

Fathers as Perpetrators

Parent-child incest, particularly between a father or stepfather and a child in the family, is the type of incest that has received the most attention in society. Such incest is a blatant abuse of power and authority. Stepfathers are much more likely than biological fathers to perpetrate incest. For example, in Russell's (1984) study, 17%, or about 1 out of every 6 women who had a stepfather as a principal figure during childhood, were sexually abused by him. In contrast, 2%, or 1 out of 40 women, were abused by their biological father. Other data suggest that stepfathers may not be more likely to have sex with their children than biological fathers (Laumann et al., 1994). Whether biological father or stepfather, female children, more than male children, are the primary targets (Bolen, 2001).

The experience of a woman who, as a child, was forced to have sexual relations with her biological father is described as follows:

> *I was around 6 years old when I was sexually abused by my father. He was not drinking at the time; therefore, he had a clear mind as to what he was doing. On looking back, it seemed so well planned. For some reason, my father wanted me to go with him to the woods behind our house to help him saw wood for the night. I went without any question. Once we got there, he looked around for a place to sit and wanted me to sit down with him. In doing so, he said, "Susan, I want you to do something for daddy." I said, "What's that, daddy?" He went on to explain that "I want you to lie down, and we are going to play mamma and daddy." Being a child, I said "okay," thinking it was going to be fun. I don't know what happened next because I can't remember if there was pain or whatever. I was threatened not to tell, and remembering how he beat my mother, I didn't want the same treatment. It happened approximately two other times. I remember not liking this at all. Since I couldn't tell mama, I came to the conclusion it was wrong and I was not going to let it happen again.*
>
> *But what could I do? Until age 18, I was constantly on the run, hiding from him when I had to stay home alone with him, staying out of his way so he wouldn't touch me by hiding in the corn fields all day long, under the house, in the barns, and so on, until my mother got home, then getting punished by her for not doing the chores she had assigned to me that day. It was a miserable life growing up in that environment. (authors' files)*

Factors contributing to father-daughter incest include extreme paternal dominance (the daughter learns to be obedient to her father), maternal disability (the mother ceases to function as an emotional and sexual partner for the husband), and imposition of the mothering role on the oldest daughter (she becomes responsible for housework and child care). An added consequence of the oldest daughter taking over the role of the mother is her belief that she is responsible for keeping the family together. This implies not only doing what the father wants, but also keeping it a secret because she or her father will be expelled from the family for disclosure.

Think About It

Although some children report having been touched inappropriately as a child, not all use the term "sexual abuse." Of 649 undergraduates, 83% of the male victims and 68% of the female victims perceived themselves as "not sexually abused" during childhood. And, more than 80% of both sexes reported that their childhood was either "average" or "very happy" (Madu, 2001). A student in the authors' classes reported that her father fondled her regularly as a child but that his doing so had no long-term negative impact on her. "He was just crazy so I figured he didn't know what he was doing" (authors' files).

Although some fathers may force themselves on their daughters (as in the example of the 6-year-old girl described earlier), incest may begin by affectionate cuddling between father and daughter. The father's motives may be sexual; his daughter's are typically nonsexual. Indeed, the daughter is often unaware of any sexual connotations of her behavior; her motive is to feel acceptance and love from her father. Ambivalent feelings often result:

> *My daddy never touched me unless he wanted to have me play with his genitals. I didn't like touching him there, but he was affectionate to me and told me how pretty I was. I was really mixed up about the whole thing. (authors' files)*

Because of her ambivalence, the daughter may continue to participate in sexual activity with her father. Not only may she derive attention and affection from the relationship, but she may also develop a sense of power over her father. As she grows older, she may even demand gifts in exchange for her silence. Mothers may be slow to act because of incomplete information. "When the mother has not actually observed the abuse, when there is no physical evidence, and when the offender or child denies the abuse, how is she to know for sure that the abuse is occurring?" (Bolen, 2001, p. 198).

Other male family members may also be perpetrators. One of our students reported the following:

> *Our family was having a family gathering with all the relatives for Thanksgiving. It was held in the back yard of my aunt's. I had to go inside the house to get something and while I was inside one of my uncles came in. At that time we were pretty close and so, at first, I didn't think anything of the following events.*
>
> *My uncle came into the kitchen where I was alone and hugged and kissed me. I kissed him back. Then he kissed me again and because we were close, I didn't think anything about the second kiss. I then moved into the walk-in pantry and my uncle followed me and wanted to hug and kiss me again.*
>
> *I then realized this was no longer a "friendly kiss." I tried to move from the pantry and he blocked me. I tried not to act scared, even though I was. Trying to dodge him, he moved quickly and knocked a glass jar off the shelf. He told me to get paper towels to clean up the mess. Then my cousin came in the kitchen so I asked her to help with the broken jar and made an excuse to get outside. That was all that happened. To this day, I get chills when I have to be around my uncle, but I'm always careful not to be alone in his presence.*
>
> *I never told anyone of this event. He is my mother's favorite and closest brother and at the time I decided not to hurt her. (author's files)*

Women as Perpetrators

Incest between mothers and sons (or daughters) occurs less frequently (about 2%) than father-daughter incest (Bolen, 2001). It rarely includes intercourse but is usually confined to various stimulating behaviors. The mother may continue to bathe her son long after he is capable of caring for himself, during which time she stimulates him sexually. Later, she may stimulate her son to ejaculation. The mother may also sleep with her son. Although no specific sexual contact may occur, she may sleep in the nude; this behavior is provocative as well as stimulating.

Although the data suggest that women are much less likely to sexually abuse their children than men, mothers "have historically been charged as co-offenders of the abuse . . . for their alleged failure to protect" (Bolen, 2001, p. 193). Indeed some treatment models for incest require that mothers apologize to their child for their inability to protect the child.

Sibling Incest

Sibling incest is more common than parent-child incest; in fact, it is probably the most common type of incest (Adler & Schultz, 1995). Pierce and Pierce (1990) identified two categories of sibling activities. One type usually begins early as mutual exploration. It may end when the children realize the behavior is not acceptable. If, however, the behavior continues into adolescence, the siblings may have distress in later sexual relationships, although this is not always the case. The other type of activity involves one sibling forcing another to participate in sexual activities. Such offenders may be imitating the sexually precocious acts of abused siblings, participating in a promiscuous family lifestyle, or acting out other problems within the family.

Adler and Schultz (1995) studied 12 male sibling sex offenders (a very small sample) and noted that they came from intact middle-class homes with no previous victimization. The researchers also noted considerable parental denial and minimization. In almost 60% of the cases, sibling incest had been previously reported to the parents, but the incest continued. The mean age difference between the offending sibling and the victim sibling was 5 years; a mean of 16 or more incidents was involved (mostly oral sex and vaginal penetration); and the average duration of the incest was 22 months. Verbal threats were used to maintain the secrecy.

Cultural Diversity 

Although brother-sister incest taboos are nearly universal across cultures, there are exceptions. Siblings in royal families in ancient Egypt, Hawaii, and the Incas of Peru were permitted to have sex to keep power invested in a small group.

17-5c Extrafamilial Child Sexual Abuse

Extrafamilial child sexual abuse Attempted or completed forced sex, before a child reaches the age of 14, by a person who is unrelated to the child by blood or marriage.

Another pattern of child sexual abuse is extrafamilial child sexual abuse, which includes sexual abuse by adults in day-care contexts, caretakers in institutional settings, same- or opposite-sex peers, and strangers. Technically, **extrafamilial child sexual abuse** is defined as attempted or completed forced sex, before a child reaches the age of 14, by a person who is unrelated to the child by blood or marriage. The nature of the sexual behavior may range from touching breasts and genitals to rape. In some states, any forced or attempted sex with an unrelated child before the age of 17 (in Japan it is age 13) constitutes extrafamilial child sexual abuse. In Russell's study (1984), the perpetrators of extrafamilial child sexual abuse were acquaintances (42%), friends (of the family, of the respondent, dates, or boyfriends; 41%), and strangers (15%).

CULTURAL DIVERSITY 

Whether sex between children and adults is considered acceptable varies across societies and historical time periods. Bullough (1990) observed that "what appears obvious from a historical overview is that adult/child and adult/adolescent sexual behavior has had different meanings at different historical times" (p. 70). For example, during the eighteenth and nineteenth centuries in England, a child of 12 could consent to sexual behavior with a middle-aged adult. Even children under 12 "could be seduced with near impunity in privacy" (p. 74).

17-5d Recovered Memories of Abuse

Before we leave this discussion on childhood sexual abuse, it is important to comment on the issue of *recovered memories of abuse;* more recently, the terms *delayed, recovered,* and *discontinuous memory* are being used (Banyard, 2000). David Clohessy is one of the 3,000 boys alleged to have been molested by his priest in the 1980s (see Box 17-2). He said that memories of his abuse were triggered when he saw the Barbra Streisand movie *Nuts,* which involved recovered memories (Hewitt et al., 2002).

A number of factors may be involved to account for the fact that traumatic memories may be "forgotten." They include failure to encode (no memory was created at the time of the event), repression (active prevention of retrieval of memory), and long-term depression (cellular changes that suppress transmission of data from certain cells to others; Roth & Friedman, 1997).

Along with discussions of how memory is affected, there is debate among professionals as well as the general public as to whether some sexual molestation charges are the product of a therapist's suggestion or the client's imagination. Laboratory research on memory has shown that children can be persuaded to "remember" a traumatic event that did not actually happen to them, such as being separated from a parent on a shopping trip (Loftus, 1993). Bruck and Ceci (1999) noted that pre-school children are particularly susceptible to suggestion that they remember things that did not occur. Parks (1999) asked adults (who had been misled as to the true purpose of the research) whether they could recall certain aspects of their childhood and adolescence. Later, when asked how recently they had thought about some of those same items, participants often seemingly forgot that they had recalled them only minutes before. Although such studies for suggestibility and memory have documented that there can be problems with the memories of children and adults, the generalizability of these results to the topic of adult survivors of child sexual abuse has been challenged. Also, research suggests that "memories for traumatic events are different in important ways from memories for non-traumatic events" (Banyard, 2000, p. 2). For example, trauma may alter a person's physical systems so that trauma is stored in sensory motor rather than narrative form, thus making the trauma less accessible to memory retrieval. Williams (1994) noted that 38% of women with documented histories of sexual victimization in childhood did not recall the abuse that had been reported 17 years earlier.

In an effort to provide a balanced report on the scientific knowledge base of the reality of repressed memories of childhood trauma, the International Society for Traumatic Stress Studies summarized the research on traumatic memory and its implications for clinical and forensic practice (Roth & Friedman, 1997). They reviewed a number of research studies that show a significant proportion (20–60%) of adult women and men with documented cases of childhood sexual abuse did not seem to recall the abuse when they were interviewed as young adults. The younger the person at the time of the trauma, the more likely he or she was to have forgotten and to report recovered memories. Such triggers as watching a television program, reading materials, talking with family or friends, or experiencing a similar event seem associated with the recovery of memories.

In fact, the majority of recovered memories do not occur during therapy. However, questions have been raised about whether some of these recovered trauma memories, although sincerely believed, may be inaccurate (so-called "false memories"). Indeed, there seems to be agreement that "memory is by nature imperfect, constructive, and subject to change over time" (Banyard, 2000, p. 2).

Cognitive psychologists and neurobiologists studying human memory processes explain that memory does not perfectly represent an event (like a photograph). Instead, the memory processes prioritize information based on what is thought to be the most important when the event occurred. Memory storage has been compared to a "spider web in which specific memories are represented by the pattern of connections among fibers in the entire network. Memory is not a process of locating intact bits of information but rather involves partially recreating a pattern of associated threads of information across an entire network" (Roth & Friedman, 1997, p. 11). In addition, there may be differences in how traumatic and nontraumatic memories are encoded, consolidated, and retrieved. Professional societies in North America, Europe, Australia, and New Zealand have produced position papers that agree on three points:

> (1) traumatic events are usually remembered in part or in whole;
>
> (2) traumatic memories may be forgotten, then remembered at some later time;
>
> (3) illusory memories can also occur. (Roth & Friedman, 1997, p.15)

Traumatic memories are related to a number of post-traumatic symptoms. Specific trauma memories may be an important focus of treatment because they are likely to be distressing and affect assumptions about one's self. Talking in detail about one's experience can be an important part of cognitive and emotional processing. However, it is important for therapists to keep in mind that memory is fallible. They should adhere to recognized principles of therapy and be cautious not to use therapeutic approaches that create or reinforce false beliefs of trauma. They should not assume that the presence of specific symptoms or symptom groups substantiate a history of trauma or abuse. Therapists can help clients explore their past and come to their own conclusions about the best course of action to take. "Whether or not there is traumatic material under discussion, improving current functioning is ultimately the major goal of treatment. While childhood traumatic experiences may always remain an important part of a survivor's identity, after successful treatment survivors are likely to be facing forward rather than looking back" (Roth & Friedman, 1997, p. 17). Hence, practitioners have moved away from aggressively pursuing the recovery of abuse memories to discussing the best way to interview child victims and providing therapy for survivors.

17-6 CONSEQUENCES OF CHILD SEXUAL ABUSE AND TREATMENT

In sections 17-6a through 17-6c, we look at the impact of—and the treatment alternatives for—child sexual abuse.

17-6a Impact of Child Sexual Abuse

Child sexual abuse is associated with negative outcomes. Chandy, Blum, and Resnick (1996a) studied 1,011 female teenagers with a history of sexual abuse and compared them with an equal number of randomly selected female teenagers from a group who did not report a history of child sexual abuse. Lower school performance, suicidal involvement, eating disorder behavior, pregnancy risk, and substance use were associated with the former. When compared with boys, girls had higher tendencies of suicidal behavior, eating disorders, and drinking problems. Boys showed higher tendencies of delinquent activities and sexual risk-taking (Chandy, Blum, & Resnick, 1996b). Adolescents who sought treatment for substance use problems had twice the rate of sexual abuse history compared to adoles-

Box 17-2 Up Close

Pedophiles in the Catholic Church

In section 16-1, "Variant Sexual Behavior: Definitions and Overview," we defined *pedophilia* as engaging in sexual behavior with a child or having a recurrent urge to do so. To be diagnosed as a pedophile, an individual must be at least 16 years old and must be at least 5 years older than the target child. Although attraction to girls is more commonly reported, individuals with pedophilia may be sexually aroused by both young girls and young boys. Those who are attracted to young boys have a higher recidivism rate (American Psychiatric Association, 2000).

Pedophiles may engage in a wide range of behaviors. On one end of the continuum are such activities as undressing the child, looking at the nude body of a child, exposing one's self to the child, masturbating in the presence of the child, and fondling the child. Alternatively, the other end of the continuum includes such behaviors as performing fellatio on the child; penetrating the child's mouth or anus with one's finger, a foreign object, or one's penis; and using various levels of force to do so.

Pedophilia received national attention with the 2002 accusation of an estimated 2,000 priests (McGeary et al., 2002) in the Catholic Church having sex with young children; 3,000 plus children have claimed abuse (Hewitt et al., 2002). Defrocked priest John Geoghan is thought to have molested 130 children and was sentenced from 9–10 years in prison for abusing a 10-year-old boy. More than $30 million has already been paid to settle more than 80 lawsuits. It is reported that priests told their victims that they had a "special relationship" with them—an effort to "convince them that molestation is some kind of holy secret that must never be disclosed" (Hewitt et al., 2002). In the wake of this horrific set of abuses, "lives have been hurt, trust damaged, and the credibility of the Church to speak on social issues tainted" (McGeary et al., 2002, p. 52).

Wilton Gregory, president of the Bishop's Conference, discusses with the press the Church's plan for dealing with priests accused of child sexual abuse.

AP/ Wide World Photos

cents in the general population (Ballon, Courbasson, & Smith, 2001). Youth who used substances to cope with sexual abuse were also more likely to have made past suicide attempts.

Negative outcomes of child sexual abuse have been observed by other researchers; they include low self-esteem, difficulty in intimate relationships, repeated victimization, and sexually transmitted diseases (Herman, 1981; Hillis, Anda, Felitti, & Marchbanks, 2001). Low self-esteem results from repeatedly engaging in behavior society labels as bad. Difficulty in intimate relationships results from the generalization of negative feelings from the incestuous relationship to other relationships, and repeated victimization results from a feeling of entrapment and accommodation: The child feels trapped by her father's control, and her only perceived alternative is to accommodate the situation.

The age at which a child experiences sex abuse is relevant to the effects of the experience. Children who experience sex abuse between the ages of 7 and 13, when they are old enough to be aware of cultural taboos, experience the highest incidence of psychopathology (Browne & Finkelhor, 1986). In addition, those women who had suffered forceful, prolonged, or highly intrusive sexual abuse (penetration) or who had been abused by their fathers or stepfathers were the most likely to report long-lasting negative effects of incest (Herman, Russell, & Trocki, 1986; Beitchman et al., 1992).

Two researchers (Morrow & Sorrell, 1989) studied adolescent girls who had been sexually abused and observed that the most devastating effects occurred when the sexual behavior was intercourse. "This finding supports the contention that sexual intercourse in a tabooed incestuous relationship, which is likely to involve the loss of virginity, is viewed as extremely negative by adolescent incest victims" (p. 683). Not only were sexually abused girls more likely to have a teenage pregnancy (Boyer, Fine, & Killpack, 1991), but they also were likely to have lower self-esteem, higher levels of depression, and greater numbers of antisocial (running away from home, illegal drug use) and self-injurious (attempted suicide) behaviors). Sarwer and Durlak (1996) also found that penetration in child sexual abuse was significantly associated with sexual dysfunction in adult women.

Case studies of eight adult men who were molested as children by their nonpsychotic mothers revealed several problems the men had as adults. These problems included difficulty establishing intimate relationships with significant others (100%), depression (88%), and substance abuse (63%) (Krug, 1989). Elliott and Briere (1992), in their review of the literature, observed that abused men develop negative self-perceptions, anxiety disorders, sleep and eating disturbances, and gastrointestinal problems. They further noted an increased incidence of sexual dysfunctions in the form of decreased sexual desire, early ejaculation, and inability to achieve an orgasm.

The sex of the adult and the child may have an additional consequence. Boys who are sexually abused by men (including relatives) tend to develop concerns about their sexual identities for years afterward. Tomeo, Templer, Anderson, and Kotler (2001) studied 942 nonclinical adults and observed that almost half (46%) of the homosexual men in contrast to 7% of heterosexual men reported homosexual molestation. Women who are molested by women may also be affected because 22% of lesbian women, in contrast to 1% of heterosexual women, reported homosexual molestation.

Child sexual abuse accommodation syndrome Phases in coping behavior (including secrecy, helplessness, accomodation, disclosure, and retraction) of children as they adjust to repeated sexual abuse.

Summit (1983) identified a **child sexual abuse accommodation syndrome** that characterizes what children experience as victims of incest. Children are threatened into secrecy and feel entrapped and helpless with no choice other than to accommodate the situation. Disclosure of the incest is delayed and often disbelieved by the nonoffending parent. Being disbelieved by the mother and feeling the extreme impending disorganization of the family, the child usually retracts the allegations of abuse. Hence, in the case of father-daughter incest, "unless there is immediate support for the child and immediate intervention to force responsibility on the father, the girl will follow the normal course and retract her complaint" (p. 182). "It is usually only when men are in treatment that they concede that the child told the truth" (p. 190).

Whether brother-sister incest is a problem for siblings depends on a number of factors. If the siblings are young (4 to 8 years of age); of the same age; have an isolated sexual episode; engage only in exploratory, nonintercourse behavior; and both consent to the behavior, there may be little to no harm. However, as we have noted, a change in any of these factors increases the chance that sibling incest may have negative consequences for the individual (depression) and her or his subsequent relationships (unsatisfying sexual relationships; Canavan, Meyer, & Higgs, 1992).

Negative consequences of adult-child sex are not inevitable (Rind, 1995). Variables influencing the outcome include the adult's use of force, the perception of the child's willingness to participate, and the child's knowledge about and values related to sex. The degree to which one feels self-blame for the sexual abuse is also associated with adjustment (McMillen & Zuravin, 1997). Hence, individuals who have experienced sex as a child with an adult should not assume dire consequences for the future.

17-6b Treatment of Sexually Abused Children and Adults Sexually Abused as Children

Because a frequent type of child sexual abuse reported to professionals is father-daughter incest or abuse by a step-father or a mother's boyfriend, we will follow the case of a girl who tells a school nurse or counselor that she is being sexually molested by her father. The counselor calls the designated child protection agency to report the suspected abuse. The child protection agency will probably involve the local law enforcement agency, and an officer may be sent to obtain an initial statement from the girl. If the community has an interdisciplinary child abuse investigation team, this reduces the number of times the child must be interviewed. If the investigation suggests sufficient evidence exists to warrant an arrest and referral to the district attorney for prosecution, the father is arrested and placed in jail or released on his own recognizance. Ideally, he is not allowed to make contact with the daughter or to return to the home until legal disposition of the case is completed and progress in therapy has been made.

Incest and step-parent abuse are viewed as a family problem in terms of assessment and intervention. Counseling begins immediately; the individuals are first seen alone and then as a family. The focus of the counseling is to open channels of communication between all family members and to develop or re-establish trust between the husband and the wife. Another aspect of the program involves the confrontation between the father and the daughter, in which the father apologizes and takes full responsibility for the sexual abuse. The ideal outcome of therapy is for the father to take complete responsibility for the sex abuse, for the mother to take responsibility for not having been more vigilant, and for the child to feel completely absolved of any guilt for having participated in the sex abuse.

In discussing the emphasis on family therapy used in treating incestuous fathers, Finkelhor (1986) noted that some family analyses have exaggerated the role of family dynamics, especially the contribution of the mother to the child's abuse. Finkelhor recommended not limiting attention to the matrix of family dynamics. He observed that many incestuous abusers "have characteristics of pedophiles and other sex offenders who have a rather autonomous proclivity to abuse" (p. 56). Finkelhor cited data from a unique study in which abusers were given absolute confidentiality; 45% of incestuous abusers of girls were sexually involved with children outside their family. These findings suggest deviant arousal patterns that could not be adequately treated without individual and group work with the offender.

Depending on the circumstances and the recommendation of the social worker, the father might face criminal proceedings. If he is convicted (usually for child molestation or statutory rape), a presentencing evaluation may be completed to assess whether incarceration or treatment is indicated. He may be sent to prison or receive a suspended sentence if he agrees to participate in a treatment program of individual, group, and family counseling. Treatment is usually prescribed to last anywhere from 18 months to 5 years (Ballard, Williams, Horton, & Johnson, 1990).

Bass and Davis (1988), in their book *The Courage to Heal,* noted that a basic step in healing from sex abuse is for survivors to have compassion for their previous choices. "Even if you didn't make the wisest, healthiest choices, you took the options you saw at the time. And now you're making better choices. Focus on that" (p. 174). Lew (1990), in *Victims No Longer,* emphasized the importance of forgiving one's self:

> *Without question, this is the most important need of all. As long as you continue to accept blame for what happened to you—as long as you buy any part of the lies that you have been told—the abuse is continuing. Although having been abused does not call for forgiveness of others, it is necessary for you to "forgive yourself." (p. 258)*

Cognitive Processing Therapy (also used for adult rape survivors) has also been applied for treatment of adults with a history of child sexual abuse (Owens, Pike, & Chard, 2001). Beyond traditional therapy is eye movement desensitization and reprocessing (EMDR). Although it is still controversial, Edmond, Rubin, and Wambach (1999) found clinical gains associated with the use of this treatment, which involves cognitive reprocessing along with eye movements or other left-right stimulation. Finally, help for sex abuse victims is available nationwide through Childhelp USA (1-800-422-4453).

17-6c Personal Choices: Children Testifying in Cases of Alleged Child Sexual Abuse

Robert Kelly was the owner and operator of the Little Rascals Day Care Center in Edenton, North Carolina. In the spring of 1992, he was found guilty on 99 of 100 counts of sexual abuse of the children in his center. Parents agonized over whether to subject their children to testifying in court, to enduring cross-examination, and to disrupting their schedules for the 6-month trial. After the verdict was read, they sighed with relief that the man charged with abusing their children had not been allowed to escape with impunity. (In 1999, Kelly appealed the conviction and the charges were dropped. He served 6 years in jail.)

In a study by Burgess, Hartman, Kelley, Grant, and Gray (1990), parents whose children testified in trials against defendants charged with committing sexual abuse in daycare centers were compared with parents whose children were also alleged to have been sexually abused but who decided not to encourage their children to testify. The parents' motivation for encouraging their child to testify was "to create safety for their child as well as other children. Safety was defined in terms of the child feeling safe to know the perpetrator was 'locked up' and that the child would be believed and protected during testifying" (Burgess et al., 1990, p. 402). When parents who encouraged their children to testify were asked if they had made the right decision, 70% said "yes."

However, for some parents, the cost of their decision was high. Parents whose children testified presented higher symptoms of psychological distress than parents whose children did not testify. Such distress involved decreased income (legal expenses, time in court), job changes, alcohol or drug abuse, and separation or divorce (Burgess et al., 1990).

Peters, Dinsmore, and Toth (1989) emphasized the importance of prosecuting alleged child sexual abuse perpetrated by family members. Although the argument for not prosecuting is to "keep the family together," there are at least two reasons to pursue prosecution vigorously:

1. Criminal prosecution clearly establishes that children are innocent victims and that the perpetrators are solely responsible for their wrongful behavior.
2. Successful prosecutions educate the public and provide community visibility for the unacceptability of child sex abuse.

Peters et al. (1989) also noted that "in the great majority of cases that are criminally prosecuted, children do not have to testify at trial" (p. 657). But if they do, the benefits may outweigh the discomfort for the children or the family.

17-7 PREVENTION OF CHILD SEXUAL ABUSE

Our society has prioritized the sexual safety of our children.

17-7a Strategies to Reduce Child Sexual Abuse

Strategies to reduce child sexual abuse include regendering cultural roles, providing specific information to children on sex abuse, improving the safety of neighborhoods, providing healthy sexuality information for both teachers and children in the public schools at regular intervals, and promoting public awareness campaigns.

From a larger societal preventive perspective, Bolen (2001) recommended that child sexual abuse should be viewed as a gendered problem. Indeed, "child sexual abuse is endemic within society and may be a result of the unequal power of males over females" (p. 249). As evidence, females are at greater risk of abuse than males, males are more likely to offend, child sexual abuse is most frequently heterosexual, etc. The implication here is that one way to discourage child sexual abuse is to change traditional notions of gender role relationships, masculinity, and male sexuality so that men respect the sexuality of women and children and take responsibility for their sexual behavior.

Adults are also helping children acquire specific knowledge and skills to protect themselves from sexual abuse. A survey of 400 school districts in the United States revealed that 85% had offered a prevention program in the past year (Davis & Gidyez, 2000). Through various presentations in the elementary schools, children are taught how to differentiate between appropriate and inappropriate touching by adults or siblings, to understand that it is okay to feel uncomfortable if they do not like the way someone else is touching them, to say "no" in potentially exploitative situations, and to tell other adults if the offending behavior occurs. While children who participate in these programs have

Box 17-3 Social Choices

Megan's Law and Beyond?

In 1994, Jesse Timmendequas lured 7-year-old Megan Kanka into his Hamilton Township house in New Jersey to see a puppy. He then raped and strangled her and left her body in a nearby park. Prior to his rape of Megan, Timmendequas had two prior convictions for sexually assaulting girls. Megan's mother, Maureen Kanka, argued that she would have kept her daughter away from her neighbor if she had known about his past sex offenses. She campaigned for a law, known as **Megan's Law**, requiring that communities be notified of a neighbor's previous sex convictions. New Jersey and 45 other states have enacted similar laws. President Clinton signed a federal version in 1996.

The law requires that convicted sexual offenders register with local police in the communities in which they live. It also requires the police to go out and notify residents and certain institutions (such as schools) that a dangerous sex offender has moved into the area. It is this provision of the law that has been challenged on the belief that individuals should not be punished forever for past deeds. Critics of the law argue that convicted child molesters who have been in prison have paid for their crime. To stigmatize them in communities as sex offenders may further alienate them from mainstream society and increase their vulnerability for repeat offenses.

In many states, Megan's Law is not operative because it is on appeal. Although parents ask, "Would you want a convicted sex offender, even one who has completed his prison sentence, living next door to your 8-year-old daughter?" the reality is that little notification is afforded parents in most states. Rather, the issue is tied up in court and will likely remain so until the Supreme Court decides. A group of concerned parents (Parents for Megan's Law) are trying to implement Megan's Law nationwide. Their web site is http://www.parentsformeganslaw.com/

In July 2002, Parents for Megan's Law sought to enact legislation for the "civil commitment for a specific group of the highest risk sexual predators who freely roam our streets, unwilling or unable to obtain proper treatment. This kind of predator commitment follows a criminal sentence and generally targets repeat sex offenders who then remain in a sexual predator treatment facility until it is safe to release them to a less restrictive environment or into the community" (http://www.parentsformeganslaw.com/html/message.lasso). Indeed, this group not only wants parents to be notified of criminal sex offenders but also to house them in treatment centers on release from prison.

Megan's Law Federal law that requires that convicted sex offenders register with local police when they move into a community.

greater knowledge of sexual abuse and learn strategies to circumvent it, "it cannot be assumed that children participating in abuse prevention programs are at lower risk for sexual abuse" (Davis & Gidyez, 2000, p. 263).

Public awareness programs include "Run, Yell, Tell," "Stranger Danger," and "Yello Dyno Safety Program." In spite of the worthwhile goals of these and other preventive programs, Reppucci and Haugaard (1989) questioned whether preschool children are capable of conceptualizing sex abuse, discriminating what is and isn't abuse, and being assertive where indicated. Furthermore, prevention programs may have unwanted negative side effects, such as making children feel uncomfortable with nonsexual contact such as tickling, wrestling, or sitting on a parent's lap. They might also interpret information from prevention programs that teaches negatives about sex—it is secret, dirty, and dangerous.

Helping to ensure that children live in safe neighborhoods where it is known if neighbors are former convicted child molesters is the basis of Megan's Law (see Box 17-3).

Think About It

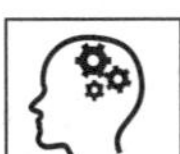

Assume that you have a young child. A convicted child molester has been released from prison and now lives in your neighborhood. What do you feel your rights are as a parent in terms of knowing about the presence of this person? What about this person's right to privacy?

17-7b Internet Safety Issues for Children

Although the Internet has become one of the most valuable information and educational tools of our society, it can be lethal if children are not properly supervised in its use. Pedophiles, posing as friends, may enter chat rooms with unsuspecting prepubescents, interact with them as though they are peers, arrange to meet them at the mall, and abduct them. Awareness of the presence of pedophiles on the Internet has become a concern for parents who want their children to become computer literate. Pedophiles have no shortage of sites. Typing "childsex" and "kiddieporn" into the AltaVista search engine yielded more than 173,000 web pages devoted to child pornography (Casanova, Solursh, Solursh, Roy, & Thigpen, 2000).

One strategy to reduce the exposure of children to pedophiles on the Internet is to not allow children to have a computer in their bedroom where they can spend long hours in isolation on the computer without the content being monitored. Rather, the computer should be placed in the living room or family room or open space where constant monitoring of content can occur. Web sites such as GetNetWise (http://www.getnetwise.org/) address safe Internet use by children. Box 17-3 presents a recommended agreement between parents and children (http://www.getnetwise.org/tools/toolscontracts.php).

Other Internet sites designed to help children remain safe on the Internet are Kidshield (http://www.kidshield.com/), Children's Guardian (http://wiasa.org/), and Cybercitizens Awareness Program (http://www.cybercitizenship.org/). The ChiBrow (http://www.chibrow.com/) site sells a browser that will prescreen "safe" sites for children.

17-8 SEXUAL HARASSMENT

Sexual harassment
Unwelcome sexual advances, requests for sexual favors, and other verbal or physical conduct of a sexual nature when submission to or rejection of this conduct explicitly or implicitly affects an individual's employment; unreasonably interferes with an individual's work performance; or creates an intimidating, hostile, or offensive work environment.

Like rape or child sexual abuse, sexual harassment is another form of sexual coercion. Sexual harassment is a form of sex discrimination that violates Title VII of the Civil Rights Act of 1964.

17-8a Definition and Incidence of Sexual Harassment

According to the Equal Employment Opportunity Commission (EEOC), **sexual harassment** is defined as unwelcome sexual advances, requests for sexual favors, and other verbal or physical conduct of a sexual nature when submission to or rejection of this conduct explicitly or implicitly affects an individual's employment; unreasonably interferes with an individual's work performance; or creates an intimidating, hostile, or offensive work environment (EEOC web site at http://www.eeoc.gov/facts/fs-sex.html, 2002). Although

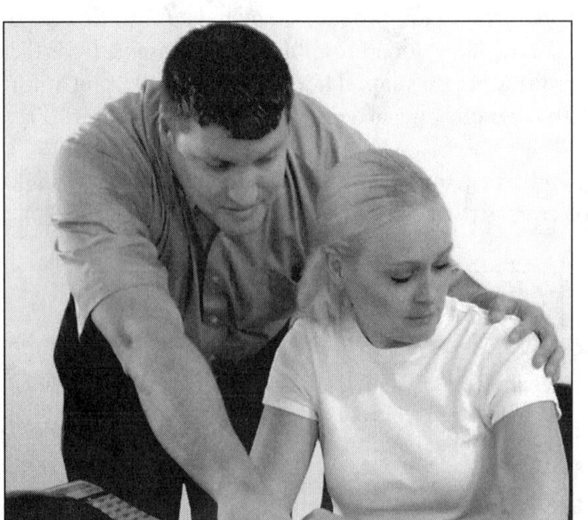

When does a behavior become sexual harassment?

Box 17-3 Up Close

Staying Safe Online—An Agreement Between Children and Parents

1. I will ALWAYS tell a parent or another adult immediately, if something is confusing or seems scary or threatening.
2. I will NEVER give out my full name, real address, telephone number, school name or location, schedule, password, or other identifying information when I'm online. I will check with an adult for any exceptions.
3. I will NEVER have a face-to-face meeting with someone I've met online. In rare cases, my parents may decide it's OK, but if I do decide to meet a cyberpal, I will make sure we meet in a public place and that a parent or guardian is with me.
4. I will NEVER respond online to any messages that use bad words or words that are scary, threatening, or just feel weird. If I get that kind of message, I'll print it out and tell an adult immediately. The adult can then contact the online service or appropriate agency. If I'm uncomfortable in a live chat room, I will use the "ignore" button.
5. I will NEVER go into a new online area that is going to cost additional money without first asking permission from my parent or teacher.
6. I will NEVER send a picture over the Internet or via regular mail to anyone without my parent's permission.
7. I will NOT give out a credit card number online without a parent present.

Young Person ______________________________ Date _______

Parent/Guardian ______________________________ Date _______

Source: Reprinted by permission of Internet Education Foundation.

definitions vary across studies and states, there seems to be agreement on two elements of the definition: Sexual harassment occurs when sexual behavior is (a) inappropriate for the context, and (b) it is unwanted by a participant or observer (Sbraga & O'Donohue, 2000).

Two types of sexual harassment have been identified. **Hostile environment sexual harassment** refers to deliberate or repeated unwanted sexual comments or behaviors that affect one's performance at work or school. **Quid pro quo sexual harassment** (*quid pro quo* means *this for that*) sets up workplace consequences contingent upon sexual favors (such as requiring sexual favors to obtain a raise or promotion, or to prevent being fired or demoted; Avina & O'Donahue, 2002). Some behaviors that have been considered sexual harassment include the following:

Hostile environment sexual harassment Environment whereby deliberate or repeated unwanted sexual comments or behaviors affect one's performance at work or school.

Quid pro quo sexual harassment Type of sexual harassment whereby the individual is provided benefits (promotions, salary raises) in exchange for sexual favors.

- Sexual comments about a woman's body or attire
- Rumoring—spreading sexual gossip behind a target's back
- Sexual graffiti or material placed on a target's desk
- Personal questions
- Sexual posturing
- Sexual touching
- Pressure for dates or relationships
- Sexual bribery

Sexual harassment can occur in a variety of circumstances, including but not limited to the following:

- The victim as well as the harasser may be a woman or a man. The victim does not have to be of the opposite sex.
- The harasser can be the victim's supervisor, an agent of the employer, a supervisor in another area, a co-worker, or a nonemployee.
- The victim does not have to be the person harassed but could be anyone affected by the offensive conduct.
- Unlawful sexual harassment may occur without economic injury to or discharge (firing) of the victim.
- The harasser's conduct must be unwelcome.

17-8b Theories of Sexual Harassment

Five theories have been advanced to explain sexual harassment (Sbraga & O'Donohue, 2000). Some of them are the same theories used to explain other types of sexual coercion:

1. The *natural/biological model* implies that sexual harassment is a natural consequence of men's sex drive. The sociobiological model fits here with the assumption that men engage in sexual harassment to increase their probability of gaining sexual access to more women.
2. The *sociocultural model* considers the social and political context of male dominance in the society. Male and female workers often act on gender roles and stereotypes at work. However, the fact that gender role socialization has become somewhat more flexible in recent years has not curbed the existence of sexual harassment .
3. The *organizational model* considers the power hierarchies, norms, and situations within an organization that may be conducive to sexual harassment. For example, there may be personal appearance demands for women, requirements for travel or working behind closed doors. This model has been criticized as not taking into consideration what the personnel bring to the workplace.
4. The *sex-role spillover model* hypothesizes that workers bring gender-biased behavior expectancies into the workplace, even if these beliefs are not appropriate for work. When the sex-role stereotypes are discrepant from the work demands, conflicts arise. Therefore, women in work roles that do not involve nurturing or being an object of sexual attention are more likely to be harassed.
5. The *fifth theory* offers a more comprehensive model. It is the four-factor model offerred by O'Hare and O'Donohue (1998). It states that for sexual harassment to occur, four factors must be present: (a) motivation to harass, (b) overcoming internal inhibitions that might suppress harassment, (c) overcoming external inhibitions, and (d) overcoming victim resistance. This model takes into consideration the complexity of a combination of factors (human predispositions, social values and norms, organizational policy, and sex-role beliefs).

17-8c Sexual Harassment in the Workplace

About half of all working women in the United States are affected by sexual harassment (Richman et al., 2001). In terms of sexual harassment in different professions, 51% of female family practice resident physicians, 64% of women in the U.S. military, 70% of female office workers, and 88% of female nurses report having been sexually harassed (Avina & O'Donohue, 2002). Although sexual harassment of men does occur, it is less common because men have greater power in society. Indeed, sexual harassment is often directed toward young, unmarried women in traditionally all-male organizations. The U.S. military and police units are contextual havens for sexual harassment.

Gay and lesbian individuals are also vulnerable to sexual harassment in the workplace. Based on a study of more than 2,000 adult workers in the United States, 41% of the gay and lesbian workers reported facing some form of hostility or harassment on the job. Almost 1 in 10 of the gay or lesbian workers stated that he or she was fired or dismissed unfairly from a previous job, or pressured to quit a job because of his or her sexual orientation (Harris Interactive & Witeck-Combs, 2002).

Due to increased visibility of sexual harassment suits in our society, various policies have been instituted for dealing with such harassment. These policies are the topic of Box 17-4.

17-8d Sexual Harassment in Educational Settings

Although sexual harassment on campus triggers visions of the faculty sexually harassing students, students may also be perpetrators. Matchen and DeSouza (2000) studied 102 faculty and 359 college students at a large Midwestern university. More than half (53%)

Box 17-4 Social Choices

Sexual Harassment Policy in the Workplace?

The Equal Employment Opportunity Commission (EEOC) of the Federal Government, major companies, and academic institutions have developed sexual harassment policies. The formal goals of these policies are to go on record as being against sexual harassment, to discourage employees from engaging in sexually harassing behavior, and to provide a mechanism through which harassment victims can inform management. The informal goals are to provide the organization with guidelines for reacting to allegations of harassment, and to protect the organization from being taken to court and being forced to pay punitive damages. Organizations and schools also offer educational programs about sexual harassment by developing and distributing brochures and conducting training workshops. Increasingly, policies emphasize the rights of the harassed and the responsibility of the organization to prevent harassment and provide mechanisms for dealing with it when it occurs.

Persons who file sexual harassment suits may encounter empathy for their experiences, or they may discover that the full weight of the organization is being used against them. Both the institution and the alleged harasser may be willing, and have the resources to be able, to launch a full-scale attack on the professional, personal, and sexual life of the complainant (Schultz & Woo, 1994). Race and gender may also become variables in a forthcoming trial. Wuensch, Campbell, Kesler, and Moore set up a simulated civil case (a female plaintiff accused a male defendant of sexual harassment) and had 161 White and 152 Black college students serve as mock jurors. Results showed that mock jurors of both races tended to favor litigants of their own race and gender. Many persons who file sexual harassment complaints end up withdrawing them.

of the faculty reported having experienced at least one sexually harassing behavior from students; 63% of the students reported engaging in potentially sexually harassing behaviors at least once toward faculty members. The students did not differ by gender in their likelihood of perpetrating sexual harassment. However, the women professors reported more unwanted sexual attention than did the men professors and were also more bothered by unwanted sexual attention. Likewise, in another campus study, in the faculty group, female faculty experienced higher rates of overall generalized workplace abuse.

Think About It

Eisenman (2002) conducted research on sexual harassment charges by students toward faculty and concluded that such cases involve vague definitions of what constitutes harassment, with faculty being denied proper hearings and being fired even if they have tenure. In fact, Eisenman noted that sexual harassment charges provide administrators a way to fire faculty with tenure, something they would like to do but are typically precluded from doing. In some cases, Eisenman found that the faculty member was as good as convicted even before any testimony was heard. How often do you feel faculty are unjustly removed over charges of sexual harassment?

On the other hand, faculty behaviors that are distressing to students are not always affirmed as harassment. An example of what some students considered sexual harassment occurred in the Criminal Law classroom of Professor Alan M. Dershowitz at Harvard Law School. A group of feminists threatened to file hostile environment charges following his spending two classes discussing false reports of rape. They ultimately decided not to do so, due to the issue of Harvard guidelines applicable to classroom discussions (Robinson, 2001).

Students also complain of being sexually harassed by their peers. In a survey (known as the "Hostile Hallways" study) of more than 2,000 public school students in grades 8–11, 80% of the students reported experiencing some form of sexual harassment (American Association of University Women, AAUW, 2001).

17-8e Consequences of Sexual Harassment

Although fraudulent charges of sexual harassment can wreck a career, sexual harassment may be devastating for its victims. Direct experiences with harassment can lead to a shattering of victims' core assumptions about the world and themselves, which, in turn, can result in considerable psychological distress. Victims complain of depression, anxiety, anger, fear, guilt, helplessness, sexual dysfunction, isolation from family/friends, and substance abuse (Fineran, 2002). In regard to the latter, sexual harassment may lead to "serious psychopathology such as problem drinking in individuals who tend to self-medicate when distressed" (Richman et al., 2001, p. 353). Sexually harassed students in the "Hostile Hallways" survey in grades 8–11 reported skipping school (16%), dropping out of a particular activity or sport (9%), and dropping a course (3%; AAUW, 2001). Although boys and girls reported experiencing harassment, girls were more likely than boys to feel self-conscious, embarrassed, and less confident as a result. They were also more likely than boys to change behaviors such as not talking as much in class (30% of girls to 18% of boys) and to avoid the person who harassed them (56% of girls to 24% of boys).

University students report having changed majors, academic programs of study, and career intentions as a result of sexual harassment (Gutek & Koss, 1997). Sexual harassment may also become a "threat to an individual's resources by threatening financial resources...losses can occur in terms of a lost job, lost status among coworkers, failure to gain a raise or promotion, lost interpersonal supports, and lost esteem regarding one's work" (Dansky & Kilpatrick, 1997, p. 156).

Although not all sexually harassing events constitute a trauma, researchers are finding that nearly a third of sexual harassment victims meet the symptom criteria for PTSD diagnosis (Avina & O'Donohue, 2002). The sexual harassment experience is often compounded by distress from office gossip, retaliation, and financial losses.

Think About It

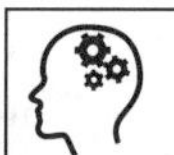

Suppose Carl, a restaurant manager, likes Shirly, a waitress at the restaurant. Carl wants to pursue a relationship with Shirly but is afraid that any suggestive comments he might make may be construed as harassment. How can Carl "flirt" with Shirly without risking an accusation of harassment? How can Shirly communicate to Carl that his behavior makes her uncomfortable and that she wants him to stop?

17-8f Responses to Sexual Harassment

Victims' most frequent response to sexual harassment is to ignore it. Unfortunately, ignoring harassment does not make it go away. Many victims try to avoid the harasser by dropping a class, changing a position, or quitting a job. These indirect strategies are not very effective and do nothing to deter the harasser from violating others. Victims are not more direct about voicing their complaints out of fear of retaliation if they do complain. In a sample of almost 3,000 women, more than half (57%) of those who had been harassed reported they felt that their chances of promotions or pay raises would be hurt if they complained (Dansky & Kilpatrick, 1997). As a result of feeling that they would experience limited gains from complaining, less than 15% of victims file formal sexual harassment complaints.

17-8g Personal Choices: Confronting Someone Who Sexually Harasses You

Aside from ignoring or avoiding the sexual harasser, a victim has at least three choices: verbal, written, or institutional/legal action. The verbal choice consists of telling the harasser what behavior he or she is engaging in that creates discomfort and asking the person to stop. The victim could soften the accusation by saying something like, "You may not be aware that some of the things you say and do make me uncomfortable...." Some harassers will respond with denial ("What are you talking about? I was just joking."); others will apologize and stop the behavior.

If direct communication is not successful in terminating the harassment, a written statement of the concerns is the next level of intervention. Such a letter should detail the sexual harassment behaviors (with dates of occurrence) and include a description of the consequences (personal distress, depression, sleeplessness). The letter should end with a statement of what the victim would like to happen in the future. For example, "I ask that our future interaction be formal and professional."

The letter should be sent immediately after it becomes clear that the offender did not take the verbal requests for change seriously. If the desired behavior is not forthcoming, the letter can be used as evidence of an attempt to alert the offender of the sexual harassment problem. Use of this evidence may be internal (inside the organization) or external (a formal complaint filed with the Equal Employment Opportunity Commission). Information for filing a complaint with the EEOC can be found at its web site.

Unfortunately, women who take the direct approach to confront the harasser are at greater risk for experiencing adverse psychological and somatic symptoms than those who attempt to solve the problem indirectly. Although the direct approach is assertive, harassment victims who speak up often encounter reprisals, counter-allegations, forced time off from work, and slander (Sbraga & O'Donohue, 2000).

Sexual harassment in educational settings is also against the law. School boards are advised to make clear what behaviors are not tolerated in the school setting, how to file a complaint, and what sanctions may be enforced against perpetrators (Russo, 2001).

SUMMARY

Sexual coercion involves depriving a person of free choice and using force (actual or threatened) to engage a person in sexual acts against that person's will. This chapter discussed rape, child sexual abuse, and sexual harassment.

Sexual Coercion: Rape and Assault

About 20% of women report having been forced to have sex. Rape occurs in homosexual as well as heterosexual relationships. Most rapes are not reported; rapists are rarely arrested, and rarely sentenced. Some rapists are falsely accused. Most rapes are conducted by someone known to the person who is raped. Data from a national sample of 204 women reported that only 4% of the rapists were strangers.

Theories of Rape

Theories of rape include evolutionary/biological theory (men are predisposed to rape women to plant their seed and reproduce), psychopathological theory (rapists have a mental disorder), feminist theory (rape is due to unequal status between men and women in society), and social learning theory (men are socialized that it is okay to rape women).

Consequences of Rape and Treatment

Rape is a traumatic experience, but treatment may help reduce symptoms of distress. Initial reactions to rape include an acute period of disorganization, helplessness, vulnerability, and anger. The person may also blame himself or herself for the incident. The most devastating aspect of rape may not be the genital contact, but rather the sense of cognitive and emotional violation. Post-traumatic stress disorder may follow, invoking terror, helplessness, and fear of loss of life. This is also a reaction experienced by some rape victims. The rape survivor may have persistent episodes of re-experiencing the event, such as flashbacks, hallucinations, or nightmares. Anger, social isolation, depressed mood, and lower self-esteem are other consequences. Rape victims who seek help quickly adjust more quickly.

Therapeutic alternatives used in the treatment of sex offenders include providing group therapy, providing medications to reduce deviant sexual arousal, and increasing arousal to appropriate stimuli.

Prevention of Rape

Rape prevention strategies for women include AAA (Assess, Acknowledge, and Act). A similar model for men is also AAA (Ask, Acknowledge, Act). Other aspects of teaching men not to rape are to alert them to rape myths.

Child Sexual Abuse

About 25% of women and half that number of men report childhood sexual abuse. A family friend is the most likely perpetrator. Theories of child abuse include that it is "natural" (Freudian theory), "learned" (social learning theory), or "socialized" (male sex role socialization theory).

Consequences and Treatment of Child Sexual Abuse

Child sexual abuse is associated with negative outcomes such as lower school performance, suicidal ideation, eating disorder behavior, pregnancy risk, and substance use. Other negatives associated include low self-esteem, difficulty in intimate relationships, repeated victimization, and sexually transmitted diseases. Treatment includes communicating to the child that he or she is not responsible for the abuse.

Prevention of Child Sexual Abuse

Strategies to reduce child sexual abuse include regendering cultural roles, providing specific information to children on sex abuse, improving the safety of neighborhoods, providing healthy sexuality information for both teachers and children in the public schools at regular intervals, and promoting public awareness campaigns. Megan's Law is an effort to make communities safe. Some advocates of Megan's Law have sought incarceration of sex offenders in treatment facilities after they are released from prison. There is debate about whether this violates the civil liberties of a person who has paid the debt for his crime.

Sexual Harassment

Sexual harassment is defined as unwelcome sexual advances, requests for sexual favors, and other verbal or physical conduct of a sexual nature when submission to or rejection of this conduct explicitly or implicitly affects an individual's employment. Both men and women of heterosexual or homosexual orientation report having been sexually harassed. University faculty and students have been both the perpetrators and victims of sexual harassment. Up to 80% of children in grades 8–11 report having experienced sexual harassment. Girls are especially likely to report embarrassment and change their behavior by not speaking in class and avoiding the harasser.

SUGGESTED WEBSITES

Note: These websites were functional when we went to press. Please access the online text for the most up-to-date URLs.

American Association of University Women:

See "How to Stop Sexual Harassment in Schools: A Guide for Students, Parents, and Teachers"
http://www.aauw.org/7000/ef/harass/pdf/models.pdf

Child Safety Programs:

Run, Yell, Tell
http://www.safechoicessafechildren.com/home_page.htm

Stranger Danger
http://polksheriff.org/community/stranger.html

Child Safety on the Internet
http://www.getnetwise.org/

Equal Employment Opportunity Commission
http://www.eeoc.gov/facts/fs-sex.html

National Center for PTSD
http://ncptsd.org/facts/specific/fs_child_sexual_abuse.html

Parents for Megan's Law
http://www.parentsformeganslaw.com/

KEY TERMS

acquaintance rape (p. 512)
child sexual abuse accomodation syndrome (p. 528)
classic rape (p. 513)
date rape (p. 512)
extrafamilial child sexual abuse (p. 524)
forced sex (p. 510)
forcible rape (p. 510)
GHB (p. 512)
hostile environment sexual harassment (p. 533)
intrafamilial child sexual abuse (p. 522)
marital rape (p. 510)
Megan's Law (p. 531)
post-traumatic stress disorder (PTSD) (p. 517)
predatory rape (p. 513)
quid pro quo sexual harassment (p. 533)
rape (p. 510)
rape myths (p. 511)
rape-supportive beliefs (p. 511)
rape trauma syndrome (p. 517)
Rohypnol (p. 512)
sexual coercion (p. 510)
sexual harassment (p. 532)
statutory rape (p. 510)

CHAPTER QUIZ

1. There ________ legal penalties for a person who falsely accuses someone of rape.
a. are
b. are no

2. Who tends to be more accepting of rape myths (or rape-supportive beliefs)?
a. women
b. men

3. In societies where rape is almost nonexistent,
a. marriage is monogamous.
b. marriage is polygynous.
c. poverty rates are low.
d. women and men have equal status.

4. Which theory of rape is concerned with the sex violence linkage effect, the modeling effect, the desensitization effect, and the "rape myth" effect?
a. evolutionary and biological theories of rape
b. psychopathological theory of rape
c. feminist theory of rape
d. social learning theory of rape

5. In a study of women who had been raped (Rothbaum et al., 1992), 3 months after the rape nearly one-half of the women presented symptoms of post-traumatic stress disorder (PTSD).
a. true
b. false

6. Data on reporting and conviction rates in Ohio reveal that of 92,490 rapes reported, ________ actually resulted in a conviction (Langan & Dawson, 1988).
a. less than 5%
b. about one quarter
c. nearly half
d. more than 90%

7. According to research cited in your text, the more forcefully a woman resists a rapist, the ________ severe the sexual abuse.
a. more
b. less

8. Having sex with an intoxicated or drugged partner ________ considered sexual assault.
a. can be
b. is not

9. According to your text, who is most likely to be the perpetrator in child abuse cases?
a. a pastor, minister, priest, or clergy
b. a parent
c. a stepparent
d. a family friend

10. Intrafamilial child sexual abuse refers to exploitative sexual contact or attempted or forced sex that occurs between relatives when the victim is
a. 12 or younger.
b. under age 16.
c. under age 18.
d. under age 21.

11. In addition to intercourse, which of the following behaviors can constitute child sexual abuse?
a. fondling of the breasts and genitals
b. oral sex
c. both a and b
d. neither a nor b

12. Which of the following type of incest is the most common?
a. mother-son incest
b. father-daughter incest
c. grandfather-grandchild incest
d. sibling incest

13. Children who experience sex abuse between the ages of 7 and 13 experience the ________ incidence of psychopathology related to the abuse.
a. lowest
b. highest

14. Megan's Law requires which of the following?
a. castration for male sex offenders who have been convicted of sexual assault three times
b. the provision of rape-prevention programs in public schools
c. men who have been convicted of adult or child sexual abuse cannot get a marriage license unless they inform their partner of their prior sex abuse convictions
d. communities must be notified of a neighbor's previous sex convictions

15. Two types of sexual harassment are hostile environment sexual harassment and ________ sexual harassment.
a. reciprocal
b. ambiguous
c. quid pro quo
d. ad hoc

16. According to your text, what is the most frequent response victims have to sexual harassment?
a. retaliation of some type
b. ignore it
c. avoid the harasser
d. file a formal complaint

REFERENCES

American Association of University Women. (2001). *Hostile hallways: bullying, teasing, and sexual harassment in school.* Washington, DC: Author.

Acierno, R., Gray, M., Best, C., Resnick, H., Kilpatrick, D., Saunders, B., et al. (2001). Rape and physical violence: Comparison of assault characteristics in older and younger adults in the National Women's Study. *Journal of Traumatic Stress, 14*, 685–695.

Adler, N. A., & Schultz, J. (1995). Sibling incest offenders. *Child Abuse and Neglect, 19*, 811–819.

American Psychiatric Association. (2000). *Diagnostic and statistical manual of mental disorders*. (4th ed., text revision). Washington, DC: Author.

Avina, C., & O'Donohue, W. (2002). Sexual harassment and PTSD: Is sexual harassment diagnosable trauma? *Journal of Traumatic Stress, 15*, 69–75.

Ballard, D. T., Williams, D., Horton, A. T., & Johnson. B. L. (1990). Offender identification and current use of community resources. In A. T. Horton, B. L. Johnson, L. M. Roundy, & D. Williams (Eds.), *The incest perpetrator: A family member no one wants to treat* (pp. 150–163). Newbury Park, CA: Sage.

Ballon, B. C., Courbasson, C., & Smith, P. D. (2001). Physical and sexual abuse among youths with substance abuse problems. *Canadian Journal of Psychiatry, 46*, 617–621.

Banyard, V. L. (2000). Trauma and memory. *PTSD Research Quarterly, 11*, 1–2.

Barron, M., & Kimmel, M. (2000). Sexual violence in three pornographic media: Toward a sociological explanation. *The Journal of Sex Research, 37*, 161–168.

Bass, E., & Davis, L. (1988). *The courage to heal.* New York: Harper and Row.

Beitchman, J. H., Zucker, K. J., Hood, J. E., daCosta, G. A., Akman, D., & Cassavia, E. (1992). A review of the long-term effects of child sexual abuse. *Child Abuse and Neglect, 16*, 101–119.

Bolen, R. M. (2001). *Child sexual abuse: Its scope and our failure.* New York: Kluwer Academic/Plenum Publishers.

Boyer, D., Fine, D., & Killpack, S. (1991, summer). Sexual abuse and teen pregnancy. *The Network*, 1–2.

Browne, A., & Finkelhor, D. (1986). Initial and long-term effects: A review of the research. In D. Finkelhor (Ed.), *A sourcebook on child sexual abuse* (pp. 143–179). Newbury Park, CA: Sage.

Bruck, M., & Ceci, S. J. (1999). The suggestibility of children's memory. *Annual Review of Psychology, 50*, 419–439.

Buddie, A. M., & Miller, A. G. (2001). Beyond rape myths: A more complex view of perceptions of rape victims. *Sex Roles: A Journal of Research, 38*, 139–162.

Bullough, V. L. (1990). History in adult human sexual behavior with children and adolescents in Western societies. In J. R. Feierman (Ed.), *Pedophilia* (pp. 69–90). New York: Springer-Verlag.

Burgess, A. W., Hartman, C. R., Kelley, S. J., Grant, C. A., & Gray, E. B. (1990). Parental response to child sexual abuse trials involving day care settings. *Journal of Traumatic Stress, 3*, 395–405.

Burgess, A. W., & Holstrom, L. L. (1974). Rape trauma syndrome. *American Journal of Psychiatry, 131*, 981–986.

Canavan, M. M., Meyer, W. J., III, & Higgs, D. C. (1992). The female experience of sibling incest. *Journal of Marital and Family Therapy, 18*, 129–142.

Carlstedt, A., Forsman, A., & Soderstrom, H. (2001). Sexual child abuse in a defined Swedish area 1993–1997: A population-based survey. *Archives of Sexual Behavior, 30*, 483–493.

Casanova, M. F., Solursh, D., Solursh, L., Roy, E., & Thigpen, L. (2000). The history of child pornography on the Internet. *Journal of Sex Education and Therapy, 25*, 245–251.

Chandy, J. M., Blum, R. W., & Resnick, M. D. (1996a). Female adolescents with a history of sexual abuse. *Journal of Interpersonal Violence, 11*, 503–518.

Chandy, J. M., Blum, R. W., & Resnick, M. D. (1996b). Gender specific outcomes for sexually abused adolescents. *Child Abuse and Neglect, 20*, 1219–1231.

Cheasty, M., Clare, A. W., & Collins, C. (2002). Child sexual abuse—A predictor of persistent depression in adult rape and sexual assault victims. *Journal of Mental Health, 11*, 79–84.

Dailey, R. M., & Claus, R. E. (2001). The relationship between interviewer characteristics and physical and sexual abuse disclosures among substance users: A multilevel analysis. *Journal of Drug Issues, 31*, 867–889.

Dansky, B. S., & Kilpatrick, D. G. (1997). Effects of sexual harassment. In W. O'Donohue (Ed.), *Sexual harassment: Theory, research, and treatment* (pp. 152–174). Needham Heights, MA: Allyn & Bacon.

Davis, M. K., & Gidyez, C. A. (2000). Child sexual abuse prevention programs: A meta-analysis. *Journal of Clinical Child Psychology, 29*, 257–266.

Dunn, P. C., Vail-Smith, K., & Knight, S. M. (1999). What date/acquaintance rape victims tell others: A study of college student recipients of disclosure. *Journal of American College Health, 47*, 213–214.

Edmond, T., Rubin, A., & Wambach, K. G. (1999). The effectiveness of EMDR with adult female survivors of childhood sexual abuse. *Social Work Research, 23*, 103–127.

Eisenman, R. (2002). Fair and unfair sexual harassment charges. *Journal of Evolutionary Psychology, 34*, 34–40.

Elliott, D. M., & Briere, J. (1992). Sexual abuse trauma among professional women: Validating the Traumatic Symptom Checklist (TSC-40). *Child Abuse and Neglect, 16*, 391–399.

Ellis, L. (1989). *Theories of rape: Inquiries into the causes of sexual aggression*. New York: Hemisphere.

Felton, L. A., Gumm, A., & Pittenger, D. J. (2001). Recipients of unwanted sexual encounters among college students. *College Student Journal, 35*, 135–142.

Fineran, S. (2002). Sexual harassment between same-sex peers: Intersection of mental health, homophobia, and sexual violence in schools. *Social Work*, *47*, 65–74.

Finkelhor, D. (1986). Sexual abuse: Beyond the family systems approach. In T. S. Trepper & M. J. Barrett (Eds.), *Treating incest: A multiple systems perspective* (pp. 55–65). New York: Haworth.

Foubert, J. D. (2000). The longitudinal effects of a rape-prevention program on fraternity men's attitudes, behavioral intent, and behavior. *Journal of American College Health*, *48*, 158–165.

Fouts, B., & Knapp, J. (2001). A sexual assault education and risk reduction workshop for college freshmen. In A. J. Ottens & K. Hotelling (Eds.), *Sexual violence on campus* (pp. 98–119). New York: Springer Publishing Co.

Frank, J. G. (1991, August 16). *Risk factors for rape: Empirical confirmation and preventive implications*. Poster session presented at the 99th annual convention of the American Psychological Association, San Francisco.

Girshick, L. B. (2002). *Woman-to-woman sexual violence: Does she call it rape?* Boston: Northeastern University Press.

Gordon, L. C. (2002, April). *Dating violence and sexual coercion as part of a general antisocial orientation*. Paper presented at the meeting of the Southern Sociological Society, Baltimore, MD.

Graupner, H. (2000). Sexual consent: The criminal law in Europe and overseas. *Archives of Sexual Behavior*, *29*, 413–461.

Gregory, J., & Lees, S. (1996). Attrition in rape and sexual assault cases. *British Journal of Criminology*, *36*, 1–17.

Groth, A. N., & Birnbaum, H. J. (1979). *Men who rape: The psychology of the male offender*. New York: Plenum Press.

Gutek, B. A., & Koss, M. P. (1997). Changed women and changed organizations: Consequences of and coping with sexual harassment. In L. L. O'Toole & J. R. Schiffman (Eds.), *Gender violence: Interdisciplinary perspectives* (pp. 151–164). New York: New York University Press.

Harris Interactive & Witeck-Combs. (2002, September). *Sexual harassment among gay and lesbian employees*. Out & Equal Workplace Conference, Orlando, FL.

Herman, J. (1981). *Father-daughter incest*. Cambridge, MA: Harvard University Press.

Herman, J., Russell, D., & Trocki, K. (1986). Long-term effects of incestuous abuse in childhood. *American Journal of Psychiatry*, *143*, 1293–1296.

Hewitt, B., Klise, K., Comander, L., Schorr, M., Hardy, A., Duffy, T., et al. (2002). Breaking the silence. *People*, *57*, 56 et passim.

Hillis, S. D., Anda, R. F., Felitti, V. J., & Marchbanks, P. A. (2001). Adverse childhood experiences and sexual risk behaviors in women: A retrospective cohort study. *Family Planning Perspectives*, *33*, 206–211.

Hotelling, K. (2001). Summary remarks: Emerging themes and implications. In A. J. Ottens & K. Hotelling (Eds.), *Sexual violence on campus* (pp. 283–293). New York: Springer Publishing Co.

Jones, L. M., Finkelhor, D., & Kopiec, K. (2001). Why is sexual abuse declining? A survey of state child protection administrators. *Child Abuse & Neglect*, *25*, 1139–1158.

Kalichman, S. C., Benotsch, E., Rompa, D., Gore-Felton, C., Austin, J., Luke, W., et al. (2001). Unwanted sexual experiences and sexual risks in gay and bisexual men: Associations among revictimization, substance use, and psychiatric symptoms. *The Journal of Sex Research*, *38*, 1–11.

Kalof, L. (2000). Ethnic differences in female sexual victimization. *Sexuality and Culture*, *4*, 75–97.

Kanin, E. (1994). False rape allegations. *Archives of Sexual Behavior*, *23*, 81–93.

Koss, M. P. (2000). Blame, shame, and community: Justice responses to violence against women. *The American Psychologist*, *55*, 1332–1342.

Krug, R. S. (1989). Adult male report of childhood sexual abuse by mothers: Case descriptions, motivations, and long-term consequences. *Child Abuse and Neglect*, *13*, 111–119.

Langan, P. A., & Dawson, J. M. (1988). Felony sentences in State Courts, 1988. Washington, DC: Bureau of Justice Statistics of the U.S. Department of Justice.

Laumann, E. O., Gagnon, J. H., Michael, R. T., & Michaels, S. (1994). *The social organization of sexuality: Sexual practices in the United States*. Chicago: University of Chicago Press.

Lew, M. (1990). *Victims no longer: Men recovering from incest and other sexual child abuse*. New York: Harper and Row.

Loftus, E. F. (1993). The reality of repressed memories. *American Psychologist*, *48*, 518–537.

Lottes, I. L. (1991). Belief systems: Sexuality and rape. *Journal of Psychology and Human Sexuality*, *4*, 37–59.

Lottes, I. L. (1998). Rape Supportive Attitudes Scale. In C. M. Davis, W. L. Yarber, R. Bauserman, G. Schreer, & S. L. Davis (Eds.), *Handbook of sexuality-related measures* (p. 504). Thousand Oaks, CA: Sage.

Lottes, I. L., & Weinberg, M. S. (1996). Sexual coercion among university students: A comparison of the United States and Sweden. *The Journal of Sex Research*, *34*, 67–76.

Madu, S. N. (2001). The prevalence and patterns of childhood sexual abuse and victim-perpetrator relationship among South African college students. *South African Journal of Psychology*, *31*, 32–38.

Marchell, T., & Cummings, N. (2001). Alcohol and sexual violence among college students. In A. J. Ottens & K. Hotelling (Eds.), *Sexual violence on campus* (pp. 30–52). New York: Springer Publishing Co.

Matchen, J., & DeSouza, E. (2000). The sexual harassment of faculty members by students. *Sex Roles*, *42*, 295–306.

McDonald, J., & Bradford, W. (2000). The treatment of sexual deviation using a pharmacological approach. *The Journal of Sex Research*, *37*, 248–257.

McGeary, J., Winters, R., Morrissey, S., Scully, S., Sieger, M., Crittle, S., et al. (2002). Can the church be saved? *Time Atlantic*, *159*, 52–62.

McMillen, C., & Zuravin, S. (1997). Attributions of blame and responsibility for child sexual abuse and adult adjustment. *Journal of Interpersonal Violence*, *12*, 30–48.

Monson, C. M., Byrd, G. R., & Langhinrichsen-Rohling, J. (1996). To have and to hold: Perceptions of marital rape. *Journal of Interpersonal Violence*, *11*, 410–424.

Morrow, R. B., & Sorrell, G. T. (1989). Factors affecting self-esteem, depression, and negative behaviors in sexually abused, female adolescents. *Journal of Marriage and the Family, 51,* 677–686.

National Clearinghouse on Child Abuse and Neglect Information. (2002). *National child abuse & neglect data system: Summary of key findings from calendar year 2000.* Retrieved March 30, 2003, from http://www.calib.com/nccanch/pubs/factsheets/canstats.cfm

Nurius, P. S., & Norris, J. (1996). A cognitive ecological model of response to sexual coercion in dating. *Journal of Psychology and Human Sexuality,* 8, 117–139.

O'Brien, J. (2001). The MVP program. Focus on student-athletes. In A. J. Ottens & K. Hotelling (Eds.), *Sexual violence on campus* (pp. 93–110). New York: Springer.

O'Hare, E., & O'Donohue, W. (1998). Sexual harassment: Identifying risk factors. *Archives of Sexual Behavior, 27,* 561–579.

O'Sullivan, C. S. (1991). Acquaintance gang rape on campus. In A. Parrot & L. Brechhofer (Eds.), *Acquaintance rape* (pp. 368–380). New York: Wiley.

Ottens, A. J. (2001). The scope of sexual violence on campus. In A. J. Ottens & K. Hotelling (Eds.), *Sexual violence on campus* (pp. 93–110). New York: Springer Publishing Co.

Owens, G. P., Pike, J. L., & Chard, K. M. (2001). Treatment effects of cognitive processing therapy on cognitive distortions of female child sexual abuse survivors. *Behavior Therapy, 32,* 413–424.

Parks, T. E. (1999). On one aspect of the evidence for recovered memories. *American Journal of Psychology, 112,* 365–369.

Peters, J. M., Dinsmore, J., & Toth, P. (1989). Why prosecute child abuse? *South Dakota Law Review, 34,* 649–659.

Pierce, L. H., & Pierce, R. L. (1990). Adolescent/sibling incest perpetrators. In A. L. Horton, B. L. Johnson, L. M. Roundy, & D. Williams (Eds.), *The incest perpetrator: A family member no one wants to treat.* Newbury Park, CA: Sage.

Rauch, S. A. M., Hembree, E. A., & Foa, E. B. (2001). Acute psychosocial preventive interventions for posttraumatic stress disorder. *Advances in Mind-Body Medicine, 17,* 187–191.

Resick, P. A., & Schnicke, M. (1993). *Cognitive processing therapy with rape victims.* New York: Sage.

Resnick, H. S., Kilpatrick, D. G., & Lipovsky, J. A. (1991). Assessment of rape-related post-traumatic stress disorder: Stressor and symptom dimensions. *Journal of Consulting and Clinical Psychology,* 3, 561–572.

Reppucci, N. D., & Haugaard, J. J. (1989). Prevention of child sexual abuse: Myth or reality. *The American Psychologist, 44,* 1266–1276.

Richman, J. A., Rospenda, K. M., Nawyn, S. J., Flaherty, J. A., Fendrich, M., Drum, M. L., et al. (2001). Sexual harassment and generalized workplace abuse. In J. K. Davidson, Sr. & Nelwyn B. Moore (Eds.), *Speaking of sexuality* (pp. 350–355). Los Angeles, CA: Roxbury Publishing Co.

Riggs, N. (2000). Analysis of 1,076 cases of sexual assault. *The Journal of the American Medical Association, 283,* 3048–3054.

Rind, B. (1995). An analysis of human sexuality textbook coverage of the psychological correlates of adult-nonadult sex. *The Journal of Sex Research, 32,* 219–233.

Robinson, D., Jr. (2001, Summer). Harassment, fairness, and academic freedom. *Academic Questions,* 25–36.

Roth, S., & Friedman, M. J. (Eds.). (1997). *Childhood trauma remembered: A report on the current scientific knowledge base and its applications.* International Society for Traumatic Stress Studies. Available from ISTSS, 60 Revere Drive, Suite 500, Northbrook, IL 60062.

Rothbaum, B. O., Foa, E. B., Riggs, D. S., Murdock, T., & Walsh, W. (1992). A prospective examination of posttraumatic stress disorder in rape victims. *Journal of Traumatic Stress,* 5, 455–475.

Rozee, P. D., & Koss, M. P. (2000). Rape: A century of resistance. *Psychology of Women Quarterly, 25,* 295–311.

Russell, B. L., & Oswald, D. L. (2001). Strategies and dispositional correlates of sexual coercion perpetrated by women: An exploratory investigation. *Sex Roles: A Journal of Research, 45,* 103–126.

Russell, D. E. H. (1984). *Sexual exploitation: Rape, child sexual abuse, and workplace harassment.* Beverly Hills, CA: Sage.

Russell, D. E. H. (1991). Wife rape. In A. Parrot & L. Bechhofer (Eds.), *Acquaintance rape: The hidden crime* (pp. 129–139). New York: Wiley.

Russo, C. J. (2001). Supreme Court update on sexual harassment in schools. *Education and the Law, 13,* 69–74.

Salter, A. (1988). *Treating child sex offenders and victims: A practical guide.* Newbury Park, CA: Sage.

Sanday, P. R. (1981). The socio-cultural context of rape: A cross-cultural study. *Journal of Social Issues, 37,* 5–27.

Sarwer, D. B., & Durlak, J. A. (1996). Childhood sexual abuse as a predictor of adult female sexual dysfunction: A study of couples seeking sex therapy. *Child Abuse and Neglect, 20,* 693–972.

Sbraga, T. P., & O'Donohue, W. (2000). Sexual harassment. *Annual Review of Sex Research, 11,* 258–285.

Scarce, M. (1997). *Male on male rape: The hidden toll of stigma and shame.* New York: Insight Books.

Schuiteman, J. (2001). Feminist approaches to addressing violence against women. In A. J. Ottens & K. Hotelling (Eds.), *Sexual violence on campus* (pp. 76–97). New York: Springer Publishing Co.

Schultz, E. E., & Woo, J. (1994, September 19). Plaintiffs' sex lives are being laid bare in harassment cases. *The Wall Street Journal,* pp. A1, A9.

Stermac, L., Sheridan, P. M., Davidson, A., & Dunn, S. (1996). Sexual assault of adult males. *Journal of Interpersonal Violence, 11,* 52–64.

Struckman-Johnson, C., & Struckman-Johnson, D. (1994). Men pressured and forced into sexual experience. *Archives of Sexual Behavior, 23,* 93–114.

Summit, R. C. (1983). The child sexual abuse accommodation syndrome. *Child Abuse and Neglect, 7,* 177–192.

Thornhill, R., & Palmer, C. T. (2000). *A natural history of rape: Biological bases of sexual coercion*. Cambridge, MA: The MIT Press.

Tjaden, P., & Thoennes, N. (1998, November). Prevalence, incidence, and consequences of violence against women: Findings from the National Violence Against Women Survey. *National Institute of Justice Centers for Disease Control and Prevention Research Brief*.

Tomeo, M. E., Templer, D. I., Anderson, S., & Kotler, D. (2001). Comparative data of childhood and adolescence molestation in heterosexual and homosexual persons. *Archives of Sexual Behavior*, *30*, 535–541.

Tuel, B. D. (2001). Sexual assault: When victims are gay, lesbian, or bisexual students. In A. J. Ottens & K. Hotelling (Eds.), *Sexual violence on campus* (pp. 190–217). New York: Springer Publishing Co.

Tyson, A. (1997). *Students' expectations for rape when alcohol is involved*. Unpublished manuscript, East Carolina University, Greenville, NC.

Ullman, S. E., & Knight, R. A. (1991). A multivariate model for predicting rape and physical injury outcomes during sexual assaults. *Journal of Consulting and Clinical Psychology*, *59*, 724–731.

Walsh, W. J., Isaacson, H. R., Rehman, F., & Hall, A. (1997). Elevated blood copper/zinc ratios in assaultive young males. *Physiology & Behavior*, *62*, 327–329.

Watts, C., & Zimmerman, C. (2002). Violence against women: Global scope and magnitude. *Lancet*, *359*, 1232–1238.

Williams, L. M. (1994). Recall of childhood trauma: A prospective study of women's memories of child sexual abuse. *Journal of Consulting and Clinical Psychology*, *62*, 1167–1176.

Wuensch, K. L., Campbell, M. W., Kesler, K. C., & Moore, C. H. (2002). Racial bias in decisions made by mock jurors evaluating a case of sexual harassment. *The Journal of Social Psychology*, *142*, 587–600.

Zorza, J. (2001). Drug-facilitated rape. In A. J. Ottens & K. Hotelling (Eds.), *Sexual violence on campus* (pp. 53–75). New York: Springer Publishing Co.

Zweig, J. M., Barber, B. L., & Eccles, J. S. (1997). Sexual coercion and well-being in young adulthood. *Journal of Interpersonal Violence*, *12*, 291–308.

18

Illness, Disability, Drugs, and Sexuality

Chapter Outline

It is normal and natural for every person with a body to express their sexuality regardless of their handicap condition or functional ability level.

—Rebecca Koller, University of Utah

♦ ♦ ♦

Disability A health condition that involves functional deficits in performing activities of daily living.

Slightly more than 12% of the U.S. population are limited in what they can do because of a chronic condition or have a **disability**—a health condition that involves functional deficits in performing activities of daily living (*Statistical Abstract of the United States: 2002*, Table 179). When individuals are born with a disability or develop one later in life, they and their families must contend with many concerns—medical care, finances, social stigma, and quality of life. Illness, disease, and disability may negatively interfere with the quality of life in relationships and sexuality. Unfortunately, health-care professionals often ignore the sexuality of individuals with disability or illness:

> *Too often, an individual's sexual health concerns are not adequately assessed or treated by their health care providers. Untreated sexual disorders may affect the individual's overall quality of life and may seriously affect their partnered relationship, leading to sexual avoidance and loss of desire and intimacy. (Fleming & Kleinbart, 2001, p. 222)*

In this chapter, we hope to bring to light some of the sexual issues and concerns facing individuals with health problems, their partners, and their health-care providers. We include information on the effects of alcohol and drugs on sexuality.

18-1 ILLNESS, DISABILITY, AND THE MYTH OF ASEXUALITY

There is little direct empirical evidence for belief that individuals with disease or disability are perceived as asexual—that is, as having no interest in sexual expression and no capacity for experiencing physical pleasure and intimacy. However, personal narratives by disabled adults and lack of attention to the sex education and sexual counseling needs of persons with disabilities provide indirect evidence that persons with illness or disability are often viewed as asexual (Milligan & Neufeldt, 2001). But this view that the disabled are asexual is a myth. Milligan and Neufeldt (2001) note that

> *For most people, both with and without disabilities, sexuality and its expression are a natural and important component of self-concept, emotional well-being, and overall quality of life. . . . Physical and mental impairments may significantly alter functioning, but do not eliminate basic drives or the desire for love, affection, and intimacy. (pp.91–92)*

For some individuals, living with a disability actually *increases* the importance of sexual expression. One man with a disability explained, "I'm even more interested in sex than most. Because of my disability, options and opportunities for outside recreation are reduced—sex is a most joyous recreation at home. So sex is a major recreation for me" (quoted in Taleporos & McCabe, 2001, p. 143).

Although people with chronic illness or disability may be sexually active and maintain sexual interests, they are at heightened risk for having sexual problems because of the physiological, psychological, and social impact of an illness, disability, or its treatment. In this chapter, we discuss aspects of illness and disability that can interfere with sexual functioning, including negative self-concept and body image, impaired sensory-motor function, impaired cognitive function, pain, fatigue, emotional responses, financial hardship, effects of medical treatment, and effects on interpersonal relationships.

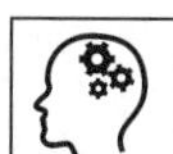

Think About It

Ward, Trigler, and Pfeiffer (2001) noted that, "Although attitudes are changing, society continues to react with discomfort to the recognition that people with disabilities are sexual beings with inherent needs for affection and intimacy as well as sexual gratification" (p. 17). To what degree does the thought of a person with a disability engaging in sexual activity create discomfort for you? If so, what might be the source of this discomfort?

18-2 EFFECTS OF ILLNESS AND DISABILITY ON SELF-CONCEPT AND BODY IMAGE

In general, persons with chronic illness or disability are vulnerable to developing a negative self-concept and body image, and viewing themselves as undesirable or inadequate romantic and sexual partners. In a focus group study of how disability affects sexuality, many participants reported believing that they were less sexually desirable than nondisabled persons (Taleporos & McCabe, 2001).

Individuals with disease or disability often struggle against the social attitude that they are "damaged goods"—that they lack sexual needs and abilities and are, therefore, unsuitable as a romantic partner. All too often, individuals with disabilities internalize these negative social attitudes, which may lead them to retreat from intimate relations and adopt a nonsexual lifestyle. Men who base their self-worth on traditional male roles of wage earner and sexual performer are vulnerable to low self-esteem if an illness or disability interferes with their ability to earn an income or have erections. Men may also withdraw emotionally and sexually if they feel ashamed by becoming dependent on others (Schover, 2000).

Persons with disabilities or disease may also view themselves as physically flawed and sexually unattractive. The use of cold, hard, metallic appliances (such as braces or wheelchairs); weight loss or gain; loss of reproductive capacity; scars and other alterations of the body due to surgery; hair loss (caused by radiation treatment of cancer); and loss of control over bodily functions (e.g., elimination of urine and stool) can also contribute to a negative body image.

Despite the challenges and obstacles, many ill and disabled individuals succeed in developing and maintaining a positive self-concept and body image. A national survey of women with disabilities found that most (78%) reported high or moderately high self-esteem (Nosek, Howland, Rintala, Young, & Chanpong, 2001). Those who had a very positive sense of self

> *tended to appreciate their own value, asserted their right to make choices that would improve their lives, felt ownership of their bodies, avoided allowing their sense of sexual self to be diminished by negative images associated with their disability, were accepting, not ashamed of their bodies, and took action to enhance their attractiveness. (p. 11)*

On average, however, the women in this study who had disabilities reported lower self-esteem than the women without disabilities.

Think About It

Illness and disability can also enhance one's self-concept. For example, some childhood cancer survivors feel stronger and more confident as a result of surviving cancer. "They may feel more independent and mature than their peers, having grown up in an adult world that presented them with life-and-death challenges" (Olivo & Woolverton, 2001, p. 176). What are some other ways in which illness and/or disability might enhance one's self-concept?

This man suffered a spinal cord injury but continues to put a positive spin on life. Every Christmas, he sends out a card reflecting his zest for life.

18-3 IMPAIRED SENSORY-MOTOR FUNCTION AND SEXUALITY

A number of neurological diseases and injuries can result in impaired sensory-motor functioning, including stroke, spinal cord injury, multiple sclerosis (MS), and cerebral palsy. The effects of sensory-motor impairment on sexuality are varied and depend, in part, on the type and severity of the illness or injury.

18-3a Stroke

Stroke Sudden disturbance in the blood supply to the brain caused by hemorrhage from rupture or blockage of a blood vessel.

Stroke refers to a sudden disturbance in the blood supply to the brain caused by hemorrhage from rupture or blockage of a blood vessel. A stroke often results in some form of paralysis to parts of the body and may also produce impaired speech, impaired cognitive function (such as memory loss and language comprehension difficulties), mood disorders (e.g., depression), and even death.

Sexual dysfunction frequently occurs after a stroke and often involves significant declines in sexual desire, erectile function, orgasmic ability, vaginal lubrication, and coital frequency (Kalayjian & Morrell, 2000). Reasons for decreased coital frequency in stroke patients and their spouses include fear of impotence, inability to discuss sexuality, and unwillingness to participate in sexual activity (Korpelainen, Nieminen, & Myllyla 1999). Some stroke patients avoid sexual activity because they fear that having sex increases their risk of having another stroke, although this risk is low (Kalayjian & Morrell, 2000).

18-3b Spinal Cord Injury

The majority of new spinal cord injuries (SCIs) in the United States each year involve men (82%) between the ages of 16 and 30. The most common causes of SCI in the United States include motor vehicle accidents (36%), violence (29%), and falls (21%; Spinal Cord Injury Resource Center, 2002).

The effect of spinal cord injury on sexual functioning depends on the level of injury and whether it is "complete" or "incomplete." A complete injury means that there is no function below the level of the injury, no sensation, and no voluntary movement. An incomplete injury means that there is some functioning below the primary level of the injury.

Quadriplegia Paralysis from the neck down.

Paraplegia Paralysis of the lower half of the body.

Cervical (neck) injuries usually result in **quadriplegia**—paralysis from the neck down. Very high cervical injuries can result in a loss of many involuntary functions including the ability to breathe, necessitating breathing aids such as mechanical ventilators. Injuries at the thoracic level and below result in **paraplegia**—paralysis of the lower half of the body.

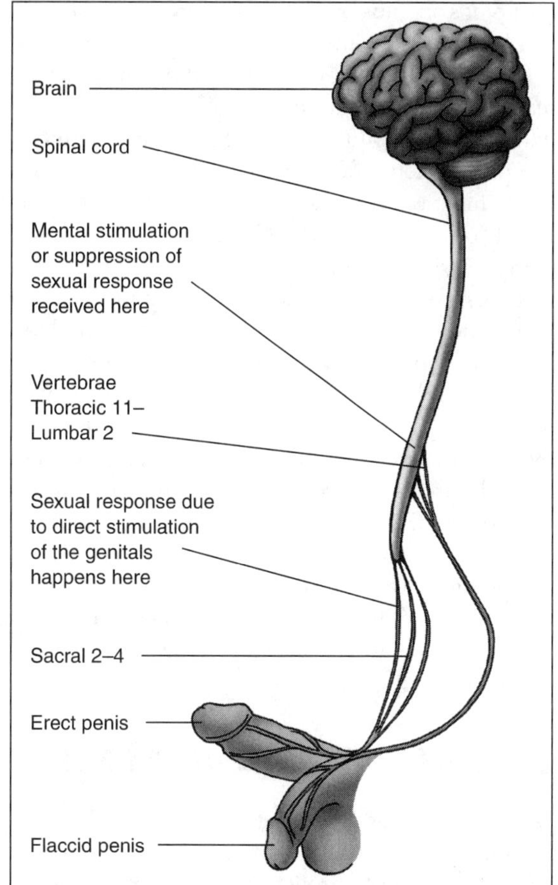

FIGURE 18-1
The Spinal Cord and Sexual Response

Some form of sexual arousal can be achieved in most spinal cord–injured patients (Kalayjian & Morrell, 2000). In one study of more than 200 quadriplegics and paraplegics, a substantial number reported feeling sensation in the genital-perineal area, and about half of the men and 60% of the women reported orgasm after their injury (Donohue & Gebhard, 1995). In spinal cord–injured persons, orgasm may occur by direct stimulation of the genitals, by mentally reassigning sensations that can be felt in other areas of the body to the genitals, and/or by erotic imagery (i.e., fantasizing; Whipple, Cerdes, & Komisaruk, 1996; Tepper, Whipple, Richards, & Komisaruk, 2001).

For spinal cord–injured men who are able to achieve erection, intercourse may take place with the partner sitting down on the erect penis. If erection is not achieved, some couples use the "stuffing technique," in which partners push the soft penis into the woman's vagina, which she then contracts to hold the penis inside her. For some spinal cord–injured men, sildenafil citrate (Viagra) or an inflatable penile prosthesis implant can be helpful in achieving erection (see Figure 18-1). Although spinal cord–injured women can have coitus in a variety of positions, they may have reduced sensation and movement, and may need to use a lubricant. Pregnancy and vaginal delivery of a baby are possible for spinal cord–injured women; however, the risk of complications is increased.

18-3c Multiple Sclerosis and Cerebral Palsy

Multiple sclerosis (MS) is a progressive disease that attacks the central nervous system. Onset of MS usually occurs between the ages of 20 and 40 and the incidence of MS is two to three times higher in women than men (Kalayjian & Morrell, 2000). Symptoms of MS, which vary from person to person, may include muscle incoordination; weakness and fatigue; tremors; spasms; stiffness; slurred speech; bladder and bowel dysfunction; impaired genital sensation; pain (stabbing pain in the face or down the spine, burning, aching,

Multiple sclerosis (MS) A progressive disease that attacks the central nervous system.

cramping, or "pins and needles" sensation); numbness in the face, body, or extremities; and cognitive impairment.

Sexual dysfunction is common among women and men with MS, and may involve reduced genital sensation, genital pain, vaginal dryness, loss of libido, erection problems, difficulty or inability to ejaculate, and difficulty reaching orgasm (National Multiple Sclerosis Society, 2001). Because of the progressive nature of the disease, symptoms of sexual dysfunction in women and men with MS tend to increase in severity and number over time (Zorzon et al., 2001). However, individuals with MS and their partners can improve marital and sexual satisfaction through counseling, communication about sexual issues with health-care providers, and interventions to improve sexual functioning such as sildenafil citrate (Viagra) for men and personal lubricating products for women (Foley, LaRocca, Sanders, & Zemon, 2001).

Cerebral palsy (CP) Condition often caused by brain damage that occurs before or during birth or in infancy, resulting in muscular impairment and sometimes speech and learning disabilities.

Cerebral palsy (CP)—a condition caused by brain damage that occurs before or during birth or in infancy—also involves symptoms that can interfere with sexual expression. Symptoms of cerebral palsy vary according to the area and degree of brain damage but generally include uncontrollable movement, lack of coordination, spasms, and speech impairment. Problems with sight and hearing may also occur. Cerebral palsy may also result in cognitive impairment (e.g., learning disabilities, mental retardation).

Adults with CP often require counseling and assistance in achieving sexual satisfaction. For example, one woman with severe spasticity due to cerebral palsy used her mouth to operate a specially designed vibrator that enabled her to reach orgasm (Donnelly, 1997).

18-4 DIABETES AND SEXUALITY

Diabetes mellitus A chronic disease in which the pancreas fails to produce sufficient insulin, which is necessary for metabolizing carbohydrates and fats.

Diabetes mellitus is a chronic disease in which the pancreas fails to produce sufficient insulin, which is necessary for metabolizing carbohydrates and fats. The symptoms, which may be controlled through injections of insulin, include excess sugar in the blood and urine; excessive thirst, hunger, and urination; and weakness. An estimated 16 million Americans, or nearly 6% of the population, have diabetes (Clement, 2002). About 1 million have type 1 diabetes (patients may be of any age, and are usually nonobese), and 15 million have type 2 diabetes (often associated with obesity in later life). Type 2 diabetes is increasing dramatically in the United States and worldwide as populations become more sedentary and obese, and about one third of Americans who have this condition are unaware of it (Clement, 2002).

In women, diabetes can result in lack of libido, diminished clitoral sensation, vaginal dryness and discomfort, and orgasmic dysfunction (Erol et al., 2002). Diabetic men may notice a progressive softening of the penis, eventually leading to the inability to perform vaginal penetration. Erectile dysfunction may be caused by physiological or psychosocial factors (Weinhardt & Carey, 1996). Physiologically, damage to the autonomic nerves is irreversible, even with the restoration of "normal" blood sugars via insulin. Psychosocial factors include anxiety and depression resulting from the perceived disability and difficulty in functioning.

18-5 IMPAIRED COGNITIVE FUNCTION AND SEXUALITY

Many illnesses and injuries result in impaired cognitive functioning, such as memory loss, language comprehension problems, learning disabilities, and confusion. Some illnesses and injuries—such as stroke, multiple sclerosis, and cerebral palsy (discussed in section 18-3c)—may involve both sensory-motor impairment as well as cognitive impairment. Next, we examine impaired cognitive function and its effects on sexuality more closely, focusing on Alzheimer's disease and other forms of dementia, traumatic brain injury, and mental retardation.

18-5a Alzheimer's Disease and Other Forms of Dementia

Dementia is a brain disorder involving memory impairment and at least one of the following: **aphasia** (impaired communicative ability); **agnosia** (loss of auditory, sensory, or visual comprehension); **apraxia** (inability to perform coordinated movements); or loss of ability to think abstractly and to plan, initiate, sequence, monitor, and stop complex behavior (Rabins et al., 2000). Other symptoms of dementia include depression, personality changes, sleep disturbances, psychosis and agitation, and incontinence.

Causes of dementia include stroke, Parkinson's disease, head trauma, brain tumor, infectious disease (HIV, syphilis), and long-term alcohol abuse. The most common cause of dementia, accounting for two thirds of all dementia cases, is **Alzheimer's disease**—a progressive and degenerative brain disease that typically progresses through stages from mild memory loss, through significant cognitive impairment, to very serious confusion and the loss of ability to manage activities of daily living, such as dressing, eating, and bathing (Moody, 2000). A person with end-stage Alzheimer's may be incontinent, unable to speak, and unable to walk.

It is not uncommon for persons with dementia to exhibit inappropriate sexual and social behavior, such as uninvited and intrusive touching and inappropriate sexual comments. For example, a hospitalized man diagnosed with Alzheimer's disease asked a female psychology student who was conducting research in the hospital to come and talk with him. "When she approached him, he immediately placed his hands on her breasts, rapidly moving one hand to his genital area while grabbing his penis through his pants, and he asked, 'Will you take care of me, and suck me?'" (Mayers, 2000, p. 145). Spouses or partners of individuals with Alzheimer's disease face a number of sexual concerns, as expressed in the following comments made by spouses of Alzheimer's patients (Shaw, 2001, p. 142):

> "Can I refuse sex with him, and if so, how?"
>
> "I feel guilty and uncaring refusing, and yet, my partner doesn't remember that we just had sex."
>
> "When I have sex just to calm my partner or to relax myself, I am doing it with a stranger, not my beloved."
>
> "I still get aroused, is it OK to initiate sex for my own good memories?"
>
> "Now that my mate is incapacitated . . . I might want to establish a sexual relationship with an outside partner but I feel torn about this because we have been happily sexual and monogamous for 30 years."

Dementia Brain disorder involving multiple cognitive deficits, including memory impairment and at least one of the following: aphasia, agnosia, apraxia, or loss of ability to think abstractly and to plan, initiate, sequence, monitor, and stop complex behavior.

Aphasia Impaired communicative ability.

Agnosia Loss of auditory, sensory, or visual comprehension.

Apraxia The inability to perform coordinated movements.

Alzheimer's disease Progressive and degenerative brain disease progressing from mild memory loss, through significant cognitive impairment, to very serious confusion and the loss of ability to manage activities of daily living, such as dressing, eating, and bathing.

18-5b Traumatic Brain Injury

Traumatic brain injury is a closed head injury that results from an exterior force and creates a temporary or enduring impairment in brain functioning. The nature of impairment varies according to the severity of the injury and the specific area of the brain that is affected. Following a traumatic brain injury, individuals may experience some type of problem in sexual functioning, such as reduced sexual drive and self-control, decreased erectile ability, and/or inability to sexually lubricate or become aroused (Gaudet, Crethar, Burger, & Pulos, 2001). They may also experience changes that affect their social interactions, such as mood swings, depression, social withdrawal, and problems with anger control.

Traumatic brain injury A closed head injury that results from an exterior force and creates a temporary or enduring impairment in brain functioning

18-5c Mental Retardation

Mental retardation, also referred to as *intellectual disability*, involves subaverage intellectual functioning and deficits in adaptive behavior. A person's degree of retardation can be described as *mild, moderate, severe*, or *profound*. Important issues regarding mental retardation and sexuality include sexual consent capacity, sterilization, and sex education.

Mental retardation A condition which involves subaverage intellectual functioning and deficits in adaptive behavior. (Also referred to as *intellectual disability*.)

Sexual Consent Capacity

Sexual consent capacity The ability to make informed and voluntary choices about sexual behavior.

Involvement of mentally retarded adults in sexual relationships raises the question of **sexual consent capacity**—the ability to make informed and voluntary choices about sexual behavior (Kennedy & Niederbuhl, 2001). Psychologists have no agreed-upon guidelines for assessing sexual consent capacity, and legal criteria vary from state to state. However, a survey of doctoral-level members of the American Psychological Association found the following factors "absolutely necessary" for determining sexual consent capacity (Kennedy & Niederbuhl, 2001):

- The individual can say or demonstrate "no."
- The individual knows that having intercourse can result in pregnancy.
- When given options, the individual can make an informed choice.
- The individual knows that having sexual relations can result in disease.
- The individual can differentiate between appropriate and inappropriate times and places to engage in intimate relations.
- The individual can differentiate between men and women.
- The individual can recognize individuals or situations that might be a threat to him or her.
- The individual will stop a behavior if another person tells him or her "no."

Sterilization and Mental Retardation

Between 1907 and 1927, 23 states enacted laws permitting sterilization of mentally retarded individuals, and by 1938, more than 27,000 people (more women than men) in the United States had undergone compulsory sterilization (Beirne-Smith, Ittenbach, & Patton, 2002). Sterilization of mentally retarded individuals was done out of concern that they could not perform in the parent role or that their children would also be retarded. In 1942, the U.S. Supreme Court declared human procreation to be a fundamental right, and obtaining authorization to sterilize individuals with mental retardation became more difficult. Today, sterilization of individuals with mental retardation involves legal and ethical considerations.

Legally, persons who are deemed to have adequate mental capacity to make decisions about their health care are entitled to do so without undue influence from others. A person who is deemed competent to make decisions about sexual behavior and reproduction cannot be sterilized (or forced to use any form of contraception) unless he or she has given consent. Thus, the first consideration in the sterilization of individuals with mental retardation involves assessing whether the person is competent to make independent decisions about health care and reproduction.

When a person is deemed legally incompetent to consent to or refuse sterilization, a parent or legal guardian may authorize the procedure to protect against unwanted pregnancy and/or medically risky pregnancy. Some guardians who seek male sterilization by castration do so to prevent impregnation of others, or with a belief that it may help prevent sexually aggressive behavior. However, there is little evidence that surgical castration accomplishes this goal (Nelson, 1999).

Many individuals with mental retardation who desire to have a child may be able to assume that responsibility if provided with adequate social support. Mentally retarded adults who are within the bounds of competency need reproductive counseling regarding the physical health of any potential children. "Does the mentally retarded individual have a condition that can be genetically transmitted?" and "Does the person take medication that is known to cause birth defects?" are important considerations (Denekens, Nys, & Stuer, 1999).

Sex Education for Individuals with Mental Retardation

Sex education for individuals with mental retardation can help prevent sexual abuse, pregnancy, and sexually transmitted diseases, and can teach individuals with mental retardation how to express their sexual needs and engage in sexual behavior in ways that are socially appropriate and safe. Such education is important because individuals with mental retardation sometimes exhibit inappropriate or offensive sexual behaviors, includ-

Box 18-1 Social Choices

Caregiver Response to Masturbation by Mentally Retarded?

Masturbation is a normal and healthy part of being human. However, individuals with mental retardation commonly masturbate inappropriately. Masturbation is inappropriate if it (a) causes injury to the genitalia; (b) occurs in the wrong time or place; (c) is done so frequently that it interferes with regular activities; (d) causes distress for others, e.g., causing hygiene problems, making excessive noise; and/or (e) causes distress for the person, e.g., frustration due to being unable to reach orgasm, extreme feelings of guilt (Walsh, 2000). When caregivers of mentally retarded individuals—such as family members, special education teachers, and staff at residential settings for the mentally retarded—observe mentally retarded individuals inappropriately masturbating, how should they respond?

Inappropriate masturbation among mentally retarded individuals frequently is either ignored or treated with ridicule, punishment, or misinformation. One group of mentally retarded men believed that masturbation would cause their penises to fall off. They learned this misinformation from caregivers who were attempting to stop the men from masturbating (Walsh, 2000). Rather than discourage masturbation altogether, caregivers of mentally retarded individuals might consider the following responses:

- Provide mentally retarded individuals with adequate unstructured time and with access to a private place that is comfortable and pleasant to be in.
- To prevent inappropriate sexual behavior that is motivated by boredom and sensory deprivation, provide recreational and social activity options and pleasant nonsexual sensory input (e.g., music, massage, swimming, physical play, bubble baths).
- Provide education about body parts and sexual functioning; the difference between public and private; and ways to masturbate safely, hygienically, and effectively. Offer access to water-based lubricant and/or sexual aids.
- Teach and encourage mentally retarded individuals to communicate needs, express emotions, and seek attention in appropriate ways.
- Avoid the word *don't*, and instead, redirect inappropriate behavior by explaining what the person can do in the situation. For example, if a mentally retarded person is masturbating in the grocery store, redirect by saying, "Jane, push the shopping cart, please." If Jane were masturbating in the kitchen at home, redirect by saying, "You can do that in your bedroom with the door shut. Go to your room, please." (p. 37)

ing (a) sex acts involving nonconsenting partners, (b) sexual behavior that is public or intrusive, and/or (c) sexual behavior that presents a danger to the individual or others, such as sexual assault and masturbation with objects that could easily cause bodily injury (Ward et al., 2001). Box 18-1 discusses caregiver responses to inappropriate masturbation among mentally retarded individuals.

18-6 MENTAL ILLNESS AND SEXUALITY

Everyone experiences problems in functioning that are not necessarily considered mental illness, unless they meet specific criteria (such as level of intensity and duration) specified in the *Diagnostic and Statistical Manual of Mental Disorders* (American Psychiatric Association, 2000). **Mental disorders** are characterized by mild to severe disturbances in thinking, mood, and/or behavior associated with distress and/or impaired functioning. **Mental illness** refers collectively to all mental disorders. There are more than 200 classified forms of mental illness.

Mental disorders Mental states characterized by mild to severe disturbances in thinking, mood, and/or behavior associated with distress and/or impaired functioning.

Mental illness A collective term for all mental disorders.

NATIONAL DATA An estimated 40% of individuals in the United States will have some type of mental disorder in their lifetime (WHO International Consortium in Psychiatric Epidemiology, 2000). On an annual basis, 22–23% of U.S. adults have a diagnosable mental disorder (U.S. Department of Health and Human Services, 1999).

18-6a Mental Illness and Sexual Dysfunction

Some mental illnesses and their treatments (e.g., medication) are associated with problems in sexual functioning. For example, major depression is associated with a higher risk of erectile dysfunction in men and low sexual desire in both women and men (Riley & May, 2001; Strand, Wise, Fagan, & Schmidt, 2002). Some antidepressant medications used to treat depression, such as Prozac and Paxil, may interfere with sexual desire and arousal.

INTERNATIONAL DATA In 1998, major depression was the leading cause of disability in developed nations, including the United States (World Health Organization, 1999).

Schizophrenia A mental disorder characterized by social withdrawal and disturbances in thought, motor behavior, and interpersonal functioning.

Persons with **schizophrenia**—a mental disorder characterized by social withdrawal and disturbances in thought, motor behavior, and interpersonal functioning—can have hallucinations of a sexual nature, delusions related to sexual identity, and hypersexualism. Antipsychotic medications can eliminate these symptoms but can cause other sexual dysfunctions, such as loss or decrease in sexual desire, erectile dysfunction and ejaculatory difficulties, and difficulty achieving orgasm (Fortier, Trudel, Mottard, & Piche, 2000).

18-6b Mental Illness and Barriers to Sexual Expression, Safer Sex, and Contraception

In residential settings for mentally ill persons, such as group homes, lack of privacy and "no sex between residents" policies limit opportunities for sexual expression (Cook, 2000). Among the noninstitutionalized mentally ill population, the formation of intimate relationships is hindered by the stigma associated with mental illness and by the impaired social skills associated with some disorders. For example, individuals with schizophrenia tend to masturbate more often and have fewer sexual relationships than the normal population because of deficits in their social and relational abilities (Fortier et al., 2000).

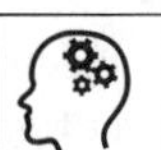

Think About It

Among individuals with schizophrenia, women are more likely than men to have a sexual partner and sexual relationships (Fortier et al., 2000). Why do you think this is so?

A major barrier to the practice of safer sex and the use of contraception among individuals with mental illness is lack of knowledge and information (Cook, 2000). Case managers and clinicians who work with mentally ill patients often feel uncomfortable discussing sexuality with their clients. A study of medical records of 56 women who were discharged from a hospital psychiatric ward found "a striking paucity of data in the notes and care plans about any aspect of sexual health . . . usage of contraception was hardly mentioned" (Cole, 2000, p. 308). The families of mentally ill patients may also disapprove of their relative's sexual activity, resulting in a lack of support from family members for using contraception and safer sex. Also, many persons with mental illness have limited incomes and cannot afford the most effective methods of contraception such as birth control pills. Finally, some individuals with mental illness may lack the social skills needed to negotiate safer sex, such as persuasion or limit-setting.

18-7 EFFECTS OF PAIN AND FATIGUE ON SEXUALITY

Persons with illness or disability often experience pain and fatigue.

18-7a Pain and Sexuality

Pain can result from a disease or injury itself and/or treatments for the disease or injury. Pain is associated with a number of health problems, including arthritis, migraine headaches, back injuries, multiple sclerosis, and cancer.

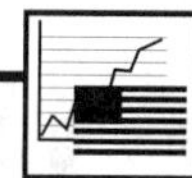

NATIONAL DATA According to a Gallup survey, 4 of 10 U.S. adults suffer pain daily ("Four of 10 Americans Suffer Pain Daily, Gallup Survey Shows," 2000).

Most people with chronic pain have pain-related difficulty with sexual activity (Ambler, Williams, Hill, Gunary, & Cratchley, 2001). Painful conditions can impair range of motion or make vigorous movement difficult during sexual activity. Pain decreases sexual desire and contributes to emotional distress, anxiety, fatigue, and depression, which, as we discuss later, interfere with sexual functioning.

To minimize the effects of pain on sexual functioning, couples can explore alternative positions for comfort and substitute noncoital sexual activity. Some sexual positions involve less physical exertion, place little or no weight on painful areas, and permit more control of depth of penetration during intercourse. When pain makes intercourse uncomfortable, couples can explore the pleasures of kissing, massage, cuddling, oral and/or manual genital stimulation.

Think About It

Has pain ever prevented you from having sex? If so, was your partner understanding?

Various medications can relieve pain, which can have a positive effect on sexuality. However, pain is often undertreated with inadequate doses of pain medication. For example, less than half of people with cancer-related pain get adequate relief of their pain (American Cancer Society, 2002a). Women are more likely than men to receive inadequate medical treatment for pain because they are sometimes viewed by doctors as exaggerating their pain (Wartik, 2002). Pain medication often has negative sexual side effects, which we discuss in section 18-8b.

18-7b Fatigue and Sexuality

In addition to pain, chronic illness and disability are often accompanied by fatigue. Persons with fatigue feel exhausted, weak, and depleted of energy. Fatigue may result from the effects of an illness or disease on the various body organs. For example, individuals with **chronic obstructive pulmonary disease (COPD)**— a collective term for diseases that affect the flow of air into the body (such as asthma, bronchitis, and emphysema)— often experience fatigue due to decreased oxygen intake and the effort involved in breathing. Because breathing is difficult for COPD patients (some require an oxygen tank), any activity that increases respiration rate, including sexual activity, may be beyond the person's physical capability.

Chronic obstructive pulmonary disease (COPD) A collective term for diseases that affect the flow of air into the body (such as a asthma, bronchitis, and emphysema). Individuals with COPD often experience fatigue due to decreased oxygen intake and the effort involved in breathing.

Fatigue may also result from medication or other medical treatments. The emotional and psychological stress that accompanies chronic illness and disability also produces fatigue, not only for patients, but for their intimate partners as well. Patients and their partners may spend a great deal of emotional energy trying to cope with the illness or disability.

When fatigue interferes with sexual interest and/or functioning, several interventions may be helpful. First, the fatigued person might engage in sexual behavior at a time when he or she feels most rested and has the most energy. Second, the person may explore different positions for sexual activity and noncoital sexual behaviors that are less demanding. Third, counseling may help a person work through the conflicts of accepting the illness or disability in an effort to reduce psychological fatigue.

18-8 EFFECTS OF MEDICAL TREATMENT ON SEXUALITY

Although medical treatments, such as medication, radiation, and surgery, can improve sexual functioning, they can also reduce sexual desire, produce erectile dysfunction or vaginal dryness, cause difficulty reaching orgasm, and/or lead to ejaculation problems.

18-8a Effects of Surgery on Sexuality

Surgery can have positive effects on sexuality when it alleviates a condition that interferes with sexual functioning. For example, a man who lacks interest in sex due to chronic back pain may find renewed libido following successful back surgery. Or, a woman who avoids sexual activity because she has **endometriosis**—the growth of endometrial tissue outside the uterus (in the Fallopian tubes or abdominal cavity)—may be free of pain and able to enjoy intercourse again following surgery to remove the endometrial tissue.

Endometriosis The growth of endometrial tissue outside the uterus (in the Fallopian tubes or abdominal cavity), which may cause pain.

However, surgical treatment of medical problems can also have a negative impact on sexuality. Surgical procedures involving the pelvic area involve high risk of damaging the pelvic autonomic nerves that affect sexual sensations and responses (Lefkowitz & McCullough, 2001). Surgery can also affect sexuality by removing a part of the body involved in sexual activity, causing negative changes in body image and self-concept, affecting hormonal levels, and causing infertility.

Hysterectomy

Surgical removal of the uterus, known as a **hysterectomy,** is the second most common surgery performed on women in the United States (after the C-section) . The loss of fertility caused by hysterectomies is often unnecessary because most hysterectomies are performed for benign conditions, and studies have found that about one in three hysterectomies is medically unnecessary (Skilling, 2000).

Hysterectomy Surgical removal of the uterus.

In nearly half of all hysterectomies, women lose both ovaries (Skilling, 2000). Surgical removal of the ovaries (**oophorectomy**) alters the estrogen levels of women, resulting in what is known as **surgical menopause.** The sudden decrease in estrogen can lead to decreased desire, vaginal dryness, and dyspareunia. Hormone replacement therapy can alleviate these sexual dysfunction symptoms (Lefkowitz & McCullough, 2001).

Oophorectomy Surgical removal of the ovaries.

Surgical menopause The sudden decrease in estrogen resulting from removal of the ovaries that can lead to decreased desire, vaginal dryness, and dyspareunia.

Following a hysterectomy, the experience of orgasm may change because the woman can no longer experience uterine contractions. However, a study of more than 1,000 women who had had a hysterectomy found that most women reported having orgasms that were as strong or stronger than before the hysterectomy (Rhodes, Kjerulff, Langenberg, & Guzinski, 1999). Most women in this study also reported increased frequency of sexual activity and decreased sexual dysfunction (low libido, dyspareunia) following hysterectomy.

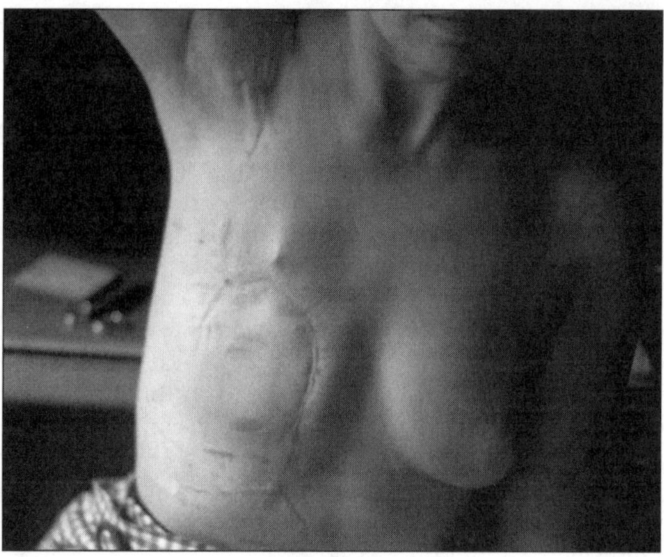

After having a mastectomy, some women still enjoy being touched around the area of the healed scar; others dislike being touched there.

Mastectomy and Lumpectomy

Women with breast cancer may have **breast-conserving therapy** (**BCT,** commonly known as **lumpectomy**), **mastectomy** (surgical removal of the breast), or **double mastectomy** (removal of both breasts). Women who have a mastectomy commonly struggle to accept their body image and may choose to wear prosthetic breasts that are inserted into a bra or glued onto the body. Alternatively, they may choose to undergo reconstruction surgery to form a new breast (or two new breasts if they have had a double mastectomy). In a reconstructed breast, feelings of pleasure from touching the breast and nipple are largely lost because the nerve that supplies feeling to the nipple is cut during surgery. For people in this situation, Schover (2001a) suggests exploring the pleasurable sensations found in other parts of the body, noting, "You may find new places to replace the pleasure you used to feel" (p. 32).

Breast-conserving therapy (BCT) The removal of the cancerous lump rather than the whole breast. (See also **lumpectomy.**)

Lumpectomy See **breast-conserving therapy.**

Mastectomy The surgical removal of one breast.

Double mastectomy The removal of both breasts.

Radical Prostatectomy, Orchiectomy, and Penectomy

Treatment for prostate cancer may involve surgical removal of the prostate (a procedure known as a **radical prostatectomy**) and/or surgical removal of the testicles (known as an **orchiectomy**). Removal of both testicles stops the production of the hormone testosterone that nourishes the cancer. These surgical procedures result in infertility. Other sexual effects of these surgeries include erection problems; low sexual desire; and lack of orgasm, dry orgasm, and weaker orgasm (Schover, 2001b).

Radical prostatectomy Surgical removal of the prostate.

Orchiectomy Surgical removal of the testicles.

Orchiectomy is also performed for testicular cancer, although in this case, the surgeon usually removes only the affected testicle, leaving the man with one testicle. Fertility, sexual desire, and sexual functioning are rarely affected when only one testicle is removed. After undergoing surgical removal of a testicle, a man can have a silicone gel-filled prosthesis surgically implanted in his scrotum to regain a more natural look.

When a man has cancer of the penis or of the bottom part of the urethra, treatment may involve **penectomy**—surgical removal of part or all of the penis. Following a partial penectomy, in which only the end of the penis is removed, the remaining shaft still becomes erect with excitement, and sexual penetration can usually be achieved. Even though the most sensitive area of the penis (the glans or "head") is gone, a man can still experience orgasm and ejaculation. A total penectomy involves removing the entire penis. The surgeon creates a new opening for the urethra, and the man expels urine from a tube between his scrotum and his anus. After a total penectomy, the man can reach

Penectomy The surgical removal of part or all of the penis.

orgasm by stimulating sensitive areas such as the scrotum and surrounding area (Schover, 2001b). The man can pleasure his partner through manual or oral stimulation, or by stimulation with a vibrator.

Ostomy Surgery

During ostomy surgery, a portion of the large or small intestine or urinary system is rerouted and brought to the skin surface of the abdomen. The resulting protruding portion of bowel is called a **stoma** (also referred to as an **ostomy**) and has a moist reddish appearance similar to the lining inside the mouth. Depending on the type of surgery, urine or stool leaves the body through the stoma and is collected in a pouch adhered to the abdomen and worn under clothing. The most common reason for **ostomy surgery** is cancer, usually of the colon, rectum, bladder, cervix, or ovaries (Turnbull, 2001).

Stoma The protruding portion of the large or small intestine (bowel) or urinary system that is rerouted and brought to the skin surface of the abdomen during ostomy surgery. (See also **ostomy.**)

Ostomy See **stoma.**

Ostomy surgery Surgery whereby a portion of the large or small intestine or urinary system is rerouted and brought to the skin surface of the abdomen where the contents are collected in a bag. Cancers of the colon, rectum, bladder, cervix, or ovaries are typical causes of ostomy surgery.

Ostomy surgery affects sexuality primarily through its negative effects on sexual self-concept and body image. A person with a stoma cannot control the elimination of urine, gas, or stool from the body. "Functions previously conducted in private (urination, defecation, and passage of gas) are now out of control in public situations, possibly accompanied by noise and odor. . . . This loss of control creates a sense of being unacceptable" (Turnbull, 2001, p. 191).

18-8b Effects of Medication and Radiation on Sexuality

Medication can improve sexual functioning either by (a) directly affecting sexual response (e.g., Viagra improves erectile functioning) or (b) alleviating the health problem that underlies the sexual dysfunction (e.g., aspirin relieves pain that interferes with sexual desire). However, many commonly prescribed medications, including antidepressants, antihypertensives (for high blood pressure), and drugs for heartburn, interfere with sexual desire and functioning ("Drugs that can sabotage your sex life," 2002). Some prescription pain medications produce sedation, constipation, and nausea—symptoms that diminish interest in sexual activity (Fleming & Paice, 2001).

Chemotherapy medication and radiation treatment for cancer patients produce nausea and fatigue, which reduce sexual desire. Hair loss, weight loss, and paleness—other common effects of cancer treatment—can reduce sexual desire by creating feelings of unattractiveness.

When a medication has a negative sexual side effect, a doctor may suggest that the patient wait to see if the problem subsides, change the drug's schedule or dosage, switch to a different drug, or take another drug to counteract or neutralize the first drug's side effect. Alternative therapies that can relieve pain without the sexual side effects associated with medication include biofeedback, hypnosis, yoga, meditation, and acupuncture.

Medications and radiation can also interfere with fertility and reproduction. For example, women who must take medication regularly to control a health condition (such as antiseizure medicine for epilepsy) are advised to avoid getting pregnant because the medication they must take could result in birth defects. Chemotherapy drugs and radiation to the pelvic area used to treat cancer can either temporarily or permanently damage ovaries, affecting fertility in women, and can slow semen production, affecting fertility in men (Schover, 2001a; Schover, 2001b).

> *Providing optimal treatment to women recovering from cervical cancer is especially important because cervical cancer is curable; women live long lives suffering with the side effects of treatment that leave an imprint on their psychological well-being and relationship functioning.*
>
> —*Andrea B. Hamilton*

Although treatments for many illnesses and injuries can negatively impact sexuality, the effects of cancer treatments, as we have seen, can be particularly devastating. Unfortunately, chances of developing cancer in one's lifetime are alarmingly high: The probability of developing cancer in one's lifetime is a little less than 1 in 2 for U.S. men; for women, the risk is a little more than 1 in 3 (American Cancer Society, 2002a). Following heart disease, cancer is the second leading cause of death in the United States, where one of every four deaths is from cancer (American Cancer Society, 2002a). One of the most important factors that determine a person's chance of surviving cancer and minimizing the negative effects of cancer treatments is early detection. Section 18-8c describes a number of cancer-screening recommendations that, when followed, can help detect certain forms of cancer in its early stages.

18-8c Personal Choices: Follow Cancer-Screening Recommendations

Breast Cancer Screening

Cancer of the breast is the most common type of cancer in women. **Mammography,** an important early detection tool, involves taking an X ray of the breasts to look for growths that may be cancerous. The American Cancer Society (2002a) recommends that women age 40 and older have a mammogram and clinical breast examination by a health-care provider each year. Women ages 20–39 should have a clinical breast examination by a health-care provider every three years. Women of all ages should perform breast self-examination (see Figure 4-5).

Mammography Procedure which involves taking an X ray of the breasts to look for growths that may be cancerous.

Uterine Cancer Screening

There are two types of uterine cancer: cancer of the cervix and cancer of the endometrium (lining of the uterus). Symptoms of uterine cancer include abnormal vaginal bleeding, spotting, or discharge, and pain, although cancerous cells can be present for years without any symptoms. Factors associated with increased risk for developing cervical cancer include young age at time of initial sexual intercourse, having multiple sexual partners, having certain types of the sexually transmitted human papillomavirus, and cigarette smoking (American Cancer Society, 2002a).

The best detection method for cervical cancer is the **Pap smear test,** a procedure in which surface cells are scraped from the vaginal walls and cervix to detect the presence of cancer (see Figure 18-2). All women who are or have been sexually active or who are 18 and older should have an annual Pap smear test and pelvic examination (American Cancer Society, 2002b). At age 35, women at risk for endometrial cancer should consider endometrial biopsy annually to screen for endometrial cancer. Women should also be encouraged to report any unusual bleeding or spotting to their physicians.

Pap smear test Procedure in which surface cells are scraped from the vaginal walls and cervix and examined under a microscope to detect the presence of cancer.

Ovarian Cancer Screening

Ovarian cancer causes more deaths than any other cancer of the female reproductive system (American Cancer Society, 2002a). The most common sign is enlargement of the abdomen, which is caused by accumulation of fluid. Other symptoms include stomach discomfort and gas that persists and cannot be explained by any other cause.

The Pap smear test, useful in detecting cervical cancer, rarely uncovers ovarian cancer. Transvaginal ultrasound may help diagnose ovarian cancer but is not routinely used for screening. An annual pelvic examination is the primary means of screening for ovarian cancer.

Prostate Cancer Screening

Prostate cancer is the second most common cancer (following skin cancer) among U.S. men (American Cancer Society, 2002b). Symptoms include difficulty with urination, frequent urination, painful urination, and blood in the urine. Men who have higher risk for prostate cancer include those who are Black and over age 65. The American Cancer Society (2002a) recommends that beginning at age 50, men should have a digital rectal exam and a prostate-specific antigen (PSA) blood test annually. African American men and men who have a close relative diagnosed with prostate cancer at a young age should begin testing at age 45.

FIGURE 18-2

Pelvic Examination and Pap Smear Test

(Appreciation is expressed to Beth Cradle, MAEd, CHES, a health education specialist in human sexuality, at East Carolina University for providing this text.)

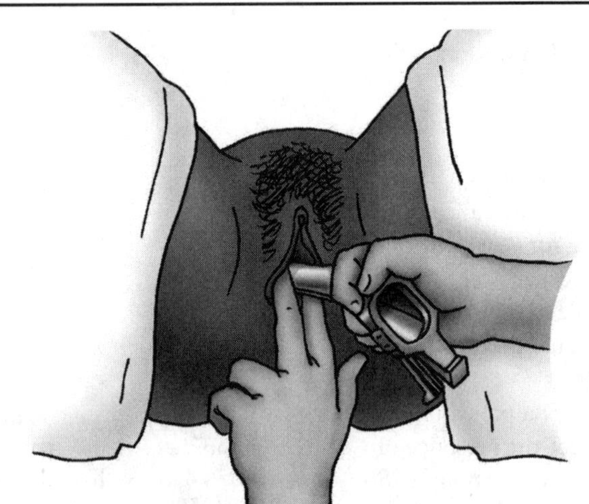

Preparing for the Exam

You will need to undress and cover yourself with a paper gown or sheet, lie down on the exam table, and rest your heels in the stirrups. The health-care provider will perform a manual breast exam (and possibly other routine checks, such as checking the thyroid glands in the neck area or listening to the heart/lungs) as well as a visual inspection of the outer genital area. He or she will use a bright light during the exam and will prepare you before touching the genital area by placing an arm or elbow on your thigh to prevent you from being startled when the exam is about to begin. If you are startled, anxious, frightened, or very nervous, the vaginal muscles can contract involuntarily around the instruments used, making the exam more difficult or possibly uncomfortable.

Speculum Examination

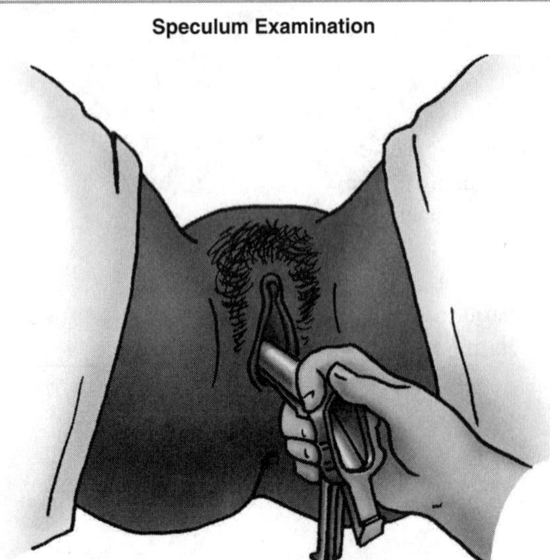

Inserting the Speculum

An instrument called a *speculum* will be used to separate and hold back the vaginal walls to give the health-care provider a clear view of the vagina. The speculum will be either plastic or metal, and a water-based lubricant will be applied to the instrument for easy insertion. The health-care provider will pull the labia (folds of skin covering the genital area) back with one hand and gently and slowly insert the speculum into the vagina at a comfortable angle. Insertion should not be painful. Different size speculums may be used for women who have never had sexual penetration, who have never had children, or who are postmenstrual. Be sure to relax, and talk to the health-care provider if adjustments need to be made to increase comfort.

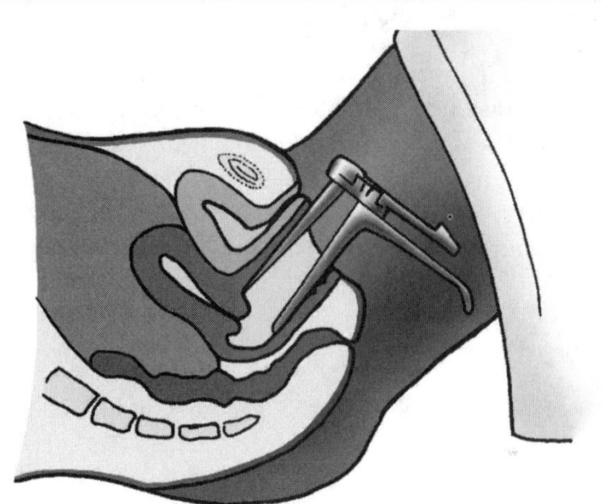

Inspecting the Cervix

To visually inspect the cervix, the bottom portion of the uterus that connects at the top of the vagina, the health-care provider will slowly rotate the speculum for the best view. There should be little or no discomfort as this occurs. The health-care provider will check the cervix for any visible signs or symptoms of infection, tearing, cysts or growths, and other health concerns.

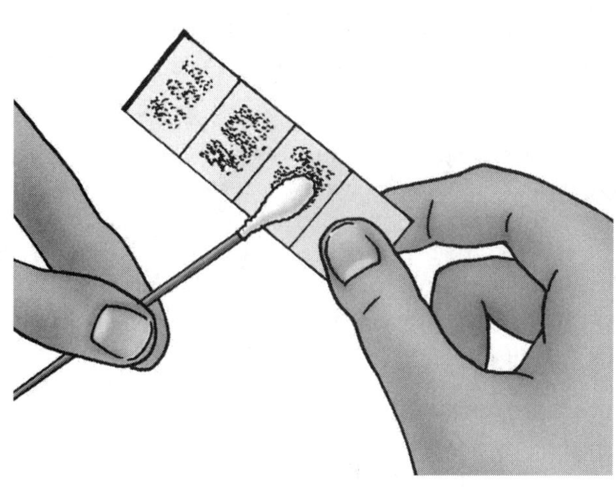

The Pap Smear Test

A researcher named Dr. George N. Papanicolau developed a medical procedure called the Pap smear test for the detection of abnormal changes in the tissue of the cervix. This procedure is capable of screening for precancerous/cancerous cells of the cervix. The Pap smear test is recommended annually for women who are 18 or older or after becoming sexually active. Women should not have sexual intercourse 24 hours prior to the exam, should avoid scheduling during the menstrual period, and should refrain from using products that change the environment of the cervix at least 48 hours prior to their screening, including douches, vaginal creams or lotions, yeast infection medications, etc., because they can distort the appearance of the cells when analyzed. While the speculum is in place, two samples of the cervical cells are collected by swabbing or rubbing the cervix with specially designed instruments. The samples are then placed on prepared slides or tubes for laboratory analysis. The health-care provider may also take samples of the natural vaginal mucus to test for certain types of infections.

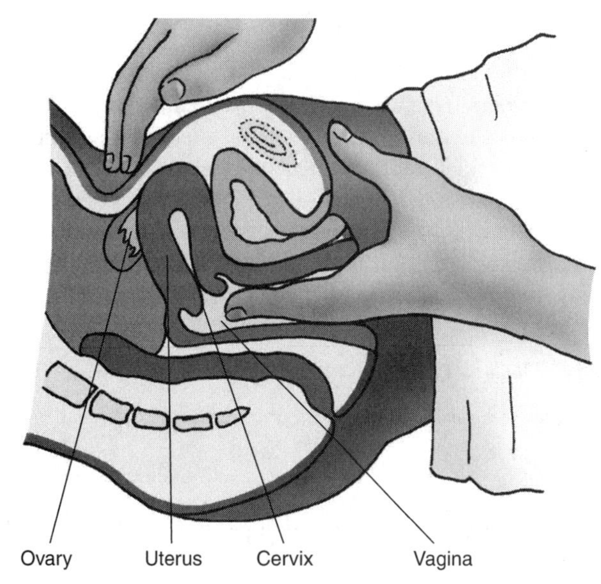

Pelvic/Bimanual Examination

After the speculum is removed, the health-care provider will perform the pelvic/bimanual exam. During this part of the exam, the health-care provider checks for growths, masses, tenderness or signs of infection, and other reproductive health concerns. Pelvic inflammatory disease, or PID, is infection in the upper reproductive system that may be diagnosed through the pelvic exam. This exam also allows the provider to ensure that the reproductive organs are of proper shape, size, position, and consistency. The provider will insert one finger into the vagina while placing his or her other hand on the outer lower abdomen. He or she will palpate, or press firmly, around the abdomen area externally (where the uterus and ovaries are located), while elevating and feeling the cervix internally. After the bimanual exam, the health-care provider may further recommend a rectal exam, where he or she places one finger into the vagina while simultaneously inserting one finger into the rectum. This exam allows the provider to check the back of the vagina and to exclude signs of rectal complications, such as colon cancer.

18-9 ALCOHOL, OTHER DRUGS, AND SEXUALITY

Substance dependence A harmful pattern of substance use involving such symptoms as increased tolerance of the substance, withdrawal, and continued use despite problems caused by the substance used.

Substance abuse Overuse or overdependence on drugs or chemicals that results in a failure to fulfill role obligations at work, school, or home. Effects include danger (e.g., driving while impaired), recurrent substance-related legal problems, and continued substance use despite its negative effect on social or interpersonal relationships.

Use of alcohol or other drugs is considered mental illness when it meets the criteria for **substance dependence** or **substance abuse** (see Table 18-1). Substance-related disorders are the most common form of mental illness, with a lifetime prevalence of about 17–24% (Hubbard & Martin, 2001). Substance abuse and dependence generally interfere with healthy functioning in all areas of life, including sexual expression and relationships. Occasional use of alcohol or other drugs for recreational or social purposes has varied effects on sexuality (see Table 18-2).

18-9a Alcohol and Sexuality

Alcohol is the most frequently used recreational drug in our society and on college and university campuses.

National Data A national study found that 62% of U.S. adults are current drinkers; 5.7% of men are heavy drinkers, consuming more than 14 drinks per week, and 3.8% of women are heavy drinkers, consuming more than 7 drinks per week (Schoenborn & Adams, 2002). A national study of more than 14,000 college students found that in the 2 weeks preceding the survey, 44% of college students had engaged in binge drinking, defined as drinking 5 or more drinks on at least one occasion (Wechsler, Lee, Kuo, & Lee, 2000).

Alcohol is a central nervous system depressant that physiologically suppresses sexual response for both women and men, and can interfere with sexual arousal, penile erection, and ability to achieve orgasm. Why then do some individuals consume alcohol to enhance sexual arousal? Research suggests that the belief or expectancy that alcohol consumption increases sexual desire and response has a strong effect on sexual arousal (Roberts & Linney, 2000). Whereas some partners consume alcohol to enhance sexual intimacy, others drink to suppress their negative feelings toward sex and/or toward their partner and to tolerate sexual relations. Long-term alcohol use in high doses can lead to cirrhosis and other diseases of the liver, and a number of other health problems that affect sexual functioning and relationships. In men, alcoholism can lead to decreases in testosterone, loss of facial hair, breast enlargement, decreased libido, and erectile dysfunction. In women, alcoholism can interfere with menstruation and ovulation, leading to early menopause (Mirin et al., 2000).

18-9b Other Recreational Drugs and Sexuality

Ecstasy A drug which has both stimulant and psychedelic effects that can result in increased energy; enhanced sense of pleasure and self-confidence; and feelings of peacefulness, acceptance, and closeness with others. Use of the drug is also associated with dangerous risks such as heart failure. (Also known as MDMA, X, or E.)

Recreational drugs are often used with the intention of enhancing sexual pleasure. For example, some individuals report that marijuana use enhances their experience of sexual pleasure. Another drug sometimes used to enhance sexual pleasure is **ecstasy,** also known as MDMA, X, or E. Ecstasy has both stimulant and psychedelic effects that can result in increased energy; enhanced sense of pleasure and self-confidence; and feelings of peacefulness, acceptance, and closeness with others. Although these effects of ecstasy can enhance sexual pleasure, ecstasy is also associated with a number of dangerous risks, including dehydration, hyperthermia, seizures, and heart or kidney failure (Mathias & Zickler, 2001).

18-9c Alcohol, Drugs, and Unsafe Sex

Many teens, as well as young adults, are mixing sex with alcohol and drugs, and putting themselves at risk.

—*Drew E. Altman*

Use of alcohol and other drugs is associated with having unprotected sex. In a national survey, nearly one quarter (23%) of sexually active teens and young adults (ages 15–24) reported having had unprotected sex because they were drinking alcohol or using drugs

TABLE 18-1

Criteria for Substance Dependence and Abuse

Substance Dependence	Substance Abuse
Drug tolerance (more and more of the drug is needed to experience the effects)	Failure to fulfill role obligations at work, school, or home due to substance use
Persistent desire or failed efforts to reduce or control substance use	Substance use in situations that are hazardous (e.g., driving while impaired)
Giving up important social, occupational, or recreational activities because of substance use	Recurrent substance-related legal problems
Continued substance use despite knowledge that such use contributes to a physical or psychological problem	Continued substance use despite its negative effect on social or interpersonal relationships

TABLE 18-2

Illicit and Abused Drugs Associated with Sexual Disorders

Substance	Sexual Disorder
Alcohol	**Acute effects: erectile disorder,*** desire disorder,*** delayed orgasm*****
	Chronic effects: erectile disorder,* desire disorder*****
Amphetamines	Low doses: may increase desire and delay orgasm*
	High doses and chronic use: **delayed or no ejaculation,***** erectile disorder,** inhibition of orgasm (men and women)*
Amyl nitrate	Decrease in arousal and lubrication; erectile disorder; delayed orgasm or ejaculation*
Barbiturates	**Decreased desire, erectile disorder, inhibited ejaculation*****
Cocaine	**Erectile disorder,*** spontaneous or delayed ejaculation, priapism***
Diazepam (Valium)	**Decreased desire, delayed ejaculation, retarded or no orgasm in women***
Marijuana	**Decreased desire, hormonal alteration***
MDMA	**Erectile disorder,**** inhibited ejaculation**** and orgasm,****** decreased desire**
Methaqualone	Erectile disorder, inhibited ejaculation, decreased desire in women*
Morphine	Decreased desire, erectile disorder, hormonal alteration*
Tobacco	Erectile disorder**

* Case reports, package insert, or uncertain frequency
** Infrequent side effect
*** Frequent side effect
**** Very frequent side effect

Note: Medications and their accompanying side effects that have been cited frequently as causing sexual disorders are in bold italic type.

Source: Reprinted with permission from Finger, W. W., Lund, M., & Slagle, M. A. (1997). Medications that may contribute to sexual disorders: A guide to assessment and treatment in family practice. *Journal of Family Practice*, *44*, 33–43. Dowden Health Media.

("Substance abuse, alcohol linked to unprotected sex," 2002). Another study found that the biggest predictor of HIV infection for both male and female injecting drug users is high-risk sexual behavior, not sharing needles used to inject drugs, as previously believed (Mathias, 2002). High-risk sexual behavior associated with substance use may result from the disinhibiting effects of the substance, the effect of the substance on judgment, or from the exchange of sex for drugs (or for money to buy drugs).

18-10 EMOTIONAL RESPONSES TO ILLNESS AND DISABILITY

Being diagnosed with a chronic illness or living with a disability can produce a number of emotional responses that can affect sexual desire and functioning.

18-10a Anxiety, Fear, and Worry

Chronically ill or disabled individuals and their partners may worry about their future: Who will take care of them? How will they pay for medical care? Will they be a burden to their families? How bad will the pain get? If the illness is fatal or life-threatening, fear of death and worries about leaving spouses and children behind are not uncommon.

Anxiety, fear, and worry can interfere with sexuality. A study of 158 men recently diagnosed with prostate cancer found that receiving the diagnosis of prostate cancer caused a significant decrease in sexual activity, sexual interest, and sexual pleasure, and an increase in erection problems (Incrocci et al., 2001). The researchers explain that "most men express anxiety after diagnosis . . . fearing a loss of erectile capacity as a result of treatment. . . . Fear of death and worries about family also can play a role in impairing sexual functioning when men are told they have cancer" (pp. 357–358). When an illness is life-threatening, "concern for survival is so great that sex is far down on the list of needs to be met. . . . Few people are interested in sex when they feel their life is being threatened" (Schover, 2001a, p. 11).

Making difficult health-care decisions can also produce fear and anxiety because people worry whether they are making the best decision. One woman with cancer described the experience she and her husband had in making treatment choices (Kramp & Kramp, 1998):

> *We started to do our own independent research on breast cancer and treatment options. . . . The number of conventional and unconventional treatments was overwhelming. . . . We were scared and unsure, especially considering we did not know the first thing about breast cancer or chemotherapy as little as thirty days prior. (pp. 124–125)*

In addition to consulting health-care providers when we face medical decisions, increasingly, consumers are turning to the Internet to find medical information and advice (see section 18-10b). Indeed, more people go online for medical advice on any given day than actually visit health professionals (Fox & Rainie, 2000). If you have used the Internet to find medical or health information, you may want to fill out the self-assessment in Box 18-2 before reading further.

18-10b Personal Choices: Use of the Internet to Find Health-Care Information and Advice

Denise has chronic back pain. Her doctor, who could find no cause for the pain, referred her to a psychiatrist, which Denise thinks is ridiculous. Denise's sister offered her some prescription muscle relaxants and recommended she see a chiropractor. A friend suggested she see a physical therapist, a co-worker said to try Yoga, and her husband advised her to find a different doctor. In the grocery store line, Denise notices a magazine article on using acupuncture for managing pain.

After being paralyzed in a car accident, Barbara assumed she would never be able to become pregnant and have a child. Her doctors have not addressed the topic of fertility and childbearing, and Barbara is too embarrassed to bring up the subject.

Box 18-2 Self-Assessment

What Type of Internet Health Consumer Are You?

Directions: When searching for health information or advice on the Internet, how often do you do the following?

a. all the time b. most of the time c. sometimes d. hardly ever e. never

___ 1. I check the source of the information to make sure it is a reliable source.
___ 2. I check the date of the information to make sure it is current and up-to-date.
___ 3. I read the website's privacy policy to make sure your privacy on that site is protected.
___ 4. I spend at least 30 minutes searching the web.
___ 5. I visit at least 4 different websites.
___ 6. I consult a health-care professional about information you find online.

Interpretation: If you answered "a" ("all the time") to each of the items, you are a very vigilant Internet health consumer, and are following the Medical Library Association's recommendations for using the Internet to find health information and advice. If you answered either "a" or "b" to each of the items, you are a concerned Internet health consumer, following most of the Medical Library Association's recommendations most of the time. However, if you answered "c," "d," or "e" for one or more of the items—especially items 1, 2, and 5—you are a risky Internet health consumer; you are not following important guidelines for finding health information on the Internet and you may be at risk for finding information that at best, can fail to help you and at worse, can hurt you.

Source: Information used to develop this self-assessment was obtained from *Vital decisions: How Internet users decide what information to trust when they or their loved ones are sick*, by Fox, S. & Rainie, L., 2002. Pew Internet & American Life Project. www.pewinternet.org/

Bill has noticed changes in the behavior and mood of Jason, his teenage son. Jason has started skipping school, is withdrawn, doesn't seem to eat much, and neglects his hygiene and appearance. In a meeting with the school nurse to discuss Bill's concern for his son, the nurse said, "There's probably nothing to worry about. Jason is just acting like a normal teenager."

Conflicting health-care advice, unmet needs for medical information, and questionable medical opinions are among the reasons that many health-care consumers are turning to the Internet for medical information and advice. A recent U.S. survey found that 72% of online women and 51% of online men have used the Internet to find health information (Fox & Rainie, 2002). Internet health consumers look for information about a particular illness or condition; nutrition, exercise, and weight control; prescription drugs; alternative or experimental treatments or medicine; mental health issues; sensitive health issues that are difficult to talk about (e.g., sexually transmitted diseases); and particular doctors or hospitals.

Overall, Internet health consumers report good results from their health information web searches: 61% say the Internet has improved the way they take care of their health either "a lot" or "some" (Fox & Rainie, 2002). Survey respondents who found health information on the Internet to be helpful said that the information affected them in the following ways (Fox & Rainie, 2002):

1. Affected a decision about how to treat an illness or condition
2. Led them to ask a doctor new questions or get a second opinion
3. Changed approach to maintaining their own health or health of someone they care for
4. Changed the way they think about diet, exercise, and stress
5. Changed the way they cope with a chronic condition or manage pain
6. Affected a decision about whether to see a doctor or not

Although the Internet can be a valuable tool for finding medical information and advice, one must be careful. In a study on Internet health consumers, 2% of respondents said they know someone who has been seriously harmed by following medical advice or health information found on the Web. If you choose to search the Internet for health information or medical advice, what can you do to ensure you are getting the best information? The Medical Library Association offers the following guidelines for using the Internet to find health and medical information and advice (see also Box 18-2):

- Check the sponsorship of the web site because this information provides an indication of the respectability and dependability of the site. Be wary of commercial web sites that are trying to sell you something. Commercial web sites have addresses that end with ".com." Rely more on web sites that have addresses that end with ".gov," ".edu," or ".org," because these web sites are sponsored by government agencies (.gov), educational institutions (.edu), and professional organizations such as scientific or research societies (.org). However, some web sites that have addresses ending with ".com" do contain reliable information. For example, the Mayo Clinic web site (www.mayoclinic.com) is one of the top health/medical web sites recommended by the Medical Library Association (other recommended health/medical web sites are listed at the end of this chapter).
- Check the date of the information to make sure it is current and up-to-date.
- Read the web site's privacy policy to make sure your privacy on that site is protected.
- Spend at least 30 minutes searching the web and visit at least four different web sites to compare information.
- Consult a health-care professional about the information you find online.

18-10c Anger and Guilt

The anger of people with disabilities is rarely understood or accepted as valid or necessary. Our anger is ignored, denied, or silenced by those who tell us how we should feel and behave.

—Nancy L. Lane

Chronic illness or disability often elicits anger in individuals and/or their loved ones. Anger may be related to grief associated with loss or may be a reaction to frustration, fear, and feelings of powerlessness. In an essay on living with disability, Lane (1999) suggests that anger can be a constructive tool for communicating needs and feelings, and that denying one's anger can cause physical and emotional health problems. "If you cannot express anger, you cannot move through it, nor can you move through the grief cycle. You remain stuck in a cycle of loss, frustration and depression" (Lane 1999, p. 179). However, it is important to avoid letting anger become abusive and destructive. "It is not necessary, nor is it always a good thing, to 'vent anger' every time we experience it. . . . Expressing that one feels angry is not the same as giving anger free reign to trample on our relationships" (Lane, 1999, p. 174).

When ill or disabled patients or their partners believe they are responsible for the illness or injury, feelings of guilt may interfere with their sexuality. Guilt can be understood as anger toward one's self. It is not uncommon, for example, for cancer patients or survivors to believe that previous sexual behavior may have led to their developing cancer (Fleming & Paice, 2001). Women with cervical cancer are especially vulnerable to feeling sexual guilt because the incidence of cervical cancer is higher among women who begin sexual relationships during their adolescence and engage in sexual intercourse with multiple partners. In addition, "guilt about such past sexual behavior as an affair, premarital sex, sex with a prostitute, or an abortion can trigger a fear that a disease is the punishment for sin. Some even use a kind of religious 'bargaining,' vowing to give up sex altogether if only they can get well or survive longer" (Schover, 2000, p. 404). Feelings of guilt are also not uncommon among cancer patients who have used tobacco. Tobacco use increases the risk for developing cancer of the lung, mouth, larynx, pharynx, esophagus, pancreas, kidney, bladder, and cervix (American Cancer Society, 2002b).

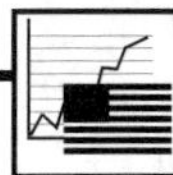

NATIONAL DATA Thirty percent of all cancer deaths in the United States can be attributed to tobacco (American Cancer Society, 2002b).

18-10d Depression

Not surprising, depression is more common in individuals with illness or disability than in the general population (Clary & Krishnan, 2001; Nosek et al., 2001). Depression may be related to a perceived social devaluation as an individual with a disability, or grief over loss of function and aspects of identity (Clifford, 2000). For example, individuals who are infertile due to illness, disability, or medical treatment may suffer profound grief over the loss of their reproductive capacity. The loss of enjoyable activities can also contribute to depression. One woman with multiple sclerosis describes grieving over the loss of enjoyable activities:

> *I mourn the loss of simple pleasures that I once took for granted. I can no longer get around, even in my own home, without the aid of my electric scooter. I am unable to walk barefoot on the beach or to dance. I mourn the loss of those pleasures. (Topf, 2002, p. 2).*

One of the classic symptoms of depression is a lack of interest in sex. For example, depression is one of the most common causes of sexual problems in people with cancer (Murphy, Morris, & Lange, 1997). Hamilton (2001) explains,

> *For many cancer survivors, sexual intimacy serves as a painful reminder of the inability to have a child. Many patients report that sadness and grief emerge during sexual experiences, leaving them vulnerable to sexual dysfunction and a sense of sexual inadequacy. The sexual estrangement from their partner is particularly troubling, because it results in a disconnection from a primary source of support at a time when this support is most needed. (p. 202)*

People with chronic illness or disabilities who suffer from depression may need assistance in working through their feelings of grief and loss associated with their illness or disability. Professional counseling, supportive interpersonal relationships, journaling, support groups, and online contact with others may be helpful. Antidepressant medications can alleviate depression but often have negative sexual side effects.

18-11 ILLNESS, DISABILITY, AND RELATIONSHIPS

Illness and disability affect the formation of sexually intimate relationships as well as preexisting marital and other intimate relationships.

18-11a Effects of Illness and Disability on the Formation of Intimate Relationships

> *When people are sick, they can go a long time without feeling the loving touch of another person, which can be terribly isolating.*
>
> —*Erin Tierney Kramp*

Establishing intimate relationships is often difficult for individuals with an illness or disability. Compared to the rest of the population, people with disabilities begin dating and experiencing sexual interaction at a later age; they are also less likely to marry (Nosek et al., 2001). Some adolescents and adults who survived childhood cancer experience discomfort with and avoidance of dating relationships because "they are unsure how they can truly feel close with someone who did not experience this life-altering period of time with them" (Olivo & Woolverton, 2001, p. 177).

The high unemployment and poverty rate among individuals with illness or disability also interferes with the formation of intimate relationships. Living with a physical or mental disability may restrict a person's ability to participate in gainful employment. The high unemployment rate among people with illness or disability means that these individuals lack access to one of the primary sources adults have for meeting people and forming relationships.

The financial hardship associated with having limited income is exacerbated by the high cost of medical care and equipment, prescription drugs, personal assistance, and assistive technologies (such as vehicles adapted for use by a spinal cord–injured person). With little money to spend, people find their options for engaging in social and recreational activities limited. One sociologist describes the relationship between financial status and sexuality: "Being sexual costs money. You need to buy clothes, to feel good about, and go places to feel good in. If you are poor . . . then it is correspondingly harder to be sexual" (Shakespeare, 2000, p. 161). In addition, "both unemployment and poverty . . . can exert a significant negative impact on a person's confidence, self-esteem, and social status, making it more difficult for him or her to take the social risks required to form new relationships" (Davidson & Stayner 1999, p. 226).

NATIONAL DATA Half of disabled Americans are poor (Shakespeare, 2000).

Social rejection also limits disabled individuals from forming sexually intimate relationships, as described in the following comments made by a disabled adult:

> *There's no question in my mind, some people don't think of me as a potential partner—or reject me outright . . . because of my disability. I've spoken to many other people with disabilities about sex and relationships, and most say the same thing. People may accept you as a friend but they won't ever consider a sexual relationship with you. (quoted in Taleporos & McCabe, 2001, p. 139)*

Some women with disabilities fear that a nondisabled person wants to date her for the "wrong reasons." For example, "a domineering man may be attracted to a woman with a disability because he perceives her as being especially helpless and vulnerable, so needy that she will put up with any kind of behavior, no matter how despicable, from him" (Howland & Rintala, 2001, p. 62).

Think About It

A **devotee** is a person who is sexually aroused and/or interested specifically in people with disabilities. Amputees are the most commonly desired disability population among devotees, but there are also devotees who are aroused by wheelchairs, crutches, braces, cerebral palsy, and other subgroups of the disability community (Aguilera, 2000). Much of the literature on devotees portrays them as predators exploiting disabled women. Aguilera (2000) suggests that although some devotees probably fit the description of exploiting others, "this view does not take into account the choice that some disabled women and men may make to participate in these relationships" (p. 261). Also, why is it socially acceptable to be attracted to someone because he or she has blue eyes or long legs, and not acceptable to be attracted to someone because he or she is missing limbs or is in a wheelchair? In the words of one self-proclaimed devotee, "it's just another physical attribute like any of the more typical that people are permitted to express attraction to" (quoted in Aguilera, 2000, p. 261).

Devotee A person who is sexually aroused and/or interested in people with disabilities.

18-11b Effects of Illness and Disability on Couples

A crisis like my accident doesn't change a marriage; it brings out what's truly there.
—Christopher Reeve

The effects of illness and disability on couples depend on many factors, including the nature of the illness or disability, when the illness or disability occurred (before or after the formation of the relationship), the quality of the relationship before the illness or disability occurred, and the couple's resources and coping abilities. When one partner becomes ill or disabled, couples often face the challenge of adjusting to changes in sexual interest and functioning. One cancer patient described her experience:

> *Since getting ill, both Doug and I have had to adjust to my lack of interest in sex following the intense chemotherapy. Even when I have felt the desire to make love to my husband, my body has been unable to handle it.... We have tried to compensate for this deficit by cuddling and touching, though even that can be a problem when I am not feeling well. Doug says that getting plenty of exercise has helped to relieve some of the strain (Kramp & Kramp, 1998, p. 94).*

When the ill or disabled individual is placed in a nursing home or other facility, or when there is 24-hour home nursing care, lack of privacy can interfere with intimate, physical expression. When an ill or disabled partner is unable to meet the sexual needs of the well partner, one option is for the well partner to masturbate. Sometimes the healthier spouse begins an affair to cope with the sexual frustration, loneliness, or stress of caregiving. However, in other cases, the well partner may end an affair when his or her partner becomes ill or disabled (Schover, 2000). When illness or disability leads to infidelity, it is not always the well partner who is unfaithful. In some cases, a partner who becomes ill or disabled may attempt to repair his or her sexual self-concept and body image by having sexual relations with others (outside the primary relationship).

Schover (2000) suggests that "despite a cultural 'myth' that illness in one partner often leads to divorce, couples in happy marriages often say that an illness has brought them closer.... It is the minority of relationships that are already fragile and conflicted that are at risk to disintegrate during the stress of an illness" (p. 410). Nevertheless, the challenges and difficulties couples face when one partner is ill or disabled can take a toll on the relationship. In a study of spinal cord–injured women, of the 11 women who were in committed (living with or married to) relationships at the time of injury, 8 believed that their injury contributed to "breaking up" those relationships (Tepper et al., 2001).

Intimate partners confronted with illness or disability may benefit from professional counseling that focuses on (a) educating the couple about the impact of their particular disease, injury, or treatment on sexual function; (b) promoting positive cognitions about body image, self-concept, and changes in their sexual functioning (see section 18-11c); (c) exploring ways to express affection and experience pleasure and intimacy given the limitations of the ill or disabled partner; (d) encouraging open communication about sexual needs and preferences; and (e) finding ways to cope with or alleviate pain, fatigue, functional disabilities, and other aspects of the illness, disability, or treatment.

> *Helping medical patients regain sexual pleasure is a victory in the face of sadness and a confirmation of the will to live and be intimate with others.*
>
> —*Leslie R. Schover*

18-11c Personal Choices: Using Cognitive Restructuring to Cope with Illness or Disability

Cognitive restructuring involves changing the way we think about something. For ill or disabled individuals and their partners, cognitive restructuring can be used to develop healthier, more positive ways to think about the illness or disability.

Cognitive restructuring Therapeutic technique that involves changing the way an individual thinks about something.

For example, Gary, a disabled man who has impaired penile function explains,

> *Because [the injury] hindered the growth of parts of my body—including my penis—it became natural for me to think of sex in different ways . . . the stereotypical male [has] the got-to-have-the-orgasm-from-the-penis-syndrome . . . I don't have that . . . men who have the "penis-focused syndrome" are missing so much because what I experience when I have sex is something that is so much deeper than I think you could ever, ever perceive. (quoted in Guldin, 2000, p.236)*

Another man, Marv, views his disability as giving him an advantage over nondisabled men:

> *Non-disabled men, says Marv, are less likely to perform and enjoy oral sex. He believes that the tongue can elicit more pleasure from a woman than the penis and he considers his tongue to be more finely-tuned than the tongues of non-disabled men who, according to Marv, only perform oral sex so the act will be reciprocated. (Guldin, 2000, p.236)*

Penny, a disabled woman, conveys a positive attitude toward the effect her disability has on her sexuality in the following comments:

> *I see my limitations only as parameters: my normality, my sexuality, to be pushed right to the edge. If you are a sexually active disabled person, and comfortable with the sexual side of your life, it is remarkable how dull and unimaginative non-disabled people's sex lives can appear. (quoted in Shakespeare, 2000, p.163)*

Individuals who choose to use cognitive restructuring to cope with their or their partner's illness or disability might consider the following questions (Hulnick & Hulnick, 1989):

1. How can we use this situation to our advancement?
2. What can we learn from our disability?
3. What might we do that might result in a more uplifting experience for everyone involved?
4. How can we relate to ourselves in a more loving way?

Assistance in cognitive restructuring is available from professional therapists who offer a form of psychotherapy known as *cognitive therapy*. A recent study funded by the National Institute of Mental Health and GlaxoSmithKline, maker of the antidepressant Paxil, found that cognitive therapy was just as effective as Paxil in alleviating depression (Begley, 2002). Psychologist Steven Hollon, a co-author of the study, noted that, "cognitive therapy has an enduring effect that protects against relapse. . . . It looks like people walk away from psychotherapy with something they can use for life" (quoted in Begley, 2002, p. B4). Whether one attempts to use cognitive restructuring on one's own, or with the assistance of a therapist, this strategy is useful for individuals coping with illness or disability.

18-12 ADDRESSING SEXUAL CONCERNS: PHYSICIAN AND PATIENT BARRIERS

Despite the negative effects that illness and disability often have on sexuality, physicians often fail to discuss sexual concerns with their patients (Schover, 2000). And even though patients want more information about sexuality, they don't always ask for what they want.

18-12a Physicians' Barriers to Addressing Sexual Concerns with Patients

In a national study of women with disabilities, 41% believed that they did not have adequate information about how their disability affects their sexual functioning (Nosek et al., 2001). Another study of 15 women with ovarian cancer found that most women thought that a health-care professional should have provided written information or discussed sexual issues with them. However, none received written information and only two received brief verbal information: A doctor told one woman that if she was having problems with sex, the hospital had creams to help her; and another woman vaguely recalled a doctor saying something, but she still was unsure about the safety of sexual activity (Stead, Fallowfield, Brown, & Selby, 2001).

It is not unusual for physicians to ignore sexual aspects of illness and disability. Physicians caring for individuals with disabilities sometimes assume that their patients are asexual. Susan Buchanan (1999), who acquired a disability at age 16, explains,

Health care providers frequently assume we do not need and are not interested in birth control or counseling on safe sex. . . . When I was sixteen, no one treating me seemed to feel it was important that I be educated when it came to sex. At an age when awakening sexuality is very much a part of a young girl's life, I was left feeling as though my questions were unimportant. (p.425)

Some health-care providers mistakenly believe that older individuals are not sexually active, so they view addressing sexual issues as unnecessary. Other barriers to health-care providers addressing sexual concerns of their patients include discomfort in discussing sexuality; lack of knowledge about the sexual consequences of an illness, disability, or treatment; and ignorance about treatments available for sexual problems (Schover, 2000).

18-12b Patients' Barriers to Addressing Sexual Concerns with Health-Care Providers

Because of physician barriers to addressing sexual concerns with their patients, sexual problems of medical patients are typically identified only when patients bring up the topic (Schover, 2000). But because patients face their own barriers to addressing sexual concerns with their doctors, many never raise the subject. When they do, it is often with allied health-care providers such as nurses, physical therapists, or social workers. Patients' barriers to asking for information and help with sexual concerns associated with their illness or disability include embarrassment in discussing sexual topics with health-care providers, lack of knowledge about treatments available for sexual problems, and finding out that insurance may not cover treatment of sexual dysfunctions (Schover, 2000).

Experiencing illness or disability in one's self or one's partner can refocus one's priorities in life on what is most important and meaningful. For many individuals, intimacy—including sexual intimacy—provides one of the most important and meaningful experiences that life has to offer. So let us vow to honor our sexual selves by attending to the sexual needs and concerns of ourselves and of others, in sickness and in health.

SUMMARY

In this chapter, we examined some of the effects of physical and mental illness, their treatments, and substance use on sexuality. This chapter brings to light some of the sexual issues and concerns facing individuals with health problems, their partners, and their health-care providers.

Illness, Disability, and the Myth of Asexuality

Although individuals with disease or disability are often perceived as being asexual, sexual intimacy, affection, and pleasure are important to most individuals with illness or disability. Indeed, for some individuals, living with a disability *increases* the importance of sexual expression. People with chronic illness or disability are, however, at heightened risk for having sexual problems because of the physiological, psychological, and social impact of an illness, disability, or its treatment.

Effects of Illness and Disability on Self-Concept and Body Image

Persons with chronic illness or disability are vulnerable to developing a negative self-concept and body image, and viewing themselves as undesirable or inadequate romantic and sexual partners. Nevertheless, many ill and disabled individuals succeed in developing and maintaining a positive self-concept and body image.

Impaired Sensory-Motor Function and Sexuality

A number of neurological diseases and injuries can result in impaired sensory-motor functioning, including stroke, spinal cord injury, multiple sclerosis (MS), and cerebral palsy. The effects of sensory-motor impairment on sexuality are varied and depend, in part, on the type and severity of the illness or injury.

Diabetes and Sexuality

Diabetes mellitus is a chronic disease in which the pancreas fails to produce sufficient insulin, which is necessary for metabolizing carbohydrates and fats. In women, diabetes can result in lack of libido, diminished clitoral sensation, vaginal dryness and discomfort, and orgasmic dysfunction. Diabetic men may notice a progressive softening of the penis, eventually leading to the inability to perform vaginal penetration.

Impaired Cognitive Function and Sexuality

Many illnesses and injuries result in impaired cognitive functioning, such as memory loss, language comprehension problems, learning disabilities, and confusion. The effects of Alzheimer's disease and other forms of dementia, traumatic brain injury, and mental retardation on sexuality depend on the severity of the impairment. Inappropriate sexual behavior is common among persons with cognitive impairment. Important issues regarding mental retardation and sexuality include sexual consent capacity, sterilization, and sex education.

Mental Illness and Sexuality

Mental disorders are characterized by mild to severe disturbances in thinking, mood, and/or behavior associated with distress and/or impaired functioning. An estimated 40% of individuals in the United States will have some type of mental disorder in their lifetime.

Some mental illnesses and their treatments (e.g., medication) are associated with problems in sexual functioning. Major depression is associated with a higher risk of erectile dysfunction in men and low sexual desire in both women and men, and some antidepressant medications used to treat depression interfere with sexual desire and arousal. In addition, individuals with mental illness face barriers to sexual expression, safer sex, and contraception.

Effects of Pain and Fatigue on Sexuality

Persons with illness or disability often experience pain and fatigue. Pain can impair range of motion or make vigorous movement difficult during sexual activity. Pain decreases sexual desire and contributes to emotional distress, anxiety, fatigue, and depression. To minimize the effects of pain on sexual functioning, couples can explore alternative positions for comfort and substitute noncoital sexual activity. Various medications can relieve pain, which can have a positive effect on sexuality. However, pain medication often has negative sexual side effects.

Fatigue may result from the effects of an illness or disease on the various body organs, from medication or other medical treatments, and/or from the emotional and psychological stress that accompanies chronic illness and disability. When fatigue interferes with sexual interest and/or functioning, the fatigued person might (a) engage in sexual behavior at a time when he or she feels most rested and has the most energy, (b) explore different positions for sexual activity and noncoital sexual behaviors that are less demanding, and (c) seek counseling to work through the conflicts of accepting the illness or disability in an effort to reduce psychological fatigue.

Effects of Medical Treatment on Sexuality

Although medical treatments, such as medication, radiation, and surgery, can improve sexual functioning, they can also reduce sexual desire, produce erectile dysfunction or vaginal dryness, cause difficulty reaching orgasm, and/or lead to ejaculation problems. Surgical procedures involving the pelvic area involve high risk of damaging the pelvic autonomic nerves that affect sexual sensations and responses. Surgery can also affect sexuality by removing a part of the body involved in sexual activity, causing negative changes in body image and self-concept, affecting hormonal levels, and causing infertility. Many commonly prescribed medications, including antidepressants, antihypertensives (for high blood pressure), and drugs for heartburn, interfere with sexual desire and functioning.

Some prescription pain medications produce sedation, constipation, and nausea—symptoms that diminish interest in sexual activity. Chemotherapy medication and radiation treatment for cancer patients produce nausea and fatigue, which reduce sexual desire. Hair loss, weight loss, and paleness—other common effects of cancer treatment—can reduce sexual desire by creating feelings of unattractiveness. Medications and radiation can also interfere with fertility and reproduction.

Alcohol, Other Drugs, and Sexuality

Alcohol is the most frequently used recreational drug in our society and on college and university campuses. Alcohol is a central nervous system depressant that physiologically suppresses sexual response for both women and men, and can interfere with sexual arousal, penile erection, and ability to achieve orgasm. However, the belief or expectancy that alcohol consumption increases sexual desire and response has a strong effect on sexual arousal. Some partners drink to suppress their negative feelings toward sex and/or toward their partner and to tolerate sexual relations. Long-term alcohol use in high doses can lead to cirrhosis and other diseases of the liver, and a number of other health problems that affect sexual functioning and relationships. Recreational drugs, such as marijuana and ecstasy, are often used with the intention of enhancing sexual pleasure. Ecstasy is associated with a number of dangerous risks, including dehydration, hyperthermia, seizures, and heart or kidney failure. Use of alcohol and other drugs is associated with having unprotected sex.

Emotional Responses to Illness and Disability

Illness and disability may produce feelings of anxiety, fear, worry, anger, guilt, and depression. These emotions can interfere with sexual functioning and relationships.

Illness, Disability, and Relationships

Illness and disability often interfere with the formation of intimate relationships due to reduced social contact, financial hardship, negative self-concept, and lack of encouragement from others. The effects of illness and disability on couples depend on many factors, including the nature of the illness or disability, when the illness or disability occurred (before or after the formation of the relationship), the quality of the relationship before the illness or disability occurred, and the couple's resources and coping abilities. A common challenge for couples when one partner becomes ill or disabled is adjusting to changes in sexual interest and functioning.

Addressing Sexual Concerns in a Medical Setting: Physician and Patient Barriers

Physicians often fail to discuss sexual concerns with their patients. Barriers to health-care providers addressing sexual concerns of their patients include discomfort in discussing sexuality; lack of knowledge about the sexual consequences of an illness, disability, or treatment; and ignorance about treatments available for sexual problems. Patients' barriers to asking for information and help with sexual concerns associated with their illness or disability include embarrassment in discussing sexual topics with health-care providers, lack of knowledge about treatments available for sexual problems, and finding out that insurance may not cover treatment of sexual dysfunctions.

SUGGESTED WEBSITES

Note: These websites were functional when we went to press. Please access the online text for the most up-to-date URLs.

The Medical Library Association recommends the following websites for health and medical information and advice:

MedlinePlus
www.medlineplus.gov

HealthFinder
www.healthfinder.gov

Mayo Clinic
www.mayoclinic.com

Medem
http://medem.com

National Women's Health Information Center
www.4women.gov/

NOAH: New York Online Access to Health
www.noah-health.org/

Oncolink: A University of Pennsylvania Cancer Center Resource
http://oncolink.upenn.edu

Centers for Disease Control and Prevention
www.cdc.gov/

HealthWeb
http://healthweb.org

HIV Insite
http://hivinsite.ucsf.edu/

KEY TERMS

agnosia (p. 551)
Alzheimer's disease (p. 551)
aphasia (p. 551)
apraxia (p. 551)
breast-conserving therapy (BCT) (p. 557)
cerebral palsy (CP) (p. 550)
chronic obstructive pulmonary disease (COPD) (p. 555)
cognitive restructuring (p. 569)
dementia (p. 551)
devotee (p. 568)
diabetes mellitus (p. 550)
disability (p. 546)
double mastectomy (p. 557)
ecstasy (p. 562)
endometriosis (p. 556)
hysterectomy (p. 556)
lumpectomy (p. 557)
mammography (p. 559)
mastectomy (p. 557)
mental disorders (p. 553)
mental illness (p. 553)
mental retardation (p. 551)
multiple sclerosis (MS) (p. 549)
oophorectomy (p. 556)
orchiectomy (p. 557)
ostomy (p. 558)
ostomy surgery (p. 558)
Pap smear test (p. 559)
paraplegia (p. 548)
penectomy (p. 557)
quadriplegia (p. 548)
radical prostatectomy (p. 557)
schizophrenia (p. 554)
sexual consent capacity (p. 552)
stoma (p. 558)
stroke (p. 548)
substance abuse (p. 562)
substance dependence (p. 562)
surgical menopause (p. 556)
traumatic brain injury (p. 551)

CHAPTER QUIZ

1. A person who has had a stroke should avoid sexual activity because having sex involves a high risk of having another stroke.
   a. True
   b. False

2. The majority of new spinal cord injuries in the United States each year involve
   a. men between the ages of 16 and 30.
   b. women under age 25.
   c. women over the age of 55.
   d. men over the age of 65.

3. What is the most common cause of dementia?
   a. spinal cord injury
   b. traumatic brain injury
   c. stroke
   d. Alzheimer's disease

4. The authors of your text make which of the following arguments?
   a. Any individual diagnosed with mental retardation cannot fulfill the role of parent and either should be sterilized or use long-term effective birth control (such as Norplant).
   b. Many individuals with mental retardation who desire to have a child may be able to assume that responsibility if provided with adequate social support.

5. Your text describes a group of mentally retarded men who believed that masturbation would cause their penises to fall off. Where did they learn this information?
   a. from their parents
   b. from one of the mentally retarded men in their group
   c. from caregivers who were attempting to stop the men from masturbating
   d. from their physician

6. According to your text, major depression is associated with low sexual desire in
   a. women.
   b. men.
   c. both a and b.
   d. neither a nor b.
7. According to your text, why do individuals with schizophrenia tend to masturbate more often and have fewer sexual relationships than the normal population?
   a. because they fear pregnancy
   b. because they lack social and relationship skills
   c. because they are physically unattractive
   d. because they are selfish
8. A study of medical records of 56 women who were discharged from a hospital psychiatric ward found that contraception was
   a. heavily emphasized.
   b. hardly mentioned.
9. According to data in your text, 4 of 10 U.S. adults suffer from pain
   a. daily.
   b. weekly.
   c. monthly.
   d. yearly.
10. Which of the following results in *surgical menopause*?
    a. oophorectomy
    b. endometriosis
    c. orchiectomy
    d. ostomy surgery
11. When a man has one of his testicles surgically removed due to cancer, fertility, sexual desire, and sexual functioning are ____________ affected.
    a. usually
    b. rarely
12. Which of the following is the most common reason for ostomy surgery?
    a. chronic obstructive pulmonary disorder
    b. motor vehicle accident
    c. endometriosis
    d. cancer
13. Which of the following is (are) the most common form of mental illness?
    a. major depression
    b. substance-related disorders
    c. phobias (including sexual phobias)
    d. anxiety disorders
14. Alcohol is a central nervous system
    a. stimulant.
    b. depressant.
15. A *devotee* is a person who
    a. remains loyal to his or her partner in sickness and in health.
    b. advocates for the rights of mentally retarded adults to have children.
    c. is sexually aroused and/or interested specifically in people with disabilities.
    d. works as a professional caregiver for individuals with disabilities.
16. Physicians routinely provide information to their clients about how illness and disability affect sexuality.
    a. True
    b. False

REFERENCES

Aguilera, R. J. (2000). Disability and delight: Staring back at the devotee community. *Sexuality and Disability, 18,* 255–261.

Ambler, N., Williams, A. C., Hill, P., Gunary, R., & Cratchley, G. (2001). Sexual difficulties of chronic pain patients. *Clinical Journal of Pain, 17*(2), 138–145.

American Cancer Society. (2002a). *Cancer facts & figures 2002.* Atlanta, GA: Author.

American Cancer Society. (2002b). *Cancer prevention & early detection.* Atlanta, GA: Author.

American Psychiatric Association. (2000). *Diagnostic and statistical manual of mental disorders* (4th ed., text rev.). Washington, DC: Author.

Begley, S. (2002, May 24). In NIMH study, therapy works as well as drugs for depression. *The Wall Street Journal,* pp. B1, B4.

Beirne-Smith, M., Ittenbach, R. F., & Patton, J. R. (2002). *Mental retardation* (6th ed.). Upper Saddle River, NJ: Merrill-Prentice Hall.

Buchanan, S. (1999). Surviving a system: One woman's experience of disability and health care. In R. P. Marinelli & A. E. Dell Orto (Eds.), *The psychological & social impact of disability* (4th ed., pp. 423–428). New York: Springer Publishing Co.

Clary, G. L., & Krishnan, K. R. R. (2001). Treatment of mood disorders in the medically ill patient. In G. O. Gabbard (Ed.), *Treatments of psychiatric disorders* (3rd ed., vol. 2., pp. 1389–1415). Washington, DC: American Psychiatric Publishing, Inc.

Clement, S. (2002). Diabetes mellitus. In M. T. McDermott (Ed.), *Endocrine secrets* (3rd ed., pp. 1–12). Philadelphia, PA: Hanley & Belfus, Inc.

Clifford, D. (2000). Caring for sexuality in loss. In D. Wells (Ed.), *Caring for sexuality in health and illness* (pp. 85–105). London: Harcourt Publishers.

Cole, M. (2000). Out of sight, out of mind: Female sexuality and the care plan approach in psychiatric inpatients. *International Journal of Psychiatry in Clinical Practice, 4,* 307–310.

Cook, J. A. (2000). Sexuality and people with psychiatric disabilities. *Sexuality and Disability, 18,* 195–206.

Davidson, L., & Stayner, D. (1999). Loss, loneliness, and the desire for love: Perspectives on the social lives of people with schizophrenia. In R. P. Marinelli & A. E. Dell Orto (Eds.), *The psychological & social impact of disability* (4th ed., pp. 220–235). New York: Springer Publishing Co.

Denekens, J., Nys, H., & Stuer, H. (1999). Sterilization of incompetent mentally handicapped persons: A model for decision making. *Journal of Medical Ethics, 25*(3), 237–242.

Donnelly, J. (1997). Sexual satisfaction for a woman with severe cerebral palsy. *Sexuality and Disability, 15,* 16.

Donohue, J., & Gebhard, P. (1995). The Kinsey Institute/Indiana University report on sexuality and spinal cord injury. *Sexuality and Disability, 13,* 7–85.

Drugs that can sabotage your sex life. (2002). *Consumer Reports on Health, 14*(3), 5.

Erol, B., Tefekli, A., Ozbey, I., Salman, F., Dincag, N., Kadioglu, A., et al. (2002). Sexual dysfunction in type II diabetic females: A comparative study. *Journal of Sex and Marital Therapy, 28,* 55–62.

Finger, W. W., Lund, M., & Slagle, M. A. (1997). Medications that may contribute to sexual disorders: A guide to assessment and treatment in family practice. *Journal of Family Practice, 44,* 33–43.

Fleming, M. P., & Kleinbart, E. (2001). Breast cancer and sexuality. *Journal of Sex Education and Therapy, 26,* 215–224.

Fleming, M. P., & Paice, J. A. (2001). Sexuality and chronic pain. *Journal of Sex Education and Therapy, 26,* 204–214.

Foley, F. W., LaRocca, N. G., Sanders, A. S., & Zemon, V. (2001). Rehabilitation of intimacy and sexual dysfunction in couples with multiple sclerosis. *Multiple Sclerosis, 7*(6), 417–421.

Fortier, P., Trudel, G., Mottard, J., & Piche, L. (2000). The influence of schizophrenia and standard or atypical neuroleptics on sexual and sociosexual functioning: A review. *Sexuality and Disability, 18,* 85–104.

Four of 10 Americans Suffer Pain Daily, Gallup Survey Shows. (2000, April 6). PRNewswire, Atlanta, GA.

Fox, S., & Rainie, L. (2002). Vital decisions: How Internet users decide what information to trust when they or their loved ones are sick. Pew Internet & American Life Project. www.pewinternet.org/

Gaudet, L., Crethar, H. C., Burger, S., & Pulos, S. (2001). Self-reported consequences of traumatic brain injury: A study of contrasting TBI and non-TBI participants. *Sexuality and Disability, 19,* 111–119.

Guldin, A. (2000). Self-claiming sexuality: Mobility impaired people and American culture. *Sexuality and Disability, 18,* 233–238.

Hamilton, A. B. (2001). Regaining sexual health after cervical cancer. *Journal of Sex Education and Therapy, 26,* 196–203.

Howland, C. A., & Rintala, D. H. (2001). Dating behaviors of women with physical disabilities. *Sexuality and Disability, 19*(1), 41–70.

Hubbard, J. R., & Martin, P. R. (2001). Substance abuse in the mentally and physically disabled: An overview. In J. R. Hubbard & P. R. Martin (Eds.), *Substance abuse in the mentally and physically disabled* (pp. 1–10). New York: Marcel Dekker, Inc.

Hulnick, M. R., & Hulnick, H. R. (1989). Life's challenges: Curse or opportunity? Counseling families of persons with disabilities. *Journal of Counseling and Development, 68,* 166–171.

Incrocci, L., Madalinska, J. B., Essink-Bot, M., Van Putten, W. L. J., Koper, P. C., & Schroder, F. H. (2001). Sexual functioning in patients with localized prostate cancer awaiting treatment. *Journal of Sex and Marital Therapy, 27,* 353–363.

Kalayjian, L. A., & Morrell, M. J. (2000). Female sexuality and neurological disease. *Journal of Sex Education and Therapy, 25,* 89–95.

Kennedy, C. H., & Niederbuhl, J. (2001). Establishing criteria for sexual consent capacity. *American Journal on Mental Retardation, 106*(6), 503–510.

Korpelainen, J. T., Nieminen, P., & Myllyla, V. V. (1999). Sexual functioning among stroke patients and their spouses. *Stroke, 30*(4), 715–719.

Kramp, E. T., & Kramp, D. H. (with McKhann, E. P.). (1998). *Living with the end in mind.* New York: Three Rivers Press.

Lane, N. J. (1999). A theology of anger when living with disability. In R. P. Marinelli & A. E. Dell Orto (Eds.), *The psychological & social impact of disability* (4th ed., pp. 173–186). New York: Springer Publishing Co.

Lefkowitz, G. K., & McCullough, A. R. (2001). Influence of abdominal, pelvic, and genital surgery on sexual function in women. *Journal of Sex Education and Therapy, 25,* 45–48.

Mathias, R. (2002). High-risk sex is main factor in HIV infection for men and women who inject drugs. *NIDA Notes (National Institute on Drug Abuse), 17*(2), 5, 10.

Mathias, R., & Zickler, P. (2001). NIDA conference highlights scientific findings on MDMA/Ecstasy. *NIDA Notes (National Institute on Drug Abuse), 16*(5), 1, 5–8.

Mayers, K. S. (2000). Inappropriate social and sexual responses to a female student by male patients with dementia and organic brain disorder. *Sexuality and Disability, 18,* 143–147.

Milligan, M. S., & Neufeldt, A. H. (2001). The myth of asexuality: A survey of social and empirical evidence. *Sexuality and Disability, 19,* 91–109.

Mirin, S. M., Batki, S. L., Bukstein, O., Isbell, P. G., Kleber, H., Schottenfeld, R. S., et al.(2000). Practice guideline for the treatment of patients with substance use disorders: Alcohol, cocaine, opioids. In American Psychiatric Association Steering Committee on Practice Guidelines (Eds.), *Practice guidelines for the treatment of psychiatric disorders* (pp. 6139–6238). Washington, DC: American Psychiatric Association.

Moody, H. R. (2000). *Aging: Concepts & controversies* (3rd ed.). Thousand Oaks, CA: Pine Forge Press.

Murphy, G. P., Morris, L. B., & Lange, D. (1997). *Informed decisions: The complete book of cancer diagnosis, treatment, and recovery.* New York: Penguin Books.

National Multiple Sclerosis Society. (2001). *The MS information sourcebook.* Information Resource Center and Library of the National Multiple Sclerosis Society. Retrieved October 15, 2002, from www.nationalmssociety.org/Sourcebook

Nelson, R. M. (1999). Sterilization of minors with developmental disabilities. *Pediatrics, 104*(2), 337–341.

Nosek, M. A., Howland, C., Rintala, D. H., Young, M. E., & Chanpong, G. F. (2001). National study of women with physical disabilities: Final report. *Sexuality and Disability, 19*(1), 5–39.

Olivo, E. L., & Woolverton, K. (2001). Surviving childhood cancer: Disruptions in the developmental building blocks of sexuality. *Journal of Sex Education and Therapy, 26,* 172–181.

Rabins, P., Blacker, D., Bland, W., Bright-Long, L., Cohen, E., Katz, I., et al. (2000). Practice guideline for the treatment of patients with Alzheimer's disease and other dementias of late life. In American Psychiatric Association Steering Committee on Practice Guidelines (Eds.), *Practice guidelines for the treatment of psychiatric disorders* (pp. 69–137). Washington, DC: American Psychiatric Association.

Rhodes, J. C., Kjerulff, K. H., Langenberg, P. W., & Guzinski, G. M. (1999). Hysterectomy and sexual functioning. *JAMA: The Journal of the American Medical Association, 282*(20), 1934–1941.

Riley, A., & May, K. (2001). Sexual desire disorders. In G. O. Gabbard (Ed.), *Treatments of psychiatric disorders* (3rd ed., vol. 2, pp. 1849–1871). Washington, DC: American Psychiatric Publishing, Inc.

Roberts, L. J., & Linney, K. D. (2000). Alcohol problems and couples: Drinking in an intimate relational context. In K. B. Schmaling & T. G. Sher (Eds.), *The psychology of couples and illness: Theory, research, & practice* (pp. 269–310). Washington, DC: American Psychological Association.

Schoenborn, C. A., & Adams, P. (2002). *Alcohol use among adults: United States, 1997–1998.* Advance Data from Vital and Health Statistics, No. 324 (Revised), April 18, 2002. Washington, DC: U.S. Department of Health and Human Services.

Schover, L. R. (2000). Sexual problems in chronic illness. In S.R. Leiblum & R. C. Rosen (Eds.), *Principles and practice of sex therapy* (3rd ed., pp. 398–422). New York: The Guilford Press.

Schover, L. R. (2001a). *Sexuality and cancer: For the woman who has cancer, and her partner.* New York: American Cancer Society.

Schover, L. R. (2001b). *Sexuality and cancer: For the man who has cancer, and his partner.* New York: American Cancer Society.

Shakespeare, T. (2000). Disabled sexuality: Toward rights and recognition. *Sexuality and Disability, 18,* 159–166.

Shaw, J. (2001). When you're asked to speak about sex, intimacy, and Alzheimer's. *Journal of Sex Education and Therapy, 26,* 140–145.

Skilling, J. (2000). *Fibroids: The complete guide to taking charge of your physical, emotional, and sexual well-being.* New York: Marlowe & Company.

Spinal Cord Injury Resource Center. (2002). http://www.spinalinjury.net/

Statistical Abstract of the United States: 2001. (2001). 121st ed. Washington, DC: U.S. Bureau of the Census.

Stead, M. L., Fallowfield, L., Brown, J. M., & Selby, P. (2001). Communication about sexual problems and sexual concerns in ovarian cancer: Qualitative study. *British Medical Journal, 323,* 836–837.

Strand, J., Wise, T. N., Fagan, P. J., & Schmidt, C. W., Jr. (2002). Erectile dysfunction and depression: Category or dimension? *Journal of Sex and Marital Therapy, 28,* 175–181.

Substance abuse, alcohol linked to unprotected sex. (2002). *Nation's Health, 32*(3), 15.

Taleporos G., & McCabe, M. P. (2001). Physical disability and sexual esteem. *Sexuality and Disability, 19*(2), 131–148.

Tepper, M. S., Whipple, B., Richards, E., & Komisaruk, B. R. (2001). Women with complete spinal cord injury: A phenomenological study of sexual experiences. *Journal of Sex and Marital Therapy, 27,* 615–623.

Topf, L. N. (2002). Good mourning. *Inside MS, 20*(2), 62–64.

Turnbull, G. B. (2001). Sexual counseling: The forgotten aspect of ostomy rehabilitation. *Journal of Sex Education and Therapy, 26,* 189–195.

U.S. Department of Health and Human Services. (1999). *Mental Health: A Report of the Surgeon General.* Rockville, MD: U.S. Government Printing Office.

Walsh, A. B. (2000). IMPROVE and CARE: Responding to inappropriate masturbation in people with severe intellectual disabilities. *Sexuality and Disability, 18,* 27–39.

Ward, K. M., Trigler, J. S., & Pfeiffer, K. T. (2001). Community services, issues, and service gaps for individuals with developmental disabilities who exhibit inappropriate sexual behaviors. *Mental Retardation, 39,* 11–19.

Wartik, N. (2002, June 23). Hurting more, helped less? *New York Times.* Retrieved June 23, 2002, from www.nytimes.com/2002/06/23/health/womenshealth/23COVER.html

Wechsler, H., Lee, J. E., Kuo, M., & Lee, H. (2000). College binge drinking in the 1990s: A continuing problem. *Journal of American College Health,* 48, 199–210.

Weinhardt, L. S., & Carey, M. P. (1996). Prevalence of erectile disorder among men with diabetes mellitus: Comprehensive review, methodological critique, and suggestions for future research. *The Journal of Sex Research, 33,* 205–214.

Whipple, B., Cerdes, C. A., & Komisaruk, B. R. (1996). Sexual response to self stimulation in women with complete spinal cord injury. *The Journal of Sex Research, 33,* 231–240.

WHO International Consortium in Psychiatric Epidemiology. (2000). Cross-national comparisons of the prevalences and correlates or mental disorders. *Bulletin of the World Health Organization*, *78*(4), 413–426.

World Health Organization. (1999). *The World Health Report* 1999. Retrieved September 1, 2002, from the World Health Organization web site at www.who.int

Zorzon, M., Zivadinov, R., Monti Bragadin, L., Morettie, R., De Masi, R., & Nasvelli, D. (2001). Sexual dysfunction in multiple sclerosis: A 2-year follow-up study. *Journal of Neurological Science*, *187*(1–2), 1–5.

Glossary

A

Abortion The deliberate termination of a pregnancy through chemical or surgical means. (See also **induced abortion.**)

Abortion rate The number of abortions per 1,000 women aged 15–44.

Abortion ratio The number of abortions per 1,000 live births.

Absolutism Belief system that is based on the unconditional power and authority of religion, law, or tradition.

Abstinence The condition of having refrained from having sexual intercourse.

Acquaintance rape Nonconsensual sex between people who know each other, are dating, or on a date. (See also **date rape.**)

Acquired dysfunction Sexual dysfunction that a person is currently experiencing but has not always experienced. (See also **secondary dysfunction.**)

Acquired Immunodeficiency Syndrome (AIDS) The last stage of HIV infection in which the immune system of a person's body is so weakened that it becomes vulnerable to disease and infection (opportunistic infections).

Acrotomophilia Paraphilia that involves deriving sexual arousal or gratification from engaging in sex with an amputee.

Adolescence The developmental period in which youth move from childhood to adulthood.

Agency adoption A type of adoption in which birth parents release their child to the adoption agency, which then places the child with a carefully selected family.

Agnosia Loss of auditory, sensory, or visual comprehension.

Alzheimer's disease Progressive and degenerative brain disease progressing from mild memory loss, through significant cognitive impairment, to very serious confusion and the loss of ability to manage activities of daily living, such as dressing, eating, and bathing.

Ambivalence Conflicting feelings that coexist, producing uncertainty or indecisiveness about a person, object, idea, or course of action.

Amenorrhea Absence of menstruation for 3 or more months when a woman is not pregnant, menopausal, or breast-feeding.

Amniocentesis Prenatal test in which a needle is inserted (usually in the 16th or 17th week of pregnancy) into the pregnant woman's uterus to withdraw fluid, which is analyzed to see if the cells carry XX (female) or XY (male) chromosomes, and to identify chromosomal defects.

Analingus Involves the licking of and/or insertion of the tongue into the partner's anus. (See also **rimming.**)

Androgen-insensitivity syndrome (AIS) Disorder caused by gene mutation in encoding androgen, resulting in feminization of external genitals and body type of XY individuals. (See also **testicular feminization syndrome.**)

Androgenital syndrome Genetic defect that causes the adrenal glands of the XX fetus to produce excessive amounts of androgens.

Androgyny Having traits stereotypically associated with both masculinity and femininity.

Antinatalism Social attitude that is anti or against children.

Aphasia Impaired communicative ability.

Aphrodisiac Any food, drink, drug, scent, or device that arouses and increases sexual desire.

Apotomnophilia Paraphilia that involves becoming sexually aroused by the thought of becoming an amputee.

Apraxia The inability to perform coordinated movements.

Areola Darkened ring around the nipple; keeps the nipples lubricated by secretions of oil during breast-feeding.

Artificial insemination The introduction of sperm into a woman's vagina or cervix by means of a syringe, rather than a penis. The sperm may be from a partner, a husband (AIH, artificial insemination by husband), or a donor (AID, artificial insemination by donor).

Asceticism Belief system based on the conviction that giving into carnal lust is wrong and that one must rise above the pursuit of sensual pleasure to live a life of self-discipline and self-denial.

Asphyxiophilia Paraphilia that involves cutting off one's air supply to enhance orgasm.

Asymptomatic Producing no symptoms or signs, or as in some STDs, yielding symptoms so mild that medical care is not sought.

Autoerotic behavior Natural, nonharmful means of sexual self-pleasuring that individuals of all ages and sexual orientations engage in. (See also **masturbation**.)

Autonepiophilia Paraphilia that involves deriving sexual arousal or gratification from wearing wet diapers.

Aversive conditioning A type of behavior therapy that involves pairing an aversive or unpleasant stimulus with a previously reinforcing stimulus; used in sex offender treatment to decrease deviant sexual arousal and reduce the probability of engaging in paraphilic behavior.

B

Bartholin's glands Located at the base of the minor lips of the female genitalia, they secrete a small amount of mucous to the inner surfaces of the labia minora.

Beliefs Mental acceptance of definitions and explanations about what is true.

Berdache A native American term often used by anthropologists in describing individuals who cross gender lines.

Bestiality Sexual activity between a human being and an animal.

Biosexology Study of the biological aspects of sexuality.

Biphobia Fearful, negative, discriminatory reactions toward bisexuals.

Bisexuality The emotional and sexual attraction to members of both sexes.

Blended orgasm Type of orgasm whereby the woman experiences both vulval contractions and deep uterine enjoyment.

Brainstorming Problem-solving strategy of suggesting as many alternatives as possible without evaluating them.

Breast-conserving therapy (BCT) The removal of the cancerous lump rather than the whole breast. (See also **lumpectomy**.)

Breech birth Delivery in which the baby's feet or buttocks come out of the vagina first.

Bundling A courtship custom among the Puritans in which the would-be groom slept in the prospective bride's bed (both fully clothed) in her parents' home. (See also **tarrying**.)

C

Candidiasis A vaginal yeast infection that tends to occur in women during pregnancy, when they are on oral contraceptives, or when they have poor resistance to disease.

Case study A research method that involves conducting an in-depth, detailed analysis of an individual, group, relationship, or event.

Celibacy The condition of refraining from sexual intercourse, especially by reason of religious vows; also used to refer to being unmarried.

Cerebral palsy (CP) Condition often caused by brain damage that occurs before or during birth or in infancy, resulting in muscular impairment and sometimes speech and learning disabilities.

Cervical cap A thimble-shaped contraceptive device made of rubber or polyethylene that fits tightly over the cervix and is held in place by suction.

Cervical ectopy An outgrowth of membranous tissue from the cervix toward the vagina.

Cervix The narrower portion of the uterus, which projects into the vagina.

Cesarean section A surgical incision made in the woman's abdomen and the uterus to deliver a fetus.

Chancroid An STD characterized by a painful ulcer in the genital region. Less common in North America than in tropical countries.

Chastity The state of not having had sexual intercourse; also implies moral purity or virtuousness in both thought and conduct.

Chicken porn Pornography depicting children involved in sexual activity (also referred to as kiddie porn).

Childhood Developmental time frame that extends from age 2 to age 12 and involves physical, cognitive, social, and sexual development.

Child sexual abuse accomodation syndrome Phases in coping behavior (including secrecy, helplessness, accomodation, disclosure, and retraction) of children as they adjust to repeated sexual abuse.

Chlamydia A common sexually transmitted infection caused by the microorganism *chlamydia trachomatis*, often asymptomatic (therefore known as "the silent disease").

Chromosomes Threadlike structures of DNA within the cell nucleus that carry the genes and transmit hereditary information.

Chronic obstructive pulmonary disease (COPD) A collective term for diseases that affect the flow of air into the body (such as a asthma, bronchitis, and emphysema). Individuals with COPD often experience fatigue due to decreased oxygen intake and the effort involved in breathing.

Circumcision Surgical procedure in which the foreskin of the penis is pulled forward and cut off. (Also known as *male genital mutilation*.)

Civil union Legally recognized status between two gay individuals that approximates but does not equal marriage. Vermont permits civil unions.

Classical conditioning Behavior modification technique whereby an unconditioned stimulus and a neutral stimulus are linked to elicit a desired response.

Classic rape Rape by a stranger which may involve a weapon. (See also **predatory rape**.)

Climacteric Term often used synonymously with menopause, refers to changes that both men and women experience at midlife.

Clitoral orgasm See **vulval orgasm**.

Clitoris Sensory organ located at the top of the labia minora of the female genitalia.

Closed adoption Traditional adoption that involves confidentiality, secrecy, and sealed adoption records; after the child is adopted, the birth parents have no further contact with the child or the adoptive family.

Closed-ended question Type of question that yields little information and can be answered in one word.

Cognitive/affective theories As related to sexuality, these theories emphasize the role of thought processes and emotions in sexual behavior.

Cognitive restructuring Therapeutic technique that involves changing the way an individual thinks about something.

Cognitive sex therapy Treatment method emphasizing that negative thoughts and attitudes about sex interfere with sexual interest, pleasure, and performance.

Cohabitation A living situation in which two heterosexual adults involved in an emotional and sexual relationship share a common residence for four nights a week for three months.

Coitus The sexual union of a man's penis and a woman's vagina. (See also **sexual intercourse**.)

Coitus interruptus The practice whereby the man withdraws his penis from the vagina before he ejaculates. (See also **withdrawal**.)

Coming out (A shortened form of "coming out of the closet") Refers to the sequence of defining one's self as homosexual in sexual orientation and disclosing one's self-identification to others.

Communication The exchange of messages between two or more people.

Complementary-needs theory Theory of mate selection which states that one tends to select mates whose needs are opposite and complementary to one's own needs.

Computer affair Emotionally intense relationship between individuals whose primary method of communication is the computer. The relationship may escalate to phone calls, meetings, and sexual behavior.

Comstock Act Law passed by Congress in 1873 prohibiting the mailing of obscene matter; this included advertisements for methods of contraception.

Conception The point at which the egg and sperm are joined. (See also **fertilization**.)

Conflict theory Sociological theory that views society as consisting of different parts competing for power and resources.

Congenital Adrenal Hyperplasia (CAH) Malfunction that causes the adrenal glands of the XX fetus to produce excessive amounts of androgens, which results in androgenital syndrome.

Contract mother See **surrogate mother**.

Coolidge effect The effect of novelty and variety on sexual arousal; when a novel partner is available, a sexually satiated male regains capacity for arousal.

Coprophilia Paraphilia that involves using feces for sexual arousal either by watching another defecate or by defecating on someone.

Corona Raised rim on the glans of the penis that is especially sensitive to touch.

Correlation Statistical index that represents the degree of relationship between two variables.

Courtship disorder A distortion of the standard sequence of interpersonal events in courtship that lead to the development of an intimate relationship; used as a theory to explain rape, the rapist short-circuits the courtship stages and progresses immediately to intercourse.

Covert sensitization Therapeutic technique that involves instructing the client to use negative thoughts as a way of developing negative feelings associated with a deviant sexual stimulus.

Cross-dresser A broad term for an individual who may dress or present himself or herself in the gender of the other sex. (See also **transvestites**.)

Cross-dressing Dressing in the clothes of the other gender, typically a man dressing in a woman's clothes.

Cryopreservation Preservation by freezing, as when fertilized eggs are frozen for possible implantation at a later time.

Cultural relativism Understanding other cultures according to the standards of the culture in which the behaviors and beliefs exist.

Culture-specific Of or relating to primary cultural attitudes, values, beliefs, and practices of diverse members of a community.

Cunnilingus Stimulation of the clitoris, labia, and vaginal opening of the woman by her partner's tongue and lips.

Curvilinear correlation Relationship that exists when two variables vary in both the same and opposite directions.

Cybersex The exchange of mutual erotic dialog via computer.

Cystitis A bladder inflammation.

D

Damiana The primary agent identified in the literature as being a sexual stimulant/aphrodisiac for women.

Date rape Nonconsensual sex between people who are dating or on a date. (See also **acquaintance rape**.)

Deductive research Sequence of research starting with a specific theory, generating a specific expectation or hypothesis based on that theory, and then gathering data that will either support or refute the theory.

Defense of Marriage Act Legislative act that denies federal recognition of homosexual marriage and allows states to ignore same-sex marriages licensed elsewhere.

Degrading pornography Sexually explicit material that degrades, debases, and dehumanizes people, typically women.

Dementia Brain disorder involving multiple cognitive deficits, including memory impairment and at least one of the following: aphasia, agnosia, apraxia, or loss of ability to think abstractly and to plan, initiate, sequence, monitor, and stop complex behavior.

Dental dam Thin piece of latex that covers the vulva during cunnilingus.

Dependent variable Variable that is measured to assess what, if any, effect the independent variable has on it.

Depo-Provera A synthetic compound similar to progesterone injected into the woman's arm or buttock that protects a woman against pregnancy for 3 months by preventing ovulation.

Descriptive research Qualitative or quantitative research that describes sexual processes, behaviors, and attitudes, as well as the people who experience them.

Determinism Belief that one's choices are largely determined by heredity and environment.

Devotee A person who is sexually aroused and/or interested in people with disabilities.

Diabetes mellitus A chronic disease in which the pancreas fails to produce sufficient insulin, which is necessary for metabolizing carbohydrates and fats.

Diaphragm A shallow rubber dome attached to a flexible, circular steel spring, 2–4 inches in diameter, that can be inserted vaginally to cover the cervix and prevent sperm from entering the uterus.

Dichotomous model (also referred to as the "either-or" model of sexuality) Way of conceptualizing sexual orientation that prevails not only in views on sexual orientation, but also in cultural understandings of biological sex (male vs. female) and gender (masculine vs. feminine).

Dilation and curettage (D&C) Abortion procedure whereby a physician uses a metal surgical instrument to scrape any remaining fetal tissue and placenta from the uterine walls after suctioning the contents of the uterus.

Dilation and evacuation (D&E) Abortion procedure during the second trimester (13 to 24 weeks' gestation) whereby the cervix is dilated and the fetal parts inside are dismembered so they can be suctioned out.

Dilation and suction (D&S) Abortion procedure during the first 12 weeks whereby the cervix is dilated before the suction procedure occurs.

Direct laboratory observation In human sexuality research, actually observing individuals engage in sexual behavior. Masters and Johnson as well as Alfred C. Kinsey observed individuals and couples engaging in sexual behavior.

Disability A health condition that involves functional deficits in performing activities of daily living.

Discrimination Behavior that involves treating categories of individuals unequally.

Double mastectomy The removal of both breasts.

Dysmenorrhea Painful menstruation.

Dyspareunia The recurrent or persistent genital pain associated with intercourse or attempts at sexual intercourse.

E

Eclectic view View that recognizes the contribution of multiple perspectives to the understanding of sexuality.

Ecstasy A drug which has both stimulant and psychedelic effects that can result in increased energy; enhanced sense of pleasure and self-confidence; and feelings of peacefulness, acceptance, and closeness with others. Use of the drug is also associated with dangerous risks such as heart failure. (Also known as *MDMA*, *X* or *E*.)

Ectopic pregnancy Condition in which a fertilized egg becomes implanted in a site other than the uterus.

Egalitarian relationships Relationships in which the partners relate to each other as equals.

Ego Freud's term for that part of an individual's psyche that deals with objective reality.

Electra complex In psychoanalysis this term refers to a daughter's (unconscious) sexual desire for her father; the term refers to the Greek myth in which Electra assists her brother in killing their mother and her lover to avenge their father's death.

Embryo The developing organism from conception to the 8th week of pregnancy.

Embryo transfer A procedure whereby a cryopreserved embryo (one's own or donated) is implanted into a woman who will carry the pregnancy to term.

Emergency contraception Contraceptive administered within 72 hours following unprotected intercourse; referred to as the "morning-after pill." (See also **postcoital contraception**.)

Empirical evidence Data that can be observed, measured, and quantified.

Endogamy The cultural expectation that one selects a marriage partner within one's own social group, such as race, religion, and social class.

Endometriosis The growth of endometrial tissue outside the uterus (in the Fallopian tubes or abdominal cavity), which may cause pain.

Ephebophilia Paraphilia that involves engaging in sexual behavior with an adolescent or having a recurrent urge to do so.

Epididymis Part of the spermatic duct system, connecting the testicles with the vas deferens.

Episiotomy Birthing procedure that involves cutting the perineum (the area between the vagina and the anus) to make a larger opening for the baby and to prevent uncontrolled tearing of the perineum.

Erotica Sexually explicit material that is neither a degrading nor violent portrayal of consensual sexual activity.

Erotophilia The propensity to have very positive views of and emotional responses to sexuality.

Erotophobia The propensity to have very negative views of and emotional responses to sexuality.

Erotophonophilia Paraphilia that involves committing lust murder, in which the partner is killed as a means of atoning for sex with that individual.

Essure A permanent sterilization procedure that requires no cutting and only a local anesthetic in a half-hour procedure that blocks the Fallopian tubes.

Ethnocentrism Judging other cultures according to the standards of one's own culture and viewing one's own culture as superior.

Ethnography The descriptive study of cultures or subcultures.

Ethnology The comparative study of two or more cultures or subcultures.

Evolutionary theories Theory that explains human sexual behavior and sexual anatomy on the basis of human evolution. (See also **sociobiological theories**.)

Exchange theory Theory of mate selection which holds that partners select each other on the basis of who offers the greatest rewards at the lowest cost.

Excitement phase Phase of sexual response cycle whereby increasing arousal is manifested by increases in heart rate, blood pressure, respiration, overall muscle tension, and vasocongestion.

Exhibitionism Paraphilia that involves an intense, recurrent sexual urge (over a period of at least 6 months), often accompanied by sexually arousing fantasies, to expose one's genitals to a stranger.

Exogamy The cultural expectation to marry outside one's own family group.

Experimental research Research methodology that involves manipulating the independent variable to determine how it affects the dependent variable.

External locus of control Perspective that successes and failures are determined by fate, chance, or some powerful external source.

Extradyadic sexual involvement Sexual relationship that occurs outside the couple, as when an individual of a dyad (couple) becomes sexually involved with someone other than the partner or mate.

Extrafamilial child sexual abuse Attempted or completed forced sex, before a child reaches the age of 14, by a person who is unrelated to the child by blood or marriage.

Extramarital Attraction of a spouse to someone other than one's mate.

F

Fallopian tubes Oviducts, or tubes, that extend about 4 inches laterally from either side of the uterus to the ovaries and that transport the ovum from an ovary to the uterus.

Family balancing Act of selecting the sex of a child before it is conceived for a "balanced" (one boy, one girl) family. One method separates sperm carrying the X and Y chromosomes.

Fellatio Oral stimulation of the man's genitals.

Female condom A lubricated, polyurethane adaptation of the male condom. It is about 6 inches long and has flexible rings at both ends—one inserted vaginally, which covers the cervix, and one external, which partially covers the labia.

Female genital mutilation (FGM) The various practices of cutting or amputating some or all of the female external genitalia—the prepuce or hood of the clitoris, the glans and shaft of the clitoris, the labia minora (small genital lips), and the labia majora (large genital lips). (See also **female genital operations**.)

Female genital operations See **female genital mutilation**.

Female infanticide The abortion or killing of females (in contrast to males) after the baby is born. (See also **sex-selective abortion**.)

Female orgasmic disorder A persistent or recurrent difficulty, delay in, or absence of experiencing orgasm following sufficient stimulation and arousal.

Female pseudohermaphrodites Individuals with androgenital syndrome who are genetically female.

Female sexual arousal disorder The persistent or recurrent inability to attain or maintain sufficient sexual excitement or a lack of genital (lubrication/swelling) or other somatic responses. (See also **sexual arousal disorder**.)

Feminist theories Perspectives that analyze discrepancies in equality between men and women, and how these imbalances affect sexuality, studies in sexuality, and sexual healthcare delivery.

Fertilization The union of a sperm and an egg resulting in a zygote. (See also **conception**.)

Fetal alcohol syndrome (FAS) The possible negative consequences (e.g., facial malformation, low birth weight) for the fetus and infant of the mother who drinks alcohol during pregnancy.

Fetally androgynized females Individuals with a condition caused by excessive androgen, whereby the clitoris greatly enlarges and the labia majora fuses together to resemble a scrotum, resulting in genitals that resemble those of a male.

Fetishism Paraphilia that involves a pattern, of at least 6 months' duration, of deriving sexual arousal or sexual gratification from actual or fantasized inanimate objects.

Formicophilia Paraphilia that involves becoming sexually aroused by ants, bugs, or other small, crawling creatures.

Fetus The developing organism from the 8th week of pregnancy forward.

Field research Method of data collection that involves observing and studying social behaviors in settings in which they occur naturally.

Fisting The insertion of several fingers or an entire closed fist and forearm (typically lubricated with a non-petroleum-based lubricant) into a partner's rectum and sometimes the lower colon.

Focus group Interviews conducted in a small group typically focused on one topic.

Folkways Customs and traditions of society.

Follicle-stimulating hormone Hormone responsible for the release of an egg from the ovary.

Forced sex Acts of sex (or attempted sex) in which one party is nonconsenting, regardless of the age and sex of the offender and victim—whether or not the act meets criteria for what legally constitutes rape.

Forcible rape Sexual force involving three elements: vaginal, oral, or anal penetration; the use of force or threat of force; and nonconsent of the victim.

Formal adoption A legal agreement consenting to adoption or relinquishing one's parental rights.

Free will Belief that although heredity and environment may influence our choices, individuals are ultimately in charge of their own destinies.

Frenulum The thin strip of skin on the underside of the head of the penis, which connects the glans with the shaft.

Frotteurism Paraphilia that involves recurring, intense, sexual urges (for at least 6 months), accompanied by fantasies of touching or rubbing, often with the genitals, against a nonconsenting person.

Fundus The broad, rounded part of the uterus.

G

G spot An alleged highly sensitive area on the front wall of the vagina 1 to 2 inches into the vaginal canal. (Also called the *Grafenb rg spot*.)

Gamete intrafallopian transfer (GIFT) A procedure whereby a physician places an egg and sperm directly into the Fallopian tube.

Gay liberation movement Social movement that increased the visibility of gay, bisexual, and transgender people as viable lifestyles of sexual orientation and identity.

Gender The social and psychological characteristics associated with being female or male.

Gender dysphoria A condition in which one's gender identity does not match one's biological sex.

Gender identity The psychological state of viewing one's self as a girl or a boy, and later as a woman or a man.

Gender postmodernism A state where there is a dissolution of male and female categories as currently conceptualized in Western capitalist society.

Gender role The social norms that dictate appropriate female and male behavior.

Gender role ideology Socially prescribed role relationships between women and men in any given society.

Gender role transcendence The abandonment of gender schema, or becoming "gender aschematic" so that personality traits, social and occupational roles, and other aspects of an individual's life become divorced from gender categories.

Gender schema theory A network of associations with the concepts of male and female (or masculinity and femininity) that organize and guide perception.

Generalized dysfunction Sexual dysfunction that occurs with all partners, contexts, and settings.

Genital herpes A viral infection that may cause blistering, typically of the genitals; it may also infect the lips, mouth, and eyes. (See also **herpes simplex virus type 2**.)

Genital warts See **human papillomavirus**.

Gerontophilia Paraphilia that involves becoming sexually aroused by elderly individuals.

GHB Gamma hydroxybutyrate, a date rape drug that may be fatal; it acts faster than Rohypnol to induce confusion, intense sleepiness, unconsciousness, and memory loss.

Glans The small rounded body of tissue on the head of the penis that can swell and harden.

Gonorrhea A bacterial infection that is sexually transmitted. (Also known as "the clap," "the drip," "the whites," and "morning drop.")

H

Hedonism Sexual value which reflects a philosophy that the pursuit of pleasure and the avoidance of pain are the ultimate values and motivation for sexual behavior.

Hepatitis B An inflammatory disease of the liver caused by a virus.

Hermaphroditism A rare condition in which individuals are born with both ovarian and testicular tissue. These individuals, called hermaphrodites, may have one ovary and one testicle, feminine breasts, and a vaginal opening beneath the penis.

Herpes simplex virus type 1 (HSV-1) A viral infection that may cause blistering, typically of the lips and mouth; it may also infect the genitals. (See also **oral herpes**.)

Herpes simplex virus type 2 (HSV-2) See **genital herpes**.

Heterosexism The belief, stated or implied, that heterosexuality is superior (e.g., morally, socially, emotionally, and behaviorally) to homosexuality.

Heterosexuality Sexual orientation whereby the predominance of emotional and sexual attraction is to persons of the other sex.

Highly active antiretroviral therapy (HAART) A combination of drugs an HIV-infected person takes to treat the virus. (Also known as "cocktail therapy.")

Homogamy theory Theory of mate selection that individuals are attracted to and become involved with those who are similar in such characteristics as age, race, religion, and social class.

Homonegativity Construct that refers to antigay responses including negative feelings (fear, disgust, anger), thoughts, and behavior.

Homophobia Negative emotional responses toward and aversion to homosexuals.

Homosexuality Sexual orientation that involves the predominance of emotional and sexual attractions to persons of the same sex.

Hookup A sexual encounter (physical interaction that might or might not include intercourse), usually lasting just one night, between two people who are strangers or just briefly acquainted.

Hormone Chemical messenger that travels from cell to cell via the bloodstream.

Hostile environment sexual harassment Environment whereby deliberate or repeated unwanted sexual comments or behaviors affect one's performance at work or school.

Human immunodeficiency virus (HIV) A virus that attacks the immune system and may lead to AIDS.

Human papillomavirus (HPV) A sexually transmitted viral disease that may produce genital warts.

Human sexuality Complex term that includes the elements of thoughts, sexual self-concept, values, emotions, anatomy/physiology, reproduction, and behaviors.

Hymen A thin mucous membrane that may partially cover the vaginal opening.

Hyperactive sexual desire disorder Very high (hyperactive) sexual interest, which influences persons to behave as though they are driven to sexual expression and the pursuit of sex, which may have negative effects on the health, relationships, or career of the individual.

Hyperventilation Abnormally heavy breathing, resulting in loss of carbon dioxide from the blood, sometimes resulting in lowered blood pressure and fainting.

Hypoactive sexual desire disorder The persistent or recurrent deficiency (or absence) of sexual fantasies/thoughts and /or desire for, or receptivity to, sexual activity, which causes personal distress.

Hypothesis A tentative and testable proposal or an educated guess about the outcome of a research study.

Hysterectomy Surgical removal of the uterus.

I

"I" statements Statements that focus on the feelings and thoughts of the communicator without making a judgment on what the other person says or does.

Id Freud's term that refers to instinctive biological drives, such as the need for sex, food, and water.

Independent adoption An adoption arranged without an agency whereby the initial contact is made directly between a pregnant woman and adoptive parents or the pregnant woman and an attorney, depending on state law.

Independent variable The variable that is presumed to cause or influence the dependent variable.

Induced abortion See **abortion**.

Inductive research Sequence of research that begins with specific empirical data, which are then used to formulate a theory to explain the data.

Infancy The first year of life following birth.

Infant mortality Deaths among infants under 1 year of age.

Infertility The inability to achieve a pregnancy after at least 1 year of regular sexual relations without birth control, or the inability to carry a pregnancy to a live birth.

Informal adoption A type of adoption most common in African American families that involves a woman placing her child with another caregiver, usually within the kinship system, without going through formal court procedures.

Inhibited male orgasm A persistent or recurrent delay in or absence of orgasm following a normal sexual excitement phase. (See also **retarded ejaculation** and **male orgasmic disorder**.)

Intact dilation and extraction (D&X) Abortion procedure involving breech delivery of fetus, except for the head, partial evacuation of the brain, resulting in the vaginal delivery of a dead fetus. (See also **partial birth abortion**.)

Internal locus of control Belief that the successes and failures in life are attributable to one's own abilities and efforts.

Intersexed infants Infants who are born with ambiguous genitals that are neither clearly male nor female.

Interview survey research Type of research in which trained interviewers ask respondents a series of questions and either take written notes or tape-record the respondents' answers. Interviews may be conducted over the telephone or face-to-face.

Intimacy The emotional closeness and bond between two individuals.

Intrafamilial child sexual abuse The exploitative sexual contact or attempted or forced sex that occurs between related individuals when the victim is under the age of 18. (Also known as *incestuous child abuse*.)

Intrauterine device (IUD) A device inserted into the uterus by a physician to prevent the fertilized egg from implanting on the uterine wall.

Introitus The vaginal opening.

In vitro fertilization Procedure that involves removing the woman's ovum and placing it in a lab dish, fertilizing it with a partner's or donor's sperm, and inserting the fertilized egg into the woman's uterus. (Also known as **test tube fertilization.**)

Involuntary abstinence Not engaging in sexual intercourse for a period of time due to lack of a partner or restricted access to a partner.

J

Jadelle® A system of rod-shaped silicone implants that are inserted under the skin in the upper inner arm to provide time-release progestin into a woman's system for contraception.

Jealousy An emotional response to a perceived or real threat to an important or valued relationship.

K

Kegel exercises Voluntarily contracting the PC muscle, as though stopping the flow of urine after beginning to urinate, several times at several sessions per day.

Klinefelter's syndrome Condition that occurs in males and results from the presence of an extra X sex chromosome (XXY), resulting in abnormal testicular development, infertility, low interest in sex (low libido), and, in some cases, mental retardation.

Klismaphilia Paraphilia that involves becoming sexually aroused by receiving an enema.

L

Labia majora ("major lips") Two elongated folds of fatty tissue that extend from the mons veneris to the perineum.

Labia minora ("little lips") Two smaller elongated folds of fatty tissue that enfold the urethral and vaginal openings.

Laparoscope A narrow, telescope-like medical instrument. One use involves inserting the instrument through an incision just below the woman's navel to view the Fallopian tubes and ovaries.

Laparoscopy A tubal ligation performed with the use of a laparoscope.

Laws Norms that are formalized and backed by political authority.

Lazarus Syndrome Psychological challenge experienced by individuals who had expected to die from AIDS but now have a new opportunity for survival due to recent treatment developments.

LesBiGay/Transgender affirmative model Way of conceptualizing sexual orientation that incorporates the insights of the multidimensional model but also affirms variations in sexual diversity and identity, and differences in the way individuals experience and express gender.

LesBiGays A term that collectively refers to lesbians, gays, and bisexuals.

Libido The craving for sexual gratification (biologically driven by estrogen and androgens) that motivates individuals to seek sexual union. (See also **sex drive** and **lust.**)

Lifelong dysfunction A sexual dysfunction that a person has always experienced; for example, a person may have always lacked sexual desire. (See also **primary dysfunction.**)

Locus of control An individual's beliefs about the source or cause (internal or external) of his or her successes and failures.

Long-term nonprogressor (LTNP) An individual who has been affirmed as HIV-seropositive but has nevertheless retained a healthy immune system.

Looking glass self The idea that the image people have of themselves is a reflection of what other people tell them about themselves

Lovemap A mental representation or template of one's idealized lover that develops early in the individual's life.

Lumpectomy See **breast-conserving therapy**.

Lunelle A hormonal method of contraception currently available; a 1-month injection must be administered by a physician.

Lust The craving for sexual gratification (biologically driven by estrogen and androgens) that motivates individuals to seek sexual union. (See also **sex drive** and **libido.**)

M

Male erectile disorder A persistent or recurrent inability to attain, or to maintain until completion of sexual activity, an adequate erection.

Male genital mutilation See **circumcision**.

Male orgasmic disorder See **inhibited male orgasm**.

Male pseudohermaphrodites Individuals who have the external genital appearance of a female (and are therefore reared as female) but whose testes are embedded in the abdomen.

Mammogram A low-dose X-ray technique used by a radiologist to detect small tumors inside the breast.

Mammography Procedure which involves taking an X ray of the breasts to look for growths that may be cancerous.

Marital rape Forcible rape by one's spouse; marital rape is now illegal in all states.

Mastectomy The surgical removal of one breast.

Masturbation A natural, common, and nonharmful means of sexual self-pleasuring that is engaged in by individuals of all ages, sexual orientations, and levels of functioning. (See also **autoerotic behavior**.)

Maternal mortality Deaths that result from complications associated with pregnancy or childbirth.

Mating gradient The tendency for husbands to be more advanced than their wives with regard to age, education, and occupational success.

Medical abortion The intentional termination of pregnancy through the use of pharmaceutical drugs. (See also **pharmaceutical abortion**.)

Medicalization of sexual dysfunctions The emphasis that sexual dysfunctions have a medical or biological basis rather than an emotional or relationship cause.

Megan's Law Federal law that requires that convicted sex offenders register with local police when they move into a community.

Menarche First menstruation.

Menopause The permanent cessation of menstruation that occurs in middle age.

Menorrhagia Excessive or prolonged menstruation.

Menstruation/menses The sloughing off of blood, mucus, and lining of the uterus.

Mental disorders Mental states characterized by mild to severe disturbances in thinking, mood, and/or behavior associated with distress and/or impaired functioning.

Mental illness A collective term for all mental disorders.

Mental retardation A condition which involves subaverage intellectual functioning and deficits in adaptive behavior. (Also referred to as *intellectual disability*.)

Microinjection Procedure whereby a physician injects sperm directly into an egg.

Middle age Time in a person's life that begins when the last child leaves home and continues until retirement or the death of either spouse; defined by the U.S. Census Bureau as age 45.

Mifepristone A synthetic steroid that effectively inhibits implantation of a fertilized egg by making the endometrium unsuitable for implantation. In effect, it aborts the fetus, and may be used within the first 7 weeks of pregnancy. (See also **RU-486**.)

Mittelschmerz Term used in reference to the pain experienced during ovulation.

Miscarriage The unintended termination of a pregnancy. (See also **spontaneous abortion**.)

Mons veneris The soft cushion of fatty tissue that lies over the pubic symphysis (joint between the left and right public bones).

Morbidity Chronic illness and disease.

Mores Norms that have a moral basis.

Mortality Death.

Muira puama Considered an aphrodisiac for men. (Also known as *erection root*.)

Multidimensional model Way of conceptualizing sexual orientation which suggests that a person's orientation consists of various independent components (including emotional feelings, lifestyle, self-identification, sexual attraction, fantasy, and behavior) and that these components may change over time.

Multigravida A woman who has experienced more than one pregnancy.

Multiple sclerosis (MS) A progressive disease that attacks the central nervous system.

Myotonia Muscle contractions.

Mysophilia Paraphilia that involves deriving sexual excitement from filthy or soiled objects.

N

Narratophilia Paraphilia that involves listening to "dirty talk" as a means of becoming sexually aroused.

Natural selection The belief that individuals who have genetic traits that are adaptive for survival are more likely to survive and pass on their genetic traits to their offspring.

Necrophilia Paraphilia that involves deriving sexual arousal or gratification from sexual activity with a dead person (or a person acting in the role of a corpse).

Negative correlation Relationship between two variables that change in opposite directions.

Nepiophilia Paraphilia that involves becoming sexually aroused by babies.

Nocturnal emission An ejaculation that results from an erotic dream. (See also **wet dream**.)

Nocturnal penile tumescence Erections that men commonly have during sleep.

Nongonococcal urethritis (NGU) An infection of the urethra—the tube that carries urine from the bladder.

Nonparticipant observation Type of research in which the investigators observe the phenomenon being studied but do not actively participate in the group or the activity.

Nonverbal messages Type of communication in which facial expressions, gestures, bodily contact, and tone of voice predominate.

Norms Socially defined rules of behavior.

Norplant The first hormonal contraceptive implant system using six flexible silicon capsules, inserted under the skin of a woman's upper arm.

NuvaRing A soft, flexible, and transparent ring approximately 2 inches in diameter that is worn inside the vagina; it provides month-long pregnancy protection.

Nymphomania Excessive sexual desire or behavior in women.

O

Object relations theory Psychodynamic theory in which early relationships with people or things (objects of an infant's drive for satisfaction) establish the blueprint for future relationships.

Obscenity Label for sexual material that meets three criteria: (a) the dominant theme of the material must appeal to a prurient interest in sex; (b) the material must be patently offensive to the community; and (c) the sexual material must have no redeeming social value.

Obsessive relational intrusion Behavior that may be pursued by a stranger or an acquaintance who repeatedly invades one's physical or symbolic privacy in his or her attempts to have an intimate relationship.

Occupational sex segregation The tendency for women and men to pursue different occupations.

Oedipal complex Freud's term based on the legend of the Greek youth Oedipus, who unknowingly killed his father and married his mother; the Oedipal complex involves the young boy's awakening sexual feelings for his mother as he becomes aware he has a penis and his mother does not.

Olfactophilia Paraphilia that involves becoming sexually aroused by certain scents.

Oligomenorrhea Irregular monthly periods.

Oophorectomy Surgical removal of the ovaries.

Open adoption Type of adoption that allows birth parents to have some control over the adoption process—selection of the adoptive parents, access to the child if desired, etc.

Open-ended question A broad question designed to elicit a great deal of information.

Open marriage A marriage in which the spouses regard their own relationship as primary but agree that each will have sexual relationships with others.

Operant learning theory An explanation of human behavior which emphasizes that the consequences of a behavior influence whether or not that behavior will occur in the future.

Operational definition Working definition; how a variable is defined in a particular study.

Operationalize Defining how a variable will be measured.

Oral herpes Sores of the lip and mouth, often caused by herpes simplex virus type I but can also be cause by herpes simplex virus type II.

Orchiectomy Surgical removal of the testicles.

Orgasm The climax of sexual excitement, experienced as a release of tension involving intense pleasure.

Ortho Evra A contraceptive transdermal patch that delivers hormones to a woman's body through skin absorption. The contraceptive patch is worn for 3 weeks (anywhere on the body except the breasts) and is changed on a weekly basis.

Ostomy See **stoma**.

Ostomy surgery Surgery whereby a portion of the large or small intestine or urinary system is rerouted and brought to the skin surface of the abdomen where the contents are collected in a bag. Cancers of the colon, rectum, bladder, cervix, or ovaries are typical causes of ostomy surgery.

Outercourse Activities that do not involve exposing a partner to blood, semen, or vaginal secretions. Outercourse includes hugging, cuddling, masturbating, fantasizing, massaging, and rubbing each other's bodies with clothes on.

Ovaries Female gonads, attached by ligaments on both sides of the uterus, that have the following two functions: producing ova and producing the female hormones estrogen and progesterone.

Ovum transfer A procedure whereby sperm is placed into a surrogate woman. When the egg is fertilized, her uterus is flushed out, and the zygote is implanted into the otherwise infertile female partner.

P

Pap smear test Procedure in which surface cells are scraped from the vaginal walls and cervix and examined under a microscope to detect the presence of cancer.

Paraphilia An overdependence on a culturally unacceptable or unusual stimulus for sexual arousal and satisfaction.

Paraplegia Paralysis of the lower half of the body.

Parental investment Any investment by a parent that increases the offspring's chance of surviving and thus increases reproductive success.

Partial birth abortion Nonmedical term used by abortion opponents to describe abortions performed very late in pregnancy in which the terminated fetus is delivered. (See also **intact dilation and extraction**.)

Partialism Paraphilia that involves deriving sexual arousal or gratification from a specific nongenital body part (such as the foot).

Partial zona drilling (PZD) Procedure that involves drilling tiny holes in the protective shell of the egg to increase the chance of it being fertilized.

Participant observation Type of research in which the researcher participates in the phenomenon being studied to obtain an insider's perspective of the people and/or behavior being observed.

Partner notification laws A set of laws that require health-care providers to advise all persons with serious sexually transmitted diseases about the importance of informing their sex or needle-sharing partner (or partners).

Patriarchy A system of social organization in which the father is the head of the family and family descent is traced through the male line.

Pelvic imflammatory disease (PID) Inflammation of the upper female reproductive system, possibly including the uterus, ovaries, Fallopian tubes, and nearby structures; the most common serious complication of STDs, causing infertility in 20% of PID patients.

Penectomy The surgical removal of part or all of the penis.

Penile supraincision A longitudinal slit through the dorsal (top) of the foreskin.

Penis The primary male external sex organ, which, in the unaroused state, is soft and hangs between the legs.

Performance anxiety Excessive concern over adequate sexual performance, which may result in sexual dysfunction.

Perineum The area of skin between the opening of the vagina and the anus.

Periodic abstinence Refraining from sexual intercourse during the 1 to 2 weeks each month when the woman is thought to be fertile. (Also known as *rhythm method*, *fertility awareness*, and *natural family planning*.)

Persistent sexual arousal syndrome (PSAS) Condition in which a woman experiences excessive and seemingly continuous arousal.

Peyronie's disease Disease that causes a painful curving or bending in the penis during erection.

Pharmaceutical abortion See **medical abortion**.

Pheromones Chemicals secreted by an animal (or person) that influence the behavior or development of others of that species.

Physiological theories Theories that describe and explain how physiological processes affect and are affected by sexual behavior.

Pictophilia Paraphilia that involves becoming sexually aroused in reference to sexy photographs.

Plateau phase Second phase of Masters and Johnson's model of the sexual response cycle, which involves the continuation of sexual arousal, including myotonia (muscle contractions), hyperventilation (heavy breathing), tachycardia (heart rate increase), and blood pressure elevation.

PLISSIT model Method of sex therapy that involves four treatment levels: permission, limited information, specific suggestions, and intensive therapy.

Polyamory A relationship of more than three individuals in a pair-bonded relationship (some of the individuals may be married to each other) who have an emotional, sexual, and parenting relationship.

Pornography Sexually explicit pictures, writing, or other images, usually pairing sex with power and violence.

Positive correlation Relationship between two variables that exists when both variables change in the same direction.

Post abortion syndrome (PAS) Term with no credibility in the scientific community, refers to symptoms following abortion such as depression, anxiety, shame, helplessness, lowered self-esteem, uncontrollable crying, alcohol or drug dependency, eating disorders, and relationship problems.

Postcoital contraception See **emergency contraception**.

Postnatal abstinence The abstaining from sexual intercourse after the baby is born.

Postpartum depression A severe depressive reaction following the birth of one's baby.

Post-traumatic stress disorder (PTSD) Mental health diagnostic category that characterizes a particular set of symptoms following traumatic events (including military combat, natural disasters, or other events that invoke terror, helplessness, and fear of loss of life), experienced by many rape victims.

Preconception care Risk assessment, interventions to reduce risk (such as treatment of infections and diseases and assistance with quitting smoking), and general health promotion (such as encouraging healthy eating, sleep, and exercise patterns; avoiding drugs; and eating a nutritional diet) to help ensure the development of a healthy baby during pregnancy. (Also called *preconception counseling*.)

Preconceptual sex selection The selection of the sex of a child before it is conceived. (See also **family balancing**.)

Predatory rape Rape by a stranger which may involve a weapon. (See also **classic rape**.)

Pregnancy State of carrying developing offspring within the woman's body.

Premature ejaculation See **rapid ejaculation**.

Premenstrual dysphoric disorder (PMDD) A proposed diagnostic category, indicating a more severe form of PMS, which interferes with the work, social activities, and relationships of the woman.

Premenstrual syndrome (PMS) Physical and psychological symptoms caused by hormonal changes from the time of ovulation to the beginning of, and sometimes during, menstruation.

Prenatal sex selection The selection of the sex of a child before the child is born.

Preorgasmia Condition which implies that the woman will be able to achieve orgasm given sufficient context, stimulation, or training.

Primacy/recency effect The tendency of individuals to remember best what occurs first and last in a sequence.

Primary dysfunction See **lifelong dysfunction**.

Primary sex characteristics Those characteristics that differentiate women and men, such as external genitalia (vulva and penis), gonads (ovaries and testes), sex chromosomes (XX and XY), and hormones (estrogen, progesterone, and testosterone).

Primigravida The condition of being pregnant for the first time.

Principle of least interest The person who has the least interest in a relationship controls the relationship.

Pronatalism Social bias in favor of having children.

Prostate gland A chestnut-sized structure in the male located below the bladder and in front of the rectum that produces much of the seminal fluid.

Prostitution The exchange of money, drugs, or goods for access to one's body for the purpose of the purchaser's pleasure or enjoyment.

Pseudohermaphroditism A condition in which an individual is born with gonads matching the sex chromosomes, but genitals resembling those of the other sex.

Psychoanalytic theory Freud's theory that emphasizes the role of unconscious processes in one's life.

Psychosexology Area of sexology focused on how psychological processes influence and are influenced by sexual development and behavior.

Puberty Developmental stage in which a youth achieves reproductive capacity.

Pubic lice The crab louse (pidiculosis) causes itching, irritated skin, usually confined to the pubic hair.

Pubococcygeus Muscle surrounding the opening to the vagina that can influence sexual functioning, in that if it is too tense, vaginal entry may be difficult or impossible.

Punishment A consequence that decreases or terminates a behavior.

Purging Act of throwing away or burning one's clothes as a desperate means of ending one's cross-dressing.

Q

Quadriplegia Paralysis from the neck down.

Quickening The stage of pregnancy in which the woman can feel movement of the fetus inside her (usually in the fourth or fifth month of pregnancy).

Quid pro quo sexual harassment Type of sexual harassment whereby the individual is provided benefits (promotions, salary raises) in exchange for sexual favors.

R

Radical prostatectomy Surgical removal of the prostate.

Rape Acts of sex (or attempted sex) in which one party is nonconsenting, regardless of the age and sex of the offender and victim.

Rape myths Generally false but widely held attitudes and beliefs that serve to justify male sexual aggression against women. (See also **rape-supportive beliefs**.)

Rape-supportive beliefs See **rape myths**.

Rape trauma syndrome Acute and long-term reorganization process that occurs as a result of forcible rape or attempted rape.

Rapid ejaculation The persistent or recurrent onset of orgasm and ejaculation—with minimal sexual stimulation—before, on, or shortly after penetration. (See also **premature ejaculation**.)

Raptophilia Paraphilia that involves becoming sexually aroused by surprise attack and violent assault.

Reductase-deficient males Individuals with XY chromosomes who also have a defective gene that creates problems with an enzyme involved in testosterone metabolism.

Reflective listening Communication technique in which one person restates the meaning of what his or her partner has said in a conversation.

Refractory period Stage in the sexual response cycle after orgasm when the person cannot be sexually aroused.

Reinforcement A consequence that maintains or increases a behavior.

Relativism Sexual value which emphasizes that sexual decisions should be made in the context of a particular situation.

Representative sample A sample the researcher studies that is representative of the population from which it is taken.

Resolution phase Final phase of Masters and Johnson's model of the sexual response cycle that describes the body's return to its pre-excitement condition.

Retarded ejaculation See **inhibited male orgasm**.

Rimming See **analingus**.

Roe v. Wade The 1973 Supreme Court decision declaring that during the first three months of pregnancy the decision to have an abortion would be between the woman and her physician.

Rohypnol (Also known as dulcitas, the "forget me drug") Drug used in date rape scenarios which causes profound and prolonged sedation, a feeling of well-being, and short-term memory loss.

RU-486 See **Mifepristone**.

S

Salpingectomy Tubal ligation or "tying of the tubes" sterilization procedure whereby the woman's Fallopian tubes are cut out and the ends are tied, clamped, or cauterized so that eggs cannot pass down the Fallopian tubes to be fertilized.

Sample A portion of the population that the researcher studies and attempts to make inferences about the whole population.

Satiation Psychological term that refers to the repeated exposure to a stimulus which results in the loss of ability of that stimulus to reinforce.

Satyriasis Excessive sexual behavior in men.

Scatalogia Paraphilia that involves becoming sexually aroused by calling a stranger on the phone and either talking about sex or making sexual sounds (breathing heavily; also called *telephonicophilia*).

Schizophrenia A mental disorder characterized by social withdrawal and disturbances in thought, motor behavior, and interpersonal functioning.

Scopophilia Paraphilia that involves recurrent, intense urges to look at unsuspecting people who are naked, undressing, or engaging in sexual behavior. (See also **voyeurism**.)

Scrotum The sac located below the penis that contains the testicles.

Secondary dysfunction See **acquired dysfunction**.

Secondary sex characteristics Characteristics that differentiate males and females that are not linked to reproduction (e.g., beard in men, high voice in women).

Self-fulfilling prophecy Behaving in such a way as to make expectations come true. For example, caustic accusations to a partner for infidelity may actually drive the partner to be unfaithful.

Semen-conservation doctrine From early Ayurvedic teachings in India, the belief that general good health in both sexes depended on conserving the life-giving power of "vital fluids" (semen and vaginal fluids).

Seminal vesicles Two small glands about 2 inches in length, located behind the bladder in the male, which secrete fluids that mix with sperm to become semen.

Seminiferous tubules Part of the spermatic duct system, located within the testicles.

Sensate focus Treatment used in sex therapy developed by Masters and Johnson whereby the partners focus on pleasuring each other in nongenital ways.

Sex Term that refers to the biological distinction between being female and being male, usually categorized on the basis of the reproductive organs and genetic makeup.

Sex drive The craving for sexual gratification (biologically driven by estrogen and androgens) that motivates individuals to seek sexual union. (See also **lust** and **libido**.)

Sexology A unique discipline that identifies important questions related to sexuality issues and finding/integrating answers from biology, psychology, and sociology based on scientific methods of investigation.

Sex roles Roles filled by women or men that are defined by biological constraints and can be enacted by members of one biological sex only—wet nurse, sperm donor, child bearer.

Sex-selective abortion An abortion that is performed because the fetus is thought to be a particular sex (usually female). (See also **female infanticide**.)

Sexual addiction Sometimes described as an intimacy disorder manifested by a compulsive cycle of preoccupation and ritualization of sexual behavior and despair.

Sexual anatomy Term referring to internal and external genitals. (Also called *sex organs*.)

Sexual arousal disorder See **female sexual arousal disorder**.

Sexual aversion disorder The persistent or recurrent phobic aversion to and avoidance of sexual contact with a sexual partner.

Sexual celibacy The state of not having sexual intercourse or activity.

Sexual coercion The use of force (actual or threatened) to engage a person in sexual acts against that person's will.

Sexual cognition A wide range of thoughts, images, and fantasies, including fleeting sexual thoughts or images, elaborate and ongoing sexual fantasies, sexual thoughts and fantasies that are engaged in deliberately, and sexual thoughts that are experienced as intrusive.

Sexual consent capacity The ability to make informed and voluntary choices about sexual behavior.

Sexual debut One's first sexual intercourse.

Sexual disorder Diagnosis that a disturbance in sexual desire or the psychophysiological components of one's sexual response cycle cause significant distress and interpersonal difficulty.

Sexual double standard One standard for women and another for men. An example of the double standard in U.S. society is that it is normative for men to have more sexual partners and women to have fewer partners.

Sexual dysfunction An impairment or difficulty that affects sexual functioning or produces sexual pain.

Sexual fantasies Cognitions, or thoughts and/or images, that are sexual in nature.

Sexual guilt Personal emotional reaction to engaging in sexual behavior that violates personal sexual values.

Sexual harassment Unwelcome sexual advances, requests for sexual favors, and other verbal or physical conduct of a sexual nature when submission to or rejection of this conduct explicitly or implicitly affects an individual's employment; unreasonably interferes with an individual's work performance; or creates an intimidating, hostile, or offensive work environment.

Sexual identity Composite term that refers to factors including one's biological sex, gender identity, gender role, and sexual orientation.

Sexual intercourse The sexual union of a man's penis and a woman's vagina. (See also **coitus.**)

Sexually transmitted disease (STD) A disease caused by any of more than 25 infectious organisms that are transmitted primarily through sexual activity.

Sexually transmitted infection (STI) An infection transmitted primarily through sexual activity. A recent term sometimes used to avoid the negative connotations sometimes associated with *STD*.

Sexual masochism Paraphilia characterized by recurrent, intense, sexual urges and sexually arousing fantasies, of at least 6 months' duration, in which sexual arousal or gratification is obtained through enacting scripts that involve experiencing suffering and pain.

Sexual orientation The classification of individuals as heterosexual, bisexual, or homosexual based on their emotional, cognitive, and sexual attractions as well as their self-identity and lifestyle.

Sexual physiology The vascular, hormonal, and central nervous system processes involved in genital functioning.

Sexual revolution Cultural openness of sexual issues and approval for intercourse between unmarried individuals.

Sexual sadism Paraphilia characterized by recurrent, intense, sexual urges and sexually arousing fantasies, of at least 6 months' duration, involving acts that hurt or humiliate the sexual partner.

Sexual self-concept The way an individual thinks and feels about his or her body, self-evaluation of one's interest in sex, and self-evaluation as a sexual partner.

Sexual values Moral guidelines for making sexual choices.

Situational dysfunction Sexual dysfunction that occurs with one partner or in one situation only.

Social learning theory Framework that emphasizes the process of learning through observation and imitation.

Social scripts Shared interpretations that have three functions: to define situations, name actors, and plot behaviors.

Sociobiological theories Framework that explains human sexual behavior and sexual anatomy as functional for human evolution. (See also **evolutionary theories.**)

Sociobiology Framework in which social behavior is viewed as having a biological basis in terms of being functional in human evolution. (See also **sociobiological theories.**)

Sociosexology Aspect of sexology that is concerned with how social and cultural forces influence and are influenced by sexual attitudes, beliefs, and behaviors.

Somnophilia Paraphilia that involves fondling a person who is sleeping so as to become sexually aroused. The person is often a stranger.

Spectatoring Self-monitoring one's own sexual responses to the point that a sexual dysfunction may occur.

Spermicide A chemical that kills sperm.

Spiritualistic dualism Term from early Christian doctrine whereby the body and spirit or mind were seen as being separate from each other.

Spontaneous abortion See **miscarriage.**

Spurious correlation Pattern that exists when two variables appear to be related but only because they are both related to a third variable.

Stalking An extreme form of obsessive relational intrusion and may involve following or watching a victim, property damage, threats, home invasion, or threats of physical harm.

Statistical model of normality A way to conceptualize prevalence; better known as the *normal curve*. This statistical presentation of the prevalence of a phenomenon reveals the distribution in a large population.

Statutory rape Sexual intercourse without use of force with a person below the legal age of consent.

Sterilization Surgical procedure that permanently prevents reproduction.

Stoma The protruding portion of the large or small intestine (bowel) or urinary system that is rerouted and brought to the skin surface of the abdomen during ostomy surgery. (See also **ostomy.**)

Stroke Sudden disturbance in the blood supply to the brain caused by hemorrhage from rupture or blockage of a blood vessel.

Structural-functional theory Framework that views society as a system of interrelated parts that influence each other and work together to achieve social stability.

Substance abuse Overuse or overdependence on drugs or chemicals that results in a failure to fulfill role obligations at work, school, or home. Effects include danger (e.g., driving while impaired), recurrent substance-related legal problems, and continued substance use despite its negative effect on social or interpersonal relationships.

Substance dependence A harmful pattern of substance use involving such symptoms as increased tolerance of the substance, withdrawal, and continued use despite problems caused by the substance used.

Suction curettage Abortion procedure performed the first 6 to 8 weeks of pregnancy whereby a hollow plastic rod is inserted into the woman's uterus where the fetal tissue is evacuated. (See also **vacuum aspiration.**)

Superego Freud's term for the conscience, which functions by guiding the individual to do what is morally right and good.

Surgical menopause The sudden decrease in estrogen resulting from removal of the ovaries that can lead to decreased desire, vaginal dryness, and dyspareunia.

Surrogate mother A woman who voluntarily agrees to be artificially inseminated, carry a baby to term, and give up the legal right to the baby at birth to a couple or individual desiring such a baby. The woman may also be implanted with a fertilized zygote from another sperm and egg so that she is not biologically related to the baby she carries to term. (See also **contract mother**.)

Surrogate sex partner therapy Treatment method that involves a person with sexual difficulties becoming sexually involved with a trained individual (other than the primary therapist) for therapeutic purposes.

Survey research Research that involves eliciting information from respondents using questions.

Swinging Agreement between the partners of one marriage or committed relationship that they will have sexual relations with the partners of another relationship. (Also referred to as *comarital sex*.)

Symbolic interaction theory Sociological theory that focuses on how meanings, labels, and definitions learned through interaction affect one's attitudes, self-concept, and behavior.

Syphilis A sexually transmitted (or congenital) disease caused by a spirochete (Treponema pallidum); if untreated, it can progress to a systemic infection through three stages and can be fatal.

Syringe-exchange programs Programs designed to reduce the transmission of HIV that is associated with drug injection by providing sterile syringes in exchange for used, potentially HIV-contaminated syringes.

Systems theory Theoretical framework that emphasizes the interpersonal and relationship aspects of sexuality.

T

Tachycardia Increased heart rate.

Tarrying A courtship custom among the Puritans in which the would-be groom slept in the prospective bride's bed (both fully clothed) in her parents' home. (See also **bundling**.)

Testes Male gonads that develop from the same embryonic tissue as the female gonads (the ovaries) and produce spermatozoa and male hormones. (Also called *testicles*.)

Testicular feminization syndrome (TFS) Disorder that involves the lack of development of male genitals in the body of a person who is genetically male (a person who has XY chromosomes). The genitals of the infant look female but the infant is biologically a male. (See also **androgen-insensitivity syndrome**.)

Theory A set of ideas designed to answer a question or explain a particular phenomenon.

Therapeutic abortion An abortion performed to protect the life or health of the woman.

Touch-and-ask rule Sexual technique whereby each touch and caress is accompanied by the question "How does that feel?" to be followed by feedback from the partner.

Toucheurism Paraphilia that involves actively using one's hands on the victim. Although the person may be distressed over the overwhelming urge to touch or rub against another, he also may act on those fantasies.

Trafficking Related to prostitution, using force and deception to transfer persons into situations of extreme exploitation.

Transgendered Term that refers to individuals who express some characteristics other than their assigned gender, which is usually based on their biological sex (male or female).

Transgendered individuals Persons who do not fit neatly into either the male or female category, or their behavior is not congruent with the norms and expectations of their sex.

Transgenderist An individual who lives in a gender role that does not match his or her biological sex but who does not surgically alter his or her genitalia (as does a transsexual).

Transsexuals Persons with the biological/anatomical sex of one gender (e.g., male) but the self-concept of the other sex (e.g., female).

Transvestic fetishism Paraphilia that involves recurrent, intense, sexual urges and sexually arousing fantasies, of at least 6 months' duration, involving cross-dressing (e.g., a man dressing in a woman's clothes).

Transvestites A broad term for individuals who may dress or present themselves in the gender of the other sex. A more pejorative term than cross-dresser; see also **cross-dresser.**

Traumatic brain injury A closed head injury that results from an exterior force and creates a temporary or enduring impairment in brain functioning.

Tribadism A form of intimacy in which two women stimulate each others' genital area (vulva, mons area, clitoris) with their own vulval area or with their fingers, hands, or other body parts such as their knee or thigh.

Tumescence A swelling or enlargement of an organ, as caused by increased blood flow to the genitals.

Turner's Syndrome Condition that occurs in females and results from the absense of an X chromosome (XO), resulting in a short, webbed neck, absence of pubic and axillary hair, and very small ovaries.

Two-spirit men Term for traditional Native American men who have both masculine and feminine traits; although they may participate in same-sex intimacy, they are less likely to identify themselves using such terms as homosexual, gay, or berdache.

U

Ultrasound scan Procedure whereby sound waves are used to project an image of the developing fetus on a video screen; used in prenatal testing.

Umbilical cord Cord which connects the developing fetus and the placenta.

Unidimensional continuum model Identification of one's sexual orientation on a scale from 0 (exclusively heterosexual) to 6 (exclusively homosexual) suggesting that most people are not on the extremes but somewhere in between.

Urethra Short tube that connects the bladder with the urethral opening.

Urethritis Inflammation of the urethra.

Uophilia Paraphilia that involves becoming sexually aroused by watching someone urinate or by urinating on someone.

Uterine orgasm In contrast to a "clitoral" orgasm, an orgasm caused by deep intravaginal stimulation and involving contractions in the uterus as well as vagina.

Uterus The womb; a hollow, muscular organ in which a fertilized egg may implant and develop.

V

Vacuum aspiration See **suction curettage**.

Vagina A 3- to 5-inch long muscular tube that extends from the vulva to the cervix of the uterus.

Vaginismus The recurrent or persistent involuntary spasm of the musculature of the outer third of the vagina that interferes with vaginal penetration.

Vaginitis Infection of the vagina.

Variable Any measurable event or characteristic that varies or is subject to change.

Vas deferens Tube from the ejaculatory ducts to the testes that transport sperm.

Vasectomy A minor surgical procedure whereby the vas deferens are cut so as to prevent sperm from entering the penis.

Vasocongestion Increased blood flow to the genital region.

Verbal messages Words individuals say to each other.

Vestibule The smooth tissue surrounding a woman's urethral opening.

Violent pornography Sexually explicit visual images of sexual violence usually directed by men against women.

Virginity Refers to not having experienced sexual intercourse.

Voluntary abstinence Foregoing sexual intercourse for a period of time by choice.

Voyeurism Paraphilia that involves recurrent, intense urges to look at unsuspecting people who are naked, undressing, or engaging in sexual behavior. (See also **scopophilia**.)

Vulva The external female genitalia.

Vulval orgasm Type of orgasm that results primarily from manual stimulation of the clitoris and is characterized by contractions of the outer third of the vagina. (See also **clitoral orgasm**.)

W

Wet dream See **nocturnal emission**.

Win-win solution Outcome of an interpersonal conflict whereby both people feel satisfied with the agreement or resolution.

Withdrawal See **coitus interruptus**.

Women's movement Social movement that supports the belief that women should have the right to make choices regarding their bodies and reproduction, thus advocating access to sex education, contraception, and abortion.

Y

Yang In Chinese thought, the male force that was viewed as active.

Yin In Chinese thought, the female force that was seen as passive.

Yohimbe Substance alleged to be a sexual stimulant for men. (Sometimes sold under the trade name of Yokon.)

"You" statements In communication theory, those statements that blame or criticize the listener and often result in increasing negative feelings and behavior in the relationship.

Z

Zoophilia Paraphilia that involves becoming aroused by sexual contact with animals. (Also known as *bestiality*.)

Zygote intrafallopian transfer (ZIFT) Procedure that involves fertilizing an egg in a lab dish and placing the zygote or embryo directly into the Fallopian tube.

Name Index

C

D

E

F

G

H

I

J

K

L

M

Q

R

S

T

Subject Index

Page numbers in italics identify an illustration.

C

D

N

O

P

R

S

T

U

V

W

Y